UNIVERSITY CASEBOOK SERIES

CASES AND MATERIALS

LOCAL GOVERNMENT LAW

FOURTH EDITION

by

LYNN A. BAKER

Frederick M. Baron Chair in Law

University of Texas School of Law

CLAYTON P. GILLETTE

Max E. Greenberg Professor of Contract Law

New York University School of Law

FOUNDATION PRESS

2010

1 New York Plaza, 34th Floor

New York, NY 10004

Phone Toll Free 1–877–888–1330

Fax (646) 424–5201

foundation–press.com

Printed in the United States of America

ISBN 978–1–59941–420–1

Mat #40654726

For Abby, for everything

—C. P. G.

For Sam, who makes everything better

—L. A. B.

PREFACE TO THE FOURTH EDITION

This edition retains the organization and general approach of the prior editions of this casebook. We continue to focus on the unique role that local governments play in the federal system, and the distinct characteristics of local governments that distinguish them from other levels of government. The larger questions that we ask remain the same: How should our local "communities" be defined in practice, and who should decide? What is and should be the relationship that states and localities have with their citizens, other states and localities, and the federal government? Which level of government (if any) should provide a particular good or service, or regulate activity in a particular area? How should the goods and services provided by states and localities be paid for, and who should decide?

This edition includes new material concerning the role of local governments in local economic development, a topic of heightened importance and controversy in light of the U. S. Supreme Court's 2005 decision in *Kelo v. City of New London*. We also discuss new developments in the relationship between the federal government and states and localities, including recent U.S. Supreme Court decisions concerning the federal preemption of state law and the scope of Congress's power under the Commerce Clause, as well as challenges to the No Child Left Behind Act and unfunded federal mandates to states and school districts.

Our students at the University of Texas School of Law and the NYU School of Law have improved this edition with their questions, comments, and suggestions. We are particularly grateful to Michael Stephan of the University of Texas School of Law, who provided valuable assistance with research and proofreading. Finally, we owe a continuing debt to our deans, Ricky Revesz at NYU and Larry Sager at the University of Texas, for their support of our projects, including this book.

LYNN A. BAKER
CLAYTON P. GILLETTE

April 2010

PREFACE TO THE THIRD EDITION

This edition continues the organization of the prior editions of this casebook, but recognizes developments that have occupied much of local government law in recent years. We have, for instance, added a section dealing with the important issue of redistribution by local governments. The enactment of living wage laws in many jurisdictions, and the inevitable challenges that these ordinances face in the courts, raise fascinating legal and policy issues about the extent to which localities can assist the poor, as well as the extent to which localities should subsidize businesses. This material also provides an effective means of discussing the more general question of how a community defines itself. We have also expanded the materials on regionalism to reflect the burgeoning literature on the extent to which cities and suburbs depend on each other in creating a regional economy. This material invites discussion about the obligations that communities owe to each other and the conflicting incentives that they face to compete and to cooperate.

Throughout these materials, we ask the questions that have been the focus of this book from its first edition: To what extent should local governments be permitted autonomously to define their objectives? Who gets which services within a community, and who should make those decisions? Who pays for the services that are provided? What kinds of legal constraints are necessary to permit one jurisdiction from exploiting another? What kinds of legal entitlements should be used to assist those who cannot easily migrate to jurisdictions that they would find more hospitable? What are the motivations of local government officials? We hope that you find these issues, and the debates that they engender, as fascinating as we do.

Numerous students at the University of Texas School of Law and NYU School Of Law assisted in the preparation of this edition. We are particularly grateful to Monica Brewer, Craig Cepler, Tracey Dingman, Claire Morris, and Leila Kimberly Thompson. Claire Morris of the University of Texas School of Law proofread the entire text and saved us from many errors. Finally, we owe a special debt to our deans, Ricky Revesz at NYU School of Law and William Powers at the University of Texas School of Law, for supporting this project as well as our other research.

LYNN A. BAKER
CLAYTON P. GILLETTE

July 2004

PREFACE TO THE SECOND EDITION

This edition retains the general approach and aims of the first: it seeks to explain local government law through an exploration of institutional design; it reflects a preference for explicating the law through the state courts rather than through federal court explanations of what localities ought to do; and it attempts to provide a basis for students to consider work from other disciplines, ranging from public finance to political philosophy, in order to encourage a more reflective critique of the legal doctrine and its consequences.

Users of the first edition will also find much—beyond the addition of a second author—that is new, however. This second edition reflects many important, post–1994 developments in local government law and scholarship, including: the increasingly problematic issues surrounding the city suburb relationship; the debate concerning the privatization of various community services; the growth of homeowners associations and other forms of "private government"; the revival of constitutional protections against federal power for states and localities embodied in United States v. Lopez and Printz v. United States; and increased attention to communitarian theories and scholarship. These materials will no doubt continue to evolve, and we welcome comments from users.

We are grateful to the many law students at the University of Virginia and the University of Texas who provided excellent research assistance: Jennifer Kraber, Craig May, Kristine Rayann Ottwaway, Jacqueline Watson, and William Wiese. Finally, we owe special thanks to our respective deans, Robert E. Scott and M. Michael Sharlot, and our colleagues for the continuing intellectual support that made this project possible.

Clayton P. Gillette
Lynn A. Baker

December 1998

PREFACE TO THE FIRST EDITION

The study of local government law has, in recent years, achieved new levels of analysis. The debates in the legal literature about liberalism and communitarianism, about the role of interest groups in the selection and passage of legislation, about the proper scope of the judiciary in allocating social resources all have implications for the issues of local competence and local autonomy that constitute the framework of local government law. At the same time, debates in the political forum about the role of local government in the federal firmament have become more important as federal funding has decreased, cities have struggled with fiscal distress, and states have imposed increased obligations on localities to address social issues ranging from environmental cleanup to the delivery of basic services. The materials in this book attempt to provide a means for studying these phenomena and for wrestling with both the theoretical and practical issues that local governments face today.

My approach to these issues consists of an investigation of the basics of what it is that we expect of local governments, of why we would or would not favor local redress for a particular social problem. My concern, therefore, is with the question of when local bodies (cities, counties, special authorities, towns) rather than some other level of government, or the marketplace, should make decisions concerning the allocation of social resources. In short, these materials explain local government law through an exploration of institutional design.

The issues that these materials address are familiar in the public law component of the law school curriculum. They involve the scope of governmental decisionmaking and the competence of the decisionmaker to render results consistent with an acceptable social objective, such as fairness or efficiency. Most public law courses, however, address these issues only at the federal level and ask whether a given decision should be made by the executive, the legislature, or the judiciary. A course in local government law adds to this matrix the issue of whether a particular decision should be made at the local, state, or federal level. Occasionally, these materials also invite the student to consider whether the good or service at issue should be provided by government at all. The materials begin from the assumption that the appropriate level of decisionmaking for any issue depends on three factors: (1) the extent to which the decision will have effects beyond the jurisdiction of the decisionmaker; (2) the possibility that decentralization will enhance or frustrate a decisionmaking procedure that is dominated by nonrepresentative interests, that is, the problem of collective action; and

(3) the desirability of creating institutions for decisionmaking that promote state of local government scholarship, it is not appropriate to address these issues as purely legal matters. Instead, the law that emerges, and the student's reaction to it, largely reflects learning from other disciplines, ranging from public finance to political philosophy. I have attempted to provide some basis for students to consider work from these other disciplines in order to encourage a more reflective critique of the legal doctrine and its consequences.

A word about the cases is in order. Many of the doctrines of local government law lack the precision and definiteness that one would like. Concepts such as "debt," "public purpose," "local affairs," and "uniform taxation" are not readily susceptible to definition. I have attempted to select cases that demonstrate the complexity inherent in these concepts and that give sufficient examples of when the particular court believes the standard at issue has or has not been satisfied. Unfortunately, cases that are successful for these purposes tend, for the same reason, to be lengthy. My apologies in advance to teachers and students. In addition, I have chosen to retain detailed discussions of the transactions that give rise to the underlying disputes in the hope that students will come to appreciate the intricate and varied contexts in which local governments interact with the state, with each other, and with their residents. Here, too, I fear, brevity must give way.

I have also attempted (with notable exceptions) to select relatively recent cases from state courts in order to give students a sense of the currency of the problems presented. The cases also reveal my preference for explicating the law through the state courts rather than through federal court explanations of what localities ought to do. In large part, this choice reflects my preference not to turn the study of local government law into an examination of "constitutional law as applied to localities." Hence, I have avoided cases that treat "first amendment law as applied to localities" or "takings law as applied to cities" in favor of cases that, at least implicitly, ask fundamental questions about the appropriate scope of municipal conduct.

These materials have evolved over a period of years, and I have no faith that the evolutionary process has ended. I welcome comments from users of the materials. That these materials and my own thinking about local government have reached this point is due in no small part to the generosity of others in conversation and commentary. I have been fortunate to have served under two remarkable deans, Bob Scott at the University of Virginia and Ron Cass at Boston University. Each has provided not only the time and resources necessary to complete this project, but also the intellectual support and engagement that has added richly to my understanding of the subject. Several individuals, Kathy Abrams, Lynn Baker, Cheryl Conner, Ann Gellis, Dan Rodriguez, and Gary Schwartz, subjected their students and themselves to all or parts of these materials in nascent form and gave me feedback that improved the content and the presentation. I owe a special debt to Gary Schwartz, who spent more hours than mere collegiality required to discuss details of the manuscript. Others took the time and effort to discuss sections of the book and contribute ideas. These include

Richard Briffault, Pam Karlan, Saul Levmore, and William Stuntz. I am also grateful to several anonymous reviewers, whose comments forced me to rethink the substance of the book.

Marian Ryerson provided substantial secretarial assistance. Legions of law students at the University of Virginia and Boston University provided excellent research assistance. I am particularly indebted to Karen Essex, David Harrington, Kari Levine, Patti Levine, Aimee Meltzer, and Holly June Stiefel. I am grateful for research support from the Class of 1957 Research Endowment at the University of Virginia School of Law. The editorial staff at Little, Brown and Co., Carol McGeehan, David Bemelmans, Betsy Kenny, and Tom Lincoln, provided both comfort and professionalism.

I was fortunate to do much of the research for this book on Westlaw, and am grateful for the advances in computer technology that have expedited the process of legal research.

Finally, my family, Abby, Jonah, and Alexander, have offered me more sacrifice and support than any one family member has the right to expect. I can only hope that the product in some small way rewards their faith.

A final note on the text: I have occasionally omitted citations within cases without designation. Where I have reprinted footnotes from cases, I have retained the original footnote numbers.

CLAYTON P. GILLETTE

February 1994

ACKNOWLEDGMENTS

The authors acknowledge the permissions kindly granted to reproduce the materials indicated below.

American Bar Association, The Challenge of Direct Democracy in a Republic: Report and Guidelines of the Task Force on Initiatives and Referenda (1993). Reprinted by permission.

Arendt, Hannah, from On Revolution by Hannah Arendt. Copyright 1963 by Hannah Arendt. Used by permission of Viking Penguin, a division of Penguin Group (USA) Inc.

Bachrach, Peter, Interest, Participation, and Democratic Theory, in NOMOS XVI: Participation in Politics. Reprinted by permission.

Baker, Lynn A., Conditional Federal Spending after Lopez. This article originally appeared at 95 Colum. L. Rev. 1911 (1995). Reprinted by permission.

Been, Vicki, Comment on Professor Jerry Frug's "The Geography of Community," 48 Stan. L. Rev. 1109 (1996). Copyright 1996 by the Board of Trustees of the Leland Stanford Junior University.

Been, Vicki, "Exit" as a Constraint on Land Use Exactions: Rethinking the Unconstitutional Conditions Doctrine. This article originally appeared at 91 Colum. L. Rev. 473 (1991). Reprinted by permission.

Bollens, Scott A., Concentrated Poverty and Metropolitan Equity Strate-gies, 8 Stan. L. & Pol. Rev. 11 (1997). Reprinted by permission.

Briffault, Richard, Our Localism, Part I: The Structure of Local Government Law. This article originally appeared at 90 Colum. L. Rev. 1 (1990). Reprinted by permission.

Bruff, Harold H., Judicial Review in Local Government Law: A Reappraisal, 60 Minn. L. Rev. 669 (1976). Reprinted by permission.

Cloe, Lyman H., and Sumner Marcus, Special and Local Legislation, 24 Ky. L.J. 351 (1936). Reprinted by permission of Kentucky Law Journal.
Elhauge, Einer R., The Scope of Antitrust Process, 104 Harv. L. Rev. 667 (1991). Copyright 1991 by The Harvard Law Review Association. Reprinted by permission.

Farber, Daniel, and Philip Frickey, Law and Public Choice: A Critical Introduction (1991). Copyright 1991 by The University of Chicago. Reprinted by permission.

Frug, Gerald, The City as Legal Concept, 93 Harv. L. Rev. 1057 (1980). Copyright 1980 by The Harvard Law Review Association and Gerald Frug. Reprinted by permission.

Frug, Gerald E., City Services, 73 N.Y.U. L. Rev. 23 (1998). Reprinted by permission.

Frug, Jerry, Decentering Decentralization, 60 U. Chi. L. Rev. 253 (1993). Copyright 1993 by The University of Chicago and Jerry Frug.

Gellis, Ann Judith, Legislative Reforms of Government Tort Liability: Overreacting to Minimal Evidence, 21 Rutgers L.J. 375 (1990). Reprinted by permission.

Gillette, Clayton P., Plebiscites, Participation,and Collective Action in Local Government Law, 86 Mich. L. Rev. 930 (1998). Reprinted by permission.

Gillette, Clayton P. and Thomas D. Hopkins, Federal User Fees: A Legal and Economic Analysis. 67 B.U.L. Review 793 (1987). Reprinted by permission.

Handlin, Oscar, and Mary Handlin. Reprinted by permission of the publisher from Commonwealth: A Study of the Role of Government in the American Economy, 1774–1861, by Oscar Handlin and Mary Handlin, pp. 240–41, Cambridge, Mass.: The Belknap Press of Harvard University Press. Copyright 1947, 1969 by the President and Fellows of Harvard College.

Haughwout, Andrew F. and Robert P. Inman, Should Suburbs Help Their Central City? 2002 Brookings–Wharton Papers on Urban Affairs. Copyright 2002. Reprinted by permission of the Brookings Institution Press.

Krane, Dale, Platon N. Rigos, and Melvin B. Hill, Jr., Home Rule in America, CQ Press. Copyright (c) 2000 by Congressional Quarterly Inc. Reprinted by permission.

Ladd, Helen F., and John Yinger, America's Ailing Cities: Fiscal Health and the Design of Urban Policy. The Johns Hopkins University Press, Baltimore/London, 1989. Reprinted by permission.

Logan, John and Harvey L. Molotch, Urban Fortunes: The Political Economy of Place. Copyright 1987 by the University of California Press. Reprinted by permission.

Miller, Gary J., Cities by Contract: The Politics of Municipal Incorporation (1981). Copyright 1981 by The Massachusetts Institute of Technology. Reprinted by permission.

Moak, Lennox L., and Albert M. Hillhouse, Local Government Finance (1975). Copyright by the Municipal Finance Officers Association.

Netzer, Dick, Economics of the Property Tax (1966). Copyright by the Brookings Institution. Reprinted by permission.

Note, Unfulfilled Promises: School Finance Remedies and State Courts, 104 Harv. L. Rev. 1072 (1991). Copyright 1991 by The Harvard Law Review Association. Reprinted by permission.

Raimondo, Henry John, Economics of State and Local Government (1992). Copyright 1992 by Henry J. Raimondo. Reprinted with permission of Greenwood Publishing Group., Inc., Westport, CT.

Reynolds, Laurie. Rethinking Municipal Annexation Powers, 24 Urb. Law. 247 (1992). Copyright 1992 American Bar Association. Reprinted by permission.

Rosenblum, Nancy, Membership & Morals. Copyright 1998 by Princeton University Press. Reprinted by permission of Princeton University Press.

Sandalow, Terrance, The Limits of Municipal Power Under Home Rule: A Role for the Courts, 48 Minn. L. Rev. 643 (1964). Reprinted by permission.

Schill, Michael H., Privatizing Federal Low Income Housing Assistance: The Case of Public Housing, 75 Cornell L. Rev. 878 (1990). Copyright 1990 by Cornell University. All Rights Reserved. Reprinted by permission.

Schumpeter, Joseph, Capitalism, Socialism and Democracy, 3rd ed. by Joseph Schumpeter. Copyright 1942, 1947 by Joseph A. Schumpeter. Reprinted by permission of HarperCollins Publishers, Inc., at page 659 infra.

Tiebout, Charles, A Pure Theory of Local Expenditures, 64 J. Pol. Econ. 416 (1956). Copyright 1956 by The University of Chicago. Reprinted by permission.

Tocqueville, Alexis de, "Absence of Administrative Centralism" from Democracy in America by Alexis de Tocqueville. Edited by J. P. Mayer and Max Lerner. Translated by George Lawrence. English translation copyright 1965 by Harper & Row, Publishers, Inc. Reprinted by permission of Harper- Collins Publishers, Inc., at page 12 infra.

Waters, M. Dane, Initiative and Referendum Almanac. Copyright 2003 by Carolina Academic Press (www.cap-press.com). Reprinted by permission.

Zelinsky, Edward A., The Once and Future Property Tax: A Dialogue with My Younger Self, 23 Cardozo L. Rev. 2199 (2002). Reprinted by permission.

SUMMARY OF CONTENTS

TABLE OF CONTENTS

CHAPTER 3 The Community's Relationship With the State 237

TABLE OF CASES

Principal cases are in bold type. Non-principal cases are in roman type. References are to Pages.

CASES AND MATERIALS

LOCAL GOVERNMENT LAW

Introduction: Local Government and Institutional Competence

A. The Question of Institutional Design

Government plays a variety of roles in the lives of all citizens. At times, government can be a source of relief, providing protection from threatened harms, goods and services not otherwise available, or aid after harms have materialized. Alternatively, government can itself be a threat to or a source of limits on the choices of individuals. Indeed, because resources are limited, protecting or assisting one group often requires placing constraints on another. Finally, government can provide opportunities for individuals to participate in decisionmaking about the protections and constraints that should be provided or imposed, about the ways in which scarce resources should be allocated.

The study of the legal processes by which we enable government to protect constituents and provide goods and services, and by which we limit the ability of government to impose threats, typically addresses the sources of governmental authority and the constitutional and statutory restrictions and mandates that we impose on government. A course in local government law necessarily addresses these issues. At the same time, it introduces an additional issue, often taken for granted in public law courses that concentrate on the federal government. That is the issue of which level of government should be involved in a given activity or should be constrained in a particular way. When we speak of government in the law school curriculum, we can too easily forget that public governments in the United States include not only the federal government and those of the 50 states; they also include the more than 87,000 political subdivisions of the states—3,000 counties, 19,000 municipal corporations, 16,000 townships, 13,000 school districts, and 35,000 special districts. Each of these entities has the ability to confer the benefits and impose the burdens that we associate with government generally, albeit over a smaller jurisdiction than the federal government. With respect to some issues, these localities may be particularly well positioned to render decisions that will satisfy the dictates of legitimacy, fairness, or efficiency that serve as the standard for proper governmental activity. With respect to other decisions, however, localities would seem to be largely incompetent. The study of local government law, therefore, necessarily requires that we consider which level of government should exercise a particular power and which limits we want to place on any given level of government. A course in local government law, in short, is in large part a course in institutional competence and institutional design.

These materials seek to answer the question: Under what circumstances should a given government decision be made by a local body? In order to allow the student to make this inquiry these materials first address, in Chapter 1, the question of what it is that we expect local governments to do that is different from other levels of government and from the private market for goods and services. This inquiry cannot, of course, be addressed exclusively, or even initially, as an issue of law. The law of local government necessarily implements a political vision that is informed by principles drawn from disciplines as diverse as political theory and economics. These principles must ultimately dictate the proper scope of local competence. There is, however, very little consensus in legal theory about the role of local government in the United States; indeed, there is little literature that addresses the legal theory of local government at all. The inquiry into the proper scope of local government, therefore, begins with consideration of what nonlawyers—political scientists, economists, and philosophers—have said about the benefits and drawbacks of decentralized government. In this part, you will be introduced to some major themes that pervade contemporary scholarship in local government law, although some of the readings themselves date back to the late eighteenth century.

These readings reveal some of the longstanding tensions that exist between competing conceptions of local government. One strain of recent scholarship views local government as a focal point for public discourse about politics, as the sole level of government that is capable of providing some semblance of participatory democracy. This strain has its contemporary applications in the literature of communitarianism and republicanism. Courts and commentators who take this view consider local units to be primarily areas of public life in which individuals can have a meaningful role in self-government. More centralized governmental units are simply too large and impersonal to admit much of a participatory role for their constituents. Localities provide opportunities for individuals to seek common ground, to interact with one another and hence to develop a sense of community and interdependence. Hence, those who view self-government and participation as a primary function of local units advocate greater degrees of local autonomy from state and federal control and more diversity among localities.

The other strain of scholarship considers local government as a mechanism for achieving a more mundane, but no less important, objective: the allocation of goods and services that are best provided collectively (through government) rather than through market mechanisms. This strain is perhaps best recognized as the legal descendant of welfare economics. Courts and commentators who take this view of local government may similarly seek local autonomy, but do so in the name of maximizing the choices of individual residents rather than empowering groups, and may evince a stronger distrust of intervention into private affairs by any level of government. Where intervention is inevitable or desirable, that level of government least likely to divert resources away from the welfare of individuals will be preferred.

These two scholarly strains are not necessarily diametrically opposed. One reason why people might want to engage in self-government, for instance, would be to have a role in choosing the goods and services for which their tax dollars are used. Nevertheless, there is sufficient tension between these two visions of local government to generate, at least occasionally, different answers to the central question about the proper scope of local government competence.

After this initial introduction into the role of local government, the materials in Chapter 2 address an issue that is central to all that will follow: Who should be considered as members of the "community" that seeks to make a particular legal decision? Our willingness to permit local institutions to act will often depend on whom we think will be affected by the local decision. Most people, for instance, would likely believe that local governments should not set national defense policy for a variety of reasons: (1) local leaders will not necessarily have sufficient information, (2) different priorities of different localities will lead to conflict (residents of Kansas might spend less on naval defense than residents of South Carolina), and (3) local officials are unlikely to consider the consequences for nonresidents of a decision reached at the local level, even though those nonresidents are affected by the local decision. But most people would likely have a different reaction to the question of whether a local government should be entitled to exclude trailer parks, which is not to say that all people would agree on what answer the local government should give to that question. Nevertheless, much of the reasoning for objecting to local decisions about defense applies to some degree to the decision about trailer parks. In the latter case, localities that are considering exclusion will probably make decisions without all relevant information before them; and, again, those localities are unlikely to consider the interests of those who will be excluded as a result of their decision. What, then, is the difference between the two issues? If we accept the need to have some decisions made locally, are we willing to permit local residents to sort themselves by any set of preferences they desire? To what extent are we willing to credit the preferences of individuals to live exclusively among others who are "like themselves," ethnically, socially, and economically? The way in which we define the "community" that is entitled to make any given decision may rest on our answers to these questions.

Once we are armed with alternative conceptions of what localities might do and have defined the proper decisionmaking community, we are prepared to examine the core questions of what localities can and should do. To consider this issue, the bulk of the materials, comprising Chapters 3–8, examines three relationships: the relationship between the community and the state, the relationship between the community and its residents, and the relationship between the community and its neighbors. As you investigate these relationships, you should ask how each of them should be structured if we wanted to implement the communitarian vision of local government, on the one hand, or the welfarist (allocational) vision on the other.

An example of the types of questions that these materials address may be helpful here. Assume that Brighton is a small, college community with

15,000 full-year residents and a local university with a student population that swells the city by an additional 10,000 persons between the months of September and June. Housing for students is somewhat restricted. Single students face particular difficulty obtaining apartments in Brighton because landlords would prefer to avoid the problems of short-term lessees, high-turnover, subletting, and maintenance that they identify with leasing housing to unmarried students. A practice has therefore developed in Brighton whereby several landlords will rent only to married couples in the belief that (a) this will mean fewer students, (b) married students are more responsible than single students, and (c) married students are more likely to remain in the area during summers and after graduation and thus will enter into long-term leases and not sublet.

Assume that in recent years, complaints from single students about this practice and the inability of single students to obtain housing near campus have reached such proportions that university officials have persuaded the Brighton City Council to consider a local ordinance that would prohibit discrimination in rental housing on the basis of marital status. Local landlords are united against such an ordinance and think that they have persuaded the City Council that their concerns—as full-time residents, taxpayers, and voters—should dominate. Assume also that Brighton is in a state the constitution and laws of which prohibit discrimination in housing on the basis of religion, race, creed, nationality, or gender, but that are silent on the question of discrimination on the basis of marital status.

Finally, assume that Brighton lies in the midst of a county that has seen an influx of single students since the discriminatory practice developed. There has subsequently developed in the county a severe housing shortage that is generally attributed to the influx of students. With the housing shortage there has arrived the inevitable increase in rents and pricing out of poorer residents. If the ordinance were passed in Brighton and single students could migrate to that city, it is believed that the county's housing shortage would be alleviated.

From a normative point of view, we could argue for hours whether such an ordinance ought to be adopted. But that is not our primary concern in an inquiry into local government law. Here, we are interested in questions of institutional design that fall along the following lines:

1. Why is this the kind of issue that requires governmental intervention at all? If landlords believe that refusal to rent to unmarried students will maximize their profits, why should government interfere?

2. Does Brighton have the authority to enact this kind of ordinance? Where did it get that authority if it has it? What importance should we attribute to the silence of the state constitution and statutes on this issue?

3. If Brighton has the power to enact this kind of ordinance, is there reason to believe that the decision of the city council will be based on some conception of the public interest, or should we be concerned that some group (either local landlords or the university) will be able to

dominate the decisionmaking process? If the latter, then how should we alter the decisionmaking process to eliminate the problem?

4. Regardless of who makes the ultimate decision on the ordinance, what role, if any, should the county have to play? Should county residents have a right to be heard on the issue before the city council? Should nonresident students have the right to be heard?

Note that these questions do not simply pose the traditional law school inquiry of what substantive legal doctrine courts should apply to decide a case. Rather the emphasis is on how the decisionmaking process is to be structured, or, more directly, at what level of government and with what participants should the ordinance be considered? The way in which we respond to this question depends in very large part on the model we have in mind for local government. If we view localities solely as functionaries of the state with a primary function of allocating public goods and services, then we might have a very different answer to these questions than if we view localities as the focal point of participation, civic virtue, and popular deliberation. If local officials are to be administrators alone, then there is little reason for them to be policymakers and to decide issues of the type involved here. If, on the other hand, localities are to be a locus of some degree of power, the question becomes more complex. Then we have to decide whether the question before the locality will generate the kind of deliberative discussion that we expect to occur before government intervenes to guide or alter private decisions. That means we must be concerned about how many sides of the issue can be represented in the discussion.

B. PUBLIC OFFICIALS AND THEIR CONSTITUENTS

As suggested above, one question of institutional design involves the question of which entity is best situated to implement the objectives we define for government. For instance, it is obvious that we would not want to assign the task of implementation to a body that is incompetent, or disinterested in satisfying the objective, or that would require more resources to satisfy the objective than some alternative body. It makes little sense, for instance, to require the national government to decide how frequently to pave streets in Portland, or to allocate to the state Department of Tourism the responsibility of drafting a "bottle return" bill.

Even where all agree that a particular governmental objective belongs within the domain of local government, however, problems of implementation may remain. These problems result from a phenomenon that, in legal and economics literature, falls under the heading of "agency costs." Basically, these are costs incurred by a principal whose interests do not coincide exactly with those of the agents employed to carry out the principal's bidding. Principals may incur a variety of costs to account for this divergence of interests. Some costs will be incurred to monitor the behavior of agents in an effort to minimize conduct that is inconsistent with the principal's interest. Additionally, costs will be incurred to bond the agent more closely to the principal, thereby making monitoring less necessary. For instance, the principal and agent may enter into contractual arrangements that make the success of the agent contingent on the success of the principal. In the private sector, this can be done by giving agents ownership interests or property in the principal's business. Other costs will be incurred in the form of losses suffered by the principal to the extent that the gap between principal and the agent interests cannot be closed.

Agency costs have been much studied in the private sector, in contexts such as the potentially divergent interests between shareholders and officers of corporations. See, e.g., Eugene F. Fama & Michael C. Jensen, Agency Problems and Residual Claims, 26 J. L. & Econ. 327 (1983); Michael C. Jensen & William H. Meckling, Theory of the Firm: Managerial Behavior, Agency Costs and Ownership Structure, 3 J. Fin. Econ. 305 (1976). Until recently, however, the topic has commanded less attention in study of the public sector. In part, this is because there has been an assumption that agency costs in the public sector are very low—that elected officials attempt to do the bidding of the public, so that the interests of public agents (elected and appointed officials) fully reflect the interests of the principals (the constituents) they serve. This assumption follows from the belief that, by and large, officials who enter public life either do so because they wish to advance public welfare or because the threat of removal by the electorate is sufficient to constrain officials who might otherwise act in a manner inconsistent with their constituents' interest. If we subscribe to this view of public officials, there is little reason to impose additional legal constraints on their behavior, as they will already be motivated to implement the desires of their constituents. On this view, legal rules affecting local government, at least the rules that primarily have intramural effects, will have a communicative purpose. These rules will attempt to create means by which constituents can indicate their desires so officials will know what policies to implement.

If we have a more pessimistic view of public officials, however, the question of agency costs becomes more complicated. This view, identified with a school of thought known as "public choice," suggests that political officials have the same motivation as nonpolitical actors who allocate goods through private markets, i.e., self-interest. The key difference between actors in the public and private sector, on this view, is that the currency of the private market is money, while that of political markets is votes. Initially, one might believe that public officials in a democracy will want to maximize the number of votes they get, and hence increase their chances of election or reelection; officials will therefore seek to serve the interests of the majority of voters. Thus, self-interested pursuit of votes by public officials will necessarily translate into conduct consistent with the public interest, assuming that public interest and majority interest are largely coextensive.

Two arguments suggest the limits of this claim. The first, consistent with traditional democratic theory, is that sometimes we do not want "raw" majoritarianism to be the basis of political action. Majorities may act in a manner that runs roughshod over minorities. Thus, at times we want public officials to temper the demands of majorities. Typically, however, we do not think of public officials who act in this way as diverging from the public interest, even though they are not literally following the will of the majority. Rather we believe that public officials should refine the views of majorities and implement the will that we attribute to an "informed" or "more rational" majority. Thus, public officials who blindly maximize votes by appealing to majorities may be described derisively as demagogues rather than as actors who pursue the public interest.

The second argument that refutes the consistency of public interest and vote maximization is more closely tied to the underpinnings of the public choice literature. Maximizing votes does not necessarily mean appealing to the largest number of constituents. Rather, it means appealing to the largest number of voters or to supporters who can help officials to influence voters. For reasons that will become clear, many potential voters do not actually cast ballots. Further, there are ways to influence officials other than by casting votes. Individuals who can contribute campaign funds or who can lobby for passage of legislation may have more influence than those who register their preferences only by voting. If some individuals, who have interests that deviate from those of the public at large, are more likely to vote or to participate in the political process than the average constituent, the political official may be able to maximize votes by appealing to those individuals (or that interest group), notwithstanding that the interests of those individuals do not coincide with the public interest. If that is the case, then the public has as much need to monitor the conduct of public officials as shareholders of private corporations have to monitor their agents.

The divergence of interests between officials and their constituents affects all levels of government. Obviously, this divergence can be limited if constituents are able to monitor the conduct of their officials and turn them out of office when the divergence becomes too great. But it is not necessarily the case that all public officials are susceptible to the same monitoring devices or that they are susceptible to monitoring devices to the same degree. Local officials may be more (or less) vulnerable to public scrutiny than state or federal officials. Similarly, local officials may have different interests than their state or federal counterparts. If we accept this view of public officials, it follows that the role of legal rules requires more than allowing constituents to communicate their preferences. Legal rules may also be necessary to restrict the discretion of local officials or to facilitate principals (the public) when they seek to check the performance of their agents. Decisionmaking at the local level would be preferred, on this model, where local constituents are better monitors of public officials than their state or federal counterparts.

Stating the role of local government in these terms, however, presents what some have seen as the dark side of public choice. If local government only involves bringing individuals together to (in the language of economics) register their preferences for goods and services, aggregating those preferences to define the local objective, and then monitoring elected officials to ensure that those preferences are satisfied, then local government may lose much of its potential for creating the interdependent community that some see as the distinguishing feature of local units.

This dichotomy between an economic model of local government and a communal, public interest model is reflected in many of the questions about the proper scope and role of local government law with which these materials are concerned. See Frank I. Michelman, Political Markets and Community Self–Determination: Competing Judicial Models of Local Government Legitimacy, 53 Ind. L.J. 145 (1977–1978). These models, however, are not as pure as their initial statement might suggest. Even if one subscribes to the "public interest" view, the fact that localities will always have scarce resources, and thus be unable to satisfy all the desires of all residents, requires discovering individual preferences at least to create a starting point for the reconciliation of competing objectives. And even if residents of a locality engage in deliberative processes and seek accommodation of conflicting views, the problem of agency costs remains when local officials attempt to implement the understanding reached by their constituents. On the other hand, the economic model cannot be implemented on a fully individualized basis. Even the most self-interested residents do not develop their values and preferences in a vacuum. They are necessarily influenced by the opinions and interests of those with whom they live and work. Perhaps more importantly, neither the public interest nor the public choice model can be perfectly realized without some form of intervention, since the conditions that each model requires (ability to express preferences, ability to participate, ability to relate one's interests for consideration by others, and, ultimately, the ability to move to a more amicable jurisdiction) do not exist uniformly throughout society or within a given locality.

If we desire to attain either of these conceptions, or some combination of them, then we must confront this inability to create the conditions that would allow realization of the model we choose. The questions of institutional design with which these materials are concerned may be considered as an attempt to find ways to compensate for that inability, and to use legal doctrine as a means of bringing us closer to the conditions necessary to achieve an environment in which individuals can express their interests, participate in the decisionmaking process, and recognize the interests of others. As you peruse the materials that follow, therefore, you should consider such issues of institutional design as: (1) If we seek to have each level of government serve the public interest, what functions are local governments best situated to perform? (2) What barriers prevent local governments from performing those functions? (3) How can the rule of law reduce those barriers and facilitate local achievement of the objectives ideally assigned to it? The theoretical perspectives on local government that follow elaborate on these questions.

CHAPTER 1

THEORETICAL PERSPECTIVES ON THE FUNCTIONS OF LOCAL GOVERNMENT

A. THE PERSPECTIVE FROM POLITICS

John Stuart Mill, Considerations on Representative Government

From the constitution of the local bodies I now pass to the equally important and more difficult subject of their proper attributions. This question divides itself into two parts: what should be their duties, and whether they should have full authority within the sphere of those duties or should be liable to any, and what, interference on the part of the central government.

It is obvious, to begin with, that all business purely local—all which concerns only a single locality—should devolve upon the local authorities. The paving, lighting, and cleansing of the streets of a town, and in ordinary circumstances the draining of its houses, are of little consequence to any but its inhabitants. The nation at large is interested in them in no other way than that in which it is interested in the private well-being of all its individual citizens. But among the duties classed as local, or performed by local functionaries, there are many which might with equal propriety be termed national, being the share, belonging to the locality, of some branch of the public administration in the efficiency of which the whole nation is alike interested: the gaols, for instance, most of which in this country are under county management; the local police; the local administration of justice, much of which, especially in corporate towns, is performed by officers elected by the locality and paid from local funds. None of these can be said to be matters of local, as distinguished from national, importance. It would not be a matter personally indifferent to the rest of the country if any part of it became a nest of robbers or a focus of demoralization, owing to the maladministration of its police; or if, through the bad regulations of its gaol, the punishment which the courts of justice intended to inflict on the criminals confined therein (who might have come from, or committed their offenses in, any other district) might be doubled in intensity, or lowered to practical impunity. The points, moreover, which constitute good management of these things are the same everywhere; there is no good reason why police, or gaols, or the administration of justice should be differently managed in one part of the kingdom and in another; while there is great peril that in things so important, and to which the most instructed minds available to the State are not more than adequate, the lower average of capacities which alone can be counted on for the service of the localities might commit errors of such magnitude as to be a serious blot upon the general administration of the country. Security of person and property and equal justice between individuals are the first needs of society and the primary ends of government; if these things can be left to any responsibility below the highest, there is nothing, except war and treaties, which requires a general government at all. Whatever are the best arrangements for securing these primary objects should be made universally obligatory and, to secure their enforcement, should be placed under central superintendence. It is often useful, and with the institutions of our own country even necessary, from the scarcity, in the localities, of officers representing the general government, that the execution of duties imposed by the central authority should be entrusted to functionaries appointed for local purposes by the locality. But experience is daily forcing upon the public a conviction of the necessity of having at least inspectors appointed by the general government to see that the local officers do their duty. If prisons are under local management, the central government appoints inspectors of prisons to take care that the rules laid down by Parliament are observed, and to suggest others if the state of the gaols shows them to be requisite; as there are inspectors of factories, and inspectors of schools, to watch over the observance of the acts of Parliament relating to the first, and the fulfillment of the conditions on which State assistance is granted to the latter.

But if the administration of justice, police and gaols included, is both so universal a concern, and so much a matter of general science independent of local peculiarities, that it may be, and ought to be, uniformly regulated throughout the country, and its regulation enforced by more trained and skillful hands than those of purely local authorities—there is also business, such as the administration of the poor laws, sanitary regulation, and others, which, while really interesting to the whole country, cannot consistently with the very purposes of local administration be managed otherwise than by the localities. In regard to such duties the question arises how far the local authorities ought to be trusted with discretionary power, free from any superintendence or control of the State.

To decide this question it is essential to consider what is the comparative position of the central and the local authorities as to capacity for the work, and security against negligence or abuse. In the first place, the local representative bodies and their officers are almost certain to be of a much lower grade of intelligence and knowledge than Parliament and the national executive. Secondly, besides being themselves of inferior qualifications, they are watched by, and accountable to, an inferior public opinion. The public under whose eyes they act, and by whom they are criticized, is both more limited in extent and generally far less enlightened than that which surrounds and admonishes the highest authorities at the capital, while the comparative smallness of the interests involved causes even that inferior public to direct its thoughts to the subject less intently, and with less solicitude. Far less interference is exercised by the press and by public discussion, and that which is exercised may with much more impunity be disregarded in the proceedings of local than in those of national authorities. Thus far the advantage seems wholly on the side of management by the central government. But, when we look more closely, these motives of preference are found to be balanced by others fully as substantial. If the local authorities and public are inferior to the central ones in knowledge of the principles of administration, they have the compensating advantage of a far more direct interest in the result. A man's neighbors or his landlord may be much cleverer than himself, and not without an indirect interest in his prosperity, but for all that his interests will be better attended to in his own keeping than in theirs. It is further to be remembered that, even supposing the central government to administer through its own officers, its officers do not act at the center, but in the locality; and however inferior the local public may be to the central, it is the local public alone which has any opportunity of watching them, and it is the local opinion alone which either acts directly upon their own conduct or calls the attention of the government to the points in which they may require correction. It is but in extreme cases that the general opinion of the country is brought to bear at all upon details of local administration, and still more rarely has it the means of deciding upon them with any just appreciation of the case. Now, the local opinion necessarily acts far more forcibly upon purely local administrators. They, in the natural course of things, are permanent residents, not expecting to be withdrawn from the place when they cease to exercise authority in it; and their authority itself depends, by supposition, on the will of the local public. I need not dwell on the deficiencies of the central authority in detailed knowledge of local persons and things, and the too great engrossment of its time and thoughts by other concerns, to admit of its acquiring the quantity and quality of local knowledge necessary even for deciding on complaints and enforcing responsibility from so great a number of local agents. In the details of management, therefore, the local bodies will generally have the advantage; but in comprehension of the principles even of purely local management, the superiority of the central government, when rightly constituted, ought to be prodigious, not only by reason of the probably great personal superiority of the individuals composing it, and the multitude of thinkers and writers who are at all times engaged in pressing useful ideas upon their notice, but also because the knowledge and experience of any local authority is but local knowledge and experience, confined to their own part of the country and its modes of management, whereas the central government has the means of knowing all that is to be learned from the united experience of the whole kingdom, with the addition of easy access to that of foreign countries.

The practical conclusion from these premises is not difficult to draw. The authority which is most conversant with principles should be supreme over principles, while that which is most competent in details should have the details left to it. The principal business of the central authority should be to give instruction, of the local authority to apply it. Power may be localized, but knowledge, to be most useful, must be centralized; there must be somewhere a focus at which all its scattered rays are collected, that the broken and colored lights which exist elsewhere may find there what is necessary to complete and purify them. To every branch of local administration which affects the general interest there should be a corresponding central organ, either a minister or some specially appointed functionary under him; even if that functionary does no more than collect information from all quarters and bring the experience acquired in one locality to the knowledge of another where it is wanted. But there is also something more than this for the central authority to do. It ought to keep open a perpetual communication with the localities: informing itself by their experience, and them by its own; giving advice freely when asked, volunteering it when seen to be required; compelling publicity and recordation of proceedings, and enforcing obedience to every general law which the legislature has laid down on the subject of local management. That some such laws ought to be laid down few are likely to deny. The localities may be allowed to mismanage their own interests, but not to prejudice those of others, nor violate those principles of justice between one person and another of which it is the duty of the State to maintain the rigid observance. If the local majority attempts to oppress the minority, or one class another, the State is bound to interpose.

Hannah Arendt, On Revolution

234–259 (1965).

No doubt only great perplexity and real calamity can explain that Jefferson—so conscious of his common sense and so famous for his practical turn of mind—should have proposed these schemes of recurring revolutions. Even in their least extreme form, recommended as the remedy against "the endless circle of oppression, rebellion, reformation," they would either have thrown the whole body politic out of gear periodically or, more likely, have debased the act of foundation to a mere routine performance, in which case even the memory of what he most ardently wished to save—"to the end of time, if anything human can so long endure"—would have been lost. But the reason Jefferson, throughout his long life, was carried away by such impracticabilities was that he knew, however dimly, that the Revolution, while it had given freedom to the people, had failed to provide a space where this freedom could be exercised. Only the representatives of the people, not the people themselves, had an opportunity to engage in those activities of "expressing, discussing and deciding" which in a positive sense are the activities of freedom. And since the state and federal governments, the proudest results of revolution, through sheer weight of their proper business were bound to overshadow in political importance the townships and their meeting halls—until what Emerson still considered to be "the unit of the Republic" and "the school of the people" in political matters had withered away—one might even come to the conclusion that there was less opportunity for the exercise of public freedom and the enjoyment of public happiness in the republic of the United States than there had existed in the colonies of British America. Lewis Mumford recently pointed out how the political importance of the township was never grasped by the founders, and that the failure to incorporate it into either the federal or the state constitutions was "one of the tragic oversights of post-revolutionary political development." Only Jefferson among the founders had a clear premonition of this tragedy, for his greatest fear was indeed lest "the abstract political system of democracy lacked concrete organs."

The failure of the founders to incorporate the township and the town-hall meeting into the Constitution, or rather their failure to find ways and means to transform them under radically changed circumstances, was understandable enough. Their chief attention was directed toward the most troublesome of all their immediate problems, the question of representation, and this to such an extent that they came to define republics, as distinguished from democracies, in terms of representative government. Obviously direct democracy would not do, if only because "the room will not hold all" (as John Selden, more than a hundred years earlier, had described the chief cause for the birth of Parliament). These were indeed the terms in which the principle of representation was still discussed at Philadelphia; representation was meant to be a mere substitute for direct political action through the people themselves, and the representatives they elected were supposed to act according to instructions received by their electors, and not to transact business in accordance with their own opinions as they might be formed in the process. However, the founders, as distinguished from the elected representatives in colonial times, must have been the first to know how far removed this theory was from reality....

Corruption and perversion are more pernicious, and at the same time more likely to occur, in an egalitarian republic than in any other form of government. Schematically speaking, they come to pass when private interests invade the public domain, that is, they spring from below and not from above. It is precisely because the republic excluded on principle the old dichotomy of ruler and ruled that corruption of the body politic did not leave the people untouched, as in other forms of government, where only the rulers or the ruling classes needed to be affected, and where therefore an "innocent" people might indeed first suffer and then, one day, effect a dreadful but necessary insurrection. Corruption of the people themselves—as distinguished from corruption of their representatives or a ruling class—is possible only under a government that has granted them a share in public power and has taught them how to manipulate it. Where the rift between ruler and ruled has been closed, it is always possible that the dividing line between public and private may become blurred and, eventually, obliterated. Prior to the modern age and the rise of society, this danger, inherent in republican government, used to arise from the public realm, from the tendency of public power to expand and to trespass upon private interests. The age-old remedy against this danger was respect for private property, that is, the framing of a system of laws through which the rights of privacy were publicly guaranteed and the dividing line between public and private legally protected. The Bill of Rights in the American Constitution forms the last, and the most exhaustive, legal bulwark for the private realm against public power, and Jefferson's preoccupation with the dangers of public power and this remedy against them is sufficiently well known. However, under conditions, not of prosperity as such, but of a rapid and constant economic growth, that is, of a constantly increasing expansion of the private realm—and these were of course the conditions of the modern age—the dangers of corruption and perversion were much more likely to arise from private interests than from public power. And it speaks for the high caliber of Jefferson's statesmanship that he was able to perceive this danger despite his preoccupation with the older and better-known threats of corruption in bodies politic.

The only remedies against the misuse of public power by private individuals lie in the public realm itself, in the light which exhibits each deed enacted within its boundaries, in the very visibility to which it exposes all those who enter it. Jefferson, though the secret vote was still unknown at the time, had at least a foreboding of how dangerous it might be to allow the people a share in public power without providing them at the same time with more public space than the ballot box and with more opportunity to make their voices heard in public than election day. What he perceived to be the mortal danger to the republic was that the Constitution had given all power to the citizens, without giving them the opportunity of *being* republicans and of *acting* as citizens. In other words, the danger was that all power had been given to the people in their private capacity, and that there was no space established for them in their capacity of being citizens....

Hence, according to Jefferson, it was the very principle of republican government to demand "the subdivision of the counties into wards," namely, the creation of "small republics" through which "every man in the State" could become "an acting member of the Common government, transacting in person a great portion of its rights and duties, subordinate indeed, yet important, and entirely within his competence." It was "these little republics [that] would be the main strength of the great one"; for inasmuch as the republican government of the Union was based on the assumption that the seat of power was in the people, the very condition for its proper functioning lay in a scheme "to divide [government] among the many, distributing to every one exactly the functions he [was] competent to." Without this, the very principle of republican government could never be actualized, and the government of the United States would be republican in name only.

Nancy Rosenblum, Membership and Morals

140–145 (1998).

States permit area residents to fix local boundaries and incorporate at will (the criterion of "community of interest" is simply deduced from the petition to incorporate).... The multiplication of cities is the result of incorporation initiatives by residents or landowners brought for pragmatic, self-regarding, usually defensive, reasons. Local governments are "frequently created and defended ... to insulate one set of local people or interests from the regulatory authority and population of another local government." States enable municipalities to ward off annexation by other cities. They insure that they are free from any obligation to "take in" or consolidate poorer contiguous areas. Once created, municipalities are protected against reorganization aimed at political or economic justice, for reasons of diversity or distribution. There is no analogue to periodic electoral redistricting....

The impetus to exclusion is mainly but not solely fiscal. Zoning is intended to give people a degree of control over "the look of the place" and who their neighbors will be.... "One need only attend a few public hearings on controversial zoning changes in suburban areas to realize that the people consider their right to pass judgment on their future neighbors as sacred." The desire to "maintain the status quo within the community" defined in terms of "life style" or "character" receives judicial support....

The extent to which cities are able to exploit their legal autonomy is another matter. "The republican tradition taught that to be free is to share in governing a political community that controls its own fate," Michael Sandel reminds us. So local autonomy depends not on its formal authority but on its actual revenues and fiscal strains. Fiscal autonomy gives reality to localism, as it does to federalism (and to freedom of association)....

So economic development takes precedence over distribution, and cities are reluctant to become attractive places for poor people to live. The realistic fear is a "race to the bottom." Paul Peterson describes a liberal Massachusetts town that offered "apartments for poor families, group homes for recovering drug and alcohol abusers, halfway homes, counseling centers, and other programs for the poor." The growing number of clients provoked complaints from town leaders and taxpayers: "We can't afford this anymore." No wonder Herbert Gans advises that if they are to avoid irreconcilable conflict, municipalities can tolerate only moderate heterogeneity: "since local institutions, including government, have little power to affect—and to ameliorate—the basic causes of such conflict, they [are] unable to handle it constructively."

These themes come together in the New Jersey supreme court decisions collected under the title *Mount Laurel*, the principal challenge to the exercise of zoning authority solely for the welfare of a particular community. The town of Mount Laurel was not antigrowth; its zoning scheme was explicitly devised to oppose development that would detract from its average wealth. In 1975, a unanimous New Jersey court reasoned that since zoning is a delegation of state police power, any scheme having an impact beyond the borders of the local community must promote the general welfare of the "affected region" rather than impair it. Significantly, the court did not resort to defining the interests of nonresidents as basic liberties. Nor did it say that local zoning authority and the desire to exclude residents were illegitimate. Only that this desire had to be balanced against the "countervailing interests" of nonresidents. In this case, the failure to make "realistically possible a variety and choice of housing" sufficed to violate state constitutional due process and equal protection.

Mount Laurel and other communities would have to do their "fair share" to meet the region's low- and moderate-income housing needs. The ruling required cities to develop "affirmative housing strategies based on private sources of housing production and subsidies." The prescriptions set by the court, and modified by the New Jersey legislature's subsequent Fair Housing Act of 1986, were modest, though, and the effects have been attenuated. The decision has not served as a precedent. There has been little change in judicial deference to localities, even in states that have taken a regional view. As the California supreme court put it, "suburban residents ... may assert a vital interest in limiting immigration to their community." After over a dozen years of litigation, Mount Laurel's mayor continues to insist, "We'd just like to see our town develop in a nice way. We should have the right to run our town." This remains the prevailing view....

James Madison, The Federalist #10

Among the numerous advantages promised by a well-constructed Union, none deserves to be more accurately developed than its tendency to break and control the violence of faction....

By a faction I understand a number of citizens, whether amounting to a majority or minority of the whole, who are united and actuated by some common impulse of passion, or of interest, adverse to the rights of other citizens, or to the permanent and aggregate interests of the community.

There are two methods of curing the mischiefs of faction: the one, by removing its causes; the other, by controlling its effects.

There are again two methods of removing the causes of faction: the one, by destroying the liberty which is essential to its existence; the other, by giving to every citizen the same opinions, the same passions, and the same interests.

It could never be more truly said than of the first remedy that it was worse than the disease. Liberty is to faction what air is to fire, an ailment without which it instantly expires. But it could not be less folly to abolish liberty, which is essential to political life, because it nourishes faction, than it would be to wish the annihilation of air, which is essential to animal life, because it imparts to fire its destructive agency.

The second expedient is as impracticable as the first would be unwise. As long as the reason of man continues fallible, and he is at liberty to exercise it, different opinions will be formed. As long as the connection subsists between his reason and his self-love, his opinions and his passions will have a reciprocal influence on each other; and the former will be objects to which the latter will attach themselves. The diversity in the faculties of men, from which the rights of property originate, is not less an insuperable obstacle to a uniformity of interests. The protection of these faculties is the first object of government. From the protection of different and unequal faculties of acquiring property, the possession of different degrees and kinds of property immediately results; and from the influence of these on the sentiments and views of the respective proprietors ensues a division of the society into different interests and parties. . . .

The two great points of difference between a democracy and a republic are: first, the delegation of the government, in the latter, to a small number of citizens elected by the rest; secondly, the greater number of citizens, and greater sphere of country, over which the latter may be extended.

The effect of the first difference is, on the one hand, to refine and enlarge the public views by passing them through the medium of a chosen body of citizens, whose wisdom may best discern the true interest of their country and whose patriotism and love of justice will be least likely to sacrifice it to temporary or partial considerations. Under such a regulation it may well happen that the public voice, pronounced by the representatives of the people, will be more consonant to the public good than if pronounced by the people themselves, convened for the purpose. On the other hand, the effect may be inverted. Men of factious tempers, of local prejudices, or of sinister designs, may, by intrigue, by corruption, or by other means, first obtain the suffrages, and then betray the interests of the people. The question resulting is, whether small or extensive republics are most favorable to the election of proper guardians of the public weal; and it is clearly decided in favor of the latter by two obvious considerations.

In the first place it is to be remarked that however small the republic may be the representatives must be raised to a certain number in order to guard against the cabals of a few; and that however large it may be they must be limited to a certain number in order to guard against the confusion of a multitude. Hence, the number of representatives in the two cases not being in proportion to that of the constituents, and being proportionally greatest in the small republic, it follows that if the proportion of fit characters be not less in the large than in the small republic, the former will present a greater option, and consequently a greater probability of a fit choice.

In the next place, as each representative will be chosen by a greater number of citizens in the large than in the small republic, it will be more difficult for unworthy candidates to practise with success the vicious arts by which elections are too often carried; and the suffrages of the people being more free, will be more likely to center on men who possess the most attractive merit and the most diffusive and established characters.

It must be confessed that in this, as in most other cases, there is a mean, on both sides of which inconveniences will be found to lie. By enlarging too much the number of electors, you render the representative too little acquainted with all their local circumstances and lesser interests; as by reducing it too much, you render him unduly attached to these, and too little fit to comprehend and pursue great and national objects. The federal Constitution forms a happy combination in this respect; the great and aggregate interests being referred to the national, the local and particular to the State legislatures.

The other point of difference is the greater number of citizens and extent of territory which may be brought within the compass of republican than of democratic government; and it is this circumstance principally which renders factious combinations less to be dreaded in the former than in the latter. The smaller the society, the fewer probably will be the distinct parties and interests composing it; the fewer the distinct parties and interests, the more frequently will a majority be found of the same party; and the smaller the number of individuals composing a majority, and the smaller the compass within which they are placed, the more easily will they concert and execute their plans of oppression. Extend the sphere and you take in a greater variety of parties and interests; you make it less probable that a majority of the whole will have a common motive to invade the rights of other citizens; or if such a common motive exists, it will be more difficult for all who feel it to discover their own strength and to act in unison with each other. Besides other impediments, it may be remarked that, where there is a consciousness of unjust or dishonorable purposes, communication is always checked by distrust in proportion to the number whose concurrence is necessary.

NOTES

1. *The Scope of Governmental Competence.* Why should the activities that Mill assigns to local government—he speaks of street lighting, paving, and cleaning—be provided by government at all? Why not assume that neighbors who prefer these services will join together to provide them for themselves? Alternatively, why not assume that private markets will provide the service?

2. Even among those services that government provides, Mill limits the scope of local activities to those that involve "purely local duties," or "business purely local." What are the characteristics of activities properly placed in these categories? How do they differ from an activity, such as the administration of justice, that Mill excludes from local jurisdiction? Certainly one of Mill's concerns is that unconstrained local governments will ignore the external effects that their activities generate. Note that those effects are not limited to the provision of services that may impose tangible costs on neighbors. They also involve principles that a locality may have and that place it at odds with the larger society. Thus, just as it "would not be a matter personally indifferent to the rest of the country if any part of it became a nest of robbers," it might not be a matter of indifference to the rest of the country if any part of it permitted discrimination on the basis of certain characteristics or became a nest of poverty.

Mill's reluctance to grant much decisionmaking authority to localities seems to reflect Madison's distrust of local bodies. But the source of the distrust appears (at least on the face of it) to be quite different. Madison is explicitly concerned with the appearance of factions that may dominate public decisionmaking and that, he asserts, are most likely to arise unopposed where government is decentralized. Is this Mill's concern as well?

When Mill speaks of the "lower grade of intelligence and knowledge" of local officials and of the "lower capacities" of the local population to monitor local affairs and officials, does he mean that these citizens (or their local officials) are ignorant? Or is he concerned that they will act in a manner contrary to the interests of the society at large? If the latter, what is the basis for such concern?

How can you make sense of Mill's objection that local officials are watched by "an inferior public opinion"? After all, don't the same people who watch local officials ultimately monitor national officials as well? If so, then what does Mill believe that this public brings to the consideration of national policies that is not brought to bear on local policies?

3. Mill seems primarily concerned with the capacity of local governments to provide goods and services to their constituents. That is certainly not Arendt's objective for local government. She seems to believe that localities can serve as a primary focal point for public involvement in politics and thus laments the absence of a role for local government in our constitutional structure. Representative government, on this view, denies individuals an opportunity to participate in public life and relegates them to the role of the represented. What role does private property play, for Arendt, in this separation between the great mass of society and the public realm?

Does Mill share any of this concern for the ability of residents to become involved in public life? What do you make of the penultimate sentence of the excerpt from Mill? Why would he think it permissible for localities to "mismanage" their own interests, as long as others are not penalized? If the central government is truly more competent, why should that level of government not also dictate policy with respect to purely local affairs?

4. Arendt appears to favor the political possibilities of small communities. Political participation, which forms the foundation of robust citizenship, is available only at that level of government. But Rosenblum highlights what might be seen as the downside of community. Rosenblum suggests that political activity of the type that Arendt favors may be directed at creating an idiosyncratic conception of community that insulates members from their neighbors or at capturing local benefits at the expense of those neighbors. If political participation at the local level were as robust as Arendt desires, are there reasons to believe that it would actually *reduce* the chances that localities would be as isolationist as Rosenblum fears? Arendt, after all, appears to see participation as a bulwark against the self-interest. If Rosenblum, who reflects Mill's concern that assigning tasks to local governments will have adverse extraterritorial consequences, is correct, what does that tell us about the relationship between relatively centralized and relatively decentralized governments?

5. The emphasis on participation and the pursuit of a communal identity that is discussed in the excerpts from Arendt and Rosenblum is representative of a school of thought best referred to as "communitarianism." Although it would be a mistake to group all communitarians under the same philosophical umbrella (distinctions among them are drawn in Stephen A. Gardbaum, Law, Politics, and the Claims of Community, 90 Mich. L. Rev. 685 (1992), with a rebuttal in Daniel R. Ortiz, Saving the Self?, 91 Mich. L. Rev. 1018 (1993)), as a general matter communitarians reject the individualization of decisionmaking that is commonly identified with liberalism. On this view, a liberal community embraces a decisionmaking process in which individuals vote their personal preferences and are motivated solely by self-interest in the formation of those preferences. Communitarian decisionmaking differs in that individuals identify with the common objectives of the community and are concerned with the interests of all members of the community in formulating those objectives. In the words of one communitarian theorist,

> [T]o say that the members of a society are bound by a sense of community is not simply to say that a great many of them profess communitarian sentiments and pursue communitarian aims, but rather that they conceive their identity—the subject and not just the object of their feelings and aspirations—as defined to some extent by the community of which they are a part. For them, community describes not just what they *have* as fellow citizens but also what they *are*, not a relationship they choose (as in a voluntary association) but an attachment they discover, not merely an attribute but a constituent of their identity.

Michael Sandel, Liberalism and the Limits of Justice 150 (1982).

Important in the communitarian critique is the understanding that individuals cannot be as autonomous as liberal theory suggests. According to this critique, liberalism based on the individual simply attempts to aggregate preferences and fails to comprehend the ways in which those preferences can be shaped or changed by membership in a group. See, e.g., Michael Walzer, The Communitarian Critique of Liberalism, 18 Pol. Theory 6, 15–16 (1989).

Some critics of communitarianism see the possibility of conformity and communal definition of the good life as a threat rather than a strength. In the communitarian ideal, conformity results from accommodation among competing interests rather than from the reluctance of some to dissent from a majority view. To these critics, community can be a source of repression rather than of a more benign "conflict avoidance." In the words of one skeptic,

> [I]f Sandel is arguing that when members of a society have settled roots and established traditions, they will tolerate the speech, religion, sexual, and associations preferences of minorities, then history simply does not support his optimism. A great deal of intolerance has come from societies of selves so "confidently situated" that they were sure repression would serve a higher cause. The common good of the Puritans of seventeenth-century Salem commanded them to hunt witches; the common good of the Moral Majority of the twentieth century commands them not to tolerate homosexuals. The enforcement of liberal rights, not the absence of settled community, stands between the Moral Majority and the contemporary equivalent of witch hunting.

Amy Gutmann, Communitarian Critics of Liberalism, 14 Phil. & Pub. Aff. 308, 319 (1985). In the legal literature, a similar theme is found in Richard Briffault, Our Localism, Parts I & II, 90 Colum. L. Rev. 1, 346 (1990), which suggests that localities, and suburbs in particular, act in a parochial manner that disserves the interests of nonresidents.

6. Madison's fear of small republics (by which he seemed to mean states, but the point applies with even greater force at the local level) lies in the ability of a faction that has an intense interest in the outcome of a specific decision to achieve its objective while ignoring the interests of opponents, who may (because they are less interested in the outcome) be less well organized or less able to make their voices heard. Typically, the ability of one group to dominate a political decision gives rise to concern about majority tyranny, i.e., the ability of the majority to implement its will, notwithstanding negative consequences for the minority. Is Madison also concerned about a faction that constitutes a "minority of the whole." How could minority tyranny arise? Why won't the majority simply outvote minority interests? Consider the questions in light of the essay on "Local Government as Provider" below at pages 31–46.

B. THE PERSPECTIVE FROM ECONOMICS—AND A RESPONSE

Charles Tiebout, A Pure Theory of Local Expenditures

64 J. Pol. Econ. 416 (1956).

Musgrave and Samuelson implicitly assume that expenditures are handled at the central government level. However, the provision of such governmental services as police and fire protection, education, hospitals, and courts does not necessarily involve federal activity. Many of these goods are provided by local governments. It is worthwhile to look briefly at the magnitude of these expenditures.

Historically, local expenditures have exceeded those of the federal government. The thirties were the first peacetime years in which federal expenditures began to pull away from local expenditures. Even during the fiscal year 1954, federal expenditures on goods and services exclusive of defense amounted only to some 15 billions of dollars, while local expenditures during this same period amounted to some 17 billions of dollars. There is no need to quibble over which comparisons are relevant. The important point is that the often-neglected local expenditures are significant and, when viewed in terms of expenditures on goods and services only, take on even more significance. Hence an important question arises whether at this level of government any mechanism operates to insure that expenditures on these public goods approximate the proper level.

Consider for a moment the case of the city resident about to move to the suburbs. What variables will influence his choice of a municipality? If he has children, a high level of expenditures on schools may be important. Another person may prefer a community with a municipal golf course. The availability and quality of such facilities and services as beaches, parks, police protection, roads, and parking facilities will enter into the decisionmaking process. Of course, non-economic variables will also be considered, but this is of no concern at this point.

The consumer-voter may be viewed as picking that community which best satisfies his preference pattern for public goods. This is a major difference between central and local provision of public goods. At the central level the preferences of the consumer-voter are given, and the government tries to adjust to the pattern of these preferences, whereas at the local level various governments have their revenue and expenditure patterns more or less set. Given these revenue and expenditure patterns, the consumer-voter moves to that community whose local government best satisfies his set of preferences. The greater the number of communities and the greater the variance among them, the closer the consumer will come to fully realizing his preference position.

A Local Government Model

The implications of the preceding argument may be shown by postulating an extreme model. Here the following assumptions are made:

1. Consumer-voters are fully mobile and will move to that community where their preference patterns, which are set, are best satisfied.

2. Consumer-voters are assumed to have full knowledge of differences among revenue and expenditure patterns and to react to these differences.

3. There are a large number of communities in which the consumer-voters may choose to live.

4. Restrictions due to employment opportunities are not considered. It may be assumed that all persons are living on dividend income.

5. The public services supplied exhibit no external economies or diseconomies between communities.

Assumptions 6 and 7 to follow are less familiar and require brief explanations:

6. For every pattern of community services set by, say, a city manager who follows the preferences of the older residents of the community, there is an optimal community size. This optimum is defined in terms of the number of residents for which this bundle of services can be produced at the lowest average cost. This, of course, is closely analogous to the low point of a firm's average cost curve. Such a cost function implies that some factor or resource is fixed. If this were not so, there would be no logical reason to limit community size, given the preference patterns. In the same sense that the average cost curve has a minimum for one firm but can be reproduced by another there is seemingly no reason why a duplicate community cannot exist. The assumption that some factor is fixed explains why it is not possible for the community in question to double its size by growth. The factor may be the limited land area of a suburban community, combined with a set of zoning laws against apartment buildings. It may be the local beach, whose capacity is limited. Anything of this nature will provide a restraint.

In order to see how this restraint works, let us consider the beach problem. Suppose the preference patterns of the community are such that the optimum size population is 13,000. Within this set of preferences there is a certain demand per family for beach space. This demand is such that at 13,000 population a 500–yard beach is required. If the actual length of the beach is, say, 600 yards, then it is not possible to realize this preference pattern with twice the optimum population, since there would be too little beach space by 400 yards.

The assumption of a fixed factor is necessary, as will be shown later, in order to get a determinate number of communities. It also has the advantage of introducing a realistic restraint into the model.

7. The last assumption is that communities below the optimum size seek to attract new residents to lower average costs. Those above optimum size do just the opposite. Those at an optimum try to keep their populations constant.

This assumption needs to be amplified. Clearly, communities below the optimum size, through chambers of commerce or other agencies, seek to attract new residents. This is best exemplified by the housing developments in some suburban areas, such as Park Forest in the Chicago area and Levittown in the New York area, which need to reach an optimum size. The same is true of communities that try to attract manufacturing industries by setting up certain facilities and getting an optimum number of firms to move into the industrially zoned area.

The case of the city that is too large and tries to get rid of residents is more difficult to imagine. No alderman in his right political mind would ever admit that the city is too big. Nevertheless, economic forces are at work to push people out of it. Every resident who moves to the suburbs to find better schools, more parks, and so forth, is reacting, in part, against the pattern the city has to offer.

The case of the community which is at the optimum size and tries to remain so is not hard to visualize. Again proper zoning laws, implicit agreements among realtors, and the like are sufficient to keep the population stable.

Except when this system is in equilibrium, there will be a subset of consumer-voters who are discontented with the patterns of their community. Another set will be satisfied. Given the assumption about mobility and the other assumptions listed previously, movement will take place out of the communities of greater than optimal size into the communities of less than optimal size. The consumer-voter moves to the community that satisfies his preference pattern.

The act of moving or failing to move is crucial. Moving or failing to move replaces the usual market test of willingness to buy a good and reveals the consumer-voter's demand for public goods. Thus each locality has a revenue and expenditure pattern that reflects the desires of its residents.

John R. Logan & Harvey L. Molotch, Urban Fortunes

41–42, 103–111 (1987).

[Logan and Molotch contend that urban areas serve both "exchange values" and "use values." The former reflects the value that urban land commands in the marketplace. The latter involves the use to which the current occupier of the land puts it. These values may be in tension in a variety of ways. Most importantly for Logan and Molotch, exchange values may fail to recognize use values that have no market price or may fail to reflect features that cause the market itself to operate inefficiently.—EDS.]

Tiebout likened towns and cities to products—packages of benefits and costs from which consumers make their choices. Each town establishes its own standards for taxes and its level and mix of services. Members of the public, as residential buyers, then choose the package that most suits their preferences....

Our critique should by now be predictable. The free, autonomous action assumed by market theories fails to acknowledge people's bonds to place, entrepreneurs' collusion, and the regulatory function—all inherent in real estate markets. To think of whole towns and cities as "products" and residents as "shoppers" truly strains the market metaphor.... Public choice theorists like Tiebout do not recognize the internal cleavages within cities or the competing designs of outsiders on the management of cities. They think of local policies as mere summations of citizen-residents' preferences—particularly of potential residents who might be attracted through the right service mix. But we find it easy enough to demonstrate that such land-use democracy is the exception rather than the rule in determining how local governments operate; the politics of place is about *whose* interests government will serve....

* * *

TYPES OF USE VALUES

Each neighborhood has its own individual mix of use values, forged through the historic development of its physical structure, ethnic and class relations, and connections to outside institutions. We discern six categories of use values—six factors that make up the basis of neighborhood.

The Daily Round

The place of residence is a focal point for the wider routine in which one's concrete daily needs are satisfied. Neighborhoods provide a place for shopping (particularly for food and other essentials), schooling, child care, and routine health needs. For some, the locality is also a place of work. For others, it is a point of departure to a work place, affording access to appropriate means of transportation. Defining a daily round is gradually accomplished as residents learn about needed facilities, their exact locations and offerings, and how taking advantage of one can be efficiently integrated into a routine that includes taking advantage of others. Routes and timings have to be carefully worked out to achieve maximum benefits. The development of an effective array of goods and services within reach of residence is a fragile accomplishment; its disruption, either by the loss of one of the elements or by the loss of the residential starting place, can exact a severe penalty.

Informal Support Networks

Place of residence is the potential source of an informal network of people who provide life-sustaining products and services. Examples range from friends and neighbors who baby-sit, do yard work, or shovel snow to friends, neighbors, and acquaintances who offer aid that can alter a way of life, such as referrals for an available job, a political connection to solve a problem, a welfare benefit, or lucrative criminal contact. Sometimes gains are achieved through an informal marketplace among proximate beneficiaries, in which money may change hands but more commonly operates according to a barter system. Reciprocity rules the loaning of cups of sugar or the minding of children. These, too, are hard-won gains; and along with other attributes of neighborhood, they form "the bonds people build with one another that enable them to rely on one another".

Especially for the poor, this income "in kind" represents a crucial resource and it is made possible only by a viable community. In order to situate themselves to capture such advantages, working-class people tend to live near their relatives and to draw their friends from a proximate group of neighbors. Though they have fewer friends than people in other classes, they seem to depend upon their network more than do people in affluent areas. Since the community of poor people is less spatially "liberated" than that of the well-to-do, poor people's use values are particularly damaged when their neighborhood is disrupted....

Security and Trust

A neighborhood also provides a sense of physical and psychic security that comes with a familiar and dependable environment. There are "eyes on the street" from friendly onlookers and a variety of "social landmarks" individuals and institutions accepted as dependable, predictable actors with known reputations. Gerald Suttles, in his effort to construct a general theory of urban life, or at least "the" social structure of the slum, portrays neighborhoods as bastions "defended" against the perceived dangers of interlopers drifting in from adjacent areas. Signs of commonality (skin color, diction, gait in walking) serve as a *prima facie,* if imperfect, basis for categorizing others as either members or nonmembers of the neighborhood circle of mutual trust.... Reassured by shared symbols, common cultures, kinship ties, and personal reputations, residents experience a sense of relative security, a sense they sorely need in the larger contexts of physical danger and, we would emphatically add to Suttles's picture, threats from the exchange system that surrounds them. Neighborhood can provide the benefit of *membership* in a social space that is viewed as orderly, predictable and protective.

Although not as dependent on the local security net as the poor, the well-to-do also have a round of routines that cannot be reproduced overnight. Again, the affluent may less often depend upon neighborhood networks to get jobs, but face-to-face interaction still has its uses. Even in the highest circles, proximity matters; that's why we find that memberships on corporate boards of directors so frequently overlap within regions, rather than across them....

For women with families, regardless of social status, neighborhood use values have special significance. Women must construct a path to appropriate schools, lessons, a job, shops, and friends. They must be "in so many places at a time." Involved are hours of daily work and a great deal of automobile driving or time on the bus. Working women's double burden of managing family life and employment makes the neighborhood resource base that much more critical. Some women are involved in the largely "invisible work" of volunteer activities, which, while providing free resources to their community, build on women's knowledge of the unmet needs in the nearby life space....

Identity

A neighborhood provides its residents with an important source of identity, both for themselves and for others. Neighborhoods offer a resident not only spatial demarcations but social demarcations as well. In the United States, people use place names to identify the general social standing of themselves and others. To do this people must have a sense of neighborhood boundaries and the connotations of names of other areas. Hunter reports that between 80 and 90 percent of his Chicago respondents were able to define clear boundaries for their place-named communities and, more important here, tended to manipulate these names and boundaries to increase or protect their own status.... As Hunter and Suttles note, "Residential identities ..., are imbedded in a contrastive structure in which each neighborhood is known primarily as a counterpart to some of the others."

This contrastive structure also means that community resources are desired not just to secure better material conditions, like nice parks, but to display success compared to other neighborhoods seeking the same resources. That is one reason why it is impossible for city governments to satisfy neighborhood claims; since public facilities are needed for competitive advantage over other areas, the needs are infinite and insatiable. Resources are needed not only to sustain a daily round but also to sustain a daily identity....

Agglomeration Benefits

A shared interest in overlapping use values (identity, security, and so on) in a single area is a useful way to define neighborhood. A neighborhood is far more than a mere collection of houses; rather, it is a shared experience of an agglomeration of complementary benefits.

The concentration of a large number of similar people stimulates the development of agglomerations especially appropriate to their needs. For example, the presence of many Mexican–Americans in one place provides the necessary base for a bodega, which then attracts still more Mexican–American residents, who then provide the still larger base needed to support a Spanish-language movie theater. These institutions become symbols of belonging and control, enhancing the feeling of turf security, which reinforces the base on which the ethnic businesses depend. Potentially at least, a successful indigenous business class can then play a supporting role in defending the neighborhood against external threats. Local business and social life become intertwined in a single support system. . . .

Ethnicity

Not infrequently, these benefits are encapsulated in a shared ethnicity. Everybody you need is a member of your ethnic group. When this occurs, ethnicity serves as a summary characterization of all the overlapping benefits of neighborhood life. Ethnicity works for these purposes because it does often accurately represent a shared life style, similar needs in the daily round, and the social boundaries for providing service and gaining interpersonal support. Ethnicity works because of its simple practicality; it neatly demarcates large numbers of people with a single term and, with greater or lesser degrees of accuracy, categorizes them on the basis of only a few gross indicators (such as skin color or diction). . . .

The Exchange Value Threats to Neighborhood

Threats to neighborhood, forces with the potential for overturning the local systems of material and psychic accomplishment, vary according to time and place. . . . For us, the major challenge to neighborhood, as a demographic-physical construct as well as a viable social network, comes from organizations and institutions (firms and bureaucracies) whose routine functioning reorganizes urban space. The stranger to fear may not be the man of different ethnicity on the street corner, but a bank president or property management executive of irrelevant ethnicity far from view. In their large-scale study of national sample of neighborhoods, Schill and Nathan found that a large proportion of movers (22%) were, in effect, forced out by rent increases, property renovation or conversion, or the landlord's sale of property. . . .

Sometimes, of course, these changes can represent a use value gain; despite initial hardships from adjustment to even forced moves, many people end up with housing they judge to be at least as good as what they started with. And some commercial manipulations contribute to use values; residents may come to value their new grocery store on the corner or the new factory down the road. Nevertheless, residents ordinarily have little control over such changes and this contributes to the general anxiety resulting from the fact that market mechanisms, as currently structured, may well serve to undermine neighborhood.

NOTES

1. Tiebout's article is a staple of local government analysis. Essentially, he claims that, under some very heroic assumptions, individuals will gravitate to localities that offer preferred goods and services at a tax price that individuals are willing to pay. Localities, in return, will "compete" for residents by offering preferred goods and services until each locality reaches its optimal size. Those residents who are unhappy with a locality's decision about what package of goods, services, and taxes to provide will "costlessly" move. The result is that the market for residence is "efficient" in that those who live in any given jurisdiction are presumed to receive the goods and services that they desire and at a price they are willing to pay.

There is a significant literature that purports to test Tiebout's theory. For summaries and argument about their implications, see William A. Fischel, The Homevoter Hypothesis 39–97 (2001). Consider the following evaluation of the literature:

> Those studies provide substantial proof that local jurisdictions do compete for residents.
>
> That is not to say that the evidence "proves" Tiebout's theory that competition among jurisdictions will force local governments to be efficient providers of public goods, however; the validity of Tiebout's positive theory remains quite controversial. First, the theory is criticized as based upon unrealistic assumptions: Tiebout assumed that all consumer-voters are fully knowledgeable about differences in the revenue and expenditure patterns of the available towns; that they are fully and costlessly mobile; and that they live on dividend income, and therefore may choose among communities solely on the basis of fiscal factors, without regard to employment opportunities. He further assumed that there are a large number of communities in which the consumer-voters can choose to live, that each community provides a given level of services, and that those services impose no externalities upon other communities. Finally, Tiebout assumed that for every package of community services, there is an optimal community size at which those services can be produced at the lowest average cost per resident. Communities below their optimum size would seek to attract new residents in order to lower the average cost of their services, while those at or above the optimum size would seek to limit growth.
>
> Second, some scholars have argued that, unlike Tiebout's model, a realistic "vote with your feet" market will not result in an equilibrium, or that any equilibrium reached will be inefficient or unstable. Others argue that the possibility that government officials may act in a self-regarding, rather than public-regarding, manner will mean that competition alone will not ensure an efficient distribution of public services. Tiebout's model also has been criticized as being grossly incomplete because consumer mobility is only one means by which consumers can seek to satisfy their demands for public services. Rather than moving to another community, consumers can use the political process to achieve a change in the level of services a community offers, or in the level of taxes it charges. Alternatively, residents can purchase additional or different services on the private market—for example, by sending their children to private schools.
>
> Despite those criticisms of Tiebout's hypothesis, Tiebout's core observation—that local jurisdictions compete for residents—enjoys wide acceptance. Evaluating the accuracy of that core proposition requires analysis of several questions. First, we must examine whether consumers have a sufficient variety of communities from which to choose to live. Second, we must analyze whether consumers choose among communities, at least in part, on the basis of such factors as the quantity and quality of public services offered and the taxes charged. If consumers choose among communities solely on the basis of

> nonfiscal factors such as accessibility to the workplace, proximity to family and friends, or the racial or other characteristics of the communities' residents, municipalities will be severely limited in their abilities to attempt to attract residents, and the "marketplace" will be competitive only in the sense that natural resources or historical factors will make some communities more attractive than others. Finally, we must examine the extent to which frictions in the market limit its competitiveness.

Vicki Been, "Exit" as a Constraint on Land Use Exactions: Rethinking the Unconstitutional Conditions Doctrine, 91 Colum. L. Rev. 473, 514–518 (1991).

2. The Tiebout model has implications for the process of drawing municipal boundaries, which we will examine in Chapter 2. A major theme in that discussion involves the inquiry into whether it is desirable to create numerous small localities that serve the preferences of residents, but that might generate substantial costs for nonresidents and frustrate efforts to achieve economies of scale or to address regional problems that transcend jurisdictional boundaries. The Tiebout model embodies a faith that numerous small localities will advance both the participatory and efficiency objectives of local government law:

> The remarkable claim made by Tiebout is that giving individuals a choice in this way serves not only to reassert individual autonomy but also to restore efficient individual autonomy, that is, the invisible hand. When faced with a choice of jurisdictions, each providing a different mix of public services, the people of a metropolitan area will sort themselves out on the basis of similar tastes for public goods. Given a wide enough range of choice, no individual need live in a jurisdiction where he obtains a set of services markedly different from what he prefers, and each jurisdiction can efficiently meet the tastes of its homogenous population.
>
> This view was in direct opposition to the traditional reform position with regard to metropolitan government. The traditional reform position was that too many governments operating in a single metropolitan area inhibited efficiency, accountability, and equity. The numerous small governments were thought to be too small to achieve economies of scale and too numerous to deal effectively with area-wide problems. Furthermore, fragmentation inhibited accountability because there were too many officials for even an alert, intelligent citizenry to keep track of. And finally, a tendency was observed for some governmental jurisdictions to have the lion's share of resources in a metropolitan area, while others were unable to meet basic service needs.

Gary J. Miller, Cities by Contract: The Politics of Municipal Incorporation 7 (1981).

3. Do Logan and Molotch properly characterize Tiebout? Do you think that Tiebout believed that cities worked in accordance with his assumptions? Or was Tiebout creating a model that would allow explanations of why we see the intralocal and interlocal disparities that exist? For instance, if "public choice theorists" believe that "tastes" or "preferences" could explain interlocal differences in a world characterized by Tiebout's assumptions, do they necessarily believe that the same factors explain those differences where Tiebout's assumptions did not hold?

4. Individuals within a city may identify themselves as members of a neighborhood as well as of the city as a whole. Communities, in fact, need not be defined by geographical boundaries at all. Individuals frequently consider themselves to be members of unions, religious groups, or social classes that transcend geography. As a result, even a local government may comprise many, potentially conflicting communities. The potential for intralocal conflict is, for instance, evident in movements to exclude chain stores from areas that local businesses have dominated and in commentaries, such as those by Logan and Molotch, that criticize the failure of markets to recognize the value of coherent neighborhoods and the subsequent diminution of communities that have a "use value" to current residents that may exceed their "exchange value" in the marketplace. Similar critiques suggest that landlords may gentrify areas because they can command high rents for new, relatively wealthy tenants, even though that means displacing long-term residents who share a socio-economic or ethnic affinity that cannot be easily replaced. See Communitarianism and Individualism (Shlomo Avineri & Avner de-Shalit, eds. 1992); William H. Simon, The Community Economic Development Movement (2001).

In order to promote some of the use values described by Logan and Molotch, a city might have to refrain from making changes or offering services that a majority of residents would otherwise prefer. For instance, through zoning or housing subsidies a municipality might preserve a stable socio-economic or ethnic neighborhood that would otherwise become more developed and have attracted new residents or tenants who could afford higher exchange values. Those higher exchange values, however, could translate into more economic growth and lower taxes for the municipality as a whole. How should the municipality evaluate the tradeoff between these different objectives?

5. The economic view of local governments tends to take people's preferences as given and suggests that local governments will attempt to satisfy their residents' preferences. The political view provides more of a role for local governments to shape the preferences of residents, largely by political debate, and to override the preferences of some, residents' preferences. What if people have "preferences" for living in socio-economically diverse communities or for the promotion of the kinds of use values that Logan and Molotch describe? Would the economic and noneconomic views of local government's function merge in such a municipality? Would we still have concerns about relatively immobile residents who wanted to satisfy the use value of their homes, but who lived in a locality in which a majority of residents did not share those preferences?

6. The excerpts from at least some of the authors you have read to this point suggest that residents of local governments will receive the goods and services in which they are most interested. Mill suggests that this will happen as long as governmental tasks are assigned to the proper level of government. Arendt implies that this could happen through the dynamics of the political process. Tiebout suggests that this can happen through the operation of the market for residence. Political markets and residential markets, therefore, appear to be substitutes for registering the interests and preferences of potential residents. Residents can indicate which characteristics they want their locality to possess either by voting and lobbying, what the economist Albert O. Hirschman referred as the exercise of "voice," or by exercising mobility, what Hirschman called "exit." See Albert O. Hirschman, Exit, Voice, and Loyalty: Responses to Decline in Firms, Organizations, and States (1970). Hirschman applies this observation largely to the private sphere. For instance, a consumer who dislikes a change in a product can either petition the manufacturer to undo the change ("voice"), or can select an alternative product in the marketplace ("exit").

But if political or residential markets are likely to provide potential residents with the goods and services that they prefer, then what function does law play in defining the functions of local government? Presumably, law is necessary when both political and residential markets are working poorly. Under those circumstances, we could not assume that the locality is providing what residents or prospective residents might desire, but the kinds of political activity or immigration and emigration that such failure should generate fails to occur. That observation, however, poses a difficulty that lies at the core of this course. Markets, both political and residential, will always suffer some failures. For instance, Madison suggests that factions may distort the political market, while Logan and Molotch imply that markets for residence may fail because residents who object to the primacy of exchange value over use value have neither political power nor the resources necessary for mobility. How much market failure is necessary, however, before it is appropriate for law to intervene? As you read the following materials, think about the likelihood that legal intervention will suffer from its own failures.

LOCAL GOVERNMENT AS PROVIDER—AN INTRODUCTION TO THE PROBLEM OF COLLECTIVE ACTION

Implicit in the work of some of the authors quoted above (most notably Mill's) is the belief that local government should provide certain goods and services to its constituents. But how do local officials determine what their constituents want? In the private market, providers of goods and services typically determine demand through the pricing mechanism. Local governments provide some goods and services in that manner, such as when they charge user fees for city parks or water. But governments provide lots of services without demanding specific payments. Rather, funding for those services, such as public education or construction of a town hall, is financed through taxes that are not explicitly linked to provision of the particular good or service. Government officials typically attempt to gauge demand by offering a package of goods and services. Constituents then use the voting mechanism to select the officials who promise the package of goods and services that the voters most prefer.

These different forms of determining demand and paying for the services that users of those services prefer suggests that markets and governments have different advantages in providing different types of goods and services. While it is possible to overemphasize the distinction, it makes sense to try to understand the conditions under which governmental, rather than market, provision is necessary or useful. Once we understand that distinction, it is possible to determine when *local* government is the proper governmental provider.

Consider first what lies behind the assumption that the market, rather than the government is, in capitalist societies, the presumptive supplier of goods and services. In the highly stylized, ideal marketplace that gives rise to this assumption, rational, self-interested individuals signal their preference for scarce resources by indicating a willingness to pay for them. Potential producers respond to these signals by entering the market to supply the desired commodities. Competitive forces within this ideal market push prices to the point where they equal the cost of production of the last unit produced (marginal cost pricing). At the same time, scarcity creates opportunities for producers to increase prices so that those who value the good most highly can outbid others. The winners in this auction, in turn, are expected to use these resources to produce additional goods and services valued by others and to capture that value in the prices they charge for the goods and services. Indeed, it is the ability of the original purchasers to use resources productively and capture their value on resale that induces the initial bids.

If markets worked perfectly, government would not have to play any "allocative" role, that is, government would not become involved in decisions about which goods were produced. (Government would still have to play a "distributive" role; for instance, government would have to decide whether to assist those who were worst off after market transactions led to an initial distribution of goods.) This idealized perfect market would allow individuals who had equal opportunities to express and bid on their preferences to enter freely into transactions, and those transactions would have no adverse consequences for parties who did not themselves have the chance to transact for redress; those with the potential to create social benefits would be willing to do so, even if their conduct created spillover effects that could not be fully captured through pricing mechanisms.

Unfortunately, the world is not so lovely. Markets fail to achieve an ideal allocation for a variety of reasons. Some have to do with initial distributions of wealth that prevent individuals to whom goods are valuable from making bids that reflect those values. Local governments may be able to contribute relatively little to the solution of that problem because residents who do not wish to participate in redistributive efforts can easily emigrate to other jurisdictions. But other sources of market failure may be more susceptible to remedy at the local level. These failures involve actors who have the capacity to enter markets (that is, they do not suffer from poverty or discrimination), but who refrain from market transactions either because they can obtain the benefits of those transactions without incurring the cost of entry (that is, they can obtain a benefit without making any contribution towards its creation as long as someone else is willing to produce the benefit, an effect known as the "free rider" problem) or because they cannot be confident that they will receive benefits in excess of the costs of entry. Alternatively, these individuals may enter particular transactions that have adverse effects on others (known as the "externalities" problem). In any of these cases, market transactions are skewed from what is socially optimal. In the first case, less of a good will be produced than is socially desirable. In the second case, more will be produced than is socially desirable. The failures most relevant to local government involve public goods, externalities, or informational disabilities.

Public Goods

Goods and services that fall within the classification of "public goods" may be undersupplied because self-interested individuals are unwilling to express their true preferences for them in the market. A review of the characteristics of "public-ness" will reveal why this is the case. Public goods tend to be *nonrival*, so that consumption of a unit by one individual does not preclude another from enjoying the same unit. (This phenomenon is also referred to as *"jointness of supply."*) It may be possible to exclude the second user, but there is little social reason to do so since that use does not interfere with the enjoyment of the initial user. (The initial user may suffer from envy or spite generated by a desire to have exclusive access to the good. But if the second user can make productive use of the good that does not interfere with the initial user's productive use, the selfish desire should not be credited.) In their classic work on the subject, Richard and Peggy Musgrave characterize as nonrival such goods as uncrowded bridges, for which tolls are feasible but counterproductive (in that they exclude users who could benefit from the bridge at no additional cost), and radio broadcasts (that could be limited to listeners with certain decoding equipment, but each of whom could be accommodated at zero marginal cost once the broadcast facility was created).[1]

Of course, even though marginal cost (the cost of accommodating an additional user) to any given user is zero, the cost of initially supplying nonrival goods may be significant. Someone must pay for erecting the bridge or broadcast facilities. In market transactions, that selection process is typically made by charging potential users a share of the original, capital cost of the product, thereby ensuring that the purchasers are those whose use of the resource creates more value than its cost. But where marginal cost is zero, standard marginal cost pricing cannot signal producers about the usefulness of these goods or the amount that should be produced. Hence, some alternative to the market is necessary.

These effects of nonrival consumption are exacerbated where the benefit of the good or service is *nonexcludable*, that is, where potential users cannot feasibly be excluded from enjoying the good, even though they

1. See Richard A. Musgrave & Peggy B. Musgrave, Public Finance in Theory and Practice 56 (3d ed. 1980).

have contributed nothing to its production. Think of controlling mosquitoes, or avoiding depletion of the ozone layer. Any action you take towards these ends will benefit me, regardless of my failure to support your efforts. Here, the assumption that actors are self-interested is crucial. An individual motivated by self-interest will take a particular action only when the personal benefits of that action exceed its personal costs. Adam Smith's invisible hand notwithstanding, where goods are nonrival and nonexcludable that calculation may lead individuals to act in a manner inconsistent with social interest.

To see why the joint effects of nonrivalness and nonexcludability may lead to socially undesirable results, assume that an entrepreneur believes that the residents of a locality would like to have piano concertos piped through the city streets. Assume further that all residents would like to have the music, or, at worst, are indifferent. (That is, none would treat the piano concertos as a form of pollution.) The entrepreneur announces a willingness to install the necessary technology in return for a promise by residents who want the service and who actually listen to the music to make a monthly payment. Obviously, once the technology is in place, each resident can enjoy the music without interfering with the listening enjoyment of others (nonrivalness). Further, the entrepreneur cannot prevent nonpaying residents from enjoying the music along with payers (nonexcludability). Knowing this, each resident is motivated to understate his or her preference for the music in order to avoid requests for payment while obtaining the same benefits as payers, as long as sufficient numbers of people are willing to pay for the service to make it profitable to the entrepreneur. But since each self-interested listener will seek to free ride on the payments of others, no one may make the payments necessary to create the good at all. Unless the benefits of piano concertos are sufficiently great that some smaller subset of the residents (perhaps only one) would be willing to incur the entire cost, the market will fail to provide the service, notwithstanding that all desire it. This can, of course, happen. Howard Hughes, an eccentric but wealthy individual, apparently purchased a television station in order to ensure that he could watch western and aviation movies during late night and early morning hours. He therefore conferred a benefit on numerous insomniacs with television sets. See Russell Hardin, Collective Action 42 (1982).

The same motivation that underlies free riding, that is, the pursuit of self-interest regardless of social effects, may be all the more dramatic where selfish action produces a social, or public, bad. Assume that Jill is on vacation and has just purchased a package of candy. When she has consumed the candy, she can either discard the package on the street or she can walk across the street to a trash can. Unless she would be crossing the street for some other reason (perhaps the museum she has come to see is located there), taking that action imposes costs on Jill. Yet she receives no benefit from the action—she will not return to this vacation spot to see the litter and, in any event, she regards her contribution to litter as infinitesimal. Thus, Jill will litter. If Harry, Joan, and Ken also litter, each following self-interest, the result is pollution, a public bad.

Note an interesting difference between the two cases we have considered to this point. In the littering case, Jill considers the personal benefits of her action and the personal costs. Her calculations are not affected by what others do. In the piano concerto case, however, the conduct of any one person depends on the conduct of others. My unwillingness to pay could be altered if I am convinced that an insufficient number of others will contribute to the provision of the concertos, so that my contribution makes the difference between having them and not having them. This concern for the conduct of others indicates that we are in the realm of *strategic behavior*. If you are willing to incur the costs related to production of a public good, then I can conceal my preference for the same good, permit you to produce it, and then take as much advantage of it as if I had paid my full share towards its provision.

To see how strategies may affect the provision of public goods, assume that Alberta (A) and Brian (B) are neighbors who live in an area affected by crime. A may propose joint patrolling of the neighborhood in order to reduce the incidence of crime. B may openly disagree in the hope that if A is sufficiently convinced of B's unwillingness to contribute, A will bear the entire costs of patrolling, notwithstanding that cooperation between them will reduce a substantially greater amount of crime. If A takes the bait, she will be unable to exclude B from the benefits, notwithstanding B's failure to contribute. If we assume that both actors possess a similar level of self-interestedness, however, then A is likely to be engaged in the same concealment of preferences as B. Neither will provide what each desires.

Understanding the consequences of strategic behavior may clarify the difficulty of obtaining public goods. Assume that patrolling the neighborhood costs a total of 100. This cost could be incurred by A or B alone, or evenly divided (50 each) between them. (Obviously, other apportionments are possible, but for the sake of simplicity we will limit ourselves to these two alternatives.) Patrolling, whether done by A *or* B or by A *and* B, creates a gain of 125 to each (a social total of 250) from avoided theft losses. Thus, it is worthwhile for each to incur the full cost of patrolling (because that person would still gain 125–100, or 25), but each comes out better if the other incurs the entire cost. If costs are evenly divided, each actor gains 125–50, or 75. The worst case obtains if neither patrols; in that situation each actor can anticipate no gain over the status quo, in which each suffers losses through theft in excess of costs that would have avoided those losses. In summary, both A and B would prefer that the other supply a public good, but if the other fails to do so, each would prefer to act rather than have neither act. In game theory, situations that bear these characteristics are often called "Chicken Games."

These choices can be summarized in the following matrix, each cell of which represents the consequences or payoffs (the sum of benefits—avoided theft losses—less payments) to each player who is preparing to choose whether to patrol or hold out. In accordance with game theory convention, the payoff for the party represented by rows (here, A) is shown first in each cell, and the party represented by columns (here, B) is shown second.

		B	
		Patrol	*Hold Out*
A	*Patrol*	75, 75	25, 125
	Hold Out	125, 25	0, 0

It is quite unclear what the parties will do in such a case. Each actor would be best off by holding out while the other patrols. Each, however, would be better off patrolling if the other holds out. A might patrol, therefore, if she believes that B will not, as A is better off if she patrols alone than if neither patrols, albeit not as well off as if B patrolled alone. B, of course, faces the same decision. If A and B have sufficient information, or make certain assumptions about the conduct of the other, then this uncertainty may be reduced. Assume, for instance, that B believes that there is a 50 percent chance that A will patrol and a 50 percent chance that A will hold out. Then the expected value to B of patrolling is 50, calculated as (.50)(75) + (.50)(25), and the expected value of holding out is 62.5, calculated as (.50)(125) + (.50)(0). If B seeks to maximize personal expected value, B will hold out. If A has the same expectations about B's behavior, then A will also hold out. Different information or speculation, e.g., a belief by one actor that the other is 90 percent likely to patrol, could alter the strategies. So Chicken Games are unstable. Pre-commitment to a particular strategy (for instance, B could announce to A that he was going on vacation for a month and would be unavailable to patrol) may make the outcome of the Chicken Game more determinate.

A small adjustment in the payoff schedule transforms the uncertainty inherent in a Chicken Game into a more certain result, but not a happier one. In this situation, known in game theory as the "Prisoner's Dilemma," each player again has the opportunity to cooperate with or defect from other players. The best result for the players taken together (the best social result) could be achieved if they cooperated. The payoff schedule of each player, however, is such that noncooperation will make the player better off than cooperating no matter what the other player does. The worst payoff for each player occurs if he or she cooperates while the other does not. Hence (and unlike the Chicken Game), from a self-interested perspective, defection *dominates* all other strategies; that is, it is best to defect no matter what the other party does. Because this result is the same for all players, however, they all have incentives to defect, notwithstanding that they could have done better had they all cooperated.

Assume, for instance, that A and B are considering whether to pave the street on which they live. Recapturing paving costs *ex post,* e.g., by charging tolls, will be prohibitively expensive. If each contributes time equally, total paving costs will equal 6, or 3 each. If only one contributes time, however, total paving costs to that party will equal 8 (it might take more than twice as long for one person to complete the task because of fatigue). Thus, A and B can agree to share costs or each can hold out in the knowledge that he or she cannot be excluded from the benefits if the other pays all paving costs. Each actor believes that if the street is paved, the personal value of the street would increase from its current level of 7 (since unpaved roads are bumpier and exact wear and tear on automobiles) to 14. Thus each actor faces the following matrix of net benefits (benefit less costs):

		B	
		Pay	*Hold Out*
A	*Pay*	4, 4	−1, 7
	Hold Out	7, −1	4, 4

The road will not get paved notwithstanding that it is worthwhile paving (value can be increased from 7 to 14 at a cost of 6). Even though each actor knows that the other will not act alone (as the marginal cost of acting alone, 8, exceeds the marginal benefit, 7), and thus it cannot free ride on the efforts of the other, each actor also knows that its own efforts will be unavailing if it cannot depend on cooperation from the other.

Externalities

Markets may also fail to allocate scarce resources ideally because a market transaction fails to reflect all the social costs and benefits it generates. Assuming that the parties to the transaction are rational and self-interested, we can expect that their transaction will achieve an optimal exchange between them. Iris will sell her law books to Fred for $100 only if Iris values her law books at less than $100 and Fred values them at no less than $100. But transactions may have implications, both positive and negative, for nonparties. These spillover or external effects will not be reflected in the transaction (assuming the transacting parties are solely self-interested) unless they are simultaneously and fully realized by the parties to the transaction. Thus, transactions that are worthwhile for the transacting parties may impose substantial costs or confer substantial benefits on others.

Consider pollution as an example. Assume I produce a good by a process that requires the discharge of pollutants into a nearby water supply. Assume further that pollution causes damage downstream in the amount of $10,000, but could be eliminated by my investment in a pollution control technology that would cost me less than $10,000. From a social perspective it is desirable that I install the technology. If I sell my products only to people who live upstream from me, however, I will not install the technology. They have no reason to induce me to reduce pollution levels, as they do not suffer its ill effects. Instead, they will be happy to pay lower prices for the goods that reflect no increase for pollution control. My failure to install the technology, then, causes me no loss of sales, while installation—and subsequent increases in prices—would presumably cause some of my buyers to purchase from others who did not have to factor the costs of pollution control into the price of their goods. Thus, transactions with my customers will fail to internalize all the costs associated with the production, sale, and purchase of the good.

If pollution simultaneously caused danger to my workers, and if they were aware of those dangers, they might bargain for higher wages that reflected their exposure to a hazardous job site. Alternatively, they might bargain for a lower wage if I installed the polluting technology. If the costs of the technology were less than the wage rates I would otherwise have to pay, presumably I would agree to install the technology, as failure to do so would cause the resignation of my (best) workers. When the workers transact with me for installation of the technology, they would be conferring an external benefit on downstream residents. Nevertheless, their transaction will not necessarily fully reflect the interests of those residents. Assume that I could install either of two technologies to reduce pollution. The first would eliminate pollution within the plant and reduce (but not eliminate) polluting discharges outside the plant. The second, more expensive, technology would eliminate adverse effects both within and without the plant. If my employees bargained for the first technology, I would accede, assuming that the related costs are less than what I would otherwise have to pay in risky wage rates. In short, I would be willing to confer the beneficial spillovers on downstream residents because I can capture the benefits of my activity through my negotiations with employees. But the employees have no incentive to bargain for the more expensive technology since (assuming they live upstream from the plant) they receive no benefit from it, and would have to sacrifice additional wages to induce me to install it. Since I cannot capture the rewards of that investment (the beneficiaries do not transact with me as customers or employees), I am unwilling to make it.

At times, my willingness to impose negative externalities may be affected by the conduct of others, just as in the case of strategic refusal to create public goods. Assume, for instance, that the downstream pollution problem was sufficiently great that it was worthwhile for downstream residents as a group to transact with me, that is, to offer to pay me to install the pollution control technology. At the same time, the polluting effects on any one resident might be too small to warrant any person's entering into the transaction with me, notwithstanding that the aggregate costs of pollution make the transaction socially desirable. Now we are back to our classic collective action problem. The costs of assembling all the residents, negotiating among them, and negotiating with me will be substantial. Indeed, the costs to any one person of building and working with a coalition will likely exceed the benefits to that person. Each potential member of the coalition might be better off attempting to free ride on the efforts of others by concealing his or her preference for pollution control in the hopes that others will make sufficient contributions without requesting funds from the holdouts. Thus, no group will form to transact with me and to induce me to internalize the external consequences of my activity.

One form of externality has significant implications for local government, because it involves multiple users of common property, such as municipally owned property. In what is known as the "Tragedy of the Commons," each party has an incentive to maximize its own net benefit from a common resource, notwithstanding that doing so imposes excessive costs on others. Each actor realizes the entire marginal benefit of the personal use, but only a pro rata share of the affiliated costs.[2] Examples include littering and other forms of pollution, deforestation, and students removing materials from the law library.

Information and Coordination

Markets allocate resources efficiently when parties to market transactions have sufficient information to engage in reasoned speculation about the desirability of a given exchange and when they have sufficient choice to avoid exchanges that they consider inopportune. Perfect information is not a requirement of operating markets, not only because it is unattainable, but because numerous market transactions are predicated on the assumption that social gains can result from speculation. If you do not know that your land contains a valuable mineral resource and I have done sufficient research to determine that fact, society as a whole may be better off if I make that information known. But the discussion about externalities suggests that I will be willing to obtain and exploit my information only if I can capture some part of the subsequent benefits. Thus, if I offer to purchase your land without disclosing my superior knowledge and would otherwise be unwilling to invest in discovering the information, we might say that your decision to sell was an informed one, notwithstanding your imperfect, indeed inferior, information.

Nevertheless, the absence of information may impede useful market transactions. Return to the example of the workers in the polluting plant. Even if they, as well as downstream residents, are adversely affected by the pollution and could bargain for installation of the pollution control technology, they are unlikely to do so unless they know of the adverse effects. That knowledge, in turn, is not simply a function of having particular factual information before them. It also involves the ability to process the information properly. As we shall see, some extra-market corrective may be necessary where parties systematically misuse information.

---

2. The Tragedy of the Commons is frequently associated with the simultaneous use by multiple parties of a resource open to all, such as fishing on a public lake or grazing cattle on a common pasture. Assume, for instance, that two herders, A and B, each graze 5 cattle on a commons that supports an optimum of 10 cattle, each of which, fattening on one-tenth of the pasture, can be sold for $100. Thus, the total value of grazing cattle at the optimum will be $1,000. Assume further that if an additional animal is permitted to graze, it will reduce the value of all cattle to $85 per head, while every additional animal added thereafter reduces the value by an additional $10 per head. The chart below demonstrates that each A and B can increase her own welfare by adding an animal, but that total social welfare is reduced by adding an animal, since the value that each receives by adding an animal is more than offset by the costs imposed on the herder who does not add an animal. The latter party, however, can retaliate by adding an animal of her own, increasing personal welfare, but—at least within a range—further reducing social welfare.

A's Value	*B's Value*	*Social Welfare*
5 × $100 = $500	5 × $100 = $500	$1,000
6 × 85 = $510	5 × $85 = $425	$935
6 × 75 = $450	6 × $75 = $450	$900
7 × 65 = $455	6 × $65 = 390	$845

A variant on the problem of information exists where individuals are willing to cooperate and, unlike the Prisoner's Dilemma, are confident that others would also like to cooperate. The problem is that they don't know what cooperation requires because there are multiple ways of coordinating with others. Assume, for instance, that A and B would each be willing to drive on the same side of the road at all times and are indifferent whether that is the right or the left. All that matters is that each selects the same side. They now face the following matrix:

		B	
		Right	*Left*
A	*Right*	50, 50	250, 250
	Left	250, 250	50, 50

Here, each party would prefer coordination, but is indifferent as between the two potential coordination points right-right and left-left. If A and B are the only relevant actors and can communicate with each other, one would imagine that they will quickly come to agree on mutual driving on one of the two sides. But if A and B are in an area with 1,000 other persons, sharing information that will allow selection of a single coordination point becomes far more complex, even if all persons within the area would be willing to coordinate and are indifferent as to which point is chosen.

Government as a Response to Collective Action Problems

The traditional response to these problems of collective action (public goods, externalities, informational gaps) has been to use government to counter self-interest and publicize information. In theory, at least, government, which represents the interests of the society at large rather than those of any individual, can allocate resources in the same manner as an operating market by determining the desired level of use, providing the good or service (or contracting with a private provider), and imposing a payment scheme that can be enforced through the use of legitimate coercion. In the easiest case of collective action problems, where all parties wish to cooperate and need only to overcome informational gaps, government may select a coordination point and publicize it. Thus, government can decree that all parties will drive on the right, and presumably will face little opposition since most parties will welcome the announcement of the way in which they are expected to cooperate.

In more difficult cases, government may raise the costs of defection or the benefits of cooperation and thus neutralize the rewards of self-interest that generate socially irrational behavior. Government may solve Chicken Games by providing the public good and then using coercive threats to obtain pro rata contributions from each beneficiary. Thus, government may pave the streets and exact fees from users or reimburse itself through taxes imposed on a class of beneficiaries. Government may minimize externalities by regulating or prohibiting the use of common resources and enforcing its edicts through fines and imprisonment. Alternatively, government may assign property rights to those adversely affected and provide a forum to hear claims that those rights have been infringed. For instance, government may create a private right of action for the victims of pollution and then create a system of courts to permit aggrieved citizens to obtain redress against polluters. Government may induce coordination among "prisoners" by facilitating communication, making bargains for cooperation enforceable, or regulating in a manner that makes defection relatively costly (changing the payoffs to each player).

But there are problems with relying on government to solve these market failures, and these problems have implications for the scope of local government law. The first problem deals with the need for any governmental intervention. In recent years, there has developed a substantial literature that seeks to demonstrate that self-interested parties can achieve solutions to problems of collective action even without government. For instance, players in a Prisoner's Dilemma may agree to cooperate if they will face each other in repeated situations. Under these circumstances, each player can feel confident that if he or she cooperates, others will also do so in order to avoid retaliation in future meetings between the parties. Assume, for instance, that Harry lives in a drought area that is experiencing a severe water shortage. All residents of the area recognize that it would be socially useful if lawn watering occurred only in the early morning and late evening hours in order to conserve water (as evaporation is less rapid during those periods). Harry may limit his lawn watering to those periods not because he seeks to promote social welfare (indeed, in this situation the reservoir of water constitutes a commons that he can exploit with few external effects, albeit the aggregation of effects if all followed that route would be catastrophic), but because neighbors will be able to monitor his activity and chastise his violation of the community norm. Obviously, the effects of reputation are likely to be more compelling where principals are likely to interact frequently. Thus, the argument may have more consequences for the need for local rather than centralized government.

The second problem lies in the observation that government itself possesses the characteristics of a public good. If I choose to govern in the public interest in order to obtain the benefits of solving the collective action problem, I cannot exclude others from the same benefits of government. Of course, on a single occasion, my act of government will create winners and losers. But if I am acting in the public interest rather than to vindicate the interests of a discrete group of actors, then the identities of winners should change over time. In addition, where government intervenes to solve pure coordination problems (e.g., on which side of the road should we drive), there should be only winners. Similarly, the act of governing exhibits characteristics of nonrivalness. If A can lead a more civil life as a result of living under a government, B can do the same.

The public good nature of government suggests some reasons to be wary of governmental intervention that take us back to the concerns of Mill and Madison. If the act of government has characteristics of nonrivalness and nonexcludability, then why would anyone become a governor? One answer, of course, is that individuals do not always act out of self-interest. Some may want to create public goods for others. An alternative response is less optimistic. Governors may get reputational benefits, including a place in history, if they do enough and rise high enough in the public view. Alternatively, they may enhance their opportunities for private sector employment after leaving public office. Or, they may enjoy a certain level of power and authority while in government. Note, however, that none of these incentives for becoming a public official is necessarily consistent with fulfilling one's duties in a manner compatible with the public interest.

Apart from the ways in which the public goods characteristics of governance affect governors, however, consider the ways in which those characteristics affect the decisions of the governed to ensure good government. We noted above that government officials, unlike their private market counterparts, determine what goods and services constituents desire by examining the results of voting. The underlying assumption is that voters are willing to reveal their preferences. But there are some difficulties with this assumption. First, some preferences might not be appropriate. Preferences that are discriminatory against certain groups or activities may be inconsistent with the laws, values, or norms of the larger community and thus should be disregarded by officials, even if their constituents actually hold them.

Second, even well-meaning public officials may misunderstand the public's preferences, and less well-meaning officials may ignore those preferences. Hence, public monitoring of officials' conduct is necessary to ensure that the public's preferences are implemented as well as registered. The problem is that registering preferences and monitoring conduct are also nonrival and nonexclusive activities. The result is that there is little incentive for any one person to undertake these tasks. The problem can be remedied by providing low-cost mechanisms for registering preferences. Voting for candidates provides such a mechanism, but a relatively imprecise one. Candidates receive votes based on the package of policies they favor rather than issue by issue. Hence, even if I am willing to incur the costs of voting (notwithstanding that my individual vote will have little significance), I have little opportunity to indicate that I agree with a candidate on school funding and street paving, but disagree on issues of low-income housing and tax rates. I can only vote my beliefs on balance.

Nor can I register the intensity of my agreement or disagreement; voting tends to be binary in nature (I vote for or against), so that if I feel very strongly for candidate A, my vote can be canceled by the vote of someone with only the mildest preference for candidate B. If we think that voting should reflect intensity of interests, maybe it is appropriate to have a costly process, so that those who are nearly indifferent about results do not participate.

As costs of voting or monitoring increase, the numbers of participants quickly diminish. One lesson to be learned from Madison, however, is that potential voters or monitors do not necessarily drop out proportionately on each side of an issue. Lobbying, vote-gathering, political contributions, and like mechanisms for indicating preferences and monitoring officials on discrete issues may be dominated by groups and persons with particular interests in outcomes. But not all potential interest groups face equal obstacles to collective action. If the benefits of political action are widely dispersed and the effects for any individual are small, then—as seen in the discussion about pollution—there is little incentive for anyone adversely affected to do anything, since any action will create more costs than benefits for the potential actor. On the other hand, if the benefits of political action are concentrated among a small group, and if that group is able to coalesce and control its membership, then the benefits to individual members of participating in collective action may exceed the costs. Thus, those who are left to vote, or to lobby for passage or defeat of proposed legislation, will be those with substantial amounts to gain or lose as a result of the ultimate decision. It is, however, by no means clear that the interests of those individuals will reflect the interests of the public at large.

In some situations, discrete and intensely interested groups will arise on all sides of an issue. Think, for instance, of disputes between tenants' unions and landlords, or the well-organized efforts on both sides of the abortion controversy. Thus, the appearance of interests is not, of itself, problematic. But if the costs or benefits of a proposed action are realized by a discrete group, while the competing benefits or costs are widely dispersed, the former should be able to organize with relative ease compared to the second.

The Scope of Local Government

If government is to play the function of allocating goods and services where markets fail, at what point should the relevant government be a decentralized, or local, entity? The message from the provision theory of government is relatively clear: The governmental entity responsible for solving the problems of market failure should be the one whose boundaries are most consonant with the spatial benefits and burdens that are the source of any misallocation that would otherwise occur. Governments best positioned to match individual and social costs and benefits are best able, in the jargon of economists, to "internalize externalities" that are at the root of market failure. A unit of government composed of self-interested individuals is likely to act in a manner consistent with its corporate self-interest. A locality that can capture all the benefits of an activity (e.g., a wealthy tax base), while externalizing the costs (e.g., housing opportunities for low-income families that require tax subsidies) to other localities, is unlikely to pay significant attention to the external burdens it imposes. Simultaneously, a locality that does not bear all the costs of its activity is likely to engage too much or too little in the activity. In short, a government charged with the supply of public goods should be of a size sufficient to recognize both the costs and benefits of provision of that good. Hence, localities are likely to be most effective for the efficient provision of public goods that have relatively narrow spatial effects, such as paving roads, patrolling streets, and providing parks. Local policies that necessarily affect outsiders are unlikely to take the interests of those outsiders into account. Think of the city of Boston making decisions about siting a nuclear waste dump or of the city of Duluth deciding which naval yards should remain open nationwide. It is, perhaps, in this spirit that Mill assigns to local governments only those objects that are of "purely local concern."

But localities may also provide less coercive mechanisms for overcoming the problems represented by the Prisoner's Dilemma. Return to the notion that reputational interest may keep individuals from antisocial, noncooperative behavior. If government can play a role in publicizing good and bad reputations, it may harness the power of reputation in neutralizing self-interest by those who would otherwise defect with impunity. The ability to monitor and publicize reputation, however, may be more significant within narrow geographical areas, in which case this appears to be a function best allocated to the local level. Reputational pull is likely to be strongest among individuals who will enjoy repeated contact with one another. In this situation, those who perceive misbehavior will have opportunities for retaliation, the fear of which deters the initial defection. Those repeated iterations, of course, are most likely where the individuals are within a limited geographical area.

NOTES

1. Issues such as littering, pollution, and police patrols are classic examples of collective action problems that can be solved by the creation of government. Can you think of others?

2. Why do public libraries tend to be free? The model of self-interested behavior outlined above suggests that individuals who use libraries will keep books out longer than is necessary and will treat books less well than books that they own. A library, in short, is an example of a commons that all are willing to overuse since no one user bears the entire cost of misuse. Would it be appropriate to charge library book users according to the amount of time a book is withdrawn and according to the condition of the book on its return? Allowing books to be used without charge makes sense if users produce benefits for nonusers and charging fees would deter use. What kinds of "external" benefits might users confer on nonusers? Are they sufficient to justify making books available without charge? To what other kinds of goods traditionally offered by local governments does this argument apply?

3. A frequent criticism of the current array of federal regulatory agencies is that, although created to serve the public interest, they ultimately serve those who were intended to be regulated. The metaphor that is often used to describe this phenomenon is "capture" of the regulators by the regulated. The argument goes something like this: Regulated industries are frequently before the regulators, while any subset of the public will only rarely benefit from appeals to the same agency. The industry members are small in number and are known to each other and thus can monitor contributions by each other to the collective effort of resisting undesirable regulation. The public, which might actually be helped by such regulation, is diffuse and anonymous; further, each member of the public can benefit without undertaking any costly action to influence regulators, as long as others contribute to the effort. Hence, relatively few will contribute to the collective effort, as compared to those in the regulated industry. Finally, the regulated can hold out to the regulators the promise of profitable careers after government service, assuming that the regulator, while a government official, was sufficiently receptive to the industry. For a general discussion of this critique, see Joseph P. Kalt & Mark A. Zupan, Capture and Ideology in the Economic Theory of Politics, 74 Am. Econ. Rev. 279 (1984); Sam Peltzman, Toward a More General Theory of Regulation, 19 J. L. & Econ. 211 (1976); Richard A. Posner, Theories of Economic Regulation, 5 Bell J. Econ. & Mgmt. Sci. 335 (1974); George J. Stigler, The Theory of Economic Regulation, 2 Bell J. Econ. & Mgmt. Sci. 3 (1971).

Local government shares some characteristics of federal regulatory agencies, but also varies significantly. Some residents (and nonresidents) frequently appear before the city council (imagine developers seeking zoning variances and permits) far more than others. Nevertheless, when an issue does galvanize the community, the limited geographical range of those affected and their smaller number may make organization easier than at the federal level. As you consider the propriety of the principles of local government law in these materials, think whether the law is necessary to overcome obstacles to collective action at the local level.

4. *Local Government and Redistribution.* Government is frequently assigned the role of redistributing wealth throughout society in order to ensure that those worst off in the society do not fall below a given baseline. The prior discussion has ignored the possibility that local government plays a significant role in performing this function. Although this possibility plays an important part in the materials that follow, particularly in Chapter 4, it is useful at this point to understand some possible limits on local redistribution. Theoretically, any governmental entity with the authority to tax could engage in redistribution. Nevertheless, there may be practical reasons to prefer that central, rather than local, governments undertake this task. While it might be nice to imagine altruistic wealthy citizens freely helping others in the community by willingly paying redistributive taxes, those who wished to avoid that burden might too easily escape if localities were the primary source of welfare payments. Relatively wealthy local residents might emigrate to localities that imposed a lower redistributive burden on them. At the same time, localities that offered substantially higher redistributive benefits might find that those in need of such benefits gravitated to those jurisdictions, with the result that the subsequent demand for redistributive services led even more residents to emigrate elsewhere.

The ability to avoid redistributive taxes is reduced as the taxing jurisdiction becomes more centralized—it is cheaper, other things being equal, to move from city to suburb, than it is to move to a new state, and cheaper still than it is to move to a new country. Does this mean that all redistribution should occur at a federal, or at least nonlocal, level? Not necessarily. If we believe that individuals will be more willing to donate to those with whom they have some affinity, then redistributive taxes that are explicitly used within the community may be more acceptable than redistributive taxes that are directed to other jurisdictions for the benefit of individuals unknown to the payers. Just as I may be more willing to donate to family members than to strangers, so may I be more willing to donate to strangers within my community than to strangers in another state, or in another country. Thus, the relevant issue is not whether local government ought to be involved in redistributive efforts, but how much and in what form?

C. THE FORMS AND STRUCTURES OF LOCAL GOVERNMENT

The most recent available census data indicate that there were 89,476 governmental units in the United States as of March 2008, excluding the federal government and the 50 state governments.[1] In addition, 96.2 percent of all elected officials in the United States are officials of local governments. The distribution of local government units is as follows:

	Number of Units
General-purpose local governments	**39,044**
County governments	3,033
Municipal governments	19,492
Town or township governments	16,519
Special-purpose local governments	**50,432**
School districts	13,051
Other special districts	37,381
Total local governments	**89,476**

1. All of the information in this section is taken from the following: U.S. Census Bureau, 2007 Census of Governments, Local Governments and Public School Systems by Type and State: 2007, available at http://www.census.gov/govs/cog/GovOrgTab03ss.html [hereinafter "2007 Census"]; U.S. Dep't of Commerce, 2002 Census of Governments: Government Organization—Government Organization (2002) [hereinafter "2002 Government Organization"]; U.S. Census Bureau, 2007 Census of Government Finance, Table 2 (Local Government Finances by Type of Government and State: 2006–07), available at http://www2.census.gov/govs/estimate/0700ussl_2.txt; U.S. Census Bureau, 2007 Census of Government Finance, Table 1 (Local Government Finances by Type of Government and State: 2006–07), available at http://www2.census.gov/govs/estimate/0700ussl_1.txt; U.S. Census Bureau, Public Education Finances: 2007 (issued 2009), available at http://www2.census.gov/govs/school/07f33.pub.pdf; U.S. Dep't of Commerce, 1992 Census of Governments: Government Organization—Popularly Elected Officials (1995); and U.S. Advisory Comm'n on Intergovernmental Relations, State Laws Governing Local Government Structure and Administration (1993).

1. County Governments

County governments are administrative arms of the state, and typically provide general government services such as roads, courts, jails, law enforcement, land records, vital statistics, welfare, and public health. Some counties also provide services more commonly provided by municipalities, including hospitals, parks, libraries, and airports. In 2006–07, the major source of county revenues nationwide was state government (28.7% of total revenue), followed by property tax receipts (23.7%), various sales and gross receipts taxes (7.6%), county hospitals (6.7%), the federal government (3.0%), local governments (1.7%), utilities (1.3%), and income taxes (1.2%). During 2006–07, the major expenditures of county governments nationwide were for education (13.9% of total expenditures), public welfare assistance (10.5%), hospitals (8.8%), health (7.4%), police (6.5%), and highways (6.1%).

County governments exist in every state except Connecticut and Rhode Island, and the District of Columbia. In Louisiana, they are called "parish" governments, and in Alaska they are called "borough" governments. The total number of county governments nationwide has scarcely changed over the last five decades, numbering 3,052 in 1952 and 3,033 in 2007.

The number of county governments per state ranges widely, from 254 in Texas to only 3 in Delaware and Hawaii. Although the average population served by a county government is approximately 83,000, Loving County, Texas, had only 67 inhabitants in 2000, while Los Angeles County, California, had more than 9.5 million. The vast majority (72%) of county governments each serve fewer than 50,000 persons.

Counties are governed by an elected body, typically a board of supervisors or a board of commissioners. The majority of these boards have three to five members, who are elected either by district or at large, and who are part-time officials. In addition, some 400 counties have an appointed county manager, and about 70 counties have a separately elected county executive. County officials may also include a sheriff, prosecuting attorney, and clerk, who are either independently elected or (increasingly) appointed by the county board.

2. Municipal Governments

"Municipal governments" for census purposes are "political subdivisions within which a municipal corporation has been established to provide general local government for a specific population concentration in a defined area, and includes all active government units officially designated as cities, boroughs (except in Alaska), towns (except in the six New England states, and in Minnesota, New York, and Wisconsin), and villages." 2002 Government Organization, supra note 1, at p. VI. All 50 states and the District of Columbia have municipal governments.

Municipalities generally lie within counties, although in Virginia the cities are separate from the counties, and a very few consolidated city-county governments exist across the country. Municipalities provide general public services in addition to those provided by counties and other units of local government. In 2006–07, the major source of municipal revenues nationwide was property taxes (16.2% of total revenue), followed by state government (15.0%), utility revenue (14.1%), sales taxes (5.8%), the federal government (4.0%), and individual income taxes (3.3%). During 2006–07, the major expenditures of municipal governments nationwide were for police protection (9.7% of total expenditures), education (9.0%), electricity (7.1%), water (6.6%), highways (6.0%), sewerage (5.5%), fire protection (4.9%), and parks and recreation (4.2%).

The total number of municipal governments nationwide has increased steadily and substantially during the last five decades, from 16,807 in 1952 to 19,492 in 2007. The number of municipalities per state varies widely, from more than 1,000 in Illinois, Pennsylvania, and Texas, to fewer than 50 in Connecticut, the District of Columbia, Hawaii, Maine, Massachusetts, Nevada, New Hampshire, Rhode Island, and Vermont. The presence of so many New England states in the latter group is explained by the fact that a town government in these states often provides urban services provided by municipal governments in other states. Slightly less than one-half of all municipalities have fewer than 1,000 inhabitants, but these municipalities account for only 2.2 percent of the total population served by municipal governments. Approximately 76 million of the 174 million people who live in areas with municipal governments live in cities of at least 100,000 people.

There are three basic forms of municipal government: mayor-council, council-manager, and commission. The mayor-council form is by far the most common, and the commission form the least common. In the mayor-council form, the council is a legislative body, typically consisting of five to seven members who serve part-time and who may be elected at large or by district. The mayor is also popularly elected and functions as the chief executive. Under a strong mayor-council plan, usually found in large cities, the mayor has broad administrative, budgetary, and appointive powers, which may include a veto power over ordinances enacted by the council. Mayors under a weak mayor-council plan typically have few independent powers.

The council-manager form of government involves an elected (usually nonpartisan) city council, a professional city manager hired by the council, and a mayor who may be either appointed by the council or elected by the voters. The council is responsible for making the budget and most policy decisions and for setting tax rates, while the manager implements the council's policies and administers the city's affairs. The mayor is the political leader of the city and is a member of the council, but does not perform executive functions. The commission form of government consists of an elected (usually nonpartisan) commission of three to five members who perform all legislative and executive functions.

3. TOWN OR TOWNSHIP GOVERNMENTS

"Town or township governments" typically serve sparsely populated areas, and exist in only 20 states in the Northeast and Midwest:

Connecticut	Illinois	Indiana
Kansas	Maine	Massachusetts
Michigan	Minnesota	Missouri
Nebraska	New Hampshire	New Jersey
New York	North Dakota	Ohio
Pennsylvania	Rhode Island	South Dakota
Vermont	Wisconsin	

They include some "plantations" in Maine and some "locations" in New Hampshire.

New England, New Jersey, and Pennsylvania townships perform functions similar to municipalities, and typically utilize a municipal form of governmental organization. Midwestern townships usually perform more limited government functions, and are commonly governed by an elected board of three to five part-time supervisors or trustees. The classic New England town, in contrast, is governed by an annual town meeting in which all residents are eligible to participate, and during which the residents enact ordinances and set the budget. The daily operations of the town are supervised by part-time selectmen. Larger towns in Connecticut and Massachusetts conduct town meetings in which only 100–150 elected representatives are eligible to vote. In 2006–07, the major sources of township revenues nationwide were property taxes (52.4% of total revenue) and state government (17.4%). The major expenditures of township governments nationwide in 2006–07 were for education (24.9% of total expenditures), highways (11.0%), police protection (8.3%), fire protection (5.0%), and sewerage (4.2%).

The total number of town and township governments nationwide has decreased steadily over the past five decades, from 17,202 in 1952 to 16,519 in 2007. The number of town or township governments per state varies widely, from 31 in Rhode Island to more than 1,400 in Illinois, Minnesota, and Pennsylvania. In 2002, some 52.4 percent of all towns or townships had fewer than 1,000 inhabitants, and only 7.1 percent (1,179) had 10,000 or more inhabitants.

Only Indiana has township governments covering its entire area and population, and all municipal governments in Indiana therefore operate within territory that is served also by township governments. There is no geographic overlap between town or township governments and municipalities in nine states: Maine, Massachusetts, New Hampshire, New Jersey, North Dakota, Pennsylvania, Rhode Island, South Dakota, and Wisconsin. There is some geographic overlap in the ten other states with town or township governments.

4. School Districts

There were 14,561 public school systems in the United States as of 2007, of which 13,051 are independent governmental entities. The remaining 1,510 "dependent" public school systems are agencies of other government units—state, county, municipal, or town or township. In 31 states, the public elementary and secondary schools are provided solely through independent school districts. In the District of Columbia and four states (Alaska, Hawaii, Maryland, and North Carolina) there are no independent school districts. In the remaining 15 states, some of the public schools are operated by independent school districts while others are operated by general purpose state or local governmental units. The number of independent school districts nationwide has decreased dramatically during the past five decades, from 67,355 in 1952 to 13,051 in 2007. The bulk of this decline occurred between 1952 and 1967, when the number of independent school districts dropped from 67,355 to 21,782.

The number of independent school districts per state (in states in which they exist at all) varies widely, from fewer than 20 in Connecticut, Delaware, Nevada, Rhode Island, Tennessee, and Virginia, to more than 1,000 in California and Texas. In 1952, there were 20 states with more than 1,000 independent school districts each. In 2007, California (1,044) and Texas (1,081) together accounted for 16 percent of all independent school districts in the nation.

More than 80 percent of all independent school districts are governed by a nonpartisan, elected board of 5 to 15 members, which sets policy and oversees administration of the schools by a professional superintendent of schools. In 2006–07, school districts nationwide relied on revenue from state sources (52.8% of total revenue), property taxes (34.3%), local sources other than property taxes (1.2%), as well as federal sources (1.0%). Per pupil expenditures on public elementary-secondary school systems in 2006–07 averaged $9,666 nationwide, and ranged from $15,981 in New York and $15,691 in New Jersey, to $5,683 in Utah and $6,625 in Idaho.

5. OTHER SPECIAL DISTRICTS

The census bureau requires that "[i]n order to be counted as a special district government, rather than be classified as a subordinate agency, an entity must possess three attributes—existence as an organized entity, governmental character, and substantial [fiscal and administrative] autonomy." 2002 Government Organization, supra note 1, at p. VII. Most special districts or special-purpose governments are called "districts" or "authorities," but many entities bearing these designations are not independent special districts. Special-purpose governments vary substantially in form, so precise characterization is difficult. Distinctions may nonetheless be made among "special districts" that provide a single service (over 90% of special-purpose governments in 2002) ranging from hospitals and fire protection to mosquito abatement and cemetery upkeep; multiple-function districts that combine two or more related services such as sewerage and water supply or conservation, irrigation, and reclamation; and "public authorities" that frequently provide services on a larger scale, such as statewide housing authorities, port authorities, and airport authorities. The functions most commonly performed (by nearly 36% of all special-purpose governments) are related to natural resources—drainage, flood control, irrigation, and soil and water conservation.

The total number of special districts nationwide has grown steadily during the past four decades, from 12,340 in 1952 to 37,381 in 2007. Special districts are by far the most rapidly growing form of local government, and the various factors thought to promote the creation of special districts are discussed infra at pp. [197–194]. Special district governments exist in every state, but there is wide variation among the states in the number of such districts each contains. As of 2007, two states—Alaska (15), and Hawaii (15)—and the District of Columbia (1) each contained fewer than 20 special districts, while thirteen states with more than 1,000 special districts accounted for nearly sixty percent of all such districts: California (2,765), Colorado (1,904), Florida (1,051), Illinois (3,249), Indiana (1,272), Kansas (1,531), Missouri (1,809), Nebraska (1,294), New York (1,119), Oregon (1,034), Pennsylvania (1,728), Texas (2,291), and Washington (1,229). The vast majority of special districts are located entirely within a single county, and approximately one-third of all special district governments have boundaries coterminous with some other local government—county, municipality, town, or township.

Special districts, like counties, are governed by a board which may be elected but is more commonly appointed by officials of the states or local government units that have joined to form the special district. The source of revenue for a special district is often determined by the function it serves, and districts may have more than one source of revenue. Forty-three percent of districts nationwide have the authority to levy property taxes (e.g., districts providing hospitals, airports, libraries, fire protection, parks, and cemeteries). Nearly 25 percent of districts are authorized to impose service charges (e.g., utility districts providing water, sewerage, and solid waste disposal). More than 30 percent rely for funding on grants, shared taxes, and reimbursements from other governmental units (e.g., soil and water conservation, housing, and community development). And other districts rely on special assessments or other taxes.

D. THE FEDERAL PERSPECTIVE ON LOCAL GOVERNMENTS

Local governments, of course, are part of a federal system, and are, from some perspectives, at the lowest point in the system. This does not mean that they are less important in the functions they fulfill; it means only that they are more likely to be subordinate to, or dependent on, "superior" levels of government (states and the federal government) in defining and implementing those functions. Thus, the extent to which localities can fulfill the objective of service provision or community building may depend on the extent to which they are allowed to act autonomously. While these materials primarily concern the relationship between local governments and the state of which they are a political subdivision, it is useful at the outset to consider the way in which the federal government perceives the position of localities in a federal system.

Recall that in the excerpt from Hannah Arendt's *On Revolution*, she noted Lewis Mumford's observation that one of the failures of the founding fathers was the omission of any place for localities in the constitutional firmament. The absence of a constitutional grounding for local autonomy, however, does not mean that the federal government plays no role in defining the scope of local autonomy. The more the federal government is permitted to regulate the affairs of localities (and the states of which they are a part), whether through specific federal programs, conditions on federal funds, or judicial application of federally defined principles to sub-national units of government, the less autonomy local governments may have with respect to the services they provide and the type of community they are allowed to embrace.

1. The Tenth Amendment and the Commerce Clause

> "The powers not delegated to the United States by the Constitution, nor prohibited by it to the States, are reserved to the States respectively, or to the people."
>
> —U.S. Const. amend. X

> "The Congress shall have Power ... [t]o regulate Commerce ... among the several States...."
>
> —U.S. Const. art. I, § 8, cl. 3.

Resolution of this trade-off between federal imposition of nationwide standards and the autonomy of individual localities and other sub-national units of government has been quite unstable during the past two decades. Something approaching Arendt's view of constitutional protection for local government seemed implicit in the version of federalism embraced by a majority of the Supreme Court in National League of Cities v. Usery, 426 U.S. 833 (1976). In that case, the Court invalidated congressional legislation that applied the minimum wage and maximum hour provisions of the Fair Labor Standards Act to employees of states and their political subdivisions. The Court held that "insofar as the challenged amendments operate to directly displace the States' freedom to structure integral operations in areas of traditional governmental functions, they are not within the authority granted Congress by [the Commerce Clause]." Id. at 852.

The Court reasoned that the Tenth Amendment to the Constitution precluded the federal government from interfering with certain functions of states and localities.

> This Court has never doubted that there are limits upon the power of Congress to override state sovereignty, even when exercising its otherwise plenary powers to tax or to regulate commerce which are conferred by Art. I of the Constitution.... The [Tenth] Amendment expressly declares the constitutional policy that Congress may not exercise power in a fashion that impairs the States' integrity or their ability to function effectively in a federal system.

Id. at 842–43. The areas of state and local freedom from federal intervention were variously defined throughout the majority opinion as areas of "integral governmental functions," "traditional governmental functions," and areas "essential" to the separate and independent existence of the states.

The lessons of *National League of Cities* quickly became muddled in attempts by the lower courts to define more concretely the areas in which nominally subordinate governmental bodies retained independence from the federal government. In 1985, a new majority of the Court declared the effort unavailing.

Garcia v. San Antonio Metropolitan Transit Authority

469 U.S. 528 (1985).

■ JUSTICE BLACKMUN delivered the opinion of the Court.

We revisit in these cases an issue raised in National League of Cities v. Usery, 426 U.S. 833, 96 S. Ct. 2465, 49 L. Ed. 2d 245 (1976).

In that litigation, this Court, by a sharply divided vote, ruled that the Commerce Clause does not empower Congress to enforce the minimum-wage and overtime provisions of the Fair Labor Standards Act (FLSA) against the States "in areas of traditional governmental functions." Id., at 852, 96 S. Ct., at 2474. Although *National League of Cities* supplied some examples of "traditional governmental functions," it did not offer a general explanation of how a "traditional" function is to be distinguished from a "nontraditional" one. Since then, federal and state courts have struggled with the task, thus imposed, of identifying a traditional function for purposes of state immunity under the Commerce Clause.

In the present cases, a Federal District Court concluded that municipal ownership and operation of a mass-transit system is a traditional governmental function and thus, under *National League of Cities*, is exempt from the obligations imposed by the FLSA. Faced with the identical question, three Federal Courts of Appeals and one state appellate court have reached the opposite conclusion.

Our examination of this "function" standard applied in these and other cases over the last eight years now persuades us that the attempt to draw the boundaries of state regulatory immunity in terms of "traditional governmental function" is not only unworkable but is also inconsistent with established principles of federalism and, indeed, with those very federalism principles on which *National League of Cities* purported to rest. That case, accordingly, is overruled. . . .

The prerequisites for governmental immunity under *National League of Cities* were summarized by this Court in [Hodel v. Virginia Surface Mining & Recl. Ass'n, 452 U.S. 264, 287–288 (1981)]. Under that summary, four conditions must be satisfied before a state activity may be deemed immune from a particular federal regulation under the Commerce Clause. First, it is said that the federal statute at issue must regulate "the 'States as States'." "Second, the statute must 'address matters that are indisputably "attribute[s] of state sovereignty." ' " Third, state compliance with the federal obligation must "directly impair [the States'] ability 'to structure integral operations in areas of traditional governmental functions.' " "Finally, the relation of state and federal interests must not be such that 'the nature of the federal interest ... justifies state submission.' " ...

The controversy in the present cases has focused on the third *Hodel* requirement—that the challenged federal statute trench on "traditional governmental functions." The District Court voiced a common concern: "Despite the abundance of adjectives, identifying which particular state functions are immune remains difficult." 557 F. Supp., at 447. Just how troublesome the task has been is revealed by the results reached in other federal cases. [The court then cited myriad cases on each side of the "traditional functions" line.—EDS. NOTE] We find it difficult, if not impossible, to identify an organizing principle that places each of the cases in the first group on one side of a line and each of the cases in the second group on the other side. The constitutional distinction between licensing drivers and regulating traffic, for example, or between operating a highway authority and operating a mental health facility, is elusive at best....

Many constitutional standards involve "undoubte[d] ... gray areas," Fry v. United States, 421 U.S. 542, 558, 95 S. Ct. 1792, 1801, 44 L. Ed. 2d 363 (1975) (dissenting opinion), and, despite the difficulties that this Court and other courts have encountered so far, it normally might be fair to venture the assumption that case-by-case development would lead to a workable standard for determining whether a particular governmental function should be immune from federal regulation under the Commerce Clause. A further cautionary note is sounded, however, by the Court's experience in the related field of state immunity from federal taxation. In South Carolina v. United States, 199 U.S. 437, 26 S. Ct. 110, 50 L. Ed. 261 (1905), the Court held for the first time that the state tax immunity recognized in Collector v. Day, 11 Wall. 113, 20 L. Ed. 122 (1871), extended only to the "ordinary" and "strictly governmental" instrumentalities of state governments and not to instrumentalities "used by the State in the carrying on of an ordinary private business." 199 U.S., at 451, 461, 26 S. Ct., at 112, 116. While the Court applied the distinction outlined in *South Carolina* for the following 40 years, at no time during that period did the Court develop a consistent formulation of the kinds of governmental functions that were entitled to immunity. The Court identified the protected functions at various times as "essential," "usual," "traditional," or "strictly governmental." While "these differences in phraseology ... must not be too literally contradistinguished," Brush v. Commissioner, 300 U.S. 352, 362, 57 S. Ct. 495, 496, 81 L. Ed. 691 (1937), they reflect an inability to specify precisely what aspects of a governmental function made it necessary to the "unimpaired existence" of the States. Collector v. Day, 11 Wall., at 127. Indeed, the Court ultimately chose "not, by an attempt to formulate any general test, [to] risk embarrassing the decision of cases [concerning] activities of a different kind which may arise in the future." Brush v. Commissioner, 300 U.S., at 365, 57 S. Ct., at 498.

If these tax-immunity cases had any common thread, it was in the attempt to distinguish between "governmental" and "proprietary" functions. To say that the distinction between "governmental" and "proprietary" proved to be stable, however, would be something of an overstatement.... It was this uncertainty and instability that led the Court shortly thereafter, in New York v. United States, 326 U.S. 572, 66 S. Ct. 310, 90 L. Ed. 326 (1946), unanimously to conclude that the distinction between "governmental" and "proprietary" functions was "untenable" and must be abandoned....

The distinction the Court discarded as unworkable in the field of tax immunity has proved no more fruitful in the field of regulatory immunity under the Commerce Clause. Neither do any of the alternative standards that might be employed to distinguish between protected and unprotected governmental functions appear manageable. We rejected the possibility of making immunity turn on a purely historical standard of "tradition" in [Transportation Union v. Long Island R. Co., 455 U.S. 678 (1982)] and properly so. The most obvious defect of a historical approach to state immunity is that it prevents a court from accommodating changes in the historical functions of States, changes that have resulted in a number of once-private functions like education being assumed by the States and their subdivisions. At the same time, the only apparent virtue of a rigorous historical standard, namely, its promise of a reasonably objective measure for state immunity, is illusory. Reliance on history as an organizing principle results in line-drawing of the most arbitrary sort; the genesis of state governmental functions stretches over a historical continuum from before the Revolution to the present, and courts would have to decide by fiat precisely how longstanding a pattern of state involvement had to be for federal regulatory authority to be defeated.

A nonhistorical standard for selecting immune governmental functions is likely to be just as unworkable as is a historical standard. The goal of identifying "uniquely" governmental functions, for example, has been rejected by the Court in the field of governmental tort liability in part because the notion of a "uniquely" governmental function is unmanageable.... Another possibility would be to confine immunity to "necessary" governmental services, that is, services that would be provided inadequately or not at all unless the government provided them. Cf. Flint v. Stone Tracy Co., 220 U.S., at 172, 31 S. Ct., at 357. The set of services that fits into this category, however, may well be negligible. The fact that an unregulated market produces less of some service than a State deems desirable does not mean that the State itself must provide the service; in most if not all cases, the State can "contract out" by hiring private firms to provide the service or simply by providing subsidies to existing suppliers. It also is open to question how well equipped courts are to make this kind of determination about the workings of economic markets.

We believe, however, that there is a more fundamental problem at work here, a problem that explains why the Court was never able to provide a basis for the governmental/proprietary distinction in the intergovernmental tax-immunity cases and why an attempt to draw similar distinctions with respect to federal regulatory authority under *National*

League of Cities is unlikely to succeed regardless of how the distinctions are phrased. The problem is that neither the governmental/proprietary distinction nor any other that purports to separate out important governmental functions can be faithful to the role of federalism in a democratic society. The essence of our federal system is that within the realm of authority left open to them under the Constitution, the States must be equally free to engage in any activity that their citizens choose for the common weal, no matter how unorthodox or unnecessary anyone else—including the judiciary—deems state involvement to be. Any rule of state immunity that looks to the "traditional," "integral," or "necessary" nature of governmental functions inevitably invites an unelected federal judiciary to make decisions about which state policies it favors and which ones it dislikes. "The science of government ... is the science of experiment," Anderson v. Dunn, 6 Wheat. 204, 226, 5 L.Ed. 242 (1821), and the States cannot serve as laboratories for social and economic experiment, see New State Ice Co. v. Liebmann, 285 U.S. 262, 311, 52 S.Ct. 371, 386, 76 L.Ed. 747 (1932) (Brandeis, J., dissenting), if they must pay an added price when they meet the changing needs of their citizenry by taking up functions that an earlier day and a different society left in private hands....

We therefore now reject, as unsound in principle and unworkable in practice, a rule of state immunity from federal regulation that turns on a judicial appraisal of whether a particular governmental function is "integral" or "traditional." Any such rule leads to inconsistent results at the same time that it disserves principles of democratic self-governance, and it breeds inconsistency precisely because it is divorced from those principles. If there are to be limits on the Federal Government's power to interfere with state functions—as undoubtedly there are—we must look elsewhere to find them. We accordingly return to the underlying issue that confronted this Court in *National League of Cities*—the manner in which the Constitution insulates States from the reach of Congress' power under the Commerce Clause.

III

When we look for the States' "residuary and inviolable sovereignty," The Federalist No. 39, p. 285 (B. Wright ed. 1961) (J. Madison), in the shape of the constitutional scheme rather than in predetermined notions of sovereign power, a different measure of state sovereignty emerges. Apart from the limitation on federal authority inherent in the delegated nature of Congress' Article I powers, the principal means chosen by the Framers to ensure the role of the States in the federal system lies in the structure of the Federal Government itself. It is no novelty to observe that the composition of the Federal Government was designed in large part to protect the States from overreaching by Congress. The Framers thus gave the States a role in the selection both of the Executive and the Legislative Branches of the Federal Government. The States were vested with indirect influence over the House of Representatives and the Presidency by their control of electoral qualifications and their role in Presidential elections. U.S. Const., Art. I, § 2, and Art. II, § 1. They were given more direct influence in the

Senate, where each State received equal representation and each Senator was to be selected by the legislature of his State. Art. I, § 3. The significance attached to the States' equal representation in the Senate is underscored by the prohibition of any constitutional amendment divesting a State of equal representation without the State's consent. Art. V.

The extent to which the structure of the Federal Government itself was relied on to insulate the interests of the States is evident in the views of the Framers. James Madison explained that the Federal Government "will partake sufficiently of the spirit [of the States], to be disinclined to invade the rights of the individual States, or the prerogatives of their governments." The Federalist No. 46, p. 332 (B. Wright ed. 1961). Similarly, James Wilson observed that "it was a favorite object in the Convention" to provide for the security of the States against federal encroachment and that the structure of the Federal Government itself served that end. 2 Elliot, at 438–439. Madison placed particular reliance on the equal representation of the States in the Senate, which he saw as "at once a constitutional recognition of the portion of sovereignty remaining in the individual States, and an instrument for preserving that residuary sovereignty." The Federalist No. 62, p. 408 (B. Wright ed. 1961). He further noted that "the residuary sovereignty of the States [is] implied *and secured* by that principle of representation in one branch of the [federal] legislature" (emphasis added). The Federalist No. 43, p. 315 (B. Wright ed. 1961). See also McCulloch v. Maryland, 4 Wheat. 316, 435 (1819). In short, the Framers chose to rely on a federal system in which special restraints on federal power over the States inhered principally in the workings of the National Government itself, rather than in discrete limitations on the objects of federal authority. State sovereign interests, then, are more properly protected by procedural safeguards inherent in the structure of the federal system than by judicially created limitations on federal power.

The effectiveness of the federal political process in preserving the States' interests is apparent even today in the course of federal legislation. On the one hand, the States have been able to direct a substantial proportion of federal revenues into their own treasuries in the form of general and program-specific grants in aid. The federal role in assisting state and local governments is a longstanding one; Congress provided federal land grants to finance state governments from the beginning of the Republic, and direct cash grants were awarded as early as 1887 under the Hatch Act. In the past quarter-century alone, federal grants to States and localities have grown from $7 billion to $96 billion. As a result, federal grants now account for about one-fifth of state and local government expenditures. The States have obtained federal funding for such services as police and fire protection, education, public health and hospitals, parks and recreation, and sanitation. Moreover, at the same time that the States have exercised their influence to obtain federal support, they have been able to exempt themselves from a wide variety of obligations imposed by Congress under the Commerce Clause. For example, the Federal Power Act, the National Labor Relations Act, the Labor–Management Reporting and Disclosure Act, the Occupational Safety and Health Act, the Employee Retirement Income Security Act, and the Sherman Act all contain express or implied exemptions for States and their subdivisions. The fact that some federal statutes such as the FLSA extend general obligations to the States cannot obscure the extent to which the political position of the States in the federal system has served to minimize the burdens that the States bear under the Commerce Clause.

We realize that changes in the structure of the Federal Government have taken place since 1789, not the least of which has been the substitution of popular election of Senators by the adoption of the Seventeenth Amendment in 1913, and that these changes may work to alter the influence of the States in the federal political process. Nonetheless, against this background, we are convinced that the fundamental limitation that the constitutional scheme imposes on the Commerce Clause to protect the "States as States" is one of process rather than one of result. Any substantive restraint on the exercise of Commerce Clause powers must find its justification in the procedural nature of this basic limitation, and it must be tailored to compensate for possible failings in the national political process rather than to dictate a "sacred province of state autonomy." . . .

Insofar as the present cases are concerned, then, we need go no further than to state that we perceive nothing in the overtime and minimum-wage requirements of the FLSA, as applied to SAMTA, that is destructive of state sovereignty or violative of any constitutional provision. SAMTA faces nothing more than the same minimum-wage and overtime obligations that hundreds of thousands of other employers, public as well as private, have to meet.

In these cases, the status of public mass transit simply underscores the extent to which the structural protections of the Constitution insulate the States from federally imposed burdens. When Congress first subjected state mass-transit systems to FLSA obligations in 1966, and when it expanded those obligations in 1974, it simultaneously provided extensive funding for state and local mass transit through UMTA. In the two decades since its enactment, UMTA has provided over $22 billion in mass-transit aid to States and localities. In 1983 alone, UMTA funding amounted to $3.7 billion. As noted above, SAMTA and its immediate predecessor have received a substantial amount of UMTA funding, including over $12 million during SAMTA's first two fiscal years alone. In short, Congress has not simply placed a financial burden on the shoulders of States and localities that operate mass-transit systems, but has provided substantial countervailing financial assistance as well, assistance that may leave individual mass-transit systems better off than they would have been had Congress never intervened at all in the area. Congress' treatment of public mass transit reinforces our conviction that the national political process systematically protects States from the risk of having their functions in that area handicapped by Commerce Clause regulation.

IV

This analysis makes clear that Congress' action in affording SAMTA employees the protections of the wage and hour provisions of the FLSA contravened no affirmative limit on Congress' power under the Commerce Clause. The judgment of the District Court therefore must be reversed.

... [T]he principal and basic limit on the federal commerce power is that inherent in all congressional action—the built-in restraints that our system provides through state participation in federal governmental action. The political process ensures that laws that unduly burden the States will not be promulgated. In the factual setting of these cases the internal safeguards of the political process have performed as intended.

These cases do not require us to identify or define what affirmative limits the constitutional structure might impose on federal action affecting the States under the Commerce Clause....

National League of Cities v. Usery, 426 U.S. 833, 96 S. Ct. 2465, 49 L. Ed. 2d 245 (1976), is overruled. The judgment of the District Court is reversed, and these cases are remanded to that court for further proceedings consistent with this opinion.

It is so ordered.

■ Justice Powell, with whom The Chief Justice, Justice Rehnquist, and Justice O'Connor join, dissenting.

... Because I believe this decision substantially alters the federal system embodied in the Constitution, I dissent.

... Despite some genuflecting in the Court's opinion to the concept of federalism, today's decision effectively reduces the Tenth Amendment to meaningless rhetoric when Congress acts pursuant to the Commerce Clause....

Today's opinion does not explain how the States' role in the electoral process guarantees that particular exercises of the Commerce Clause power will not infringe on residual state sovereignty. Members of Congress are elected from the various States, but once in office they are Members of the Federal Government.[8] Although the States participate in the Electoral College, this is hardly a reason to view the President as a representative of the States' interest against federal encroachment....

The Court apparently thinks that the State's success at obtaining federal funds for various projects and exemptions from the obligations of some federal statutes is indicative of the "effectiveness of the federal political process in preserving the States' interests...." Ante, at 1018. But such political success is not relevant to the question whether the political processes are the proper means of enforcing constitutional limitations. The fact that Congress generally does not transgress constitutional limits on its power to reach state activities does not make judicial review any less necessary to rectify the cases in which it does do so. The States' role in our system of government is a matter of constitutional law, not of legislative

8. One can hardly imagine this Court saying that because Congress is composed of individuals, individual rights guaranteed by the Bill of Rights are amply protected by the political process. Yet, the position adopted today is indistinguishable in principle. The Tenth Amendment also is an essential part of the Bill of Rights....

grace. "The powers not delegated to the United States by the Constitution, nor prohibited by it to the States, are reserved to the States, respectively, or to the people." U.S. Const., Amdt. 10.

More troubling than the logical infirmities in the Court's reasoning is the result of its holding, i.e., that federal political officials, invoking the Commerce Clause, are the sole judges of the limits of their own power. This result is inconsistent with the fundamental principles of our constitutional system....

In our federal system, the States have a major role that cannot be pre-empted by the National Government. As contemporaneous writings and the debates at the ratifying conventions make clear, the States' ratification of the Constitution was predicated on this understanding of federalism. Indeed, the Tenth Amendment was adopted specifically to ensure that the important role promised the States by the proponents of the Constitution was realized.

Much of the initial opposition to the Constitution was rooted in the fear that the National Government would be too powerful and eventually would eliminate the States as viable political entities. This concern was voiced repeatedly until proponents of the Constitution made assurances that a Bill of Rights, including a provision explicitly reserving powers in the States, would be among the first business of the new Congress.

The Court maintains that the standard approved in *National League of Cities* "disserves principles of democratic self-governance." Ante, at 1016. In reaching this conclusion, the Court looks myopically only to persons elected to positions in the Federal Government. It disregards entirely the far more effective role of democratic self-government at the state and local levels. One must compare realistically the operation of the state and local governments with that of the Federal Government.... The administration and enforcement of federal laws and regulations necessarily are largely in the hands of staff and civil service employees. These employees may have little or no knowledge of the States and localities that will be affected by the statutes and regulations for which they are responsible. In any case, they hardly are as accessible and responsive as those who occupy analogous positions in state and local governments.

... [M]embers of the immense federal bureaucracy are not elected, know less about the services traditionally rendered by States and localities, and are inevitably less responsive to recipients of such services, than are state legislatures, city councils, boards of supervisors, and state and local commissions, boards, and agencies. It is at these state and local levels—not in Washington as the Court so mistakenly thinks—that "democratic self-government" is best exemplified....

Although the Court's opinion purports to recognize that the States retain some sovereign power, it does not identify even a single aspect of state authority that would remain when the Commerce Clause is invoked to justify federal regulation....

As I view the Court's decision today as rejecting the basic precepts of our federal system and limiting the constitutional role of judicial review, I dissent.

■ JUSTICE O'CONNOR, with whom JUSTICE POWELL and JUSTICE REHNQUIST join, dissenting.

... It has been difficult for this Court to craft bright lines defining the scope of the state autonomy protected by *National League of Cities.* Such difficulty is to be expected whenever constitutional concerns as important as federalism and the effectiveness of the commerce power come into conflict. Regardless of the difficulty, it is and will remain the duty of this Court to reconcile these concerns in the final instance. That the Court shuns the task today by appealing to the "essence of federalism" can provide scant comfort to those who believe our federal system requires something more than a unitary, centralized government. I would not shirk the duty acknowledged by *National League of Cities* and its progeny, and I share Justice REHNQUIST's belief that this Court will in time again assume its constitutional responsibility.

I respectfully dissent.

■ [The dissenting opinion of JUSTICE REHNQUIST is omitted.]

NOTES

1. *State and Local Autonomy and the Protections of the Federal Political Process.* The *Garcia* majority contends that "[s]tate sovereign interests, then, are more properly protected by procedural safeguards inherent in the structure of the federal system than by judicially created limitations on federal power." 469 U.S. at 552. Do you find the *Garcia* majority persuasive on this important point? Can you formulate a reply to the counterarguments offered by Justice Powell in his *Garcia* dissent?

Prior to the Court's decision, several legal scholars had made this argument at greater length. See, e.g., Jesse H. Choper, Judicial Review and the National Political Process: A Functional Reconsideration of the Role of the Supreme Court (1980); Herbert Wechsler, The Political Safeguards of Federalism: The Role of the States in the Composition and Selection of the National Government, 54 Colum. L. Rev. 543 (1954); and D. Bruce La Pierre, The Political Safeguards of Federalism Redux: Intergovernmental Immunity and the States as Agents of the Nation, 60 Wash. U.L.Q. 779 (1982). The debate on this issue has continued into the present, much of it spawned by Larry Kramer's 2000 article, Putting the Politics Back into the Political Safeguards of Federalism, 100 Colum. L. Rev. 215 (2000). See, e.g., Lynn A. Baker, Putting the Safeguards Back into the Political Safeguards of Federalism, 46 Vill. L. Rev. 951 (2001); Neal Devins, The Judicial Safeguards of Federalism, 99 Nw. U.L. Rev. 131 (2004); Marci A. Hamilton, Why Federalism Must Be Enforced: A Response to Professor Kramer, 46 Vill. L. Rev. 1069 (2001); Gregory P. Magarian, Toward Political Safeguards of Self–Determination, 46 Vill. L. Rev. 1219 (2001); John O. McGinnis & Ilya Somin, Federalism v. States' Rights: A Defense of Judicial Review in a Federal System, 99 Nw. U.L. Rev. 103 (2004); Robert A. Mikos, The Populist Safeguards of Federalism, 68 Ohio St. L.J. 1669 (2007); Note, The Lesson of *Lopez*: The Political Dynamics of Federalism's Political Safeguards, 119 Harv. L. Rev. 609 (2005).

2. The *Garcia* majority contends that the Court's attempt in *National League of Cities* "to draw the boundaries of state regulatory immunity in terms of 'traditional governmental function' " was "unworkable." Does that conclusion necessarily lead to the result in *Garcia*? If not, how do you explain the result in that case? Do you think that drawing "workable" lines, capable of judicial application, in this area is, in fact, more difficult than drawing those lines in other areas of constitutional law? (Does Justice O'Connor seem to think so?) If not, how do you explain the greater willingness of the Court in *Garcia* to declare defeat with regard to that task? See Lynn A. Baker & Ernest A. Young, Federalism and the Double Standard of Judicial Review, 51 Duke L.J. 75 (2001).

Notwithstanding its decision in *Garcia*, the Court since 1985 has intermittently provided increased protection for the autonomy of states and their political subdivisions under both the Tenth Amendment and the Commerce Clause. For discussion of the impact that some of these decisions have actually had on the lower courts and Congress, see Lynn A. Baker, The Revival of States' Rights: A Progress Report and a Proposal, 22 Harv. J.L. & Pub. Pol'y 95 (1998); Randy E. Barnett, Three Federalisms, 39 Loy. U. Chi. L.J. 285 (2008); Erwin Chemerinsky, The Assumptions of Federalism, 58 Stan. L. Rev. 1763 (2006); Richard H. Fallon, Jr., The Conservative Paths of the Rehnquist Court's Federalism Decisions, 69 U. Chi. L. Rev. 433 (2002); Calvin Massey, Federalism and the Rehnquist Court, 53 Hastings L.J. 431 (2002); J. Mitchell Pickerill, Leveraging Federalism: The Real Meaning of the Rehnquist Court's Federalism Jurisprudence for the States, 66 Alb. L. Rev. 823 (2003); Peter J. Smith, Federalism, Instrumentalism, and the Legacy of the Rehnquist Court, 74 Geo. Wash. L. Rev. 906 (2006); Kathleen M. Sullivan, From States' Rights Blues to Blue States' Rights: Federalism after the Rehnquist Court, 75 Fordham L. Rev. 799 (2006); Mark Tushnet, What Is the Supreme Court's New Federalism?, 25 Okla. City U.L. Rev. 927 (2000).

The first of the post-*Garcia* federalism decisions, New York v. United States, 505 U.S. 144 (1992), involved provisions of the Low-Level Radioactive Waste Policy Amendments Act of 1985, which were intended to facilitate the disposal of low-level radioactive waste. The challenged provisions created a series of incentives and regulations that were intended to induce each state to participate in the disposal effort. The Court found only one set of these incentives, the "take title" provision, to be problematic:

> The take title provision offers state governments a "choice" of either accepting ownership of waste or regulating according to the instructions of Congress. Respondents do not claim that the Constitution would authorize Congress to impose either option as a freestanding requirement. On one hand, the Constitution would not permit Congress simply to transfer radioactive

> waste from generators to state governments. Such a forced transfer, standing alone, would in principle be no different than a congressionally compelled subsidy from state governments to radioactive waste producers. The same is true of the provision requiring the States to become liable for the generators' damages. Standing alone, this provision would be indistinguishable from an Act of Congress directing the States to assume the liabilities of certain state residents. Either type of federal action would "commandeer" state governments into the service of federal regulatory purposes, and would for this reason be inconsistent with the Constitution's division of authority between federal and state governments. On the other hand, the second alternative held out to state governments—regulating pursuant to Congress' direction—would, standing alone, present a simple command to state governments to implement legislation enacted by Congress. As we have seen, the Constitution does not empower Congress to subject state governments to this type of instruction.
>
> Because an instruction to state governments to take title to waste, standing alone, would be beyond the authority of Congress, and because a direct order to regulate, standing alone, would also be beyond the authority of Congress, it follows that Congress lacks the power to offer the States a choice between the two. Unlike the first two sets of incentives, the take title incentive does not represent the conditional exercise of any congressional power enumerated in the Constitution. In this provision, Congress has not held out the threat of exercising its spending power or its commerce power; it has instead held out the threat, should the States not regulate according to one federal instruction, of simply forcing the States to submit to another federal instruction. A choice between two unconstitutionally coercive regulatory techniques is no choice at all. Either way, "the Act commandeers the legislative processes of the States by directly compelling them to enact and enforce a federal regulatory program," ... an outcome that has never been understood to lie within the authority conferred upon Congress by the Constitution.
>
> ... Whether one views the take title provision as lying outside Congress' enumerated powers, or as infringing upon the core of state sovereignty reserved by the Tenth Amendment, the provision is inconsistent with the federal structure of our Government established by the Constitution.

505 U.S. at 175–177.

Three years later, in United States v. Lopez, 514 U.S. 549 (1995), the Court held for the first time in nearly 60 years that a federal law exceeded Congress's power under the Commerce Clause.

United States v. Lopez

514 U.S. 549 (1995).

■ CHIEF JUSTICE REHNQUIST delivered the opinion of the Court.

In the Gun–Free School Zones Act of 1990, Congress made it a federal offense "for any individual knowingly to possess a firearm at a place that the individual knows, or has reasonable cause to believe, is a school zone." 18 U.S.C. § 922(q)(1)(A) (1988 ed., Supp. V). The Act neither regulates a commercial activity nor contains a requirement that the possession be connected in any way to interstate commerce. We hold that the Act exceeds the authority of Congress "[t]o regulate Commerce ... among the several States...." U.S. Const., Art. I, § 8, cl. 3....

... [W]e have identified three broad categories of activity that Congress may regulate under its commerce power. *Perez, supra,* at 150, 91 S.Ct., at 1359; see also *Hodel, supra,* at 276–277, 101 S.Ct., at 2360–2361. First, Congress may regulate the use of the channels of interstate commerce. See, *e.g., Darby,* 312 U.S., at 114, 61 S.Ct., at 457; *Heart of Atlanta Motel, supra,* at 256, 85 S.Ct., at 357 (" '[T]he authority of Congress to keep the channels of interstate commerce free from immoral and injurious uses has been frequently sustained, and is no longer open to question.' " (quoting *Caminetti v. United States,* 242 U.S. 470, 491, 37 S.Ct. 192, 197, 61 L.Ed. 442 (1917))). Second, Congress is empowered to regulate and protect the instrumentalities of interstate commerce, or persons or things in interstate commerce, even though the threat may come only from intrastate activities. See, *e.g., Shreveport Rate Cases,* 234 U.S. 342, 34 S.Ct. 833, 58 L.Ed. 1341 (1914); *Southern R. Co. v. United States,* 222 U.S. 20, 32 S.Ct. 2, 56 L.Ed. 72 (1911) (upholding amendments to Safety Appliance Act as applied to vehicles used in intrastate commerce); *Perez, supra,* at 150, 91 S.Ct., at 1359 ("[F]or example, the destruction of an aircraft (18 U.S.C. § 32), or ... thefts from interstate shipments (18 U.S.C. § 659)"). Finally, Congress' commerce authority includes the power to regulate those activities having a substantial relation to interstate commerce, *Jones & Laughlin Steel,* 301 U.S., at 37, 57 S.Ct., at 624, *i.e.,* those activities that substantially affect interstate commerce, *Wirtz, supra,* at 196, n. 27, 88 S.Ct., at 2024, n. 27.

Within this final category, admittedly, our case law has not been clear whether an activity must "affect" or "substantially affect" interstate commerce in order to be within Congress' power to regulate it under the Commerce Clause. Compare *Preseault v. ICC,* 494 U.S. 1, 17, 110 S.Ct. 914, 924–925, 108 L.Ed.2d 1 (1990), with *Wirtz, supra,* at 196, n. 27, 88 S.Ct., at 2024, n. 27 (the Court has never declared that "Congress may use a relatively trivial impact on commerce as an excuse for broad general regulation of state or private activities"). We conclude, consistent with the great weight of our case law, that the proper test requires an analysis of whether the regulated activity "substantially affects" interstate commerce.

We now turn to consider the power of Congress, in the light of this framework, to enact § 922(q). The first two categories of authority may be quickly disposed of: § 922(q) is not a regulation of the use of the channels of interstate commerce, nor is it an attempt to prohibit the interstate transportation of a commodity through the channels of commerce; nor can § 922(q) be justified as a regulation by which Congress has sought to protect an instrumentality of interstate commerce or a thing in interstate commerce. Thus, if § 922(q) is to be sustained, it must be under the third category as a regulation of an activity that substantially affects interstate commerce.

... [W]e have upheld a wide variety of congressional Acts regulating intrastate economic activity where we have concluded that the activity substantially affected interstate commerce. Examples include the regulation of intrastate coal mining; *Hodel, supra,* intrastate extortionate credit transactions, *Perez, supra,* restaurants utilizing substantial interstate supplies, *McClung, supra,* inns and hotels catering to interstate guests, *Heart of Atlanta Motel, supra,* and production and consumption of homegrown wheat, *Wickard v. Filburn,* 317 U.S. 111, 63 S.Ct. 82, 87 L.Ed. 122 (1942). These examples are by no means exhaustive, but the pattern is clear. Where economic activity substantially affects interstate commerce, legislation regulating that activity will be sustained. . . .

Section 922(q) is a criminal statute that by its terms has nothing to do with "commerce" or any sort of economic enterprise, however broadly one might define those terms. . . . Section 922(q) is not an essential part of a larger regulation of economic activity, in which the regulatory scheme could be undercut unless the intrastate activity were regulated. It cannot, therefore, be sustained under our cases upholding regulations of activities that arise out of or are connected with a commercial transaction, which viewed in the aggregate, substantially affects interstate commerce. . . .

The Government's essential contention, *in fine,* is that we may determine here that § 922(q) is valid because possession of a firearm in a local school zone does indeed substantially affect interstate commerce. Brief for United States 17. The Government argues that possession of a firearm in a school zone may result in violent crime and that violent crime can be expected to affect the functioning of the national economy in two ways. First, the costs of violent crime are substantial, and, through the mechanism of insurance, those costs are spread throughout the population. See *United States v. Evans,* 928 F.2d 858, 862 (CA9 1991). Second, violent crime reduces the willingness of individuals to travel to areas within the country that are perceived to be unsafe. Cf. *Heart of Atlanta Motel,* 379 U.S., at 253, 85 S.Ct., at 355. The Government also argues that the presence of guns in schools poses a substantial threat to the educational process by threatening the learning environment. A handicapped educational process, in turn, will result in a less productive citizenry. That, in turn, would have an adverse effect on the Nation's economic well-being. As a result, the Government argues that Congress could rationally have concluded that § 922(q) substantially affects interstate commerce.

We pause to consider the implications of the Government's arguments. The Government admits, under its "costs of crime" reasoning, that Congress could regulate not only all violent crime, but all activities that might lead to violent crime, regardless of how tenuously they relate to interstate commerce. See Tr. of Oral Arg. 8–9. Similarly, under the Government's "national productivity" reasoning, Congress could regulate any activity that it found was related to the economic productivity of individual citizens: family law (including marriage, divorce, and child custody), for example. Under the theories that the Government presents in support of § 922(q), it is difficult to perceive any limitation on federal power, even in areas such as criminal law enforcement or education where States historically have been sovereign. Thus, if we were to accept the Government's arguments, we are hard pressed to posit any activity by an individual that Congress is without power to regulate....

Admittedly, a determination whether an intrastate activity is commercial or noncommercial may in some cases result in legal uncertainty. But, so long as Congress' authority is limited to those powers enumerated in the Constitution, and so long as those enumerated powers are interpreted as having judicially enforceable outer limits, congressional legislation under the Commerce Clause always will engender "legal uncertainty." *Post,* at 1664....

The possession of a gun in a local school zone is in no sense an economic activity that might, through repetition elsewhere, substantially affect any sort of interstate commerce. Respondent was a local student at a local school; there is no indication that he had recently moved in interstate commerce, and there is no requirement that his possession of the firearm have any concrete tie to interstate commerce.

To uphold the Government's contentions here, we would have to pile inference upon inference in a manner that would bid fair to convert congressional authority under the Commerce Clause to a general police power of the sort retained by the States. Admittedly, some of our prior cases have taken long steps down that road, giving great deference to congressional action. See *supra,* at 1629. The broad language in these opinions has suggested the possibility of additional expansion, but we decline here to proceed any further. To do so would require us to conclude that the Constitution's enumeration of powers does not presuppose something not enumerated, cf. *Gibbons v. Ogden, supra,* at 195, and that there never will be a distinction between what is truly national and what is truly local, cf. *Jones & Laughlin Steel, supra,* at 30, 57 S.Ct., at 621. This we are unwilling to do.

For the foregoing reasons the judgment of the Court of Appeals is

Affirmed.

■ [The dissenting opinion of JUSTICE BREYER, and the concurring opinions of JUSTICES O'CONNOR, KENNEDY, and THOMAS are omitted.]

NOTE

1. Five years after *Lopez,* the U.S. Supreme Court decided United States v. Morrison, 529 U.S. 598 (2000), and reaffirmed the "three broad categories of activity that Congress may regulate under its commerce power" that it had set forth in *Lopez.* Id. at 608–09. At issue in *Morrison* was the constitutionality of 42 U.S.C. § 13981, which provided a federal civil remedy for victims of gender-motivated violence. En route to concluding that Congress lacked constitutional authority to enact the civil damages remedy, the *Morrison* Court, 529 U.S. at 611–619, observed:

> *Lopez's* review of Commerce Clause case law demonstrates that in those cases where we have sustained federal regulation of intrastate activity based upon

the activity's substantial effects on interstate commerce, the activity in question has been some sort of economic endeavor....

Gender-motivated crimes of violence are not, in any sense of the phrase, economic activity. While we need not adopt a categorical rule against aggregating the effects of any noneconomic activity in order to decide these cases, thus far in our Nation's history our cases have upheld Commerce Clause regulation of intrastate activity only where that activity is economic in nature....

In contrast with the lack of congressional findings that we faced in *Lopez,* § 13981 *is* supported by numerous findings regarding the serious impact that gender-motivated violence has on victims and their families. See, *e.g.,* H.R. Conf. Rep. No. 103–711, p. 385 (1994), U.S.Code Cong. & Admin.News 1994, pp. 1803, 1853; S.Rep. No. 103–138, p. 40 (1993); S.Rep. No. 101–545, p. 33 (1990). But the existence of congressional findings is not sufficient, by itself, to sustain the constitutionality of Commerce Clause legislation. As we stated in *Lopez,* " '[S]imply because Congress may conclude that a particular activity substantially affects interstate commerce does not necessarily make it so.' " 514 U.S., at 557, n. 2, 115 S.Ct. 1624 (quoting *Hodel,* 452 U.S., at 311, 101 S.Ct. 2389 (REHNQUIST, J., concurring in judgment)). Rather, " '[w]hether particular operations affect interstate commerce sufficiently to come under the constitutional power of Congress to regulate them is ultimately a judicial rather than a legislative question, and can be settled finally only by this Court.' " 514 U.S., at 557, n. 2, 115 S.Ct. 1624 (quoting *Heart of Atlanta Motel,* 379 U.S., at 273, 85 S.Ct. 348 (Black, J., concurring))....

Given these findings and petitioners' arguments, the concern that we expressed in *Lopez* that Congress might use the Commerce Clause to completely obliterate the Constitution's distinction between national and local authority seems well founded. See *Lopez, supra,* at 564,115 S.Ct. 1624. The reasoning that petitioners advance seeks to follow the but-for causal chain from the initial occurrence of violent crime (the suppression of which has always been the prime object of the States' police power) to every attenuated effect upon interstate commerce....

Petitioners' reasoning, moreover, will not limit Congress to regulating violence but may, as we suggested in *Lopez,* be applied equally as well to family law and other areas of traditional state regulation since the aggregate effect of marriage, divorce, and childrearing on the national economy is undoubtedly significant....

We accordingly reject the argument that Congress may regulate noneconomic, violent criminal conduct based solely on that conduct's aggregate effect on interstate commerce. The Constitution requires a distinction between what is truly national and what is truly local. *Lopez,* 514 U.S., at 568, 115 S.Ct. 1624 (citing *Jones & Laughlin Steel,* 301 U.S., at 30, 57 S.Ct. 615).

Printz v. United States

521 U.S. 898 (1997).

■ JUSTICE SCALIA delivered the opinion of the Court.

The question presented in these cases is whether certain interim provisions of the Brady Handgun Violence Prevention Act, Pub.L. 103–159, 107 Stat. 1536, commanding state and local law enforcement officers to conduct

background checks on prospective handgun purchasers and to perform certain related tasks, violate the Constitution.

I

The Gun Control Act of 1968 (GCA), 18 U.S.C. § 921 *et seq.*, establishes a detailed federal scheme governing the distribution of firearms....

In 1993, Congress amended the GCA by enacting the Brady Act. The Act requires the Attorney General to establish a national instant background-check system by November 30, 1998, Pub.L. 103–159, as amended, Pub.L. 103–322, 103 Stat. 2074, note following 18 U.S.C. § 922, and immediately puts in place certain interim provisions until that system becomes operative. Under the interim provisions, a firearms dealer who proposes to transfer a handgun must first: (1) receive from the transferee a statement (the Brady Form), § 922(s)(1)(A)(i)(I), containing the name, address, and date of birth of the proposed transferee along with a sworn statement that the transferee is not among any of the classes of prohibited purchasers, § 922(s)(3); (2) verify the identity of the transferee by examining an identification document, § 922(s)(1)(A)(i)(II); and (3) provide the "chief law enforcement officer" (CLEO) of the transferee's residence with notice of the contents (and a copy) of the Brady Form, §§ 922(s)(1)(A)(i)(III) and (IV). With some exceptions, the dealer must then wait five business days before consummating the sale, unless the CLEO earlier notifies the dealer that he has no reason to believe the transfer would be illegal. § 922(s)(1)(A)(ii)....

Under a separate provision of the GCA, any person who "knowingly violates [the section of the GCA amended by the Brady Act] shall be fined under this title, imprisoned for not more than 1 year, or both." § 924(a)(5).

Petitioners Jay Printz and Richard Mack, the CLEOs for Ravalli County, Montana, and Graham County, Arizona, respectively, filed separate actions challenging the constitutionality of the Brady Act's interim provisions....

II

. . .

Petitioners here object to being pressed into federal service, and contend that congressional action compelling state officers to execute federal laws is unconstitutional. Because there is no constitutional text speaking to this precise question, the answer to the CLEOs' challenge must be sought in historical understanding and practice, in the structure of the Constitution, and in the jurisprudence of this Court....

III

. . .

A

It is incontestible that the Constitution established a system of "dual sovereignty." *Gregory v. Ashcroft,* 501 U.S. 452, 457, 111 S.Ct. 2395, 2399,

115 L.Ed.2d 410 (1991); *Tafflin v. Levitt,* 493 U.S. 455, 458, 110 S.Ct. 792, 795, 107 L.Ed.2d 887 (1990). Although the States surrendered many of their powers to the new Federal Government, they retained "a residuary and inviolable sovereignty," The Federalist No. 39, at 245 (J. Madison).... Residual state sovereignty was also implicit, of course, in the Constitution's conferral upon Congress of not all governmental powers, but only discrete, enumerated ones, Art. I, § 8, which implication was rendered express by the Tenth Amendment's assertion that "[t]he powers not delegated to the United States by the Constitution, nor prohibited by it to the States, are reserved to the States respectively, or to the people."

. . .

This separation of the two spheres is one of the Constitution's structural protections of liberty. "Just as the separation and independence of the coordinate branches of the Federal Government serve to prevent the accumulation of excessive power in any one branch, a healthy balance of power between the States and the Federal Government will reduce the risk of tyranny and abuse from either front." 501 U.S., *supra,* at 458, 111 S.Ct., at 2400....

IV

.... Federal commandeering of state governments is such a novel phenomenon that this Court's first experience with it did not occur until the 1970's, when the Environmental Protection Agency promulgated regulations requiring States to prescribe auto emissions testing, monitoring and retrofit programs, and to designate preferential bus and carpool lanes....

[L]ater opinions of ours have made clear that the Federal Government may not compel the States to implement, by legislation or executive action, federal regulatory programs....

When we were at last confronted squarely with a federal statute that unambiguously required the States to enact or administer a federal regulatory program, our decision should have come as no surprise. At issue in *New York v. United States,* 505 U.S. 144, 112 S.Ct. 2408, 120 L.Ed.2d 120 (1992), were the so-called "take title" provisions of the Low-Level Radioactive Waste Policy Amendments Act of 1985, which required States either to enact legislation providing for the disposal of radioactive waste generated within their borders, or to take title to, and possession of, the waste—effectively requiring the States either to legislate pursuant to Congress's directions, or to implement an administrative solution. *Id.,* at 175–176, 112 S.Ct., at 2428. We concluded that Congress could constitutionally require the States to do neither. *Id.,* at 176, 112 S.Ct., at 2428. "The Federal Government," we held, "may not compel the States to enact or administer a federal regulatory program." *Id.,* at 188, 112 S.Ct., at 2435.

The Government contends that *New York* is distinguishable on the following ground: Unlike the "take title" provisions invalidated there, the background-check provision of the Brady Act does not require state legislative or executive officials to make policy, but instead issues a final directive to state CLEOs. It is permissible, the Government asserts, for Congress to command state or local officials to assist in the implementation of federal law so long as "Congress itself devises a clear legislative solution that regulates private conduct" and requires state or local officers to provide only "limited, non-policymaking help in enforcing that law." "[T]he constitutional line is crossed only when Congress compels the States to make law in their sovereign capacities." Brief for United States 16.

The Government's distinction between "making" law and merely "enforcing" it, between "policymaking" and mere "implementation," is an interesting one.... Executive action that has utterly no policymaking component is rare, particularly at an executive level as high as a jurisdiction's chief law enforcement officer. Is it really true that there is no policymaking involved in deciding, for example, what "reasonable efforts" shall be expended to conduct a background check?....

Even assuming, moreover, that the Brady Act leaves no "policymaking" discretion with the States, we fail to see how that improves rather than worsens the intrusion upon state sovereignty. Preservation of the States as independent and autonomous political entities is arguably less undermined by requiring them to make policy in certain fields than (as Judge Sneed aptly described it over two decades ago) by "reduc[ing] [them] to puppets of a ventriloquist Congress," *Brown v. EPA,* 521 F.2d, at 839. It is an essential attribute of the States' retained sovereignty that they remain independent and autonomous within their proper sphere of authority. See *Texas v. White,* 7 Wall., at 725. It is no more compatible with this independence and autonomy that their officers be "dragooned" (as Judge Fernandez put it in his dissent below, 66 F.3d, at 1035) into administering federal law, than it would be compatible with the independence and autonomy of the United States that its officers be impressed into service for the execution of state laws....

The Government also maintains that requiring state officers to perform discrete, ministerial tasks specified by Congress does not violate the principle of *New York* because it does not diminish the accountability of state or federal officials. This argument fails even on its own terms. By forcing state governments to absorb the financial burden of implementing a federal regulatory program, Members of Congress can take credit for "solving" problems without having to ask their constituents to pay for the solutions with higher federal taxes. And even when the States are not forced to absorb the costs of implementing a federal program, they are still put in the position of taking the blame for its burdensomeness and for its defects. See Merritt, Three Faces of Federalism: Finding a Formula for the Future, 47 Vand. L. Rev. 1563, 1580, n. 65 (1994). Under the present law, for example, it will be the CLEO and not some federal official who stands between the gun purchaser and immediate possession of his gun. And it will likely be the CLEO, not some federal official, who will be blamed for any error (even one in the designated federal database) that causes a purchaser to be mistakenly rejected....

Finally, the Government puts forward a cluster of arguments that can be grouped under the heading: "The Brady Act serves very important purposes, is most efficiently administered by CLEOs during the interim period, and places a minimal and only temporary burden upon state officers." There is considerable disagreement over the extent of the burden, but we need not pause over that detail. Assuming *all* the mentioned factors were true, they might be relevant if we were evaluating whether the incidental application to the States of a federal law of general applicability excessively interfered with the functioning of state governments. See, *e.g.*, *Fry v. United States*, 421 U.S. 542, 548, 95 S.Ct. 1792, 1796, 44 L.Ed.2d 363 (1975); *National League of Cities v. Usery*, 426 U.S. 833, 853, 96 S.Ct. 2465, 2475, 49 L.Ed.2d 245 (1976) (overruled by *Garcia v. San Antonio Metropolitan Transit Authority*, 469 U.S. 528, 105 S.Ct. 1005, 83 L.Ed.2d 1016 (1985)); *South Carolina v. Baker*, 485 U.S. 505, 529, 108 S.Ct. 1355, 1370, 99 L.Ed.2d 592 (1988) (REHNQUIST, C.J., concurring in judgment). But where, as here, it is the whole *object* of the law to direct the functioning of the state executive, and hence to compromise the structural framework of dual sovereignty, such a "balancing" analysis is inappropriate.... It is the very *principle* of separate state sovereignty that such a law offends, and no comparative assessment of the various interests can overcome that fundamental defect. Cf. *Bowsher*, 478 U.S., at 736, 106 S.Ct., at 3192–3193 (declining to subject principle of separation of powers to a balancing test); *Chadha*, 462 U.S., at 944–946, 103 S.Ct., at 2780–2782 (same); *Plaut v. Spendthrift Farm, Inc.*, 514 U.S. 211, 239–240, 115 S.Ct. 1447, 1462–1463, 131 L.Ed.2d 328 (1995) (holding legislated invalidation of final judgments to be categorically unconstitutional). We expressly rejected such an approach in *New York*, and what we said bears repeating:

> Much of the Constitution is concerned with setting forth the form of our government, and the courts have traditionally invalidated measures deviating from that form. The result may appear 'formalistic' in a given case to partisans of the measure at issue, because such measures are typically the product of the era's perceived necessity. But the Constitution protects us from our own best intentions: It divides power among sovereigns and among branches of government precisely so that we may resist the temptation to concentrate power in one location as an expedient solution to the crisis of the day.

505 U.S., at 187, 112 S.Ct., at 2434.

We adhere to that principle today, and conclude categorically, as we concluded categorically in *New York*: "The Federal Government may not compel the States to enact or administer a federal regulatory program." *Id.*, at 188, 112 S.Ct., at 2435. The mandatory obligation imposed on CLEOs to perform background checks on prospective handgun purchasers plainly runs afoul of that rule.

V

. . .

* * *

We held in *New York* that Congress cannot compel the States to enact or enforce a federal regulatory program. Today we hold that Congress cannot circumvent that prohibition by conscripting the State's officers directly. The Federal Government may neither issue directives requiring the States to address particular problems, nor command the States' officers, or those of their political subdivisions, to administer or enforce a federal regulatory program. It matters not whether policymaking is involved, and no case-by-case weighing of the burdens or benefits is necessary; such commands are fundamentally incompatible with our constitutional system of dual sovereignty. Accordingly, the judgment of the Court of Appeals for the Ninth Circuit is reversed.

It is so ordered.

■ JUSTICE STEVENS, with whom JUSTICE SOUTER, JUSTICE GINSBURG, and JUSTICE BREYER join, dissenting.

.... As we explained in *Garcia v. San Antonio Metropolitan Transit Authority,* 469 U.S. 528, 105 S.Ct. 1005, 83 L.Ed.2d 1016 (1985): "[T]he principal means chosen by the Framers to ensure the role of the States in the federal system lies in the structure of the Federal Government itself. It is no novelty to observe that the composition of the Federal Government was designed in large part to protect the States from overreaching by Congress." *Id.,* at 550–551, 105 S.Ct., at 1017. Given the fact that the Members of Congress are elected by the people of the several States, with each State receiving an equivalent number of Senators in order to ensure that even the smallest States have a powerful voice in the Legislature, it is quite unrealistic to assume that they will ignore the sovereignty concerns of their constituents. It is far more reasonable to presume that their decisions to impose modest burdens on state officials from time to time reflect a considered judgment that the people in each of the States will benefit therefrom.

Indeed, the presumption of validity that supports all congressional enactments ... has added force with respect to policy judgments concerning the impact of a federal statute upon the respective States. The majority points to nothing suggesting that the political safeguards of federalism identified in *Garcia* need be supplemented by a rule, grounded in neither constitutional history nor text, flatly prohibiting the National Government from enlisting state and local officials in the implementation of federal law.

Recent developments demonstrate that the political safeguards protecting Our Federalism are effective. The majority expresses special concern that were its rule not adopted the Federal Government would be able to avail itself of the services of state government officials "at no cost to itself." *Ante,* at 2378; see also *ante,* at 2382 (arguing that "Members of Congress can take credit for 'solving' problems without having to ask their constituents to pay for the solutions with higher federal taxes"). But this specific problem of federal actions that have the effect of imposing so-called "unfunded mandates" on the States has been identified and meaningfully addressed by Congress in recent legislation.[18] See Unfunded Mandates Reform Act of 1995, Pub.L. 104–4, 109 Stat. 48.

The statute was designed "to end the imposition, in the absence of full consideration by Congress, of Federal mandates on State ... governments without adequate Federal funding, in a manner that may displace other essential State ... governmental priorities." 2 U.S.C. § 1501(2) (1994 ed., Supp. II). It functions, *inter alia,* by permitting Members of Congress to raise an objection by point of order to a pending bill that contains an "unfunded mandate," as defined by the statute, of over $50 million.... The mandate may not then be enacted unless the Members make an explicit decision to proceed anyway. See Recent Legislation, Unfunded Mandates Reform Act of 1995, 109 Harv. L. Rev. 1469 (1996) (describing functioning of statute). Whatever the ultimate impact of the new legislation, its passage demonstrates that unelected judges are better off leaving the protection of federalism to the political process in all but the most extraordinary circumstances....

Perversely, the majority's rule seems more likely to damage than to preserve the safeguards against tyranny provided by the existence of vital state governments. By limiting the ability of the Federal Government to enlist state officials in the implementation of its programs, the Court creates incentives for the National Government to aggrandize itself. In the name of State's rights, the majority would have the Federal Government create vast national bureaucracies to implement its policies. This is exactly

18. The majority also makes the more general claim that requiring state officials to carry out federal policy causes States to "tak[e] the blame" for failed programs. *Ante,* at 2382. The Court cites no empirical authority to support the proposition, relying entirely on the speculations of a law review article. This concern is vastly overstated.

Unlike state legislators, local government executive officials routinely take action in response to a variety of sources of authority: local ordinance, state law, and federal law. It doubtless may therefore require some sophistication to discern under which authority an executive official is acting, just as it may not always be immediately obvious what legal source of authority underlies a judicial decision. In both cases, affected citizens must look past the official before them to find the true cause of their grievance. See *FERC v. Mississippi,* 456 U.S. 742, 785, 102 S.Ct. 2126, 2151, 72 L.Ed.2d 532 (1982) (O'CONNOR, J., concurring in part and dissenting in part) (legislators differ from judges because legislators have "the power to choose subjects for legislation"). But the majority's rule neither creates nor alters this basic truth.

The problem is of little real consequence in any event, because to the extent that a particular action proves politically unpopular, we may be confident that elected officials charged with implementing it will be quite clear to their constituents where the source of the misfortune lies. These cases demonstrate the point. Sheriffs Printz and Mack have made public statements, including their decisions to serve as plaintiffs in these actions, denouncing the Brady Act. See, *e.g.,* Shaffer, Gun Suit Shoots Sheriff into Spotlight, Arizona Republic, July 5, 1994, p. B1; Downs, Most Gun Dealers Shrug off Proposal to Raise License Fee, Missoulian, Jan. 5, 1994. Indeed, Sheriff Mack has written a book discussing his views on the issue. See R. Mack & T. Walters, From My Cold Dead Fingers: Why America Needs Guns (1994). Moreover, we can be sure that CLEO's will inform disgruntled constituents who have been denied permission to purchase a handgun about the origins of the Brady Act requirements. The Court's suggestion that voters will be confused over who is to "blame" for the statute reflects a gross lack of confidence in the electorate that is at war with the basic assumptions underlying any democratic government.

the sort of thing that the early Federalists promised would not occur, in part as a result of the National Government's ability to rely on the magistracy of the States. See, *e.g.,* The Federalist No. 36, at 234–235 (A. Hamilton); *id.,* No. 45, at 318 (J. Madison).[21]

* * *

The provision of the Brady Act that crosses the Court's newly defined constitutional threshold is more comparable to a statute requiring local police officers to report the identity of missing children to the Crime Control Center of the Department of Justice than to an offensive federal command to a sovereign State. If Congress believes that such a statute will benefit the people of the Nation, and serve the interests of cooperative federalism better than an enlarged federal bureaucracy, we should respect both its policy judgment and its appraisal of its constitutional power.

Accordingly, I respectfully dissent.

NOTES

1. What is the constitutional basis for the "anti-commandeering" doctrine set forth in *Printz*? Could the Court have reached the result it did in *Printz* without this doctrine? If so, how and why? For discussion of *Printz* see, e.g., Matthew D. Adler & Seth F. Kreimer, The New Etiquette of Federalism: *New York*, *Printz*, and *Yeskey*, 1998 Sup. Ct. Rev. 71; Evan H. Caminker, *Printz*, State Sovereignty, and the Limits of Formalism, 1997 Sup. Ct. Rev. 199; Roderick M. Hills, Jr., The Political Economy of Cooperative Federalism: Why State Autonomy Makes Sense and "Dual Sovereignty" Doesn't, 96 Mich. L. Rev. 813 (1998); Vicki C. Jackson, Federalism and The Uses and Limits of Law: *Printz* and Principle?, 111 Harv. L. Rev. 2180 (1998); Jason Mazzone, The Commandeerer in Chief, 83 Notre Dame L. Rev. 265 (2007); Timothy Meyer, Federalism and Accountability: State Attorneys General, Regulatory Litigation, and the New Federalism, 95 Cal. L. Rev. 885 (2007); Neil S. Siegel, Commandeering and Its Alternatives: A Federalism Perspective, 59 Vand. L. Rev. 1629 (2006).

2. In 2000, the Supreme Court decided Reno v. Condon, 528 U.S. 141 (2000), which involved a challenge to the Driver's Privacy Protection Act of 1994 ("DPPA"), 18 U.S.C. §§ 2721–2725. The Act establishes a regulatory scheme that restricts the states' ability to disclose and sell a driver's personal information (e.g., address, phone number, Social Security number, medical information, and vehicle description) without the driver's consent. South Carolina filed suit alleging, inter alia, that the DPPA violates the Tenth Amendment to the U.S. Constitution. The Supreme Court unani-

---

21. The Court raises the specter that the National Government seeks the authority "to impress into its service . . . the police officers of the 50 States." *Ante,* at 2378. But it is difficult to see how state sovereignty and individual liberty are more seriously threatened by federal reliance on state police officers to fulfill this minimal request than by the aggrandizement of a national police force. The Court's alarmist hypothetical is no more persuasive than the likelihood that Congress would actually enact any such program.

mously held that the DPPA "is consistent with the constitutional principles enunciated in *New York* and *Printz*." 528 U.S. at 151.

> The United States asserts that the DPPA is a proper exercise of Congress' authority to regulate interstate commerce under the Commerce Clause, U.S. Const., Art. I, § 8, cl. 3. The United States bases its Commerce Clause argument on the fact that the personal, identifying information that the DPPA regulates is a "thin[g] in interstate commerce," and that the sale or release of that information in interstate commerce is therefore a proper subject of congressional regulation. *United States v. Lopez,* 514 U.S. 549, 558–559, 115 S.Ct. 1624, 131 L.Ed.2d 626 (1995). We agree with the United States' contention. The motor vehicle information which the States have historically sold is used by insurers, manufacturers, direct marketers, and others engaged in interstate commerce to contact drivers with customized solicitations. The information is also used in the stream of interstate commerce by various public and private entities for matters related to interstate motoring. Because drivers' information is, in this context, an article of commerce, its sale or release into the interstate stream of business is sufficient to support congressional regulation. . . .
>
> We agree with South Carolina's assertion that the DPPA's provisions will require time and effort on the part of state employees, but reject the State's argument that the DPPA violates the principles laid down in either *New York* or *Printz.* We think, instead, that this case is governed by our decision in *South Carolina v. Baker,* 485 U.S. 505, 108 S.Ct. 1355, 99 L.Ed.2d 592 (1988). In *Baker,* we upheld a statute that prohibited States from issuing unregistered bonds because the law "regulate[d] state activities," rather than "seek[ing] to control or influence the manner in which States regulate private parties." *Id.,* at 514–515, 108 S.Ct. 1355. . . .
>
> Like the statute at issue in *Baker,* the DPPA does not require the States in their sovereign capacity to regulate their own citizens. The DPPA regulates the States as the owners of data bases. It does not require the South Carolina Legislature to enact any laws or regulations, and it does not require state officials to assist in the enforcement of federal statutes regulating private individuals. We accordingly conclude that the DPPA is consistent with the constitutional principles enunciated in *New York* and *Printz.*

Id. at 148–151. Are you persuaded that the DPPA *is* in fact "consistent with the constitutional principles enunciated in *New York* and *Printz*?" What do you think the best arguments are that it might not be?

Gonzales v. Raich

545 U.S. 1 (2005).

■ JUSTICE STEVENS delivered the opinion of the Court.

California is one of at least nine States [including, as of December 1, 2004, Alaska, Arizona, Colorado, Hawaii, Maine, Montana, Nevada, Oregon, Vermont, and Washington] that authorize the use of marijuana for medicinal purposes. The question presented in this case is whether the power vested in Congress by Article I, § 8, of the Constitution "[t]o make all Laws which shall be necessary and proper for carrying into Execution" its authority to "regulate Commerce with foreign Nations, and among the several States'' includes the power to prohibit the local cultivation and use of marijuana in compliance with California law.

I

. . . In 1996, California voters passed Proposition 215, now codified as the Compassionate Use Act of 1996. The proposition was designed to ensure that "seriously ill" residents of the State have access to marijuana for medical purposes, and to encourage Federal and State Governments to take steps toward ensuring the safe and affordable distribution of the drug to patients in need. The Act creates an exemption from criminal prosecution for physicians, as well as for patients and primary caregivers who possess or cultivate marijuana for medicinal purposes with the recommendation or approval of a physician. A "primary caregiver" is a person who has consistently assumed responsibility for the housing, health, or safety of the patient.

Respondents Angel Raich and Diane Monson are California residents who suffer from a variety of serious medical conditions and have sought to avail themselves of medical marijuana pursuant to the terms of the Compassionate Use Act. They are being treated by licensed, board-certified family practitioners, who have concluded, after prescribing a host of conventional medicines to treat respondents' conditions and to alleviate their associated symptoms, that marijuana is the only drug available that provides effective treatment. . . .

Respondent Monson cultivates her own marijuana, and ingests the drug in a variety of ways including smoking and using a vaporizer. Respondent Raich, by contrast, is unable to cultivate her own, and thus relies on two caregivers, litigating as "John Does," to provide her with locally grown marijuana at no charge. These caregivers also process the cannabis into hashish or keif, and Raich herself processes some of the marijuana into oils, balms, and foods for consumption.

On August 15, 2002, county deputy sheriffs and agents from the federal Drug Enforcement Administration (DEA) came to Monson's home. After a thorough investigation, the county officials concluded that her use of marijuana was entirely lawful as a matter of California law. Nevertheless, after a 3-hour standoff, the federal agents seized and destroyed all six of her cannabis plants.

Respondents thereafter brought this action against the Attorney General of the United States and the head of the DEA seeking injunctive and declaratory relief prohibiting the enforcement of the federal Controlled Substances Act (CSA), 84 Stat. 1242, 21 U.S.C. § 801 *et seq.,* to the extent it prevents them from possessing, obtaining, or manufacturing cannabis for their personal medical use. . . . Respondents claimed that enforcing the CSA against them would violate the Commerce Clause, the Due Process Clause of the Fifth Amendment, the Ninth and Tenth Amendments of the Constitution, and the doctrine of medical necessity. . . .

... The case is made difficult by respondents' strong arguments that they will suffer irreparable harm because, despite a congressional finding to the contrary, marijuana does have valid therapeutic purposes. The question before us, however, is not whether it is wise to enforce the statute in these circumstances; rather, it is whether Congress' power to regulate interstate markets for medicinal substances encompasses the portions of those markets that are supplied with drugs produced and consumed locally. Well-settled law controls our answer. The CSA is a valid exercise of federal power, even as applied to the troubling facts of this case....

II

[I]n 1970, after declaration of the national "war on drugs," federal drug policy underwent a significant transformation ..... [P]rompted by a perceived need to consolidate the growing number of piecemeal drug laws and to enhance federal drug enforcement powers, Congress enacted the Comprehensive Drug Abuse Prevention and Control Act.

... The main objectives of the CSA were to conquer drug abuse and to control the legitimate and illegitimate traffic in controlled substances. Congress was particularly concerned with the need to prevent the diversion of drugs from legitimate to illicit channels.

To effectuate these goals, Congress devised a closed regulatory system making it unlawful to manufacture, distribute, dispense, or possess any controlled substance except in a manner authorized by the CSA. 21 U.S.C. §§ 841(a)(1), 844(a). The CSA categorizes all controlled substances into five schedules. § 812....

In enacting the CSA, Congress classified marijuana as a Schedule I drug. 21 U.S.C. § 812(c).... Schedule I drugs are categorized as such because of their high potential for abuse, lack of any accepted medical use, and absence of any accepted safety for use in medically supervised treatment. § 812(b)(1).... By classifying marijuana as a Schedule I drug, as opposed to listing it on a lesser schedule, the manufacture, distribution, or possession of marijuana became a criminal offense, with the sole exception being use of the drug as part of a Food and Drug Administration preapproved research study. §§ 823(f), 841(a)(1), 844(a); see also *United States v. Oakland Cannabis Buyers' Cooperative,* 532 U.S. 483, 490, 121 S.Ct. 1711, 149 L.Ed.2d 722 (2001)....

III

Respondents in this case do not dispute that passage of the CSA, as part of the Comprehensive Drug Abuse Prevention and Control Act, was well within Congress' commerce power. Brief for Respondents 22, 38. Nor do they contend that any provision or section of the CSA amounts to an unconstitutional exercise of congressional authority. Rather, respondents' challenge is actually quite limited; they argue that the CSA's categorical prohibition of the manufacture and possession of marijuana as applied to the intrastate manufacture and possession of marijuana for medical purposes pursuant to California law exceeds Congress' authority under the Commerce Clause....

Our case law firmly establishes Congress' power to regulate purely local activities that are part of an economic "class of activities" that have a substantial effect on interstate commerce. See, *e.g., Perez,* 402 U.S., at 151, 91 S.Ct. 1357; *Wickard v. Filburn,* 317 U.S. 111, 128–129, 63 S.Ct. 82, 87 L.Ed. 122 (1942)....

In assessing the scope of Congress' authority under the Commerce Clause, we stress that the task before us is a modest one. We need not determine whether respondents' activities, taken in the aggregate, substantially affect interstate commerce in fact, but only whether a "rational basis" exists for so concluding. *Lopez,* 514 U.S., at 557, 115 S.Ct. 1624; see also *Hodel v. Virginia Surface Mining & Reclamation Assn., Inc.,* 452 U.S. 264, 276–280, 101 S.Ct. 2352, 69 L.Ed.2d 1 (1981); *Perez,* 402 U.S., at 155–156, 91 S.Ct. 1357; *Katzenbach v. McClung,* 379 U.S. 294, 299–301, 85 S.Ct. 377, 13 L.Ed.2d 290 (1964); *Heart of Atlanta Motel, Inc. v. United States,* 379 U.S. 241, 252–253, 85 S.Ct. 348, 13 L.Ed.2d 258 (1964). Given the enforcement difficulties that attend distinguishing between marijuana cultivated locally and marijuana grown elsewhere, 21 U.S.C. § 801(5), and concerns about diversion into illicit channels, we have no difficulty concluding that Congress had a rational basis for believing that failure to regulate the intrastate manufacture and possession of marijuana would leave a gaping hole in the CSA. Thus, as in *Wickard,* when it enacted comprehensive legislation to regulate the interstate market in a fungible commodity, Congress was acting well within its authority to "make all Laws which shall be necessary and proper" to "regulate Commerce ... among the several States." U.S. Const., Art. I, § 8. That the regulation ensnares some purely intrastate activity is of no moment. As we have done many times before, we refuse to excise individual components of that larger scheme.

IV

To support their contrary submission, respondents rely heavily on two of our more recent Commerce Clause cases. In their myopic focus, they overlook the larger context of modern-era Commerce Clause jurisprudence preserved by those cases. Moreover, even in the narrow prism of respondents' creation, they read those cases far too broadly.

Those two cases, of course, are *Lopez,* 514 U.S. 549, 115 S.Ct. 1624, and *Morrison,* 529 U.S. 598, 120 S.Ct. 1740. As an initial matter, the statutory challenges at issue in those cases were markedly different from the challenge respondents pursue in the case at hand. Here, respondents ask us to excise individual applications of a concededly valid statutory scheme. In contrast, in both *Lopez* and *Morrison,* the parties asserted that a particular statute or provision fell outside Congress' commerce power in its entirety. This distinction is pivotal for we have often reiterated that "[w]here the class of activities is regulated and that class is within the reach of federal power, the courts have no power 'to excise, as trivial, individual instances' of the class." *Perez,* 402 U.S., at 154, 91 S.Ct. 1357 (quoting *Wirtz,* 392 U.S., at 193, 88 S.Ct. 2017 (emphasis deleted)); see also *Hodel,* 452 U.S., at 308, 101 S.Ct. 2352....

Unlike those at issue in *Lopez* and *Morrison,* the activities regulated by the CSA are quintessentially economic. "Economics" refers to "the production, distribution, and consumption of commodities." Webster's Third New International Dictionary 720 (1966). The CSA is a statute that regulates the production, distribution, and consumption of commodities for which there is an established, and lucrative, interstate market. Prohibiting the intrastate possession or manufacture of an article of commerce is a rational (and commonly utilized) means of regulating commerce in that product....

... One need not have a degree in economics to understand why a nationwide exemption for the vast quantity of marijuana (or other drugs) locally cultivated for personal use (which presumably would include use by friends, neighbors, and family members) may have a substantial impact on the interstate market for this extraordinarily popular substance. The congressional judgment that an exemption for such a significant segment of the total market would undermine the orderly enforcement of the entire regulatory scheme is entitled to a strong presumption of validity. Indeed, that judgment is not only rational, but "visible to the naked eye," *Lopez,* 514 U.S., at 563, 115 S.Ct. 1624, under any commonsense appraisal of the probable consequences of such an open-ended exemption....

V

... As the Solicitor General confirmed during oral argument, the statute authorizes procedures for the reclassification of Schedule I drugs. But perhaps even more important than these legal avenues is the democratic process, in which the voices of voters allied with these respondents may one day be heard in the halls of Congress. Under the present state of the law, however, the judgment of the Court of Appeals must be vacated. The case is remanded for further proceedings consistent with this opinion.

It is so ordered.

■ JUSTICE O'CONNOR, with whom THE CHIEF JUSTICE and JUSTICE THOMAS join as to all but Part III, dissenting.

* * * *

This case exemplifies the role of States as laboratories. The States' core police powers have always included authority to define criminal law and to protect the health, safety, and welfare of their citizens. *Brecht v. Abrahamson,* 507 U.S. 619, 635, 113 S.Ct. 1710, 123 L.Ed.2d 353 (1993); *Whalen v. Roe,* 429 U.S. 589, 603, n. 30, 97 S.Ct. 869, 51 L.Ed.2d 64 (1977). Exercising those powers, California (by ballot initiative and then by legislative codification) has come to its own conclusion about the difficult and sensitive question of whether marijuana should be available to relieve severe pain and suffering. Today the Court sanctions an application of the federal Controlled Substances Act that extinguishes that experiment, without any proof that the personal cultivation, possession, and use of marijuana for medicinal purposes, if economic activity in the first place, has a substantial effect on interstate commerce and is therefore an appropriate subject of federal regulation. In so doing, the Court announces a rule that gives Congress a perverse incentive to legislate broadly pursuant to the Commerce Clause—nestling questionable assertions of its authority into comprehensive regulatory schemes—rather than with precision. That rule and the result it produces in this case are irreconcilable with our decisions in *Lopez, supra,* and *United States v. Morrison,* 529 U.S. 598, 120 S.Ct. 1740, 146 L.Ed.2d 658 (2000). Accordingly I dissent....

II

A

... Today's decision suggests that the federal regulation of local activity is immune to Commerce Clause challenge because Congress chose to act with an ambitious, all-encompassing statute, rather than piecemeal. In my view, allowing Congress to set the terms of the constitutional debate in this way, *i.e.,* by packaging regulation of local activity in broader schemes, is tantamount to removing meaningful limits on the Commerce Clause....

Today's decision allows Congress to regulate intrastate activity without check, so long as there is some implication by legislative design that regulating intrastate activity is essential (and the Court appears to equate "essential" with "necessary") to the interstate regulatory scheme. Seizing upon our language in *Lopez* that the statute prohibiting gun possession in school zones was "not an essential part of a larger regulation of economic activity, in which the regulatory scheme could be undercut unless the intrastate activity were regulated," 514 U.S., at 561, 115 S.Ct. 1624, the Court appears to reason that the placement of local activity in a comprehensive scheme confirms that it is essential to that scheme. *Ante,* at 2209–2210. If the Court is right, then *Lopez* stands for nothing more than a drafting guide: Congress should have described the relevant crime as "transfer or possession of a firearm anywhere in the nation"—thus including commercial and noncommercial activity, and clearly encompassing some activity with assuredly substantial effect on interstate commerce. Had it done so, the majority hints, we would have sustained its authority to regulate possession of firearms in school zones....

B

... Even if intrastate cultivation and possession of marijuana for one's own medicinal use can properly be characterized as economic, and I question whether it can, it has not been shown that such activity substantially affects interstate commerce. Similarly, it is neither self-evident nor demonstrated that regulating such activity is necessary to the interstate drug control scheme....

The Court uses a dictionary definition of economics to skirt the real problem of drawing a meaningful line between "what is national and what is local," *Jones & Laughlin Steel,* 301 U.S., at 37, 57 S.Ct. 615. It will not do to say that Congress may regulate noncommercial activity simply because it may have an effect on the demand for commercial goods, or because the noncommercial endeavor can, in some sense, substitute for commercial activity. Most commercial goods or services have some sort of privately producible analogue. Home care substitutes for daycare. Charades games substitute for movie tickets. Backyard or windowsill gardening substitutes for going to the supermarket. To draw the line wherever private activity affects the demand for market goods is to draw no line at all, and to declare everything economic. We have already rejected the result that would follow—a federal police power. *Lopez, supra,* at 564, 115 S.Ct. 1624.

In *Lopez* and *Morrison,* we suggested that economic activity usually relates directly to commercial activity. See *Morrison,* 529 U.S., at 611, n. 4, 120 S.Ct. 1740 (intrastate activities that have been within Congress' power to regulate have been "of an apparent commercial character"); *Lopez,* 514 U.S., at 561, 115 S.Ct. 1624 (distinguishing the Gun–Free School Zones Act of 1990 from "activities that arise out of or are connected with a commercial transaction"). The homegrown cultivation and personal possession and use of marijuana for medicinal purposes has no apparent commercial character....

Even assuming that economic activity is at issue in this case, the Government has made no showing in fact that the possession and use of homegrown marijuana for medical purposes, in California or elsewhere, has a substantial effect on interstate commerce. Similarly, the Government has not shown that regulating such activity is necessary to an interstate regulatory scheme. Whatever the specific theory of "substantial effects" at issue (*i.e.,* whether the activity substantially affects interstate commerce, whether its regulation is necessary to an interstate regulatory scheme, or both), a concern for dual sovereignty requires that Congress' excursion into the traditional domain of States be justified....

There is simply no evidence that homegrown medicinal marijuana users constitute, in the aggregate, a sizable enough class to have a discernable, let alone substantial, impact on the national illicit drug market—or otherwise to threaten the CSA regime. Explicit evidence is helpful when substantial effect is not "visible to the naked eye." See *Lopez,* 514 U.S., at 563, 115 S.Ct. 1624. And here, in part because common sense suggests that medical marijuana users may be limited in number and that California's Compassionate Use Act and similar state legislation may well isolate activities relating to medicinal marijuana from the illicit market, the effect of those activities on interstate drug traffic is not self-evidently substantial....

The Court recognizes that "the record in the *Wickard* case itself established the causal connection between the production for local use and the national market" and argues that "we have before us findings by Congress *to the same effect.*" *Ante,* at 2208 (emphasis added). The Court refers to a series of declarations in the introduction to the CSA saying that (1) local distribution and possession of controlled substances causes "swelling" in interstate traffic; (2) local production and distribution cannot be distinguished from interstate production and distribution; (3) federal control over intrastate incidents "is essential to the effective control" over interstate drug trafficking. 21 U.S.C. §§ 801(1)–(6). These bare declarations cannot be compared to the record before the Court in *Wickard*.

They amount to nothing more than a legislative insistence that the regulation of controlled substances must be absolute. They are asserted without any supporting evidence—descriptive, statistical, or otherwise. "[S]imply because Congress may conclude that a particular activity substantially affects interstate commerce does not necessarily make it so." *Hodel v. Virginia Surface Mining & Reclamation Assn., Inc.*, 452 U.S. 264, 311, 101 S.Ct. 2352 (1981) (REHNQUIST, J., concurring in judgment). Indeed, if declarations like these suffice to justify federal regulation, and if the Court today is right about what passes rationality review before us, then our decision in *Morrison* should have come out the other way. In that case, Congress had supplied numerous findings regarding the impact gender-motivated violence had on the national economy. 529 U.S., at 614, 120 S.Ct. 1740; *id.*, at 628–636, 120 S.Ct. 1740 (SOUTER, J., dissenting) (chronicling findings). But, recognizing that " ' "[w]hether particular operations affect interstate commerce sufficiently to come under the constitutional power of Congress to regulate them is ultimately a judicial rather than a legislative question," ' " we found Congress' detailed findings inadequate. *Id.*, at 614, 120 S.Ct. 1740 (quoting *Lopez, supra,* at 557, n. 2, 115 S.Ct. 1624, in turn quoting *Heart of Atlanta Motel, Inc. v. United States,* 379 U.S. 241, 273, 85 S.Ct. 348, 13 L.Ed.2d 258 (1964) (Black, J., concurring)). If, as the Court claims, today's decision does not break with precedent, how can it be that voluminous findings, documenting extensive hearings about the specific topic of violence against women, did not pass constitutional muster in *Morrison,* while the CSA's abstract, unsubstantiated generalized findings about controlled substances do? . . .

The Government has not overcome empirical doubt that the number of Californians engaged in personal cultivation, possession, and use of medical marijuana, or the amount of marijuana they produce, is enough to threaten the federal regime. Nor has it shown that Compassionate Use Act marijuana users have been or are realistically likely to be responsible for the drug's seeping into the market in a significant way. . . . Piling assertion upon assertion does not, in my view, satisfy the substantiality test of *Lopez* and *Morrison.*

III

. . . Relying on Congress' abstract assertions, the Court has endorsed making it a federal crime to grow small amounts of marijuana in one's own home for one's own medicinal use. This overreaching stifles an express choice by some States, concerned for the lives and liberties of their people, to regulate medical marijuana differently. If I were a California citizen, I would not have voted for the medical marijuana ballot initiative; if I were a California legislator I would not have supported the Compassionate Use Act. But whatever the wisdom of California's experiment with medical marijuana, the federalism principles that have driven our Commerce Clause cases require that room for experiment be protected in this case. For these reasons I dissent.

■ [The concurring opinion of JUSTICE SCALIA and the dissenting opinion of JUSTICE THOMAS are omitted.]

NOTE

1. Which do you find more persuasive? The *Raich* dissent's claim that the majority's holding "gives Congress a perverse incentive to legislate broadly pursuant to the Commerce Clause ... rather than with precision" and is "irreconcilable" with the Court's decisions in *Lopez* and *Morrison*? Or the majority's assertion that the statutory challenges at issue in those cases were markedly different from the challenge in *Raich,* because "in both *Lopez* and *Morrison,* the parties asserted that a particular statute or provision fell outside Congress' commerce power in its entirety," while in *Raich* respondents asked the Court "to excise individual applications of a concededly valid statutory scheme"?

2. What is the response of the *Raich* majority to the dissent's question regarding the seemingly different approach to empirical findings taken by the Court in *Raich* versus *Lopez* and *Morrison*: "If, as the Court claims, today's decision does not break with precedent, how can it be that voluminous findings, documenting extensive hearings about the specific topic of violence against women, did not pass constitutional muster in *Morrison,* while the CSA's abstract, unsubstantiated generalized findings about controlled substances do?" Do you find the dissent's claim persuasive?

3. Scholars agree that the Court's decision in *Raich* did not advance, and almost certainly undercut, the *Lopez* Court's revival of limits on the commerce power. Those concerned to limit federal power, however, are far from united in their prescriptions for the future evolution of the Court's commerce clause doctrine. See, e.g., Randy E. Barnett, Foreword: Limiting *Raich*, 9 Lewis & Clark L. Rev. 743 (2005); Thomas W. Merrill, Rescuing Federalism after *Raich*: The Case for Clear Statement Rules, 9 Lewis & Clark L. Rev. 823 (2005); Glenn H. Reynolds & Brannon P. Denning, What Hath *Raich* Wrought? Five Takes, 9 Lewis & Clark L. Rev. 915 (2005); Ilya Somin, A False Dawn for Federalism: Clear Statement Rules after *Gonzales v. Raich*, 2006 Cato Sup. Ct. Rev. 113; Ernest A. Young, Just Blowing Smoke? Politics, Doctrine, and the Federalist Revival after *Gonzales v. Raich*, 2005 Sup. Ct. Rev. 1.

2. THE SPENDING POWER

Although advocates of state and local autonomy may cheer the Court's decisions in *New York*, *Lopez*, and *Printz*, these cases must be viewed in the context of the Court's 1987 decision in South Dakota v. Dole, 483 U.S. 203 (1987), that provided Congress a seemingly easy end run around any restrictions the Constitution might impose on its ability to regulate the states or their political subdivisions. For extended discussions of this point, see, e.g., Lynn A. Baker, Conditional Federal Spending after *Lopez*, 95 Colum. L. Rev. 1911 (1995); Lynn A. Baker, The Spending Power and the Federalist Revival, 4 Chap. L. Rev. 195 (2001); Lynn A. Baker & Mitchell N. Berman, Getting off the *Dole*: Why the Court Should Abandon Its Spending Doctrine, and How a Too–Clever Congress Could Provoke It to Do So, 78 Ind. L.J. 459 (2003); Erwin Chemerinsky, Protecting the Spending Power, 4 Chap. L. Rev. 89 (2001); Neil S. Siegel, Dole's Future: A Strategic Analysis, 16 Sup. Ct. Econ. Rev. 165 (2008); Ilya Somin, Closing the Pandora's Box of Federalism: The Case for Judicial Restriction of Federal Subsidies to State Governments, 90 Geo. L.J. 461 (2002).

South Dakota v. Dole

483 U.S. 203 (1987).

■ CHIEF JUSTICE REHNQUIST delivered the opinion of the Court.

Petitioner South Dakota permits persons 19 years of age or older to purchase beer containing up to 3.2% alcohol. S.D.Codified Laws § 35–6–27 (1986). In 1984 Congress enacted 23 U.S.C. § 158 (1982 ed., Supp. III), which directs the Secretary of Transportation to withhold a percentage of federal highway funds otherwise allocable from States "in which the purchase or public possession . . . of any alcoholic beverage by a person who is less than twenty-one years of age is lawful." The State sued in United States District Court seeking a declaratory judgment that § 158 violates the constitutional limitations on congressional exercise of the spending power and violates the Twenty-first Amendment to the United States Constitution. The District Court rejected the State's claims, and the Court of Appeals for the Eighth Circuit affirmed. 791 F.2d 628 (1986).

In this Court, the parties direct most of their efforts to defining the proper scope of the Twenty-first Amendment. . . .

Despite the extended treatment of the question by the parties, however, we need not decide in this case whether that Amendment would prohibit an attempt by Congress to legislate directly a national minimum drinking age. Here, Congress has acted indirectly under its spending power to encourage uniformity in the States' drinking ages. As we explain below, we find this legislative effort within constitutional bounds even if Congress may not regulate drinking ages directly.

The Constitution empowers Congress to "lay and collect Taxes, Duties, Imposts, and Excises, to pay the Debts and provide for the common Defence and general Welfare of the United States." Art. I, § 8, cl. 1. Incident to this power, Congress may attach conditions on the receipt of federal funds, and has repeatedly employed the power "to further broad policy objectives by conditioning receipt of federal moneys upon compliance by the recipient with federal statutory and administrative directives." *Fullilove v. Klutznick,* 448 U.S. 448, 474, 100 S.Ct. 2758, 2772, 65 L.Ed.2d 902 (1980) (opinion of Burger, C.J.). See *Lau v. Nichols,* 414 U.S. 563, 569, 94 S.Ct. 786, 789, 39 L.Ed.2d 1 (1974); *Ivanhoe Irrigation Dist. v. McCracken,* 357

U.S. 275, 295, 78 S.Ct. 1174, 1185, 2 L.Ed.2d 1313 (1958); *Oklahoma v. Civil Service Comm'n,* 330 U.S. 127, 143–144, 67 S.Ct. 544, 553–554, 91 L.Ed. 794 (1947); *Steward Machine Co. v. Davis,* 301 U.S. 548, 57 S.Ct. 883, 81 L.Ed. 1279 (1937). The breadth of this power was made clear in *United States v. Butler,* 297 U.S. 1, 66, 56 S.Ct. 312, 319, 80 L.Ed. 477 (1936), where the Court, resolving a longstanding debate over the scope of the Spending Clause, determined that "the power of Congress to authorize expenditure of public moneys for public purposes is not limited by the direct grants of legislative power found in the Constitution." Thus, objectives not thought to be within Article I's "enumerated legislative fields," *id.,* at 65, 56 S.Ct., at 319, may nevertheless be attained through the use of the spending power and the conditional grant of federal funds.

The spending power is of course not unlimited, *Pennhurst State School and Hospital v. Halderman,* 451 U.S. 1, 17, and n. 13, 101 S.Ct. 1531, 1540 n. 13, 67 L.Ed.2d 694 (1981), but is instead subject to several general restrictions articulated in our cases. The first of these limitations is derived from the language of the Constitution itself: the exercise of the spending power must be in pursuit of "the general welfare." See *Helvering v. Davis,* 301 U.S. 619, 640–641, 57 S.Ct. 904, 908–909, 81 L.Ed. 1307 (1937); *United States v. Butler, supra,* at 65, 56 S.Ct., at 319. In considering whether a particular expenditure is intended to serve general public purposes, courts should defer substantially to the judgment of Congress. *Helvering v. Davis, supra,* at 640, 645, 57 S.Ct., at 908–909.[2] Second, we have required that if Congress desires to condition the States' receipt of federal funds, it "must do so unambiguously ..., enabl[ing] the States to exercise their choice knowingly, cognizant of the consequences of their participation." *Pennhurst State School and Hospital v. Halderman, supra,* at 17, 101 S.Ct., at 1540. Third, our cases have suggested (without significant elaboration) that conditions on federal grants might be illegitimate if they are unrelated "to the federal interest in particular national projects or programs." *Massachusetts v. United States,* 435 U.S. 444, 461, 98 S.Ct. 1153, 1164, 55 L.Ed.2d 403 (1978) (plurality opinion). See also *Ivanhoe Irrigation Dist. v. McCracken, supra,* 357 U.S., at 295, 78 S.Ct., at 1185, ("[T]he Federal Government may establish and impose reasonable conditions relevant to federal interest in the project and to the over-all objectives thereof"). Finally, we have noted that other constitutional provisions may provide an independent bar to the conditional grant of federal funds. *Lawrence County v. Lead–Deadwood School Dist.,* 469 U.S. 256, 269–270, 105 S.Ct. 695, 703–704, 83 L.Ed.2d 635 (1985); *Buckley v. Valeo,* 424 U.S. 1, 91, 96 S.Ct. 612, 669, 46 L.Ed.2d 659 (1976) *(per curiam); King v. Smith,* 392 U.S. 309, 333, n. 34, 88 S.Ct. 2128, 2141, n. 34, 20 L.Ed.2d 1118 (1968).

South Dakota does not seriously claim that § 158 is inconsistent with any of the first three restrictions mentioned above. We can readily conclude that the provision is designed to serve the general welfare, especially in

---

2. The level of deference to the congressional decision is such that the Court has more recently questioned whether "general welfare" is a judicially enforceable restriction at all. See *Buckley v. Valeo,* 424 U.S. 1, 90–91, 96 S.Ct. 612, 668–669, 46 L.Ed.2d 659 (1976) *(per curiam).*

light of the fact that "the concept of welfare or the opposite is shaped by Congress. . . ." *Helvering v. Davis, supra,* at 645, 57 S.Ct., at 910. Congress found that the differing drinking ages in the States created particular incentives for young persons to combine their desire to drink with their ability to drive, and that this interstate problem required a national solution. The means it chose to address this dangerous situation were reasonably calculated to advance the general welfare. The conditions upon which States receive the funds, moreover, could not be more clearly stated by Congress. See 23 U.S.C. § 158 (1982 ed., Supp. III). And the State itself, rather than challenging the germaneness of the condition to federal purposes, admits that it "has never contended that the congressional action was . . . unrelated to a national concern in the absence of the Twenty-first Amendment." Brief for Petitioner 52. Indeed, the condition imposed by Congress is directly related to one of the main purposes for which highway funds are expended—safe interstate travel. See 23 U.S.C. § 101(b). This goal of the interstate highway system had been frustrated by varying drinking ages among the States. A Presidential commission appointed to study alcohol-related accidents and fatalities on the Nation's highways concluded that the lack of uniformity in the States' drinking ages created "an incentive to drink and drive" because "young persons commut[e] to border States where the drinking age is lower." Presidential Commission on Drunk Driving, Final Report 11 (1983). By enacting § 158, Congress conditioned the receipt of federal funds in a way reasonably calculated to address this particular impediment to a purpose for which the funds are expended.

The remaining question about the validity of § 158—and the basic point of disagreement between the parties—is whether the Twenty-first Amendment constitutes an "independent constitutional bar" to the conditional grant of federal funds. *Lawrence County v. Lead–Deadwood School Dist., supra,* at 269–270, 105 S.Ct., at 702–703. . . .

. . . [T]he "independent constitutional bar" limitation on the spending power is not, as petitioner suggests, a prohibition on the indirect achievement of objectives which Congress is not empowered to achieve directly. Instead, we think that the language in our earlier opinions stands for the unexceptionable proposition that the power may not be used to induce the States to engage in activities that would themselves be unconstitutional. Thus, for example, a grant of federal funds conditioned on invidiously discriminatory state action or the infliction of cruel and unusual punishment would be an illegitimate exercise of the Congress' broad spending power. But no such claim can be or is made here. Were South Dakota to succumb to the blandishments offered by Congress and raise its drinking age to 21, the State's action in so doing would not violate the constitutional rights of anyone.

Our decisions have recognized that in some circumstances the financial inducement offered by Congress might be so coercive as to pass the point at which "pressure turns into compulsion." *Steward Machine Co. v. Davis, supra,* 301 U.S., at 590, 57 S.Ct., at 892. Here, however, Congress has directed only that a State desiring to establish a minimum drinking age lower than 21 lose a relatively small percentage of certain federal highway funds. Petitioner contends that the coercive nature of this program is evident from the degree of success it has achieved. We cannot conclude, however, that a conditional grant of federal money of this sort is unconstitutional simply by reason of its success in achieving the congressional objective.

When we consider, for a moment, that all South Dakota would lose if she adheres to her chosen course as to a suitable minimum drinking age is 5% of the funds otherwise obtainable under specified highway grant programs, the argument as to coercion is shown to be more rhetoric than fact. As we said a half century ago in *Steward Machine Co. v. Davis:*

> [E]very rebate from a tax when conditioned upon conduct is in some measure a temptation. But to hold that motive or temptation is equivalent to coercion is to plunge the law in endless difficulties. The outcome of such a doctrine is the acceptance of a philosophical determinism by which choice becomes impossible. Till now the law has been guided by a robust common sense which assumes the freedom of the will as a working hypothesis in the solution of its problems.

301 U.S., at 589–590, 57 S.Ct., at 891–892.

Here Congress has offered relatively mild encouragement to the States to enact higher minimum drinking ages than they would otherwise choose. But the enactment of such laws remains the prerogative of the States not merely in theory but in fact. Even if Congress might lack the power to impose a national minimum drinking age directly, we conclude that encouragement to state action found in § 158 is a valid use of the spending power. Accordingly, the judgment of the Court of Appeals is

Affirmed.

■ [The dissenting opinions of JUSTICES O'CONNOR and BRENNAN are omitted.]

NOTES

1. At the time that the Supreme Court decided *Dole*, it could cite only one instance in which it had found that a congressional enactment did not meet the requirement that Congress state any conditions on the states' receipt of federal funds " 'unambiguously[,] . . . enabl[ing] the States to exercise their choice knowingly, cognizant of the consequences of their participation.' " 483 U.S. at 207. Some twelve years later, however, in Davis v. Monroe County Board of Education, 526 U.S. 629 (1999), Justice Kennedy, joined by Chief Justice Rehnquist and Justices Scalia and Thomas, all in dissent, made clear that, in their view, this prong of the *Dole* test had bite:

> A vital safeguard for the federal balance is the requirement that, when Congress imposes a condition on the States' receipt of federal funds, it "must do so unambiguously." *Pennhurst State School and Hospital v. Halderman,* 451 U.S. 1, 17, 101 S.Ct. 1531, 67 L.Ed.2d 694 (1981). . . .
>
> Our insistence that "Congress speak with a clear voice" to "enable the States to exercise their choice knowingly, cognizant of the consequences of their

> participation," *ibid.,* is not based upon some abstract notion of contractual fairness. Rather, it is a concrete safeguard in the federal system. Only if States receive clear notice of the conditions attached to federal funds can they guard against excessive federal intrusion into state affairs and be vigilant in policing the boundaries of federal power. Cf. *Dole, supra,* at 217, 107 S.Ct. 2793 (O'CONNOR, J., dissenting) ("If the spending power is to be limited only by Congress' notion of the general welfare, the reality, given the vast financial resources of the Federal Government, is that the Spending Clause gives 'power to the Congress to tear down the barriers, to invade the states' jurisdiction, and to become a parliament of the whole people, subject to no restrictions save such as are self-imposed' " (quoting *Butler, supra,* at 78, 56 S.Ct. 312)). . . .

Thus, the four dissenting justices, unlike the *Davis* majority, would not have read Title IX to authorize a private action for damages against a school board in cases of student-on-student harassment. The dissenters' concern was that the statute had not given grant recipients "clear and unambiguous notice that they would be liable in money damages for failure to remedy discriminatory acts of their students," 526 U.S. at 657.

In Jackson v. Birmingham Board of Education, 544 U.S. 167 (2005), the same four justices, again in dissent, reaffirmed their view that the "clear notice" provision of the *Dole* doctrine has bite. Unlike the majority, the *Jackson* dissenters would not have interpreted Title IX to authorize a private right of action for claims by an individual that he suffered retaliation because he complained about "sex discrimination," finding that the statute was insufficiently clear on the issue of "retaliation liability."

In the handful of cases in which a majority of the Court has shown that there are teeth to *Dole*'s requirement that states receiving federal funds be given clear notice of any attached conditions, the issue posed has not been the constitutionality of the funding condition. Rather, like *Davis* and *Jackson*, nearly all of those cases have been brought by third-party beneficiaries of the funding statute (§ 1983) who are seeking a private cause of action against the state for its noncompliance with the condition imposed on the federal funds. In those cases, the Court has repeatedly held that "unless Congress 'speak[s] with a clear voice,' and manifests an 'unambiguous' intent to confer individual rights, federal funding provisions provide no basis for private enforcement by § 1983," Gonzaga Univ. v. Doe, 536 U.S. 273, 280 (2002) (declining to authorize private enforcement of Family Educational Rights and Privacy Act); see also Suter v. Artist M, 503 U.S. 347 (1992) (declining to authorize private enforcement of Adoption Assistance and Child Welfare Act of 1980); Blessing v. Freestone, 520 U.S. 329 (1997) (declining to authorize private enforcement of Title IV–D of the Social Security Act regarding federal child-welfare funds). See also Arlington Central School Dist. Bd. of Ed. v. Murphy, 548 U.S. 291, 299 (2006) (interpreting Individuals with Disabilities Education Act (IDEA) not to authorize the recovery of non-attorney expert's fees for services rendered to prevailing parents in litigation under the IDEA because "the terms of the IDEA fail to provide the clear notice that would be needed to attach such a condition to a state's receipt of IDEA funds").

For discussion of the "clear notice" (or *Pennhurst*) prong of the *Dole* doctrine, see, e.g., Lynn A. Baker, Federalism and the Spending Power from *Dole* to *Birmingham Board of Education*, in The Rehnquist Legacy (ed. Craig M. Bradley, 2006); Lynn A. Baker, South Dakota v. Dole, in Encyclopedia of the Supreme Court of the United States (David Tanenhaus, ed., 2009); David Freeman Engstrom, Drawing Lines between *Chevron* and *Pennhurst*: A Functional Analysis of the Spending Power, Federalism, and the Administrative State, 82 Tex. L. Rev. 1197 (2004); Brian Galle, Getting Spending: How to Replace Clear Statement Rules with Clear Thinking about Conditional Grants of Federal Funds, 37 Conn. L. Rev. 155 (2004); Peter J. Smith, *Pennhurst*, *Chevron*, and the Spending Power, 110 Yale L.J. 1187 (2001).

2. In 2001, the Washington Supreme Court in Guillen v. Pierce County, 31 P.3d 628, held, inter alia, that a federal law exceeded Congress's power under the Spending Clause. It therefore presented the Rehnquist Court a rare opportunity both to re-examine its 1987 decision in *Dole*, and to address the challenges that current Spending Clause doctrine pose for state (and local) autonomy and current federalism doctrine more broadly.

At issue was 23 U.S.C. § 409, which protects information "compiled or collected" by state and local governments in connection with certain federal highway safety programs from being discovered or admitted in certain federal or state trials. The U.S. Supreme Court granted certiorari, but held that the challenged statute fell within Congress's power under the Commerce Clause. Thus, notwithstanding the rare opportunity afforded it, the Court never reached the spending power issue. For a critique of the U.S. Supreme Court's decision in *Guillen*, see, e.g., Lynn A. Baker & Mitchell N. Berman, Getting off the *Dole*: Why the Court Should Abandon Its Spending Doctrine, and How a Too–Clever Congress Could Provoke It to Do So, 78 Ind. L.J. 459 (2003); Mitchell N. Berman, *Guillen* and Gullibility: Piercing the Surface of Commerce Clause Doctrine, 89 Iowa L. Rev. 1487 (2004).

For a proposed reinterpretation of the Spending Clause that would enable it to work in tandem, rather than at odds, with the Court's post–*Garcia* readings of the Tenth Amendment and the Commerce Clause, see Lynn A. Baker, Conditional Federal Spending After *Lopez*, 95 Colum. L. Rev. 1911 (1995). For other critiques of *Dole* and discussions of Congress's spending power, see, e.g., Mitchell N. Berman, Coercion without Baselines: Unconstitutional Conditions in Three Dimensions, 90 Geo. L.J. 1 (2001); Reeve Bull, The Virtue of Vagueness: A Defense of *South Dakota v. Dole*, 56 Duke L.J. 279 (2007); Laurence Claus, "Uniform throughout the United States": Limits on Taxing as Limits on Spending, 18 Const. Comment. 517 (2001); John C. Eastman, Restoring the "General" to the General Welfare Clause, 4 Chap. L. Rev. 63 (2001); David E. Engdahl, The Spending Power, 44 Duke L.J. 1 (1994); Thomas R. McCoy & Barry Friedman, Conditional Spending: Federalism's Trojan Horse, 1988 Sup. Ct. Rev. 85; Neil S. Siegel, *Dole*'s Future: A Strategic Analysis, 16 Sup. Ct. Econ. Rev. 165 (2008).

3. *State and Local Autonomy and the Protections of the Federal Political Process.* Consider again the discussion in Part 1 above regarding the contention of the *Garcia* majority that "[s]tate sovereign interests, then, are more properly protected by procedural safeguards inherent in the structure of the federal system than by judicially created limitations on federal power." 469 U.S. at 552. In addition to the counter-arguments offered by Justice Powell in his *Garcia* dissent, consider the following counter-argument put forward in the context of conditional federal spending:

> While the state-based apportionment of representation within the federal government may well ensure that "*state interests as such*" are protected against federal oppression, *federal* oppression is not the problem. The problem, rather, lies in the ability of *some states* to harness the federal lawmaking power to oppress *other states*. Not only can the state-based allocation of congressional representation not protect states against this use of the federal lawmaking power, it facilitates it.
>
> ... [A] conditional offer of federal funds to the states implicitly divides them into two groups[: (1) states that already comply, or without financial inducement would happily comply, with the funding condition(s), and for which the offer of federal money therefore poses no real choice; and (2) states that find the funding condition(s) unattractive and therefore face the choice of foregoing the federal funds in order to avoid complying with the condition(s), or submitting to undesirable federal regulation in order to receive the offered funds]. One would therefore expect such conditional funding legislation to be enacted only if a (substantial) majority of states fall within the first group.... Few congressional representatives, after all, should be eager to support legislation that gives the states money only if they comply with a condition that a majority of their own constituents would independently find unattractive.

Lynn A. Baker, Conditional Federal Spending After *Lopez*, 95 Colum. L. Rev. 1911, 1940–1941 (1995).

Why would a state's congressional representatives ever prefer to enact a conditional rather than an unconditional offer of federal funds to the states, including their own? Consider the following possibilities: (a) in order to "entice" outlier states into amending or adopting some provision(s) of state constitutional or statutory law; (b) in order to win the votes of rationally self-interested constituents who believe that certain activities in another state impose negative externalities on them; (c) in the hope that some states(s) might decline the offer of federal funds; (d) in order to secure majority support for legislation whose only goal is distributing federal funds for the states to use for some specified purpose. For discussion of each of these possibilities, see id. at 1942–1947.

4. *Unfunded Mandates*. It is one thing to say that the federal constitution imposes certain obligations on states and their political subdivisions when they seek to engage in a particular activity, e.g., one that constitutes a taking. It is quite another matter for the federal government to impose on a state or its political subdivisions a requirement to engage in an activity, but not to provide the funds necessary to pay for it. In the latter situation, subordinate political bodies are constrained from engaging in activities that they would prefer because allocating resources to federally compelled activities leaves fewer resources for activities preferred by local residents.

Nevertheless, there has been substantial growth in these areas of mandated expenses. If the theory of *Garcia* is correct, states should have little complaint about mandated expenses, because representatives of the states, as agents of their constituencies, would simply be imposing these obligations on their principals. Dissatisfied principals (voters) could refuse to return their representatives to office. Are there reasons to believe that representatives will impose obligations on their constituents that those constituents would oppose? Return to the problem of collective action, discussed earlier in this chapter. Consider the following explanations for mandated programs that are disfavored by a majority.

(1) Pro-mandate forces can form a cohesive unit to lobby for the program, since they will receive concentrated benefits, while anti-mandate forces have difficulty in forming a coalition, since the costs of the mandate to any opponent are less than the costs of opposing it. In addition, if the number of potential opponents is sufficiently high, each potential opponent can attempt to free ride on the efforts of others in classic Chicken Game fashion.

(2) Legislators can gain the support of constituents by voting for programs, but to the extent that they can shift the costs of the programs to other levels of government and have the costs hidden in general taxes (e.g., federal income taxes or local property taxes), those same legislators will not be held responsible for increasing expenditures.

(3) Even if legislators are held responsible for the costs of the program, voters who oppose these programs will not retaliate against legislators. The electorate will not have an opportunity to approve or disapprove the legislator's performance on every issue, but will have to cast a single vote either to return the legislator to office or to turn the legislator out. As long as the legislator is viewed as doing a good job on average, a voter is unlikely to vote against that legislator because of a position on any single issue, as long as that issue is not salient to the voter. Thus, as long as the legislator does not vote in favor of a mandate that is salient to and opposed by many voters, he or she can obtain the support of pro-mandate supporters (to whom the mandate may well be salient, as evidenced by their lobbying for it), without losing votes of those who oppose it.

Is any of these explanations a "political process failure" as that phrase is used in *Garcia*? If so, would it be appropriate for a court to intervene to invalidate legislative mandates on subordinate levels of government?

The problem of unfunded mandates is not simply one that exists at the federal level. State legislators face the same opportunities to deflect costs to localities. See pages 503–514 infra. See also Daniel H. Cole & Carol S. Comer, Rhetoric, Reality, and the Law of Unfunded Federal Mandates, 8 Stan. L. & Pol'y Rev. 103 (1997); A. Raymond Randolph & Edward A. Zelinsky, Accountability and Mandates: Redefining the Problem of Federal Spending Conditions, 4 Cornell J.L. & Pub. Pol'y 482 (1995); Edward A. Zelinsky, Unfunded Mandates, Hidden Taxation, and the Tenth Amendment: On Public Choice, Public Interest, and Public Services, 46 Vand. L. Rev. 1355 (1993); Edward A. Zelinsky, The Unsolved Problem of the Unfunded Mandate, 23 Ohio N.U. L. Rev. 741 (1997); Robert W. Adler, Unfunded Mandates and Fiscal Federalism: A Critique, 50 Vand. L. Rev. 1137 (1997); Patricia T. Northrop, The Constitutional Insignificance of

Funding for Federal Mandates, 46 Duke L.J. 903 (1997); David A. Dana, The Case For Unfunded Environmental Mandates, 69 S. Cal. L. Rev. 1 (1995); Julie A. Roin, Reconceptualizing Unfunded Mandates and Other Regulations, 93 Nw. U. L. Rev. 351 (1999). Do the explanations for federal imposition of mandates on states apply with equal force when we are speaking of state imposition of mandates on localities?

5. *The Unfunded Mandates Reform Act of 1995.* Congress enacted the Unfunded Mandates Reform Act of 1995 ("UMRA") in a proclaimed attempt to address the problem of the federal government imposing increasing numbers of unfunded mandates on state and local governments. Under the UMRA, proposed legislation is out of order and any member of Congress can object to its consideration if it lacks a cost estimate or includes certain unfunded intergovernmental mandates. Any objection, however, is subject to waiver by a simple majority of the chamber. In addition, the UMRA contains numerous loopholes. First, an intergovernmental mandate is defined as a provision that "would impose an enforceable duty upon State, local, or tribal governments, except a condition of Federal assistance." Thus, Congress can continue to impose obligations, as long as they are structured as conditional aid which is unlikely to be refused. Second, the UMRA contains seven broadly phrased exceptions that make it inapplicable, for instance, to any provision that "enforces constitutional rights of individuals," or "is necessary for the national security or the ratification or implementation of the international treaty obligations," or "requires compliance with accounting or auditing procedures with respect to grants ... provided by the Federal Government." For additional explanation and critique, see Elizabeth Garrett, Enhancing the Political Safeguards of Federalism? The Unfunded Mandates Reform Act of 1995, 45 U. Kan. L. Rev. 1113, 1141 (1997) (indicating that, by one estimate, two-thirds of the unfunded federal mandates enacted during the 1980s would have fallen under one of the UMRA's exceptions); Daniel E. Troy, The Unfunded Mandates Reform Act of 1995, 49 Admin. L. Rev. 139 (1997). Since the adoption of the UMRA in 1995, a variety of proposals seeking to further protect state and local fiscal autonomy from federal encroachment have been put forward in Congress, but none has been enacted into law. For one perspective on why such "process reforms" are difficult to enact, see John Dinan, Strengthening the Political Safeguards of Federalism: The Fate of Recent Federalism Legislation in the U.S. Congress, 34 Publius 55 (2004).

6. *Unfunded Mandates and the No Child Left Behind Act of 2001.* The No Child Left Behind Act ("NCLBA") was signed into law in 2001 in order to "ensure that all children have a fair, equal, and significant opportunity to obtain a high-quality education." 20 U.S.C. § 6301. The Act provides for federal educational grants to states in order to promote academic accountability and educational attainment. A state's participation in the NCLBA is voluntary, but a state that chooses to accept the federal funds that accompany the Act must comply with NCLBA requirements. One such requirement is that participating states each must submit a plan to the Secretary of Education that includes annual testing in math and reading/language arts for students in grades three through eight, as well as high school students, 20 U.S.C. § 6311(b)(3). The participating states must report the results of these tests, as measured against an "Annual Yearly Progress" benchmark, to the Secretary of Education. Id. § 6311(b)(2)(B) & § 7325. Schools or districts that fail to make appropriate progress must undertake corrective measures and face progressively severe sanctions for continued noncompliance, including permitting students in a noncomplying school to transfer to any school within the district that has met the benchmark and, ultimately, replacing the majority of the failing school's staff. Id. § 6316(b)(1)–(8). The Act provides federal funds to assist states in developing and administering the tests required by the Act, and includes an "Unfunded Mandates Provision," id. § 7907(a), which states:

> Nothing in this chapter shall be construed to authorize an officer or employee of the federal Government to mandate, direct, or control a State, local educational agency, or school's curriculum, program of instruction, or allocation of State or local resources, or mandate a State or any subdivision thereof to spend any funds or incur any costs not paid for under this chapter.

Since its adoption, the NCLBA, especially including the Unfunded Mandates Provision, has been controversial, with some states contending that this provision means that the Act "does not require school districts to comply with the Act's educational requirements if doing so would require the expenditure of state and local funds to cover the additional costs of compliance." School District of the City of Pontiac v. Secretary of the U.S. Department of Education, 584 F.3d 253, 259 (6th Cir. 2009) (en banc). Those states have also argued, in the alternative, that "the Act is ambiguous as to whether school districts are required to spend their own funds, and that imposing such a requirement would violate the ['clear notice' provision of the] Spending Clause [of the United States Constitution]." Id. The Secretary of Education, in contrast, has argued that the Unfunded Mandates Provision "merely prevents officers and employees of the federal government from imposing additional, unauthorized requirements on the participating States," and that "this section simply emphasizes that State participation in NCLB is entirely voluntary, but that once a State chooses to participate, it must comply fully with NCLB requirements regardless of whether federal funding is adequate to cover the cost of compliance." Id. at 273.

The only federal appellate court to have ruled on this issue thus far is the Sixth Circuit sitting en banc, which divided evenly (8 to 8), thereby affirming the judgment of the district court. In his opinion affirming the judgment of the district court and granting the Secretary of Education's motion to dismiss, Judge Sutton held that the Act "clearly requires the States (and school districts) to comply with its requirements, whether doing so requires the expenditure of state and local funds or not. A contrary interpretation is implausible and fails to account for, and effectively eviscerates, numerous components of the Act." Id. at 285 (Sutton, J., concurring in the order):

> The [Act] might be described in many ways.... But one thing it is not is ambiguous, at least when it comes to the central tradeoff presented to the States: accepting flexibility to spend significant federal funds in return for (largely) unforgiving responsibility to make progress in using them.... Here, unlike prior education funding programs, Congress did not exercise [its] control by telling the schools how to spend the money but by telling them to get results with it. Time will tell whether Congress was wise to move from conditioning federal funds on "adequate" additional local funding to conditioning federal funds on "adequate" local progress. But no state official who read the Act could plausibly think that Congress intended to impose *neither* condition.
>
> ... It is the political branches, not the judiciary, that must make any changes, because the Act's requirements are clear, making them enforceable upon participating States and their school districts.

Id. at 295–296 (Sutton, J. concurring in the order).

For discussions of the NCLBA and other litigation surrounding it, see, e.g., Connecticut v. Spellings, 453 F. Supp. 2d 459 (D. Conn. 2006); Michael Heise, The Political Economy of Education Federalism, 56 Emory L.J. 125 (2006); Nicole Liguori, Leaving No Child Behind (Except in States that Don't Do as We Say): Connecticut's Challenge to the Federal Government's Power to Control State Education Policy through the Spending Clause, 47 B.C. L. Rev. 1033 (2006); Note, No Child Left Behind and the Political Safeguards of Federalism, 119 Harv. L. Rev. 885 (2006); Michael L. Pendell, How Far Is Too Far?: The Spending Clause, the Tenth Amendment, and the Education State's Battle Against Unfunded Mandates, 71 Alb. L. Rev. 519 (2008); Robert A. Schapiro, Toward a Theory of Interactive Federalism, 91 Iowa L. Rev. 243 (2005).

3. FEDERAL PREEMPTION OF LOCAL AND STATE LAWS

In addition to what are commonly considered to be the central "federalism" provisions of the Constitution (e.g., the Commerce Clause and the Tenth Amendment), preemption doctrine importantly regulates the relationship between the federal and sub-national units of government. See Ernest A. Young, The Rehnquist Court's Two Federalisms, 83 Tex. L. Rev. 1 (2004). Federal preemption of state and local regulations occurs pursuant to the Supremacy Clause of Article VI, Section 2 of the U.S. Constitution, which states that "This Constitution and the Laws of the United States which shall be made in Pursuance thereof; ... shall be the supreme Law of the Land; ... any Thing in the Constitution or Laws of any State to the Contrary notwithstanding." Thus, so long as Congress or an authorized federal agency acts within its constitutional powers, it may require that a federal regulatory scheme supplant any existing state or local scheme in the same area.

Federal preemption of state and local regulation is a relatively common phenomenon, and the issues confronted by the courts are readily divided into two major groups, each exemplified by one of the cases excerpted in this section: questions involving the interpretation of express preemption clauses in federal laws (see *Riegel v. Medtronic*, below), and questions of "implied" preemption, involving either claims that Congress has "occupied the field" or other seeming conflicts between state/local regulations and federal laws (see *Crosby v. National Foreign Trade Council*, below).

Donna S. Riegel, individually and as administrator of the Estate of Charles R. Riegel, Petitioner v. Medtronic, Inc.

552 U.S. 312 (2008).

■ JUSTICE SCALIA delivered the opinion of the Court.

We consider whether the pre-emption clause enacted in the Medical Device Amendments of 1976, 21 U.S.C. § 360k, bars common-law claims challenging the safety and effectiveness of a medical device given premarket approval by the Food and Drug Administration (FDA).

I

A

The Federal Food, Drug, and Cosmetic Act (FDCA), 52 Stat. 1040, as amended, 21 U.S.C. § 301 *et seq.*, has long required FDA approval for the introduction of new drugs into the market. Until the statutory enactment at issue here, however, the introduction of new medical devices was left largely for the States to supervise as they saw fit. See *Medtronic, Inc. v. Lohr*, 518 U.S. 470, 475–476, 116 S.Ct. 2240, 135 L.Ed.2d 700 (1996).

The regulatory landscape changed in the 1960's and 1970's, as complex devices proliferated and some failed. Most notably, the Dalkon Shield intrauterine device, introduced in 1970, was linked to serious infections and several deaths, not to mention a large number of pregnancies. Thousands of tort claims followed. R. Bacigal, The Limits of Litigation: The Dalkon Shield Controversy 3 (1990). In the view of many, the Dalkon Shield failure and its aftermath demonstrated the inability of the common-law tort system to manage the risks associated with dangerous devices. See, *e.g.*, S. Foote, Managing the Medical Arms Race 151–152 (1992). Several States adopted regulatory measures, including California, which in 1970 enacted a law requiring premarket approval of medical devices. 1970 Cal. Stats. ch. 1573, §§ 26670–26693; see also Leflar & Adler, The Preemption Pentad: Federal Preemption of Products Liability Claims After *Medtronic*, 64 Tenn. L. Rev. 691, 703, n. 66 (1997) (identifying 13 state statutes governing medical devices as of 1976).

Congress stepped in with passage of the Medical Device Amendments of 1976 (MDA), 21 U.S.C. § 360c *et seq.*, which swept back some state obligations and imposed a regime of detailed federal oversight. The MDA includes an express pre-emption provision that states:

> "Except as provided in subsection (b) of this section, no State or political subdivision of a State may establish or continue in effect with respect to a device intended for human use any requirement—

"(1) which is different from, or in addition to, any requirement applicable under this chapter to the device, and

"(2) which relates to the safety or effectiveness of the device or to any other matter included in a requirement applicable to the device under this chapter."§ 360k(a).

The exception contained in subsection (b) permits the FDA to exempt some state and local requirements from pre-emption....

Although the MDA established a rigorous regime of premarket approval for new Class III devices, it grandfathered many that were already on the market. Devices sold before the MDA's effective date may remain on the market until the FDA promulgates, after notice and comment, a regulation requiring premarket approval. §§ 360c(f)(1), 360e(b)(1). A related provision seeks to limit the competitive advantage grandfathered devices receive. A new device need not undergo premarket approval if the FDA finds it is "substantially equivalent" to another device exempt from premarket approval. § 360c(f)(1)(A). The agency's review of devices for substantial equivalence is known as the § 510(k) process, named after the section of the MDA describing the review. Most new Class III devices enter the market through § 510(k). In 2005, for example, the FDA authorized the marketing of 3,148 devices under § 510(k) and granted premarket approval to just 32 devices. P. Hutt, R. Merrill, & L. Grossman, Food and Drug Law 992 (3d ed.2007).

Premarket approval is a "rigorous" process....

The FDA spends an average of 1,200 hours reviewing each application, ... and grants premarket approval only if it finds there is a "reasonable assurance" of the device's "safety and effectiveness," § 360e(d). The agency must "weig[h] any probable benefit to health from the use of the device against any probable risk of injury or illness from such use." § 360c(a)(2)(C). It may thus approve devices that present great risks if they nonetheless offer great benefits in light of available alternatives....

The premarket approval process includes review of the device's proposed labeling. The FDA evaluates safety and effectiveness under the conditions of use set forth on the label, § 360c(a)(2)(B), and must determine that the proposed labeling is neither false nor misleading, § 360e(d)(1)(A)....

Once a device has received premarket approval, the MDA forbids the manufacturer to make, without FDA permission, changes in design specifications, manufacturing processes, labeling, or any other attribute, that would affect safety or effectiveness. § 360e(d)(6)(A)(i). If the applicant wishes to make such a change, it must submit, and the FDA must approve, an application for supplemental premarket approval, to be evaluated under largely the same criteria as an initial application. § 360e(d)(6); 21 CFR § 814.39(c).

After premarket approval, the devices are subject to reporting requirements. § 360i.... The FDA has the power to withdraw premarket approval based on newly reported data or existing information and must withdraw approval if it determines that a device is unsafe or ineffective under the conditions in its labeling. § 360e(e)(1); see also § 360h(e) (recall authority).

B

... The device at issue is an Evergreen Balloon Catheter marketed by defendant-respondent Medtronic, Inc. It is a Class III device that received premarket approval from the FDA in 1994; changes to its label received supplemental approvals in 1995 and 1996.

Charles Riegel underwent coronary angioplasty in 1996, shortly after suffering a myocardial infarction. App. to Pet. for Cert. 56a. His right coronary artery was diffusely diseased and heavily calcified. Riegel's doctor inserted the Evergreen Balloon Catheter into his patient's coronary artery in an attempt to dilate the artery, although the device's labeling stated that use was contraindicated for patients with diffuse or calcified stenoses. The label also warned that the catheter should not be inflated beyond its rated burst pressure of eight atmospheres. Riegel's doctor inflated the catheter five times, to a pressure of 10 atmospheres; on its fifth inflation, the catheter ruptured. Complaint 3. Riegel developed a heart block, was placed on life support, and underwent emergency coronary bypass surgery.

Riegel and his wife Donna brought this lawsuit in April 1999, in the United States District Court for the Northern District of New York. Their complaint alleged that Medtronic's catheter was designed, labeled, and manufactured in a manner that violated New York common law, and that these defects caused Riegel to suffer severe and permanent injuries....

II

Since the MDA expressly pre-empts only state requirements "different from, or in addition to, any requirement applicable ... to the device" under federal law, § 360k(a)(1), we must determine whether the Federal Government has established requirements applicable to Medtronic's catheter. If so, we must then determine whether the Riegels' common-law claims are based upon New York requirements with respect to the device that are "different from, or in addition to" the federal ones, and that relate to safety and effectiveness.§ 360k(a)....

Premarket approval ... imposes "requirements" under the MDA as we interpreted it in *Lohr*. Unlike general labeling duties, premarket approval is specific to individual devices. And it is in no sense an exemption from federal safety review—it *is* federal safety review. Thus, the attributes that *Lohr* found lacking in § 510(k) review are present here. While § 510(k) is " 'focused on *equivalence,* not safety,' " *id.,* at 493, 116 S.Ct. 2240 (opinion of the Court), premarket approval is focused on safety, not equivalence. While devices that enter the market through § 510(k) have "never been formally reviewed under the MDA for safety or efficacy,"*ibid.,* the FDA may grant premarket approval only after it determines that a device offers a reasonable assurance of safety and effectiveness, § 360e(d). And while the FDA does not "require" that a device allowed to enter the market as a substantial equivalent "take any particular form for any particular reason," *ibid.*, at 493, 116 S.Ct. 2240, the FDA requires a device that has received premarket approval to be made with almost no deviations from the specifications in its approval application, for the reason that the FDA has determined that the approved form provides a reasonable assurance of safety and effectiveness.

III

We turn, then, to the second question: whether the Riegels' common-law claims rely upon "any requirement" of New York law applicable to the catheter that is "different from, or in addition to" federal requirements and that "relates to the safety or effectiveness of the device or to any other matter included in a requirement applicable to the device." § 360k(a). Safety and effectiveness are the very subjects of the Riegels' common-law claims, so the critical issue is whether New York's tort duties constitute "requirements" under the MDA.

A

In *Lohr,* five Justices concluded that common-law causes of action for negligence and strict liability do impose "requirement[s]" and would be pre-empted by federal requirements specific to a medical device. See 518 U.S., at 512, 116 S.Ct. 2240 (opinion of O'Connor, J., joined by Rehnquist, C. J., and SCALIA and THOMAS, JJ.); *id.*, at 503–505, 116 S.Ct. 2240 (opinion of BREYER, J.). We adhere to that view....

Congress is entitled to know what meaning this Court will assign to terms regularly used in its enactments. Absent other indication, reference to a State's "requirements" includes its common-law duties. As the plurality opinion said in *Cipollone,* common-law liability is "premised on the existence of a legal duty," and a tort judgment therefore establishes that the defendant has violated a state-law obligation. *Id.*, at 522, 112 S.Ct. 2608. And while the common-law remedy is limited to damages, a liability award " 'can be, indeed is designed to be, a potent method of governing conduct and controlling policy.' " *Id.*, at 521, 112 S.Ct. 2608.

In the present case, there is nothing to contradict this normal meaning. To the contrary, in the context of this legislation excluding common-law duties from the scope of pre-emption would make little sense. State tort law that requires a manufacturer's catheters to be safer, but hence less effective, than the model the FDA has approved disrupts the federal scheme no less than state regulatory law to the same effect. Indeed, one would think that tort law, applied by juries under a negligence or strict-liability standard, is less deserving of preservation. A state statute, or a regulation adopted by a state agency, could at least be expected to apply cost-benefit analysis similar to that applied by the experts at the FDA: How many more lives will be saved by a device which, along with its greater effectiveness, brings a greater risk of harm? A jury, on the other hand, sees only the cost of a more dangerous design, and is not concerned with its benefits; the patients who reaped those benefits are not represented in court. As Justice BREYER explained in *Lohr,* it is implausible that the MDA was meant to "grant greater power (to set state standards 'different from, or in addition to' federal standards) to a single state jury than to state officials acting through state administrative or legislative lawmaking processes." 518 U.S., at 504, 116 S.Ct. 2240. That perverse distinction is not required or even suggested by the broad language Congress chose in the MDA, and we will not turn somersaults to create it.

B

The dissent would narrow the pre-emptive scope of the term "requirement" on the grounds that it is "difficult to believe that Congress would, without comment, remove all means of judicial recourse" for consumers injured by FDA-approved devices. *Post,* at 1015 (opinion of GINSBURG, J.) (internal quotation marks omitted). But, as we have explained, this is exactly what a pre-emption clause for medical devices does by its terms. The operation of a law enacted by Congress need not be seconded by a committee report on pain of judicial nullification. See, *e.g., Connecticut Nat. Bank v. Germain,* 503 U.S. 249, 253–254, 112 S.Ct. 1146, 117 L.Ed.2d 391 (1992). It is not our job to speculate upon congressional motives. If we were to do so, however, the only indication available—the text of the statute—suggests that the solicitude for those injured by FDA-approved devices, which the dissent finds controlling, was overcome in Congress's estimation by solicitude for those who would suffer without new medical devices if juries were allowed to apply the tort law of 50 States to all innovations....

IV

State requirements are pre-empted under the MDA only to the extent that they are "different from, or in addition to" the requirements imposed by federal law. § 360k(a)(1). Thus, § 360k does not prevent a State from providing a damages remedy for claims premised on a violation of FDA regulations; the state duties in such a case "parallel," rather than add to, federal requirements. *Lohr,* 518 U.S., at 495, 116 S.Ct. 2240; see also *id.,* at 513, 116 S.Ct. 2240 (O'Connor, J., concurring in part and dissenting in part). The District Court in this case recognized that parallel claims would not be pre-empted, see App. to Pet. for Cert. 70a–71a, but it interpreted the claims here to assert that Medtronic's device violated state tort law notwithstanding compliance with the relevant federal requirements, see *id.,* at 68a....

* * * *

■ JUSTICE GINSBURG, dissenting.

The Medical Device Amendments of 1976 (MDA or Act), 90 Stat. 539, as construed by the Court, cut deeply into a domain historically occupied by state law. The MDA's preemption clause, 21 U.S.C. § 360k(a), the Court holds, spares medical device manufacturers from personal injury claims alleging flaws in a design or label once the application for the design or label has gained premarket approval from the Food and Drug Administration (FDA); a state damages remedy, the Court instructs, persists only for claims "premised on a violation of FDA regulations." *Ante,* at 1011. I dissent from today's constriction of state authority. Congress, in my view, did not intend § 360k(a) to effect a radical curtailment of state common-law suits seeking compensation for injuries caused by defectively designed or labeled medical devices....

I

... Preemption analysis starts with the assumption that "the historic police powers of the States [a]re not to be superseded ... unless that was the clear and manifest purpose of Congress." *Rice v. Santa Fe Elevator Corp.,* 331 U.S. 218, 230, 67 S.Ct. 1146, 91 L.Ed. 1447 (1947). "This assumption provides assurance that 'the federal-state balance' will not be disturbed unintentionally by Congress or unnecessarily by the courts." *Jones v. Rath Packing Co.,* 430 U.S. 519, 525, 97 S.Ct. 1305, 51 L.Ed.2d 604 (1977) (citation omitted).

The presumption against preemption is heightened "where federal law is said to bar state action in fields of traditional state regulation." *New York State Conference of Blue Cross & Blue Shield Plans v. Travelers Ins. Co.,* 514 U.S. 645, 655, 115 S.Ct. 1671, 131 L.Ed.2d 695 (1995). Given the traditional "primacy of state regulation of matters of health and safety," *Lohr,* 518 U.S., at 485, 116 S.Ct. 2240, courts assume "that state and local regulation related to [those] matters ... can normally coexist with federal regulations," *Hillsborough County v. Automated Medical Laboratories, Inc.,* 471 U.S. 707, 718, 105 S.Ct. 2371, 85 L.Ed.2d 714 (1985).

Federal laws containing a preemption clause do not automatically escape the presumption against preemption. See *Bates v. Dow Agrosciences LLC,* 544 U.S. 431, 449, 125 S.Ct. 1788, 161 L.Ed.2d 687 (2005); *Lohr,* 518 U.S., at 485, 116 S.Ct. 2240. A preemption clause tells us that Congress intended to supersede or modify state law to some extent. In the absence of legislative precision, however, courts may face the task of determining the substance and scope of Congress' displacement of state law. Where the text of a preemption clause is open to more than one plausible reading, courts ordinarily "accept the reading that disfavors pre-emption." *Bates,* 544 U.S., at 449, 125 S.Ct. 1788....

II

* * * *

C

Congress' experience regulating drugs ... casts doubt on Medtronic's policy arguments for reading § 360k(a) to preempt state tort claims. Section 360k(a) must preempt state common-law suits, Medtronic contends, because Congress would not have wanted state juries to second-guess the FDA's finding that a medical device is safe and effective when used as directed. Brief for Respondent 42–49. The Court is similarly minded. *Ante,* at 1008–1009.

But the process for approving new drugs is at least as rigorous as the premarket approval process for medical devices. Courts that have considered the question have overwhelmingly held that FDA approval of a new drug application does not preempt state tort suits. Decades of drug regulation thus indicate, contrary to Medtronic's argument, that Congress did not regard FDA regulation and state tort claims as mutually exclusive.

III

Refusing to read § 360k(a) as an automatic bar to state common-law tort claims would hardly render the FDA's premarket approval of Medtronic's medical device application irrelevant to the instant suit. First, a "preemption provision, by itself, does not foreclose (through negative implication) any possibility of implied conflict preemption." *Geier v. American Honda Motor Co.,* 529 U.S. 861, 869, 120 S.Ct. 1913, 146 L.Ed.2d 914 (2000) (brackets and internal quotation marks omitted). See also *Freightliner Corp. v. Myrick,* 514 U.S. 280, 288–289, 115 S.Ct. 1483, 131 L.Ed.2d 385 (1995)....

Second, a medical device manufacturer may be entitled to interpose a regulatory compliance defense based on the FDA's approval of the premarket application. Most States do not treat regulatory compliance as dispositive, but regard it as one factor to be taken into account by the jury. See Sharkey, Federalism in Action: FDA Regulatory Preemption in Pharmaceutical Cases in State Versus Federal Courts, 15 J. Law & Pol'y 1013, 1024 (2007). See also Restatement (Third) of Torts § 16(a) (Proposed Final Draft No. 1, Apr. 6, 2005). In those States, a manufacturer could present the FDA's approval of its medical device as evidence that it used due care in the design and labeling of the product.

The Court's broad reading of § 360k(a) saves the manufacturer from any need to urge these defenses. Instead, regardless of the strength of a plaintiff's case, suits will be barred *ab initio*. The constriction of state authority ordered today was not mandated by Congress and is at odds with the MDA's central purpose: to protect consumer safety.

* * *

For the reasons stated, I would hold that § 360k(a) does not preempt Riegel's suit....

■ [The opinion of JUSTICE STEVENS concurring in part and concurring in the judgment is omitted.]

Crosby v. National Foreign Trade Council

530 U.S. 363 (2000).

■ JUSTICE SOUTER delivered the opinion of the Court.

The issue is whether the Burma law of the Commonwealth of Massachusetts, restricting the authority of its agencies to purchase goods or services from companies doing business with Burma, is invalid under the Supremacy Clause of the National Constitution owing to its threat of frustrating federal statutory objectives. We hold that it is.

I

In June 1996, Massachusetts adopted "An Act Regulating State Contracts with Companies Doing Business with or in Burma (Myanmar)," 1996 Mass. Acts 239, ch. 130 (codified at Mass. Gen. Laws §§ 7:22G–7:22M, 40 F. 1/2 (1997)). The statute generally bars state entities from buying goods or services from any person (defined to include a business organization) identified on a "restricted purchase list" of those doing business with Burma. §§ 7:22H(a), 7:22J.... There are three exceptions to the ban: (1) if the procurement is essential, and without the restricted bid, there would be no bids or insufficient competition, § 7:22H(b); (2) if the procurement is of medical supplies, § 7:22I; and (3) if the procurement efforts elicit no "comparable low bid or offer" by a person not doing business with Burma, § 7:22H(d), meaning an offer that is no more than 10 percent greater than the restricted bid, § 7:22G. To enforce the ban, the Act requires petitioner Secretary of Administration and Finance to maintain a "restricted purchase list" of all firms "doing business with Burma," § 7:22J.

In September 1996, three months after the Massachusetts law was enacted, Congress passed a statute imposing a set of mandatory and conditional sanctions on Burma.... The federal Act has five basic parts, three substantive and two procedural.

First, it imposes three sanctions directly on Burma. It bans all aid to the Burmese Government except for humanitarian assistance, counternarcotics efforts, and promotion of human rights and democracy....

Second, the federal Act authorizes the President to impose further sanctions subject to certain conditions....

Third, the statute directs the President to work to develop "a comprehensive, multilateral strategy to bring democracy to and improve human rights practices and the quality of life in Burma." § 570(c)....

As for the procedural provisions of the federal statute, the fourth section requires the President to report periodically to certain congressional committee chairmen on the progress toward democratization and better living conditions in Burma as well as on the development of the required strategy. § 570(d). And the fifth part of the federal Act authorizes the President "to waive, temporarily or permanently, any sanction [under the federal Act] ... if he determines and certifies to Congress that the application of such sanction would be contrary to the national security interests of the United States." § 570(e).

On May 20, 1997, the President issued the Burma Executive Order, Exec. Order No. 13047, 3 CFR 202 (1997 Comp.). He certified for purposes of § 570(b) that the Government of Burma had "committed large-scale repression of the democratic opposition in Burma" and found that the Burmese Government's actions and policies constituted "an unusual and extraordinary threat to the national security and foreign policy of the United States," a threat characterized as a national emergency. The President then prohibited new investment in Burma "by United States persons," Exec. Order No. 13047, § 1, any approval or facilitation by a

United States person of such new investment by foreign persons, § 2(a), and any transaction meant to evade or avoid the ban, § 2(b). The order generally incorporated the exceptions and exemptions addressed in the statute. §§ 3, 4. Finally, the President delegated to the Secretary of State the tasks of working with ASEAN and other countries to develop a strategy for democracy, human rights, and the quality of life in Burma, and of making the required congressional reports. § 5.

II

Respondent National Foreign Trade Council (Council) is a nonprofit corporation representing companies engaged in foreign commerce; 34 of its members were on the Massachusetts restricted purchase list in 1998. *National Foreign Trade Council v. Natsios,* 181 F.3d 38, 48 (C.A.1 1999). Three withdrew from Burma after the passage of the state Act....

In April 1998, the Council filed suit in the United States District Court for the District of Massachusetts, seeking declaratory and injunctive relief against the petitioner state officials charged with administering and enforcing the state Act (whom we will refer to simply as the State). The Council argued that the state law unconstitutionally infringed on the federal foreign affairs power, violated the Foreign Commerce Clause, and was preempted by the federal Act. After detailed stipulations, briefing, and argument, the District Court permanently enjoined enforcement of the state Act, holding that it "unconstitutionally impinge[d] on the federal government's exclusive authority to regulate foreign affairs." *National Foreign Trade Council v. Baker,* 26 F.Supp.2d 287, 291 (D.Mass. 1998).

The United States Court of Appeals for the First Circuit affirmed on three independent grounds. 181 F.3d, at 45. It found the state Act unconstitutionally interfered with the foreign affairs power of the National Government under *Zschernig v. Miller,* 389 U.S. 429, 88 S.Ct. 664, 19 L.Ed.2d 683 (1968), see 181 F.3d, at 52–55; violated the dormant Foreign Commerce Clause, U.S. Const., Art. I, § 8, cl. 3, see 181 F.3d, at 61–71; and was preempted by the congressional Burma Act, see *id.,* at 71–77.

The State's petition for certiorari challenged the decision on all three grounds and asserted interests said to be shared by other state and local governments with similar measures.[5] ... We granted certiorari to resolve these important questions, 528 U.S. 1018, 120 S.Ct. 525, 145 L.Ed.2d 407 (1999), and now affirm.

III

A fundamental principle of the Constitution is that Congress has the power to preempt state law. Art. VI, cl. 2; *Gibbons v. Ogden,* 9 Wheat. 1, 211, 6 L.Ed. 23 (1824); *Savage v. Jones,* 225 U.S. 501, 533, 32 S.Ct. 715, 56 L.Ed. 1182 (1912); *California v. ARC America Corp.,* 490 U.S. 93, 101, 109

5. "At least nineteen municipal governments have enacted analogous laws restricting purchases from companies that do business in Burma." *Id.,* at 47; Pet. for Cert. 13 (citing N.Y.C. Admin. Code § 6–115 (1999); Los Angeles Admin. Code, Art. 12, § 10.38 *et seq.* (1999); Philadelphia Code § 17–104(b) (1999); Vermont H.J. Res. 157 (1998); 1999 Vt. Laws No. 13).

S.Ct. 1661, 104 L.Ed.2d 86 (1989). Even without an express provision for preemption, we have found that state law must yield to a congressional Act in at least two circumstances. When Congress intends federal law to "occupy the field," state law in that area is preempted. *Id.*, at 100, 109 S.Ct. 1661; cf. *United States v. Locke,* 529 U.S. 89, 115, 120 S.Ct. 1135, 146 L.Ed.2d 69 (2000) (citing *Charleston & Western Carolina R. Co. v. Varnville Furniture Co.,* 237 U.S. 597, 604, 35 S.Ct. 715, 59 L.Ed. 1137 (1915)). And even if Congress has not occupied the field, state law is naturally preempted to the extent of any conflict with a federal statute. *Hines v. Davidowitz,* 312 U.S. 52, 66–67, 61 S.Ct. 399, 85 L.Ed. 581 (1941); *ARC America Corp., supra,* at 100–101, 109 S.Ct. 1661; *Locke, supra,* at 109, 120 S.Ct. 1135. We will find preemption where it is impossible for a private party to comply with both state and federal law, see, *e.g., Florida Lime & Avocado Growers, Inc. v. Paul,* 373 U.S. 132, 142–143, 83 S.Ct. 1210, 10 L.Ed.2d 248 (1963), and where "under the circumstances of [a] particular case, [the challenged state law] stands as an obstacle to the accomplishment and execution of the full purposes and objectives of Congress." *Hines, supra,* at 67, 61 S.Ct. 399. What is a sufficient obstacle is a matter of judgment, to be informed by examining the federal statute as a whole and identifying its purpose and intended effects:

"For when the question is whether a Federal act overrides a state law, the entire scheme of the statute must of course be considered and that which needs must be implied is of no less force than that which is expressed. If the purpose of the act cannot otherwise be accomplished—if its operation within its chosen field else must be frustrated and its provisions be refused their natural effect—the state law must yield to the regulation of Congress within the sphere of its delegated power." *Savage, supra,* at 533, 32 S.Ct. 715, quoted in *Hines, supra,* at 67, n. 20, 61 S.Ct. 399.

Applying this standard, we see the state Burma law as an obstacle to the accomplishment of Congress's full objectives under the federal Act. We find that the state law undermines the intended purpose and "natural effect" of at least three provisions of the federal Act, that is, its delegation of effective discretion to the President to control economic sanctions against Burma, its limitation of sanctions solely to United States persons and new investment, and its directive to the President to proceed diplomatically in developing a comprehensive, multilateral strategy toward Burma.

A

First, Congress clearly intended the federal Act to provide the President with flexible and effective authority over economic sanctions against Burma....

... It is simply implausible that Congress would have gone to such lengths to empower the President if it had been willing to compromise his effectiveness by deference to every provision of state statute or local ordinance that might, if enforced, blunt the consequences of discretionary Presidential action.

And that is just what the Massachusetts Burma law would do in imposing a different, state system of economic pressure against the Burmese political regime. As will be seen, the state statute penalizes some private action that the federal Act (as administered by the President) may allow, and pulls levers of influence that the federal Act does not reach.... Quite simply, if the Massachusetts law is enforceable the President has less to offer and less economic and diplomatic leverage as a consequence....

B

Congress manifestly intended to limit economic pressure against the Burmese Government to a specific range. The federal Act confines its reach to United States persons, § 570(b), imposes limited immediate sanctions, § 570(a), places only a conditional ban on a carefully defined area of "new investment," § 570(f)(2), and pointedly exempts contracts to sell or purchase goods, services, or technology, § 570(f)(2). These detailed provisions show that Congress's calibrated Burma policy is a deliberate effort "to steer a middle path," *id.,* at 73, 61 S.Ct. 399.

The State has set a different course, and its statute conflicts with federal law at a number of points by penalizing individuals and conduct that Congress has explicitly exempted or excluded from sanctions....

The conflicts are not rendered irrelevant by the State's argument that there is no real conflict between the statutes because they share the same goals and because some companies may comply with both sets of restrictions. See Brief for Petitioners 21–22. The fact of a common end hardly neutralizes conflicting means, see Gade v. National Solid Wastes Management Assn., 505 U.S. 88, 103, 112 S.Ct. 2374, 120 L.Ed.2d 73 (1992), and the fact that some companies may be able to comply with both sets of sanctions does not mean that the state Act is not at odds with achievement of the federal decision about the right degree of pressure to employ....

C

Finally, the state Act is at odds with the President's intended authority to speak for the United States among the world's nations in developing a "comprehensive, multilateral strategy to bring democracy to and improve human rights practices and the quality of life in Burma." § 570(c)....

Again, the state Act undermines the President's capacity, in this instance for effective diplomacy. It is not merely that the differences between the state and federal Acts in scope and type of sanctions threaten to complicate discussions; they compromise the very capacity of the President to speak for the Nation with one voice in dealing with other governments....

IV

The State's remaining argument is unavailing. It contends that the failure of Congress to preempt the state Act demonstrates implicit permission. The State points out that Congress has repeatedly declined to enact express preemption provisions aimed at state and local sanctions, and it calls our attention to the large number of such measures passed against South Africa in the 1980's, which various authorities cited have thought were not preempted. The State stresses that Congress was aware of the state Act in 1996, but did not preempt it explicitly when it adopted its own Burma statute. The State would have us conclude that Congress's continuing failure to enact express preemption implies approval, particularly in light of occasional instances of express preemption of state sanctions in the past.

The argument is unconvincing on more than one level. A failure to provide for preemption expressly may reflect nothing more than the settled character of implied preemption doctrine that courts will dependably apply, and in any event, the existence of conflict cognizable under the Supremacy Clause does not depend on express congressional recognition that federal and state law may conflict, *Hines,* 312 U.S., at 67, 61 S.Ct. 399. The State's inference of congressional intent is unwarranted here, therefore, simply because the silence of Congress is ambiguous. Since we never ruled on whether state and local sanctions against South Africa in the 1980's were preempted or otherwise invalid, arguable parallels between the two sets of federal and state Acts do not tell us much about the validity of the latter.

V

Because the state Act's provisions conflict with Congress's specific delegation to the President of flexible discretion, with limitation of sanctions to a limited scope of actions and actors, and with direction to develop a comprehensive, multilateral strategy under the federal Act, it is preempted, and its application is unconstitutional, under the Supremacy Clause....

■ [The opinion of JUSTICE SCALIA concurring in the judgment is omitted.]

NOTES

1. *Express versus implied pre-emption*. The U.S. Supreme Court has stated that "pre-emption may be either expressed or implied, and is 'compelled whether Congress' command is explicitly stated in the statute's language or implicitly contained in its structure and purpose.' " Gade v. National Solid Wastes Management Assoc., 505 U.S. 88, 98 (1992) (quoting Jones v. Rath Packing Co., 430 U.S. 519 (1977).

The resolution of "express pre-emption" cases is often complex, notwithstanding the presence of an explicit "preemption clause" in the relevant federal statute. The U.S. Supreme Court in Lorillard Tobacco Company v. Reilly, 533 U.S. 525, 541–42 (2001), described the court's role as follows:

> In these cases, our task is to identify the domain expressly pre-empted, see *Cipollone, supra,* at 517, 112 S.Ct. 2608, because "an express definition of the pre-emptive reach of a statute ... supports a reasonable inference ... that Congress did not intend to pre-empt other matters," *Freightliner Corp. v. Myrick,* 514 U.S. 280, 288, 115 S.Ct. 1483, 131 L.Ed.2d 385 (1995). Congressional purpose is the "ultimate touchstone" of our inquiry. *Cipol-*

> *lone, supra,* at 516, 112 S.Ct. 2608.... Because "federal law is said to bar state action in [a] fiel[d] of traditional state regulation," ..., see *Packer Corp. v. Utah,* 285 U.S. 105, 108, 52 S.Ct. 273, 76 L.Ed. 643 (1932), we "wor[k] on the assumption that the historic police powers of the States [a]re not to be superseded by the Federal Act unless that [is] the clear and manifest purpose of Congress." *California Div. of Labor Standards Enforcement v. Dillingham Constr., N. A., Inc.,* 519 U.S. 316, 325, 117 S.Ct. 832, 136 L.Ed.2d 791 (1997).... See also *Medtronic, Inc. v. Lohr,* 518 U.S. 470, 475, 116 S.Ct. 2240, 135 L.Ed.2d 700 (1996).

In the absence of explicit pre-emptive language in a statute, the U.S. Supreme Court has

> recognized at least two types of implied pre-emption: field pre-emption, where the scheme of federal regulation is " 'so pervasive as to make reasonable the inference that Congress left no room for the States to supplement it,' " [Fidelity Fed. Sav. & Loan Assn. v. De la Cuesta, 458 U.S. 141, 153 (1982)] (quoting Rice v. Santa Fe Elevator Corp., 331 U.S. 218, 230 ... (1947)), and conflict pre-emption, where "compliance with both federal and state regulations is a physical impossibility," Florida Lime & Avocado Growers, Inc. v. Paul, 373 U.S. 132, 142–143 ... (1963), or where state law "stands as an obstacle to the accomplishment and execution of the full purposes and objectives of Congress," Hines v. Davidowitz, 312 U.S. 52, 67 ... (1941)....

Gade, 505 U.S. at 98. Notwithstanding the above, one scholar has argued that "there is no such thing as implied preemption," and that "[i]f Congress wishes to exercise its preemption power, it must say so by speaking directly to the issue." Stephen Gardbaum, Congress's Power to Preempt the States, 33 Pepp. L. Rev. 39, 40, 52 (2005).

2. *Intent to pre-empt.* In cases in which the federal statute at issue does not have an explicit pre-emption clause, the court's inquiry often focuses on whether Congress (or the relevant federal agency) intended to pre-empt the state/local regulation. This is also often the focus of the court's inquiry in express pre-emption cases in which the court must determine the scope of the relevant law's express pre-emption clause.

Gade v. National Solid Wastes Management Ass'n., 505 U.S. 88 (1992), was an implied pre-emption case, in which the Court found that the federal Occupational Safety and Health Act impliedly pre-empted state licensing of workers at hazardous waste facilities. The federal Act permitted states to submit state plans that would substitute for federal regulations; the Court concluded, *id* at 98–99, that this authorization was intended to pre-empt state hazardous worker safety regulations that had not been submitted for approval:

> Our ultimate task in any pre-emption case is to determine whether state regulation is consistent with the structure and purpose of the statute as a whole. Looking to "the provisions of the whole law, and to its object and policy," *Pilot Life Ins. Co. v. Dedeaux*, 481 U.S. 41 ... (1987) ..., we hold that nonapproved state regulation of occupational safety and health issues for which a federal standard is in effect is impliedly pre-empted as in conflict with the full purposes and objectives of the OSH Act.... The design of the statute persuades us that Congress intended to subject

employers and employees to only one set of regulations, be it federal or state, and that the only way a State may regulate an OSHA-regulated occupational safety and health issue is pursuant to an approved state plan that displaces the federal standards.

The scope of an express pre-emption clause was the focus in both *Cipollone* and *Altria*. In Cipollone v. Liggett Group, Inc., 505 U.S. 504 (1992), a majority of the Court found that express congressional pre-emption of warnings on cigarette advertisements did not also pre-empt the availability of state tort actions. The majority determined that, in light of a substantial presumption against pre-emption, congressional language that pre-empted any "requirement or prohibition ... imposed under State law ... with respect to advertising and promotion," id. at 524, did not preclude common law tort claims that arose out of express warranties made by manufacturers or fraud and misrepresentation, but did preclude tort actions based on state law obligations, such as a state-imposed duty to warn.

Altria Group, Inc. v. Good, 129 S.Ct. 538 (2008) involved the related question of whether a fraudulent advertising claim against a cigarette manufacturer brought under a state Unfair Trade Practices Act was pre-empted by the Federal Cigarette Labeling and Advertising Act. As in *Cipollone*, at issue was the federal Act's express pre-emption provision which provides that "[n]o requirement or prohibition based on smoking and health shall be imposed under State law with respect to the advertising or promotion of any cigarettes the packages of which are labeled in conformity with the provisions of this chapter." Id. at 544. A majority of the Court held that "fidelity to the [federal] Act's purposes does not demand the pre-emption of state fraud rules," id. at 545. Thus, smokers were permitted to bring state-law causes of action that a cigarette manufacturer's claims that its product was "light" and had "lowered tar and nicotine" were misleading and fraudulent.

Wyeth v. Levine, 129 S.Ct. 1187 (2009), involved numerous, inter-related issues of express and implied pre-emption. The core question presented was "whether the FDA's drug labeling judgments 'preempt state law product liability claims premised on the theory that different labeling judgments were necessary to make drugs reasonably safe for use.' " Id. at 1193. When Congress enacted an express pre-emption provision for medical devices in 1976, it did not enact a similar provision for prescription drugs. Id. at 1196. In 2006, however, in the preamble to a "regulation governing the content and format of prescription drug labels," id. at 1200, "the FDA declared that [federal law] establishes 'both a "floor" and a "ceiling," ' so that 'FDA approval of labeling ... preempts conflicting or contrary State law.' " Id. The preamble also stated "that certain state-law actions, such as those involving failure-to-warn claims, 'threaten FDA's statutorily prescribed role as the expert Federal agency responsible for evaluating and regulating drugs.' " Id. A majority of the Court observed that "an agency's mere assertion that state law is an obstacle to achieving its statutory objectives" was not alone dispositive, and that the "weight [the Court] accord[s] the agency's explanation of state law's impact on the federal scheme depends on its thoroughness, consistency, and persuasiveness." Id.

at 1201. In affirming the Vermont Supreme Court's finding that Levine's state law tort claims were not preempted, the Court held:

> the FDA's 2006 preamble does not merit deference. . . .
>
> [It] is at odds with what evidence we have of Congress' purposes, and it reverses the FDA's own longstanding position without providing a reasoned explanation, including any discussion of how state law has interfered with the FDA's regulation of drug labeling during decades of coexistence. . . .
>
> . . . Congress has repeatedly declined to pre-empt state law, and the FDA's recently adopted position that state tort suits interfere with its statutory mandate is entitled to no weight. Although we recognize that some state-law claims might well frustrate the achievement of congressional objectives, this is not such a case.

Id. at 1201–1204.

3. *Federal floors versus ceilings.* Consider *Medtronic* and *Crosby* in light of Professor William Buzbee's recent argument that "there is a principled rationale for distinguishing federal floors and ceilings":

> Principled rationales exist to distinguish and embrace a protective federal one-way ratchet of floor preemption, or at least to see floor preemption as less institutionally problematic than the new breed of ceiling preemption that [I refer] to as "unitary federal choice preemption." Unitary federal choice preemption, by definition, precludes additional state and local protections and eliminates institutional diversity that is preserved (though limited) by floor preemption. Unitary federal choice preemption is, upon closer examination, a regulatory choice that in operation runs counter to many of the most valuable elements of federalist schemes. In contrast, federal floors retain the benefits of multiple regulatory voices, protections, and diverse regulatory modalities. These factors serve as important antidotes to common forms of regulatory dysfunction.

William W. Buzbee, Asymmetrical Regulation: Risk, Preemption, and the Floor/Ceiling Distinction, 82 NYU. L. Rev. 1547, 1554–55 (2007). Do you find Professor Buzbee's analysis persuasive? If so, can you reconcile the Court's decisions in *Medtronic* and *Crosby* with Buzbee's position?

4. *A presumption against preemption?* Professor William Buzbee (see Note 3 immediately above) ultimately

> embraces the presumption against preemption, especially where the preemptive power claimed involves ceiling preemption that constitutes a final, unitary federal choice. Policymakers and courts assessing such ceiling preemption should be sensitive to inevitable associated losses of institutional diversity and heightened risks of regulatory failure. Not all federal standard setting is the same.

Buzbee, supra, at 1619. Professor Rick Hills also favors an "anti-preemption default rule," but of a broader sort, and for different reasons:

> . . . As the number of interest groups increases and as political parties weaken, the capacity to muster a majority becomes more difficult. As the ratio of appointed experts to elected generalists grows larger, the latter use the former to protect their incumbency from political risk taking. Both of these conditions afflict the federal government more than state govern-

> ments to the extent that the conditions are a function of population size and interest group heterogeneity.
>
> What has any of this to do with preemption? I suggest an unfamiliar (and obviously partial) palliative to the tyranny of the status quo—a "clear statement" anti-preemption rule of construction that would discourage federal judicial preemption of state tort and regulatory law.... My suggestion rests on three hypotheses. First, specific action from Congress on specific legislation can mobilize public opinion, thus diminishing the tyranny of the status quo. Second, state regulation of business for the sake of health, safety, or environmental quality gives regulated interests an incentive to put broad issues of health, safety, and environmental quality on the congressional agenda, in the form of legislation that would preempt state regulation. Third, those regulated industries that support preemption have a greater capacity to elicit a specific congressional response to a bill—either a floor vote or committee hearings—than the interest groups that oppose preemption. Therefore, if the goal is to mobilize the public to focus its attention on Congress, then it makes sense to choose a default rule that places the burden on the regulated industries to lobby for preemptive legislation, rather than one that places the burden on those anti-preemption interests to lobby for a waiver of preemption.
>
> ....
>
> One does not need to love federalism in order to hate preemption. Even if one distrusts state politicians, there is reason to believe that they can break congressional gridlock that can be just as costly as state incompetence. Courts can help states perform this function by refusing to find preemption absent clear evidence that state law announces policies that contradict policy judgments contained in federal statutes. Lacking such evidence, the courts would be well advised to leave state law unpreempted, secure in the knowledge that congresspersons will have strong incentives to strengthen the statutes' preemptive force if this is the wish of their constituents.

Roderick M. Hills, Jr., Against Preemption: How Federalism Can Improve the National Legislative Process, 82 NYU L. Rev. 1, 16–17, 68 (2007). The costs and benefits of a presumption against preemption, whether narrow or broad, has been the focus of much scholarly discussion. See, e.g., Erwin Chemerinsky, Empowering States When It Matters: A Different Approach to Preemption, 69 Brook. L. Rev. 1313 (2004); David A. Dana, Democratizing the Law of Federal Preemption, 102 Nw. U.L. Rev. 507 (2008); Mary J. Davis, Unmasking the Presumption in Favor of Preemption, 53 S.C. L. Rev. 967 (2002); Federal Preemption: States' Powers, National Interests (Richard A. Epstein & Michael S. Greve eds. 2007); Michael S. Greve & Jonathan Klick, Preemption in the Rehnquist Court: A Preliminary Empirical Assessment, 14 Sup. Ct. Econ. Rev. 43 (2006); Caleb Nelson, Preemption, 86 Va. L. Rev. 225 (2000); Note, New Evidence on the Presumption against Preemption: An Empirical Study of Congressional Responses to Supreme Court Preemption Decisions, 120 Harv. L. Rev. 1604 (2007); Alan Schwartz, Statutory Interpretation, Capture, and Tort Law: The Regulatory Compliance Defense, 2 Am. L. & Econ. Rev. 1 (2000); Symposium, Ordering State–Federal Relations Through Federal Preemption Doctrine, 102 Nw. U.L. Rev. (Issue 2) (2008).

5. *Federal pre-emption of local versus state regulations.* In Wisconsin Public Intervenor v. Mortier, 501 U.S. 597 (1991), the Court considered whether the Federal Insecticide, Fungicide, and Rodenticide Act (FIFRA) pre-empted local regulation of pesticides. One provision of FIFRA permitted states to regulate the sale or use of pesticides, so long as the state regulation did not permit a sale or use prohibited by federal law. The case concerned a local ordinance that imposed permit requirements on certain users of pesticides in a manner not directly addressed by federal law. Mortier, who was granted a use permit subject to restrictions imposed by the locality, claimed that the ordinance was pre-empted by FIFRA. The Court determined that FIFRA did not expressly supersede local regulation of pesticide use. It then rejected the claim that statutory language indicated pre-emptive intent. The Court first concluded that provisions of the statute that permitted states to regulate pesticides did not necessarily disable local governments, even though the latter were not included within FIFRA's definition of "state." States could re-delegate their authority to political subdivisions. Any pre-emption of local regulation, the Court opined, would have to meet the standard of "clear and manifest" intention to pre-empt. "Mere silence cannot suffice to establish a clear and manifest purpose to pre-empt local authority." 501 U.S. at 607. The Court further rejected any finding of pre-emptive intent in the legislative history of FIFRA (a process and result with which Justice Scalia, concurring in the judgment, vehemently disagreed). Instead, the Court discovered conflicting evidence in committee reports concerning the permissible scope of local regulation. Finally, the Court rejected the argument that FIFRA regulated pesticides so comprehensively as to constitute implied preemption of local regulation.

The Supreme Court again demonstrated significant latitude towards local regulation in City of Columbus v. Ours Garage and Wrecker Service, Inc., 536 U.S. 424 (2002). Federal law expressly pre-empts both state and local regulation of motor carriers, but reserves to "States" the authority to impose safety regulations on carriers. In *City of Columbus*, the Court held that states could delegate that authority to political subdivisions, notwithstanding the absence of an explicit exception to the express pre-emption of local authority. A majority of the Court concluded that the explicit allusion to "political subdivisions" elsewhere in the statute was not intended to alter the general principle that states are able to delegate governing authority to localities. The court confirmed the view expressed in *Mortier* that an inference of Congressional intent to supplant local authority requires a "clear and manifest indication."

In Engine Manufacturers Assn. v. South Coast Air Quality Management Dist., 541 U.S. 246 (2004), however, the Court held that Fleet Rules adopted by a political subdivision of California responsible for air pollution control in the Los Angeles Metropolitan area and parts of surrounding counties were pre-empted by the Clean Air Act ("CAA"). The Fleet Rules at issue prohibited the purchase or lease by various public and private fleet operators of vehicles that did not comply with stringent emission requirements. Section 209(a) of the CAA prohibited any "State or any political subdivision thereof" from "adopt[ing] or attempt[ing] to enforce any standard relating to the control of emissions from new motor vehicles or new motor vehicle engines," and further prohibited a State from requiring any certification or "other approval relating to the control of emissions . . . as condition precedent to the initial retail sale" of a motor vehicle, id. at 252. The Court held that the Fleet Rules were "standard[s]" within the meaning of Section 209(a) and were therefore pre-empted by the CAA. The court in Metropolitan Taxicab Bd. of Trade v. City of New York, 2008 WL 4866021 (S.D.N.Y.), relied partially on the analysis in *Engine Manufacturers* to hold that plaintiffs had shown a likelihood of success in prevailing on a claim that federal law pre-empted New York City's efforts to dictate minimum mileage per gallon requirements for new taxicabs.

Lower courts, both state and federal, have been reluctant to find federal pre-emption of local ordinances. In Penn Advertising of Baltimore, Inc. v. Mayor and City Council, 63 F.3d 1318 (4th Cir. 1995) vacated, 518 U.S. 1030 (1996), modified, adhered to, 101 F.3d 332 (4th Cir. 1996), the Fourth Circuit applied the *Cippollone* case in determining that a Baltimore ordinance prohibiting cigarette advertising on billboards was not preempted by the Federal Cigarette Labeling and Advertising Act. The ordinance prohibited the placement of any sign that "advertises cigarettes in a publicly visible location," or on "outdoor billboards, sides of building[s], and free standing signboards." 63 F.3d at 1321. Penn Advertising argued that because the ordinance's prohibition was "based on smoking and health," it was pre-empted by the federal statute. The court determined that the Baltimore ordinance did not address the content, but rather the location of the billboards. Thus the court found that the ordinance did not impose a duty, nor relieve a burden, on cigarette advertisers based on smoking and health, as was necessary to fall within the scope of the federal statute.

In City of New York v. Job–Lot Pushcart, 666 N.E.2d 537 (N.Y. 1996), cert. denied sub nom. JA–RU v. City of New York, 519 U.S. 871 (1996), the New York Court of Appeals found that a New York City Administrative Code provision, which outlawed the sale, possession, or use of any toy or imitation gun that substantially resembles an actual firearm, was not pre-empted by the 1988 Federal Toy Gun Law. Plaintiff, a national distributor and marketer of toy guns, represented that its products complied with the regulations for toy guns approved by the Secretary of Commerce pursuant to the Federal Toy Gun Law. Plaintiff further contended that the federal statute comprehensively regulated the area. The court, again applying *Cipollone*, interpreted the provisions of the federal law to pre-empt only state regulation of the sale or manufacture of specifically mentioned items, leaving New York City free to regulate in areas not expressly pre-empted by Congress.

In Banner Advertising v. City of Boulder, 868 P.2d 1077 (Colo. 1994), however, the Colorado Supreme Court invalidated a local ordinance prohibiting commercial signs towed by aircraft, holding the ordinance to be in conflict with, and pre-empted by, regulations and authorization certificates of the Federal Aviation Administration.

The U.S. Court of Appeals for the Seventh Circuit decided two pre-emption cases in the same week, each involving the National Labor Relations Act ("NLRA"). In the first, Metropolitan Milwaukee Assoc. of Commerce v. Milwaukee County, 431 F.3d 277 (7th Cir. 2005), the Court unanimously held that the NLRA pre-empted a county ordinance requiring "firms that have contracts with the County for the provision of transportation and other services for elderly and disabled County residents to negotiate 'labor peace agreements' with any union that wants to organize employees who work on County contracts." Id. at 277–78. The Court found a "mismatch between the interest in uninterrupted service and the requirement of labor-peace agreements," and concluded that the County's motivating concern was not preventing service interruptions but instead impermissibly substituting "its own labor-management philosophy" for that of the NLRA, id. at 280–81. Four days later, in Northern Illinois Chapter of Associated Builders and Contractors, Inc. v. Lavin, 431 F.3d 1004 (7th Cir. 2005), the Seventh Circuit upheld an Illinois statute that conditioned the state's grants for the construction and renovation of renewable-fuel plants on the grant recipient's willingness to enter into a "project labor agreement" that establishes wages and benefits and must include a no-strike clause. Id. at 1005. The court held that "the NLRA was intended to supplant state labor *regulation*, not all legitimate state activity that affects labor," and concluded that "[b]ecause Illinois has limited its condition to the project financed by the subsidy, it has not engaged in 'regulation' ... and its conditions are not preempted by federal labor law." Id. at 1006–07.

CHAPTER 2

DEFINING THE COMMUNITY

A. THE VARIETY OF COMMUNITIES

In this Chapter, we introduce a recurring theme of this book. One of the primary objectives of local government law is to establish the appropriate scope of local autonomy. Much of the reading in Chapter 1 suggests that broad local autonomy is desirable because political participation can be enriching and is more likely occur in decentralized jurisdictions, and because the existence of a wide variety of local governments that offer different bundles of goods and services enhances the ability of prospective residents—at least those who are mobile—who have different preferences to migrate to jurisdictions that they find most hospitable. Some individuals will seek large, urban areas close to workplaces, public gardens, and cultural events. Others will want rural environments, or the relatively large lots and tranquility of suburban life. There will be "property owners who want to preserve the existing community and property owners who want to profit from development or gentrification; people who fear the dangers of city life and people who love living in cities; parents who feel that the suburbs are 'a great place to raise a family' and kids who consider the suburbs vacuous; women who feel trapped by living in the suburbs and women who feel protected by living there; activists seeking to rid their neighborhoods of 'undesirables' and the undesirables themselves." Jerry Frug, Decentering Decentralization, 60 U. Chi. L. Rev. 253, 291 (1993). The result is the possibility that localities will form around particular characteristics that attract individuals who cannot obtain the environment that they desire from other jurisdictions. For example, recent efforts to create new localities include a town that would cater to the deaf and encourage use of American Sign Language, see As Town for Deaf Takes Shape, Debate on Isolation Re–Emerges, New York Times, March 21, 2005, available at http://www.nytimes.com/2005/03/21/national/21deaf.html?_r=1&scp=1&sq=town% 20deaf% 20iso lation&st=cse; a town created by Domino's Pizza founder Tom Monaghan to house a university dedicated to Catholic perspectives in higher education, see http://www.avemaria.com/Default.aspx?ID=18; and a town that consists solely of a 2,300 acre resort, hotels, gift shops, a rodeo arena, restaurants, gas stations, a grocery store, and areas for campers and recreational vehicles, see In Utah, a "Company Town" Means Just That, New York Times, July 24, 2007, available at http://www.nytimes.com/2007/07/24/us/24bryce.html?scp=1&sq=utah+company+town&st=nyt.

A moment's reflection, however, reveals that, even if the assumptions that underlie a fully operating Tieboutian market for residence could be achieved, there are multiple problems with this simple story of individuals seeking different visions of the good life. First, we are not prepared to allow even like-minded individuals to create any kind of community that they desire. The more we allow localities to exercise autonomy, the more some jurisdictions will seek to attract or to exclude potential residents on grounds that members of the larger society find inappropriate or offensive for a governmental entity. Even if localities do not formally exclude individuals, localities may signal the characteristics that they seek to attract or deter residents by favoring or banning certain activities. One recent example that has gained significant publicity involved the efforts of different localities to take measures that either attract or discourage undocumented immigrants. Hazelton, Pennsylvania enacted ordinances that barred landlords within the city from knowingly leasing to or permitting occupancy by illegal aliens, and required apartment dwellers to obtain an occupancy permit by presenting proof that they were citizens or lawful residents. The ordinances also banned employment of undocumented aliens. In a federal lawsuit, the court concluded that the ordinances were preempted by federal immigration laws. Lozano v. City of Hazleton, 496 F.Supp.2d 477 (M.D. Pa. 2007). The city of Valley Park, Missouri enacted ordinances prohibiting local businesses from knowingly employing unauthorized aliens and creating procedures for lodging complaints against alleged violators. See Gray v. City of Valley Park, 567 F.3d 976 (8th Cir. 2009). Other cities have taken the opposite position by enacting ordinances that have transformed them into "sanctuary cities" for illegal immigrants. These cities, for instance, have instructed police not to inquire about immigrants' status and have issued identification cards that permit access to city services without proof of citizenship. See A Haven Indeed: One City Devises Its Own Immigration Policy, The Economist, August 2, 2007, available at http://www.economist.com/world/unitedstates/displaystory.cfm?story_id=E1_JVRSRQP.

The reactions to these ordinances suggest that there is significant variation in the extent to which local autonomy interferes with the preferences or values of the broader society of which the locality is a member. Some ways of defining the community will be prohibited, some activities will not be allowed even though a majority of residents prefers them, and some means of attracting or discouraging residents will not be permitted. Many of the legal doctrines that we study in this course implicitly or explicitly define the scope of local autonomy and the extent to which localities will be able to use certain characteristics to create a market for residence. Obviously, federal anti-discrimination laws and constitutional principles prohibit ordinances that violate widely shared values about prohibited bases of discrimination, such as race, religion, and national origin. But other doctrines, such as the preemption doctrines addressed in Chapter 1, the bases for incorporation of a local government, the scope of legislative delegation to localities, and the doctrines used to resolve interlocal conflicts implicitly define the extent to which a locality can define itself in a distinctive manner, even when that definition is inconsistent with judgments made at more centralized levels of government.

Our purpose in the first part of this Chapter is not to discuss the substance of anti-discrimination laws or other doctrines that restrict or allow local variation. Rather, our objective here is to address directly why some manifestations of local autonomy are permitted, indeed desirable, while others are prohibited or deterred. The extent to which we are willing to allow localities to pursue residents' visions of a good life, the obligations we impose on localities with respect to their residents, to their neighbors, and to more centralized jurisdictions all follow to some degree from these basic questions about the scope of local identity. Thus, we use the first part of this chapter to introduce the problem of permissible local characteristics and the contexts in which the issue might arise. Subsequent parts of this chapter indicate how legal rules permit the formal creation of municipalities within specific geographical boundaries in order to achieve the functions that the community defines for itself. Implicit in what follows is the possibility that not all regulation should share the same geographic scope. Some regulations may be appropriate at the national, or indeed, international level. Other regulations, however, may be discretionary with the jurisdiction. As one example,the fact that legal tests for obscenity that falls outside the protection of the First Amendment incorporates "community standards," Miller v. California, 413 U.S. 15 (1973), indicates that at least some constitutional guarantees can be tailored to local circumstances. It is less clear, however, when that kind of tailoring is permissible. For a recent argument about the permissibility of local differences in the scope of rights, see Mark D. Rosen, The Surprisingly Strong Case for Tailoring Constitutional Principles, 153 U. Penn. L. Rev. 1513 (2005); Richard C. Schragger, The Role of the Local in the Doctrine and Discourse of Religious Liberty, 117 Harv. L. Rev. 1810 (2004).

As evidenced in the Tiebout model, in its strongest form the exercise of local autonomy imposes few costs because those who disagree with local policies can exit to other jurisdictions. In reality, of course, even when a municipality is entitled to define itself according to the choices of residents, the fact that individuals are not perfectly mobile means that the community is likely to contain some residents who do not share the interests of the majority and who lack the capacity to emigrate to other localities. There will be occasions on which it may be important to protect those in the minority against the imposition or prohibition of activities or lifestyles that are preferred by the majority. Nevertheless, there may be times when those in the minority cannot easily be accommodated. In those cases, legal institutions must determine what, if any, protections should be available to the minority.

While these limitations on autonomy involve the internal dynamics of local government, an additional limitation involves the extraterritorial effects of local action. Municipalities may permit activities or pursue an identity the consequences of which cannot be contained within local boundaries. The decisions of one municipality may be in direct conflict with the preferences of its neighbors. Under those circumstances, either some form of compromise will be necessary, or one locality will have to subordinate its own interests to that of the other.

These themes of the proper scope of local autonomy pervade this entire course. While we focus first on the ability of a locality to pursue the choices of residents, later chapters explore in greater depth how the general principles that you might derive from the materials in this Chapter affect a locality's relations with the state, with its residents, and with neighboring localities.

1. RESTRICTING ACTIVITIES IN THE COMMUNITY

Schad v. Borough of Mount Ephraim

452 U.S. 61 (1981).

■ JUSTICE WHITE delivered the opinion of the Court, in which BRENNAN, STEWART, MARSHALL, BLACKMUN, and POWELL, JJ., joined.

[In 1973, Appellants opened an adult bookstore in the commercial zone of the borough of Mount Ephraim. Three years later the store installed a coin-operated mechanism permitting the customer to view a live dancer, usually nude, performing behind a glass panel. Appellee brought suit, claiming that the bookstore had violated a zoning ordinance that the Court construed as prohibiting all live entertainment, including nude dancing. The ordinance permitted a number of other commercial uses in the same area, such as offices, banks, taverns, restaurants, car dealerships, and retail stores. The majority concluded that the ordinance violated the First and Fourteenth Amendments to the Constitution.—EDS.]

The power of local governments to zone and control land use is undoubtedly broad and its proper exercise is an essential aspect of achieving a satisfactory quality of life in both urban and rural communities. But the zoning power is not infinite and unchallengable.... [W]hen a zoning law infringes upon a protected liberty, it must be narrowly drawn and must further a sufficiently substantial governmental interest.

[The Court then determined that the proffered interests of limiting the commercial zone in the Borough to the supply of residents' "immediate needs" did not justify the ordinance, since permitted uses included enterprises that fell outside the quoted category. Similarly, the Court found that the prohibition on live entertainment did not necessarily reduce problems such as "parking, trash, police protection, and medical facilities" any more than permitted uses within the commercial zone.—EDS.]

Accordingly, the convictions of these appellants are infirm, and the judgment of the Appellate Division of the Superior Court of New Jersey is reversed and the case is remanded for further proceedings not inconsistent with this opinion.

■ CHIEF JUSTICE BURGER, with whom JUSTICE REHNQUIST joins, dissenting.

The Borough of Mount Ephraim is a small borough in Camden County, N.J. It is located on the Black Horse Turnpike, the main artery connecting Atlantic City with two major cities, Camden and Philadelphia. Mount

Ephraim is about 17 miles from the city of Camden and about the same distance from the river that separates New Jersey from the State of Pennsylvania.

The Black Horse Turnpike cuts through the center of Mount Ephraim. For 250 feet on either side of the turnpike, the Borough has established a commercial zone. The rest of the community is zoned for residential use, with either single- or multi-family units permitted. Most of the inhabitants of Mount Ephraim commute to either Camden or Philadelphia for work.

The residents of this small enclave chose to maintain their town as a placid, "bedroom" community of a few thousand people. To that end, they passed an admittedly broad regulation prohibiting certain forms of entertainment. Because I believe that a community of people are—within limits—masters of their own environment, I would hold that, as applied, the ordinance is valid.

At issue here is the right of a small community to ban an activity incompatible with a quiet, residential atmosphere. The Borough of Mount Ephraim did nothing more than employ traditional police power to provide a setting of tranquility. This Court has often upheld the power of a community "to determine that the community should be beautiful as well as healthy, spacious as well as clean, well-balanced as well as carefully patrolled." . . .

The Court depicts Mount Ephraim's ordinance as a ban on live entertainment. But, in terms, it does not mention any kind of entertainment. As applied, it operates as a ban on nude dancing in appellants' "adult" bookstore, and for that reason alone it is here. Thus, the issue in the case that we have before us is not whether Mount Ephraim may ban traditional live entertainment, but whether it may ban nude dancing, which is used as the "bait" to induce customers into the appellants' bookstore. When, and if, this ordinance is used to prevent a high school performance of "The Sound of Music," for example, the Court can deal with that problem.

An overconcern about draftsmanship and overbreadth should not be allowed to obscure the central question before us. It is clear that, in passing the ordinance challenged here, the citizens of the Borough of Mount Ephraim meant only to preserve the basic character of their community. It is just as clear that, by thrusting their live nude dancing shows on this community, the appellants alter and damage that community over its objections. As applied in this case, therefore, the ordinance speaks directly and unequivocally. It may be that, as applied in some other case, this ordinance would violate the First Amendment, but, since such a case is not before us, we should not decide it. . . .

The fact that a form of expression enjoys some constitutional protection does not mean that there are not times and places inappropriate for its exercise. The towns and villages of this Nation are not, and should not be, forced into a mold cast by this Court. Citizens should be free to choose to shape their community so that it embodies their conception of the "decent life.'' This will sometimes mean deciding that certain forms of activity—factories, gas stations, sports stadia, bookstores, and surely live nude shows—will not be allowed. That a community is willing to tolerate such a commercial use as a convenience store, a gas station, a pharmacy, or a delicatessen does not compel it also to tolerate every other ''commercial use,'' including pornography peddlers and live nude shows.

NOTES

1. What is the permissible scope of a community's ability to exclude activities of which current residents disapprove? In what ways is Chief Justice Burger's argument that the people of Mount Ephraim, by excluding nude dancers, ''meant only to preserve the basic character of their community'' more compelling than a similar argument used to justify exclusionary zoning that has the effect of preventing low-income families from residing in a ''community''? If citizens are free to choose to shape a community ''to reflect their conception of the 'decent life' '' free from seeing pornography, why not a conception free from seeing poverty?

Is there something incongruous about Chief Justice Burger's assertion that those who offer live nude dancing are ''thrusting'' their views on the good residents of Mount Ephraim? The Chief Justice concluded that the borough is ''a small community on the periphery of two major urban centers where this kind of entertainment may be found acceptable.'' Given this finding, whom do you think is patronizing these establishments? If patrons are members of the Mount Ephraim community, is Chief Justice Burger correct in assuming that nude dancing is inconsistent with community values? Given the proximity of the borough to urban centers where adult entertainment might more readily be available, one might believe that nonresidents would not flock to a hostile community to find entertainment. Thus, if residents do not value these shows, why won't the market take care of the problem, i.e., why won't they close for lack of patronage? Does it matter if the Black Horse Turnpike is frequented by transients, e.g., interstate truck drivers?

2. *Community Restrictions on Nude Dancing.* The Court's holding in *Schad* was subsequently restricted in City of Renton v. Playtime Theatres, Inc., 475 U.S. 41 (1986). In that case, the Court upheld an ordinance that restricted the location of adult motion picture theaters within 1,000 feet of certain other land uses, including residential districts, schools, or churches. The Court concluded that the Renton ordinance was narrowly tailored to affect only theatres that were shown to produce unwanted secondary effects. In Barnes v. Glen Theatre, Inc., 501 U.S. 560 (1991), the Court, in a 5–4 decision, held that a state public indecency statute requiring dancers to wear pasties and a G-string did not violate the First Amendment. Chief Justice Rehnquist, writing for the plurality, claimed that ''[p]ublic indecency statutes such as the one before us reflect moral disapproval of people appearing in the nude among strangers in public places.... This and other public indecency statutes were designed to protect morals and public order." Because of the state's inherent police power to provide for public health, safety, and morals, and because the statute was narrowly tailored to preclude only public nudity, the Court found it constitutionally permissible. Justice Scalia, in a concurring opinion, stated that the statute was not subject to First Amendment scrutiny at all since nudity was not a form of expression. Justice Souter, also concurring, rested his holding on the state's "substantial interest in combatting the secondary effects of adult entertainment establishments of the sort typified by respondents' establishments."

In City of Erie v. Pap's A.M., 529 U.S. 277 (2000), the Court clarified its reasoning in *Barnes*. The Court reversed a decision of the Pennsylvania Supreme Court that had invalidated a public indecency ordinance prohibiting nude dancing. The Court concluded that because the ordinance prohibited all public nudity, and did not single out nudity directed at expression, the ordinance could be analyzed under an intermediate level of review, rather than under the standard of strict scrutiny. In this case, the Court opined, the city had asserted that the ordinance was intended to combat the secondary "impacts on public health, safety, and welfare" that the Court had previously concluded were related to the presence of nude dancing establishments. The Court accepted the findings of the Erie City Council that "certain lewd, immoral activities carried on in public places for profit are highly detrimental to the public health, safety and welfare, and lead to the debasement of both women and men, promote violence, public intoxication, prostitution and other serious criminal activity." The Court relied on the City's summary conclusions, without requiring any empirical basis for them. Instead, the Court contended that the complaining establishment had failed to contest the findings. The Court also suggested that Erie could rely on similar findings in other jurisdictions. If a locality contends that it has a unique character or suffers unique effects from permitting activities that it desires to prohibit, should it be required to demonstrate the accuracy of its claims? Or is its desire to retain a particular character, regardless of effects, sufficient?

More recently, in City of Los Angeles v. Alameda Books, Inc., 535 U.S. 425 (2002), the Court upheld an ordinance that prohibited the establishment or maintenance of more than one adult entertainment business in the same building. The city had enacted the ordinance in an effort to reduce crime after a study that it conducted concluded that concentrations of adult businesses are associated with higher crime rates. The majority concluded that the ordinance was reasonably directed at the reduction in crime, in which government has a substantial interest. Justice Scalia again asserted that reliance on secondary effects was sufficient but not necessary, because "the Constitution does not prevent those communities that wish to do so from regulating, or indeed entirely suppressing, the business of pandering sex." For recent cases involving municipal restrictions based on alleged secondary effects of sexually oriented material, see, e.g., East Brooks Books, Inc. v. Shelby County, 588 F.3d 360 (6th Cir. 2009); Annex Books, Inc. v. City of Indianapolis, 581 F.3d 460 (7th Cir. 2009).

3. *Community and Religious Character.* There have been occasional attempts to create municipalities that have a religious purpose, or that signal a willingness to accommodate the practices of certain religions. To what extent should First Amendment restrictions on government establishment of religion or interference with the free exercise of religion preclude such signals? Is it appropriate to apply the same strictures to local accommodations as to statewide or federal accommodations? In 1981, the Bhagwan Shree Rajneesh and several hundred followers moved to a 64,000–acre ranch in central Oregon. The residents of the ranch soon voted to incorporate the area as the City of Rajneeshpuram. After several years of litigation, in which the incorporation was challenged under state land use statutes as well as constitutional provisions, a federal district court ruled that incorporation of a city dedicated to a religious purpose violated the Establishment Clause of the First Amendment. See State of Oregon v. City of Rajneeshpuram, 598 F.Supp. 1208 (D. Or. 1984). For a discussion of the Rajneeshpuram community, see Frances Fitzgerald, Cities on a Hill 247–382 (1981).

In Board of Education of Kiryas Joel Village School District v. Grumet, 512 U.S. 687 (1994), the Supreme Court invalidated the creation of a school district comprising a village in which the only residents were Hasidic Jews, an orthodox group that "make[s] few concessions to the modern world and go[es] to great lengths to avoid assimilation into it." Id. at 690. The district was created to accommodate Hasidic children who had previously received special education in the public schools of another school district, the boundary lines of which had no relationship to any religious group. The children had difficulty adjusting their religious training to the secular school district. In response, the legislature established the new district, which operated a public special education program. All other village children attended religious schools within the community. A majority of the Court concluded that carving out the school district favored one religion and granted the Hasidim a unique benefit, in violation of the neutrality principle of the First Amendment. A plurality of the Court concluded that the delegation of the state's discretionary authority over schools to a group defined by a common religion impermissibly "fused" government and religious functions. While the New York statute at issue did not delegate the power by express reference to the religious nature of the community, the Court found that the delegation of power to a village that purposely contained only members of that religion was equivalent to the state granting the power because of the group's religious nature.

In Tenafly Eruv Ass'n, Inc. v. Borough of Tenafly, 309 F.3d 144 (3d Cir. 2002), cert. denied, 539 U.S. 942 (2003), plaintiffs had constructed an *eruv* within the boundaries of the Borough. An *eruv* is a space within which Orthodox Jews may engage in activities that their religious convictions otherwise deny to them on the Sabbath. The space was demarcated by placing strips, indistinguishable from nonreligious symbols, around utility poles with the consent and participation of Borough officials. Some Borough residents opposed the *eruv* on the grounds that it would encourage Orthodox Jews to move to Tenafly. After construction of the *eruv* with the consent of a county official, the Borough instructed the owners of the utility poles to remove the demarcating strips. The Borough predicated its action on an ordinance that prohibited the placing of signs or other matters on poles, but that had been disregarded in the past. Plaintiffs brought an action to enjoin the removal. The court concluded that placement of the strips did not constitute expressive speech protected under the Free Speech Clause of the First Amendment, because the strips did not communicate any message. The court found, however, that the selective removal of the strips, while permitting other postings on the poles, violated the Free Exercise Clause of the First Amendment.

For decisions that permit a municipality to grant the right to create an *eruv* without violating the Establishment Clause of the First Amendment, see ACLU of New Jersey v. City of Long Branch, 670 F.Supp. 1293 (D.N.J. 1987); Smith v. Community Bd. No. 14, 128 Misc.2d 944, 491 N.Y.S.2d 584 (N.Y. Sup. Ct. 1985).

Do the same principles that preclude a locality from accommodating a religious practice within the community also preclude a locality from prohibiting a practice? In Church of the Lukumi Babalu Aye, Inc. v. City of Hialeah, 508 U.S. 520 (1993), the Court invalidated a local ordinance that prohibited ritual slayings of animals for purposes other than food consumption. The petitioner church followed practices that the ordinance prohibited. The Court concluded that the ordinance was not neutral, but was directed at the petitioner's religious practice. Furthermore, the ordinance could not be justified by the city's asserted compelling interest in health and safety, which could have been satisfied by regulations that imposed fewer restrictions on religious practice.

4. *Federal Legislation and Community Accommodation of Religion.* In 1993, Congress enacted the Religious Freedom Restoration Act ("RFRA"), which permitted government to burden religious practices only in furtherance of a compelling state interest and where the contested law was the least restrictive means of accomplishing that end. The law applied to zoning ordinances of general applicability when directed at religious institutions. In City of Boerne v. Flores, 521 U.S. 507 (1997), the Court invalidated the RFRA on the grounds that Congress had exceeded its powers under Section 5 of the Fourteenth Amendment in enacting it. The majority concluded that RFRA defined rights rather than created a mechanism for enforcing them, which Section 5 permitted. The Court acknowledged that laws of general applicability could burden religion, but permitted such results if the burden is incidental. Congress responded in 2002 by enacting the Religious Land Use and Institutionalized Persons Act, 42 USC § 2000cc ("RLUIPA"). RLUIPA provides that no government shall discriminate against a religious institution in imposing or implementing a land use regulation unless the government's law passes a strict scrutiny analysis. In order to avoid the ruling in *Boerne*, the law applies only where the federal government has control under its commerce or spending powers. Under this scheme, Congress is not bound by the limits of the Section 5 analysis of *Boerne*. RLUIPA provides that in establishing land use systems, a locality may not place religious institutions on "less than equal" terms as nonreligious institutions. Additionally, governments may not discriminate between religious denominations, nor entirely exclude religious institutions from a jurisdiction, nor unreasonably limit religious institutions within a jurisdiction. For application of these principles, see Christopher Serkin & Nelson Tebbe, Condemning Religion: RLUIPA and the Politics of Eminent Domain, 85 Notre Dame L. Rev. 1 (2009).

In Civil Liberties for Urban Believers v. City of Chicago, 342 F.3d 752 (7th Cir. 2003), the court defined a "land-use regulation that imposes a substantial burden on religious exercise" as "one that necessarily bears direct, primary, and fundamental responsibility for rendering religious exercise—including the use of real property for the purpose thereof within the regulated jurisdiction generally—effectively impracticable." The court found that zoning ordinances that adversely affected the ability of churches to find suitable sites did not create a substantial burden on their free exercise, both because the zoning requirements were generally applied to all land developers, and because the churches eventually found sites within the city. In World Outreach Conference Center v. City of Chicago, 591 F.3d 531 (7th Cir. 2009), the same court concluded that a landmark designation that prohibited demolition of a building owned by a religious organization did not substantially burden religious exercise because the organization could have sold the building and used the proceeds to finance construction of its preferred use in another location.

5. *Homeowner Associations and Community Character.* To what extent can residents create explicit contractual arrangements prohibiting activities that allegedly affect the community's character? Of course, we might think of zoning ordinances as implicit contracts that define the character of the community and that prohibit uses or activities inconsistent with that character. But in some instances, residents of a subcommunity may desire to augment governmental zoning with additional restrictions. This occurs most commonly when homeowner associations are created to govern multiunit residential developments. These associations tend to be governed by a series of covenants, conditions, and restrictions (often referred to as CC & Rs) created by the initial developer of the property. As in the cases of cooperative or condominium associations, homeowner associations may contain fewer than 10 residents, but may easily comprise city-sized developments with thousands of residents. They emulate local governments in that they encompass significant geographical areas, hold property in common for their residents, and either provide or contract out for the provision of services ranging from the most common municipal functions (such as security patrols and street maintenance) to golf courses and community centers.

The application of CC & Rs and subsequently adopted regulations has increasingly become the subject of litigation. The proper level of judicial deference to the application of CC & Rs by governing boards has been a matter of some debate. Many courts have suggested that deference to association decisions about enforcement of their covenants is appropriate in light of the contractual or consensual nature of those arrangements. A frequently quoted justification for providing associations with broad discretion is found in Hidden Harbour Estates, Inc. v. Norman, 309 So.2d 180, 181–182 (Fla. Dist. Ct. App. 1975):

> [I]nherent in the condominium concept is the principle that to promote the health, happiness, and peace of mind of the majority of the unit owners since they are living in such close proximity and using facilities in common, each unit owner must give up a certain degree of freedom of choice which he might otherwise enjoy in separate, privately owned property. Condominium unit owners comprise a little democratic subsociety of necessity more restrictive as it pertains to use of condominium property than may be existent outside the condominium organization.

See, e.g., Citizens for Covenant Compliance v. Anderson, 906 P.2d 1314 (Cal. 1995) (upholding restriction that would prohibit winery and llamas on property); Nahrstedt v. Lakeside Village Condominium Ass'n, Inc., 878 P.2d 1275 (Cal. 1994) (upholding a covenant barring pets from residential units). Courts and commentators frequently contend that these subsocieties offer benefits that their residents could not otherwise obtain. These benefits include the ability to obtain goods and services that might not be desired by the entire community or the increased capacity to participate in decentralized governance. After all, if one justification for dividing a nation into states, and states into political subdivisions is to allow people with preferences for certain public goods to aggregate, then why shouldn't decentralization continue to a finer level of neighborhoods or homeowner associations? See Robert C. Ellickson, New Institutions for Old Neighborhoods, 48 Duke L.J. 75 (1998). At the same time, several commentators have expressed concern that these private governments will become insulated from the rest of the community and will fail to support public financing of goods and services that association members can fund for themselves, but that non-members cannot afford to finance privately.

The more we view homeowner associations as private governments, the more we may be wary of significant judicial deference to the association's interpretation of its "contract" with residents. There are, of course, difficult issues about what constitutes private versus public associations. See, e.g., Boy Scouts of America v. Dale, 530 U.S. 640 (2000) (application of public accommodations law to Boy Scouts violates group's First Amendment right of expressive association); New York State Club Ass'n v. City of New York, 487 U.S. 1 (1988) (upholding city law prohibiting discrimination by clubs which provided benefits to business entities and to persons other than their own members on grounds that they had lost "private" characteristic). The "public" nature of the services that homeowner associations typically provide suggests, for some commentators, that these organizations should be subject to constraints similar to those imposed on governmental entities. If, for instance, a covenant against the posting of signs is the functional equivalent of a zoning regulation adopted by a city council, is there reason to distinguish the two on the basis of the public or private nature of the decisionmaker? See Bryan v. MBC Partners, L.P., 541 S.E.2d 124 (Ga. App. 2000). It would be somewhat odd for a court to enforce a local ordinance or state statute on the grounds that residents had consented to the law by virtue of their decision to live in the jurisdiction that had adopted it. For discussion of contractual justifications for CC & Rs and the limits of those justifications, see, e.g., Stewart E. Sterk, Minority Protection in Residential Private Governments, 77 B.U.L. Rev. 273 (1997).

For general treatments of the proper scope of association autonomy, see, e.g., Robert Jay Dilger, Neighborhood Politics (1992); Gregory S. Alexander, Dilemmas of Group Autonomy: Residential Associations and Community, 75 Cornell L. Rev. 1 (1989); Robert Ellickson, Cities and Homeowners Associations, 130 U. Pa. L. Rev. 1519 (1982); Lee Ann Fennell, Contracting Communities 2004 U. Ill. L. Rev. 829; Gerald Frug, Cities and Homeowners Associations: A Reply, 130 U. Pa. L. Rev. 1589 (1982); Clayton P. Gillette, Courts, Covenants, and Communities, 61 U. Chi. L. Rev. 1375 (1994); Roderick M. Hills, Jr., The Constitutional Rights of Private Governments, 78 N.Y.U.L. Rev. 144 (2003); Lior Jacob Strahilevitz, Exclusionary Amenities in Residential Communities, 92 Va. L. Rev. 437 (2006).

2. RESTRICTING MEMBERSHIP IN THE COMMUNITY

D & M Country Estates Homeowners Ass'n v. Romriell

59 P.3d 965 (Idaho 2002).

■ TROUT, CHIEF JUSTICE.

Appellants, various individuals and business entities involved in owning and managing nursing home facilities, appeal from the district judge's order permanently enjoining them from converting a single-family residence and operating a group home for the elderly in violation of the neighborhood subdivision's restrictive covenants. The district judge's order is affirmed.

Sometime prior to September 2000, the Appellants, Dwight G. and Denise B. Romriell, Dannis M. and Ruth N. Adamson, the Aspen Grove Assisted Living General Partnership, and E–Riter, L.L.C. (collectively, "the Romriells"), purchased the real property at issue located in the D & M Subdivision, Chubbuck, Idaho and subject to certain restrictive covenants ("Covenants"). At the time of purchase, a single-family residence was located on the property. Respondent, D & M Estates Home Owner's Association Board ("D & M"), a non-profit association of homeowners, is entitled to enforce these covenants.

The most important Covenant at issue restricts the construction on each lot to only one dwelling to be used by no more than two families. The Covenant states, "[n]o more than one dwelling shall be erected on any one lot and all such dwellings shall be limited to not more than two families." A second Covenant provides a procedure for allowing exceptions to the Covenants: "[e]xceptions to the present restrictive covenants applicable to property in D & M Estates shall be permitted upon written approval by signatures of at least 2/3 of the property owners and by the Architectural Control Committee: provided that such exceptions shall comply with any applicable laws or zoning regulations."

The Romriells planned to use the residential property at issue for operating a group home for the elderly. In order to accommodate the proposed use, the Romriells planned to remodel the single-family home and convert it from a three-bedroom, two-bath residence to an eight-bedroom, eight-bath residence for use by a maximum of eight, unrelated adults.

The Romriells sought approval for their proposed group home through the procedure provided in the Covenants for granting exceptions. As part of this process, the Romriells sent an undated, open letter to the homeowners in the D & M Subdivision both describing the process for granting exceptions to the Covenants and requesting approval from the homeowners for a proposed renovation of the property for the purpose of developing a group home for the elderly. Both the D & M Estates Water and Architectural Board ("Board") and the homeowners rejected the Romriells' proposal.

Nevertheless, in January 2001, the Romriells began remodeling the residence. The Romriells believed they were legally justified in doing so, claiming that D & M had unlawfully refused their proposal and could not enforce the applicable Covenants due to I.C. §§ 67–6530 and 6531. Those statutory provisions set forth the policy in Idaho relating to the use of real property for the care of the elderly.

On January 23, 2001, D & M filed a complaint with the district court alleging violation of the D & M Covenants. On February 8, 2001, a preliminary injunction was granted. On February 9, 2001, the Romriells responded to the complaint with an answer, counterclaim, and third party complaint. The counterclaim sought damages, attorneys fees and costs based on alleged violations of public policy and lost investment costs of $250,000. The third party complaint named each member of D & M and the Board personally alleging claims of breach of contract and unlawful discrimination.

On February 14, 2001, following a two-day evidentiary hearing, the district judge granted D & M a permanent injunction against the Romriells. The court's key rulings held the Covenants (1) are valid, enforceable, and unambiguous; (2) prohibit the Romriells' proposed group home for the elderly; (3) are not invalidated by I.C. §§ 67–6530 and 6531, which only limit zoning regulations; and (4) are not unlawfully discriminatory and have not been enforced in an unlawfully discriminatory manner. Pursuant to I.R.C.P. 54(b), the Judgment was certified final for the purposes of appeal.

* * *

A. The D & M Covenants Unambiguously Prohibit the Construction of a Group Home.

Holding

The district judge did not err in determining, as a matter of law, the Covenants unambiguously prohibit the construction and operation of a group home for eight, unrelated adults. A plain reading of the Covenants shows they clearly prohibit use of residential structures by more than two families.

Idaho recognizes the validity of covenants that restrict the use of private property. *Nordstrom v. Guindon,* 135 Idaho 343, 345, 17 P.3d 287, 290 (2000)(citing *Brown v. Perkins,* 129 Idaho 189, 192, 923 P.2d 434, 437 (1996)). When interpreting such covenants, the Court generally applies the same rules of construction as are applied to any contract or covenant. Id. However, because restrictive covenants are in derogation of the common law right to use land for all lawful purposes, the Court will not extend by implication any restriction not clearly expressed. *Post v. Murphy,* 125 Idaho 473, 475, 873 P.2d 118, 120 (citing *Thomas v. Campbell,* 107 Idaho 398, 404, 690 P.2d 333, 339 (1984)). Further, all doubts are to be resolved in favor of the free use of land. Id.

Beginning with the plain language of the covenant, the first step is to determine whether or not there is an ambiguity. *Brown v. Perkins,* 129 Idaho at 193, 923 P.2d at 437 (citing *City of Chubbuck v. City of Pocatello,* 127 Idaho 198, 201, 899 P.2d 411, 414 (1995)). "Words or phrases that have established definitions in common use or settled legal meanings are not rendered ambiguous merely because they are not defined in the document where they are used." *City of Chubbuck v. City of Pocatello,* 127 Idaho at 201, 899 P.2d at 414. Rather, a covenant is ambiguous when it is capable of more than one reasonable interpretation on a given issue. To determine whether or not a covenant is ambiguous, the court must view the agreement as a whole.

The second step in contract or covenant construction depends on whether or not an ambiguity has been found. If the covenants are unambiguous, then the court must apply them as a matter of law. *City of Chubbuck v. City of Pocatello*, 127 Idaho at 201, 899 P.2d at 414. "Where there is no ambiguity, there is no room for construction; the plain meaning governs." *Post v. Murphy*, 125 Idaho at 475, 873 P.2d at 120. Conversely, if there is an ambiguity in the covenants, then interpretation is a question of fact, and the Court must determine the intent of the parties at the time the instrument was drafted. *Brown v. Perkins*, 129 Idaho at 193, 923 P.2d at 438.

The Covenants at issue clearly provide for only one dwelling unit per lot to be used by no more than two families. Article IV of the Covenants states, "[n]o more than one dwelling shall be erected on any one lot and all such dwellings shall be limited to not more than two families." The Romriells' proposed use of their lot violates this prohibition because housing up to eight unrelated adults in an institutionalized setting violates the restriction against use by more than two families. For this reason, this Court determines the district judge was not in error, and the Romriells' proposed use of the residence in the D & M Subdivision violates the Covenants as a matter of law.

B. Idaho Code §§ 67–6530 and 6531 Do Not Affect D & M's Covenants.

Upon review, this Court determines, as a matter of law, I.C. §§ 67–6530 and 6531 do not apply to private covenants and the district judge correctly determined the unambiguous meaning of the statute.

Determining the meaning of a statute and its application is a matter of law subject to plenary review. The starting point for any statutory interpretation is the literal wording of the statute. To determine the meaning of a statute, the Court applies the plain and ordinary meaning of the terms used. Where the language of a statute is unambiguous, there is no need to consult extrinsic evidence.

Here, the trial court analyzed the statutes in question and correctly determined I.C. §§ 67–6530 and 6531 do not invalidate or render unenforceable D & M's Covenants because, by their own terms, these statutes apply only to zoning laws, ordinances and similar regulations.

Idaho Code § 67–6530 provides:

> The legislature declares that it is the policy of this state that ... elderly persons are entitled to live in normal residential surroundings and should not be excluded therefrom because of their ... advanced age, and in order to achieve statewide implementation of such policy it is necessary to establish the statewide policy that the use of property for the care of eight (8) or fewer ... elderly persons ... is a residential use of such property *for the purposes of local zoning.* (Emphasis added)

In addition, Idaho Code § 67–6531 defines "single family dwelling" as follows:

> *For the purposes of any zoning law, ordinance or code,* the classification of "single family dwelling" shall include any home in which eight (8) or fewer unrelated ... elderly persons reside; and which is supervised. (Emphasis added).

Thus, by their clear terms, these statutes apply only to zoning regulations. This plain meaning should prevail since there is no evidence that the legislature intended a different meaning and, contrary to the Romriells arguments, the plain meaning does not result in absurd results. In addition, the plain meaning is also supported by two standard rules of statutory construction. Under the first, *expressio unius est exclusio alterius,* where a statute specifies certain things, designation of the specific excludes other things not mentioned. Thus, the reference to "zoning" specifically excludes the statute's application to private restrictive covenants, which were not mentioned. The second applicable rule of statutory construction is that courts must construe a statute under the assumption that the legislature knew of all legal precedent and other statutes in existence at the time the statute was passed. Because this Court has long upheld the validity and enforceability of restrictive covenants, the legislature would have clearly stated if it wished to void them. Therefore, both the plain meaning of the statute and accepted rules of statutory construction support the district judge's view that I.C. §§ 67–6530 and 6531 do not invalidate or render unenforceable the D & M Covenants.

The Romriells' also argue the trial court's Findings of Fact do not support the Conclusions of Law. The Romriells essentially argue for this Court to adopt the reasoning of the Washington Supreme Court in *Mains Farm Homeowners v. Worthington,* 121 Wash.2d 810, 854 P.2d 1072 (1993), and request additional findings to support the district judge's Conclusions. This argument is in error, because, as discussed above, where the statute's plain meaning is clear, the Court should apply the meaning without consulting extrinsic evidence. The types of findings the Romriells believe the court should have made include (1) whether the need for elderly group housing is being met; (2) whether other efforts have been undertaken to meet this need; and (3) a determination of the effect such a policy will have on existing contractual rights and the concomitant question of a governmental taking. Such findings are unnecessary where, as here, the statute's plain meaning and narrow application are clear.

* * *

CONCLUSION

Romriell's proposed use of the residence at issue for the purposes of operating a group home was in violation of the D & M Covenants. The Covenants are unambiguous as applied to this particular issue, and the district judge applied them correctly as a matter of law. Furthermore, the Covenants are not rendered invalid or unenforceable as a result of I.C. §§ 67–6530 and 6531, which, by their own terms, are limited in application to zoning regulations alone and do not apply to restrictive covenants. We award costs, but not fees, to Respondents D & M on appeal.

■ JUSTICES SCHROEDER, WALTERS, KIDWELL, and EISMANN concur.

NOTES

1. Is it as clear and unambiguous to you as it was to the court that "housing up to eight unrelated adults in an institutionalized setting violates the restriction against use by more than two families"? The scope of the restriction presumably turns on the definition of the term "family." How is the court defining that term? What is the basis for its definition? In Hill v. Community of Damien of Molokai, 911 P.2d 861 (N.M. 1996), members of a homeowner association sought to prevent a dwelling within the association from being used as a group home for patients with AIDS. The members claimed that the group home would violate a covenant and restriction that lots within the association could only be used for "single family residence purposes." The court upheld the use of the group home. The court concluded that there was nothing in the covenant to suggest that its drafters intended to limit the term "single family" to "a discrete family unit comprised only of individuals related by blood or by law." Instead, the court indicated that the drafters must have intended their covenant to incorporate the meaning of the term under a local zoning ordinance, which defined the term to include up to five unrelated persons living in a dwelling. Given the state law definition of "single family dwelling" in *D &*

M Country Estates, why wouldn't the court believe that the drafters of the restrictive covenant meant to include that definition?

2. Community restrictions on residence were at issue in Village of Belle Terre v. Boraas, 416 U.S. 1 (1974). That case involved an ordinance that restricted land use to one family dwellings and defined the word "family" to include "(*o*)ne or more persons related by blood, adoption, or marriage, living and cooking together as a single housekeeping unit, exclusive of household servants." Owner-landlords challenged the ordinance after they were prohibited from renting a house to more than two unrelated students. Their wide-ranging challenge alleged that the ordinance

> interferes with a person's right to travel; that it interferes with the right to migrate to and settle within a State; that it bars people who are uncongenial to the present residents; that it expresses the social preferences of the residents for groups that will be congenial to them; that social homogeneity is not a legitimate interest of government; that the restriction of those whom the neighbors do not like trenches on the newcomers' rights of privacy; that it is of no rightful concern to villagers whether the residents are married or unmarried; that the ordinance is antithetical to the Nation's experience, ideology, and self-perception as an open, egalitarian, and integrated society.

416 U.S. at 6. The Supreme Court upheld the ordinance as a permissible exercise of the zoning power. Justice Douglas concluded:

> A quiet place where yards are wide, people few, and motor vehicles restricted are legitimate guidelines in a land-use project addressed to family needs. This goal is a permissible one within Berman v. Parker, supra. The police power is not confined to elimination of filth, stench, and unhealthy places. It is ample to lay out zones where family values, youth values, and the blessings of quiet seclusion and clean air make the area a sanctuary for people.

416 U.S. at 9.

Justice Marshall dissented. He contended that while zoning could properly deal with numbers of dwellings or persons, it could not dictate who those persons were or their characteristics. In his view, the ordinance was unconstitutional because it

> discriminates on the basis of just such a personal lifestyle choice as to household companions. It permits any number of persons related by blood or marriage, be it two or twenty, to live in a single household, but it limits to two the number of unrelated persons bound by profession, love, friendship, religious or political affiliation, or mere economics who can occupy a single home. Belle Terre imposes upon those who deviate from the community norm in their choice of living companions significantly greater restrictions than are applied to residential groups who are related by blood or marriage, and compose the established order within the community. The village has, in effect, acted to fence out those individuals whose choice of lifestyle differs from that of its current residents.

416 U.S. at 16–17.

Belle Terre, however, may also have constituted the highwater mark for community restrictions on living arrangements. In Moore v. City of East Cleveland, 431 U.S. 494 (1977), the Court invalidated a local housing ordinance that limited occupation of dwelling units to members of a single family, defined as "a number of individuals related to the nominal head of the household or to the spouse of the nominal head of the household living together as a single housekeeping unit in a single dwelling unit." The ordinance also recognized as a "family" only a few categories of related individuals. Inez Moore's "family" fell into none of these categories. Ms. Moore, who lived with her son and two grandsons, was convicted for violating the ordinance because the two grandsons were cousins rather than brothers. The Supreme Court overturned the conviction finding that the ordinance denied Moore her constitutional liberty protected by the Fourteenth Amendment. Justice Powell, author of the four-Justice plurality opinion, distinguished the case from *Belle Terre* by noting that Belle Terre's ordinance "affected only *unrelated* individuals" while East Cleveland had chosen to regulate residence "by slicing deeply into the family itself." Id. at 498. Furthermore, the Court noted in *Belle Terre* that the ordinance fostered "family needs" and "family values" while East Cleveland criminalized "a grandmother's choice to live with her grandson." Id. at 498–499. Powell concluded that such intrusive regulation of "family living arrangements" threatened the liberty protected by the Fourteenth Amendment and thus required careful examination of "the importance of governmental interests advanced and the extent to which they are served by the regulation." Id. at 499.

The City attempted to justify its ordinance as a way to minimize crowding, traffic congestion, and the burdens placed on the City's schools. Justice Powell noted, however, that the ordinance would permit a family consisting of "a half dozen licensed drivers, each with his or her own car" but would not allow "an adult brother and sister to share a household, even if both faithfully use public transportation." Id. at 500. Finding that the ordinance had "but a tenuous relation" to the stated goals, Powell concluded that the ordinance was invalid as it restricted a liberty interest in family life protected by the Fourteenth Amendment. Justice Stevens concurred in the judgment, but argued that the decision should be predicated on Ms. Moore's right to use her property.

The federal Fair Housing Act prohibits discrimination in housing on the basis of a number of characteristics. One section of the Act provides an exemption for "any reasonable local, State, or Federal restrictions concerning the maximum number of occupants permitted to occupy a dwelling." 42 U.S.C. § 3607(b)(1). In City of Edmonds v. Oxford House, Inc., 514 U.S. 725 (1995), the Court considered whether the exemption applied to a local zoning code that restricted a residential area to "single-family" dwellings and defined "family" as "persons [without regard to number] related by genetics, adoption, or marriage, or a group of five or fewer [unrelated] persons." The Court concluded that the inclusion of traditional families, regardless of size, meant that the provision did not qualify as the type of "total occupancy limit" that the exemption was intended to cover. Justice Thomas, writing in dissent, contended that the exemption should apply because the local provision constituted a "five-occupant limit," with an exception for traditional families.

3. It is conceivable that a community's definition of itself changes over time. The result may be that a group that once was included within a community-wide definition subsequently finds itself at odds with the community's new sense of itself. Should that development alter that analysis of the ability of the community to exclude?

In Poletown Neighborhood Council v. City of Detroit, 304 N.W.2d 455 (Mich. 1981), the court upheld, against a takings challenge, the use of eminent domain, pursuant to state statute, to permit Detroit to level 1,200 homes and displace 3,500 residents of an area of the City known as Poletown and occupied predominantly by Polish–Americans. The area was to be used by General Motors to modernize its operations. General Motors had threatened to leave the City unless it could find an appropriate site for a modern manufacturing plant. A majority of the court concluded that, given the City's economic dependence on the automobile industry and the fiscal disaster that would attend a departure of General Motors, taking of the property satisfied a public use. The City of Detroit paid $62 million in compensation to those displaced. Which "community" should have been entitled to make the decision whether these costs (human, neighborhood, and financial) were worth incurring? Residents of Poletown? Residents of Detroit? Employees of General Motors? If the city council believed that the city as a whole would be better off by favoring General Motors over the displaced residents, why should a court second guess that determination? The Supreme Court of Michigan subsequently changed its view about the use of eminent domain for purposes of providing land to private entities that promised economic development of the community as a whole. In County of Wayne v. Hathcock, 684 N.W.2d 765 (2004), the court overruled *Poletown*. The court concluded that a county's proposed condemnation of land to be transferred to private entities in a business and technology park did not satisfy the state's constitutional requirement that eminent domain could be employed only to "advance public use." The court concluded that the proposed transferees would only be pursuing their own financial interests once they obtained the land, and the generalized economic benefit of alleviating unemployment and revitalizing the economic base of the community would be insufficient to justify the transfer.

Why should Mt. Ephraim be unable to keep uses out, while the City of Detroit, at least prior to *Hathcock*, was enabled to dislocate residents who were already members of the Detroit community? Is it relevant that one case deals with people while the other deals with activities? Does it matter that those who might be adversely affected by the Mt. Ephraim decision are not able to be heard, while those who are affected by the Detroit decision can make their concerns known to representative decisionmakers? Assuming for the moment that the legitimacy of the decision to destroy Poletown should be measured by examining whether affected parties had an opportunity to be heard, what was the likelihood that those adversely affected by the decision, Poletown residents, were adequately represented in the decisionmaking process? Note that an activist citizens' group sent five staff people to fight the General Motors project, that the Catholic churches in the area became intensely involved in the effort to save Poletown (numerous churches were destroyed in the redevelopment effort), and that residents were able to organize numerous protests. See Jeanie Wylie, Poletown: Community Betrayed (1989). Does this capacity for collective action suggest that those adversely affected were sufficiently represented? Or does the fact that those who were to be dislocated constituted only a small minority of Detroit residents mean that it was impossible for them to have their concerns adequately represented? If they have been represented in the decisionmaking process, does that end the scope of judicial inquiry into the propriety of the decision? Recall that the mere fact that a minority is systematically outvoted does not (necessarily) mean that the majority decision is illegitimate. As Professor Briffault has suggested:

> Majority actions may be inconsistent with the best interests—the public interest—of the community. But if majority rule, in the sense of local decisions that reflect the true and active support of current majorities, does not define the local public interest, then what does? How are we to know the local public interest apart from the interest of local majorities—and apart from our own personal biases with respect to the "right" outcomes of particular local issues?

Richard Briffault, Home Rule, Majority Rule, and Dillon's Rule, 67 Chi.-Kent L. Rev. 1011, 1018 (1991).

4. *Homeowner Associations and Residence Controls.* The court in *D & M Country Estates* notes that the state had prevented localities from enacting zoning ordinances that would have had the same effect as the restrictive covenant that it upheld. Thus, the court implies that private associations are allowed a greater degree of control over their character than are governmental units. In Clem v. Christole, Inc., 582 N.E.2d 780 (Ind. 1991), owners in a residential subdivision sought to exclude a group home for developmentally disabled individuals. Covenants that governed the subdivision prohibited the use of "business or commercial purposes of any kind" and restricted the use of lots to "single-family and two-family dwellings." A state statute explicitly invalidated such covenants as applied to the developmentally disabled or mentally ill. A majority of the court declared that the statute violated the contracts clause of the state constitution insofar as the law was applied retroactively. See Mains Farm Homeowners Ass'n v. Worthington, 854 P.2d 1072 (1993).

In the absence of a statutory or constitutional limitation on the right of private parties to discriminate, how extensively may homeowners' associations restrict membership? In Mulligan v. Panther Valley Property Owners Ass'n., 766 A.2d 1186 (N.J. App. Div. 2001), the membership of a private common-interest residential community consisting of more than 2000 homes adopted an amendment to its by-laws that prohibited any individual registered as a Tier 3 offender under New Jersey law from residing in the community. In order to be classified as a Tier 3 registrant, an individual must be a sex-offender who has been deemed by the state to pose a high risk of committing additional similar offenses. Tier 3 offenders, which include those who commit sex offenses against children, must also give more widespread notice of their residence than other offenders. Plaintiff contended that the amendment unlawfully restricted her ability to sell her home. The court concluded that amendments to by-laws should be reviewed by reference to a "reasonableness" standard, which presumably permitted more judicial scrutiny than an alternative "business judgment" standard. The court believed that the greater degree of scrutiny was necessary to protect residents who had not consented to the terms of the amendment when they initially purchased their homes. But the court declined to pass on the validity of the amendment on the grounds that the parties had not created a sufficient record. The court noted that there were only 80 Tier 3 offenders in the state and therefore expressed skepticism as to whether the amendment "unreasonably" limited plaintiff's right of alienation. But the court contended that it was unaware of how many common interest communities within the State had adopted comparable restrictions. Thus, the court could not determine whether the result of such provisions "is to make a large segment of the housing market unavailable to one category of individual and indeed perhaps to approach 'the ogre of vigilantism and harassment,' the potential dangers of which the Supreme Court recognized even while upholding the constitutionality" of the law creating the Tier 3 requirements. 766 A.2d at 1192–93. The court also concluded that the record did not sufficiently reveal the extent to which the development performed municipal functions that might subject its conduct to the same restrictions that would apply to governments.

Why should the ability of one community to exclude certain people depend on the conduct on other communities? What do you make of the following argument:

> Group homes ... may be considered undesirable by most municipalities. Hence, if we allow a municipality to reject siting of such land uses, most municipalities will prohibit them. Under these circumstances, municipalities that might accept a "fair share" of such homes would fear that they will end up accepting all of them if other localities proscribe such uses. Thus, even municipalities otherwise willing to accept their "fair share" have incentives to join in the ban. Universal prohibition on such bans may therefore be necessary in order to locate group homes anywhere.... In the absence of a requirement that all parts of the locality accept group homes, any neighborhood, including those willing to accept a "fair share" of the homes, will seek to prohibit them for fear that others will do so. The fact that communities with covenant regimes will have an easier time avoiding such uses than other parts of the locality may mean that associations suffer fewer undesirable land uses.... Judicial refusal to enforce covenants that have such effects serves as a mechanism for breaking out of the prisoner's dilemma that exists where numerous localities or areas of the same locality would, if left to their own devices, reject the same individuals. Conversely, judicial enforcement of covenants that affect nonresidents may be appropriate where there remain "enough" areas to which those excluded by the covenant can migrate.

Clayton P. Gillette, Courts, Covenants, and Communities, 61 U. Chi. L. Rev. 1375, 1437–38 (1994).

5. *Subcommunities within Municipalities.* Where a municipality contains several communities (i.e., those who reside in residential associations and those who do not or who reside in residential associations governed by other regulations), the interests of those communities may conflict. Does it make a difference that a group traditionally excluded from the larger community wishes to maintain a geographic subcommunity rather than become integrated? In Asian Americans for Equality v. Koch, 527 N.E.2d 265 (N.Y. 1988), plaintiffs challenged a zoning plan for a special district encompassing the Chinatown area of New York City that would have displaced low-income residents of that area, largely of Chinese descent, and created mixed-income residences. Although the plan admittedly would have had certain beneficial effects for the Chinatown area and the city in general, plaintiffs demanded that the plan be altered to "assure that the present residents who wish to stay in Chinatown are able to do so." Plaintiffs claimed that the new development would "force them from their homes and, because the change in zoning favors construction of mixed-income apartments, present structures will be replaced by living accommodations they cannot afford. They note that the constitutional validity of zoning rests on the exercise of the police power for the general welfare and that the general welfare is no more abused by zoning which excludes the poor from a community than by zoning which forces them out of the community." The court affirmed a dismissal of the plaintiffs' complaint:

> [The plaintiffs] have adopted in this court the position of the Appellate Division dissenters that the *Berenson* rule prohibiting exclusionary zoning must be modified to define the "community" for zoning purposes as the 14–block area of the Special Manhattan Bridge District. [In Berenson v. Town of New Castle, 341 N.E.2d 236 (N.Y. 1975), the New York Court of Appeals held that a zoning ordinance would be annulled if it did not include districts for housing of a type required by the socioeconomic demands of the community and region.—EDS.]
>
> *Berenson* cannot reasonably be extended to the facts presented here. The City is the governing authority, not the District and this action challenges its laws. When enacting them, City officials must address the needs of the broader community and must act not only for benefit of the District and its residents, but for the benefit of the City as a whole. Requiring City planners to include particular uses in every district may be truly obnoxious to the City's over-all development, however, and applying the *Berenson* rule to a district as small as this 14–block area could defeat the intended purpose of special district zoning. The interpretation plaintiffs seek also runs counter to the rationale underlying the *Berenson* decision. That holding was deemed necessary to avoid the parochialism of elected local officials in communities which excluded minorities and socioeconomic groups from undeveloped areas of their municipalities to cater to a favored constituency. But here the question of exclusion relates to a Special District in the most highly developed municipality in the Nation, one which already has made extensive allowance for a variety of housing opportunities within its boundaries.

527 N.E.2d at 272.

Does it matter that the area sought to be preserved in the *Asian Americans* decision was only part of the city rather than the entire city?

6. Cases brought under the federal Voting Rights Act reveal solicitude for certain communities within the boundaries of traditional political subdivisions. The concept of "vote dilution" applies to cases in which plaintiffs claim that voting district boundaries within a jurisdiction have been drawn in a manner that prevents a particular group from forming a majority within any district. This may occur by drawing districts in a way that divides the group among several districts, so that group members form a minority in each of several districts rather than a majority in their own district. Alternatively, the electoral system may require that all municipal officials are elected "at large," by all voters within the locality, so that a group that constitutes a distinct minority is unable to elect its members to any position. In either case, members of the minority claim that their votes have been "diluted" by district line drawing. In Board of Estimate v. Morris, 489 U.S. 688 (1989), however, the Supreme Court found claims to subcommunity membership insufficient to relax the one-person, one-vote principle. In that case, the Court struck down the voting methods of the New York City Board of Estimate which treated the five boroughs of the City with relative equality, although populations among the boroughs (which arguably constitute very separate communities within New York City) ranged from 2.2 million to 350,000. The Court concluded that the interest in maintaining some integrity for the individual boroughs did not justify the deviation from population equality in the case. For a discussion of the relationship between the *Morris* case and vote dilution principles, see M. David Gelfand & Terry Allbritton, Conflict and Congruence in One–Person, One–Vote and Racial Vote Dilution Litigation: Issues Resolved and Unresolved by *Board of Estimate v. Morris,* 6 J.L. & Pol. 93 (1989).

3. COMMUNITY EFFECTS ON NONMEMBERS—WHO GETS TO DECIDE?

Holt Civic Club v. City of Tuscaloosa

439 U.S. 60 (1978).

■ MR. JUSTICE REHNQUIST delivered the opinion of the Court.

Holt is a small, largely rural, unincorporated community located on the northeastern outskirts of Tuscaloosa, the fifth largest city in Alabama. Because the community is within the three-mile police jurisdiction circumscribing Tuscaloosa's corporate limits, its residents are subject to the city's "police [and] sanitary regulations." Ala. Code § 11–40–10 (1975). Holt residents are also subject to the criminal jurisdiction of the city's court, Ala. Code § 12–14–1 (1975), and to the city's power to license businesses, trades, and professions, Ala. Code § 11–51–91 (1975). Tuscaloosa, however, may collect from businesses in the police jurisdiction only one-half of the license fee chargeable to similar businesses conducted within the corporate limits. Ibid.

In 1973 appellants, an unincorporated civic association and seven individual residents of Holt, brought this statewide class action in the United States District Court for the Northern District of Alabama, challenging the constitutionality of these Alabama statutes. They claimed that the city's extraterritorial exercise of police powers over Holt residents, without a concomitant extension of the franchise on an equal footing with those residing within the corporate limits, denies residents of the police jurisdiction rights secured by the Due Process and Equal Protection Clauses of the Fourteenth Amendment. . . .

Appellants focus their equal protection attack on § 11–40–10, the statute fixing the limits of municipal police jurisdiction and giving extraterritorial effect to municipal police and sanitary ordinances. Citing Kramer v. Union Free School Dist., 395 U.S. 621, 89 S. Ct. 1886, 23 L. Ed. 2d 583 (1969), and cases following in its wake, appellants argue that the section creates a classification infringing on their right to participate in municipal elections. The State's denial of the franchise to police jurisdiction residents, appellants urge, can stand only if justified by a compelling state interest.

At issue in Kramer was a New York voter qualification statute that limited the vote in school district elections to otherwise qualified district residents who (1) either owned or leased taxable real property located within the district, (2) were married to persons owning or leasing qualifying property, or (3) were parents or guardians of children enrolled in a local district school for a specified time during the preceding year. Without deciding whether or not a State may in some circumstances limit the franchise to residents primarily interested in or primarily affected by the activities of a given governmental unit, the Court held that the statute was not sufficiently tailored to meet that state interest since its classifications excluded many bona fide residents of the school district who had distinct and direct interests in school board decisions and included many residents whose interests in school affairs were, at best, remote and indirect

On the same day, in Cipriano v. City of Houma, 395 U.S. 701, 89 S. Ct. 1897, 23 L. Ed. 2d 647 (1969), the Court upheld an equal protection challenge to a Louisiana law providing that only "property taxpayers" could vote in elections called to approve the issuance of revenue bonds by a municipal utility system. Operation of the utility system affected virtually every resident of the city, not just property owners, and the bonds were in no way financed by property tax revenue. Thus, since the benefits and burdens of the bond issue fell indiscriminately on property owner and nonproperty owner alike, the challenged classification impermissibly excluded otherwise qualified residents who were substantially affected by and directly interested in the matter put to a referendum. The rationale of *Cipriano* was subsequently called upon to invalidate an Arizona law restricting the franchise to property taxpayers in elections to approve the issuance of general obligation municipal bonds. Phoenix v. Kolodziejski, 399 U.S. 204, 90 S. Ct. 1990, 26 L. Ed. 2d 523 (1970).

Appellants also place heavy reliance on Evans v. Cornman, 398 U.S. 419, 90 S. Ct. 1752, 26 L. Ed. 2d 370 (1970). In *Evans* the Permanent Board of Registry of Montgomery County, Md., ruled that persons living on the grounds of the National Institutes of Health (NIH), a federal enclave located within the geographical boundaries of the State, did not meet the residency requirement of the Maryland Constitution. Accordingly, NIH residents were denied the right to vote in Maryland elections. This Court rejected the notion that persons living on NIH grounds were not residents of Maryland....

Thus, because inhabitants of the NIH enclave were residents of Maryland and were "just as interested in and connected with electoral decisions as they were prior to 1953 when the area came under federal jurisdiction and as their neighbors who live off the enclave," id., at 426, 90 S. Ct. at 1757, the State could not deny them the equal right to vote in Maryland elections.

From these and our other voting qualifications cases a common characteristic emerges: The challenged statute in each case denied the franchise to individuals who were physically resident within the geographic boundaries of the governmental entity concerned.... No decision of this Court has extended the "one man, one vote" principle to individuals residing beyond the geographic confines of the governmental entity concerned, be it the State or its political subdivisions. On the contrary, our cases have uniformly recognized that a government unit may legitimately restrict the right to participate in its political processes to those who reside within its borders.... Bona fide residence alone, however, does not automatically confer the right to vote on all matters, for at least in the context of special interest elections the State may constitutionally disfranchise residents who lack the required special interest in the subject matter of the election. See Salyer Land Co. v. Tulare Lake Basin Water Storage Dist., 410 U.S. 719, 93 S. Ct. 1224, 35 L. Ed. 2d 659 (1973); Associated Enterprises, Inc. v. Toltec Watershed Improvement Dist., 410 U.S. 743, 93 S. Ct. 1237, 35 L. Ed. 2d 675 (1973).

Appellants' argument that extraterritorial extension of municipal powers requires concomitant extraterritorial extension of the franchise proves too much. The imaginary line defining a city's corporate limits cannot corral the influence of municipal actions. A city's decisions inescapably affect individuals living immediately outside its borders. The granting of building permits for high rise apartments, industrial plants, and the like on the city's fringe unavoidably contributes to problems of traffic congestion, school districting, and law enforcement immediately outside the city. A rate change in the city's sales or ad valorem tax could well have a significant impact on retailers and property values in areas bordering the city. The condemnation of real property on the city's edge for construction of a municipal garbage dump or waste treatment plant would have obvious implications for neighboring nonresidents. Indeed, the indirect extraterritorial effects of many purely internal municipal actions could conceivably have a heavier impact on surrounding environs than the direct regulation contemplated by Alabama's police jurisdiction statutes. Yet no one would suggest that nonresidents likely to be affected by this sort of municipal action have a constitutional right to participate in the political processes bringing it about. And unless one adopts the idea that the Austinian notion of sovereignty, which is presumably embodied to some extent in the authority of a city over a police jurisdiction, distinguishes the direct effects of limited municipal powers over police jurisdiction residents from the indirect though equally dramatic extraterritorial effects of purely internal municipal actions, it makes little sense to say that one requires extension of the franchise while the other does not. . . .

B

Thus stripped of its voting rights attire, the equal protection issue presented by appellants becomes whether the Alabama statutes giving extraterritorial force to certain municipal ordinances and powers bear some rational relationship to a legitimate state purpose. San Antonio Independent School Dist. v. Rodriguez, 411 U.S. 1, 93 S. Ct. 1278, 36 L. Ed. 2d 16 (1973). . . .

Government, observed Mr. Justice Johnson, "is the science of experiment," Anderson v. Dunn, 6 Wheat. 204, 226, 5 L. Ed. 242, 247 (1821), and a State is afforded wide leeway when experimenting with the appropriate allocation of state legislative power. This Court has often recognized that political subdivisions such as cities and counties are created by the State "as convenient agencies for exercising such of the governmental powers of the state as may be entrusted to them." Hunter v. Pittsburgh, 207 U.S. 161, 178, 28 S. Ct. 40, 46, 52 L. Ed. 151 (1907). . . .

The extraterritorial exercise of municipal powers is a governmental technique neither recent in origin nor unique to the State of Alabama. See R. Maddox, Extraterritorial Powers of Municipalities in the United States (1955). In this country 35 States authorize their municipal subdivisions to exercise governmental powers beyond their corporate limits. Comment, The Constitutionality of the Exercise of Extraterritorial Powers by Municipalities, 45 U. Chi. L. Rev. 151 (1977). Although the extraterritorial municipal powers granted by these States vary widely, several States grant their cities more extensive or intrusive powers over bordering areas than those granted under the Alabama statutes.

In support of their equal protection claim, appellants suggest a number of "constitutionally preferable" governmental alternatives to Alabama's system of municipal police jurisdictions. For example, exclusive management of the police jurisdiction by county officials, appellants maintain, would be more "practical." From a political science standpoint, appellants' suggestions may be sound, but this Court does not sit to determine whether Alabama has chosen the soundest or most practical form of internal government possible. Authority to make those judgments resides in the state legislature, and Alabama citizens are free to urge their proposals to that body. See, e.g., Hunter v. Pittsburgh, 207 U.S., at 179, 28 S. Ct., at 46. Our inquiry is limited to the question whether "any state of facts reasonably may be conceived to justify" Alabama's system of police jurisdictions, Salyer Land Co. v. Tulare Lake Basin Water Storage Dist., 410 U.S., at 732, 93 S. Ct., at 1231, and in this case it takes but momentary reflection to arrive at an affirmative answer.

The Alabama Legislature could have decided that municipal corporations should have some measure of control over activities carried on just beyond their "city limit" signs, particularly since today's police jurisdiction may be tomorrow's annexation to the city proper. Nor need the city's interests have been the only concern of the legislature when it enacted the police jurisdiction statutes. Urbanization of any area brings with it a number of individuals who long both for the quiet of suburban or country living and for the career opportunities offered by the city's working environment. Unincorporated communities like Holt dot the rim of most major population centers in Alabama and elsewhere, and state legislatures have a legitimate interest in seeing that this substantial segment of the population does not go without basic municipal services such as police, fire, and health protection. Established cities are experienced in the delivery of such services, and the incremental cost of extending the city's responsibility in these areas to surrounding environs may be substantially less than the expense of establishing wholly new service organizations in each community.

Nor was it unreasonable for the Alabama Legislature to require police jurisdiction residents to contribute through license fees to the expense of services provided them by the city. The statutory limitation on license fees to half the amount exacted within the city assures that police jurisdiction residents will not be victimized by the city government....

In sum, we conclude that Alabama's police jurisdiction statutes violate neither the Equal Protection Clause nor the Due Process Clause of the Fourteenth Amendment. Accordingly, the judgment of the District Court is affirmed....

■ MR. JUSTICE BRENNAN, with whom MR. JUSTICE WHITE and MR. JUSTICE MARSHALL join, dissenting....

There is no question but that the residents of Tuscaloosa's police jurisdiction are governed by the city. Under Alabama law, a municipality exercises "governing" and "law-making" power over its police jurisdiction. City of Homewood v. Wofford Oil Co., 232 Ala. 634, 637, 169 So. 288, 290 (1936). Residents of Tuscaloosa's police jurisdiction are subject to license fees exacted by the city, as well as to the city's police and sanitary regulations, which can be enforced through penal sanctions effective in the city's municipal court. See Birmingham v. Lake, 243 Ala. 367, 372, 10 So. 2d 24, 28 (1942). The Court seems to imply, however, that residents of the police jurisdiction are not governed enough to be included within the political community of Tuscaloosa, since they are not subject to Tuscaloosa's powers of eminent domain, zoning, or ad valorem taxation. Ante, at 391 n.8. But this position is sharply contrary to our previous holdings. In Kramer v. Union Free School Dist., 395 U.S. 621, 89 S. Ct. 1886, 23 L. Ed. 2d 583 (1969), for example, we held that residents of a school district who neither owned nor leased taxable real property located within the district, or were not married to someone who did, or were not parents or guardians of children enrolled in a local district school, nevertheless were sufficiently affected by the decisions of the local school board to make the denial of their franchise and local school board elections a violation of the Equal Protection Clause. Similarly, we held in Cipriano v. City of Houma, 395 U.S. 701, 89 S. Ct. 1897, 23 L. Ed. 2d 647 (1969), that a Louisiana statute limiting the franchise in municipal utility system revenue bond referenda to those who were "property taxpayers" was unconstitutional because all residents of the municipality were affected by the operation of the utility system. See Phoenix v. Kolodziejski, 399 U.S. 204, 90 S. Ct. 1990, 26 L. Ed. 2d 523 (1970).

The residents of Tuscaloosa's police jurisdiction are vastly more affected by Tuscaloosa's decisionmaking processes than were the plaintiffs in either Kramer or Cipriano affected by the decisionmaking processes from which they had been unconstitutionally excluded. Indeed, under Alabama law Tuscaloosa's authority to create and enforce police and sanitary regulations represents an extensive reservoir of power "to prevent, an anticipation of danger to come, ... and in so doing to curb and restrain the individual tendency." Gilchrist Drug Co. v. Birmingham, 234 Ala. 204, 208, 174 So. 609, 612 (1937). See Cooper v. Town of Valley Head, 212 Ala. 125, 126, 101 So. 874, 875 (1924). A municipality, for example, may use its police powers to regulate, or even to ban, common professions and businesses. "In the exertion and application of the police power there is to be observed the sound distinction as to useful and harmless trades, occupations and businesses and as to businesses, occupations and trades recognized as hurtful to public morals, public safety, productive of disorder or injurious to public good. In applying it to the class last mentioned it may be exerted to destroy." Chappell v. Birmingham, 236 Ala. 363, 365, 181 So. 906, 907 (1938). The Court today does not explain why being subjected to the authority to exercise such extensive power does not suffice to bring the residents of Tuscaloosa's police jurisdiction within the political community of the city. Nor does the Court in fact provide any standards for determining when those subjected to extraterritorial municipal legislation will have been "governed enough" to trigger the protections of the Equal Protection Clause....

The criterion of geographical residency is thus entirely arbitrary when applied to this case. It fails to explain why, consistently with the Equal Protection Clause, the "government unit" which may exclude from the franchise those who reside outside of its geographical boundaries should be composed of the city of Tuscaloosa rather than of the city together with its police jurisdiction. It irrationally distinguishes between two classes of citizens, each with equal claim to residency (insofar as that can be determined by domicile or intention or other similar criteria), and each governed by the city of Tuscaloosa in the place of their residency.

The Court argues, however, that if the franchise were extended to residents of the city's police jurisdiction, the franchise must similarly be extended to all those indirectly affected by the city's actions. This is a simple non sequitur. There is a crystal-clear distinction between those who reside in Tuscaloosa's police jurisdiction, and who are therefore subject to that city's police and sanitary ordinances, licensing fees, and the jurisdiction of its municipal court, and those who reside in neither the city nor its police jurisdiction, and who are thus merely affected by the indirect impact of the city's decisions. This distinction is recognized in Alabama law, cf. Roberson v. City of Montgomery, 285 Ala. 421, 233 So. 2d 69 (1970), and is consistent with, if not mandated by, the very conception of a political community underlying constitutional recognition of bona fide residency requirements.

NOTES

1. What is the nature of the complaint of the appellants in *Holt*? Are they contending that their perspective is not heard or seriously considered when Tuscaloosa officials make decisions? Or are they contending that they are not represented by officials of their own choosing in the decisionmaking process? If the former, then are there reasons to believe that, even if nonresidents are denied the vote, their interest will be represented by residents of Tuscaloosa? If that is the case, would that be sufficient to allay any fears about local decisionmaking? Or is the distinction between being represented by representatives of one's choosing and being represented through surrogates elected by others similar to Hannah Arendt's concern (expressed in Chapter 1) that "the people are not admitted to the public realm" so that "the business of government has become the privilege of the few?"

In Burba v. City of Vancouver, 783 P.2d 1056 (Wash. 1989), nonresidents challenged the inclusion of a city utility tax in the rates they paid for water and sewer services provided by a city utility. The nonresidents claimed that they had no voice in the decision to create or levy the utility tax. The court concluded that the utility tax was analogous to a business and occupation tax that a city could impose on a retailer who sold to both resident and nonresident customers. The court determined that as long as a taxable event occurred within the city, it was appropriate to impose a tax on those who benefited from that event. In this situation, those beneficiaries included the nonresident customers of the utility. But the court also concluded that nonresidents were not without meaningful representation in the decision to impose the tax:

> The plaintiffs are provided with procedural safeguards, including the right to attend and participate in public hearings, which satisfy constitutional due process requirements. In addition, the courts protect nonresidents from any potentially discriminatory, arbitrary, or unreasonable rates imposed by the Utility. Plaintiffs' inability to vote in Vancouver's municipal elections does not render the tax unconstitutional. Bona fide residential requirements placed on the right to vote do not violate the equal protection clause even where a tax levied on services provided imposes an indirect burden on nonresident customers.

Id. at 1059.

A municipality, however, may wish to expand the franchise to nonresidents. Does the fact that it does not have to extend voting rights mean that it can restrict extraterritorial voting rights any way that it desires? In Brown v. Board of Commissioners of the City of Chattanooga, 722 F.Supp. 380 (E.D. Tenn. 1989), the court upheld a state statute that permitted nonresidents to vote in a municipality in which they owned property. The court found, however, that at least 78 percent of the nonresident property holders who registered to vote under that provision were white, while the City of Chattanooga was 32 percent black. The court also found that the city had permitted as many as 23 nonresidents to register to vote as owners of a single piece of property in the city. The court determined that while the state statute satisfied a "reasonable relationship," the Chattanooga charter provision that implemented the statute and that permitted a nonresident who owned a trivial amount of property to vote in municipal elections did not serve any rational governmental interest. Thus, the court concluded that the charter provision violated the equal protection clause of the Fourteenth Amendment. The Tennessee law currently limits to two the number of nonresident owners of any parcel who can vote in a municipality based on property ownership, regardless of the number of owners of the parcel. See Tenn. Code Ann. § 2–2–107(a)(3).

2. *Denial of Voting Rights to Nonresidents.* In Pure Water Committee of Western Maryland v. Mayor and City Council of Cumberland, 2003 WL 22095654 (D. Md. 2003), plaintiffs were nonresident customers of water systems located in municipalities that had recently voted to fluoridate their water supply. Plaintiffs contended that they were subjected to fluoride without having the right to vote. The court concluded that plaintiffs failed to show an injury because they did not have a right to vote in the municipalities involved in the action. Similarly, in Mixon v. State of Ohio, 193 F.3d 389 (6th Cir. 1999), the court cited *Holt* for the proposition that states could limit the right to vote in municipal elections to residents if the restriction was rationally related to a reasonable state purpose. In that case, only residents were permitted to vote for mayor of Cleveland, even though the mayor appointed board members of a school district that included nonresidents. The court concluded that the state had reasonably acted "to improve the established school system that was failing the City of Cleveland and its schoolchildren."

In Herriman City v. Swenson, 521 F.Supp.2d 1233 (D. Utah 2007), cities entered into an interlocal agreement to form a new school district to be carved from existing school districts. The issue was subject to a ballot election in which only residents of the proposed new district were entitled to vote. Residents of a city that was part of an existing district, but that was not included in the proposed new district, were not eligible to vote under the statutory scheme. After reviewing the history of voting rights recited in *Holt*, the court found that states are free to restrict elections to those who reside within the jurisdiction holding the vote as long as the restrictive statute is rationally related to a legitimate governmental purpose. This was so because states have wide discretion in structuring the affairs of their political subdivisions, especially where the election involves a limited issue, such as creation of a school district, rather than a general election. In addition, the distinction at issue involved only geographical location, not "an improper consideration, such as race, wealth, tax status, or other considerations." Here, it was rational to distinguish between the different interests of the geographic areas involved insofar as the legislature could rationally determine that the residents of the proposed new school district are most directly affected by the creation of the new district, and the statutory scheme was rationally related to the improvement of education through the promotion of community-based schools.

3. Justice Rehnquist in *Holt* states that "no one would suggest that nonresidents likely to be affected by [the indirect extraterritorial effects of municipal action] have a constitutional right to participate in the political processes bringing it about." Professor Jerry Frug responds:

> Well, I'm suggesting something of this sort, albeit not on constitutional grounds. In the ageographical city, residency within invisible boundary lines should not determine who can use schools, hospitals, addiction treatment centers or the like. Local services should be open to all local people. The problem is to decide who they are and how to do so.

Jerry Frug, Decentering Decentralization, 60 U. Chi. L. Rev. 253, 324–325 (1993). Frug suggests changing the rules of inclusion within a "locality" in ways that would transcend geographical boundaries and recognize that individuals have connections to communities that are nongeographic. He suggests, for instance, that individuals might receive a fixed number of votes to be cast in whatever local elections they feel affect their interests. Nonresident workers, shoppers, and property owners, for instance, might cast votes in communities in which they have an intense interest, notwithstanding that they do not live there. Our "boundary-fixation" has already been undermined, he suggests, by the multitude of legally defined jurisdictions that do not correlate to city borders, such as school districts, park districts, transportation districts, and redevelopment authorities.

B. DEFINING "COMMUNITY" IN PRACTICE: MUNICIPAL BOUNDARIES AND DECIDING WHO DECIDES

1. CONSTITUTIONAL CONSTRAINTS ON BOUNDARY MAKING

Moorman v. Wood

504 F.Supp. 467 (E.D. Ky. 1980).

Memorandum Opinion

■ BERTELSMAN, DISTRICT JUDGE.

FACTS

The court is here presented with a constitutional attack on a state annexation statute. The exact counterpart of this controversy has apparently not been the subject of any other judicial decision. The 1980 session of the Kentucky General Assembly enacted K.R.S. 81A.430 which authorizes any city to designate for annexation a contiguous part of another city. If there is an objection, the matter can be placed on the ballot and the citizens of the annexation area then vote on the matter and a majority of those voting decide the issue.

Plaintiffs here are citizens of the City of Covington, portions of which are sought to be annexed by the defendants, the smaller cities of Ft. Wright and Crescent Springs. Plaintiffs seek to block the annexation on the ground that K.R.S. 81A.430 is unconstitutional in that it contravenes their right to equal protection under the Fourteenth Amendment to the Constitution of the United States. They contend that the law must fall because it does not permit all of the voters of Covington to vote on what amounts to the deannexation of part of their city, a matter in which they claim a substantial interest. The rationale of the 1980 annexation statutes cannot be understood in a vacuum. Some background is essential. Annexation wars have been rife in Kentucky for generations. They have been the subject of particularly bitter controversies in the northern area of the state in which this court sits. This northern area is composed of some 50 cities, contained in three counties. The largest of the cities, Covington, has a population of about 50,000 and the smallest contains only a few hundred residents.

It is important to an understanding of the statutes here involved and of this decision to grasp that these disputes have no racial overtones. Nor do they usually involve conflicting class interests of wealth and poverty.

Although the plaintiffs here claim that the annexations are the result of the efforts of two "affluent subdivisions" to attempt to avoid their fair share of urban problems, this is not always, nor even usually the case in local annexation controversies. The court has known citizens of an unincorporated area with no municipal services whatever and a blue collar population to resist annexation to an affluent city of 15,000 and, in another case, a ferocious court battle to be waged to resist annexation to a city with a population of 3,000 or less, where neither the annexors nor the annexees could be described as affluent.

Although, of course, there may be some desire to escape higher taxes and urban problems, in many instances, the motivation for resisting annexation in this vicinity is that many of the people like to live in their small towns where they can know the mayor, city council members and other officials personally, and where they can live their lives, as they see it, relatively free from regulation and have a direct voice in such municipal matters as zoning or the granting of a liquor license.

Where financial considerations are a primary motive in opposing annexations, frequently they involve a conscious desire to accept fewer municipal services as a trade off for lower taxes. For example, many of the smaller communities, both incorporated and unincorporated, keep taxes rather low by utilizing volunteer fire departments, part-time police forces, septic tanks instead of sewers, no city manager or engineer, etc. From this point of view, the prevention of annexation enables those with limited financial resources better to own their own homes. To such people terms like "metro government" and "annexation" are calls to a holy war of resistance.

The annexing cities, on the other hand, are often motivated by a desire to expand their tax base and a perceived need to end the confusion and inefficiency which they contend results from the profusion of small government entities. The court expresses no opinion as to the wisdom of either of these positions. They are described here solely to explain the emotionally charged dilemma with which the legislature was presented.

It is out of this history that the present controversy arises. In 1962 the City of Covington, certain citizens of which are individual plaintiffs here, commenced efforts to annex extensive unincorporated areas of Kenton County. At that time annexations were resisted in Kentucky by remonstrance suits, under which the state court in the context of an equitable action determined, under prescribed statutory tests, whether an annexation was appropriate.

The 1962 annexation litigation worked its tortuous way through the courts until it finally concluded in 1979, with a decision in favor of the annexing City of Covington. The proceedings are too complicated even to attempt to describe here. In 1979 Covington was ultimately successful in finalizing the annexation of these large unincorporated areas. Some of this territory which went to Covington at the conclusion of this 18 years of forensic hostilities is now sought to be detached from Covington and joined to Crescent Springs and Ft. Wright by what amounts to a preemptive strike.

This was made possible because such bitter animosities had been engendered by the prolonged conflict that the vanquished citizens of these areas, refusing to accept their defeat, set up a type of underground resistance movement, sought aid from the General Assembly of the Commonwealth and induced it to repeal the old annexation statutes and enact the one at issue here.

These citizens, who regard themselves as freedom fighters of a sort, then formed an alliance with the smaller cities of Ft. Wright and Crescent Springs to annex them away from Covington under the new law. The annexation was challenged by the filing of appropriate petitions, and the issue scheduled to be placed on the ballot at the general election of November 4, 1980, pursuant to the new statute. The plaintiffs here as citizens of Covington attacked the new law and sought to enjoin the holding of the election, claiming the statute violated their equal protection rights in that it did not permit all the citizens of Covington to vote in the annexation election, although all had a substantial interest in the result.

A preliminary injunction was sought from, but denied by this court, and the election held. There were other annexation issues on the ballot, through which Covington was attempting to annex certain unincorporated areas of Kenton County. The results are in the margin. In interpreting them, it must be recalled that a vote for the Ft. Wright and Crescent Springs annexation is actually an anti-annexation vote with respect to the City of Covington.[1] As these results show, popular local enthusiasm for annexation to Covington is somewhat restrained.

1. ARE YOU IN FAVOR OF BEING ANNEXED TO THE CITY OF FT. WRIGHT?

Fort Wright Ordinance 204–180
YES 504 votes
NO 18 votes

ISSUE

Thus the issue is presented:

Does a violation of the Equal Protection Clause of the Fourteenth Amendment result from the efforts of the legislature of the Commonwealth of Kentucky to resolve the difficult political problems of annexation by providing that the residents of an annexation area, to the exclusion of other affected citizens, decide by popular referendum the city in which they shall live?

The resolution of this issue involves both the equal protection doctrine and principles of federalism. This court holds that the legislature's solution to the annexation quandary is not unconstitutional.

JUSTICIABILITY

Defendants suggest that this case involves a non-justiciable controversy under the doctrine of Hunter v. City of Pittsburgh. As the discussion which follows shows, the court does not regard that decision as one relating to the justiciability doctrine, but as one applying principles of federalism. Therefore, the court holds that this case is justiciable.

PRINCIPLES OF FEDERALISM

It has been said that the division of powers between the branches of the federal government and between federal and state government is "the most central tenet of American constitutionalism."

In the infancy of our Republic, great emphasis was placed on the autonomy of the states as a "barrier against the enterprises of ambition." . . .

In the context of municipal government, this principle is best exemplified by Hunter v. City of Pittsburgh. *Hunter* was an annexation case,

---

Fort Wright Ordinance 217–1980
YES 494 votes
NO 15 votes
ARE YOU IN FAVOR OF BEING ANNEXED TO THE CITY OF CRESCENT SPRINGS?
Crescent Springs Ordinance 1980–38
YES 108 votes
NO 2 votes
Crescent Springs Ordinance 1980–39
YES 16 votes
NO 2 votes
ARE YOU IN FAVOR OF BEING ANNEXED TO THE CITY OF COVINGTON?
Edgewood, Kentucky
YES 48 votes
NO 3,783 votes
Liberty Construction
YES 2 votes
NO 189 votes
Decoursey Pike
YES 6 votes
NO 349 votes

exhibiting some of the conflicting policy problems found in the case at bar. There, the court held a statute of the State of Pennsylvania, providing for the merger of contiguous cities, constitutional under the Fourteenth Amendment, where the votes of both the larger and smaller cities were pooled, thus in effect giving the larger city the right to annex the smaller one contrary to the will of a majority of its citizens. In language that has been much quoted and frequently construed, the Court said:

> We think the following principles ... have become settled doctrines of this court, to be acted upon wherever they are applicable. Municipal corporations are political subdivisions of the State, created as convenient agencies for exercising such of the governmental powers of the State as may be entrusted to them. For the purpose of executing these powers properly and efficiently they usually are given the power to acquire, hold, and manage personal and real property. The number, nature and duration of the powers conferred upon these corporations and the territory over which they shall be exercised rests in the absolute discretion of the State. Neither their charters, nor any law conferring governmental powers, or vesting in them property to be used for governmental purposes, or authorizing them to hold or manage such property, or exempting them from taxation upon it, constitutes a contract with the State within the meaning of the Federal Constitution. The State, therefore, at its pleasure may modify or withdraw all such powers, may take without compensation such property, hold it itself, or vest it in other agencies, expand or contract the territorial area, unite the whole or a part of it with another municipality, repeal the charter and destroy the corporation. All this may be done, conditionally or unconditionally, with or without the consent of the citizens, or even against their protest. In all these respects the State is supreme, and its legislative body, conforming its action to the state constitution, may do as it will, unrestrained by any provision of the Constitution of the United States. Although the inhabitants and property owners may by such changes suffer inconvenience, and their property may be lessened in value by the burden of increased taxation, or for any other reason, they have no right by contract or otherwise in the unaltered or continued existence of the corporation or its powers, and there is nothing in the Federal Constitution which protect them from these injurious consequences. The power is in the State and those who legislate for the State are alone responsible for any unjust or oppressive exercise of it.

The judicial exegesis on the text of *Hunter* has been inconsistent. Some courts have considered *Hunter* as a political question decision, similar to the decisions of the Supreme Court prior to Baker v. Carr. These courts have implied that the case is a dead letter, because of the decision in *Baker* and others which have developed its doctrine.

Other cases have stated that the thrust of *Hunter* is negated by subsequent voting rights and discrimination cases.

Many recent cases, however, have rejuvenated *Hunter*. In Holt Civic Club v. Tuscaloosa, the Supreme Court stated that, although *Hunter* was subject to the voting right cases, it "continues to have substantial constitutional significance in emphasizing the extraordinarily wide latitude that states have in creating the various types of political subdivisions and conferring authority upon them."

This court's reading of *Hunter* is not that it concerned political questions in the sense of the justiciability doctrine, but rather that it has to do with the principles of division of powers between the state and federal government, and is a "political question" decision only in that sense. *Hunter's* holding was not that an annexation question is non-justiciable under the Federal Constitution, but—in more modern constitutional parlance—that there is no property right or liberty interest in living within a particular political subdivision. Thus, a state statute directly placing a citizen in a particular city or county, or changing by the redrawing of boundary lines the political subdivision in which he resides, or providing some procedure where that may be done, may not be attacked under the due process or equal protection clauses of the Fourteenth Amendment, except in certain very restricted circumstances.

As standing for this precept, *Hunter* is still good law, except where its force may be overcome by the counterthrust of the voting rights decisions, or those involving the realignment of political subdivisions for invidious racial motives or in other situations involving a clear denial of due process or equal protection. As applied to annexation elections, an analysis of the facts of all the cases cited by the parties or found by the court indicates that, so long as the residents of the affected areas are treated alike within those areas, statutory provisions for a wide variety of voting schemes will be upheld against an equal protection attack, and the vote of one area may be given more weight than that of the other, or the franchise may even be granted to one area and denied to another if a rational basis exists for so providing.[25] These cases dovetail with the view of the voting rights cases that residence is a legitimate criterion for limiting the right to vote, as discussed in the next section of this opinion.

In the last analysis, what these cases are saying is that annexation has its pros and cons, and is a political question in the sense that under our Constitution's principles of federalism, it is the prerogative of the individual states to resolve the conflicting interests involved in annexation disputes as they see fit. It is true that the prerogative is subject to limitations of equal protection and due process, but *Hunter* requires that these limitations be interpreted in the light of that federalism.

---

25. See Hunter v. City of Pittsburgh, 207 U.S. 161, 28 S. Ct. 40, 52 L. Ed. 151 (1907) (larger city could annex smaller, votes of both being pooled); Hayward v. Edwards, 456 F. Supp. 1151 (D.S.C. 1977), *aff'd,* Hayward v. Clay, 573 F.2d 187 (4th Cir. 1978) (annexing and annexed areas voted separately, approval of voters of each could be required, but freeholders of annexed area could not be given veto); Murphy v. Kansas City, 347 F. Supp. 837 (W.D. Mo. 1972) (annexing city only has vote, citizens of area to be annexed have no vote). In cases involving annexation schemes where no election was provided, courts have invoked a similar principle in upholding various statutory plans. See Deane Hill Country Club v. City of Knoxville, 379 F.2d 321 (6th Cir. 1967), *cert. den.,* 389 U.S. 975, 88 S. Ct. 476, 19 L. Ed. 2d 467 (1967); Berry v. Bourne, 588 F.2d 422 (4th Cir. 1978); Wilkerson v. City of Coralville, 478 F.2d 709 (8th Cir. 1973); Jimenez v. Hidalgo County (S.D. Tex. 1975); Adams v. City of Colorado Springs, 308 F. Supp. 1397 (D. Col. 1970), *aff'd,* 399 U.S. 901, 90 S. Ct. 2197, 26 L. Ed. 2d 555 (1970).

As the next section of this opinion shows, equal protection rights have not been violated, and the resolution the Commonwealth of Kentucky has made of the conflicting political interests involved in annexation controversies, by submitting the matter to a plebiscite of the residents of the annexation area, must be respected by this court.

EQUAL PROTECTION

Plaintiffs present this case as a voting rights case. They argue that the fact that the new annexation statute permits only the residents of the areas sought to be annexed to vote on an annexation violates plaintiffs' right of equal protection. Plaintiffs' rationale is that, as citizens of the City of Covington, they are substantially affected by the loss of these areas to that city, and that the statute is unconstitutional in depriving them of a right to vote on the matter. But in all the voting cases, it was conceded that the right to vote could be limited to the residents of the governmental unit or area concerned.

Plaintiffs contend that the right to vote is a fundamental right, the denial of which is subject to the equal protection strict scrutiny test, rather than the less stringent rational basis test. In annexation elections, this is true in regard to classifying residents of a given area, but in granting the franchise to residents of one area, and denying it to those of another area, or giving the votes of different areas different weight, the less stringent rational basis test is the test that has been employed. . . .

Not only a rational basis, but a compelling state interest for the new statute is found in the following considerations. First, annexation battles, in this part of the state at least, were tearing the community apart and generating hostility to such a degree that some solution had to be found. The point had been reached where, even after it had been determined that an area was to be annexed to a particular city, harmony was destroyed, and the annexed citizens were devoting substantial civic energies to reversing the annexation. The procedure of committing annexation problems to the judiciary had not worked. The judiciary, the legislature apparently concluded, was not suited for the task of regulating annexations. There was no reason to believe an administrative procedure would work any better, and it would only result in returning the matter to the judiciary once again, because the Constitution of Kentucky guarantees judicial review of administrative action.

Therefore, the state had a compelling interest in finding some way to provide a fast, certain answer to annexation controversies. Experience demonstrated that such an immediate, certain solution, which would avoid years of litigation and uncertainty as to the status of a given area, was more desirable than one which nicely balanced all the relevant theoretical considerations of political science, but at the cost of decade-long, bitterly divisive court battles.

The legislature determined that voting is a workable answer. Having chosen voting as the best available, though certainly not a perfect solution to the problem of resolving annexation controversies, the state also had a compelling interest in limiting the right to vote in annexation elections to residents of the geographic area of the proposed annexation. The answer to plaintiffs' argument that all of the residents of the City of Covington must be given the right to vote, because they are substantially affected, is the same as that given by the Court in Holt Civic Club v. Tuscaloosa, supra, to a similar argument, that is, that such an argument proves too much.

Many persons other than residents of the annexation areas have a substantial interest at least equal to that of the citizens of Covington in the outcome of these annexations. A non-resident who works in an area may be subjected to or relieved from a substantial payroll tax. A non-resident who owns a valuable piece of real property in an area may find the tax rate imposed on it substantially altered by the annexation. In the present case, the citizens of the cities to which the annexed areas are sought to be attached have a substantial interest. In the annexation of an unincorporated area, the citizens of the county would have a very real interest. In fact, since the three counties of Northern Kentucky are in essence one integral metropolitan area, all of its citizens may be more than minimally affected by the results of these annexations. Once you go beyond the residents of the annexation area, where are you going to stop?[40] . . .

CONCLUSION

It can be argued that liberal annexation is the most practical solution to our pressing urban problems and that to permit people to fence themselves off in suburban enclaves is to guarantee lack of interest in these problems, to facilitate the erosion of the core areas, and to promote urban blight and racial and class strife. Those who oppose such arguments contend that size in municipal government is no guarantor of efficiency, that smaller towns or unincorporated communities are more in accord with democracy, and indeed that almost pure democracy, as exemplified by the New England town meeting, can be approached there. They cite stories of illegal public employee strikes and the inefficiencies inherent in bureaucratic government in support of their opposition to metropolitan government. In short, there is much to be said both for and against liberal annexation procedures. Plaintiffs here claim that the statute under attack authorizes a war of attrition by the smaller surrounding cities against the core city, but this assumes that the outlying areas of Covington are eager to be detached from it. Perhaps the legislature believed that submitting annexation questions to a vote would require the core cities to do a better selling job, and indeed be

---

40. The court has considered the comment in Note, The Right to Vote in Municipal Annexations, 88 Harv. L. Rev. 1571, 1609 (1975), and Note, Annexation Elections and the Right to Vote, 20 U.C.L.A. L. Rev. 1093 (1973) and has found many of the considerations pointed out there helpful in reaching this decision. Both generally agree that it is impractical, if not impossible, to find some manner in which everyone who has a substantial stake in the outcome of an election, residents and non-residents alike, may be permitted to vote. This court, however, disagrees with the conclusions of the articles that elections cannot be employed for this reason. Rather, this court holds that the inability to formulate a practical way to permit all of those who have a substantial stake in the outcome of an annexation election to vote therein, provides a compelling state interest for limiting the voting to the residents of the annexation area.

more efficient. The legislature might also have meant to encourage cities to work out plans for consolidation of services. It should be noted that in the annexation of unincorporated territory, the legislature weighted the scales heavily in favor of annexation, requiring a vote of 75 percent of all the registered voters in an area to defeat it. This again exemplifies a nice balancing of conflicting political interests with which a federal court has no authority to interfere. Advocates of each side of this controversy are unlikely to be convinced by the arguments of those of the opposing persuasion. What *Hunter* and the similar cases cited herein are saying is that these difficult policy problems of local government are matters for the individual states to resolve, and the federal courts should stay out of them if principles of due process and equal protection are observed, as construed in light of federalism. The Constitution of the United States enacts neither principles of consolidated metropolitan government nor those of decentralized government in villages and small towns. It is silent on these subjects. It grants the federal courts no power to construct solutions to urban blight or suburban sprawl, or to invalidate solutions reached by a state, if racial discrimination or some other unconstitutional factor is not involved.

Under such principles of federalism, the strictures of equal protection having been observed, the new annexation procedure of the Commonwealth of Kentucky, as it concerns the annexation of part of one city by another, cannot be struck down by this court. Therefore, the complaint must be dismissed.

A judgment to that effect is this day entered.

NOTES

1. *The Rule of* Hunter. In Hunter v. City of Pittsburgh, 207 U.S. 161 (1907), relied on by the court in *Moorman*, plaintiffs sought to avoid a consolidation of the cities of Pittsburgh and Allegheny authorized by a legislative act. Plaintiffs claimed that the consolidation would impair the obligation of contract existing between themselves and their city, Allegheny, that taxes imposed on plaintiffs would only be used for that city's purposes. They also complained, on due process grounds, that they had already funded improvements in Allegheny and would now be required to pay off debts incurred by Pittsburgh to improve services in that city. The Court rejected these contentions, holding, in the language quoted in *Moorman*, that the state possessed plenary power over its political subdivisions, even if inhabitants of those subdivisions were injured.

Subsequent Supreme Court decisions have affirmed the view that localities possessed no Fourteenth Amendment rights against their creator, the state. See Williams v. Mayor of Baltimore, 289 U.S. 36 (1933); City of Trenton v. New Jersey, 262 U.S. 182 (1923). In *Williams,* the Court concluded: "A municipal corporation, created by a state for the better ordering of government, has no privileges or immunities under the Federal Constitution which it may invoke in opposition to the will of its creator." 289 U.S. at 40.

Some courts have cast doubt on the continuing vitality of the rule barring municipal lawsuits against the state. In Rogers v. Brockette, 588 F.2d 1057, 1067–1071 (5th Cir.), cert. denied, 444 U.S. 827 (1979), a school district sought to invalidate state legislation requiring participation in a subsidized breakfast program. The state claimed that it could not be sued by the district. The court concluded that, while some precedent seemed to support a flat bar, *Hunter* and *City of Trenton* were best interpreted as decisions that the federal courts would not interfere with a state's "internal political organization," and were not decisions concerning standing. Instead, the court held, those cases concluded only that the municipalities had no rights under the substantive constitutional clauses there invoked. Thus, the school district could proceed against the state, as its substantive claim was that Congress had affirmatively prohibited the state from denying political subdivisions the right not to participate in breakfast programs. See also Charleston v. Public Service Commission, 57 F.3d 385, 390 (4th Cir. 1995) (noting that "doubts have been expressed as to whether the 'broad dicta' that 'a political subdivision may never sue its maker on constitutional grounds' is really 'the rule' ").

Does this principle disable a municipality from asserting constitutional rights against parties other than the state of which it is a political subdivision? In Township of River Vale v. Town of Orangetown, 403 F.2d 684 (2d Cir. 1968), the plaintiff, a municipal corporation of New Jersey, claimed that a zoning ordinance adopted by a neighboring municipal corporation of New York State caused a depreciation in value of property in the former locality. The defendant township argued that, as a political subdivision, the New Jersey township could assert no rights under the federal Constitution's Due Process Clause. The court disagreed. It held the dictates of *Hunter's* successors to be limited to cases in which a municipality challenged the actions of its "creator" state and hence irrelevant where the municipality asserted rights against any other entity.

2. *The Status of the* Hunter *Rule.* It is tempting to consider *Hunter* as a relic of nineteenth-century formalism rather than a reflection of contemporary views of the relationship between the state and its political subdivisions. But *Moorman* is not alone in following the dictates of *Hunter*, at least as far as boundary decisions are concerned. In City of Tucson v. Pima County, 19 P.3d 650 (Ariz. App. Div. 2001), appellants challenged a state statute that permitted residents of certain areas to incorporate as a city or town only if they could obtain the consent of a neighboring municipality. Appellants claimed that granting the neighboring municipality a veto over the incorporation decision unconstitutionally burdened their right to vote. The court denied that there was a fundamental right to vote for incorporation, citing *Hunter* for the proposition that "the state has very broad powers to establish municipalities and manage their growth because the cities and towns are no more than political entities created as the legislature deems wise." The court found that the legislature had acted reasonably to avoid a "proliferation of small towns within a short distance of large cities and the attendant inefficient and uneconomical provision of government services."

In Board of Supervisors v. Local Agency Formation Commission, 838 P.2d 1198 (Cal. 1992), *cert. denied,* 507 U.S. 988 (1993), the court upheld, against an equal protection challenge, a statutory scheme that permitted incorporation elections where only residents of the proposed municipality were eligible to vote. The court determined that restrictions on the right to vote in elections involving municipal organization were governed by a rational relationship standard rather than a strict scrutiny standard since, under *Hunter,* "individual interests in voting are much attenuated by the state's plenary power to oversee and regulate the formation of its political subdivisions." 838 P.2d at 1205. The court concluded that restricting incorporation votes to those most directly affected by the election, those who would reside in the new municipality, would foster the legislatively articulated objective of encouraging orderly growth and development of local boundaries and would enhance political participation.

In Murphy v. Kansas City, 347 F.Supp. 837 (W.D. Mo. 1972), the court upheld Missouri constitutional and statutory provisions governing annexation of unincorporated areas. Plaintiffs, residents of an unincorporated area subject to annexation by Kansas City, alleged that they were denied equal protection because only city residents were entitled to vote on the annexation and because Missouri statutes created different annexation schemes for different annexees. The court found that the Missouri schemes were all rationally based. Plaintiffs contended that the state's procedures for annexation should be upheld only if they satisfied the more stringent standard of promoting a compelling state interest, and argued that they fell within the mandate of voting rights cases that used the latter standard. The court responded:

> In the instant case plaintiffs are *not residents* of the City of Kansas City being denied the right to vote in that city's elections on the grounds of race, wealth, ownership of property, tax status, military status, or period of residency. Rather, plaintiffs are residents of an unincorporated area in Platte County, Missouri. They have no statutory or constitutional right to participate in the governmental processes of the City of Kansas City, for they do not reside within the boundaries of that governmental subdivision. In annexing adjacent territory, the City of Kansas City, Missouri is exercising power entrusted to it by the State of Missouri. The case of Hunter v. City of Pittsburgh, supra, establishes that the State of Missouri is empowered to alter municipal boundaries "with or without the consent of the citizens, or even against their protests." The City of Kansas City, as an agency of the state exercising this power, has, as a part of its internal governmental process, a method by which its electorate exercises a vote on the matter of whether or not to extend its city limits and numerous city services to an adjacent area. This in no way violates the principles of the voting rights cases relied on by plaintiffs.

347 F.Supp. at 844. The Missouri annexation procedure permitted residents of an area proposed for annexation to vote, and to have veto power over the annexation, in two situations: (1) where a constitutional charter city (such as Kansas City) sought to annex incorporated territory, and (2) where a constitutional charter city within the boundaries of a first class chartered county sought to annex unincorporated territory. No vote was given to potential annexees where (as in *Murphy*) a constitutional charter city

sought to annex unincorporated territory in a county that had not obtained a first class charter. What explains the relationship between resident voting power and the form of government in which the annexees reside? Are the interests of residents of an unincorporated area within a first class county greater than those of residents of an unincorporated area of other counties? Could first class counties have had more leverage before the state legislature and have exercised it to protect their residents from unwanted annexations? The court determined that first class charter counties, unlike other counties, perform municipal functions in unincorporated areas and thus have an interest in controlling annexation of territory. As for the right of a city to annex unincorporated rather than incorporated land, the court concluded that the state had an interest in preserving existing municipal corporations and ensuring that their destruction is accomplished only with the consent of their citizens. Do the distinctions drawn by the court seem compelling?

State courts have also invoked *Hunter* to uphold annexation schemes. In Mid–County Future Alternatives Committee v. City of Portland, 795 P.2d 541 (Or.), *cert. denied,* 498 U.S. 999 (1990), the court upheld a statutory scheme described as "triple-majority" annexation. Under this scheme, a metropolitan area local boundary commission could approve, without a vote of affected residents, annexation of territory to a city that received a request for annexation signed by more than half the land owners in the proposed annexation area, if the signers owned more than half the land in the proposed annexation area, and if land owned by the signers represents more than half the assessed value of all land in the proposed annexation area. Plaintiffs, opponents of a proposed annexation to the City of Portland, contended that they were constitutionally entitled to vote on the annexation. The court cited *Hunter* for the proposition that there exists no federal constitutional right to vote on municipal annexations. See also Hardin County v. City of Adamsville, 1993 WL 8377 (Tenn. App.).

3. *The Search for an Ideal Voting Procedure.* Is there a single voting scheme that would satisfy all those interested in the outcome of an annexation decision? A scheme that required only a majority vote of the annexees could allow a relatively small population to veto the preferences of the larger annexing locality. A scheme that required an aggregate majority of both annexors and annexees could permit the former to override the preferences of the latter, even if the annexees were more directly affected by the annexation. A concurrent majority scheme (in which separate majorities of both annexees and annexors had to approve the annexation) could also create veto power for a small segment of the affected population, the annexees. Obviously, none of these solutions is perfect. Consider, in addition, the effects of annexation on those who are neither annexed nor city residents. As they lose taxpayers to the annexing city, they may have to pay more to support services previously funded, in part, by the annexees. Nevertheless, as nonresidents and nonannexees, they are unlikely to have any voice in the outcome of the annexation decision. What does the absence of any ideal scheme say about the conclusion that any proposed voting scheme is constitutionally mandated?

For consideration of the advantages and drawbacks of concurrent majorities, consider the arguments of John C. Calhoun. Calhoun believed that a concurrent majority system was preferable to a numerical majority for purposes of determining the validity of imposing federal legislation on the states. He believed that only through securing concurrent majorities at both levels could oppression by the numerical majority against a smaller community be avoided. To the claim that government would be unable to perform any task under such a system, Calhoun replied that the ability of a community to nullify within its borders the acts of the numerical majority would foster compromise between majority and community interests. He concluded:

> The concurrent majority, on the other hand, tends to unite the most opposite and conflicting interests and to blend the whole in one common attachment to the country. By giving to each interest, or portion, the power of self-protection, all strife and struggle between them for ascendancy is prevented, and thereby not only every feeling calculated to weaken the attachment to the whole is suppressed, but the individual and the social feelings are made to unite in one common devotion to country. Each sees and feels that it can best promote its own prosperity by conciliating the good will and promoting the prosperity of the others.

John Calhoun, A Disquisition on Government 37–38 (C. Post ed., 1953).

Is there reason to believe that these arguments (which basically elevate the community's interests over those of the larger population) are more compelling when applied to the relationship between state and political subdivision than when applied to the relationship between federal government and state?

In Town of Lockport v. Citizens for Community Action at the Local Level, Inc., 430 U.S. 259 (1977), the Supreme Court upheld a New York State procedure that required concurrent majorities to approve a change in the form of county governance. The New York procedure made a proposed strengthening of county regulatory powers dependent on approval in a referendum of city residents and noncity residents within the affected county. A proposed new county charter for Niagara County won the approval of a majority of city residents as well as a majority of all voters. A majority of noncity voters, however, rejected the proposal. In an equal protection challenge to the concurrent majority requirement, the Court noted that the new form of county government could have differential impacts on city and noncity voters within the county. The different interests of these groups justified a state requirement that the change occur only when each group believed that the charter served its welfare, since the mere fact that passage would create closer ties between the groups was insufficient to guarantee "one community of interest." 430 U.S. at 271.

4. Notwithstanding the survival of *Hunter* in boundary cases, other provisions of the federal constitution may impinge directly on the ability of the state to create or abolish local governments. The next case suggests how *Hunter*'s analysis may be limited by explicit constitutional restrictions.

Gomillion v. Lightfoot

364 U.S. 339 (1960).

■ MR. JUSTICE FRANKFURTER delivered the opinion of the Court.

This litigation challenges the validity, under the United States Constitution, of Local Act No. 140, passed by the Legislature of Alabama in 1957, redefining the boundaries of the City of Tuskegee.

Petitioners, Negro citizens of Alabama who were, at the time of this redistricting measure, residents of the City of Tuskegee, brought an action in the United States District Court for the Middle District of Alabama for a declaratory judgment that Act 140 is unconstitutional, and for an injunction to restrain the Mayor and officers of Tuskegee and the officials of Macon County, Alabama, from enforcing the Act against them and other Negroes similarly situated. Petitioners' claim is that enforcement of the statute, which alters the shape of Tuskegee from a square to an uncouth twenty-eight-sided figure, will constitute a discrimination against them in violation of the Due Process and Equal Protection Clauses of the Fourteenth Amendment to the Constitution and will deny them the right to vote in defiance of the Fifteenth Amendment.

The respondents moved for dismissal of the action for failure to state a claim upon which relief could be granted and for lack of jurisdiction of the District Court. The court granted the motion, stating, "This Court has no control over, no supervision over, and no power to change any boundaries of municipal corporations fixed by a duly convened and elected legislative body, acting for the people in the State of Alabama." 167 F. Supp. 405, 410. On appeal, the Court of Appeals for the Fifth Circuit, affirmed the judgment, one judge dissenting. 270 F.2d 594. We brought the case here since serious questions were raised concerning the power of a State over its municipalities in relation to the Fourteenth and Fifteenth Amendments. 362 U.S. 916, 80 S. Ct. 669, 4 L. Ed. 2d 737.

At this stage of the litigation we are not concerned with the truth of the allegations, that is, the ability of petitioners to sustain their allegations by proof. The sole question is whether the allegations entitle them to make good on their claim that they are being denied rights under the United States Constitution. The complaint, charging that Act 140 is a device to disenfranchise Negro citizens, alleges the following facts: Prior to Act 140 the City of Tuskegee was square in shape; the Act transformed it into a strangely irregular twenty-eight-sided figure as indicated in the diagram appended to this opinion. The essential inevitable effect of this redefinition of Tuskegee's boundaries is to remove from the city all save four or five of its 400 Negro voters while not removing a single white voter or resident. The result of the Act is to deprive the Negro petitioners discriminatorily of the benefits of residence in Tuskegee, including, inter alia, the right to vote in municipal elections.

These allegations, if proven, would abundantly establish that Act 140 was not an ordinary geographic redistricting measure even within familiar abuses of gerrymandering. If these allegations upon a trial remained uncontradicted or unqualified, the conclusion would be irresistible, tantamount for all practical purposes to a mathematical demonstration, that the legislation is solely concerned with segregating white and colored voters by fencing Negro citizens out of town so as to deprive them of their preexisting municipal vote.

It is difficult to appreciate what stands in the way of adjudging a statute having this inevitable effect invalid in light of the principles by which this Court must judge, and uniformly has judged, statutes that, howsoever speciously defined, obviously discriminate against colored citizens. "The (Fifteenth) Amendment nullifies sophisticated as well as simple-minded modes of discrimination." Lane v. Wilson, 307 U.S. 268, 275, 59 S. Ct. 872, 876, 83 L. Ed. 1281.

The complaint amply alleges a claim of racial discrimination. Against this claim the respondents have never suggested, either in their brief or in oral argument, any countervailing municipal function which Act 140 is designed to serve. The respondents invoke generalities expressing the State's unrestricted power—unlimited, that is, by the United States Constitution—to establish, destroy, or reorganize by contraction or expansion its political subdivisions, to wit, cities, counties, and other local units. We freely recognize the breadth and importance of this aspect of the State's political power. To exalt this power into an absolute is to misconceive the reach and rule of this Court's decisions in the leading case of Hunter v. City of Pittsburgh, 207 U.S. 161, 28 S. Ct. 40, 52 L. Ed. 151, and related cases relied upon by respondents.

The *Hunter* case involved a claim by citizens of Allegheny, Pennsylvania, that the General Assembly of that State could not direct a consolidation of their city and Pittsburgh over the objection of a majority of the Allegheny voters. It was alleged that while Allegheny already had made numerous civic improvements, Pittsburgh was only then planning to undertake such improvements, and that the annexation would therefore greatly increase the tax burden on Allegheny residents. All that the case held was (1) that there is no implied contract between a city and its residents that their taxes will be spent solely for the benefit of that city, and (2) that a citizen of one municipality is not deprived of property without due process of law by being subjected to increased tax burdens as a result of the consolidation of his city with another. Related cases, upon which the respondents also rely, such as City of Trenton v. State of New Jersey, 262 U.S. 182, 43 S. Ct. 534, 67 L. Ed. 937; City of Pawhuska v. Pawhuska Oil & Gas Co., 250 U.S. 394, 39 S. Ct. 526, 63 L. Ed. 1054, and Laramie County Comrs. v. Albany County Comrs., 92 U.S. 307, 23 L. Ed. 552, are far off the mark. They are authority only for the principle that no constitutionally protected contractual obligation arises between a State and its subordinate governmental entities solely as a result of their relationship.

In short, the cases that have come before this Court regarding legislation by States dealing with their political subdivisions fall into two classes: (1) those in which it is claimed that the State, by virtue of the prohibition against impairment of the obligation of contract (Art. I, § 10) and of the

Due Process Clause of the Fourteenth Amendment, is without power to extinguish, or alter the boundaries of, an existing municipality; and (2) in which it is claimed that the State has no power to change the identity of a municipality whereby citizens of a preexisting municipality suffer serious economic disadvantage.

Neither of these claims is supported by such a specific limitation upon State power as confines the States under the Fifteenth Amendment. As to the first category, it is obvious that the creation of municipalities—clearly a political act—does not come within the conception of a contract under the *Dartmouth College* case. 4 Wheat. 518, 4 L. Ed. 629. As to the second, if one principle clearly emerges from the numerous decisions of this Court dealing with taxation it is that the Due Process Clause affords no immunity against mere inequalities in tax burdens, nor does it afford protection against their increase as an indirect consequence of a State's exercise of its political powers.

Particularly in dealing with claims under broad provisions of the Constitution, which derive content by an interpretive process of inclusion and exclusion, it is imperative that generalizations, based on and qualified by the concrete situations that gave rise to them, must not be applied out of context in disregard of variant controlling facts. Thus, a correct reading of the seemingly unconfined dicta of *Hunter* and kindred cases is not that the State has plenary power to manipulate in every conceivable way, for every conceivable purpose, the affairs of its municipal corporations, but rather that the State's authority is unrestrained by the particular prohibitions of the Constitution considered in those cases.

The *Hunter* opinion itself intimates that a state legislature may not be omnipotent even as to the disposition of some types of property owned by municipal corporations, 207 U.S. at pages 178–181, 28 S. Ct. at pages 46–47. Further, other cases in this Court have refused to allow a State to abolish a municipality, or alter its boundaries, or merge it with another city, without preserving to the creditors of the old city some effective recourse for the collection of debts owed them. Shapleigh v. City of San Angelo, 167 U.S. 646, 17 S. Ct. 957, 42 L. Ed. 310; Port of Mobile v. United States *ex rel.* Watson, 116 U.S. 289, 6 S. Ct. 398, 29 L. Ed. 620; Town of Mount Pleasant v. Beckwith, 100 U.S. 514, 25 L. Ed. 699; Broughton v. City of Pensacola, 93 U.S. 266, 23 L. Ed. 896. For example, in Port of Mobile v. United States *ex rel.* Watson the Court said:

> Where the resource for the payment of the bonds of a municipal corporation is the power of taxation existing when the bonds were issued, any law which withdraws or limits the taxing power, and leaves no adequate means for the payment of the bonds, is forbidden by the constitution of the United States, and is null and void.

Port of Mobile v. United States *ex rel.* Watson, supra, 116 U.S. at page 305, 6 S. Ct. at page 405.

This line of authority conclusively shows that the Court has never acknowledged that the States have power to do as they will with municipal corporations regardless of consequences. Legislative control of municipalities, no less than other state power, lies within the scope of relevant limitations imposed by the United States Constitution. The observation in Graham v. Folsom, 200 U.S. 248, 253, 26 S. Ct. 245, 247, 50 L. Ed. 464, becomes relevant: "The power of the state to alter or destroy its corporations is not greater than the power of the state to repeal its legislation." In that case, which involved the attempt by state officials to evade the collection of taxes to discharge the obligations of an extinguished township, Mr. Justice McKenna, writing for the Court, went on to point out, with reference to the Mount Pleasant and Mobile cases:

> It was argued in those cases, as it is argued in this, that such alteration or destruction of the subordinate governmental divisions was a proper exercise of legislative power, to which creditors had to submit. The argument did not prevail. It was answered, as we now answer it, that such power, extensive though it is, is met and overcome by the provision of the Constitution of the United States which forbids a state from passing any law impairing the obligation of contracts. . . .

200 U.S. at pages 253–254, 26 S. Ct. at page 247.

If all this is so in regard to the constitutional protection of contracts, it should be equally true that, to paraphrase, such power, extensive though it is, is met and overcome by the Fifteenth Amendment to the Constitution of the United States, which forbids a State from passing any law which deprives a citizen of his vote because of his race. The opposite conclusion, urged upon us by respondents, would sanction the achievement by a State of any impairment of voting rights whatever so long as it was cloaked in the garb of the realignment of political subdivisions. "It is inconceivable that guaranties embedded in the Constitution of the United States may thus be manipulated out of existence." Frost & Frost Trucking Co. v. Railroad Commission of California, 271 U.S. 583, 594, 46 S. Ct. 605, 607, 70 L. Ed. 1101.

The respondents find another barrier to the trial of this case in Colegrove v. Green, 328 U.S. 549, 66 S. Ct. 1198, 90 L. Ed. 1432. In that case the Court passed on an Illinois law governing the arrangement of congressional districts within that State. The complaint rested upon the disparity of population between the different districts which rendered the effectiveness of each individual's vote in some districts far less than in others. This disparity came to pass solely through shifts in population between 1901, when Illinois organized its congressional districts, and 1946, when the complaint was lodged. During this entire period elections were held under the districting scheme devised in 1901. The Court affirmed the dismissal of the complaint on the ground that it presented a subject not meet for adjudication. The decisive facts in this case, which at this stage must be taken as proved, are wholly different from the considerations found controlling in *Colegrove*.

That case involved a complaint of discriminatory apportionment of congressional districts. The appellants in *Colegrove* complained only of a dilution of the strength of their votes as a result of legislative inaction over a course of many years. The petitioners here complain that affirmative legislative action deprives them of their votes and the consequent advantages that the ballot affords. When a legislature thus singles out a readily isolated segment of a racial minority for special discriminatory treatment, it violates the Fifteenth Amendment. In no case involving unequal weight in voting distribution that has come before the Court did the decision sanction a differentiation on racial lines whereby approval was given to unequivocal withdrawal of the vote solely from colored citizens. Apart from all else, these considerations lift this controversy out of the so-called "political" arena and into the conventional sphere of constitutional litigation.

In sum, as Mr. Justice Holmes remarked, when dealing with a related situation, in Nixon v. Herndon, 273 U.S. 536, 540, 47 S. Ct. 446, 71 L. Ed. 759, "Of course the petition concerns political action," but "The objection that the subject-matter of the suit is political is little more than a play upon words." A statute which is alleged to have worked unconstitutional deprivations of petitioners' rights is not immune to attack simply because the mechanism employed by the legislature is a redefinition of municipal boundaries. According to the allegations here made, the Alabama Legislature has not merely redrawn the Tuskegee city limits with incidental inconvenience to the petitioners; it is more accurate to say that it has deprived the petitioners of the municipal franchise and consequent rights and to that end it has incidentally changed the city's boundaries. While in form this is merely an act redefining metes and bounds, if the allegations are established, the inescapable human effect of this essay in geometry and geography is to despoil colored citizens, and only colored citizens, of their theretofore enjoyed voting rights. That was no *Colegrove v. Green*.

When a State exercises power wholly within the domain of state interest, it is insulated from federal judicial review. But such insulation is not carried over when state power is used as an instrument for circumventing a federally protected right. This principle has had many applications. It has long been recognized in cases which have prohibited a State from exploiting a power acknowledged to be absolute in an isolated context to justify the imposition of an "unconstitutional condition." What the Court has said in those cases is equally applicable here, viz., that "Acts generally lawful may become unlawful when done to accomplish an unlawful end, United States v. Reading Co., 226 U.S. 324, 357, 33 S. Ct. 90, 57 L. Ed. 243, and a constitutional power cannot be used by way of condition to attain an unconstitutional result." Western Union Telegraph Co. v. Foster, 247 U.S. 105, 114, 38 S. Ct. 438, 439, 62 L. Ed. 1006. The petitioners are entitled to prove their allegations at trial.

For these reasons, the principal conclusions of the District Court and the Court of Appeals are clearly erroneous and the decision below must be *Reversed*.

■ MR. JUSTICE DOUGLAS, while joining the opinion of the Court, adheres to the dissents in Colegrove v. Green, 328 U.S. 549, 66 S. Ct. 1198, 90 L. Ed. 1432, and South v. Peters, 339 U.S. 276, 70 S. Ct. 641, 94 L. Ed. 834.

■ MR. JUSTICE WHITTAKER, concurring.

I concur in the Court's judgment, but not in the whole of its opinion. It seems to me that the decision should be rested not on the Fifteenth Amendment, but rather on the Equal Protection Clause of the Fourteenth Amendment to the Constitution. I am doubtful that the averments of the complaint, taken for present purposes to be true, show a purpose by Act No. 140 to abridge petitioners' "right ... to vote," in the Fifteenth Amendment sense. It seems to me that the "right ... to vote" that is guaranteed by the Fifteenth Amendment is but the same right to vote as is enjoyed by all others within the same election precinct, ward or other political division. And, inasmuch as no one has the right to vote in a political division, or in a local election concerning only an area in which he does not reside, it would seem to follow that one's right to vote in Division A is not abridged by a redistricting that places his residence in Division B if he there enjoys the same voting privileges as all others in that Division, even though the redistricting was done by the State for the purpose of placing a racial group of citizens in Division B rather than A.

But it does seem clear to me that accomplishment of a State's purpose—to use the Court's phrase—of "fencing Negro citizens out of" Division A and into Division B is an unlawful segregation of races of citizens, in violation of the Equal Protection Clause of the Fourteenth Amendment, Brown v. Board of Education, 347 U.S. 483, 74 S. Ct. 686, 98 L. Ed. 873; Cooper v. Aaron, 358 U.S. 1, 78 S. Ct. 1401, 3 L. Ed. 2d 5, and, as stated, I would think the decision should be rested on that ground—which, incidentally, clearly would not involve, just as the cited cases did not involve, the *Colegrove* problem.

APPENDIX TO THE OPINION OF THE COURT
Chart showing Tuskegee, Alabama, Before and After Act 140

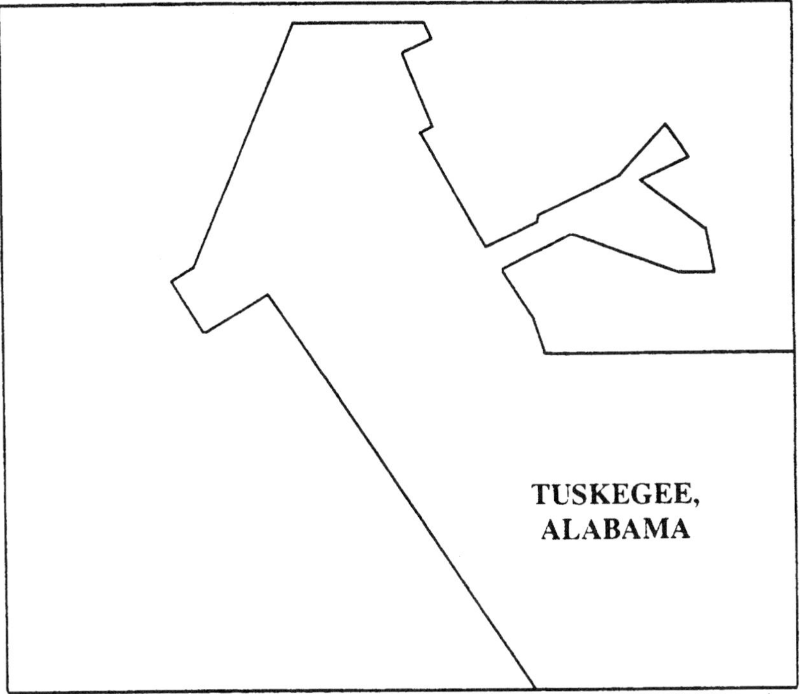

(The entire area of the square comprised the City prior to Act 140. The irregular black-bordered figure within the square represents the post-enactment city.)

NOTES

1. Why is Justice Whittaker so insistent on using a Fourteenth Amendment analysis in *Gomillion* rather than a Fifteenth Amendment analysis, given that he agrees with the result reached by the majority? Perhaps he believed that the majority's Fifteenth Amendment analysis was too casual. Professors Frank Michelman and Terrance Sandalow have asked what result would obtain if the Alabama legislature had detached the white areas from the redrawn city of "Tuskegee." See Frank I. Michelman & Terrance Sandalow, Government in Urban Areas 555 (1970). Alternatively, what if the legislature had maintained white dominance of the local political process by annexing suburban white populations rather than detaching black ones? Could the plaintiffs then claim that they were denied the right to vote in Tuskegee? If not, then should the constitutional principle at stake depend on the cleverness of the state legislature in deciding which political subdivision should maintain the name of the locality that previously housed all interested parties? Certainly the outcome should not rest on such a formality. But if we adopt this counterfactual situation and the Fifteenth Amendment does not apply, what is left for the plaintiffs but a claim that they have been denied equal protection under the Fourteenth Amendment? And isn't *Hunter* a complete answer to that claim?

On one reading of *Gomillion,* plaintiffs establish a Fifteenth Amendment violation by proving that a boundary change was enacted purely out of racial motivations. If that is the case, then the fact that black former citizens of Tuskegee retained the full, unhindered right to vote either in a new jurisdiction or in a reformed Tuskegee would not preclude a finding of a constitutional infirmity in those cases. In City of Mobile v. Bolden, 446 U.S. 55 (1980), the Court considered a challenge to the system for electing members of the Mobile City Commission. Under the challenged system, all candidates ran on an "at large" basis, that is, all voters voted for all three positions on the City Commission. Plaintiffs claimed that an at-large system diluted the voting power of black citizens of Mobile, who constituted a minority of the city's population, and impaired their ability to elect a representative of their choice in violation of the Fifteenth Amendment and Section 2 of the federal Voting Rights Act. Plaintiffs requested that the city commission be abolished and replaced with a mayor and a city council with members elected from single-member districts, some of which presumably would contain a majority of black citizens.

The Court rejected the plaintiffs' contentions. Justice Stewart, writing for a plurality of the Court, found that racially discriminatory motivation is a necessary ingredient of a Fifteenth Amendment violation. That showing could not be made in this case, however, since black residents could vote on an unhindered, equal basis with other citizens of Mobile. See also Wright v. Rockefeller, 376 U.S. 52 (1964). Should one infer that it would have been sufficient to establish a Fifteenth Amendment violation if plaintiffs had been able to demonstrate that the at-large system was intended to dilute the votes of black residents? If so, does that mean that changes in municipal boundaries, which (unlike voting district boundaries) presumably serve purposes unrelated to voting, are also subject to Fifteenth Amendment challenges when they are instituted for racial purposes? How would you frame the holding of Gomillion v. Lightfoot in order to have it control the hypothetical cases suggested above? Did the Court need to stretch its decision in *Hunter* in order to find a constitutional violation in *Gomillion*?

See Jo Desha Lucas, Dragon in the Thicket: A Perusal of Gomillion v. Lightfoot, 1961 Sup. Ct. Rev. 194, where the author suggests that, although "the facts of *Gomillion* do not present an ideal case for intervention," an alternative decision would have frustrated attempts to desegregate municipal services, as localities could have redrawn boundaries to create ethnic jurisdictions with "white school and black school, white golf course and black golf course, white swimming pool and black swimming pool." Id. at 242.

In Shaw v. Reno, 509 U.S. 630 (1993), the Court endorsed Justice Whittaker's analysis of *Gomillion* and applied it to prohibit the creation of voting districts with "bizarre" boundaries that evinced a motive to consider only race in redistricting decisions. In that case, plaintiffs contended that North Carolina's effort to create a congressional voting district that contained a majority of black voters, and that resulted in a district of dramatically irregular shape, constituted an unconstitutional racial gerrymander. The Court described one of the challenged districts as follows: "It is approximately 160 miles long and, for much of its length, no wider than the I–85 corridor. It winds in snake-like fashion through tobacco country, financial centers, and manufacturing areas 'until it gobbles in enough enclaves of black neighborhoods.' [Shaw v. Barr, 808 F.Supp. 461] at 476–477 [E.D.N.C. 1992] (Voorhees, C.J., concurring in part and dissenting in part). Northbound and southbound drivers on I–85 sometimes find themselves in separate districts in one county, only to 'trade' districts when they enter the next county." 509 U. S. at 635–36.

The Court concluded that, while race-conscious redistricting is not impermissible in all circumstances, "redistricting legislation that is so extremely irregular on its face that it rationally can be viewed only as an effort to segregate the races for purposes of voting, without regard for traditional districting principles and without sufficiently compelling justification" offended equal protection principles. The Court concluded that an allegation that the state had considered none of the traditional nonracial bases for districting decisions—such as commonality of interests, contiguity, or political cohesiveness—stated a claim upon which relief could be granted under the Equal Protection Clause.

In the course of its opinion, the Court noted that in *Gomillion*: "[t]he majority resolved the case under the Fifteenth Amendment.... Justice Whittaker, however, concluded that the 'unlawful segregation of races of citizens' into different voting districts was cognizable under the Equal Protection Clause.... This Court's subsequent reliance on *Gomillion* in other Fourteenth Amendment cases suggests the correctness of Justice Whittaker's view.... *Gomillion* thus supports appellants' contention that district lines obviously drawn for the purpose of separating voters by race require careful scrutiny under the Equal Protection Clause regardless of the motivations underlying their adoption." 509 U.S. at 645.

Should it matter that the North Carolina legislation that was challenged in Shaw v. Reno constituted an attempt to enhance, rather than dilute the voting power of minority voters? The majority rejected this proposition on the grounds that racial distinctions in creating voting districts necessarily amounted to "political apartheid." In dissent, Justices Souter and White suggested that a constitutionally cognizable harm in a voting rights case must consist of either dilution of group power (which was not present here) or abridgment of the right to vote (again, not present here). The result was that the Court was willing to allow the judiciary to reexamine the political process in ways that the Court had previously eschewed. Note that there was no claim in *Reno* that the group allegedly disadvantaged by the way in which district boundaries were drawn was unrepresented or underrepresented in the state legislature's redistricting process.

In Miller v. Johnson, 515 U.S. 900 (1995), the Supreme Court added to *Shaw* a burden of proof requirement regarding legislative intent. The Court determined that a plaintiff must show that "race was the predominant factor motivating the legislature's decision to place a significant number of voters within or without a particular district" and that "the legislature subordinated traditional race-neutral districting principles ... to racial considerations." 515 U.S. at 916. According to the Court, the plaintiff may submit this proof through "circumstantial evidence of a district's shape and demographics" or through "more direct evidence going to legislative purpose." Id.

In Bush v. Al Vera, 517 U.S. 952 (1996), the Supreme Court found that the redistricting boundaries of three Texas congressional districts were not narrowly tailored to serve a compelling state interest. In applying the intent requirement of *Miller*, the Court found the Texas Legislature was motivated by concerns for incumbency protection and other factors as well as race in redrawing district lines. Nevertheless, because racial motivations were "predominant," the redistricting was unlawful.

Bush and *Miller* suggest it is feasible for the Court to uphold a redistricting decision at least partially motivated by race. In Easley v. Cromartie, 532 U.S. 234 (2001), the Supreme Court explicitly affirmed the implication of *Bush* and *Miller* that racial motivations in drawing boundaries are not *per se* unconstitutional if they do not predominate over traditional districting principles. Id. at 241. The state claimed that the redistricting plan at issue was drawn according to voting behavior, which happened to correlate very highly with racial identity. Id. at 242. The Court upheld the plan despite its apparent racial basis. While plaintiffs had shown that the *effect* of the plan was to separate voters by race, they failed to prove that the legislature *intended* such an effect. Id. at 249. Consistent with *Bush,* the Court held that mere correlation did not offend equal protection principles. Id. at 243 (quoting Bush v. Vera, 517 U.S. 952, 968 (1996) (O'Connor, J., principal opinion)). In *Cromartie,* the Court adopted the "demanding" burden of proof requirement from Justice O'Connor's concurrence in *Miller*. That standard incorporates the policy of judicial deference to state redistricting decisions. As long as the defendant is able to articulate a legitimate political objective for the redistricting, a plaintiff may defeat the plan only by proving that a different district could have been drawn that was more consistent with traditional districting principles *and* was better balanced racially than the plan proffered by the state. Id. at 242, 257–58. This standard makes successful challenges to redistricting plans unlikely, because legislators will almost always be able to meet the threshold requirement of asserting a legitimate purpose for the redistricting, thereby shifting the burden to the plaintiff to disprove the articulated reason and prove racial motivation instead.

In Georgia v. Ashcroft, 539 U.S. 461 (2003), the Court concluded that the Voting Rights Act does not require jurisdictions that must receive "preclearance" of new voting districts to draw boundaries in a manner that maximizes the number of districts with a majority of minority voters. Jurisdictions may satisfy their obligations under the Act by creating more districts in which minorities have influence or can join in winning coalitions, even if, standing alone, they cannot elect minority representatives.

2. *Limitations on* Hunter. What situations other than racial distinctions give rise to a limitation on the principle of *Hunter*? Port of Mobile v. United States *ex rel.* Watson, 116 U.S. 289 (1886), discussed by the Court in *Gomillion*, demonstrates the selfish motives that state legislatures may have in creating and dissolving municipal corporations, and hence suggests the need for some federal constitutional limits on the *Hunter* doctrine. In *Port of Mobile*, plaintiff had purchased a bond issued by the City of Mobile and secured by that entity's promise to levy a tax sufficient to pay principal and interest. After suffering financial distress, the City became unable to pay the plaintiff's debt and obviously did not wish to increase local taxes. The legislature came to the rescue. It dissolved the City and disposed of its assets without ensuring any means for payment of the debt owed plaintiff. The legislature then created a new municipality, called the Port of Mobile, that encompassed basically the same territory and assets of the City of Mobile, but which was intended by the legislature not to be responsible for the latter's debts. In an opinion that appeared to be rooted in the Contracts Clause of the federal Constitution, which prohibits a state from impairing the obligation of contracts, the Supreme Court held that the new locality was bound to pay the debts of the old:

> We are of opinion, upon this state of the statutes and facts, that the Port of Mobile is the legal successor of the City of Mobile, and liable for its debts. The two corporations were composed of substantially the same community, included within their limits substantially the same taxable property, and were organized for the same general purposes.
>
> Where the legislature of a State has given a local community, living within designated boundaries, a municipal organization, and by a subsequent act or series of acts repeals its charter, and dissolves the corporation, and incorporates substantially the same people as a municipal body under a new name for the same general purpose, and the great mass of the taxable property of the old corporation is included within the limits of the new, and the property of the old corporation used for public purposes is transferred without consideration to the new corporation for the same public uses, the latter, notwithstanding a great reduction of its corporate limits, is the successor in law of the former, and liable for its debts; and if any part of the creditors of the old corporation are left without provision for the payment of their claims, they can enforce satisfaction out of the new.

116 U.S. at 300–301. Was the Court assuming that the legislature was not acting in a manner consistent with the interests of its constituents? If the legislature was seeking to rescue its citizens, then why should the Court invalidate its action?

A claim that a proposed annexation discriminated between those annexed and those omitted from the annexation on the basis of wealth was rejected under the rule of *Hunter* in Baldwin v. City of Winston–Salem, 710 F.2d 132 (4th Cir. 1983). Landowners outside the city claimed that municipalities had acted arbitrarily and capriciously in annexing prosperous areas but not poorer ones. The court determined that annexations were only subject to judicial review under the due process clause of the Fourteenth

Amendment if a fundamental right or suspect classification was at issue. Finding neither involved in this case, the court dismissed the suit.

In Hussey v. City of Portland, 64 F.3d 1260 (9th Cir.), cert. denied, 516 U.S. 1112 (1996), the Ninth Circuit invalidated a Portland ordinance that required nonresidents to consent to annexation as a condition to receiving a subsidy for sewer connections. The city had been required by the state to provide sewer services to the area and was prohibited from making annexation a condition to the service. The state's statutory scheme allowed annexation of an area through a conventional election by a majority of the ballots cast; or by the written consent of a majority of all voters registered in the territory to be annexed, and the written consent of owners of a majority of the land in that territory—the so-called "double majority" method. The plaintiffs alleged that the city's use of the subsidy to induce consent to annexation imposed financial distress on annexation opponents and violated equal protection. The court determined that the consents of the voters and owners were the equivalent of traditional votes; thus, the same principles that govern voting should apply to the consents. The court agreed with the city that there was no constitutional right to vote on annexation at all. It concluded, however, that once the city had granted a right to vote (or its equivalent), whether required to or not, that vote was subject to the same constitutional requirements as mandated votes. The court concluded that the Portland ordinance "unreasonably interferes with the right to vote" by conditioning the subsidy on the way the "voter" cast his or her "ballot." Finally, the court asserted that the ordinance "created a classic Prisoner's Dilemma, thereby subverting the process through which citizens consent to be governed." Who were the prisoners? What was their dilemma? Or did the Ninth Circuit simply misunderstand the concept?

The Supreme Court of Washington upheld a scheme that gave owners who held a supermajority of the assessed value of property in the area proposed for annexation the right to control consideration of an annexation petition in Grant County Fire Protection District No. 5 v. City of Moses Lake, 83 P.3d 419 (Wash. 2004) (en banc). The statute was challenged under a state constitutional provision that invalidated a law that granted to any citizen or class of citizens privileges or immunities that did not equally belong to all citizens. The court construed this provision as an effort to prevent a small class of citizens from obtaining special benefits at the expense of the majority. The court determined that "privileges and immunities" referred to in the constitution meant only the fundamental attributes of citizenship and did not entail all legislatively created entitlements. Annexation did not fall within that category. Since the legislature had plenary control over annexation, and could authorize annexation without the consent of residents, it could condition annexation free of the constraints in the state constitutional clause. Moreover, the "privileged" landowners could only recommend an annexation; the ultimate decision was made by the city. Finally, the court appeared to disagree with *Hussey* on the issue of the equivalence between annexation petitions and voting. The court in *Grant County* held that a right to petition for annexation was not akin to fundamental rights to vote, as evidenced by the holding in

Hunter that no federal constitutional right was implicated in annexation. In an earlier decision, which the en banc panel in Grant County vacated, the court had explicitly disagreed with *Hussey* and concluded that the statutory scheme was reasonably related to the objective of giving resident and nonresident owners a voice in the annexation process. Moreover, the legislature "could have concluded that highly valued property owners had a greater interest in annexation than those with lower valued property."

3. Professor Richard Epstein argues that while the rationale of *Gomillion* is wanting, the analysis would be improved if the Court recognized that it had decided *Hunter* improperly. He argues that the implicit shift of Pittsburgh tax burdens to Allegheny constituted a taking by the state that was not permissible without compensation. Similarly, blacks in Tuskegee "enjoyed a bundle of goods and services for which they paid taxes. If the net level of benefits after the forced dissociation was negative, then there is a similar imbalance of benefits and burdens as in *Hunter* itself. But the Court decided not to treat this imbalance as a matter of economic deprivation but as a sheer matter of racial hostility." Richard A. Epstein, Tuskegee Modern, or Group Rights under the Constitution, 80 Ky. L.J. 869, 873 (1992). Is there reason to be skeptical of the takings analysis? What if some (or all) of the black residents of Tuskegee were not landowners and had not paid taxes to Tuskegee? Or what if Tuskegee agreed to continue to provide the same level of services to the black citizens even though they no longer were residents? Would the takings claim continue to have the force that Epstein attributes to it? If it does not, should the case be decided differently than it was?

4. In Caserta v. Village of Dickinson, 672 F.2d 431 (5th Cir. 1982), the court rejected an effort to invalidate an incorporation of a village on the grounds that it violated the Fourteenth and Fifteenth Amendments by excluding Hispanic and black residents of the area from which village boundaries were drawn. The court found that the incorporators had originally attempted to include all residents of the unincorporated area, but were unsuccessful in obtaining an affirmative vote of the residents because an area of that size would have too much taxing power. Thus, the court concluded, racial motivations did not determine the ultimate boundary lines.

2. STANDARDS FOR INCORPORATION AND THE JUDICIAL ROLE

Apart from federal constitutional restrictions, states retain complete latitude to design procedures for local boundary drawing. Two separate issues arise in attempting to decide how that latitude should be exercised: (1) Under what conditions should incorporation be permitted? (2) Who should decide whether those conditions have been satisfied? The first issue involves the substantive standards that the decisionmaker ought to apply in deciding whether to permit the formation (or incorporation) of a new governmental entity. While some standards permit little discretion—e.g., a requirement that the proposed municipality have a minimum population, or a petition signed by a specified number or percentage of residents within the proposed municipality—other substantive criteria require interpretation. Typical requirements of this sort include a finding that there exists a "community" that has sufficient common interests to warrant its recognition as a separate entity, and the capacity of the community to be self-sufficient with respect to the kinds of goods and services typically identified with local government, e.g., utilities, educational facilities, and public amenities. Even in the absence of specific substantive criteria, courts have determined that incorporation cannot occur where municipal services cannot be made available to the area under consideration. For instance, in Chesapeake & Ohio Ry. v. City of Silver Grove, 249 S.W.2d 520 (Ky. 1952), the court refused to incorporate an area including railroad property that was not susceptible to any municipal services or development. Notwithstanding the absence of any explicit legislative criteria that would have required such uses, the court concluded:

> The Legislature has provided by statute a general plan under which towns may be incorporated. The statute does not attempt to define the character of the property that may be incorporated, but we will not assume the Legislature intended to authorize the incorporation into a municipality of property incapable of any municipal use, except to the extent that the incorporation of such property is incidental to the incorporation of other property which is or may be adaptable to that purpose. The words "city" and "town" imply that the real estate incorporated should be reasonably susceptible to municipal development, and that some benefits will be returned to the incorporated area.

249 S.W.2d at 522.

This is not to say that all localities must provide the same services. It is, however, to say that the concept of a municipality carries with it a connotation of providing services within a common range. It is not necessary that every locality have a public park, a public swimming pool, a fire department, a police force, public schools, public garbage collection, a recycling program, and a road maintenance program. Yet it would be odd to imagine a locality that provided none of these services. When a locality seeks recognition as a separate political entity, however, it does not necessarily begin to provide the desired services for the first time. In the absence of incorporation, residents may have access to services supplied by the county (e.g., water supply or police services), by volunteers (e.g., a volunteer fire department or rescue squad), or private contract (e.g., garbage collection). In State ex rel. Johnson v. Allen, 569 N.W.2d 143 (Iowa 1997), for instance, the court interpreted state statutes to require a city to provide police services, but left to the city council the question of whether to employ police or to contract with another municipality for those services. See Fred S. McChesney, Government Prohibitions on Volunteer Fire Fighting in Nineteenth–Century America: A Property Rights Perspective, 15 J. Legal Stud. 69 (1986). Moreover, the choice between incorporation and no incorporation does not carry with it the implication of the choice between service and no service. Thus, the mere ability of a proposed municipality to provide services to its residents does not, without more, justify its incorporation. Something beyond existing service provision must underlie the desire of a proposed municipality to carve itself out from the remainder of the unincorporated area. Of course, that "something" may be a selfish desire of the proposed incorporators to take advantage of a resource that must, under current political arrangements, be shared with others in the unincorporated area. Or it may involve a desire to avoid a burden that is imposed on residents of the unincorporated area. See, e.g., Board of Supervisors v. Local Agency Formation Commission, 838 P.2d 1198 (Cal. 1992), *cert. denied,* 507 U.S. 988 (1993) (financially distressed counties fear adverse effects if wealthy districts within counties seek to incorporate as cities). The desire to act in this way does not necessarily mean that the proposed incorporation is improper. It does, however, suggest that the decision about the overall propriety of the proposed incorporation is not simply a technical one of adopting the preferences of a majority of the residents in the proposed municipality.

The fact that the substantive criteria may allow for some discretion gives rise to the second issue that is relevant to defining standards for incorporation: Who decides whether the substantive criteria for incorporation have been satisfied? The process for approving or disapproving the incorporation varies widely among jurisdictions. In some states, boundary commissions that are independent of any existing governmental entity determine whether a proposed incorporation satisfies substantive statutory requirements. See, e.g., Alaska Const. art. X, § 12; Alas. Stat. § 44.33.810–.828 (2009). In other states, officials of the county from which the proposed municipality would be carved make the initial determination. Alternatively, a court having jurisdiction over the unincorporated area from which the new municipality will be carved will determine the propriety of the incorporation. Approval by the proper administrative body will often be followed by an election within the proposed municipality. In each case, the decision is subject to judicial review. Judicial review, however, may reflect either substantial deference to the initial decisionmaker or something closer to de novo review. The position that the reviewing court takes on this issue necessarily reflects a level of faith in the capacity of the initial decisionmaker to exercise its discretion in a manner that accomplishes the legislative intent in creating substantive criteria.

At one level, concentrating on the decisionmaker seems superfluous. One might conclude that as long as the incorporators are willing to incur the costs of incorporation and can gain the support of the proposed residents, there is no reason for judicial intervention in the incorporation decision. These individuals, after all, have determined that they share enough in common to create a community as they define it, and it seems odd to invite substantial review of that decision. This conclusion, however, assumes that the incorporators and residents of the proposed municipality will absorb ("internalize") all the costs of incorporation as well as the benefits. If that were the case, then the incorporation would presumably reflect the welfare of the society at large, since the incorporators would not incur costs unless they (and, hence, society) enjoyed net benefits as a result of the incorporation. If, however, incorporation imposes costs on others who are not represented by the incorporators, then it may be that even though the costs to incorporators are outweighed by benefits to incorporators, the additional costs to others make the incorporation undesirable. Since those others are not represented in the decision, however, the costs imposed on them may not be taken into consideration. In this situation, some form of intervention, typically judicial intervention, may be appropriate to test whether the total benefits of the incorporation decision outweigh total social costs.

The same point can be made within the communitarian or civic republican perspective on local government. The unincorporated area constitutes a community out of which the incorporators propose to extract a subcommunity. There may be reasons why that subcommunity would be better able to foster the kind of participation and deliberation that would bring about the results that decentralization is supposed to accomplish. As the court stated in Board of Supervisors v. Local Agency Formation Commission, 838 P.2d 1198 (Cal. 1992), *cert. denied,* 507 U.S. 988 (1993), "community residents and landowners often prefer to govern their local affairs insofar as possible, and cityhood provides them with greater opportunities for self-determination than does residence or ownership in a more amorphous unincorporated area." But the subcommunity enhances those opportunities only at the expense of the larger community. In addition, carving out the subcommunity is likely to decrease the diversity of the larger community, and thus frustrate efforts to reconcile conflicting interests.

To reach the conclusion that courts should take an active role in incorporation decisions, however, one must also believe that courts enjoy an advantage in comparing the costs and benefits of a particular incorporation proposal. If courts are not very good at performing that calculus, then they are likely to approve incorporations that are, in fact, undesirable and reject incorporations that are, in fact, desirable. The relevant question, then, is whether courts or unregulated incorporation will lead to a greater amount of "erroneous" incorporation decisions. Of course, there may be other decisionmaking institutions that could make the incorporation decision. As you read the following materials, consider what kind of factors are relevant to a decision about the propriety of a proposed incorporation and the capacity of various institutions to define and quantify those factors.

PROBLEM I

The Board of Supervisors of Paradise County has received and approved a duly signed petition for the incorporation of the town of Pleasant Valley. Opponents of the incorporation, who would be residents of the incorporated town, have appealed the Board's approval, alleging that the proposed town fails to comply with state statutes relating to incorporation. Those statutes provide:

9–101. Incorporation

A. When two-thirds of the real property taxpayers residing in a community containing a population of five hundred (500) or more inhabitants petition the board of supervisors, setting forth the metes and bounds of the community, and the name under which the petitioners desire to be incorporated, and praying for the incorporation of the community into a city or town, and the board is satisfied that two-thirds of the real property taxpayers residing in the community have signed the petition, it shall, by an order entered of record, declare the community incorporated as a city or town.

B. For purposes of this section, the word community shall mean a locality in which a body of people reside in more or less proximity having common interests in such services as public health, public protection, fire protection, and water which bind together the people of the area and where the people are acquainted and mingle in business, social, educational, and recreational activities.

The proposed town consists of approximately 2.85 square miles within which there are no retail stores, no businesses or industries, no professional or governmental offices, and no public transportation facilities. Indeed, an aerial photograph admitted into evidence suggests that the corporate lines were drawn to exclude such areas. The opponents contend that the proposed town fails to meet the requirements of a community, so that the Board, as a matter of law, could not be satisfied that the statutory requirements have been met. You represent the incorporators of the proposed town. What response will you make to the opponents' contentions?

Selected Incorporation Statutes

Ala. Code § 11–41–1. Authority; Petition to Probate Judge for Order of Incorporation

When the inhabitants of an unincorporated community, which has a population of not less than 300, constituting a body of citizens whose residences are contiguous to and all of which form a homogeneous settlement or community, desire to become organized as a municipal corporation, they may apply to the probate judge of the county in which such territory is situated, or the greater portion thereof if it is situated in two or more counties, for an order of incorporation, by a petition in writing signed by not less than 15 percent of the qualified electors residing within the limits of the proposed municipality and by the persons, firms, or corporations owning at least 60 percent of the acreage of the platted or unplatted land of the proposed municipality.... An unincorporated community lying within or partly within the boundaries of a county having a population of 600,000 or more, according to the most recent federal decennial census, shall not be incorporated under this section if the territory proposed to be incorporated has a total population of less than 1,000 or if the territory or any part of its perimeter lies within three miles of the corporate limits of any existing city or town.... [Exceptions omitted. EDS.]

The petition for incorporation shall be submitted by the persons seeking the incorporation referendum to the judge of probate by a verified application, which shall state the proposed name of the municipality, have attached thereto and as a part thereof an accurate plat of the territory proposed to be embraced within the corporate limits, including all subdivisions into lots, blocks, streets, and alleys, within the territory, if any, and have accurate description by metes and bounds of the boundary of the territory. . . .

Ky. Rev. Stat. Ann. § 81.060. Standards for Incorporation—Court Considerations—Judgment—Certification to Secretary of State

(1) At the hearing the court shall, if the proper notice has been given or publication made, and no defense is interposed, enter a judgment establishing a city as requested by the petition, filed pursuant to KRS 81.050, if the court finds as a matter of law that the following standards have been met:

(a) At least three hundred (300) persons reside in the territory sought to be incorporated;

(b) Incorporation constitutes a reasonable way of providing the public services sought by the voters or property owners of the territory, and there is no other reasonable way of providing the services;

(c) The territory is contiguous;

(d) The territory is able to provide necessary city services to its residents within a reasonable period after its incorporation; and

(e) The interest of other areas and adjacent local governments is not unreasonably prejudiced by the incorporation.

(2) In determining whether the standards for incorporation have been met, the court shall consider, but shall not be limited to the consideration of the following criteria:

(a) Whether the character of the territory is urban or rural;

(b) The ability of any existing city, county or district to provide needed services;

(c) Whether the territory and any existing city are interdependent or part of one (1) community;

(d) The need for city services in the territory;

(e) The development scheme of applicable land-use plans;

(f) The area and topography of the territory; and

(g) The effect of the proposed incorporation on the population growth and assessed valuation of the real property in the territory.

(3) Defense may be made to the petition by any inhabitant of the proposed city, and if defense is made, the court shall hear and determine the same, and render a judgment establishing or refusing to establish a city, as may seem proper.

(4) If the court renders judgment granting the petition, the order shall set out the name of the city, a metes and bounds description of its boundaries, the population contained therein and the class to which the city shall be assigned by reason of its population. The order shall appoint the officers appropriate to the class of the new city, who shall hold their respective offices until the next regular election at which city officers are elected, at which time officers shall be elected by the residents of the new city.

(5) Whenever any city shall be established in the manner above provided, the court shall in the judgment direct the clerk of the court wherein such judgment is entered to, not later than ten (10) days thereafter, certify a copy thereof to the secretary of state, whose duty it shall be to properly index and file the same as a permanent record in his office.

Minn. Stat. § 414.02. Exclusive method of municipal incorporation

Subdivision 1. Initiating the proceedings. This section provides the exclusive method of incorporating a municipality in Minnesota. Proceedings for incorporation of a municipality may be initiated by petition of 100 or more property owners or by resolution of the town board within an area which is not included within the limits of any incorporated municipality and which area includes land that has been platted into lots and blocks in the manner provided by law. The petition or resolution shall be submitted to the chief administrative law judge and shall state the proposed name of the municipality, the names of all parties entitled to mailed notice under section 414.09, the reason for requesting incorporation, and shall include a proposed corporate boundary map.

Subd. 1a. Notice of intent to incorporate. (a) At least 30 days before submitting the petition or resolution to the chief administrative law judge under this section, the township must serve the clerk of each municipality and each township that is contiguous to the township by certified mail a notice of the township's intent to incorporate.

(b) If the proceedings for incorporation are initiated by the requisite number of property owners, the notice of intent to incorporate must be served by the property owner or owners or designee in the manner required under this paragraph. The property owner or owners or designee must serve a notice of intent to incorporate on the town board of the township containing the area proposed for incorporation. The property owner or owners or designee must also serve the clerk of each municipality and each township that is contiguous to the area proposed for incorporation by certified mail a notice of intent to incorporate.

Subd. 2. Hearing time, place. Upon receipt of a petition or resolution made pursuant to subdivision 1, the chief administrative law judge shall designate a time and place for a hearing in accordance with section 414.09.

Subd. 3. Relevant factors, order. (a) In arriving at a decision, the chief administrative law judge shall consider the following factors:

(1) present population and number of households, past population and projected population growth for the subject area;

(2) quantity of land within the subject area; the natural terrain including recognizable physical features, general topography, major watersheds, soil conditions and such natural features as rivers, lakes and major bluffs;

(3) present pattern of physical development, planning, and intended land uses in the subject area including residential, industrial, commercial, agricultural, and institutional land uses and the impact of the proposed action on those uses;

(4) the present transportation network and potential transportation issues, including proposed highway development;

(5) land use controls and planning presently being utilized in the subject area, including comprehensive plans, policies of the metropolitan council; and whether there are inconsistencies between proposed development and existing land use controls;

(6) existing levels of governmental services being provided to the subject area, including water and sewer service, fire rating and protection, law enforcement, street improvements and maintenance, administrative services, and recreational facilities and the impact of the proposed action on the delivery of the services;

(7) existing or potential environmental problems and whether the proposed action is likely to improve or resolve these problems;

(8) fiscal impact on the subject area and adjacent units of local government, including present bonded indebtedness; local tax rates of the county, school district, and other governmental units, including, where applicable, the net tax capacity of platted and unplatted lands and the division of homestead and nonhomestead property; and other tax and governmental aid issues;

(9) relationship and effect of the proposed action on affected and adjacent school districts and communities;

(10) whether delivery of services to the subject area can be adequately and economically delivered by the existing government;

(11) analysis of whether necessary governmental services can best be provided through the proposed action or another type of boundary adjustment;

(12) degree of contiguity of the boundaries of the subject area and adjacent units of local government; and

(13) analysis of the applicability of the State Building Code.

(b) Based upon these factors, the chief administrative law judge may order the incorporation on finding that:

(1) the property to be incorporated is now, or is about to become, urban or suburban in character; or

(2) that the existing township form of government is not adequate to protect the public health, safety, and welfare; or

(3) the proposed incorporation would be in the best interests of the area under consideration.

(c) The chief administrative law judge may deny the incorporation if the area, or a part thereof, would be better served by annexation to an adjacent municipality.

(d) The chief administrative law judge may alter the boundaries of the proposed incorporation by increasing or decreasing the area to be incorporated so as to include only that property which is now, or is about to become, urban or suburban in character, or may exclude property that may be better served by another unit of government. The chief administrative law judge may also alter the boundaries of the proposed incorporation so as to follow visible, clearly recognizable physical features for municipal boundaries.

(e) In all cases, the chief administrative law judge shall set forth the factors which are the basis for the decision.

(f) Notwithstanding any other provision of law to the contrary relating to the number of wards which may be established, the chief administrative law judge may provide for election of council members by wards, not less than three nor more than seven in number, whose limits are prescribed in the chief administrative law judge's order upon a finding that area representation is required to accord proper representation in the proposed incorporated area because of uneven population density in different parts thereof or the existence of agricultural lands therein which are in the path of suburban development, but after four years from the effective date of an incorporation the council of the municipality may by resolution adopted by a four-fifths vote abolish the ward system and provide for the election of all council members at large as in other municipalities....

Gary J. Miller, Cities by Contract: The Politics of Municipal Incorporation

35–40 (1981).

There are three steps in providing local services: demand articulation, funding, and actual delivery of the service. In the United States, local governments have historically been responsible for all three.

Are any of these functions especially relevant to the proponent of incorporation? When the incorporationist says he favors incorporation to gain "local control," over which function does he wish to gain control? It is possible that the incorporationist wants to gain control over the agencies which actually deliver the services. That is, Lakewood, for instance, might have incorporated because its citizens felt that the Long Beach police and fire departments, as large bureaucracies, would provide their services in an unresponsive or inefficient manner. However, Lakewood and almost all other cities incorporated as contract cities, which means that the same county agencies provided essentially the same services before and after incorporation. Furthermore, these bureaucracies were at least as large as the Long Beach bureaucracies, and (at least with the county sheriff's office) subject to at least as many charges of bureaucratic unresponsiveness. While one incorporation (Downey's) did result in the creation of locally controlled service delivery agencies, the motivation for the creation of these agencies can be attributed to the funding aspect of local government. Local control of service delivery was clearly not the primary motivator of contract city incorporation.

Demand articulation is a function completely separate from that of service delivery. Local governments, in the form of elected representatives of the population, make authoritative decisions about the combination of services to be delivered to the population, and arrange for their delivery (either by creating a service delivery bureaucracy or contracting with an existing agency).

[One argument about the distribution of municipal services] ... is based on the centrality of the demand articulation function. That is to say, different groups and communities of people have different levels of demand for local services, but a single government can normally decide on a single mix of services. Therefore, if two different communities exist within a single government structure, one or another, or both, communities will be unhappy with the level of services provided. A community that is annexed is faced with the prospect of having its preferences absorbed (and ignored) by the larger community. Incorporation, on the other hand, lets a community articulate its distinct preferences with regard to local services. As Robert Bish applies this argument, the incorporation of the Lakewood Plan cities was advantageous "because their preferences for municipal goods and services were quite different from those of neighboring areas, and they wanted to meet these demands as efficiently as possible." The explanation for these new cities, according to [this] interpretation, is that "families with similar tastes locate together, and often, incorporate as a municipality."

However, the main argument of this and the next chapter is that this "demand articulation" interpretation of the Lakewood Plan cities is of secondary importance, and that the primary motivation for the Lakewood Plan cities has followed from the way in which local services are funded. American municipalities have traditionally been responsible for funding the services they provide through "local" resources. That is to say, the state grants local governments a "property right" to locally owned property. These governments can tax locally owned property to provide the services to that property. The Bradley–Burns sales tax act of 1956 used the same "point of origin" mode of distributing sales tax revenue to localities. The localities were viewed as having an autonomous right to a share of the sales tax revenue generated within their borders, rather than (for instance) receiving funds through statewide distribution to localities on a per capita basis.

Both the sales tax and property tax generated an intense competition for resources among local governments. Indeed, the renewal of intense annexation wars among the cities of Los Angeles County after World War II was due not so much to the "booster" mentality of earlier decades, but to a very simple calculation. Obtaining new sources of funding local services was at the root not only of the annexationist intentions of Long Beach, but also of the incorporationist motivations of Lakewood.

The explanation for municipal incorporations lies not in differences in tastes among individuals for public services, requiring local autonomy over demand articulation units; rather, it lies in the basic similarity of individuals summarized by the economic notions of price and income elasticity of demand. Incorporating around a considerable revenue resource allows inhabitants to procure services at a low tax price. Even incorporations around a small tax base can be explained in terms of the centrality of the revenue function and the relative redistributional advantage of incorporating as opposed to being annexed to another community....

One of the first high-resource incorporations was that in Downey, in the rapidly developing east-central portion of the county between Long Beach and Whittier. In the 1950s Downey experienced both the rapid residential growth and industrial development that were the fate of this region. Located between the San Gabriel and Los Angeles rivers, it was one of the few regions in the county with an excellent ground water supply. This, along with its location, was one of the reasons industries (including aerospace, chemical, and fertilizers) were attracted to Downey. It had achieved a population of almost 50,000, mostly newcomers since World War II.

This area was naturally plagued with problems, including a high crime rate. The city was reportedly one of the centers for narcotics trafficking in California. In addition, fire protection was poor because of fragmented water delivery. Although there were over fifty water districts in the area, many served only a half-dozen houses. Many bits of land had no water, and many others were served by wooden water mains. In addition, the county served the area with only two patrol cars and a single fire station, for its 12.5 square miles.

A rapidly rising demand for more services was one of the clear motivations for incorporation. At first, this would seem to be indicative of a clear "demand articulation" effect. The citizens of Downey were unique among the citizens of unincorporated areas because they demanded more in the way of municipal services. Their preference structure was different, and the municipal incorporation election allowed them to reveal this difference.

However, is this accurate? When an individual votes (with a ballot or with his feet) for a new jurisdiction, does this always say something about that individual's distinct tastes for public goods? ...

Thus, a group of people may seek incorporation because they are uniquely endowed with a resource base, rather than because of differences in tastes for municipal services. This is exactly what happened in the creation of the city of Downey. Downey's per capita assessed valuation was high enough so that Downey could afford more services at a lower tax price by erecting institutional barriers around its property tax base. Before incorporation, the community paid a tax rate of $.85 for the county fire district, and for that they had the benefit of one station with one pumper. The strong tax base in Downey was diluted by being pooled in a jurisdiction that included many areas with much weaker tax bases. After incorporation, the citizens of Downey withdrew from the county fire district and created their own fire department. They paid a municipal tax of $.29 per hundred and acquired four fire stations, and a 100–man police department as well. "Our assessed valuation was tremendous. We never wanted for money."

The incorporation of Downey says nothing about the preference structure (i.e., the structure of indifference curves) of the citizens who voted for it, or who subsequently moved to the town. It does say something about the relatively inexpensive per unit tax price facing these people, given their location in a resource-rich community. It is not clear that the individuals of Downey have a greater interest in police and fire protection than the citizens of resource-poor Willowbrook and East Los Angeles, who have tried and failed to incorporate on numerous occasions. Presumably, the citizens of these latter areas dislike being robbed or burned out of their homes just as much as the more affluent citizens of Downey. But, the citizens of Downey were located in such a way as to make it possible for them to procure protection from these threats at less cost. The incorporation reveals something about a difference in means, not a difference in tastes.

In addition, only months before the incorporation election, the League of California Cities had pushed the Bradley–Burns sales tax through the legislature. This made it possible for every city to tax 1 percent of the sales revenue within the city limits, without fearing that local business would relocate in a neighboring city where the sales tax burden would be smaller. By 1960, this tax resulted in more than $1 million in revenue a year within the city limits. That money made it possible to provide even better services; without incorporation, the money would have gone to the county, where the rich sales tax potential of Downey would have been diluted over such a broad population that it would have had no significant effect on the quality of services within Downey itself.

Because of this, the city council candidates and the incorporation committee ran a 1956 campaign based on the promise of providing more services at a smaller tax cost through municipal departments. Downey was to be the only city to incorporate after 1954 with its own complete set of service departments, rather than with a set of contracts with the county.

In re Incorporation of the Borough of Glen Mills

558 A.2d 592 (Pa. Commw. Ct. 1989).

■ CRAIG, JUDGE.

The Glen Mills School appeals a decision of Judge Howard F. Reed, Jr., of the Court of Common Pleas of Delaware County, that denied the school's Petition for Incorporation as a borough, out of Thornbury Township, which is here as appellee. We affirm.

As provided in the Borough Code, Act of February 1, (1965) 1656, as amended, 202, 53 P.S. 45202, freeholders may apply for the incorporation of their property as a borough. Glen Mills School is the sole freeholder involved in this borough incorporation petition, and the only one who signed it. The Code requires the common pleas court to appoint an advisory committee to make findings of fact and conclusions regarding the desirability of incorporation. The Glen Mills advisory committee held three hearings, made findings of fact, and ultimately recommended that the court of common pleas should deny the petition.

Glen Mills operates as a school for the education and rehabilitation of court-committed boys. The school is a nonprofit corporation, governed by a board of managers, which owns the 779 acres which the school seeks to have designated as a borough. The school provides for its own drinking water and trash removal, and also has an on-site sewage disposal system. Although Glen Mills maintains an informal security force, the school must rely on the Pennsylvania State Police and volunteer fire companies for protection. Additionally, aside from the state roads which pass through Glen Mills' property, the school maintains its own roads, and provides for snow removal in winter.

Glen Mills proposes that the school's employees and their families, who live in school-owned dwellings, will be the borough's citizens. The school suggests that, once incorporated, the borough can operate, and provide services that the school presently does not make available, through the one-percent wage tax the school's employees now pay to the township. That tax, however, generates only about $25,000 a year.

The school argues that the trial court improperly considered factors not listed in the Borough Code's provisions relating to applications for incorporation. Subsections 202(c) and (d) of the Code state:

> (c) Such committee shall ... advise the court in relation to the establishment of the proposed borough. In particular, the committee shall render expert advice and findings of fact relating to the desirability of such an incorporation, including, but not limited to, advice as to:
>
> (1) the proposed borough's ability to obtain or provide adequate and reasonable community support services....;
>
> (2) the existing and potential commercial, residential and industrial development of the proposed borough; and
>
> (3) the financial or tax effect on the proposed borough and existing governmental unit or units.
>
> (d) The court, if it shall find, after hearing and advice of the committee, that the conditions prescribed by this section have been complied with, shall certify the question to the board of elections of the county for a referendum vote of the residents of the proposed borough.

53 P.S. 45202(c), (d).

The school suggests, as a matter of statutory interpretation, that the trial court should consider only factors (1)–(3) of subsection (c) and that, once the court is satisfied that the proposed borough can comply with those factors, the court must certify the question of borough incorporation to the board of elections for a referendum vote. We disagree with that interpretation.

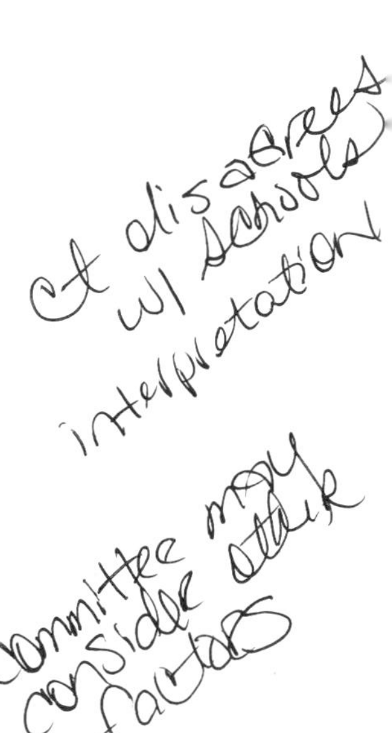

Subsection (c) specifically says that the advisory committee's consideration of the desirability of the proposed borough shall include, but not be limited to, the three factors listed in that subsection. Thus, an advisory committee properly may consider other factors, and the trial court which reviews the committee's findings and conclusions may evaluate the petition on the basis of those other considerations which the Code does not specify. See Borough of Bridgewater Petition, 87 Pa. Commonwealth Ct. 599, 488 A.2d 374 (1985).

Judge Reed correctly considered a factor not specifically described in 4502(c)(1)–(3)—the geographic integrity of the proposed borough—in reaching his decision. This concept is reflected in the existing case law that recognizes as a pertinent factor in examining incorporation petitions whether the proposed borough will constitute "a harmonious whole." Bear Creek Township v. Penn Lake Park Borough, 20 Pa. Commonwealth Ct. 77, 84, 340 A.2d 642, 645 (1975).

As the township points out, Glen Mills borough, by excluding from the proposed borough certain properties which the school does not own, would create three isolated islands of Thornbury Township area surrounded by territory of the borough or of another township. One of the properties is an unused parcel of land next to railroad tracks which run through the township and the proposed borough. Another isolated area is the federal post office that the township residents use. The third island is the unused township field house which is surrounded on three sides by the proposed borough and by Concord Township on the fourth side.

Although the school argues that isolating those portions from the rest of Thornbury Township would not affect those areas or the township, we do not believe the Borough Code prevents the trial court from considering that aspect of the incorporation petition.

Regardless of the fact that township residents would still have access to, and use of, these properties, we believe the present and future use of those areas, however insignificant, and their location within township jurisdiction, remain matters of concern for the township. Conceivably, Glen Mills could sell its land or change its zoning. Such changes could adversely affect the township. The township has a rational justification to maintain a linkage with all land within its jurisdiction.

Furthermore, the creation of the borough, as approved, would isolate a sizeable segment of land in the southeastern region of the township which is zoned residential. The record includes testimony and a map which show that this residential area would not be contiguous to any portion of the township except for a narrow connection at the northeastern neck of this area.

Although the school claims that the residents in that area would experience only psychological isolation because of geographical separation from the rest of the township, we believe the concerns discussed above are also applicable regarding this area.

For example, if the proposed borough ever changed the land uses northwest of those township residents' property, the value or utility of that property may be affected. The owners, whose collective properties would be surrounded on all sides by municipalities other than Thornbury Township, formerly protected by the township's comprehensive zoning scheme, would have no voice in determining the treatment of the substantial area (the proposed borough) lying between them and the rest of the township.

In our opinion, preventing the creation of swiss-cheese configurations within municipalities, which might interfere with the surrounding municipality's functions, is a valid concern of the judicial administration of the borough incorporation law. We note that the facts involved in this case are not similar to borough incorporation petitions that only carve out an enclave in an existing township. In this case, the creation of the borough would unjustifiably leave isolated portions of the existing township within the borough limits and isolate substantial portions of Thornbury in which township residents live. We do not believe the Borough Code contemplates such a result.

The trial court did not err by considering the geographical impact that borough incorporation would have on the township's territorial integrity. Judge Reed noted that all the residents of the proposed borough are employees of Glen Mills. Accordingly, this court approves and adopts Judge Reed's opinion stating:

> The concept here presented strikes at the very root and concept of government, most certainly democratic government as we understand it in America, which always rests upon the union of a group of freeholders into a self governing unit, wherein divergent groups and people through the vote express their majority will and voice.
>
> Here we have one land owner who now says I want to separate and govern myself.
>
> If this were allowed, how far would it go: colleges, universities, sundry institutions, corporations, larger land owners, perhaps smaller too, would break-off at will from Townships and into multi-separate boroughs. Each borough going its own way to create a mix of perhaps harmonious, perhaps antagonistic, but incongruous zoning or development patterns, and as well conflicting and often inconsistent services. The potential for exclusion, exploitation and overreaching becomes real and ever present.
>
> Suppose Glen Mills School sold its property and moved, one whole Borough would then be bought, and available for unbridled and unrestricted control except as the Borough Code might provide....
>
> In the end we have not come so far in our evolving history to now go backward toward creating what would ultimately become feudal-like estates. This is certainly not the acceptable or reasonable basis and approach to local government.

We hold that Judge Reed properly exercised his discretion under section 202 in denying Glen Mills' Petition to Incorporate. Affirmed.

NOTES

1. Test your cartographic skills. Can you draw a map of the proposed municipality and its surroundings from the court's description of the area?

2. According to Pennsylvania statute, the Committee that advises the court must consist of two residents of the proposed borough, two residents of the township outside of the proposed borough, and one resident of the county not residing in either area who shall serve as Committee chairperson. What does this membership suggest about the incentives of the Committee to approve or deny the petition for incorporation? Should the scope of review depend on whether the Committee has approved or denied the petition? The Committee, for instance, seems relatively balanced between those who might have incentives to approve the incorporation (members who are residents of the proposed city) and those who might have incentives to reject it (members who are residents of the area from which the new city would be carved). But consider a situation in which the initial decisionmaker is a board of county commissioners, as in Problem I. Is there reason to believe that such a body would systematically approve or deny petitions for incorporation? If, for instance, commissioners have tendencies to deny petitions because incorporations reduce their jurisdiction, should a court begin with a stronger presumption of propriety when the commissioners actually approve a petition? Does this mean that the court should have a different presumption when it is reviewing a decision made by a court or other independent body, such as a local boundary commission? See, e.g., Petitioners for Incorporation of City and Borough of Yakutat v. Local Boundary Commission, 900 P.2d 721 (Alaska 1995) (local boundary commission "has broad authority to decide what the most appropriate boundaries of the proposed borough would be" and reviewing court will uphold determination if there is "a reasonable basis of support for the Commission's reading of the standards and its evaluation of the evidence").

3. Does the court's appeal to "geographic integrity" or the statutory direction to consider the proposed borough's susceptibility to "adequate and reasonable community support services" suggest a concern for the residents of the proposed borough or for the effects of the incorporation on nonresidents? The requirement that a municipality be able to provide its residents with municipal services is common in both the statutory criteria for incorporation and the caselaw. See, e.g., City of Sunland Park v. Santa Teresa Concerned Citizens Assn., 792 P.2d 1138 (N.M. 1990); Daniel Mandelker, Standards for Municipal Incorporations on the Urban Fringe, 36 Tex. L. Rev. 271, 275 (1958). To the extent that the susceptibility of the proposed municipality to services concerns residents, why won't market forces be sufficient to address any adverse effects? For instance, individuals who believe that the municipality is unlikely to provide the goods and services that they desire will choose not to live (or work) there. Those who live in the locality at the time of the proposal and have this fear will vote against incorporation. Judicial inquiry into the provision of services seems paternalistic, unless the court believes that some residents of the newly incorporated area will be taking advantage of others (the latter being a minority that was numerically unable to block the incorporation in the first place). Is there reason to believe that the boundary lines in *Glen Mills* were drafted in a way to permit such taking advantage? Alternatively, the court might be concerned that incorporation was sponsored by a small percentage of the residents with an intense interest in the result, so that a small elite was able to impose the costs of incorporation on others, none of whom considered it personally worthwhile to fight the effort. Certainly it is true that incorporation proceedings are likely to begin through the activity of those who would benefit disproportionately from the jurisdictional change. Nevertheless, does the presence of special interests in the incorporation effort necessarily mean that the incorporation did not serve the interests of the residents of the new municipality? Consider the following argument:

> I fully agree that the organizational costs of an incorporation campaign are extremely large, and that without the external forces of developers, firefighters, PR consultants, and the ability of these external actors to work together as a team, virtually none of the Lakewood Plan cities would have been successfully incorporated, and there would now be approximately forty-five large, fiscally similar cities in the county, instead of eighty-one diverse cities of various sizes.
>
> However, the fact that the local citizenry did not voluntarily take on the organizational costs of an incorporation campaign does not necessarily mean that they were exploited, or irrational, or unaware of their best interests, or even that they were controlled like puppets by outside forces. On the contrary, since the creation of a city government is a nonexcludable, public good, it is in fact rational for most citizens to act as "free riders," allowing others to bear the organizational costs associated with incorporation, even if they themselves would benefit by it. Each individual is likely to feel that his or her own contribution to an incorporation campaign is tiny compared to the total organizational costs involved. The small probability of making a difference in the outcome and the fact that each individual will enjoy the benefits of incorporation if it succeeds whether or not he or she contributed to its success combine to make it unprofitable for most individuals in a community to undertake the start-up costs associated with incorporation.

Gary J. Miller, Cities by Contract: The Politics of Municipal Incorporation 31–32 (1981).

4. The mix of concern for external and internal effects of incorporation was also an issue in the case of In re Incorporation of Borough of New Morgan, 590 A.2d 274 (Pa.), *cert. denied,* 502 U.S. 860 (1991). In that case, a limited partnership that owned 3,700 acres sought to incorporate in order to develop the land with a landfill, a trash-to-steam plant, a tourist attraction called Victorian Village, a golf course, a cultural center, a mixed use center, commercial areas, agricultural areas, and open space areas. Only six occupied homes existed in the proposed borough. The court upheld a finding that the area (unlike Glen Mills) constituted a "harmonious whole with common interests and problems which can be properly served by borough government." This harmony was found, notwithstanding the diverse interests that residents would presumably be able to pursue:

> After hearing from planners, developers, architects and others, the committee and the trial court determined that the proposed borough was a harmonious whole. The plan, in sum, is to create a large landfill, a trash-to-steam generator plant, a national tourist attraction which would draw 25,000 visitors per day, a 1,000 room luxury hotel, a residential area complementing the Victorian theme of the tourist attraction, open spaces, and commercial areas. The cost of building the plan would approximate $800,000,000. Over 12,000 persons would be employed and a permanent population of 9,000 would emerge.

590 A.2d at 278. Does the fact that the incorporators anticipated attracting a population of 9,000, when there are currently only six occupied homes in the area, suggest anything about the desired level of court intervention to ensure that the area constitutes a "harmonious whole"?

The court also indicated that any external effects of incorporation, such as increased road maintenance and reduced tax revenues, had to be balanced against the benefits of incorporation. On this criterion, the court concluded, the incorporators' interests outweighed the financial impact incorporation would have on surrounding townships.

A more recent case reveals greater concern for the proliferation of small, specialized localities. In In re Incorporation of Borough of Pocono Raceway, 646 A.2d 6 (Pa. Commw. Ct. 1994), the court affirmed a trial court's dismissal of a petition for incorporation by putative residents of the proposed borough. The proposed borough would have contained approximately 11 residents, most of whom were members of a family who owned a raceway to be located within borough boundaries. The advisory committee had recommended in favor of the incorporation. The court noted that the legislature had recently enacted a statute requiring a minimum population of 500 in any new borough. Alluding to the decision in *Glen Mills* that permitted consideration of factors other than the explicit statutory criteria, the court concluded: "In the end we have not come so far in our evolving history to now go backward toward creating what would ultimately become feudal-like estates. This is certainly not the acceptable or reasonable basis and approach to local government." The court indicated particular solicitude for adjoining nonresidents of the proposed borough "whose thin, isolated strip of land would be virtually surrounded by the proposed Borough, [and who] would have no control over zoning and proposed development in the Borough."

5. If the Pennsylvania statute on incorporation does not specifically address the issue of "geographic integrity," what business does the court have adding this requirement to the approval process? Note that some of the other statutes do speak to factors that seem related to "geographic integrity." Does this mean that the Pennsylvania legislature specifically rejected such a requirement?

Citizens of Rising Sun v. Rising Sun City Development Committee

528 N.W.2d 597 (Iowa. 1995).

■ MCGIVERIN, CHIEF JUSTICE.

Iowa Code chapter 368 (1993) establishes procedures and conditions for incorporation of a territory into a city. One condition for incorporation is that citizens seeking to incorporate must show an ability "to provide customary municipal services within a reasonable time." The respondent city development committee found and determined that petitioner Citizens of Rising Sun failed to meet this burden. On judicial review, the district court concluded substantial evidence supported the committee's decision disapproving the Citizens of Rising Sun's petition to incorporate their territory into a city. We agree and thus affirm the district court's judgment.

I. *Background facts and proceedings.* In 1992, Citizens of Rising Sun (Rising Sun) submitted a petition to the City Development Board, see Iowa Code section 368.9, to incorporate the territory known as Rising Sun into a city. See id. § 368.11. The proposed new city of Rising Sun is located adjacent to the eastern boundary of the city of Pleasant Hill in eastern Polk County and consists of approximately five square miles. The estimated population of the area is 1,022 persons who live in single family residences on small acreages and farms.

In order to consider Rising Sun's proposal, the Rising Sun City Development Committee (Committee) was formed pursuant to Iowa Code section 368.14. The Committee consisted of five permanent members of the City Development Board who had been appointed by the governor, see id. section 368.9, and one local representative from the territory involved who was appointed by the county board of supervisors, see id. section 368.14(1).

Once formed, the Committee held a public hearing on Rising Sun's petition for incorporation. See id. § 368.15. Aware of Iowa Code section 368.17(1)'s requirement that it must show an ability to provide customary municipal services, Rising Sun submitted evidence of the types of services it would provide and the methods by which it would provide them.

Rising Sun produced evidence that it would be able to provide most customary municipal services, including law enforcement, fire protection and rescue, road maintenance and construction, library, and some administration, through contracts with other governmental entities pursuant to Iowa Code chapter 28E.

Rising Sun also presented evidence of other services, such as natural gas, electricity, water, garbage, and sewer services, that would be provided through franchise agreements, individual contracts, or by the residents themselves.

Finally, Rising Sun stated that it would provide certain services itself. These included city clerk services, legal services, and cemetery services.

As Rising Sun admitted, the provision of the majority of these services would remain essentially the same after the proposed incorporation as they had been before the proposed incorporation. Also, Rising Sun emphasized that it sought to maintain the mostly residential and agricultural character of the area, and that it did not have any plans for a centralized commercial district or for industrial development.

Two other governmental entities from Polk County appeared at the public hearing: Polk County and the city of Pleasant Hill. Polk County did not take any position for or against the incorporation.

Pleasant Hill, however, opposed the incorporation. Pleasant Hill had twice attempted to involuntarily annex, pursuant to chapter 368, all or portions of the Rising Sun territory into its city during the past few years, but had been unsuccessful.

After the public hearing, the Committee held its decisional meeting and subsequently filed its findings, conclusions, and determination. See Iowa Code § 368.19. The Committee found and concluded that the proposed city could not provide customary municipal services within a reasonable time. In particular, the Committee reasoned that indefinitely contracting for all services does not constitute the provision of municipal services. Also, the Committee found and concluded that the proposed incorporation was not in the public interest. See id. § 368.16. The Committee, therefore, disapproved Rising Sun's petition. See id. § 368.17(1).

Rising Sun filed a petition for judicial review with the district court. See id. § 368.22. The district court ruled that both Committee conclusions and its final decision were supported by substantial evidence. See id.

Rising Sun appealed, see id. section 17A.20, contending that the Committee erred in determining that contracting, either privately or through chapter 28E agreements, for municipal services cannot satisfy section 368.17(1)'s requirement that it show the proposed city would "provide customary municipal services within a reasonable time." Rising Sun also contends that the Committee erred in concluding that the incorporation of Rising Sun was not in the public interest as required by section 368.16.

II. *Scope of review.* Our review of a city development committee's decision to deny or approve a petition for incorporation is limited generally under Iowa Code section 17A.19 and specifically under section 368.22. Section 368.22 provides in pertinent part that:

> The judicial review provisions of this section and chapter 17A shall be the exclusive means by which a person or party who is aggrieved or adversely affected by agency action may seek judicial review of that agency action. *The court's review on appeal of a decision is limited to questions relating to* jurisdiction, regularity of proceedings, and *whether the decision appealed from is* arbitrary, unreasonable, or *without substantial supporting evidence.* The court may reverse and remand a decision of a ... committee, with appropriate directions.

(Emphasis added.)

Section 368.22 then states that certain portions of section 17A.19's general judicial review provisions are not applicable to chapter 368 actions. These include subsection 17A.19(8) which sets forth several reasons a reviewing court may grant relief from other agencies' actions.

Accordingly, section 368.22 and the contentions as submitted by the parties limit our review in this incorporation case to the sole question of whether there is substantial supporting evidence for the Committee's decision. See Iowa Code § 368.22; see also Des Moines v. City Dev. Bd., 473 N.W.2d 197, 199 (Iowa 1991). To make this determination, we ask whether a reasonable person would find the evidence adequate to reach the decision made by the committee; if a reasonable person would find the evidence adequate to reach the same decision as the committee, it is "substantial" for purposes of our review. See Dickinson County v. City Dev. Comm., 521 N.W.2d 466, 469 (Iowa 1994) (citation omitted).

III. *Relevant incorporation statutes.* Incorporation law is purely statutory. See Iowa Code ch. 368; see also Des Moines v. City Dev. Bd., 473 N.W.2d at 199. The legislature prescribes procedures and conditions under which citizens may incorporate a territory as a city, see Iowa Code section 368.1(13), and we are bound by those legislative prescriptions. See id. ch. 368; see also Des Moines v. City Dev. Bd., 473 N.W.2d at 199.

The legislative prescriptions for incorporation which are the focus of this case are sections 368.16 and 368.17(1). Section 368.16 provides in part: "*[s]ubject to section 368.17,* the committee shall approve any proposal which it finds to be in the public interest." (Emphasis added.) Several factors the committee may consider in determining the public interest are then set forth in subsections 368.16(1) through (7).

Section 368.17(1) provides: "The committee may not approve: 1. An incorporation unless it finds that the city to be incorporated *will be able to provide customary municipal services within a reasonable time.*" (Emphasis added.)

The Committee found that the petitioner Rising Sun did not comply with either section 368.16 or section 368.17(1). However, if substantial evidence supports the Committee's findings and conclusion concerning section 368.17(1), we need not consider the section 368.16 issue because section 368.16 makes fulfillment of section 368.17(1)'s requirements a condition precedent to consideration of section 368.16.

Thus, the main question is whether substantial evidence supports the Committee's findings and determination that Rising Sun will not "be able to provide customary municipal services within a reasonable time" as required by section 368.17(1).

IV. *Rising Sun's showing regarding provision of customary municipal services.* Rising Sun had the burden to establish by a preponderance of the evidence that it could provide customary municipal services within a reasonable time. See Iowa Code §§ 368.11, 368.17(1). The burden of proving such an allegation requires an affirmative showing that Rising Sun is capable of furnishing such services and benefits.

At the public hearing held by the Committee, Rising Sun produced evidence of both its ability to provide the proposed municipality with several services and the methods by which it would provide them. Rising Sun submitted that it would provide most services through intergovernmental contractual agreements authorized by chapter 28E of the Iowa Code. The services to be provided in this manner were:

- *Law Enforcement.* The Polk County Sheriff's Department would provide dispatch, patrol, accident investigation, criminal investigation, narcotics task force, community programs such as DARE and Neighborhood Watch, a liaison officer specially assigned to Rising

Sun, a monthly activity report and record keeping, detective services, and all other law enforcement services offered by Polk County.

- *Fire Protection and Rescue Services.* The Camp Township and Altoona Fire Departments would provide these services.
- *Road Maintenance and Construction.* Polk County would provide these services, including road repair, weed control, snow removal, road-ditch maintenance, shoulder maintenance, sanding, and related road services.
- *Library Services.* The Des Moines Public Libraries would provide Rising Sun residents with access to the largest public library in Iowa, computer assisted data and technical support services, fine art and record collections, and related services.
- *Administrative Services.* Polk County would perform building inspections, animal control, and plan and zoning services.

Additionally, the petitioner offered evidence of the following services which would be provided on a franchise or an individual, contractual basis:

- *Natural Gas and Electricity.* Midwest Gas and Midwest Power would provide natural gas and electricity, respectively, pursuant to franchise agreements identical to those required of other municipalities.
- *Water Service.* Individual consumers would purchase water service directly from the Southeast Polk Rural Water District.
- *Garbage Collection.* Individual customers would make payments for garbage collection directly to a private hauler.
- *Sewer Services.* Rising Sun would not provide a central sewage system. Sewer services would initially be continued by private septic systems.

Finally, Rising Sun stated that it would provide certain services itself. These included:

- *Administrative Services.* City clerk services, legal services, and insurance would be provided by Rising Sun.
- *Cemetery Services.* Rising Sun would maintain the local cemetery.

Neither chapter 368 nor Iowa case law defines the phrase "[provision of] customary municipal services within a reasonable time." Cf. Iowa Code 368.11(8) (defining "existing municipal services"). Further, all found case law interpreting chapter 368 and its requirements involve chapter 368's conditions for annexation of a territory, found in section 368.17(4), rather than its conditions for incorporation of a territory, found in section 368.17(1). See, e.g., Dickinson County, 521 N.W.2d at 469 (interpreting section 368.17(4)'s phrase "substantial municipal services and benefits not previously enjoyed" to require the petitioner to prove that the territory did not previously enjoy the proposed services and benefits); Des Moines v. City Dev. Bd., 473 N.W.2d at 201–202 (concluding substantial evidence supported decision that the annexing city met section 368.17(4)'s requirement that it "provide substantial municipal services and benefits not previously enjoyed" to the annexed territory); City of Decorah v. Peterson, 203 N.W.2d 629, 631–632 (Iowa 1973) (defining "municipal services" in context of an annexation proceeding to include police protection, fire protection, street maintenance and construction, water services, sewage services, and administrative services).

These annexation cases do not serve as precedent for incorporation cases, but they do demonstrate that incorporation and its requirements under section 368.17(1) are different than annexation and its requirements under section 368.17(4). The annexation cases also show that the section 368.17(1) requirements are less stringent than their counterparts in section 368.17(4). But even if the incorporation statute is less demanding than the annexation statute, we believe the incorporation statute still requires a petitioner to demonstrate a sound economical reason for incorporation of a territory into a city and a reasonable plan for the city itself to furnish substantial municipal services within a reasonable time.

The Committee found that petitioner had shown neither a sound economical reason for incorporation nor a reasonable plan for the provision of customary services to the proposed city of Rising Sun. In its findings of fact, the Committee stated that "[w]ith the current population density, it is cost prohibitive to provide a high level of urban services that would justify incorporation to the territory." The Committee also "found that the petitioners proposed to leave most of the services exactly as they have been [with] [t]he same parties provid[ing] the services and the City contracting for these services." The Committee then stated that "[c]ontracting for all of the services does not constitute the provision of customary municipal services."

Based on these findings, the Committee concluded that "the proposed city would not provide customary municipal services to the territory within a reasonable time," and that it was "barred from approving the proposed incorporation pursuant to section 368.17(1) of the Iowa Code."

Substantial evidence supports the Committee's determination. Petitioner did not anticipate directly furnishing any services to the territory, except a part-time city clerk and legal services needed to establish and maintain contracts for services. Instead, petitioner admitted in its petition for incorporation that all services would remain essentially in the status quo, continuing to be provided by the county, townships, adjacent cities or private businesses. Also, the petitioner failed to include a contingency plan for staffing or funding to provide municipal services if the contracts could not be maintained, or a comprehensive plan for the independent provision of substantial municipal services in the future. Finally, Rising Sun emphasized in its petition for incorporation that it sought to maintain the mostly residential and agricultural character of the area and that it did not have any plans for a centralized commercial district or for industrial development.

Based on this evidence in the record, a reasonable person could conclude, as did the Committee, that Rising Sun would not be able to provide customary municipal services within a reasonable time to the proposed territory as required for municipal incorporation under section 368.17(1).

V. *Conclusion.* Because substantial evidence supports the decision of the Committee to disapprove the petitioner's incorporation petition, we need not discuss whether substantial evidence also supported the Committee's alternative conclusion that petitioner's proposal to incorporate was not in the public interest as required by section 368.16.

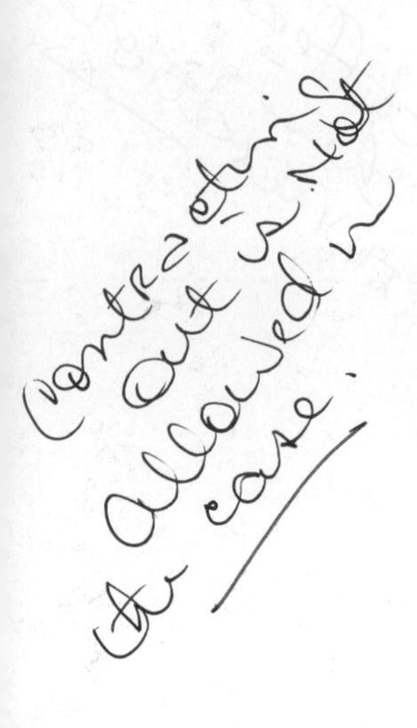

Under our view of the case, we also need not discuss other issues raised by intervenor Pleasant Hill....

AFFIRMED.

NOTES

1. Why do you think the residents of the proposed city wanted to incorporate if they were going to obtain the same services that they currently enjoyed? What do you make of the court's statement that the city of Pleasant Hill had twice been unsuccessful in attempting to annex the area that comprised the proposed city of Rising Sun?

Note the requirements in some incorporation statutes that no municipality may be incorporated within a certain distance of an existing municipal corporation. These requirements respond to the threat of "defensive incorporations" undertaken to prevent one municipality from growing through annexation of surrounding areas. Annexation is typically limited to unincorporated land, so a city would be precluded from absorbing a resistant population if the latter could incorporate. These pockets of resistance, however, could frustrate efforts to address metropolitan or regional problems, or to solve central city overcrowding and to internalize costs that suburbs impose on central cities. See Daniel R. Mandelker, Standards for Municipal Incorporations on the Urban Fringe, 36 Tex. L. Rev. 271 (1958). In Town of Ouita v. Heidgen, 448 S.W.2d 631 (Ark. 1970), the court upheld the invalidation of an order of incorporation where the area proposed to be incorporated consisted of open farmland, pastureland, or timberland, with no urban territory and where representatives of the incorporators testified that the incorporation was intended to avoid restrictive municipal ordinances and taxes that would apply to them if a pending proposal to annex them to a nearby city were implemented. Why isn't the desire of a rural area to avoid regulation and taxation sufficient to constitute a "community" for incorporation purposes?

2. Assume that the only reason for the proposed incorporation was to avoid ultimate annexation to Pleasant Hill. Should the motive for incorporation be relevant to the decision of whether the statutory requirements have been satisfied?

Even where motive is not explicitly recognized as a factor in an incorporation decision, it is conceivable that a court will take motive into account in applying relatively vague statutory standards of incorporation. In In re Incorporation of Borough of Bridgewater, 488 A.2d 374 (Pa.

Commw. Ct. 1985), petitioners sought to incorporate a 92–acre area as a borough within an unincorporated township. Pursuant to statute, the trial court appointed a borough advisory committee, which—by a divided vote—recommended against incorporation. On review of the committee's report, the trial court similarly concluded that incorporation of the borough would be destructive of the remainder of the township and denied incorporation. On appeal, the court set forth the statutory standards for incorporation, which included the ability of the proposed borough to provide services to its residents, the existing and potential commercial and residential development of the proposed borough, and the "financial and tax effects" of the proposed borough on existing governmental units. Other than the financial and tax effects, the statute did not direct the court to consider the implications of the proposed incorporation on existing governments. The court upheld the denial of the petition on the grounds that the trial court had not abused its discretion in reaching its decision. The court described the trial judge's decision as based on the following:

> Of the factors considered by the trial court, we find several to be significant. The current racial composition of the Township is fifty-nine percent (59%) white and forty-one percent (41%) non-white. The composition of the proposed borough would be eighty-two point five percent (82.5%) white and seventeen point four percent (17.4%) non-white. The remaining portion of the Township would be twenty-six point six percent (26.6%) white and seventy-three percent (73%) non-white. The trial court found that the motivation for the proposed Borough was to segregate it from the rest of the Township.
>
> Additionally, the trial court listed the several debts accumulated by the Township and concluded that the proposed Borough sought to escape supporting the financially troubled Township. In addition to its debts, the portion of the Township which would remain intact after the proposed incorporation would carry the responsibility for all of the low-income housing currently supported by the entire Township.
>
> The proposed Borough is comprised wholly of privately owned residential units, with little or no existing or potential area for commercial or industrial growth. While acknowledging that the proposed Borough would probably be able to take care of itself financially, by imposing a real estate tax, the trial court held that the remainder of the Township would be deprived of the "support and balance which is essential to preserve and develop a complete, integrated and, yet, diverse community of population, interests, and uses; all of which are essential to the stability and growth of a suburban municipality."
>
> We cannot fault the trial court in its concern for preserving the diversity of the Township necessary to support it financially and socially. Therefore, we hold that the trial court properly exercised its discretion under Section 202 in denying the Petition to Incorporate.

488 A.2d at 376–377. If the appellate court credited the trial court's concern "for preserving the diversity of the Township," but did not believe that diversity was necessary to support the Township "financially," would it have been appropriate to find that the trial court had not abused its discretion? Given the statutory standards, of what relevance is the finding that preserving diversity was necessary to support the Township? If the

court believed that the incorporation petition was racially motivated, would it have been better for the court to have said so directly?

3. The proposal of an area to incorporate, rather than accept annexation to an existing municipality, may be motivated by the proposed annexees' fears of higher taxes or more government regulation if they become part of the central city. In what ways could these fears be reduced by bargains between annexors and annexees?

4. What basis is there for concluding that the statutory requirement that services be provided can only be satisfied by public production rather than by public contracting with outside providers? Assume that the city proposed to provide all the listed services with its own employees, except that it proposed to permit residents to contract privately for garbage collection. Would that be acceptable? If one service can be provided through private contract, then at what point does the proposed city violate the statute by providing for multiple services through private contract? Would it matter if the proposed municipality can demonstrate that privatization of services reduces costs?

NOTES ON SPECIAL PURPOSE GOVERNMENTS: CREATION AND VOTING RIGHTS

1. *The Nature and Creation of Special Purpose Governments.* The most familiar local government bodies—cities, towns, counties, and villages—are general purpose governments; that is, they provide a wide array of services to their constituents. As we discussed supra at pp. 49–51, however, there also exist a large number of special purpose governments that are created to provide a particular service. These governments, including school districts, which usually fall under the category of special districts or authorities, are frequently created because the service they provide can be more effectively provided by an entity that crosses traditional local government boundaries. For instance, a sewer district may be able to deal with problems of a segment of a locality or with problems of multiple localities more efficiently than an existing city because the sewage problems that need to be addressed are not coextensive with municipal boundaries. Although historically created to provide services in rural areas that were not yet part of a city or county, a special district today is as likely to result from an existing locality's financial inability to provide the service. In order to accomplish its purpose, a special purpose government is granted limited governmental authority that frequently includes the power to incur debt, set user fees, levy taxes, or receive funds from state and federal government. Some special purpose governments have additional powers such as eminent domain.

Special purpose governments are created by one of four different methods. Frequently, special districts are created locally under a general act of the state legislature that grants counties or municipalities the authority to create special governments either singly or in combination with another local government. See, e.g., Neb. Rev. Stat. § 18–401 to 18–

411; Pa. Stat. Ann. tit. 53, § 5603; Mich. Comp. Laws Ann. § 124.404. Establishment usually requires submission of a petition by affected landowners to the county board of supervisors for publication. A public hearing is held to decide if the district should be created. In some cases, a petition can be denied if the board decides the district is not needed. Peters v. Frye, 223 P.2d 176 (Ariz. 1950).

Special purpose governments can also be created by a special act of the state legislature. Typically this procedure is used when the government is created to encompass a large area or will require significant amounts of financing. Authorities are frequently created by this method. See, e.g., Cal. Water Code App. § 85–23; N.Y. Pub. Auth. Law § 2040–c.

A third procedure involves the passage of a general act of the legislature allowing the electorate of a region to authorize creation. These statutes frequently require a request for the creation of a special district to be backed by a petition signed by a certain percentage of registered voters, or taxpayers owning at least 50 percent of the property in a proposed area. See, e.g., Cal. Health & Safety Code §§ 8900–8941 (cemetery district); Vt. Stat. Ann. tit. 20, § 2481 (fire district).

Finally, authorities can be created by executive order if first authorized by the legislature. See Alex E. Rogers, Clothing Governmental Entities With Sovereign Immunity: Disarray in the Eleventh Amendment Arm-of-the-State Doctrine, 92 Colum. L. Rev. 1243, 1245 (1992); Comment, An Analysis of Authorities: Traditional and Multicounty, 71 Mich. L. Rev. 1376, 1380 n.25 (1976).

The increased popularity of special purpose governments, discussed supra at p. 51, has led to substantial debate about their comparative advantages and disadvantages. As we will discover in our discussion of debt restrictions, infra at page 618, many states and municipalities are subject to statutory or constitutional limits on the amount of taxpayer financed debt that can be incurred to finance general community needs such as police and fire departments, schools, water and wastewater treatment, and transportation. Since special purpose governments are operationally and financially independent, their debts are not included in those of the local governments whose constituency they serve. Thus, a local government may create special districts to finance community needs without consuming any of its current debt capacity. While this ability has permitted localities to finance projects that might otherwise be unavailable, it has also led to suggestions that special purpose governments are employed primarily to circumvent constitutional restrictions on localities rather than to ensure a more efficient provision of service. See, e.g., Annmarie Hauck Walsh, The Public's Business: The Politics and Practices of Government Corporations 22–24 (1978); Stewart E. Sterk & Elizabeth S. Goldman, Controlling Legislative Short–Sightedness: The Effectiveness of Constitutional Debt Limitations, 1991 Wis. L. Rev. 1302; Robert H. Bowmar, The Anachronism Called Debt Limitations, 52 Iowa L. Rev. 863 (1967).

Another advantage of a special district is its unique ability to provide services only to the area of need without regard to existing governmental boundaries. Since special districts can transcend jurisdictional boundaries, they can realize economies of scale in the provision of services that might otherwise be offered by individual localities. While these advantages are most apparent in metropolitan areas where a central city shares resources with surrounding suburbs, the advantage can also be captured by unincorporated areas where there is no municipal government providing the service. Jurisdictional flexibility is especially important for soil conservation and water districts. Information on the history and benefits provided by water and soil conservation districts as well as the extent of state and federal regulation of such districts can be found in Daniel R. Mandelker, Controlling Nonpoint Source Water Pollution: Can it be Done?, 65 Chi.–Kent L. Rev. 479 (1989); Bryan J. Wilson, Westlands Water District and Its Federal Water: A Case Study of Water District Politics, 7 Stan. Envtl. L. J. 187 (1987–1988); and James L. Arts & William L. Church, Soil Erosion—The Next Crisis, 1982 Wis. L. Rev. 535 (1982).

These advantages, however, are offset by criticisms directed at the use and conduct of special purpose governments. Much of this criticism is directed at the immunity that these governmental entities enjoy from restrictions placed on private firms without commensurate accountability of the type that usually justifies those immunities. Benefits such as tax exemptions are granted to special districts as long as the property is used for the provision of a public service. Thus, it has been held that land leased by an authority for the generation of revenue was unrelated to the provision of a public service and therefore subject to property tax. Borough of Moonachie v. Port of New York Authority, 185 A.2d 207 (N.J. 1962). In addition, several authorities have generated excess revenues through the provision of public services and have used these revenues to finance projects unrelated to the central purpose of the authority rather than using the money to lower user fees or pay property taxes.

Further, the efficiency that special purpose governments can theoretically attain is difficult to confirm. Their independent status frustrates the ability of outsiders to maintain a close watch on the operation. Groups such as bondholders are not necessarily good surrogates for the constituency of the special purpose government since bondholders' interests are not necessarily co-extensive with those of the recipients of the service. Because special purpose governments typically are monopolists with respect to the services they provide, they are as exempt from competitive forces that might create incentives for efficient operation as are general purpose governments. Hence, it is difficult for a community to compare the cost and quality of service provided by a special district with the cost and quality that would result if the service were provided by a private party either independently of the district or under contract with the district. Many of the cost advantages enjoyed by special purpose governments, for instance, may relate to exemptions from property taxes, avoidance of certain laws, or the grant of monopoly power rather than from efficient operation.

In some areas, the proliferation of special districts with overlapping boundaries that do not coincide with jurisdictional boundaries has perhaps created as many problems as the districts were intended to solve. The San Francisco Bay Area is an example of one such region where the vast number of special districts has contributed to the inability of jurisdictions within the area to cooperate to solve mutual concerns. Many districts providing the same service have overlapping boundaries and frequently compete for revenue. Kenneth A. Brunetti, Note, It's Time to Create a Bay Area Government, 42 Hastings L.J. 1103 n.13 (1991) (citing Heyman, Symposium: The San Francisco Bay Area—Regional Problems and Solutions, 55 Calif. L. Rev. 695, 698 (1967)).

2. *Voting Rights in Special Purpose Government Elections.* For the most part, voting in local government elections is subject to the principle of one-person, one-vote. That principle, first established in Reynolds v. Sims, 377 U.S. 533 (1964), requires that all citizens of a state have "an equally effective voice" in state popular elections. Id. at 579. In *Reynolds,* the Court found that a plan to reapportion the Alabama legislature based on 60-year-old census figures violated principles of equal protection, as subsequent shifts in population had led to vastly different ratios of representatives to constituents in different districts. As stated in *Reynolds,* equal protection principles require that voting schemes ensure "uniform treatment of persons standing in the same relation to the governmental action questioned or challenged." Id. at 565.

The one-person, one-vote requirement was extended to local government elections in Avery v. Midland County, 390 U.S. 474 (1968). The plaintiff in *Avery* claimed that unequal population distribution among county districts violated equal protection because each district was represented by one commissioner to the County Commissioners Court and the populations of the four districts varied from 67,906 to 414. The Court stated that when power delegated to a local government by the state provides for local election of district officials, the state "must insure that those qualified to vote have the right to an equally effective voice in the election process" Id. at 480. Furthermore, the court found "little difference, in terms of the application of the Equal Protection Clause and of the principles of Reynolds v. Sims, between the exercise of state power through legislatures and its exercise by elected officials in the cities, towns, and counties." Id. at 481. Noting that the powers of the Commissioners Court included the ability to set the tax rate, issue bonds, and make other significant decisions that affected the development of the entire county, the Court held that "the Constitution permits no substantial variation from equal population in drawing districts for units of local government having general governmental powers over the entire geographic area served by the body." Id. at 484–485.

The same concern that governments providing a broad range of services and exercising substantial governmental powers afford representation in strict accordance with the one-person, one-vote principle similarly led to invalidation of a statutory scheme in Hadley v. Junior College District, 397 U.S. 50 (1970). The statute at issue in that case apportioned representation to a Junior College District among the eight existing school districts on the basis of the number of residents in each district between the ages of six and 20 years. Under this scheme, residents of the Kansas City School district were entitled to elect only three of the Junior College District's six trustees, even though the district contained approximately 60 percent of all persons between the ages of six and 20 who resided in the Junior College District. The Court found that the scheme "necessarily results in a systematic discrimination against voters in the more populous school districts," id. at 57, above and beyond "the inherent mathematical complications in equally apportioning a small number of trustees among a limited number of component districts," id. at 58. Finding that the elected officials at issue had powers, including the authority to tax, issue bonds, and condemn property, that "are general enough and have sufficient impact throughout the district" to warrant application of the one-person, one-vote principle, id. at 53–54, the Court invalidated the scheme. En route to this holding, however, the Court noted that "[i]t is of course possible that there might be some case in which a State elects certain functionaries whose duties are so far removed from normal governmental activities and so disproportionately affect different groups that a popular election in compliance with [the one-person, one-vote requirement of] *Reynolds* ... might not be required...." Id. at 56.

Similarly, in Board of Estimate of the City of New York v. Morris, 489 U.S. 688 (1989), the Court held that the one-person, one-vote principle applied to a New York City board consisting of three members elected at large and each of the elected presidents of the city's five boroughs. The Court observed that the board members were elected rather than appointed, that the board engaged in a "significant range of functions common to municipal governments," and that it had "considerable authority to formulate the city's budget." 489 U.S. at 694–696. Because the borough presidents each had one vote on the board despite the significant differences in the size of their respective boroughs, the Court held the board's apportionment of representation to be unconstitutional.

The Court in *Avery* had also indicated the existence of an exception to the one-person, one-vote rule as applied to local governments. In a passage that reflects a desire for substantial autonomy for localities to structure their internal affairs, the Court concluded that neither the Constitution nor judicial decisions should be viewed as "roadblocks in the path of innovation, experiment, and development among units of government." 390 U.S. at 485. Yet no local government electoral scheme that deviated from one-person, one-vote passed constitutional muster until Salyer Land Co. v. Tulare Lake Basin Water Storage District, 410 U.S. 719 (1973). In that case, the Court held that the right to vote in an election for the board of directors of a water storage district could be limited to landowners. The election procedures for district directors were established by the California Water Code which allocated one vote per each $100 worth of land located in the district whether owned by an individual or a corporation. The court noted that the district was created to "provide for the acquisition, storage, and distribution of water for farming" and provided "no other general public services." Id. at 729. Furthermore, the district's exercise of limited authority "disproportionately" affected landowners as the benefits of the district accrued primarily to landowners and were financed by landowners in accordance with the amount of land owned. Id. Finding that the district had a "special limited purpose" and a "disproportionate effect on landowners as a group," the Court concluded that the district's election procedures were an example of an exception to the one-person, one-vote rule contemplated in *Hadley*. Id. at 728.

The Court found that lessees denied the right to vote under the *Salyer* scheme were not denied equal protection of the laws. Id. at 733. Significantly, the Court indicated that because the district had a limited function and disproportionately affected landowners, its restrictions on the vote did not have to survive a strict scrutiny analysis that is typically applied to infringements of fundamental rights, like voting. Instead, the Court was willing to uphold the restrictions as long as they bore a rational relationship to a legitimate state interest. The Court found that the state's decision could be justified on the ground that the state may have "felt that landowners would be unwilling to join in the forming of a water storage district if short-term lessees whose fortunes were not in the long run tied to the land were to have a major vote in the affairs of the district." Id. at 732. Furthermore, because the state allowed voting in the district by proxy, a lessee always had the opportunity to bargain with the landlord for the right to vote. Id. at 733.

The *Salyer* exception to the one-person, one-vote rule was further clarified eight years later in Ball v. James, 451 U.S. 355 (1981), where the court discussed the importance of the issues of finance and degree of district power. In *Ball*, the right to vote for directors of the Salt River Project Agricultural Improvement and Power District was limited to landowners by a state statute that apportioned votes in accordance with the number of acres owned. The Court noted that the services provided by the district were "more diverse" and affected "far more people than those of the Tulare Lake Basin Water Storage District." Id. at 365. In particular, the district had actually exercised its authority to generate and sell electric power (unlike the district in *Salyer*), and the district area included almost half the state. Furthermore, approximately 15 percent of the water provided by the district was provided for nonagricultural purposes in farming areas and another 25 percent was provided for urban use. Id. at n.9. Despite these characteristics and the fact that the majority of the district's costs were covered through the sale of power as opposed to assessments on property, the Court found that the district fell within the *Salyer* exception to the one-person, one-vote principle because the district exercised limited governmental powers and its purpose was "relatively narrow," notwithstanding the broad geographical area in which it exercised those powers. Id. at 366, 367. As a result, the restrictions on voting could be upheld if they were rationally related to a legitimate state interest, a test that the Court found satisfied in the relationship between the acreage ownership and the costs and benefits of the district's operations.

In distinguishing *Ball* from its predecessors, the Court relied on the fact that the district could not "impose ad valorem property taxes or sales taxes" nor could it "enact any laws governing the conduct of citizens." Id. at 366. In addition, the district did not perform "normal functions of government [such] as the maintenance of streets, the operation of schools, or sanitation, health, or welfare services." Id. Furthermore, the Court concluded that the district's powers were "relatively narrow" and related to its primary purpose. Id. at 367. The fact that much of the district's water was delivered for nonagricultural use did not matter as "[t]he constitutionally relevant fact is that all water delivered by the Salt River District, like the water delivered by the Tulare Lake Basin Storage District, is distributed according to land ownership, and the District does not and cannot control the use to which the landowners who are entitled to the water choose to put it." Id. at 367–368. The Court also noted that the size and degree of power exercised by the district were not relevant to the finding that the district exercised limited powers and thus could not be relied upon to characterize the district as possessing general governmental power. "Nothing in the *Avery, Hadley,* or *Salyer* cases suggest that the volume of business or the breadth of economic effect of a venture undertaken by a government entity as an incident of its narrow and primary governmental public function can, of its own weight, subject the entity to the one-person, one-vote requirements of the *Reynolds* case." Id. at 370.

In a dissent joined by three other Justices, Justice White argued that the Court misapplied the principles of *Salyer* in finding that "the provision of water and electricity to several hundred thousand citizens is a 'peculiarly narrow function.'" Id. at 374 (J. White, dissenting). White argued that the powers and benefits granted to the district, as a municipal corporation established under the laws of Arizona, clearly indicated the "governmental nature of the District's function." Id. at 378. These powers included the power of eminent domain, the right to contract, and the authority to veto any surface water transfer. In addition, the district enjoyed other privileges granted to municipal corporations such as exemptions from taxation of property. Justice White also objected to the Court's characterization of the district's electric power generation as "incidental" to its primary purpose of storing and delivering water for agricultural purposes. Unlike the district in *Salyer,* the benefits and burdens of the Salt River District did not rest entirely with property owners. At one point in time, 98 percent of the district's income was derived from the sale of electricity, not property taxes. In addition, 40 percent of the water provided by the district was provided to nonagricultural users. Justice White concluded that these facts made it clear "that the burdens placed upon the lands within the District are so minimal that they cannot possibly serve as a basis for limiting the franchise to property owners." Id. at 383.

After *Ball*, as after *Salyer*, state courts have frequently upheld restrictions on voting in special purpose government elections. See, e.g., Southern California Rapid Transit Dist. v. Bolen, 822 P.2d 875 (Cal.), *cert. denied sub nom.* Atchison, Topeka & Santa Fe Ry. Co. v. Southern California Rapid Transit Dist., 505 U.S. 1220 (1992) (upholding statute limiting right to vote in municipal bond elections to owners of commercial real property within the proposed bond assessment district, and further weighting votes on the basis of the assessed value of the property); Lane v. Town of Oyster Bay, 603 N.Y.S.2d 53, 54 (N.Y. App. 1993) (upholding statute providing that "a proposition to extend an improvement district into a new portion of a town 'must be approved by the affirmative vote of a majority of the owners of taxable real property situate in the proposed ... extended district ...,'" and invalidating referendum pursuant to this provision that was not limited to qualified electors who owned taxable real property); Polk County Bd. of Supervisors v. Polk Commonwealth Charter Commission, 522 N.W.2d 783 (Iowa 1994) (upholding proposed Mayors' Comm'n that apportioned one vote to, among others, "the mayor of each commonwealth member, and the mayor of other cities having fifty percent or more of their population or area within the commonwealth," id. at 787, notwithstanding wide variation in the populations of the affected cites, on the ground that the Commission's powers "to study, evaluate, and recommend the transfer of municipal services to the control of the Commonwealth," id., are not the "general governmental powers" necessary for the one-person, one-vote principle to apply, id. at 790).

There have also been some intriguing post-*Ball* exceptions to the nonapplicability of the one-person, one-vote principle to special purpose government elections, however. Most notably, in Fumarolo v. Chicago Board of Education, 566 N.E.2d 1283 (Ill. 1990), the Illinois Supreme Court invalidated on equal protection grounds the Chicago School Reform Act's voting scheme for electing members of the local school councils because the scheme "denie[d] an equal vote in local school council elections to large portions of the electorate." Id. at 1286. Under the Act, each grammar and high school in the Chicago public school system would have its own "school council" composed of the school principal and ten elected members. Six of the ten elected members of each council were to be parents of currently enrolled students, and only parents of currently enrolled students were permitted to vote for these members. Two members were to be residents of the attendance area served by the school who would be elected by all the residents of that area. The remaining two members were to be teachers at the school who would be elected solely by the school staff.

The court held that even though the councils "cannot levy taxes, appropriate money, enter into contracts, issue bonds, acquire property, or set basic educational policy at the district level," id. at 1295–1296, the "councils perform functions which are at the heart of a traditional and vital governmental function: the operation of public education," id. at 1296. The court went on to find that because "the cost of operating the community's schools falls directly or indirectly on virtually all community residents" through property taxes, id. at 1298, and because the "benefits resulting from the election of competent and efficient local school councils are far from limited to parents with children in the public schools," id., "[i]t simply cannot be said that the activities and the performance of the local school council have a sufficiently disproportionate effect on those parents with children in current attendance at the public school," id. at 1298–1299.

Thus, the court concluded that "because the local school councils perform a general governmental function which affects the entire community," the one-person, one-vote principle would apply and the scheme at issue would be subject to strict scrutiny rather than rational basis review. Id. at 1299. The court concluded that "it is unreasonable and not necessary for purposes of the Act that those citizens who do not, at the time, have children in the public schools are denied an equal voice in the selection of local school council members." Id. at 1300.

On occasion, local government voting restrictions that would be acceptable under the federal Constitution may be found invalid under the state constitution. In Foster v. Sunnyside Valley Irrig. Dist., 687 P.2d 841 (Wash. 1984), the Washington Supreme Court concluded that a district that did not possess general governmental powers, and that thus was not subject to the federal one-person, one-vote principle, was required under the state constitution to ensure that those who "are significantly affected by district elections be given an opportunity to vote." Thus, "whether the right to vote is in fact so apportioned is subject to strict judicial scrutiny" and landowners residing in the district who were "directly and significantly affected by the district's operation" could not be denied the right to participate in the election. Id. at 849, 850. The same court further clarified its holding in Fakkema v. Island County Public Transportation Benefit Area, 722 P.2d 90 (Wash. 1986), by noting that nonresidents of a district could be excluded from the vote if they were "at most indirectly affected by a sales tax levied in a neighboring public transportation benefit area." Id. at 94.

Are restrictions on voting rights more consistent with communitarian or service provision models of local government? At first glance, they might appear to be inconsistent with a communitarian model, insofar as members of the community are disenfranchised, and thus excluded, or at least deterred, from the political debate that the community is supposed to foster. But local autonomy may also be intended to permit individuals with similar interests to gravitate to a community that is attentive to their needs, and allocating voting rights in a manner that reflects differential needs may help create communities of individuals who share similar interests.

This latter rationale is obviously consistent with the service provision model of local government. Electoral voting has the effect of levelling the interests of all voters, so those with an intense interest in outcome have no more say than those with only a mild interest in outcome. One effect of weighting votes is to allow those with the greatest interest to be able to register the intensity of their preference. Of course, the legitimacy of such a scheme depends heavily on whether the interests being weighted are related to an appropriate function of government. It would, for instance, be considered illegitimate to give members of one race or religion weighted votes because members of the favored group were considered to have a greater interest in the outcome of an election than persons not of that group. Restrictions on voting rights to landowners or the weighting of votes in an election for directors of an irrigation district according to amounts of real property owned may allow those who have the greatest interest in how land is irrigated to have the most say in irrigation decisions. Hence, restrictions on voting may allow preferences to be registered more accurately than under the one-person, one-vote principle. The result may be that localities will provide services more in line with the preferences of their constituents, taking intensity of preference into account. But are those effects sufficiently related to other, more dubious discriminants, e.g., wealth, to render the procedure nonetheless invalid?

Should it matter whether the restrictive voting procedures are enacted as part of a statutory scheme or whether they are enacted by the special district itself? If the restrictions are enacted by the state legislature, and the legislature itself is apportioned in accordance with the one-person, one-vote standard, are district residents denied the right to vote in matters affecting the special district nonetheless afforded a voice in district affairs by their representatives in the legislature? Does that mean that district residents eligible to vote on district matters and residents denied the vote ultimately have equal influence? Are there other avenues through which district residents ineligible to vote could influence policies of the district?

Before you conclude that all deviations from the one-person, one-vote principle are necessarily employed to preserve existing distributions of political influence or wealth, think how similar voting schemes might be employed to ensure more adequate representation of historical minorities who, notwithstanding intense preferences for municipal services, may have been consistently outvoted by a majority that is inattentive to their interests. See, e.g., Lani Guinier, The Tyranny of the Majority (1994); Samuel Issacharoff, et al., The Law of Democracy: Legal Structure of the Political Process (2d ed. 2002); Richard Briffault, Lani Guinier and the Dilemmas of American Democracy, 95 Colum. L. Rev. 418 (1995); Richard H. Pildes & Kristen A. Donoghue, Cumulative Voting in the United States, 1995 U. Chi. Legal F. 241.

For a general discussion and critique of the one-person, one-vote principle as applied to local government, see, e.g., Leon R. Weaver, The Rise, Decline, and Resurrection of Proportional Representation in Local Governments in the United States, in Electoral Laws and Their Political Consequences 139 (Bernard Grofman & Arend Lijphart eds. 1986); Richard Briffault, Who Rules at Home?: One Person/One Vote and Local Government, 60 U. Chi. L. Rev. 339 (1993); Grant M. Hayden, The False Promise of One Person, One Vote, 102 Mich. L. Rev. 213 (2003).

3. ANNEXATION AND BOUNDARY ADJUSTMENTS

PROBLEM II

The City of Wilberger decided to construct a landfill on a parcel located in the county approximately 12 miles east of the Wilberger border to dispose of trash generated by city residents. Concerns soon arose among interested parties about adverse effects that the landfill would have for county residents. After failed negotiations with county officials, the Wilberger City Council decided to annex the land on which the landfill would be located.

State law provides for the addition of land to a city, but imposes certain restrictions on the annexation procedure. The city council may, at its discretion, annex territory adjacent to the city, provided that it obtains the written consent of the owners of a majority of the land to be added. An exception to the consent requirement permits annexation without consent when three sides of the property to be added are adjacent to the city.

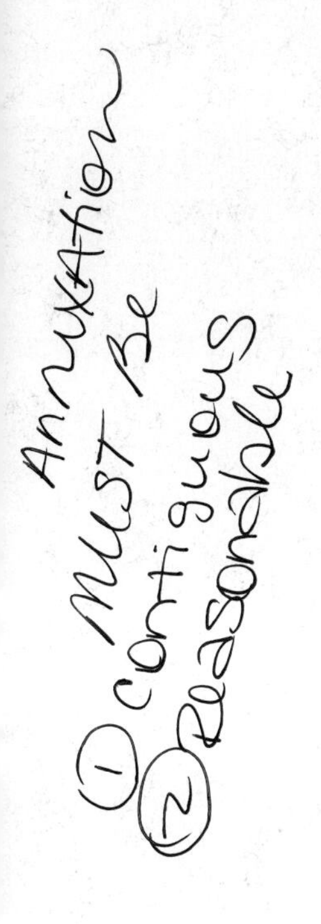

The Wilberger City Council enacted a series of ordinances purporting to annex the land on which the landfill was to be sited. First, the council obtained the consent of the owners of a strip of land 60 feet wide extending from the current southeastern border of the city limits 12 miles due east and then five miles north and passed an ordinance annexing this strip to the city. This formed a cul-de-sac around the property on which the landfill would be located. The council then passed an ordinance purporting to annex the enclosed area formed by the first annexation pursuant to that part of the statute that permitted annexation without consent when the property to be annexed was surrounded on three sides by city property.

You represent the county, which wishes to challenge the validity of the annexation. What arguments can you make on the county's behalf? What responses do you anticipate? Who should prevail? See In re Village of South Barrington, 289 N.E.2d 1 (Ill. App. Ct. 1972); Botsford v. City of Norman, 354 F.2d 491 (10th Cir. 1965).

Laurie Reynolds, Rethinking Municipal Annexation Powers

24 Urb. Law. 247, 249–250, 260–262, 266–267 (1992).

Annexation battles are typically fought in one of two contexts: when neighboring municipalities are competing for the same piece of land; or when a municipality is seeking to annex land from its unincorporated environs. In the first type of battle, occurring mainly in developed areas where municipalities are frequently adjacent or nearly so, the result will determine which municipal government will win the prize of annexation. In this situation, the two potential annexors may have sharply different ideas about the proper land-use classification for the land to be annexed. Moreover, both municipalities may claim that the land lies within each of their natural paths of development. In most states, the first municipality to initiate annexation proceedings will be the victor.

In the second type of annexation conflict, the stakes are somewhat different. The result will determine whether the land will become part of a municipal government's jurisdiction at all or, in the alternative, remain in the unincorporated county. This conflict most frequently involves residential subdivisions whose owners prefer to remain in the county with its lower tax rates, even though, to the uninformed observer, the subdivision already forms a part of the municipality whose annexation it is resisting.

Unfortunately, most state annexation procedures do not adequately respond to the variety of interests at issue in the two very different contexts described above. As this Article argues, the protection and importance currently afforded to the desires of the residents and landowners on the fringe of the municipality unwisely thwart the municipality's ability to annex urbanized territory. Moreover, when the annexation conflict is between two municipalities, most state statutory schemes reward the municipality that was the first to initiate proceedings, thereby putting a premium on quick rather than reasoned action....

State statutes create five basic types of annexation procedures: (1) by petition of affected landowners; (2) by municipal ordinance; (3) by judicial determination; (4) by independent appointed or elected boundary review boards or commissions; and (5) by state legislative action. Most states combine several different methods, thus creating a variety of possible annexation procedures. In some states, the result is cumbersome and complicated statutory procedures; in others the choices are well-defined and the methods for each type of annexation clearly delineated.

A survey of these statutes reveals, however, that even with the wide variety of methods available for annexation, most states impose an overlay of self-determination on all proceedings. Thus, whether the annexation entails a hearing before a boundary commission, or whether it is initiated by municipal ordinance, consent of those to be annexed is frequently an absolute prerequisite to annexation. As a result, in nearly all states, objections by owners or residents immunize many tracts of contiguous urbanized territory from annexation. Self-determination remains the preferred, and frequently exclusive, means by which a municipality can expand its borders. Even in those states that do grant unilateral annexation powers to municipal governments, stringent statutory provisions usually limit involuntary annexations to very narrow circumstances....

Perhaps the strongest motivating force in determining the shape of state annexation statutes is the notion that individuals should have the right to choose the government under which they live. Close examination, however, reveals that the principle simply does not justify granting virtual veto power to residents in outlying areas who object to municipal annexation. Those who live on the fringe of a municipality have in fact exercised their right of self-determination; they have chosen to live in and be a part of an urban area. Having made that choice, the municipality's exercise of its annexation power would merely confirm the reality that this land is already urban. The nonresidents on the fringe should no more have the power to opt out of the responsibilities of urban life than should city residents be able to claim an exemption from taxes to support services they do not use. In many instances, then, the self-determination principle merely provides nonresidents a way to protect themselves from assuming the burdens, while letting them enjoy the benefits, of being part of a municipality. Moreover, the self-determination principle has unwisely elevated and declared inviolable the wishes of a few residents to the possible detriment of the interests of the broader municipality. The one-sidedness of the self-determination principle cannot be justified; as the North Carolina Municipal Government Study Commission concluded: "We do not believe that an individual who chooses to buy a lot and build a home in the vicinity of a city thereby acquires the right to stand in the way of action which is deemed necessary for the good of the entire urban area." Rejection of the self-determination principle in no way implies that the residents should be subject to unbridled and standardless municipal power to annex, but rather the judgment that residents on the fringe should not have a veto power over the course of municipal growth. At the same time, the state should adopt legislative standards to protect the rights of annexed citizens. Unfortunately, the self-determination principle has mistakenly protected the desire to avoid municipal obligations and at the same time ignored the wide range of other interests that are involved.

Finally, analysis of the current role of the self-determination principle in shaping municipal annexation practices reveals that the principle is unevenly and incompletely applied. That is, the states do not guarantee that only willing individuals will be annexed. Virtually all states allow annexation upon petition by a majority of landowners in a territory and/or annexation upon majority vote of the residents in the areas. Although at first blush this approach appears to be nothing more than adherence to democratic majoritarian principles, the municipality's ability to manufacture majority consent by carefully picking and choosing the territory to be included in the annexation petition frequently results in de facto involuntary annexation. As currently applied in all states, then, the self-determination principle allows for creative machinations to achieve that majority consent, thus subverting one owner's opposition to annexation to the desires of willing individuals. Because most states do not require annexation by petition to comply with urbanization standards or other statutory prerequisites, current schemes allow for far more potentially abusive annexation practices than those that would be permissible under a system establishing clear contiguity and urbanization prerequisites to involuntary municipal annexation.

Clayton P. Gillette, Voting with Your Hands: Direct Democracy in Annexation

78 S. Cal. L. Rev. 835, 839–41, 844, 854, 857 (2005).

The broad variety of annexation procedures is not surprising. The absence of a single ideal procedure that could accommodate all interests involved in the annexation suggests that different jurisdictions will resolve the inevitable conflicts among these parties differently. Annexors, annexees, and the remaining residents of the area from which annexation will occur all have a valid claim to representation in the annexation decision. Annexors will be concerned whether tax and fee revenues from the proposed annexation will be sufficient to offset the cost of providing municipal services to the new residents. Annexees may bear new tax burdens for urban services from which they receive insufficient benefit and that were not governmentally provided by the jurisdiction of which they were previously residents. Alternatively, they may be concerned that they will be required to utilize services, such as public schools, that were previously governed by the source jurisdiction's authority, rather than the annexor's, and will lose the opportunity to participate in the governance of a small autonomous jurisdiction. The source jurisdiction may face additional tax burdens if the annexed area provides a disproportionately high percentage of the tax base within that jurisdiction or if removal of the annexees adversely affects the area's political, economic, or ethnic composition. In theory, therefore, each of these groups could legitimately claim a voice in the annexation decision.

The difficulty arises in attempting to translate these effects into a decisionmaking mechanism that both recognizes the various interests of these groups, and simultaneously permits arrangement of local government boundaries in a manner that addresses regional welfare. There is no single, inexorable manner for balancing all of these competing interests. . . .

. . . . Aggregating the votes of all affected individuals essentially delegates the decision to the electorate of the annexor, which will certainly outnumber the electorate of the annexees and may well outnumber the combined electorate of the annexees and the source jurisdiction. Thus, where there is significant division between the interests of annexors and annexees, vote aggregation will essentially amount to a right of unilateral annexation and will necessarily assign to annexors a veto power over the decision of others affected by the proposed annexation.

Allowing annexees the sole authority to vote, on the other hand, necessarily tolerates minority veto of majority preferences, given that annexors are likely to be more numerous and to have significant interests in the outcome of the annexation decision. That violation of a majoritarian norm in democratic politics seems dubious enough. More objectionably, minority veto invites strategic behavior on the part of annexees. Presumably, annexation will be desirable where it creates a regional surplus over existing arrangements. Minority veto induces proposed annexees to hold out for a disproportionately large share of that surplus. Allowing those remaining in the source jurisdiction to vote may have similar effects since they will not be governed by the resulting jurisdiction and thus have incentives to vote solely on the compensation they might obtain for "releasing" the annexees, rather than on any regional benefits that might materialize as a consequence of the annexation. These competing interests suggest that legislation adopted by any state to regulate annexation is likely to reflect the relative political power of the competing groups rather than any principle so inexorable as to receive universal acceptance or to be enshrined in a constitutional mandate.

The absence of an ideal procedure, therefore, does not mean that all plausible procedures will generate equal effects. Indeed, the procedures that a state adopts apparently affect the frequency, as well as the outcome, of annexation....

The very possibility that annexation will generate a regional surplus suggests that elections should be perceived as a bargaining process in which municipalities propose annexation of a particular scope, annexees have an opportunity to accept or reject the proposed terms, and both have opportunities to amend their initial positions in light of the expected reaction of the other....

Bargains, of course, exist against background default rules that assign entitlements to each party. Assigning a veto to potential annexees essentially confers on them an entitlement to remain within their own jurisdiction. This entitlement, however, is not inalienable. Rather it is protected by a property rule that permits another who values that right more highly than the initial entitlement holder to purchase it in a voluntary exchange.... Thus, initial assignment of the entitlement simply provides a means of initiating a bargain between the holder of the entitlement and those who would prefer to have it.... [T]he ultimate objective may be to generate a situation in which the entitlement is ultimately held by the party who values it most highly.

Since it is the existence of transactions costs that makes the initial entitlement matter in the first instance, the choice of rules ultimately may depend on whether annexors or annexees are better able to bargain for the entitlement initially misallocated to the other....

To speak of a bargain in this situation may initially appear somewhat anomalous. The very collective action difficulties that preclude annexees from coalescing to purchase an entitlement of unilateral annexation from the annexors should also frustrate explicit bargaining with the municipality. That limitation, however, does not necessarily preclude bargaining between annexors and annexees. Rather, it means that the municipality that seeks to attract annexees must anticipate the service and tax package that a majority of them would accept rather than enter express negotiations with multiple parties. The bargain, therefore, is implicit rather than explicit. The process of annexor proposal followed by annexee acceptance or rejection is thus more likely to deviate from an optimal bargain in which parties explicitly negotiate terms and tend to internalize the consequences of their agreement. Nevertheless, it may produce a process that is superior to both aggregate majorities and unilateral voting by either annexors or annexees.

NOTES

1. Professor Reynolds argues for broader use of involuntary annexations. Is her phrase "self-determination" useful in analyzing the competing interests at stake? After all, the annexors could claim that their efforts are undertaken in the name of "self-determination" to have a larger municipality, while potential annexees could claim that they have exercised their right of "self-determination" to avoid living in urban areas. Is this necessarily an invidious choice? Return to the court's explanation for avoiding annexation in Moorman v. Wood, p. 144 supra. What are the other values that lead legislatures to give annexees a stronger role in annexation decisions?

Professor Reynolds identifies four primary arguments to allow annexation even where annexees do not consent: (1) it would allow municipalities to provide superior services to the area to be annexed; (2) the municipality needs to grow as its population increases; (3) the municipality has an interest in maintaining adequate zoning and regulation at the urban fringe; (4) nonresidents who work, shop, and entertain themselves in the city should be required, as are city residents, to contribute to the maintenance of the city. Why isn't the following a complete response? (1) residents of unincorporated areas that desire "superior" municipal services can contract for them, or indicate through their residence, that such services are relatively unimportant to them; (2) the municipal desire to grow should not be given greater weight than the preference of noncity residents to live in suburban areas; (3) suburban or rural land-use and regulatory efforts that have substantial effects on localities can and should be handled through state agencies without annexation; (4) nonresidents who work, shop, and are entertained in the locality typically make substantial contributions to the city through payment of sales taxes, parking fees, highway tolls, and meal taxes; any additional contributions can be obtained through similar fees and taxes without the need for annexation.

2. A dated, but still useful survey of annexation practices can be found in Frank S. Sengstock, Annexation: A Solution to the Metropolitan Problem (1962). Sengstock starts with the assumption that a multiplicity of local governments constitutes a problem because areas on the urban fringe are less heavily regulated than cities and create planning and zoning policies that are inconsistent. The suburban area, Sengstock argues, also pits "the city against the rest of the metropolitan area and vice versa to obtain undeserving tax advantages." Are there reasons to disfavor Sengstock's predilection for larger urban areas? To the extent that you agree with Sengstock's analysis, what is the proper decisionmaking body to pass on the propriety of a proposed annexation? One might imagine that Sengstock would prefer decisions made by a body that represented all affected parties, such as the legislature. Nevertheless, Sengstock concludes,

> The desirability of legislative determination as a means of annexation is questionable. All the evils attendant upon special legislation are present. Interference by the state in the specific problems of local government is objectionable as being contrary to the philosophy of home rule. Grass roots democracy is by-passed. Long range community planning is an impractical possibility. Legislative determination as a means of solving metropolitan area problems is dubious because legislatures, through gerrymandering methods, are generally weighed predominantly in favor of rural interests; representatives of those problems may not be disposed to consider metropolitan area problems with either understanding or favor. Where it has existed as an exclusive method of annexation, legislative determination has in fact in recent years failed to produce any kind of substantial annexation activity.

Id. at 12. Sengstock favors instead the legislative promulgation of specific procedures to be applied by the affected localities. He, like Reynolds, particularly endorses unilateral annexation by municipalities, notwithstanding recognition that this procedure can generate "land grabs" and may not lead to efficient metropolitan government where the municipality is reluctant to annex undesirable territory. See David Rusk, Cities Without Suburbs (2d ed. 1995).

3. Professor Reynolds raises a question that is implicit in much of the study of local government: As between central cities and their suburbs, who is taking advantage of whom? Reynolds suggests that it is the suburbanites who are engaged in free riding. In her view, residents on the urban fringe are attempting to obtain the benefits of urban life without incurring the commensurate burdens of taxes and urban problems. Thus, central cities should have greater latitude to bring suburbanites within their jurisdiction through involuntary annexation. If the central city is subsidizing suburbs, are there ways to compensate without annexation? Presumably, localities could either increase the benefits of urban life, and hence make urban living more attractive to potential suburbanites, or decrease the burdens. One way to increase the benefits of urban living would be to shift costs incurred by the city to suburbanites who are believed to be the cause of those costs. For instance, if overcrowdedness or street decay is attributed to commuters, the city might impose toll roads, parking taxes, or income taxes. If central cities imposed these taxes, what would be the response of suburbanites? If you believe that they would come into the city less frequently (to work, to shop, because the high costs of commuting could be avoided with suburban shopping centers and commercial/industrial parks), would that make the city better off or worse off? If you think that the city would be worse off without the suburbanites than with them, does that suggest that suburbanites are bearing more of their share of the urban burden than Reynolds suggests, e.g., by providing a workforce and an expanded tax base? Even if so, annexation might cause a more accurate internalization of burdens and benefits. Would the threat of involuntary annexation lead to the same results as taxation of nonresidents, i.e., drive them further from the central city?

4. Why does annexation require the complex voting or consent schemes that we saw in *Moorman* and that are discussed in the Reynolds article? Do you find persuasive Gillette's claim in the excerpt above that the process of annexor proposal followed by annexee acceptance or rejection may be the voting rule most likely to increase the aggregate welfare of the annexor and the annexee? Why wouldn't annexation issues best be resolved by creating a flat rule that urban areas can always annex whatever areas they want, and allow annexors and annexees to bargain around this rule? Under which rule does one expect to see greater collective action problems that could inhibit the ability of annexees to join together to decide what would be necessary to induce them to become part of the annexing city?

Notwithstanding the problems of collective action, there are occasional successes in residential coalition building. An article in the New York

Times from 1985 recounts the organization of 144 homeowners into a corporation to sell their aggregate 85.5 acres of parcels to developers of a proposed office complex at a price approximately twice the cumulative appraised value of the homes. See Homeowners Unite in Selling to Developers, New York Times, Jan. 16, 1985, at p. 1, col. 3.

5. What if the problem is not potentially expropriative annexation of neighboring land by an existing municipality, but rather an issue known to urban geographers as "municipal underbounding: annexation policies and practices in which cities grow around or away from low-income minority communities, thus excluding them from voting rights in city elections and, in many cases, municipal services." Michelle Wilde Anderson, Mapped Out of Local Democracy, 62 Stan. L. Rev. 931, 938 (2010). Is annexation the best way to meet the needs in these unincorporated urban areas? If so, what voting rule or annexation procedure is most likely to be effective? For a thoughtful discussion of these issues see also Michelle Wilde Anderson, Cities Inside Out: Race, Poverty, and Exclusion at the Urban Fringe, 55 UCLA L. Rev. 1095 (2008).

In the Matter of the Enlargement and Extension of the Municipal Boundaries of the City of Jackson, Mississippi: Bunch v. City of Jackson

691 So.2d 978 (Miss. 1997).

■ ROBERTS, JR., JUSTICE, for the Court:

Jackson, Mississippi's mayor, Kane Ditto, recommended to the City Council that the City annex a total of 24.25 square miles of territory made up of two tracts of land lying south and southwest, respectively, of Jackson's existing corporate limits. The City's Planning Department presented the Planning Board and the City Council a four page document outlining their recommendation for annexing the area. On April 21, 1992, the City Council adopted an ordinance approving the proposed annexation, and a petition of annexation was filed in the Chancery Court of the First Judicial District of Hinds County the next day on April 22, 1992.

Municipalities within three miles of the proposed annexation area were served with process. The only named defendants to file answers were the City of Raymond, which objected, and the Town of Terry, which did not. Although the City of Raymond filed an answer objecting to the proposed annexation, it did not appear at trial. [Four] individuals also filed objections to the proposed annexation by the City of Jackson....

... On May 14, 1993, the lower court issued a twenty-six page typed opinion, finding the annexation by the City of Jackson of the entire proposed area reasonable.... Final judgment in favor of the City of Jackson was filed on June 4, 1993. At that time, several of the individual objectors, ("Objectors"), perfected an appeal to this Court....

After careful review of the record and evidence in this case, we find the chancellor to be manifestly wrong in holding the proposed annexation of

Byram by the City of Jackson to be reasonable at this time. Accordingly, we reverse and render.

STANDARD OF REVIEW

This Court, in *In the Matter of the Enlargement and Extension of the Municipal Boundaries of the City of Madison, Mississippi: The City of Jackson, Mississippi v. City of Madison*, 650 So.2d 490 (Miss. 1995), gave the following discussion on the chancery court's duty in annexations, and this Court's standard of review in such cases:

> While "[a]nnexation is a legislative affair," confirmation of annexations is in the province of the chancery court. *Matter of the Boundaries of City of Jackson*, 551 So.2d 861, 863 (Miss. 1989); Miss. Code Ann. 21–1–33 (1972). The role of the judiciary in annexations is limited to one question: whether the annexation is reasonable. *City of Jackson*, 551 So.2d at 863. Courts are "guided" in this determination of reasonableness by twelve factors previously set forth by this Court. This Court recently reaffirmed these twelve "indicia of reasonableness," but held "that municipalities must demonstrate through plans and otherwise, that residents of annexed areas will receive something of value in return for their tax dollars in order to carry the burden of showing reasonableness." *In the Matter of the Extension of the Boundaries of the City of Columbus*, 644 So.2d 1168, 1172 (Miss. 1994).
>
> The twelve indicia of reasonableness are: (1) the municipality's need to expand, (2) whether the area sought to be annexed is reasonably within a path of growth of the city, (3) potential health hazards from sewage and waste disposal in the annexed areas, (4) the municipality's financial ability to make the improvements and furnish municipal services promised, (5) need for zoning and overall planning in the areas, (6) need for municipal services in the areas sought to be annexed, (7) whether there are natural barriers between the city and the proposed annexation area, (8) past performance and time element involved in the city's provision of services to its present residents, (9) economic or other impact of the annexation upon those who live in or own property in the proposed annexation area, (10) impact of the annexation upon the voting strength of protected minority groups, (11) whether the property owners and other inhabitants of the areas sought to be annexed have in the past, and in the foreseeable future unless annexed will, because of their reasonable proximity to the corporate limits of the municipality, enjoy economic and social benefits of the municipality without paying their fair share of taxes, and (12) any other factors that may suggest reasonableness. See *Matter of Boundaries of City of Jackson*, 551 So.2d 861, 864 (Miss. 1989).
>
> These twelve factors are not separate, independent tests which are conclusive as to reasonableness. *Western Line Consol. School Dist. v. City of Greenville*, 465 So.2d 1057, 1059 (Miss. 1985). Rather, these factors are "mere indicia of reasonableness." "[T]he ultimate determination must be whether the annexation is reasonable under the totality of the circumstances." [citations omitted]. An annexation is reasonable only if it is fair. Western Line, 465 So.2d at 1060. In making this determination, the annexation must be viewed "from the perspective of both the city and the landowner[s]" of the proposed annexation area. Id. at 1059–1060.... [I]f the chancellor employed the correct legal standards, this Court's standard of review is limited. Reversal of the chancellor's findings regarding reasonableness of the annexation is warranted only if

> the chancellor is manifestly wrong and his findings are not supported by substantial credible evidence....

City of Jackson v. City of Madison, 650 So.2d at 494–495....

DISCUSSION OF THE ISSUES

... The Objectors argue that when evaluating the twelve factors there is a lack of substantial credible evidence to support the chancellor's finding that the proposed annexation is reasonable. The City of Jackson, of course, argues that there is more than substantial evidence in the record to support such a finding. The chancellor in her opinion and supplemental opinion discussed the evidence presented at trial concerning each of the twelve indicia of reasonableness set out by this Court in prior case law. The chancellor then concluded that Jackson's annexation of the entire proposed area was reasonable.

We disagree with the chancellor's findings but, deeming it unnecessary to do so, will not address the indicia separately as our explanation otherwise is adequate.

There was considerable undisputed evidence presented at trial that the population of the City of Jackson is decreasing and, that although there is considerable vacant, developable land within the City, applications for both residential and commercial building permits have decreased considerably over the last few years. While it is true that this Court has allowed annexations even though there is no significant population growth and/or a relatively high percentage of undeveloped land within the existing city limits, this presence of these factors should, at the very least, be an impediment to annexation....

Evidence shows 40.15 square miles of vacant land within the City in 1990. The City's population has declined from 202,888 in 1983 to 196,637 in 1990 with an out-migration from Jackson of 26,532 people. Mayor Ditto admitted at trial that Jackson had no need to expand to accommodate "anticipated growth within its boundaries." The City admits in its brief that it is not trying to annex Byram because it has outgrown its existing boundaries, but argues that there are other factors that indicate its need to expand.

Michael Bridge, the Objectors' expert in urban and regional development, testified that, "the vacant land resources of the city are the most dominant resources of the land resources within the city. It comprises some 25,700 vacant acres, or 37 percent of the total land area within the existing city." Bridge testified, as follows, concerning the effect of a large amount of vacant and developable land within a city:

> When you have vacant developable land that's not put into productive urban use, then it essentially tends to be a drain on the economy and the fiscal structure of the city. Vacant land—normally to go from developed area to vacant land to another developed area, you have to have roads. The utilities have to extend through that vacant area. So the city is in a position where they have expended in many instances significant resources to extend infrastructure into vacant areas and through vacant areas, and if the area does not develop or

> is not encouraged to develop, then it becomes a drain on the city because they have to extend those lines further and further. Those are not in productive uses. When those vacant lands go into productive uses, then they tend to strengthen the tax base. The converse, when you continually stretch the rubber band, you know, ultimately it will break. The concept of strengthening the tax base by ignoring the vacant land resources within the existing city is on the simplest basis just totally wrong. . . .

Bridge went on to discuss the concept of urban sprawl and its effect on the City of Jackson:

> Urban sprawl is essentially the development of properties at an extremely low density. The properties are not necessarily characterized by excessively large, vacant parcels interdispersed between the development, but that the development tends to have some continuity but such a low density that it becomes extremely costly for the city to provide the municipal level services and facilities to that area. . . .

According to Bridge, annexation would increase the City of Jackson's problems with urban sprawl.

The City at trial and in its brief has not been at all hesitant to state that it wants the revenues annexation would provide by expanding its tax base. Numerous witnesses testified at trial that the City was in need of expanding its tax base in order to continue providing the same level of services. Although it has been held that a city's need to maintain or expand its tax base, especially as growth and development occurs on its perimeters, is a factor to be considered when determining the reasonableness of a proposed annexation, *City of Jackson*, 551 So.2d at 865, this Court has in the past, been very critical of annexations which are in effect "tax grabs."

Over ninety years ago this Court held that "[m]unicipalities are not designed for the purpose solely, nor chiefly, of raising revenue. The power of extending corporate limits is granted not to be resorted to for the purpose alone of increasing the income of the municipality. . . ." *Forbes v. City of Meridian*, 86 Miss. 243, 38 So. 676, 678 (1905). Much more recently, Justice Smith in his dissenting opinion in *In the Matter of the Enlargement of the City of Gulfport*, 627 So.2d 292, 296 (Miss. 1993), stated, "[c]ities should be required to demonstrate other valid reasons for annexation other than mere tax base increases."

From studying the record and briefs, especially the testimony of city officials, we believe that the City of Jackson's primary motivation for the proposed annexation is to expand its tax base. Whether or not the taxes garnered by annexing Byram would be beneficial to the City of Jackson when compared to the expenditures that would result from the annexation is debatable. Bridge testified for the Objectors that it would not. . . .

We tend to agree with Mr. Bridge's assessment. Before the City of Jackson annexes more land and residents for which it has had to extend infrastructure and provide services, it should make an effort to extend that infrastructure to the vacant, developable land within the existing boundaries and take steps to encourage development in those areas.

The City of Jackson maintains that if the city experiences a decline it will have an adverse affect on the entire metropolitan area, including the proposed annexation area.... It is a fact that Jackson is the capital of the state and its largest city, and for these and other reasons the City's prosperity affects more than just the city itself. These things are validly taken into consideration; however, it is not a "super-factor" whereby whatever Jackson wants, Jackson gets.... We believe the chancellor placed too much importance on this so-called "Jackson factor."

The City failed to prove that the current services in the proposed annexation area are inadequate.... The City of Jackson produced no Byram resident, other than Ted Somers, Jackson's Public Works Director, who was not satisfied with the current level of services currently provided in the proposed annexation area. Instead, all residents who testified expressed concern about a decrease in the level of services, especially police protection, if annexation occurred....

... Bridge testified that "this is the only instance in all the annexation cases I've ever been involved in where I've seen that the county level of service in terms of street maintenance and right-of-way maintenance has been noticeably better than the city."

... The Objectors concede that "theoretically Jackson has the financial ability to make the expenditures it proposes." However, they argue that the City's desire or will to make promised improvements should be considered in light of the City's past performance of failing to furnish the promised improvements to the 1976 and 1989 annexed areas.

The Objectors produced a number of Jackson residents, mostly from the 1976 annexation area, who testified unfavorably about the level of services provided by the City. Their main complaints dealt with the City's police and fire protection, road maintenance and sewer service. There was testimony concerning slow response time of the Jackson Police Department and their failure to sufficiently investigate crimes. There was also testimony concerning the lack of fire hydrants and insufficient water flow to adequately fight fires in South Jackson....

Louis Armstrong, Jackson City Council member from Ward 2, which includes the 1989 annexation area, testified that many of the promises made by the City prior to the 1989 annexation had not been met....

The testimony concerning the City's past performance in previously annexed areas compel us to restate that this Court feels that the City of Jackson should make an effort to extend the infrastructure and enhance services and facilities within its existing boundaries in order to encourage development and expand its tax base....

There are over 1200 students that would be affected by the annexation. The evidence presented at trial shows that [the Jackson Public School District ("JPSD")] is reluctant to except [sic] the students from the proposed annexation area and has no proposed plan in place if the school districts' boundaries were to change. Dr. Benjamin Cannada, then JPSD Superintendent, testified that JPSD was "not seeking any new students to come into the system." Cannada testified that he thought JPSD could accommodate the additional students but admitted that with the exception of possibly two schools, all of JPSD's schools were already operating at or above capacity and that no thought had been given to where the annexed students would attend school. Dr. Cannada also testified that the funding of a building program that the schools had received from a recent bond issue was based on current enrollment and growth and the possibility of annexation had not been taken into account.

Dr. Leslie Johnson, [Hinds County School District ("HCSD")] Superintendent, testified that if the proposed annexation area was to be incorporated into the JPSD it would be a "very devastating situation" for the HCSD. He stated that HCSD would lose approximately 25% of its student population and about 50% of its students in that area of the county.

The effect of annexation on the school districts involved is a serious consideration which should be addressed. Although the chancellor had case law to support her decision that the school districts would not be affected at this time, the law is not clear as to how the school districts in an annexed area will be treated. To allow the annexation to proceed prior to a decision by the District Court for the District of Columbia would be most unreasonable.

* * *

The City also maintains that if the annexation is denied then there will most likely be a renewed effort to incorporate the proposed annexation area, which if successful will effectively cut off one of the City's two remaining paths of growth. The fact that none of the named defendants in this case appeared at trial to contest the annexation does not necessarily weigh in favor of the reasonableness of the proposed annexation. In fact it could be considered as a factor indicating unreasonableness since one of the City's last potential paths of growth is not being threatened by annexation from other municipalities. Furthermore, this Court is not encouraging the incorporation of the Byram area, nor are we saying that Jackson's annexation of this area would not be reasonable at a later time. We merely find that the record does not support annexation at this time....

The objectors argue that the chancellor failed to consider the totality of the circumstances, as required, when considering the evidence and making her decision. For the reasons hereinabove stated, we agree....

... [W]e find that at this time the City of Jackson's proposed annexation is unfair to the residents of the proposed annexation area and fails to meet the test of reasonableness. The proof before this Court does not sustain the chancellor's decision and, accordingly, we reverse....

■ PRATHER, PRESIDING JUSTICE, dissenting:

I respectfully dissent. In my view, the chancellor's ruling was supported by substantial evidence and should be affirmed. The record clearly indicates that the chancellor carefully considered the various factors relating to reasonableness, and her findings were clearly supported by evidence in the record. One particular concern I have is with regard to the City's need to expand its tax base. The objectors would have this Court place little if any importance on this issue, but, it is clearly essential that the City be able to gain revenue from those citizens who so often enjoy the benefits of its services. As to the City's needs in this regard, the chancellor found that:

> The City's evidence of need to expand was more than adequate. As the economic, governmental, and cultural center of Mississippi, Jackson's continued economic well being is important to the central portion of Mississippi and the entire state. One of the indicators of a declining tax base in Jackson is the fact that real property assessed valuation in Jackson has declined in the past three years, indicating a clear trend toward stagnant tax revenues. A substantial portion of Jackson's overall revenue comes from its real property tax revenues, making a decline of such revenue quite significant.

This Court has held that City of Jackson's need to maintain or expand its tax base, especially as growth and development occurs on its perimeters, is a factor to be considered under the "need to expand" factor. In *Matter of Extension of Boundaries of City of Jackson*, 551 So.2d 861 (Miss. 1989), this Court wrote that:

> Jackson's need for an expanded tax base is reasonable as well. As a matter of fact, recent years reflect a gradual recession of Jackson's (economic) life blood to the various surrounding communities. These communities have experienced meteoric growth, most of them with a planned development. They have drained off and continue to drain off the life of the city's flow of wealth in people, culture and dollars. Indeed, the very statistics recited by the Court below are the product of the flight of so many persons from Jackson's corporate limits, not so far as to deprive themselves of full access to the economic, social and cultural benefits Jackson has to offer but only so far as to sever their relationship with Jackson's assessor and tax collector. Barring a wholly unanticipated act of altruism by Ridgeland, Madison, Flowood, Pearl, Richland, Florence or Clinton—not to mention unincorporated western Rankin County, Jackson faces the certainty of a slow but sure erosion of its tax base by the unilateral actions of these selfish former citizens.

City of Jackson, 551 So.2d at 865. The words of this Court in *City of Jackson* are equally applicable today. I find it ironic that representatives of areas which have grown largely out of a desire to avoid taxation for the services which they enjoy in City of Jackson should accuse the City of attempting a "tax grab" out of considerations of greed.

In the case of City of Jackson, the need for tax dollars is more a matter of survival than greed. As the home of many government buildings, City of Jackson is faced with the burden of having much of its real estate occupied by tax-exempt entities, and the City has recently seen a flight of important tax-paying businesses to surrounding areas. This Court has given some, but, in my view, insufficient, consideration to City of Jackson's need for physical expansion outside of its current boundaries, but the welfare of our capital city depends upon more than available land. Tax-paying citizens are indeed the lifeblood of a modern city, and allowing City of Jackson the physical area it needs to expand while depriving it of the economic lifeblood it needs to survive would be tantamount to allowing the City to wither on the vine....

Although revenue considerations constitute one of City of Jackson's most pressing problems at this time, the fact remains that the majority's opinion will also serve to place in jeopardy one of City of Jackson's two remaining paths of growth. The chancellor noted that City of Jackson's ability to expand towards the east, north, northeast, and west have been cut off by surrounding communities, and the majority's opinion places the area to the south/south-west in increasing danger of being cut off as well. It is clear that Byram lies in one of City of Jackson's few remaining potential paths of growth, and this Court noted in *City of Jackson* that it need only be shown that the area to be annexed is, "in a path of growth, not necessarily the most urgent or even the city's primary path of growth." *City of Jackson*, 551 So.2d at 865.

Although City of Jackson has not been experiencing growth in the last few years, the potential for growth nevertheless remains. That potential for growth will be seriously and adversely affected, however, if this Court allows the gradual encirclement of our capital city to continue. This Court wrote in *City of Jackson* that:

> This is not an ordinary annexation case. Much more is at stake than whether a large municipality may annex 4.92 square miles along its northern border. Rather, we must decide whether Mississippi's largest and capital city, already largely landlocked by a plethora of bedroom communities, will have another nail driven in the coffin which, if closed, will doom it to the fate already experienced by so many central cities around the nation. It is patently unreasonable that this should occur.

City of Jackson, 551 So.2d at 862. I find unpersuasive the objectors' argument that the City has no need to expand based on the fact that it is not experiencing a population growth. In previous cases, this Court has allowed annexations in cases in which there was no significant population growth and/or a relatively high percentage of undeveloped land within the existing city limits. See *Matter of Enlargement of Corp. Limits of City of Hattiesburg*, 588 So.2d 814, 819–821 (Miss. 1991); *City of Greenville v. Farmers, Inc.*, 513 So.2d 932, 934 (Miss. 1987); *Extension of Boundaries of Horn Lake v. Renfro*, 365 So.2d 623, 625 (Miss. 1979).

This Court should not permit the annexation without a showing that the citizens in the annexation area would receive value for their tax dollars. *Matter of Extension of Boundaries of City of Columbus*, 644 So.2d 1168 (Miss. 1994). In this regard, the chancellor found that the increased taxes that would be imposed on residents in the annexation area would be offset by increased services and a reduction in fire insurance premiums and water rates. As both parties agree, the City of Jackson has the financial ability to make improvements and furnish necessary services. Although the City's past performance in its previous annexed areas has at times been less than exemplary, the evidence does show that City of Jackson has provided numerous services and improvements in annexed areas.

A continuation in City of Jackson's decline will have an adverse effect on the entire metropolitan area, including the proposed annexation area. If the annexation is denied, there will most likely be a renewed effort to incorporate the proposed annexation area which, if successful, would effectively cut off one of the City of Jackson's two remaining paths of growth. In my view, the chancellor properly gave serious consideration to the needs of our capital city in concluding the annexation to be reasonable, and I would affirm her ruling. Accordingly, I dissent.

■ BANKS, J., joins this opinion.

NOTES

1. *Judicial Determinations of Reasonableness.* Where questions of annexation are decided by election or by authority to engage in unilateral annexation, the role of the judiciary may be quite limited. The court need only consider whether the procedural criteria for the annexation have been satisfied. See In re Petition to Annex Certain Territory to the Village of North Barrington, 579 N.E.2d 880 (Ill. 1991); Superior Oil Co. v. City of Port Arthur, 628 S.W.2d 94 (Tex. Ct. App. 1981), *app. dismissed,* 459 U.S. 802 (1982). As the *City of Jackson* case indicates, however, courts may be explicitly charged with reviewing the reasonableness of a proposed annexation. See, e.g., Ark. Code Ann. § 14–40–603 (2009) (judicial investigation into whether annexation is "right and proper"); Miss. Code Ann. § 21–1–33 (2009); N.Y. Gen. Mun. Law § 712 (McKinney's 2009) (judicial determination of whether annexation is in "over-all public interest"); Tenn. Stat. Ann. § 6–51–103 (2009). See M. G. Woodroof III, Systems and Standard of Municipal Annexation Review: A Comparative Analysis, 58 Geo. L.J. 743 (1970). Do the factors considered by the Mississippi court reflect all the factors that might be considered in determining the reasonableness of a proposed annexation? Where there is doubt about the application of one of the factors, should the court presume reasonableness or unreasonableness?

The Mississippi court applied the multi-factor "reasonableness" test in great detail in In re Extension of Boundaries of City of Hattiesburg, 840 So.2d 69 (Miss. 2003). There the court emphasized that it had limited authority to review annexation decisions and would only reverse a chancery court's findings as to the reasonableness of an annexation if they were "manifestly wrong and ... not supported by substantial and credible evidence." The court thus upheld the reasonableness of a proposed annexation, notwithstanding some reservations about its effect on the cohesiveness of one of the annexed communities, including that community's championship high school football team. See 840 So.2d at 94 n.23. The court applied a rigorous analysis of each of the 12 factors that informed reasonableness, but ultimately determined that there was no basis for overturning the chancellor's findings. See also In re Enlarging, Extending, and Defining the Corporation Limits of the City of Brookhaven, 957 So.2d 382 (Miss. 2007); In re Enlargement and Extension of Municipal Boundaries of City of D'Iberville, 867 So.2d 241 (Miss. 2004).

2. *Annexation by Jackson.* The principal case does not involve Jackson's first effort to expand its boundaries. In 1989, the Mississippi Supreme Court upheld as reasonable an annexation by the city of 4.92 square miles along its northern border. City of Jackson v. City of Ridgeland, 551 So.2d 861 (Miss. 1989). The area was largely undeveloped, although it included a few commercial establishments, two churches, and a college. The court concluded that Jackson's need for expansion and the absence of other available outlets outweighed any costs of urbanization that would inevitably occur in the annexed area. A dissenting judge disagreed:

> Many good citizens move to get out of the city. Many have lived outside all of their lives and have no desire to come into a city. They are governed by county government. They may be satisfied with it or, perhaps, feel that one local government is bad enough, without having to put up with two. Some are ordinary folk, living on fixed incomes, who are unable to pay the additional taxes. They are not selfish persons who have moved just far enough to escape taxes, while remaining close enough to enjoy the cultural benefits afforded by the city. Many probably prefer the murmur of the pines, the hum of insects, the early evening call of the whippoorwills, to the sounds of the symphony or the opera, and choose the light of the moon, the beauty of the stars and the flight of the fireflies to theater and ballet. They prefer, perhaps, rabbits to switch blades, petunias to "pot," and mocking birds to sirens. If some did, indeed, flee to the country, why should they be pursued? If city life is so advantageous and socially desirable as to be forced upon the people by judicial decree, why is there so much litigation in opposition to city expansion? Why are the people not clamoring for these advantages?
>
> ... New concepts of community are emerging and these may well require different governmental patterns, the combining of county and city governments and the elimination of waste involved in the duplication of jurisdiction and often overlapping efforts. The dinosaurs are gone. Cities, as we have known them may be on the way out. It is not the duty of the courts to attempt to stem the tide.

551 So.2d at 869–870 (Blass, J. dissenting).

In 1997, the Supreme Court of Mississippi deannexed most of the 4.92 square miles annexed in *City of Jackson*. In re the Exclusion of Certain Territory from the City of Jackson, 698 So.2d 490 (Miss. 1997). The court found that the controverted area was not reasonably within the growth path of Jackson; that the residents of the annexed area had not received benefits necessary to balance their fair share of the taxes paid; and that the other citizens of Jackson would be forced to bear the heavy burden of providing new services should the annexation be enforced.

3. *Administrative Approval and Judicial Review.* Decisions in Kansas suggest an alternative mechanism for review of annexation decisions. Cities in Kansas may annex land where specific conditions for unilateral annexation are not satisfied, as long as the city successfully petitions the relevant board of county commissioners for permission. See Kan. Stat. Ann. § 12–521. The statutes provide that "the action of the board of county commissioners shall be quasi-judicial in nature." The state supreme court confronted the meaning of "quasi-judicial" in City of Topeka v. Shawnee

County Board of Commissioners, 845 P.2d 663 (Kan. 1993). Topeka sought to annex approximately 2,500 acres of residential land that was bordered by the city on two sides. The board of county commissioners denied the annexation on the grounds that the increase in taxes and reduction in services provided to the annexees constituted manifest injury. The board also found that the city would suffer no such injury should the annexation be denied.

On appeal from a district court opinion, the supreme court affirmed the denial. Topeka argued that the board had applied the wrong standard of review, and had treated the question as a legislative rather than a "quasi-judicial" one. As evidence of this error, the city cited the board's consideration of the effect the annexation would have on a community outside the area proposed for annexation. The supreme court responded that the statute directed the board to consider the impact of annexation on the entire community. Hence, the court found, no "legislative/advisability" review (which presumably would fall outside the jurisdiction of the board) had been undertaken in this case.

What facts would a board be prevented from considering under a "quasi-judicial" analysis that would be allowable if the board had "legislative" authority? See Cedar Creek Properties, Inc. v. Board of County Commissioners of Johnson County, 815 P.2d 492 (Kan. 1991), in which the supreme court, in reviewing a proposed annexation under another statute, reversed a trial court decision that limited judicial investigation into the effects of annexation on growth. The trial court considered such an investigation to be tantamount to substituting judicial findings for legislative judgment. The court concluded that "a finding that annexation will not hinder proper growth is more than just a legislative decision that annexation is advisable. It is analogous to finding that annexation will not cause manifest injury, which is a judicial finding." 815 P.2d at 498.

Town of Mt. Pleasant v. City of Racine

127 N.W.2d 757 (Wis. 1964).

■ DIETERICH, JUSTICE.

The case was tried upon stipulated facts. The annexed property comprises an area of approximately 145 acres, almost all of which was devoted to agricultural purposes on the date the annexation ordinance was passed. The map showing the boundaries of the annexed area was made a part of the plaintiff's complaint, and a copy of this map is reproduced in the opinion.

The property touches upon the Racine city limits only by a corridor approximately 1,705 feet long, and varying in width from approximately 306 feet to 152 feet. The corridor is 153 feet wide where it touches the southwest corner of the Racine city limits, and also where it connects with the boundaries of the annexed area. At the time of the passage and approval of the annexation ordinance, there was no dedicated street in existence through the corridor—although such a street was established on March 18, 1963—and there were no other city streets giving access thereto. The main portion of the annexed property was platted for 328 residential lots with an expected future population of 1,148 persons. Prior to the annexation the town had entered into a contract with the city providing for sewage disposal, in the area and a sewerage system was under construction. The town had also received authorization from the Public Service Commission to construct water public utility service to the area, with water supplied by the city. The town of Mt. Pleasant maintains a police force, is part of a school district, has street grade ordinances, an agreement for fire protection with the city and an adjacent village, and all the usual incidents of municipal corporations.

The annexed area was a part of the town of Mt. Pleasant and lies wholly within three miles of the corporate limits of the city of Racine. Neither Racine county, which employs a full time planner, nor the town, has ever approved the plat. Prior to the passage of the annexation ordinance, the Racine common council had received a report from the planning division of the Wisconsin Department of Resource Development, which, among other things, found that the annexation was not against the public interest.

The trial court's findings of fact were that the corridor contains a full width street; that the area within the corridor will contain or provide all of the necessary services to the entire annexed area; that the corridor provides a natural and practical connection whereby the area as a whole may be developed as an integral and homogeneous part of the city of Racine; and that the city has a need for additional residential and shopping areas to provide for its expanding population. The trial court concluded that the statutory requirements for annexation were complied with; that the tract in question is contiguous to the city of Racine; and that the tract is reasonably suitable or adaptable to city uses and needs.

The major issue raised on the appeal is whether the annexation was void because the area proposed to be annexed is not contiguous to the city of Racine within the requirements of sec. 66.021(2)(a), par. 2, Stats.[1] That section limits direct annexation to land "contiguous" to the annexing city or village.

The statement of agreed facts indicates that the 145 acre tract sought to be annexed touches upon the Racine city limits only by a 1,705 foot-long corridor, varying in width from approximately 152 feet to approximately 306 feet.

---

1. "(2) *Methods of annexation*. Territory contiguous to any city or village may be annexed thereto in the following ways:

"(a) *Direct annexation*. A petition for direct annexation may be filed with the city or village clerk signed by: . . .

"2. If no electors reside in such territory, by a. the owners of one-half of the land in area within such territory, or b. the owners of one-half of the real property in assessed value within such territory."

There is a decided lack of Wisconsin authority on the question of the validity of "corridor" or "strip" annexations. There is, however, no lack of out-of-state authority holding such annexation void.

This court has authority to review the annexation of territory to a city or village, and apply "the test of reason," which test is applicable to the inclusion, as well as the exclusion of land by internal or external boundaries. Town of Fond du Lac v. City of Fond du Lac (1964), 22 Wis. 2d 533, 126 N.W.2d 201. This court in the *Fond du Lac* Case made it clear that the discretionary power to a city to determine its own boundaries is not wholly without limitations. The question is not whether a city can have only one continuous boundary line, but whether the proposed boundary lines are reasonable in the sense that they were not fixed arbitrarily, capriciously, or in the abuse of discretion. The precise holding of the *Fond du Lac* Case is not directly in point, for there it was held that a city could not, by annexation, create a small "island" bounded on three sides by the annexed territory, and on the fourth by the city's existing boundary. However, the principles involved and stated in the *Fond du Lac* Case for determination of the validity of proposed annexations are binding.

The legal as well as the popular idea of a municipal corporation in this country, is that of oneness—a collective body, not several bodies. So, as to territorial extent, the idea of a city is one of unity, and not of plurality; of compactness or contiguity, not separation or segregation.

Shoestring or gerrymander annexation is not a rare phenomenon. The tendency of subdividers to reach far out into the countryside for vacant land, and their desire to attach it to the city of services, is natural; however, this can lead to annexations which in reality are no more than isolated areas connected by means of a technical strip a few feet wide. Such a result does not coincide with legislative intent, and tends to create crazy-quilt boundaries which are difficult for both city and town to administer. See Cutler, "Characteristics of Land Required for Incorporation or Expansion of a Municipality," 1958 Wisconsin Law Review, 6, 33.

A thorough review of the record, and application thereto of the rule of reason as set forth in the *Fond du Lac* Case, compels us to conclude that the annexation of the area in question does not meet the statutory requirement of contiguity. It follows that the judgment of the trial court declaring the proceedings valid must be reversed.

The judgment is reversed, and cause remanded with instructions to the trial court to enter judgment declaring the annexation ordinance adopted by the city of Racine on March 7, 1963, void and of no effect.

■ WILKIE, JUSTICE (dissenting).

Annexation proceedings are purely statutory. The only statutory requirement as to the contiguity of territory proposed to be annexed is set forth in sec. 66.021(2), Stats., which reads as follows:

> Methods of annexation. Territory contiguous to any city or village may be annexed thereto in the following ways:

There is no further statutory definition of what the term "contiguous" means.

The majority has engrafted onto the statute the additional requirement that a proposed annexation is subject to review under the "rule of reason" to determine whether the proposed boundary lines are "reasonable in the sense that they were not fixed arbitrarily, capriciously, or in abuse of discretion."

I see no basis for superimposing this additional requirement. The statute merely requires that the property proposed to be annexed be "contiguous" to the annexing city or village. There is no requirement as to the extent or degree of contiguity. There is no statutory prohibition against a "corridor" or "strip" annexation. We have found no previous case in this state that defines the term "contiguous" as applied to municipal annexations. Decisions of this court dealing with school district attachment proceedings have approved "strip" or "corridor" attachments.

In the instant case the trial court found that the proposed annexed territory was contiguous to the city and that the requirements of the statute had been met. The record also shows that, prior to enactment of the annexation ordinance, the Racine Common Council had received a report from the planning division of the Wisconsin Department of Resource Development, finding that the annexation was not against the public interest. This report was submitted pursuant to sec. 66.021(11)(c), pars. 1 and 2, Stats., which orders the planning division in part to consider whether the proposed territory to be annexed is "contiguous."

Under present law cities or villages must consider proposed annexations as presented by petitioners on a "take it or leave it" basis. They may not initiate proposed annexations of territory that they consider should properly be annexed in the orderly development of the urban community. The procedure that is entirely laid out by statute has been evolved over many years by the legislature, which, in almost every biennium, is asked to give careful consideration to changes in these statutes. Especially in view of this legislative history, I do not think that this court should now attach this court-made modification of the requirement of "contiguity."

If the "rule of reason" is to be engrafted onto sec. 66.021(2), Stats., in regard to whether or not the proposed annexed area is "contiguous," then certainly the trial court should have a chance to enter findings on whether the proposed boundary lines were "reasonable in the sense that they were not fixed arbitrarily, capriciously, or in abuse of discretion."

I must respectfully take strong exception to the majority's conclusion that the proposed boundary lines were unreasonable as a matter of law. I would affirm.

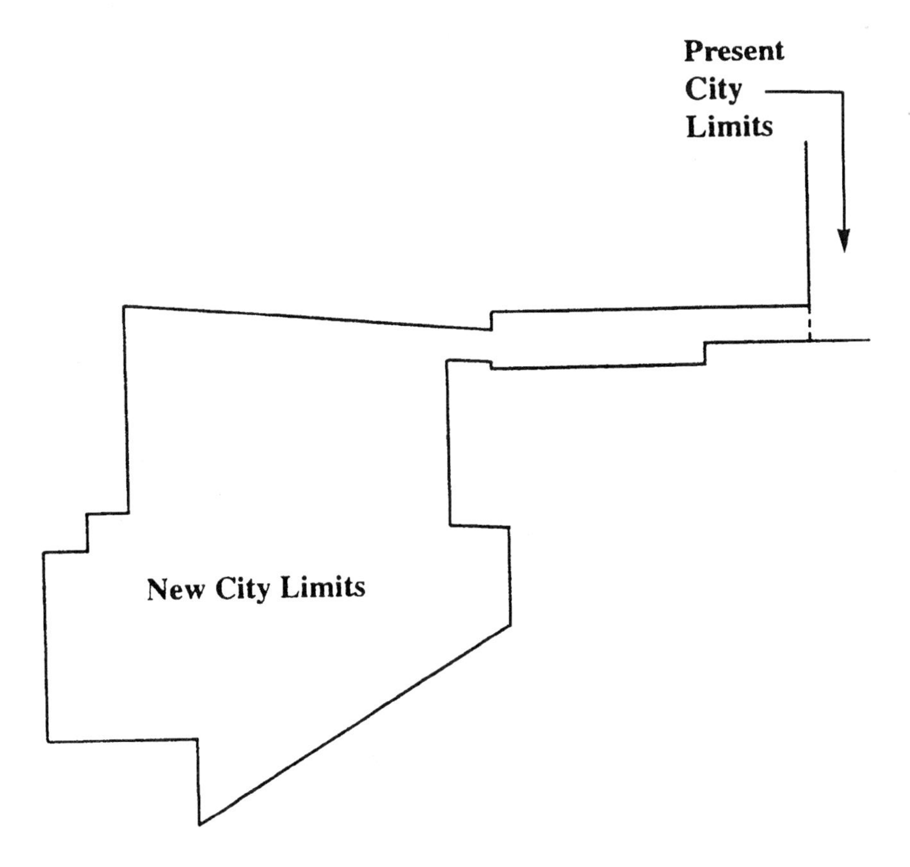

NOTES

1. The requirement that annexed land be contiguous to the annexor is a near-universal criterion. See Note 4 infra. At first glance, it seems almost too obvious to require justification. Before jumping to the conclusion that governing bodies should always be restricted to contiguous jurisdictions, however, consider the fact that the United States has noncontiguous jurisdictions. Does it matter that the relationship there is between the federal and state governments rather than between different parts of a locality?

There are numerous justifications for a contiguity requirement. First, requiring the annexor to be geographically proximate to the annexee discourages a locality from annexing distant wealthy unincorporated areas while excluding "undesirable" areas that might constitute a substantial drain on the central city's tax base. Second, contiguity serves as a rough measure of the annexor's ability to provide services to the annexed area. Third, contiguity also serves as a rough check to ensure that new residents will be close enough to take advantage of the central city. Finally, contiguity may be a surrogate for fiscal fairness by ensuring that new residents who must pay for municipal services benefit from those services. The annexation of noncontiguous property, especially if not initiated by the persons to be annexed, may be a proxy for a "land grab" or "tax grab" by the annexing jurisdiction. In these situations, annexors may select the neighboring areas that provide the most significant tax base, while omitting areas that require more municipal services.

Of course, a state may permit noncontiguous annexation if it so desires. See, e.g., N.C. Stat. Ann. § 160A–58.1, which permits certain cities to annex noncontiguous property located not more than three miles from the annexing city, as long as the city can provide annexees with the same services that it provides within its primary corporate limits. But in ambiguous cases, there may be reasons to presume that noncontiguous annexation was not intended. In Board of County Com'rs of County of Laramie v. City of Cheyenne, 85 P.3d 999 (Wyo. 2004), landowners had petitioned the City to annex their land, presumably in order to obtain City services for their planned development. The City agreed. The County, however, sought to declare the annexation void because the property was more than one-quarter of a mile from the nearest City boundary. The state annexation statute required that annexed land be "contiguous with or adjacent to" the annexor. Wyo. Stat. Ann. § 15–1–402(a)(iv). The City claimed that the use of the words "contiguous" and "adjacent" in the same statute meant that they must have different meanings, and thus permitted annexation of land "nearby," as well as of land "touching" the City. The court resolved the apparent ambiguity by concluding that the legislature intended to give the terms their common meaning: "that is, the lands to be annexed must geographically touch the municipality to some extent, with the contiguity requirement being satisfied by the slighter touching contemplated by the word 'adjacent.'" 85 P.3d at 1007. The court relied both on construction of the entire annexation statute and on decisions of other jurisdictions interpreting a contiguity requirement. But the court also agreed with the policy underlying the requirement:

> The element of contiguity helps to preserve the economic and political viability of municipal government. The costly package of services provided by municipal government can be economically maintained only within the compact boundaries fostered by the contiguity requirement. Conversely, the requirement of contiguity discourages prohibitively expensive extension of municipal services to noncontiguous areas where municipal services cannot be economically supplied. Moreover, it goes without saying that, from a political standpoint, a compact, contiguous area is more easily governed than one split into diverse, noncontiguous enclaves. Vicinity engenders a unified sense of community identity which facilitates the formation of the consensus essential to effective government.

Id. at 1009.

2. Given the justifications for the requirement, should technical satisfaction of "contiguity" be enough? Or should a court investigate the sufficiency of the contiguity to determine whether it satisfies the underlying justifications? In City of Rapid City v. Anderson, 612 N.W.2d 289 (S.D. 2000), the court invalidated the City's annexation of an airport. The statute permitted annexation where "[t]he governing body of a municipality, upon receipt of a written petition describing the boundaries of any territory, contiguous to that municipality sought to be annexed to that municipality, may by resolution include such territory or any part thereof within such municipality if the petition is signed by not less than three-fourths of the registered voters and by the owners of not less than three-fourths of the value of the territory sought to be annexed to the municipality." S.D.C.L. § 9–4–1. The annexed airport was situated approximately 4.7 miles from the pre-existing boundary of Rapid City, and was connected by a 200–foot–wide right-of-way and railway frontage along Highway 44 for the 4.7 mile distance. The court observed that "[i]n the annexation context, 'contiguity' and 'best interest' include more than common boundaries. [citations omitted]. There must also be a showing of a community of interest flowing from one of the justifications for a natural and reasonable annexation discussed above." 612 N.W.2d at 293. Where does the court's "best interest" test come from?

In In re Village of Glen Carbon, 264 N.E.2d 283 (Ill. App. Ct. 1970), the court described territory that was the subject of an annexation petition as resembling "an index finger bent 90 degrees at both of its joints." Objecting landowners within the territory contended that the contiguity requirement was not satisfied both because of the irregular boundaries and because "contiguity requires a community of interest and facilities" and the only service immediately to be obtained from the annexor was water. The objectors contended that the annexor would be unable to afford any services to the annexed residents. The court found that, notwithstanding the irregular shape, there were no "mere strips of land used as a subterfuge to reach outlying areas of land." As for the commonality of interest, the court found that the annexing village could subsequently deliver additional services to the annexed territory and thus the fact that "the immediate need of petitioners is only for water services does not negate the existence of a community of purpose and facilities." Given that the governing Illinois statute permitted annexation of any territory "which is contiguous to a municipality," on what theory could the court make the inquiry into the existence of a "community" of land that was admittedly contiguous? If it turns out that the annexor could not or did not extend the promised services, what remedy would be available to the annexees? See Waite Development, Inc. v. City of Milton, 866 So.2d 153 (Fla. App. 2004) (allowing cause of action for breach of contract where annexing city allegedly failed to pay cost of installing water and sewer lines in annexed subdivision as agreed).

The ability to provide city services was also at issue in Hughes v. Town of Oak Island, 580 S.E.2d 704 (N.C. App. 2003). The court in that case affirmed the invalidation of a "shoestring" annexation on the grounds that the annexed land was insufficiently contiguous. The court found that the annexation areas included several income-producing, high-value properties, but excluded other tracts that were surrounded by included areas and thus were equally in need of municipal services. The court concluded that "[l]iteral compliance with [the contiguity requirement] is not sufficient ... where it would result in the subversion of the purpose underlying the contiguity requirement—to ensure that the essential governmental services are provided to 'residents within compact borders.' " 580 S.E.2d at 709.

In Amick v. Town of Stallings, 382 S.E.2d 221 (N.C. App. 1989), the court found that annexation of subdivisions connected to a town by a 1,500 foot corridor which was itself being annexed for no purpose other than to satisfy a statutory contiguity requirement would create a result "which would clearly contravene the purpose of the [annexation] statute." Id. at 226. The court, therefore, refused to approve the annexation and remanded the annexation ordinance to the Town for amendment of its proposed boundaries.

3. In whose interest is the court intervening in the principal case? Certainly not the interests of the City, as it desires the annexation. Similarly, the landowners in the area to be annexed have petitioned for annexation. As in *Glen Mills*, it appears that the court is concerned with the ability of residents in the affected area to obtain the goods and services that they desire. At first glance, it appears that the court is even more justified in representing those interests in *Mt. Pleasant*, since those who will reside in the annexed area do not currently live there and thus cannot represent their own views in the annexation proceedings. But on reflection, doesn't the fact that the annexed area does not currently contain the "expected future population of 1,148 persons" weaken the case for judicial intervention? If the city does not make services available to the annexed area, presumably individuals who desire those services will not migrate there. Thus, market forces will resolve the issue without judicial intervention. Alternatively, those who move to the area notwithstanding the lack of services will be readily able to organize and petition the city officials for preferred services. Thus, service issues that are not resolved through market forces will be resolved through political forces.

Maybe the court believed that it was vindicating the interests of the Town of Mt. Pleasant. Should the use to which the annexed land will be put affect the level of judicial intervention in the annexation decision? Are there reasons to believe that the town's interest in avoiding the annexation should receive less credit in this situation than if, for instance, the city wanted to use the annexed area as a nuclear waste dump? What if the developer sought to become annexed to the city because, even though the town had been willing to accept a residential zone in the annexed area, the proposed construction was of a less sturdy type than permitted under the town's zoning law?

4. Judicial inquiry into the satisfaction of a contiguity requirement leaves open the possibility of erroneous decisions (finding contiguity where the underlying policies are not satisfied or rejecting such a finding where the policies are satisfied) and imposes the costs of litigation. In Daugherty v. City of Carlsbad, 905 P.2d 1120 (N.M. App.), *cert. denied*, 904 P.2d 1061 (N.M. 1995), the majority expressed such a concern. The plaintiffs in that case challenged a proposed annexation on the ground that the property sought to be annexed was not "contiguous" to the City limits, as required by the New Mexico statute, and argued that the City could not meet this contiguity requirement merely by annexing the "shoestring" comprising plaintiffs' property.

The failure of the New Mexico Legislature to require that petitioners show more than proof of physical contiguity creates a temptation for judicial intervention when annexation might appear to produce poor urban planning or an apparent lack of suitable community cohesiveness. Such intervention, however, deprives the process of predictability and does not produce provably better results than the political process established by our Legislature. Professor Clayton Gillette recently discussed policies in favor of judicial restraint on such a political question:

> A clear contiguity rule that reduces the role of judicial review requires those affected by a proposed annexation to take advantage of political opportunities to influence the shape and structure of the proposal. The incentives created by a nebulous rule are just the opposite—to invite courts into the business of drawing boundaries and hence restructuring a transaction, thereby advancing the annexees' objective of using protracted litigation to delay consummation of the proposed annexation. This strategy, of course, may be applied any time an annexation is proposed, not just in those cases in which annexations in fact abuse the technical contiguity requirement. If, as seems to be the case, we cannot be certain that "better" decisions will result from judicial intervention, at the very least we can minimize the costs of decision making, an objective that technical application of the contiguity requirement appears to satisfy.

Clayton P. Gillette, Expropriation and Institutional Design in State and Local Government Law, 80 Va. L. Rev. 625, 684 (1994).

This does not leave the judiciary without a meaningful role in reviewing annexation by petition. While the process is political, it does not, of course, allow abrogation of annexees' constitutional rights. The proper role of the judiciary in reviewing such an annexation is to resolve constitutional challenges to the political process involved. See Torres v. Village of Capitan, 92 N.M. 64, 69–70, 582 P.2d 1277, 1282–1283 (1978); see generally 56 Am. Jur. 2d Municipal Corporations 57 (1971). That is why, in *Dugger*, this Court made it clear that no constitutional objection had been raised to those annexations. *Dugger*, 114 N.M. at 53–54, 834 P.2d at 430–431. Nor has any constitutional objection been raised in the present case.

905 P.2d at 1124. What do you think of Professor Gillette's suggestion, quoted in *Daugherty*, that "technical application of the contiguity requirement" can at least "minimize the costs of decision making" in contexts where "we cannot be certain that 'better' decisions will result from judicial intervention"? Is the contiguity requirement at issue in *Mt. Pleasant* capable of "technical application"? What about a requirement that required the annexed area to share a specified amount of contiguous border with the annexor?

In this vein, consider the North Carolina statute governing annexation, N.C. Gen. Stat. § 160A–36, which reads in part,

> (a) A municipal governing board may extend the municipal corporate limits to include any area which meets the general standards of subsection (b), and which meets the requirements of subsection (c).
>
> (b) The total area to be annexed must meet the following standards:

(1) It must be adjacent or contiguous to the municipality's boundaries at the time the annexation proceeding is begun, except if the entire territory of a county water and sewer district created under G.S. 162A-86(b1) is being annexed, the annexation shall also include any noncontiguous pieces of the district as long as the part of the district with the greatest land area is adjacent or contiguous to the municipality's boundaries at the time the annexation proceeding is begun.

(2) At least one eighth of the aggregate external boundaries of the area must coincide with the municipal boundary.

(3) No part of the area shall be included within the boundary of another incorporated municipality.

For a discussion of recent interpretations of the North Carolina statutes on annexation, see Steven W. Blevins, Municipal Annexation in North Carolina: A Look at the Past Decade, 14 Camp. L. Rev. 135 (1992). See also Kan. Stat. Ann. § 12–520c (2009) (annexation of land not adjoining city).

NOTE ON SECESSION AND DISANNEXATION

A problem related to annexation involves attempts by one part of an established locality to secede from the larger body. During the last several years, municipal secession movements have formed with increasing frequency, and variable success, in a wide range of locations, including Boston, Massachusetts; Los Angeles, California; Staten Island, New York; Long Island, Maine; West Seattle, Washington; "the Valley" in Los Angeles, California; and Michigan's Upper Peninsula.

Why do you think a group would attempt to secede from an existing municipality? What might the costs of secession be for the group seeking secession? Should the motivation(s) of the group seeking to secede be considered in a determination of whether or not the secession should be permitted? What about the costs of secession for the rest of the municipality? Disannexation may be appropriate where the land in question does not receive any services from the municipality. See, e.g., Ramey v. City of Blackfoot, 580 P.2d 1289 (Idaho 1978); Town of Satellite Beach v. State, 122 So.2d 39 (Fla. Dist. Ct. App. 1960). More difficulty arises, however, where residents seek disannexation not because they are not receiving services, but because they believe that they can provide services for themselves at lower costs or of higher quality, or can create an environment more suitable to their own interests, if they form an independent entity. Often, moreover, disannexation may mean excising the wealthier segments of a municipality, leaving the remainder of the locality with an impoverished tax base. Should the attempt by a largely white part of town to secede from largely minority residents be viewed differently from an attempt by members of a racial minority to secede from their largely white neighbors?

In a modern classic, Exit, Voice, and Loyalty: Responses to Decline in Firms, Organizations, and States (1970), Albert O. Hirschman suggested that a deterioration in the performance of any firm or organization, typically in terms of the perceived quality of the product or service provided consumers or the organization's members, is likely to generate either "exit" or "voice." Id. at 4. Under the exit option, members leave the organization or customers stop buying the firm's product. Under the voice option, "[t]he firm's customers or the organization's members express their dissatisfaction directly to management ... or through general protest addressed to anyone who cares to listen...." Id. Hirschman posits that a consumer/member's

> decision whether to exit will often be taken *in the light of the prospects for the effective use of voice.* If customers are sufficiently convinced that voice will be effective, then they may well *postpone* exit.... [I]f deterioration is a process unfolding in stages over a period of time, the voice option is more likely to be taken at an early stage. Once you have exited, you have lost the opportunity to use voice, but not vice versa; in some situations, exit will therefore be a reaction of *last resort* after voice has failed.

Id. at 37. What does Hirschman's analysis suggest about the relative needs for, and benefits of, a fixed, formal procedure for secession and for annexation or incorporation? Is the "voice" option likely to be more or less effective with a clear "exit" option in place?

What do you think the optimal standard or voting rule for secession is? Which groups should be afforded a voice in any proposed secession? Should the decision lie solely with those who seek detachment from the city, or also with the city from which the detachment would occur? How much voice should each of these groups have relative to other groups? Consider the fates of two recent secession movements. Sections of Los Angeles, California considered secession from the city. The agency that had jurisdiction over such matters, the Local Agency Formation Commission for Los Angeles County, determined that two of the areas, the San Fernando Valley and Hollywood sections of the city, satisfied the relevant financial and other statutory criteria required for secession. In November 2002, a vote was held to determine whether the secession would occur. Secession would have required a majority vote both by voters in the area seeking detachment and by voters in the City of Los Angeles as a whole. See Gerald E. Frug, Is Secession from the City of Los Angeles a Good Idea?, 49 UCLA L. Rev. 1783 (2002). At the election 50.7 percent of San Fernando voters favored secession for their area, but only 33.1 percent of Los Angeles voters approved. Of Hollywood voters, 31.5 percent voted for secession of their area, but only 28.7 percent of citywide voters approved. Thus, both efforts failed. See http://www.losangelesalmanac.com/topics/Election/el22.htm.

In 1990, the New York Court of Appeals, New York's highest court, permitted the residents of Staten Island, a borough of New York City, to hold a legislatively authorized referendum, largely advisory in nature, on whether the borough should pursue secession from the City and become a separate municipality. City of New York v. State of New York, 562 N.E.2d 118 (N.Y. 1990) (per curiam). In November 1990, 83 percent of Staten Island voters opted to explore secession, and in November 1993, Staten Island voters approved a new charter for Staten Island as an independent city by a margin of 2–to–1. In its 1990 decision, the New York Court of

Appeals stated that a voter-approved "charter . . . for the City of Staten Island can become law only if the Legislature enacts legislation enabling Staten Island to disengage and separate from the City of New York." Id. at 119. The Court expressly declined to rule, however, on "whether genuine secession legislation, if ever it were to come before the Legislature, would require a home rule message," i.e., formal permission from New York City. Id. at 120.

In 1994, secession legislation was introduced before the New York Legislature, but the Home Rule Counsel of the State Assembly determined that a home rule message was required before the bill could be reported out of committee. The Speaker of the Assembly, a Manhattan representative and opponent of secession, concurred. Both the New York City Council President at the time and Mayor Rudolph Giuliani were known to oppose secession, and the City was therefore highly unlikely to grant the permission that the court required. Several Staten Island assemblymen subsequently sued to overturn the Speaker's decision, but the lower court ruled that the Speaker's decision was immune from judicial review under the Speech or Debate Clause of the New York Constitution. Straniere v. Silver, 637 N.Y.S.2d 982 (N.Y. App. Div. 1996). Several months later, this decision was affirmed by the state's highest court, Straniere v. Silver, 675 N.E.2d 1222 (N.Y. 1996), leaving New York City with unilateral veto power over secession by Staten Island or any other of the City's boroughs.

Writing in 1992, Professor Richard Briffault expressed the view that New York City should not be permitted to veto secession, but also that secession should not be able to occur without New York City's formal participation in the process:

> Instead, a secession procedure should recognize the presence of substantial state and local interests—and two sets of local interests—here. An appropriate formula for holding together all three interests and their overlapping commitments to local self-determination is suggested by the state constitutional provision for annexations: (i) conduct a referendum in the area seeking to secede in order to get an authoritative statement of the views of the people who would obtain municipal independence; then (ii) require the consent of the municipality from which they seek to secede, since that municipality would be directly and significantly affected by secession and ought to be allowed to participate in the process to protect its municipal integrity; but then (iii) provide for a state-level review of the action of the existing municipality, a review that could overturn the denial of consent to secession on the basis of the "overall public interest" of the region.

Richard Briffault, Voting Rights, Home Rule, and Metropolitan Governance: The Secession of Staten Island as a Case Study in the Dilemmas of Local Self-Determination, 92 Colum. L. Rev. 775, 818–819 (1992). What are the advantages and disadvantages of Professor Briffault's proposal relative to the two alternatives that he finds unsatisfactory? Should his "state-level review of the action of the existing municipality" be conducted by the state legislature or the courts? What sorts of evidence would Staten Island have needed to provide the reviewing body in order to show that secession was in the " 'overall public interest' of the region"?

Note that Professor Briffault expressly modeled his proposed secession standard on the "state constitutional provision for annexations." Should different standards be applied to disannexation (secession) or disincorporation than to annexation or incorporation? What does Hirschman's analysis suggest that the answer to this question should be? If the function of local government is to provide public goods efficiently, then it would seem that the same inquiry about whether a particular government structure accomplishes that objective would be relevant to both the creation of new boundary lines and the dissolution of existing ones. Once boundaries existed for purposes of providing these services, it would presumably be difficult to break these boundaries apart absent a showing that a more efficient provision could be made under some alternate division of governmental responsibilities. If, however, localities are intended to bring together individuals who share a sense of community, a very different result might exist. Individuals who are so situated as to facilitate common provision of goods and services, but who are otherwise (by class, ethnicity, interests) disparate from each other would appear to have less likelihood of forming a meaningful "community." Dissolution of boundary lines would appear to be a means of accomplishing these objectives for localities—unless one believed that by forcing individuals with initially disparate interests to live together, common ground could be obtained. Perhaps the concern that individuals would break into subcommunities that exclude on the basis of invidious discriminants—race, religion, etc.—should lead us to reject any view that too readily permits subdivision of political entities. See Kathryn Abrams, Law's Republicanism, 97 Yale L.J. 1591 (1988); Jerry Frug, Decentering Decentralization, 60 U. Chi. L. Rev. 253 (1993).

In an interesting twist on the disannexation issue, the town of Killington, Vermont voted in March 2004 to secede from the state of Vermont and join New Hampshire, which is located 25 miles from the town boundary. Secession proponents claimed that the town contributed $20 million in taxes to the state annually and received only $1 million annually in state aid for education and other local assistance. The residents were apparently particularly concerned with a new method of financing education statewide through property taxes that increased the burden on wealthy communities, such as Killington. Neither Vermont nor New Hampshire has yet approved the change.

NOTE ON BOUNDARY CHANGES AND THE VOTING RIGHTS ACT OF 1965

The federal Voting Rights Act of 1965, as amended, 42 U.S.C. § 1973, is intended to protect the right of minority citizens to vote. Section 5 of the Act, 42 U.S.C. § 1973c, purports to prevent the adoption of discriminatory election regulations by prohibiting a covered state or political subdivision from modifying any law, practice, or procedure that affects voting unless it has first obtained clearance of the proposal from the United States Attorney General or secured a declaratory judgment from the federal district court for the District of Columbia. To receive approval, the applicant must prove, by a preponderance of the evidence, City of Port Arthur v. United States, 517 F.Supp. 987 (D.D.C 1981), *aff'd*, 459 U.S. 159 (1982), that the change in any voting "qualification, prerequisite, standard, practice, or procedure does not have the purpose and will not have the effect of denying or abridging the right to vote on account of race or color...." Id. A state or political subdivision is subject to the preclearance requirement of § 5 if it previously applied particular prerequisites for voting that have been identified with discriminatory practices. For a discussion of the states and political subdivisions that have been subject to § 5 preclearance at various times, see Samuel Issacharoff, et al., The Law of Democracy: Legal Structure of the Political Process 546–672 (2d ed. 2002).

In Perkins v. Matthews, 400 U.S. 379, 388 (1971), the Supreme Court held that annexation constituted "the change of a 'standard, practice, or procedure with respect to voting' " within the meaning of § 5. The revision of local boundaries affects voting both by redefining who may vote in a municipal election, and by diluting the weight of the vote of residents of the preannexation municipality. The Court concluded that "§ 5 was designed to cover changes having a potential for racial discrimination in voting, and such potential inheres in a change in the composition of the electorate affected by an annexation." Id. at 388–389.

A few years later, in City of Richmond v. United States, 422 U.S. 358, 368 (1975), the Court acknowledged that annexations raise particularly problematic questions under the Voting Rights Act, because "it would be difficult to conceive of any annexation that would not change a city's racial composition at least to some extent; and we did not hold in *Perkins* that every annexation effecting a reduction in the percentage of [blacks] in the city's population is prohibited by § 5." Presumably, annexations are sometimes undertaken for economic and other reasons entirely independent of the effect on racial groups' relative voting strengths. In *Richmond*, the Court further delineated the post-*Perkins* § 5 requirement that an annexation have "neither the purpose nor the effect of denying or abridging the right to vote" on account of race or color. Id. at 362.

At issue in *Richmond* was an annexation by the City of Richmond, Virginia, of 23 square miles of land that caused the city's black population to decline from 52 percent to 42 percent. Richmond was governed by a nine-member city council elected at large, but as part of the post-*Perkins* preclearance procedure arrived at a plan with the Attorney General under which each council member would be elected from a separate ward. Four of the wards were to have substantial black majorities, four would have substantial white majorities, and the ninth ward would be approximately 59 percent white and 41 percent black. The Court stated that "[a]s long as the ward system fairly reflects the strength of the Negro community as it exists after the annexation, we cannot hold, without more specific legislative directions, that such an annexation is nevertheless barred by § 5." Id. at 371. The Court further found that the proposed "plan does not undervalue the black strength in the community after annexation," id. at 372, even though an alternative ward plan had been proposed "which would have improved the chance that Negroes would control five out of the nine wards." Id. at 367.

Even if no discriminatory effect is found to result from a boundary change, § 5 also requires that the proponent of the change demonstrate an absence of discriminatory purpose. Thus, the *Richmond* Court remanded the case for further proceedings to determine whether there were "objectively verifiable, legitimate reasons for the annexation" other than diluting the weight of Richmond blacks' votes. Id. at 375. In City of Pleasant Grove v. United States, 479 U.S. 462 (1987), the Court faced a challenge to the annexation by an historically all-white Alabama city of 450 acres of vacant land and a 40–acre parcel occupied by a single, extended white family. Notwithstanding the obvious absence of any immediate discriminatory (or other) effect of the annexation on black citizens' right to vote, the lower court found that the City's simultaneous failure to annex any of several neighboring black areas that petitioned for annexation was "racially motivated," id. at 469. The Supreme Court did not determine that these findings were "clearly erroneous," notwithstanding the City's protestations that its annexation decisions were based on "economic considerations." Id. at 469–470.

What would constitute "objectively verifiable, legitimate reasons" for a boundary change? In *City of Pleasant Grove,* the city attempted to prove that its prior annexation decisions were based on economic self-interest. To support its contention, the city produced evidence that two committees investigating the potential annexation of a local black neighborhood found that the annexation would produce net costs to the city. This conclusion was based on claims of lost development fees and the cost of providing health and safety services to the new areas. The Court rejected the claim. The Court found that all the supporting economic studies were conducted after decisions not to annex had been made. Further, the studies exaggerated the costs of annexing the black neighborhood, e.g., by including the expense of police and fire services that the city already provided to the black neighborhood without charge. In City of Port Arthur v. United States, 517 F.Supp. 987 (D.D.C. 1981), *aff'd,* 459 U.S. 159 (1982), however, the court approved a boundary change involving the consolidation of two communities and the annexation of another. The court found indicia of discriminatory purpose in the historical background of the consolidation. Nevertheless, the court concluded that legitimate reasons for the changes could be found in the subsequent reduction of tax burden for the localities and qualification for federal revenue sharing. The city would also be able to achieve economies of scale with respect to municipal services and to attract businesses and jobs. Do these decisions suggest that the inclusion of new communities will be upheld more readily than the refusal to include?

Between 1965 and 1982, virtually all voting rights litigation raised claims under § 5 of the Act. In 1982, however, § 2 of the Act was amended to no longer merely track the language of the Fifteenth Amendment, and since then most of the racial vote dilution litigation has taken place under § 2 rather than under § 5 or the Constitution. As amended, § 2 continued to prohibit states and political subdivisions from imposing or applying any "voting qualification or prerequisite to voting or standard, practice, or procedure" which results in the denial or abridgment of the right to vote of any citizen on the basis of race or color or membership in a "language minority group." The amendments to § 2, however, specified that, unlike under § 5, the burden of proof would rest with the challenger and no proof of discriminatory purpose would be required. A violation would be found "if, based on the totality of the circumstances, it is shown that the political processes leading to nomination or election in the State or political subdivision are not equally open to participation by members of a [protected] class of citizens ... in that its members have less opportunity than other members of the electorate to participate in the political process and to elect representatives of their choice." 42 U.S.C. § 1973(b). Importantly, the amendments to § 2 included express language that "nothing in this section establishes a right to have members of a protected class elected in numbers equal to their proportion in the population." Id.

Section 2 challenges most frequently arise in the context of the apportionment of representation. See, e.g., pages 164–166 supra; League of United Latin American Citizens v. Perry, 548 U.S. 399 (2006); Johnson v. De Grandy, 512 U.S. 997 (1994); Thornburg v. Gingles, 478 U.S. 30 (1986); Gomez v. City of Watsonville, 863 F.2d 1407 (9th Cir. 1988), cert. denied, 489 U.S. 1080 (1989); McNeil v. Springfield Park Dist., 851 F.2d 937 (7th Cir.), cert. denied, 490 U.S. 1031 (1989). In at least one instance, however, LeBlanc–Sternberg v. Fletcher, 781 F.Supp. 261 (S.D.N.Y. 1991), plaintiffs used § 2 to challenge an incorporation. In that case, the local Orthodox Jewish community asserted that boundary lines for a new village had been designed to exclude Orthodox Jews, thereby diluting the voting power that they had previously exercised with respect to matters such as zoning and taxation. The court ruled that since the members of the community had no right, should redistricting occur, to be left in a single district for purposes of selecting representatives, they similarly had no right to be included in the new village. The court implied, however, that plaintiffs would have a valid § 2 claim if they were able to demonstrate discriminatory intent and denied a motion to dismiss in order to permit plaintiffs to prove their claims. It is unclear from the opinion why the court concentrated on the congressionally discarded "intent" test rather than the more recent "effects" test.

For useful examinations of the evolution of voting rights jurisprudence in the local government context, see, e.g., Quiet Revolution in the South (Chandler Davidson & Bernard Grofman eds. 1994); Samuel Issacharoff, Groups and the Right to Vote, 44 Emory L.J. 869 (1995); Richard H. Pildes, The Politics of Race, 108 Harv. L. Rev. 1359 (1995). For discussions of the kind(s) of "political participation" the Voting Rights Act protects, e.g., traditional acts of voting, lobbying, grassroots politics, running for office, see, e.g., Kathryn Abrams, "Raising Politics Up": Minority Political Participation and Section 2 of the Voting Rights Act, 63 N.Y.U. L. Rev. 449 (1988); Pamela S. Karlan, Maps and Misreadings: The Role of Geographic Compactness in Racial Vote Dilution Litigation, 24 Harv. Civ. Rts.–Civ. Lib. L. Rev. 173 (1989).

CHAPTER 3

THE COMMUNITY'S RELATIONSHIP WITH THE STATE

A. THE STATE'S PLENARY POWER AND THE INHERENT RIGHT TO SELF-GOVERNMENT

1. HISTORICAL OVERVIEW

In this chapter we explore the relationship between a locality and the state of which it is a political subdivision. We will be addressing issues such as whether a municipality can regulate its residents or others without first receiving permission from the state, whether a locality can avoid obligations that the state desires to place on it, and whether state statutes or local ordinances prevail in the event of a conflict. These questions are at the heart of the debate over the proper scope of *local autonomy*, that is, the extent to which localities can implement policies unencumbered (at least legally) by the effects of their choices on others. The answers to these questions have shifted over time and among jurisdictions. At one extreme is the view that localities have an inherent right of self-government. One important implication of this right is that localities can initiate legislation without the prior permission of the state. Conversely, an inherent right of self-government implicitly limits the capacities of the state to create, alter, or eliminate municipal boundaries and powers. If the relationship between the state and its political subdivisions is grounded in a right of local self-government, then the provisions of the state constitution that address that relationship should be interpreted in the same manner as one would interpret provisions of the federal Constitution that address the relationship between the federal government and the states. The accepted reading of the federal Constitution is that it is a document of grant rather than of limitation. Hence, Congress cannot engage in any activity not granted to it within the Constitution. While the concept of what constitutes a "grant" sufficient to authorize congressional action may receive a broad reading in our federal jurisprudence, the baseline that some provision must be found to ground congressional action remains intact.

Application of this interpretation to the relationship between a state and its localities requires the state to find some textual basis in its constitution before it can regulate its political subdivisions. This position was promoted by early advocates of municipal autonomy who saw state control as a threat to community freedom. See, e.g., E. McQuillin, Constitutional Right of Local Self–Government of Municipalities, 35 Am. L. Rev.

510 (1901). In People ex rel. Le Roy v. Hurlbut, 24 Mich. 44 (1871), Judge Cooley, writing for the Michigan Supreme Court, ruled that the state legislature lacked authority to appoint full-term members to the board of public works for the City of Detroit. Cooley found justification for the holding in the history of city-state relations, which, he concluded, demonstrated that limits on legislative discretion in regard to local governments rest on "fundamental principles." These principles indicated that while the state legislature could modify the structure of local governments, "local government is [a] matter of absolute right." Id. at 108. To Cooley, this absolute right was an essential guarantee of liberty because "a centralized government, though by representatives freely chosen, must be despotic, as any other form of centralization necessarily is." Id. at 98. Cooley also expressed concerns about the political implications of subjecting the selection of local officials to state control. If the state legislature could make such appointments, he concluded, these jobs would become "spoils of party," and officeholders would have no common interest with city residents.

Those who adhered to this inherent right of local self-government believed that the authority of municipalities did not derive from written constitutions and was not conferred by central authorities. Rather, localities could exercise intrinsic power that emanated from the principle that "the nearer the officers are to the people over whom they have control, the more easily and readily are reached the evils that result from political corruption and the more speedy and certain the cure." E. McQuillin, The Law of Municipal Corporations § 70 at 155–156 (1970). Local charters, far from being initial grants of authority to municipalities, simply confirmed existing rights that originated in English common law and that were necessarily adopted in American jurisprudence, in so far as American municipalities antedated central (colonial) government. See Hendrik Hartog, Public Property and Private Power: The Corporation of the City of New York in American Law 1730–1870 (1983); Joan C. Williams, The Invention of the Municipal Corporation: A Case Study of Legal Change, 34 Am. U. L. Rev. 369 (1984).

To those who adhere to the contrary view, the state has full power over its political subdivisions. This view has come to dominate local government law, and is embodied in a rule of statutory construction, known as Dillon's Rule, that severely restricts the scope of local autonomy under certain circumstances and requires localities to obtain state legislative permission before it can perform desired functions. See pages 281–313 infra. For those who subscribed to this position at the turn of the twentieth century, colonial history was too ambiguous to support a contrary conclusion on historical grounds, and state constitutional law had evolved to confer on the state plenary power over all subjects except those over which state power was explicitly or implicitly surrendered or restricted. See Howard Lee McBain, The Doctrine of an Inherent Right of Local Self-Government, 16 Colum. L. Rev. 190 (1916). This view entails that the state constitution is properly considered as a document of limitation that restricts state power over its localities, not one that grants it. As a result, the state can exercise any power that it desires over its political subdivisions, unless something in the state constitution prevents it from doing so. See, e.g., Hornbeck v. Somerset County Bd. of Educ., 458 A.2d 758 (Md. 1983). Professor Frug summarizes the position of these commentators as follows:

> Howard Lee McBain, a noted municipal law authority of the time, argued that most courts had properly rejected the right of self-government. In discounting the thesis, McBain seized upon the weak links in the way proponents framed the right. He denounced the idea of an "implied limitation" on legislative power as dangerous and unworkable and argued that, even if the right to local self-government were a common law right, it would not therefore be beyond the legislative power to change the common law. He also denied that there was in fact an historical right to self-government, at least if interpreted as the right to democratic, popular control of local officials.
>
> McBain's arguments were cleverly aimed at the phrasing, and not the substance, of the Cooley–Eaton–McQuillin thesis. The proponents of the thesis could have responded that the power of public corporations was a "liberty" interest expressly protected by the due process clause in the same way that the "property" interests of private corporations were protected. They could also have explained that this liberty interest was not the democratic control of corporations as understood in the nineteenth century, but instead the kind of local autonomy all corporations had exercised before the ideas of property and sovereignty were separated in the late eighteenth and the nineteenth centuries. But they did not do so. Nor would it have mattered. By the time of McBain's attack, courts were not willing to eliminate the distinction between public and private corporations—even Cooley, Eaton and McQuillin did not challenge that distinction. That state power over cities was different from state power over corporations had become an automatically accepted part of legal thought.
>
> In 1923, William Munro, in his classic work, The Government of American Cities, stated that Dillon's position on state control of cities was "so well recognized that it is not nowadays open to question." McQuillin's thesis, on the other hand, has been substantially revised even in his own treatise by its current editor:
>
>> [The] municipal corporation is a creature of the legislature, from which, within constitutional limits, it derives all its rights and powers. Distinction should be made between the right of local self-government as inherent in the people, and the right as inherent in a municipal corporation; while as to the people, the right has quite commonly been assumed to exist, but as to the municipal corporation the right must be derived, either from the people through the constitution or from the legislature.

Gerald E. Frug, The City as a Legal Concept, 93 Harv. L. Rev. 1057, 1114–1115 (1980).

One reaction by advocates of broad local autonomy to the triumph of this "plenary power" position was to insert into state constitutions explicit limits on the powers that the state could exercise over its localities. The more important reaction, however, was to insert into state constitutions provisions that permit localities to engage in a broad array of activities without first obtaining explicit authority from the state legislature. As we will see, these constitutional vary significantly among the states, though they all fall under the amorphous classification of "home rule." Moreover, although many of these provisions were intended primarily to enhance the scope of local autonomy, there is some support for the proposition that many of them were initially proposed to limit the capacity of legislators to permit localities to engage in certain kinds of behavior that were either redistributive, and thus imposed obligations on property holders, or that interfered with "good government" principles. See David J. Barron, Reclaiming Home Rule, 116 Harv. L. Rev. 2255, 2288–2321 (2003). These different objectives for home rule are today reflected in the various forms that home rule takes and in the different interpretations of home rule that courts have advanced when structuring the relationship between localities and the state. But perhaps the important lesson to be learned from this history is that there is nothing either inevitable or immutable about the relationship between the states and their political subdivisions. Even those jurisdictions that begin with a presumption of state plenary power may ultimately carve out so many exceptions to that rule that localities effectively attain substantial independence. And even those jurisdictions that nominally grant a significant scope of "home rule" authority to their localities may ultimately define the areas of autonomy so narrowly as to permit legislative control of local activity in most areas of substantive importance.

2. POWERS OF INITIATION AND OF IMMUNITY

As you proceed through this chapter, it is important to keep separate two related issues that define the scope of local autonomy. The first of these involves the initiation of local legislation. A locality that possesses authority to initiate legislation without prior authorization could enact ordinances concerning civil rights, business regulations, or zoning, notwithstanding that state statutes were silent on these issues. If the locality can initiate local legislation only with the prior consent of the legislature, then enactment of those ordinances must await legislative permission. Dillon's Rule speaks to this issue most explicitly insofar as it precludes a locality from engaging in any activity without receiving prior authority from the state. As we will see, the primary effect of home rule is to grant the power to initiate local legislation to localities and thus to avoid the strictures of Dillon's Rule.

The fact that a locality has authority to initiate local legislation, however, does not end the matter. It is conceivable that a legislature could authorize localities to engage in certain activities, but then enact a statute that affected the same activity. At that point, there exists a question of whether the local ordinance or the state statute applies. This raises the second issue of local autonomy, the issue of local immunity from state regulation. "The power of immunity is essentially the power of localities to act without fear of the supervisory authority of higher tiers of the state.... An example of immunity would be local government's regulating land use (in accordance with their right to do so), without any outside review agency." Gordon L. Clark, Judges and Cities 68 (1985). The most favorable version of home rule, from the locality's perspective, would not only allow the locality to regulate without prior legislative authority, but also to trump any state legislation that attempted to regulate the same activity in a different manner.

The combined inquiries into the scope of local initiative and local immunity define the boundaries of local autonomy. Those boundaries thus determine the extent to which a locality will be able to become a unique community or be required to conform to standards imposed by others. The greater the scope of initiative and immunity, the easier it will be for those who share a common vision of the public interest or the good life to gravitate to a locality where they can pursue that vision, free from interference by the state or other intermediaries. Broad initiative and immunity, however, also reduce the obligations that any locality may have to surrounding communities.

Note how the boundaries of initiative and immunity also affect the political process by which local and state governments enact laws that affect local government. If localities have an inherent right of self-government and thus can initiate legislation without authorization from the state, groups that have an organizational advantage at the local level are more likely to see their agenda for local legislation enacted. Assume, for instance, that the relationship between a locality and the state is such that the locality can initiate legislation without prior authorization from the state, but that state legislation prevails over conflicting local ordinances. Assume further that a group, call it *X*, desires to have the locality pass Ordinance A. Another group, *Y*, opposes the ordinance. If *X* has a greater ability to organize at the local level than *Y*, perhaps because the members of *X* are more concentrated geographically than the members of *Y*, then *X* has a better chance of winning at the local level than *Y*. That may be true even though *X* would not have been able to convince the state legislature to grant the locality the right to exercise the power authorized in Ordinance A. If, however, *Y* is better able than *X* to organize at the state level, then *Y* may be able to convince the state legislature to deny the locality the authority to enact Ordinance A. But *Y* will have to obtain that specific denial. *Y* may be unsuccessful if, for instance, the matter is considered beyond the state's authority over its political subdivisions.

If, on the other hand, localities had no authority to initiate legislation without prior state authorization, then *X* would have had to ask the state legislature to grant the locality permission to enact Ordinance A. If *Y* is better able to organize at the state level than *X*, then *Y* might have been able to prevent the locality from receiving authority to legislate in the area in the first instance. We would expect each group to address that legislative body in which it has an organizational advantage. For instance, if bottling companies (who want to maximize demand for their product) are better able to organize at the state level, while environmentally aware consumers are better able to organize at the local level, one would expect to see bottle deposit ordinances passed locally, and to see efforts to override those ordinances introduced at the state level. But that means that the initial assignment of authority, either to the locality or to the state, may determine whether the locality is able to exercise certain powers. For an analogous discussion of how groups might select to pursue their goals at the federal or state level, see Jonathan R. Macey, Federal Deference to Local Regulators and the Economic Theory of Regulation: Toward a Public Choice Explanation of Federalism, 76 Va. L. Rev. 265 (1990).

Of course, one group that may be very effective at the state level is the group of municipal officials. After all, state legislators typically represent districts carved from municipal corporations, so it is in the interests of those legislators to provide benefits sought by municipalities. Thus, initially there is reason to believe that localities will be able to obtain legislation that they desire. Nevertheless, not all municipalities have identical interests, and not all municipalities have interests that conflict with those of other groups. Moreover, where municipalities do have consistent interests, it is not clear that they will always coalesce to pursue those interests. Presumably, the lobbying effort to obtain a grant of authority from the legislature (or to oppose a burden that the legislature is considering imposing on municipalities) is time consuming and costly. Costs may take the form not only of the direct effort, but also of providing representatives with certain benefits (electoral support, promises to support other projects preferred by the representative) in order to induce them to pursue the locality's agenda. Passage of the measure (or defeat of the unwanted measure), however, benefits the entire group of municipalities, regardless of whether they have contributed to the lobbying effort. If the interests of several municipalities converge, each may attempt to avoid these costs by free riding on the efforts of the others, with the result that an insufficient effort is exercised by the group as a whole.

Presumably, legislation that serves the public interest rather than the interest of a small group is more likely to emerge when all sides are adequately represented in a deliberative lawmaking process. That is Madison's lesson in Federalist No. 10. See pages 16–18 supra. One question that is relevant to the decision about the proper relationship between the state and the locality, therefore, is which forum is most likely to be accessible to multiple sides of an issue. To the extent that we believe that the local forum is more likely to represent all sides of an issue (possibly because no side will have an advantage in gaining access to the city council, while one side would have such an advantage in the state legislature), we might wish to increase local autonomy with respect to that issue.

One might initially conclude that this analysis confirms Mill's view that localities should have authority only over those matters "of purely local concern." Nonresidents are likely to have little access to local legislative bodies, and thus their interests in the extraterritorial effects of local action is likely to be disregarded. As a result, local activity that generates substantial external effects should perhaps be regulated by the state. But on reflection, one might conclude that representation of nonresidents need not take the form of appearances by the nonresidents themselves in order for their interests to be considered. Residents may often serve as proxies or surrogates for those interests. Think, for instance, of a city resident who owns a private bus service that transports commuters from outlying suburbs to workplaces in the city's downtown district. If the city proposes a "commuter tax," commuters themselves may have little access to hearings on the issue. But the resident owner of the bus service (along with resident owners of businesses that depend on commuting employees and who fear that they will have to pay wages that offset the new tax or lose their best employees to suburban employers) have incentives to represent the commuters' interests before the city council. That is not to say, of course, that the tax will or should be rejected. It is only to say that a decision can be made with all perspectives on the issue before the city council, even though the people directly affected might initially be considered to have been isolated from the decisionmaking process.

As you read the following materials, consider the way in which the court in each case envisions the relationship between the state and its political subdivisions. What groups in each case are likely to gain or lose from the local ordinance or state law at issue and how likely were those groups to be represented in the legislative (state or local) process? What images of the role of localities must the judges have to reach their decisions?

PROBLEM III

You represent the City of Brookville, which has filed a declaratory judgment action to invalidate a recently enacted state statute. The statute reads as follows:

> Whenever any employee member of a fire or police department of a municipal corporation or other political subdivision of the state shall be sued for damages arising out of the performance of his official duties and while engaged in the course of his employment by such governmental agency, such governmental agency shall be authorized and required to provide defense counsel for such employee in such suit and to indemnify him from any judgment rendered against him in such suit; provided, however, that such indemnity shall not extend to any judgment for punitive damages or for damages arising out of any willful wrongdoing by said employee; and provided, further, that such municipal corporation or other political subdivision shall have notice of such suit.

Brookville's elected officials believe that the financial burden imposed by this requirement will severely restrict its ability to fund other goods and services that it believes are desired by its residents. Indeed, they have polled residents and have discovered that there is little support in Brookville for the expenditures required by the statute. You have perused the constitution of the state and found no clause that expressly permits the state to require any of its political subdivisions to make expenditures for a particular purpose. What arguments can you make to have the statute declared invalid under the state constitution? What is the likelihood of success? See City of Chattanooga v. Harris, 442 S.W.2d 602 (Tenn. 1969). Would your argument be the same if Congress had passed a similar law requiring all states to provide defense counsel and indemnity to state police officers? See, e.g., Printz v. United States, 521 U.S. 898 (1997); New York v. United States, 505 U.S. 144 (1992).

Would it matter if the state constitution included a provision that "[n]o law of general application shall impose increased expenditure requirements on cities and counties unless the General Assembly shall provide that the state share in the cost"? Would such a provision be desirable?

Sanitation District No. 1 of Shelby County v. Shelby County

964 S.W.2d 434 (Ky. App. 1998).

■ JOHNSON, JUDGE.

The Sanitation District No. 1 of Shelby County, Kentucky (the Sanitation District) has appealed from the judgment of the Shelby Circuit Court entered on June 24, 1996, which upheld the constitutionality of Kentucky Revised Statutes (KRS) 220.035 (the statute). We affirm.

The Sanitation District is a political subdivision, or municipal corporation, of the Commonwealth of Kentucky, created on February 28, 1974, and organized pursuant to the provisions of KRS Chapter 220 *et seq.* KRS 220.020 vests the Secretary of the Natural Resources and Environmental Protection Cabinet (the Cabinet) with the authority "to establish sanitation districts within any county of the Commonwealth[,]" so as to address several concerns relating to sewage disposal and water pollution, all of which are enumerated in KRS 220.030. The Sanitation District is governed by a board of directors (KRS 220.140 and 220.170) which is empowered to "control and manage the affairs of the district" and which is charged with devising a plan "for the improvements for which the district was created." KRS 220.140 and 220.220. All plans prepared by the Sanitation District's board are submitted to the Cabinet for approval. KRS 220.240.

Although the Cabinet has been the entity designated to establish sanitation districts where needed, and has been given extensive supervisory and oversight responsibilities over these districts, the statutory scheme has historically given certain authority over the sanitation districts to the fiscal court or courts in the county or counties in which the sanitation districts are located. ["Fiscal courts" in Kentucky are county entities that have certain legislative and administrative authority. EDS.] For example, the county judge executive was given the authority by the Legislature to appoint the members of a district's board (KRS 220.140). Further, a sanitation district must file its annual budget with the county judge executive. KRS 220.080(4).

In 1984, the Legislature enacted KRS 220.035, the pertinent parts of which provide as follows:

(1) A fiscal court may:

(a) Review and approve, amend or disapprove proposed district land acquisitions;

(b) Review and approve, amend or disapprove proposed district construction of capital improvements;

(c) Review and approve, amend or disapprove proposed service charges or user fees; and

(d) Review and approve, amend or disapprove the district's proposed budget.

(2) In order to exercise any or all of the powers enumerated in subsection (1) of this section, the fiscal court shall adopt a county ordinance explicitly stating which of the powers the fiscal court intends to exercise and setting forth the procedures by which the sanitation district shall submit plans and documentation for review and approval, amendment or disapproval. The exercise of such powers shall become effective thirty (30) days following the effective date of the ordinance. In the case of districts lying in two (2) or more counties, no fiscal court shall exercise the powers enumerated in subsection (1) of this section until each fiscal court has adopted conforming ordinances stating the powers to be exercised.

Pursuant to subsection (2) of the statute, the appellee, the Fiscal Court of Shelby County (the Fiscal Court) passed an ordinance in January 1995, assuming all the powers enumerated in subsection (1) with the exception of (1)(c), the right to review charges or fees.

The Sanitation District and its president, Loyd Cheak, filed a petition on February 1, 1995, requesting that the Shelby Circuit Court declare KRS 220.035 unconstitutional and void and further asking the court to enjoin Shelby County and the Fiscal Court from "exercising any of the powers purportedly delegated to them under KRS 220.035[.]" In its final judgment, the trial court found that the "General Assembly ha[d] not exceeded its authority by enacting the Statute[,]" and that the statute "is a valid and constitutional exercise by the General Assembly of its powers over sanitation districts." It dismissed the petition for declaration of rights and denied the Sanitation District's request for injunctive relief. This appeal followed.

* * *

It is settled, as the trial court observed, that as a creation of the Legislature, the Sanitation District's continued existence and the purview of its authority are dependent upon the will and discretion of the Legislature. This principal was succinctly stated in *Allen v. Hollingsworth,* 246 Ky. 812, 816, 56 S.W.2d 530, 531 (1933), as follows:

> Apart from restraints of the organic law, the Legislature has plenary powers in respect to the establishment and regulation of the government of municipalities, and such divisions of government possess only those powers that the state, through the Legislature, has conferred upon them, expressly or impliedly, and those granted powers may be enlarged or diminished in the discretion of the superior body, for the municipalities are derivative creations.

Likewise, in *Covington Bridge Commission v. City of Covington,* 257 Ky. 813, 820, 79 S.W.2d 216, 219 (1934), the Court stated that the power to create a political subdivision "necessarily" included "the right[s] to amend, abridge, or repeal[,]" citing *City of Pineville v. Meeks,* 254 Ky. 167, 171, 71 S.W.2d 33, 35 (1934).

We agree with the Sanitation District that the powers to review, approve, amend, or disapprove its acquisition of realty, capital improvements and its budget as provided in KRS 220.035, result in a significant shift in authority between the Sanitation District and the Fiscal Court. Nevertheless, there is nothing in the Kentucky Constitution that specifically safeguards these powers in the Sanitation District. Clearly, the Legislature may "transfer the power and duties of one office from one body of local officers to another local body[.]" *Covington Bridge Commission, supra* at 220. *See also Candler v. Blevins,* Ky., 922 S.W.2d 376 (1996); *Fiscal Court of Jefferson County v. City of Anchorage,* Ky., 393 S.W.2d 608 (1965); and *Adams v. Burke,* 308 Ky. 722, 215 S.W.2d 531 (1948). Thus, despite the Sanitation District's insistence that these cases are "mostly irrelevant," we believe they address the very essence of the dispute and we conclude that the trial court was correct in its determination that KRS 220.035 is a valid exercise of the Legislature's power over one of its creations.

* * *

Accordingly, the judgment of the Shelby Circuit Court is affirmed.

NOTES

1. *The State's Plenary Power*. The decision in *Shelby County* incorporates two related but distinct principles. The first principal is that the state legislature can exercise plenary power over its municipal corporations, subject only to specific constraints found in the state constitution (and, of course, any federal constitutional constraints). This principle is well entrenched in state constitutional law. In Independent School Dist. v. Pfost, 4 P.2d 893 (Idaho 1931), the plaintiff school district claimed that a gasoline tax imposed by the legislature was not authorized by a state constitutional clause that expressly permitted the legislature to impose property taxes, license taxes, and per capita taxes. The court concluded that express mention of these taxes did not preclude enactment of additional taxes. Instead, the court held that any legislative act is legal "when the Constitution contains no prohibition against it." More recently, a North Carolina court construed the state constitution in a manner that allowed the legislature to impose restrictions on a city's practice of billing higher water rates to nonresidents and imposed liability on the city for failure to serve those customers. The court began its analysis with an exegesis on the relationship between the state and its political subdivisions: " 'All power which is not expressly limited by the people in our State Constitution remains with the people, and an act of the people through their representatives in the legislature is valid unless prohibited by that Constitution.' 'The members of the General Assembly are representatives of the people. The wisdom and expediency of a statute are for the legislative department, when acting entirely within constitutional limits.' Nonetheless, 'we are aware that . . . [i]t is well settled in this State that the courts have the power, and it is their duty in proper cases, to declare an act of the General Assembly unconstitutional—but it must be plainly and clearly the case.' 'If there is any reasonable doubt, it will be resolved in favor of the lawful exercise of their powers by the representatives of the people' " (internal citations omitted). City of Asheville v. State, 665 S.E.2d 103 (N.C.App. 2008). Although the court determined that certain state constitutional provisions limited the scope of the state's plenary power, it concluded that none of those restrictions applied to the challenged legislation.

The court in *Shelby County* notes that "there is nothing in the Kentucky Constitution that *specifically* safeguards these powers in the Sanitation District" (emphasis added). How explicit must a constitutional prohibition be in order to limit the legislature's plenary power? In Dwyer v. Omaha–Douglas Public Building Commission, 195 N.W.2d 236 (Neb. 1972), the legislature authorized a city and county to establish a building commission. The commission was entitled to levy a tax, separate from that already levied by the city and county, to finance the construction of governmental buildings. Plaintiffs complained that the legislation was invalid because the state constitution placed a tax limitation on counties, and the tax imposed by the new commission, combined with pre-existing county taxes, would exceed that limitation. The court disagreed. It concluded that nothing in the state constitution, including the tax limitation, limited the legislature's ability to remove functions (such as office construction) from the county, delegate them to a new entity (such as the commission), and grant the power of taxation to the new entity. The tax limitation applied only to counties, not to overlapping instrumentalities of the state. Note that the effect of the court's decision is to require that any prohibition on legislative action be express. The court was unwilling to infer from the expression of specific forms of taxation that all other forms were implicitly prohibited (or at least the court required stronger evidence of implied limitations). In the *City of Asheville* case, cited above, the state constitution precluded legislation that dealt with health or sanitation, or that regulated trade. The court concluded that the enactments at issue were local in nature, but concerned neither of those categories and thus were permissible.

2. *The State Constitution as a Document of Limitation.* The second principle implicit in *Shelby County* is that a state constitution is a document of limitation, not a document of grant. The defendant county did not have to point to a specific constitutional clause giving the legislature the right to enact the statute. Rather, the sanitation district had to (and could not) point to an explicit constitutional clause preventing the legislature from exercising its power. This is the generally accepted view in state constitutional law. Thus, in City of Fort Oglethorpe v. Boger, 480 S.E.2d 186 (Ga. 1997), the court permitted the state legislature to annex noncontiguous property to a city, even though a statute prohibited cities from themselves annexing noncontiguous areas.

In City of Chicago v. Holland, 795 N.E.2d 240 (Ill. 2003), the court addressed the validity of a statute that expanded the authority of the state's Auditor General. The state constitution permitted audits of "public funds of the state." The legislature authorized the Auditor General to exceed that limitation and undertake audits of the City of Chicago's operation of its airports. This statute admittedly exceeded the category of "public funds of the state." Although it held that audit of the City's airports was invalid on other grounds, the court upheld the legislative expansion of the Auditor General's authority. The court reasoned as follows:

> Our court regards the language in the constitution as a limitation upon the legislature's authority, not as a grant of power. Based on that view, our court has held that the General Assembly is free to enact any legislation that the constitution does not expressly prohibit. Where, however, the constitution specifically addresses the authority of constitutional officers or the power of the General Assembly to enact particular legislation, basic principles of constitutional and statutory interpretation still apply. The court must ascertain the plain and ordinary meaning of the relevant constitutional and statutory provisions in the constitutional and legislative contexts in which they appear. Constitutional officers may not act in contravention to the constitutional and statutory authority conferred on them. Action by a constitutional officer that is not authorized by the constitutional provisions creating his position and defining his powers or by legislation promulgated under authority of such constitutional provisions is impermissible.

795 N.E.2d at 246. Nevertheless, the court concluded that the legislative enactment was consistent with, rather than more expansive than, the constitutional authorization for the Auditor General to audit all funds appropriated or authorized by the legislature. For a broader interpretation of a constitutional limitation on the legislature, see Gerberding v. Munro, 949 P.2d 1366 (Wash. 1998), where the court found that express statements of qualifications for state office impliedly precluded the imposition of additional qualifications by a legislative act.

Notice how this principle of state constitutional law differs from its federal counterpart. The federal Constitution is considered a document of grant, so that the federal government cannot act with respect to the states unless it can find a specific textual referent, such as the Commerce Clause, that permits federal action. Is there a logical, rather than historical, reason for the different starting points? Recall from the Supreme Court's opinion in Garcia v. San Antonio Metropolitan Transit Authority, supra at page 53, that the Court believed the political process would save the states from undue interference by Congress since Congress was composed of representatives from the states. Couldn't the same argument be made with respect to state legislatures and the localities from which representatives are drawn? Conversely, if we fear that failures in the national political process will lead Congress to impose unwanted and improper burdens on the states, should we be less concerned that states could improperly burden their localities?

3. *State Constitutional Protection for Local Governments*. Article IX of the Nebraska Constitution was cited by the court in Dwyer v. Omaha–Douglas Public Building Commission, 195 N.W.2d 236, 245 (Neb. 1972), for the proposition that the legislature "probably cannot substantially destroy the counties by removing all or substantially all of their functions while merely respecting their territorial integrity." In fact, Article IX provides that counties cannot be reduced in area below a certain limit and cannot be subdivided without a vote of the electorate. If a court is willing to infer substantive restrictions on the legislature's ability to define county powers from constitutional provisions creating counties, should the court be similarly willing to infer from a constitutional tax limitation the existence of substantive restrictions on the legislature's ability to impose taxes? Was the court in *Dwyer* simply trying to salvage some vestige of an inherent right of local self-government?

4. *Local Option Legislation.* The fact that a legislature possesses plenary power does not require that the legislature use it. In some jurisdictions, the legislature has shared power with localities by passing substantive, "authorizing" legislation, the effect of which in a locality is contingent on local acceptance of the measure. On occasion, local option legislation has been considered to be an unconstitutional delegation of authority to localities. See Arlan's Department Stores, Inc. v. Kelley, 130 N.W.2d 892 (Mich. 1964). The contemporary position on the issue is stated in Shetters v. Alaska, 832 P.2d 181 (Alaska Ct. App. 1992):

> It is the state legislature that has enacted the local option laws; the local voters have no authority to pass state laws, but merely elect whether the state laws will take effect within their communities. Shetters does not argue that AS 04.11.496 or any other statute of the local option law was not constitutionally enacted by the legislature and subject to veto by the governor. The voters of Kiana could vote to adopt this option without submitting their election results to the state government for enactment. It is not an unconstitutional delegation of legislative power to grant local communities the choice of whether to adopt the state law.... The fact that the local community is not itself enacting a state law when it holds a local option election disposes of Shetters' other arguments that local options are unconstitutionally enacted. It does not violate due process for local voters to elect to adopt a state law regulating alcoholic beverages without the opportunity to specifically vote on all the provisions of the state law. Nor does the possibility that a community might frequently change its local option establish an unlimited delegation of legislative power.

Common uses of local options involve the imposition of local sales taxes and the decision of a municipality to allow gambling or, as in *Shetters*, the decision of a municipality to allow the sale or importation of alcoholic beverages. See, e.g., Outpost Travel Centers, L.L.C. v. Webster Parish Police Jury, 17 So. 3d 1045 (La. App. 2009); Dalton v. Fortner, 125 S.W.3d 316 (Ky. App. 2003); Edmonds Shopping Center Associates v. City of Edmonds, 71 P.3d 233 (Wash. App. 2003). The availability of local option legislation is occasionally incorporated into a constitutional provision. See, e.g., Ky. Const. Art. 61.

Why would a state legislature permit a locality an option on the implementation of state legislation? One explanation is consistent with the view that the legislature is acting in the best interests of localities, i.e., that it is responsive to the fact that different localities have different needs and a statewide rule may not best serve the interests of individual jurisdictions. An alternative, and less flattering, explanation suggests that the state legislature would use the local option when it does not want to confront a difficult or divisive issue that is likely to create animosity toward legislators regardless of the decision. By allocating decisionmaking responsibility to localities, the state legislature can deflect animosity without being accused of an unwillingness to address the issue at all. Given the situations in which local option legislation has been used, which of these explanations is more convincing?

5. *Explicit Grants of Legislative Power.* Notwithstanding the general claim that state constitutions are documents of limitation, several state constitutions contain explicit grants of power to the legislature. Why would these be necessary if the general proposition of plenary legislative power is correct? One explanation is that these grants are included to override judicial decisions denying the state the right to engage in a particular activity or to avert any ambiguity about the scope of state competence. See Robert F. Williams, State Constitutional Law Processes, 24 Wm. & Mary L. Rev. 169 (1983).

B. CONSTITUTIONAL RESTRICTIONS ON THE LEGISLATURE'S PLENARY POWER: SPECIAL COMMISSION PROHIBITIONS

The previous materials established that contemporary legal thought defines the relationship between the state and its political subdivisions as one in which the state can exercise plenary power over municipalities, subject to limits in the state constitution. Provisions of the state constitution may have either of two effects on this relationship. First, they may prevent the legislature from imposing unwanted burdens on localities. The existence of such provisions ensures a degree of local autonomy notwithstanding the general proposition that municipalities are subordinate bodies of the state. One may interpret these provisions as embodiments of a view that states should refrain from imposing on political subdivisions obligations to which they did not specifically consent and for which they should bear no burden greater than that of the rest of the state. By insulating localities from obligations to use their resources in ways dictated by the state, the constitution permits localities to pursue their constituents' conceptions of what the community should look like. Simultaneously, these provisions make it more difficult for state legislators to threaten localities with the imposition of additional burdens unless certain "rents" are paid to the legislators. But these same provisions might frustrate state attempts to control local activities that create adverse effects beyond local boundaries. Where this is the case, the provisions might best be explained under a public choice model that suggests that one group of municipalities has dominated the state legislature to avoid sharing what is properly treated as a statewide burden. For instance, some commentators argue that suburban legislators dominate the state legislature and prevent the imposition of burdens that would assist residents of central cities. See, e.g., Sheryll D. Cashin, Drifting Apart: How Wealth and Race Segregation are Reshaping the American Dream, 47 Vill. L. Rev. 595 (2002); James E. Ryan & Michael

Heise, The Political Economy of School Choice, 111 Yale L.J. 2043 (2002). Since either of these explanations might be possible in many settings, the way in which a court interprets a constitutional restriction may depend on whether the court believes that the provision reflects a public interest, as opposed to a public choice perspective.

Alternatively, these provisions may prevent the legislature from conferring entitlements on certain localities. For instance, in Hurd v. City of Buffalo, 343 N.Y.S.2d 950 (N.Y. App. Div. 1973), aff'd, 311 N.E.2d 504 (N.Y. 1974), the legislature passed a statute declaring that pension payments made by certain financially distressed cities, including Buffalo, had a useful life of more than one year. The effect of the statute was to exclude these payments from the constitutional limit on real property taxes, so that Buffalo was able to impose $17.7 million more in real property taxes than it otherwise would have been allowed. The court held that the legislation violated the constitutional provision on the theory that a contrary holding would justify a similar argument for almost all of the city's expenditures, with the result that "the constitutional restriction would be meaningless." At first glance, prohibitions on the grant of benefits might seem difficult to justify. If a locality seeks a benefit or release from an obligation, why would a legislature composed primarily of representatives from other localities not be enabled to grant it? While local exercise of a power might create some externalities, legislative passage of the measure suggests a judgment that statewide benefits outweighed total costs. One response may be that every burden can be recast as a benefit, so that allowing legislatures to confer benefits more freely than burdens would invite legislative machinations. For instance, is relief from a constitutional tax limitation a benefit conferred on the locality, because it can fund projects that otherwise would have been unavailable, or a burden, because local residents are now subject to higher tax rates? See, e.g., Dwyer v. Omaha–Douglas Public Building Commission, 195 N.W.2d 236 (Neb. 1972). This rationale suggests that the legislature may not be acting in the interests of the locality, even though the legislative intervention appears to be beneficial.

Another justification for limiting the legislative conferral of benefits would assume that the legislature is, in fact, acting at the behest of local officials, but that those officials are not acting in the interest of their constituents. Instead, those officials may be trying to attain benefits that advance their own agenda, such as appealing to particular interest groups, but that disserve the public at large. This might be the case where the burden falls disproportionately on unrepresented or underrepresented constituents. For instance, constitutional restrictions might be appropriate where short-term benefits are offset by long-term costs, but where future residents who will have to bear those costs cannot represent their interests.

Finally, constitutional limits on legislative conferral of benefits might be appropriate where the local officials accurately represent the preferences of their constituents, but there is a paternalistic reason not to permit localities to exercise the power. On this view, constitutional provisions may be pre-commitment devices by which constituents bind themselves not to engage in certain activities, even if they later change their minds. Return, for example, to the case of the constitutional tax limitation. Taxpayers may believe that a current expenditure is worth incurring, even though it requires exceeding the tax limits, because the expenditure will generate sufficient revenues in the future that the long-term effects of tax increases will be minimal. Or, the same taxpayers may simply discount by too much the future cost of a desired good or service, and hence incur an obligation with insufficient attention to the need to pay for it when the tax bill comes due. (We will discuss this at greater length when we reach the issue of constitutional debt limitations.) In these cases, constitutional provisions protect local residents from themselves by preventing legislators from acceding to ill-considered preferences.

As you read the following materials, think about which explanation for the constitutional provision at issue makes sense. Should the justification for the provision affect the judicial interpretation of its scope? Should courts be more willing to intervene in legislative decisions where constitutional provisions appear to protect localities from outside interference than where provisions appear to protect localities from their own officials, since constituents have a form of political redress against their own officials?

PROBLEM IV

The city of Putnam is one of the largest municipalities in the state. It has long been more tolerant of "adult" activities than other municipalities in the state. Parts of the city have been zoned for "adult entertainment," and there has been some feeling in other parts of the state that city officials have been overly tolerant of illicit prostitution in these areas. The legislature has recently enacted legislation creating a bureau of public morals within any city that has a population in excess of 100,000 (of which Putnam is one). The bureau is charged with investigating and acting on questions and conditions arising from prostitution in each city. The law provides that each bureau is to have a board of seven directors appointed by the mayor and confirmed by the council of the city. The directors are subject to removal by the mayor and are required to elect one of their members to serve as superintendent of the bureau. The enabling legislation grants the bureau of each city the authority to enforce laws against prostitution and prosecute violations, and therefore permits each bureau to require assignment of police officers from the regular police force of the city. The city's director of public safety must comply with the requisition, but has discretion in approving the individual officers in the detail.

The Putnam city council has enacted an ordinance to appropriate $45,000 to pay the salary of the superintendent of the bureau of public morals in the city of Putnam. Warren, a taxpayer residing in Putnam, has brought an action to enjoin the city controller from paying any part of the appropriation on the grounds that the bureau of public morals violates the state constitution. A provision of that document states that "The General Assembly shall not delegate to any special commission any power to perform any municipal function whatever." You serve as city attorney for Putnam. What attacks do you anticipate against the ordinance and statute? How will you respond? See Moll v. Morrow, 98 A. 650 (Pa. 1916).

Specht v. City of Sioux Falls

526 N.W.2d 727 (S.D. 1995).

■ AMUNDSON, JUSTICE.

City of Sioux Falls appeals the trial court's peremptory writ of prohibition and declaratory judgment holding that SDCL ch. 34–11B is unconstitutional. We affirm.

FACTS

The 1992 South Dakota Legislature enacted SDCL ch. 34–11B authorizing municipalities to establish a regional emergency medical services authority (EMS authority). After public hearings, the Sioux Falls City Commission (Commission) passed Resolution 408–92 creating the Sioux Falls Regional Emergency Medical Services Authority (SFREMSA). On January 4, 1993, Commission appointed commissioners to SFREMSA and, soon thereafter, it was issued a certificate of incorporation from the South Dakota Secretary of State. On July 19, 1993, Commission passed Resolution 241–93 authorizing SFREMSA to borrow funds.

On July 30, 1993, Michael Specht and the Sioux Falls Fire Fighters Association (Specht) served the City of Sioux Falls (City) with an alternative writ of prohibition challenging Resolution 241–93. At that time, City was also served with an application for writ of prohibition alleging, among other things, that SDCL ch. 34–11B was unconstitutional....

Specht challenged SFREMSA and SDCL ch. 34–11B which authorized it under Article III, § 26 and § 1, of the South Dakota Constitution.[1] Specht argued SFREMSA and its enabling statutory scheme (SDCL ch. 34–11B) violates Article III, § 26, because it creates a special commission whose powers, defined by SDCL ch. 34–11B, involve an improper delegation of municipal functions. After considering written and oral arguments, the trial court agreed. Accordingly, the trial court issued a peremptory writ of prohibition and independently ruled SDCL 34–11B unconstitutional. City appeals....

City claims the trial court incorrectly declared SDCL ch. 34–11B unconstitutional. City has four grounds for its argument, namely: (1) SFREMSA is not engaging in a "municipal function" as prohibited by Article III, § 26; (2) SFREMSA is not a "special commission"; (3) SFREM-

---

1. S.D. Const. art. III, § 26, provides:

The legislature shall not delegate to any special commission, private corporation or association, any power to make, supervise, or interfere with any municipal improvement, money, property, effects, whether held in trust or otherwise, or levy taxes, or to select a capital site, or to perform any municipal functions whatever.

SA is subject to local control and oversight; and (4) SFREMSA's power to tax is constitutional. These arguments will be addressed in order....

A. *Is SFREMSA engaging in a "municipal function"? ...*

This court has never ruled what constitutes a nondelegable "municipal function" under Article III, § 26. Here, the trial court specifically found that "municipalities are better able to govern ambulance and emergency medical services because of the wide diversity between communities and ... resources within [those] communities." The trial court found that municipalities have historically performed and are better able to perform ambulance and emergency medical service. We agree. The trial court also observed that although oversight and regulation of ambulance service and prehospital emergency care may affect some interests of people beyond the boundaries of Sioux Falls, its main concern is a city-wide function protecting the local interest only.

Based on these findings, the trial court concluded that SFREMSA was engaged in a municipal function in violation of Article III, § 26. Although City claims that the trial court's findings are erroneous and SFREMSA is not engaged in a municipal function, it has not designated which of the trial court's findings, if any, are clearly erroneous. Instead, City argues that, since the statutes allow more than one municipality to participate in an EMS authority, it is not a municipal function. This argument rings hollow. The fact that the statutory scheme allows only municipal corporations to participate in such EMS authorities supports the trial court's conclusion that this is a municipal function.[8]

City further alleges that SFREMSA is not engaged in a municipal function because the state issues licenses to EMS authorities, like it does to physicians, surgeons, practitioners of healing arts, physicians' assistants, advanced life support personnel, registered and practical nurses, medical assistants, respiratory care practitioners, ambulances, and hospitals. We are not persuaded by such argument. Were we to adopt City's position, the only true "municipal function" would be one that is independent of state license or regulation. Just because people subject to these regulations are required to obtain licenses from the state does not render the function nonmunicipal. Therefore, we affirm the trial court's holding that SFREMSA is engaged in a municipal function.

B. *SFREMSA is a "special commission" prohibited by Article III, § 26.*

The trial court found that SFREMSA was a special commission in conflict with Article III, § 26. City argues that this is erroneous.

To support its position, City cites Tribe v. Salt Lake City Corporation, 540 P.2d 499, 502–503 (Utah 1975), where the Utah Supreme Court defined a special commission as "some body or group separate and distinct

---

8. SDCL 34–11B–2 allows only municipal corporations with populations of fifty thousand or more to create EMS authorities. At the time of enacting SDCL ch. 34–11B, only two communities in South Dakota had a population of more than fifty thousand and these communities are more than three hundred miles apart.

from municipal government." City's reliance on this case is misplaced. SDCL ch. 34–11B defines an EMS authority as "an *independent* public body." (Emphasis added.) SFREMSA by statute, and City's definition of "special commission," are one and the same. Therefore this argument lacks merit.

Further, as noted by the trial court, the effect was that the legislature was creating a special commission; it did not appoint the commission, but it defined its powers. Unfortunately, the legislation does not provide specific standards to guide the EMS authority in the broad exercise of its power.

C. The SFREMSA is not subject to local control or oversight.

As the trial court found, the most significant constitutional problem with the legislation "is the extent to which [it] will intrude upon the ability of the [municipality's citizens] to control through their elected officials the substantive policies that affect them uniquely."

City also asserts the trial court erred in finding SFREMSA not subject to local control, asserting that it is accountable because municipal corporations are not required to create an EMS authority. This argument is confusing. Whether or not a community creates an EMS authority is irrelevant and completely distinct from whether SFREMSA is accountable for its actions. We agree this entity is optional, but must examine its amenability to local control after it has been created. Our review indicates that once commissioned, the SFREMSA is beyond the control or supervision of any outside source.

City argues that SFREMSA is accountable to the citizens because the commissioners of the authority are appointed by the City Commission for a definite term. This argument is fatally flawed however, because SDCL ch. 34–11B has no provision for removing commissioners. Theoretically, commissioners can remain in their appointed positions forever. The trial court found that City had no power to remove the commissioners once appointed, or to control the taxing authority of those commissioners once the taxing authority had been granted. City has not effectively disputed this finding.

Another example of Commission's power is that its authority cannot be decreased unless all the commissioners consent to same in conjunction with the city commissioners. SDCL 34–11B–12. Furthermore, Commission's authority to act cannot be diminished if "the authority has any bonds outstanding ... unless one hundred percent of the holders of the bonds consent in writing." Id. Related to this issue, Specht also points out that SDCL 34–11B–31 allows SFREMSA to sell bonds without an election. This ability to unilaterally sell municipal bonds contradicts SDCL 6–8B–2, which requires a 60 percent majority vote in favor of issuance, before a public body may so act. By dispensing with the election requirement, the public has no control over this bonding authority.

Additionally, City is not free to withdraw from SFREMSA if it is in debt; yet SFREMSA is permitted to borrow money for any of its purposes, without any independent supervision or permission. SDCL 34–11B–12 &

31. Consequently, City is subject to SFREMSA's unsupervised, unaccountable financial practices.

City, in reality, has little or no control over the SFREMSA after its creation. From that point on, SFREMSA has the statutory authority to become a self-propelled, unaccountable, bureaucratic freight train. The trial court did not err in finding improper control of the organization....

The trial court's judgment is affirmed in all respects, since Specht proved beyond a reasonable doubt that the statute in question violated Article III, 26, of the South Dakota Constitution.

■ MILLER, C.J., SABERS, J., and WUEST and HENDERSON, RETIRED JUSTICES, concur.

NOTES

1. *Origins and Objectives of "Ripper Clauses."* Constitutional prohibitions on the creation of special commissions to act in the area of municipal affairs, often called "ripper clauses," followed perceived legislative "abuses" of municipal autonomy in the late nineteenth century. These included state replacement of municipal police departments, fire departments, park commissions, and rapid transit commissions with state entities, as well as legislative imposition of local taxes to pay for these bodies. On one account, these enactments were perceived as a burden placed on cities by a legislature dominated by representatives of rural areas. Thus, one would imagine that these prohibitions would have been favored by city officials, since they prevent the state from decreasing local autonomy. Occasionally, however, the prohibited commissions were created at the behest of a local interest group concerned about its ability to retain political power in the face of an influx of immigrants to urban areas. In a thorough study of the clauses, David Porter suggests that commissions were created to control the phenomenon "that many eastern cities were being challenged by immigrant ethnic groups which came to outnumber the native Protestants. This was the case in Boston after 1890. Reluctant to relinquish their dominant position, the natives sought to control the city from the statehouse. Boston's police commissioner became a gubernatorial appointee, and state-controlled licensing and finance boards were created." David O. Porter, The Ripper Clause in State Constitutional Law: An Early Urban Experiment—Part I, 1969 Utah L. Rev. 287, 300. On other accounts, however, these clauses were inserted at the behest of "good government" groups concerned about high levels of corruption in city government. These groups appealed to their local delegations in the state legislature to introduce bills that authorized state commissions to conduct local functions. See Jon C. Teaford, The Unheralded Triumph: City Government in America, 1870–1900 83–102 (1984). If the legislature was simply deferring to the local delegations, it is more difficult to classify these commissions as evidence of the state's abuse of its plenary authority over localities. Of course, these two stories are not necessarily inconsistent; one person's corruption may be another person's normal politics. Are there legitimate reasons why a state might intervene to shift authority over a particular subject matter from localities to the state? If so, how should a court determine whether there has been a violation of a clause prohibiting legislative appointment of a "commission"? Porter's study of the history and effect of these clauses concludes that their judicial construction encompasses three basic principles:

> (1) the legislature cannot delegate legislative power unless such power is delegated to an elected municipal body; (2) the legislature may not delegate the taxing power except to such an elective body on the ground that "taxation without representation is tyranny"; and (3) local governments are inherently better suited than the state legislature to determine the scope and depth of their activities and services.

David O. Porter, The Ripper Clause in State Constitutional Law: An Early Urban Experiment—Part II, 1969 Utah L. Rev. 450, 481. See also David O. Porter, The Ripper Clause in State Constitutional Law: An Early Urban Experiment—Part I, 1969 Utah L. Rev. 287.

If the state intervened only to address matters that affected nonresidents of the regulated locality, why wouldn't the special commission be appropriate? If localities are permitted to engage in activities that adversely affect nonresidents, is there less "tyranny" than exists where nonresidents are entitled to impose taxes on residents? Could the constitutional provisions serve as evidence that the localities had captured the constitution-making process to obtain an advantage that they could not obtain through the state legislature?

2. *Questions on* Specht. The constitutional prohibition on special commissions reinvests localities with some right of local self-government with which the legislature cannot interfere. Thus, it limits the plenary power of the state as articulated in *Shelby County*. The prohibition necessarily implicates the allocation of government power between the state and the locality. But one would imagine that the question of who holds power is a matter of concern only where one entity (e.g., the state) wants the locality to engage in an activity that the other entity (e.g., the locality) resists. Note that in *Specht*, the legislature did not create an authority, but only permitted the city to create one. Sioux Falls implemented the state law by passing a resolution that created the SFREMSA. If the constitutional prohibition was intended to protect localities from state interference, why isn't the requirement that the locality implement the law in this manner sufficient protection for local autonomy? Are there reasons why Sioux Falls might have acted even if it believed that creation of the authority was a threat to its capacity for self-government?

3. In Tribe v. Salt Lake City Corporation, 540 P.2d 499 (Utah 1975), plaintiffs challenged the constitutionality of the Redevelopment Agency of Salt Lake City, which had been created pursuant to the Utah Neighborhood Development Act. Under the Act, the Board of Commissioners of Salt Lake City was also to serve as the Redevelopment Agency of the city. (Any conflict of interest here?) The city approved a plan to have the agency redevelop a downtown area through the issuance of bonds. The bonds were to be paid from revenue generated by the commercial enterprises that would occupy the "redeveloped" area. The enabling legislation was enacted by the state legislature to deal with what the court considered the "statewide" problem of blight. All the agency's activities were to be located in the city. To a claim that the agency constituted a special commission, barred by the state constitution, the court replied:

> It appears clear that the agency here concerned is a quasi-municipal corporation, and not a special commission. A quasi-municipal corporation has been defined as a public agency created by the legislature to aid the state in some public work for the general welfare, other than to perform as another community government. A municipal corporation is a body politic and corporate, created to administer the internal concerns of the district embraced within its corporate limits, in matters peculiar to such place and not common to the state at large. A special commission is some body or group separate and distinct from municipal government. Such a commission is not offensive to the constitution by its creation, but only when such a commission is delegated powers which intrude into areas of purely municipal concern.
>
> The success of plaintiff's challenges depends upon the character of the agency created by the legislature. If the legislative enactment authorizes the performance of activities, which qualify as a function appropriately performed by a state agency, the constitutional interdiction of Article VI, Section 28, is not applicable. This section applies only to municipal functions, the performance of which are constitutionally limited to the units of local government. The problem of "urban blight" we recognize as one of statewide concern, and not merely a local or municipal problem. The agency for that reason does not run counter to Article VI, Section 28. The agency is a quasi-municipal corporation, a public agency created for beneficial and necessary public purposes. It is not a true municipal corporation, having power of local government, but an agency of the state designed for state purposes. Since it is a quasi-municipal corporation, formed for public purposes, it is within the discretion of the legislature to grant it any powers, not expressly prohibited by the constitution, to further such purposes, including the power of taxation. The public purposes for which the agency is organized inures to the benefit of the public generally, therefore the public may be charged for such benefits through general taxation. The agency is separate and apart from the city government, and yet is administered by a legislative body responsible to the local electorate.

540 P.2d at 502–503. Does the state/municipal distinction developed in *Tribe* explain the different results in that case and *Specht*? The proposed development was to occur entirely within the downtown area of Salt Lake City. To characterize this as a statewide concern, one would have to believe that urban blight in that area had substantial adverse consequences beyond the city's boundaries. Would the services at issue in *Specht* be less likely to be contained within the jurisdictional boundaries of Sioux Falls?

Even if one is skeptical of the state/municipal distinction, there may be a justification for the different results in *Tribe* and *Specht*. The majority opinions in both cases arguably seek to increase the scope of local autonomy with which the state cannot interfere and hence recapture for localities some of what is surrendered through abrogation of an inherent right of local self-government. The decision in *Specht* does this directly by invalidating a state entity that arguably could exercise discretion on behalf of a city. But the legislation in *Tribe* may also enhance city power because it effectively increased the bonding power of Salt Lake City and thus enhanced its ability to perform municipal functions preferred by city residents. Recall that agency officials also served as city officials, so it was unlikely that the agency would undertake projects that were unpopular with residents. Given the history of the ripper clause, does it make sense to distinguish between state actions that enhance and those that detract from municipal power? The Pennsylvania Supreme Court in Local 22, Philadelphia Fire Fighters' Union v. Commonwealth, 613 A.2d 522 (Pa. 1992), appeared to be making this distinction when it upheld the state's Intergovernmental Cooperation Authority Act against a special commission challenge. The Act created a special agency, composed of financial experts, to assist cities in financial planning and obtaining access to capital markets. The agency offered help to cities that agreed to accept certain financial restraints. The court rejected the claim that the agency constituted a special commission, concluding that the agency could only enter agreements with cities that voluntarily requested assistance. Thus, "the authority cannot impose its imperial will upon a hapless city." Id. at 526. Presumably, a city would only request assistance when doing so would not decrease its political or financial position.

C. CONSTITUTIONAL RESTRICTIONS ON THE LEGISLATURE'S PLENARY POWER: SPECIAL LEGISLATION PROHIBITIONS

PROBLEM V

The Dyspepsia Improvement District has been created in a state the constitution of which bars the enactment of special laws. The state legislature has enacted a law that permits any first-class city in the state that has a population in excess of 250,000 to create a local improvement district to construct internal improvements within the municipality. One provision of the law allows the local improvement district to issue bonds. Another provision permits the local improvement district to impose taxes and fees to pay for the improvements it constructs. The legislation, however, permits such cities to create local improvement districts only in areas with a population of less than 4,000 persons and only where the district is surrounded by an area that contains, within a three-mile radius of the district's boundaries, a population at least seven times as large as that of the district itself.

The legislature has previously allowed localities to form other types of districts and has itself created special districts to perform certain governmental functions. These districts have traditionally been granted the right to issue bonds to finance their objectives and have been authorized to impose fees or service charges to pay the bonds. No other form of district, however, has been granted the power to tax.

The city of Dyspepsia, which is a first-class city and which has a population in excess of 250,000, created the Dyspepsia Improvement District last year. It is the only local improvement district that has been formed in the state. The current population that resides within the district is 2,500. The population of the area within the surrounding three-mile radius exceeds 20,000. The District now seeks to issue bonds, the proceeds of which will be used to construct a parking lot. Drivers would be able to use the parking lot without charge. The bonds will be paid for by the imposition of a tax on all residents and businesses in the District.

Oxnard, a resident of the District, has filed an action to enjoin issuance of the bonds on the grounds that the authorizing legislation constitutes a special law. What result? Would it make a difference if there is no other first-class city in the state with a population in excess of 250,000? Would it make a difference if there existed other first-class cities with the requisite population, but none that contained an area in need of improvements with a population of less than 4,000 that was surrounded by a population at least seven times as large within a three-mile radius?

PROBLEM VI

The General Assembly has enacted an "Education Empowerment Act" (the "Act") to improve education in the State. The Act requires the State Department of Education to maintain a list of school districts with a history of low test performance. School districts on the list receive state aid and authority to replace district administrative personnel, establish charter schools, and adjust the normal rules for operation of schools within the district. At the same time, the Department of Education plays a more significant role in the operation of school districts on the list than it does with respect to other school districts. If the initial remedial programs do not sufficiently improve the performance of a school district on the list for a three-year period, the Act requires the Department of Education to assume control of the district through creation of an education "empowerment district" that replaces the local school board.

The Act creates one exception to this scheme. Section 17 of the Act provides:

> For a school district of the second class [state legislation frequently classifies municipalities by population—EDS.] which has a history of extraordinarily low test performance, which is coterminous with a city of the third class that has opted to be governed by a mayor-council form of government and which has a population in excess of forty-five thousand, the Secretary of Education shall waive the inclusion of the school district on the education empowerment list and immediately certify the school district as an education empowerment district. The mayor of the city in which the district is located shall appoint a Board of Control to consist of five members of the community who serve at the mayor's pleasure, and exercises essentially the same powers as a Board of Control appointed by the Secretary. The mayor shall also appoint a school district empowerment team to develop a district improvement plan. A district certified under this provision shall be governed by the mayor's Board of Control

for at least five years. No school district shall be certified under this section later than December 31, 2008.

The effect of this provision is to allow immediate transfer of control of a qualifying school district from the board of education to the mayor of the city in which the school district is located.

At the current time, only the Harrisburg School District, located in the City of Harrisburg, qualifies for treatment under Section 17. The mayor of Harrisburg has appointed a board of the Harrisburg Empowerment District to exercise authority over the City's schools. The Board of Education of the Harrisburg School District now seeks to enjoin the creation of the Harrisburg Empowerment District. It claims that establishment of the District violates Article IV of the State Constitution, which provides "The General Assembly shall pass no local or special law regulating the affairs of counties, cities, townships, wards, boroughs or school districts."

Does Section 17 of the Act violate Article IV of the Constitution? Does Section 17 advantage or disadvantage the City of Harrisburg relative to all other jurisdictions in the State? See Harrisburg School District v. Zogby, 828 A.2d 1079 (Pa. 2003).

Lyman H. Cloe & Sumner Marcus, Special and Local Legislation

24 Ky. L.J. 351, 375–381 (1936).

With the exception of four New England states the constitutions of all others contain restrictions upon local and special legislation. Uniformity in such provisions is lacking. They range in style and effect from these which appear to be no more than a declaration of policy or procedural requirement to the inclusive type which not only places an absolute prohibition on such legislation in certain named instances, but in all other cases where a general law can be made applicable....

Regardless of the form of the constitutional provision in issue, as the purpose of the prohibition was to secure uniformity, the problem is presented in each case whether the statute in question is general or special, that is, whether there has been a reasonable classification of its objects.

There is no serious conflict between the courts in the statement of the law whereby general acts are separated from local and special. A law is general when the persons or things upon which it operates are reasonably classified. It may operate only within a single place or apply to but few persons or things. Universality is immaterial so long as those affected are reasonably different from those excluded and for the purpose of the act there is a logical basis for treating them in a different manner. When the operation of the law is limited by the presence or absence of features which are inconsequential to the object of the statute—which creates an artificial class of those affected—it is special or local. No two things are exactly identical and the constitutional provisions are not to be avoided by basing the operation of a law upon unimportant distinctions. Thus, a statute was held special which prohibited the establishment of a cemetery within one mile of a city of the first class, the drainage from which emptied into a stream from which the water supply was obtained. The features named have no relation to the establishment of a cemetery within a mile of a city.

As the distinctions which are drawn must relate to the purpose of the statute, a classification for one purpose may be entirely irrelevant for another....

Patently these rules are not difficult. Their inadequacy becomes evident only when we turn to the individual case for an examination of the purpose of the law and the distinctions which are drawn and ask whether there are those outside its operation sufficiently similar to those included so that it is arbitrary to treat them in a different manner.

In making this decision it has been suggested that the legislature has broad discretion in establishing a class, that it is not necessary for the court to understand all of the distinctions. In some instances it has been said that inquiry will be made as to the "good faith" of the legislature or that the court will consider whether the classification creates greater uniformity or diversity in the existing law.

In practice these "principles" appear to be no more than bolstering statements; they are used when in accord with the court's conclusion and otherwise ignored. In many of the cases it does not appear that the court has granted any discretion to the legislature. In Indiana a law regulating the use of trade-marked bottles, syphons, cans, kegs, barrels, hogsheads, and other enclosures made of glass, metal and wood was held to be special because it did not include rubber, earthenware, and pasteboard enclosures.

The "good faith" of the legislature is a nebulous thing. Certainly the courts do not mean that a law otherwise general is special because its enactment was the result of a desire to provide for a particular situation. There are cases where the court has "felt" that the legislature was attempting to take advantage of a technicality, but there is no universal rule that a thing which cannot be accomplished by one method may not be performed in another if the latter is valid....

In deciding the reasonableness of the selection of persons or things it has been often suggested that the classification should be "open," that theoretically others should be able to enjoy the benefits of the law by attaining the prescribed qualifications. Ordinarily "closed" classes occur where the differentiation is according to past events, as an auto license act which distinguished between present owners and subsequent purchasers. Many municipal statutes have been held special which classified according to population at a prior time. However, it does not appear to be an infallible rule that classification by past events renders a class special. A statute applying to public officers was held general though exempting present incumbents.

The "open" class rule has been extended to situations where the time for the operation of the law was so restricted that in practical effect only those would be able to comply who then possessed the described qualifications. The remote possibility of others entering an "open" class has been considered in holding it special, but ordinarily statutes are held general although applying only to cities with a large population and there is small prospect of any other city reaching the high population requirement.

The courts have frowned upon classifications which employ more than one distinguishing feature. Each additional element rapidly narrows the present class and makes the possibility of others qualifying extremely remote; the effect is the same as though one object was specified. For example, laws have been held special which applied to cities of a certain class in counties of a certain population. However, recently a statute was held general which applied to counties of a population between 250,000 and 400,000 and having three or more cities of over 50,000. . . .

Municipalities are ordinarily classified according to population. Where the maximum and minimum population requirements present too narrow a figure the class is held special, but it is impossible to name a required amount of variance. In Tennessee it has been held that for the purpose of legislation allowing dogs to run at large counties may be classified as those between 29,946 and 29,975. In Indiana it was held that a variation of 8,000 in the population of counties for the purpose of building a war memorial was too narrow.

Usually population is determined according to the last preceding federal census, but the legislature may specify some other means which will give an accurate result, though whatever means is selected must be consistently used.

Geographic features of a municipality are often specified as a basis of distinction, and while these are often tantamount to a "closed" class, it has been held that for the purpose of sewage disposal cities may be distinguished according to their location on streams which constitute a natural outlet and that for the purpose of fire protection counties may be classed according to their acreage of timber. Still other municipal classifications have been made according to assessed valuation, the issuance of bonds, duties of officers, and the miles of roads.

NOTES

1. *Open Classification*. The "openness" requirement is best understood as a means to ensure that the legislature is addressing a problem intrinsic to any jurisdiction that has the characteristics described in the legislation, rather than simply trying to impose a burden or confer a benefit on a particular jurisdiction. For instance, classifications based on population might make sense for legislation concerning traffic control. Larger localities are more likely to have issues concerning traffic that are not shared with smaller localities. The Oklahoma Supreme Court concluded that larger localities might have different organizational structures and resources for dealing with their employees than small localities, so that a statute allowing collective bargaining in cities with a population greater than 35,000 was not invalid. City of Enid v. Public Employees Relations Board, 133 P.3d 281

(Okla. 2006). Even if the classification only describes one locality at the time it is enacted, it is likely that other localities will suffer the same traffic problems as their populations grow so that they fit the statutory classification.

Nevertheless, a legislature could attempt to disguise its efforts to address a single locality by drafting the legislation in terms that are general but that, in fact, do not and could not easily apply to more than one jurisdiction. If localities cannot enter and exit the statutory classification, the "openness" requirement is defeated. Perhaps the highwater mark of such efforts can be found in City of Fort Worth v. Bobbitt, 36 S.W.2d 470 (1931). In that case, the Texas legislature had passed a law permitting cities that satisfied certain requirements to issue certain forms of indebtedness free from legal limitations that would otherwise apply. The cities covered by the legislation included those "having not less than 106,000 and not more than 110,000 inhabitants, according to the United States Census of 1920." The legislation was enacted in 1930. Only the city of Fort Worth satisfied the population requirements under the 1920 Census. Since the time to satisfy those requirements was locked into a time period that had already passed, it was impossible for any other city ever to fall within the statutory permission. The court invalidated the statute. The court concluded that "this act is confined in its application to the city of Ft. Worth only, just as clearly, and just as effectively, as if the stipulation with reference to population had been omitted and the name 'Ft. Worth' written therein in its stead."

The argument that a classification by population was intended to address a problem unique to municipalities within the classification, rather than to apply only to particular localities, seems weaker as the relevant population range becomes smaller. In Hixson v. Burson, 43 N.E. 1000 (Ohio 1896), the court considered legislation that authorized road construction in counties that, by the last federal census or any subsequent census, had a population between 35,150 and 35,200. Not surprisingly, this restriction made the Act applicable to a single jurisdiction. The court invalidated the Act as special legislation. For a general discussion, see John M. Winters, Classification of Municipalities, 57 Nw. U. L. Rev. 279 (1962).

2. *Presumption Against Finding Special Legislation.* Given the ambiguity of the test for special legislation, with what presumption should a court begin and how may a court determine whether that presumption has been rebutted? Usually, of course, courts presume that the legislature has acted reasonably. Judicial willingness to rebut this presumption may correlate with the specificity of the legislation at issue, since specificity suggests that legislative classifications are responses to very local situations rather than to problems of a general class of municipalities. In Owen v. Dalton, 757 S.W.2d 921 (Ark. 1988), the Arkansas Supreme Court considered an ordinance that altered the method in which the City of Little Rock elected its board of directors. The ordinance was authorized by a statute that mandated or authorized particular forms of government and election for a variety of local governments. The court looked on the authorizing legislation with suspicion:

> The Act carves out so many exceptions that its general purpose has become an empty statement. First, all cities with a population of less than 15,000 are excluded; that means most cities in Arkansas. The Act is then made applicable to all cities between 15,000 and 15,999, but not to cities with populations between 16,000 and 16,700. Cities located in counties with less than 34,000 people are excluded, as are cities whose form of government was established pursuant to Act 498 of 1973. As it stands after the amendment in 1987, two cities for certain, Little Rock and Hot Springs, with a city manager form of government and populations of over 30,000 have the option of being exempt from the Act or passing an ordinance like the one in question.

757 S.W.2d at 922–923. The court struck down the legislation as a violation of the state constitutional prohibition on special or local legislation.

Some courts, however, appear to go to substantial lengths to uphold legislation against a challenge as a special law. In Bopp v. Spainhower, 519 S.W.2d 281 (Mo. 1975), the court upheld a law that authorized enactment of a sales tax by any city not within a county, any first class county not containing a city with a population of over 400,000, and any city with a population greater than 400,000 and situated within a county. Plaintiff contended that there existed only one first class county that did not contain a city of over 400,000. The next smallest county contained a city, Kansas City, with a population in excess of 500,000. Plaintiff argued that, since the law required that the tax be imposed within the succeeding six and one-half months, the legislation was special. The court disagreed: "In the six and one-half months that elapsed between the effective date of this Act and January 1, 1974, it was possible, though concededly not likely, that said population [of Kansas City] could have been reduced to less than 400,000. This could have occurred by reason of war or an extensive fire or an epidemic of serious proportions or other unforeseen disaster." 519 S.W.2d at 285.

The Missouri Supreme Court seems to have changed its approach. In Tillis v. City of Branson, 945 S.W.2d 447 (Mo. 1997), plaintiffs challenged the validity of state legislation that enabled the city to enact a municipal tourism tax. The statute authorized the tax to be imposed by "any municipality of the fourth classification with a population of more than three thousand inhabitants but less than five thousand inhabitants and with more than five thousand hotel and motel rooms inside the municipal limits and which is located in a county that borders the state of Arkansas." 945 S.W.2d at 448. The description applied only to the city of Branson. The Missouri court determined that special laws were presumed unconstitutional, and thus the party defending the legislation bore the burden of proving validity. While the statute's classification based on population could be considered open, the court found the classifications based on geography (the location in counties bordering Arkansas) involved an immutable characteristic and therefore constituted a facially special law. Because the city did not meet its burden of demonstrating substantial justification for the geographical classification, the court found that the presumption of invalidity stood.

Maple Run at Austin Municipal Utility Dist. v. Monaghan

931 S.W.2d 941 (Tex. 1996).

■ PHILLIPS, CHIEF JUSTICE.

Section 43.082 of the Texas Local Government Code, enacted in 1995 and expiring on the last day of 1996, purportedly authorizes certain municipal utility districts lying within a municipality's extraterritorial jurisdiction to dissolve, requiring the affected municipality to take ownership of the district's assets and assume its debts. Because of extremely specific requirements about the amount and character of outstanding debt and other factors, Maple Run at Austin Municipal Utility District is the only district in the state qualifying for the special treatment under section 43.082. The parties stipulate to this fact, and they further stipulate that the Legislature intended for the statute to apply only to this district. In this direct appeal, we must decide whether section 43.082 violates the Texas Constitution. The trial court invalidated the statute and enjoined its enforcement. Because we hold that section 43.082 is an invalid local law under Article III, Section 56, we affirm the judgment of the trial court.

I

Maple Run at Austin Municipal Utility District (hereinafter "Maple Run" or "the District") was formed in 1983 in an area south of the City of Austin to provide utility service to the area's residents. The District, created under Chapter 54 of the Texas Water Code, is authorized to, among other things, construct and operate plants and facilities for supplying water and wastewater services. See Tex. Water Code § 54.201. The District is a political subdivision of the state, with the power to incur bonded indebtedness and levy ad valorem taxes. See Tex. Water Code §§ 54.501, 54.601.

Because Maple Run lies within the City of Austin's extraterritorial jurisdiction, the Maple Run landowners were required under section 54.016 of the Texas Water Code to obtain consent from the City to create the district. In connection with the City's grant of consent, the District and the City entered into a written agreement concerning the creation and operation of the District (the "Consent Agreement"). This agreement recognizes that the District lies within the City's extraterritorial jurisdiction, and that its area "is scheduled for annexation by the City in accordance with the Annexation Plan of the City." It further requires all parties to "use their best efforts to bring about the conclusion of [the annexation] process...."

The Consent Agreement also provides that, upon annexation, the District will dissolve and the City will immediately take title to the District's assets and assume its liabilities. The District is required to obtain the City's prior approval as to the amount, terms, and conditions of all bonds issued by the District, and the City has the right to approve all plans and specifications for construction of the District's facilities. The agreement also mandates that real estate development in the District comply with the City's land use ordinances.

The District subsequently issued $20,900,000 in "contract revenue bonds," repayable out of revenues from the District's utility operations. See Tex. Water Code § 54.503(2). The District also issued $3,750,000 in "combination tax and revenue bonds," repayable out of a combination of ad valorem taxes and revenues. Id. at § 54.503(3). All facilities for which the District issued its bonds have been constructed. Based on its projected use of the District facilities, the City agreed to bear 84.83 percent of the debt service for the contract revenue bonds. The City assumed no liability, prior to annexation, for the remaining part of the contract revenue bonds, or any part of the combination tax and revenue bonds.

Real estate development did not occur in Maple Run as expected. The District initially anticipated that as many as 2,000 single family and multifamily units would be developed, as well as a substantial number of commercial projects. Since 1983, however, only about 450 homes have been built, and there has been no multi-family or commercial development. Accordingly, revenues from water and wastewater services have been much lower than expected, forcing the District to assess relatively high taxes and monthly surcharges to homeowners. Despite these high rates, the District contends that it is still experiencing serious financial trouble.

In 1995, the Legislature passed Senate Bill 1261, which was codified as section 43.082 of the Texas Local Government Code. This act authorizes the municipal utility district that meets its specific requirements to dissolve upon resolution of the district's board, without consent from the adjacent municipality, and upon dissolution requires the municipality to assume the assets and liabilities of the district.

When a district dissolves under section 43.082, the municipality is required to provide full municipal services to the area, and the municipality may annex the district by simple resolution, without following the normal notice and hearing procedures. See Tex. Local Gov't Code § 43.082(b), (c). The municipality may assess a $25 monthly surcharge on utility customers in the former district and, importantly, may also assess a platting fee surcharge on developers desiring to subdivide land in the former district. The surcharge may be in an amount sufficient to offset the financial burden imposed on the municipality from assuming the district's indebtedness. See id. at § 43.082(e).

The application of section 43.082 is restricted as follows:

> (a) This section applies to any district created in or after 1983 within the extraterritorial jurisdiction of a municipality with written consent by ordinance or resolution as required by Section 42.042 if the district has:
>
> (1) issued not less than $17 million nor more than $21 million in bonds, excluding refunding bonds, repayable in a manner authorized under Section 54.503(2), Water Code;

(2) issued at least $3.5 million of bonds repayable in a manner authorized under Section 54.503(3), Water Code, before June 1, 1993; and

(3) constructed all of the facilities for which the bonds were issued prior to December 31, 1991.

Tex. Local Gov't Code § 43.082(a). The parties stipulate that Maple Run is the only district in the State meeting these criteria, that only Maple Run requested its enactment, and that the Legislature intended for section 43.082 to apply only to Maple Run. In other words, while Maple Run is not mentioned by name in the statute, the Legislature selected the criteria for the purpose of restricting the statute solely to that district. Moreover, because section 43.082 expires on December 31, 1996, there is no chance that it will ever apply to any other districts. The legislative history accompanying Senate Bill 1261 confirms that the statute was enacted to relieve the financial problems of Maple Run. See Bill Analysis of S.B. 1261 (May 11, 1995).

In January 1996, the Maple Run board of directors adopted a resolution dissolving the District in accordance with section 43.082, effective May 10, 1996. Prior to dissolution, Maple Run landowners James G. Monaghan, Maple Run Joint Venture and S.R. Ridge Limited Partnership (collectively "Monaghan") sued the District and the City of Austin seeking to enjoin enforcement of section 43.082, contending that it violated the Texas Constitution. Monaghan argued that section 43.082 was a special or local law prohibited by Article III, Section 56, a grant of public money and credit prohibited by Article III, Sections 50, 51, and 52, and an extinguishment of public debt prohibited by Article III, Section 55. The City filed a cross-claim against the District raising a similiar constitutional challenge, thus aligning itself with Monaghan on this issue. Although receiving notice of the constitutional challenge, the Attorney General declined to intervene in the proceedings. See Tex. Civ. Prac. & Rem. Code § 37.006(b). After stipulating to the essential underlying facts, the parties filed cross motions for summary judgment directed solely to the constitutional issues.

On May 6, 1996, the trial court, without stating its reasons, signed a final judgment declaring the statute unconstitutional and permanently enjoining its operation. The District perfected a direct appeal to this Court, challenging this ruling. See Tex. Gov't Code § 22.001(c); Tex. R. App. P. 140. Monaghan and the City are aligned as appellees, arguing in support of the trial court's judgment. We took jurisdiction over the appeal. See Tex. R. App. P. 140(b).

II

A

Article III, Section 56 of the Texas Constitution provides in relevant part:

LOCAL AND SPECIAL LAWS. The Legislature shall not, except as otherwise provided in this Constitution, pass any local or special law ... [r]egulating the affairs of counties, cities, towns, wards or school districts.... And in all other

> cases where a general law can be made applicable, no local or special law shall be enacted....

While the terms "local law" and "special law" have at times been used interchangeably, a local law is one limited to a specific geographic region of the State, while a special law is limited to a particular class of persons distinguished by some characteristic other than geography. See 1 George D. Braden, the Constitution of the State of Texas: an Annotated and Comparative Analysis 273–277 (1977).

The purpose of Section 56 is to "prevent the granting of special privileges and to secure uniformity of law throughout the State as far as possible." Miller v. El Paso County, 136 Tex. 370, 150 S.W.2d 1000, 1001 (1941). In particular, it prevents lawmakers from engaging in the "reprehensible" practice of trading votes for the advancement of personal rather than public interests. Id.

A law is not a prohibited local law merely because it applies only in a limited geographical area. We recognize the Legislature's broad authority to make classifications for legislative purposes. See Miller, 150 S.W.2d at 1001. However, where a law is limited to a particular class or affects only the inhabitants of a particular locality, "the classification must be broad enough to include a substantial class and must be based on characteristics legitimately distinguishing such class from others with respect to the public purpose sought to be accomplished by the proposed legislation." Miller, 150 S.W.2d at 1001–1002. "The primary and ultimate test of whether a law is general or special is whether there is a reasonable basis for the classification made by the law, and whether the law operates equally on all within the class." Rodriguez v. Gonzales, 148 Tex. 537, 227 S.W.2d 791, 793 (1950).

For example, in County of Cameron v. Wilson, 160 Tex. 25, 326 S.W.2d 162 (1959), we upheld a law providing for the development of public parks that applied only in counties "border[ing] on the Gulf of Mexico within whose boundaries is located any island, part of an island, or islands, suitable for park purposes." 326 S.W.2d at 165. We held that "[t]he coastal geography of Texas affords a reasonable distinction between the island park on the one hand and the mainland park on the other," noting that the "demand for the conveniences usually provided by county parks may be greater along the coast than in many inland areas." Id. at 166.

Similarly, in Robinson v. Hill, 507 S.W.2d 521 (Tex. 1974), the Court upheld a law imposing special bail bond regulations in counties with a population of 150,000 or more. We held that there was a reasonable basis for this classification, concluding that

> [t]he Legislature in this instance may well have concluded that bail bondsmen in the more populous counties should be regulated and required to secure their obligations because of the high incidence of crime and the difficulties involved in enforcing bond forfeitures ..., but that the same safeguards and procedures were not necessary and would be unduly burdensome in more sparsely populated areas.

Id. at 525. See also Smith v. Davis, 426 S.W.2d 827, 830–832 (Tex. 1968) (upholding special ad valorem tax rules for hospital districts in counties with a population greater than 650,000 and operating a teaching hospital).

On the other hand, we have struck down several laws under Section 56 where no reasonable basis supported the classification. For example, in Miller, we invalidated a law authorizing an economic development tax that applied only in counties

> having a population of not less than 125,000 nor more than 175,000 inhabitants, and containing a city having a population of not less than 90,000 inhabitants, as shown by the last preceding Federal census.

150 S.W.2d at 1002. We held that these population brackets, which included only El Paso County, bore no substantial relation to the objects sought to be accomplished by the act.

Similarly, in City of Fort Worth v. Bobbitt, 121 Tex. 14, 36 S.W.2d 470, 471–472 (1931), the Court struck down a public works law that applied only in cities with a population between 106,000 and 110,000. The Court held that the bracket advanced no legitimate purpose, but rather was simply a means of singling out one city for special treatment.

Likewise, in Bexar County v. Tynan, 128 Tex. 223, 97 S.W.2d 467 (1936), the Court invalidated an act reducing the compensation of certain officers in counties with a population between 290,000 and 310,000, which included only Bexar County. The Court concluded that

> the attempted classification is unreasonable and arbitrary to such degree as to indicate beyond doubt that the purpose of the Legislature was to single out one county and to attempt to legislate upon the question of the compensation of its officers, and not upon the subject generally. . . .

Id. at 470. See also Smith v. Decker, 158 Tex. 416, 312 S.W.2d 632, 636 (1958) (striking down act imposing special bail bond rules in counties with a population between 73,000 and 100,000); Rodriguez v. Gonzales, 148 Tex. 537, 227 S.W.2d 791, 793–794 (1950) (invalidating act providing for special procedures for collecting ad valorem taxes applicable only in certain counties along the Mexican border); Anderson v. Wood, 137 Tex. 201, 152 S.W.2d 1084, 1087 (1941) (invalidating act authorizing the employment of special traffic officers which excluded counties with a population between 195,000 and 205,000, such exclusion covering only Tarrant County).

Here, there is no dispute that the Legislature singled out Maple Run for special treatment. No one contends that the brackets selected by the Legislature have anything to do with the purpose of the statute; rather, these brackets serve solely to restrict section 43.082 to the District without actually identifying it by name. Further, the District offers no legitimate reason, and none appears in the record, why the statute is limited to Maple Run. The parties have stipulated that there are other districts in the state (1) with serious financial troubles, (2) with tax rates higher than Maple Run, (3) with annual debt service higher than Maple Run, and (4) with overall indebtedness higher than Maple Run.

Because the Legislature singled out the District for special treatment without any reasonable basis for doing so, section 43.082 has all the appearances of a local law within the meaning of Article III, Section 56.

B

The District argues, however, that section 43.082 is not a local law because it affects a matter of statewide interest. This argument, as framed by the District, consists of three components: (1) section 43.082 serves a conservation purpose; (2) Article XVI, Section 59 of the Texas Constitution mandates that conservation of our natural resources is of statewide importance; and (3) laws affecting matters of statewide importance are by definition not local or special laws. We conclude that this approach is flawed.

We assume for purposes of this discussion that section 43.082 does in fact serve a conservation purpose. The District relies on Article XVI, Section 59 of the Texas Constitution for the general proposition that conservation of our natural resources is a matter of statewide importance. Section 59 provides in relevant part:

> The conservation and development of all the natural resources of this State, including the control, storing, preservation, and distribution of its storm and flood waters, the waters of its rivers and streams, for irrigation, power and all other useful purposes, ... are each and all hereby declared public rights and duties; and the Legislature shall pass all such laws as may be appropriate thereto.

Tex. Const. art. XVI, § 59(a). While we agree that all Texans have an interest in protecting this State's natural resources, we disagree that one may simplistically conclude that any law having a conservation purpose is ipso facto, not a local or special law. The District relies on a series of cases in which this Court has espoused the principle that a law is not local, even if its operation is restricted to a specific area, if it affects a matter of statewide interest. See Lower Colorado River Authority v. McCraw, 125 Tex. 268, 83 S.W.2d 629, 636 (1935); Stephensen v. Wood, 119 Tex. 564, 34 S.W.2d 246, 248 (1931); Reed v. Rogan, 94 Tex. 177, 59 S.W. 255, 257 (1900); Clark v. Finley, 93 Tex. 171, 54 S.W. 343, 346 (1899). The statutes involved in these cases, however, affected a substantial class of persons over a broad region of the state, as opposed to section 43.082, which applies to one municipal utility district. Moreover, our later cases have clarified that the ultimate question under Article III, Section 56 is whether there is a reasonable basis for the Legislature's classification. See, e.g., Robinson v. Hill, 507 S.W.2d 521, 525 (Tex. 1974); Rodriguez v. Gonzales, 148 Tex. 527, 227 S.W.2d 791, 793 (1950); Miller v. El Paso County, 136 Tex. 370, 150 S.W.2d 1000, 1001 (1941). The significance of the subject matter and the number of persons affected by the legislation are merely factors, albeit important ones, in determining reasonableness:

> Where the operation or enforcement of a statute is confined to a restricted area, the question of whether it deals with a matter of general rather than purely local interest is an important consideration in determining its constitutionality. When a statute grants powers to or imposes duties upon a class of

> counties, the primary and ultimate test is whether there is a reasonable basis for the classification and whether the law operates equally on all within the class.

County of Cameron v. Wilson, 160 Tex. 25, 326 S.W.2d 162, 165 (1959). For example, in City of Irving v. Dallas/Fort Worth Int'l Airport Bd., 894 S.W.2d 456, 467 (Tex. App.–Fort Worth 1995, no writ), the court upheld legislation giving certain municipal airport authorities the exclusive power to make land-use decisions for property within the geographic boundaries of the airport. Because the statute applied only to airports operated jointly by two cities with a population exceeding 400,000, only D/FW Airport qualified. The court upheld this classification as reasonable, however, noting the tremendous statewide importance of the facility and the special zoning conflicts that can arise for a jointly operated airport. It does not follow, however, that any legislation having some incidental effect on the environment must be upheld, regardless of whether there was any legitimate basis for the classification drawn by the Legislature. This would seriously undermine the purpose of Article III, Section 56.

Because section 43.082 singles out one specific municipal utility district for special treatment without any reasonable basis for doing so, we hold that it is a local law within the meaning of Section 56.

NOTES

1. Can you imagine a legitimate reason why the Texas legislature would have singled out Maple Run for favorable treatment, presumably against the wishes of the City of Austin? Our examination of collective action problems suggests that governmental entities, as well as individuals, have incentives to free ride on the efforts of others. Thus, it should not be surprising that other districts, even financially distressed districts, would not join in the effort to obtain favorable legislation, since they would all benefit if some other district did all the work of drafting and lobbying for the law, and would not have to incur the related costs. Is that the state of affairs here however? Who receives the benefits of the legislation at issue, and who bears the costs? Which part of the statute offends the special legislation prohibition in the *Maple Run* case? Is it that the District alone requested the relief? Is it that the District alone falls within the category described by the statute? If the classification is open, the fact that it currently comprises only a single locality should not be decisive, since those criteria may still indicate a condition that would likely apply to any other locality that subsequently satisfied those criteria.

Is the offensive part of the statute its limitation to districts that had completed construction of all projects for which bonds had been issued by December 31, 1991? That seems to be a more difficult requirement to explain if the legislature was attempting to address a generic problem. Nevertheless, do you believe that the court would have reached a contrary decision had this part of the statute been omitted? Perhaps the court believes that the criteria set forth in the statute do not serve as a good proxy for the problem that the legislation purports to address. If, as the court indicates, other districts face similar financial distress but cannot resolve their problems in similar ways because they do not satisfy the statutory criteria, that seems to indicate that the legislature was not attempting to address the problem at hand, but rather to serve the interests of one particular district.

The fact that the other criteria do not correspond perfectly with districts that need assistance should not, however, mean that the legislation is necessarily invalid. A legislature can either create broad standards (such as by writing legislation that applies to all "financially distressed" districts) and leave their application to ad hoc judicial inquiry, or the legislature can develop a rough, but imperfect, proxy for the situations in which relief of the sort provided here would be appropriate. Any legislative proxy is likely to create problems of underinclusiveness and overinclusiveness; but ad hoc judicial inquiry is also likely to lead to erroneous decisions. Unless it is clear that judicial error through ad hoc adjudication of the vague standard is likely to be less than legislative error through improper line drawing, why should the court distrust the legislative decision?

2. *Constitutional Permission for Special Legislation.* Do the following provisions provide a better way than the provision of the Texas Constitution quoted in *Maple Run* of dealing with the issue of special legislation? Note that both of these provisions permit special legislation that confers benefits on the affected locality (at least one would assume that the locality would not adopt or urge the passage of proposed legislation that imposed particular burdens on itself).

Minn. Const. art. XII

2. Special laws; local government

Sec. 2. Every law which upon its effective date applies to a single local government unit or to a group of such units in a single county or a number of contiguous counties is a special law and shall name the unit or, in the latter case, the counties to which it applies. The legislature may enact special laws relating to local government units, but a special law, unless otherwise provided by general law, shall become effective only after its approval by the affected unit expressed through the voters or the governing body and by such majority as the legislature may direct. Any special law may be modified or superseded by a later home rule charter or amendment applicable to the same local government unit, but this does not prevent the adoption of subsequent laws on the same subject. The legislature may repeal any existing special or local law, but shall not amend, extend or modify any of the same except as provided in this section.

Mass. Const. amend. art. 89, § 8

The general court shall have the power to act in relation to cities and towns, but only by general laws which apply alike to all cities, or to all towns, or to all cities and towns, or to a class of not fewer than two, and by special laws enacted (1) on petition filed or approved by the voters of a city or town, or the mayor and city council, or other legislative body, of a city, or the town meeting of a town, with respect to a law relating to that city or town; (2) by a two-thirds vote of such branch of the general court following a recommendation by the governor; . . .

3. *The Objectives of the Special Legislation Prohibition: Logrolling.* Insofar as these provisions permit special legislation that benefits a single locality, they seem to be at odds with the objective that the court in the principal cases attributes to the special legislation prohibition. Recall that the court identifies the purpose of the prohibition as "to 'prevent the granting of special privileges and to secure uniformity of law throughout the State as far as possible.' " Under that interpretation, special legislation that confers special benefits is more problematic than special legislation that imposes unique burdens on a locality. Other courts have defined the function of the prohibition as preventing both the conferral of special benefits and the imposition of special burdens. See, e.g., In re Belmont Fire Protection District, 489 N.E.2d 1385 (Ill. 1986) ("A special law confers 'some special right, privilege or immunity or impose(s) some particular burden upon some portion of the people of the State less than all' ").

Should it matter whether the locality is burdened or benefited? Following the rationale of the "special commission" cases in Chapter 2, one might be concerned that the rest of the state would "gang up" on one locality, and one thus might want to avoid legislation that imposed special burdens on a particular locality. On this rationale, the prohibition serves to prevent state interference with local autonomy. Particularly where the local activity threatens few external effects, legislative intervention seems unnecessary. See Belin v. Secretary of the Commonwealth, 288 N.E.2d 287 (Mass. 1972) (striking down law that required only cities that vote by proportional representation or preferential voting for city officials to consider alternative voting schemes, where the law would apply in practice to a single city).

But why should anyone complain if the rest of the state agrees to confer a benefit on one locality? One might contend that the legislature should not be spending its time attending to the limited interests of a single jurisdiction. Some courts have employed this justification to invalidate statutes that confer special privileges:

> State constitutional provisions regulating private, local, and special legislation were adopted in response to the changing conditions in which 19th century state legislatures found themselves. State legislatures were under pressure from their constituents to act on a multitude of subjects. The volume of laws drastically increased, and private or local laws dramatically outnumbered the general laws. The proliferation of laws of limited applicability created the specter of favoritism and discrimination and diverted the legislature's attention from matters of public, state-wide importance. The constitutional proscriptions against special, private or local legislation were intended to prevent the granting of special privileges or the imposition of special disabilities and to encourage the legislature to devote its time to the interests of the state at large.

Soo Line R.R. Co. v. Department of Transp., 303 N.W.2d 626, 630 (Wis. 1981).

But why not leave to the legislature the question of when legislation has a sufficiently statewide appeal to warrant the legislature's attention? Courts would not appear to have any advantage in determining that legislation is "special" where that term means the legislature would spend "too much" time on matters that return purely parochial benefits.

The Texas court in the principal case, however, provides a different justification for prohibiting the conferral of special benefits. The court says that the constitutional provision "prevents lawmakers from engaging in the 'reprehensible' practice of trading votes for the advancement of personal rather than public interests." This rationale is also explicit in other judicial discussions of special legislation. In Municipal City of South Bend v. Kimsey, 781 N.E.2d 683, 685–86 (Ind. 2003), the court observed:

> Limits on "special legislation" are found, "in some form or other, in most state constitutions." Osborne M. Reynolds, *Local Government Law* 85–86 (1982). Their purpose is "to prevent state legislatures from granting preferences to some local units or areas within the state, and thus creating an irregular system of laws, lacking state-wide uniformity." Id. at 86. This "irregularity" is not in itself the only perceived evil. In the view of the proponents of these provisions, if special laws are permitted, the result is perceived to be "a situation in which it [becomes] customary for members of the legislature to vote for the local bills of others in return for comparable cooperation from them (a practice often termed 'logrolling')." Id. In simple terms, these anti-logrolling provisions are grounded in the view that as long as a law affects only one small area of the state, voters in most areas will be ignorant of and indifferent to it. As a result, many legislators will be tempted, some would say expected, to support the proposals of the legislators from the affected area, even if they deem the proposal to be bad policy that they could not support if it affected their own constituents.

There are two questionable claims implicit in this justification. First, it implies that vote trading is a bad idea. Second, it implies that legislators will trade votes on legislation to confer local benefits even though the result is the imposition of statewide burdens. Typically, we would believe that legislators who voted in this way would face electoral rebuke. Thus, this justification makes sense only if legislators can impose the costs of advancing their "personal" interests with impunity.

The possibility that the court's implicit beliefs are accurate is evident from the literature on logrolling, or vote trading. Assume that there exist within a state two pending bills and a legislature composed of one representative from each of three localities. Passage of each bill would return net gains or losses to the representatives' jurisdictions as indicated below.

Locality	Bill 1	Bill 2
A	−2	−2
B	+6	−3
C	−1	+7

Ideally, each of these bills should pass, because each returns benefits to the state as a whole in excess of costs (+3 for Bill 1, +2 for Bill 2). Yet, assuming the representatives act solely according to the interests of their constituents, without vote trading or logrolling neither will pass, because in each case a majority of those voting will lose more than they gain through an affirmative vote. A and C will vote against Bill 1, while A and B will vote against Bill 2. Notice, however, that it is possible for representatives to bring about the result that benefits the state as a whole by allowing vote trading. Representative B could agree with Representative C that they will each support both bills, thus creating a majority. B will get what it wants (enactment of Bill 1) and C will get what it wants (enactment of Bill 2), although each will give up something in the process (B will lose 3, but will gain 6, and C will lose 1, but gain 7). Thus, in this instance, logrolling facilitates socially optimal results.

If logrolling always generated socially optimal results, applying the special legislation prohibition to deny net benefits would seem anomalous. But now assume the following net gains and losses in the same jurisdiction.

Locality	Bill 1	Bill 2
A	−4	−8
B	−1	+3
C	+3	−1

Now we would prefer that neither bill passes, as both generate losses in excess of gains (−2 in the case of Bill 1, −6 in the case of Bill 2). But B and C still have incentives to trade, since each comes out ahead by doing so, even though the state as a whole loses if that trade occurs and both bills pass. Indeed, A has an incentive to trade in order to prevent a bargain between B and C. For instance, A might agree with C to support Bill 1 if C agrees not to trade with B on Bill 2. That way A will come out better than if both bills pass, even though A would prefer that both bills fail. This procedure obviously involves substantial transaction costs as representatives seek to form coalitions and block others from forming competing coalitions. Thus, in this instance, logrolling brings about socially undesirable results.

Note that Bill 1 and Bill 2 in this second case do create benefits for a locality, but only for a single locality. Thus, these bills appear to fit the definition of special legislation. Further, that benefit is created at the expense of the remainder of the state. Nevertheless, representatives of the nonbenefited localities have incentives to pass such legislation, as long as they can trade for legislation that benefits their own localities and that would otherwise not obtain majority support. Considered in this light, the constitutional prohibition on special legislation should apply to legislation that confers benefits on a particular locality, as well as to legislation that imposes burdens on a particular locality. Indeed, if we believe that logrolling is more likely to occur in instances like the second case, where the logroll leads to net negative results from the state's perspective, than in instances like the first case, where the logroll leads to net positive results, then we could consider the special legislation prohibition as a form of precommitment device by all representatives not to engage in this kind of behavior at all.

We can model the problem of vote trading as a Prisoner's Dilemma, of the sort discussed on pages 36–37, supra. The state as a whole would be best off if no localities attempted to gain benefits that were exceeded by losses visited on the remainder of the state. Each locality, however, does best if it procures beneficial legislation (defects), while other localities try to keep total state costs to a minimum (cooperate) by not seeking legislation that costs others more than it benefits the locality. Since all localities face the same preferences, however, all are likely to defect. The Dilemma can be avoided by imposing a prohibition on the activity, a result that the bar on special legislation purports to accomplish. Are there reasons to believe that logrolling is more likely to generate net negative than net positive results? See James M. Buchanan & Gordon Tullock, The Calculus of Consent, 134–145 (1965); Lynn A. Baker, Direct Democracy and Discrimination: A Public Choice Perspective, 67 Chi.-Kent L. Rev. 707 (1991); Clayton P. Gillette, Expropriation and Institutional Design in State and Local Government Law, 80 Va. L. Rev. 625, 642–657 (1994). On the use of logrolling rather than other signaling mechanisms to allocate social benefits to those who value them most highly, see Saul Levmore, Just Compensation and Just Politics, 22 Conn. L. Rev. 285 (1990). For an argument that logrolling should be presumed to generate net benefits and tends to promote transparency in the political process by packaging legislative tradeoffs, see Michael D. Gilbert, Single Subject Rules and the Legislative Process, 67 U. Pitt. L. Rev. 803 (2006). Professor Gilbert, however, distinguishes between logrolling and "riders," which may be attached to a bill at the behest of a single legislator who has disproportionate authority. He suggests that riders may presumptively be detrimental from a social perspective, even if they benefit the sponsoring legislator.

4. *Special Legislation Prohibition on Local Government.* To this point, we have been discussing prohibitions that prevent the state legislature from enacting special legislation that affects a subset of localities. But state constitutional prohibitions may also bind localities themselves from enacting legislation that affects only a subset of residents. The same analysis we have been considering would be applied to determine the propriety of an ordinance challenged as special legislation. In Hug v. City of Omaha, 749 N.W.2d 884 (Neb. 2008), the city council had adopted an ordinance that prohibited smoking in most public places, but deferred application of the ordinance for bars, keno establishments, and horseracing simulcasting locations, and exempted tobacco retail outlets. Plaintiffs contended that the exemptions transformed the ordinance into special legislation. The city justified the distinctions in the ordinance as a means of protecting public health and welfare in public gathering places and places of employment and of guaranteeing a right to breathe smoke-free air. The court concluded that "[n]othing in the ordinance's stated purpose would explain why employees of the exempted facilities or members of the public who wish to patronize those establishments are not entitled to breathe smoke-free air or to have their health and welfare protected." In the absence of evidence of a substantial difference between covered and exempted establishments, the court invalidated the exemptions as arbitrary and unreasonable classifications. But the court allowed the ordinance without the exemptions to stand on the grounds that the exemptions were severable. A concurring judge concluded that invalidation of the exemptions was appropriate to prevent a preferred group of businesses from obtaining a significant economic benefit.

5. *Geographical Limitations on Regulation of Private Activity*. Legislators may also use geographical limitations to limit the application of regulations on private actors, rather than on political subdivisions. These regulations are subject to the same analysis that would apply if the legislation was directed at the localities. In Illinois Hotel and Lodging Ass'n v. Ludwig, 869 N.E.2d 846 (Ill. App. 2007), the court considered state legislation that required employers to provide hotel room attendants with two 15–minute breaks and one 30–minute meal period in each workday in which the room attendant worked at least seven hours, and imposed significant penalties for violations. But the legislation applied only to hotel room attendants employed in counties with a population greater than 3 million, which meant only in Cook County. The court noted that the special legislation clause prohibits only arbitrary regulations, and applied a rational basis test to determine arbitrariness. The court concluded that the legislature could have found that Cook County hotels employed a majority of hotel room attendants statewide and could better absorb the costs of the regulations than employers elsewhere in the state. Indeed, the plaintiff had lobbied against statewide application of the measure on the grounds that imposition of rules that might pertain in Chicago would be less suitable "downstate." Thus, the legislation was constitutional.

6. *Single–Subject Requirements*. Other common state constitutional provisions also reflect antipathy towards logrolling. One such provision requires all state legislation to embrace a "single subject" or "single object." The rationale and application for the rule was explained in Porten Sullivan Corp. v. State, 568 A.2d 1111 (Md. 1990). That case invalidated a statute that authorized a county to impose certain taxes, but also imposed certain "ethics" requirements on county officials. The court described the evolution and application of the single-subject requirement:

> One reason for the relatively limited discussion, in Maryland constitutional history, of the reasons for the single-subject rule may be that it is one that has been applied for centuries. During Roman times, there was a prohibition against proposing laws that contained more than one subject. Corwin, The "Higher Law" Background of American Constitution Law, 42 Harv. L. Rev. 149, 160 n.36 (1928); Ruud, "No Law Shall Embrace More Than One Subject," 42 Minn. L. Rev. 389, 389 (1958)....
>
> As of 1982, "forty-one state constitutions provide[d] that an act shall not embrace more than one subject or object." Sutherland Statutory Construction 17.01 (4th ed. 1985). Many states recognize that a purpose of the one-subject rule is "to prevent 'riders' from being attached to bills that are popular and so certain of adoption that the rider will secure adoption not on its own merits, but on the merits of the measure to which it is attached." Ruud, supra, at 391. See, e.g., Gellert v. State, 522 P.2d 1120, 1122 (Ala. 1974) (purpose of one-subject requirement is to prevent logrolling); Floridians Against Casino Takeover v. Let's Help, 363 So.2d 337, 339 (Fla. 1978) (single-subject rule allows

people to express separate approval or disapproval of statutory sections); Kane County v. Carlson, 116 Ill.2d 186, 214, 107 Ill.Dec. 569, 580, 507 N.E.2d 482, 493 (1987) (purpose of rule is to prohibit combining of provisions which on their own may not have enough support to pass)....

An additional purpose of the single-subject rule is to "protect the integrity of the governor's veto power." Williams, State Constitutional Limits on Legislative Procedure: Legislative Compliance and Judicial Enforcement, 48 U. Pitt. L. Rev. 797, 809 (1987). In Brown v. Firestone, the Supreme Court of Florida said that a purpose of the one-subject rule is to prevent

> a practice under which the legislature could include in a single act matters important to the people and desired by the Governor and other matters opposed by the Governor or harmful to the welfare of the state, with the result that in order to obtain the constructive or desired matter the Governor had to accept the unwanted portion. The veto power of the chief executive [would] thereby [be] severely limited if not destroyed and one of the intended checks on the authority of the legislature [would be] able to be negated in practice.

382 So.2d 654, 663–664 (Fla. 1980) (quoting Green v. Rawls, 122 So.2d 10, 13 (Fla. 1960))....

The ethics legislation requiring the disqualification of Prince George's County Council members as prescribed by Chapter 244 is similarly distinct from those portions of the Act that extend certain taxing authority for one year. The "ethics" provisions are unrelated to raising revenue for county government operations. Moreover, while the "tax" provisions are grants of authority to the County Council, the "ethics" provisions are not. Except for minor details about filing affidavits and reports by the Council's clerk, the "ethics" portion of the Act does not deal with authority or discretionary activity by the Council; it simply imposes the "ethics" requirements on that body as well as on applicants (as defined in the Act), their agents, spouses, and children.

This legislation does not deal, in any general way, with the County Council. It contains two unrelated and disparate sets of provisions, one imposing mandatory "ethical" requirements on Council members and certain entities that appear before the Council in zoning matters; the other extending the Council's authority to impose certain taxes. The two disparate subjects are not transformed into one merely because there is authority in the Act to spend some of the tax revenues on "funding of the public ethics provisions," authority that to a considerable extent would have existed even without the language of Chapter 244. See Article 24, § 9–603(f)(2) as added by Chapter 244, Acts of 1989, and Section 3 of that statute. No one has been able to point to any particular county funding provision that requires money to be used for "ethics" measures. If any exists, it seems that it is de minimis.

568 A.2d at 1116–19. Would a statute enacting the Uniform Commercial Code pass muster under the "single subject" standard? The Maryland court decided that it did since "[t]he U.C.C., extensive as it is, deals with but one general subject—commercial transactions—in its many related aspects." Madison Natl. Bank v. Newrath, 275 A.2d 495, 504 (Md. 1971). Is it possible to contend that the provision in *Porten Sullivan* dealt generally with the county's government? The court rejected that assertion. Instead, the court found that the statute exhibited just the kind of logrolling that the constitutional provision was intended to avoid. The court traced the

history of the bill's passage through the legislature and determined that what had begun as a tax bill subsequently had the ethics provisions added to it in a manner that required the county's representatives to agree to those provisions in order to obtain the taxing authority.

One tool that courts may use to determine the "subject" of a bill is to examine the title that is assigned to it. In Trout v. State, 231 S.W.3d 140 (Mo. 2007)(en banc), the court reversed the trial court's determination that a bill contained more that a single subject. Violation of the prohibition, under the court's test, depended on whether all sections of the bill related to the same "general core purpose." The trial court had determined that different subjects were involved because the bill addressed issues of campaign finance, but also contained provisions relating to disqualification from running for office. The supreme court, however, concluded that the "general core purpose" as recited in the title of the bill was "ethics," and that both the campaign finance and disqualification provisions related to that core purpose.

The single-subject rule also serves to avoid "cycling" and instability within legislative bodies. Cycling occurs when voters must choose among multiple alternatives and have different preferences. For instance, faced with three alternatives, A, B, and C, voters 1, 2, and 3 may have the following preferences:

Voter 1	A, B, C
Voter 2	B, C, A
Voter 3	C, A, B

If voters are asked to decide between alternatives A and B first, A will win. If voters are then asked to decide between alternatives A and C, C will win. Thus, C will be selected, even though, had the first vote been between B and C, B would have won. Instability results because a measure that could be enacted into law when co-joined with another matter could subsequently be repealed by a vote taken on the same measure in isolation. The incorporation of multiple subjects into a single law raises the same issue by creating a situation in which a provision is enacted into law even though it is not preferred by a majority. Thus, Farber and Frickey summarize the effect of the single-subject requirement:

> One legislative rule that seems trivial, but whose significance is shown by public choice, is the "single subject" rule—a common state constitutional requirement that legislation may embrace only one subject, which must be expressed in its title. This rule has at least three purposes: (a) to limit logrolling, (b) to keep surprises from being hidden in bills, and (c) to prevent use of irrelevant riders to dilute the governor's veto power.... Many state courts construe the rule flexibly to avoid interference with legislative processes. Yet the purposes of the rule are worthy, and more rigorous enforcement may well be in order. Enforcement of the rule is particularly attractive when substantive riders have been attached to appropriations legislation.
>
> Even under a single subject rule, the complexity of many bills leaves room for legislative cycling. Nevertheless, if multiple, unrelated subjects are covered

> in the same bill, the possibility of cycling is greatly enhanced. Hence, the single subject rule promotes stability.

Daniel A. Farber & Philip P. Frickey, Law and Public Choice 127–128 (1991). For an argument that the single-subject rule should be applied differently, depending on whether the challenged proposal is embodied in regular legislation or in an initiative enacted through direct democracy, see Michael D. Gilbert & Robert D. Cooter, A Theory of Direct Democracy and the Single Subject Rule, 110 Colum. L. Rev. ___ (2010). The authors contend that the bargaining that occurs in legislatures, and that thus might justify the combining of multiple subjects in one legislative proposal, cannot exist in initiatives.

D. STATUTORY POWERS—HEREIN OF "DILLON'S RULE"

PROBLEM VII

Sutterville has adopted an ordinance that prohibits any establishment that has been granted a liquor license and that also permits dancing on its premises from denying admission to any person on the basis of sexual orientation. Scuggs, who claims that the ordinance grants a private right of action to anyone suffering injury by virtue of its violation, has brought an action against Sandy's Bar on the grounds that he and his male companion were subjected to harassment and forced to leave the bar, which is primarily frequented by heterosexual men and women. Sandy's has raised as a defense to the action the incapacity of Sutterville to adopt the ordinance at issue. State statutes include the following provision:

> Sec. 4321. Any municipal corporation within the state may license, tax, and regulate restaurants, eating houses, lodging houses, and taverns.

During the most recent session of the legislature, both the state senate and the state house of representatives held hearings on a bill that would make it illegal for establishments open to the public to discriminate with respect to patrons or employees on the basis of sexual orientation. The bill did not pass either chamber.

As attorney for Scuggs, what arguments will you make to support your contention that Sutterville possessed authority to pass the ordinance? What responses do you anticipate? See Arlington County v. White, 528 S.E.2d 706 (Va. 2000); Women & Infants Hospital v. City of Providence, 527 A.2d 651 (R.I. 1987); Nance v. Mayflower Tavern, Inc., 150 P.2d 773 (Utah 1944); Chicago Real Estate Board v. City of Chicago, 224 N.E.2d 793 (Ill. 1967); Marshall v. Kansas City, 355 S.W.2d 877 (Mo. 1962); Michael A. Woods, Comment, The Propriety of Local Government Protections of Gays and Lesbians from Employment Discrimination Practices, 52 Emory L.J. 515 (2003).

John F. Dillon, 1 Commentaries on the Law of Municipal Corporations

448–451 (5th ed. 1911).

237. **Extent of Power. Limitations; Canons of Construction.**—It is a general and undisputed proposition of law that *a municipal corporation possesses and can exercise the following powers, and no others:* First, those granted in *express words;* second, those *necessarily or fairly implied* in or *incident* to the powers expressly granted; third, those essential to the accomplishment of the declared objects and purposes of the corporation,Cnot simply convenient, but indispensable. Any fair, reasonable, substantial doubt concerning the existence of power is resolved by the courts against the corporation, and the power is denied. Of every municipal corporation the charter or statute by which it is created is its organic act. Neither the corporation nor its officers can do any act, or make any contract, or incur any liability, not authorized thereby, or by some legislative act applicable thereto. All acts beyond the scope of the powers granted are void. Much less can any power be exercised, or any act done, which is forbidden by charter or statute. *These principles are of transcendent importance, and lie at the foundation of the law of municipal corporations.* Their reasonableness, their necessity, and their salutary character have been often vindicated, but never more forcibly than by the learned Chief Justice Shaw, who, speaking of municipal and public corporations, says: "*They can exercise no powers* but those which are conferred upon them by the act by which they are constituted, or such as are necessary to the exercise of their corporate duties, and the accomplishment of the purposes of their association. This principle is derived from the nature of corporations, the mode in which they are organized, and in which their affairs must be conducted"

Southern Constructors, Inc. v. Loudon County Board of Education

58 S.W.3d 706 (Tenn. 2001).

OPINION

■ WILLIAM M. BARKER, J., delivered the opinion of the court, in which FRANK F. DROWOTA, III, C.J., and E. RILEY ANDERSON, ADOLPHO A. BIRCH, JR., and JANICE M. HOLDER, JJ., joined.

[The Loudon County Board of Education ("Board") contracted with Southern Constructors, Inc. ("SCI"), for additions and renovations to two county school buildings. The Board withheld payments from SCI to pay for removal of mold and mildew growth in an area of the school that had been deprived of electricity because of the acts of a subcontractor for SCI. SCI demanded payment of the withheld amount, and the parties agreed to submit their claims to arbitration. The arbitrator rendered a decision in favor of the Board, but he awarded a small portion of the withheld amount to SCI. SCI subsequently filed a complaint seeking to set aside the arbitration award on the basis that the Board, "as a governmental entity[,] had no authority to enter into an agreement to arbitrate and its act in doing so was ultra vires."—EDS.]

The question before the Court is whether the Loudon County Board of Education possesses the authority under the laws of the State of Tennessee to arbitrate disputes arising out of a school construction contract. If the Board possesses no such authority, then its agreement to arbitrate the dispute in this case, along with the ultimate award, are void as *ultra vires.* The Board urges this Court, under several legal theories, to find that it possesses the authority to enter into such arbitration agreements, and SCI urges this Court to apply Dillon's Rule and to strictly construe the statutory powers of county school boards against having any such authority....

I. DILLON'S RULE AND THE SCOPE OF LOCAL GOVERNMENTAL AUTHORITY IN TENNESSEE

At its most basic level, Dillon's Rule is a canon of statutory construction that calls for the strict and narrow construction of local governmental authority....

As in many jurisdictions throughout the nation, Dillon's Rule has been applied in this state for more than a century to determine the scope of local governmental authority. Beginning with *Mayor & City Council v. Linck,* 80 Tenn. (12 Lea) 499 (1883), this Court has recognized that municipal governments in Tennessee derive the whole of their authority solely from the General Assembly and that courts may reasonably presume that the General Assembly "has granted in clear and unmistakable terms all [power] that it has designed to grant...." Id. at 505 (citation omitted). To this end, the *Linck* Court held that municipal governmental authority should be strictly construed, and it stated that a municipal government may exercise a particular power only when one of the following three conditions is satisfied: (1) the power is granted in the "express words" of the statute, private act, or charter creating the municipal corporation; (2) the power is "*necessarily or fairly implied* in, or *incident* to[,] the powers expressly granted"; or (3) the power is one that is neither expressly granted nor fairly implied from the express grants of power, but is otherwise implied as "essential to the declared objects and purposes of the corporation." *See id.* at 504 (emphases in original). Consistent with other articulations of Dillon's Rule, we also stated that " '[a]ny fair, reasonable doubt concerning the existence of the power is resolved by the courts against the corporation and the power is denied.' " Id. (quoting 1 John F. Dillon, *Commentaries on the Law of Municipal Corporations* 173 (1st ed. 1872)).

Although a discussion of the numerous applications of Dillon's Rule in this state is unnecessary, the Rule has been consistently applied to all forms of local government, including those of cities, counties, and special districts. Despite this wide application, however, many legal commentators, and some courts, have criticized the Rule as needlessly depriving local governments of the ability to deal with, and respond to, changing local situations and needs. *See, e.g.*, Gerald E. Frug, *The City as a Legal Concept,* 93 Harv. L. Rev. 1059 (1980); *State v. Hutchinson,* 624 P.2d 1116, 1121 (Utah 1980). Indeed, the Board in this case cites many of these same concerns as reasons to abrogate Dillon's Rule in Tennessee.

We are not unmoved by some of these criticisms, but while Dillon's Rule is essentially only a canon of construction, it continues to reflect the constitutional realities of local government in this state. Article II, section 3 of our Constitution confers upon the General Assembly the whole of the state's legislative power, and with limited exception, *see Gibson County Special Sch. Dist. v. Palmer,* 691 S.W.2d 544, 550 (Tenn.1985), the General Assembly has the sole and plenary authority to determine whether, and under what circumstances, portions of that power should be delegated to local governments. As this Court has previously acknowledged, local governments have never possessed the inherent right to autonomous self-government, and all local governmental authority "has always been interpreted as a matter of constitutional entitlement or legislative delegation of authority." Plainly stated, then, without some form of constitutional authorization, local governments in Tennessee possess only those powers and authority as the General Assembly has deemed appropriate to confer upon them.

It is from this rationale—that local governments have no inherent right to autonomous self-government—that the rule of strict construction of local governmental authority arises in this state.... Far from being an irrational interpretive canon, the doctrine of strict, but reasonable, construction of delegations of state legislative power seeks only to give effect to the practical nature of local governmental authority in Tennessee....

Nevertheless, although the constitutional structure of local government in Tennessee provides a sound basis for the continued strict construction of local governmental authority, we also recognize that several important exceptions to Dillon's Rule have diminished its practical importance. For example, the General Assembly itself can mitigate any unwanted effects of strict construction by supplying direct evidence of its intent to grant broad local governmental powers when it chooses to do so. Importantly, strict construction of local governmental power is only appropriate when legislative intent as to the proper scope of that power is absent or otherwise ambiguous, and an intent to have local powers broadly construed may be expressed either in the language granting the particular power itself or in a separate statute applying to all grants of power generally. Because Dillon's Rule is essentially only a canon of construction used to ascertain the intention of the General Assembly, the Rule must necessarily yield when a contrary intent plainly appears.

As an important corollary to this principle, where the General Assembly grants comprehensive governmental power to the local authority without either enumerating the powers or expressly limiting the scope of the authority, that "general provision [will] be *liberally* construed." *See Linck,* 80 Tenn. (12 Lea) at 508 (emphasis in original). One example of a comprehensive grant of power may be seen in the charter government provisions for counties authorized by Article VII, section 1 of the Tennessee Constitution and Tennessee Code Annotated sections 5–1–201 to 5–1–214. . . .

Further, courts have not taken a narrow view of local governmental power when the General Assembly has conferred general welfare authority to protect the citizens' health, convenience, and safety. In the same decision that recognized Dillon's Rule as a rule of construction in this state, this Court stated that where the legislature grants local governments broad authority to provide for the general welfare, Dillon's Rule cannot be used to challenge the exercise of that authority as beyond the scope of the delegated power. *See Linck,* 80 Tenn. (12 Lea) at 509–10. Because the very nature of general police powers demands that such authority receive a broad construction to accomplish its purposes, the *Linck* Court held that so long as ordinances adopted under a grant of general welfare authority are not "unreasonable or oppressive[,] they are valid, and will be maintained." Id. at 510. We continue to concur in that assessment.

Finally, an exception to Dillon's Rule necessarily arises when the issue concerns the authority of home rule municipalities. [The consequences of home rule for narrow interpretation of local autonomy are discussed in Section E of this Chapter infra—EDS.]

Subject to these important exceptions, we hold that the courts of this state should continue to strictly, but reasonably, construe the scope of local governmental authority delegated by the General Assembly. The legislature has relied upon the continued existence of this presumption in delegating its power to local authorities, and it has displayed a noted ability to abrogate the Rule when necessary to accomplish its desired objectives. While Dillon's Rule is essentially only a judicial rule of statutory construction, and is therefore within our power to abrogate, we acknowledge that the Rule is generally necessary to give effect to the constitutional realities of local government in this state. Consequently, we retain Dillon's Rule, subject to its exceptions, as a rule of construction to determine the scope of local governmental authority.

II. APPLICATION OF DILLON'S RULE IN THIS CASE

Although we have found no case in Tennessee expressly holding that Dillon's Rule applies in construing the authority of county boards of education, we nevertheless conclude that it is proper to do so. Just as the Constitution grants the General Assembly plenary authority to structure and provide for local government, Article XI, section 12 of the Constitution also grants the General Assembly plenary and exclusive authority to "provide for the maintenance, support and eligibility standards of a system of free public schools." . . . .

Consequently, if Dillon's Rule is generally applied to determine the scope of municipal and county governmental authority, it seems only appropriate, in the absence of any exception, to apply this rule of construction to determine the scope of local school board authority as well. . . .

Our first inquiry, then, in applying Dillon's Rule in this case is whether the General Assembly has expressly conferred upon county school boards the power to arbitrate disputes arising out of a construction contract. The authority to enter into construction contracts is granted by Tennessee Code Annotated section 49–2–203(a)(4), which confers upon county school boards the authority to "[p]urchase all supplies, furniture, fixtures and material of every kind through the executive committee." Through subsections (C)(1), (C)(2), and (D) of this provision, the General Assembly has given the local school boards the authority to "contract for the construction of school buildings or additions to existing buildings," and it has emphasized that "[n]o board of education shall be precluded from purchasing materials and employing labor for the construction of school buildings or additions thereto." However, no part of section 49–2–203 expressly mentions any authority to enter into arbitration agreements, either to confer the power or to deny it.

Because the General Assembly has not expressly conferred upon county school boards the power to arbitrate disputes arising out of construction contracts, our next inquiry is whether that power is fairly implied from the powers expressly granted. The law implies powers from express grants of authority because the General Assembly can hardly be expected to specify in minute detail the incidents of power conferred upon local governments. However, in finding the existence of an implied power, courts must remember that "[i]mplied powers do not exist independently of the grant of express powers[,] and the only function of an implied power is to aid in carrying into effect a power expressly granted." *City of Flagstaff v. Associated Dairy Prods. Co.,* 75 Ariz. 254, 255 P.2d 191, 193 (1953). Consequently, we examine closely the express powers of the county boards of education to determine what authority is also conferred as fairly implied from those powers.

Upon examination of the powers given to boards of education by section 49–2–203, we conclude that the power to arbitrate is fairly implied from the express power to contract in the first instance. Although no case from this Court has specifically held that the power to arbitrate a contract dispute is fairly implied from the power to contract itself, the veracity of this proposition cannot be reasonably doubted. As the Wisconsin Supreme Court has articulated the principle of law, " 'It is well established that a city has the power to submit to arbitration any claim asserted by or against it, whether based on contract or tort, in the absence of a statutory prohibition. This power is based on the right to contract and the right to maintain and defend suits.' " *City of Madison v. Frank Lloyd Wright Found.,* 20 Wis.2d 361, 122 N.W.2d 409, 416 (1963) (quoting *Power of a Municipal Corporation to Submit to Arbitration,* 40 A.L.R. 1370, 1372 (1926)). Wisconsin is not alone in this view, and decisions in several states reflect similar holdings.

This Court held long ago that "when the law gives the power and right to contract, the right to enforce such contract necessarily and as a matter of course follows. . . ." *Uhl v. Board of Comm'rs,* 74 Tenn. (6 Lea) 610, 614

(1881). The power to enforce that contract not only includes the authority to seek full judicial determination of the respective rights and obligations of the parties, but it must also necessarily include the ability to seek other reasonable avenues of dispute resolution, including settlement, mediation, and arbitration. It is not for this Court to decide which is the better course for a local government to pursue in resolving a contract dispute. *Cf. Mitchell v. Garrett,* 510 S.W.2d 894, 898 (Tenn.1974) (stating that discretionary actions of an education board or superintendent are presumed to be reasonable and fair, "unless there is clear evidence to the contrary"). Consequently, because the legislature has not provided for a specific method to be used in resolving contract disputes, that decision is more properly made by those entrusted with ensuring the overall well-being of each county school system.

In response, and citing an unreported case from the Court of Appeals, SCI urges this Court to reject the notion that the power to arbitrate is fairly implied from the power to contract. In *Chattanooga Area Regional Hamilton County Transp. Authority v. Parks Construction Co.,* [1999 WL 76074 (Tenn.Ct.App.)—EDS.] the intermediate court held that municipalities lack the implied power to arbitrate disputes, relying exclusively upon a federal decision that reached the same conclusion by applying Virginia law. *See Schlosser Co. v. School Bd.,* 980 F.2d 253 (4th Cir.1993). In *Schlosser Co.,* the court held that a local school board under Virginia law has no authority to arbitrate a dispute arising out of a construction contract. The school board argued that the power to arbitrate is implied from the power to contract, and while the court noted that this argument was not "without force," it viewed the Virginia Public Procurement Act as reflecting a policy to withhold from local governments the power to arbitrate disputes. *See* 980 F.2d at 256. We note that even were we to agree with the general rationale used by the *Schlosser Co.* Court, we find no evidence of a similar policy in Tennessee to generally withhold arbitration from local governments as an avenue of dispute settlement. Consequently, to the extent that the *Parks Construction Co.* Court did not note this apparent distinction between the general policies of our state and that of Virginia, its persuasive value as an accurate reflection of Tennessee law is significantly weakened. *Cf.* Tenn. Sup.Ct. R. 4(H)(1).

In any event, given that the general rule of law is that the power to contract necessarily includes the power to settle disputes arising under that contract, one would reasonably expect the General Assembly to expressly withhold the ability to arbitrate disputes if that avenue of dispute resolution were not available. We can find no express prohibition in this regard, however, and we must therefore conclude that the power to arbitrate disputes is fairly implied from the power to contract in the first instance. Accordingly, we hold that the Board possessed the authority to arbitrate its construction contract dispute with SCI as a power fairly implied from its authority to contract with that party in the first instance. Having so concluded, it is unnecessary for us to inquire further as to whether the power to arbitrate is otherwise so essential to the declared objects and purposes of county boards of education that it must be within the scope of their authority.

* * *

Early Estates, Inc. v. Housing Board of Review of Providence

174 A.2d 117 (R.I. 1961).

■ PAOLINO, JUSTICE.

This is a petition for certiorari to review the decision of the housing board of review of the city of Providence denying the petitioner's appeal from a compliance order of the director of the division of minimum housing standards pursuant to the provisions of chapter 1040 of the ordinances of said city, entitled the Minimum–Standards Housing Ordinance. Pursuant to the writ the board has certified the pertinent records to this court.

The petitioner owns a three-tenement house. Public Laws 1956, chap. 3715, is the enabling act which authorizes the city of Providence to enact a minimum standards housing ordinance. The question presented by this petition is whether the act as written vests the city with power to enact an ordinance requiring petitioner to provide a rear hallway light in its premises and to install hot water facilities in the third-floor tenement, and, if so, whether such requirements are valid.

Sections 7 and 8 of article 4 of the act delegate to the city council power to enact minimum housing standards. Section 7 provides that: "The city council of the city of Providence is authorized to pass, ordain, establish and amend ordinances, rules and regulations for the establishment and enforcement of minimum standard for dwellings." In defining this general grant of power the legislature provided as follows in sec. 8:

> Without limiting the generality of the foregoing, such ordinances, rules and regulations may include:
>
> (a) Minimum standards governing the conditions, maintenance, use and occupancy of dwellings and dwelling premises deemed necessary to make said dwellings and dwelling premises safe, sanitary and fit for human habitation.

Pursuant to the provisions of the enabling act the city council enacted chapter 1040, the Minimum–Standards Housing Ordinance.

The provisions involved in the instant proceeding are subsecs. 8.8, entitled "Lighting of Public Spaces," and 6.4, entitled "Hot Water."

Subsection 8.8 provides that:

> Every public hall and common stairway used primarily for egress or ingress in connection with two or more dwellings units shall be supplied with a proper amount of natural or electric light at all times; provided that such public halls and common stairways in structures containing not more than three dwelling units shall be deemed to have fulfilled such requirement if they are properly supplied with conveniently located switches, controlling an adequate electric lighting system which may be turned on when needed; and provided that all

> common stairways not used primarily for egress or ingress in all dwellings shall be properly supplied with such switches.

Subsection 6.4 provides that:

> Within three (3) years following the effective date of this Ordinance every kitchen sink, lavatory basin, and bathtub or shower bath required under the provisions of Subsections 6.1, 6.2 and 6.3 of this section shall be properly connected to hot as well as cold water lines.

The petitioner concedes that subsecs. 8.8 and 6.4, if valid, apply to its premises. However, with respect to the requirements of 8.8, it contends that under the common law of this state as declared in Capen v. Hall, 21 R.I. 364, 43 A. 847, and followed by other later cases, there is no duty on a property owner to provide artificial light or switches in common hallways and stairways. The petitioner also contends that the council, absent legislative authority, is without power to change the common law relating to hallway lights; that the act as written contains no language vesting the council with such power; and that consequently subsec. 8.8 is invalid and the director's compliance order requiring such hallway light is null and void.

After careful consideration it is our opinion that the enabling act clearly vests the council with power to legislate on the subject of lighting for common hallways and stairways. The legislature therein declared in art. 2, sec. 2, that "the establishment of minimum standards for dwellings is essential to the protection of the public health, safety, morals and general welfare." Such language clearly indicates a legislative intent to vest in the council power to require minimum standards dealing with factors relating to safety.

Again, in carrying out such intent, the legislature provided in art. 4, sec. 8, that the ordinances which the council was empowered to enact might include, without limiting the generality of the language in sec. 7, minimum standards governing the conditions, maintenance, use and occupancy of dwellings and dwelling premises deemed necessary to make said dwellings and dwelling premises safe, sanitary and fit for human habitation. The use of such language makes it abundantly clear that the legislature clearly intended to vest the council with power to require hallway lights as a safety measure. We are satisfied that the council had legislative authority to enact subsec. 8.8 and that the requirements therein are reasonable and therefore are a proper exercise of the police power. See Palombo v. Housing Board of Review, R.I., 169 A.2d 613. The cases cited by petitioner are not in point and require no discussion.

We come now to a consideration of the provisions of subsec. 6.4 requiring the installation of hot water facilities in the third-floor tenement of petitioner's property. Its principal contentions with respect thereto are that the act is silent on the subject of hot water; that there is no language therein vesting the council with power to legislate on the subject; and that therefore the council acted in excess of its jurisdiction.

At this point we are not concerned with the wisdom or desirability of the requirements in question. It may very well be that hot water facilities in a dwelling are convenient and desirable, but the only question before us is whether the act as written vests the council with power to require the installation of such facilities. The act contains no express grant of such power.

In art. 2 the legislature declares that it has found that there exist in the city of Providence numerous dwellings which are substandard due to "uncleanliness" and lack of adequate "sanitary" facilities, and that the establishment of minimum standards for dwellings is essential to the protection of the public health, safety, morals and general welfare. Under sec. 8 the council is vested with power to enact minimum standards governing the conditions, maintenance, use and occupancy of dwellings deemed necessary to make said dwellings safe, sanitary and fit for human habitation.

In the absence of an express grant of legislative authority, the determination of the issue raised by petitioner's instant contentions depends wholly upon the question whether the statutory language discussed in the preceding paragraph indicates a clear legislative intent to delegate the power in question. In other words, is the use of such language equatable to a grant of power to the council empowering it to require the installation of hot water facilities? Is the requirement of hot water facilities related to the "uncleanliness" of dwellings and dwelling premises? Is such requirement related to sanitation or public health and welfare?

Keeping in mind that chap. 3715 involves a delegation of power relating to minimum housing standards, can it reasonably be said that by empowering the council to enact minimum standards necessary to make dwellings and dwelling premises "fit for human habitation," the legislature meant that the installation of hot water facilities is necessary to achieve the desired purpose? Can it be said that dwellings and dwelling premises lacking such facilities are unfit for human habitation?

Prior to the enactment of chap. 3715, in the absence of contractual obligations to the contrary there was no duty on a property owner to provide hot water facilities under the law of this state. After careful consideration it is our opinion that the act contains no language indicating a legislative intent to create such a duty or to vest the council with power to enact an ordinance requiring the installation of hot water facilities. The requirement of those facilities is not necessarily related to sanitation or public health and welfare, nor is such requirement reasonably necessary to make dwellings and dwelling premises fit for human habitation. We cannot read into the act that which is not there.

From what we have stated, it is clear that in enacting subsec. 6.4 the council exceeded its jurisdiction. That portion of the ordinance is therefore invalid and the decision of the board based thereon is in error. In view of this result it becomes unnecessary to discuss or consider the petitioner's other contentions.

The petition for certiorari is granted insofar as it relates to the decision of the board with respect to the order requiring the installation of hot water facilities and that part of the board's decision is quashed. Insofar as it relates to the decision of the board with respect to the rear hallway light the petition is denied and dismissed and to such extent the writ heretofore issued is quashed.

■ ROBERTS, JUSTICE (dissenting).

I am unable to agree with the conclusion of the majority of the court that the action of the city council in providing in chap. 1040, subsec. 6.4, of the city ordinance that in all dwelling units kitchen sinks, lavatory basins, and bathing facilities be connected with hot as well as cold water lines was in excess of the authority conferred upon it by the pertinent provisions of the enabling act, P.L. 1956, chap. 3715, art. 4, sec. 8(a).

The enabling act confers upon the city council authority to establish by ordinance minimum standards for dwellings. In art. 4, sec. 8 thereof, after expressly stating it to be the legislative policy that the generality of the grant of such authority is not limited thereby, the legislature provided that such an ordinance could set out certain specific provisions, among which were included "Minimum standards governing the conditions, maintenance, use and occupancy of dwellings and dwelling premises deemed necessary to make said dwellings and dwelling premises safe, sanitary and fit for human habitation."

Clearly, it was the intention of the legislature to confer upon the city council comprehensive authority to provide minimum standards for dwelling premises. The subsequent enumeration of norms to be observed by the city council in its exercise of the police power thus delegated to it was not intended to diminish the scope of that authority. Because the legislature intended to bestow upon the city council such a broad power to provide for minimum dwelling standards, I am persuaded that the legislature also intended to leave to the discretion and judgment of the local legislature the nature of the precise minimum standards to be established. If the specific requirements thus prescribed as minimum standards by the city council bear a reasonable relationship to the public health, morals, and welfare, the enactment thereof constituted a valid exercise of the police power delegated to it.

I am unable to perceive that the action of the city council requiring the connecting of kitchen sinks, lavatory basins, and bathing facilities to hot water lines was violative of the norms set out in art. 4, sec. 8(a), of the enabling act. Nor do I think it reasonable to conclude that the providing of lines which would serve to give the occupant of the dwelling access to an appliance that would, if utilized, make available to him a supply of hot water may not be deemed necessary to promote sanitation in dwelling premises or to render such premises fit for human habitation.

That a definite relationship exists between the maintenance of an adequate condition of sanitation in a community and the availability of access to a supply of hot water in the dwelling units in that community has been given judicial recognition in City of Newark v. Charles Realty Co., 9 N.J. Super. 442, 74 A.2d 630. In that case, on the basis of the evidence adduced, the court found that where a supply of hot water is not readily available in dwellings by reason of a failure to have access to facilities for supplying such hot water, the danger of production and spread of disease in the community tends to increase. Without intending to unduly extend this dissenting opinion, I quote in part from that case at page 452 of 9 N.J. Super., at page 635 of 74 A.2d: "For instance, as to gastro-intestinal diseases, there have been 'outbreaks of that disease because hot water was not available for that purpose,' the testimony instancing as typical, the spread of such disease throughout the city from a restaurant, an employee of which fails to properly wash his hands due to the lack of hot water at home, and thus spreads this diarrheal disease." While it may be possible to maintain adequate sanitation in a community where there is a lack of readily available supplies of hot water for use in personal hygiene by the residents thereof, it is manifestly clear that a high degree of sanitation would be promoted and more effectively maintained when access to adequate supplies of hot water is provided for in the dwellings in that community.

Neither do I believe that the requirement of subsec. 6.4 for the connecting of hot water lines to kitchen sinks, lavatory basins, and bathing facilities may not reasonably be deemed necessary to render a dwelling fit for human habitation. To attribute to the legislature an intention to use the phrase "fit for human habitation" as meaning any structure that suffices to give one shelter from the elements so as to survive the vicissitudes and hardships of life in a climate such as ours is to attribute to the legislature an intent to have its enactment result in an absurdity. It is my belief that a dwelling fit for human habitation within the contemplation of the legislature was a dwelling so built and equipped as to afford the occupants thereof access to those conveniences and amenities that, in this day of social enlightenment, are considered as the responsibility of the property owner to the welfare of the community. When the city council included within the ordinance provisions requiring the connecting of kitchen sinks, lavatory basins and bathing facilities with hot water lines, it was acting well within the norm inherent in the legislative phrase "fit for human habitation."

To so construe the pertinent section of the enabling act does not, in my opinion, have the effect of bringing the legislation within the purview of any constitutional inhibition. Such a construction does not obscure the clear purpose of this legislation, that is, to confer upon the city council a comprehensive authority with which to act effectively to eradicate existing blighted areas and to prevent any further spread of such blighted areas within the community. Neither does such construction nullify the validity of the norms prescribed therein by the legislature for the guidance of the city council. That there is a reasonable relationship between these purposes and the health, morals, and welfare of the public is self-evident, in my opinion, and the legislature in its enactment thereof is engaged in a valid exercise of the police power. Robinson v. Town Council, 60 R.I. 422, 199 A.

308. Because I take this view, it is my opinion that the petition for certiorari should have been denied and dismissed and the decision of the respondent board affirmed.

■ FROST, J., concurs in the dissenting opinion of ROBERTS, J.

NOTES

1. *The Subsequent History of Early Estates.* In 1962, the Rhode Island General Assembly added the following paragraph to § 8(a) of ch. 3715:

> Such minimum standards may require, among other things, as part of the facilities of any dwelling, a kitchen sink, flush toilet and lavatory basin, bath tub or shower bath. Provision may also be required for the installation of facilities to heat hot water and to require the connection of such hot water in addition to cold water, to such kitchen sink, lavatory basin, bath tub or shower bath. This provision shall not in any way limit the city of Providence in establishing other minimum standards.

Public Law ch. 122 (1962). Does this result suggest that the Rhode Island legislature thought that the majority opinion in Early Estates was as silly as the dissenting opinion suggests? Does the statute suggest that tenant groups were able to organize successfully at the state level to overcome an adverse judicial decision? See Note 3 infra.

2. *Private Corporations Compared.* The general rule for interpretation of the authority of private corporations provides:

> In determining the powers of a corporation, courts follow the general rules of statutory construction that provisions of the laws of the state of incorporation and the articles of incorporation should be given a fair and reasonable construction with due regard to the purposes of the corporation.... Where the power exercised is not wholly inconsistent with the powers granted or with the object or purpose of the corporation and the power has been exercised for a long period of time, any doubt regarding the construction of a grant of power should be resolved in favor of the corporation.

6 William M. Fletcher, Cyclopedia of the Law of Corporations § 2483. Why should there be different rules for interpreting the powers of municipal and private corporations? Does it matter that one exercises governmental powers and one does not? Assume that two adjoining municipalities receive electrical energy from different sources. The first receives it from a municipally owned power plant. The second receives its energy from a privately owned utility. Both the municipally owned plant and the privately owned utility now seek to construct a nuclear power plant. The charters of both the municipality and the private utility provide that they may undertake construction of projects "useful in the generation of electrical energy." What justification is there for using different legal standards to interpret the powers of each of these utilities?

Would it help in answering the above question to consider the relative opportunities for residents (of municipal corporations) and shareholders (of private corporations) to monitor their representatives? What are their incentives to monitor to ensure that those representatives are acting in the interests of the residents or shareholders? Ideally, residents monitor their local officials closely. But return to Mill's observation about the capacity of the local electorate to watch over their representatives. Even a properly concerned citizen may disregard an official's failure to serve that constituent's interest in one area if the official provides an overall adequate level of services. Do officials of private corporations similarly escape scrutiny? Are shareholders more attentive to the conduct of their agents than residents of a municipality are to theirs? Do these distinctions help to justify the difference in the legal rule interpreting the scope of the corporations' powers?

3. *Dillon's Rule and Interest Group Capture.* It seems "clear," to use a term that seems to be the majority's major tool for analysis in *Early Estates*, that landlords would oppose the ordinance enacted in Providence. Tenants and prospective tenants might be mixed in their reaction to the proposed ordinance, depending on whether they thought landlords would be able to pass on the costs of improvements. Electricians and plumbers would likely favor the ordinance, as it would increase their job opportunities. Which of these groups do you think would have the best access to the decisionmakers in Providence? If those who disfavored the ordinance had the best access to the city council, is the fact that the ordinance passed nonetheless some evidence that the ordinance was not intended to cater to special interests? What would be the implications of such a finding for the scope of judicial review? For discussion of whether application of Dillon's Rule should depend on the susceptibility of the local decision to dominance by an interest group, see Clayton P. Gillette, In Partial Praise of Dillon's Rule, or, Can Public Choice Theory Justify Local Government Law?, 67 Chi.–Kent L. Rev. 959 (1991); Gary Schwartz, Reviewing and Revising Dillon's Rule, 67 Chi.–Kent L. Rev. 1025 (1991).

4. Return to the argument in *Southern Constructors* that "given that the general rule of law is that the power to contract necessarily includes the power to settle disputes arising under that contract," the legislature would have expressly withheld the ability to arbitrate if that had been its intention. Was it clear prior to that decision that the rule of law was as the court stated? After all, an intermediate court of the state had, the court indicated, reached a contrary conclusion about the power to arbitrate two years earlier. Can the legislative enactment of a statutory right to enter into contracts without simultaneously explicitly permitting arbitration constitute sufficient evidence of a denial of an implied power rather than confirmation of it?

5. Dillon's Rule remains a primary maxim for judicial construction of statutes that authorize municipalities to engage in a particular activity. Notwithstanding the court's willingness to interpret statutory authority broadly in *Southern Constructors, Inc.*, Tennessee courts have recently applied the rule to deny municipalities the authority to initiate legislation without an explicit grant. In Allmand v. Pavletic, 292 S.W.3d 618 (Tenn. 2009), the court held that employment contracts for the superintendent of the city's gas and electric department that permitted post-termination compensation were not authorized by general statutes concerning the creation or governance of public utility plants or statutes governing gas, sewers, and waterworks. In Entertainer 118 v. Metropolitan Sexually Oriented Business Licensing Bd., 2009 WL 2486195 (Tenn.Ct.App.), the court concluded that a licensing board did not have authority under state law to assess a fine for violation of a local ordinance.

Other jurisdictions, however, have explicitly repudiated the Rule. See, e.g., Ind. St. § 36–1–3–3, which provides:

> (a) The rule of law that any doubt as to the existence of a power of a unit shall be resolved against its existence is abrogated.
>
> (b) Any doubt as to the existence of a power of a unit shall be resolved in favor of its existence. This rule applies even though a statute granting the power has been repealed.

Judge Dillon's home state of Iowa repudiated the rule when it adopted a home rule provision in its constitution. See Berent v. City of Iowa City, 738 N.W.2d 193 (Ia. 2007). North Carolina has adopted N.C.G.S.A. § 160A–4, which provides:

> It is the policy of the General Assembly that the cities of this State should have adequate authority to execute the powers, duties, privileges, and immunities conferred upon them by law. To this end, the provisions of this Chapter and of city charters shall be broadly construed and grants of power shall be construed to include any additional and supplementary powers that are reasonably necessary or expedient to carry them into execution and effect.

But Dillon's Rule still is injected into interpretations of state statutes that grant power to municipal corporations. Notwithstanding the North Carolina statute, an appellate court in that state invalidated a county ordinance that prohibited mobile homes more than ten years old from being brought into the county. The court concluded that the county's statutory authority to protect property values, preserve the integrity of the community, and promote the health, safety, and welfare of residents did not authorize the ordinance, which was predicated in part on increasing the county's tax base. Five C's, Inc. v. County of Pasquotank, 672 S.E.2d 737 (N.C. App. 2009). In a controversial opinion that led to the default of $2.2 billion in municipal bonds, the Supreme Court of Washington invalidated contracts entered into between municipalities in that state and the Washington Public Power Supply System. Under the contracts the municipalities agreed to make payments to the Supply System sufficient to pay debt service on bonds issued to construct two nuclear power plants. The municipalities anticipated receiving electrical energy from the plants, but were obligated to make the payments even if the plants were neither completed nor operating. The court determined that the statutory authority granted to municipalities to purchase electricity did not include authority to purchase a chance of obtaining electricity. Chemical Bank v. Washington Public Power Supply System, 666 P.2d 329 (Wash. 1983).

The rule is frequently employed when courts invalidate ordinances as unauthorized by or in conflict with state law, see e.g., Premium Standard

Farms, Inc. v. Lincoln Township, 946 S.W.2d 234 (Mo. 1997); Jachimek v. Superior Court, 819 P.2d 487 (Ariz. 1991). Would you expect to find patterns of broad interpretation or narrow interpretation, depending on the subject matter of the ordinance? For instance, is there reason to believe that localities will be found to have more discretion when enacting ordinances relating to roadway construction than in the area of regulating condominium conversion? For an argument that broad zoning authorization has rendered the rule obsolete (at least in the area of land use), see Carol Rose, The Ancient Constitution vs. the Federalist Empire: Anti–Federalism from the Attack on "Monarchism" to Modern Localism, 84 Nw. U. L. Rev. 74, 99 (1990). For an opinion that interprets a zoning ordinance in light of Dillon's Rule, see Hawthorne v. Village of Olympia Fields, 765 N.E.2d 475 (Ill. App. 2002) (non-home rule municipality may not use zoning ordinance to bar day care facilities in light of state Child Care Act, which regulates child care facilities throughout the state).

Tabler v. Board of Supervisors of Fairfax County

269 S.E.2d 358 (Va. 1980).

■ I'ANSON, CHIEF JUSTICE.

In this appeal, we must determine whether the Board of Supervisors of Fairfax County (the County Board) possessed legislative authority to enact an ordinance requiring a minimum cash refund value on containers for nonalcoholic beverages.

On December 8, 1975, the County Board enacted the Beverage Container Ordinance, Fairfax County Code 111–1–1 to 111–3–4. Section 111–3–1 of that Code, as amended on June 6, 1977, provides that every container in which nonalcoholic beverages are sold or offered for sale in Fairfax County must have a cash refund value of not less than five cents. The ordinance became effective on September 1, 1977.

On August 23, 1977, Charles Tabler, trading as Foodarama Supermarket, and a group of corporations engaged in the business of bottling and distributing soft drinks (the appellants) instituted a suit challenging the validity of the ordinance and requesting both temporary and permanent injunctive relief against its enforcement. The petition for a temporary injunction was denied by the trial court in August 1977 and by this court in September 1977. In May 1978, the chancellor entered a decree holding that the County Board was authorized to enact the ordinance and dismissing the appellants' bill of complaint. We granted an appeal, limited to considering whether the County Board possessed legislative authority to enact the Beverage Container Ordinance.

As noted in several recent decisions, Virginia follows the Dillon Rule of strict construction concerning the legislative powers of local governing bodies. See, e.g., Commonwealth v. Arlington County Bd., 217 Va. 558, 573, 232 S.E.2d 30, 40 (1977). The Dillon Rule provides that local governing bodies have only those powers that are expressly granted, those that are necessarily or fairly implied from expressly granted powers, and those that are essential and indispensable. . . .

The appellees note that the General Assembly has expressly authorized counties to enact ordinances requiring property owners to remove garbage and litter, Code 15.1–11; regulating the dumping of trash on a public highway, Code 33.1–346(e); and providing for the health, safety, and welfare of county residents, Code 15.1–510. These Code sections clearly do not, however, provide express authority to adopt the provisions of the ordinance at issue. Thus, we must determine whether the County Board was impliedly authorized to enact such legislation.

Questions concerning implied legislative authority of a local governing body are resolved by analyzing the legislative intent of the General Assembly. Arlington County Bd., 217 Va. at 577, 232 S.E.2d at 42. This court has consistently refused to imply powers that the General Assembly clearly did not intend to convey. "(W)hen legislative intent is plain, our duty is to respect it and give it effect." 217 Va. at 579, 232 S.E.2d at 43. In determining legislative intent, we have looked both to legislation adopted and bills rejected by the General Assembly. For example, in *Arlington County Bd.*, holding that localities lacked the implied power to enter into collective bargaining agreements, we noted the General Assembly's adoption of a resolution rejecting such a power and the General Assembly's consistent rejection of proposed legislation altering that policy. 217 Va. at 564–65, 577–78, 232 S.E.2d at 35, 42.

In their briefs and in oral argument, the parties have discussed Acts 1978, c. 765 (codified as Code 10–213.1) and House J. Res. 174, Acts 1978, at 1991–92. Although Code 10–213.1 preempts any local ordinance requiring a deposit on a disposable bottle, the General Assembly provided in clause 2 that "this act shall not affect the validity of any local ordinance adopted and in litigation" as of March 4, 1978, "or any adjudication thereon." Acts 1978, c. 765, cl. 2. Because the Fairfax ordinance meets the criteria specified in clause 2, the appellees argue that clause 2 is an implicit acknowledgment of the County Board's authority to enact such legislation. The appellants suggest that clause 1 indicates the General Assembly never intended to confer such a power. Both arguments require a consideration of the provisions of the act, contrary to the terms of clause 2, which reflects the legislature's long-standing policy of not interfering with pending litigation. Because of the directive found in this clause, we shall not consider the provisions of this statute in passing upon the validity of the ordinance.

The General Assembly's actions in regard to proposed legislation concerning beverage containers indicate that the legislature did not intend to confer upon local governing bodies the power to set a minimum refund value for such containers. In the 1972 legislative session, the General Assembly did not enact either of two bills proposing a ban on nonreturnable bottles. In the 1974, 1975, and 1976 sessions, the General Assembly rejected bills which would have placed a tax upon nonreturnable beverage containers. In several recent sessions, the General Assembly has refused to adopt proposed legislation which would have set a minimum refund value on beverage containers. Moreover, in the 1971 and 1976 sessions, while considering several proposed amendments to the charter for the City of Alexandria, the General Assembly rejected proposed amendments explicitly granting Alexandria the power to regulate or prohibit the sale or use of disposable containers. These actions by the General Assembly indicate clearly and unambiguously that the legislature did not intend to grant local governing bodies the power to regulate or prohibit the sale or use of disposable containers. Accordingly, we hold that the County Board did not have legislative authority to enact legislation setting forth a minimum cash refund value on containers for nonalcoholic beverages and that the trial court erred in upholding those provisions of the ordinance.

The decree of the trial court will therefore be reversed and a final decree will be entered here in favor of the appellants.

Reversed and final decree.

NOTES

1. *Legislative Rejection as a Basis of Interpretation.* The court in *Tabler* finds substantial support for its conclusion in the failure of the legislature to enact legislation that would have set a minimum refund value on beverage containers or that would have permitted Alexandria the power to regulate the sale or use of disposable containers. Is it appropriate to draw such inferences from legislative failure to enact legislation? Assume that the state legislature consists of 100 representatives, 40 of whom voted for these bills and 60 of whom voted against. Assume further, however, that the latter group is composed of 45 representatives who voted against the bill because they opposed the concept of return bottle requirements, and 15 representatives who voted against the bill because they thought its provisions were insufficiently strong. Under these assumptions, the court's conclusion is more difficult to justify. To make the case against inferences from legislative inaction even stronger, assume that of the 60 representatives who voted against the legislation, 40 did so because they believed that the issue should be left to local discretion. Even if the other 20 believed that there should be no bottle bill legislation passed by any level of government, it would be difficult to assume on these facts that the defeat of the measure served as evidence of legislative intent not to permit local measures in this area.

Nevertheless, there may be situations in which inferences can properly be drawn from legislative inaction. In the context of inferences to be drawn from the failure of Congress to pass legislation, William Eskridge, Jr. and Philip Frickey write:

> [T]he [Supreme] Court in construing tax statutes, in particular, presumes that Congress is actively aware of judicial and administrative interpretations of the Internal Revenue Code and that when Congress amends or re-enacts provisions that have been the subject of interpretation Congress is implicitly acquiescing in those interpretations.... Moreover, the Supreme Court most often relies on Congressional inaction when there has been active deliberation in response to

> administrative or judicial interpretations of statutes—so that the "inaction" is arguably a reasoned acquiescence and not one borne of simply lethargy or inattention.

William N. Eskridge, Jr. & Philip P. Frickey, Cases and Materials on Legislation: Statutes and the Creation of Public Policy 773 (1988). Professor Eskridge elaborates on the arguments for and against making inferences from the failure to pass legislation in William N. Eskridge, Jr., Interpreting Legislative Inaction, 87 Mich. L. Rev. 67 (1988).

In Heck v. Commissioners of Canyon County, 853 P.2d 587 (Idaho Ct. App. 1992), appellants sought to invalidate a county ordinance that restricted the sale of fireworks. Appellants claimed that the ordinance conflicted with a state fireworks law. The state statute included a provision that permitted cities to impose additional regulations on the sale, use, and possession of fireworks within their corporate limits. Appellants claimed that this provision, by excluding counties, intended to preclude counties from adopting prohibitions on the sale of fireworks more restrictive than those in the state law. Appellants introduced evidence that the legislature had rejected an amendment that would have included counties in the provision. The court rejected this argument, concluding that the legislative history "indicates simply that the proposed amendments were not passed, not the reason for the legislature's rejection of the amendments." After review of the history of the state law, the court concluded:

> Looking at the history of the Fireworks Act, there appears to be no legislative intent to differentiate the regulatory authority of counties from that of cities. Examining I.C. § 39–2629A in the context of the remainder of the Act, it is apparent that any authority that is extended to a city is also extended to counties. In addition, there is no obvious or even obscure rationale for prohibiting counties from regulating the sale and use of fireworks inside their territorial limits. In light of this, the omission of the word "county" in I.C. § 39–2629A appears to be merely an oversight.

Id. at 593. On appeal, the Supreme Court of Idaho reversed. That court concluded that the state statute preempted any county regulation of the retail sale of certain fireworks. With respect to the provision that permitted additional city regulation, the court concluded:

> If the legislature had this authority in mind in 1970 when it enacted I.C. § 39–2629A, why was it necessary for the legislature to recognize specifically the authority of cities to enact restrictions beyond those contained in the fireworks law? The only reasonable answer is that the legislature intended the fireworks law to preempt the authority of both cities and counties to regulate the sale, use, and possession of fireworks and wanted to grant cities, but not counties, the authority to enact restrictions beyond those contained in the fireworks law. The commissioners ask us to read into I.C. § 39–2629A a grant to counties to enact restrictions beyond those contained in the fireworks law. The statute grants authority to cities only. The reading the commissioners suggest is not reasonable.

Heck v. Commissioners of Canyon County, 853 P.2d 571, 573 (Idaho 1993).

2. Assume in *Tabler* that those who favored a bottle return bill (a citizens' group) were well organized at the local level but not at the state level.

Assume further that those opposed to the bill (bottlers and store owners) were not well organized at the local level, but were well represented by trade groups at the state level. This alignment could explain how similar proposals could pass at the local level but be defeated as a statewide measure. If this explains the action of local and state legislative bodies in *Tabler*, is it appropriate to conclude from the state legislature's rejection of bottle bill legislation that the locality was not authorized to pass an ordinance on the same subject?

3. If the concern that underlies Dillon's Rule is that localities will be insufficiently diverse to allow all sides of an issue to be represented in the decisionmaking process, hence triggering the Madisonian fear of minority factions, does it make sense to apply the rule with equal force to all political subdivisions of the state? Does it make sense to relax the rule as the decisionmaking process becomes more centralized? See, e.g., Resource Conservation Management, Inc. v. Board of Supervisors of Prince William County, 380 S.E.2d 879 (Va. 1989) (county ordinance prohibiting specific uses of land subject to Dillon's Rule, but permissible under state waste management act). Should the rule apply at all to special districts? See Cohen v. Board of Water Commissioners, 585 N.E.2d 737 (Mass. 1992) (fire district considered subject to Dillon's Rule).

Gerald E. Frug, The City as a Legal Concept

93 Harv. L. Rev. 1057, 1109–1110 (1980).

I. *Dillon's Treatise*.—The legal doctrine that cities were subject to state authority was enthusiastically endorsed by John Dillon, who in 1872 wrote the first and most important American treatise on municipal corporations. Dillon did not seek to disguise the values he thought important in framing the law for municipal corporations. In speeches, law review articles, and books, Dillon eloquently defended the need to protect private property from attack and indicated his reservations about the kind of democracy then practiced in the cities.

It would be a mistake, however, to read Dillon's defense of strict state control of cities as simply a crude effort to advance the interests of the rich or of private corporations at the expense of the poor inhabitants of cities. Instead, it is more plausible to interpret Dillon as a forerunner of the Progressive tradition; he sought to protect private property not only against abuse by democracy but also against abuse by private economic power. To do so, he advocated an objective, rational government, staffed by the nation's elite—a government strong enough to curb the excesses of corporate power and at the same time help those who deserved help. It is important to understand how Dillon could consider state control of cities as a major ingredient in accomplishing these objectives.

According to Dillon, a critical impediment to the development of a government dedicated to the public good was the intermingling of the public and the private sectors. Strict enforcement of a public/private distinction was essential both to protect government from the threat of domination by private interests and to protect the activities of the private economy from being unfairly influenced by government intervention. Moreover, to ensure its fully "public" nature, government had to be organized so that it could attract to power those in the community best able to govern. Class legislation in favor of either the rich or the poor had to be avoided—neither a government of private greed nor one of mass ignorance could be tolerated. Instead, it was the role of the best people to assume responsibility by recognizing and fulfilling their communal obligations: "It is a duty of perpetual obligation on the part of the strong to take care of the weak, of the rich to take care of the poor."

PROBLEM VIII

The Town of Rydell has been authorized by state statute to regulate structures and the use of land within its boundaries through the adoption of zoning ordinances. Ordinances adopted pursuant to this authorization are required by state law to be

> in accordance with a comprehensive plan and designed for one or more of the following purposes: to lessen congestion in the streets; secure safety from fire, panic and other dangers; promote health, morals or the general welfare; provide adequate light and air; prevent the overcrowding of land or buildings; avoid undue concentration of population. Such regulations shall be made with reasonable consideration, among other things, to the character of the district and its particular suitability for particular uses, and with a view towards conserving the value of property and encouraging the most appropriate use of land throughout such municipality.

Claiming authorization under the zoning statute, Rydell has enacted an ordinance that prohibits any citizen from maintaining "any clothesline, drying rack, pole, or other similar device for hanging clothes, rags, or other fabrics in a front yard or side yard abutting the street." Darin is a resident who has been cited for violation of the ordinance and fined $50 for hanging clothing on a clothesline erected in his front yard. Darin claims that the ordinance has been enacted solely for aesthetic purposes, a fact that the town concedes, and that an ordinance that serves such a purpose is not authorized by the zoning statute. You represent the town. How will you respond to Darin's argument? On aesthetic zoning generally, see J. J. Deukminier, Jr., Zoning for Aesthetic Objectives: A Reappraisal, 20 Law & Contemp. Probs. 218 (1955); 23 Geo. Wash. L. Rev. 730; Luczynski v. Temple, 497 A.2d 211 (N.J. Super. Ct. 1985); People v. Miller, 416 A.2d 821 (N.J. 1980). On the constitutionality of ordinances that have aesthetic purposes, see Metromedia, Inc. v. City of San Diego, 453 U.S. 490 (1981) (protection of appearance of city a substantial governmental goal sufficient to support billboard ordinance, but distinction between commercial and noncommercial billboards would constitute infringement of free speech).

PROBLEM IX

You serve on the City Council of the City of Stubley, which has a population of approximately 7,000. There is pending before the Council a proposed ordinance that would provide for fluoridation of water furnished to residents of the city through its municipal water works. You are convinced that fluoridation of the water supply would benefit your constituents, but you are unsure whether Stubley is empowered to enact the ordinance. Passage of the ordinance will undoubtedly generate a lawsuit from opponents of fluoridation. You do not wish to vote for an ordinance that will require the city to incur substantial litigation costs unless you are also convinced that the city can defeat a challenge to its authority to enact the ordinance. Perusal of the state statutes and constitution reveals the following provisions:

> State Code 397. Cities and towns shall have the power to purchase, establish, construct, maintain, and operate waterworks with all the necessary reservoirs, mains, filters, streams, trenches, pipes, and other requisites of such works or plants.
>
> State Code 466. Municipal corporations shall have the power to make and publish ordinances, not contrary to the general laws of the State, as shall seem necessary and proper to provide for the safety, preserve the health, promote the prosperity, and improve the morals, order, comfort, and convenience of such corporations and the inhabitants thereof.

How will you vote on the proposed ordinance? Why? See Hall v. Bates, 148 S.E.2d 345 (S.C. 1966); Wilson v. City of Council Bluffs, 110 N.W.2d 569 (Iowa 1961).

State of Utah v. Hutchinson

624 P.2d 1116 (Utah 1980).

■ STEWART, JUSTICE:

Defendant, a candidate for the office of Salt Lake County Commissioner, was charged with having violated § 1–10–4, Revised Ordinances of Salt Lake County, which requires the filing of campaign statements and the disclosure of campaign contributions....

A complaint charged defendant in two counts: (1) failure to report the name and address of a $6,000 contributor to his election campaign, and (2) failure to file supplemental campaign disclosures of the discharge of campaign debts and obligations.

Defendant filed a motion in a city court to dismiss the complaint on the ground that the ordinance was in violation of the Utah Constitution. The court granted the motion and held that Salt Lake County was without constitutional or statutory authority to enact the ordinance under which defendant was charged and dismissed the complaint.

An appeal was taken to a district court which affirmed the dismissal....

Defendant contends that because the Legislature has not specifically authorized counties to enact ordinances requiring disclosure of campaign contributions in county elections, Salt Lake County had no power to enact the ordinance in question....

Concededly, the district court was correct in holding that the Legislature has not expressly authorized enactment of an ordinance requiring disclosure of campaign contributions in county elections. However, the Legislature has conferred upon cities and counties the authority to enact all necessary measures to promote the general health, safety, morals, and welfare of their citizens. Section 17–5–77, U.C.A. (1953), as amended, provides:

> The board of county commissioners may pass all ordinances ... not repugnant to law ... necessary and proper to provide for the safety, and preserve the health, promote the prosperity, improve the morals, peace and good order, comfort and convenience of the county and the inhabitants thereof, ... and may enforce obedience to such ordinances ... by fine in any sum less than $300 or by imprisonment not to exceed six months, or by both such fine and imprisonment....

The Legislature has made a similar grant of power to the cities.

The specific issue in this case is whether § 17–5–77 by itself provides Salt Lake County legal authority to enact the ordinance for disclosure of campaign contributions, or whether there must be a specific grant of authority for counties to enact measures dealing with disclosures of campaign financing to sustain the ordinance in question. Defendant claims that the powers of municipalities must be strictly construed and that because Salt Lake County did not have specific, delegated authority to enact the ordinance in issue, the ordinance is invalid.

The rule requiring strict construction of the powers delegated by the Legislature to counties and municipalities is a rule which is archaic, unrealistic, and unresponsive to the current needs of both state and local governments and effectively nullifies the legislative grant of general police power to the counties. Furthermore, although the rule of strict construction is supported by some cases in this State, it is inconsistent with other cases decided by this Court—a situation that permits choosing between conflicting precedents to support a particular result.

Dillon's Rule, which requires strict construction of delegated powers to local governments, was first enunciated in 1868. The rule was widely adopted during a period of great mistrust of municipal governments and has been viewed as "the only possible alternative by which extensive governmental powers may be conferred upon our municipalities, with a measurable limit upon their abuse."

The courts, in applying the Dillon Rule to general welfare clauses, have not viewed the latter as an independent source of power, but rather as limited by specific, enumerated grants of authority.... More recently, however, reasoned opinion regarding the validity of the rule has changed. One authority has noted the harmful effects that the rule of strict construction has had upon the effective exercise of appropriate municipal authority:

> Any vestige of inherent powers or liberality in construing delegated powers was soon swept away by the Dillon Rule. This rule was formulated in an era when farm-dominated legislatures were jealous of their power and when city

> scandals were notorious. It has been the authority, without critical analysis of it, for literally hundreds of subsequent cases.
>
> As it arose, the strict construction doctrine applied to municipal corporations but it has been extended to local government generally and it must be faced in any approach to liberalizing local powers. This rule sends local government to State legislatures seeking grants of additional powers; it causes local officials to doubt their power, and it stops local governmental programs from developing fully. The strict construction rule stimulated home rule efforts and is largely responsible for the erosion of home rule. Because of its importance the rule should be examined critically from time to time.

As pointed out in Frug, The City As A Legal Concept, 93 Harvard L. Rev. 1059, 1111 (1980):

> Most troubling of all to Dillon, cities were not managed by those "*best fitted* by their intelligence, business experience, capacity and moral character." Their management was "too often both unwise and extravagant." A major change in city government was therefore needed to achieve a fully public city government dedicated to the common good. [Footnotes omitted.] [Emphasis in original.]

If there were once valid policy reasons supporting the rule, we think they have largely lost their force and that effective local self-government, as an important constituent part of our system of government, must have sufficient power to deal effectively with the problems with which it must deal. In a time of almost universal education and of substantial, and sometimes intense, citizen interest in the proper functioning of local government, we do not share the belief that local officials are generally unworthy of the trust of those governed. Indeed, if democratic processes at the grassroots level do not function well, then it is not likely that our state government will operate much better....

The fear of local governments abusing their delegated powers as a justification for strict construction of those powers is a slur on the right and the ability of people to govern themselves. Adequate protection against abuse of power or interference with legitimate statewide interests is provided by the electorate, state supervisory control, and judicial review. Strict construction, particularly in the face of a general welfare grant of power to local governments, simply eviscerates the plain language of the statute, nullifies the intent of the Legislature, and seriously cripples effective local government.

There are ample safeguards against any abuse of power at the local level. Local governments, as subdivisions of the State, exercise those powers granted to them by the State Legislature, Ritholz v. City of Salt Lake, 3 Utah 2d 385, 284 P.2d 702 (1955), and the exercise of a delegated power is subject to the limitations imposed by state statutes and state and federal constitutions. A state cannot empower local governments to do that which the state itself does not have authority to do. In addition, local governments are without authority to pass any ordinance prohibited by, or in conflict with, state statutory law. Salt Lake City v. Allred, 20 Utah 2d 298, 437 P.2d 434 (1968). Also, an ordinance is invalid if it intrudes into an area which the Legislature has preempted by comprehensive legislation intended to blanket a particular field.

In view of all these restraints and corrective measures, it is not appropriate for this Court to enfeeble local governments on the unjustified assumption that strict construction of delegated powers is necessary to prevent abuse. The enactment of a broad general welfare clause conferring police powers directly on the counties was to enable them to act in every reasonable, necessary, and appropriate way to further the public welfare of their citizens.

The ultimate limitation upon potential abuses by local governments is the people themselves. It is their vigilance and sound judgment by which all democratic governments in the end, are restricted and directed. Officials who abuse the powers with which they have been entrusted ought not to be, and usually are not, long tolerated.

In short, we simply do not accept the proposition that local governments are not to be trusted with the full scope of legislatively granted powers to meet the needs of their local constituents. On the contrary, the history of our political institutions is founded in large measure on the concept at least in theory if not in practice that the more local the unit of government is that can deal with a political problem, the more effective and efficient the exercise of power is likely to be. . . .

The wide diversity of problems encountered by county and municipal governments are not all, and cannot realistically be, effectively dealt with by a state legislature which sits for sixty days every two years to deal with matters of general importance. Thus the manner in which the Legislature operates militates in favor of a rule of judicial construction which permits localities to deal with their problems by local legislative action.

The general welfare provision, § 17–5–77, grants county commissioners of each county two distinct types of authority. In the first instance, power is given to implement specific grants of authority. Second, the counties are granted an independent source of power to act for the general welfare of its citizens. Thus § 17–5–77 provides authority to "pass all ordinances and rules and make all regulations, not repugnant to law, necessary for carrying into effect or discharging the powers and duties conferred by this title. . . ." The second part of that section empowers counties to pass ordinances that are "necessary and proper to provide for the safety, and preserve the health, promote the prosperity, improve the morals, peace and good order, comfort and convenience of the county and the inhabitants thereof, and for the protection of property therein."

Nothing in § 17–5–77 or in Title 17 suggests that the general welfare clause should be narrowly or strictly construed. Its breadth of language demands the opposite conclusion. Moreover, the Constitution does not allow the Legislature unlimited discretion to deal with local government. The broad delegation of power by the Legislature to the counties is consistent with constitutional provisions which establish counties as governmental entities and place certain aspects of county government beyond the power of the Legislature. Article XI, § 1 gives constitutional status to the counties as they existed at the time of adoption of the Constitution, and they are "recognized as legal subdivisions of this State. . . ." Sections 2 and 3 of that article restrict the Legislature with respect to the changing of county seats and county lines. In addition, it should be noted that charter cities have even more specific and wide-ranging powers established by the Constitution in Article XI, § 5. . . .

These decisions are consistent with our basic framework of government. This Court in State v. Standford, 24 Utah 148, 66 P. 1061 (1901), stated:

> [T]he Constitution implies a right of local self-government to each county, and a right to establish a system of county government is expressly recognized and enjoined. The power is given to create the county government, not to administer to such a system when created. The right of the Legislature was to provide for and put in action, not to run and operate, the machinery of the local government to the disfranchisement of the people. People v. Hurlbut, 24 Mich. 44, 9 Am. Rep. 103. When the county government is established separate from the state, each is compelled to bear its own burdens, and not assume those of the other. (24 Utah at 158–59, 66 P. at 1062.)

The reason for providing appropriate protection for local government was stated in State v. Eldredge, 76 P. 337 (Utah 1904):

> The fact is that every provision of the Constitution relating to this important subject appears to manifest an intention to bring those through whom power is to be exercised as close as possible to the subjects upon whom the power is to operate to preserve the right of local self-government to the people, and to restrict every encroachment upon such right. And, as has been seen, this is in harmony with history, with our American constitutional law, with our notions of decentralization of power, and with the spirit and genius of our institutions. (27 Utah at 485, 76 P. at 340.)

More recently, this Court, in accord with that philosophy, has expressly held a reasonable latitude of judgment and discretion is essential for a county commission to exercise its express and implied powers. Gardner v. Davis County, Utah, 523 P.2d 865 (1974); Cottonwood City Electors v. Salt Lake County Board of Commrs., 28 Utah 2d 121, 499 P.2d 270 (1972).

The courts of other states have also held that a general welfare clause confers power in addition to and beyond that granted by specific statutory grants. . . .

These cases state the rule which we adopt in this case. When the State has granted general welfare power to local governments, those governments have independent authority apart from, and in addition to, specific grants of authority to pass ordinances which are reasonably and appropriately related to the objectives of that power, i.e., providing for the public safety, health, morals, and welfare. Salt Lake City v. Allred, 20 Utah 2d 298, 437 P.2d 434 (1968). And the courts will not interfere with the legislative choice of the means selected unless it is arbitrary, or is directly prohibited by, or is inconsistent with the policy of, the state or federal laws or the constitution of this State or of the United States. Specific grants of authority may serve to limit the means available under the general welfare clause, for some limitation may be imposed on the exercise of power by directing the use of power in a particular manner. But specific grants should generally be construed with reasonable latitude in light of the broad language of the general welfare clause which may supplement the power found in a specific delegation....

Local power should not be paralyzed and critical problems should not remain unsolved while officials await a biennial session of the Legislature in the hope of obtaining passage of a special grant of authority. Furthermore, passage of legislation needed or appropriate for some counties may fail because of the press of other legislative business or the disinterest of legislators from other parts of the State whose constituencies experience other, and to them more pressing, problems. In granting cities and counties the power to enact ordinances to further the general welfare, the Legislature no doubt took such political realities into consideration.

We therefore hold that a county has the power to preserve the purity of its electoral process. The county was entitled to conclude that financial disclosure by candidates would directly serve the legitimate purpose of achieving the goal that special interests should not be able to exercise undue influence in local elections without their influence being brought to light....

In sum, the Dillon Rule of strict construction is not to be used to restrict the power of a county under a grant by the Legislature of general welfare power or prevent counties from using reasonable means to implement specific grants of authority. County ordinances are valid unless they conflict with superior law; do not rationally promote the public health, safety, morals and welfare; or are preempted by state policy or otherwise attempt to regulate an area which by the nature of the subject matter itself requires uniform state regulation. Of course a specific power delegated to municipalities may imply a restriction upon the manner of exercise of that power, but the restriction on the exercise of such power is to be construed to permit a reasonable discretion and latitude in attaining the purpose to be achieved....

We do not judge the wisdom, effectiveness, or practicality of the ordinance in question, or concern ourselves with the factual issues which underlie the allegations against defendant in this case. We rule only that the ordinance under which this action is brought is constitutional.

The judgment of the lower court is reversed, and the case is remanded for a trial on the merits.

■ MAUGHAN, JUSTICE (dissenting):

For the following reasons, I dissent....

The analysis of the majority opinion utilizes the familiar technique of erecting a straw man, in this case, the abstract principle of law identified as Dillon's Rule, and throttling it with the evocative shibboleth of local control. The majority then interprets Section 17–5–77 as a carte blanche delegation of the state police power to local government, unless there be a specific and direct conflict between state and local law. This interpretation is inconsistent with the multiple statutes, wherein the legislature confers specific powers and duties on local government, and distorts the nature of the police power.

The State is the sole and exclusive repository of the police power, neither the federal nor local government has any such inherent power. The police power is awesome, for it confers the right to declare an act a crime and to deprive an individual of his liberty or property in order to protect or advance the public health, safety, morals, and welfare. The decision of whether a problem should be deemed one of local concern and should be regulated under the police power should initially be decided by the legislature representing all the citizens of this state. The legislature may then elect to delegate the power to local government to deal with the specific area of concern. It is equally a legislative judgment to deny delegating this power to local government.

The palliative suggested by the majority opinion that local citizens can change the law by electing new officials provides no relief for the individual previously convicted and avoids the basic issue of whether the police power has, in fact, been delegated under the specific circumstance. All exercise of the police power by local government is derivative, none is inherent, and it is the exclusive prerogative of the State to establish the conditions under which it will be exercised. If local government discerns a condition which merits control through the police power, this matter should be submitted to the legislature so that representatives of the entire state may resolve whether the problem should be addressed on a local level....

NOTES

1. If the legislature, in enacting a general welfare clause, intended to authorize localities to enact ordinances to exercise powers not granted elsewhere, then what is the function of statutes that expressly permit localities to exercise particular powers? Wouldn't the former render the latter superfluous?

The Utah Supreme Court subsequently interpreted Hutchinson to require broad interpretation of the "general contracting powers" of local governments unless the legislature has "clearly limited them." In Utah County v. Ivie, 137 P.3d 797 (Utah 2006), a city had been denied the authority to condemn land for street construction outside its boundaries because it lacked statutory extraterritorial authority. The city then entered into a contract with the county in which the land was situated. The contract provided that the county would condemn the land and the city would reimburse all the county's expenses. The city and county acted pursuant to an interlocal cooperation act ("ICA"). Plaintiffs contended that the ICA only allowed localities to act together to engage in conduct that each could have done individually. Since the city could not condemn the land directly, plaintiffs argued, they could not contract to have the land condemned. But the court interpreted the ICA to permit cooperation as long as each locality only performed an act for which it had authority. Since the city was only committing acts, such as appropriating money for the "safety, health, prosperity, ... or convenience" of its residents, that its general contracting power authorized it to undertake, the requirements of the ICA were satisfied.

2. In Williams v. Town of Hilton Head Island, 429 S.E.2d 802 (S.C. 1993), the court considered an ordinance imposing a real estate transfer fee adopted by the town without express legislative authority. The state legislature had recently enacted a series of statutes pursuant to a state constitutional amendment that provided that "all laws concerning local government shall be liberally construed in their favor. Powers, duties, and responsibilities granted local government subdivisions by this Constitution and by law shall include those fairly implied and not prohibited by this Constitution." S.C. Const. art. VIII, § 17. Subsequently, the legislature enacted a statute that provided, in pertinent part: "Each municipality of the State ... may enact regulations, resolutions, and ordinances, not inconsistent with the Constitution and general law of this State, including the exercise of powers in relation to roads, streets, markets, law enforcement, health and order in the municipality or respecting any subject which appears to it necessary and proper for the security, general welfare, and convenience of the municipality or for preserving health, peace, order and good government in it, including the authority to levy and collect taxes on real and personal property and as otherwise authorized in this section, make assessments, and establish uniform service charges relating to them...." Appellants contended that Dillon's Rule, which had previously provided the controlling standard of judicial construction with respect to municipal powers, survived passage of the general welfare statute. The court disagreed.

> This issue has been considered by other jurisdictions with subsequently enacted "Home Rule" legislation. The Iowa Supreme Court in Kasparek v. Johnson County Bd. of Health, 288 N.W.2d 511 (Iowa 1980), held that Dillon's Rule is no longer valid following adoption of home rule amendments. Alaska's Court of Appeals considered the continued applicability of Dillon's Rule in Simpson v. Municipality of Anchorage, 635 P.2d 1197 (1981), and noted the consistency of the holding that home rule constitutional provisions were adopted in order to abrogate traditional restrictions on the exercise of local autonomy. Id. at 1200.
>
> This Court concludes that by enacting the Home Rule Act, S.C. Code Ann. § 5–7–10, et seq. (1976), the legislature intended to abolish the application of Dillon's Rule in South Carolina and restore autonomy to local government. We are persuaded that, taken together, Article VIII and Section 5–7–30, bestow upon municipalities the authority to enact regulations for government services deemed necessary and proper for the security, general welfare and convenience of the municipality or for preserving health, peace, order and good government, obviating the requirement for further specific statutory authorization so long as such regulations are not inconsistent with the Constitution and general law of the state.

Williams v. Town of Hilton Head Island, 429 S.E.2d at 805.

For examples of the different constructions of general welfare clauses, compare Williams v. Blue Cross Blue Shield of North Carolina, 581 S.E.2d 415 (N.C. 2003), with Square Lake Hills Condominium Assn. v. Bloomfield Township, 471 N.W.2d 321 (Mich. 1991). In *Williams*, the court determined that state statutes that permitted a county to enact ordinances that "define, regulate, prohibit, or abate acts, omissions, or conditions detrimental to the health, safety, or welfare of its citizens and the peace and dignity of the county," did not authorize a county to enact an ordinance that (1) prohibited discrimination in employment on the basis of race, color, religion, sex, national origin, age, disability, marital status, familial status, and veteran status; (2) authorized the county Human Relations Commission to investigate alleged offenses; and (3) permitted private actions against employers whom the Commission reasonably believed had discriminated. The court indicated that the grant in the ordinance that permitted private causes of action exceeded the authority granted the county by the general welfare clause. In *Square Lake Hills*, a town used its statutory authority to "protect the general welfare" in order to enact an ordinance regulating boat docking and launching. The court noted that the state constitution effectively reversed Dillon's Rule and provided for liberal construction of statutes concerning the powers of municipal corporations. See Mich. Const. Art. VII, § 34. The court found that the challenged ordinance regulated an activity rather than land use, and thus was a "general welfare" ordinance rather than a zoning ordinance. The court concluded that the ordinance was a reasonable exercise of the police power necessary to avoid a nuisance, protect natural resources, maintain property values, and avoid risks to public health. The court indicated that the legislature had drafted the "general welfare" statute in a manner that indicated a desire to allow municipalities to address local issues without additional statutory authority. A dissenting judge suggested that the ordinance was a zoning ordinance and thus could be enacted only pursuant to, and in accordance with, a state zoning act.

3. Note that the effect of Dillon's Rule is to require municipalities to seek specific authority from the state legislature. The Utah Supreme Court in *Hutchinson*, in recognition of this fact, points out that the state legislature only meets for 60 days every two years. Should the frequency with which the legislature meets affect the judicial construction of local powers? Most state legislatures (including Utah's) now meet annually, although some (including Texas's) still meet biennially. Several state legislatures operate for constitutionally limited periods that may be as short as 30 or 60 days. See, e.g., Ala. Const. art. IV, § 48; Fla. Const. art. III, § 3(d); Ky. Const. § 36. Special sessions may be called to extend the period of a legislative session.

4. In *Hutchinson*, the Utah Supreme Court indicates that there exist at least three mechanisms for avoiding abuse of local authority: the legislature, the judiciary, and the electorate. If any of these mechanisms is effective, the need for a rule of law or of statutory interpretation that constrains local autonomy would appear to be superfluous. Indeed, if alternative checks on abuse are available, a rule of law that frustrates local initiative may actually discourage novel local activity that is potentially beneficial. Thus, it makes sense to determine the accuracy of the court's observation about the effectiveness of these checks on local excess.

Begin with consideration of candidate elections. The court assumes that local officials who do not serve the public interest will be rejected at the next election and that the threat of defeat will be sufficient to deter abuse. Is this a realistic perspective? Consider two counterarguments. First, local officials whose misconduct adversely affects nonresidents, e.g., by imposing discriminatory taxes or who site waste management facilities at the edge of town, will not necessarily suffer rebuke at the polls since those who are distressed do not have a vote. Second, abuse on a particular issue is unlikely to bring about electoral rebuke if the official's overall performance is satisfactory. Voters in elections face a binary choice. They can only vote for or against a candidate. They cannot register content or discontent with individual parts of the candidate's record. Thus, even a voter who is disgruntled about an official's lack of evenhandedness in the award of city contracts, for example, is likely to vote for the official if the voter finds that the schools are satisfactory, that the garbage is collected on time, and that taxes are relatively low, as long as those issues are of greater importance to the voter. In short, no one act of favoritism or misfeasance by a particular official is likely to be pivotal for a majority of voters, and many voters may be persuaded to reelect an official who has delivered on a matter of salient importance to them, even if the same official has granted wasteful, less salient favors to other groups.

Legislative review of local abuse is likely to fail for reasons that by now should be familiar. State legislators are likely to respond to local problems only when confronted by a group that possesses sufficient influence and interest to command the legislative ear. The general problem of collective action suggests that a (typically small) group that desires a concentrated benefit is far more likely to satisfy these conditions than a (typically much larger) group, each member of which will suffer a small loss if the local government exploits them. This is true even if the total losses suffered by the latter group exceed the total benefits to the former group. If the group that is the victim of the expropriative legislation could form an effective coalition, moreover, it is likely that it would be able to appeal to the local legislative body and prevent the abuse from occurring in the first instance. Thus, the court's assumption that state legislative oversight can deter local lawmaking abuses requires the existence of a group that has substantial influence in the state legislature even though it has little influence at the local level. What kinds of groups fit this description? Is state legislation enacted at the behest of such groups more likely to serve the public interest than local legislation that adversely impacts such groups?

Judicial supervision of local activity suffers from a different limitation. Judicial intervention can occur only when a local act is challenged. But, given the difficulty of organizing a group to oppose the interests that passed the local legislation, there is little reason to believe that, once the legislation is passed, a particular litigant would invest the time, effort, and money necessary to bring a successful lawsuit challenging the ordinance. Thus, the very problem that makes the judicial solution necessary also renders it insufficient. Here, two counterarguments must be mentioned. The first is that litigation does occasionally materialize. Cases like *Hutchinson* in Utah and *Early Estates* in Rhode Island demonstrate the willingness of litigants occasionally to come forward. It is true that, as in all collective action problems, a subgroup with a sufficiently intense interest may overcome the tendency for inertia. In the Utah case, the issue was whether a candidate for public office had committed a criminal offense by violating a local campaign expenditure ordinance. Obviously, the personal benefit of initiating the lawsuit to avoid criminal conviction was sufficiently high to justify the costs of litigating the ordinance's validity. But this occasional creation of public goods through litigation may occur too infrequently to serve as a benchmark for the appropriate legal rule. Can we expect a similarly willing creator of public goods to arise in more mundane situations? When an individual does have a sufficiently intense interest to challenge a local act as being outside the proper scope of municipal autonomy, what is the likelihood that the litigant will represent the public good? Assume, for instance, that a locality wishes to subsidize a shopping center with tax breaks in order to attract potential employers. An existing shopping mall owner may challenge the legitimacy of the subsidy out of fear that the plan will put his operation at a competitive disadvantage. Is the public interest adequately represented in the ensuing contest?

Before dismissing the majority's rationale in *Hutchinson*, however, keep in mind that state legislators also may permit local officials to "abuse" the public trust. A state statute that permits local officials to engage in activities that are not consistent with the interests of (a majority of) their constituents is as harmful as a local ordinance that has the same effect. Thus, if we are concerned about reducing local abuse, the relevant question is whether state or local lawmaking bodies are more likely to make decisions that are inconsistent with their constituents' interests. Dillon's Rule, of course, implicitly suggests that local governments are less trustworthy in this respect. Dillon's Rule might be justifiable, therefore, if we believed that the state legislature better protects the local public interest than local officials do. It is not immediately apparent, however, that this proposition is correct. Consider the constraints on public officials that the majority in *Hutchinson* addresses. It is not clear that the local electorate has any greater ability to control state officials than it has over local officials. First, only a limited number of state legislators will be interested in the local affairs of any particular municipality. Second, members of the local electorate will have more difficulty getting the attention of state legislators. The local electorate will face more competition for the legislators' time, and will have to bear higher costs of traveling to the state legislature to lobby for their interests.

Nevertheless, there may be some reason to believe that the state legislature may be less easily captured by a particular interest group. Bicameralism, which is rarely found at the local level, increases the costs of lobbying at the state level and thus diminishes its likelihood. See Saul

Levmore, Bicameralism: When are Two Decisions Better than One?, 12 Intl. Rev. L. & Econ. 145 (1992). Fear of the executive veto similarly raises the costs of legislative conduct contrary to the "general welfare." Finally, the prevalence of legislative committees at the state level may increase both the costs of passing legislation and the probability that schemes contrary to the "general welfare" will be exposed as such.

The fact that the costs of procuring legislation at the state level are likely to be higher than at the local level, however, may have more insidious effects. Even if all sides of an issue are organized at the state level, so that the state legislature is, at least in theory, able to hear all voices, some groups may have greater financial ability than others to incur the costs related to the existence of bicameral decisionmaking, legislative committees, and distant representatives. Thus, there may be instances in which the increased costs of decisionmaking at the state level means that well-financed interest groups will have a distinct advantage in passing favorable legislation.

E. THE CONCEPT(S) OF "HOME RULE"

PROBLEM X

The City of Butterworth is authorized by the state constitution to "make and enforce within its limits all local, police, sanitary, and other regulations with respect to all municipal affairs." The state has enacted a Labor Code that establishes minimum wages and maximum hours for employees in the state. The city has adopted a charter that fully embodies the constitutional prerogative. Pursuant to that charter, the city has enacted an ordinance establishing a pay scale for municipal employees that is lower than the minimum pay scale required by the state Labor Code.

Fitch is employed by Butterworth as an electrician. She consults you on the possibility of bringing an action against the city for damages and an injunction on the grounds that the city has failed to pay its electricians the minimum wage dictated by state law. She asks you whether the city had authority to enact the challenged ordinance. How will you respond? See Bishop v. City of San Jose, 460 P.2d 137 (Cal. 1969).

Dale Krane, Platon N. Rigos, & Melvin B. Hill, Jr., Home Rule in America

10–14 (2001).

The Home Rule Movement

In the decades just before and after the Civil War, reformers sought to end the problems caused by "local privilege" legislation and to end or minimize state legislative interference in municipal operations. Rather than subjecting municipalities to state legislative control, these reformers sought state constitutional grants that would permit cities to write and amend their own charters. [These charters, tantamount to a "constitution" for a municipality, would permit municipalities to define their own powers and therefore to exercise authority without first obtaining permission from the legislature.—EDS.] This reform strategy was known as the home rule movement and originally was conceived as a means for ending the interference of local state legislative delegations in municipal affairs. Over time, the movement became associated with the larger idea of broad grants of local government autonomy.

* * *

After the Civil War, those who sought to provide cities with constitutional protections from state legislative abuse understood that it would be impossible to confer substantive powers on cities without also conferring on them the power to write their own charters. When Missouri wrote its 1875 constitution, it included the first-ever state constitutional provision to permit the drafting of municipal charters. Howard McBain, in his seminal work *The Law and the Practice of Municipal Home Rule,* published in 1916, declared that the Missouri action "marked the most important step that had ever been taken in the United States in the direction of securing home rule to cities through the medium of a constitutional provision." Several other states soon followed Missouri's lead and gave positive grants of authority to municipalities via various forms of general enabling laws and the option for home rule charters. The list includes California (1879), Washington State (1889), Minnesota (1896), Colorado (1902), Virginia (1902), Oregon (1906), Oklahoma (1907), Michigan (1908), Arizona (1912), Ohio (1912), Nebraska (1912), and Texas (1912). The constitutional language in these thirteen states shared the common feature of establishing home rule through the use of a locally drafted charter which was to be ratified by local voters (or in one case, the city council).

Advocates of home rule benefited from association with the Populist and Progressive reformers who sprung up on the Great Plains after the Civil War. The aggrieved farmers who made up the Populist movement attacked a wide range of private and public abuses of power, and in the process spawned a series of important changes in government at all levels—for example, the secret ballot, direct election of U.S. senators, a public fund deposit law, initiative, referendum, recall, and the end of free railroad passes for elected officials. Whereas the Populists were primarily agrarians, the Progressives, who came a bit later, were primarily urban dwellers, but the two movements shared a similar reform impulse: breaking the alliance between big business and party officials. In particular, the Progressives sought to constrain the abuses of boss rule, state legislative interference in local governments, and the spoils system. With their emphasis on efficiency, economy, and professionalism, the Progressives pushed for "good government," defined as making it more "business-like." At the local government level, the Progressives urged the adoption of city-commission and city-manager forms of government, unified executive budgets, regional planning, and a merit-based civil service system.

The First Half of the Twentieth Century

The Progressive Movement, with its emphasis on business-like government, became the vehicle for further efforts to reform government after World War I, and the home rule idea continued to spread. In the 1920s "good government" associations such as the National Municipal League disseminated model constitutional provisions that included home rule concepts. This modest campaign continued for the next three decades with incremental advances. A good example of this effort is H.S. Gilbertson's book *The County: The "Dark Continent" of American Politics,* which leveled damning indictments at county and township governments. Gilbertson called for the reform of county governments and urged other states to emulate the 1911 California County Home Rule Constitutional Amendment and the 1912 Los Angeles County Charter. Richard Childs, one of the most influential of the Progressive reformers in the National Municipal League, was impressed by the success of the League's Model City Charter in spreading the adoption of the city manager form of government. In 1930, along with others, Childs proposed the "Principles of a Model County Government" as well as a Model County Manager Law.

After the U.S. Supreme Court in 1923 upheld Dillon's Rule for a second time, the home rule movement waned, coming to a standstill by the middle of the Great Depression. By 1937, only twenty-one states had opted for some form of home rule charter authority. States adopting home rule were Maryland (1915), Pennsylvania (1923), New York (1923), Nevada (1924), Wisconsin (1924), Utah (1932), Ohio (1933), and West Virginia (1936).

The home rule movement, in its campaign for municipal and county charters, broached the crucial question: What powers should be granted to local jurisdictions? If the purpose of a home rule charter is threefold—"(1) to prevent [state] legislative interference with local government, (2) to enable cities [and counties] to adopt the kind of government they desire, and (3) to provide cities [and counties] with sufficient powers to meet the increasing needs for local services"—then the fundamental question in home rule becomes where should the line between "local affairs" and "state government interests" be drawn? New York State addressed this question in 1923 when it adopted a constitutional amendment that included a lengthy list of items regarded as essentially "local," which thus were placed under local control. Other states, such as Utah, also adopted this strategy of enumerating "local affairs," because they thought this approach would clarify the line between state and local interests, and as a consequence, would reduce the number of lawsuits that were filed immediately after the adoption of a home rule charter.

It is easy to understand the attraction of this strategy, which parallels the enumeration clause in the U.S. Constitution. This period was still under the influence of the doctrine of "dual federalism," which held that national and state governments possessed separate spheres of authority and that neither plane of government should be permitted to interfere with the other's responsibilities. The National Municipal League supported this "dual federalism" approach by arguing for the concept of *Imperium in Imperio,* or the establishment of a state within a state. The device of a constitutional list of specified local government powers, because of the legal rule of exclusion, would not only enumerate the areas of local activity but would also reserve to state governments those activities not on the list, and thus the list was believed to be a clear statement that could be adhered to by state legislators and state judges. The *Imperium* approach suffers from the inflexibility of constitutions. Once the list of state versus local powers becomes part of the state constitution, it is very difficult to amend. As a result, state courts, through their decisions in lawsuits challenging state or local exercise of some power, become the arbiters of the scope of local authority.

However, just as sorting out national versus state interests has been a quixotic quest, so also has been the effort to do so between states and localities.... State courts soon found themselves embroiled in numerous lawsuits asking for rulings as to whether some activity such as public health, street repair, or liquor licenses were matters of local or state interest. The frustration of finding a clear line was expressed by the Wisconsin Supreme Court in a 1936 ruling on home rule: "When is an enactment of the legislature of state wide concern? We find no answer to this question in any decision of any court in this country." Despite the logical difficulties of this strategy, vestiges of it continue to the present day, and the matters that state courts consider to be "local affairs" vary from state to state.

Last Half of the Twentieth Century

The American Municipal Association, forerunner to the National League of Cities, hired Jefferson B. Fordham in 1952 to analyze state-local relations and to make recommendations for a new approach. Fordham was professor and dean of the College of Law at Ohio State University and was the author of *Local Government Law: Text, Cases & Other Materials.* His book, according to the American Bar Association, "revolutionized the teachings of this field." Fordham's report suggested a European-style "devolution of powers" plan in which a state legislature would grant local discretionary authority via the adoption of a municipal charter. The charter, under the Fordham plan, would allow municipalities to supersede special state laws and many general laws applicable to municipal corporations. In its essence, the Fordham "devolution of powers" plan proposed a reversal of Dillon's Rule:

> A municipal corporation which adopts a home rule charter rule may exercise any power or perform any function which the legislature has power to devolve upon a non-home rule charter municipal corporation and which is not denied to all home rule charter municipal corporations by statute and is within such limitations as may be established by the statute.

Instead of exercising only those powers explicitly granted to them, municipalities under Fordham's plan could act unless explicitly prohibited by state law. Twelve states adopted the plan, but, as with the original home rule movement, enthusiasm waned for the "devolution powers" model.

This model of home rule authority is sometimes referred to as "legislative home rule."

* * *

Despite the enlargement of local government discretion by state legislatures during the last half of the twentieth century, the actions of the state legislatures have often been negated by state courts that have been reluctant to drop the catechism of Dillon's Rule. Crabbed judicial interpretations have continued to construe local government power very narrowly, even when the legislature has indicated that it has a contrary intent. "Even in *imperio* states, where local ordinances are supposed to govern in municipal matters," Richard Briffault asserts, "the difficulties state courts experience in defining exclusive areas of local interest erode the legal protection of autonomy." Consequently, in many states, a narrow interpretation of Dillon's Rule prevails, and "this means that a city cannot operate a peanut stand at the city zoo without first getting the state legislature to pass an enabling law, unless, perchance, the city's charter or some previously enacted law unmistakably covers the sale of peanuts."

State constitutional provisions, statutes, court decisions, and advisory rulings by state attorneys general and by other state officers (auditors, for example) continue to define, refine, and redefine the parameters of local government authority in each state. For example, Illinois, when it rewrote its constitution in 1970, modified the devolution-of-powers model by moving in the direction of the enumeration strategy that had been tried during the "good government" era. That is, the Illinois Constitution set forth complex decision rules related to the establishment of home rule; the writing and adoption of charters; the specific areas of local affairs, including powers to regulate health, safety, morals, and welfare; and powers to tax and incur debt. Equally important, the Illinois Constitution went to the heart of Dillon's Rule by telling state legislators and judges how to interpret the list of local powers—"the powers and functions of home rule units shall be construed liberally." By contrast, non-home rule units and limited-purpose governments (such as special districts, townships) "shall have only powers granted by law."

The Illinois approach is significant because it has established what might be labeled as a new model of home rule—the "liberal construction" model. By reaching back to the "sorting out" strategy and then wrapping the list of local powers within the cloak of reasonably clear language that state courts and the legislature must follow, Illinois tried to clarify the conditions under which the state government could preempt a local government charter.

Lynn A. Baker & Daniel B. Rodriguez, Constitutional Home Rule and Judicial Scrutiny

86 Denver U. L. Rev. 1337, 1364–1371 (2009).

We have seen in Part III the various ways that the state courts have drawn lines between the state and local spheres of authority. In this Part we consider whether and to what extent that project has been a success. Such an assessment, we believe, has implications not only for state constitutionalism and home rule, but also for the appropriate role of the courts in demarcating and enforcing federal constitutional boundaries of state regulatory immunity.

The long and rich history of state courts crafting doctrines and working through, case by case, the adjudicatory problems posed by home rule provisions in the state constitution stands in stark contrast to the U.S. Supreme Court's holding in *Garcia v. San Antonio Metropolitan Transit Authority* that the courts could not usefully, and should not, play a role in disputes under the Tenth Amendment concerning the boundaries of state immunity from federal regulation. The fact that the U.S. Supreme Court has declared impossible a task that lesser state courts regularly undertake underscores the importance and value of critically evaluating the state courts' work. If the state courts are in fact doing a good job, it would suggest that the task is far from impossible and, indeed, that the U.S. Supreme Court might do well to follow the state courts' lead. If, instead, a close examination causes one to question the quality or feasibility of the state courts' work, then those courts might do well to adopt the *Garcia* Court's approach and abandon this particular line-drawing project.

In order to evaluate the state courts' home rule doctrines and decisions, one must first agree upon a metric or baseline against which to measure them. This fact is surprisingly often overlooked by commentators and appellate courts when they engage in such critiques. In addition, it is important to note that there are two possible focuses of any evaluation of the work of the courts: the judicially crafted doctrine or test, and the court's application of that doctrine or test to the facts of individual cases.

By what standard should one evaluate the state courts' tests for distinguishing between "local affairs" and "matters of state-wide concern"? Should one ask, for example, whether such a test, in the abstract, is coherent? Draws distinctions that are logical? Treats like cases alike? Is likely to yield predictable results? Or appears to be an efficient means toward a proclaimed policy goal? Similarly, one might ask by what standard one should judge a state court's application of its home rule doctrine to the facts of individual cases: Are like cases treated alike? Are the results predictable? Are plausible justifications given for the distinctions that are drawn?

We do not propose to resolve these important questions involving the baselines that should be used in evaluating either aspect of the courts' work. We raise them largely to underscore the fact that one cannot properly assess the quality or success of a legal doctrine or judicial decision in a vacuum or against an unspecified ideal. In the absence of an appropriate, agreed-upon metric, we will nonetheless in the remainder of this Part attempt to evaluate the work of the state courts by closely examining several criticisms that logically might be levied against the *imperio* home rule doctrines that the courts have devised. These criticisms, not surprisingly, echo those discussed by the U.S. Supreme Court in the context of its efforts, pursuant to the Tenth Amendment, to protect traditional state functions, "the functions essential to separate and independent existence of the states," from federal regulation.

First, one might contend that the doctrines that the courts have crafted pursuant to the *imperio* home rule provisions of their states' constitutions are unworkable. The claim is that one cannot distinguish between matters of "local" or "municipal" concern versus matters of "statewide" concern with sufficient consistency nor define these terms with sufficient coherence. This claim must be further parsed, however. The project of distinguishing between local/municipal and statewide matters of concern is mandated by the text of many state constitutions' home rule provisions. The Colorado Constitution, for example, authorizes any home rule city to make the laws governing "all its local and municipal matters," and further stipulates that such local laws "shall supersede within the territorial limits and other jurisdiction of said city or town any law of the state in conflict therewith." Thus, any perceived problems with the coherence or "workability" of the larger project, including the defining or identifying of such "local and municipal matters," are the fault of the drafters and ratifiers of the constitution's home rule provision rather than of the courts.

If the claim, rather, is that the doctrines that the courts have crafted to explicate the distinction between local and statewide concerns and to guide the ensuing line-drawing are not capable of coherent or consistent application, then several other questions arise: Against what baseline is "coherence" or "consistency" in this context usefully measured? How is a coherent or consistent application of *any* doctrine to be identified? What is an example of a judicial doctrine that *is* capable of the requisite level of coherence and consistency in its application? In this area, as in all others in which courts engage in constitutional interpretation, there is substantial, beneficial doctrinal path dependence that mitigates against large, abrupt, unexpected changes as a doctrine evolves. Can one ask more of a system of case-by-case adjudication than that it produce a roughly consistent and sensible pattern of cases that carry out the larger objectives of a defensible public policy?

In this regard, it should be noted that no less an authority than New York's Chief Justice Cardozo affirmed some 80 years ago that drawing these lines was surely possible, although he did not answer any of the preceding questions in reaching that conclusion....

One need not simply defer, however, to Chief Justice Cardozo's implicit assessment that the courts are quite capable of drawing appropriate and principled lines between matters of state and local concern. The claim that the courts' *imperio* home rule doctrines are not capable of coherent or consistent application is problematic in several independent respects. First, in the absence of an agreed baseline against which various doctrines might be measured and compared, there is no reason to think that judicial linedrawing in this area is any less coherent or consistent than in other doctrinal areas. Second, one implication of concerns about the coherence or consistency of these doctrines is that the courts should play no role at all unless they can do so with some (unspecified) level of jurisprudential purity. The further implication is that judicial abstinence in this context is preferable to arguably imperfect judicial review.

Is there support for such a claim? Perhaps judicial review in this context is not in fact necessary or preferable. What if the state legislature were simply left to make its own determinations of what matters are of statewide versus local concern, without judicial oversight or interference? In enacting laws, the legislature in an *imperio* home rule state could be understood to have made a determination, implicitly or explicitly, that the matter at issue is of statewide concern. If the role of the courts under *imperio* home rule provisions is to correct any errors in these determinations by the legislature, such judicial review would arguably be unnecessary if either there were no legislative errors for the courts to correct or if the likelihood of subsequent judicial errors were at least as great as the likelihood of an initial legislative error. We take up each of these possibilities in turn.

Can the state legislature reasonably be expected *not* to encroach into areas of local concern? The argument, analogous to that set out by the *Garcia* majority in the federalism context, would be that to the extent that localities and municipalities are represented in the state legislature, the state lawmaking process will inevitably and naturally protect their interests. In fact, however, representation in state legislatures does not respect the geographic boundaries of municipalities, let alone provide municipalities any analogue to the representation of states in the U.S. Senate. Thus, for example, the city of Austin is represented by two members of the Texas Senate, each of whom represents a portion of the city, and each of whom also represents various neighboring cities. The city of Austin has six Representatives in the Texas House, each of whom represents a different part of the city, and all but one of whom also represents some or all of several neighboring municipalities. This structure of representation can offer no reassurance to those who contend that municipalities *could* protect themselves adequately within a state's political process, in the absence of any judicial review, *if* each municipality were represented within that process as a whole and separate municipality. That is, if one's concern, as embodied in *imperio* home rule provisions of state constitutions, is to ensure that home rule jurisdictions have a realm of autonomy from state regulation, the existing allocation of representation gives one no reason to think that the members of the state legislature will be especially keen to abstain from regulating in areas of "local concern."

It must be noted, however, that the *absence* of an analogue to the U.S. Senate within state legislatures may nonetheless protect localities from legislative encroachments on their autonomy in a different way. Since at least 1964, when the U.S. Supreme Court held in *Reynolds v. Sims* that "the Equal Protection Clause requires that both houses of a state legislature be apportioned on a population basis," representation in each house of every state's legislature has been allocated among districts of equal population. This means that small and large municipalities receive equivalent representation, relative to their shares of the state's population. And this further means that the gains from any legislation that the state legislature passes are highly likely to be distributed across municipalities in proportion to their relative shares of the state's population.

This state of affairs differs markedly from that surrounding the U.S. Senate, which affords large and small states equal representation, without regard to population. As one of us has demonstrated in previous work, the disproportionately great representation that the Senate affords small population states, relative to their shares of the nation's population, results in small population states wielding disproportionately great power in Congress as a whole. This in turn can be shown, both theoretically and empirically, to result in small states receiving a disproportionately large slice, and large states a disproportionately small slice, of the federal "pie." This systematic redistribution of wealth from the larger states to the smaller ones cannot be explained by systematically greater poverty in the smaller states, nor can it be justified by any moral or economic theory. In sum, the equal representation afforded states by the Senate systematically encroaches on the autonomy of the larger population states, to the benefit of the smaller states.

The thoroughly proportional structure of representation in state legislatures, combined with the absence of municipality-based representation, means that a subset of cities within a state are unlikely to be able systematically to harness the state lawmaking power to infringe on the autonomy of other cities. At the same time, however, the absence of municipality-based representation may give the state legislature no particular reason to respect, and to refrain from legislating in, areas of "local concern." In sum, the structure of representation within the state legislature, taken alone, does not provide a persuasive argument that the state legislature can reasonably be expected *not* to encroach into areas of local concern.

If state legislatures cannot be presumed consistently to "get right" the divide between matters of local versus statewide concern, the question then becomes whether the addition of judicial review will reduce or increase the rate of errors in this area. In essence, the question is one of comparative institutional competence between state courts and state legislatures in the area of ensuring constitutionally mandated local autonomy.

At one level, this inquiry simply returns us to a variant of the questions with which we began: by what baseline or metric should one measure the competence of the court in this area? And what is the purpose of constitutional home rule provisions? If one looks beyond these questions to potentially relevant differences between courts and legislatures, however, it seems likely that judicial review will reduce rather than increase the rate of errors in identifying areas of local concern. Judicial norms can be expected to cause the courts to strive for continuity over time in deciding what is or is not a matter of local concern. Although this respect for precedent might be construed as resulting in "regressive" or "backward looking" decisions, it means that there is likely to be a predictability to those decisions. Appellate courts, especially, are likely to be attentive to the temporal "big picture" in a particular doctrinal area. The legislature, by contrast, operates under very different norms. The preferences of current interest groups and constituencies are likely to substantially affect legislative outcomes. In sum, as compared to the legislature, the courts seem to have relatively little incentive to be biased in their decisionmaking in favor of any particular interest group or constituency, and to be relatively more likely to be impartially concerned with the larger, theoretical question of what is a matter of local concern.

Finally, without regard to the persuasiveness of the above, some might contend that there is no reason for the courts to review legislation under the state constitution's home rule provision because the courts are also reviewing legislation under a variety of other constitutional provisions designed to reign in plenary legislative power. Such provisions include prohibitions against special and local legislation, prohibitions on special commissions, and "public purpose" requirements for the issuance of debt and the spending of public funds. Although the effect of some of these provisions in particular instances may be to prevent legislative encroachments on local autonomy, none of these other provisions has that as its focus. Consistent with that fact, at the time of their adoption, *imperio* home rule provisions were quite obviously not considered to be redundant with concurrently adopted or pre-existing constitutional constraints on plenary legislative power.

NOTE

The preceding materials do not simply suggest that home rule takes different forms in different jurisdictions. They also suggest that the form of home rule matters. Different grants of home rule create different relationships between states and their local subdivisions. Thus, the scope of local autonomy should vary with the form of home rule that prevails in a given state. Baker and Rodriguez provide a thorough description of the home rule provisions of different states. See Lynn A. Baker & Daniel B. Rodriguez, Constitutional Home Rule and Judicial Scrutiny, 86 Denver U. L. Rev. 1337, 1374–1424 (2009). The distinguish between those states that have what they call "legislative home rule" provisions—which authorize municipalities to exercise only those powers not prohibited by the legislature—and *imperium in imperio* provisions—which provide an area within which local governments are shielded from state intervention. The scope of that shield, however, and thus the meaning of the *imperio* provisions, varies from state to state, as the following materials indicate. As you read the following materials, consider what kind of relationship the constitutional grant of home rule embodies; does it neatly divide government functions between state and local governments, or does it create a more complicated arrangement in which state and local governments share authority? Regardless of the arrangement, do you find that courts pay attention to the constitutional structure of relationship in deciding the scope of local authority?

City of Atlanta v. McKinney

454 S.E.2d 517 (Ga. 1995).

■ FLETCHER, JUSTICE.

These appeals involve a challenge to City of Atlanta ordinances that prohibit discrimination on the basis of sexual orientation, establish a domestic partnership registry for jail visitation, and extend insurance and other employee benefits to domestic partners of city employees. The trial court ruled that the city exceeded its powers in enacting the domestic partnership ordinances, but dismissed the claims challenging the anti-discrimination laws. We hold that the city has the power to enact the anti-discrimination and registry ordinances, but exceeded its authority in extending employee benefits to persons who are not dependents under state law. We affirm in part and reverse in part the trial court's grant of judgment on the pleadings to the plaintiffs in S94A1610 and affirm the grant of the city's motion to dismiss in S94X1612.

The Atlanta City Council in 1986 amended its charter's bill of rights and its code of ordinances to prohibit discrimination on the basis of sexual orientation. See Ordinance 86–0–0190 & 86–0–0308. The ordinances prohibit sexual orientation discrimination in city employment, artist selection, festival admission, Atlanta Civic Center exhibitors, licensed alcohol beverage establishments, and vehicles for hire. "Sexual orientation" is defined as "the state of being heterosexual, homosexual, or bisexual."

In June 1993, the city council passed an ordinance providing for the establishment of a domestic partnership registry in the city's business license office. Ordinance 93–0–0776 defines "domestic partners" as "two people of the opposite or same gender who live together in the mutual interdependence of a single home and have signed a Declaration of Domestic Partnership." The declaration is a city form in which the partners "agree to be jointly responsible and obligated for the necessities of life for each other." The ordinance extends visitation rights to city jails to domestic partners and their family. In August 1993, the city council adopted an ordinance that extended employee benefits to domestic partners.

> The City of Atlanta recognizes domestic partners as a family relationship and not a marital relationship and shall provide sick leave, funeral leave, parental leave, health and dental benefits, and any other employee benefit available to a City employee in a comparable manner for a domestic partner, as defined herein, as for a spouse to the extent that the extension of such benefits does not conflict with existing laws of the State of Georgia.

Ordinance 93–0–1057, § 3.

State representative Billy McKinney, two city council members, a city taxpayer, a city employee, and a retired city employee filed a declaratory judgment action seeking to have the four ordinances declared invalid and unconstitutional and seeking damages. The city moved to dismiss the complaint for failure to state a claim. After a hearing, the trial court granted the plaintiffs a partial judgment on the pleadings under OCGA § 9–11–12(c), declaring the domestic partnership ordinances ultra vires, void, and unconstitutional under the Georgia Municipal Home Rule Act and the Georgia Constitution, but dismissed the plaintiffs' claims related to the anti-discrimination ordinances and damages. The city appeals the judgment invalidating the domestic partnership ordinances in S94A1610. McKinney appeals the dismissal of the claims challenging the anti-discrimination ordinances and seeking damages in S94X1612.

S94A1610. Domestic Partnership Ordinances

1. "Municipal corporations are creations of the state and possess only those powers that have been expressly or impliedly granted to them." Porter v. City of Atlanta, 259 Ga. 526, 384 S.E.2d 631 (1989). The Municipal Home Rule Act of 1965 grants a city the legislative power to adopt ordinances "relating to its property, affairs, and local government for which no provision has been made by general law and which are not inconsistent with the Constitution." OCGA § 36–35–3(a) (1993). In determining the validity of an ordinance, this court must decide whether the city had the power to enact the ordinances and whether the exercise of its power is clearly reasonable. Porter, 259 Ga. at 526, 384 S.E.2d 631.

The city argues that the registry ordinance merely provides for an internal list of city residents and employees who have entered into written agreements similar to the one that this court upheld in Crooke v. Gilden, 262 Ga. 122, 414 S.E.2d 645 (1992), and grants domestic partners visitation rights to city jails. The ordinance states that it does not attempt to alter state laws regulating private or civil relationships.

> Rights and Duties Created. Neither this ordinance nor the filing of a Declaration of Domestic Partnership shall create any legal rights or duties from one of the parties to the other, except those which specifically refer to Domestic Partnership. Nothing herein shall be construed to explicitly or implicitly create a marital relationship. This ordinance does not attempt to alter or affect the laws in the State of Georgia that regulate any private or civil relationships.

Ordinance 93–0–0776, § 2(A).

Courts have a duty to construe a statute to sustain it if its language is susceptible to more than one construction. Mayor & Council v. Anderson, 246 Ga. 786, 272 S.E.2d 713 (1980). Following this rule, we construe the registry ordinance as creating only a registration system and not any legal rights. Under this construction, the ordinance is valid. First, the city possesses the power to grant visitation rights to the city jail to registered persons. The Atlanta City Charter gives the city the power to "operate, maintain, regulate, [and] control . . . corrective, detentional, penal and medical institutions, agencies and facilities." 1973 Ga. Laws 2188, 2256. Second, the registry ordinance is a reasonable exercise of the city's power. The registry is merely the mechanism by which the city can identify the residents and employees who may exercise their jail visitation rights because of their declaration as domestic partners. Because the registry and jail visitation law as construed is a reasonable ordinance related to the city's affairs, we reverse the trial court's grant of judgment on the pleadings concerning this ordinance.

2. The Georgia Constitution prohibits cities from enacting special laws relating to the rights or status of private persons. Ga. Const. Art. III, Sec. VI, Par. IV(c); see also id. (a) (prohibiting a city from enacting a local or special law for which provision has been made by general law). The home rule act also precludes cities from taking "any action affecting the private or civil law governing private or civil relationships, except as is incident to the exercise of an independent governmental power." OCGA § 36–35–6(b). Although the meaning of this provision is ambiguous, it indicates that the state does " 'not wish to give our cities the power to enact a distinctive law of contract.' " See Marshal House, Inc. v. Rent Review and Grievance Bd. of Brookline, 357 Mass. 709, 260 N.E.2d 200, 204 (1970) (quoting Fordham, "Home Rule–AMA Model," 44 Nat'l Municipal Review 137, 142). At a minimum, it means that cities in this state may not enact ordinances defining family relationships. The Georgia General Assembly has provided for the establishment of family relationships by general law. See, e.g., OCGA §§ 19–3–1 to 19–5–17 (1991); see also City of Bloomington v. Chuckney, 165 Ind. App. 177, 331 N.E.2d 780, 783 (1975) ("a city should not be able to enact its own separate law of contracts or domestic relations since these areas are unsuited to less than statewide legislation").

The Municipal Home Rule Act specifically grants cities the authority to provide insurance benefits for a city's "employees, their dependents, and their survivors." OCGA § 36–35–4(a). The issue here is whether the city impermissibly expanded the definition of dependent to include domestic partners. Although the home rule act does not define the term "dependent," other state statutes define a dependent either as a spouse, child, or one who relies on another for financial support. Compare OCGA § 20–2–886 (granting right to health insurance coverage to the spouse and dependent children of public school employees), OCGA § 45–18–8 (1990) ("spouse and dependent children" may be included in the health care coverage of state and other public employees), and OCGA § 34–9–13(a) & (b) (1993) (under workers' compensation statute a wife, husband, or child is "presumed to be the next of kin wholly dependent for support upon the deceased employee") with OCGA § 48–7–26 (Supp. 1994) (adopting the Internal Revenue Code's definition of dependent as an individual who receives half of his or her support from the taxpayer and is a member of the taxpayer's household). Domestic partners do not meet any of these statutory definitions of dependent.

The powers of cities must be strictly construed, and any doubt concerning the existence of a particular power must be resolved against the municipality. City of Macon v. Walker, 204 Ga. 810, 812, 51 S.E.2d 633 (1949); City of Doraville v. Southern Railway Co., 227 Ga. 504, 510, 181 S.E.2d 346 (1971). We conclude that the city exceeded its power to provide benefits to employees and their dependents by recognizing domestic partners as "a family relationship" and providing employee benefits to them "in a comparable manner ... as for a spouse." Accord Lilly v. City of Minneapolis, 527 N.W.2d 107 (Minn. Ct. App. 1995) (LEXIS, States, Minn.). Since it is beyond the city's authority to define dependents inconsistent with state law, we affirm the trial court's ruling invalidating the benefits ordinance as ultra vires under the home rule act and the Georgia Constitution.

[The discussions upholding the city's authority to enact an ordinance prohibiting discrimination in municipal hiring under the city's police power, and denying damages are omitted.—EDS.]

Judgment affirmed in part and reversed in part in Case No. S94A1610.

■ CARLEY, JUSTICE, concurring in part and dissenting in part.

I concur in the affirmance of the trial court's ruling invalidating the "benefits" ordinance and the trial court's dismissal of all damages claims. However, upon consideration of the Municipal Home Rule Act of 1965 and the Georgia Constitution of 1983, I cannot agree with the reversal of the trial court's ruling invalidating the "registry" ordinance and the affirmance of the trial court's dismissal of the claims related to the "sexual orientation" ordinances. Accordingly, I concur in Divisions 2 and 4 and dissent to Divisions 1 and 3.

1. The registry ordinance begins with many requirements for recognition as a domestic partnership: living together for at least six months, a mutually interdependent relationship intended to be lifelong, an agreement to be jointly obligated for the necessities of life for each other, not married to anyone else, 18 years of age or older, competency to contract, not related by blood closer than would bar marriage, no other domestic partner, filing of a termination of the domestic partnership if any of these facts change, and termination of any prior domestic partnership. The registry ordinance further states that any entity which requires evidence of the existence of a domestic partnership shall accept a Declaration of Domestic Partnership as complete proof, and provides that such declaration is reasonable proof for qualifying for any present or future domestic partner benefits that private corporations or public institutions offer. Another portion of the registry ordinance gives domestic partners jail visitation privileges which are identical to those of a spouse or other immediate family members. Finally, the registry ordinance provides for termination of the domestic partnership by written notice, death, or no longer meeting the qualifications for domestic partnership.

The registry ordinance is much more than "merely the mechanism by which the city can identify the residents and employees who may exercise their jail visitation rights because of their declaration as domestic partners." (Majority opinion, p. 520) Rather, the City's exercise of its power to grant jail visitation rights is merely one portion of the much broader registry ordinance. Thus, the registry ordinance is not "incident to the exercise of an independent governmental power." OCGA § 36–35–6(b). And, by requiring private entities which recognize domestic partnerships to accept a Declaration of Domestic Partnership as complete proof of the existence of a domestic partnership, the ordinance certainly "*affect[s]* the private or civil law governing private or civil relationships. . . ." (Emphasis supplied.) OCGA § 36–35–6(b). Therefore, in my opinion, the registry ordinance violates Georgia's Home Rule Act.

Furthermore, by defining in detail a new relationship which is very similar to marriage, see OCGA §§ 19–3–1, 19–3–2, and by providing a ready means of proof of that relationship, the registry ordinance is a proscribed "special law *relating to* the rights or *status* of private persons...." (Emphasis supplied.) Ga. Const. of 1983, Art. III, Sec. VI, Par. IV(c); Giles v. Gibson, 208 Ga. 850, 851–852, 69 S.E.2d 774 (1952) (a municipal ordinance is a special law). See also Att'y Gen. Op. 93–26. And, as a special law, the registry ordinance is preempted by this state's general law of marriage and divorce. Ga. Const. of 1983, Art. III, Sec. VI, Par. IV(a); OCGA § 36–35–6(a). Georgia's law of marriage already provides for "registration" of relationships of the same general type as that defined in the registry ordinance, OCGA § 19–3–30 et seq., and limits such "registration" to couples of opposite sex. The constitutional provision on special laws

> was intended to insure that once the legislature entered a field by enacting a general law, that field must thereafter be reserved exclusively to general legislation and could not be open to special or local laws. The terms of the constitution do not limit this rule to those fields and subjects which have been completely exhausted by a general law. It embraces every field and subject which has been covered, though superficially, by a general law.

City of Atlanta v. Hudgins, 193 Ga. 618, 623(1), 19 S.E.2d 508 (1942). See also Lomax v. Lee, 261 Ga. 575, 579(3), 408 S.E.2d 788 (1991).

The registry ordinance does not augment or strengthen the general law of marriage. Compare Grovenstein v. Effingham County, 262 Ga. 45, 47(1), 414 S.E.2d 207 (1992). That general law provides that "[m]arriage is encouraged by the law. Every effort to restrain marriage ... shall be invalid and void...." OCGA § 19–3–6. The registry ordinance tends to discourage marriage by providing alternative official recognition of a relationship akin to marriage, but without many of the restrictions found in Georgia's marriage law. See Sims v. Sims, 245 Ga. 680, 682(5), 266 S.E.2d 493 (1980). For example, termination of a domestic partnership is far easier to accomplish than is termination of a marriage.

Section 2(A) of the registry ordinance, quoted in the majority opinion, denies that it creates legal rights or duties, "*except* those which specifically refer to Domestic Partnership." (Emphasis supplied.) Section 2(A) also disclaims any creation of a marital relationship and any attempt to alter or affect Georgia laws regulating any private or civil relationships. However, semantics cannot save an ordinance which violates the constitutional provision on special laws.

> This provision of the constitution would be nullified if by play upon words and definitions the courts should hold valid a special law when there existed at the time of its enactment a general law covering the same subject-matter.

City of Atlanta v. Hudgins, supra, 193 Ga. at 623(1), 19 S.E.2d 508. If in fact the ordinance does not purport to alter or affect Georgia law regulating private or civil relationships, it would seem unnecessary to expressly provide, in Section 7, that any person may seek enforcement of the ordinance in law or equity in the "State Court of Fulton County or the Superior Court of Fulton County (or the appropriate courts in DeKalb County for residents of the City of Atlanta in DeKalb County)." Those courts are, of course, state courts of record and of general jurisdiction.

Crooke v. Gilden, 262 Ga. 122, 414 S.E.2d 645 (1992) is in no way relevant to this case. In Crooke, this court upheld the validity of a real estate contract providing for mutual contribution toward improvement of the real estate and sharing of expenses and assets. No official status of the kind contemplated by the registry ordinance was at issue in Crooke.

2. The sexual orientation ordinances prohibit discrimination, because of sexual orientation, on the part of the City, many alcoholic beverage licensees, and drivers of vehicles for hire. The ordinances also require affirmative action on the part of the City, "to promote the full realization of equal employment opportunity through a positive, continuing program in each department and agency of the City government." Ordinance 86–0–0308, § 1.

Georgia law, like federal law, recognizes and protects certain classifications of people from discrimination. Ga. Const. of 1983, Art. I, Sec. I, Par. II (state equal protection), Par. IV (religious discrimination in holding public office or trust); OCGA §§ 34–1–2 (age discrimination in employment); 34–5–1 et seq. (sex discrimination in employment); 34–6A–1 et seq. (discrimination against handicapped in employment). By these general laws, Georgia has clearly entered the field of anti-discrimination law, yet has not included a person's sexual orientation among the proscribed bases of discrimination. Therefore, the sexual orientation ordinances, like the registry ordinance, are preempted by the general law of this state.

The sexual orientation ordinances neither augment nor strengthen general anti-discrimination law. Compare Grovenstein v. Effingham County, supra, 262 Ga. at 47(1), 414 S.E.2d 207. To the contrary, general anti-discrimination law is diluted by expansion of the number of protected classes which public or private entities are required to consider.

The majority relies on the powers given to municipal corporations by OCGA § 36–34–2. While this statute may authorize ordinances prohibiting discrimination against a class protected by federal or state law, it does not authorize the expansion of protected classes. OCGA § 36–34–2 does not and cannot give a municipal corporation the power to enact an ordinance in violation of the constitutional provision on special laws, Ga. Const. of 1983, Art. III, Sec. VI, Par. IV(a). City of Atlanta v. Myers, 240 Ga. 261, 263–264(2), 240 S.E.2d 60 (1977). The Fair Employment Practices Act of 1978, also relied upon by the majority, prohibits employment discrimination by the State because of race, color, religion, national origin, sex, handicap, or age. OCGA §§ 45–19–22, 45–19–29. I agree that a municipality may pass a law on the same subject matter which is not inconsistent with the State's version. OCGA § 45–19–21(c). In my opinion, however, an ordinance which protects more classes than does the Fair Employment Practices Act is inconsistent with the Act. However, even if the sexual orientation ordinances were consistent with the Fair Employment Practices Act, the other provisions of general law enumerated above, which apply to the City and private employers as well as the State, preempt the sexual orientation ordinances.

The registry ordinance creates a parallel institution to marriage, and the sexual orientation ordinances expand the classes of people protected from discrimination by state and federal law. Thus, in enacting these ordinances, the City exceeded its authority under the Georgia Constitution and under Georgia's Home Rule Act.

NOTES

1. *City Charters and Their Construction.* The court indicates that Atlanta has amended its charter and enacted the ordinance. A charter of a home rule city serves essentially as the city's constitution. See City of Tulsa v. Public Employees Relations Board, 845 P.2d 872 (Okla. 1990). The charter outlines the powers that a home rule city has assigned to itself pursuant to the home rule authority granted by the state constitution. Thus, the scope of charter provisions is subject to interpretation, just as legislation and constitutional provisions are. In Midwest Employers Council, Inc. v. City of Omaha, 131 N.W.2d 609 (Neb. 1964), plaintiffs sought to invalidate a city ordinance that made it unlawful for employers to discriminate on the basis of race, religious creed, color, national origin, or ancestry in hiring decisions. The court opined that the Omaha city charter was a document of grant, not of limitation, and that in the absence of an explicit charter grant of authority to enact a civil rights ordinance, the city could not validly enact the challenged regulation without legislative authority. The Florida Supreme Court similarly invalidated a rent control ordinance not explicitly authorized in a city charter in City of Miami Beach v. Fleetwood Hotel, Inc., 261 So.2d 801 (Fla. 1972).

The Supreme Court of California interpreted a home rule city's charter more liberally in Domar Electric, Inc. v. City of Los Angeles, 885 P.2d 934 (Cal. 1994). The court determined that a city charter requirement that contracts subject to competitive bidding be awarded to the "lowest and best regular responsible bidder" did not preclude the Los Angeles Board of Public Works from implementing an outreach program, authorized by mayoral executive directive, to equalize opportunities for all businesses, particularly minority and women-owned businesses, to compete for city contracts. In reaching its decision, the California Supreme Court found that the city charter "represents the supreme law of the City, subject only to conflicting provisions in federal and state constitutions and to preemptive state law." 885 P.2d at 938. According to the California court, the city charter "operates not as a grant of power, but as an instrument of limitation and restriction on the exercise of power over all municipal affairs which the city is assumed to possess and the enumeration of powers does not constitute an exclusion or limitation." Id. As long as the outreach program was not expressly forbidden, and was consistent with the charter's objective of securing the best work at the lowest price practicable, its passage was within the authority given to home rule cities.

A dissenting judge found that the outreach program was intended to promote social policy, not competition, and the program requirement of good faith outreach efforts was incompatible with the charter mandate that contracts for city work be awarded to the lowest and best regular responsible bidder.

Note that invalidation of an ordinance enacted under home rule authority does not necessarily entail a narrow scope of the power to initiate legislation. It may instead involve a situation in which the locality has broad powers to initiate legislation, but those powers are subject to defeasance by the state if the ordinance involves matters outside of or in addition to those that affect the municipality. Constitutional grants of home rule may permit localities to act within a specific area, denominated as "local affairs" or "municipal affairs," but still allow the state to trump local ordinances within that area by enacting conflicting statutes with statewide application. Invalidation of the ordinance in such a case does not deny that the municipality had the authority to enact the ordinance; rather it provides that even within its range of competence, municipal activity is subject to state supremacy.

Is the court in *McKinney* saying that Atlanta did not have the authority to enact the ordinance because the subject matter was not one of local concern, or is the court saying that Atlanta could enact the ordinance because it was a matter of local concern, but that the ordinance was invalid because it conflicted with state statutes? Can you imagine circumstances in which it made a difference which of these lines of reasoning the court followed?

2. *Municipal Regulation of Domestic Partner Insurance Coverage.* After the decision in *McKinney*, the Atlanta city council enacted a new ordinance that provided insurance benefits for dependents of city employees registered as domestic partners under the registry upheld in that case. The ordinance defined "dependent" as "one who relies on another for financial support," but did not purport to create any family relationship between the employee and the dependent party. In City of Atlanta v. Morgan, 492 S.E.2d 193 (Ga. 1997), the court found this definition consistent with other statutory definitions and with common, dictionary definitions of the term. The court rejected the contention that the registration requirement constituted an improper expansion of the concept of "dependent," holding that the requirement simply restricted which dependents of the employee were entitled to benefits.

Multiple other home rule jurisdictions have enacted domestic partner ordinances with mixed results. In Lilly v. City of Minneapolis, 527 N.W.2d 107 (Minn. Ct. App. 1995), the court invalidated a local ordinance enacted by a home-rule municipality that extended health care benefits to same-sex domestic partners of city employees. As in *McKinney*, the court in *Lilly* rejected the ordinance on the grounds that the statute that authorized cities to provide health insurance coverage limited beneficiaries to municipal employees and a defined set of dependents that did not include domestic partners. But the court went further and found that the city could not enact an ordinance with broader coverage under its home rule authority because the provision of insurance coverage by cities was a matter of statewide, not local, concern. After the decision in *Lilly*, the city of Minneapolis enacted an ordinance that required certain private contractors with the city to provide benefits to their employees' domestic partners. Thus, the city required employers to provide benefits that the city could not provide to its own employees. Is such an ordinance valid after *Lilly*? See Chad Bayse, Comment: Pulling *Lilly* from the Pond? Minneapolis Wades into Domestic Partner Benefits Legislation Once Again, 30 Wm. Mitchell L. Rev. 931 (2004).

Other decisions denying localities the capacity to confer health benefits on domestic partners have not been based on the extent of a locality's home rule authority. The Supreme Court of Virginia invalidated an ordinance that granted benefits to domestic partners on the grounds that classification of unmarried partners as "dependents" was *ultra vires* for a county that did not have home rule authority. In National Pride at Work, Inc. v. Governor of Michigan, 748 N.W.2d 524 (Mich. 2008), the court determined that an amendment to the state constitution that proclaimed "the union of one man and one woman in marriage shall be the only agreement recognized as a marriage or similar union for any purpose" prohibited public employers from providing health-insurance benefits to their employees' qualified same-sex domestic partners.

Various other home rule local governments, however, including Montgomery County, Maryland, and the cities of Vancouver (Washington), Philadelphia, Chicago, and New York, had more success in asserting that they had home rule authority to expand health benefits to the same-sex domestic partners of local government employees. Recent decisions to this effect include Devlin v. City of Philadelphia, 862 A.2d 1234 (Pa. 2004) (which upheld ordinances creating a "life partnership" as a marital status and extending employee benefits to "life partners," but invalidated ordinances concerning discrimination against couples registered as "life partners" and an exemption for "life partners" from the real estate transfer tax); Tyma v. Montgomery County, 801 A.2d 148 (Md., 2002); Heinsma v. City of Vancouver, 29 P.3d 709 (Wash., 2001); Crawford v. City of Chicago, 710 N.E.2d 91 (Ill. App.), *appeal denied*, 720 N.E.2d 1090 (1999); Schaefer v. City and County of Denver, 973 P.2d 717 (Colo. App. 1998), *cert. denied* (1999) and Slattery v. City of New York, 179 Misc.2d 740 (N.Y. Misc. 1999). The Massachusetts Supreme Court held that Boston possessed the authority to enact such an ordinance under its home rule power, but that an ordinance nonetheless was invalid because it conflicted with express state law that defined the scope of "dependents." Connors v. City of Boston, 714 N.E.2d 335 (Mass. 1999). For an early analysis of domestic partner ordinances, see Craig A. Bowman & Blake M. Cornish, Note, A More Perfect Union: A Legal and Social Analysis of Domestic Partner Ordinances, 92 Colum. L. Rev. 1164 (1992).

The California Supreme Court concluded that city and county officials lacked the authority to issue marriage licenses to, solemnize marriages of, and register certificates of marriage for same-sex couples, even if the mayor concluded that a state statute limiting marriage to heterosexual couples was unconstitutional. Lockyer v. City and County of San Francisco, 95 P.3d 459 (Cal. 2004). Is there an argument that decisions concerning the scope of marriage should be made at the local level? See Richard C. Schragger, Cities as Constitutional Actors: The Case of Same–Sex Marriage, 21 J. L. & Pol. 147 (2005).

3. The majority in *McKinney* states that the Georgia Home Rule Act prevents a city from adopting "any action affecting the private or civil law governing private or civil relationships." But the majority stops short of holding (although it strongly implies) that the definition of "dependents" for insurance purposes entails such a relationship. We will study the "private or civil law" exception to home rule shortly. For the moment, consider what function is served by this exception, and whether it is possible to classify the definition of "dependents" of city employees as a matter that affects public rather than private or civil law.

The *McKinney* court notes that the Home Rule Act authorizes cities to provide insurance for their employees and their dependents, but does not define the latter phrase. The court thus looks to other statutes for a definition. Are there reasons not to incorporate the definition from other statutes into the insurance statute? Would it matter whether the state or the locality paid for the insurance?

4. What is the effect of the court's holding on the scope of the municipal initiative under the Home Rule Act? The court concludes that the city's ordinance extending health benefits is invalid because it conflicts with state law. Is this a holding that the city's definition of "dependents" is not a matter "relating to its property, affairs, and local government"? Since those are the matters as to which the state Home Rule Act grants localities home rule authority, such a finding would mean that the city had no right to enact the ordinance, regardless of what the state had done. Or is the court holding that it would have upheld the ordinance, but for the existing state statutes defining "dependents"? Assume, for instance, that the state had not defined "dependents" in any statutory provision. Would Atlanta still be precluded from adopting a definition for purposes of providing insurance to city employees and their dependents? Or is the court holding that the definition is invalid only if state law exists on the same subject? If so, what would be the result if the state repealed its statutes on the subject and Atlanta reenacted the ordinance? Note that if a home rule ordinance is trumped by state intervention, the result does not necessarily imply any general restriction on the scope of the local initiative power. The result might instead follow from a determination that even where matters of municipal affairs are concerned, they are subject to defeasance by state intervention if the state shares with the locality an interest in the subject matter of the ordinance. Alternatively, restrictions on the initiative power may result from a determination that the ordinance is beyond the scope of any level of government. See, e.g., State ex rel. Hill v. Smith, 305 S.E.2d 771 (W. Va. 1983). For example, a determination of unconstitutionality may not be a restriction on local authority, but on governmental authority generally.

5. Notice that the *McKinney* court construes the home rule power in classic Dillon's Rule terms. It states that "powers of cities must be strictly construed, and any doubt concerning the existence of a particular power must be resolved against the municipality." This is a different interpretation than the one found in *Domar Electric, Inc.*, supra page 329 where the California court stated that the city's charter "represents the supreme law of the City, subject only to conflicting provisions in the federal and state Constitutions and to preemptive state law." As support for its position, the Georgia court in *McKinney* turns to a 1949 case. Why is that case relevant to the construction of a Home Rule Act enacted in 1965? What was the purpose of the 1965 Act if not to overturn the cases construing the powers of localities narrowly? The court in *McKinney* also cites a 1971 case. That case precluded a city from construction or operation of a railroad switching yard on the grounds that the Home Rule Act specifically exempted from cities' home rule power the ability to regulate any business activity, such as railroads, regulated by the Public Service Commission. Is that case distinguishable from *McKinney*?

6. *Civil Rights Ordinances and Home Rule*. Municipalities have generally had mixed success in their efforts to use home rule authority to enact ordinances dealing with civil rights. For a narrow construction of the home rule authority in this context, see H.P. White Laboratory v. Blackburn, 812 A.2d 305 (Md. 2002). That case involved construction of the grant of home rule in Maryland's constitution. That provision permits a county that has adopted a home rule charter to enact "local laws ... upon all matters covered by the express powers granted" by the General Assembly. Md. Const. art. XI–A, § 3. The challenged ordinance prevented certain discriminatory practices in employment, prohibited employer retaliation against employees who filed complaints alleging discriminatory practices, and authorized civil and criminal actions for violations of the prohibitions. The ordinance purported to regulate only employers and employment practices located within the county. The court relied on prior case law that invalidated local ordinances concerning employment discrimination and the creation of private causes of action. Those cases concluded that employment discrimination was a statewide problem and that creation of causes of action had "been the province of state agencies." In the earlier cases, the court had distinguished a local law, which is "confined in its operation to prescribed territorial limits," from a general law, which "deals with the general public welfare, a subject which is of significant interest not just to any one county, but rather to more than one geographical subdivision, or even to the entire state." McCrory Corp. v. Fowler, 570 A.2d 834 (Md. 1990). For a contrary view, permitting a local civil rights ordinance to create a cause of action, see Sims v. Besaw's Café, 997 P.2d 201 (Or. App. 2000). In Baker v. City of Iowa City, 750 N.W.2d 93 (Ia. 2008), the court concluded that the city's effort to cover small employers in its anti-discrimination ordinance conflicted with state law and was thus invalid, but its addition of marital status as a prohibited basis of discrimination only expanded on classes protected by state law and thus was permissible.

State *ex rel.* Haynes v. Bonem

845 P.2d 150 (N.M. 1992).

■ MONTGOMERY, JUSTICE.

We issued an alternative writ of prohibition in this case to consider an important question relating to the legislative powers of home rule municipalities under New Mexico law: whether a home rule municipality may provide for a different number of members of its governing body than the number prescribed by the Municipal Code. More specifically, the question is whether the City of Clovis, a home rule municipality that has adopted a commission-manager form of government, is bound by the provisions of NMSA 1978, Sections 3–10–1(B) and 3–14–6(A) (Repl. Pamp. 1985), to constitute its city commission with five members, or may instead provide for a different number as set out in its charter.

We hold that neither Section 3–10–1(B) nor Section 3–14–6(A) is a general law that expressly denies to a home rule municipality the power to provide for a different number of city commissioners than that fixed in those statutes. More broadly, we hold that the purpose of the home rule amendment to our Constitution—to provide for maximum local self-government—would be frustrated by applying the statutes to a home rule municipality, because the subject of the legislation (composition of the municipal government) is a matter of local concern; and, even if the subject is regarded as a matter of statewide concern, the legislature has not expressly denied the power to enact a composition different from that set out in the Municipal Code.

I

The City of Clovis adopted its home rule charter in 1971. The charter provides that the City is to be governed by a commission-manager form of government and calls for a seven-member city commission, with four commissioners to be elected from four single-member districts and three commissioners to be elected at large.

In 1985, two residents of Clovis sued the City in the United States District Court for the District of New Mexico for alleged violations of the federal Voting Rights Act. The lawsuit resulted in a judgment by consent decree on July 18, 1986. The consent decree changed the number of members on the city commission and the method of their election. It ordered that the commission be composed of eight members, to be elected from four dual-member districts. The consent decree set forth a specific districting plan for the City and stated that the districting plan would "remain in effect" until the Clovis City Commission had the responsibility or opportunity to redistrict based on the 1990 census. It further provided that "[a]fter that time, any claim that any districting plan employed by the Clovis City Commission violates federal law or the law of the State of New Mexico must be pursued, if at all, through a new and different lawsuit or other legal proceeding."

Following entry of the federal court judgment, the City of Clovis implemented the new districting plan in accordance with the terms of the consent decree. That plan remained in effect until 1991, when the City began redistricting to comport with the 1990 census. While the City was considering various redistricting plans, the petitioners in this case requested that the City change the composition of the Commission from eight members, elected from four dual-member districts, to five members, elected from five single-member districts. The petitioners based their request on various provisions of the Municipal Code, including Section 3–10–1(B), which states that the elective officers of a commission-manager form of government shall include five commissioners, and Section 3–14–6(A), which provides that the governing body of a commission-manager form of government shall district the municipality into five single-member districts.

The Clovis City Commission refused petitioners' request and instead adopted a redistricting plan that retained four dual-member districts. Subsequently, petitioners filed a petition for a writ of mandamus in the District Court of Curry County, requesting that the court order the City Commission to adopt a plan providing for five single-member commissioner districts....

[The district court] concluded that mandamus was not appropriate because the City of Clovis was not required to comply with Sections 3–10–1(B) and 3–14–6(A). The court distinguished Casuse v. City of Gallup, 106 N.M. 571, 746 P.2d 1103 (1987), in which this Court held that NMSA 1978, Section 3–12–1.1 (Cum. Supp. 1992), which requires that members of municipal governing bodies reside in and be elected from single-member districts, applies to home rule municipalities. The district court stated that it found no legislative intent that Sections 3–10–1(B) and 3–14–6(A) should apply to home rule municipalities and that therefore, while *Casuse* requires that the city commissioners be elected from single-member districts, the law does not otherwise require the number of commissioners to be five....

II

Resolution of the issue in this case requires an understanding of municipal home rule and the distinction between home rule and non-home-rule municipalities. Prior to 1970, municipal home rule did not exist in New Mexico. At that time, all municipalities in the state depended on the state legislature for their power to act. They looked to state statutes for express or implied grants of authority, and if they did not find such authority, they could not act. Thus, the state exercised plenary control over municipal governments except as limited by the state or federal constitutions.

In 1970, New Mexico adopted a home rule amendment to our Constitution and thereby authorized a change in the then existing relationship between state and local governments. That amendment establishes the right of the citizens of a municipality to adopt a home rule charter. N.M. Const. art. X, § 6. A municipality adopting such a charter becomes a "home rule municipality" and may then "exercise all legislative powers and perform all functions not expressly denied by general law or charter." Id. 6(D). Thus, home rule municipalities do not look to the legislature for a grant of power to legislate, but only look to statutes to determine if any express limitations have been placed on that power. Apodaca [v. Wilson, 525 P.2d 876 (N.M. 1974)]. Those municipalities that choose not to adopt a home rule charter must still depend on the legislature for their power to act.

The purpose of municipal home rule is to "enable municipalities to conduct their own business and control their own affairs, to the fullest possible extent, in their own way." *Apodaca*, 86 N.M. at 520, 525 P.2d at 880 (quoting Fragley v. Phelan, 126 Cal. 383, 58 P. 923, 925 (1899)). Our home rule amendment states that "[t]he purpose of this section is to provide for maximum local self-government" and that "[a] liberal construction shall be given to the powers of municipalities." N.M. Const. art. X, § 6(E).

Additionally, the New Mexico Municipal Charter Act, NMSA 1978, Sections 3–15–1 to –16 (Repl. Pamp. 1985 & Cum. Supp. 1992), which supplements and implements the home rule amendment, provides that:

> The charter may provide for any system or form of government that may be deemed expedient and beneficial to the people of the municipality, including the manner of appointment or election of its officers, the recall of the officers and the petition and referendum of any ordinance, resolution or action of the municipality; provided, that the charter shall not be inconsistent with the constitution of New Mexico.

NMSA 1978, § 3–15–7 (Repl. Pamp. 1985).

With this background, we may now consider the specific issue before us. Stated again, that issue is whether Sections 3–10–1(B) and 3–14–6(A) bind a home rule municipality and preclude it from adopting a governmental structure that is inconsistent with those provisions. To resolve this issue we must determine whether either Section 3–10–1(B) or Section 3–14–6(A) is (1) a "general law" that (2) "expressly denies" to a home rule municipality the right to establish the structure (and especially, in this case, the number of commissioners) of a commission-manager form of government.

III

The first question is whether the statutes at issue are "general laws." A general law is "a law that applies generally throughout the state, or is of statewide concern as contrasted to 'local' or 'municipal' law." *Apodaca*, 86 N.M. at 521, 525 P.2d at 881. Petitioners, relying on Casuse v. City of Gallup, assert that Sections 3–10–1(B) and 3–14–6(A) are general laws because Section 3–10–1(B) applies to all municipalities in the state and Section 3–14–6(A) applies to all municipalities with populations over 10,-000.

In *Casuse*, this Court held that Section 3–12–1.1 of the Municipal Code is a general law because it applies to all municipalities in the state with populations over 10,000. However, that holding was founded on a statewide concern for the principle of single-member districting in general, and we do not believe *Casuse* holds that the form of a law determines whether the law should be characterized as "general" for purposes of Article X, Section 6 (the home rule amendment) of the Constitution. See *Apodaca*, 86 N.M. at 522, 525 P.2d at 882 ("A law general in form cannot, under the Constitution, deprive cities of the right to legislate on purely local affairs germane to the purposes for which the city was incorporated.") (quoting City of Portland v. Welch, 154 Or. 286, 59 P.2d 228, 232 (1936)). Even if a statute applies to all municipalities throughout the state, it is not necessarily a general law if it does not relate to a matter of statewide concern.

The proposition just stated may at first blush seem inconsistent with the definition of "general law" in *Apodaca* as a law applying generally throughout the state or one of statewide concern. In the context of the home rule amendment, however, we believe there is no inconsistency. In defining the term "general law" as used in the home rule amendment, this Court in *Apodaca* was attempting to impart the basic notion, applied across the country, that in order for a statute to override an enactment of a home rule municipality, the statute must relate to a matter of statewide concern. See, e.g., 2 Eugene McQuillin, The Law of Municipal Corporations § 4.80, at 180 (3d ed. rev. vol. 1988) ("A home-rule city's ordinance will supersede a conflicting state statute on the same subject matter in areas of strictly local concern. Conversely, a state statute will supersede a conflicting municipal charter or ordinance on a matter of exclusively statewide concern." (footnote omitted)). We might as easily have said, for example, that the term "general law" means a law that applies generally throughout the state and is of statewide concern as contrasted to "local" or "municipal" law. Or we could have said that a general law is one that applies generally throughout the state or (*in other words*) is of statewide concern, as contrasted to a local or municipal law. The disjunctive "or" does not exclude the conjunctive "and" unless the context so requires.

Our opinion in *Apodaca* made clear that in order for a general law to supersede a home rule municipality's charter or ordinance, " 'the subject matter of the general legislative enactment must pertain to those things of general concern to the people of the state.' " *Apodaca*, 86 N.M. at 522, 525 P.2d at 882 (quoting *City of Portland*, 59 P.2d at 232). Similarly, we have in other cases focused on the impact of the law and whether it implicates matters of statewide concern, as opposed to matters of purely local concern, in characterizing the law as "general" for the purpose of determining which of two conflicting enactments, legislative or municipal, should be given primacy. . . .

Determining whether a matter is of statewide or local concern is not always an easy task. "[T]here is a twilight zone within which it is difficult to discern with positive assurance what is a matter of general concern as distinguished from a matter of local or municipal concern." McQuillin, supra, § 4.85, at 207–208. Because of this difficulty, some courts have eschewed altogether any attempt to lay down a firm rule as to what is a matter of general, statewide concern and what is a matter of only local or municipal concern. See id. 4.85 (referring to courts' unwillingness or inability to designate line dividing municipal and state affairs). While we likewise do not feel it necessary to lay down a fixed guiding principle that will in all cases distinguish between the two areas of concern, we do believe that our own case law provides considerable assistance in this regard. In *Apodaca*, we quoted from *City of Portland*, which in turn quoted from McQuillin, as follows:

> "The purpose (referring to the home rule amendments) was to give local communities full power in matters of local concern, that is, in those matters which peculiarly *affected* the inhabitants of the locality, not in common with the inhabitants of the whole state. Those matters which *affected* all of the inhabitants of the state were viewed as state matters, and therefore subject to state control, but those things which did not concern inhabitants of the state other than those residing in the particular community, were sought to be differentiated as local concerns, which under these constitutional provisions were to be regarded as exclusively matters of local self-government...."

Apodaca, 86 N.M. at 522, 525 P.2d at 882 (quoting *City of Portland*, 59 P.2d at 232, and McQuillin, supra, § 93 (2d ed.) (emphasis added)). Thus, the test, or at least a test, is the effect of a legislative enactment—whether it affects all, most, or many of the inhabitants of the state and is therefore of statewide concern, or whether it affects only the inhabitants of the municipality and is therefore of only local concern.

In the present case, the statutes at issue, Sections 3–10–1(B) and 3–14–6(A), contain two basic requirements: that the governing bodies of commission-manager forms of government shall be composed of five commissioners and that the commissioners shall be elected from single-member districts. Because petitioners have chosen not to pursue a claim that the City of Clovis must restructure itself into single-member districts, we do not address that potential claim. Rather, we focus on their argument that the City Commission must consist of five, rather than seven (or eight), commissioners. Accordingly, we must consider whether the number of commissioners in a commission-manager form of government is a matter of statewide or of local concern—i.e., whether that matter affects the inhabitants of this state outside the City of Clovis or affects only the City's residents.

Considering this issue in light of the purpose of our home rule amendment, we rather easily conclude that the subject is of local concern. As we have said, the purpose of our home rule amendment is to delegate to municipalities autonomy in matters concerning their local community, as opposed to matters of statewide concern or interest. We believe that the present subject—the number of commissioners in the governing body—is precisely the sort of matter intended to fall within the decisionmaking power of a home rule municipality. It is a subject that is predominantly, if not entirely, of interest to the citizens of the City of Clovis. To paraphrase a rhetorical question in *Apodaca*, 86 N.M. at 523, 525 P.2d at 883: Of what concern is it statewide what the City's residents decide as to the number of commissioners they wish to serve on their city commission?

IV

Having concluded that neither Section 3–10–1(B) nor Section 3–14–6(A) is a "general law" within the meaning of Article X, Section 6, of the Constitution, we need not consider the second question noted above—whether either section "expressly denies" the power to a home rule municipality to provide for a different number of city commissioners than that prescribed by the statutes. The legislature is not constitutionally empowered to deny to home-rule municipalities their powers of local governance. However, a few words on the meaning of the phrase "expressly denies" may be helpful in resolving future cases. Although we said in *Apodaca* that the phrase "not expressly denied" means "that some express statement of the authority or power denied must be contained in such general law in order to be applicable," 86 N.M. at 521, 525 P.2d at 881, we have since qualified this statement by noting that a negation of the power *in haec verba* is not necessary; words or expressions which are tantamount or equivalent to such a negation are equally effective. In *Casuse*, we said that "any New Mexico law that clearly intends to preempt a governmental area should be sufficient without necessarily stating that affected municipalities must comply and cannot operate to the contrary." 106 N.M. at 573, 746 P.2d at 1105....

We find no indication that either Section 3–10–1(B) or Section 3–14–6(A) clearly intends to preempt (to the legislature) the governmental area of fixing the number of city commissioners and to restrict home rule municipalities from adopting a different number. Similarly, we see in neither of these sections a limitation that the number of commissioners may be set at only a stated number, nor do we find a grant of authority to some other governmental body or agency that would make a city's exercise of its power to establish the structure of its governing body so inconsistent with such a grant of authority that the grant could properly be deemed equivalent to an express denial.

V

For either of these reasons, then—that is, because neither Section 3–10–1(B) nor Section 3–14–6(A) is a general law of statewide concern, and/or because neither section expressly denies to a municipality the power to constitute its city commission with a different number of commissioners than that prescribed in the statutes—we hold that these sections, insofar as they provide for five city commissioners in a commission-manager form of government, do not override the inconsistent provisions of the Clovis Municipal Charter. We do not read these sections out of our Municipal Code; they retain vitality as default provisions governing municipalities that choose not to become home rule municipalities....

Accordingly, we reaffirm our previous order quashing our alternative writ of prohibition in this case.

It is so ordered.

■ RANSOM, C.J., and FRANCHINI, J., concur.

NOTES

1. Can you reconcile the court's opinion with its earlier decision in the *Apodaca* case it cites? Why didn't the court just overrule its earlier decision and announce a new standard for home rule?

2. In Cottrell v. Santillanes, 901 P.2d 785 (N.M. App.), cert. denied, 900 P.2d 962 (N.M. 1995), the New Mexico Court of Appeals revisited the limits of municipal home rule raised in *Haynes* to determine whether the City of Albuquerque, a home rule municipality, could limit its city councilors to no more than two elected terms. The court found that the clause of the state constitution which sets out the requirements for persons to hold state elective office precluded a home rule municipality from adopting additional qualifications. The city argued that the home rule amendment provided that, absent a clear denial in general law of the home rule municipality's power to legislate, a municipality's enactments cannot be overridden. The city relied on *Haynes* for that proposition and asserted that constitutional qualifications for office are not general laws. The court found this argument unpersuasive and held that, like the districting law at question in Casuse v. City of Gallup, 746 P.2d 1103 (N.M. 1987), distinguished in *Haynes*, "the Qualifications Clause is a general law with important statewide ramifications that would prohibit a municipal charter from acting to abrogate it." 901 P.2d at 787.

Town of Telluride v. Lot Thirty–Four Venture, L.L.C.

3 P.3d 30 (Colo. 2000).

■ JUSTICE KOURLIS delivered the Opinion of the Court.

This case concerns the scope of the state prohibition on rent control contained in section 38–12–301, 10 C.R.S. (1999). Specifically, we must determine whether a local affordable housing measure constitutes rent control prohibited by the statute, and whether a home rule municipality may exercise its authority over matters of local concern to regulate rents despite the state rent control statute.

* * *

In September 1994, the Town Council of the Town of Telluride (Town Council) adopted Ordinance 1011, which amends the Telluride Land Use Code to add "affordable housing" mitigation requirements. The Town Council enacted the ordinance to address concerns generated by the pressures of new development in the area. The ordinance requires owners engaging in new development to mitigate the effects of that development by generating affordable housing units for forty percent of the new employees created by the development....

Ordinance 1011 provides developers with four general options, or a combination thereof, to satisfy the affordable housing requirement. They may (1) construct new units and deed-restrict them as affordable housing, (2) deed restrict "existing free market units" as affordable housing, (3) pay fees in lieu of deed restricted housing, or (4) convey land to the Town of Telluride with a fair market value equivalent to the fee paid under option three.

* * *

Thirty–Four Venture challenged the affordable housing provisions of Ordinance 1011 in San Miguel County District Court. Thirty–Four Venture sought to enjoin the Town from enforcing the ordinance, arguing that it constitutes rent control, and therefore, violates section 38–12–301, 10 C.R.S. (1999), which precludes municipalities from "enact[ing] any ordinance ... which would control rents on private residential property."

We granted certiorari to consider whether Ordinance 1011 is a form of "rent control" within the purview of section 38–12–301, and if so, whether section 38–12–301, enacted by the General Assembly in 1981, constitutionally supersedes Ordinance 1011.

II.

The first issue on appeal requires us to determine whether Telluride's affordable housing scheme falls within section 38–12–301's prohibition of "rent control." The statute is titled "Local Control of Rents Prohibited" and states,

> The general assembly finds and declares that the imposition of rent control on private residential housing units is a matter of statewide concern; therefore, no county or municipality may enact any ordinance or resolution which would control rents on private residential property. This section is not intended to impair the right of any state agency, county, or municipality to manage and control any property in which it has an interest through a housing authority or similar agency.

§ 38–12–301.

* * *

"Rent control statutes come in all types, shapes and sizes." Richard A. Epstein, *Rent Control and the Theory of Efficient Regulation,* 54 Brook. L. Rev. 741, 742 (1988). Generally, however, rent control statutes peg allowable rent to the historic rent in an area at some fixed point in time, and permit increases in rent payments only on the basis of the consumer price index or some other neutral yardstick. *See id.* at 743. Rent control statutes do not isolate particular units for special treatment, but usually apply to a broad class of rental properties. *See id.* at 745. "Every rent control statute has only one raison d'etre to insure that the landlord's rent is kept below the fair market rental of the property." Id. at 746. The result is that such statutes effectively compel a landlord to convey a portion of his property interest to the tenant for the tenant's benefit. *See id.* at 744.

We find the term "rent control" to be clear on its face. Rent control is commonly understood to mean allowable rent capped at a fixed rate with only limited increases. *See* Epstein, *supra,* at 742. Because Ordinance 1011 sets a base rental rate per square foot and then strictly limits the growth of the rental rate, the ordinance constitutes rent control. The scheme as a whole operates to suppress rental values below their market values. Therefore, the court of appeals correctly concluded that the ordinance restricts the property owner's ability to develop his land as he sees fit.

Although the ordinance has the laudable purpose of increasing affordable housing within the communities where lower income employees work, the ordinance nevertheless violates the plain language of the state prohibition on rent control. The prohibition in section 38–12–301 on rent control is unambiguous and complete, encompassing "*any* ordinance or resolution which would control rents." (Emphasis added.) The term "rent control" is not used as a term of art, and the broad language of the statute plainly encompasses any mandate that would operate to control rents.

Were we to hold that Ordinance 1011 does not constitute rent control, we effectively would create an exception to the statute that the General Assembly has not debated or adopted. Of course, our holding today that Ordinance 1011 constitutes rent control does not prevent the General Assembly from amending the rent control statute to permit local ordinances such as Ordinance 1011. In short, we hold that the Town's remedy must be with the legislature.

* * *

The fact that the ordinance offers developers several options for satisfying the "affordable housing requirement" does not change the character of, or redeem, the rent control provisions. Either the provisions constitute rent control and cannot be enforced, or they do not. What we examine here is whether the options for constructing new housing or deed restricting existing housing constitute rent control. *See* Ordinance 1011, §§ 3–750.B.2.a to 3–750.B.2.d, 3–750.B.3.a to 3–750.B.3.d. Whether the balance of the ordinance is severable and remains enforceable is not an issue that was before the court of appeals or before us. Therefore, we do not address it.

Once owners decide to develop their property, they must engage in a program that effectively redistributes the value of the rental property from landlord to tenant—a hallmark of rent control. Because Ordinance 1011 imposes a base price for rental values, and thereafter limits the rate growth, we conclude that the ordinance constitutes rent control within the plain meaning of section 38–12–301.

III.

Because we hold that Ordinance 1011 is a form of rent control, we must address the second question presented for review: whether Telluride may nonetheless impose rent control because it is a home rule municipality. . . .

The statute prohibiting rent control applies to all counties and municipalities. *See* § 38–12–301. The statute defines municipality to include "any city, town, or city and county which has chosen to adopt a home rule charter." § 38–12–302, 10 C.R.S. (1999).

The Town of Telluride is a home rule municipality. Home rule cities are granted plenary authority by the constitution to regulate issues of local concern. *See* Colo. Const. art. XX, § 6.[1] If a home rule city takes action on a matter of local concern, and that ordinance conflicts with a state statute, the home rule provision takes precedence over the state statute. *See id.; see also City & County of Denver v. State,* 788 P.2d 764, 767 (Colo.1990) (finding a state statute unconstitutional because it conflicted with a local initiative on a matter of local concern). If the matter is one of statewide concern, however, home rule cities may legislate in that area only if the constitution or a statute authorizes the legislation. Otherwise, state statutes take precedence over home rule actions. If the matter is one of mixed local and statewide concern, a home rule provision and a state statute may coexist, as long as the measures can be harmonized. If the home rule action conflicts with the state legislature's action, however, the state statute supersedes the home rule authority.

Whether Telluride is authorized to impose rent controls, therefore, turns on the question of whether rent control should be characterized as a local, statewide, or mixed issue. Further, whether a matter is one of state or local concern is a legal issue. We, therefore, must conduct a de novo review.

"There is no litmus-like indicator for resolving whether a matter is of local, statewide, or mixed concern." *National Adver. Co. v. Department of Highways,* 751 P.2d 632, 635 (Colo.1988). Courts should take the totality of the circumstances into account in reaching this legal conclusion. As part of the totality of the circumstances, this court has considered a number of issues, all directed toward weighing the respective state and local interests implicated by the law. We have looked at whether the General Assembly declared that the matter is one of statewide or local concern. *See National Adver. Co.,* 751 P.2d at 635 (holding that a declaration of statewide policy should be afforded "great weight"). Although such a declaration is not conclusive, *see City & County of Denver,* 788 P.2d at 768, n. 6 (noting that the General Assembly's declaration is not binding), it will be afforded deference in recognition of the legislature's authority to declare the public

1. [Colo. Const. art. XX, § 6 reads as follows:

Home rule for cities and towns. The people of each city or town of this state, having a population of two thousand inhabitants as determined by the last preceding census taken under the authority of the United States, the state of Colorado or said city or town, are hereby vested with, and they shall always have, power to make, amend, add to or replace the charter of said city or town, which shall be its organic law and extend to all its local and municipal matters.

Such charter and the ordinances made pursuant thereto in such matters shall supersede within the territorial limits and other jurisdiction of said city or town any law of the state in conflict therewith....—EDS.]

policy of the state in matters of statewide concern, *see National Adver. Co.,* 751 P.2d at 635.

Even if a home rule city has considerable local interests at stake, a particular issue may be characterized as "mixed" if sufficient state interests also are implicated. *See Denver & Rio Grande W. R.R. Co. v. City & County of Denver,* 673 P.2d 354, 358 (Colo.1983). In determining whether the state interest is sufficient to justify preemption of home rule authority, this Court has articulated various factors that drive the analysis. These include: (1) the need for statewide uniformity of regulation; (2) the impact of the measure on individuals living outside the municipality; (3) historical considerations concerning whether the subject matter is one traditionally governed by state or local government; and (4) whether the Colorado Constitution specifically commits the particular matter to state or local regulation. All of these factors are intended to assist the court in measuring the importance of the state interests against the importance of the local interests in order to make the ad hoc decision as to which law should prevail.

Having concluded that Telluride's ordinance is, in fact, rent control under the terms of the statute, we must now apply these factors to the analysis of whether the state statute prohibiting rent control impacts Telluride's ordinance.

We begin with two general propositions. First, courts must avoid making decisions that are intrinsically legislative. It is not up to the court to make policy or to weigh policy. If we determine that the issue is legitimately one over which the General Assembly has authority, then our inquiry must end.

Second, we note that the General Assembly here did announce that the preclusion of rent control is a matter of statewide concern. *See* § 38–12–301. As we have indicated, this pronouncement is not dispositive, but it is instructive.

We turn then to the specific factors. The first consideration is whether the state has a pervading interest in statewide uniform regulation. For example, in *National Advertising Co.,* this court found a need for statewide uniform regulation of highway advertisements in order to prevent the loss of federal funding and to achieve statewide safety, recreational, aesthetic, and fiscal goals. 751 P.2d at 636. This court also has found uniform access to markets throughout the state to be an important state concern. *See Century Elec. Serv. & Repair, Inc. v. Stone,* 193 Colo. 181, 184, 564 P.2d 953, 955 (1977) (holding that a state statute superseded home rule authority regarding the licensing of electricians because "[t]he state has a clear concern in ensuring that Colorado electricians have free access to markets throughout the state").

Here, both the municipality and the state have significant interests in maintaining the quality and quantity of affordable housing in the state. Ordinances like Telluride's can change the dynamics of supply and demand in an important sector of the economy—the housing market. A consistent prohibition on rent control encourages investment in the rental market and the maintenance of high quality rental units. Although economic conditions may vary in housing markets across the state, the legislature has seen fit to enact a uniform ban on rent control as a matter of public policy.

In addition, the rent control statute is part of the state statutory scheme regulating landlord and tenant relations. *See* §§ 38–12–101, to—302, 10 C.R.S. (1999). Landlord-tenant relations is an area in which state residents have an expectation of consistency throughout the state. Uniformity in landlord-tenant relations fosters informed and realistic expectations by the parties to a lease, which in turn increases the quality and reliability of rental housing, promotes fair treatment of tenants, and could reduce litigation.

The second factor is the closely related question of whether the home rule municipality's action will have any extraterritorial impact. An extraterritorial impact is one involving state residents outside the municipality. In *Denver & Rio Grande Western Railroad Co.,* this court looked at the potential ripple effect from a local ordinance that directed the construction of a viaduct and apportioned the costs for the project. 673 P.2d at 358–59. The court realized that the municipality's efforts to impose costs on the railroads could impact the railroads' overall ability to serve their customers, resulting in a reduction, or even termination, of service in areas outside the municipality. *See id.* Because of the potential impact beyond the municipality's borders, the court concluded that the ordinance presented a matter of mixed local and statewide concern.

The findings in Telluride's ordinance itself recite that the issue is one that impacts other communities: "Maintaining permanent and long-term housing in proximity to the source of employment generation serves to maintain the community, reduce regional traffic congestion, and minimize impacts on adjacent communities." *See* Ordinance 1011, § 3–710.A. The General Assembly recognized the potential extraterritorial impact of rent control when it passed section 38–12–301. Representative Chaplin, the sponsor of the bill in the House of Representatives stated: "We're facing future disasters. Any rent control lowers the availability of housing stock.... This would have a disastrous effect, and a rippling effect throughout our entire state of Colorado." House Bill 1604–81: Discussion Before the Senate Comm. on Local Government, 42d Legis., 1st Reg. Sess. (Apr. 21, 1981). Managing population and development growth is among the most pressing problems currently facing communities throughout the state. Restricting the operation of the free market with respect to housing in one area may well cause housing investment and population to migrate to other communities already facing their own growth problems. Although such a ripple effect may well be minimal in Telluride because of its geographic isolation, it is absolutely true that the growth of other mountain resort communities has impacted neighboring communities greatly. The fact that the Telluride ordinance is an affirmative effort to mitigate that impact does not change the fact that the growth of the one community is tied to the growth of the next, thereby buttressing the need for a regional or even statewide approach.

The third factor inquires as to whether the matter traditionally has been regulated at the state or the local level. Because our courts have not yet confronted the characterization of the state's interest in rent control, we can look only to other states to determine how they regulate rent control. A number of other state legislatures have prohibited rent control. Some of these states specifically have concluded that rent control is an issue of statewide concern. *See* Ariz.Rev.Stat. § 33–1329 (2000); Mass. Gen. Laws ch. 40P, § 5 (2000); Or.Rev.Stat. § 91.225 (1999); *City of New York v. State,* 31 N.Y.2d 804, 339 N.Y.S.2d 459, 291 N.E.2d 583, 584 (1972).

The fourth factor similarly focuses on whether the constitution commits the matter either to state or local regulation. The constitution does not assign the issue of rent control, or economic regulation generally, either to state or local regulation.

Where does this analysis lead us, then, in assessing and measuring the various interests at stake? The state's interests include consistent application of statewide laws in a manner that avoids a patchwork approach to problems. Further, the state has a legitimate interest in preserving investment capital in the rental market, ensuring stable quantity and quality of housing, maintaining tax revenues generated by rental properties, and protecting the state's overall economic health. Telluride, on the other hand, has a valid interest in controlling land use, reducing regional traffic congestion and air pollution, containing sprawl, preserving a sense of community, and improving the quality of life of the Town's employees.

On the whole, we cannot conclude that this matter is so discretely local that all state interests are superseded. Given the legitimacy of both the state interests and Telluride's interests, we conclude that rent control represents an area of mixed state and local concern. . . .

In conclusion, we hold that Ordinance 1011 constitutes rent control because the options for constructing new employee housing or deed restricting existing housing are within the commonly understood meaning of rent control. The propriety of rent control is an issue that has both local and statewide implications and impact, and we conclude that it falls within an area of mixed state and local concern and interest. Given the broad language of the statute, we find that Ordinance 1011 clearly conflicts with the state prohibition on rent control contained in section 38–12–301. As a result, we hold that Ordinance 1011 is invalid and that section 38–12–301 does not violate the home rule amendment to the constitution.

■ CHIEF JUSTICE MULLARKEY, dissenting.

* * *

I disagree with the majority's analysis of the state and municipal interests implicated by Ordinance 1011. The majority ultimately concludes that "rent control represents an area of mixed state and local concern." Maj. op. at 39. Narrowly construed, I agree that rent control may be an area of mixed concern. Broadly construed, however, it is not. This ordinance is on the fringe of the majority's extraordinarily broad understanding of rent control. As so applied, it passes beyond the mixed area and into the area of local concern. I would hold that Ordinance 1011 is of local concern, and therefore, the ordinance supersedes section 38–12–301 to the extent that they conflict.

The crux of my disagreement with the majority is its characterization of Ordinance 1011. The majority finds Ordinance 1011 to be economic legislation: "Even though the measure amended the Telluride Land Use Code, the ordinance does not dictate permissible uses of real property; rather, it dictates the rate at which the property may be used for a permissible purpose. It is, therefore, properly characterized as economic legislation." Maj. op. at 39 n.9. To the contrary, I contend that Ordinance 1011 is fundamentally a land use regulation, an area that the General Assembly and this court have consistently recognized to be a matter of local concern.

The majority rests its characterization of Ordinance 1011 on an overly restrictive concept of the definitional scope of "land use policy" by relying on the fact that Ordinance 1011 "does not dictate permissible uses of real property; rather, it dictates the rate at which the property may be used for a permissible purpose." Id. Land use policy, however, is not limited to the mere definition of permissible uses; rather, land use policy encompasses conditions implemented within the rubric of zoning and planning decisions. Dedications, for example, have been classified as a land use policy despite the fact that dedications do not "dictate permissible uses of real property."

Several considerations compel me to view Ordinance 1011 as a land use regulation. As the majority recognizes, Ordinance 1011 amended Telluride's Land Use Code. While I acknowledge that the existence of this fact is not dispositive, it is indicative of the intended functioning of Ordinance 1011 as a component of the city's overall land use policy.

* * *

With this distinction in mind, I now turn to the factors established under *City & County of Denver* to ascertain whether Ordinance 1011 is a matter of state, local, or mixed concern. The majority's finding of a state interest in the first factor, the need for uniformity, is contrary to the General Assembly's consistent refusal to consider land use regulations as requiring statewide legislation. This is set forth clearly in the Land Use Control Act, *see* § 29–20–102, and has been implicitly recognized by this court, *see, e.g., Voss v. Lundvall Bros.*, 830 P.2d 1061, 1064–65 (Colo.1992) (discussing a home rule city's authority to control land use policy). Under the specific facts of this case, Ordinance 1011, to the extent that one can construe it as a rent control measure, is integrated into the larger context of Telluride's land use policy—an area demonstrably within the purview of local governmental regulation. As such, the state's interest in uniformity in this area is minimal. There may be a need for uniformity as the majority suggests, but the legislature has yet to assert that need in the area of land use policy.

With respect to the second factor, the extraterritorial impact, the majority raises the specter of a "ripple effect" produced on surrounding communities. Maj. op. at 39. Specifically, the majority argues that "[r]estricting the operation of the free market with respect to housing in one area may well cause housing investment and population to migrate to other communities already facing their own growth problems." Id. I find the majority's argument unpersuasive for several reasons.

First, in *City & County of Denver,* this court considered the extraterritorial impact of a city-imposed residency requirement for city employees. We rejected the state's argument that focused on the adverse economic impacts accruing outside of the city, primarily because of the speculative nature of the argument. *See id.* I view the majority's extraterritoriality analysis to suffer from the same speculative defects.

Second, the majority's extraterritoriality analysis strikes at the fundamental premise of land use planning, zoning, and development regulations by exalting free operation of the housing market over the police power of local government to shape the design of a community. The majority's rationale ignores the fact that the General Assembly, when considering the role of local government in land use control, has consistently decided in favor of local prerogative to employ market restrictions to manage growth. *See, e.g.,* §§ 29–20–102, 104 (Local Government Land Use Control Enabling Act of 1974). The majority's reasoning countermands the express finding and declaration of the General Assembly in the Colorado Land Use Act that Colorado's rapid growth and development demands new and innovative measures to encourage planned and orderly land use development and plan for the needs of residential communities. *See* § 24–65–102(1); *see also* § 29–20–102.

Third, the majority characterizes Telluride's effort to reasonably mitigate the impacts of new development on its community as if it were imposing a burden on other communities. Yet, Telluride's ordinance is aimed directly at mitigating the effects on other localities of an ever-increasing public problem in mountain resorts. Workers cannot afford to live where they work because the housing market left to itself prices out the laborers in favor of tourists and second home owners. Enabling people to live where they work is a key concept in reducing pollution, congestion, and demand on transportation infrastructure, such as new or expanded roads or transit to carry workers from their overnight abodes to where they earn their wages.

The majority misanalyzes the extraterritorial impact of Telluride's ordinance. It has precisely the opposite impact: it attempts to contain the effects of growth within Telluride. The ordinance assists the livability of people and communities in the areas surrounding the city of Telluride by addressing the particular concerns that its geography and demographics present. This positive effect is of a different character than the negative effects previously recognized by this court to support a state concern determination.

An analysis of the third factor also favors recognizing a local concern. As discussed *supra,* Ordinance 1011 is properly classified as a land use regulation. This court has consistently recognized that land use regulations are within the province of the local government.

The *City & County of Denver* factors do not support the majority's conclusion that the state's interest rises to such a level as to require the legal determination that the matter before us is one of mixed concern. On the other hand, and as stated by the majority, the Town of Telluride has significant interests in this mitigation measure: "Telluride . . . has a valid interest in controlling land use, reducing regional traffic congestion and air pollution, containing sprawl, preserving a sense of community, and improving the quality of life of the Town's employees." Maj. op. at 39.

Because Telluride's interests so significantly outweigh those of the state, I would hold that Ordinance 1011 constitutes legislation of a matter of local concern. Therefore, to the extent that section 38–12–301 conflicts with the ordinance, the statutory provision is unconstitutional in violation of article XX, section 6. Telluride validly exercised its powers as a home rule city in enacting and enforcing Ordinance 1011. Therefore, I respectfully dissent from the majority's holding in section III.

■ [The dissent of JUSTICE HOBBS is omitted.—EDS.]

NOTES

1. Distinguish between the following uses of home rule: (a) to permit a municipal corporation to initiate legislation without first receiving a grant of authority from the legislature or the constitution; (b) to create an area in which only a municipal corporation, and not the state legislature, can act. The first might be considered the investing function of home rule, while the second might be considered the divesting function of home rule. Should the area in which a locality is invested with authority be equivalent to the area from which the state is divested of the power to act? Assume, for instance, that a locality wishes to use its home rule power to pass an ordinance requiring deposits on returnable bottles. Is a finding that the ordinance is a "municipal affair" for purposes of allowing the locality to enact this ordinance necessarily equivalent to a finding that the ordinance is a "municipal affair" for purposes of preventing the state legislature from passing a statewide bottle bill? Or does the scope of the phrase depend on the context in which it is used?

The extent to which home rule divests the state of the power to intervene in "municipal affairs," of course, varies with the constitutional provisions. Assume that the Georgia legislature, subsequent to the *McKinney* case, enacted a law prohibiting localities from adopting ordinances that require charging of deposits on returnable bottles. There can be little doubt that a subsequently enacted local ordinance requiring such deposits would be invalid, since the state's Home Rule Act explicitly subjects even those ordinances that concern local affairs to conflicting state law. But what if the same sequence occurs in Colorado? Now a very different analysis follows, even if the terminology is similar. Even if it is clear that bottle deposit ordinances are within the scope of municipal affairs, it does not necessarily follow that the local ordinance is subject to state override. That will depend on the factors set forth in the *Telluride* case.

2. Given the differences between the *Telluride* majority and the dissent in the analysis of the multifactor analysis for determining the existence of a statewide interest, how much predictability does such an approach provide to localities? As the majority indicates, it developed the tests for distinguishing between local and statewide concerns in City and County of Denver v. State of Colorado, 788 P.2d 764 (Colo. 1990). In that case, the court held that an ordinance imposing residency requirements on municipal employees prevailed over a state law that forbade municipalities from adopting residency requirements. The court determined that the state had not asserted any particular state interest in uniformity of regulation with respect to residency requirements and that the court itself could perceive none. The court then opined that such requirements would impose few adverse economic impacts beyond the borders of the particular municipalities, in part because new municipal employees might be expected to move into the city in any event. Finally, the court concluded that cities had an interest in imposing residency requirements to ensure employees' availability in an emergency, to increase employees' investment in the city in which they would pay taxes, and to "instill a sense of pride in their work." Since the court defined employee residency as a matter of local concern, it concluded that the ordinance trumped the conflicting state statute.

In Fraternal Order of Police, Colorado Lodge #27 v. City and County of Denver, 926 P.2d 582 (Colo. 1996), the issue was whether the deputy sheriffs serving in the city and county should be governed by the state's Peace Officers Standards and Training (POST) Act, which sets qualifications for the training of peace officers. The court first found that there was insufficient state interest in having uniform training for all peace officers. While statewide uniformity of training for police officers was a legitimate state public safety interest because of police officers' ability to "exercise arrest authority" and their "continuous interaction with citizens on public and private property," the majority found the duties of the deputy sheriffs were limited to the "local" activities of serving process, acting as bailiffs, or attending to Denver detention facilities. The local nature of the officers' duties also led the court to determine that there was no significant extraterritorial impact, rejecting the claim that safety concerns regarding the transportation and incarceration of persons in Denver's detention facilities created statewide effects. In applying the third factor, other state interests, the court found that the Denver deputy sheriffs did not have authority substantially to impact public safety outside of Denver. Addressing the fourth factor, local interests, the court concluded that Denver had a substantial interest in the qualifications of its own public officers.

A dissenting opinion contended that the *Denver* principles required application of the state law. The dissent found that deputy sheriffs were in constant contact with prisoners held under state criminal charges; were responsible for preventing prison escapes and apprehending escaped prisoners; were in possession of firearms and had to be certified in the use of weapons; were charged with protecting the general public in the course of transporting criminal defendants to and from court; and were required to serve process, testify in court, advise prisoners of proceedings, and interact in other ways with the criminal court system. These duties led the dissenting justice to determine that uniformity was needed, extraterritorial impact was present, and the issue, while certainly important to localities, was a matter of substantial state interest.

3. *Home Rule and the Exercise of Extraterritorial Authority.* The Colorado Supreme Court gave a very broad interpretation to "municipal affairs" under article XX when it permitted the town of Telluride to condemn property outside its boundaries, notwithstanding a state statute that prohibited that power. Town of Telluride v. San Miguel Valley Corporation, 185 P.3d 161 (Colo. 2008). Telluride sought to condemn 572 acres of real property located adjacent to its borders for open space and park purposes. The owners of the property contended that a statute, recently enacted after lobbying by the landowners of the property subject to condemnation, explicitly prohibited home rule municipalities from condemning property outside municipal boundaries for parks, recreation, open space, or other similar purposes. A majority of the court concluded that the statute abrogated Telluride's constitutional home rule authority to condemn property for open space and park purposes. The court first concluded that the condemnation of property for open space and park purposes fell within the scope of the eminent domain power granted to home rule municipalities in article XX of the Colorado Constitution. Article XX gives all municipalities the right to exercise eminent domain "within or without its territorial limits" for certain "public works." The majority argued that the purposes specified in Article XX were "merely examples of a broader grant of power, namely the power to condemn property for any lawful, public, local, and municipal purpose." The court then contended that the issue at stake in *Lot Thirty-Four Venture*, whether a power was being exercised pursuant to a purely local affair, was relevant where a state statute conflicted with an independently adopted local ordinance. But, the court said, the weighing of competing state and local concerns of the type involved in that case was not appropriate where a municipality was exercising a power, such as extraterritorial condemnation, that the state constitution specifically allocated to it. Finally, the court concluded that the exercise of eminent domain for park or open space purposes was a municipal purpose within the constitutional grant of the condemnation authority to home rule municipalities. Thus, the legislative act had impermissibly abrogated a power that the constitution had specifically granted to home rule localities. A dissenting judge would have limited superseding ordinances to those that had effects within the enacting municipality's boundaries.

Does the majority's reading of article XX confuse the issue of whether the locality had the authority to condemn with the question of whether the locality's extraterritorial exercise of that authority could trump a state statute? How should we think about the consequences of a decision to allow home rule localities to exercise extraterritorial authority immune from state interference? In the wake of the *San Miguel* decision, should we think of the property owners as sympathetic nonresidents of Telluride who were subjected to the abusive whims of that locality without any representation? Or should we think of them as powerful outsiders who were able to obtain favorable legislation at the state level, even though they were imposing significant externalities on Telluride residents who preferred open spaces to gaudy development at the urban fringe? For discussion of the broad and common exercise of extraterritorial authority by home rule municipalities, see Richard Briffault, *Town of Telluride v. San Miguel Valley Corp.: Extraterritoriality and Local Autonomy*, 86 Den. U. L. Rev. 1311 (2009).

4. In a rare opinion that recognized (at least implicitly) the distinction between the investive and divestive uses of home rule, the California Supreme Court upheld a state statute that nullified a city business license tax. California Federal Savings & Loan Association v. City of Los Angeles, 812 P.2d 916 (Cal. 1991), involved an interpretation of the California Constitution's grant of home rule. That provision both permits cities to "make and enforce all ordinances and regulations in respect to municipal affairs, subject only to restrictions and limitations provided in their several charters" and allows city charters to "supersede any existing charter, and with respect to municipal affairs shall supersede all laws inconsistent therewith." Calif. Const. art. XI, § 5(a). Los Angeles imposed a business license tax on the plaintiff, notwithstanding a statute that imposed a state income tax on financial corporations and declared that tax to be in lieu of all other taxes, including local taxes. The court determined that taxation was a municipal affair for purposes of determining whether the city had the initial authority to impose the tax. The court concluded, however, that in cases of genuine conflict between state and local law, the state statute prevails where "the court is persuaded that the subject of the state statute is one of statewide concern and that the statute is reasonably related to its resolution." Under those circumstances, "the conflicting charter city measure ceases to be a 'municipal affair' pro tanto and the Legislature is not prohibited . . . from addressing the statewide dimension." 812 P.2d at 925. The court understood that the designation of a government activity as "local" or "state" was not intended to recognize a static allocation of authority, but was

> a means of adjusting the political relationship between state and local governments in discrete areas of conflict. When a court invalidates a charter city measure in favor of a conflicting state statute, the result does not necessarily rest on the conclusion that the subject matter of the former is not appropriate for municipal regulation. It means, rather, that under the historical circumstances presented, the state has a more substantial interest in the subject than the charter city.

> A corollary of that proposition is that every decision sustaining a state statute over a charter city measure does not mean that if the former were repealed, charter cities would remain incompetent to legislate in the area. Nor does a decision favoring a charter city measure preclude superseding state legislation in a later case if the fact-bound justification—the statewide dimension—is subsequently demonstrated.

812 P.2d at 926. Ultimately, the court determined that the state interest in the operation and regulation of financial institutions was sufficiently great as to make their taxation an issue of statewide, rather than municipal, concern.

In Johnson v. Bradley, 841 P.2d 990 (Cal. 1992), the same court confronted a claim that a state statute prohibiting public funding of election campaigns preempted a Los Angeles municipal code provision permitting public funding for political candidates. The court held that the state had a legitimate interest in achieving the statute's objective of preserving the "integrity of the electoral process." The court determined, however, that its decision in the *California Federal* case also required that any preemptive statute bear a reasonable relation to the state's legitimate interest and be narrowly tailored to the pursuit of that goal. Relying on the holding in Buckley v. Valeo, 424 U.S. 1 (1976), which prevented Congress from imposing spending limitations on campaigns without a corresponding offer of public funds, the court reasoned that the state statutory combination of limits on campaign spending and prohibition on public funding would frustrate efforts to protect the integrity of the electoral process. Thus, the statute, although concerned with a legitimate state interest, was not sufficiently tailored toward that goal to preempt the efforts of Los Angeles to limit spending and provide partial funding for political candidates. For a discussion of the constitutional relationship between states and localities under the California Constitution, see Daniel B. Rodriguez, State Supremacy, Local Sovereignty: Restructuring State/Local Relations Under the California Constitution, in Constitutional Reform in California 401 (Bruce E. Cain and Roger C. Noll eds. 1995).

The California Constitution art. XI, § 5(b)(4), allows home rule cities to adopt charters with "plenary authority" over "the manner in which, the method by which, the times at which, and the terms for which the several municipal officers and employees whose compensation is paid by the city shall be elected or appointed, and for their removal, and for their compensation, and for the number of deputies, clerks and other employees that each shall have, and for the compensation, method of appointment, qualifications, tenure of office and removal of such deputies, clerks and other employees." The court in *Johnson* did not rest its decision on this constitutional clause. On prior interpretations of the California Constitution, see Sho Sato, "Municipal Affairs" in California, 60 Calif. L. Rev. 1055 (1972).

In County of Riverside v. Superior Court, 66 P.3d 718 (Cal. 2003), the California Supreme Court invalidated an act of the state legislature that allowed unions representing public safety employees to declare an impasse in labor negotiations and require a locality to submit unresolved economic issues to binding arbitration. The Sheriff's Association of Riverside County invoked the legislation to compel arbitration of its negotiations with the county. The court concluded that the legislation violated two provisions of the California Constitution that guaranteed autonomy to counties. The first provision authorized counties to provide for the compensation of employees. The second precluded the delegation of county affairs or the performance of a municipal function to a private body. The Sheriff's Association maintained that the legislation was valid because the legislature determined that mandated arbitration addressed a "statewide concern" against strikes by public sector employees. The court concluded that the judiciary was the ultimate arbiter of the division of power between local government and the state legislature, and that, while the legislature could regulate the relationship between local governments and their employees, it could not deprive a county of the authority to set employee salaries. The constitutional commitment of authority for employee compensation to counties rendered that activity a municipal affair.

5. *Captured in Colorado.* What do you imagine was the motivation for town officials in *Telluride* to enact the affordable housing ordinance? What groups within the town would have supported such a measure? Why couldn't those same groups prevail at the state level to prevent the state from enacting a prohibition on "rent control," or at least to prevent enactment of a prohibition that included this type of ordinance within the definition of "rent control"? Would groups adversely affected by the affordable housing ordinance receive a more sympathetic hearing from state legislators than from town officials? Are there extralegal constraints on localities that limit their willingness to enact ordinances that restrict development? If so, are those constraints sufficient to make legal constraints superfluous?

PROBLEM XI

The state constitution provides that cities within the state may "exercise any legislative power or perform any function unless denied by charter or general statute," but provides an exception that prohibits the enactment of ordinances that relate to "private or civil law relationships." The City of Brimstone, which has adopted a home rule charter pursuant to the constitutional provision, has enacted an ordinance that requires property owners within the city who wish to excavate on their property to do so in a manner that would "fully protect adjacent land and buildings." Common law in the state requires excavation to be undertaken in a manner that leaves adjacent land "as stable as before," but is silent with respect to adjacent buildings. Nembish owns a parcel of land that adjoins land and a home belonging to Mellon. Nembish has recently excavated a foundation for a house that he hopes to construct on his property. Within two weeks of the time that the excavation was completed, Mellon's home began to show serious cracks which Mellon attributes to the work done by Nembish. Mellon has brought an action for damages against Nembish, based in part on rights that Mellon claims were established by the passage of the ordinance. Nembish has moved for summary judgment with respect to that part of Mellon's complaint, alleging that the ordinance is invalid insofar as it exceeds the city's home rule power under the state constitution.

You serve as the law clerk to the judge deciding the case. The judge has requested that you provide a memorandum outlining the arguments for and against the validity of the ordinance. Please respond in a concise, but comprehensive manner. See Young v. Mall Investment Co., 215 N.W. 840 (Minn. 1927).

New Mexicans for Free Enterprise v. City of Santa Fe

126 P.3d 1149 (N.M. 2005).

■ FRY, J.

Plaintiffs New Mexicans for Free Enterprise, the Santa Fe Chamber of Commerce, and several local business owners challenge an ordinance enacted by the City of Santa Fe mandating certain city-based businesses to pay a minimum wage higher than the current state and federal minimum hourly wage. Plaintiffs contend that the ordinance is beyond the power of a home rule municipality to enact and that the state minimum wage law preempts local policymaking in this area. [The home rule amendment to the New Mexico Constitution provides: "A municipality which adopts a charter may exercise all legislative powers and perform all functions not expressly denied by general law or charter. This grant of powers shall not include the power to enact private or civil laws governing civil relationships except as incident to the exercise of an independent municipal power"—Eds.]

* * *

The significant facts in this case are those surrounding the processes by which the City passed the ordinance as well as the particular provisions of the ordinance. In 2002, the City passed the first version of the ordinance setting a minimum wage above that of the federal and state minimum wages for its own workers, contractors doing substantial business with the City, and other businesses directly receiving city benefits. Santa Fe, N.M., Wage Requirements: Minimum Wage Payment Requirements, ch. XXVIII, § 1.5 (2003). The City also established a Living Wage Roundtable that was directed to "explore and develop" an amendment to the 2002 ordinance that would mandate a living wage for the entire city. The Roundtable reviewed a substantial amount of information regarding local wages, cost of living, the daily challenges faced by both workers and employers in Santa Fe, and the costs and benefits of minimum wage requirements. The Roundtable consisted of nine members representing both labor and business management....

The city council then held public hearings on the amended ordinance proposed by the Roundtable majority, and received input from over 150 speakers on both sides of the issue. Several economists provided input on the impact minimum wage increases would have upon the local economy, businesses, and workers. One economist represented to the city council that the federal and state minimum wage has declined significantly in real dollars.

The council and the Roundtable both had information detailing the Santa Fe employment scene, including figures of how many low-wage workers worked in particular businesses. Early versions of the amended ordinance excluded small businesses, which they defined as those employing fewer than ten workers. On the night that the council was to vote on the amendments to the ordinance, the council expanded the small business exemption by requiring compliance by only those businesses with twenty-five or more workers. The councilor making the proposal noted that expanding the exemption for small businesses would approximately cut in half the number of private businesses impacted while reducing the percentage of Santa Fe low-wage workers benefitting from the higher wage from around 75 percent to around 58 percent.

The amendments to the ordinance passed by a vote of seven to one. The ordinance as amended requires for-profit businesses or non-profit entities that are registered or licensed in Santa Fe and that employ twenty-five or more workers (either full-time or part-time) to pay a minimum hourly wage of $8.50. Id. § 1.5(A)(4), (C). This wage increases to $9.50 in 2006 and to $10.50 in 2008; thereafter, the hourly wage is to be increased in tandem with increases in the Consumer Price Index. . . .

In passing the amendments to the ordinance, the council issued legislative findings, including a finding that many workers in Santa Fe earn wages insufficient to support themselves and their families and that the community bore the burden when workers could not meet basic needs such as housing, food, shelter, and health care. Santa Fe, N.M., Wage Requirements: Legislative Findings ch. XXVIII, § 1.2(B), (H) (2003). The council also found that the cost of living in Santa Fe is 18 percent higher than the national average, while average earnings in Santa Fe are 23 percent below the national average. Id. § 1.2(E). In finding that Santa Fe housing is substantially more expensive than in most of New Mexico and that low-wage workers must spend a disproportionate portion of their income for housing in Santa Fe, the city council concluded:

A. The public welfare, health, safety and prosperity of Santa Fe require wages and benefits sufficient to ensure a decent and healthy life for workers and their families. . . .

D. Minimum wage laws promote the general welfare, health, safety and prosperity of Santa Fe by ensuring that workers can better support and care for their families through their own efforts and without financial governmental assistance. . . .

I. It is in the public interest to require certain employers benefiting [sic] from city actions and funding, and from the opportunity to do business in the city, to pay employees a minimum wage, a "living wage[,]" adequate to meet the basic needs of living in Santa Fe.

* * *

3. THE ORDINANCE IS A PRIVATE OR CIVIL LAW

Plaintiffs contend that the ordinance is a private or civil law governing the civil relationship of employer and employee because it "seeks to establish legal duties between private businesses and their private employees, and it establishes a new cause of action against private businesses that do not pay the wage." We agree. While there are no bright-line divisions between public law and private law, Terrance Sandalow, *The Limits of Municipal Power Under Home Rule: A Role for the Courts,* 48 Minn. L. Rev. 643, 674 [hereinafter Sandalow], private law has been defined as consisting "of the substantive law which establishes legal rights and duties between and among private entities, law that takes effect in lawsuits brought by one private entity against another." Gary T. Schwartz, *The Logic of Home Rule and the Private Law Exception,* 20 UCLA L. Rev. 671, 688 [hereinafter Schwartz] (internal footnotes omitted). That definition certainly applies to the ordinance, which sets a mandatory minimum wage term for labor contracts between private parties that the employee may enforce by bringing a civil action against the employer. The fact that the city administrator may punish violation of the ordinance as a misdemeanor does not convert the ordinance into "public law" nor does it alter the basic nature of the ordinance, which is to set and enforce a key contract term between private parties. *See Marshal House, Inc. v. Rent Review & Grievance Bd. of Brookline,* 357 Mass. 709, 260 N.E.2d 200, 206 (1970) (noting that public enforcement is not dispositive of the private law nature of an ordinance). The relationship between private employer and employee has been described as a civil relationship because it is governed by the civil law of contracts. *See New Orleans Campaign for a Living Wage v. City of New Orleans,* 02–0991 at p. 11, 825 So.2d at 1117 (Weimer, J., concurring) (concluding that a private employee-employer relationship is both a private and civil relationship and that a minimum wage ordinance is attempting to regulate that relationship). We conclude that the ordinance is a private or civil law governing civil relationships within the meaning of the home rule amendment.

4. THE ORDINANCE IS WITHIN THE INDEPENDENT POWERS EXEMPTION

Although the ordinance is a private law, nonetheless the home rule amendment permits a municipality to enact such a law if it is "incident to the exercise of an independent municipal power." N.M. Const. art. X, § 6(D). Both commentators and courts have noted the ambiguity of this independent power exemption. For example, Professor Schwartz observed that while its "precise legal meaning can be questioned ... [it] clearly attempts to express the idea that cities have a substantial stake in private law insofar as that law may advance or support the cities' 'independent' (i.e. public law) programs or enactments." Schwartz, *supra,* at 718 (internal footnote omitted).

Also noting the vagueness of the private law exception overall, the Massachusetts Supreme Judicial Court held in *Marshal House, Inc.* that for an ordinance to fall within the independent power exemption, a municipality must point to an "individual component of the municipal police power" that provides it authority to act; otherwise, the private law exception might have "a very narrow range of application." 260 N.E.2d at 206–07. The court held that the municipality failed to do this in connection with a provision establishing a rent-control and review board. The court rejected the municipality's claims that its objective in controlling rents was to provide for the public welfare. Id. While the court recognized the link between affordable housing and the public welfare, it stated that "[r]ent control, however, is also an objective in itself designed to keep rents at reasonable levels." Id. at 206. The court held that "it would be, in effect, a contradiction (or circuitous) to say that a by-law the *principal objective* ... of which is *to control rent payments,* is also merely incidental to the exercise of an independent municipal power to control rents." Id. at 207 (emphasis added).

Plaintiffs urge us to follow *Marshal House, Inc.* by requiring that the City point to an "individual component" of its police power providing the power to pass the ordinance. We decline to adopt the reasoning in *Marshal House, Inc.* for two reasons. First, the court in that case provided a specious answer to the question "What is the object of the regulation?" by concluding the object was "to control rent payments." There, the stated "principal objective" of the municipality was not to control rent payments as an end itself, but to provide for the general health and welfare of residents by providing sufficient affordable housing. Second, because New Mexico municipalities have been delegated a generic police and general welfare power, we think that forcing a municipality to point to an "individual component" of its police power puts an unduly restrictive gloss on the exemption and reads words into the home rule amendment that are not there.

The exemption refers to an "independent municipal power," which we conclude means any power other than home rule. There is no indication in the phrase "independent municipal power" that such a power must be in some way particularized or tailored; as long as there is a power granted by the legislature that is independent from home rule power, that is enough. We take the view that as long as a municipality can point to a power that the legislature has delegated to it, and the regulation of the civil relationship is reasonably incident to, and clearly authorized by that power, the exemption can apply.

The only additional limitation on a municipality's power, which we have gleaned from the commentators, is the need for uniformity that informs any consideration of the private law exception and independent powers exemption. *See* Howard McBain, *The Law and the Practice of Municipal Home Rule* (1916) 673 (noting that, "[b]y common understanding such general subjects as crime, domestic relations, wills and administration, mortgages, trusts, contracts, real and personal property, insurance, banking, corporations and many others have never been regarded by any one, least of all by the cites themselves, as appropriate subjects of local control"); Schwartz, *supra,* at 720–47 (proposing three underlying rationales for the private law exception, including "the need to retain uniformity in private law"); Sandalow, *supra,* at 678–79 (stating that "chaos would ensue" if all home rule municipalities could "adjust contract, property and the host of other legal relationships between private individuals"). Given this concern for uniformity, we conclude there are two prerequisites to a municipality's regulation of a civil relationship. Where a municipality has been given powers by the legislature to deal with the challenges it faces, those may be sufficiently independent municipal powers to allow regulation of a civil relationship as long as (1) the regulation of the civil relationship is reasonably "incident to" a public purpose that is clearly within the delegated power, and (2) the law in question does not implicate serious concerns about non-uniformity in the law. This rule allows a home rule municipality to regulate a civil relationship as far as necessary within its delegated powers to address local public concerns, while preventing the harm at which the private law exception is primarily aimed. *See* Schwartz, *supra,* at 752 (stating "[h]avoc would be occasioned if city corporation codes and blue sky ordinances were enforced against corporations which engage in operations or sell securities throughout the state or nation"). *See also City of Baltimore v. Sitnick,* 254 Md. 303, 255 A.2d 376, 384 (Md.1969) (concluding that unique local conditions, such as higher cost of living and housing problems, justified additional city regulation of the minimum wage). This rule is also sufficiently flexible to allow a fact-intensive evaluation of any given municipal action by balancing the municipality's pursuit of the public interest to address local issues against the need for stability and uniformity in the law across the state. *See* Schwartz, *supra,* at 747 (describing some non-uniformity as "a price we willingly pay in order to achieve the benefits of local democracy"). This rule is consistent with the home rule amendment and Municipal Code, both of which provide for liberal construction in favor of granting power to cities for a "maximum local self-government." N.M. Const. art. X, § 6(E); § 3–15–13(B) (repeating this rule of construction).

In light of this holding, we apply the rule and evaluate (1) whether the ordinance's regulation of the civil relationship is reasonably "incident to" a public purpose that is clearly within the legislature's delegation of specific, independent powers, and (2) whether the ordinance implicates serious concerns about non-uniformity in the law. With respect to public purpose within a municipality's delegated powers, the legislature has given all municipalities the power to provide for the general welfare of their residents by the general welfare clause in Section 3–17–1(B). In addition, the legislature has given all municipalities the police power to "protect generally the property of its municipality and its inhabitants" and to "preserve peace and order within the municipality" by Section 3–18–1(F) and (G). While these are separate powers, they may be treated as one. *Biswell,* 81 N.M. at 780, 473 P.2d at 919 (stating that these two powers "if independent of one another, tend to merge"). We consider these powers to be independent municipal powers within the meaning of the home rule amendment because they are powers delegated to municipalities completely independent from the home rule amendment.

The connection between wages and the general welfare of workers is well established in American jurisprudence and is clearly within the police power of a state to regulate. In *West Coast Hotel Co. v. Parrish,* 300 U.S. 379, 57 S.Ct. 578, 81 L.Ed. 703 (1937), the United States Supreme Court upheld against a freedom of contract challenge a state court decision that the police power of the state permitted setting a minimum wage. Id. at 413–14, 57 S.Ct. 578. The Court concluded that wages insufficient to support basic needs are a public problem due to the impact on the entire community. Id. at 399, 57 S.Ct. 578. This conclusion was presaged by Justice Stone's dissent in *Morehead v. New York ex rel. Tipaldo,* 298 U.S. 587, 56 S.Ct. 918, 80 L.Ed. 1347 (1936), *overruled on other grounds by Olsen v. Nebraska ex rel. W. Reference & Bond Ass'n, Inc.,* 313 U.S. 236, 61 S.Ct. 862, 85 L.Ed. 1305, (1941) when he noted:

> We have had opportunity to perceive more clearly that a wage insufficient to support the worker does not visit its consequences upon him alone; that it may affect profoundly the entire economic structure of society and, in any case, that it casts on every taxpayer, and on government itself, the burden of solving the problems of poverty, subsistence, health and morals of large numbers in the community. Because of their nature and extent these are public problems.

Morehead, 298 U.S. at 635, 56 S.Ct. 918 (Stone, J., dissenting). Given this authority, we conclude that setting a minimum wage is unquestionably a public purpose and that such legislation is within the police and general welfare power of a New Mexico municipality.

As to whether the City is acting incident to the exercise of an independent municipal power, there is little conclusive authority on the subject. In *Marshal House, Inc.,* the court held that regulating the landlord-tenant relationship by setting the rental price term was a direct, rather than incidental, regulation of the relationship, yet it would have allowed regulation of the relationship for safety or health codes, such as fire prevention or hallway lighting, which it viewed as incidental to the police power. 260 N.E.2d at 206.

The rationale of *Marshal House, Inc.,* appears to allow comparatively minor intrusions by an ordinance into a civil relationship, but bars greater intrusions. Yet we fail to see how regulating a private relationship in terms of health and building safety codes is "indirect" while regulating a more central or important aspect, such as the rental term in *Marshal House, Inc.,* is "direct." Such a principle would lead to arcane inquiries into the relative importance of different aspects of an agreement. Is building safety or rent more important to the landlord-tenant relationship? Is worker health and safety less critical than wages or hours? We read "incident to an exercise of an independent municipal power" as simply limiting the circumstances in which a municipality may pass a private or civil law, not as barring certain types of private or civil law or limiting the degree of their intrusion into the relationship. Id. We conclude that as long as the intrusion into the private relationship is in pursuit of the public interest and clearly within the independent municipal power, that is sufficient to permit the municipality to pass a private or civil law regulating that relationship as long as the law does not generate non-uniformity issues. We focus on whether there is a public purpose or objective for the exercise of the independent municipal power. Here, there clearly is a public purpose as described by the myriad authorities holding that a minimum wage protects the general welfare of the community....

We now turn to the second prong of the rule permitting regulation of a civil relationship and consider whether the ordinance seriously implicates concerns about non-uniformity. Commentators and courts have expressed concern about home rule municipalities creating a patchwork quilt of law that would hamper business transactions and unfairly upset parties' expectations, and we have concluded that this is the primary evil at which the private law exception is aimed. We view the inquiry, then, as whether the ordinance disrupts or confuses New Mexico law to an unacceptable degree.

The nature of the ordinance is central in determining whether it implicates serious concerns about non-uniformity. For example, substantial disorder and confusion would result if the City rejected the Uniform Commercial Code, adopted a contributory negligence regime, or if it imposed heightened burdens on corporate boards of directors for companies doing business in the City. Leaving aside potential conflicts with state law (which will often bar such local laws), these types of private or civil law changes would frustrate and confuse even the most diligent consumer, businessperson, or lawyer. Those contracting with city parties, corporations doing business there, or those injured by tortfeasors in the City would have little reason to know of these special rules and each would cause notice, compliance, and choice of law issues. Our task is to determine whether such issues are so pervasive that the ordinance disrupts or confuses New Mexico law.

Here, the ordinance does not raise serious concerns about non-uniformity in the way that any of the prior examples would. Any concerns about inefficiency in terms of high notice and compliance costs are allayed by the limited application of the ordinance-it applies only to employers who are registered or licensed in the City. We presume that those entities with more than twenty-five employees seeking city business licenses are doing so purposefully (and with at least some deliberation), and we doubt that they are unaware of such a high-profile ordinance. In addition, the burden on a regional or national business of discovering and applying a higher wage for city workers is modest at most. Presumably, extra-local businesses can identify their own locations and workers licensed in the City and set their hourly wage.

Given modern technology and administration, the cost of discovering and complying with the City's law is minimal. We would be much more concerned if the City were attempting to set a minimum wage term for any contracts for labor "entered into" within the City or for any "labor provided" in the City. Such provisions would raise more serious questions regarding the cost of discovering and complying with the ordinance and the overall disruption of employment contract terms. *See* Madison, Wisc., Officials, Boards, Employees, & Public Records ch. 3, § 3.45(2)(k), *abro-*

gated by, Wis. Stat. Ann. § 104.001(2) (2005) (setting a living wage above the state minimum wage, and defining the term "employee" to mean anyone who "performs at least two hours of compensable work" per calendar week to any employer in Madison). In light of the ordinance's requirements, we doubt that the ordinance will generate confusion in the law of contracts in New Mexico, produce great inefficiency among the businesses that are required to comply with the ordinance, or cause choice of law problems. Thus, the ordinance does not implicate any serious concerns about generating non-uniformity in New Mexico law.

We emphasize that our conclusion is informed by the circumstances of this case, in which the City has made a showing that it was addressing a serious local problem and where the particular regulation of the employer/employee relationship has long been considered a reasonable exercise of the police power. Were a home rule municipality to enact a private or civil law regulating a civil relationship at the borders of its delegated powers, clearly engaging in overreaching, or implicating substantial non-uniformity issues, we think a different result could obtain. We disagree with Plaintiffs' contention that allowing a home rule municipality to rely on its police power to enact private or civil law governing civil relationships would render the private law exception in the home rule amendment "meaningless." We conclude that our construction is a straightforward application of the language in the home rule amendment as well as consistent with the model version of the private law exception. *American Municipal Association: Model Constitutional Provisions for Municipal Home Rule,* 21, at cmt. 5 (1953) (stating that "[i]t is the theory of the draft that a proper balance can be achieved by enabling cities to enact private law only as an incident to the exercise of some independent municipal power").

NOTES

1. The Massachusetts Supreme Judicial Court interpreted its earlier decision in *Marshal House*, cited in the principal case, to invalidate a local ordinance intended to regulate the conversion of residential rental units to condominiums in CHR General, Inc. v. City of Newton, 439 N.E.2d 788 (Mass. 1982). The court concluded that the ordinance affected "private or civil law governing civil relationships" because it impinged on the landlord-tenant relationship and on the owner's freedom of choice as to the buyers for converted units. The ordinance also required extension of the lease for substantial periods; restricted evictions; mandated a right of purchase in the tenant; and imposed other duties on a landlord seeking to convert rental housing units into condominiums. The court further concluded that the ordinance could not be upheld as incident to the exercise of either its police or its zoning powers. That an ordinance was enacted pursuant to the city's broad police power was insufficient; instead, the constitutional exception required that it be enacted pursuant to some individual component of that broad power. The city's independent zoning authority was irrelevant, because that power dealt with the use of property rather than ownership of property, which was the subject of the contested ordinance. The same court found that a condominium conversion ordinance improperly governed civil relationships in Bannerman v. City of Fall River, 461 N.E.2d 793 (Mass. 1984). The court rejected the claim that the ordinance was passed incident to the city's power to operate water and sewage systems or to regulate traffic and city streets.

The Louisiana Constitution, art. VI, 9, provides that, with stated exceptions, "no local governmental subdivision may enact an ordinance governing private or civil relationships." In Hildebrand v. City of New Orleans, 549 So.2d 1218 (La. 1989), cert. denied sub nom. Hirsch v. City of New Orleans, 494 U.S. 1028 (1990) the court considered a challenge to a series of ordinances enacted by the city to impose taxes on property of decedents and their heirs and legatees. The court found that the city was authorized to levy an inheritance tax that was not otherwise prohibited by or inconsistent with the state constitution. No violation of the "private or civil relationships" clause existed because the ordinances merely served as revenue-raising devices imposed on the transmission and receipt of an estate. Even though the court found that the effect of the tax was to reduce the value of the inheritance, the relationships protected by the constitutional clause were those between the decedent and heirs or legatees, and these relationships were not regulated by the ordinances.

2. What rationale could justify the "private law" exception to the home rule power? That exception was embodied in the model of home rule promulgated by Professor Jefferson Fordham and the National League of Cities, as discussed in the reading from Krane, Rigos, and Hill. The objective of the National League of Cities Model was to free municipalities from judicial restraints on local autonomy. The scope of home rule depended on successful lobbying by cities to prevent the state legislature from enacting anti-home rule legislation. But where does the general prohibition on "private law" fit in this scheme? Here are three possible explanations; does any of them justify a different result in *New Mexicans for Free Enterprise*?

(1) *The transaction costs explanation.* Discovering the law of neighboring jurisdictions is costly. Some individuals will avoid entering into transactions that they would otherwise find efficient (worth entering into) because the costs of investigating the underlying law makes the total costs of the transaction too high. In order to reduce costs, and thus induce people to enter into otherwise efficient transactions, the law governing these transactions should be uniform across broad geographical areas, i.e., states rather than localities. A prohibition on local regulation of these transactions achieves that objective. For an elaboration of this justification, see Gary Schwartz, The Logic of Home Rule and the Private Law Exception, 20 U.C.L.A. L. Rev. 670 (1973).

(2) *The public choice explanation.* Within a particular locality, interest groups may form that would not be large or organized enough to persuade the state legislature to deviate from the public interest, but that might have enough influence to control a local legislature. For instance, landlords seeking to avoid rent control statutes might be offset by tenant groups at

the state level, but might be effective in a particular locality where tenant groups are atypically weak. A requirement that such legislation be enacted at the state level reduces the effectiveness of local interest groups. At the same time, the requirement enhances the effectiveness of interest groups that have an advantage in forming statewide coalitions.

(3) *The local circumstances explanation.* A particular locality may suffer or enjoy unique conditions that make generally applicable regulations inappropriate. Home rule permits such localities to respond quickly and directly to idiosyncratic circumstances. But the circumstances that would justify a unique local response rarely involve private law situations. While one can easily imagine, for instance, a local need for particular control over zoning, pollution, or provision of water or sewage services, it is difficult to imagine why one locality would need a rule of offer and acceptance that differs from that of any other locality within the state.

F. CONFLICT AND PRE-EMPTION

PROBLEM XII

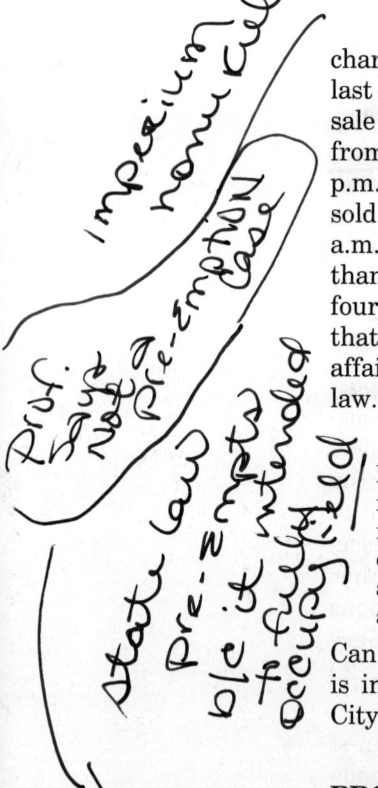

You represent Kirkland, a resident of the City of Delmore, who is charged with selling fireworks to an undercover police officer on July 5 of last year. The charge was filed under a local ordinance that proscribed the sale or offering for sale of fireworks "within the City of Delmore except from twelve o'clock noon on the twenty-eighth day of June to eleven o'clock p.m. on the fourth day of July of each year. No common fireworks may be sold or discharged between the hours of eleven o'clock p.m. and nine o'clock a.m. Any violation of this ordinance is punishable by a fine of not more than $500." Kirkland admits to the sale, which took place at approximately four o'clock in the afternoon. Delmore is a first-class municipality in a state that permits such localities to exercise home rule with respect to municipal affairs, "provided that such ordinances are not in conflict with general law."

You have discovered a state statute that provides:

> No common fireworks shall be sold or discharged within this state except from twelve o'clock noon on the twenty-eighth of June to twelve o'clock noon on the sixth of July of each year. No common fireworks may be sold or discharged between the hours of eleven o'clock p.m. and nine o'clock a.m. Any violation of this provision is punishable by a fine of up to $5,000 and 30 days imprisonment.

Can you argue that the local ordinance under which your client is charged is invalid? What response do you anticipate from the city? See Brown v. City of Yakima, 807 P.2d 353 (Wash. 1991).

PROBLEM XIII

Several years ago, the State legislature enacted a series of protections for residential tenants occupying apartment buildings that were being converted to condominiums (the "Act"). These protections included notice rights, lease extensions, rights of first refusal to purchase, and relocation assistance. The Act extended these rights only to tenants (1) who occupied a unit within the building at the time a master deed for the condominium conversion was filed with the locality in which the building was located, or (2) who moved into the building before the initial sale of a condominium unit. The Act also permitted cities in the State to provide additional regulations to protect tenants in the event of the conversion of apartments to condominium or cooperative forms of ownership. Last year, the State legislature reversed course and passed a new statute (the "Revision") that prohibited rent control or the regulation of "evictions, condominium conversion and the removal of properties from rent control." The Revision, however, expressly excluded from its coverage any local rent control regulation authorized under the previous enabling Act. The City of Glinda has enacted an ordinance for the stated purpose of "preserving a reasonable balance in the city's housing stock and a reasonable supply of rental housing, particularly for those who are elderly, handicapped, or of low– or moderate–income." The ordinance, which provides extensive rent control and eviction regulations, applies to all tenants of condominiums, including those who occupy condominiums as tenants after the initial sale of the relevant unit. The Greater Glinda Real Estate Board, which represents local landlords, has retained you to challenge the validity of the ordinance. What arguments will you make on behalf of your client? What responses do you anticipate? See Greater Boston Real Estate Board v. City of Boston, 705 N.E.2d 256 (Mass. 1999).

Miller v. Fabius Township Bd.

114 N.W.2d 205 (Mich. 1962).

■ KAVANAGH, JUSTICE.

Plaintiff filed a bill of complaint in chancery in the circuit court for the county of St. Joseph naming the Fabius township board as defendant under the Michigan declaratory judgment statute, Comp. Laws 1948, 691.501 et seq. He sought a decree finding the following ordinance adopted by defendant board to be void and unconstitutional:

> Effective August 25, 1959, powerboat racing and water skiing shall be prohibited on Pleasant lake in Fabius township, St. Joseph county, Michigan each day after the hour of 4:00 p.m. until the following day at 10:00 a.m. Any person who violates, disobeys or refuses to comply with or who resists the enforcement of the provisions of this ordinance shall upon conviction, be fined not less than $25 nor more than $100 for such offense, or imprisonment in the county jail until such fine and costs shall be paid and such imprisonment shall be for a period not to exceed 30 days.

Defendant board appeared and filed an answer to the bill of complaint alleging that the ordinance in question was valid and praying for dismissal of the bill of complaint.

Plaintiff claims he is one of a number of people who own land or cottages on the shores of Pleasant lake and who enjoy the sport of water skiing during the summer months.

Plaintiff alleges that he, like many other summer lake vacationers, due to employment, is unable to arrive at his property on Pleasant lake until after 5:00 p.m. He desires to take advantage of the recreational facilities of Pleasant lake and participate in the sport of water skiing during the daylight hours, which last until approximately 9:00 p.m.

Plaintiff claims he is deprived of water skiing by reason of the ordinance adopted by the local township board.

In 1959 the Michigan legislature enacted Act 55, P.A. 1959, amending Act 246, P.A. 1945, the title of which reads as follows:

> An act to authorize the township boards of certain townships to adopt ordinances and regulations to secure the public peace, health, safety, welfare and convenience; to provide for the establishment of a township police department; to provide for policing of townships by the county sheriff; to provide penalties; and to repeal all acts and parts of acts in conflict therewith.

Section 1 of the act, as amended, reads in pertinent part as follows:

> The township board of any township may, at any regular or special meeting by a majority of the members elect of such township board, adopt ordinances regulating health and the safety of persons and property therein . . .

The case came on for hearing in the circuit court for St. Joseph county. After proofs and briefs, the trial court in his opinion found the ordinance constitutional and valid and entered an order dismissing the bill of complaint.

Plaintiff appeals claiming the ordinance is void because the statutes—Act 215, P.A. 1931 and Act 310, P.A. 1957—have preempted the field of regulating motorboating and water skiing on Michigan's inland lakes.

Plaintiff alleges the ordinance is void because it prohibits that which the State statutes permit and exceeds the powers granted townships by Act 246, P.A. 1945, as amended. Plaintiff also claims the ordinance is void because it treats motorboating and water skiing as a local regulatory problem when, in fact, such activities are not local but are State-wide in scope and require uniform State-wide regulation.

Plaintiff argues that in 1931 the legislature undertook regulation of motorboating and water skiing activities on inland lakes when it enacted section 1 of Act 215, P.A. 1931. The act required motorboats and other watercraft to be equipped with mufflers and other devices to deaden the sound. It also purported to regulate the speed and use of motorboats on inland lakes.

Plaintiff further alleges that 26 years later a second statute—Act 310, P.A. 1957—was enacted by the legislature which recognized the need for more comprehensive regulation of boating and water activities on our inland lakes. This statute made certain changes in the regulation of motorboating and provided limitations on water skiing activities.

Section 3 of the 1957 act relates to persons operating watercraft under the influence of intoxicating liquor or narcotic drugs. Section 4 of the act relates to the speed of watercraft. Section 5 of the act as amended by Act 208, P.A. 1958, for the first time took recognition of the problem of water skiing and other water surface sports, and provides as follows:

> Any person who operates any watercraft, or who navigates, steers or controls himself while being towed on water skis, water sleds, surfboards or similar contrivances, upon any of the waterways of this state carelessly and heedlessly in disregard of the rights or safety of others, or without due caution and circumspection and at a speed or in a manner so as to endanger or be likely to endanger any person or property, shall be guilty of reckless operation of a watercraft and upon conviction shall be punished as provided in section 16 of this act.

Section 8 of the act specifically relates to restrictions on the periods when water skiing is prohibited and reads as follows:

> No operator of any watercraft shall have in tow or shall otherwise be assisting in the propulsion of a person on water skis, water sled, surfboard, or other similar contrivance during the period 1 hour after sunset to 1 hour prior to sunrise. Any person permitting himself to be towed on water skis, water sleds, surfboards or similar contrivances in violation of any of the provisions of this act shall be guilty of a misdemeanor.

It is contended the 1957 act was to cover on a State-wide basis the entire field of prohibitory regulation of motorboating and water skiing on our inland lakes.

The trial court rejected plaintiff's claim in this regard. On appeal we are asked to determine whether the ordinance conflicts with the State statutes.

Concerning this problem, 37 Am. Jur., Municipal Corporations, 165, p. 790, states the following:

> It has been held that in determining whether the provisions of a municipal ordinance conflict with a statute covering the same subject, the test is whether the ordinance prohibits an act which the statute permits, or permits an act which the statute prohibits....
>
> The mere fact that the state, in the exercise of the police power, has made certain regulations does not prohibit a municipality from exacting additional requirements. So long as there is no conflict between the two, and the requirements of the municipal bylaw are not in themselves pernicious, as being unreasonable or discriminatory, both will stand. The fact that an ordinance enlarges upon the provisions of a statute by requiring more than the statute requires creates no conflict therewith, unless the statute limits the requirement for all cases to its own prescription. Thus, where both an ordinance and a statute are prohibitory and the only difference between them is that the ordinance goes further in its prohibition, but not counter to the prohibition under the statute, and the municipality does not attempt to authorize by the ordinance what the legislature has forbidden or forbid what the legislature has expressly licensed, authorized, or required, there is nothing contradictory between

> the provisions of the statute and the ordinance because of which they cannot coexist and be effective. Unless legislative provisions are contradictory in the sense that they cannot coexist, they are not deemed inconsistent because of mere lack of uniformity in detail.

This Court has followed the above rule holding portions of a field not covered by State law are open to local regulation. . . .

The rule has long been recognized that municipalities are not divested of all control even where the legislature has enacted laws.

This Court said in People v. McGraw, supra (p. 238, 150 N.W. p. 837):

> . . . the municipality retains reasonable control of its highways, which is such control as cannot be said to be unreasonable and inconsistent with regulations which have been established, or may be established, by the state itself with reference thereto. This construction allows a municipality to recognize local and peculiar conditions, and to pass ordinances, regulating traffic on its streets, which do not contravene the state laws. The congested condition of traffic on many of the streets of the city of Detroit is a matter of common knowledge, and these conditions make it absolutely necessary, for the protection of pedestrians and the drivers of vehicles, to enact rules and regulations peculiarly adapted to the conditions there found, and to enact ordinances to diminish the danger. . . .

The question we have to determine, then, is whether the State has so pre-empted the field that it would be unconstitutional for the township to attempt to regulate water skiing by ordinance.

The legislation relied upon by plaintiff merely relates to various phases of the operation of watercraft, including its speed and use upon inland lakes. Section 8 of the 1957 statute only prohibits water skiing during the period 1 hour after sunset to 1 hour before sunrise. It, therefore, certainly cannot be said that the legislature intended to pre-empt the entire field or activity of water skiing. If the legislature so intended, it could have expressly stated pre-emptive control. It logically follows, then, that the portions of the township ordinance which endeavor to regulate water skiing, if not in conflict with the State law, are valid so far as the pre-emption doctrine is concerned.

It is obvious the ordinance was enacted to prevent the many dangers and alleviate the congested local conditions that existed on Pleasant lake.

In City of Howell v. Kaal, supra, this Court held that an ordinance may not invade a field completely occupied by statute but may enter an area not pre-empted by the State act, and further held that what the State law expressly permits an ordinance may not prohibit.

Since the cited statutes do not expressly control the period of regulation covered by the ordinance, it must be concluded there is no conflict. The ordinance speaks only where the statutes are silent. . . .

While the general problem with reference to water skiing and motorboating and the use of our inland lakes by different classes of sportsmen are State-wide problems, there are peculiar circumstances that are local in character—such as the number of boat users on the lake; the amount of fishing on the lake; the congestion and conflict between fishermen and water skiers; the location of the lake to densely populated areas—which the 1959 amendment authorizes townships to deal with under the "health and safety of persons and property" clause.

A comparison might be made between traffic ordinances of a city and the State traffic statutes. Densely populated cities with large numbers of automobiles require more local regulation, even to a greater reduction in speed, than do rural communities. The State prescribes by its statutes the general provisions with respect to problems, and this Court has upheld the right of municipalities to further regulate as long as there is no conflict between the State statute and the municipal ordinance. We believe this rule of law equally applicable to the regulation of boating and water skiing on inland lakes.

The trial court reached a correct conclusion in finding the ordinance was valid as having a reasonable relation to the health and safety of persons and property of the area involved.

Under the facts in this particular case, we do not find the ordinance unconstitutional or invalid for the reasons claimed by plaintiff.

The decree of the lower court is affirmed. A public question being involved, no costs are allowed.

■ SOURIS, JUSTICE (for reversal).

I read the township ordinance to prohibit from 4:00 p.m. until one hour before sunset and from one hour after sunrise to 10:00 a.m. that which the state statute permits to be done during a period which includes those hours. The ordinance conflicts with the statute and, therefore, necessarily is invalid. People v. McDaniel, 303 Mich. 90, 5 N.W.2d 667, and National Amusement Co. v. Johnson, 270 Mich. 613, 259 N.W. 342.

I would reverse, but would not award costs.

■ SMITH, J., concurred with SOURIS, J.

NOTES

1. *Relative Harshness of the Local Regulation.* Back at the dawning of the Age of Aquarius, the city of Ann Arbor, Michigan, adopted an ordinance that made possession of an ounce or less of marijuana punishable by a fine of $25 for the first offense, $50 for the second offense, and $100 for the third offense. Under state law, possession of the same amount of marijuana was punishable by a fine of up to $1,000 and imprisonment for up to one year. Did the ordinance conflict with state law? Would it matter that, under double jeopardy principles, state prosecution would be barred by an earlier prosecution under the ordinance? See Note, The Concurrent State and Local Regulation of Marijuana: The Validity of the Ann Arbor Marijuana Ordinance, 71 Mich. L. Rev. 400 (1972); Note, Conflict Between State Statutes and Municipal Ordinances, 72 Harv. L. Rev. 737 (1959).

Should it matter that the ordinance in Ann Arbor is less harsh than the state statute? In City of North Charleston v. Harper, 410 S.E.2d 569 (S.C. 1991), the court struck down an ordinance that imposed a mandatory 30–day sentence for possession of a controlled substance. State law permitted the imposition of a 30–day sentence, but also permitted a judge to impose lesser sanctions. The court concluded that the ordinance contravened a constitutional provision that prohibited localities from setting aside state criminal laws and penalties for their violation, and conflicted with a state law giving municipal judges discretion in the sentencing of offenders. Harsher local penalties might be justified on the grounds that proscribed conduct raises particular concern within a locality where it is more frequent or especially abhorrent to residents. This argument, however, needs to be balanced against the desire to provide notice to residents and transients of the consequences of proscribed behavior. See In re Hubbard, 396 P.2d 809 (Cal. 1964). Some courts have concluded that harsher local regulation is invalid because the legislature has impliedly permitted what it has not prohibited. See, e.g., Town of Boaz v. Jenkins, 25 So.2d 394 (Ala. Ct. App. 1946) (statute that prohibited gambling in public places impliedly permitted gambling in private, and thus invalidated local regulation to the contrary). Can this rationale be reconciled with the opinion in *Miller v. Fabius Township*? What reasons might exist for allowing a locality to impose lesser sanctions on criminals but not harsher ones?

Whether an ordinance is more or less stringent than the state statute is sometimes a matter of controversy. In Michigan Restaurant Association v. City of Marquette, 626 N.W.2d 418 (Mich. App. 2001), the court considered a pre-emption challenge to a Marquette city ordinance that placed a total ban on smoking in restaurants. Plaintiffs contended that the ordinance was in conflict with a state statute that provided that restaurants "may designate" a certain percentage of their seating capacity as seating for smokers. The majority invalidated the ordinance, reasoning that it "does something more than expanding the state statute to make it more stringent. The ordinance creates a general prohibition on smoking as opposed to, for example, creating a higher percentage of nonsmoking tables." Id. at 420. The majority added that the "ordinance is in direct conflict with a food service establishment's right under [the state statute] to designate a certain percentage of its seating capacity as seating for smokers. The question whether there should be a total ban on smoking in restaurants must be left to the legislature." Id. at 422. The dissenting judge, however, read the intent of the state statute to be guaranteeing nonsmoking, not smoking, space in restaurants, and concluded that because the "ordinance provides for more, not less, nonsmoking space, it is not preempted" by the state law. Id. at 423. But see Tri–Nel Management, Inc. v. Board of Health of Barnstable, 741 N.E.2d 37, 44 (Mass. 2001) (holding that state statutes prohibiting smoking in various locations and permitting smoking in large restaurants only in designated smoking areas did not preempt municipal regulation prohibiting smoking in all restaurants and bars because the local ban "furthers, rather than frustrates [state legislative] intent").

2. *Relative Harshness and Conflict.* In BeeRite Tire Disposal/Recycling, Inc. v. City of Rhodes, 646 N.W.2d 857 (Iowa App. 2002), the court considered a local ordinance that imposed more stringent restrictions on a tire disposal business than did applicable state statutes. The court accepted that a local law is irreconcilable with a state law when it prohibits an act permitted by statute. The court concluded, however, that a local ordinance that imposed harsher restrictions, but that did not "revise the statutory scheme," could co-exist with the state law. In *BeeRite Tire*, the city required a permit for storage of a smaller number of tires than the state requirements, increased permit fees, imposed stricter limits on space dedicated to tire storage, and limited storage of processed tires beyond the limitations of state law. The court determined that the city had only imposed further restrictions on activities already restricted by state law, thus "further promoting the underlying policy of that statute, but with greater force." Id. at 860. The city had not impermissibly "bypassed, contradicted, or overridden" the state regulatory scheme. Does the distinction between a stricter restriction and a restriction of a previously unregulated activity make sense? But see Iowa Grocery Industry Association v. City of Des Moines, 712 N.W.2d 675 (Iowa 2006) (invalidating Des Moines ordinance that imposed an additional "administrative fee" on applications for liquor licenses to be processed pursuant to state law on the ground that the ordinance conflicts with the state regulatory scheme and "does more than merely increase the details of regulation").

3. Does it matter why Fabius Township passed the ordinance at issue in *Miller*, above? Assume that the state statute was passed for safety reasons, while the local ordinance was passed to minimize noise during late afternoon and early evening hours. Would that indicate that the state and municipality were not in conflict, since they were regulating for different purposes?

Now assume that the ordinance was passed in order to discourage absentee ownership and those summer vacationers who, like plaintiff Miller, who would be unable to use the lake before 5:00 p.m. due to employment. If this were the case, you might conclude that residents who encouraged passage of an ordinance for these reasons had captured the local decisionmaking process and improperly imposed costs on unrepresented nonresidents. But even if you reach the conclusion that the ordinance was intended to disfavor absentees, it does not follow that the ordinance resulted in capture. There are, after all, ways in which the interests of absentee owners or nonresidents can be represented before the township board. Presumably, those who rent their homes to summer vacationers and businesses that depend on them would want to retain a hospitable atmosphere for vacationers and nonresidents. How could a court determine whether representation actually occurred in the decisionmaking process? Should the motivations that led to passage of the ordinance matter? How could a court become aware of those motivations?

PROBLEM XIV

The State Constitution, art. 89, § 6, provides in part that "(a)ny city or town may, by the adoption, amendment, or repeal of local ordinances or by by-laws, exercise any power or function which the general court [the state legislature] has power to confer upon it which is not inconsistent with the Constitution or laws enacted by the general court...." The Town of Dighton, for which you serve as counsel, has used this power to remedy a situation created by the operation of a dog racing track within the town by the plaintiff Taunton Greyhound Association. On nights when races are run, several thousand patrons converge on the small town, threatening the pastoral setting and the peace of mind of its residents. The town has passed a by-law that requires any sponsor of a gathering to which the public is invited for a consideration and at which attendance exceeds 400 to request the Chief of Police of the town to assign one police officer for every 400 persons in attendance and to pay for such officers.

Plaintiff, in a suit to declare the by-law invalid, argues that any ordinance affecting the presence of police officers at the racetrack has been preempted by the statute creating the State Racing Commission. That statute includes a provision that directs the Commission, when it deems necessary, to apply to the Department of Public Safety or to the police department of a city or town in which a "racing meeting" is to be held, to furnish a police detail in such numbers as the Commission may require. The agency applied to is then obligated to furnish the detail, which the Commission assigns to duty at the "meeting." The Commission has never assigned a detail to the Dighton race track.

Other sections of the statute in question provide for licensing of horse and dog racing, supervision of wagering, periodic inspection of installations and facilities operated by licensees, rulemaking procedures of the State Racing Commission, regulation of drug use to affect the speed of dogs or horses, penalties for affecting the outcome of a race, and exclusion of certain persons from racing premises.

How will you respond to the plaintiff's argument?

Envirosafe Services of Idaho, Inc. v. County of Owyhee

735 P.2d 998 (Idaho 1987).

■ HUNTLEY, JUSTICE.

Owyhee County appeals the trial court's writ of prohibition and order prohibiting it from enforcing its Ordinance No. 83–02, wherein the county sought to regulate the disposal of hazardous and non-hazardous wastes and materials (including polychlorinated biphenyls (PCBs)) and establish user fees.

On April 9, 1984, the Owyhee County Board of Commissioners enacted "the third amended Owyhee County Catastrophic and Emergency Preparedness Hazardous Waste and Materials Disclosure and Fee Ordinance" (hereinafter Ordinance No. 83–02). The ordinance adopted standards delineated in the Resource Conservation Recovery Act (RCRA) 42 U.S.C. § 6901 et seq., and Toxic Substance Control Act (TSCA), 15 U.S.C. § 2601 et seq., which included requiring the operators of hazardous waste facilities in

Owyhee County to file disclosure forms indicating truck delivery routes, the kinds of wastes and materials received, and the names of the generators of the waste. A fee of one cent per pound of waste deposited in the county was also imposed. Enforcement was by civil penalty. The ordinance was directed at Envirosafe Services of Idaho, Inc. (ESI), the plaintiff/respondent in this case, which operates two hazardous waste management facilities in Owyhee County. . . .

The trial court found that the Idaho Legislature, by enacting the Hazardous Waste Management Act of 1983 (HWMA), I.C. §§ 39–4401–4432, intended to fully occupy the field of hazardous waste disposal and, thus, Ordinance No. 83–02 was preempted by state law and void. The trial court also found the provisions of Ordinance 83–02 regarding PCB disposal to be preempted by the HWMA and state regulations. . . .

I. The Standards of Preemption Analysis

Prior to any discussion of the merits of appellants' contention that the State has neither preempted the field of hazardous waste disposal, nor the field of PCB disposal, a discussion of the salient standards governing such an analysis is appropriate.

The Idaho Constitution, art. 12, § 2, provides that county ordinances may not conflict with state statutes. . . .

The concept of "conflict" broadens when put in the context of a determination of state preemption over a field of regulation. Of course, direct conflict (expressly allowing what the state disallows, and vice versa) is "conflict" in any sense. State v. Musser, 67 Idaho 214, 176 P.2d 199 (1946). Additionally, a "conflict" between state and local regulation may be implied. This state firmly adopted the doctrine of implied preemption in Caesar v. State, 101 Idaho 158, 610 P.2d 517 (1980).

Where it can be inferred from a state statute that the state has intended to fully occupy or preempt a particular area, to the exclusion of [local governmental entities], a [local] ordinance in that area will be held to be in conflict with the state law, even if the state law does not so specifically state. . . .

The doctrine of implied preemption typically applies in instances where, despite the lack of specific language preempting regulation by local governmental entities, the state has acted in the area in such a pervasive manner that it must be assumed that it intended to occupy the entire field of regulation.

"The [local governmental entity] cannot act in an area which is so completely covered by general law as to indicate that it is a matter of state concern." *Caesar*, 101 Idaho at 161, 610 P.2d at 520. . . .

Owyhee County argues that *Caesar*, supra, is an anomalous case which has been abrogated by more recent case law. Specifically, Owyhee County cites Benewah County Cattlemen's Association, Inc. v. Board of County Commissioners of Benewah County, 105 Idaho 209, 668 P.2d 85 (1983), as the more orthodox precedent. Any reliance by Owyhee County on *Benewah*

County, supra, is misplaced. In that case, the doctrine of implied preemption was in no way abrogated. Rather, this Court simply could not find *any* intent to preempt by the legislature, since it had not occupied the field at issue (livestock control)....

Moreover, the underpinnings for the doctrine of implied preemption are principles of long-standing in this state. In Clyde Hess Distributing Co. v. Bonneville County, 69 Idaho 505, 210 P.2d 798 (1949), this Court acknowledged the ability of the legislature to implicitly preempt local regulation by occupying the field of regulation. In that case, we found that the legislature "did not intend to occupy the whole field of hours of sale of beer, thereby making any regulation by the county necessarily inconsistent with the general law." *Clyde Hess*, 69 Idaho at 510, 210 P.2d at 800. Our failure to find the field preempted in *Clyde Hess* was due to the fact that express intent not to preempt was found in the same statute which had been alleged to preempt the field. (I.C. §§ 23–1014–15.) (See also, State v. Poynter, 70 Idaho 438, 220 P.2d 386 (1950).)

With these standards in mind, we turn now to the case at hand.

II. The Field of Hazardous Waste Disposal

The HWMA contains no express language indicating intent to preempt local regulation; nor does it expressly grant to localities the right to regulate. However, I.C. § 39–4404 provides:

> The legislature intends that the State of Idaho enact and carry out a hazardous waste program that will enable the state to assume primacy over hazardous waste control from the federal government.... By the provisions of this chapter, the legislature desires to avoid the existence of duplicative, overlapping or conflicting state and federal regulatory systems....

I.C. § 39–4405 further provides that the Board of Health and Welfare "adopt such rules and regulations as are necessary and feasible for the management of post generation handling, collection, transportation, treatment, storage and disposal of hazardous wastes within the state."

Importantly, I.C. § 39–4419 reads:

> The director [of the Idaho Department of Health and Welfare] shall have the power and the duty to encourage cooperative activities between the department and other states for the improved management of hazardous wastes, and so far as is practical, to provide for uniform state regulations and for interstate agreements relating to hazardous waste management.

All of the above-cited code sections evince a strong legislative intent that regulation of the field of hazardous waste disposal be regulated by means of one, uniform statewide scheme enabling this state to enter into meaningful interstate agreements. Taken alone, this clear legislative intent is more than sufficient to preempt the field and preclude local governmental regulation of the subject matter.

However, even were such not the case, the HWMA, in and of itself, is a comprehensive statutory scheme of the kind which implicitly evidences legislative intent to preempt the field. The HWMA provides for regulation, trip permits and a manifest system for those who transport hazardous waste (I.C. §§ 67–2929–30 and I.C. § 39–4410); it further regulates a permit system for hazardous waste facilities (I.C. § 39–4409) and provides recording and reporting requirements for generators and facilities (I.C. § 39–4411, 39–4429); fee systems and dedicated funds for emergency responses, and monitoring (I.C. §§ 39–4417, 4410 and 39–4427) are also provided. There are also code sections dealing with citizen suits (I.C. § 39–4416), local governmental notice (I.C. § 39–4418), interstate cooperation (I.C. § 39–4419), employment security (I.C. § 39–4420), as well as broad enforcement provisions (I.C. § 39–4413).

The HWMA speaks for itself. This state's legislature has acted in an all-encompassing fashion towards regulating the field of hazardous waste disposal. Such is also readily apparent from a reading of the ordinance. Ordinance 83–02 is largely duplicative of the HWMA. In fact, the county itself concedes that the bulk of Ordinance 83–02 is entirely duplicative of the HWMA and, necessarily, the RCRA. Such extensive duplication leads to the inescapable conclusion that the area has already been fully regulated and the fields sought to be covered by the ordinance already occupied by the HWMA....

Most importantly, we also note that the very subject matter here involved, the field of hazardous waste disposal, is fraught with such unique concerns and dangers to both the state and the nation that its regulation demands a statewide, rather than local, approach. We are not the only state to so decide. In Stablex Corp. v. Town of Hooksett, 122 N.H. 1091, 456 A.2d 94 (1982), the Town of Hooksett enacted ordinances regulating the siting and construction of hazardous waste facilities. The New Hampshire Supreme Court noted that "state and federal hazardous waste legislation was ... enacted against a background that can only be termed a state and national emergency...." *Stablex,* 456 A.2d at 96. That court further concluded that the New Hampshire state statutes regulating hazardous waste comprised a "comprehensive and detailed program of statewide regulation" which preempted any local action in the field. (See also, Applied Chemical Technology, Inc. v. Town of Merrimack, 126 N.H. 45, 490 A.2d 1348 (1985)).

Equally compelling and nearly identical reasoning was employed in Township of Cascade v. Cascade Resource Recovery Inc., 118 Mich. App. 580, 325 N.W.2d 500 (1982).

> [T]he safe management and disposal of hazardous wastes is clearly an area which demands uniform, statewide treatment.... Michigan is extremely limited in the number of facilities that handle this waste properly. This is due partly because no community wants hazardous waste facility in its vicinity. Thus, local interests strongly want to retain their control. However, the same reasoning easily justifies state control. The legislature recognized that hazardous waste disposal areas evoke such strong emotions in localities that the decision as to where a landfill should go should not be given to the locality, which is far more swayed by parochial interests than the state. The legislature, instead, gave the power to a centralized deci-

> sionmaker who could act uniformly and provide the most effective means of regulating hazardous waste.

325 N.W.2d at 504.

It is important to note that the same considerations which permeated the holding in *Township of Cascade* are equally applicable here. The state of Idaho is limited to very few facilities which handle hazardous waste. Additionally, the treatment and storage of hazardous waste is a subject which inspires a unique amount of interest and concern from this state's citizenry. We recognize the unique importance of and benefit derived from local government regulation and that, ordinarily, local problems are best solved by local regulation, since local governmental entities are uniquely suited to fashioning workable solutions by virtue of their proximity to, and direct awareness of, the issues involved. By our ruling here, we in no way denigrate the function of local government. Instead, we acknowledge the unique importance and complexity of the subject matter. (See also, Rollins Environmental Services of Louisiana Inc. v. Iberville Parish Police Jury, 371 So. 2d 1127 (La. 1979)). . . .

For the reasons stated, the trial court correctly found the field of hazardous waste disposal is uniquely susceptible of, and appropriate for, uniform statewide regulation, which regulation has, in fact, been effected through the provisions of the HWMA rendering Ordinance 83–02 void.

III. The Field of PCB Disposal

Although PCBs have not been specifically identified as "hazardous waste" by the State Department of Health and Welfare and are not identified as "hazardous waste" in the RCRA, upon which this state's HWMA is patterned, their regulation has not been ignored by this state. Last year, the legislature enacted House Bill 660, 1986 Sess. Law, ch. 324, amending I.C. § 39–4403 and defining "restricted hazardous waste" to include "liquid hazardous wastes containing polychlorinated biphenyls at concentrations greater than or equal to fifty parts per million. . . ." (I.C. § 39–4403(14)(a)(iv)). Implicit in such a definition is the concept of PCBs as "hazardous waste," which concept lends credence to the argument that the legislature has intended that PCBs be regulated via the HWMA.

Also of import is the fact that Idaho's definition of "hazardous waste" is broader than that found in the RCRA (42 U.S.C. § 6903(5)). . . . That PCBs are included in this definition of "hazardous waste," taken from the TSCA, is evidenced from the listing of PCBs in 40 C.F.R. § 261 (Appendix VIII "Hazardous Constitutions") which includes only "toxic, carcinogenic, mutagenic or teratogenic" substances. Therefore PCBs are, indeed, included in the definition of "hazardous waste" under the HWMA. Accordingly, our analysis, in Part I herein, of preemption of the subject matter is wholly applicable to the narrower field of PCB disposal.

Further evidencing this state's strong intent to fully regulate the disposal of PCBs are the Department of Health and Welfare's solid waste management regulations, 16 IDAPA § 1–6001–6014, wherein authority to regulate PCBs through "conditional use permits" is granted. These regulations, in and of themselves, "have the force and effect of law." I.C. § 39–107(8). The regulations evidence intent that the Department of Health and Welfare and not, implicitly, other governmental entities, has primacy over such regulation. "Solid wastes and post-consumer products shall be managed as determined by the department, ..." 16 IDAPA § 1–6004.01....

For the foregoing reasons, we hold that the state has fully occupied and preempted both the fields of hazardous waste disposal and PCB disposal and, therefore, Ordinance No. 83–02 was properly voided by the trial court.

Affirmed.

American Financial Services Association v. City of Oakland

104 P.3d 813 (Cal. 2005).

■ BROWN, JUSTICE.

"Predatory lending" is a term generally used to characterize a range of abusive and aggressive lending practices, including deception or fraud, charging excessive fees and interest rates, making loans without regard to a borrower's ability to repay, or refinancing loans repeatedly over a short period of time to incur additional fees without any economic gain to the borrower. Predatory lending is most likely to occur in the rapidly growing "subprime" mortgage market, which is a market generally providing access to borrowers with impaired credit, limited income, or high debt relative to their income. Mortgages in this market tend to be in smaller amounts, and with faster prepayments and significantly higher interest rates and fees, than "prime" mortgages.

In 2001, California enacted legislation to combat predatory lending practices that typically occur in the subprime home mortgage market. (Fin. Code, §§ 4970–4979.8 (Division 1.6).) Eight days before Division 1.6 was signed into law by the Governor, the City of Oakland adopted an ordinance regulating predatory lending practices in the Oakland home mortgage market.

... We conclude that the Ordinance is preempted by Division 1.6....

I. FACTUAL AND PROCEDURAL BACKGROUND

On October 15, 2001, American Financial Services Association (AFSA) filed this action against the City of Oakland and the Redevelopment Agency of the City of Oakland (City) seeking a declaration that the Ordinance was preempted by state law, and an injunction against its enforcement....

II. DISCUSSION

A. Background

According to its legislative history, the purpose of Division 1.6 was to regulate and thereby curtail predatory lending practices that typically occur in the subprime mortgage market....

... Division 1.6 and the Ordinance are similar in that they regulate the same subject matter, i.e., predatory lending practices in home mortgages. However, Division 1.6 and the Ordinance differ in significant respects with regard to how they regulate these predatory practices. For example, ... Division 1.6 permits prepayment penalties under certain conditions during the first 36 months of the loan; the Ordinance prohibits them for all high-cost and certain refinanced home loans, and limits them for other home loans. (Fin. Code, § 4973, subd. (a); Oak. Mun. Code, § 5.33.040(A).) In addition, Division 1.6 requires that borrowers be encouraged in writing to seek loan counseling; the Ordinance prohibits a high-cost home loan being made without either the borrower receiving loan counseling or giving the credit counselor a written waiver of counseling. (Fin. Code, § 4973, subd. (k)(1); Oak. Mun. Code, § 5.33.050(A).)

In addition to other enforcement mechanisms, Division 1.6 and the Ordinance both allow for civil and criminal penalties and for civil enforcement by borrowers, including punitive damages. (Fin. Code, §§ 4975, subd. (c), 4977, subds. (b), (c), 4978, subds. (a), (b)(2); Oak. Mun. Code, §§ 5.33.080, 5.33.100.) However, Division 1.6 imposes civil penalties up to $25,000 per violation; the Ordinance imposes such penalties up to the amount of $50,000. (Fin. Code, § 4977, subd. (b); Oak. Mun. Code, § 5.33.080(D).) Under Division 1.6, the amounts collected from such civil penalties are to be used by the "licensing agency, subject to appropriation by the Legislature, for the purposes of education and enforcement in connection with abusive lending practices." (Fin. Code, § 4977, subd. (g).) The amounts collected by the Ordinance presumably simply go into the city coffers....

We now turn to the question of whether these similarities and differences may coexist or, if instead, the Ordinance is preempted by Division 1.6.

B. Analysis

"Under article XI, section 7 of the California Constitution, '[a] county or city may make and enforce within its limits all local, police, sanitary, and other ordinances and regulations not in conflict with general laws.'" (*Sherwin–Williams Co. v. City of Los Angeles* (1993), 4 Cal.4th 893, 897, 16 Cal.Rptr.2d 215, 844 P.2d 534 (*Sherwin–Williams*).) In addition, charter cities such as Oakland may adopt and enforce ordinances that conflict with general state laws, provided the subject of the regulation is a "municipal affair" rather than one of "statewide concern." (Cal. Const., art. XI, § 5; Oak. City Charter, § 106; see *Johnson v. Bradley* (1992) 4 Cal.4th 389, 399, 14 Cal.Rptr.2d 470, 841 P.2d 990.) Here, however, the City reasonably concedes regulation of predatory practices in mortgage lending is one of statewide concern. Under these circumstances, the parties agree that if the Ordinance conflicts with state law, it is preempted.

A conflict between state law and an ordinance exists if the ordinance duplicates or is coextensive therewith, is contradictory or inimical thereto, or enters an area either expressly or impliedly fully occupied by general law. (*Sherwin–Williams, supra,* 4 Cal.4th at pp. 897–898, 16 Cal.Rptr.2d

215, 844 P.2d 534.) Relying solely on the Legislature's failure to include express preemption language and the unique local interests of Oakland, the City contends that Division 1.6 sets only "statewide minimum standards, not statewide uniform standards, for subprime home mortgage lending." We conclude that in enacting Division 1.6 the Legislature has impliedly fully occupied the field of regulation of predatory practices in home mortgage lending, and hence the Ordinance is preempted on this ground.

"[I]t is well settled that local regulation is invalid if it attempts to impose additional requirements in a field which is fully occupied by statute." (*Tolman v. Underhill* (1952) 39 Cal.2d 708, 712, 249 P.2d 280(*Tolman*).) "[L]ocal legislation enters an area that is 'fully occupied' by general law when the Legislature has expressly manifested its intent to 'fully occupy' the area [citation], or when it has impliedly done so in light of one of the following indicia of intent: '(1) the subject matter has been so fully and completely covered by general law as to clearly indicate that it has become exclusively a matter of state concern; (2) the subject matter has been partially covered by general law couched in such terms as to indicate clearly that a paramount state concern will not tolerate further or additional local action; or (3) the subject matter has been partially covered by general law, and the subject is of such a nature that the adverse effect of a local ordinance on the transient citizens of the state outweighs the possible benefit to the' locality [citations]." (*Sherwin-Williams, supra,* 4 Cal.4th at p. 898, 16 Cal.Rptr.2d 215, 844 P.2d 534.)

Here, of course, there is no express preemption language in Division 1.6. However, there are clear indications of the Legislature's implicit intent to fully occupy the field of regulation of predatory lending tactics in home mortgages.

"Where the Legislature has adopted statutes governing a particular subject matter, its intent with regard to occupying the field to the exclusion of all local regulation is not to be measured alone by the language used but by the whole purpose and scope of the legislative scheme." (*Tolman, supra,*). . . .

. . . Division 1.6 comprehensively regulates predatory lending practices in home mortgages. It delineates at length what mortgages are covered, what lending acts are prohibited, who can be held liable for violations of Division 1.6, the various enforcement mechanisms available, who may invoke such enforcement mechanisms, and defenses to such violations. The provisions of Division 1.6 "are so extensive in their scope that they clearly show an intention by the Legislature to adopt a general scheme for the regulation of" predatory lending tactics in home mortgages. (*Lane, supra,* 58 Cal.2d at p. 103, 22 Cal.Rptr. 857, 372 P.2d 897.)

Moreover, in regulating such lending tactics in home mortgages, the Legislature was not suddenly entering an area previously governed by municipalities and unexplored at a statewide level. To the contrary, as the City acknowledges, regulation of mortgage lenders has historically occurred at the state, not the municipal, level. . . .

Indeed, when asked at oral argument, the City could point to no other instance in over 150 years of state history where a municipality had attempted to regulate mortgage lending. Thus, state activity in the area of regulation of mortgage lending was not only historically dominant, it was exclusive....

We therefore conclude that through the enactment of Division 1.6, the Legislature has fully occupied the field of regulation of predatory tactics in home mortgages.... [T]he Ordinance is not supplementary legislation that in other contexts might be allowed, but a line item veto of those policy decisions by the Legislature with which the City disagrees. In revisiting this area fully occupied by state law, the Ordinance undermines the considered judgments and choices of the Legislature, and is therefore preempted.

In drafting Division 1.6, the Legislature balanced two compelling and competing considerations, i.e., the need to protect particularly vulnerable consumers from predatory lending practices and the concern that homeowners not be unduly hindered in accessing the equity in their own homes. (See, e.g., Sen. Judiciary Com., analysis of Assem. Bill No. 489 (2001–2002 Reg. Sess.) as amended June 21, 2001, p. 2....).... Severe regulation of subprime lending might cause lenders to cease making such loans in California, or preclude borrowers from obtaining a loan based on equity in their home even though such loans can serve a legitimate need. (Dept. of Real Estate, enrolled bill rep. on Assem. Bill No. 489 (2001–2002 Reg. Sess.) Sept. 27, 2001, p. 7.) Moreover, increased regulation generally entails additional cost, decreasing further the availability of loan funds to subprime borrowers. Thus, the Legislature was aware [that] regulation of certain predatory practices in mortgage lending, practices which occur most often in the subprime market, could have the unintended consequence of hurting those the legislation was intended to help, and sought to balance these competing concerns. The Ordinance, and the possibility of other divergent and competing local measures throughout California, upsets that balance. By analogy to federal preemption law, the Ordinance " 'stands as an obstacle to the accomplishment and execution of the full purposes and objectives' " of the Legislature.

Thus, contrary to the City's and the dissent's assertion, Division 1.6 does not set "statewide minimum" standards beyond which municipalities are free to regulate. (Dis. opn., *post,* 23 Cal.Rptr.3d at p. 478, 104 P.3d at p. 833; id. at p. 481, 104 P.3d at p. 836.)....

The City and the dissent [also] essentially assert, however, that Oakland has a higher incidence of subprime lending and the predatory tactics associated with such lending than other areas of the state, and hence may suffer more than other parts of California the resulting blight and poverty such tactics can foster. (Dis. opn., *post,* 23 Cal.Rptr.3d at pp. 475–478, 481, 104 P.3d at pp. 831–833, 836.) Assuming this is correct, and while these would be important local concerns, they do not give the City a license to regulate a highly complex financial area comprehensively addressed by state law. Such an approach would mean that any city which claimed to experience a disproportionate number of foreclosures, or instances of securities fraud, could simply write its own measures regardless of any confusion these competing measures may foster. Rather, the state's interest in uniformity in the area of mortgage lending law demonstrably transcends the concerns of a particular municipality, and is a "convincing basis for legislative action ... based on sensible, pragmatic considerations." (*Calif. Fed., supra,* 54 Cal.3d at p. 18, 283 Cal.Rptr. 569, 812 P.2d 916.) In this situation, the City must "defer to legislative estimates regarding the significance of a given problem and the responsive measures that should be taken toward its resolution." (Id. at p. 24, 283 Cal.Rptr. 569, 812 P.2d 916.)....

... [T]he Legislature's failure to include an express preemption provision in Division 1.6 does not ineluctably mean there is no implied preemption.... Indeed, the City does not point out for us any state mortgage lending law that has an express preemption provision.

The City and the dissent rely on testimony at a Senate subcommittee hearing held shortly before the passage of Division 1.6, urging inclusion of an express preemption provision, and the fact that several members of the Legislature had a brief conversation regarding preemption at that subcommittee hearing, in asserting Division 1.6 does not impliedly preempt the Ordinance. (Dis. opn., *post,* 23 Cal.Rptr.3d at pp. 473–474, 104 P.3d at pp. 829–830.)

Taken to its logical extreme, the City's and the dissent's approach would eliminate the doctrine of implied preemption at least to the extent someone somewhere ever suggested to the Legislature an express preemption clause would be useful, and the Legislature declined to adopt that suggestion. Such a standard would be easily manipulable, and would punish constituents who attempt to educate the Legislature about their concerns to the extent their concerns were not addressed in the precise manner proposed to the Legislature.... While we cannot know the reasons for the absence of express preemption language, the Legislature is deemed to be aware of existing law, and may have comfortably assumed that given such state dominance in mortgage lending regulation, and having omitted express preemption provisions in other mortgage lending laws without such an omission being read as a license for local regulation, that an express preemption provision was unnecessary. Indeed, unlike the dissent, we are reluctant to reward the opponents of preemption when nothing in the statutory language or history suggests they persuaded the Legislature to consider relinquishing its historical control of this particular regulatory field and to tolerate municipal, and possibly conflicting, regulation....

... [W]e conclude the Ordinance is preempted because by enacting Division 1.6 the Legislature has fully occupied the field of regulation of predatory practices in home loans....

■ BAXTER, J., WERDEGAR, J. and CHIN, J., concurred with BROWN, J.

■ GEORGE, CHIEF JUSTICE, dissenting.

I respectfully dissent.

Past California cases establish that a general statewide statute will be held to preempt all local legislative measures only when the state legislation, explicitly or impliedly, "clearly indicates" that the Legislature intended to fully occupy the field and preclude all local regulation. (*Sherwin-Williams Co. v. City of Los Angeles,* (1993) 4 Cal.4th 893, 898, 16 Cal. Rptr.2d 215, 844 P.2d 534.) Here, the Legislature consciously considered including express preemption language in the statewide statute (division 1.6 of the Financial Code, sections 4970–4979.8), but ultimately omitted any such language from the statute as one of the essential elements of a compromise that led to the enactment of the legislation. In view of this legislative background—which demonstrates that the statute does not "clearly indicate" a legislative intent to preempt all local legislation—and the distinctive local interest that the City of Oakland has in adopting stringent and effective measures to protect its residents from the predatory lending practices at issue, I cannot agree with the majority that Division 1.6 properly may be found to preempt the Ordinance in its entirety. * * * *

II

The majority's emphasis on state uniformity and historical regulation patterns ... fails to acknowledge properly the respect this court traditionally has accorded to localities regarding issues that have a unique local impact. As we stated in *Fisher v. City of Berkeley* (1984) 37 Cal.3d 644, 707, 209 Cal.Rptr. 682, 693 P.2d 261, "[w]e will be reluctant to infer legislative intent to preempt a field covered by municipal regulation where there is a significant local interest to be served that may differ from one locality to another." ...

... The record reflects that the Oakland City Council, in passing the ordinance in question, found that the predatory lending problem in Oakland was particularly aggravated "because of the high number of minority and low income homeowners in Oakland, and the pressures of gentrification in certain neighborhoods that increase property values and home equity," which have led to a situation in which "Oakland residents in low income areas have been perceived to be 'the house rich and the cash poor' and thus are prime targets for predatory lending practices." ...

... Oakland's particular interest in regulating subprime loans goes beyond merely protecting its particularly vulnerable citizens. As one amicus curiae points out, "predatory lending is not just a consumer protection issue; it is a *community development* issue, because it threatens the stability of lower income homeowning neighborhoods.... Predatory home mortgage lending has enormous impacts on targeted neighborhoods. Predatory lending practices, particularly the phenomenon of 'asset based lending,' contribute to an increase in the number of foreclosures. This can result in abandoned houses and blighted neighborhoods and contribute to the physical and economic deterioration of lower-income, minority, and inner city communities...."

The Legislature was free to conclude that treatment of predatory lending requires statewide uniformity. Alternatively, however, it could conclude that only a statewide minimum standard of conduct is necessary, and that local jurisdictions have some freedom to additionally regulate predatory lenders pursuant to the municipal police power to prevent urban decay and neighborhood blight. Because of the local, varying nature of the problem, this is not a case in which having differing local standards is wholly illogical.... All we can be certain of is that Division 1.6 was the product of a legislative compromise, and that the compromise included deliberate silence on the matter of preemption....

.... Although our numerous preemption cases resist easy harmonization, one theme that emerges is that those municipal ordinances that have been found to be preempted have been seen as subverting, in some tangible way, the purpose and intent of the state statute....

... The Ordinance does not appear to undermine any of the stated goals of Division 1.6. To the contrary, the ordinance grants borrowers additional rights not afforded under state law, such as restrictions on prepayment penalties, mandatory credit counseling, and the opportunity to present defenses to secondary buyers of their mortgages if the borrowers have been victimized by predatory lending practices. Far from subverting Division 1.6, the Ordinance furthers the stated goal of the state legislation by providing additional protections to the low-income borrowers in Oakland who are especially vulnerable to predatory lending practices.

The majority argues, however, that the Ordinance *does* disrupt the balance struck by the Legislature in enacting Division 1.6....

The majority's implicit assumption is that Oakland's Ordinance, by providing for stricter regulation of certain areas of subprime lending, necessarily will cause lenders to cease making loans in Oakland and in California as a whole. (Maj. opn., *ante,* at pp. 466–467, 104 P.3d at pp. 824–825.) Had a majority of the Legislature agreed with that proposition, however, it could be expected that the legislation would have included a provision expressly preempting local legislation. The conscious omission of an explicit preemption provision demonstrates that the Legislature could not agree that local legislation would undermine or impair the objectives of the state legislation. Furthermore, should the undesirable consequences forecast by the majority come to pass, the Legislature, of course, would be free to step in and add an express preemption provision to Division 1.6.

The majority also places great emphasis on the city's admission that in more than 150 years of California history, no municipality has attempted to regulate mortgage lending. (Maj. opn, *ante,* at p. 464, 104 P.3d at p. 822.) But we never have required a locality to prove a historical practice of regulation to establish the validity of a local regulation....

... [T]he Ordinance provides added protections for its citizens that will not result in uncertainty or confusion, and absent a clearly evident legislative intent I believe the Ordinance is not preempted.

I would affirm the judgment of the Court of Appeal, upholding the validity of Oakland's antipredatory lending ordinance.

■ KENNARD, J., and MORENO, J., concurred with GEORGE, C.J.

NOTES

1. *State–Wide Uniformity Versus Local Variation.* During the 1990's state courts faced a spate of cases alleging that state regulations of hazardous waste disposal preempted local ordinances that imposed similar kinds of restrictions. See, e.g., IT Corp. v. Solano County Board of Supervisors, 820 P.2d 1023 (Cal. 1991) (no preemption); Fondessy Enterprises, Inc. v. Oregon, 492 N.E.2d 797 (Ohio 1986) (no preemption); Northern States Power Co. v. City of Granite Falls, 463 N.W.2d 541 (Minn. 1990) (preemption). Is the need for state-wide uniformity or for a centralized decision-maker in the area of hazardous waste disposal compelling? Or is the attendant danger so likely to differ from locality to locality that municipal attention to the issue is warranted or preferred? Is it possible to generalize about the issue? Are your answers to each of these questions the same if the regulatory area is subprime lending rather than hazardous waste disposal? In particular, how persuasive do you find the arguments of the dissent in *American Financial Services Association* that the City of Oakland has a "more significant" interest than both the state as a whole and most other localities, in strictly regulating certain subprime lending? For a discussion of the issues surrounding possible *federal* regulations limiting *state* predatory lending laws, see Nicholas Bagley, The Unwarranted Regulatory Preemption of Predatory Lending Laws, 79 N.Y.U. L. Rev. 2274 (2004). The Supreme Court of Ohio invalidated an ordinance of the City of Cleveland that sought to regulate "predatory home mortgage lending" on the ground that it impermissibly conflicted with state law insofar as it prohibited loans that state law permitted. American Financial Services Ass'n v. City of Cleveland, 858 N.E.2d 776 (2006).

2. *Legislative Intent and Pre-emption.* How can the court know whether the legislature has acted in a manner sufficiently pervasive to constitute implied pre-emption of a field? The legislature cannot consider every contingency that might relate to the field. A court, therefore, would appear to have substantial latitude in deciding either that a series of statutory provisions was pre-emptive of an entire field, or that specific provisions were intended to constitute the only area of state interest, an application of the maxim of statutory construction *expressio unius est exclusio alterius*, or the expression of one principle implies the exclusion of others. This is not to suggest that courts will narrowly construe the conditions from which it will infer a legislative intent of preemption. In Township of Cascade v. Cascade Resource Recovery, Inc., 325 N.W.2d 500 (Mich. Ct. App. 1982), cited in *Envirosafe*, above, the court found that the legislature had acted pervasively in the field of hazardous waste when it replaced a 10–provision statutory scheme with a 51–provision one. The court held that enactment of "a detailed plan which provides for the safe management and disposal of hazardous wastes" necessarily precluded local regulation of the same area. At the same time, the court recognized that the state act considered local concerns and concluded that:

> The inclusion of local input further indicates that the Legislature has preempted the field. To hold otherwise could completely upset the balance between state and local interests since a municipality could veto the state's decision to issue a permit or license even though the state took the municipality's concerns into consideration.

325 N.W.2d at 504.

Another effort to discern legislative intent from legislative history can be found in Sherwin–Williams Co. v. City of Los Angeles, 844 P.2d 534 (Cal. 1993), discussed in *American Financial Services Association*, above. In 1981, the California legislature, in order to control graffiti, enacted legislation restricting the sale of aerosol paints. The Act contained a provision that expressly pre-empted local ordinances regulating the sale of aerosol paint containers. Although the substantive regulations of the Act were codified in the state Penal Code, the express pre-emption provision was not. Instead, the Penal Code contained a general provision, § 594.5, denying any pre-emptive intent. In 1988, the legislature amended the substantive provision to expand its coverage. The 1988 enactment contained no express pre-emptive provision. In 1990, the City of Los Angeles adopted an ordinance that required retailers of aerosol paint cans and marking pens to display such items out of reach of the public. The motion that became the ordinance indicated awareness of the state statute, but recognized the need for "additional safeguards" against theft of devices capable of use for defacing property. Notwithstanding the city's characterization of the ordinance as a deterrent to theft, the court considered both the statute and the ordinance to be concerned with the control of graffiti. In an action brought by aerosol paint manufacturers, the court determined that the statute did not preempt the ordinance. The court concluded that the express preemption in the 1981 Act did not carry over to the 1988 amendment since the 1988 amendment contained no such provision. The court also held that failure to reenact a pre-emption provision in 1988 implied an intent to revert to the prior rule of non-pre-emption.

A dissenting judge disagreed. He suggested that the 1988 amendment was intended only to expand the substantive prohibition of the 1981 Act and was not intended to address the question of preemption at all. Hence, the 1981 statement of the legislature on the issue should remain intact. The dissent continued:

> The majority opinion's grudging view of the efficacy of the 1981 preemption provision is inappropriate for another reason. Unlike the more common situation in which courts must attempt to divine from extrinsic sources the legislative intent concerning a particular statute, "where the main purpose of the statute is expressed[,] the courts will construe it so as to effectuate that purpose by reading into it what is necessary or incident to the accomplishment of the object sought." Here, we have an express statement of the Legislature's intent in this case to preempt local regulation. Thus, courts should interpret that statement generously and defer to

> such legislative judgment, viewing the legitimacy of local regulation of aerosol paint with a more critical eye so as to effectuate the clear intention of the Legislature (citations omitted).

844 P.2d at 544.

In Smith v. Los Angeles County Board of Supervisors, 128 Cal.Rptr.2d 700 (Cal. App. 2002), plaintiffs challenged a program in the county that made home visits by government employees a condition of a resident's eligibility for welfare benefits. Plaintiffs claimed that the state statutory and regulatory scheme for determining eligibility implied an intent to fully occupy the field and preclude additional local regulation. The state regulatory scheme, however, delegated to counties the responsibility for gathering evidence necessary to determine eligibility. The court concluded that the express authorization for counties to gather information "disposes of any argument that a legislative intent to occupy the area may be implied." Id. at 710–11.

3. *Pre-emption in Fiscal Matters*. States may have a need to coordinate statewide fund-raising in order to achieve equitable distribution of tax burdens and benefits. At the same time, fiscal independence is likely to be vital to any locality's ability to accomplish the objectives that define it as a community. For an argument that courts should be more reluctant to find preemption in the fiscal area, see George D. Vaubel, Toward Principles of State Restraint Upon the Exercise of Municipal Power in Home Rule, 24 Stetson L. Rev. 417 (1995).

4. *Pre-emption Presumptions and Default Rules*. If the tests for implied pre-emption are too ambiguous to provide courts reliable guidance as to legislative intent, should pre-emption be restricted to cases of express pre-emption? Courts could, for instance, declare that they will never find pre-emption in the absence of an explicit legislative statement of pre-emptive intent. Would such an absolute presumption be an improvement on the legislative intent standard put forth by the dissent, and criticized by the majority in *American Financial Services Association* as "easily manipulable" and likely to "punish constituents who attempt to educate the Legislature about their concerns to the extent their concerns were not addressed in the precise manner proposed to the Legislature"?

In People v. Llewellyn, 257 N.W.2d 902 (Mich. 1977), cert. denied sub nom. East Detroit v. Llewellyn, 435 U.S. 1008 (1978), the court struck down a local anti-obscenity ordinance on the grounds that it was impliedly pre-empted by state statute governing criminal obscenity offenses. In dissent, Justice Ryan stated "this Court has always demonstrated an express showing of the Legislature's intent to exclusively occupy the field before invalidating an ordinance on pre-emptive grounds." 257 N.W.2d at 911. Hence, the judge was endorsing a rebuttable presumption against pre-emption. But why not use the contrary presumption, i.e., courts could declare that they will always find pre-emption in the absence of a legislative statement of intent *not* to pre-empt local regulation? Which presumption is preferable? It might be possible to use some majoritarian default rule to determine whether the legislature, when it passes legislation, typically intends to pre-empt local legislation in the same field. If it does not, then the presumption should be in favor of no pre-emption. If it does, then the presumption should be in favor of pre-emption. Creating the presumption in this manner would minimize the need for the legislature to be explicit, since it would have to do so only on the infrequent occasions when the legislature wanted to opt out of the majority rule. (It would nonetheless be helpful, of course, for the legislature and/or the courts at least occasionally to state explicitly what the "majoritarian default rule" is understood to be.) A default rule reduces the ability of the legislature to avoid the issue of pre-emption—failure to add an explicit clause would necessarily lead to application of the default rule. This may be a good thing, insofar as it reduces the ability of the legislature to avoid difficult issues of pre-emption. But it may be desirable to give the legislature some leeway, for instance, by allowing the legislature to remain agnostic about the pre-emptive effects of its legislation until subsequent events provide some evidence of whether pre-emption is warranted. Courts are not of a single mind about the proper presumption to entertain. Compare New York State Club Association, Inc. v. City of New York, 505 N.E.2d 915 (N.Y. 1987), aff'd, 487 U.S. 1 (1988) (legislative intent to pre-empt need not be express), with Ticonderoga Farms, Inc. v. County of Loudoun, 409 S.E.2d 446 (Va. 1991) (political subdivision may legislate on same subject as state, unless legislature has expressly pre-empted the field).

Professor Paul Diller has expressed some reservations about an "express-only" preemption rule, on the grounds that cities may use their home rule powers for parochial or exclusionary ends rather than to engage in experimentation that could redound to the benefit of other jurisdictions. Professor Diller suggests that courts have the capacity to determine on an *ad hoc* basis whether the costs of local activity sufficiently interfere with state interests to warrant a rule of implied preemption. Since state judges are less likely to view themselves as representatives of geographical interests in the state, Professor Diller argues, they will have a more objective view of the proper balance of state and local interests than do legislators. See Paul Diller, Intrastate Preemption, 87 B.U.L. Rev. 1113 (2007).

The Illinois Constitution appears to require express pre-emption, at least with respect to home rule localities. Article VII, § 6(i) of that document provides:

> Home rule units may exercise and perform concurrently with the State any power or function of a home rule unit to the extent that the General Assembly by law does not specifically limit the concurrent exercise or specifically declare the State's exercise to be exclusive.

The Illinois Supreme Court has held that the state constitutional scheme requires that pre-emption of local ordinances occur by express statement and cannot be implied by enactment of a comprehensive regulation of an activity that would otherwise fall within the home rule power of a locality. See Village of Bolingbrook v. Citizens Utilities Co., 632 N.E.2d 1000 (Ill. 1994).

5. *Playing the "Field."* Notice that the court in *Envirosafe* had to determine whether regulation of PCBs fits within the "field" of hazardous wastes whose regulation has been pre-empted by the state. Similarly, the court (and the dissent, which believed that pre-emption had occurred) in the *Sherwin–Williams* case had to wrestle with whether the state statute regulated "graffiti prevention," "aerosol paint sales," or "aerosol paint possession." And Judge Mullarkey's dissent in *Telluride* at page 347 supra suggests that the ordinance at issue involved land use regulation, which is traditionally a matter of local concern, rather than economic regulation, which the majority concluded was a matter of statewide concern. This inquiry into the relevant "field" involves the most difficult inquiry to be made in a preemption case, and one that typically determines whether preemption exists. The inquiry is similar to the one involved in trying to discover which line of precedent a case fits. Assume, for instance, that a pitcher is sued for assault by a hitter who claims the pitcher intentionally threw a ball at his head during an organized baseball game. Two potential lines of precedent exist. In one, a player who injured another while following the rules of an organized game was found not liable for battery. In the other, a child who threw a rock at another child with intent to cause contact was found liable for battery. The difficulty the judge faces in deciding the batter versus pitcher case is determining whether it is governed by the first line of precedent or the second. Similarly, the court in *Envirosafe* must decide the field in which the activity at issue lies. Is there any alternative to classifying PCBs as "hazardous waste"? What if they are classified as "chemicals"—is it clear that state law preempts what the locality has done?

In O'Connell v. City of Stockton, 162 P.3d 583 (Cal. 2007), a city ordinance allowed for the forfeiture of a vehicle upon proof by a preponderance of evidence that it have been used "to attempt to acquire" any amount of any controlled substance. A state statute set penalties for unlawful possession and distribution of controlled substances, and allowed forfeiture only upon proof beyond a reasonable doubt of the vehicle's use to facilitate certain serious drug crimes. The court held that the statute "occupies the field of penalizing crimes involving controlled substances, thus impliedly preempting the City's forfeiture ordinance...." What if the city had argued that the ordinance was directed at the field of simple possessory drug offenses, as to which state law was silent? How should the court decide which field is the appropriate one? For an analogous argument, see Arthur Goodhart, Determining the Ratio Decidendi of a Case, 40 Yale L.J. 161 (1930).

Even express pre-emption does not eliminate the difficult inquiry of defining the scope of the relevant field. The State of Washington enacted the Uniform Controlled Substances Act, including a provision that stated, "The state of Washington fully occupies and pre-empts the entire field of setting penalties for violations of the controlled substances act. Cities, towns, and counties ... may enact only those laws and ordinances relating to controlled substances that are consistent with this chapter." In City of Tacoma v. Luvene, 827 P.2d 1374 (Wash. 1992), the court upheld a conviction for drug loitering defined under a city ordinance. The court concluded that the language of the statute indicated that "[o]nly the setting of penalties for violations of the controlled substance statutes is preempted, not the ability of local governments to criminalize drug-related activity."

6. *Pre-emption and the Prisoner's Dilemma.* Note the language quoted by the court in *Envirosafe*, above, from the decision of the Michigan court in *Township of Cascade*: "no community wants [a] hazardous waste facility in its vicinity. Thus, local interests strongly want to retain their control. However, the same reasoning easily justifies state control." The problem referred to by the court, in which no jurisdiction wants to host an activity that all jurisdictions want to be provided by someone, is known as a NIMBY (or "Not In My Back Yard") problem. On reflection, you should see that this problem can be modelled as a Prisoner's Dilemma of the sort referred to in Chapter 1. Each locality, pursuing its own self-interest, would prefer not to contribute to the disposal of hazardous waste by housing a disposal facility. Each locality, however, would also prefer to have some other locality house the facility, and to share the benefits created by the presence of that facility. In order to discourage the siting of waste disposal plants within its jurisdiction, each locality has incentives to increase the level of regulation, so that potential facilities (which seek minimal regulation) will locate elsewhere. The solution to the problem, as indicated in *Envirosafe*, is to pass pre-emptive regulation at a more centralized (that is, the state) level, hence eliminating competition among localities for the harshest restrictions. For interesting discussions of the relative willingness and abilities of states and the federal government to regulate environmental hazards, see Richard L. Revesz, Federalism and Environmental Regulation: A Public Choice Analysis, 115 Harv. L. Rev. 553 (2001); Richard L. Revesz Rehabilitating Interstate Competition: Rethinking the "Race-to-the-Bottom" Rationale for Federal Environmental Regulation, 67 N.Y.U. L. Rev. 1210 (1992); Peter P. Swire, The Race to Laxity and the Race to Undesirability: Explaining Failures in Competition among Jurisdictions in Environmental Law, 14 Yale J. Reg. 67 (1996); Richard L. Revesz, The Race to the Bottom and Federal Environmental Regulation: A Response to Critics, 82 Minn. L. Rev. 535 (1997).

7. *Federal Versus State Pre-emption.* Recall the discussion of federal pre-emption of state and local regulation in Chapter 1. Although the concept of federal and state pre-emption of laws enacted by their constituent jurisdictions is similar, the sources of pre-emption vary. Federal pre-emptive authority is derived from the Supremacy Clause of the federal Constitution, which invalidates "any Thing in the Constitution or Laws of any State" which is contrary to federal law. State pre-emptive power depends on the scope of municipal autonomy granted to localities by the state constitution or statute. As we have noted, many home rule grants limit municipal autonomy to actions that do not conflict with state law, a concept that seems related to federal pre-emption of state and local acts contrary to federal law. How closely do the tests for pre-emption of local ordinances by state legislation parallel the tests for pre-emption of state/local regulations by federal legislation? Are there reasons for courts to be more restrictive (or more liberal) in finding that a state has filled a field that a locality seeks to occupy than in finding that the federal government has filled a field that a state or locality seeks to occupy? One might claim that the federal government has more expertise and that federal legislation is more often enacted only following the development of extensive legislative history, and that its enactments therefore should receive more deference from state and local political bodies. On the other hand, federal legislation is often introduced to address matters already regulated by the states, and the situations in which a federal regulation must be applied may have greater variety than the situations in which a state regulation must be applied. Hence, we may want to allow more latitude for local circumstances in applying a federal regulation than a state one.

CHAPTER 4

THE COMMUNITY'S RELATIONSHIP WITH ITS RESIDENTS—THE SELECTION OF SERVICES

A. THE PROVISION OF SERVICES—WHAT OUGHT THE COMMUNITY TO DO?

Communities are often defined by the goods and services that they provide. This is not to say that all communities do or should provide similar services. Indeed, different localities distinguish themselves by offering different packages of goods and services. Recall from Chapter 1 Charles Tiebout's *A Pure Theory of Local Expenditures*. To the extent that localities differentiate themselves, it is possible to speak of a market for local public goods that resembles markets for private goods. One locality may be known for the quality of its schools, another for easy access to places of work, a third for providing substantial shopping or welfare services. Since each municipality has only limited resources, officials must determine what the local basket of goods and services will contain. In theory, the potential array of packages offered by localities allows each individual to gravitate to the jurisdiction that best satisfies his or her preferences for public goods. If this objective could be achieved in practice, those who view localities primarily as providers of local public goods would have little complaint. Those who view localities as focal points for community might initially be disgruntled at the individualist perspective that this model of residence selection entails. But those who seek to foster community in order to allow like-minded people to pursue their vision of the good life might also agree that, in offering a particular menu of public goods and services, localities enable those who share a common view of what government should provide to gravitate to a hospitable location. Finally, those who find in local communities an opportunity for participation in public life should also focus on the selection of goods and services, since the nature and quantity of those services, and the mechanism of paying for them, will typically constitute the subject matter around which much public debate revolves.

In this chapter, we investigate the difficulties that might emerge in creating localities that are able to provide the services that their residents prefer. If we assume that local officials are publicly interested in that they seek to satisfy their constituents' preferences for particular services, then the objective of the law (and judicial review) may be limited to ensuring that constituents' preferences are easily registered. Officials could then act on the signals that they receive to provide the desired services. Signaling of preferences can occur in various ways. Most obviously, residents of a community may express satisfaction or dissatisfaction through voting or other mechanisms of complaint or praise, such as letters or telephone calls to officials or local media. Alternatively, when individuals move to or from a locality they implicitly register satisfaction or dissatisfaction with the package of goods and services in their new and old communities. In the economics literature, as was discussed supra at page 231, the first option is often referred to as "voice" and the second as "exit," a vocabulary taken from Albert O. Hirschman, Exit, Voice, and Loyalty: Responses to Decline in Firms, Organizations, and States (1970). This distinction has played a role in the literature about monitoring corporate behavior, as shareholders can either sell shares (exit) or express concerns at shareholder meetings (voice). But the same analysis has recently been adopted in much of the legal literature that discusses the capacity of residents to monitor the conduct of local officials. See, e.g., Robert C. Ellickson, Cities and Homeowners Associations, 130 U. Pa. L. Rev. 1519 (1982); Carol M. Rose, Planning and Dealing: Piecemeal Land Controls as a Problem of Local Legitimacy, 71 Cal. L. Rev. 837 (1983); Vicki Been, "Exit;" as a Constraint on Land Use Exactions: Rethinking the Unconstitutional Conditions Doctrine, 91 Colum. L. Rev. 473 (1991); Clayton P. Gillette, Plebiscites, Participation, and Collective Action in Local Government Law, 86 Mich. L. Rev. 930 (1988); Richard Briffault, Our Localism, 90 Colum. L. Rev. 1, 346 (1990); Michael H. Schill, Uniformity or Diversity: Residential Real Estate Finance Law in the 1990s and the Implications of Changing Financial Markets, 64 S. Cal. L. Rev. 1261 (1991); Richard C. Schragger, The Limits of Localism, 100 Mich. L. Rev. 371 (2001); Daniel B. Rodriguez, Localism and Lawmaking, 32 Rutgers L.J. 627 (2001). As long as local officials interested to satisfy their constituents' preferences can receive signals about their constituents' desires, the municipal budget will be allocated to fund the goods and services most consistent with those preferences.

In theory, exit and voice may be substantial substitutes for each other. Each one provides the publicly interested official with information about residents' satisfaction with the performance of local officials. Thus, a group that did not have substantial ability to leave the jurisdiction would not necessarily be captive to the interests of other residents if it had substantial voice in the local decisionmaking process. Alternatively, those who had little opportunity to express their preferences through voting could still receive substantial benefits from the municipality if they had the opportunity to leave and their threatened departure would cause harm to residents who remained. This is not to say that having the right to vote or having mobility has no inherent value. It is only to say that exit and voice are independent and equally effective means to an end of obtaining a share of the local budget, and that the ability to achieve that objective through either means reduces the need for legal intervention.

Law becomes more important, however, under either of two conditions. First, individuals may lack opportunities for the use of either exit or voice. Individuals who are either disabled from expressing their views or whose views are systematically discounted in the decisionmaking process (perhaps because of poverty, immobility or ethnicity) have no effective opportunity for making their preferences known. Some residents may have less ability than others to lobby for a favored level of service (for instance, because they cannot overcome obstacles to forming coalitions, such as incentives to free ride). Other residents may have preferences that are so formed by their environment that they have difficulty considering alternatives. Residents who are members of groups that have easier access to local officials or who can offer officials greater benefits in the form of votes, campaign support, or assistance with future jobs in or out of government may have an advantage in convincing officials to offer particular goods or services. Note that the benefits that are offered to officials by constituents may be perfectly legal. Indeed, given that we want citizens to become involved in the political process, we should welcome participation even in the form of campaign contributions and lobbying. Nevertheless, these aspects of the political process disfavor those who are disabled for any reason (for instance, lack of wealth) from providing local officials benefits or otherwise expressing their views on local action. If these same individuals lack mobility, either because they have insufficient wealth or because other restrictions exist on the number of localities to which these individuals can plausibly move, they cannot send meaningful signals to their local officials that they are dissatisfied with the level of goods and services they are receiving. Hence, even a benevolent government will not have an accurate picture of resident preferences. Here, law may be necessary or useful in reducing obstacles to voice (by removing constraints on participation in the political process) or to exit (by removing barriers to mobility).

Second, officials may fail to respond to signals, either because the officials are not, in fact publicly interested, or because they face impediments to implementing the preferences of their constituents. Assume, for instance, that residents want the locality to construct more capital improvements. Even officials who are aware of this desire may fail to provide the service, either because they would prefer to dedicate the necessary dollars to some other project that they believe will provide greater personal benefit, or because they face legal constraints on doing what their constituents desire. Such a legal constraint, for instance, may take the form of a limitation on the amount of debt the locality would have to incur to undertake the project, or may consist of the locality's having insufficient legal authority to provide the service preferred by residents. Where constituents' preferences can be ignored, law may be necessary and useful to constrain officials from undertaking projects that serve personal rather than public interests. Where law creates the barrier to local action, it will be necessary to determine whether the law should be changed or whether the legal barrier should be construed in a manner that permits the locality to undertake the desired project.

The materials that follow pose the issue of when legal intervention is appropriate to require the locality to reconsider the package of goods and services that it has decided to provide to some or all of its residents. As you examine these materials, it may be useful to consider whether you believe that those who challenge the existing package had other mechanisms for persuading the locality to provide the package they desire. If the answer to that question is unclear, it may be useful to consider what advantage(s) a court has in determining the proper package of goods and services to be provided by a given local government. For instance, in a world in which Tiebout's assumptions hold true, what should be the role of the judiciary (or law in general) in ensuring that a municipality provides residents with their preferred services? Arguably, the judiciary should play no role in this process, since dissatisfied residents can costlessly emigrate to a more congenial jurisdiction. Thus, judges can only get in the way of a perfectly operating market for residents by mandating that municipalities offer services that are not "really" in the best interest of residents. But what does this hypothesis say about the role of courts in the world in which Tiebout's assumptions do not hold true? Should the function of the judiciary be to enforce legal rules that compensate for our inability to create a world in which Tiebout's assumptions do hold true? For instance, should legal rules that govern the delivery of municipal services compensate for the inability of people to move costlessly?

In many ways, the materials that follow imply that the primary function of localities is to provide local public goods. Nevertheless, performing that function does not necessarily suggest that individuals should be isolated from each other or that they do or should care only about satisfying material wants. A large part of what follows should be read to assume that individuals seek a community that satisfies a desire to live among and interact with others who share a certain socio-economic status, particular values, or a political perspective. As you read the materials, you may want to consider what forms of homogeneity are desirable, what forms are injurious, and how the judiciary (or law in general) might foster the former category and impede the latter.

Charles Tiebout, A Pure Theory of Local Expenditures

64 J. Pol. Econ. 416 (1956).

[See excerpt at pages 21–23 supra.]

Reid Development Corp. v. Parsippany–Troy Hills Township

89 A.2d 667 (N.J. 1952).

■ HEHER, J.

By this civil action in lieu of mandamus, plaintiff seeks to compel the defendant township to extend its water mains laid in Intervale Road through an intersecting street known as Fairway Place, for a distance of 600 feet, "under the usual terms and conditions," to provide water for lands of plaintiff on either side of Fairway Place in process of development for residential uses.

Plaintiff applied for the extension on April 26, 1950, and again on May 31 ensuing; and not long thereafter, on June 14, it was advised in writing by the local governing body that the township then had "a more than ample supply of lots" having a frontage of less than 100 feet; that the Intervale Lake area, which includes plaintiff's lands, "deserves lots of 100 feet frontage," and "In order to benefit the township by having your development built up in 100 foot lots, ... we are willing to reduce your improvement costs by supplying all the labor for installing whatever mains, hydrants, fittings, etc. are needed on your land for a water system, and by rebating to you over a period of years out of water rental received from your parcels fronting on the said water system thus installed on your land the cost of the materials needed in such system—providing you revise your map in 100 feet frontage lots approved by the Planning Board." Reference was made to "said cesspool and septic tank experiences in several parts of the Township where, before the adoption of a Zoning Law, lots smaller than 100 foot frontage have been built on." Plaintiff rejected the condition and thereupon brought this proceeding. The Superior Court ruled that "the extension of a water main by a municipality is a governmental function" calling for "the exercise of a degree of discretion on the part of the municipality," and there was no abuse of discretion here. We have a different view.

The action taken by the local authority was arbitrary and unreasonable. The water facility is a municipally-owned public utility established under legislative authority. R.S. 40:62–47 et seq., N.J.S.A. The provision of water for the public and private uses of the municipality and its inhabitants is the exclusive province of the local agency; and it is elementary that the exercise of the power must be in all respects fair and reasonable and free from oppression. There can be no invidious discrimination in the extension of the service thus undertaken by the municipality as a public responsibility. Equal justice is of the very essence of the power. Impartial administration is the controlling principle. The rule of action must apply equally to all persons similarly circumstanced. There is a denial of the equal protection of the laws unless the water service be available to all in like circumstances upon the same terms and conditions, although the rule of equality may have a pragmatic application. Persons situated alike shall be treated alike....

There are cases holding that the establishment of a water system and its operation for protection against fire and other dangers to the public health and safety constitute a governmental function comprehended in the police power of the municipality.... But there is general agreement that the distribution of water by a municipality to its inhabitants for domestic and commercial uses is a private or proprietary function which in its exercise is subject to the rules applicable to private corporations....

A public water company is under a duty as a public utility to supply water to all inhabitants of the community who apply for the service and tender the usual rates. The obligation includes the establishment of a distributive plant adequate to serve the needs of the municipality and the enlargement of the system to meet the reasonable demands of the growing community. The utility is under a duty to serve all within the area who comply with fair and just rules and regulations applicable to all alike. The obligation is enforceable by mandamus.... While it has been held that a municipality so engaged exercises a governmental discretion as to the extension of the water mains, governed largely by the extent of the need and economic considerations, the discretionary authority must be fairly and reasonably used; and the remedial process of mandamus may be invoked for an abuse of discretion if the extension be arbitrarily refused.... It would seem that no sound distinction can be made, in respect of the extension of the service, between a municipality which has undertaken to provide water to the community and a water company performing the function of a public utility. In City of Chicago v. Northwestern Mut. Life Ins. Co., 218 Ill. 40, 75 N.E. 803, 804, L.R.A., N.S., 770 (Sup. Ct. 1905), it was held that when a municipal corporation not obliged to furnish water to its inhabitants undertakes to do so, it proceeds "not by virtue of the exercise of the power of sovereignty," but rather engages in "a business which is public in its nature, and belongs to that class of occupations or enterprises upon which public interest is impressed," and is under a duty to act reasonably and not arbitrarily in the fulfillment of that function and to "serve all who may apply on equal terms."

Here, the provision of water to the plaintiff landowner was conditioned not by a circumstance of action or being reasonably bearing upon the exercise of the function, but rather by wholly alien considerations related to planning and zoning; and this was not within the province of the governing body. Compare Magnolia Development Co. v. Coles, 10 N.J. 223, 89 A.2d 664 (1952). There was then no suggestion that the enlargement of the service was indefensible on economic grounds. The need was not denied; nor was it asserted that the cost would be prohibitive or greatly disproportionate to the return. Indeed, the municipality offered to "reduce the landowner's improvement costs" by supplying labor at the outset and by rebating over a period of years out of water rentals accruing from the extension the cost of materials required for the installation of a water system on plaintiff's lands. And no question is made now as to the need.

The stipulation of facts and the proofs reveal that it has been the practice of the municipality to provide extensions of the water system under the same or similar circumstances. While not a formula common to all cases, the enlargement was usually granted on terms that the land developer would bear the initial cost of the installation and be reimbursed to the extent of 75% of the outlay from the water revenues collected for taps on the added water line during a given period, the remaining 25% to be retained by the township for "its maintenance and pumping charges for furnishing water" to the new facility....

The ordinance provides thus: extensions of the water distribution system, at the instance of "developers of tracts approved by and through" the local planning board "and consented" to by the local governing body, shall be constructed pursuant to the rules and regulations of the planning board and under the supervision of the township's engineer and the superintendent of public works, "at the developer's own cost and expense," and shall be dedicated to the public use with title vested in the township. An "individual" may, in the discretion of the governing body, have an extension to serve his "individual property," also at his own expense. Again, it is provided that the township is under no obligation "to permit any requested extension"; the granting of the extension "shall rest solely within the discretion" of the governing body, and the township shall not be under the duty of reimbursement "for all or any part of the cost thereof." But the township may construct such extensions "as a general township obligation in such streets, avenues or roads where, in its discretion, it deems the public interest will be best served by the making of such extensions."

On the reargument the ordinance was defended as a valid exercise of the power granted by R.S. 40:62–47, N.J.S.A., and R.S. 40:62–77, N.J.S.A., but it was finally conceded that the regulation is null for want of a norm or standard governing the exercise of the discretionary authority. This concession is well founded. Under the principle cited supra, the regulation is ultra vires. It purports to vest in the governing body a naked and arbitrary power to grant or withhold consent to the expansion of the service. The discretion is absolute. The extension may be at the expense of the landowner in the one case and the township in another, depending upon the mere will of the governing body. There is no standard to insure impartial action. Access to water facilities is not a matter of grace. Rights of persons and of property cannot by legislative fiat be made subject to the will or unregulated discretion of another. It matters not whether the facility is in the hands of the municipality or a privately-owned public utility. Arbitrary use of the power contravenes fundamental law and is not within the legislative province. See, in addition to the cases cited supra, P. J. Ritter Co. v. Bridgeton, 135 N.J.L. 22, 50 A.2d 1 (Sup. Ct. 1946), affirmed 137 N.J.L. 279, 59 A.2d 422 (E. & A. 1948); Lipkin v. Duffy, 119 N.J.L. 366, 196 A. 434 (E. & A. 1937). The virtue of an ordinance in the given circumstances lies in the formulation of a standard of action that precludes the exercise of arbitrary power.

It is vigorously urged that the extension of water mains by a municipality involves the exercise of a legislative or governmental discretion which precludes the remedy of mandamus. Where, as here, there was a plain abuse of authority, mandamus will lie to command performance of what under the clearly established or admitted facts constitutes a peremptory duty. Under Article VI, Section V, paragraph 4 of the Constitution of 1947 and the implementing Rule 3:81, review, hearing and relief in lieu of prerogative writs shall be afforded as of right. Where there has been an abuse of discretion, the action may be vacated and fulfillment directed of what the law deems an imperative obligation. The discretion beyond control by mandamus is that exercised under the law, and not contrary to law.... Where there is an omission to do what the law clearly and unmistakably directs as an absolute duty, mandamus is an appropriate remedy. If by reason of a mistaken view of the law or otherwise, there has been in fact no actual and bona fide exercise of discretion, e.g. where the discretion turned upon matters not contemplated by the law, mandamus will lie. This is a recognized exception to the general rule. Riesland v. Bailey, 146 Or. 574, 31 P.2d 183, 92 A.L.R. 1207 (Sup. Ct. 1934).

Here, wholly extraneous considerations governed the exercise of the discretionary authority. On the admitted facts, the extension of the water facilities was plaintiff's right; and it was an abuse of discretion to use the grant as a means of coercing the landowner into acceptance of the minimum lot-size restriction upon his lands, however serviceable to the common good. Such benefits are to be had through the channels prescribed by the law. Johnson v. Belmar, 58 N.J. Eq. 354, 44 A. 166 (Ch. 1899); Magnolia Development Co. Inc. v. Borough of Magnolia, cited supra. There is no statutory authority for this condition. Planning and zoning powers may not be exerted by indirection; the exercise of these functions must needs be in keeping with the principles of the enabling statutes. Mansfield & Swett, Inc. v. West Orange, 120 N.J.L. 145, 198 A. 225 (Sup. Ct. 1938); Schmidt v. Board of Adjustment of City of Newark, 9 N.J. 405, 88 A.2d 607 (1952)....

The judgment is reversed; and the cause is remanded for further proceedings conformably to this opinion.

NOTES

1. Implicit in Tiebout's analysis of local government expenditures is an assumption that potential residents select a place to live based on the services that the locality purports to provide. If that is the case, we might infer that all residents within a locality will receive "equal services." At the very least, a locality should, perhaps, bear the burden of explaining why it is providing a particular service to some residents and not to others. What kinds of reasons would be acceptable for unequal service provision? In Reid Development Corp. v. Parsippany–TroyHills Township, 107 A.2d 20 (N.J.Super. 1954), which is unrelated to the facts of the principal case, the court upheld the municipality's refusal to extend certain of its water mains, at its expense, some 3,000 feet to plaintiff's land. The court held that the municipality did not abuse its discretion in denying plaintiff's request because

> There is proof that the municipal water company is operating at a deficit; that it has little money for further investments in main extensions on speculation; that in the serviceable area there are many other developments and some with upwards of 500 homes that have not been fully developed. Furthermore, there is questionable proof of immediate need; there are no consumers in the area for which plaintiff seeks main extensions and no assurance of a likely customer return in the reasonably proximate future.

Id. at 23.

2. Does it matter why the township in the principal case concluded that it had "a more than ample supply of lots" having a frontage of less than 100 feet? One explanation could be that the township desired to maintain the community as an enclave for the relatively wealthy. An alternative explanation could be that the township desired an economic mix of residents, and already had an optimal number of persons who could afford these homes, given the economic status of the remainder of the community. Does the choice of explanation alter the proper judicial reaction to the township's action? If so, what ability does the judiciary have to make the relevant inquiries into the locality's objective and its achievement of that objective?

Veach v. City of Phoenix

427 P.2d 335 (Ariz. 1967).

■ Udall, Justice:

Plaintiffs seek recovery from the City of Phoenix and others (hereinafter referred to as defendants) for the sum of $66,826.56 as damages to plaintiffs' property caused by fire. Defendants filed a motion to dismiss plaintiffs' second amended complaint for failure to state a claim, which was granted and judgment was entered from which plaintiffs appeal.

In essence, the amended complaint alleged that on January 23, 1962, a fire broke out in plaintiffs' market and completely destroyed it. That part of the City of Phoenix's function as a municipal corporation is the "furnishing, supplying and distributing of water for the benefit of the (city's) inhabitants" but that defendant city "failed to distribute, supply and provide water for fighting fires at or near the location of said market"; and "That on said date when said fire broke out, there was no available supply of water with which to fight said fire, thereby causing and resulting in injury and damage to Plaintiffs." It was also alleged that previous to January 23, 1962, plaintiffs had requested of defendant that it "provide, install, maintain and supply a fire hydrant for the distribution and supplying of water at or near said location for fire protection purposes, but said Defendant negligently failed to do so."

The trial court, in ordering the dismissal of plaintiffs' complaint, found that defendant city was operating in a governmental capacity in furnishing water for the fighting of fires and that there was no duty on the part of defendant to supply water for fire protection. Plaintiffs contend the lower court erred in so holding.

There is no doubt that the trial judge ruled in accord with the general rule in the United States.... However, the majority of cases from the various jurisdictions which hold that a city has no duty to provide such service base their holding upon the conclusion that the maintenance and operation of a municipal fire department is a governmental function and in the exercise of such function, the municipality is immune to liability. In recent years, though, there has been a growing dissatisfaction with the decisions upholding municipal immunity from tort liability. The dissatisfaction of this Court with the rule of governmental immunity and the distinction between governmental and proprietary functions culminated in the landmark case of Stone v. Arizona Highway Commission, 93 Ariz. 384, 381 P.2d 107. We held therein that the doctrine of governmental immunity from tort liability was abolished and that the distinction between proprietary and governmental functions is no longer valid as a method of allocating municipal liability in this state.

This being so, whether defendant city is acting in a governmental capacity in providing water to extinguish fires is of no consequence in the disposition of this appeal. The sole question for decision is whether defendant has a legal duty to furnish water for fire protection purposes to the city's inhabitants.

The record shows that defendant owns the municipal water distribution system in the City of Phoenix; we have held that in operating a water system, a city is a public service corporation. Town of Wickenburg v. Town of Sabin, 68 Ariz. 75, 200 P.2d 342. It also appears to be the rule that a public service corporation is under a legal obligation to render adequate service impartially and without discrimination to all members of the general public to whom its scope of operation extends. . . .

In the instant case, plaintiffs alleged in the complaint that they had requested of defendant that it install a fire hydrant for the supplying of water at or near plaintiffs' property. Thus, it may be said that defendant had notice that plaintiffs required service. The basic question therefore, is whether defendant held itself out to serve in the general area within the City of Phoenix in which plaintiffs' property is located; if so, since defendant may not discriminate between members of the general public to whom its scope of operation extends, defendant would owe a legal duty to supply water for fire protection purposes to plaintiffs.

Defendant maintains that although it allegedly and admittedly served the area in question with water for domestic use, there is no allegation that the City of Phoenix did or attempted to serve any portion of the area with water for fire protection and this being so, plaintiffs' amended complaint was correctly dismissed. We do not agree.

It is the settled law of this state that if the complaint sets forth facts showing plaintiff is entitled to relief under any theory susceptible of proof, the trial court should not dismiss the complaint. The test to be applied in resolving the question of whether the complaint set forth facts showing plaintiff is entitled to relief under any theory susceptible of proof is whether, in the light most favorable to plaintiff and with every intendment regarded in her favor, the complaint was sufficient to constitute a valid claim. . . . We are of the opinion that when the amended complaint in the case at bar is read in the manner stated above it sufficiently sets forth a claim upon which relief may be granted and the trial court erred in dismissing it.

In order to avoid misunderstanding we want to make it clear that under the rule we have adopted a municipality has no absolute duty to provide water for fire protection purposes to its inhabitants. However, when a city assumes the responsibility of furnishing fire protection, then it has the duty of giving each person or property owner such reasonable protection as others within a similar area within the municipality are accorded under like circumstances. A municipality has discretion, governed by the extent of need and other economic considerations, to determine what is a reasonable protection for each area—but this discretion cannot be arbitrary, and must be fairly and reasonably exercised. Hence, in suits such as the instant one, a city is entitled to assert as a defense the reasonableness of its exercise of discretion.

It is impossible to delineate specific criteria by which a municipality should be guided in providing reasonable protection. When challenged in an action such as this, it is a question for the determination of the jury as to whether the municipality has acted reasonably in setting up an ordinance, regulation or the activities of its agents under the circumstances of the case in the light of the rule herein pronounced.

Reversed.

NOTES

1. *The Governmental/Proprietary Distinction.* Does the distinction between services provided in a "governmental" or "proprietary" capacity help to explain the discretion that a locality has in deciding the terms on which to provide a good or service to particular residents? Note that the court in *Reid* describes the distribution of water by a municipality as "a private or proprietary function," while the trial court in *Veach* described furnishing of water to fight fires as a governmental function. We will see the governmental/proprietary distinction raised in other contexts, but do not expect more in the way of consistency. For a history and critique of the distinction, see Janice C. Griffith, Local Government Contracts: Escaping from the Governmental/Proprietary Maze, 75 Iowa L. Rev. 277 (1990).

2. *Equal Service Provision.* Both *Reid* and *Veach* suggest that a municipality must provide any service to all residents on an equal basis. In *Reid*, for instance, the court opines that equal protection is denied unless a "service be available to all in like circumstances upon the same terms and conditions. . . ." The court in *Veach* imposes an obligation to provide such services as "others within a similar area within the municipality are accorded under like circumstances." What is the rationale for such a rule? The court in *Reid* suggests that the rule is predicated on an analogy to the "rules applicable to private corporations" and to public utilities. Public utilities, often described as "affected with a public interest," typically hold monopolies within a geographical range. As indicated in the introduction to public goods at page 33 supra, monopolistic provision of utility services (water, electricity) may make sense because the capital costs associated with such services are sufficiently great that firms might avoid engaging in the activity if they feared competition would prevent rapid recovery of their investment. Once granted a monopoly to provide the service, however, the utility has little reason to avoid using its monopoly power to charge higher prices than it could if competition existed. Thus, government regulation is typically introduced to control utility rates and charges. In short, private provision with public regulation is an alternative to public provision of public goods.

How does this argument affect the need for a legal rule that requires a duty to serve all on equal terms when the municipality, rather than the private utility, is the provider? If government, which presumably does not seek monetary profits at all, is to be trusted to regulate the private utility in the public interest, then why can't government be trusted to provide the proper level of service without the intervention of a judicial rule? Maybe one way to address this issue is to ask whether equal service would be provided to all residents of a community in a world that satisfied Tiebout's assumptions. For an historical and legal argument that localities must provide equal service to all residents, see Charles M. Haar & Daniel W. Fessler, The Wrong Side of the Tracks: A Revolutionary Rediscovery of the Common Law Tradition of Fairness in the Struggle Against Inequality (1986). Is there reason to believe that citizens of Phoenix who were dissatisfied with water service could not register an effective complaint with city officials or emigrate to a more hospitable jurisdiction? Is there reason to believe that every citizen of Phoenix would want a level of water service equal to that of co-residents?

3. Does the obligation in *Veach* to provide such services as "others within a similar area within the municipality are accorded under like circumstances" mean that as long as everyone in the northeast section of town has the same level of fire protection, that level may still diverge from the level provided to residents of the southwest section of the same town? Why would it be permissible to allow divergence of service among sections of the same city, but not within sections? If a particular service need not be provided equally throughout the municipality, is there still a need to have a roughly equal amount of the municipal budget spent on each section of the city? That is, would it be permissible to spend more on schools in the northeast section, as long as an equivalent amount is spent on additional garbage collection in the southwest section?

4. In Mlikotin v. City of Los Angeles, 643 F.2d 652 (9th Cir. 1981), the court granted a motion to dismiss a civil rights claim brought by plaintiffs who asserted that their neighborhood had received inadequate municipal services at a time when it was inhabited by poorer residents. As a result, plaintiffs alleged, their property was of lower value than it otherwise would have been. (Do you think that the plaintiffs, who did not claim that they were receiving inadequate services, paid a price for their property that reflected the lower level of services at the prior time?) The court concluded that there was no constitutional right to municipal services and no allegation that the municipality had distributed services based on an invidious or irrational classification. Nor had the plaintiffs argued that services had been allocated unequally to similarly situated persons.

5. The exercise of "voice" in the context of local government law is typically associated with the capacity of the electorate to register complaints about the delivery of municipal services or, if matters get sufficiently drastic, to change officials at the next election. If all beneficiaries of a service registered complaints or praise, one would anticipate that decisions about service levels would essentially reflect the preferences of constituents. If, on the other hand, only a small percentage of individuals exercise the "voice" option, there may be less reason to believe that decisions made in response to those vocal citizens actually reflect the preferences of the electorate at large. We have already seen why "free rider" or other collective action problems might inhibit the use of voice. But even if groups can overcome those problems and express dissatisfaction or "throw the bums out of office," are there reasons to believe that insufficient change will materialize? Consider the following argument:

> We already suggested certain limitations of the electoral system as a demand-registering system. Any standard checklist could include low voter turnout, limited choice . . ., the "volunteerism" of local elected officials and the limited opportunity for electoral reprisal, the impact of nonpartisanship, and the like. But there is a further problem with elections as a "voice" to change the delivery of urban services. Changing the big fish rarely changes the small ones. Mayors and council members come and go; bureaucracies and their decision-rules are more permanent. We have not argued that the council's role in allocative decisions is nil. Where a new library should be built, what route a highway should take, how revenue sharing funds should be allocated, and the like are all council-dominated questions. But the day-to-day allocations of valued urban services is more accurately called a bureaucratic phenomenon. The "reach" of elections as voice is shorter than assumptions of traditional democratic theory imply.

Robert L. Lineberry, Equality and Urban Policy: The Distribution of Municipal Services 173–174 (1977). Is there reason to believe that some groups will be better able to exercise the voice option with respect to permanent bureaucracies than others and that, of those who exercise the option, some groups will be more readily heard than others?

6. *Judicial Intervention in Allocating Municipal Budgets.* Assume that the provision of a particular service within a locality is decidedly unequal and that those residents who receive a below-average amount of the service desire to equalize service provision. Is there still a reason to be wary of judicial intervention to correct the situation? Note that if the municipal budget is relatively fixed, i.e., revenues cannot be increased, provision of one service, or provision of a higher level of a service, will require less provision of another service or provision of fewer services. One can think of this problem by imagining a budget pie in which the slices are divided by the municipal budget process. For instance, initial allocations of an over-simplified municipal budget might look something like this:

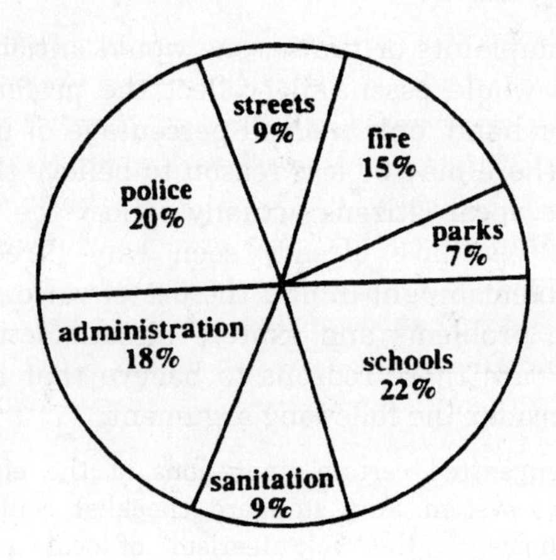

Now assume that some residents claim that they are receiving an insufficient amount of police protection, and that remedying the situation would require increasing the percentage of the budget dedicated to police services to 22 percent. The extra funds would have to come from some other, unidentified service. But deciding how to pay for the extra police services requires not only deciding to take money from another service, but also deciding how the increase in police services affects other relationships among services. Residents may be willing to have a set amount (20 percent) spent on police services because they already have a particular level of fire or school services. Once the police budget is altered, that might affect the mix of other services that are related to police. Thus the issue involves not simply a substitution of funds from some other service, but a total reallocation of the municipal budget, since each other part of the budget may depend on how much is dedicated to police services.

To make this clearer, think of the analogous situation of assigning professors to teach first-year law students in a law school with multiple first-year sections. A section with a contracts professor who relies heavily on law and economics methodology should perhaps be matched with a torts professor who teaches from a law and humanities perspective and a civil procedure professor whose emphasis is on traditional legal doctrine. If the torts professor suddenly becomes unavailable to teach, and the replacement professor teaches from a law and economics perspective, it might be desirable to change the contracts professor as well in order to provide the students in that section with the same mix of methodologies. And the new contracts professor may require a change in the civil procedure professor.

Both the curriculum staffing problem and the allocation of the municipal budget create what has been called a "polycentric" or "many-centered" problem, in which changing one part of the existing allocation creates tensions with other parts of a complicated pattern. These problems may be particularly unsuited to adjudication. Judges may be very good at deciding issues of winner-take-all among a small number of parties, each of whom can represent its interests. Polycentric problems, however, are characterized by multiple parties, compromise, and substantially divergent interests among those affected by the outcome. For instance, a decision to increase the police budget may adversely affect the parks budget; but while those who demand more police services will have substantial incentives to argue their claims before the court, it is less certain that those who will suffer from cutbacks in parks services will have either the incentive or the legal standing to represent their claims. The proper forum for these decisions, therefore, looks more like a legislative committee or political process in which the multiple centers can engage in exchange and consider the claims of others rather than an adjudicative forum. As a matter of institutional design, courts, which specialize in resolving single disputes between two parties by declaring victory for one and a loss for the other, do not appear to have a comparative advantage in resolving these issues. See Lon L. Fuller, The Forms and Limits of Adjudication, 92 Harv. L. Rev. 353 (1978).

Nevertheless, judicial deference to nonadjudicative decisionmaking processes assumes that those processes will operate in a manner that allows each of the interests that occupies one of the "centers" to have a role in the allocation made by the political process. Deference becomes more problematic where particular interests are systematically disabled from participation. It is to that possibility that we next turn.

Gerald E. Frug, City Services

73 N.Y.U. L. Rev. 23, 25–26, 28–33 (1998).

These days, the academic literature discusses city services predominantly in the language of economics: whether a city should provide any particular service is thought to turn on analysis of the concept of "public goods." Public goods, according to the standard definition, are either the kind of goods that one person can consume without diminishing anyone else's ability to do so (they are "nonrival") or the kind that cannot easily be allocated solely to those who pay for them (they are "nonexcludable"). The examples of public goods regularly referred to in the literature are national defense and lighthouses. People can benefit from services such as these no matter how many other people are also doing so. Moreover, it would be unreasonably expensive to try to stop anyone from taking advantage of them. Thus they are services that the market cannot properly apportion and, consequently, that government can legitimately offer. As the proponents of the theory of public goods recognize, however, American cities do not protect the national defense or build lighthouses. Instead, they provide services—like police, fire, sanitation, and education—that not only can be allocated to some people at the expense of others but often are. As a result, the theory of public goods, when applied to local governments, largely consists of arguments about whether, and to what extent, it is efficient for cities to supply these kinds of "mixed" or "impure" public goods.

Those engaged in this argument usually take Charles Tiebout's influential article, A Pure Theory of Local Expenditures, as a starting point....

I do not rely on the theory of public goods.... The literature as a whole, Tiebout's original article included, is based on two assumptions that

I reject—one about the nature of city services and one about the nature of cities. First of all, the public goods tradition treats city services as objects of consumption. Tiebout, for example, portrays people shopping for a city in which to live just like they shop for any other consumer good: they choose a city by determining whether the package of services it provides is worth the price charged for it in taxes. The only difference from private market transactions that Tiebout allows is that consumers make their choice not by handing over a credit card but by moving to the location where they get the best deal. Along with others who work within the public goods tradition, Tiebout also assumes that a city is similar to a voluntary association, such as a political organization, church, or chat group. People are seen as choosing a city in which to live in the way they choose a country club: what attracts them is the fact that they share interests in common with others making the same choice. Indeed, this homogeneity is said to promote efficiency; since the rich and poor tend to want different levels of services, both groups are thought to be better off if they move to homogeneous cities. . . .

This consumer-oriented vision of city services has significant undesirable consequences. First of all, by definition, it abandons for public services the notion of equality traditionally associated with the public sector, replacing the one-person, one-vote principle associated with democracy with the one-dollar, one-vote rule of the marketplace. It thus has a built in bias in favor of the rich. Everyone knows that those with more money not only can afford more consumer goods than those with less money but are considered entitled to them. Indeed, it is because of this inherent bias that market-based allocations are commonly rejected for the public sphere. It is considered unacceptable, for example, to treat voting rights, jury duty, and military service as commodities available for sale, just as it is considered unfair to allocate many city services, such as admission to public schools or public parks, according to the ability to pay. In fact, it is a crime to pay a police officer to protect oneself rather than to protect someone too poor to make such a payment. Moreover, again by definition, the consumer-oriented vision of city services equates the concept of freedom of choice with that of freedom of consumer choice. By doing so, it perpetuates a pervasive, but false, justification for the radical differences that now exist between the quality of city services available in different parts of America's metropolitan regions. The public goods literature is filled with rhetoric about how public services in America are allocated in accordance with differences in people's "preferences" or "tastes." And many suburbanites say that they moved to their particular suburb because they (unlike others?) cared about the quality of education for their children. Yet it seems odd indeed to suggest that division of America's metropolitan areas into areas with good schools and safe neighborhoods and areas with deteriorating schools and high crime rates is explicable in terms of people's differing "tastes." People who live in unsafe neighborhoods or send their children to inadequate schools don't do so because they have taste for them. They do so because they feel they have no other choice.[31] If they had a choice (and I am not using the word to mean "consumer choice"), they would prefer better schools and less crime.

These two defects can be understood simply as illustrations of a third, more fundamental, problem with the consumer-oriented vision of city services. Once again by definition, it radically limits the aspect of the self considered relevant in the design and implementation of public services. Consumption is an activity centered on the individual: spurred by their own economic interest, individuals buy consumer goods person by person (or family by family) with little concern about the impact of their purchase on those living nearby. As a result, values commonly associated with democracy—notions of equality, of the importance of collective deliberation and compromise, of the existence of a public interest not reducible to personal economic concerns—are of secondary concern, or no concern at all, to consumers. Yet it is widely recognized, in political theory as well as daily life, that reducing human experience to the act of consumption falsifies it. It is commonly said, for example, that human beings see themselves not simply as consumers but also as citizens—and that they think differently in these two different roles. As Mark Sagoff puts it,

> Last year, I fixed a couple of tickets and was happy to do so since I saved fifty dollars. Yet, at election time, I helped to vote the corrupt judge out of office. I speed on the highway; yet I want the police to enforce laws against speeding.... I love my car; I hate the bus. Yet I vote for candidates who promise to tax gasoline to pay for public transportation.[34]

The consumer-oriented understanding of city services makes this distinction disappear by collapsing citizens into "consumer-voters." The impact of this disappearance is not simply on the outcome of government decisionmaking, important as that is. It affects the evolution of American society itself and, thereby, the forces that shape and nurture consumer preferences. The consumer-oriented vision of public services strengthens the consumptive aspect of self over alternatives: consumer preferences help generate a social world that, in turn, shapes consumer preferences. By doing so, it narrows the definition of "human flourishing" that city services have the potential to foster.

NOTES

1. Professor Frug contends that the services provided by American cities "not only can be allocated to some people at the expense of others but often are," and that these services therefore do not exhibit the nonrivalness and

---

31. This lack of choice is not attributable simply to the lack of money. The poor are more dependent than the rich on neighbors, friends, and family for maintaining a support network and, therefore, are less mobile. See John R. Logan & Harvey L. Molotch, Urban Fortunes: The Political Economy of Place 42–43 (1987).

34. Mark Sagoff, At the Shrine of Our Lady of Fatima or Why Political Questions Are Not All Economic, 23 Ariz. L. Rev. 1283, 1286 (1981).

nonexcludability that characterize "public goods." Can you give examples of city services that are neither nonrival nor nonexcludable? If Frug is correct that most city services do not exhibit these characteristics, why do cities provide these services at all? That is, why is the provision of these services not simply left to the private market? If Frug is correct that the consumer-oriented vision of city services "has a built in bias in favor of the rich," would that bias necessarily affect all city services equally? That is, might the rational self-interest of the rich still cause them to support the provision of some (perhaps many) city services on some basis other than ability to pay? If so, which services might these be?

2. Frug argues that the "consumer-oriented vision" of city services "abandons for public services the notion of equality traditionally associated with the public sector, replacing the one-person, one-vote principle associated with democracy with the one-dollar, one-vote rule of the marketplace." Are there good reasons to allocate some city services on the basis of ability to pay, even if one agrees with Frug that other city services should not be allocated on this basis for the same reason that we "do not treat voting rights, jury duty, and military service as commodities available for sale"? How should a community decide which city services to allocate on the basis of ability to pay and which to allocate on some other basis? Will the democratic process, operating under "the one-person, one-vote principle," necessarily result in a non-wealth-based (or non-race-based) allocation of city services? If not, do the courts have a particularly important role to play in the allocation of city services? Will the role of the courts be more problematic when confronting claims of wealth discrimination or race discrimination in the provision of city services? Why?

3. For an extended account of Frug's views on service provision, see Gerald E. Frug, City Making: Building Communities without Building Walls (1999). For critiques of Frug's position, see, e.g., Laurie Reynolds, Local Governments and Regional Governance, 39 Urb. Law. 483 (2007); Richard Thompson Ford, Bourgeois Communities: A Review of Gerald Frug's *City Making*, 56 Stan. L. Rev. 231 (2003); Laurie Reynolds, Intergovernmental Cooperation, Metropolitan Equity, and the New Regionalism, 78 Wash. L. Rev. 93 (2003); Martha A. Lees, Expanding Metropolitan Solutions through Interdisciplinarity, 26 N.Y.U. Rev. L. & Soc. Change 347 (2000–2001); Roderick M. Hills, Romancing the Town: Why We (Still) Need a Democratic Defense of City Power, 113 Harv. L. Rev. 2009 (2000).

4. Even if one believes that it is appropriate to treat city services, or at least some of them, as a response to residents' demand for particular public goods, there may be situations in which that "market" fails. Local residents presumably register their "tastes" by voting for local officials who promise to satisfy them. What might prevent residents from registering preferences or officials from satisfying those preferences that are registered? And when that happens, what is the role of law? It is to those questions that we turn next.

B. Discrimination in Service Provision

Mount Prospect State Bank, Trustee v. Village of Kirkland

467 N.E.2d 1142 (Ill. App. 1984).

■ Reinhard, Justice.

Plaintiff, Mount Prospect State Bank, as trustee under a land trust, appeals from an order of the trial court granting the motion to dismiss of defendant, the village of Kirkland. Plaintiff raises the following issues on appeal: (1) whether it was a denial of equal protection to deny plaintiff refuse collection service where the service was provided to other village residents and paid from general tax revenues; (2) whether monies paid by plaintiff to provide its own service or tax monies retained by the government without providing the service are recoverable as compensatory damages; and (3) whether punitive damages are recoverable for defendant's exclusion of plaintiff from refuse collection....

Plaintiff owns a parcel of property in the village of Kirkland known as Congress Lake Estates, which contains 70 to 77 mobile homes. This is the only mobile home park in the village and only plaintiff, not the individual mobile homeowners, is a party to this suit. Defendant, pursuant to a contract, commencing May 1, 1982, and terminating April 30, 1985, with Saturn Disposal Systems, Inc. (Saturn), provides refuse collection service to residences within the village. Defendant pays for these services with general village tax receipts. The contract provides, in pertinent part, that Saturn "shall make one weekly unlimited pick-up of garbage * * * from each residence in the VILLAGE." The contract defines "residence" as including "each occupied single family dwelling and each occupied unit or apartment situated in a multiple family apartment building or separate apartments in single family dwellings converted to multiple family use." "Residence" expressly does not include "mobile homes located in Congress Lake Estates." The contract specifies that there are 317 residences in the village as of the date of the contract....

In its order granting defendant's motion to dismiss, the trial court noted that the parties had agreed that plaintiff's facility was the only mobile home park in the village. The court concluded that while naming and excluding the mobile home park specifically in the contract might raise an equal protection argument, the agreed fact was that this was the only mobile home park in the village and plaintiff was not being discriminated against with respect to any other such mobile home parks in the village. The court further found, *inter alia,* that it did not violate equal protection to exclude plaintiff's property from refuse collection services.

Plaintiff argues on appeal that it has been unconstitutionally denied equal protection of the laws because the defendant's refuse collection policy arbitrarily discriminates against mobile home parks. It maintains that the exclusion of its mobile home park from refuse collection unfairly classifies it with "second class status." Plaintiff claims no rational basis exists for treating it differently than other residential taxpayers and that this different treatment, which requires it to pay for refuse collection service through its payment of general property taxes without receiving the collection service provided to other village residents, is therefore a denial of equal protection. Plaintiff argues it is entitled to mandamus ordering the village to provide plaintiff with this service.

A government may "differentiate between persons similarly situated as long as the classification bears a reasonable relationship to a legitimate legislative purpose." (*Kujawinski v. Kujawinski* (1978), 71 Ill.2d 563, 578, 17 Ill.Dec. 801, 376 N.E.2d 1382.) The parties generally agree that the legislative classification here is created by the contract between defendant and Saturn and that the validity of this classification is governed by the law controlling classifications created by statute or ordinance. There is a presumption of validity of these legislative classifications and the burden is on the party challenging the classification to establish its invalidity.... Where no fundamental right or suspect class is involved, the classification "need have only a rational relationship to a legitimate State purpose to be upheld." *People v. Gurell* (1983), 98 Ill.2d 194, 204, 74 Ill.Dec. 516, 456 N.E.2d 18....

No fundamental right to garbage collection exists (*Goldstein v. City of Chicago* (7th Cir. 1974), 504 F.2d 989, 991), and mobile home park owners are not among the "suspect" classes recognized by the courts. (*Illinois Housing Development Authority v. Van Meter* (1980), 82 Ill.2d 116, 119–20, 45 Ill.Dec. 18, 412 N.E.2d 151; *San Antonio Independent School District v. Rodriguez* (1973), 411 U.S. 1, 61, 93 S.Ct. 1278, 1311, 36 L.Ed.2d 16, 59 (Stewart, J., concurring).) Thus, the classification challenged here will be upheld if it bears a rational relationship to a legitimate governmental purpose.... If the court can discern any reasonable basis for the classification, it will be upheld.... This test for constitutional validity is often referred to as the "rational basis" test.

It has been held that under the rational basis test, the court may on its own initiative, and independent of the parties, articulate facts necessary to justify the classification.... The question whether a rational basis for the classification exists has been considered to be a question of law.... Thus, it is appropriate, on a motion to dismiss, for a court on its own initiative to consider whether a rational basis exists for the classification, which would overcome an equal protection challenge.... After considering the arguments of plaintiff and defendant and considering the record before us, we conclude that a rational basis for the classification exists here and that the trial court, therefore, properly granted defendant's motion to dismiss.

It has been held that a distinction between multiple-family structures and single-family residences may be made with a municipality providing garbage service to single-family residences while excluding multiple-family structures. (*Szczurek v. City of Park Ridge* (1981), 97 Ill.App.3d 649, 659,

52 Ill.Dec. 698, 422 N.E.2d 907.) The reasons given in *Szczurek* included the "more demanding needs" of multiple-family structures and "the greater amount of refuse generated by them." (97 Ill.App.3d 649, 657–59, 52 Ill.Dec. 698, 422 N.E.2d 907.) Similar reasons can be conceived here. Plaintiff's property contains between 70 and 77 mobile homes. With such a large number of mobile homes existing on plaintiff's property, it is reasonable to conclude that the refuse collection needs of this property would vary significantly from the needs of other residents of the village. In fact, as of the date of the contract, there were only 317 residences in the village that would receive refuse pickup service. Including plaintiff's property with some 70 to 77 mobile homes in the refuse pickup contract would substantially increase the amount of refuse to be picked up resulting in a significant expense to the village. Also, greater flexibility and frequency of refuse pickup than the village could provide may be necessary to meet the needs of the residents of this mobile home park.... Additionally, a mobile home park may provide greater problems of access for refuse trucks than residences located on city streets.

We further note that the contract, by its inclusion of only residences, excludes commercial enterprises within the village from refuse collection service. Plaintiff's property, with its 70 to 77 mobile homes, has more the character of commercial property than it does residential, which we believe is a rational basis for a classification in view of greater refuse generally generated by a commercial enterprise.

Plaintiff's complaint only generally alleges an arbitrary classification and does not allege facts which would indicate that no rational basis for the distinction between it and residences in the village exist. It does not allege specific facts, for example, that apartment buildings with comparable numbers of units exist in the village and receive refuse collection service, or that other mobile homes similarly situated in the village receive the service. For the foregoing reasons, the presumption of validity of the village's actions has not been overcome, and a rational basis for the classification has been shown....

Because we conceive facts that justify the exclusion of plaintiff's mobile home park from refuse collection, we hold that plaintiff's complaint only generally alleging an equal protection violation was properly dismissed. Since the other two issues plaintiff raises on appeal are premised on a holding that plaintiff was denied equal protection, they necessarily fail because of our holding that equal protection was not denied....

AFFIRMED.

■ UNVERZAGT and LINDBERG, JJ., concur.

Ammons v. Dade City

783 F.2d 982 (11th Cir. 1986).

■ Before FAY and JOHNSON, CIRCUIT JUDGES, and HOFFMAN, SENIOR DISTRICT JUDGE.

■ PER CURIAM:

Appellants Dade City, Florida and its public officials, William F. Brewton, Agnes Lamb, Charles McIntosh, Jr., William L. Dennis and D.L.

Williams, appeal the judgment of the district court that they intentionally discriminated in violation of the fourteenth amendment in the provision of street paving, street resurfacing and maintenance, and storm water drainage facilities to the black community of Dade City. We find that the district court's finding that appellants' conduct constituted intentional racial discrimination in the provision of these municipal services is amply supported by the record evidence and not clearly erroneous. Accordingly, we affirm.

Background

On February 23, 1981 appellees, a class of black citizens of Dade City, Florida filed this action patterned after the municipal services equalization cases of Hawkins v. Town of Shaw, 437 F.2d 1286 (5th Cir. 1971), aff'd on rehearing, 461 F.2d 1171 (5th Cir. 1972) (en banc); and Johnson v. City of Arcadia, 450 F. Supp. 1363 (M.D. Fla. 1978). Appellees alleged in their complaint that Dade City, its Mayor and four city commissioners deprived black citizens of equal municipal services in violation of the thirteenth and fourteenth amendments, and sought that the qualitative and quantitative disparities between the municipal services provided to the black and white residential communities be eliminated.

[In addition to the information set forth at footnote 8 infra, the following information, taken from the district court opinion, may be helpful. Dade City had a population of 4,923 in 1980. Approximately 23.5 percent of the population was black, and 90 percent of the blacks lived in an area in the eastern quadrant of the city. All key city positions, for instance, city manager, finance director, city engineer, public works superintendent, police chief, and fire chief, were held by whites. No black city employee earned a salary greater than $12,900 per year. Eight of the 12 blacks in the city's work force of 84 employees worked in service or maintenance positions. Only one black was ever elected to the City Commission, in 1974. He died before his term expired, and his widow was appointed to the position. After her death, a black minister completed the term. The city had set aside land for a "negro subdivision" in 1948. In 1951, the city informed the Negro Civic Committee that residents of the division would have to pay in advance for street paving, a requirement that had never been imposed on other sections of the city. Indeed, although most paving was performed on the understanding that subsequent assessments against benefited property holders would be imposed and paid over a 10–year period, about half the improvements were either never assessed at all or were adjusted in a manner that effectively cancelled outstanding lien obligations—EDS.]

A three day non-jury trial was held during July 13–15, 1983. At the conclusion of trial the court reserved ruling and allowed both parties to submit proposed findings and post-trial memoranda. On September 21, 1984 the district court entered final judgment for appellees on the basis of its findings of fact and conclusions of law which determined that street paving, street resurfacing and maintenance, and storm water drainage facilities were provided inadequately and unconstitutionally to the black community of Dade City. Ammons v. Dade City, 594 F. Supp. 1274 (M.D. Fla. 1984). The district court consequently enjoined appellants from providing the three contested municipal services in a racially discriminatory manner and from initiating any new municipal services or improvements, other than customary and regular maintenance work, in the white residential community until the services in issue in the black residential community were on a par with those in the white community. Id. at 1305–06. Appellants were also directed to submit a plan to the district court for the elimination of the disparities in services which were found to have existed. Id. at 1306.

Issues

The basic issue on appeal is whether the district court erred in finding that Dade City and its public officials intentionally discriminated against the City's black residents in the provision of street paving, street resurfacing and maintenance, and storm water drainage facilities. Appellants in particular cite the following as error: (1) the district court's inclusion in the overall municipal services disparity analysis of certain streets in the black residential community that were annexed into Dade City in 1982, subsequent to the filing of the lawsuit; (2) the district court's inclusion in the overall municipal services disparity analysis of certain streets that although located in the white residential community of Dade City, were owned and maintained by state and county authorities; and (3) the district court's conclusion that Dade City did not have a non-discriminatory uniform special assessment policy for street paving purposes.

Discussion

As we stated in the municipal services equalization case of Dowdell v. City of Apopka, 698 F.2d 1181, 1184–85 (11th Cir. 1983) (citing Washington v. Davis, 426 U.S. 229, 96 S. Ct. 2040, 48 L. Ed. 2d 597 (1976)), in order "[t]o trigger strict scrutiny analysis under the fourteenth amendment, preliminary findings of both disparate impact and discriminatory intent are required." Accordingly, in reviewing the district court's decision in this case we focus on its findings of disparate impact and discriminatory intent. We address these findings seriatim.

We are mindful at the outset that while conclusions of law are freely reviewable, we are bound under Fed. R. Civ. P. 52(a) by the district court's factual findings, including its finding of intentional discrimination, unless clearly erroneous. See Pullman–Standard v. Swint, 456 U.S. 273, 287–90, 102 S. Ct. 1781, 1789–91, 72 L. Ed. 2d 66 (1982). For a finding to be clearly erroneous the reviewing court, looking at all the evidence, must be "left with the definite and firm conviction that a mistake has been committed." United States v. United States Gypsum Co., 333 U.S. 364, 395, 68 S. Ct. 525, 542, 92 L. Ed. 746 (1948). As the Supreme Court instructed this past term in Anderson v. City of Bessemer City, 105 S. Ct. 1504, 1512, 84 L. Ed. 2d 518 (1985) (citations omitted):

> If the district court's account of the evidence is plausible in light of the record viewed in its entirety, the court of appeals may not reverse it even though convinced that had it been sitting as the trier of fact, it would have weighed the evidence differently. Where there are two permissible views of the evidence, the factfinder's choice between them cannot be clearly erroneous.
>
> This is so even when the district court's findings do not rest on credibility determinations, but are based instead on physical or documentary evidence or inferences from other facts.

A. Disparate Impact

The district court's methodology in reaching its findings of disparate impact was to first analyze appellees' evidence on the racial and demographic characteristics of Dade City.[5] On the basis of this evidence the court found that the City's black residential community is comprised of two adjoining areas that are geographically segregated "on the other side of the railroad tracks." *Ammons*, 594 F. Supp. at 1278 (footnote omitted). Having thus determined the existence of racially identifiable neighborhoods in Dade City, the court then analyzed a wealth of statistical, documentary and testimonial evidence[7] introduced by appellees relating to the distribution and financing of the three contested City provided services. This evidence amply supports the district court's findings of a significant disparity between the races in the provision of street paving, street resurfacing and maintenance, and storm water drainage facilities.[8]

---

5. The district court explained in detail how this demographic data was compiled through a statistical compilation admitted into evidence under Fed. R. Evid. 1006. See *Ammons*, 594 F. Supp. at 1278 n.5. We note that appellants contested the appellees' demographic data as it related to the description of the geographical boundaries of the City's black community. Appellants proposed instead a boundary description that would "include all the areas described by [appellees] plus additional parts of the City encompassing census block districts with a minimum of ten percent black residents." Id. at 1279 n. 6. As the district court found, however, appellants offered no census, planning, engineering or legal standard to support their proposed boundary description. Appellees' description, on the other hand, was found to be "accurate," id., and we cannot conclude that the district court's findings on this matter are clearly erroneous.

7. For an account of the evidence from which the district court derived its findings of disparate impact in, respectively, street paving, street resurfacing and maintenance, and storm water drainage facilities, see *Ammons*, 594 F. Supp. at 1285, 1290, 1292–93 (footnotes omitted).

8. The district court found the following statistically significant disparities: 1. *street paving*—at the commencement of trial on July 13, 1983, 29.5% of the street footage in the black community was unpaved as compared to 18.1% in the white community and 31.1% of the residences in the black community fronted on unpaved streets as compared to 13.8% of the residences in the white community. Id. at 1285. 2. *street resurfacing and maintenance*—between 1956 to 1980 out of the total street footage resurfaced, 9.7% of the resurfacing was done in the black residential community as compared to 90.3% done in the white residential community. Street resurfacing and maintenance "is financed entirely from City funds," and out of the total monies, $117,154.24, spent for street resurfacing during that same 1956 to 1980 period, 10% was spent for resurfacing in the black residential community as compared to 90% spent for resurfacing in the white residential community. Id. at 1290. Moreover, the court

In so holding, we reject appellants' arguments challenging the validity of the statistical data base from which the district court derived its findings. As stated earlier, appellants cite as error the district court's inclusion in the overall disparity analysis of: (1) streets in the black residential community that were annexed into the City in 1982 during the course of the litigation; and (2) streets in the white residential community that were owned and maintained by state and county authorities. Appellants contend, as they did at trial, that this statistical evidence has no materiality to the instant lawsuit, alleging intentional discrimination in the provision of municipal services, because the City is responsible only for providing services to areas within its municipal limits that are owned by the City.

We do not, however, understand the district court to have ruled that a city has an obligation to annex black residential areas or to service areas outside of its municipal limits, or that it has the power or duty to service areas owned by other governmental authorities. Rather, what the district court determined, as a factual matter, was that it was equitable in this case that these two categories of streets be included in the statistical data base for the purpose of calculating disparate impact. This determination was premised on a number of subsidiary factual findings which we find persuasive and, at the very minimum, not clearly erroneous.

First, as regards the inclusion of residential streets in the 1982 annexed area, the court determined that, "the relationship between the area annexed in 1982 and the City is sufficient to constitute part of the black community for the purposes of a present disparity analysis," id. at 1287, based on the following factual findings: (1) the 1982 area is part of the general black community wedged west of the railroad tracks and "for years previously, [had] functioned as an integral part of the City," id. at 1286, and as part of the black community; (2) that geographically, according to the uncontraverted testimony of appellees' planning expert, it "is essentially engulfed by and contiguous with the City limits," id. at 1287;

found that the disparity in street resurfacing and maintenance was not "rebutted by the City with any explanation, policy or practice which could support a conclusion that it exists for any other reason other than race considerations." Id. at 1292. 3. *storm water drainage facilities*—storm water drainage in Dade City is provided through both an above-ground facility network as well as an underground system of piping. Id. at 1293. At the commencement of trial on July 13, 1983, 50.1% of the street footage in the black residential community had no above-ground drainage device as compared to 28.3% in the white residential community, id. at 1294, and 50% of the residences in the black residential community fronted on streets with no above-ground drainage device as compared to 25.5% of the residences in the white residential community. Id. at 1295. Analysis of the underground drainage system revealed a "fairly extensive system throughout the City's white residential community," id. at 1293, while, other than a "small two block area" on one street, there was no underground system in the entire black residential community. Id. While appellants continue to assert on appeal, as they did at trial, that the black residential community does not need any more drainage facilities, the court properly found this assertion as being "totally without merit." Id. at 1295. The record supports the court's finding that appellants' assertion is "in direct conflict [with] the testimony of [appellees'] expert, . . . other black community witnesses, and in fact in conflict with observations of [appellants'] own city manager and finance director." Id. (footnote omitted).

and (3) that the equities compel inclusion, given the City's past active participation and encouragement of annexing white residential areas into the City, particularly through its sharing of the expenses in paving of those new white residential areas, id., as contrasted to the lack of "evidence that the [C]ity took any steps to initiate the annexation process for [the 1982 annexed area]." Id.

Second, as regards the inclusion of City residential streets owned by the state and county, the district court properly determined that "[t]o not calculate the state/county owned residential streets in the disparity analysis would reward the City for its racially segregated practices," id. at 1288, based on findings that:

> [t]he City's racially discriminatory practices ... forced blacks to live on the "other side of the tracks," an area geographically set apart from the white residential neighborhoods which enjoy the benefits of the state/county owned paved streets.This occurred through a series of City actions—beginning with the 1914 ordinance prohibiting the intermingling of the races and continuing through the City's actions in the post-World War II era in developing the racially segregated Mickens–Harper Subdivision. Id.

Another finding dictating the court's determination to include these residential streets in the disparity analysis was the City's "intimate[ ]" involvement through its repeated requests, over three decades, to have these streets maintained and paved. Id.

Appellants also take issue with the district court's conclusion that appellants did not have a non-discriminatory uniform special assessment program for street paving purposes. In Hadnott v. City of Prattville, 309 F. Supp. 967 (M.D. Ala. 1970), the court held that the City of Prattville had paved streets and provided other services upon the basis of a uniform and non-racially discriminatory assessment policy and although, due to economic factors, this resulted in a disparity in the providing of paving in the black residential areas as compared to white residential areas, it was not constitutionally discriminatory.

The district court in this case found, however, that Dade City's assessment practice did not present a defense to the findings of disparity between the City's black and white residential neighborhoods "since the facts presented in [*Hadnott*] so significantly and materially differ from this action that the *Hadnott* principle has no application." *Ammons*, 594 F. Supp. at 1289. We agree. The district court's conclusion rests on the following factual findings, all amply supported by the record evidence: (1) the City's assessment policy was "non-uniform in nature in that many paved streets were never assessed at all," id. at 1299; (2) as to a significant portion of streets that were assessed, assessment liens were frequently never collected, id.; and (3) the assessment policy had been applied in a racially discriminatory manner "in that black citizens were required, when attempting to develop the major black Mickens–Harper Subdivision, to pay their assessment in advance of the paving which is contrary to City policy and never required in any white residential neighborhood." Id. We cannot say that these factual findings regarding the City's assessment policy are clearly erroneous nor do we find the district court's conclusion that the City's assessment practice presents no bar or defense to appellees' constitutional claims in error.

B. Discriminatory Intent

After finding a disparity in the provision of street paving, street resurfacing and maintenance, and storm water drainage facilities, the district court proceeded with its "constitutional inquiry", id. at 1300, as to whether the inequality in the three services resulted from a discriminatory intent or purpose. There must be a "correlation between municipal service disparities and racially tainted purposiveness to mandate a finding of discriminatory intent." See Dowdell v. City of Apopka, 698 F.2d 1181, 1185–86 (11th Cir. 1983).The district court's analysis and findings of intentional discrimination in this case parallel those previously found by this court in *Dowdell* as constituting "[n]early every factor which has been held to be highly probative of discriminatory intent." Id. at 1186.Those factors found by the district court and discussed in detail, *Ammons*, 594 F. Supp. at 1300–03, include discriminatory impact; foreseeability; legislative and administrative history; and knowledge. We now consider the district court's findings as to each of these four factors.

First, with respect to the factor of discriminatory impact the district court properly found that although "official act[ion] is not necessarily unconstitutional solely because it has a racially disproportionate impact," *Ammons*, 594 F. Supp. at 1301 (citing Washington v. Davis, 426 U.S. 229, 239, 96 S. Ct. 2040, 2047, 48 L. Ed. 2d 597 (1976) and Village of Arlington Heights v. Metropolitan Housing Development Corp., 429 U.S. 252, 264–65, 97 S. Ct. 555, 562–63, 50 L. Ed. 2d 450 (1977)), due to the "(1) size of the disparity, and (2) nature of the practices at issue in this case," *Ammons*, 594 F. Supp. at 1301, impact alone does give rise to "an inference of discriminatory intent." Id. Appellants, as previously discussed supra, offered extensive evidence concerning the magnitude of the disparities in municipal services between the races which amply supports the district court's finding. The magnitude of the disparities in services in this case is, as we similarly found in *Dowdell*, 698 F.2d at 1186 (citations omitted), "explicable only on racial grounds."

Second, when it is foreseeable, as the evidence reflects in this case, that the allocation of greater resources to the white residential community at the expense of the black community will lead to the "foreseeable outcome of a deprived black residential community," *Ammons*, 594 F. Supp. at 1302 (citing *Dowdell*, 698 F.2d at 1186), then a discriminatory purpose as found by the district court is properly shown. Third, in tracing the history and development of Dade City, particularly with respect to race relations, for its connection to present discrimination in the provision of the contested municipal services, the district court correctly relied upon a large body of constitutional jurisprudence which recognizes that the historical context of a challenged activity may constitute relevant evidence of intentional discrimination. See *Ammons*, 594 F. Supp. at 1302–03. The district court's findings in this case of a "legislative and administrati[ve] history of racial discrimination in general and in the allocation and distribution of the contested municipal services in particular," id. at 1303, are supported by a multitude of documentary and testimonial evidence covering practically every aspect of municipal conduct in Dade City throughout its history. See id. at 1279–84. Finally, the district court's findings as regards the factor of knowledge are amply supported by the evidence:

> That their actions [City's] would result in a discriminatory impact on the residents of the black community was not unknown to defendants. A brief visit to the black community makes obvious the need for street paving and storm water drainage control.

Id. at 1303, (brackets in *Ammons*) (quoting Dowdell v. City of Apopka, 511 F. Supp. 1375, 1383 (M.D. Fla. 1981), aff'd in part, rev'd in part, remanded in part, 698 F.2d 1181 (11th Cir. 1983)).

Although none of these four factors is "necessarily independently conclusive," "the totality of the relevant facts," *Dowdell*, 698 F.2d at 1186 (quoting Washington v. Davis, 426 U.S. at 242, 96 S. Ct. at 2049), "amply supports the district court's findings that appellants' course of conduct manifests discriminatory intent 'which is the cause and reason for the present disparity in (1) street paving, (2) street resurfacing [and maintenance], and (3) storm water drainage services.' " *Ammons*, 594 F. Supp. at 1303 (footnote omitted). In sum, the finding of intentional discrimination by the district court is not clearly erroneous.

The judgment of the district court is affirmed.

NOTES ON DISCRIMINATION IN SERVICE PROVISION

1. Can you distinguish the decision in *Village of Kirkland* from that in *Veach*? Is refuse collection service provided by a municipality in its "governmental" or "proprietary" capacity? What responses were available to the adversely affected residents in *Village of Kirkland* in the face of their municipality's discriminatory service provision? In *Veach*?

2. Why do you think the Village of Kirkland explicitly excluded the mobile homes in Congress Lake Estates from the Village-funded garbage collection service? Are you persuaded that the Village had a "rational basis" for denying the mobile homes this service, even though all other residences in the Village, including apartment buildings, received the service? Would the court's analysis—and ultimate decision—in the case have been different if the residents of the mobile homes were disproportionately black?

3. What is the effect of the *Ammons* court's finding of an intent to discriminate? In the important municipal services case of Hawkins v. Town of Shaw, 437 F.2d 1286 (5th Cir. 1971), aff'd on reh'g, 461 F.2d 1171 (5th Cir. 1972) (en banc), cited by the court in *Ammons*, black plaintiffs similarly brought an action to remedy an alleged unequal distribution of municipal services based on race in the Town of Shaw. Shaw had a population of 1,500 black residents and 1,000 white, but had only recently elected the first black member of the town council. The record in the case indicated a substantial failure in Shaw to achieve a world that approximates the results that one would anticipate under the Tiebout model, in that there was a substantial disparity in street lighting, street paving, storm drainage, and sewers in the black and white areas of the town. For instance, 99 percent of white residents were served by a sanitary sewer system, while nearly 20 percent of the black population was not so served; 97 percent of all those who lived in homes fronting on unpaved streets were black; and the town had only installed medium and high intensity mercury vapor street lighting fixtures in white neighborhoods. Nevertheless, the court found no evidence of intent to discriminate. Under the law existing at that time, however, the court determined that no finding of intent was necessary to establish an equal protection violation. The court instead found that, regardless of intent, no compelling state interest existed to justify the discriminatory results of Shaw's administration of municipal services, and that finding was sufficient to establish an equal protection violation. Wary of federal judicial intervention into the provision of municipal services, the original federal court panel required the town to submit a plan for the court's approval detailing how the town itself proposed to remedy the discriminatory provision of municipal services.

On an en banc rehearing, the Fifth Circuit, in a per curiam opinion, affirmed the judgment entered by the original panel of the court. Hawkins v. Town of Shaw, 461 F.2d 1171 (5th Cir. 1972) (en banc). The panel stressed that not "every disparity of services between citizens of a town or city creates a right of access to the federal courts for redress." It also noted that the town had appointed a bi-racial committee to advise the town with respect to the provision of city services, and that a black citizen had been elected to the city council. Do these actions suggest a greater likelihood that service provision in the town will more likely reflect the results that would be obtained if the assumptions of the Tiebout model held true? What are the implications of these findings for the propriety of judicial intervention to redirect municipal appropriations for municipal services?

The role of intent in equal protection jurisprudence has changed significantly since the Fifth Circuit's decisions in *Shaw*, causing at least one commentator to term those decisions "the high-water mark in judicial efforts to secure equality in the provision of municipal services for communities of color." Jon C. Dubin, From Junkyards to Gentrification: Explicating a Right to Protective Zoning in Low-Income Communities of Color, 77 Minn. L. Rev. 739, 779 (1993). In Washington v. Davis, 426 U.S. 229 (1976), the Supreme Court held that evidence of a discriminatory intent was necessary to subject the challenged governmental scheme to strict scrutiny under the Fourteenth Amendment. *Shaw* was among the decisions that the *Davis* Court expressly disapproved on the ground that it "rested on or expressed the view that proof of discriminatory racial purpose is unnecessary in making out an equal protection violation." 426 U.S. at 245 n.12. See also Village of Arlington Heights v. Metropolitan Housing Development Corp., 429 U.S. 252 (1977). Thus, the court in *Ammons* could reach its conclusion only after making a finding that the requisite intent to discriminate existed. As the court in *Ammons* indicates, a similar conclusion of intent to discriminate was reached in Dowdell v. City of Apopka, 698 F.2d 1181, 1184–1185 (11th Cir. 1983). Evidence in that case established that 42 percent of the street footage in the black community was unpaved, compared to 9 percent in the white community; 33 percent of the black residences fronted on unpaved streets while only 7 percent of the white community did; and 60 percent of the residential streets in the white community had curbs and gutters for storm drainage, while none existed in the black community. The court applied the following test of intent:

> First, the magnitude of the disparity, evidencing a systematic pattern of municipal expenditures in all areas of town except the black community, is explicable only on racial grounds. Second, the legislative and administrative pattern of decision-making, extending from nearly half a century in the past to Apopka's plans for future development, indicates a deliberate deprivation of services to the black community. A municipal ordinance restricting blacks to living only on the south side of the railroad tracks remained in force in Apopka until 1968. The ordinance contributed to the ghetto-like qualities of the black residential area. Blacks continue to be significantly under-represented in administrative and elective positions, and their requests for improved municipal services continue to be ignored while substantial funds are expended to annex and develop the new predominantly white sections of town. Third, the continued and systematic relative deprivation of the black community was the obviously foreseeable outcome of spending nearly all revenue sharing monies received on the white community in preference to the visibly underserviced black community. While voluntary acts and "awareness of consequences" alone do not necessitate a finding of discriminatory intent, foreseeable and anticipated disparate impact are relevant evidence to prove the ultimate fact, "forbidden purpose."
>
> Although none of these factors is necessarily independently conclusive, "the totality of the relevant facts," amply supports the finding that the City of Apopka has engaged in a systematic pattern of cognitive acts and omissions, selecting and reaffirming a particular course of municipal services expenditures that inescapably evidences discriminatory intent.

698 F.2d at 1186 (citations omitted).

In Committee Concerning Community Improvement v. City of Modesto, 2007 WL 2204532 (E.D. Cal.), plaintiffs claimed that defendants discriminated against Latino neighborhoods in funding and constructing public infrastructure, including sewers, storm drains, curbs and gutters, and sidewalks. Plaintiffs did not present any evidence of racial considerations or motive in the preparation of an infrastructure "priorities list" that allegedly was discriminatory. The court granted a motion to dismiss Equal Protection and Civil Rights Acts claims. It concluded:

> Plaintiffs present no evidence that the placement on the Priorities List was, in any way, the result of discriminatory motive. They argue that their neighborhoods' needs are greater. However, the undisputed evidence is that *all* the neighborhoods on the Priorities List have infrastructure needs for which there is not enough money. Indeed, plaintiffs neighborhoods are not the only unincorporated areas that lack storm drains, sidewalks, curbs and gutters. A facially neutral law is not invalid under the Equal Protection Clause merely because it has a greater impact upon members of one

> race than another. *Washington v. Davis,* 426 U.S. 229, 239, 96 S.Ct. 2040, 48 L.Ed.2d 597 (1976). Accordingly, the *effect,* if any, is insufficient to raise a reasonable inference of discriminatory *impact*....
>
> Plaintiffs' request for a remedy untethered to a constitutional violation, though sincere, misunderstands the nature of the judicial power. The courts are not empowered generally to "make things right." *Knight v. Alabama,* 476 F.3d 1219, 1229 (11th Cir. 2007). To avoid summary judgment, plaintiffs must "produce evidence sufficient to permit a reasonable trier of fact to find by a preponderance of the evidence that [the] decision ... was racially motivated." ...
>
> In this case, a series of events unconnected to the racial considerations required the Board to make a large number of choices relating to type of infrastructure, method of payment, costs, geographic considerations, among other considerations, in deciding which infrastructures would be prioritized. The parties present a long history and explanation of funding requirements, shortfalls in county budgets, restrictions on funding, infrastructure deficiencies and planning and related problems. State-wide changes in financial resources of local entities impacted funding for infrastructure. The County's actions can be explained by a myriad of community and planning concerns having nothing to do with the ethnicity.

2007 WL 2204532 at *9–*12.

See also Baker v. City of Kissimmee, 645 F.Supp. 571 (M.D. Fla. 1986). On intent to discriminate, see Daniel Ortiz, The Myth of Intent in Equal Protection, 41 Stan. L. Rev. 1105 (1989); Richard A. Primus, Equal Protection and Disparate Impact: Round Three, 117 Harv. L. Rev. 493 (2003); Deborah Hellman, The Expressive Dimension of Equal Protection, 85 Minn. L. Rev. 1 (2000); Darren Lenard Hutchinson, "Unexplainable on Grounds Other Than Race": The Inversion of Privilege and Subordination in Equal Protection Jurisprudence, 2003 U. Ill. L. Rev. 615.

4. What explanations might be available to a municipality that seeks to justify a disparity in services? Would it be sufficient if the locality could demonstrate that the black sections of Dade City received a disproportionate amount of the municipal budget devoted to redistributional services, such as welfare programs, child care, and elderly care, so that allocating the services at issue in *Ammons* disproportionately to the white side of town only equalized each section's portion of the total municipal budget? In answering this question, ask how important race is in justifying a disparity in services. Assume that the facts of *Ammons* are the same, but that all residents are of the same race. The disparity in services simply reflects disparate wealth within the locality, so that wealthy residents receive amenities not available to the poor. (Keep in mind that wealth itself is not a suspect classification for Fourteenth Amendment equal protection purposes. San Antonio Independent School District v. Rodriguez, 411 U.S. 1 (1973). See Clayton P. Gillette, Equality and Variety in the Delivery of Municipal Services, 100 Harv. L. Rev. 946 (1987) (book review); Martin A. Schwartz, Municipal Services Litigation After Rodriguez, 40 Brook. L. Rev. 93 (1973); Note, Equalization of Municipal Services: The Economics of *Serrano* and *Shaw*, 82 Yale L.J. 89 (1972).)

5. In an opinion concurring in the en banc affirmance of *Shaw*, Judge Wisdom appeared to embrace a somewhat broader right of equal service. He interpreted the court's decision as establishing "the right of every citizen regardless of race to equal municipal services." 461 F.2d at 1171. Does this mean that every citizen is entitled to an equal amount of the same service offered by the municipality? To this claim, Judge Roney responded in dissent:

> If everyone has a constitutional right to equal services then the class broadens to include both races, because in Shaw there are both whites and blacks who have less than equal municipal services of various kinds.... The correct principle would appear to be that every citizen has a right not to be denied services because of race, and that any denial of services must have occurred only as a result of the nonracial resolution of all of the competing influences in the politics of self-government.

Id. at 1182.

6. How would one implement an equal right to municipal services? Would it entail equality of expenditure or equality of result or something else? See, e.g., Carl S. Shoup, Rules for Distributing a Free Government Service Among Areas of a City, 42 Nat'l Tax J. 103 (1989); Carl S. Shoup, Distribution of Benefits from Government Services: Horizontal Equity, 43 Pub. Fin. 1 (1988). In Beal v. Lindsay, 468 F.2d 287 (2d Cir. 1972), black and Puerto Rican plaintiffs claimed that the city park in their neighborhood was maintained at a level lower than that of other city parks. The court determined that the city had invested equal resources in park maintenance in plaintiffs' neighborhood, but the condition of the park had deteriorated due to vandalism. The court concluded that the city was not obligated "to go beyond equal effort in order to redeem Crotona Park." 468 F.2d at 291.

Note that there are some restrictions on the capacity of a municipality to favor certain groups. In City of Richmond v. J. A. Croson Co., 488 U.S. 469 (1989), the Supreme Court invalidated under the Fourteenth Amendment a plan to require primary contractors to whom the city awarded construction contracts to subcontract at least 30 percent of the dollar amount of the contract to minority businesses. Proponents of the program indicated that while the population of Richmond was 50 percent black, only 0.67 percent of the city's primary contracts had been awarded to minority businesses in recent years. Nevertheless, the Court found no evidence of discrimination by the city in awarding prior contracts. Instead, the Court found that states and political subdivisions have less power than Congress to redress social discrimination, since Section 5 of the Fourteenth Amendment (authorizing enforcement of the dictates of the Amendment) is directed only to Congress. 488 U.S. at 490. A municipal program based on race, therefore, could only be adopted if necessary to remedy private discrimination within the locality's own jurisdiction or if the city could show that it had become a "passive participant" in a system of racial exclusion practiced by private parties who did business within the locality. In the absence of such a compelling state interest, racial classifications could not survive. Further, the mere disparity between population percentages and the percentage of minority businesses that had received construction contracts was not, of itself, sufficient evidence of past discrimination. Indeed, the lower court had implied that the disparity indicated that the set-aside program had been motivated by a desire to provide special benefits to a substantial interest group rather than to provide remediation for past misconduct. See 488 U.S. at 485, 506. Finally, the Court determined that any appropriate remedy would have to be narrowly tailored to the past discrimination that had occurred, and that the Richmond program was too broad-ranging to satisfy that criterion, insofar as any alleged past discrimination was visited on blacks while the program provided benefits to all minorities.

7. What if the locality's response to equal services cases is to offer only services that residents of a particular area request and agree to pay for? In this case, the municipality truly becomes little more than a mechanism for solving free rider problems. The result would likely be no different than the results in Dade City or the Town of Shaw, with poor sections of each locality receiving substantially fewer services than relatively wealthy sections. Yet, would the facts permit the inference of a constitutional violation? In Hadnott v. City of Prattville, 309 F.Supp. 967 (M.D. Ala. 1970), discussed in *Ammons*, the court found no constitutional violation in a city policy to pave only streets fronting on property where at least 51 percent of the property owners petitioned the city for paving and were willing to be assessed an amount sufficient to defray the costs. The result of the policy was that only 3 percent of the city's white residents lived along unpaved streets, compared to approximately 35 percent of black residents.

8. *Social Science Research and the Allocation of Municipal Services.* In an article published in 1989, Carl Shoup summarized a number of statistical studies of urban service distribution by political scientists and economists. He reported that earlier findings of political scientists suggested that urban services were distributed in "unpatterned inequalities" determined chiefly by bureaucratic decision rules rather than by racial or income class biases of officials. Shoup found that more recent surveys, however, yielded findings that were markedly different, at least with respect to some services. One survey of New York City, for instance, concluded that tax contribution per capita was the major factor that determined the allocation of property-related services such as police, fire, and sanitation. A study of Boston, however, found a statistically significant correlation between residents' race and the level of services provided, and a study of Baltimore revealed a willingness of the local government to sacrifice some productivity in the provision of police services in order to achieve a more equitable distribution of service outcomes. At most, these studies appear to demonstrate that different research methodologies may yield different results, that levels of equality may vary from jurisdiction to jurisdiction, and that (in Shoup's terms) the "allocation of urban services among areas is not, usually, haphazard without thought of general rules to be followed...." Carl S. Shoup, Rules for Distributing a Free Government Service Among Areas of a City, 42 Nat'l Tax J. 103, 116 (1989).

Compare the findings of Robert Inman and Daniel Rubinfeld. From their review of the empirical evidence, they conclude that expenditures for services that improve the environment, such as street repairs, sanitation, and parks, are pro-rich. Municipal health care budgets, on the other hand, are pro-poor. Spending on police and fire protection, they contend, is either equal between rich and poor or favorable to the rich, who have more property in need of protection. They indicate, however, that these results vary from city to city, although for all local services combined, municipal spending on services tends to increase with family income. See Robert P. Inman & Daniel L. Rubinfeld, The Judicial Pursuit of Local Fiscal Equity, 92 Harv. L. Rev. 1662 (1979).

C. Local Redistribution of Wealth

New Orleans Campaign for a Living Wage v. City of New Orleans

825 So.2d 1098 (La. 2002).

■ Kimball, Justice.

These consolidated cases are before the court on direct appeal from a judgment of the district court declaring unconstitutional La. R.S. 23:642, which prohibits a local governmental subdivision from establishing a minimum wage which a private employer would be required to pay employees. At the same time, the district court upheld the validity of Ordinance No. 20376, an amendment to the home rule charter of the City of New Orleans that establishes a minimum wage for individuals employed and performing work in the City of New Orleans. For the reasons that follow, we find La. R.S. 23:642 is a legitimate exercise of the police power and therefore constitutional. We also find that Ordinance No. 20376 abridges the police power of the state and is unconstitutional. Consequently, we reverse the judgment of the district court.

Facts and Procedural History

Effective August 15, 1997, Act 317 of 1997 prohibits local governmental subdivisions from establishing a minimum wage rate which a private employer would be required to pay employees. In passing this Act, which became La. R.S. 23:642, the legislature found that in order for Louisiana businesses to remain competitive and to attract and retain the highest caliber of employees, and thereby to remain sound, a business must work in an environment of uniform minimum wage rates. The legislature further found that local variation in mandated minimum wages would lead to economic instability and decline and to a decrease in the standard of living for Louisiana's citizens.

In September 2001, the New Orleans City Council passed Ordinance No. 20376, an ordinance placing on the ballot for vote by the electorate of

New Orleans a proposal to add a new Chapter 5 to Article IX of the home rule charter of the City of New Orleans (the "City"). The proposed Charter Amendment (the "minimum wage law") establishes a minimum wage to be paid to employees performing work in the City of New Orleans of $6.15 per hour, or $1.00 above the prevailing federal minimum wage, whichever is greater. The ordinance does not apply to employees who are currently exempted from coverage under certain enumerated provisions of the Fair Labor Standards Act of 1938, 29 U.S.C. 201 et seq., to city or state civil service employees whose wages are regulated by a civil service commission, or to persons employed on any public works contracts governed by the Louisiana Public Bid Law. Employers who fail to comply with the minimum wage law commit a misdemeanor "punishable by a fine of up to $200 for each day and each employee that wages are paid in violation thereof."

On Saturday, February 2, 2002, New Orleans voters approved the proposed Charter Amendment. The following day, Sunday, February 3, 2002, the New Orleans Campaign for a Living Wage, joined by two individuals, Jean Matthews and Philomenia Johnson (collectively the "Proponents"), instituted a declaratory judgment proceeding against the City, its mayor and City Council, and the State of Louisiana, seeking a declaration of the validity of the City's new minimum wage law. In addition, petitioners sought a declaration that La. R.S. 23:642, the state law that prohibits local governmental subdivisions from establishing a minimum wage, is unconstitutional as applied to the City of New Orleans, a pre 1974 home rule charter city.

* * *

As explained above, the instant case is before this court on direct appeal because La. R.S. 23:642 was declared unconstitutional by the district court. We must therefore begin with an analysis of this statute. Although the district court declared La. R.S. 23:642 wholly unconstitutional on its face, the Proponents argue only that the statute is unconstitutional as applied to the City, a pre 1974 home rule government. Specifically, the Proponents contend that the Opponents have not borne their burden of proving adequate constitutional grounds for the State to deny the City the power to adopt this particular minimum wage ordinance. In response, the Opponents argue that the statute's regulation of minimum wages is a valid exercise of the state's police power as it was enacted for the purpose of protecting the general economic welfare of the state as a whole and, therefore, an inconsistent ordinance cannot stand.

Local governmental autonomy or home rule exists only to the extent that the state constitution endows a local governmental entity with two interactive powers: the power to initiate local legislation and the power of immunity from control by the state legislature. The City is governed by a home rule charter that was enacted prior to the 1974 constitution. This preexisting home rule charter was continued, and essentially constitutionalized, by La. Const. art. VI, § 4.

Article VI, § 4 of the 1974 Louisiana Constitution grants the City both the power of initiation and the power of immunity. That provision states:

> Every home rule charter or plan of government existing or adopted when this constitution is adopted shall remain in effect and may be amended, modified, or repealed as provided therein. Except as inconsistent with this constitution, each local governmental subdivision which has adopted such a home rule charter or plan of government shall retain the powers, functions, and duties in effect when this constitution is adopted. If its charter permits, each of them also shall have the right to powers and functions granted to other local governmental subdivisions.

A preexisting home rule charter's grant of the power of initiation is limited by Article VI, § 4 only by its provision that the local government may not exercise that power inconsistently with the constitution. Thus, although "home rule" does not entail complete autonomy, "in affairs of local concern, a home rule charter government possesses 'powers which within its jurisdiction are as broad as that of the state, except when limited by the constitution, laws permitted by the constitution, or its own home rule charter.' " *Smith & Wesson Corp.*, 00–1132 at p. 16, 785 So.2d at 14 (*quoting Francis v. Morial,* 455 So.2d 1168, 1171 (La.1984)).

* * *

Article VI, however, also contains a provision in Section 9(B) that ensures the powers granted to home rule governments will not be used to deprive the state government of its inherent powers. This section, entitled "Limitations of Local Government Subdivisions," provides:

> Notwithstanding any provision of this Article, the police power of the state shall never be abridged.

This provision was adopted "as a principle of harmonizing the replete home rule powers granted local governments with a basic residuum of the state's power to initiate legislation and regulation necessary to protect and promote the vital interests of its people as a whole." *City of New Orleans v. Board of Comm'rs of Orleans Levee Dist.,* 93–0690 at p. 19–20, 640 So.2d at 249.

The police power of the state is best defined on a case-by-case basis; however, it has been generally described as the state's "inherent power to govern persons and things, within constitutional limits, for promotion of general health, safety, welfare, and morals." The police power extends only to measures that are reasonable. A reasonable measure taken under the state's police power is one in which the action taken is, under all the circumstances, reasonably necessary and designed to accomplish a purpose properly falling within the scope of the police power. To sustain an action under the state's police power, a court must be able to determine that its operation tends in some degree to prevent an offense or evil or otherwise to preserve public health, safety, welfare or morals. Further, the state's exercise of its police power must not interfere with constitutional rights to an extent that is entirely out of proportion to any benefit redounding to the public.

In the instant case, La. R.S. 23:642 itself purports to be an action taken under the state's police power. The statute provides:

[The statute concluded that "local variation in legally required minimum wage rates would threaten many businesses with a loss of employees to areas which require a higher minimum wage rate and many other businesses with the loss of patrons to areas which allow for a lower wage rate. The net effect of this situation would be detrimental to the business environment of the state and to the citizens, businesses, and governments of the various local jurisdictions as well as the local labor market." The statute thus concluded that business competition and the need to retain employees required "a uniform environment with respect to minimum wage rates." It concluded that local variation in wage rates would create economic instability and a decrease in living standards. The statute thus prohibited local subdivisions from establishing a minimum wage rate for private employers.—EDS.]

* * *

These findings are supported by the legislative history of the statute. Dr. Tim Ryan, an economist and Dean of the College of Business Administration at the University of New Orleans, testified before the house committee considering the bill that became La. R.S. 23:642 that the latest wage survey conducted in 1990–1991 showed that unemployment increased after an increase in the federal minimum wage. Dr. Ryan further explained that an increase in a local minimum wage creates a competitive situation between localities and leads to businesses locating in areas with lower minimum wages. *Minutes of the House Committee on Labor and Industrial Relations,* April 25, 1997, p. 15. Additionally, several individuals appeared before the committee, some in favor of the bill and others in opposition to it. Those in favor of the measure opined that higher minimum wage requirements would be detrimental to their businesses and to small business owners and would lead to layoffs. Persons appearing in opposition to the bill stated the economic data presented to the committee was "garbage" and people were moving out of New Orleans because they could not make enough money. *Minutes of the House Committee on Labor and Industrial Relations,* April 25, 1997, pp. 15–18. After hearing this testimony, the House Committee on Labor and Industrial Relations voted in favor of the bill that became La. R.S. 23:642 and the bill was ultimately passed by both the House and the Senate and signed by the governor on June 18, 1997.

In enacting La. R.S. 23:642, the legislature determined the policy of the State of Louisiana with respect to minimum wage requirements. It prescribed that minimum wage policy decisions should be made by the state to preserve consistency in the wage market. It is the role of the legislature to make such policy decisions for our state. In making this policy determination, the legislative history reveals that the legislature relied on the expert opinion of a local economist and the opinions of citizens and local businesses. These are precisely the types of opinions the legislature should consider in setting statewide policy and, based on the opinions presented, we find the legislature's policy choice is a reasonable one.

At the trial before the district court, the Proponents presented the testimony of two expert economists who voiced disagreement with the findings of the legislature regarding the need for statewide consistency in regulation of minimum wage rates in La. R.S. 23:642 and with the expert testimony presented by Dr. Ryan. We recognize these expert opinions, but conclude they represent a disagreement among experts regarding the necessity of statewide regulation of minimum wage policy. Both sides of the issue appear to be backed by legitimate concerns and it is the legislature's function to fashion policy from these competing viewpoints. The legislature chose to require statewide regulation of minimum wage laws to maintain consistency in the wage market, and we find this policy choice to be reasonable in light of the evidence presented. The reasons for judgment assigned by the district judge indicate that the judge found the testimony of Dr. Ryan to be biased and the testimony of the Proponents' experts more compelling. In reaching this conclusion, the district court overstepped its role. The legislature has "broad scope to experiment with economic problems," and "courts do not substitute their social and economic beliefs for the judgment of legislative bodies, who are elected to pass laws." *Ferguson v. Skrupa,* 372 U.S. 726, 730, 83 S.Ct. 1028, 1031, 10 L.Ed.2d 93. By choosing to give the evidence presented by one side more weight than that presented by the other, the district court improperly second-guessed the reasoned policy choice of the legislature. Instead, the court should have evaluated whether the legislature's policy choice was reasonable in light of the evidence presented.

While the legislature is the branch of government responsible for the enactment of laws designed to foster the policy of the state, the judicial branch must ensure that the legislature's actions comport with the dictates of the constitution as adopted by the people of this state. Thus, even when legislative statements indicate an action was taken pursuant to the police power, this mere assertion does not make it so. Rather, the judicial branch must apply the analysis set forth above to determine whether an action is a reasonable exercise of the state's police power. Clearly, the legislature's determination regarding the exercise of police power must be given great weight and the judicial branch should not substitute its opinion for the choice made by the legislature. Rather, the judicial branch should analyze the legislature's choice to determine whether there is support for the legislative determination that a measure constitutes a reasonable exercise of the police power.

Additionally, the district court was apparently persuaded by the "empirical data" presented by the Proponents' expert, Dr. Pollin, who testified regarding a study he conducted in 1999 based on the economic impact of the proposed minimum wage ordinance. Based on this study, Dr. Pollin testified that a one dollar increase in the minimum wage in New Orleans would not significantly affect the average firm's overall operating cost. Dr. Pollin opined the business economy of the state would not be negatively impacted by a one dollar increase in the City's minimum wage. In light of this "empirical data," which the district court found was uncontroverted, the trial judge declared La. R.S. 23:642 unconstitutional. While it is clear from the procedural posture of this case why the district court focused on the provisions of the ordinance at issue, we nevertheless find the district court fell into analytical error by concentrating on the minimum wage ordinance and basing its decision on the projected effect of a one dollar increase in the City's minimum wage. The issue to be decided is whether the state can prohibit all local governments from regulating minimum wage rates pursuant to a reasonable exercise of the police power. The fact that a one dollar increase in one municipality's minimum wage rate may or may not have an impact on the state's economy as a whole is irrelevant. The relevant inquiry is whether the legislature was reasonable in concluding that it would be detrimental to the state's interest if several municipalities increased their minimum wages and, if so, whether the statute they enacted to further this interest is reasonably necessary and designed to accomplish this purpose.

Turning to the relevant issue, we note this court has previously found that "the power to set or prescribe a minimum wage is regarded as an exercise of the police power because a minimum wage is generally intended to insure employment at fair and reasonable wages and to stimulate the economy." *Louisiana Associated Gen. Contractors v. Calcasieu Parish Sch. Bd.*, 586 So.2d 1354, 1366 (La.1991). In this case, we find, as the statute sets forth, that state regulation of minimum wage rates is of vital interest to the citizens of Louisiana, and that statewide regulation of minimum wage rates tends to preserve the public welfare. The legislature determined as a matter of policy that minimum wage policy decisions should be made by the state to preserve consistency in the wage market. We find La. R.S. 23:642 is reasonably necessary in light of this policy determination by the legislature and is designed to promote economic stability and growth of the state, and thereby to promote the welfare of Louisianans. Moreover, we find the provisions of La. R.S. 23:642 are necessary to protect the vital interest of the state as a whole and do not constitute such an interference with the City's constitutional rights that the statute must be held unenforceable against the City. Consequently, we conclude that La. R.S. 23:642 constitutes a reasonable exercise of the state's police power, is constitutional, and is applicable to the City.

Because we find La. R.S. 23:642, prohibiting local governmental subdivisions from establishing a minimum wage rate which a private employer would be required to pay employees, is a legitimate exercise of the state's police power, we conclude the City's minimum wage law, which sets a minimum wage rate private employers are required to pay their employees, abridges the police power of the state. Therefore, we find the minimum wage law invalid.

* * *

REVERSED.

■ [The concurring opinion of CHIEF JUSTICE CALOGERO is omitted.—EDS.]

■ WEIMER, J., concurring in the result.

While I agree with the majority's conclusion that Ordinance No. 20376, the Increased Minimum Wage Charter Amendment, is unconstitutional, I write separately to express my view that there exists a more appropriate avenue for resolving the constitutional conflict that presents itself in this case than the majority's resort to the provisions of Article VI, § 9(B). In my view, it is not necessary to reach the issue of whether the state's police power trumps that of the City of New Orleans, a pre–1974 home rule charter entity, because the Constitution, in Article VI, § 9(A), denies to any local governmental subdivision the power to enact legislation governing private or civil relationships unless the legislature by general law confers upon the local governmental unit the express authority to act. Because Ordinance No. 20376, which establishes a minimum wage that a private employer would be required to pay its employees working in the City of New Orleans, is an ordinance that governs a private and civil relationship, and because the State, through the enactment of LSA R.S. 23:642, has expressly denied to the City the authority to legislate with respect to the minimum wage paid by private employers, Ordinance No. 20376 cannot withstand constitutional scrutiny and must be stricken as an unlawful attempt by the City to legislate in an arena expressly reserved to the State by the 1974 Constitution.

This case arises from the attempt of a local governmental subdivision to increase the minimum wage within its jurisdiction despite a state statute prohibiting such action. Whether it is wise or prudent to raise the minimum wage is not an issue for this court to decide. It is not the role of this court to make such a policy determination, especially given the compelling social and economic objectives advanced on both sides of this debate over which reasonable and rational individuals could differ in their ultimate conclusions. The policy determination must be resolved by those entrusted with the weighty responsibility of serving in other areas of government. The role of this court is more limited. In a case in which two sovereigns—the City of New Orleans and the State of Louisiana—have enacted diametrically different regulations regarding the same subject matter, it is the role of this court to determine which has exceeded the boundaries of its constitutional authority. This constitutional conflict must be resolved by evaluating the provisions of the 1974 Louisiana Constitution.

* * *

The City's minimum wage ordinance, which purports to regulate an important aspect of the private and civil employment relationship, is an unconstitutional encroachment upon matters expressly reserved to the State in the 1974 Constitution. Unless, pursuant to the constitution, the legislature delegates to the City the authority to enact legislation in this private arena, the ordinance is unconstitutional. With the passage of LSA–R.S. 23:642, the legislature has not only failed to delegate authority to enact minimum wage legislation to the City of New Orleans, it has expressly denied such authority. As a result, Ordinance No. 20376 cannot withstand constitutional scrutiny and must be stricken as an unlawful attempt by the City of New Orleans to legislate in an arena expressly reserved to the State by the 1974 Louisiana Constitution.

* * *

■ JOHNSON, J., dissenting.

* * *

In a long line of jurisprudence, we have recognized the right of home rule entities to regulate their affairs with minimum interference from state government, limited only by the police power of the state, which shall never be abridged. "Police power" can only be defined on a case by case basis. In *Francis, supra,* this Court defined police power as "the inherent power of the State to govern persons and things, within constitutional limits, for the promotion of the general security, health, morals, and welfare." Id. at 1172. In that case, this Court recognized that the State's police power does not justify interference with constitutional rights which is entirely out of proportion to any public benefit. Id. at 1173. It follows then, that the State legislature does not have ***unqualified*** power to withdraw, preempt, or overrule a local law. . . .

When it enacted LSA R.S. 23:642, the legislature declared economic welfare a vital state interest and concluded that economic stability required a consistent minimum wage state-wide. The questions we must resolve are these: Does LSA–R.S. 23:642 protect a vital or compelling state interest? If so, can that state interest be achieved through less drastic alternatives?

Dr. Timothy Ryan testified as an expert for the State. In Dr. Ryan's opinion, minimum wage legislation is counter-productive by making Louisiana less attractive to businesses. Dr. Ryan conducted no studies of the impact a minimum wage increase would have in Orleans Parish. It is significant to note that Dr. Ryan expressed opposition to the ***federal minimum wage,*** as well as minimum wage legislation in any form. He testified that every increase in the federal minimum wage has resulted in increased unemployment. Dr. Ryan concluded that the impact of the local variation and mandated higher minimum wage would result in economic instability and decline, as well as a decrease in the standard of living.

Dr. Robert Pollin testified on behalf of plaintiffs. In contrast to Dr. Ryan's testimony before the legislature, Dr. Pollin testified that there is no statistical correlation over time between changes in the national minimum wage and employment in the United States.

In 1999, Dr. Pollin conducted a study of the business industry in New Orleans. The study revealed that, for the average firm, the cost due to the $1.00 increase in the minimum wage would result in an additional 0.9% increase in overall operating costs. The cost of labor includes everyone, including managers and supervisors, and ***minimum wage laborers are not a significant percentage of costs.*** Small firms with one to nine employees would see a 0.5% impact. Firms with one to twenty-four employees would have 0.6% impact. According to the study, the two industries that would face the largest average cost increases are the restaurant industry (2.2% cost increase) and the hotel industry (1.7% cost increase). Dr. Pollin concluded that this small increase in the firms' operating budget would not induce restaurants or hotels to incur the costs of relocating. Therefore, plaintiffs were able to show that the $1.00 increase in the minimum wage would have a negligible effect on the economy.

Additionally, plaintiffs' expert, Dr. Thomas Weiss Kopf, was of the opinion that the city-wide minimum wage would lead to an increase, rather than a decrease, in the standard of living of citizens. He opined that far from causing economic instability and decline, a city-wide minimum wage would lead to greater stability in the New Orleans labor market, and a stronger business base in the city and state.

There is no empirical evidence to support the State's conclusion that a variation in the minimum wage would be detrimental to the State's interests. In fact, there is overwhelming evidence to the contrary. In my mind, the State has failed to show that LSA–R.S. 23:642 is "necessary" to protect the vital interest of the state as a whole. The City's effort to insure that a working family has the ability to live above the poverty line, without relying on government subsidies (food stamps, etc.), is a legitimate exercise of its authority under the Home Rule Charter.

For the aforementioned reasons, I dissent.

NOTES

1. Recall the discussion at pages 45–46 about the role of local government in redistribution. There it was noted that there are limits on the capacity of localities to redistribute wealth to the relatively poor because relatively wealthy residents who would pay redistributive taxes could too easily exit to jurisdictions that promised not to impose similar burdens. Even if all residents do not satisfy Tiebout's assumption of perfect mobility, some residents will have more mobility than others. If the relatively wealthy are also relatively mobile, and if localities compete for the relatively wealthy, then a locality that imposes redistributive taxes may lose in the competition for residents. As the wealthy move out, the burden of local redistribution falls increasingly on the less wealthy, until they too exit in a continuing spiral of emigration by those most able to bear the burden of supporting the poor. Local redistributive efforts, therefore, may tend to result in enclaves of the rich and poor. Thus, standard theories of urban economics suggest that redistributive taxes should be imposed by more centralized levels of government, such as the state or the federal government. Residents will have more difficulty avoiding redistributive payments if they have to leave the state or the country to do so. See Wallace E. Oates, Fiscal Federalism 131–40 (1972); Paul E. Peterson, City Limits 182–83 (1981). See, e.g., Helen F. Ladd and Fred C. Doolittle, Which Level of Government Should Assist Poor People?, 35 Natl. Tax. J. 323, 331 (1982). It is important to note that this is not an argument against redistribution. Instead it is an argument against imposing too much redistributive burden on localities rather than other levels of government.

While taxation is a common form of achieving redistribution, governments may create other policies that have the same effect. When governments set minimum prices, such as the prices for labor, and those prices deviate from those that would otherwise prevail in the marketplace, the result is to redistribute wealth from those who would be paying a lower wage rate to those who receive the higher wage rate. But just as in the case of residence, the standard theory of urban economics suggests that local governments cannot easily impose such burdens on employers. If they do, the theory suggests, employers who must pay redistributive taxes will emigrate to nearby jurisdictions that do not impose redistributive taxes. The result will be a downward spiral in which fewer payers will be available to bear the redistributive burden. Thus, when courts address these issues, although they do so through doctrinal mechanisms such as local authority, the scope of home rule, and pre-emption analysis, they are implicitly accepting or rejecting the traditional theory on the capacity of local government to redistribute wealth.

Notwithstanding its theoretical implications, redistribution for the poor is very popular in some localities. See Kirk J. Stark, City Welfare: Views from Theory, History, and Practice, 27 Urb. Lawyer 495 (1995); Elaine B. Sharp and Steven Maynard–Moody, Theories of the Local Welfare State, 35 Am. J. Pol. Sci. 934 (1991). Local redistribution takes several forms. Historically, rent control or rent stabilization ordinances constituted a form of redistribution, though very few localities currently retain any strong form of rent control. Alternatively, localities may redistribute wealth by making certain services available to the relatively poor at little or no cost, or may impose progressive income taxes.

Why would a locality enact redistributive programs? In some instances, the state imposes redistributive obligations on localities. For instance, Connecticut requires the town of an indigent person's residence to provide support, Conn. Gen. Stat. Ann. § 17b–116, and New York state law requires local governments to pay 10 to 25 percent of Medicaid costs for their residents. Obviously, this was not the case with the living wage ordinance enacted by New Orleans, since the state explicitly banned the locality from redistributing wealth in this manner.

But localities may also voluntarily initiate redistribute programs that they believe will create local benefits that could not easily be obtained from more centralized redistribution. In some situations, for instance, the positive effects of redistribution occur within a small geographic area, so that more centralized governments will be less successful at gauging the appropriate level. See Mark V. Pauly, Income Redistribution as a Local Public Good, 2 J. Pub. Econ. 35 (1972). For instance, if a locality desires to demonstrate that it is more concerned about the welfare of its citizens than the average locality in the more centralized jurisdiction, it may wish to redistribute wealth from local sources rather than rely on the state or federal government. Alternatively, individuals may wish to live in socio-economically diverse localities, and thus wish to encourage migration of individuals who require some assistance to live in the locality. Cities, for instance, may wish to attract the relatively poor in order to fill important roles in the local economy or to live in housing that might otherwise become dilapidated. Several cities, for instance, have attempted to attract immigrants by offering redistributive services to them. Less altruistically, the relatively wealthy in a locality may be more willing to support local redistribution in the belief that their own personal welfare and property are more at risk from the geographically proximate poor. Local redistribution, therefore, may constitute a form of "bribe" to the relatively poor in order to maintain urban peace. Finally, redistribution at the local level may have a less benign objective. Local officials may redistribute wealth to reward or attract political supporters. At the extreme, local redistribution may constitute an explicit effort to induce those who pay redistributive taxes to exit the city, thus consolidating the support of current officials among the recipients of local largesse, notwithstanding that the net effects on the locality is to reduce revenues. For claims about the use of this strategy, see Edward L. Glaeser and Andrei Shleifer, The Curley Effect: The Economics of Shaping the Electorate, 21 J. L. Econ. & Org. 1 (2005).

Regardless of the reason for local redistribution, should courts or the state interfere if a locality decides that it does want to redistribute wealth? Can courts distinguish between relatively appropriate and inappropriate local redistributive programs? See Clayton P. Gillette, Local Redistribution, Living Wage Ordinances, and Judicial Intervention, 101 Nw. U. L. Rev. 1057 (2007). If the standard theory of urban economics suggests that local redistribution is contrary to local self-interest, wouldn't any efforts to redistribute wealth locally necessarily be evidence of altruistic activity that we should encourage, rather than prohibit? If New Orleans is willing to risk the possibility that it will lose employers as a result of mandating higher wages, should it be prohibited from taking that risk? Are you convinced by the arguments that local redistribution will have negative effects elsewhere in the state?

2. One would imagine that employers within the locality would tend to oppose living wage ordinances, while employees or advocacy groups, acting on behalf of employees, would support them. Does it appear that either of these groups has an advantage in presenting its case to city officials? If so, which group has that advantage? Is there reason to think that the advantaged group is likely to reflect the views of the community at large on this issue?

3. Consider two different types of living wage ordinances. The first requires the locality or any employer who contracts with the locality to pay a "living wage" in excess of the prevailing minimum wage to its employees. The second requires any employer in the locality to pay such a wage, regardless of whether the locality does business with that employer. Is there a difference in the extent to which these ordinances can be expected to reflect the beliefs of local residents about the desirability of a living wage ordinance? Who ultimately pays the higher wages in the first instance? In the second?

4. *Local Minimum Wage Ordinances.* Minimum wage ordinances have had mixed success in the courts. In Mayor and City of Baltimore v. Sitnick, 255 A.2d 376 (Md. 1969), the court upheld a Baltimore ordinance that set the minimum wage higher than the state required, and applied it to employers who were exempt from the state wage law. The Court first ruled that the power to set a minimum wage was within the city's home rule police powers. Next, the Court declared that the city law "neither conflicts nor is inharmonious" with the explicit or implicit intent of the state. The court reached a similar result that a local minimum wage could "augment and strengthen" a state minimum wage law in City of Atlanta v. Associated Builders and Contractors, 242 S.E.2d 139 (Ga. 1978). But an appellate court in New York invalidated a minimum wage ordinance that exceeded the state's minimum wage law in Wholesale Laundry Board of Trade v. City of New York, 234 N.Y.S.2d 862 (N.Y. App. Div. 1962). The court concluded that the ordinance prohibited payment of a wage that state law permitted, and that the state legislature had intended to occupy the field of wage rates. More recently, an appellate court upheld a Santa Fe living wage ordinance that required business with 25 or more employees to pay a wage higher than the federal or state mandated minimum. New Mexicans for Free Enterprise v. City of Santa Fe, 126 P.3d 1149 (N.M. Ct. App. 2005). See page 355 supra. The court rejected claims that the ordinance violated the "private law" exception of the state constitutional home rule provision or otherwise fell outside the competence of the locality. A New Jersey court upheld such an ordinance in Visiting Homemaker Servs. v. Board of Chosen Freeholders, 883 A.2d 1074, 1080–85 (N.J. Super. Ct. App. Div. 2005), and a divided panel in the United States Court of Appeals rejected a federal constitutional challenge to the Berkeley, California living wage ordinance in RUI One Corp. v. City of Berkeley, 371 F.3d 1137 (9th Cir. 2004). In an unreported decision, a Missouri appellate court held that state law preempted a living wage ordinance for St. Louis. See Note, Rachel I. Rosen, The Rise and Potential Fall of Living Wage Laws: Missouri Hotel and Motel Ass'n v. City of St. Louis, 21 J. L. and Comm. 131 (2001).

5. *Recent Enactment of Living Wage Ordinances.* One of the major advocacy groups for living wage ordinances is the Association of Community Organizations for Reform Now, or ACORN. As of February 2004, the group reported that 116 localities had enacted some form of living wage ordinance. See http://www.livingwagecampaign.org/victories.php. For legal and economic analysis of these ordinances, see Rachel Harvey, Labor Law: Challenges to the Living Wage Movement: Obstacles in a Path to Economic Justice, 14 U. Fla. J. L. and Pub. Pol. 229 (2003); William Quigley, Full–Time Workers Should Not Be Poor: The Living Wage Movement, 70 Miss. L.J. 889 (2001); Georgette C. Poindexter, Economic Development and Community Activism, 32 Ur. Law. 401 (2000).

NOTE ON FEDERAL INTERVENTION INTO THE DELIVERY OF MUNICIPAL SERVICES

The limited ability of local governments effectively to redistribute wealth provides one justification for federal involvement in setting redistributive policy for local governments. Federal administration and funding of assistance to the poor is also justified by the inability of local governments to confine the benefits and burdens of an assistance program to current residents. Just as taxpayers can move to avoid the burden of assistance, the poor can move to capture increased benefits provided by another region. The ability of the poor to travel has historically led states to adopt minimum length of residency requirements before new residents are eligible for assistance. The Supreme Court, however, has limited the ability of states to impose on the poor durational residency requirements of one year or more. See Shapiro v. Thompson, 394 U.S. 618 (1969); Graham v. Richardson, 403 U.S. 365 (1971); Memorial Hospital v. Maricopa County, 415 U.S. 250 (1974); Saenz v. Roe, 526 U.S. 489 (1999). See also Lynn A. Baker, The Prices of Rights: Toward a Positive Theory of Unconstitutional Conditions, 75 Cornell L. Rev. 1185, 1240–1242 (1990); Roderick M. Hills, Jr., Poverty, Residency, and Federalism: States' Duty of Impartiality Toward Newcomers, 1999 Sup. Ct. Rev. 277. A federal program providing a uniform level of support would remove the incentives to move and thus states would not be tempted to cut back their programs in order to prevent attracting new needy residents.

While this line of reasoning supports some form of federal intervention to ensure redistribution of municipal services, doctrines of federalism and comity require some respect for local choices in the allocation of local services and the implementation of those choices. Federalism considerations may be so strong that courts are reluctant to intervene in too heavy-handed a way, even where they find intent to discriminate. In *Shaw*, the original appellate panel expressed concern about judicial intervention (especially by a federal court) in municipal governance, notwithstanding the constitutional violation. The court concluded:

> We feel that issuing a specific order outlining exactly how the equalization of municipal services should occur is neither necessary nor proper in the context of this case. We do require, however, that the Town of Shaw, itself, submit a plan for the court's approval detailing how it proposes to cure the results of the long history of discrimination which the record reveals. We are confident that the municipal authorities can, particularly because they so staunchly deny any racial motivation, propose a program of improvements that will, within a reasonable time, remove the disparities that bear so heavily on the black citizens of Shaw.

437 F.2d at 1293.

Other federal courts, typically armed with findings of intent, have been more intrusive. Note that in *Ammons*, the district court enjoined Dade City from initiating new municipal services or improvements in the white residential community until the services in the black residential community were "on a par with those in the white community." See also Baker v. City of Kissimmee, 645 F.Supp. 571, 589–590 (M.D. Fla. 1986). In Dowdell v. City of Apopka, 698 F.2d 1181, 1184–1185 (11th Cir. 1983), the court went even further. The court impounded funds that had been received by the defendant city from federal revenue sharing programs and allowed expenditure of the funds only to pay for capital improvements to the black part of the city. The court found that 90 percent of funds received through federal revenue sharing had been used for capital improvements to the white section of the city.

Several cases demonstrate the Supreme Court's efforts to strike a balance between protecting the rights of citizens, on the one hand, and maintaining some comity between the federal government and the states (and their political subdivisions), on the other. In Missouri v. Jenkins, 495 U.S. 33 (1990), the Court held that an order issued by a federal district judge that imposed a tax on the Kansas City, Missouri, school district to finance a desegregation plan violated principles of federal/state comity. The tax would have required the school district to raise property taxes from $2.05 to $4.00 per $100 of assessed property value. That measure would have violated a state constitutional tax limit that required approval of two-thirds of district voters before taxes could be raised above $3.25 per $100 of assessed property value. District voters had already rejected a similar tax increase in an election ordered by the court. The Supreme Court upheld the district court's financing plan designed to increase integration by upgrading facilities, reducing class size, and attracting nondistrict students, but ruled that the district court should have ordered the school district itself to levy the necessary tax.

The Court was concerned that the federal judiciary not usurp the legislative authority of a local government, although the court could require the local legislature to decide for itself how to fund compliance with federal desegregation laws. To facilitate the school district's ability to raise funds, the Court suggested that the lower court enjoin the application of state constitutional and statutory restrictions on the district's ability to raise funds. Such an order, in the Supreme Court's opinion, would not violate the Tenth Amendment or Article III of the Constitution, and would remove state restrictions that hindered the ability of local governments to correct federal constitutional wrongs.

Five years later in the same case, the State challenged, inter alia, several post–1990 district court orders requiring the State to fund salary increases for the Kansas City School District's instructional and non-instructional staff. The Supreme Court agreed that these orders were beyond the district court's remedial authority and did not sufficiently "take into account the interests of state and local authorities in managing their own affairs, consistent with the Constitution." Missouri v. Jenkins, 515 U.S. 70, 98 (1995) (quoting Milliken v. Bradley, 433 U.S. 267, 280–281 (1977)). The Court emphasized that "local autonomy of school districts is a vital national tradition," 505 U.S. at 99, and stated that "[o]n remand, the District Court must bear in mind that its end purpose is not only 'to remedy the violation' to the extent practicable, but also 'to restore state and local authorities to the control of a school system that is operating in compliance with the Constitution.' " Id. at 102.

In Spallone v. United States, 493 U.S. 265 (1990), the Court was similarly faced with an order of a federal district judge who had imposed substantial fines on the City of Yonkers, New York, and on individual members of the city council for failure to remedy the practice of locating public housing only in areas of the city populated largely by minorities. The district court had ordered the city to pass remedial ordinances and assessed contempt fines when city council members failed to oblige. The Supreme Court held that the fines imposed against individual council members were inappropriate in light of a federal judicial policy to employ the least possible power adequate to achieve a specified end. The Court determined that distinctions had to be maintained between the city and individual members of the council as the latter had not demonstrably been implicated in discriminatory conduct. The Court held that no action against the individuals should have been considered until all possible sanctions against the city had been exhausted.

Writing for the four-member dissent, Justice Brennan argued that the Court should have deferred to the opinion of the district court judge who was intimately familiar with the city and the council members. He argued that the district court had ample evidence that fines against the city alone would not compel compliance with the order. Brennan indicated that the Court should defer to the district judge's finding that only sanctions against individual council members would compel the desired result as each council member "had a very strong incentive to play 'chicken' with his colleagues by continuing to defy the Contempt Order, while secretly hoping that at least one colleague would change his position and suffer the wrath of the electorate." Id. at 294.

Brennan also argued that the Court should have considered the speed with which any proposed solution would achieve the desired results. While fines against individual members would hasten compliance, fines against the City, "by design, impede the normal operation of local government" and hinder the City's ability to comply with the order. Id. at 296.

Finally, Justice Brennan disagreed with the Court's finding that imposing sanctions on individual council members was more intrusive than imposing sanctions on the government itself. While noting that the Court had a valid interest in not interfering with traditional legislative actions, Brennan argued that when legislatures are subject to a federal court order designed to remedy constitutional violations, the legislators are no longer acting in their traditional field. Under these circumstances, the Court's desire to preserve the legislative process is "misguided."

CHAPTER 5

THE COMMUNITY'S RELATIONSHIP WITH ITS RESIDENTS—PAYING FOR THE SERVICES PROVIDED

A. CONSTITUTIONAL RESTRICTIONS

1. DUE PROCESS

City of Pittsburgh v. Alco Parking Corporation

417 U.S. 369 (1974).

■ MR. JUSTICE WHITE delivered the opinion of the Court.

The issue in this case is the validity under the Federal Constitution of Ordinance No. 704, which was enacted by the Pittsburgh, Pennsylvania, City Council in December 1969, and which placed a 20% tax on the gross receipts obtained from all transactions involving the parking or storing of a motor vehicle at a nonresidential parking place in return for a consideration. The ordinance superseded a 1968 ordinance imposing an identical tax, but at the rate of 15%, which in turn followed a tax at the rate of 10% imposed by the city in 1962. Soon after its enactment, 12 operators of offstreet parking facilities located in the city sued to enjoin enforcement of the ordinance, alleging that it was invalid under the Equal Protection and Due Process Clauses of the Fourteenth Amendment, as well as Art. VIII, 1, of the Pennsylvania Constitution, which requires that taxes shall be uniform upon the same class of subjects. It appears from the findings and the opinions in the state courts that, at the time of suit, there were approximately 24,300 parking spaces in the downtown area of the city, approximately 17,000 of which the respondents operated. Another 1,000 were in the hands of private operators not party to the suit. The balance of approximately 6,100 was owned by the Parking Authority of the city of Pittsburgh, an agency created pursuant to the Parking Authority Law of June 5, 1947, Pa. Stat. Ann., Tit. 53, 341 et seq. (1974). The trial court also found that there was then a deficiency of 4,100 spaces in the downtown area.

The Court of Common Pleas sustained the ordinance. Its judgment was affirmed by the Commonwealth Court by a four-to-three vote, 6 Pa. Cmwlth. 433, 291 A.2d 556 (1972), on rehearing, 6 Pa. Cmwlth. 433, 295 A.2d 349 (1972); but the Pennsylvania Supreme Court reversed, also four to three. 453 Pa. 245, 307 A.2d 851 (1973). That court rejected challenges to the ordinance under the Pennsylvania Constitution and the Equal Protection Clause, but invalidated the ordinance as an uncompensated taking of property contrary to the Due Process Clause of the Fourteenth Amendment. Because the decision appeared to be in conflict with the applicable decisions of this Court, we granted certiorari, 414 U.S. 1127, 94 S. Ct. 863, 38 L. Ed. 2d 751 (1974), and we now reverse the judgment.

In the opinion of the Supreme Court of Pennsylvania, two aspects of the Pittsburgh ordinance combined to deprive the respondents of due process of law. First, the court thought the tax was "unreasonably high" and was responsible for the inability of nine of 14 different private parking lot operators to conduct their business at a profit and of the remainder to show more than marginal earnings. 453 Pa., at 259–260, 307 A.2d. at 859–860. Second, private operators of parking lots faced competition from the Parking Authority, a public agency enjoying tax exemption (although not necessarily from this tax) and other advantages which enabled it to offer offstreet parking at lower rates than those charged by private operators. The average all-day rate for the public lots was $2 as compared with a $3 all-day rate for the private lots. Ibid. The court's conclusion was that "[w]here such an unfair competitive advantage accrues, generated by the use of public funds, to a local government at the expense of private property owners, without just compensation, a clear constitutional violation has occurred...." "[T]he unreasonably burdensome 20 percent gross receipts tax, causing the majority of private parking lot operators to operate their businesses at a loss, in the special competitive circumstances of this case constitutes an unconstitutional taking of private property without due process of law in violation of the Fourteenth Amendment of the United States Constitution." Id., at 267, 269–270, 307 A.2d. at 863, 864.

We cannot agree that these two considerations, either alone or together, are sufficient to invalidate the parking tax ordinance involved in this case. The claim that a particular tax is so unreasonably high and unduly burdensome as to deny due process is both familiar and recurring, but the Court has consistently refused either to undertake the task of passing on the "reasonableness" of a tax that otherwise is within the power of Congress or of state legislative authorities, or to hold that a tax is unconstitutional because it renders a business unprofitable.

In Magnano Co. v. Hamilton, 292 U.S. 40, 54 S. Ct. 599, 78 L. Ed. 1109 (1934), the Court sustained against due process attack a state excise tax of 15per pound on all butter substitutes sold in the State. Conceding that the "tax is so excessive that it may or will result in destroying the intrastate business of appellant," id., at 45, 54 S. Ct. at 602, the Court held that "the due process of law clause contained in the Fifth Amendment is not a limitation upon the taxing power conferred upon Congress," that no different rule should be applied to the States, and that a tax within the lawful power of a State should not "be judicially stricken down under the due process clause simply because its enforcement may or will result in restricting or even destroying particular occupations or business." Id. at 44,

54 S. Ct. at 601. The premise that a tax is invalid if so excessive as to bring about the destruction of a particular business, the Court said, had been "uniformly rejected as furnishing no juridical ground for striking down a taxing act." Id. at 47, 54 S. Ct., at 602. Veazie Bank v. Fenno, 8 Wall. 533, 548, 19 L. Ed. 482 (1869); McCray v. United States, 195 U.S. 27, 24 S. Ct. 769, 49 L. Ed. 78 (1904) and Alaska Fish Salting & By-Products Co. v. Smith, 255 U.S. 44, 41 S. Ct. 219, 65 L. Ed. 489 (1921), are to the same effect.

In *Alaska Fish*, a tax on the manufacture of certain fish products was sustained, the Court saying, id., at 48–49, 41 S. Ct., at 220: "Even if the tax should destroy a business it would not be made invalid or require compensation upon that ground alone. Those who enter upon a business take that risk.... We know of no objection to exacting a discouraging rate as the alternative to giving up a business, when the legislature has the full power of taxation."

Neither the parties nor the Pennsylvania Supreme Court purports to differ with the foregoing principles. But the state court concluded that this was one of those "rare and special instances" recognized in *Magnano* and other cases where the Due Process Clause may be invoked because the taxing statute is "so arbitrary as to compel the conclusion that it does not involve an exertion of the taxing power, but constitutes, in substance and effect, the direct exertion of a different and forbidden power, as, for example, the confiscation of property." 292 U.S., at 44, 54 S. Ct., at 601.

There are several difficulties with this position. The ordinance on its face recites that its purpose is "[t]o provide for the general revenue by imposing a tax ...," and in sustaining the ordinance against an equal protection challenge, the state court itself recognized that commercial parking lots are a proper subject for special taxation and that the city had decided, "not without reason, that commercial parking operations should be singled out for special taxation *to raise revenue* because of traffic related problems engendered by these operations." 453 Pa., at 257, 307 A.2d, at 858 (emphasis added).

It would have been difficult from any standpoint to have held that the ordinance was in no sense a revenue measure. The 20% tax concededly raised substantial sums of money; and even if the revenue collected had been insubstantial, Sonzinsky v. United States, 300 U.S. 506, 513–514, 57 S. Ct. 554, 555–556, 81 L. Ed. 772 (1937), or the revenue purpose only secondary, Hampton & Co. v. United States, 276 U.S. 394, 411–413, 48 S. Ct. 348, 352–353, 72 L. Ed. 624 (1928), we would not necessarily treat this exaction as anything but a tax entitled to the presumption of the validity accorded other taxes imposed by a State.

Rather than conclude that the 20% levy was not a tax at all, the Pennsylvania court accepted it as such and merely concluded that it was so unreasonably high and burdensome that, in the context of competition by the city, the ordinance had the "effect" of an uncompensated taking of property. 453 Pa., at 269, 307 A.2d, at 864. The court did not hold a parking tax, as such, to be beyond the power of the city but it appeared to hold that a bona fide tax, if sufficiently burdensome, could be held invalid under the Fourteenth Amendment. This approach is contrary to the cases already cited, particularly to the oft-repeated principle that the judiciary should not infer a legislative attempt to exercise a forbidden power in the form of a seeming tax from the fact, alone, that the tax appears excessive or even so high as to threaten the existence of an occupation or business. Magnano Co. v. Hamilton, supra, at 47, 54 S. Ct., at 602; *Child Labor Tax Case*, supra, at 40–41, 42 S. Ct., at 451–452; Veazie Bank v. Fenno, supra, at 548.

Nor are we convinced that the ordinance loses its character as a tax and may be stricken down as too burdensome under the Due Process Clause if the taxing authority, directly or through an instrumentality enjoying various forms of tax exemption, competes with the taxpayer in a manner thought to be unfair by the judiciary. This approach would demand not only that the judiciary undertakes to separate those taxes that are too burdensome from those that are not, but also would require judicial oversight of the terms and circumstances under which the government or its tax-exempt instrumentalities may undertake to compete with the private sector. The clear teaching of prior cases is that this is not a task that the Due Process Clause demands of or permits to the judiciary. We are not now inclined to chart a different course.

In *Veazie Bank*, supra, a 10% tax on state bank notes was sustained over the objection of the dissenters that the purpose was to foster national banks, instrumentalities of the National Government, in preference to private banks chartered by the States. More directly in point is Puget Sound Power & Light Co. v. Seattle, 291 U.S. 619, 54 S. Ct. 542, 78 L. Ed. 1025 (1934), where the city imposed a gross receipts tax on a power and light company and at the same time actively competed with that company in the business of furnishing power to consumers. The company's contention was that "constitutional limitations are transgressed ... because the tax affects a business with which the taxing sovereign is actively competing." Id., at 623, 54 S. Ct., at 544. Calling on prior cases in support, the Court rejected the contention, holding that "the Fourteenth Amendment does not prevent a city from conducting a public waterworks in competition with private business or preclude taxation of the private business to help its rival to succeed." Id., at 626, 54 S. Ct., at 546. See also Madera Water Works v. Madera, 228 U.S. 454, 33 S. Ct. 571, 57 L. Ed. 915 (1913). The holding in Puget Sound remains good law and, together with the other authorities to which we have already referred, it is sufficient to require reversal of the decision of the Pennsylvania Supreme Court.

Even assuming that an uncompensated and hence forbidden "taking" could be inferred from an unreasonably high tax in the context of competition from the taxing authority, we could not conclude that the Due Process Clause was violated in the circumstances of this case. It was urged by the city that the private operators would not suffer because they could and would pass the tax on to their customers, who, as a class, should pay more for the services of the city that they directly or indirectly utilize in connection with the special problems incident to the twice daily movement of large numbers of cars on the streets of the city and in and out of parking garages. The response of the Pennsylvania Supreme Court was that competition from the city prevented the private operators from raising their prices and recouping their losses by collecting the tax from their customers. On the record before us, this is not a convincing basis for concluding that the parking tax effected an unconstitutional taking of respondents' property. There are undisturbed findings in the record that there were 24,300 parking places in the downtown area, that there was an overall shortage of parking facilities, and that the public authority supplied only 6,100 parking spaces. Because these latter spaces were priced substantially under the private lots it could be anticipated that they would be preferred by those seeking parking in the downtown area. Insofar as this record reveals, for the 20% tax to have a destructive effect on private operators as compared with the situation immediately preceding its enactment, the damage would have to flow chiefly, not from those who preferred the cheaper public parking lots, but from those who could no longer afford an increased price for downtown parking at all. If this is the case, we simply have another instance where the government enacts a tax at a "discouraging rate as the alternative to giving up a business," a policy to which there is no constitutional objection. Alaska Fish Salting & By–Products Co. v. Smith, 255 U.S., at 49, 41 S. Ct., at 220; Magnano Co. v. Hamilton, 292 U.S., at 46, 54 S. Ct., at 602.

The parking tax ordinance recited that "[n]on-residential parking places for motor vehicles, by reason of the frequency rate of their use, the changing intensity of their use at various hours of the day, their location, their relationship to traffic congestion and other characteristics, present problems requiring municipal services and affect the public interest, differently from parking places accessory to the use and occupancy of residences." By enacting the tax, the city insisted that those providing and utilizing nonresidential parking facilities should pay more taxes to compensate the city for the problems incident to offstreet parking. The city was constitutionally entitled to put the automobile parker to the choice of using other transportation or paying the increased tax.

The judgment of the Pennsylvania Supreme Court is reversed.

Judgment reversed.

■ MR. JUSTICE POWELL, concurring.

The opinion of the Court fully explicates the issue presented here, and I am in accord with its resolution. I write briefly only to emphasize my understanding that today's decision does not foreclose the possibility that some combination of unreasonably burdensome taxation and direct competition by the taxing authority might amount to a taking of property without just compensation in violation of the Fifth and Fourteenth Amendments.

To some extent, private business is inevitably handicapped by direct governmental competition, but the opinion of the Court makes plain that the legitimate exercise of the taxing power is not to be restrained on this account. It is conceivable, however, that punitive taxation of a private industry and direct economic competition through a governmental entity enjoying special competitive advantages would effectively expropriate a private business for public profit. Such a combination of unreasonably burdensome taxation and public competition would be the functional equivalent of a governmental taking of private property for public use and would be subject to the constitutional requirement of just compensation. As the opinion of the Court clearly reveals, ante ... no such circumstance has been shown to exist in the instant case.

NOTES ON TAXATION AND REGULATION

1. The principal case reflects the Supreme Court's general unwillingness to inquire into the "fairness" or propriety of a particular tax imposed by a state or locality on its constituents. The Court has continued to apply minimum scrutiny to tax schemes challenged under the federal Constitution. Most recently, the Court rejected an equal protection challenge to Iowa laws that taxed revenues from slot machines located at racetracks at rates up to 36 percent, but that taxed revenues from slot machines located on excursion riverboats at a maximum rate of 20 percent. Fitzgerald v. Racing Association of Central Iowa, 539 U.S. 103 (2003). The Court began its analysis by indicating that a scheme of differential taxation would survive an equal protection challenge "so long as there is a plausible policy reason for the classification, the legislative facts on which the classification is apparently based rationally may have been considered to be true by the governmental decision maker, and the relationship of the classification to its goal is not so attenuated as to render the distinction arbitrary or irrational." A law would be valid under this analysis as long as it served the general objective of the legislature, such as assisting racetracks, even if it contained other provisions that served additional or inconsistent ends. Here, the law authorizing slot machines at racetracks was intended to advance the racetracks' economic interests. The fact that revenues were taxed did not preclude achievement of that objective. Moreover, rational legislators could have desired to provide even a greater level of assistance to operators of riverboat excursions, and thus subjected them to a lower rate of taxation.

In Nordlinger v. Hahn, 505 U.S. 1 (1992), discussed at page 547 infra, the Court upheld a California property tax that was based on the value of property at the time the current owner acquired it rather than its fair market value at the time the tax is levied. The Court rejected a claim that a system that resulted in different taxation for parcels of equal current fair market value violated the Equal Protection Clause of the Fourteenth Amendment. The Court concluded that the Equal Protection Clause was satisfied so long as there was a plausible policy reason for the classification, and found such rational justification for the California system in the state's desire to preserve neighborhood stability and to honor the reliance interest of owners against significant increases in taxes once they purchased property.

The minimal scrutiny that courts apply to taxation may be justified by arguments that should now be familiar from the Tiebout model. If we want localities to offer different packages of goods and services, then we might similarly want localities to offer different "financing terms" or revenue-raising mechanisms to pay for these goods and services. Those who prefer a particular financing package can gravitate to the jurisdictions that most closely satisfy their preferences. Thus, it is difficult to conceive of any benefits accruing from a single, constitutionally required means of raising revenue. By contrast, constitutional protections would seem to be necessary for situations in which the combination of immobility and political impotence preclude a group on whom a financing burden is placed from effectively protecting itself from exploitation.

2. Even where it appears that a locality has imposed an exploitative tax on one segment of its constituency, or on those outside its jurisdiction, the Supreme Court has been reluctant to intervene. In the classic exception to this principle, Myles Salt Co. v. Board of Commissioners, 239 U.S. 478 (1916), two Louisiana parishes had formed a drainage district that was authorized to issue bonds, the proceeds of which would be used to construct drainage projects. All land within the drainage district was to be taxed to pay the bonds. The plaintiff contended that its land was situated in such a manner that it could not possibly receive any benefit from the district and that its land had been included in district boundaries solely to generate additional revenues for the district. The Court held that, assuming plaintiff's allegations to be correct, imposition of assessments on plaintiff's land to pay for district improvements would constitute a deprivation of property without due process of law. Nevertheless, it is difficult to find any other decision that applies constitutional standards to invalidate the imposition of a tax as exploitative. See, e.g., State ex rel. Pan American Production Co. v. City of Texas City, 303 S.W.2d 780 (Tex. 1957), *appeal dismissed*, 355 U.S. 603 (1958), where the court upheld an annexation against a claim that plaintiff's property was not suitable or necessary for current or foreseeable city needs, but was annexed only to obtain additional tax revenue for the city. Does this suggest either an unwillingness or an inability on the part of courts to distinguish between situations in which a majority has illicitly exploited a minority interest and situations in which a majority properly overcomes minority disapproval?

3. Perhaps a stronger claim might be made against the tax in *Alco*. That tax was nominally imposed by the city on those using parking lots. Who are the likely users of these lots? Will they be residents of the city? If you believe that the primary users of the lots will be commuters who come into the city to work or shop, then your initial reaction might be that this tax is being imposed on individuals who are not represented in the decisionmaking process. That possibility gives rise to a stronger claim of impropriety than is available in the traditional cases where the Supreme Court has avoided review, because there is a strong likelihood that representatives will attempt to place heavy tax burdens on outsiders rather than on their own constituents.

Nevertheless, there may be reasons to believe that the city council would have taken the interests of suburban commuters into account in deciding to impose the parking tax, even though those commuters had no direct representation in the decisionmaking process. If those interests were represented, albeit not by the commuters who had to pay the tax, there is less reason to believe that the city was attempting to exploit nonresidents, and hence greater justification for the federal courts' unwillingness to consider constitutional objections. Consider, for instance, the role of parking lot owners, the employers of nonresident employees who park in the parking lots, and the shopowners whose nonresident customers park in the parking lots. These businesses likely have access to the city council, whether as residents or as substantial taxpayers of the city. To the extent that their interests are aligned with those of commuters, these businesses may serve as surrogates for nonresidents. Indeed, given that the impact of the tax on parking lot owners will be significant, while the impact on any given commuter may be small, parking lot owners may be in a superior position to overcome obstacles to collective action that make lobbying efforts by commuters improbable. Similarly, while the number of parking lot owners may be small, one might expect that business owners and employers in the downtown area of Pittsburgh would, in general, want to avoid taxes that might cause suburban shoppers and employees to shop and work elsewhere. The claim here is not that these resident groups would have prevented imposition of the tax on nonresidents. Rather, the claim is that the ability of these groups to serve as proxies for nonresidents suggests that the tax is less likely to be exploitative. In imposing the tax, Pittsburgh presumably would consider both the ability of nonresidents to exit (by shopping and working outside Pittsburgh where parking taxes are lower or nonexistent) and the "voice" exercised in the political process by residents on behalf of the excluded nonresidents.

Before making too much of the ability of (certain) residents adequately to represent the interests of (certain) nonresidents, however, recall that ensuring that all points of view are heard does not satisfy all conceptions of local government. The reading from Hannah Arendt in Chapter 1 suggested that it was a failure of the federal Constitution to give "power to the citizens, without giving them the opportunity of *being* republicans and of *acting* as citizens." Under this conception, the essence of citizenship consists of participating in governmental decisionmaking, not of being represented. Some level of representation is necessary because "the room will not hold all." But, for purposes of Arendt's concerns, there is a difference between being represented by individuals elected by their constituents, and being represented by individuals who are "representatives" only in the sense that they have interests that overlap with one's own. The civic virtues that might be taught where representatives are accountable to their constituents, although not as substantial as the virtues that would accompany becoming personally involved in the process of governing, still far exceed the virtues that can be taught through the passive processes of surrogacy.

4. *Taxes and Subsidies. Alco* involves taxation that is imposed on a subset of the community that, as a result, bears a higher burden than competitors. The same economic effect can be imposed on a subgroup if its competitors receive a subsidy funded from tax revenues. In Edwards v. County of Erie, 932 A.2d 997 (Pa. Comm. Ct. 2007), hotel owners contended that they had been denied due process after the Erie County Convention Center Authority proposed to construct a publicly owned hotel as part of a convention center complex. The project was to be funded by revenues from a county hotel room tax. In effect, the private hotel owners were generating revenues to fund their competition. The owners contended, among other things, that the plan violated due process under the state and federal constitutions. The court rejected the claim, citing *Alco* for the conclusion that there "is no authority for the proposition that tax subsidized competition from a public entity that intrudes on the profits of private enterprise is per se improper." The court also upheld findings that the private owners would actually benefit from the proposed convention center, and thus could not complain about the related burden they faced to finance it.

5. *Taxing Non–Residents.* In Route One Liquors, Inc. v. Secretary of Administration and Finance, 785 N.E.2d 1222 (Mass. 2003), parking lot operators and owners brought an action to invalidate a state law that imposed an aggregate annual tax of $400,000 on all commercial operators licensed to provide parking within a three-mile radius of a stadium used by a professional football team and for other events. The proceeds of the tax were to be deposited into the general fund of the state, but the provision creating the tax was part of an Act that provided funds to improve the stadium and infrastructure in its vicinity. The Act did not indicate how the burden of the aggregate annual tax was to be allocated among the affected parking lot owners. The plaintiffs complained, among other things, that the tax was unreasonable and unequal. The court rejected the claims and noted that there was nothing in the record to indicate that the tax denied plaintiffs the economically beneficial or productive use of their land or that the plaintiffs would be unable to pass the tax on to their customers. The court concluded that "plaintiffs have failed to distinguish their situation from the case of *Pittsburgh v. Alco Parking Corp.*" Id. at 1230. For other examples of taxes or fees that likely will fall disproportionately on nonresidents, see Bold Corp. v. County of Lancaster, 801 A.2d 469 (Pa. 2002) (hotel room rental tax); Ace Rent–A–Car, Inc. v. Indianapolis Airport Authority, 612 N.E.2d 1104 (Ind. Ct. App. 1993) (exaction on car rental revenues). Should these impositions be upheld only if they reflect the value of the services that the nonresident obtains from the locality and that residents pay for through property taxes?

6. The Court in *Alco* characterizes the tax as one intended to raise revenues and to place the costs related to traffic congestion during commuter rush hours on the drivers who create those costs. Would it make a difference if the tax were instead characterized as having a regulatory function rather than a revenue raising or distributive one? Assume that the city council in Pittsburgh passed an ordinance that prohibited use of privately owned parking lots until the public lots were completely full.

Would this regulation of parking have constituted a compensable taking of the property of private lot owners? One would imagine that automobile drivers would now have a systematic tendency to use the less-expensive public lots before private ones. Should the fact that the same behavior is brought about by a tax incentive rather than by direct regulation make a difference in legal result or legal analysis? If you believe that the direct regulation would be subject to greater scrutiny, then why does the Court permit the city council to do indirectly (through a tax) what it could not have done directly (through regulation)?

Alternatively, assume that the City of Pittsburgh determined that there was an optimal number of cars that could be handled in the downtown area during rush hours. Call this number X. The city has a variety of ways to ensure that no more than X cars are allowed in the area at these times: It could set up barriers and only allow X cars to enter on a first-come, first-served basis; it could auction off X places and allow the highest bidders to obtain the parking places; it could set a fee on parking at a level that all but X drivers would find prohibitive. Assuming that each of these approaches would be equally effective, should it make a constitutional difference which method the city uses to accomplish its purpose?

These cases might become more difficult if we changed one fact in *Alco*. Assume that the number of available parking spaces in the city exceeded demand. Now if the locality either raises (through taxation) the cost of parking or places a flat restriction on the number of cars allowed into the downtown area, some parking lots may no longer be economically viable. Under the analysis in *Alco*, that result would not make a difference for the validity of a tax. But a regulation that had the same effect looks more vulnerable, although its ultimate resolution is uncertain. In Lucas v. South Carolina Coastal Council, 505 U.S. 1003 (1992), the Supreme Court held that a regulation would constitute a "taking" if the owner of the regulated property is deprived of all economically beneficial or productive use of the land or if the government physically invades the land. Such a regulatory taking would require compensation unless the owner had no preexisting right to engage in the proscribed enterprise. The Court clarified this view in Tahoe–Sierra Preservation Council, Inc. v. Tahoe Regional Planning Agency, 535 U.S. 302 (2002). In that case, an agency had placed a 32–month moratorium on development in the Lake Tahoe Basin while it formulated a more comprehensive land-use plan for the area. The Court held that the existence of a regulatory taking would be determined by an ad hoc inquiry based on careful examination and a weighing of all the relevant circumstances rather than on a categorical rule that any deprivation of economic use, however temporary, required compensation. The Court limited *Lucas* to the extraordinary case in which a regulation permanently deprives property of all economic use. As a result, the existence of a compensable taking would depend on such factors as the length of the deprivation, the character of the regulatory action and nature and extent of the interference with property rights, the extent of the diminution in value, the extent of interference with investment-backed expectations, the alternatives available to the regulating government, and the scope of the

benefits and burdens created by the regulation. See also Penn Cent. Transp. Co. v. City of New York, 438 U.S. 104 (1978). Would the flat regulation on automobiles in the downtown area constitute a "taking" under this test?

2. PUBLIC PURPOSE

Localities are not permitted to spend public monies without constraint. Virtually every state constitution restricts governmental spending to those activities that serve a "public purpose." This inherently ambiguous phrase has been defined by courts in terms such as "a purpose or use necessary for the common good and welfare of the people," Kearney v. City of Schenectady, 325 N.Y.S.2d 278, 280 (N.Y. App. Div. 1971), or as an activity that "confers direct benefit of reasonably general character . . . as distinguished from a remote or theoretical benefit," Opinion of the Justices to the House of Representatives, 197 N.E.2d 691, 693 (Mass. 1964). The materials that follow indicate how courts have applied and analyzed this nebulous concept.

Many of the cases involving the public purpose doctrine arise where either a municipal corporation or the state proposes to issue debt, typically in the form of bonds that are publicly sold, and to use the proceeds of the borrowing to finance the activity at issue. It is useful for this discussion, and as a prelude to the discussion of debt limitations that follows later in these materials, to distinguish between two types of government debt. Debts for capital projects frequently take the form of bonds, which are securities issued by the municipality as evidence of indebtedness. Where *general obligation bonds* are involved, the issuing state or local government secures its promise to make payments on its debt with all its revenue raising power. Thus, the purchasers of the bonds (the creditors of the state or local government) rely on the general taxing power of the issuer for payment. Should the specific project financed with bond proceeds not operate as expected, the bondholders are still entitled to payment from taxes on other revenue sources of the issuer. Where *revenue bonds* are involved, the issuer secures its promise to make payments on its debt only with some specified source of revenue, typically the revenues that are generated by operation of the facility financed with bond proceeds. Should the project not operate as expected, the bondholders have no recourse against any other revenue source of the locality. Thus, construction of a new city hall is likely to be financed with general obligation bonds, as the building generates no revenues. Bondholders will be paid out of the general fund of the municipality. A toll bridge or toll road is more likely to be constructed with proceeds of revenue bonds. Bondholders will be paid solely out of revenues generated by the collection of tolls from users of the bridge or road. Should the new city hall burn to the ground while bonds are still outstanding, the issuing municipality would remain liable for payments out of its general revenues. Should the toll bridge collapse and never generate any revenues, the bondholders would be unable to obtain payment from any other municipal revenue source.

As we will see, there are many variations on these basic categories. One variation, at issue in the *WDW Properties* case infra, involves use of the state or locality's borrowing power to provide funds for commercial or industrial development. To finance these projects, governments may issue debt and use the proceeds to acquire or construct commercial or industrial facilities that are subsequently leased to private users. Revenues paid by the private users to the issuing localities in the form of lease payments service the debt. The legality of these arrangements under state constitutions often depends on whether the use of publicly raised funds to assist private owners of commercial or industrial enterprises constitutes a "public" purpose.

Why don't the private owners simply borrow funds on their own? The answer lies in the intricacies of the Internal Revenue Code. Creditors of states or their political subdivisions do not have to pay federal (and typically state) income taxes on interest payments made by the governmental debtor. See 26 U.S.C. § 103. Hence, creditors of these governmental entities are willing to lend money (purchase bonds) that bear a lower rate of return than would be the case if the interest income was taxable. States and localities can borrow money at these lower interest rates and pass those savings on by charging the private enterprises that use these facilities relatively low lease payments. The Internal Revenue Code, however, dramatically curtails the availability of the tax exemption for commercial and industrial projects. See 26 U.S.C. §§ 141–148.

For an overview of the subject of public purpose, see Robert S. Amdursky & Clayton P. Gillette, Municipal Debt Finance Law §§ 3.1–3.7 (1992).

PROBLEM XV

The state legislature has enacted legislation that permits the State Housing Finance Authority ("SHFA") to implement an Urban Area Mortgage Program aimed at preventing the deterioration of urban areas and encouraging the development of communities containing persons of all income levels. The legislature acted after finding that "there exists in urban areas of the state a critical and growing need to maintain and to encourage a proper balance of housing, industrial, commercial, and recreational facilities and to restore urban areas as desirable places for persons of all income levels to live, shop, work, and enjoy the amenities of town living and meeting." The legislation declares that "in order to encourage the development of a balanced community of all income levels in urban areas it is necessary and appropriate that mortgage financing for construction, reconstruction, purchase, and refinancing of housing in urban areas for all levels of income more readily be made available."

Under the Urban Area Mortgage Program, SHFA makes funds available to participating financial institutions that are willing to make mortgages on properties in eligible urban areas. Funds for the purchase of such mortgages are obtained through the issuance and sale of SHFA's bonds.

Bondholders will be repaid from mortgage payments made by recipients of mortgages funded through the SHFA. Because SHFA bonds are issued by a governmental entity, interest on them is exempt from taxation under the Internal Revenue Code. As a result, mortgage loans made with the proceeds of SHFA bonds can be made at lower interest rates than is the case with conventional mortgages obtained through traditional mortgagees such as banks or mortgage companies.

Under the Program, mortgages are made by participating financial institutions without regard to the cost of the house or income of the mortgagor. Mortgages will be made both to those who currently live in urban areas and to those who move into urban areas from rural or suburban areas. SHFA also predicts that more than 80 percent of the people who receive mortgage commitments through the program will have family incomes less than $100,000, while less than 10 percent of the new home buyers will have incomes in excess of $150,000.

The state constitution provides that "public funds, property, or credit shall be used only for public purposes." Does the Urban Area Mortgage Program satisfy that standard? What role do the legislative findings play in making that determination?

PROBLEM XVI

Hallmark Development Corporation owns an undeveloped parcel of property in Inglewood Township. Hallmark has been negotiating for BigBox Superstores to enter into a long-term lease for the parcel. Under the proposed terms of the lease, Hallmark would construct a facility suitable for a BigBox Superstore and lease it to BigBox for thirty years. BigBox would use the facility for one of its discount department stores, in which it sells household items, clothing, food, and appliances at deep discounts. BigBox is known for aggressive pricing of its goods, which benefits consumers, but also for paying relatively low wages to its workers. Because BigBox can obtain a high volume of goods from suppliers, it can achieve economies in its supply chain. Largely because it faces low costs and pays low wages, BigBox has a reputation for forcing smaller, local competitors to drop their prices. As a result, many local competitors go out of business within two years of the arrival of a BigBox Superstore in a commercial area.

BigBox has indicated that it will only locate in Inglewood if the property owned by Hallmark receives a significant tax abatement that is passed through to BigBox in the form of lower monthly rental payments. Hallmark has also asked the Township Board to finance construction of the proposed BigBox facility with $12 million in revenue bonds. These bonds would be issued by the Township, but would be payable exclusively from rents paid by BigBox for use of the facility. No Inglewood revenues would be pledged to payment of the bonds.

BigBox would employ approximately 300 people once it was operating. It is also predicted that BigBox would bring significant new revenue to Inglewood, because there is no similar store within a 20–mile radius of the proposed location. There are, however, numerous small chain stores and independently owned stores in the area that sell groceries, appliances, clothing, and household goods.

You serve as counsel to the Township Board. The Board has requested your advice on both the propriety and the legality of the proposed tax abatement and bond issue. The constitution of the State permits taxes to be levied and expenditures to be made only for "purposes that advance the public good and welfare." How will you respond to the Board's request?

WDW Properties v. City of Sumter

535 S.E.2d 631 (S.C. 2000).

■ WALLER, JUSTICE:

WDW Properties (WDW) brought a declaratory judgment action challenging the legitimacy of a program in which the proceeds of tax-exempt bonds issued by a state agency would be loaned to a developer renovating retail and commercial properties in a blighted area of the city of Sumter (City). A master-in-equity rejected WDW's claims after a bench trial and WDW appeals.

FACTS

The parties have stipulated to the following facts. The Internal Revenue Code authorizes the use of federally tax-exempt local government bonds that finance business enterprises in designated urban "empowerment zones." *See* 26 U.S.C. §§ 1391–1392 (Supp. 1999). The secretary of the United States Department of Housing and Urban Development (HUD), at the request of local government officials, in 1998 declared about 18 square miles located in Richland and Sumter counties as an urban empowerment zone. The governing body of City in 1999 declared its downtown to be a "slum and blight area" and designated it as a "redevelopment project area" located in the empowerment zone.

Uptown Synergy plans to develop the Hampton at Main Project, located in the redevelopment project area. The $4.3 million project consists of interior and exterior renovations of three adjoining historic buildings, which would be leased for commercial office and retail space. The project is expected to create twenty full-time jobs, and the developer hopes to target low—and moderate-income persons for employment at the various offices and retail businesses. In its application for financing to the South Carolina Jobs–Economic Development Authority (JEDA), Uptown Synergy stated the project would "serve as the cornerstone for the revitalization of downtown Sumter and the surrounding communities."

JEDA's governing board adopted a resolution in which it pledged to seek authorization from the state Budget and Control Board to issue $2.5 million in economic development revenue bonds that would be exempt from state and federal income taxation. Under loan documents executed in 1999, JEDA would loan the bond proceeds to Uptown Synergy to finance about

58 percent of the project's cost. Uptown Synergy would repay the loan with revenue from the project. No tax money is involved or pledged with regard to the project. However, the tax-exempt nature of the bonds would result in lower interest costs to Uptown Synergy than it would pay if it had to obtain conventional financing.

WDW, a general partnership, owns and leases Liberty Square, which includes mini-warehouse units, retail businesses, and commercial office space. Liberty Square is not located in the empowerment zone and is not eligible for government-sponsored financing. Uptown Synergy's project would compete with Liberty Square for tenants and patrons. The apparent reason for WDW's lawsuit is its belief that government-sponsored financing gives Uptown Synergy an unfair economic advantage in the competition for tenants and patrons. . . .

Argues there is NO Public benefit

DISCUSSION

WDW contends the master erred in ruling that the JEDA loan program at issue in this case serves a public purpose through the redevelopment of blighted urban areas. The master erred by reading *Carll v. South Carolina Jobs–Economic Development Authority,* 284 S.C. 438, 327 S.E.2d 331 (1985), to mean that so long as the issuance of a given series of bonds is authorized by the JEDA Act, then the issuance of such bonds necessarily serves a required public purpose. *Carll* should be interpreted only to hold that the issuance of revenue bonds to finance industrial facilities serves a public purpose, a principle previously established by this Court, WDW argues.

WDW bases its argument on the fact that, when *Carll* was decided in 1985, JEDA regulations prohibited loans to retail or food establishments. Current JEDA regulations allow economic development bond loans to commercial businesses in certain situations, including downtown redevelopment and in economically distressed areas. WDW believes those regulatory changes mean *Carll* is not dispositive.

WDW urges us to follow the views expressed in *State ex rel. McLeod v. Riley,* 276 S.C. 323, 278 S.E.2d 612 (1981), and *Anderson v. Baehr,* 265 S.C. 153, 217 S.E.2d 43 (1975). In *McLeod,* this Court considered amendments to the Industrial Revenue Bond Act that allowed the issuance of revenue bonds for the benefit of commercial and retail facilities. The Court also considered a statute allowing the State to issue general obligation bonds to finance an alcohol fuel development program. The Court struck down both the amendments and the statute as unconstitutional, ruling, among other things, that neither primarily served a public purpose.

The *McLeod* Court stated that revenue bonds for retail and commercial businesses would provide only a "remote or indirect public benefit." Such businesses would not alleviate the pervasive problems of lack of industry and employment, would provide a minuscule number of jobs compared to industrial projects, and would merely result either in the relocation of existing businesses or importation of national chains to compete with existing businesses. *McLeod,* 276 S.C. at 332, 278 S.E.2d at 617. Approving the issuance of revenue bonds for retail and commercial businesses would "permit local governments to effectually promote undertakings to compete in free enterprise with other businesses which do not have the advantage which the Act would give." Id. at 333, 278 S.E.2d. at 617.

In *Anderson, supra,* the city of Spartanburg intended to issue revenue bonds in order to purchase property in blighted areas (through condemnation if necessary), find an interested developer, and lease or sell the property to the developer in the hope that such payments would cover repayment of the city-issued bonds. The Court held that the act, which it described as allowing the city to "join hands" with unknown private developers, did not serve a public purpose because the benefit to the developer would be substantial, while the benefit to the public would be negligible and speculative. The Court also noted the Legislature had not made any findings of public purpose in the act. *Anderson,* 265 S.C. at 159–63, 217 S.E.2d at 46–47.

In response, City argues that *Carll, supra,* is dispositive. City further asserts that the views expressed in *McLeod* and *Anderson* have been implicitly rejected by later cases in which this Court has taken a broader view of public purpose and exhibited greater deference to the legislative determinations regarding public purpose. The public purpose doctrine "is an evolving concept that reflects the changing needs of society." Even if *Carll* is not dispositive, the JEDA loan program in this case serves a public purpose, City asserts.

Revenue bonds such as those that JEDA would issue in this case are payable solely from the revenues of the particular project or enterprise, not from taxpayer funds. Revenue bond debt, as well as general obligation debt incurred by the government and repaid by government funds, may be incurred only for a public purpose. S.C. Const. art. X, § 13(9); *Elliott,* 250 S.C. at 86, 156 S.E.2d. at 427 (holding that Industrial Revenue Bond Act serves a public purpose as required by state constitution); *Feldman & Co. v. City Council of Charleston,* 23 S.C. 57, 62–63 (1885) (holding that a law authorizing taxation for any purpose other than a public purpose is void).

In *Carll,* we rejected several constitutional challenges to the 1983 act creating JEDA. In discussing whether the Act served a public purpose, we explained that

> [a]ll legislative action must serve a public rather than a private purpose. In general, a public purpose has for its objective the promotion of the public health, morals, general welfare, security, prosperity, and contentment of all the inhabitants or residents within a given political division.... It is a fluid concept which changes with time, place, population, economy and countless other circumstances. It is a reflection of the changing needs of society.

Carll, 284 S.C. at 442–43, 327 S.E.2d at 334 (citations omitted).... We held that the JEDA Act served a public purpose because its provisions were reasonably related to the legitimate public goals of economic development and job creation. We observed the Legislature's findings regarding the State's economic development problems were "detailed and comprehensive." Id.

We agree with WDW that *Carll* is not dispositive. *Carll* did not involve any particular bond issue or loan, but was an attack on the facial validity of the act creating JEDA. More importantly, regulations then in existence prohibited JEDA from making government-sponsored loans to retail or commercial businesses. JEDA regulations were amended in 1987 to allow such loans in certain situations. A statutory or regulatory change could transform a previously constitutional loan program into one that violates the public purpose doctrine. Therefore, *Carll* should not be read to foreclose challenges to JEDA programs simply because a given loan does not violate JEDA's statutory or regulatory framework as it exists when the loan is proposed or made.

However, we hold that the JEDA loan program in this case serves a public purpose as required by the constitution. We adhere to the views espoused in *Carll* and *Nichols v. South Carolina Research Authority,* 290 S.C. 415, 351 S.E.2d 155 (1986).

In *Nichols,* we upheld a statute authorizing a state agency to issue revenue bonds in order to provide financial assistance to advanced technology businesses. We overruled *Byrd v. County of Florence,* 281 S.C. 402, 315 S.E.2d 804 (1984), in which we had struck down on public purpose grounds Florence County's proposal to issue general obligation bonds to acquire and develop an industrial park to be used to attract industrial investment. In *Nichols,* we extensively discussed the public purpose doctrine and its inconsistent application in various cases over the years. We explained that

> [t]imes change. The wants and necessities of the people change.... On the one hand, what could not be deemed a public use a century ago may, because of *changed economic and industrial conditions,* be such today.
>
> The consensus of modern legislative and judicial thinking is to broaden the scope of activities which may be classed as involving a public purpose. It reaches perhaps its broadest extent under the view: that *economic welfare* is one of the main concerns of the city, state and the federal governments [sic].
>
> The views we express here reflect the decisions of multiple other jurisdictions which recognize industrial development as a public purpose.
>
> Finally, legislation may subserve a public purpose even though it (1) benefits some more than others and, (2) results in profit to individuals. Legislation does not have to benefit all of the people in order to serve a public purpose. At the same time legislation is not for a private purpose merely because some individual makes a profit as a result of the enactment.

Nichols, 290 S.C. at 425–26, 351 S.E.2d at 161 (emphasis in original) (citations and internal quotes omitted).

We emphasized anew that "[i]t is uniformly held by courts throughout the land that the determination of public purpose is one for the legislative branch.... The question of whether an Act is for a public purpose is primarily one for the Legislature." Id.

We reached a similar conclusion in *Wolper,* decided the year before *Nichols.* In *Wolper,* we upheld the constitutionality of a statute that allows cities to incur debt to revitalize deteriorating areas, with the debt service to be provided from the increased increments of property tax revenue resulting from the redevelopment project. We concluded that elimination of decaying and unhealthy areas within a city directly benefits the public, although private parties within the area also may benefit incidentally. *Wolper,* 287 S.C. at 216, 336 S.E.2d at 875.

Although we overruled *Byrd, supra,* in *Nichols,* we adopted the four-part test from *Byrd* to use in determining whether the public purpose doctrine is violated. "The Court should *first* determine the ultimate goal or benefit to the public intended by the project. *Second,* the Court should analyze whether public or private parties will be the primary beneficiaries. *Third,* the speculative nature of the project must be considered. *Fourth,* the Court must analyze and balance the probability that the public interest will be ultimately served and to what degree." *Nichols,* 290 S.C. at 429, 351 S.E.2d at 163 (emphasis in original).

Accordingly, we apply the *Nichols* test in this case. First, the ultimate benefits to the public are to increase the number of available jobs, improve the appearance of rundown buildings in Sumter's downtown, attract new businesses, and reinvigorate a downtown area that has been classified by the local and federal governments as economically distressed. Second—deferring to the Legislature's determination in establishing the JEDA program—the public will be the primary beneficiary, although the developers certainly will benefit from a more favorable loan rate. Third, the project is speculative, as is any redevelopment effort, but it is not so speculative that it violates the public purpose doctrine. And fourth, the public interest is likely to be served to a substantial degree through the creation of jobs, the reinvigoration of the downtown area, and benefits, both tangible and intangible, that should result from that reinvigoration.

We conclude that our opinion in *Nichols* implicitly overruled *McLeod*'s holding that revenue bonds may not be issued on behalf of retail or commercial businesses. We now take a broader view of the public purpose doctrine and give substantial weight to legislative determinations of the issue.

We find *Anderson, supra,* distinguishable from the present case. The Legislature did not make specific findings regarding the public purpose of the Act at issue in *Anderson,* while the Legislature has made such findings in the JEDA Act. The power of eminent domain was involved in *Anderson,* but not in this case. The city would have played a major role in the revitalization process in *Anderson,* leading the Court to conclude that the "Act undertakes to permit the city to effectually promote business undertakings to compete in free enterprise with other businesses which do not have the advantage which the Act would give. We think it a fair conclusion to say that benefit to the developer or entrepreneur, would be substantial, and the benefit to the public would be negligible and speculative." *Anderson,* 265 S.C. at 163, 217 S.E.2d at 47. In contrast, the role of City and JEDA in this case is more limited in that neither is actively promoting business undertakings to compete in free enterprise with other local businesses.

CONCLUSION

We affirm the master's ruling that the JEDA loan program serves a public purpose as required by the state constitution. We overrule *McLeod,* 276 S.C. 323, 278 S.E.2d 612, to the extent it conflicts with the views expressed in *Carll, supra, Nichols, supra,* and this opinion. We find *Anderson,* 265 S.C. 153, 217 S.E.2d 43, distinguishable from this case.

AFFIRMED.

CLEAN v. State of Washington

928 P.2d 1054 (Wash. 1996).

■ ALEXANDER, JUSTICE.

We granted review of an order of the Thurston County Superior Court dismissing two separate challenges to an act of the Legislature that provides a means of financing the construction of a publicly owned major league baseball stadium in King County. One of the challenges to the measure is by Frank Ruano and John Scannell (jointly referred to as Ruano). The other is by Jordan Brower and a non-profit corporation called CLEAN, Citizens for Leaders with Ethics and Accountability Now (jointly referred to as CLEAN). CLEAN contends that the aforementioned act violates several provisions of Washington's constitution. Specifically, it contends that the act: (1) funds a private project contrary to Wash. Const. art. VII, § 1; (2) constitutes a gift or lending of the State's credit to a private enterprise, thereby violating Wash. Const. art. VIII, §§ 5, 7; (3) invests public funds in a private enterprise in violation of Wash. Const. art. VIII, § 7; and (4) violates Wash. Const. art. II, § 28 as "special" as opposed to "general" legislation. CLEAN and Ruano both assert that what they claim is the act's invalid emergency clause wrongly circumvents the people's right to referendum as provided by Wash. Const. art. II, § 1 (amend. 72). We conclude that the act survives all of these challenges and, consequently, affirm the trial court's order dismissing both lawsuits.

The Seattle Mariners, one of 28 major league baseball clubs, has been playing its home games in Seattle's domed stadium, the Kingdome, since 1977 when it first became a major league team. In recent years, the management of the Mariners has, on several occasions, expressed concern about the viability of the Kingdome as a facility for major league baseball. On these occasions, it indicated that in order for the Mariners to achieve financial stability and to become financially competitive with other major league baseball clubs, the Mariners needed a state of the art outdoor baseball facility as its home field.

In 1995, in an apparent effort to address the problem identified by the Mariners and to enhance the survival of major league baseball in the Seattle area, the Washington State Legislature adopted legislation that authorized King County to impose, subject to voter approval, a 0.1 percent addition to the sales and use taxes imposed in King County. Laws of 1995, 1st Spec. Sess., ch. 14, §§ 6, 7. The money obtained from such a tax increase was to be used by the county to finance the construction of a new county owned major league baseball stadium. Following passage of that legislation, the King County Council sought approval by King County's voters of an increase in the sales and use taxes imposed in King County. By a narrow margin, the proposed tax increase was rejected.

Following defeat of the proposed tax increase, John Ellis, the Mariners' Chief Executive Officer, sent a letter to King County Executive, Gary Locke, in which he stated that without a new stadium, the Mariners would "offer the team for sale" after October 30. Clerk's Papers at 20, Appellants' Am. Br. at 69.

On October 11, 1995, Governor Mike Lowry called the Legislature into special session solely for "the purpose of addressing matters related to stadium financing." Clerk's Papers at 146. At that session the Legislature considered Engrossed House Bill 2115, a bill sponsored by Representatives Van Leuven and Appelwick. This measure was designed to ensure the survival of major league baseball in King County. On the day following Governor Lowry's call for a special session, public hearings on the proposal were conducted in both the Trade and Economic Development Committee of the House of Representatives and the Ways and Means Committee of the Senate. Governor Lowry testified in support of the bill at both hearings. In addition, numerous citizens testified for and against the measure. Among those testifying in support of EHB 2115 were several Seattle business persons who indicated that the presence of the Seattle Mariners was essential to the success of their businesses, and that departure of the team would adversely affect them. Robbie Stern, Special Assistant to the President of the Washington State Labor Council, expanded on the view of the business persons, stressing the broader impact of the Mariners on the state's economy, saying, "Here is an opportunity to use tax money to create family wage jobs and some service jobs that have health care and pension benefits; it's a good use of economic development funds." Senate Ways and Means Committee hearing tape 2 (Senate) (Oct. 12, 1995). Governor Lowry echoed these themes in his testimony before the committee of the House of Representatives, stating that the presence of the Mariners was of economic benefit to the entire state.

The Governor also stressed what he described as a "true family value question" indicating that: "Everywhere I've gone in the State, every kid has come up [to me] and said 'save baseball.' " House Trade and Economic Development Committee meeting (House) tape 1 (Oct. 12, 1995). Other witnesses spoke to what they opined was the importance of major league baseball to the fabric of the community. For example, Vincent "New York Vinnie" Richichi, a Seattle sports radio talk show host, described the value of the Mariners to the community in this way: "We also have something that's an intangible here, that's our kids and a way of life. Baseball has something to do with all of that. It's a commerce for some people, it's a part of culture for some people, and for others it's a way of life." House tape 1 (Oct. 12, 1995)....

The special session concluded on October 17, with the Legislature adopting EHB 2115 (hereinafter referred to as the Stadium Act), by a vote of 66 to 24 in the House of Representatives and 25 to 16 in the Senate. Laws of 1995, 3rd Spec. Sess., ch. 1. The Stadium Act authorized the creation of a public facilities district (District) in "a county with a population of one million or more," and empowered it to "acquire, construct, own, remodel, maintain, equip, reequip, repair, and operate a baseball stadium[.]" Laws of 1995, 3rd Spec. Sess., ch. 1, §§ 201(1) at 4, 201(4)(b) at 5. The act also provided that three members of the governing board of the District would be appointed by the Governor with the remaining members appointed by the county executive, subject to ratification by the county legislative authority. Laws of 1995, 3rd Spec. Sess., ch. 1, § 302, at 10.

Significantly, the Stadium Act provided a means by which King County and the State of Washington could generate additional revenues to be allotted to the District in order to defray the major portion of the costs of constructing the new baseball stadium. The act provided that moneys collected under it may only be used to pay on the bonds issued to construct the stadium. Laws of 1995, 3rd Spec. Sess., ch. 1, §§ 101(3) at 2, 103(3) at 3, 105(5) at 4, 201(3) at 5, 203(3)(a) at 9. It also stated that the "taxes authorized [by the act] shall not be collected after June 30, 1997" unless a major league baseball team has agreed to "[c]ontribute forty-five million dollars toward the reasonably necessary preconstruction costs" of the stadium and has contracted to "[p]lay at least ninety percent of its home games in the stadium for a period of time not shorter than the term of the bonds issued to finance the initial construction of the stadium." Laws of 1995, 3rd Spec. Sess., ch. 1, § 201(4)(a), (b) at 5. The Stadium Act also required the major league tenant to share a portion of any profits generated by the baseball club from the operation of the franchise for a period equal to the term of the bonds issued to finance construction of the stadium. Under this provision, shared profits were to be defined by an agreement between the stadium tenant and the District and these profits were to be used to help retire the bonds and thereafter were to go directly to the District. While the Stadium Act provided that the District was to consult with the management of the Mariners on matters such as the design, location, specifications, and budget for the baseball stadium, the ultimate decision making authority as to those issues resided with the District. Laws of 1995, 3rd Spec. Sess., ch. 1, § 301(1)–(5).

Governor Lowry signed the act into law within hours of its approval by both houses of the Legislature....

As noted above, CLEAN contends that the Stadium Act is violative of article VII, section 1 of the Washington Constitution, a provision that all taxes "shall be levied and collected for public purposes only." CLEAN asserts that public development of a baseball stadium as a home field for the Seattle Mariners Baseball Club does not serve a public purpose, but rather serves only the interests of the Seattle Mariners Baseball Club, a private for-profit business.

CLEAN correctly observes that public funds cannot be used to benefit private interests when the public interest is not primarily being served. Public expenditures must, therefore, further public purposes. "An expenditure is for a public purpose when it confers a benefit of reasonably general character to a significant part of the public." In re Marriage of Johnson, 96 Wash.2d 255, 258, 634 P.2d 877 (1981). "Where it is debatable as to whether or not an expenditure is for a public purpose, we will defer to the judgment of the legislature." Anderson v. O'Brien, 84 Wash.2d 64, 70, 524 P.2d 390 (1974).

Although no Washington case has decided whether or not a public purpose is served when the State or one of its subdivisions constructs a stadium to be leased to a professional sports franchise for use as its home field, the overwhelming majority of courts from other jurisdictions confronting this issue have determined that construction of a publicly owned stadium to be leased to professional sports teams serves a public purpose. See, e.g., Martin v. City of Philadelphia, 420 Pa. 14, 215 A.2d 894, 896 (1966) ("A sports stadium is for the recreation of the public and is hence for a public purpose."); Kelly v. Marylanders for Sports Sanity, Inc., 310 Md. 437, 530 A.2d 245, 257 (1987) ("the State's authorization for the financial support of stadium facilities [including a baseball stadium at the Camden Yards site in Baltimore] for professional sports in furtherance of public recreational activities is of long standing"); Rice v. Ashcroft, 831 S.W.2d 206, 210 (Mo. App. 1991) ("[a]ny benefits to private persons ... are incidental and do not take away from the primary purpose of legislation—to increase convention and sports activity in the St. Louis City–County area"); Libertarian Party v. State, 199 Wis.2d 790, 546 N.W.2d 424, 434 (1996) ("the fact that a private entity such as the [Milwaukee] Brewers will benefit from the Stadium Act does not destroy the predominant public purpose of this act").

On the other hand, public funding for facilities for professional sports teams has been rejected in at least two jurisdictions. In Brandes v. City of Deerfield Beach, 186 So.2d 6 (Fla. 1966), the Florida Supreme Court ruled that construction of a spring training facility for the Pittsburgh Pirates Baseball Club did not survive a challenge that it violated a provision in the Florida Constitution allowing taxes to be imposed only for "municipal purposes, and for no other purposes." Fla. Const. art. VII, § 9 n. 39 (West 1995). In reaching its decision, the court stated that " 'municipal purposes' means ... a purpose intended to embrace some of the functions of the governmental agency." *Brandes*, 186 So.2d at 12.

Similarly, in Opinion of the Justices, 356 Mass. 775, 250 N.E.2d 547 (1969), the Supreme Judicial Court of Massachusetts was called upon to issue an advisory opinion as to the constitutionality of a proposal that was then pending in the Massachusetts Legislature. The proposal, if passed, would have provided a means for public financing of the construction of a general purpose sports stadium in that state. Although the Massachusetts court noted that a public purpose could, in certain instances, be served by developing a professional sports stadium, it concluded that it was "unable to advise that the stadium complex and the arena will be for a public purpose." Opinion of the Justices, 250 N.E.2d at 560. It did so, however, because it concluded that the standards governing user fees and availability of the proposed facility were not adequate.

Although we are somewhat reluctant to rely too heavily on the interpretation that the highest court of another state places on a provision in its state constitution, particularly when the provision is not identical to the pertinent provision of our constitution, we are satisfied that the cases from the jurisdictions which have held that development of a publicly owned sports stadium serves a public purpose are instructive. Significant to our determination is that Washington's standard for determining public purpose, like Pennsylvania's, Maryland's, Wisconsin's and Missouri's, is broad. As we have noted, public expenditures in Washington need only confer a benefit of reasonably general character to a significant part of the public in order to survive a challenge that they do not serve a public purpose.

The above cited cases from Florida and Massachusetts, while on the surface appearing to provide solace to CLEAN, are not fundamentally inconsistent with the cases from the other jurisdictions. The Massachusetts court, in Opinion of the Justices, did not reject the argument that development of a public stadium as a home for professional sports teams serves a public purpose. The opinion, rather, turned on other grounds. In the *Brandes* case, the Florida Supreme Court concluded only that "municipal purposes" were not served by constructing a spring training facility that was to be leased to a major league team. In reaching its decision, the court emphasized that the primary purpose of the proposed facility was to provide a "training" facility for a single team and that opportunities for spectators were only incidental. It is not surprising, therefore, that the Florida court concluded that this purpose did not fall within the narrow category of a function of the governmental agency. Whether that court would have reached the same conclusion about the construction of a stadium for regular and post season major league baseball games remains an open question. Significantly, at least one other court has held that making the distinction between a spring training facility and a stadium serving as a home field for regular and post season games of a professional team is important in determining whether construction of a sports stadium serves a public purpose. See Lifteau v. Metropolitan Sports Facilities Comm'n, 270 N.W.2d 749, 753 n. 5 (Minn. 1978) (in which the court approved public construction of a professional sports stadium holding that "[t]he public interest in spring training games of a single team is obviously less than the public interest in a multi-purpose stadium to be used for professional (regular season and post season) and nonprofessional athletic events and nonathletic events").

We are satisfied, after reviewing the record here, that construction of a major league baseball stadium in King County confers a benefit of reasonably general character to a significant part of the public in King County, as well as other persons in the region, to survive a challenge that it is violative of article VII, section 1 of the Washington Constitution. In reaching this conclusion, we are not unmindful of the fact that the Seattle Mariners may also reap benefits as the principal tenant of the publicly owned stadium that will be built as a consequence of the passage of the Stadium Act. That fact is not fatal to the act, however, as long as a public purpose is being served. The fact that private ends are incidentally advanced is immaterial to determining whether legislation furthers a public purpose. United States v. Town of North Bonneville, 94 Wash.2d 827, 834, 621 P.2d 127 (1980).

Our conclusion that the Stadium Act does not run afoul of article VII, section 1 recognizes, as have the majority of courts around the nation, that public provision of a venue for professional sports franchises serves a public purpose in that the presence in a community of a professional sports franchise provides jobs, recreation for citizens, and promotes economic development and tourism. Having said that, we are aware that an argument can and has been made that few opportunities for recreation and little positive economic impact flow to a community from the presence of a major league baseball team. That argument merely underscores the fact that the degree to which the economy and quality of life of King County and the surrounding area will be enhanced by the development of a major league stadium to house the Seattle Mariners is debatable. The disagreement that underlies that debate, however, is best resolved by the people's elected representatives in the Legislature. In our judgment, they are in a superior position to evaluate the extent to which a public purpose is served by the realization of the perceived benefits. In deciding this question, we believe it was appropriate for the Legislature to consider that the concept of what is public purpose is not a static concept. Rather, it is a concept that must necessarily evolve and change to meet changing public attitudes. See *Bonneville*, 94 Wash.2d at 833, 621 P.2d 127. The Legislature with its staff and committees is the branch of government better suited to monitor and assess contemporary attitudes than are the courts.

CLEAN also asserts that the Stadium Act violates Wash. Const. art. VIII, §§ 5 and 7. It alleges, in that regard, that development of a major league stadium constitutes a gift or a loan of the State's credit in aid of a private business, the Seattle Mariners. The aforementioned constitutional provisions are as follows: "The credit of the state shall not, in any manner be given or loaned to, or in aid of, any individual, association, company or corporation." Wash. Const. art. VIII, § 5.

> No county, city, town or other municipal corporation shall hereafter give any money, or property, or loan its money, or credit to or in aid of any individual, association, company or corporation, except for the necessary support of the poor and infirm, or become directly or indirectly the owner of any stock in or bonds of any association, company or corporation.

Wash. Const. art. VIII, § 7. Although these two provisions are worded slightly differently, this court has held that they have identical meaning, as well as the same prohibitions and exceptions. "The manifest purpose of these provisions ... is to prevent state funds from being used to benefit private interests where the public interest is not primarily served." Japan Line, Ltd. v. McCaffree, 88 Wash.2d 93, 98, 558 P.2d 211 (1977).

A two-pronged analysis is employed to determine whether a gift of state funds has occurred. First, the court asks if the funds are being expended to carry out a fundamental purpose of the government? If the answer to that question is yes, then no gift of public funds has been made. The second prong comes into play only when the expenditures are held to not serve fundamental purposes of government. The court then focuses on the consideration received by the public for the expenditure of public funds and the donative intent of the appropriating body in order to determine whether or not a gift has occurred.... Although we have concluded above that a public purpose is served by construction of a baseball stadium, it cannot be seriously contended that the development of a baseball stadium for a major league team is a "fundamental purpose" of state government. Our inquiry must concentrate, therefore, on donative intent and consideration.

CLEAN primarily relies on Johns v. Wadsworth, 80 Wash. 352, 141 P. 892 (1914) as support for its argument that construction of a publicly funded baseball stadium to be leased to the Seattle Mariners amounts to an unconstitutional gift of public funds. In *Johns*, we held that a Pierce County ordinance appropriating money to a private association to enable it to put on the Western Washington Fair violated Wash. Const. art. VIII, § 7, notwithstanding the fact that the appropriation was "to a private corporation organized for a worthy purpose, educational in its nature." *Johns*, 80 Wash. at 355, 141 P. 892.

CLEAN's attempt to equate *Johns* to the instant case is not persuasive. The expenditure of public money that was scrutinized in that case went directly to a private fair association, the county maintaining no direct control over how the money was to be spent. Furthermore, although any building that was erected with the appropriated funds was to become the property of the county, there was no requirement in the ordinance that any of the appropriated money be devoted to the construction of buildings. Here, on the other hand, a stadium must be built with the public funds generated by the Stadium Act, and it will be owned and managed by the District, a public entity. Furthermore, any tenant, including the Mariners, will be required to pay reasonable rent to the District for the privilege of conducting its activities in the stadium. In our judgment, a plain reading of the Stadium Act reveals no intent by the Legislature to donate public funds to the Seattle Mariners....

In sum, we are satisfied that construction of a baseball stadium with a view to leasing it to a major league team does not amount to a gift of state funds nor a lending of the State's credit. If, as amicus Citizens For More Important Things suggests, the District should enter into an agreement with the Mariners that would permit the ball club to play its games in the stadium for only nominal rent, then the constitutional prohibitions against making a gift of state funds might be implicated. Such a circumstance is not now apparent and we will not speculate about the future. In the unlikely event that this prediction should come true, the issue can then be raised in an appropriate manner.

[Discussion of other challenges to the stadium financing plan are omitted.—EDS.]

NOTES

1. *Judicial Deference to Legislative Findings.* Note that the court in *WDW Properties* concludes that the judiciary should defer to the legislature on the question of whether a proposed project satisfies a public purpose. Then why have a public purpose requirement at all? Why not assume that elected officials who misperceive how their constituents want public revenues spent will be voted out of office and rely on statutes prohibiting conflicts of interest and graft to deter inappropriate expenditures?

Consider the following justification: Those who will benefit from the expenditure have a sufficiently intense interest to make it worth their while to seek support from officials for their projects. Although the projects may adversely affect others in the locality, e.g., by making bond issues for general local purposes more expensive or by placing competitors of the project's owners at a financial disadvantage, no one current resident will incur sufficient costs to justify the investment of time and money necessary to lobby against the project. Thus, a locality will be under substantial pressure to proceed with a special-interest project and under little competing pressure to prevent it. Judicial intervention is thus necessary to reduce the likelihood that spending decisions will favor a dominant interest group. Does this argument explain the decisions in *WDW Properties* and *CLEAN*?

How competent are courts to make the inquiries that would be required to determine that one group had dominated the political debate about a proposed bond issue? Can courts investigate the process by which the legislation was enacted? Would it be enough to invalidate the program that there are tendencies for one subgroup of the locality to capture the decisionmaking process, even if no concrete evidence of capture existed? See, e.g., Einer R. Elhauge, Does Interest Group Theory Justify More Intrusive Judicial Review?, 101 Yale L.J. 31 (1991); Daniel A. Farber & Philip P. Frickey, The Jurisprudence of Public Choice, 65 Tex. L. Rev. 874 (1987); Hans Linde, Due Process of Lawmaking, 55 Neb. L. Rev. 197 (1976).

If you are concerned that broad interpretation of "public purpose" could lead to an increase in political "pork," consider City of Guymon v. Butler, 92 P.3d 80 (Okla. 2004). The city had established a tax increment district to finance construction of a privately owned pork processing facility. A county that was obligated under the financing plan to make payments to the city from ad valorem property taxes withheld funds on the ground that the project served no public purpose. The court, however, concluded that the project "served public purposes by increasing the tax base, bringing new jobs to the City of Guymon and Texas County, elevating the median family income, bringing more children into the school district, and stimulating additional businesses within the Guymon Industrial Park."

2. *Revenue Bonds and Public Purpose.* The court in *WDW Properties* also notes that the bonds that will be issued to subsidize commercial development will be paid from revenues generated by operation of the financed enterprises, "not from taxpayer funds." Should satisfaction of the public purpose test be measured by the same standard regardless of whether the challenged projects are to be financed with general obligation bonds or with revenue bonds? If the function of the test is to protect the public treasury, and if—as in the case of revenue bonds—the only funds available for repayment of the bonds are revenues generated by the operation of the project financed with bond proceeds, then why should the court care about the object of the project? See Anderson v. Baehr, 217 S.E.2d 43 (S.C. 1975); Uhls v. State ex rel. City of Cheyenne, 429 P.2d 74 (Wyo. 1967).

Perhaps it would be appropriate to apply a public purpose doctrine even to activities that do not implicate the public treasury if the doctrine is intended to limit the scope of governmental activity. At an early part of the course, it was suggested that local government involvement was appropriate to cure market failures. Does it follow that local government activity is inappropriate where markets are *operating successfully*? For instance, would the doctrine properly be used to prevent a locality from opening a governmentally owned grocery store or factory where privately owned businesses of the same sort already existed? What about using the doctrine to prohibit municipal tax subsidies to attract a branch of a national bookstore chain to a community that is already served by numerous independent bookstores?

This approach to public purpose assumes that there exist separate and distinct spheres of activity for public and private entities. Government may enter the first, but not the second. For explicit judicial statements of this approach, see McClelland v. Mayor of Wilmington, 159 A.2d 596 (Del. Ch. 1960); State ex rel. Beck v. City of York, 82 N.W.2d 269 (Neb. 1957). The highwater mark of this position can be found in Village of Moyie Springs v. Aurora Mfg. Co., 353 P.2d 767, 775 (Idaho 1960). In that case, the Idaho Supreme Court rejected a proposal for a municipality to acquire industrial property that would be leased to a private firm. The purpose of the plan was to attract industry and thereby increase employment in the area. The court concluded:

> If the state-favored industries were successfully managed, private enterprise would of necessity be forced out, and the state, through its municipalities, would increasingly become involved in promoting, sponsoring, regulating and controlling private business, and our free private enterprise economy would be replaced by Socialism. The constitutions of both state and nation were founded under a capitalistic private enterprise economy and were designed to protect and foster private property and private initiative. Socialism is as foreign to our constitutional, political and economic system as our private enterprise system is to the socialist system of Russia.

Does this division of the public and private seem appropriate? Why shouldn't a state permit a locality to define itself as allowing governmental intervention in working markets and therefore, for example, to operate a city-owned supermarket that competes with private supermarkets? See, e.g., Siegel v. City of Branson, 952 S.W.2d 294 (Mo. App. 1997), in which the court upheld the city's authority to operate a campground, even though it competed with privately operated campgrounds.

3. *Financing Commercial Activities with Business Incentives*. The use of financial incentives to attract business and industry to a locality remains controversial for reasons beyond the involvement of government in market transactions. We explore this issue below in Section G of this Chapter. For the moment, consider two effects that might lead one to question whether localities should provide tax breaks or make tax-exempt financing available to firms that promise to locate within a municipality's boundaries. The first is the question of competitive advantage raised in *WDW Properties*. Firms within the municipality that did not receive tax-exempt financing will have to compete with new firms that did receive it. The former firms may have incurred debt at non-subsidized, commercial rates. See, e.g., Mayor and Members of City Council v. Industrial Dev. Auth. of Rockbridge County, 275 S.E.2d 888 (Va. 1981). Moreover, the firms that receive municipal inducements to locate, such as subsidized financing, tend to be national chains that can add to the job base of the subsidizing municipality. See, e.g., Council of the City of New Orleans v. All Taxpayers, Property Owners, et al., 841 So.2d 72 (La. App. 2003) (industrial development bonds issued to finance Wal–Mart store); State ex rel. Brown v. City of Warr Acres, 946 P.2d 1140 (Okla. 1997) (financial incentives to attract Wal–Mart store). These chains may displace locally owned stores that do not have the same access as chain stores to national supply networks or advertising. Is it a full response that national chains are more efficient? That the local legislature apparently favored the national chain over the local store? That the national chain increases employment in the locality? Do established, local firms that face competition from subsidized newcomers have any recourse to avoid "unfair" competition? One might think, for instance, that established firms have existing contacts with political officials and certainly have an incentive to make their concerns known to those officials when subsidies for potential competitors are proposed. Assume that local legislators are willing to offer subsidies to new firms, notwithstanding the strident opposition of existing firms. Should legislative approval be sufficient to overcome any argument that subsidies for new commercial or retail firms fail to provide sufficient jobs or other economic benefits to the locality at large to constitute a public purpose?

Second, some commentators suggest that business incentives ultimately impose more social costs than benefits, especially where multiple localities are competing for the same business. The locality that "wins" the competition may ultimately promise more in subsidies than the economic benefits generated by the firm it attracts. Even if the locality that "wins" the business gains, other localities may lose. If one locality lures a firm from another locality, the net effect for the firm might be positive (why else would the firm make the transition?), but the net effect for the economy may not be. The locality from which the firm migrated might lose more economically than the new locality gained, especially if the firm was a major employer in its initial location. And if all localities are engaged in the practice of luring firms from each other, then one would imagine that even a locality that sometimes attracts a firm will also occasionally lose a firm to another locality. Thus, interlocal competition looks like a classic prisoner's dilemma in which each player would do better if the competition did not occur at all. See Peter D. Enrich, Saving the States from Themselves: Commerce Clause Constrains on State Tax Incentives for Business, 110 Harv. L. Rev. 377 (1996); Walter Hellerstein & Dan Coenen, Commerce Clause Restraints on State Business Development Incentives, 81 Cornell L. Rev. 789 (1996). Are there reasons to believe that localities will successfully compete for firms only if the locality as well as the firm will reap net benefits from attracting the firm? See Clayton P. Gillette, Business Incentives, Interstate Competition, and the Commerce Clause, 82 Minn. L. Rev. 447 (1997).

4. *Prohibitions on Lending of Credit.* The plaintiffs in *CLEAN* challenged the Stadium Act under the state's constitutional provision prohibiting the lending of credit by the state or its political subdivisions, as well as under the public purpose doctrine. The constitutions of a majority of states contain similar provisions that preclude governmental involvement in private ventures by prohibiting gifts or loans of credit to individuals, associations, or corporations. Like public purpose clauses, these provisions grew out of antipathy to the use of governmental credit to guarantee the success of private ventures in the late nineteenth century. Prior to that time, state and local governments had used their credit to raise capital for industries, particularly railroads, by guaranteeing obligations of these enterprises, or by incurring their own debt and donating the proceeds to private enterprises, or by using bond proceeds to purchase stock in the firm that was to construct the railroad or other improvement. When, as was all too often the case, the promised railroad or improvement never materialized, taxpayers of the issuing jurisdiction were faced with a financial obligation and no offsetting benefit to show for it. See Charles Fairman, History of the Supreme Court of the United States, Reconstruction and Reunion: 1864–1888, at 918–1116 (1971).

Notwithstanding the popularity of these prohibitions, their interpretation and details vary from state to state. Some state constitutions expressly permit electoral or legislative override of the prohibition. See Del. Const. art. VIII, 4; Tenn. Const. art. 2, § 29. Even in the absence of express exceptions, however, courts have been imaginative in avoiding the absolute language of the prohibition. Most jurisdictions generally do not consider revenue bonds to constitute a gift or loan of credit since they are not repayable from the public treasury. See State v. Inland Protection Financing Corp., 699 So.2d 1352 (Fla. 1997); Denver Urban Renewal Authority v. Byrne, 618 P.2d 1374 (Colo. 1980). But see Gaylord v. Beckett, 144 N.W.2d 460 (Mich. 1966).

The court in *CLEAN* holds that the lending of credit prohibition is irrelevant if the underlying project serves a "fundamental purpose." The Oklahoma Supreme Court concluded that the use of bond proceeds to assist industrial plants located in the state did not violate the lending of credit prohibition because the beneficiary would be conferring benefits on the state in the form of retained jobs, new jobs, and increased business activity in the state. See In re Oklahoma Development Finance Authority, 89 P.3d 1075 (Okla. 2004). Other courts have similarly found that there is no prohibition on lending credit if the project satisfies a public purpose. See, e.g., Tosto v. Pennsylvania Nursing Home Loan Agency, 331 A.2d 198 (Pa. 1975). Presumably, any governmental activity must serve a public purpose. Thus, even a permitted loan of credit would have to satisfy that criterion. Wouldn't prohibitions on loans of credit be superfluous if they were applicable only where the loan failed to satisfy a public purpose? If both provisions are found in the state constitution, perhaps the prohibition on lending credit should be seen as restricting governmental exposure even where a public purpose is satisfied. See Comment, State Constitutional Provisions Prohibiting the Loaning of Credit to Private Enterprise—A Suggested Analysis, 41 U. Colo. L. Rev. 1135 (1969). For a detailed discussion of the prohibition and its application, see Robert S. Amdursky and Clayton P. Gillette, Municipal Debt Finance Law: Theory and Practice § 3.7 (1992).

Not every extension of credit by a governmental entity falls within the constitutional prohibition. Given that the provision is intended to guard the public treasury, courts have generally analyzed the issue in terms of the treasury's exposure to pay another's debt. Thus, a jurisdiction will violate the prohibition if it acts as guarantor for another. See, e.g., State ex rel. Thomson v. Giessel, 72 N.W.2d 577 (Wis. 1955). But the clause has been found not to be implicated where the lender receives contemporaneous consideration for the conveyance of property or credit, Cremer v. Peoria Housing Authority, 78 N.E.2d 276 (Ill. 1948), or where the alleged lender of credit is not legally obligated to pay the debt, as in the case of revenue bonds. See, e.g., Brashier v. South Carolina Dept. of Transportation, 490 S.E.2d 8 (S.C. 1997).

5. *The Dynamism of Public Purpose.* As the court in *CLEAN* notes, interpretation of the public purpose doctrine has not been static. Today, local government activities upheld under the doctrine include financing of hotels, Purvis v. City of Little Rock, 667 S.W.2d 936 (Ark. 1984); alternative energy sources, Minnesota Energy and Economic Development Authority v. Printy, 351 N.W.2d 319 (Minn. 1984); and the purchase of stock in a bank, Opinion of the Justices, 358 A.2d 705 (Del. 1976). In a heroic move, however, the Georgia Supreme Court concluded that construction of a public golf course with the proceeds of revenue bonds did not satisfy the "public purpose of developing trade, commerce, and industry." Haney v. Development Authority of Bremen, 519 S.E.2d 665 (Ga. 1999).[ ]

The dynamic nature of public purpose can be seen in a series of cases from one jurisdiction (Massachusetts) addressing the public financing of residential housing. In 1872, after a conflagration destroyed a large section of Boston, the Massachusetts legislature authorized the city to issue $20 million in bonds and lend the proceeds to owners of buildings destroyed in the fire. On a challenge to the validity of the legislation, the Supreme

Judicial Court, in the case of Lowell v. Boston, 111 Mass. 454 (1873), was adamant and unanimous: "The promotion of the interest of individuals, either in respect of property or business, although it may result incidentally in the advancement of the public welfare, is, in its essential character, a private and not a public object." 111 Mass. at 461. The fact that public money, ultimately repayable from taxation, was made available directly to private mortgagors was conclusive. That the cumulative individual benefits would be significant was insufficient to create an inference of any "public" benefit. Relying upon the decision in *Lowell*, the court in Opinion of the Justices, 211 Mass. 624, 98 N.E. 611 (1912), opined that a bill to create a state commission to purchase land and construct homes for "mechanics, laborers or other wage-earners" and to ease congestion in housing would not constitute a public use. The same court subsequently invalidated a bill to establish a public corporation that would insure private lending institutions against loss from defaults on home mortgages, and lend funds directly to the mortgagors. See Opinion of the Justices, 291 Mass. 567, 195 N.E. 897 (1935).

A significant change in the court's analysis of state participation in housing occurred when the court upheld the constitutionality of the state housing authority law in Allydonn Realty Corp. v. Holyoke Housing Authority, 304 Mass. 288, 23 N.E.2d 665 (1939). Under this state law, local housing authorities were empowered to finance the construction of low-rent housing as a means of eliminating slum areas. In *Allydonn*, the court looked past the private benefit that would accrue to builders and tenants of the projects and seized on the purported social benefit of eradicating slums. The court found that the objective of slum clearance provided a means of distinguishing its prior cases on public housing assistance. However, given that the putative beneficiaries resembled those of previously rejected programs, it is clear that the court had simply changed its mind in a post-Depression atmosphere that made governmental intervention in the housing market both acceptable and necessary.

The court's decisions following *Allydonn* continued to find public purpose in local housing legislation: A law enabling housing authorities to displace persons from a "substandard area" was approved, Stockus v. Boston Housing Authority, 304 Mass. 507, 24 N.E.2d 333 (1939); public purpose was found sufficiently broad to permit the use of bond proceeds to acquire land and construct dwellings for rental or sale to veterans at lowered prices, Opinion of the Justices, 321 Mass. 766, 73 N.E.2d 886 (1947); and the doctrine expanded to permit housing for "elderly persons of low income" even though the program would not eliminate slums or unsafe or unsanitary dwellings, Opinion of the Justices, 331 Mass. 771, 120 N.E.2d 198 (1954).

Notwithstanding the expansion of the public purpose doctrine to include some government involvement in the funding of housing, the court maintained restrictions on aid to those who could not otherwise afford sanitary dwellings. Thus, in 1966, the court opined that a bill to create a mortgage authority that would issue tax-exempt bonds to provide low-interest loans for construction of low-and moderate-income housing would fail to satisfy a public purpose. Opinion of the Justices, 351 Mass. 716, 219 N.E.2d 18 (1966). A distinction between families of moderate means and those who lived in "slums" appeared to be determinative. Nevertheless, three years later, in Massachusetts Housing Finance Agency v. New England Merchants National Bank, 356 Mass. 202, 249 N.E.2d 599 (1969), the court, less concerned with the "economic standing of the beneficiaries" and more with limiting its role as the ultimate arbiter of governmental activity, approved a similar program. Because the legislature could have rationally believed the project would be socially beneficial, the court found that a public purpose was satisfied.

Finally, in Massachusetts Home Mortgage Finance Agency v. New England Merchants National Bank, 376 Mass. 669, 382 N.E.2d 1084 (1978), the court found—without any suggestion of infidelity to *Lowell*—that a program financed with state authority for making loans to lenders who re-loaned the proceeds to mortgagors of single-family homes would satisfy a public purpose. Although the mortgagors were almost certain to be of moderate means and it was doubtful any slum clearance would be effected, the court again deferred to the legislative judgment.

One might assume from this history that any dynamism in the public purpose doctrine is one-directional, that is, the array of activities that serve public purposes has continuously expanded. See, e.g., Ullrich v. Board of County Commissioners, 676 P.2d 127, 133 (Kan. 1984). Conceptions of the proper scope of governmental competence, and of relationships between government and business have undergone contraction as well as expansion, however. In the Ante–Bellum period, for instance, state and local governments committed significant resources to enterprises that helped to develop local economies. The form of these commitments ranged from grants of funds, lands, licenses, or monopoly rights to private enterprises all the way to government operation of enterprises (such as liquor sales and the operation of banks) that could also have been conducted (and today are primarily conducted) by private firms. Even as government withdrew from direct involvement in these activities, it retained a regulatory role. But when private enterprises proved incapable of maintaining public facilities, such as in the operation of bridges or transportation networks, state or local governments took them over. As urban needs expanded, government operation of utilities previously within the private domain, such as waterworks, increased in scope and frequency. These changing needs, and government reactions to them, suggested the difficulty of drawing boundary lines between public and private. The historians Oscar and Mary Handlin reveal that the issue was troublesome in the mid–19th century:

> Bridges and waterworks, the flats, and roads fell directly into the province of government when the simple passage of regulatory laws did not achieve a balance of contending interests. Though the transition often seemed acceptable to all concerned, it was shadowed with doubts about where the Commonwealth would find limits to its activity. To draw a stalwart line of principle was difficult or impossible. If the agricultural college and grammar schools were public, why not universities and academies; if the sale of liquor, why not of

> bread? In 1851 Josiah Quincy, a member of the Athenaeum, stated categorically, "Our government, from its nature, does not comprise within its cares" the support of libraries. But not long before, that society had asked financial aid of the city of Boston, and within the decade a rival municipal institution was in active operation.
>
> If it was difficult to draw the line with reference to libraries or schools, how much more so with reference to economic activities close to the purses of the citizenry? If bridges and roads were "fit for the action of government," would anyone "be so hardy as to attempt to make a distinction between . . . a bridge and a railroad?" Indeed, Massachusetts retained the right to purchase all lines after twenty years, and regulation often reflected an intention to do so. But if the state by design undertook such enterprises, how would it answer the sponsors of a government-owned mine who pointed out: "Not an argument can be produced in favor of constructing Canals and Rail Roads for the public good, at the public expense, which is not equally applicable to the object of developing the minerals of the country, at the expense of the government, and especially that of Coal."
>
> As yet these were questions, not threats. Businessmen were uneasy lest the alternative of free government operation nibble away the limited security from political interference. In the absence of a clear distinction between "what the People must do as a *state* & what they may safely & advantageously do in their looser capacity, as a society bound together by common national ties," any enterprise, individual or corporate, might now find some hulking public exigency, unmindful of private profits, ponderously, blindly, opening a breach for direct action by the Commonwealth.
>
> A vague consciousness of the possibility of remote consequences gave added point to doubts about the proper sphere of regulation. By 1860 uncertainty was characteristic. It was as if, imperceptibly, all the familiar metes and bounds that marked off one man's estate from another's vanished, to leave a vast and open space, familiar but with the old landmarks gone. Somewhere, everyone knew, the state could act directly, somewhere it could legislate as arbiter, and somewhere it had no place at all. But where one field ended and another began, no one knew; the master map was not yet drawn. With many issues still unformulated, consistency, even in theory, was beyond the reach of any group of citizens. In practice a society that found "a disposition in the people to manage their own affairs" also witnessed a remarkable extension of government interference with the personal lives of its members.

Oscar Handlin and Mary Flug Handlin, Commonwealth: A Study of the Role of Government in the American Economy, Massachusetts 1774–1861 240–41 (1969). For additional discussions of the entanglements between local government and the economy, see, e.g., Hendrik Hartog, Public Property and Private Power: The Corporation of the City of New York in American Law, 1730–1870 (1983).

6. *Tax Me Out to the Ballgame.* Public financing for stadiums intended to attract or retain professional sports teams has recently been a subject of substantial litigation. For the most part, these decisions have approved government financing. In Friends of Parks v. Chicago Park District, 786 N.E.2d 161 (Ill. 2003), the court rejected a challenge to a state law that created the Illinois Sports Facilities Authority and authorized it to finance, construct, own, and operate sports facilities in the City of Chicago. The legislature had concluded that modern sports facilities would stimulate economic activity and create jobs in the state. The Authority entered into an agreement to issue bonds, the proceeds of which would be used to rehabilitate a facility that had previously been used by a professional football team and that would continue to be used by the team subsequent to the renovation. The agreement gave the team substantial control over use of the facility. The court noted that it was obligated to defer to legislative findings of public purpose unless it could detect legislative "evasion." In this case, the long history of the facility's use to host events that "incidentally" benefited private parties, and prior financing of a similarly situated stadium belied any inference of evasion.

In Ragsdale v. City of Memphis, 70 S.W.3d 56 (Tenn. Ct. App. 2001), a Tennessee appellate court concluded that city and county financing of a new arena for a professional basketball team satisfied a public purpose and was therefore exempt from constitutional restrictions on lending the government's credit to private enterprises. The court found that the legislature intended for the challenged activities to be "identified as a public purpose," and expressed its willingness to defer to the legislature's judgment. The court independently concluded that the financing scheme was appropriate to facilitate the community's ability to pursue its "municipal spirit," even if the National Basketball Association would also be a primary beneficiary. Nevertheless, the court, perhaps skeptical of the financial propriety of those same arrangements, went on to indicate that its legal holding "should not be construed as approving the business decisions made by the governmental authorities as reflected in the executed agreements."

The court in *Ragsdale* quoted the following language from Justice Musmanno of the Pennsylvania Supreme Court, upholding government involvement in the financing of a stadium for professional football and baseball teams in Pittsburgh:

> If a well governed city were to confine its governmental functions merely to the task of assuring survival, if it were to do nothing but provide "basic services" for an animal survival, it would be a city without parks, swimming pools, [a] zoo, baseball diamonds, football gridirons and playgrounds for children. Such a city would be a dreary city indeed. As man cannot live by bread alone, a city cannot endure on cement, asphalt and sewer pipes alone. A city must have a municipal spirit beyond its physical properties, it must be alive with an esprit de corps, its personality must be such that visitors—both business and tourist—are attracted to the city, pleased by it and wish to return to it. That personality must be one to which the population contributes by mass participation in activities identified with that city.

Conrad v. City of Pittsburgh, 218 A.2d 906, 914 (Pa. 1966) (Musmanno, J., concurring). With equal zeal, if less literary panache, Chief Justice Starcher of the Supreme Court of Appeals of West Virginia recently responded to an attack on government involvement in financing economic development with the following:

> I will personally state my belief that [plaintiffs'] explicit argument that helping to build projects like baseball parks and to refurbish downtown shopping area with public funds in unconstitutional—because those are not "public

> purposes"—is hogwash. I can think of few more public purposes than bringing people together for the convivial recreation of live local sporting events.

State ex rel. West Virginia Citizens Action Group v. West Virginia Economic Development Grant Committee, 580 S.E.2d 869, 896 (W.Va. 2003) (Starcher, C.J., concurring). Do these statements suggest that the public purpose doctrine properly takes into account interests other than economic ones? If a locality would take pride in sponsoring activities that will generate no economic benefit, should that be sufficient to satisfy the requirement? Under what circumstances would the judiciary ever have a basis for invalidating government financing of any activity?

See also Libertarian Party of Wisconsin v. State, 546 N.W.2d 424, 435 (Wis. 1996); Poe v. Hillsborough County, 695 So.2d 672 (Fla. 1997). In the *Poe* case, the court refused to examine whether the terms of the transaction (particularly a clause permitting the team to retain the first $2 million annually from nonteam events) was "too sweet." Instead, the court concluded that, once the project was determined to satisfy a paramount public purpose, the terms of the transaction were beyond the scope of judicial competence to micromanage. Massachusetts appears to be a lone holdout from the trend of stadium financing, although it has assisted professional sports teams by funding infrastructure improvements in the vicinity of stadiums. See Note, Stadium Funding in Massachusetts: Has the Commonwealth Found the Balance in Private vs. Public Spending?, 51 Cath. L. Rev. 655 (2002).

As in the case of business incentives generally, there is some debate about whether professional sports stadiums aid local economies. Some economists suggest that there is little evidence that expenditures on sports teams have significant positive economic impact, in part because spectators who attend events would simply substitute other activities if they could not attend sporting events. Others, consistent with Justice Musmanno's sentiment, suggest that professional sports teams provide an element of civic pride and quality of life that cannot easily be monetized, but that might attract other industries and residents and thus positively affect economic activity. See, e.g., Roger Noll & Andrew Zimbalist (eds.), Sports, Jobs, and Taxes: The Economic Impact of Sports Teams and Stadiums (1997); John Siegfried & Andrew Zimbalist, A Note on the Local Economic Impact of Sports Expenditures, 3 J. Sports Econ. 361 (2002); Jordan Rappaport and Chad Wilkerson, What are the Benefits of Hosting a Major League Sports Franchise?, Federal Reserve Bank of Kansas City Economic Review 55 (Fall 2001), available at http://www.kc.frb.org/publicat/econrev/PDF/1q01rapp.pdf.

B. RESTRICTIONS ON EXPENDITURES

The public purpose doctrine places constitutional restraints on the purposes for which public funds can be spent. It does not, however, impose any procedural or other requirements on public officials who decide which of the myriad projects that would satisfy the public purpose requirement should actually be financed. The number of public purpose projects available for funding at any given time could easily exceed the financial resources of the locality. Thus, some mechanism for ordering priorities among competing projects is necessary. In addition, most projects that do receive appropriations could be funded at a variety of levels.

Given a fixed budget, the more that is spent on any one project, the less that will be available for competing projects. In the absence of some sort of constraint, there is reason to expect that expenditure levels, both for individual projects and for the local budget as a whole, will be higher than desired by a majority of constituents. Indeed, there is a basis for believing that the specific projects for which appropriations are made would not be those supported by a majority of voters. At first glance, these statements seem illogical. Why would public officials spend money (and hence have to raise taxes or forgo other projects) in excess of what is desired or for purposes not supported by those (resident taxpayers) who will have to foot the bill?

Theories to explain overexpenditure by public officials abound. One account is apparent from the earlier discussion of logrolling (see page 247–77 supra). Assume a municipality with 100,000 taxpayers in which the legislative body consists of 10 Representatives (A through J), one from each of 10 equally populated districts. Assume further that expenditure decisions are made by majority vote of the legislative body. Representatives A through F each have a proposal that will require an expenditure by the locality of $100,000, essentially all the benefits of which will accrue to residents in that Representative's district (e.g., local parks, street paving, improvements to the district school). Assume that the taxpayers in these districts are unwilling to fund these programs by themselves, an indication that the cost exceeds the offsetting benefits to those taxpayers. For instance, a proposed improvement to a park in Representative A's district will cost $100,000, or $10 per constituent in that district, but will only return $8 worth of benefit to each constituent. Thus, those constituents would not fund the improvement by themselves. Nevertheless, Representative A understands that if the cost of her district's project can be spread across the city as a whole, her constituents will end up paying only one-tenth of the cost, or $1 per constituent, and will receive the entire benefit of $8 per constituent. The balance will be paid by constituents of other districts. Of course, Representative A is unlikely to obtain majority support among legislators for her district's project. If Representative A can agree with Representatives B through F to support her project in return for her support of their projects of equal size, however, she can spread the cost of the project through the city and receive a substantial subsidy. Her constituents will have to pay $1 for their project, plus $1 for each of the five projects proposed by Representatives B through F. Nevertheless, this total cost of $6 is less than the $10 that those constituents would have to pay if they funded the improvement by themselves, and less than the $8 in benefits they will receive from getting majority approval of their local project. Thus, the trade will be worth making. Note that projects that were not worth financing if beneficiaries alone had to pay the related costs will be financed under this system. It is in this sense that we may consider the projects funded through the creation of the coalition as an overexpenditure.

Of course, Representatives G through J will get nothing from this trade. Their constituents, however, will have to pay for the projects that benefit districts A through F. Thus, they will attempt to create trades that benefit their constituents at the expense of other districts. They may, for instance, attempt to form a coalition and entice Representatives B and C to join them in a new majority for a new set of projects. The resulting snowball effect is to create expenditures in excess of what would have occurred under a majority system without logrolling. Note that each Representative would be acting rationally in supporting projects from which his or her constituents received no direct benefit. For further analysis of this scenario, see James M. Buchanan and Gordon Tullock, The Calculus of Consent 135–145 (1962).

The following excerpt suggests additional reasons, inherent in the organization of local government, why municipal decisionmakers are susceptible to overexpenditures. The cases that follow the excerpt illustrate legal doctrines that affect the budgetary process. Can these doctrines successfully be explained as creating constraints to neutralize the tendencies of public officials towards overexpenditure?

Henry J. Raimondo, Economics of State and Local Government

76–82 (1992).

The Political Process and the State–Local Expenditure Decision

This discussion of a model of state-local government expenditure decisions began with a comparison of state and local governments to the individual consumer. That comparison holds in many respects. One important respect in which it does not hold is that the state-local government expenditure decision is collective in nature. Unlike the individual consumer, state and local government expenditure decisions must work their way through a political process: a vote of the people, school board, city council, or legislature.

This study of the political process and its impact on public decision making is the field of public choice theory. This field touches upon far more than can be reviewed in this section. Several public choice concepts are especially useful in explaining variations in state-local expenditures. These public choice considerations take their place alongside demand, production, costs, and finance in determining state-local expenditure levels.

Voting Rules

In any government decision, the ideal is for everyone to agree on a course of action. In that way no one is forced to do what they do not want to. A rule of unanimity requires that all voters consent to a specific action.

Unanimity is difficult to disagree with. Groups of people, especially large groups, rarely achieve it. Part of the reason that unanimity is often beyond a voting group's reach is that the cost of complete agreement on any action, in terms of time, information, and organizational resources can be prohibitive. So unanimity is not the usual voting rule that governing bodies or popular elections follow.

When unanimous agreement is put aside, what takes its place? The most popular voting rule is majority rule. Majority rule means that a government action is consented to if more than 50 percent of the voters approve. Figure 5–2 illustrates the majority rule. Five people called A, B, C, E, F (to protect their identities) in a hypothetical town are voting to determine how many additional streetlights should be installed in the town. The largest number that the majority of voters agree to will be installed. Each voter has a demand curve for streetlights (DA, DB, DC, DE, and DF); each voter pays a fixed amount for this installation (the tax price); and very significantly, each voter will not support more streetlights than his/her preferred amount, but will support less.

Figure 5-2
Majority Rule and the Median Voter Hypothesis

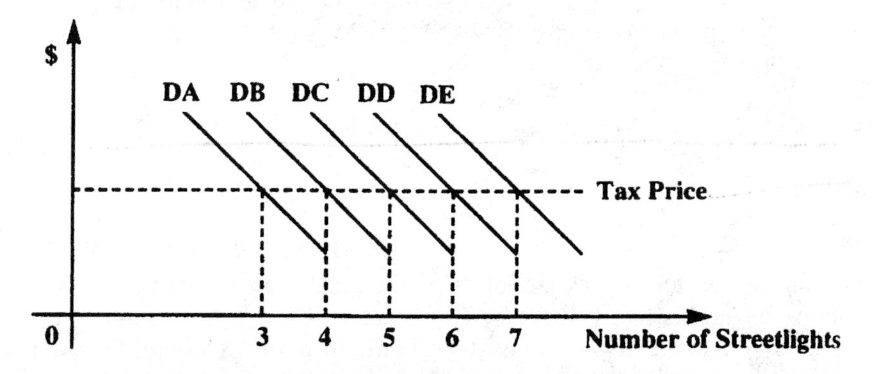

With the above assumptions, the vote would be 5–0 for three streetlights (unanimity rule); 4–1 for four streetlights; 3–2 for five streetlights; 2–3 for six streetlights; and 1–4 for seven streetlights (someone is afraid of the dark). The largest number of streetlights that the majority of voters agree to is five (3–2 vote). Something besides light comes out of this vote. When the majority rule is in effect as described above, the outcome can be predicted by the median voter. This is called the median voter hypothesis. For these purposes, the median voter hypothesis states that a vote on any level of government expenditure will be the amount preferred by the median voter. The median voter wants more spent than half the remaining voters (the median voter is excluded from the total) and less spent than the other half of the remaining voters. In the example above, person C in Figure 5–2 is the median voter and the outcome is five streetlights, the amount person C preferred.

Many, but not all empirical studies have found evidence that is consistent with the median voter hypothesis. Usually these studies conclude that median income is associated with a given level of a public good. Other studies have looked at the distribution of voters in referenda results and found that the referenda results were in line with median voters' preferences.

In addition to the median voter hypothesis, another important conclusion emerges from this simple example. The outcome of a collective choice does not have to satisfy each individual's preference. While a majority were willing to support five streetlights, that number matched only one person's desired amount. Two people actually opposed the choice, but had to go along with it.

Voting Problems

This last point concerning the lack of correspondence between a collective outcome and individual preferences raises the issue of problems with voting in general and the majority rule in specific. Voting usually does not capture the depth of a voter's feeling about an issue (called intensity); does not guarantee an efficient allocation of collective resources; and does not always produce consistent outcomes. Tables 5–5 and 5–6 illustrate these three points.

TABLE 5–5

Hypothetical Distribution of Benefits and Costs of a Public Good/Service for a Five–Person Jurisdiction

Part (a)

Individuals	*Dollar Value of Benefits*	*Tax Levied on Each Person*	*Net Benefit or Net Cost*	*Vote*
A	$400	$200	+$200	Yea
B	300	200	+100	Yea
C	250	200	+50	Yea
D	100	200	–100	Nay
E	50	200	–150	Nay
Total	$1100	$1000	+$100	Yea

Part (b)

Individuals	*Dollar Value of Benefits*	*Tax Levied on Each Person*	*Net Benefit or Net Cost*	*Vote*
A	$280	$200	+$80	Yea
B	260	200	+60	Yea
C	220	200	+20	Yea
D	100	200	–100	Nay
E	0	200	–200	Nay
Total	$860	$1000	-$140	Yea

TABLE 5–6

Hypothetical Distribution of Benefits and Costs of Three Services for a Five–Person Jurisdiction

	Sanitation			*Police*			*Education*			*Total*		
Individuals	*Benefits*	*Cost*	*Vote*	*Benefits*	*Cost*	*Vote*	*Benefits*	*Cost*	*Vote*	*Benefits*	*Cost*	*Vote*
A	$240	$200	Yea	$500	$400	Yea	$100	$800	Nay	$840	$1400	Nay
B	240	200	Yea	100	400	Nay	100	800	Nay	440	1400	Nay
C	240	200	Yea	500	400	Yea	1000	800	Yea	1740	1400	Yea
D	100	200	Nay	100	400	Nay	1000	800	Yea	1200	1400	Nay
E	100	200	Nay	500	400	Yea	1000	800	Yea	1600	1400	Yea
Total	$920	$1000	YEA	$1700	$2000	YEA	$3200	$4000	YEA	$5820	$7000	NAY

Table 5–5 shows the majority rule in operation in a five-person jurisdiction attempting to decide on a specified amount of a public good/service. To simplify the example, several assumptions are made. Voters determine their position on the public good/service based on the net benefits they receive (the difference between how they value the public good/service and the taxes paid). The tax levied on each of the five people is fixed at $200. If a person's net benefit is positive, then he/she votes for (yea) the public good/service. If it is negative, then he/she votes against (nay) the public good/service.

Part (a) of Table 5–5 shows the case where the majority rule produces an efficient decision, but intensity of feeling does not matter. Three individuals have net benefits greater than zero (i.e., A, B, and C) and two do not (i.e., D and E). The proposition to provide the public good/service carries 3–2. Fortunately, the production of the public good/service is efficient; that is, the total dollar value of benefits exceeds the total taxes levied ($1,100 vs. $1,000). Of course, each person has one vote. For person A that vote spells $200 in net benefits, for person E it spells –$150 in net benefits. Under the "one person, one vote" scheme, there is no way to differentiate these differences in net benefits or intensity. The inability to do exactly that can lead to inefficient outcomes.

Part (b) of Table 5–5 shows how the majority rule coupled with a "one person, one vote" scheme that does not capture intensity of voters' feelings can lead to an inefficient outcome. Back in the five-person jurisdiction, individual voters still make decisions based on net benefits. Again, three voters have net benefits greater than zero (i.e., A, B, and C); and two do not (i.e., D and E). However, since the magnitude of the gain or the cost to the individual voter is not accounted for, an inefficient decision results. The public good/service is supported even though total benefits are less than total costs ($860 vs. $1,000). The government undertakes a project which loses $140 for the five-person jurisdiction.

Inconsistency is the next gremlin for the majority rule. Under the majority rule, rational voters can make inconsistent choices. This result is often called the paradox of voting. Table 5–6 gives a display of the paradox of voting in action. The five-person jurisdiction now has three public goods/services to vote up or down—sanitation, police, and education. If the public goods/services are taken separately, then each would be passed even though each is inefficient based on the comparison of total benefits to total costs. It is the problem of intensity again. To be consistent the five voters who supported each service separately would be expected to support a budget consisting of the three identical services. They do not! They vote it down by a margin of 3–2. All the decisions are very logical based on the distribution of net benefits, but they lead to very inconsistent results.

So voting under the majority rule fails to match individual preferences with collectively arrived at choices; capture intensity of voters' feelings; and produce consistent results. These are some of the problems in relying on the majority rule to determine levels of state-local expenditures. Differences in levels of state-local government expenditures can be traced, in part, to these foibles of the voting process.

Political Players

The majority voting rule and the median voter certainly help to determine the levels of state-local government expenditures and state-local spending variations. While the Tiebout model creates competition among subnational governments within and across state lines so that they are efficient, some economists have argued that the nature of the political process generates pressure for increased state and local spending. In simple terms, here is how the public choice economists see the budget process.

Consumer/voters will support public action that they believe is in their interest. All too often, however, consumer/voters do not realize what action benefits them most, if at all. There is a reason. Most consumer/voters have fragmentary information concerning public issues. Learning the issues is a costly, time-consuming task. We trust our officials, the thirty-minute TV news report, or the weekly national news magazines to keep us informed. But that's simply not enough. We are not very well informed. This dereliction of duty is called the "rational ignorance effect." Lobbyists, politicians, and bureaucrats exploit our rational ignorance for their advantage.

Politicians are elected government officials. Their motivation is simple: get reelected. Public choice economists contend that politicians are determined to maximize their popular votes on election day, although vote maximization is not necessary to get reelected. Governors, state legislators, mayors, members of the city council, and members of the school board will strive to appeal to the uninformed positions of the median voter in their jurisdiction and the requests of the special interest lobbying groups, since that is where the votes are. If a politician refuses to support popular and/or lobbyists' causes, then a political competitor could well replace him/her.

There is a private market analogy. If a producer neglects to maximize his/her profits, then he/she runs the risk of failure. If a politician neglects to maximize votes, then he/she runs the risk of political defeat. This process of searching for the median voter and catering to the lobbyists increases state-local expenditures.

Bureaucrats are the next culprits in this process. They are nonelected state-local government officials who manage government programs. Their motivation is job security. Job security comes with control over public resources, the budget. The sequence works like this: the larger the slice of the budget, the greater the control, and the greater the job security.

Bureaucrats have several distinct advantages in the political process: they often control the information about state-local programs; they rarely must respond directly to the voting public; they can act as if they were monopoly suppliers since the state-local government is often the exclusive supplier of a public good/service; and there is no bottom line in the public domain to which the bureaucrat can be held. These advantages serve the bureaucrats' motivation to increase their job security because they allow the bureaucrats to push for increases in the state-local budget unchecked by the voter and encouraged by the politician.

The result is that the political process introduces a dynamic budgeting process that may not automatically combat inefficiency and may encourage growth in state-local expenditures. Suppose a local government introduces a program that will generate benefits for a minority of residents in the jurisdiction, but will be paid for by all the residents in the jurisdiction. The cost per taxpayer is small. The benefits to the select few are significant. The political imperative for the select few is to organize and lobby the consumer/voters and the politicians.

Following the principle of rational ignorance, the consumer/ voters have little incentive to understand the issues surrounding the program since the tax cost to the individual taxpayer is small relative to the cost of understanding the consequences of implementing the program. The select few will lobby the politician with promises/threats concerning his/her reelection. So the politician will have every incentive to support the program and convince the electorate to do the same. The bureaucracy welcomes this expansion of the local government, so there will be no opposition from them. The politician supports the program publicly; bureaucrats endorse it; and consumer/voters approve it (without knowing why). Local government expands its services and its taxes.

In this way, state-local expenditure decisions are part of a push-pull process. The Tiebout model of community choice, production, costs, and finance considerations ... create incentives to push the process toward an efficient spending decision. The voting rules, voting problems, and political players create incentives to pull the process toward an inefficient, expanding state-local budget.

People ex rel. Korzen v. Brewster

304 N.E.2d 46 (Ill. App. Ct. 1973).

■ BURMAN, PRESIDING JUSTICE.

Appellant, W. E. Brewster, as a taxpayer, filed objections to the 1969 tax rate levied pursuant to the annual appropriation ordinance adopted by the Chicago Park District. After considering the stipulation of facts entered into by the parties and the briefs and argument of counsel, an order was entered overruling the objections from which Brewster appeals.

The sole issue on appeal is whether the Chicago Park District appropriation for "Custodial Care—Chicago Board of Education School Facilities," item 522 in the 1969 appropriation ordinance in the amount of $816,000, is vague, indefinite, and insufficiently itemized.

The challenged appropriation is described in the ordinance as follows:

Department of Recreation

Responsible for programing and activating all recreational activities throughout the Park District, requiring consultation and cooperation with other community agencies when planning, developing, and directing recreation programs; supervision of technical staff in organizing and administering such programs; supervision and operation of beaches and swimming pools, together with such other related duties as provided in the Code or directed by the Board of Commissioners.

Code	EXPENSE CLASSIFICATIONS	Amount Appropriated
500	Contractual Services	
522	Custodial Care—Chicago Board of Education School Facilities	$816,000

The taxpayer's objection to this appropriation is that it is vague, indefinite, unintelligible, and does not state its object or purpose as required by the applicable statute and therefore is invalid. The trial court overruled the taxpayer's objection upon the ground that the object and purpose of the appropriation are plain upon its face and we find that the record supports this conclusion. The appropriation is not subject to the criticism that it is indefinite and uncertain.

The statutory requirements for the 1969 Chicago Park District Budget were set forth in section 17 of the Chicago Park District Act (Ill. Rev. Stat. 1967, ch. 105, par. 333.17) the pertinent part of which is as follows:

> The statement of proposed expenditures shall show separately the amounts for ordinary recurring expenses, for extraordinary expenditures, for debt service, and for capital outlays, and shall be accompanied by detailed estimates of expenditure requirements setting forth the objects of expenditure such as personal service, contractual services, supplies and materials, and the like, and showing such further classification, by character, object, or purpose as may be required by the system of expenditure accounts adopted by the commission.

We agree with appellant that a taxpayer has a right to have the purpose of an appropriation stated in a sufficiently clear and intelligible manner, so that he can understand, from reading it, what it is for, and so that he may have basis for determining its propriety. The appropriation ordinance of any taxing body must comply with the terms of the applicable statute and must be neither unduly vague nor insufficiently itemized.... With regard to the degree of itemization required, the Supreme Court in People ex rel. Wilson v. Wabash Ry. Co., 368 Ill. 497, 14 N.E.2d 650, cited by appellant, stated at page 502, 14 N.E.2d at page 653, that

> (t)he taxpayer's right to have separately stated the purposes for which public money is appropriated or expended is a substantial right of which he may not be deprived. Where it cannot be determined what purposes are embraced in a fund levied, we have held that it falls within the condemnation of uncertain, vague, and indefinite levies.

However, the Court went on to say:

> On the other hand, if an item in a levy is sufficiently specific to advise the taxpayer of a single general purpose for which the money is to be expended, it is valid.

368 Ill. at 502, 14 N.E.2d at 653.

The initial question then is whether or not the appropriation in question here denotes a "single general purpose," and although the cases contain no definitive guidelines, it seems clear to the us that it does. In the Wabash case quoted from above the Court held invalid omnipurpose appropriations for "board of health," as a levy for a department of government, and for "park fund" and "cemetery fund," since it could not be determined whether the fund in either case was to be used for purchasing land, for improvements, for salaries, or for other expenses. 368 Ill. at 503, 14 N.E.2d at 653. In the same case however, the Court sustained the validity of appropriations for "street lighting fund," "sidewalk fund," "salary fund," and "street and alley fund" since the word "fund" in these contexts is readily understood. 368 Ill. at 502–503, 14 N.E.2d at 653. An appropriation for "Custodial Care" relating to certain facilities in the case at bar is considerably more specifically itemized than any of these foregoing appropriations.

The appellant most strenuously seeks to demonstrate that the appropriation is nevertheless vague and unintelligible. He stresses that it might conceivably mean either custodial care in school facilities, thus perhaps referring to supervisory care of children, a kind of day care operation, or custodial care of school facilities, in which case several alternative meanings are possible—depending upon what meaning is attributed to "school facilities." We are not so persuaded. It is well settled that itemization requirements of a taxing statute must be accorded a practical and commonsense construction.... And courts will not adopt strained constructions in order to invalidate a tax, the burden resting with the objector to show its invalidity.... Here the Park District appropriation for "Custodial Care—Chicago Board of Education School Facilities" appears under the general subheading "DEPARTMENT OF RECREATION," followed by a brief description of the department's function as including responsibility "for programing and activating all recreational activities throughout the Park District, requiring consultation and cooperation with other community agencies when planning, developing, and directing recreation programs...." A further subheading refers to the appropriation as arising from contractual services. A practical and common-sense construction, rather than a strained one, would indicate to the taxpayer that the appropriation relates to custodial care of Chicago Board of Education facilities used under a contractual agreement for Chicago Park District recreational activities. The taxpayer is entitled to no more. The fact that the Park District is authorized to lease real property from other municipal corporations for park purposes (Ill. Rev. Stat. 1967, ch. 105, par. 333.15) and that the provision of recreational activities is a proper park purpose ... establishes the legality of the appropriation.

The appellant further contends that there is no clue why the Park District should appropriate money for custodial care of Board of Education facilities. The fact that the appropriation does not specifically refer to the existence of the leasing agreements from which the expenditure arose does not render it invalid. Faced with an analogous situation in Continental Ill. Natl. Bank and Trust Co. v. Village of Park Forest, 4 Ill. App. 3d 811, 282 N.E.2d 167, the Appellate Court for the Third District, in upholding the validity of a municipality's appropriation for "Construction of Sanitary Sewers (Contract)—$400,000.00," stated at page 820, 282 N.E.2d at page 174:

> Appropriation ordinances cannot be required to minutely particularize expenditures, such as, in the case before us, by specifying the routes of a proposed sewer facility. It is enough that the appropriation ordinance advises the taxpayer of the type of expenditure which will be made, so that he may make further specific inquiry with regard thereto should he so desire.

Thus a reasonable reading of the Park District appropriation in light of the more general heading and subheadings gives sufficient notice to the taxpayer of the type of expenditure, and provides him sufficient information to inquire as to its validity.

Appellant cites the case of People ex rel. Schlaeger v. Bunge Bros. Coal Co., 392 Ill. 153, 64 N.E.2d 365, for the proposition that the word "facilities" in the context of the Park District appropriation is vague. In *Bunge*, the Supreme Court sustained an objection to a City of Chicago appropriation for: "City contribution to W.P.A. project in connection with construction of Terminal building and facilities." The Court said at page 165, 64 N.E.2d at page 371:

> In the case before us, the appropriation was of funds to be contributed in connection with the construction of a terminal building and facilities. The term "facilities" is vague and indefinite. It does not apprise the taxpayer how much of the appropriation is for the building and how much is for facilities. Nor is there anything stated in the appropriation as to what shall constitute facilities.

In *Bunge* then there was no means for distinguishing "building" from "facilities,"—how to determine where one ended and the other began. We do not feel that the case stands for the bald proposition that the mere use of the word "facilities" renders a tax appropriation void and vague. It is admitted that "(t)he word 'facilities' is not a technical word but one in common use, and its meaning is to be found in the sense attached to it by approved usage." 392 Ill. at 164, 64 N.E.2d at 370. But here the meaning, as explained by the words "school" and "custodial care," is made sufficiently clear if the appropriation is read in a common-sense way. As we have noted, the ambiguity of the word "fund" in a tax appropriation depends on the context in which it is found. (People ex rel. Wilson v. Wabash Ry. Co., 368 Ill. 497, 502–503, 14 N.E.2d 650, 653.)

Appellant also relies on People ex rel. Wangelin v. Pitcairn, 371 Ill. 616, 21 N.E.2d 753, where the Court held invalid an appropriation "for drainage ways—work supported by government aid, $125,000" as being "uncertain, vague and indefinite in the extreme," it being unclear whether the fund was to be used for acquisition, improvements, salaries, or other expenses. 371 Ill. at 621, 21 N.E.2d at 756. This case does not support appellant's contention here where a single general purpose is clearly described. In People ex rel. Hempen v. B. & O.R.R. Co., 379 Ill. 543, 42 N.E.2d 69, also cited by the appellant, the Court invalidated a road and bridge tax levy for "buildings." The Court stated at page 550, 42 N.E.2d at page 74: "We think this item is too indefinite, as it is not apparent that this comes within any of the designated road and bridge purposes."

This decision is likewise inapposite to the instant case, since the use and care of Board of Education facilities under a contractual agreement is plainly proper in connection with Park District recreational activities.

In sum, we believe that the record discloses that taxpayers were sufficiently informed of the purpose for which the money in item 522 is to be spent. The Court correctly overruled the objections to that expenditure and the judgment is therefore affirmed.

Affirmed.

■ ADESKO and DIERINGER, JJ., concur.

NOTES

1. One way to limit expenditures is to place explicit restrictions on how much a locality can spend. This procedure, however, is not very common. Idaho imposes a 3 percent limitation on annual budget increases when the source of the funds is property tax revenues. Idaho Code § 63–802(1)(a). One commentator, however, reports that a combination of exceptions to this form of expenditure limit has essentially swallowed the rule, so that expenditures by local units nominally covered by the requirement virtually quadrupled during a 10–year period. See M. David Gelfand, Seeking Local Government Financial Integrity Through Debt Ceilings, Tax Limitations, and Expenditure Limits: The New York City Fiscal Crisis, the Taxpayer's Revolt, and Beyond, 63 Minn. L. Rev. 545, 575–578 (1979).

Procedural restrictions such as the itemization requirement can be understood as efforts to achieve indirectly the same objective as an expenditure limit by controlling the manner rather than the amount of appropriations. The principal case indicates that the itemization requirement is intended to give sufficient publicity to appropriations that constituents can effectively monitor the use of public funds. In theory, at least, itemization reduces the costs to the public or their surrogates, such as newspaper reporters, of discovering how municipal revenues are being allocated. Lower "search costs" should translate into greater scrutiny of public expenditures. Thus, itemization requirements demonstrate that concerns about local budgets do not involve simply "how much" is being spent, but also "on what?" But the increased availability of monitoring comes at its own cost. A requirement to specify each expenditure when budgets are made reduces the ability of the locality to adjust spending priorities during the budget cycle. Given the inability of local officials to predict expenses during the budget cycle, we would presumably want officials to retain substantial flexibility. In addition, the very act of specification is time-consuming, and thus expensive. The success of expenditure restrictions such as itemization, therefore, depends on the ability of those who implement them, both local officials and courts, to strike a balance among these concerns.

2. How specific must an itemization be in order to satisfy statutory requirements? In People ex rel. Brenza v. Morrison Hotel Corp., 123 N.E.2d 488 (Ill. 1954), a municipality had enacted an ordinance showing appropriations for the purchase of sites and buildings in the amount of $100,000, for the construction and equipment of buildings in the amount of $335,000, and for the repair and alteration of "buildings equipment" in the amount of $110,000. The objector claimed that the ordinance was insufficiently itemized to justify an appropriation for a library building fund. The court disagreed, concluding:

> The right of a taxpayer to have stated separately the purposes for which public money is appropriated does not mean that the city must itemize its appropriations to a point burdensome upon it. It is unnecessary to specify each particular item of expense for which the levy is made.... The appropriations specified with sufficient certainty the purposes for which the money was to be expended.

123 N.E.2d at 492.

3. To what extent can a locality transfer funds itemized for one purpose to another purpose? In Jarvis v. Bloodgood, 102 Cal.Rptr. 212 (Cal. Ct. App. 1972), the court upheld a county appropriation to contract with a nonprofit corporation to provide opera in the county's Music Center. After a budget hearing at which taxpayers had protested the expenditure, the Board of Supervisors of Los Angeles County deleted from the proposed budget an appropriation of $100,000 to provide opera at the county's Music Center. Later the same month, the county transferred funds from the county's Capital Fund for land acquisition to replace the deleted opera appropriation. In response to a taxpayer challenge, the court stated that "[n]othing in [the] Government Code ... states or even implies that, after the Board has specifically rejected for inclusion in the final budget an appropriation for a particular purpose, upon taxpayer protest, the Board has lost its statutory power, during the fiscal year, to provide for that purpose, if it can raise money by valid appropriation transfer pursuant to [the] Government Code." Id. at 215. The Government Code prohibits transfers of funds from "appropriations for contingencies" as well as from funds that are irrevocably committed. As the Board's transfer did not involve contingencies and "the inclusion of an item in the budget does not bind the Board to proceed with the contemplated transaction," the court upheld the transfer of funds.

In Westly v. Picur, 562 N.E.2d 1025 (Ill. App. Ct. 1 Dist. 1990), the plaintiff challenged the city's transfer of funds between line items of the city's annual appropriation ordinance without first receiving permission from the city council. Illinois law provided eight categories of proper appropriation purposes: personal services, contractual services, travel, commodities, equipment, permanent improvements, land, and contingencies. During any fiscal year, the statute provided that funds may be transferred from one purpose to another within the same department of municipal government if first approved by the city council. While the city's budget identified appropriations within the eight purposes with "item-by-item specificity, including dollar amounts," the court found that such itemization was not required and concluded that "a detailed breakdown of the spending is neither required nor should it be confused with an appropriation." Id. at 1027. The court concluded that the city's practice of transferring appropriations between line items within a single purpose did not violate the statute.

4. If local officials can extract substantial "rents" by making governmental funds available, then one would predict that officials will seek to avoid any legal constraints on their ability to appropriate public funds. What kinds of avoidance techniques might officials attempt in response to expenditure limits? One possibility is to fund projects through political entities that have their own budgets but that are less susceptible to voter scrutiny. Off-budget enterprises—including authorities, commissions, agencies, and boards—may finance their activities through nontax revenues that do not require voter approval. As a result, voters have less opportunity, and less incentive, to monitor the activities of these entities.

Nevertheless, off-budget enterprises frequently receive substantial subsidies from other units of government, such as grants or loans from general treasury funds of localities. Expenditures that have an impact on local budgets may consequently be hidden from public view. Some commentators who have studied the effects of tax and expenditure limitations have concluded that their effects have been diluted by off-budget enterprises given that the rate of increase in state and local public spending subsequent to implementation of these limits has been far greater than anticipated. See, e.g., James T. Bennett & Thomas J. Dilorenzo, Off-Budget Activities of Local Government: The Bane of Tax Revolt, 39 Public Choice 333 (1982). See also Helen F. Ladd, An Economic Evaluation of State Limitations on Local Taxing and Spending Powers, 31 Natl. Tax J. 1 (1978).

Another possible means of reducing the transparency of public funding is to reduce the obligations of the favored resident or taxpayer through tax abatements or waivers that are not included in the budget process. For discussion of tactics of "fiscal illusion" that local officials may employ, see, e.g., Geoffrey K. Turnbull, The Overspending and Flypaper Effects of Fiscal Illusion: Theory and Empirical Evidence, 44 J. Urb. Econ. 1 (1998); Bruno Heyndels & Carine Smolders, Fiscal Illusion at the Local Level: Empirical Evidence for the Flemish Municipalities, 80 Pub. Choice 325 (1994).

PROBLEM XVII

The charter of the City of Jonesboro provides:

> The said City of Jonesboro created by this Act may make and enact through its mayor and council, such ordinances, rules and regulations, and resolutions for the transaction of the business and the welfare and proper government of said

> city as to the said city council may seem best. The mayor and council shall have special power to make all contracts which they may deem necessary for the welfare of the city or its citizens. They shall have full control and power over streets, lanes and alleys of the city.

Several of the sidewalks of Jonesboro have recently fallen into a state of disrepair, a condition that has led to vocal complaints from residents. The city council solicited bids from area construction companies for repair of several blocks of concrete sidewalk and received a low bid of $16,000 from Riever Construction Co. Before the city entered into a formal contract with Riever Construction Co., however, a fire occurred at the local high school. While most of the fire damage was covered by insurance, the city's insurance policy carried a substantial deductible. As a result, the city council determined that it would be appropriate to defer the sidewalk repair work. The mayor, however, continued to receive numerous telephone calls from residents about the condition of city sidewalks. Both because he considered the large (and loud) volume of complaints to be indicative of a "mandate" from the electorate, and because he feared that sidewalk accidents could expose the city to liability, the mayor had the city's corporation counsel draw up a contract between the city and Riever Construction Co. to perform the repair work. The mayor signed the contract, as did Riever, and Riever completed the work within three weeks. Riever has submitted numerous invoices in the amount of $16,000, all of which the city treasurer has refused to pay. The treasurer has admitted that the work was performed satisfactorily, but contends that she has no authority to make payment because the city charter requires both the mayor and the city council to be signatories to any municipal contract.

You represent Riever Construction Co. Your client has informed you that, even if the treasurer's interpretation of the charter is correct, it was unaware of the requirement and relied on the implicit representation of the mayor that the contract was properly awarded. What arguments can you make to obtain payment for your client? What responses will you anticipate? What is the likelihood that you will prevail if you bring suit to recover the $16,000?

Bozied v. City of Brookings

638 N.W.2d 264 (S.D. 2001).

■ KONENKAMP, JUSTICE (on reassignment).

This is a taxpayer challenge to the legality of certain change orders executed by the City of Brookings on its Agri–Plex project. The circuit court granted summary judgment to the taxpayer, ruling that the change orders were void for violating statutory competitive bidding requirements.... We affirm in part, reverse in part, and remand for trial.

A.

Background

In August 1997, the City of Brookings devised plans to build the Brookings Agri–Plex. It was to consist of an exhibition structure with an attached building for county offices and a separate agricultural research building. To fulfill this plan, business leaders and community officials formed various project committees. John Mills, owner of Mills Construction, Inc., chaired the designing and planning committee. This committee was responsible for estimating the approximate cost of the project and developing a project package to fit within the proposed budget. Brookings then advertised for bids.

Several bids were submitted, including one from Mills Construction. John Mills resigned from the planning committee when his company submitted its bid. As the Mills bid was $635,000 lower than the next lowest bid, Brookings awarded Mills the construction contract in September 1997. The contract called for the south parking lot to be graveled. For the research building, only 5,000 square feet would be finished. The contract called for no other improvements to the remaining 25,000 square feet. Project planners were actively searching for long-term tenants and anticipated that interior improvements would eventually be needed to accommodate these tenants. Planners also expected that the south parking lot would be paved when funds became available.

After the contract was awarded and the construction began, Brookings issued a series of twelve change orders. Change order #1, dated October 22, 1997, stated, "YOU ARE DIRECTED TO MAKE THE FOLLOWING CHANGES IN THE CONTRACT." Issued by the architect, it instructed Mills to pave the south parking lot at an increased cost of $107,000. The other change order in question here, #12, was issued on July 17, 1998. This one directed $441,000 of tenant improvements for the unfinished section of the research building because Brookings had secured two tenants for the building. Neither change was advertised for bid. Mills and Brookings signed the change order forms, agreeing to the contract changes. . . .

In an audit report dated October 16, 1998, the State Auditor concluded that the change orders were unlawful. Bozied then sought to enjoin Brookings from paying Mills until a judicial determination regarding the legality of the change orders could be obtained. In response, the City adopted Ordinance 25–98, allowing Brookings to proceed even if the change orders were later judicially declared unlawful and void under SDCL 5–18–19. Noting that most of the contract money had already been expended, the circuit court denied Bozied's motion for a preliminary injunction in a letter decision dated December 23, 1998. The parties then moved for summary judgment. Following a hearing, the court granted summary judgment to Bozied.

The court ruled as a matter of law that the major portion of change order #1 and all of change order #12 violated SDCL ch. 5–18. It also concluded that Brookings City Ordinance 25–98 was invalid, as a violation of the South Dakota Constitution and established law. The court held that the defense of equitable estoppel was unavailable to Mills and ordered the company to refund amounts paid under the two unlawful change orders. . . . Mills and Brookings appeal.

* * *

C.

City Ordinance—Home Rule

After Bozied sought to enjoin work on the change orders, the Brookings City Council passed Ordinance 25–98....

This ordinance, in sum, allows the City to honor void contracts, overriding SDCL 5–18–19. The City believes it is empowered to enact such an ordinance because it holds a home rule charter, authorized by the South Dakota Constitution in Article IX § 2....

Although the power granted to home rule cities may be great, it is not absolute. The South Dakota Legislature limited home rule powers when it enacted SDCL 6–12–5:

> Neither charter nor ordinances adopted thereunder may set standards and requirements which are lower or less stringent than those imposed by state law, but they may set standards and requirements which are higher or more stringent than those imposed by state law, unless a state law provides otherwise.

The City's ordinance is less stringent than state law. Under South Dakota law, parties cannot be paid under void contracts. Not even the Legislature can enact statutes allowing such payments. The South Dakota Constitution Article XII § 3 provides:

> The Legislature shall never grant any extra compensation to any public officer, employee, agent or contractor after the services shall have been rendered or the contract entered into, *nor authorize the payment of any claims or part thereof created against the state, under any agreement or contract made without express authority of law, and all such unauthorized agreements or contracts shall be null and void....* (Emphasis added.)

* * *

D.

"Circumstances Not Reasonably Foreseeable"

Mills argues that it was legitimate to accomplish the paving and tenant improvements by change order instead of advertising for bids. The question is governed by SDCL 5–18–18.3:

> Any amendment or change order to an existing construction contract need not be bid if the contract contains unit prices for the same type or class of work, or the change or extra work is necessitated by circumstances not reasonably foreseeable at the time the underlying contract was let and the change or extra work is necessary to the completion of the project.

* * *

In most instances, foreseeability is a question of fact. *E.P. v. Riley,* 1999 SD 163, ¶ 33, 604 N.W.2d 7, 16. Foreseeability is determined under the "totality of the circumstances." *Small v. McKennan Hosp.,* 403 N.W.2d 410, 413 (S.D.1987) (Small I). According to SDCL 5–18–18.3, two factual determinations must be made: (1) whether "the change or extra work is ... not reasonably foreseeable," and (2) whether "the change or work is necessary to the completion of the project." Mills argues that the work authorized under the two change orders was unforeseeable because obtaining tenants at such an early date was unexpected. And because of the early arrival of unexpected tenants, the additional work inside the building and the paving of the parking lot were unforeseen. For summary judgment purposes, we must view the facts in a light favorable to the nonmoving party. SDCL 15–6–56(c). Under the totality of circumstances, we conclude that the fact finder must decide whether such events were not reasonably foreseeable.

Likewise, the fact finder must decide whether the improvements were "necessary" to complete the project.... These are disputed facts. After all, the City's attorney opined that the changes were unforeseen and the State Auditor concluded just the opposite. The fact finder must hear the rationales behind these varying conclusions and only then determine the question....

E.

Void Contracts—Remedies

This brings us to the crux of our case, to what Justice Henderson once called that "gnawing, aching question of conscience." *Carr Co. v. City of Sioux Falls,* 416 N.W.2d 602, 604 (S.D.1987) (Henderson, J., concurring specially). The circuit court concluded that, in accordance with our precedent, equitable remedies were unavailable to Mills because the change orders were void. Since we are remanding this matter for fact determinations, this question may arise again if the fact finder rules that the change orders were not "necessitated by circumstances not reasonably foreseeable" and not "necessary to the completion of the project." SDCL 5–18–18.3.

This Court has held that "under the proper circumstances" taxpayers may institute actions on behalf of themselves and other taxpayers to recover funds paid to a contractor under a void or illegal contract. *Sioux Falls Taxpayers Ass'n v. City of Sioux Falls,* 69 S.D. 93, 7 N.W.2d 136, 140 (1943). Though the issue in *Sioux Falls Taxpayers* was not before the Court, it recognized that the trial court in that case allowed the contractor "to retain what it thought was a reasonable value of the materials furnished, and the work and labor performed." Id. at 141. Consequently, there was not a complete forfeiture in *Sioux Falls Taxpayers.*

Bozied seeks to recover money the contractor previously received. As the circuit court recognized when it denied Bozied's motion for a preliminary injunction, "most of the moneys have already been expended." Imposing a forfeiture of over a half-million dollars on a contractor is a harsh and perhaps devastating consequence. In denying any relief to contractors in cases of this sort, we have held steadfastly to the notion that "contractors who do business with public entities do so at their peril. They are charged with the duty to be familiar with the statutory requirements and to adhere to them." *Carr,* 416 N.W.2d at 604. Government integrity and public protection warrant this inflexible rule. The rule enjoys the virtues of simplicity and rectitude, but unfortunately, it suffers the vices of rigidity and injustice. Today, we reexamine this court-fashioned rule. In the end, we conclude that the rule should prevail; however, it should apply to both sides of a void public contract.

Typically, when a contract is within a city's power to enter, but the contract is later declared void for violating some statutory requirement, a contractor who performs in good faith will end up suffering all the adverse consequences, while the public entity unjustly receives all the benefits from the contractor's performance.[6] Judges have long struggled with this question. Some courts take the position that no matter how innocent a contractor may be, there can be no recovery on a void contract, even to right a gross injustice. That has been our rule, and we continue to adhere to it. However, a contrary result may be warranted where a contractor has already been paid and a taxpayer seeks to recover the payment on behalf of a government entity.

Several courts faced with this situation have allowed a contractor to retain funds already paid but not to recover additional funds. *Elview Construction Co., Inc. v. North Scott Comm. School Dist.*, 373 N.W.2d 138, 144 (Iowa 1985); *Gamewell Co. v. City of Phoenix,* 216 F.2d 928, 941 (9th Cir. 1955); *Tobin v. Town Council of Sundance,* 45 Wyo. 219, 17 P.2d 666, 676 (1933); *Village of Pillager, Cass County v. Hewitt,* 98 Minn. 265, 107 N.W. 815, 816 (1906). *See generally* 33 ALR3d 397 (1970). This rule has been applied absent a showing of "haste, fraud, undue influence, or collusion, in the making of the payment." These jurisdictions recognize the same principle promoted in many of our decisions and most memorably in the case of *Norbeck & Nicholson Co. v. State,* 32 S.D. 189, 142 N.W. 847 (1913) (*Norbeck I*). There, our Court recited what has now become a familiar refrain: the law leaves parties to illegal contracts where it finds them and gives them no assistance in extricating themselves from the situation in which they have placed themselves—no recovery can be had on an express or implied contract or on quantum meruit. *Norbeck I,* 142 N.W. at 849. Requiring Mills to pay a refund contravenes this precept. It places the City and the taxpayers in a far better position than they were before the contract: the City of Brookings has its new Agri–Plex structure but would receive a refund for its improvements.

This principle of leaving the parties where they stand is well illustrated in the case of *Ellefson v. Smith,* 182 Wis. 398, 196 N.W. 834 (1924). That case was a taxpayer suit to recover from a builder the amount paid on a contract for the construction of a reservoir. The contract was let without competitive bidding. The court affirmed judgment for the builder upon proof that the City had the power to enter the contract: the reservoir was a public necessity; the contract was for a fair price; city officials believed the welfare of the City would best be served by letting the contract without

---

6. Many courts recognize two types of ultra vires contracts: (1) contracts ultra vires in the absolute sense because a government authority had no power at all to enter into them; and (2) contracts that a government authority was empowered to enter, but failed to execute in a lawful manner. When a public contract is ultra vires in the absolute sense, no equitable principle will extricate a contractor.

waiting for bids; and the work was done in full public view. In denying recovery against the contractor, the court said that equity does not exist to inflict punishment.

Leaving the parties as we find them is consistent with our longstanding jurisprudence. In *Hoiten v. City of Canistota,* 1998 SD 44, 579 N.W.2d 12, the contractor sued to recover for services performed on a contract not in compliance with competitive bidding requirements. We refused to enforce the contract and thus left the parties where we found them. Likewise, in *Bak v. Jones County,* 87 S.D. 468, 210 N.W.2d 65 (1973), we cited an Iowa case, *Horrabin Paving Co. v. City of Creston,* 221 Iowa 1237, 262 N.W. 480 (1935), for the rule that a contractor cannot recover against a municipality on an invalid contract. Here we have the inverse situation. Just as a contractor cannot recover on an invalid contract against a city, so too a city, or one acting on its behalf, cannot recover money it paid on such a contract. To hold otherwise under these facts, we would rescue the City and punish the contractor when both violated the law.

A contractor who fully performs a contract of this character and then receives payment should not be compelled to refund the money. Such a conclusion, will by necessity, be tempered by the facts of each case. However, where there is no showing that the amount paid was unreasonable, and the invalidity of the contract results, at least in part, from the City's own actions, repayment should not be ordered. *Elview,* 373 N.W.2d at 143 (citing *Miller,* 122 N.W. at 232 (Iowa 1909)). If, however, the evidence shows fraud, undue influence, or collusion, then a different result would be required.

This Court has emphasized on numerous occasions that the law "abhors a forfeiture." *BankWest v. Groseclose,* 535 N.W.2d 860, 864 (S.D. 1995). "Forfeitures are considered odious in the law and are not favored by the courts." *BankWest,* 535 N.W.2d at 864 (citations omitted). In the absence of collusion, fraud, or other impropriety, we cannot condone a forfeiture of $548,001.

To say that the taxpayers here are the ones truly aggrieved is to embrace a pious fable. The City was lawfully going to incur this expense or something close to it in any event. That had already been decided. Another contractor would have completed the improvements at issue had Mills not finished the job. In the end, what loss would the taxpayers have suffered? By forcing Mills to repay the City, we excuse the City from an expense it was going to incur anyway. Why should the taxpayers obtain free what otherwise would have required a substantial expenditure?

On the other hand, whether these change orders were occasioned by fraud, undue influence, or collusion remains to be decided in trial.

* * *

■ GILBERTSON, CHIEF JUSTICE, AMUNDSON, JUSTICE, and MILLER, RETIRED CHIEF JUSTICE, concur.

■ VON WALD, CIRCUIT JUDGE, sitting for SABERS, JUSTICE, disqualified, dissents.

■ VON WALD, CIRCUIT JUDGE (dissenting).

I respectfully dissent from the majority's holding on its decision to remand for a trial on the issue of foreseeability (section D), and on the holding regarding remedies under a void contract (Section E).

* * *

Void Contracts—Remedies

Did the trial court err in rejecting the defense of equitable estoppel?

The circuit court concluded that equitable remedies, in particular the defense of equitable estoppel, was unavailable to Mills because the change orders were void. This decision follows a long line of jurisprudence from this court. *See Norbeck & Nicholson Co. v. State,* 32 S.D. 189, 142 N.W. 847, 849 (1913) (court denying recovery on theory of quantum meruit due to contract being void and illegal); *Carlson v. City of Faith,* 75 S.D. 432, 67 N.W.2d 149, 151 (1954) ("equity and the rules of natural justice cannot be applied to 'interfere in the enforcement of a positive statute enacted for the protection of the public in the safeguarding of public funds.' "); *Simpson v. Tobin,* 367 N.W.2d 757 (S.D.1985) (court denying equitable defenses of laches, estoppel and quantum meruit due to void contract).

The majority has determined that the denial of equitable remedies now applies to both sides of a void public contract; that when a contract is determined to be void, the court leaves the parties as they find them. The majority reconciles the past decisions with this one by reasoning that never before has a contractor completely forfeited the entire price of the changes ordered. Also noted is the fact that Mills was "ordered" by the City to make these changes, and that City can not now gain a benefit from that order; that City's hands are not clean.

This Court previously ruled that because the contract entered into is against public policy and in violation of law, City must be permitted to recover into the public treasury funds paid out to the contractor. *See Sioux Falls Taxpayers Ass'n v. City of Sioux Falls,* 69 S.D. 93, 7 N.W.2d 136, 140 (1942) (where a contract was null and void for failure to follow the proper bidding laws, city had no authority to enter into contract or pay contractor). The general rule of illegal contracts is stated succinctly in *Norbeck and Nicholson Co.,* 32 S.D. 189, 142 N.W. 847. The majority cites the passage which says that "the law leaves the parties to illegal contracts where it finds them...." Exceptions to this rule must be pointed out as well. "exception is where the parties are not in pari delicto, in which case the party not participating in the wrong may recover his consideration but not the other party." Id. at 849. In this case Bozied brings this action on behalf of the taxpayers of the City of Brookings as authorized by this Court since 1896 as an exception to the "real party in interest" rule. *Stumes v. Bloomberg,* 1996 SD 93, 551 N.W.2d 590, 592 (citing *State ex rel. Adkins v. Lien,* 9 S.D. 297, 299, 68 N.W. 748, 749 (1896)). The taxpayers themselves are not parties to the illegal contracts.

Because Brookings taxpayers are not in pari delicto, or equally at fault, with city officials and Mills, it mandates recovery of consideration already paid. The taxpayers, specifically Bozied, gave notice at city council meetings that they believed the actions of City and Mills were illegal. That recognition by the taxpayers does not make them a party to the illegal contract and therefore they should recover those payments made illegally. "The allegation that City and its residents were not harmed but rather profited because of the illegal contract is completely irrelevant." *Himrich v. Carpenter,* 1997 SD 116, 569 N.W.2d 568 (citing *Norbeck and Nicholson Co.,* 32 S.D. 189, 142 N.W. 847). Even the best of motives do not give vitality to a contract which is void from its inception.

* * *

Even though Mills and the City both perhaps did gain time and money from executing the change orders in that fashion, that is no excuse for violating the procedures set in place by statute, requiring compliance with the public bidding laws of this state. The forfeiture of all the money paid under the illegal change orders may seem harsh in this instance; but I believe the remedy to the taxpayers is appropriate if the public bidding laws of the State of South Dakota are to have any real meaning in the future. As one renowned treatise has explained:

> The provisions of statutes, charters and ordinances requiring competitive bidding in the letting of municipal contracts are for the purpose of inviting competition, to guard against favoritism, improvidence, extravagance, fraud and corruption, and to secure the best work or supplies at the lowest price practicable, and they are enacted for the benefit of property holders and taxpayers, and not for the benefit or enrichment of bidders, and should be so construed and administered as to accomplish such purpose fairly and reasonably with sole reference to the public interest. These provisions are strictly construed by the courts, and will not be extended beyond their reasonable purpose. Competitive bidding provisions must be read in the light of the reason for their enactment.

10 McQuillan, Municipal Corporations (3rd rev. ed. 1999) § 29.29 at 364 (footnotes omitted).

With these notes of disagreement from the majority's opinion, I respectfully give my dissent on those two issues.

S. T. Grand, Inc. v. City of New York

298 N.E.2d 105 (N.Y. 1973).

■ JASEN, JUDGE.

The primary issue presented on this appeal is whether a criminal conviction is conclusive proof of its underlying facts in a subsequent civil action. If such a conviction is conclusive, the second issue is whether the equitable remedy which this court fashioned in Gerzof v. Sweeney (22 N.Y.2d 297, 292 N.Y.S.2d 640, 239 N.E.2d 521) is available to the appellant.

In November, 1966, plaintiff-appellant, S. T. Grand, Inc., entered into a contract with the defendant-respondent, City of New York, for the cleaning of the Jerome Park Reservoir. No bidding was required, since James Marcus, the city's Commissioner of Water Supply, Gas and Electricity, let the contract pursuant to the "public emergency" exception to the general bidding requirements for municipal contracts. (General Municipal Law, 103, subd. 4.) The entire cleaning has been performed.

Subsequently, the appellant and its president were convicted in Federal court of conspiracy to use interstate facilities with intent to violate the New York State bribery laws. The conviction was based upon a series of events which culminated in an agreement by the appellant to pay a "kickback" to Marcus, in return for Marcus' award of the cleaning contract to the appellant.

When the appellant sued the city for the unpaid balance of $148,735 due on the cleaning contract, the city claimed, as a defense, that the contract was illegal by reason of the bribery of Marcus, and asserted a counterclaim for the $689,500 which it had previously paid under the contract.

The city moved for summary judgment upon appellant's cause of action for the unpaid balance and upon the counterclaim. Special Term denied the city's motion for summary judgment, not on the ground that it found triable issues of fact, but because the court was of the opinion that the case of Gerzof v. Sweeney, 22 N.Y.2d 297, 292 N.Y.S.2d 640, 239 N.E.2d 521, supra, "furnishes compelling authority for holding plaintiff not completely foreclosed from recovery or retaining the amount paid by (the city)."

The Appellate Division modified and directed judgment for the city upon both its counterclaim and appellant's claim for the unpaid balance. The Appellate Division, 330 N.Y.S.2d 594, was of the opinion that there were no issues of fact here and that the unique circumstances which were present in *Gerzof* were not present in this case so that it would not offend the conscience to allow a complete forfeiture of money previously paid or to be paid under the illegal contract.

We turn first to the question of whether the criminal conviction of appellant for bribery conclusively establishes the illegality of the "emergency" cleaning contract with the city.... [The court held that the criminal conviction is conclusive proof of appellant's bribery of Marcus, and that, consequently, the illegality of the "emergency" cleaning contract was established, as a matter of law.—EDS.]

Turning to the question of remedy, the rule is that where work is done pursuant to an illegal municipal contract, no recovery may be had by the vendor, either on the contract or in quantum meruit. (Gerzof v. Sweeney, 22 N.Y.2d 297, supra, at p. 304, 292 N.Y.S.2d 640, at pp. 643–44, 239 N.E.2d 521 at p. 523; Jered Contr. Corp. v. New York City Tr. Auth., 22 N.Y.2d 187, 192, 292 N.Y.S.2d 98, 102, 239 N.E.2d 197, 200; 15 Williston, Contracts (3d ed.), 1786A; Ann., Municipality—Quasi-Contract Liability, 33 A.L.R.3d 1164, 1172; Restatement, Contracts, 598.) We have also declared that the municipality can recover from the vendor all amounts paid under the illegal contract. (Gerzof v. Sweeney, supra, at p. 305, 292 N.Y.S.2d at p. 644, 239 N.E.2d at p. 523.)

The reason for this harsh rule, which works a complete forfeiture of the vendor's interest, is to deter violation of the bidding statutes. (Gerzof v. Sweeney, supra, at p. 304, 292 N.Y.S.2d at pp. 643–44, 239 N.E.2d at p. 523; Jered Contr. Corp. v. New York City Tr. Auth., supra, at pp. 192, 193, 292 N.Y.S.2d at pp. 102, 103, 239 N.E.2d at pp. 200–201.) As we said in *Jered*:

> The continuing growth of our cities and the expansion of governmental services on all levels has necessitated, over the years, the letting of greater numbers of public contracts. While the amount of money involved in these contracts was relatively small a few decades ago, today the amount is astronomical. It is, therefore, a matter of grave public concern that there be absolute honesty in the procuring of a public contract. If we are to effectively deter the unscrupulous practice of fraudulent and collusive bidding on public contracts, we cannot look alone to existing penal sanctions. The nature of the wrong is such that it is not easily discovered but, when it is, we make it quite clear that courts of this State will decline to lend their aid to the fraudulent bidder who seeks recovery.

(at p. 193, 292 N.Y.S.2d at p. 103, 239 N.E.2d at p. 201).

However, in *Gerzof* we created an exception to the general rule, based upon the unusual circumstances of that case. There, the Village of Freeport, having decided to increase the capacity of its power plant, advertised for bids on a contract for the purchase and installation of a new electrical generator. Two bids were received, one from Enterprise for $615,685, and one from Nordberg for $673,840. The Village Water and Light Commission recommended that the Village Board of Trustees accept the Enterprise bid. Before the board of trustees could act, a new Mayor and two new trustees were elected, and upon the request of the former, the matter was deferred. When the reconstituted board of trustees met, it summarily dismissed the members of the Water and Light Commission, accepted Nordberg's higher bid and awarded the contract to Nordberg. Enterprise brought suit and succeeded in having the award set aside. Despite the court's direction to "award the contract as provided by law," the board of trustees, over the objection of the majority of Water and Light Commission, whose members had been reinstated by court order, had new specifications drawn up for a larger generator. These specifications were prepared with the active assistance of a representative of Nordberg and were so slanted as to make it impossible for anyone but Nordberg to bid on them. Accordingly, Nordberg was the only bidder, and its bid of $757,625 was accepted. After the generator had been installed and the contract price paid, a taxpayer's action was brought to annul the contract.

Our court concluded that the contract was illegal and void (16 N.Y.2d 206, 264 N.Y.S.2d 376, 211 N.E.2d 826) and directed Nordberg to return $178,636 of the contract price of $757,625 to the village. This figure represented the damage which the village suffered by having to take Nordberg's larger and more expensive generator. The damage figure was arrived at by adding to the difference between the contract price and Enterprise's original low bid ($141,940), the increased cost of installation of the larger generator ($36,696). In short, the village was put in the position it would have been in had the original Enterprise low bid been accepted.

The equitable remedy which we fashioned for Nordberg in *Gerzof* is not available to the appellant. In *Gerzof*, we had a fair idea of the damage which the village had suffered because of Nordberg's machinations, since the village had already determined that it needed a new generator and there had been one round of legitimate bidding, from which there developed a responsible low bid. In the case before us, there was neither an untainted determination that the Jerome Park Reservoir needed to be cleaned, nor a round of competitive bidding from which the damages to the city could be computed. Moreover, in *Gerzof*, the vendor's illegality infected only the final stages of the municipal contracting process, while in the instant case, the illegality goes to the origins of that process.

Thus, we conclude that the general rule of complete forfeiture should be applied here, rather than the equitable exception of *Gerzof*. The result may be harsh, but it is necessary in cases where the bribery of municipal officials is confirmed. As we recognized in *Gerzof*, "the application of the law to particular cases may not, of course, vary with the sums involved." (at p. 306, 292 N.Y.S.2d at p. 645, 239 N.E.2d at p. 524). If we would decree a complete forfeiture of an $8,000 contract, then justice demands that there be a complete forfeiture of an $800,000 contract.

Accordingly, we affirm the order of the Appellate Division.

■ Fuld, C.J., and Burke, Breitel, Gabrielli, Jones and Wachtler, JJ., concur.

Order affirmed, with costs.

NOTES

1. *Failure to Comply with Prerequisites*. The principal cases set forth the complicated rules about the effect of invalid municipal contracts. The sources of invalidity, however, may vary substantially. In *Grand*, the contract was invalid because a public official had engaged in illegal conduct. In *Bozied*, the invalidity was the result of a failure to comply with procedural requirements. Should the consequence of invalidity be the same in both cases? Should it matter whether the party against whom the invalidity is being asserted could have become aware of the underlying violation of law?

In Urban Transport, Inc. v. Mayor of Boston, 369 N.E.2d 1135 (Mass. 1977), the plaintiff bus company sought an order to compel the mayor and other Boston officials to approve and execute a three-year school bus transportation contract. A state statute provided that "[a]ll contracts made by any department of the city of Boston ... shall, when the amount involved is two thousand dollars or more, ... be in writing; and no such contract shall be deemed to have been made or executed until the approval of the mayor of said city has been affixed thereto in writing." The mayor had refused to approve the transportation contract because of alleged irregularities and violations of law in regard to Urban's bid and the school committee vote awarding the contract. While the allegations were being investigated, Urban began providing the contracted service. The allegations were ultimately demonstrated to be untrue and Urban sought compensation for its services and an order that the mayor sign the contract. The court found for the mayor. The court held that the requirement of the mayor's signature was not simply ministerial. Rather, "(t)he purpose of such legislative enactments is to limit the power of public officials in making contracts, so as to unify the control of the city's commercial transactions, and guard against waste by departments in the government. To accomplish this purpose, the mayor must be able to exercise his 'practical wisdom in the administration of the affairs of the city.' " [Citations omitted.] 369 N.E.2d at 1138. The court concluded: "The mayor here exercised his judgment by refusing to give his statutory approval to the contract. Absent bad faith, fraud, arbitrariness or capriciousness, we are unwilling to substitute our judgment for the good faith judgment of the mayor.... Even if the master was of opinion that the city's best interests are served by requiring the award of a contract to Urban, this subjective judgment alone is not sufficient to support an order compelling approval.... The ongoing criminal investigation, although essentially uncovering no wrongdoing on Urban's part, appears to be an adequate basis, devoid of whim or caprice, for the mayor's decision." 369 N.E.2d at 1139. Hence, the company was not entitled to recover for services provided when no contract was in effect.

In Boston Edison Co. v. City of Boston, 459 N.E.2d 1231 (Mass. 1984), the city of Boston relied on the same statute to argue that it was not required to pay interest for late payments to a utility company because the mayor had never signed a contract for the provision of service. Although the court cited the *Urban Transport* case, it concluded that the city could not use the statute to avoid the payments: "None of the reasons for requiring the safeguards of a written contract approved by the mayor is applicable here. The city must have electricity, and unless it generates its own, Edison is the only possible source. Since Edison has a legislatively sanctioned monopoly, there could never be competitive bidding. The rates themselves are set legislatively and cannot be altered by the parties.... When a utility wants to change its rates, it must file a schedule with the department. A consumer's challenge to a rate must be filed through the department, not the courts. Thus there can be no negotiation between the parties as to rate. The result of regulation this extensive is that it 'takes that subject out of the realm of ordinary contract in some respects, and places it upon the rigidity of a quasi statutory enactment.' " [Citations omitted.] The city also contended that interest payments were precluded by a state statute that prohibited the expenditure by any official of an amount in excess of lawful appropriations by the city council. Again, the court found the statute inapplicable to the situation at issue:

> The purpose of this requirement, like that of the contract requirement, is to prevent individual officials from incurring indebtedness for which the city

> has not provided and "to place the supervision and control of the expenditure of [public] funds upon the [city] through the medium of a budgetary system." Like the contract requirement, this requirement is strictly enforced, even when the result is that the city is unjustly enriched.... Like the contract requirement the purposes of this requirement would not be served by applying it here. The city would have no control over the amount allocated for electricity in any event. As noted above, the price is nonnegotiable and it would be impossible for the city to predict how much electricity it would need for a year. Even if it were possible to appropriate an amount based on the previous year's usage, if the department were then to allow a rate increase, the appropriation would be obsolete.

459 N.E.2d at 1235.

2. *Quantum Meruit Recoveries.* The court in the *Grand* case states that quantum meruit recoveries are not available for illegal contracts. What if the contract was invalid for failure to comply with statutory procedures rather than for criminal conduct? In Vrooman v. Village of Middleville, 458 N.Y.S.2d 424 (N.Y. App. Div. 1982), the court set forth the conditions under which a party may recover from a municipality under a theory of quantum meruit. The Village of Middleville hired Vrooman Engineers to aid in the design and planning of a wastewater treatment plant but refused to pay for the services after they were provided. At trial, the Village did not dispute the value of the services rendered, but raised belatedly several affirmative defenses. The Village claimed, inter alia, that the agreement with Vrooman was unenforceable because the Village had not followed the proper statutory contracting procedures, including prior appropriation of contract funds. On appeal, the court found that Vrooman would be entitled to recovery even if the affirmative defenses had been properly raised. In general, a party contracting with a municipality cannot recover under the theory of quantum meruit if the original contract was formed in violation of proper statutory contracting procedures. Such a rule ensures that taxpayers will not be held responsible for extravagant or collusive actions by public officials. The court however, stressed the policy behind the general rule in declaring its inapplicability to the case.

> The Village was ordered by the State to develop a sewage treatment system and the services provided by plaintiff were essential to effectuate that directive. There is no dispute as to their value and no harm to the taxpayers. To absolve the municipality from liability, particularly when it has been significantly benefitted by plaintiff's services, would encourage disregard of the statutory safeguards by municipal officials.

458 N.Y.S.2d at 426. Thus, the court held that Vrooman could recover damages as Vrooman entered into the contract in good faith, the Village had authority to contract, the contract did not violate public policy, and the Village would be unjustly enriched absent recovery. Is the court correct that absolving the municipality from liability would encourage disregard of statutory safeguards? If a municipality can receive benefits and then avoid paying for them by asserting some procedural invalidity, it would appear that municipal officials would, in fact, have incentives to ignore procedural requirements. Are there other incentives that would induce the locality to

attend to proper procedures? If no such conflicting incentives exist, would you favor a rule that permitted quantum meruit recoveries more easily? Imagine two kinds of procedural violations. In the first, the municipality fails to give proper notice of the meeting at which the contract is awarded. In the second, the mayor never signed the contract as required by statute. Is there a basis for reaching different results in these cases?

In Gill, Korff and Associate v. County of Onondaga, 544 N.Y.S.2d 393 (N.Y. App. Div. 1989), the same court denied recovery to an engineering firm because the taxpayers did not benefit from the services provided. The county hired an architectural engineering firm to provide services for the county's resource recovery facility, but failed to pay for the work provided. The court denied any contractual recovery for the firm because the county had failed to follow proper contracting procedures, which required prior appropriation or authorization of borrowing for the contract. The court also noted that, unlike Vrooman, the county was not required to construct a resource recovery facility and the county legislature had voted against its construction. Finding that the firm's services did not benefit the taxpayers nor unjustly enrich the county, the court denied recovery in quantum meruit.

3. Both principal cases indicate that courts presume private parties know the scope of authority of the municipality with which they are contracting. In City of Zanesville v. Mohawk Data Sciences Corporation, 468 N.Y.S.2d 271 (N.Y. App. Div. 1983), the court held that a city could cancel a contract without paying damages if the contract was not properly authorized or bid in accordance with state statutory requirements. Mohawk leased computer hardware to the city in exchange for monthly payments for one year before being advised by the city treasurer that the city would discontinue payments as the contract was invalid under state laws. Ohio law required that contracts over $5,000 be authorized by ordinance and awarded by competitive bid to the lowest bidder. The contract was signed by the city's assistant director of administration, but not authorized by ordinance or awarded by competitive bid. Even though the city failed to follow its own procedures, the court noted that the risk of loss should rest with Mohawk:

> Those dealing with officers or agents of municipal corporations must at their peril see to it that such officers or agents are acting within their authority . . . and they have no right to presume that the persons with whom they are dealing are acting within the line of their authority. . . . Since the authority of such officers and agents is a matter of public record, there is a conclusive presumption that persons dealing with them know the extent of their authority. . . . Although application of this rule results in occasional hardship, it has been held that the loss should be ascribed to the negligence of the person who failed to ascertain the authority vested in the public agency with whom he dealt and "statutes designed to protect the public should not be annulled for his benefit." (McCloud & Geigle v. City of Columbus, 54 Ohio St. 439, 453, 44 N.E. 95). Common sense dictates this course of action since statutory requirements could otherwise be nullified at the will of public officials to the detriment of the taxpaying public, and funds derived from public taxation could be subjected to waste and dissipation.

468 N.Y.S. at 273. The court concluded that the city council's failure "to approve the expenditure was not a mere technical irregularity but went to

the heart of the contract's validity.'' Id. at 273. Therefore, the contract was void and the court refused to uphold the arbitration clause contained in the lease.

Is this rule consistent with the general principle of contract law that losses should lie with those in the best position to avoid them? If it is not, what purpose is served by the rule? Even if the rule protects the public treasury, it does so by diluting incentives that municipal officials have to ensure that legal prerequisites are satisfied. Would it be better to enforce contracts entered into in violation of statutory requirements and leave the defalcating officials to meet their fate before the electorate?

4. *Bidding Requirements.* As the cases above suggest, local government contracts are frequently subject to competitive bidding requirements. These requirements are designed ''to protect against a variety of ills that might befall the government procurement process: sloth, lack of imagination or carelessness on the part of those who award public contracts; inadequate notice to potential bidders, causing contracting officers to act on the basis of ignorance or misinformation; and, perhaps most important of all, insufficient competition to assure the government gets the most work for the least money.'' Associated General Contractors of California, Inc. v. City of San Francisco, 813 F.2d 922 (9th Cir. 1987). See also Land Construction Co. v. Snohomish County, 698 P.2d 1120 (Wash. Ct. App. 1985) (bidding serves dual purposes of protecting general public and providing fair forum for those interested in undertaking a public project).

Competitive bidding requirements may be found in state constitutions, statutes, or local home rule charters. Occasionally a municipality will impose competitive bidding requirements by local ordinance. In the absence of some constitutional or legislative requirement, however, municipalities are not obligated to obtain competitive bids. Case–Bros. Co. v. City of Ottawa, 602 P.2d 1316 (Kan. 1979).

The provisions that create competitive bid requirements typically require the award of a local contract to the ''lowest bidder,'' the ''lowest responsible bidder,'' or the ''lowest and best bidder.'' See, e.g., Cal. Pub. Con. Code § 20128 (2010); Okla. Stat. Title 61, § 103 (2009). Even where the ''lowest bidder'' criterion is used, courts have interpreted the phrase to allow some test of contractor responsibility in the award of the contract. See, e.g., Advance Tank and Construction Co. v. Arab Water Works, 910 F.2d 761 (11th Cir. 1990) (second lowest bidders were lowest responsible bidders); Pflueger v. City and County of Honolulu, 674 P.2d 1019 (Haw. Ct. App. 1984) (city could impose additional requirements regarding experience and competence to requirements set forth in legislation). The ''responsibility'' requirement permits the municipality to consider the contractor's judgment, skill, ability, capacity, integrity, and financial resources. Prote Contracting Co. v. New York City School Construction Auth., 670 N.Y.S.2d 562 (App. Div. 1998). But see Owen of Georgia, Inc. v. Shelby County, 648 F.2d 1084 (6th Cir. 1981) (county's preference for hiring local contractors and consideration of minority employment record did not satisfy county's ''good cause'' requirements for awarding contract to other than lowest bidder).

Frequently, local governments will reserve the right to reject all bids on advertised contracts. Some courts require reasonable grounds for rejection, while others allow rejection for any reason as long as there is no fraud or arbitrariness. See, e.g., Conduit and Foundation Corp. v. Metropolitan Transportation Authority, 485 N.E.2d 1005 (N.Y. 1985) (rejection of all bids justified as lower bids could reasonably be expected).

Exceptions to competitive bid requirements are provided in the applicable legislation. Judicial decisions, however, have grafted additional exceptions onto these provisions. Contracts for the purchase of products or services provided only by one source, such as a specific tract of land or utility service, are exempt, since competitive bidding does not increase the number of potential bidders. See, e.g., Wright v. Wagner, 175 A.2d 875 (Pa. 1961), cert. denied, 369 U.S. 849 (1962); Telecom Systems, Inc. v. Lauderdale County Board of Supervisors, 405 So.2d 119 (Miss. 1981) (contract for provision of public telephone service not subject to competitive bid requirements since telephone company was a public utility and public interest was protected by utility regulation). Contracts for professional services such as the hiring of engineers, lawyers, or accountants are exempt as open negotiations presumably provide a more accurate mechanism for judging the quality of work. See, e.g., Layman's Security Co. v. Water Works and Sewer Board, 547 So.2d 533 (Ala. 1989) (security services fell within exception to competitive bid requirements covering contracts with individuals "possessing a high degree of professional skill"). Emergencies may also justify suspension of competitive bidding requirements if the costs incurred while waiting to award the contract by competitive bid outweigh the advantages provided by the process. See, e.g., Reynolds Construction Co. v. County of Twin Falls, 437 P.2d 14 (Idaho 1968).

The underlying objectives of competitive bidding also inform the procedural requirements of the process. Thus, local governments may not restrict competition by allowing an unreasonably short period of time for response to the request for bids. Legislation typically specifies the manner of notice, such as publication in a newspaper of general circulation, as well as the length of time necessary to allow bidders the opportunity to examine bid requirements and submit complete responses. In addition, contracts must be awarded on the ability of bidders to comply with published bid requirements. Local governments may not supply additional bid information that is not available to all potential bidders. See Brewer Environmental Industries, Inc. v. A.A.T. Chemical, 832 P.2d 276 (Haw. 1992).

5. *Ratification of Invalid Contracts*. A municipality may desire to enforce the terms of a contract that was initially awarded in violation of statutory requirements. In such a situation, the municipality may ratify the contract by complying with the original requirements. In Eckert v. Pierotti, 553 A.2d 114 (Pa. Commw. Ct. 1989), a township had selected an engineering firm to revise the township's sewage plan as required by the state Department of Environmental Protection. Although the official minutes of the township's meetings revealed no formal vote or resolution accepting the engineering firm, one of the township supervisors entered into a contract for engineering services with the firm. After a citizen protest was filed against construction of the proposed system, the township formally approved and ratified the agreement with the firm, as well as all expenditures that the township had made pursuant to the agreement. The court upheld the validity of the agreement. It concluded that "a municipal corporation may ratify contracts which are within its corporate powers and made by its officers without authority, or in excess of their authority. In other words, the municipal corporation may waive the irregularity of a municipal contract and ratify that contract." 553 A.2d at 118. Of course, ratification may only occur with respect to actions that the municipality had authority to undertake initially, but failed to implement through proper procedures. Ratification may not cure action that the municipality lacked the authority to undertake.

Where the municipality has not acted ultra vires, moreover, the act of ratification may be implied rather than express. In City of Kenai v. Filler, 566 P.2d 670 (Alaska 1977), the court held that a city had ratified modifications to a contract even though the city had not complied with its own technical requirements for ratification. The city had hired Filler to aid in the design of a convention center not to exceed a cost of $1.6 million. After public disapproval of the proposed plans, the city requested, and Filler submitted, an alternative with an estimated cost of $2.4 million. At Filler's request, the city manager sent Filler a letter stating that the original contract was amended to incorporate the more expensive design. Filler finalized the new plans for review by the city council, which then authorized payment for the plans. After the project was canceled due to insufficient funds, Filler sought to recover the remaining payment due to him. The city claimed that no additional payment was due, as it had never followed the procedures necessary to approve the modification. The court concluded that any requirement of formality "would place a premium on technical requirements and ignore actual circumstances." 566 P.2d at 675. It found that Filler had performed his contractual duties under the direction of the city manager, that the city council was aware of the changed plans, and that the city council never expressed disapproval of the city manager's actions. The court also rejected the city's claim that Filler had responsibility to know and follow proper city contracting procedures, concluding instead that such responsibility exists only in relationship to a municipality's attempt to exceed its proper contracting power and enter into illegal contracts. Thus, the city's actions, including partial payment based on an estimated cost higher than the original plans, and the receipt by the city of benefits in the form of bids issued in response to a request based on Filler's work, were sufficient to find that the city had ratified the modification.

C. State-Imposed Mandates

PROBLEM XVIII

State Route 9 traditionally served as the major thoroughfare from Lucky Lake, through the Town of Wells, to the interstate. As a result, traffic in the Town of Wells could be very heavy, especially in summer months. In order to alleviate this problem, the state constructed a Route 9 Bypass, which permits drivers going from Lucky Lake to the interstate to circumnavigate Wells. After completion of the Bypass, the state Commissioner of the Department of Transportation reclassified that segment of Route 9 that traversed Wells from a Class I state highway to a Class V local highway. The effect of the reclassification is to make Wells responsible for undertaking and paying for maintenance of that part of Road 9 that lies within its jurisdictional boundaries. Prior to the reclassification, the state was responsible for maintenance and its costs. The state has provided no additional funding to Wells in respect of the reclassification. The state has a longstanding practice, authorized by statute, of maintaining a state highway system of roads that are heavily traveled by nonresidents of the communities through which they pass. But the state also has a longstanding practice, also authorized by statute, of requiring localities to maintain roads that are primarily used by local residents. Both the state's reclassification of the relevant segment of Route 9 and the state's decision not to provide Wells financial assistance are consistent with these practices and statutes.

You serve as the Town Attorney for Wells. A recent amendment to the state constitution, codified as Article 28A, provides that "The State shall not mandate or assign any new, expanded or modified programs or responsibilities to any political subdivision in such a way as to necessitate additional local expenditures by the political subdivision unless such programs or responsibilities are fully funded by the State or unless such programs or responsibilities are approved for funding by the local legislative body of the political subdivision." No vote in Wells has approved funding for maintaining the relevant segment of Route 9. You would like to invalidate the Commissioner's decision to require Wells to defray the costs of maintaining the reclassified segment. Does Article 28A have that effect? See Town of Wells v. Town of Ogunquit, 775 A.2d 1174 (Me. 2001); Town of Nelson v. New Hampshire Dept. of Transportation, 767 A.2d 435 (N.H. 2001).

Board of Education of Maine Township v. State Board of Education

487 N.E.2d 1053 (Ill. App. Ct. 1985).

■ BILANDIC, JUSTICE:

This is the first judicial test of the State Mandates Act. (Ill. Rev. Stat. 1983, ch. 85, par. 2201 et seq.) Plaintiffs are 15 local school districts that filed a declaratory judgment action against defendants, the State Board of Education and the State Superintendent of Education. Count I sought to declare P.A. 83–913 (Nurses' Pay Bill) void in its entirety because a "fiscal note" was not prepared in accordance with section 8(b)(2) of the State Mandates Act. (Ill. Rev. Stat. 1983, ch. 85, par. 2208(b)(2).) In Count II, plaintiffs asserted alternatively that the Nurses' Pay Bill is unenforceable under section 8(a) of the State Mandates Act (Ill. Rev. Stat. 1983, ch. 85, par. 2208(a)), unless sufficient State appropriations were made available to reimburse them for the cost of complying with the bill, which required plaintiffs to raise the salaries of their certified school nurses. Count III was identical to Count II except that it challenged the enforceability of P.A. 83–876 (Certified Service Personnel Pay Bill) unless sufficient State appropriations were made to reimburse plaintiffs for the cost of compliance. P.A. 83–876 required plaintiffs to raise salaries of holders of school service personnel certificates, including nurses....

In order to more easily comprehend the legal issues presented in this case, we must review briefly the historical background of some pertinent facts. Prior to 1981, special interest groups would lobby the State legislature to require local governments to provide new or expanded programs or benefits. Because the State would not be required to pay for such costs incurred, legislators often yielded to the temptation to respond favorably and thereby gain popularity or political advantage. However, local taxpayers and elected officials had to shoulder the ever-increasing burden by raising taxes in order to pay for these State-imposed mandates.

Much to its credit, the Illinois General Assembly recognized this inequity and enacted the State Mandates Act. (Ill. Rev. Stat. 1983, ch. 85, par. 2201 et seq., eff. January 1, 1981.) It provides that the State must reimburse units of local government, including school districts, for their increased costs caused by State laws creating new programs or expanding existing ones. Because of the State Mandates Act, units of local government are able to set a budget with the knowledge that additional programs or expenses mandated by the State will be paid by the State.

The enactment of the State Mandates Act was a major reform that the legislature voluntarily imposed on itself by an overwhelming majority. During the debates, the legislators emphasized the State Mandates Act would "make us more responsible" because "it's our own money we're spending and not someone else's." S.B. 696, 81st General Assembly, May 16, 1979, 44th Legislative Day, p. 108 (remarks of Sen. Knuppel, the sponsor).

In general, the State Mandates Act requires the General Assembly to reimburse units of local government for the added costs of certain types of State-imposed mandates and relieves local governments of the obligation to implement such mandates if State reimbursement is not provided.

Some unnecessary confusion was created in this case when counsel used the words "exclusion" and "exemption" interchangeably in their briefs. For purposes of the State Mandates Act, "exclusion" and "exemption" are significant and should be used precisely. For example, there are only five recognized "exclusions" under the Act:

> § 8. ... (a) Exclusions: Any of the following circumstances inherent to, or associated with, a mandate shall exclude the State from reimbursement liability under this Act. If the mandate (1) accommodates a request from local governments or organizations thereof; (2) imposes additional duties of a nature which can be carried out by existing staff and procedures at no appreciable net cost

> increase; (3) creates additional costs but also provides offsetting savings resulting in no aggregate increase in net costs; (4) imposes a cost that is wholly or largely recovered from Federal, State or other external financial aid; (5) imposes additional annual net costs of less than $1,000 for each of the several local governments affected or less than $50,000, in the aggregate, for all local governments affected.

Ill. Rev. Stat. 1983, ch. 85, par. 2208(a).

Unlike "exclusions," "exemptions" are not limited to any specific situations. Sections 8.1 through 8.8 of the State Mandates Act provide for exempt mandates. (Ill. Rev. Stat. 1983, ch. 85, pars. 2208.1–2208.8 (1984 and 1985 supp.).) The General Assembly can exempt any mandate without any limitation by so identifying the mandate, as in sections 8.1–8.8. The net result is an amendment of the State Mandates Act for that particular purpose.

During its 1983 session, the legislature enacted the two laws at issue that created personnel mandates, P.A. 83–876 and P.A. 83–913. This occurred over two years after the enactment of the State Mandates Act.

P.A. 83–876 dealt with holders of a service personnel certificate. It raised their benefits to the level of those holding teaching certificates. Local school boards were directed by the State to raise those benefits. This mandate was not accompanied by an appropriation bill as required by section 8(b)(4) of the State Mandates Act (Ill. Rev. Stat. 1983, ch. 85, par. 2208(b)(4)); was not excluded from reimbursement under section 8(a) (Ill. Rev. Stat. 1983, ch. 85, par. 2208(a)); and was not declared an exempt mandate under sections 8.1–8.8 (Ill. Rev. Stat. 1983, ch. 85, pars. 2208.1–2208.8 (1984 and 1985 supp.)).

P.A. 83–913 raised certified nurses' salaries to the level of certified teachers' salaries. As in P.A. 83–876, local school boards were mandated to raise the nurses' salaries. Similarly, the mandate for nurses in P.A. 83–913 did not have a companion appropriation bill; was not excluded from reimbursement; and was not declared an exempt mandate. . . .

It is conceded that neither public act followed the provisions of the State Mandates Act. The fiscal note requirement was disregarded and the appropriation, exclusion and exemption provisions were not followed. The trial court held that P.A. 83–876 was unenforceable for failure to comply with the State Mandates Act. Defendants did not appeal this issue, so P.A. 83–876 is not involved directly in this appeal.

The issues thus presented are: (1) whether the Nurses' Pay Bill, P.A. 83–913, is enforceable against local school districts without a companion State appropriation, exclusion or exemption; and (2) whether the bill is void in its entirety for lack of a fiscal note.

I

Plaintiffs contend that the following declaration, which was incorporated as section 2 of the Nurses' Pay Bill, does not legally avoid the requirements of the State Mandates Act:

> The General Assembly hereby finds and declares that this amendatory Act does not require reimbursement by the State under the "State Mandates Act."

In enacting the State Mandates Act, the legislature imposed restraints on itself. It could not compel school districts to raise nurses' salaries without a companion appropriation (Ill. Rev. Stat. 1983, ch. 85, par. 2208(b)(4)), unless the Nurses' Pay Bill was excluded from the Act (Ill. Rev. Stat. 1983, ch. 85, par. 2208(a)), or an exemption created (Ill. Rev. Stat. 1983, ch. 85, pars. 2208.1–2208.8 (1984 and 1985 supp.)).

No appropriation was made by the State for the nurses' salary increases. None of the permitted exclusions was invoked and no exemption was created.

A

The issue, therefore, is whether the declaration in section 2 of the Nurses' Pay Bill avoids the legislative requisite of the State Mandates Act. Section 2 fails to assert any one of the five reasons for exclusion permitted by section 8(a) of the State Mandates Act. (Ill. Rev. Stat. 1983, ch. 85, par. 2208(a).) If any one of the five authorized exclusions of the Mandates Act was asserted, there would be no dispute about the legality of the Nurses' Pay Bill. The State Mandates Act is clear and unambiguous in defining the types of legislative mandates that are excluded from the reimbursement requirements of the Act. The question here is whether to give effect to the clear and unambiguous intent of the State Mandates Act, or to give effect to section 2 of P.A. 83–913.

Defendants assert that section 2 is a clear and unambiguous exclusion or exemption from the reimbursement requirements. Defendants fail to acknowledge, however, that the State Mandates Act, with equal if not greater clarity, defines the precise circumstances under which subsequently enacted "mandates" may be excluded from its reimbursement requirements. Two things are necessary for a mandate to be excluded from the reimbursement requirements. First, at least one of the five exclusions set forth in section 8(a) of the Act must be applicable. Second, the applicable exclusions must be "explicitly stated in the Act establishing the mandate." (Ill. Rev. Stat. 1983, ch. 85, par. 2208(a).) In the absence of an amendment or repeal of the State Mandates Act itself, this is the only circumstance under which a "mandate" can be excluded from the reimbursement requirements of the Act.

In this case, it is clear that none of these circumstances exist to exclude P.A. 83–913 from the State Mandates Act. None of the five statutory exclusions are applicable to P.A. 83–913, and no party to this litigation has ever suggested that they are. It is equally beyond dispute that none of the statutory exclusions are "explicitly stated" in P.A. 83–913.

Consequently, in the absence of an amendment or repeal of the State Mandates Act itself, section 2 of P.A. 83–913 is simply ineffective to exclude that law from the Mandates Act. . . .

B

The Nurses' Pay Bill, P.A. 83–913, was passed during the 1983 session of the General Assembly. There is no dispute about the fact that the General Assembly could exclude or exempt a bill from the provisions of the Mandates Act. In fact, the General Assembly exercised that right on at least 25 occasions during the same session.

However, in this case, the General Assembly chose not to exclude or exempt, as it properly could, under sections 8 and 8.1 through 8.8 of the Mandates Act. (Ill. Rev. Stat. 1983, ch.85, pars. 2208, 2208.1–2208.8 (1984 and 1985 supp.).) Instead, it merely made a declaration in section 2 of the Nurses' Pay Bill. This is an isolated instance in which intent is used in lieu of exclusion or exemption. The briefs of the parties and the three amici fail to disclose any other similar attempt by the legislature to use a declaration of intent as an exclusion or exemption.

We are not disposed to raise a declaration of intent to the level of an exclusion or exemption. Having properly exercised its power to exclude or exempt under the express provisions of the Mandates Act, the legislature could have easily done so one more time. The declared intent never was executed and must therefore fail as a vehicle to avoid the restraints that the legislature imposed on itself by enacting the Mandates Act. . . .

While this is a case of first impression in Illinois, two recent California cases support the conclusion that P.A. 83–913 must be declared unenforceable in the absence of State reimbursement. In County of Los Angeles v. State of California (2d Dist. 1984), 153 Cal. App. 3d 568, 200 Cal. Rptr. 394, two counties sued the State of California under a California statute that required reimbursement by the State for certain State-imposed costs. In its ruling in favor of the counties, the California Appellate Court held that although one legislature cannot restrict its own power or that of successor legislatures, a mandate does not restrict legislative power. "The Legislature remains free to amend or repeal" the mandate, the court said. "Until that time, the Legislature must not ignore the requirements of existing legislation." 153 Cal. App. 3d 568, 573, 200 Cal. Rptr. 394, 397.

The same reasoning is applicable to this case. The Illinois legislature was free to repeal or amend the State Mandates Act. It did neither. Therefore, P.A. 83–913 is unenforceable in the absence of State reimbursement.

City of Sacramento v. State of California (3d Dist. 1984), 156 Cal. App. 3d 182, 203 Cal. Rptr. 258, supports the same conclusion. In that case, California enacted a statute requiring public employees to be covered by the State unemployment insurance law. In mandating local public employees into the system, the legislature added a provision similar to section 2 of our Nurses' Pay Bill and attempted to keep the additional cost to local governments from State reimbursement under the California Mandates Act. The City of Sacramento and County of Los Angeles sued to obtain reimbursement.

The California Appellate Court held the State was required to reimburse the units of local government in spite of the legislature's disclaimer of liability. In reasoning equally applicable to this case, the court stated:

> The legislative disclaimers ... are merely legislative characterizations of that enactment. The interpretation of statutory language is a judicial function [citation]. While legislative declarations and characterizations are a factor we may consider in construing legislation, they are not binding [citation]. *This is particularly true when the characterization is the product of an attempt to avoid the imposition of a financial responsibility.* The Legislature's effort to label Chapter 2 a "federal mandate" is unavailing. (Emphasis added.)

156 Cal. App. 3d 182, 196–97, 203 Cal. Rptr. 258, 266.

Defendants seek to distinguish both of these California cases by arguing that at the time these cases were decided, California had a State Mandates Act provision incorporated into the State constitution. That is true, but also irrelevant because the cases all turned on the enforceability of pre-existing statutory mandates provisions.

Defendants' refusal to acknowledge that the General Assembly can bind and limit subsequent General Assemblies is inconsistent with their decision not to appeal the circuit court ruling on P.A. 83–876. That Act included the same mandated salary increases that are contained in P.A. 83–913. In addition, P.A. 83–876 contained no provision comparable to section 2 of P.A. 83–913. Indeed, P.A. 83–876 made no reference to the State Mandates Act. When the circuit court ruled that the relevant provisions of P.A. 83–876 were unenforceable in the absence of State reimbursement, the court adopted plaintiffs' position, and the position adopted by the California courts in analogous cases, that the legislature is bound by the requirements of existing legislation unless and until it is amended or repealed.

The same principle compels a ruling in plaintiffs' favor on P.A. 83–913. Until the legislature amends or repeals the provisions of the Mandates Act, the courts are duty bound to follow its clear and unambiguous directives. Defendants have never offered a principled distinction to explain why P.A. 83–876 should be ruled unenforceable while P.A. 83–913 should be held enforceable. The State Mandates Act addresses directly and clearly the unenforceability of each, and we therefore conclude that P.A. 83–913 is unenforceable in the absence of a State reimbursement.

II

Plaintiffs contend that P.A. 83–913 is void in its entirety because defendant State Superintendent of Education failed to file a "fiscal note" as provided in section 8(b)(2) of the Mandates Act. (Ill. Rev. Stat. 1983, ch. 85, par. 2208(b)(2).) Plaintiffs further contend that section 8(b)(2) provides that a "bill shall remain on second reading until a fiscal note is filed." A fiscal note was not filed; nevertheless, the bill proceeded to third reading in both the House and Senate and was enacted. This procedural flaw, according to plaintiffs' theory, renders the bill void.

What plaintiffs overlook is the fact that section 8(b)(2) of the Mandates Act itself provides that it "shall be subject to" the Fiscal Notes Act. (Ill.

Rev. Stat. 1983, ch. 85, par. 2208(b)(2).) The language of section 3 of the Fiscal Notes Act (Ill. Rev. Stat. 1983, ch. 63, par. 42.31 et seq.) leads to the conclusion that the preparation of a fiscal note is directory and not mandatory. Section 3 provides:

> Whenever the sponsor of any measure is of the opinion that *no fiscal note is necessary*, any member of either house may thereafter request that a note be obtained, and in such case the matter shall be decided by majority vote of those present and voting in the house of which he is a member. (Emphasis added.)

Ill. Rev. Stat. 1983, ch. 63, par. 42.33. Undeniably, the sponsors of P.A. 83–913 did not deem it necessary to have a fiscal note prepared, nor did any member of either House request that such a note be obtained.

Plaintiffs' argument runs contrary to the express language of the Fiscal Notes Act, as incorporated into the State Mandates Act, and runs contrary to the intent of the legislature with respect to the preparation of a fiscal note.

We conclude that the trial court correctly held that the Nurses' Pay Bill, P.A. 83–913, was not void in its entirety for lack of a fiscal note. However, the trial court erred in holding the Nurses' Pay Bill enforceable against the local school districts without an appropriation of State funds to cover the cost of the mandate.

Accordingly, the judgment of the circuit court of Cook County is affirmed in part and reversed in part.

Affirmed in part; reversed in part.

■ STAMOS, P.J., and HARTMAN, J., concur.

NOTES

1. *State Mandates*. State governments frequently direct local and special governments to act (or refrain from acting) pursuant to state-imposed standards. These mandates require subordinate levels of government to provide new services or increased levels of service. The imposition of the obligation itself may not significantly disrupt other expenditure decisions made by the locality. The disruption increases dramatically, however, where the mandate is "unfunded," that is, where the state imposes the obligation on the locality but does not appropriate funds or authorize use of a funding source with which to meet the accompanying financial obligation.

Unfunded state mandates would appear to require localities to deviate from the Tiebout model insofar as spending decisions will vary from what residents in that model would have preferred. If residents had desired the mandated services, presumably they would have voted for them and no state-imposed requirement would have been necessary. But we have also learned that localities may deviate from the Tiebout model if local spending decisions are unresponsive to the demands of those within the local community who are both politically powerless (who lack "voice") and who are relatively immobile (who cannot readily "exit"). Conceivably, those who cannot exercise voice or exit options at the local level may find it easier to coalesce at the state level. This could happen, for instance, if the number of parties interested in a program is small in each locality, but significant throughout the state, and if those geographically diverse parties can form a coalition at the state level. Social workers, for instance, might be too few to have much impact at the local level, but numerous enough statewide to mount a campaign for particular benefits for themselves or their clients. Thus, one could tell either a benign or malign story about mandates. According to the benign story, the state is the forum for those who are excluded from the local decisionmaking process. A state-imposed mandate that all localities provide a certain level of remedial education to non-English speaking students may be an example. Alternatively, a benign story could explain mandates to require localities to offer programs that generate significant positive externalities. Since the localities do not obtain the benefit of these externalities, they have no incentive to fund the activities as fully as the state would like. According to this story, mandates cause localities to look beyond their own interests and to act in a manner more consistent with the welfare of the larger state.

According to the malign story, however, mandates are imposed when those who will receive the benefits of the mandated service are better able to organize at the state level than at the local level, and those who oppose the mandated service are less able to organize at the state level. Mandates enacted by this process will not necessarily bear any relationship to social welfare at the state or local level. A requirement that localities provide certain employees with certain vacation benefits may be of this nature. Again, if the benefits of the program to the locality exceeded its costs, the locality presumably would have adopted it without any mandate from the state. Thus, one's response to unfunded mandates should depend on whether one believes that they are imposed on a local body that has been unresponsive to the demands of politically powerless constituents who would benefit from the mandate, or whether they are imposed at the behest of special interests that have attained substantial influence at the state level.

If state legislators have "benign" motivations in imposing mandates, then why would the legislature not also provide a funding source? A 1990 study by the Advisory Commission on Intergovernmental Relations (ACIR) revealed that the increasing tendency of state governments to impose obligations on localities (which the ACIR denominated a "mandate revolution") resulted from several factors. While the number of policy demands from local governments, courts, and interest groups has continued to grow, recent tax revolts and cutbacks in federal spending have forced states to shift the financial responsibility for new demands to local governments. Mandates offer an attractive way to satisfy policy demands while minimizing the financial or administrative burdens placed on state governments. ACIR, Mandates: Cases in State–Local Relations (1990). A more cynical approach would suggest that state legislators vote for unfunded mandates to obtain credit for implementation of a program, and thus receive the gratitude of the benefited group, while shifting the accompanying financial burden and political costs to local officials, who must raise taxes or cut other services to pay for the mandated program. It is not necessarily the case, however, that state mandates are disfavored by local officials. Local officials who desire to make expenditures or to enforce standards that are unpopular with influential constituents or interests may benefit from the ability to claim that their action is required by superior levels of government. See Jerry Mashaw & Susan Rose–Ackerman, Federalism and Regulation, in The Reagan Regulatory Strategy, An Assessment 111 (G. Eads & M. Fix eds., 1984). For a discussion of the roles of local officials in reacting to mandates, see Edward A. Zelinsky, Unfunded Mandates, Hidden Taxation, and the Tenth Amendment: On Public Choice, Public Interest, and Public Services, 46 Vand. L. Rev. 1355 (1993).

2. *Restrictions on Mandates*. Concern about the "malign" use of unfunded mandates has led numerous states to adopt constitutional restrictions on their use. These restrictions typically appear in one of three forms. First, states may specify procedural requirements for the adoption of mandates. For instance, states may permit unfunded mandates to be enacted only by a legislative supermajority. New Jersey allows only those unfunded mandates that have been enacted by a three-quarters majority of the legislature, and only after a public hearing with notice that an unfunded mandate will be considered. See N.J. Const. Art. VIII, § 2, par. 5(c)(6) (2010). Florida requires that the legislature make a determination that any mandate fulfills "an important state interest" and enacts the mandate by a two-thirds vote of each house. Fla. Const. art. VII, § 18(a) (2009). In Lewis v. Leon County, 15 So.3d 777 (Fla. 2009), the state supreme court invalidated legislation that imposed on counties the obligation to fund costs of "Regional Conflict Counsel." Proponents of the statute maintained that no particular process was required to satisfy the "important state interest" requirement. The court concluded that, although the legislature had deemed the law "necessary," the constitutional restriction required an explicit legislative statement that it fulfilled the requisite important state purpose. But not every legislative act that imposes incidental costs on localities will fall within the constitutional restriction. In Opinion of the Justices, 949 A.2d 670 (N.H. 2008), the New Hampshire Supreme Court concluded that a bill that would reduce the minimum voting age for party presidential primaries or state primaries did not create an unfunded mandate, because the changed voter registration requirements did not create any new program or require municipalities to accept new programs, even if local costs increased.

These restrictions often carry some exceptions, such as mandates voluntarily accepted by the locality or those necessary to comply with federal rules or that implement the state's constitutional obligations. See, e.g., Mass. Gen. Stat. Ann. ch. 29, 27C (2010); N.H. Const. Pt. 1, Art. 28–a (2009). Are there also implicit exceptions? In Durant v. State, 566 N.W.2d 272 (Mich. 1997), defendants contended that the state did not have to reimburse localities for mandated special education programs because the state mandate was imposed pursuant to federal law that prohibited discrimination against disabled students. The court concluded that the state constitutional limitation on mandates contained no exception for state mandates imposed pursuant to federal law. The court found that the state-mandated programs in the case before it existed independent of federal law. But the court went on to conclude that a "federal-mandate" exception to the state's funding obligation for locally required programs "can only be found by a 'dark or abstruse' reading" of the state constitution's restriction on unfunded mandates.

Second, some states have adopted disclosure provisions, such as a requirement that any mandate be accompanied by a "fiscal note" that summarizes the mandate's estimated costs to local governments. These procedures may provide a basis for objections to legislative action. As the principal case indicates, however, the preparation of a fiscal note may be necessary only under certain circumstances or may be waived by a supermajority of the legislature. See, e.g., Conn. Gen. Stat. Ann. § 2–24–a (2009).

How do such requirements fulfill their disclosure function? If fiscal notes are intended to lower the costs to potential anti-mandate forces of searching for information about the effects of mandates, and thus reduce the advantages that discrete groups have in lobbying in favor of mandates, why would the Illinois provision permit such requirements to be "directory" as opposed to "mandatory?" One explanation reinforces the "malign" interpretation of mandates. Perhaps legislators can accommodate anti-mandate forces in general by the inclusion of such requirements. At the same time, there may be instances in which the benefits that a discrete group can offer to legislators are so substantial that the legislature would be willing to impose the mandate if it could successfully obscure the effects of its action. In such a situation, the legislature presumably would want to be able to avoid a requirement, such as the fiscal note requirement, that reduced information costs to anti-mandate forces. A "directory" requirement thus allows the legislature to have it both ways. Is there a plausible "benign" interpretation for not making the requirement mandatory?

Finally, states may enact provisions that define state "funding" of a mandate. Florida law considers a mandate to be funded if the legislature either appropriates sufficient funds for localities or authorizes them to use a new source of funding. Fla. Const. art. VII, § 18(a) (2009). Michigan, however, places the full responsibility for collection and distribution of mandate funding on the state. Mich. Const. art. 9, § 29 (2010) provides:

> A new activity or service or an increase in the level of any activity or service beyond that required by existing law shall not be required by the legislature or any state agency of units of Local Government, unless a state appropriation is made and dispersed to pay the unit of Local Government for any necessary increased costs.

While limitations on unfunded mandates are frequently embodied in state constitutions, the limitation in the principal case is found in a legislatively enacted State Mandates Act. If the malign story about mandates is true, and if legislators can obtain significant benefits by imposing mandates, why would a legislature ever place restrictions on its ability to impose mandates on localities? One explanation might be that legislators recognize the adverse effects of mandates, but don't want to vote against mandates that might be favorable to their own constituents as long as other legislators are willing to vote for mandates that are favorable to those other legislators' constituents. Under this analysis, restrictions on all mandates become a self-binding mechanism against becoming involved in a situation that leads to worse results for all—a traditional solution to the Prisoner's Dilemma. Can you think of an example of an unfunded mandate that might be viewed with favor by a particular legislator's constituents?

3. Exceptions to the prohibition on unfunded mandates provide the legislature with some discretion over how to structure legislation to require local funding. Note, for instance, the statement by the Illinois court that the legislature had exempted mandates from the provisions of the Mandates Act on 25 occasions. Assume, for instance, that the legislature wants localities to provide a specific service, but does not wish to provide funds for that service. The legislature might enact an unfunded mandate requiring localities to provide the service by including an exemption in the legislation. But if the legislature is prohibited from doing that, or prefers not to create the exemption, it might try to accomplish the same objective through alternative means, such as by taxing local entities that do not act in the desired way, or by enacting "regulations" that apply broadly and thus are not considered mandates imposed on local governments. Think, for instance, of regulations such as minimum wage laws or requirements to accommodate the disabled, that apply to local governments, but not exclusively, and that are not funded by the regulating government. Does it make a difference which type of legislation is used? Legislative avoidance of anti-mandate provisions may be considered tolerable if you believe that unfunded mandates require localities to incur the costs of programs that either serve a state interest or that are necessary to overcome the opposition of local interest groups. If, however, you believe that mandates improperly allow interest groups with substantial influence at the state level to benefit by imposing costs on recalcitrant localities, then legislative avoidance seems less savory. For an argument that unfunded mandates may actually be superior to the alternative of regulation for purposes of ensuring an appropriate level of local expenditure and a matching of benefits and burdens, see Julie A. Roin, Reconceptualizing Unfunded Mandates and Other Regulations, 93 Nw. U.L. Rev. 351 (1999). Other useful discussions of mandates can be found in Elizabeth Garrett, Enhancing the Political Safeguards of Federalism? The Unfunded Mandates Reform Act of 1995, 45 U. Kan. L. Rev. 1113 (1997); David E. Dana, The Case for Unfunded Environmental Mandates, 69 S. Cal. L. Rev. 1 (1995).

D. SOURCES OF REVENUE

1. AD VALOREM PROPERTY TAXES

Local governments that wish to provide a particular good or service must, of course, find a mechanism to pay for it. In the materials that follow, we will investigate a variety of common forms of payment: local property taxes, user fees, and special assessments. In addition, we will investigate the issue of who ought to make these payments, regardless of form. This latter inquiry will focus on the questions of whether local goods and services should be paid by those who benefit from the services or by those most capable of paying for them, and whether payment should be made from current revenues or through the issuance of debt that is repaid over a series of years.

The existence of a variety of payment schemes implies that one form of payment is superior to another in a given situation. For example, there may be reasons to pay for construction and operation of a municipal swimming pool through one form of exaction and to pay for construction and operation of a new city hall through another, even if the general population that has access to the two facilities is the same.

At the same time, all forms of exaction may be measured by some general standards to determine whether they are desirable. There is, for instance, presumably a reason why virtually all jurisdictions have gravitated to the same forms of payment rather than to alternatives, e.g., a system by which only those selected by lottery pay for services that are available to everyone in the jurisdiction. If we could identify those standards of a "good" exaction, we would have some basis for evaluating the desirability of these common systems of payment and the propriety of using any of them to pay for a particular good or service.

The literature of public finance is helpful in this inquiry. Although there exists the inevitable debate about the proper criteria for evaluating a "tax," we can discern some characteristics that would exist in any form of exaction that commanded substantial scholarly and political support. First, such a tax should bear a reasonable relationship to a desired end. The specific end to which the exaction is a means, however, may vary. In some cases, that desired end may be matching the incidence of benefits and burdens related to the exaction. In this way, those who obtain certain services will be required to pay for them, and those who pay for them will get them in return. The resulting elimination of subsidies may prevent goods and services from being oversupplied or undersupplied relative to social demand. If, for instance, I need not pay the full cost of a service that is available to me, I have an incentive to consume an amount greater than would be the case if I had to incur the entire cost. This is simply an application of the collective action problem that we saw early in the course when we explored why decentralized levels of government might more efficiently produce local public goods than centralized levels of government.

Not all rational tax schemes seek to match benefits and burdens, however. Considerations of equity and distributional concerns may favor linking the receipt of some benefits to ability to pay rather than to willingness to pay. In many cases, ability to pay and the matching of benefits and burdens will lead to the same result. For instance, relatively wealthy citizens may be more likely to own private automobiles and to use them on the city streets more frequently; hence, a payment mechanism for street maintenance that exacted more from the relatively wealthy would be justifiable under either standard. In other cases, however, the "ability to pay" rationale may be used to impose an exaction that is explicitly redistributional, e.g., that places the payment burden on those who are not receiving any direct benefits from the service provided. Exactions that are used to provide municipal homeless shelters are of this nature, although it may be argued that the relatively wealthy receive substantial indirect benefits from these payments. Payment mechanisms that satisfy the ability to pay criterion entail the concept of "vertical equity," i.e., the concept that those who have more wealth should contribute a larger percentage of their assets to the creation of public goods than those who have less wealth.

A second criterion for a "good" tax is the presence of horizontal equity. Essentially, this principle requires that similarly situated payors pay similar amounts. This principle implies that we be able to define what it means to be "similarly situated." That inquiry must be resolved by reference to the objective we are trying to achieve. If we were agreed that city water should be paid for in a manner that equated benefits and burdens, then horizontal equity would require that two homeowners, each of whom used 100 cubic feet of water per month pay the same amount, even though one homeowner was significantly wealthier than the other. If we were agreed, however, that municipal day care should be paid for on a schedule that depended on family income, horizontal equity might require that two families with incomes under $15,000 pay the same amount, even though one family had one child in day care and the other family had three. The "situation" whose similarity we were measuring would now be income rather than benefits received.

A third criterion for evaluating a tax system is its efficiency. Exactions are supposed to raise money. But the costs of administration and compliance may be significant. A tax system that used 30 cents of every dollar collected for operating costs would be subject to substantial criticism on the grounds of inefficiency. Some tradeoff between costs and collections is necessary. We do not seek perfect compliance with a system because the costs of ensuring full payment by each obligated payor are likely to exceed the benefits. Similarly, when we administer the system of exactions, we do not seek to measure precisely benefits received or ability to pay precisely because doing so would consume too much of the revenues. Instead, we seek rough surrogates for benefits and ability to pay, such as value of certain property, size of property, or consumption of particular goods.

Finally, a "good" exaction is one that avoids the problem of "excess burden." "What we want is a set of taxes that extracts the needed revenues but has no undesirable side effects on the operation of the economic system. A tax system that introduces distortions into the functioning of the economy typically imposes a loss of welfare on consumers over and above that resulting from the tax payments themselves; this extra welfare loss is the excess burden of the tax." Wallace E. Oates, Fiscal Federalism 121–122 (1972). For instance, if the locality imposed a tax on municipal swimming pools, but not on municipal tennis courts, and if swimming and playing tennis were largely substitutes for one another, we would expect to see a distortion in behavior in that people who might otherwise swim will now play tennis. The result will be the overuse of municipal tennis courts and the underuse of municipal swimming pools.

As you examine the following materials, consider the extent to which each of these payment mechanisms does or does not satisfy these criteria. Are the courts that decide the propriety of using a specific form of exaction in a particular setting either explicitly or implicitly applying these criteria?

For further reading, see Richard A. Musgrave & Peggy B. Musgrave, Public Finance in Theory and Practice (3d ed. 1980); Stewart E. Sterk & Mitchell L. Engler, Property Tax Reassessment: Who Needs It?, 81 N.D. L. Rev. 1037 (2006); John A. Swain, The Taxation of Private Interests in Public Property: Toward a Unified Theory of Property Taxation, 2000 Utah L. Rev. 421; Louis Kaplow, Horizontal Equity: Measures in Search of Principle, 42 Nat. Tax J. 139 (1989).

Dick Netzer, Economics of the Property Tax

3–8, 173–176 (1966).

Property taxation has been the major fiscal resource of American local governments since seventeenth century colonial days. During the first two centuries of its existence, the property tax gradually became a general tax measured by the value of all types of privately owned assets, with all assets taxed at a uniform rate. However, in the last hundred years, it has become less general in coverage, in large part because of the difficulty of administering so universal a tax uniformly in an increasingly complex society. In most of the states the tax is now one chiefly on real estate and business equipment and inventories. Although the property tax is no longer virtually the sole support of state-local government in the United States as it was at the turn of the twentieth century, it remains the single most important factor in state-local finance, by a wide margin.

Critics of the Tax

There have been waves of criticism associated in time with the changing fortunes of the property tax: savage across-the-board attacks in the late nineteenth century; a somewhat more moderate tone and a quest for ways to make the institution work more effectively in the 1920's; renewed broadsides in the 1930's; and what can be best described as a "new complacency" regarding the property tax in the last decade. . . .

One strand of the nineteenth century criticism, of course, was the single-tax movement. Taxes on the value of site improvements, structures, and personal property, as well as commodity taxes, were denounced as inequitable and a deterrent to investment. Seligman in his celebrated 1895 essay on "The General Property Tax" summarized the main academic strand of criticism. First, the tax, according to Seligman, was simply not administrable: "Practically, the general property tax as actually administered is beyond all doubt one of the worst taxes known in the civilized world." He classed the administrative defects as inherent rather than correctible. But he also held that, even if the administrative problems could be overcome, the tax was intolerable on theoretical grounds.

The main counts in Seligman's indictment were twofold. First, because of the heterogeneity of property in a modern complex economy and the distinction between rights and claims in property and the physical thing itself, the tax was not one on personal wealth but an erratically double-counting tax on gross assets with virtually no theoretical underpinnings. Second, the tax had almost no relationship to ability to pay, for property had been replaced by product as evidence of such ability. While, over time, asset values do tend to reflect capitalized income, income flows are not necessarily coincident with asset values for particular taxpayers at particular dates. Moreover, property ownership is an incomplete measure of income potentials, since investment in human capital and differences in exertion are not reached by the property tax.

In addition, the property tax worked out in practice to be quite regressive in incidence; that is, the tax as a percentage of the incomes of those who bear the ultimate burden declines as income rises. Other critics supported the regressivity argument with empirical evidence, and found that the incidence of the tax was not only regressive but also poorly related to the benefits received from public expenditure financed by the property tax. Yet another serious shortcoming was considered to be the tax's discouragement of investment in that social necessity, housing.

The early wave of criticism of the tax no doubt contributed to two significant developments: first, the narrowing of the coverage of the tax by constitutional and statutory changes; and second, after 1910, the increasingly widespread adoption by state governments of income, consumption, and highway-user taxes, thus reducing state government dependence on the property tax. In the 1920's, however, the property tax seemed to gain a new lease on life. Rapid population increase, growing urbanization, and the lengthening of the period of compulsory school attendance produced a sharp increase in local government spending, and the funds for this were produced by the property tax without apparent difficulty.

This rising productivity of the property tax led to a different line of analysis: the revenues were substantial and no substitute for the tax was in sight; therefore it was unlikely to disappear no matter how deficient. Could anything be done to make it work better? Conventional solutions offered were narrowing the tax base to those classes of property which could be most easily discovered, realty and business personalty (or, alternatively, classifying intangibles and some tangible personalty for taxing at special low rates); improving local assessment administration via larger primary assessment units, better staff at the local level, and more state participation in the form of central assessment, equalization of differences in assessments among counties, and the like; and adopting supplementary state nonproperty taxes to lessen dependence on the property tax....

Since public expenditures have been increasing and are expected to continue to increase more rapidly at the local level than elsewhere, a major tax producer, the revenues from which appear to be responsive to economic growth, is not without its friends. One group of friendly critics is represented by the Advisory Commission on Intergovernmental Relations: the viewpoint is essentially that the property tax is really not so bad if adequately administered; and reasonably high standards of administration, although infrequently found, are attainable goals. The problem, according to these critics, is one of "rehabilitation" of the tax, not fundamental reform—language which suggests that there was a Golden Age in property tax administration in some earlier period. Another approach has been taken by Jesse Burkhead and other investigators at Syracuse University. They maintain that the dire economic effects theoretically expected do not seem to be of major consequence empirically. Their statistical findings also suggest that, "at least in suburban areas, it is a fairly adequate surrogate for a local income tax, since a high relationship has been found between property values and income levels." Thus Burkhead concludes:

> On the whole ... the property tax is a far better fiscal instrument than most of its critics have allowed. There is every reason to believe that it will continue to hold its relative fiscal importance in state-local public finance structures.... Although the property tax has long been condemned by students of fiscal affairs, its recent behavior suggests that it would be far better to strengthen this levy than to plan for its eradication.

Property Tax Administration

A tax institution may be found to be meritorious on distributional and efficiency grounds, or at least less harmful than alternatives which would be equally productive of revenue, and still be a highly defective means of financing government if it cannot be administered reasonably well—that is, equitably and at moderate cost....

The details of the indictment of assessment administration need not be reviewed here. Essentially, the criticism reduces to three salient points. First, there is conclusive evidence that, within most individual assessment jurisdictions, even the most common, least heterogeneous properties—single-family nonfarm houses—are assessed at widely varying fractions of market value. Presumably, the variation is even greater for more complicated types of property. Second, within individual jurisdictions, owners of differing types of property are treated differently by assessors, sometimes systematically, albeit extralegally, but often quite erratically. Third, assessment practices and levels differ among assessment jurisdictions within a single county or state. This matters because some property levies apply over an area larger than a single assessment jurisdictions (for example, county levies where there are separate city, town, and village assessors), and because assessed values are often used for other purposes such as determination of state aid amounts and tax rate and debt limits.

The continued volume and strident nature of the criticism for so many years suggest that the quality of assessment administration has not improved much over the years, or at least has improved at an unacceptably slow rate. This in turn suggests the possibility that the fault may not lie in the obstinacy and ignorance of public officials and legislators; instead, acceptable assessment administration simply may not be attainable, at least at costs which are at all reasonable.

Is this in fact the case? Is the pursuit of uniformity in assessments quixotic or even downright harmful? The answer would clearly be positive if it can be demonstrated that the achievement of uniformity would involve unacceptably high administrative costs. The evidence on the present cost of property tax administration is sketchy, but it appears to be quite low relative to tax collections, which is to be expected in view of the generally poor quality of the administrative job. Apparently, local assessment administration seldom costs as much as 1 percent of collections in the larger jurisdictions: in New York City, the assessment and review process involves expenditures of only about $4 million, with collections of slightly more than $1 billion. But there is some indication that better quality assessment is substantially more costly. It is generally agreed that the quality of assessment is relatively high in general in California and Wisconsin, as compared to, say, New York State; California and Wisconsin local and state governments appear to spend substantially more for property tax administration than those in New York State. A similar comparison can be made of the City of Milwaukee and New York City, the former having relatively high grade and high cost administration and the latter showing much poorer results for a relatively smaller administrative outlay.

Cost of "Good" Administration

If the assessment quality achieved in the best performing jurisdictions currently is the target, it may be entirely possible to get "good" property tax administration in the larger jurisdictions at a cost of no more than, say, 1.5 percent of tax collections, which is probably acceptable when compared to sales and income tax administration costs. But this standard and these levels of costs raise real problems for smaller jurisdictions. If the assessment function is to be handled by a full-time professional staff, as has been repeatedly recommended over the years, even a minimal size jurisdiction is likely to have an annual budget of $60,000 to $70,000. This budget will be less than 1.5 percent of tax collections only in jurisdictions with revenue of $4 million or more, which implies an average minimum population size of 40,000–50,000, since per capita property tax revenue currently averages about $100. In contrast, there are currently more than 18,000 primary assessment jurisdictions in the nation, with an average population of only about 10,000. The problem would not be solved by eliminating assessment districts smaller than the county in size since less than a fifth of the nation's counties have a population of 50,000 or more, and many of these appear to have total property tax revenues (including the revenues of all governments within the county) of less than $4 million. This minimum size standard appears to be met by fewer than 500 counties and cities outside counties, and suggests that multi-county or state-wide assessment districts would be necessary in many places.

This may be eminently reasonable, but does some violence to the notion that one of the main virtues of the property tax is that it is suitable for use and administration by even small local governments. If local self-government, autonomy, and self-respect require local administration of the major revenue source, then it is clear that the property tax is unsuitable on administrative grounds; local autonomy is inconsistent with acceptable standards of administration at acceptable costs of administration, except for rather large local government units. Contemporary friends of the property tax (but apparently not legislators and local officials) would answer that assessment administration can be centralized without impairing local autonomy. After all, in England and Wales, valuation for the property tax (the rates) is done by the Inland Revenue, a central government agency, and English local governments are at least as autonomous vis—vis the central government in Westminster as are American local governments vis—vis their state governments.

Helen F. Ladd & John Yinger, America's Ailing Cities: Fiscal Health and the Design of Urban Policy

126–128 (1989).

All central cities in the United States are permitted to use the property tax as a revenue source. Many, however, are not allowed to use other broad-based taxes such as earnings or income taxes or general sales taxes. Because revenue diversification typically raises revenue-raising capacity, cities have an incentive to take advantage of whatever revenue sources they are permitted to use....

At one extreme are the 29 cities that use no broad-based taxes other than the property tax. This group includes 16 cities—primarily in New England, New York, New Jersey, and North Carolina—in which the property tax accounted for 90 percent or more of all tax revenues, and 13 cities that supplemented property tax revenues with sizable revenues from selective, rather than general, sales taxes and miscellaneous other taxes. At the other extreme are 6 cities, namely Kansas City, Missouri, New York, St. Louis, San Francisco, Washington, D.C., and Birmingham, Alabama, that use both income and sales taxes along with the property tax.

Currently, only 18 of the 86 cities use some form of earnings tax, defined broadly to include earnings, payroll, and income taxes. Six of the 18 are in Ohio, where local governments rely heavily on earnings taxes. The first city earnings tax was adopted by Philadelphia in 1939. Others were adopted throughout the next three decades, the most recent being the adoption by Newark, New Jersey, of the payroll tax in 1971. Many of the 18 cities supplement the personal income or earnings tax with a tax on corporate income....

Many more cities, but still only 45 of the 86, use a general sales tax. A clear regional pattern emerges here; general sales taxes are quite common in the West and South but are used by only a few cities in the Northeast and Midwest. About one-half of the cities with a general sales tax raise more revenue from it than from the property tax.

What effect does access to a tax have on a city's revenue-raising capacity? Recall that a particular tax source influences a city's capacity through its impact on the city's ability to export tax burdens to nonresidents. Hence, we measure the impact of access to a tax by its effect on tax exporting. Consider, for example, a city that is authorized to use a property tax but not an earnings tax. If the export ratio (that is, the burden that can be shifted to nonresidents per dollar of burden on residents) for the prohibited earnings tax is greater than the export ratio for the property tax, the prohibition is binding and reduces the city's revenue-raising capacity. If, in contrast, the export ratio for the prohibited earnings tax is smaller than that for the property tax, the prohibition probably has little effect on the city's revenue-raising capacity.

A comparison across cities of export ratios for the three potential broad-based taxes shows that the earnings tax dominates property and sales taxes in most cities for most years of this study. The property tax is the most exportable tax in at most 7 of the 86 cities. Six of these 7 (all but Toledo, Ohio) rely more heavily on the property tax than on any other. In only 4 cities does the sales tax have the highest export rate. Three of the 4 use sales taxes; Honolulu, the fourth, has no general sales tax but does employ selective sales taxes.

Our analysis indicates that 60 of the 68 cities not permitted to use an earnings tax would be able to export a higher fraction of their tax burdens to nonresidents if a standard earnings tax were authorized. Moreover, the tendency ... for export ratios of the earnings tax to grow over time indicates that prohibitions against the use of such a tax are becoming relatively more restrictive.

NOTES

1. Municipalities have a variety of fiscal tools from which to select in deciding how to pay for a municipal good or service. The property tax remains the most common source of municipal revenues. According to the U.S. Census Bureau, local governments raised about $354.4 billion through taxes during the 2000–2001 fiscal year. Of this amount, $253.3 billion was raised through property taxes. The balance was raised through a combination of sales taxes, corporate and individual income taxes, motor vehicle licenses, and gross receipts taxes. See http://www.census.gov/govs/estimate/01sl00us.html. School districts continue to be especially dependent on property taxes. In 2000–2001, these special purpose governments raised $117.1 million in taxes, $112.5 million of which was attributable to property taxes. See http://www.census.gov/govs/estimate/01sp00us.html. In Chapter 8 we will explore the distributional implications of school districts' reliance on the property tax.

A simplified model of how the amount of property tax is calculated per landowner looks something like this: An assessor places a value on each parcel of taxable property within the taxing jurisdiction. The municipal budget is calculated independently, and those parts of the budget anticipated to be funded from sources other than the property tax (state and federal grants, user fees, other taxes) are subtracted. A millage rate for the jurisdiction can then be calculated by dividing the municipal budget to be funded from the property tax by the total assessed value of all taxable property within the jurisdiction. The quotient indicates the tax rate that can be applied to determine the tax attributable to each parcel. For instance, assume a municipal budget of $1,000,000 in a jurisdiction that comprises property with a total assessed valuation of $200,000,000. The tax rate would be $1,000,000 divided by $200,000,000, or .005 (5 mills). If I owned a parcel assessed at $125,000, my tax would be $125,000 x .005 or $625.

A moment's reflection will indicate that the workability of this scheme depends on a variety of factors: the accuracy of the individual assessment, the consistency of assessments across similarly situated property, the accuracy of projections for municipal expenditures, and the ability of residents to pay the amounts derived through these calculations, to name a few. Valuations may be calculated by different formulas, and the results of each may vary substantially from results obtained under different methods. Under the cost approach, assessors must separate the cost of buildings and improvements from the cost of the land. Replacement costs of the buildings and improvements are then calculated, and reduced to take depreciation into account. This result is then added to the raw land cost to determine the full value of each parcel. Under the market approach, the assessor considers the market price of parcels that have recently been sold and applies those values to comparable properties that have not recently been on the market. The income approach requires the assessor to estimate the value of income producing real property. The assessor must determine the net income of a property and apply a capitalization rate (which translates future earnings into present income).

The complexity of the valuation process, and hence the susceptibility of the process both to official discretion and to unintentional error, is evident in a Hawaii case that illuminates both the assessment methodology and the principles that guide it. In City and County of Honolulu v. Steiner, 834 P.2d 1302 (Haw. 1992), the taxpayer objected to an assessment imposed on her oceanfront parcel. The city and county appealed from an adverse decision in the state tax court. In the course of reversing the tax court, the supreme court of the state indicated the rationale and mechanism for the assessment:

> The Department of Finance has established more specific guidelines for real property valuation in the Procedure and Reference Manual of the Real Property Assessment Division, Department of Finance, City and County of Honolulu (Procedure and Reference Manual or Manual). The Manual provides two basic methods of land valuation, the market data approach and the income approach (used for income generating properties). Procedure and Reference Manual §§ 991.00–912.00. The market data approach is described as follows:
>
> > [T]his method involves obtaining all available sales data, qualifying these as being transacted at "arms-length" conditions or being "bona fide" transactions, and comparing these recently sold properties to the one being

> appraised, making adjustments as necessary for comparisons. Unit prices demonstrated by actual sales, either adjusted or unadjusted, provide valid estimates of market value. Adjustments for dissimilarities in the market data approach to value are made by plus or minus of dollar amount or percentages, from the comparable parcels to the subject, benchmark or typical parcel in the neighborhood. The major factors which should be considered in the adjustments include the time of sale, terms of sale, location of compared parcels, differences in physical characteristics among them, and all other factors which might have been significant so as to influence the prices paid for the properties.

Procedure and Reference Manual § 911.00.

Section 941.31 of the Manual directs assessors to consider three general factors affecting the value of urban and suburban residential lands: location, neighborhood characteristics and site characteristics. Site characteristics include: (1) size and shape of lot; (2) topography and soil conditions; (3) landscaping; and (4) accessibility. Another section of the Manual notes that the "topography may be such that expensive excavations are required." Procedure and Reference Manual § 913.00. Under these circumstances the appraiser is instructed to note any adjustments for these conditions on the appraisal card as a percentage reduction in the value of the affected parcel. Id.

In assessing shoreline properties, the "most important factor of value" is the quality of the shoreline itself. Procedure and Reference Manual § 941.34. Appraisers are advised to consider "the amount, kind, and quality of shoreline, the quality and condition of the surf and water, the view, and the accessibility to the shore, and including the hazards or detriments because of the natural wave action." Id. . . .

The primary method used by the City tax appraiser to value the Steiner property was to establish (1) a "typical" lot size and (2) a "benchmark" value, in dollars per square foot, for the particular neighborhood or area. The benchmark value was calculated by reviewing the sales data for ocean-front property in the surrounding areas from the year before last (e.g. 1986 sales data for the 1988 tax year). If, as in the case of the Steiner property, a lot were larger than the typical lot, the excess area or "overage" would be valued per square foot at a percentage of benchmark value. If a lot were smaller than the typical lot, the benchmark would be adjusted upward to reflect the greater value per square foot.

For the 1988 and 1989 tax years, the City assessed the property based on a typical lot size of 20,000 sq. ft. The assessor, Irene Nakamura, applied the Black Point benchmark to 20,000 sq. ft. and 50% of benchmark to the remaining 26,707 sq. ft. The benchmark value, based on comparable sales data, was $75 per sq. ft. for 1988 and $95 per sq. ft. for 1989 in the Black Point area. Based on this formula, she assessed the property as follows:

1988		
100% × $75 × 20,000 sq. ft	=	$1,500,000
50% × $75 × 26,707 sq. ft.	=	1,001,513
		$2,501,513

1989		
100% × $95 × 20,000 sq. ft.	=	$1,900,000
50% × $95 × 26,707 sq. ft.	=	1,268,583
		$3,168,583

> For the 1988 benchmark, the City relied heavily on the 1986 sales of three Black Point properties which it considered comparable to the Steiner property. These properties were calculated to have land values of $83.66, $110.27 and $82.56 per sq. ft. The City also considered sales of ocean-front properties in the Diamond Head and Kahala areas that ranged from $81.08 to $155.53 per sq. ft. From these sales data, the City determined that the benchmark should be $75 per sq. ft. for the Black Point area. Ms. Nakamura testified that the Black Point benchmark also reflected a discount for the topography in the Black Point area; she made no other adjustments to the valuation of the Steiner property based on its topography.
>
> Similarly, the 1989 Black Point benchmark of $95 per sq. ft. was based on 1987 sales in the surrounding areas, including the sale of one Black Point property.
>
> The City used the same 50% (of benchmark) overage factor for all ocean-front lots which exceeded 20,000 sq. ft. in both the Black Point and Kahala Beach areas. No adjustment was made based on the topography or usability of the overage area. Thus, level (buildable) beach-front overage on Kahala Avenue was valued at only $10 per sq. ft. more than steep, boulder strewn (unbuildable) overage with no beach access such as on the Steiner parcel.

834 P.2d at 1306–1308. The court concluded that the methodology used to arrive at the benchmark was consistent with the market data approach required by statute, that the assessor had properly integrated recent sales data into the benchmark, and that the assessor had properly made adjustments to the benchmark to account for differences in topography. In reaching this conclusion, the court determined that the assessor's adherence to the department manual was an indication of fairness in assessment, insofar as it increased the likelihood that similar procedures would be applied to all taxpayers.

2. *Property Tax Exemptions.* One longstanding critique of the property tax has been that it may prove burdensome for people who live on low or fixed incomes during periods when real estate prices increase rapidly. These residents may live in housing that was affordable at the time of purchase, but the property taxes on which have come to exceed their ability to pay. While residents in these positions may have a significant asset, the house in which they live, it is questionable whether it is appropriate to require that they sell that asset or incur significant debt (for instance, by taking a mortgage against the real estate) in order to pay escalating property taxes. Several states create certain forms of exemption to assist persons in this position.

Initially, these exemptions took the form of homestead exemptions from a certain amount of property valuation. See, e.g., W. Va. Const. art. X, sec. 1b, subsec. C (authorizing the legislature to adopt an exemption up to $20,000 for residence of nonelderly, nondisabled homeowners). Homestead exemptions were attacked, however, because they were available regardless of the income of the recipient. In the post-World War II period, state and local governments began to enact "circuit breakers" (so-called because property taxes can be said to financially "overload" the elderly), providing refunds, tax credits, or exemptions to low-income, disabled, or elderly individuals, or to other groups of special need or desert. Arizona, for instance, provides exemptions to honorably discharged members of the armed forces, and to poor widows or widowers, regardless of their age. (Ariz. Const. Art. 9, §§ 2, 2.1). In many states, taxpayers are provided with a state exemption from a portion of the assessed property tax and the state provides reimbursements to the localities for the amount of the revenue lost. Connecticut's exemption for veterans is typical of the type and format of circuit breakers in other states. In Connecticut, a property tax exemption of $1,000 is granted to all veterans. (Conn. Gen. Stat. Ann. § 12–81(19)). Servicemen and veterans having disability ratings are provided exemptions of $3,000; veterans with severe disabilities are afforded a $10,000 exemption. (Conn. Gen. Stat. Ann. § 12–81(20)). Various other exemptions are provided for surviving spouses, children, and parents. (Conn. Gen. Stat. Ann. § 12–81 (21)(b), (22)–(26)). In addition to these statewide exemptions, municipalities are given the option to create additional exemptions for veterans with incomes below a certain level with a state promise of reimbursement to the locality for the lost revenue. (Conn. Gen. Stat. Ann. § 12–81(g)(c)). Nearly every state has enacted some form of homestead exemption or circuit breaker with wide variation in eligibility and the size of the exemption or credit from state to state.

In Glenn Fisher, The Worst Tax? 193–194, (1996), the author concluded that in Florida more than 3.1 million beneficiaries received exemptions valued at $1.6 billion at the time of his report. Exemptions in Florida were available for the first $25,000 of assessed value of owner-occupied homes and all the assessed value for disabled veterans. Fla. St. Ann. §§ 196.031, 196.081. In California, approximately 196,000 beneficiaries received an average benefit of $92.12 in circuit breakers for blind, disabled, and elderly homeowners and renters with incomes of less than $13,200. California's homestead exemption provided another 4.8 million recipients with an exemption on the first $7,000 of the full cash value of owner-occupied residences. A few states have given elderly homeowners a deferral of property taxes until death, with accumulated taxes serving as a lien on the property.

Given the conditions under which exemptions are granted, and the fact that those who receive exemptions are effectively subsidized by others within the relevant state or locality, which is the better explanation for their existence: (1) they reflect a communitarian view of local government, in which exemptions allow individuals with ties to the locality to remain during periods of fiscal distress or constitute rewards for prior service to the community, or (2) they reflect lobbying by organized interest groups capable of capturing significant benefits for themselves?

3. The excerpt from Ladd and Yinger suggests that state legislatures have been reluctant to permit localities to use revenue-raising mechanisms that permit the imposition of payment obligations on nonresidents. At first glance, this might seem an obvious and desirable means of constraining localities from externalizing fiscal burdens. Left to their own devices, one might imagine, local officials would prefer to place these burdens on parties to whom the officials are not accountable. Thus, legislative restrictions on taxation properly restrict local officials from requiring nonresidents to pay for local services. Before concluding that "exportable" taxes should be rejected, however, consider the extent to which nonresidents are able to free ride on expenditures made by a municipality's residents. Do nonresidents obtain value from proximity to cultural or job-related offerings in the municipality? Do nonresidents take advantage of municipal services (police, fire, water) to which they do not contribute? Are these benefits offset by other contributions that nonresidents make to the municipality (owning businesses that create jobs, providing customers to municipal businesses)? If nonresidents utilize more in the way of city services than they contribute, then exportable taxes may be desirable. Think, for instance, about municipal taxes imposed on hotel rooms. Do they represent efforts to expropriate from transients who are not represented in the local decision-making process? Or can they be justified as a means of recapturing from business visitors and tourists some of the value of city services that are dedicated to the protection and convenience of these transients? Legislative reluctance to permit such taxes, then, may be less indicative of legislative concern about a central city's imposition of fiscal obligations on nonresidents than of suburban domination of the legislature. As you consider the different payment mechanisms employed in the materials that follow, therefore, you may want to consider the relationship between who pays for municipal services and who receives them. That is not to say that payment for all services ought to be linked to the beneficiaries of the services. Some municipal goods are distinctly redistributive. But it is useful to determine whether the relationship between payment and service in any given case is consistent with some neutral principle, or results from nothing more than the successful exercise of political power by a group that is eager to export a payment obligation onto others.

State Board of Tax Commissioners v. Town of St. John

702 N.E.2d 1034 (Ind. 1998).

■ DICKSON, JUSTICE.

The State Board of Tax Commissioners ("State Board") appeals from the Indiana Tax Court's judgment regarding the validity of the Indiana property tax assessment system. We affirm in part and reverse in part.

This case initially arose in the Indiana Tax Court on individual petitions by three taxpayers from Marion County, James K. Gilday, Dimple Clarine Shelton, and William E. Wise, and a petition by the Town of St. John on behalf of a class of approximately fifty-seven of its residents. The Tax Court consolidated the petitions, conducted a bench trial in July of 1995, and found that Indiana's current statutory system of property taxation was unconstitutional. Upon appeal by the State Board, we affirmed the Tax Court's holding that the General Assembly must provide for a uniform and equal rate of property assessment and taxation based on property wealth, noted that legislative discretion in the selection of valuation method is subject to judicial review, reversed the Tax Court's conclusion that the Indiana Constitution exclusively requires an absolute and precise fair market value system, and returned the case to the Tax Court to resume consideration of the remaining issues. On remand, the Tax Court issued a preliminary opinion finding that components of Indiana's property tax valuation system violated the constitutional requirements, and it ordered the State Board to "make future real property assessments for purposes of taxation under a system that incorporates an objective reality." *Town of St. John v. State Bd. of Tax Comm'rs*, 690 N.E.2d 370, 398 (Ind. Tax 1997) ("*St. John III*"). Following a hearing to determine an appropriate deadline for bringing the assessment system into constitutional compliance, the Tax Court entered its final judgment which ordered the State Board to consider all competent evidence of property wealth in appeals filed with the county review boards on or after May 11, 1999, and remanded to the State Board for further consideration of the specific claims of the petitioners. *Town of St. John v. State Bd. of Tax Comm'rs*, 691 N.E.2d 1387, 1390 (Ind.Tax 1998) ("*St. John IV*"). . . .

* * *

The authority and limitations regarding Indiana's system of property assessment and taxation are found in the Property Taxation Clause of the Constitution of Indiana:

> The General Assembly shall provide, by law, for a uniform and equal rate of property assessment and taxation and shall prescribe regulations to secure a just valuation for taxation of all property, both real and personal.

Ind. Const. art. X, § 1(a). To discharge this constitutional responsibility, the General Assembly created an administrative agency, the State Board, and delegated to it the responsibility for establishing rules to classify and assess tangible property according to its "true tax value." The legislature does not explicitly define the term "true tax value" but delegates to the State Board the authority to define the term. However, it must be based upon specified statutory factors "and any other factor that the board determines by rule is just and proper." [The statutory factors include property classification, size, location, use, depreciation, cost of improvements, and productivity or earning capacity of land.—EDS.] Thus, the assessment regulations and schedules prescribed by the State Board determine "true tax value."

1. Constitutionality of the Statute

* * *

Applying the Property Taxation Clause, the Tax Court found "the present system is unconstitutional" because, according to the State Board's own admission, "it [is] impossible under the present system to determine the system's compliance with the uniformity provision." *St. John III*, 690 N.E.2d at 376–77. The Tax Court further found that, "[b]ecause the present system does not allow comparison of assessments to objective data, it cannot satisfy the constitutional requirements of uniformity and equality in the property assessment." Id. at 378. The court observed, "True Tax

Value is a figure produced by the application of a closed set of self-referential rules and formulas contained in Title 50. Everything needed to calculate True Tax Value is set forth in Title 50; evidence of value external to Title 50 is irrelevant." Id. at 374. Emphasizing its belief that the Indiana Constitution "requires a system of property assessment and taxation based upon a real world, objective measure of property wealth," the Tax Court concluded that "Indiana's True Tax Value system of property taxation under *section 6–1.1–31–6(c)* and Title 50 violates the Indiana Constitution...." *Id. at 398.* In its implementing judgment entry in *St. John IV,* the Tax Court expressly characterized its prior opinion in *St. John III* as holding that the statutory provision, *Indiana Code section 6–1.1–31–6(c),* "is unconstitutional." *St. John IV, 691 N.E.2d at 1388.*

We first observe that the clear thrust and rationale of the Tax Court's general determination of unconstitutionality is directed at the Title 50 regulatory system implementing "true tax value," not the statute itself. The statutory provision expressly referenced by the Tax Court in its finding of unconstitutionality states:

> (c) With respect to the assessment of real property, true tax value does not mean fair market value. True tax value is the value determined under the rules of the state board of tax commissioners.

Ind.Code § 6–1.1–31–6(c). This subsection appears in the context of *Indiana Code section 6–1.1–31–6* which establishes the standards for the State Board's real property assessment regulations. Although the Tax Court in *St. John III* does not explicitly identify the constitutional infirmity it finds in subsection 6(c), the language of this provision suggests that the Tax Court may understand *Indiana Code section 6–1.1–31–6(c)* to be contrary to this Court's decision in *St. John II.* We stated:

> While a careful and accurate fair market value assessment may well be the system closest to our constitution's requirements for uniform and equal rates of assessment and taxation and for just valuation, a system based solely upon strict fair market value is not expressly required either by the text of the constitution, by the purpose and intent of its framers, or by the subsequent case law.

St. John II, 675 N.E.2d at 327.

If interpreted as an absolute prohibition upon considering fair market value as "true tax value," subsection 6(c) would be constitutionally infirm. However, we observe that the language of this subsection is not unambiguous. Two reasonable interpretations are possible. It may be read either to command that "true tax value" may never consist of fair market value or to instruct that "true tax value" is not exclusively or necessarily identical to fair market value.

Other statutory provisions are instructive. With respect to the classification of both real property and improvements, the State Board regulations must provide for consideration of "[a]ny other factor that the board determines by rule is just and proper." *Ind.Code §§ 6–1.1–31–6(a)(1)(ix), 6–1.1–31–6(a)(2)(viii).* In addition, the legislature requires that the Board's assessment rules include instructions for determining "[t]he true tax value of real property based on the factors listed in this subsection and any other factor that the board determines by rule is just and proper." *Ind.Code § 6–1.1–31–6(b)(7).* Similarly, in its orders to local assessing officials, the legislature instructs that "the township assessors may consider factors in addition to those prescribed by the state board of tax commissioners if the use of the additional factors is first approved by the board." *Ind.Code § 6–1.1–31–5(b)* (emphasis added). Clearly, the legislature intends for the State Board regulations to accommodate unenumerated factors that it finds just and proper.

Because a reasonable, constitutional interpretation of this statute is available, we construe *Indiana Code section 6–1.1–31–6(c)* to mean that "true tax value" is not exclusively or necessarily identical to fair market value. This provision does not prohibit the State Board from promulgating regulations in which "true tax value" is based, in whole or in part, upon property wealth. The apparent failure of the State Board's present regulations to have determined that fair market value is "just and proper" does not render the statutory provision unconstitutional.

We reverse the Tax Court's determination that *Indiana Code section 6–1.1–31–6(c)* is unconstitutional.

2. Constitutionality of Cost Schedules

The State Board contends that the Tax Court's conclusion that the Board's cost schedules are unconstitutional is clearly erroneous. The Tax Court concluded that the schedules violate the Property Tax Clause of the Indiana Constitution because they do not result in a uniform and equal rate of property assessment and taxation and do not accurately measure property wealth.

In *St. John II*, this Court approved of the Tax Court's determination that " 'the framers of *Article 10, § 1* intended that each taxpayer's property wealth bear its proportion of the overall property tax burden.' " *St. John II, 675 N.E.2d at 324* (quoting *St. John I, 665 N.E.2d at 970*). However, we recognized that varying methods of valuation could be used and that uniformity of assessment method is not required, provided that the resulting valuations are just and the burdens are distributed with uniformity. *St. John II, 675 N.E.2d at 327.* We found:

> [T]he Indiana Constitution requires that our property tax system achieve substantially uniform and equal rates of property assessment and taxation and authorizes the legislature to allow a variety of methods to secure such just valuation.

Id. The uniform and equal rate of property assessment and taxation, we held, must be "based on property wealth." *Id. at 328.* However, we also emphasized that our state constitution does not require the property taxation system to be based solely on a fair market value. *Id. at 327.* Collectively, these principles require that the system provide rates of assessment that are substantially uniform and equal based on property wealth.

While expressly foregoing any appeal of the Tax Court's invalidation of the subjective elements of the present rule (e.g., neighborhood, condition, grade, obsolescence), the State Board argues that no evidence in the record supports the Tax Court's ruling that the basic design of the cost schedules is unconstitutional.

The State Board's real property assessment rules are required by statute to include instructions for determining various factors, one of which is "the cost of reproducing improvements." *Ind.Code § 6–1.1–31–6(b)(5).* Pursuant to rules adopted by the State Board, this cost is determined by application of its cost schedules. Ind. Admin. Code tit. 50, r. 2.2–2–2(b) (assessing officials must follow the State Board's rules in assessing real property). The cost of reproduction to be applied in assessments is not the actual cost of reproducing an item, but rather the "reproduction cost" as specified in the State Board's cost schedules. *St. John III, 690 N.E.2d at 373.* As the Tax Court noted, the cost schedules are "the heart of the True Tax Value system." *Id. at 377.*

* * *

The foundation for the Tax Court's decision is its conclusion that the assessment system must be based on objectively verifiable data to enable a review of the assessment system to ensure uniformity and equality, and to ensure that individual taxpayers have a means to assert a personal "right of uniformity and equality" as to individual assessments. *St. John III, 690 N.E.2d at 376 & n. 12.* Upon this latter point, the Tax Court emphasized its view that, because the existing system precludes evidence of any value which is not found in the cost schedules or otherwise approved by the State Board, assessors are prevented from considering other relevant evidence of property wealth, thus undermining the system's ability to achieve uniformity and equality as applied to individual assessments.

By instructing the General Assembly to "provide, by law, for a uniform and equal rate of property assessment and taxation" and to "prescribe regulations to secure a just valuation for taxation of all property," the Property Taxation Clause requires the creation of a uniform, equal, and just system. However, the constitutional text does not expressly provide a personal right of absolute uniformity and equality in assessment rate. We also note that this provision is not located in Article 1 of our state constitution, which generally protects individual liberty rights and limits government action.

As we noted in *St. John II,* when *Article X* was under consideration at the Constitutional Convention of 1850–51, the delegate who proposed it, Daniel Read, acknowledged the aspirational nature of the provision's language and implied "that he did not expect the full achievement of absolute and precise exactitude." *St. John II, 675 N.E.2d at 323.* Delegate Read emphasized, " 'The rule will be a part of the organic law, and the people and the Legislature will endeavor to work up to a rule so manifestly just and equitable.' " *Id. at 323* (quoting 1 REPORT OF THE DEBATES AND PROCEEDINGS 946 (Dec. 4, 1850) (comments of Delegate Read)).

* * *

We conclude that the Property Taxation Clause requires the General Assembly to provide for a system of assessment and taxation characterized by uniformity, equality, and just valuation based on property wealth, but the Clause does not require absolute and precise exactitude as to the uniformity and equality of each individual assessment. The system must also assure that individual taxpayers have a reasonable opportunity to challenge whether the system prescribed by statute and regulations was properly applied to individual assessments, but the Clause does not create a personal, substantive right of uniformity and equality. It does not establish an entitlement to individual assessments for abstract evaluation of property wealth, nor does it mandate the consideration of independent property wealth evidence in individual assessments or tax appeals.

As we noted in *St. John II*, legislative discretion to provide regulations to secure just valuation is limited by the constitutional requirements of uniform and equal rate of property assessment and taxation, and compliance with such limitations is subject to judicial review. *St. John II, 675 N.E.2d at 328.* Such judicial relief is available when the assessment system fails adequately to provide for uniformity and equality in general. For this reason, the Tax Court is correct to require that the State Board's assessment regulations be based on objectively verifiable data to enable review of the system to assure that it generally provides uniformity and equality based on property wealth.

The State Board argues that the requirement of objectively verifiable data "euphemistically mandates adoption of market value." Brief of Appellant at 16. The State Board contends that the Tax Court is incorrect if its decision, announced in *St. John III* and *St. John IV,* means that the assessment system must incorporate all three standard market-value measures of value noted by the Tax Court (comparable sales, reproduction cost minus depreciation, and income capitalization). The Board represents that its planned revisions of the assessment system would not satisfy such a standard. The Tax Court declared: "The State Board must measure property wealth in order to meet the dictates of the Indiana Constitution. This can only be done through the application of objective data and an application of real world factors affecting property values." *Id. at 382.* Observing the three recognized valuation methods, the Tax Court acknowledges that "some valuation methods are inappropriate for some types of property." *Id. at 382 n. 27.* It authorizes the State Board to "assess certain property by certain methods to the exclusion of others." Id. The State Board's regulations are not required to use all three standard market-value measures of value in its assessment system.

However, as noted above, the system must provide rates of assessment that are substantially uniform and equal based on property wealth, and this requires that the regulations be grounded on objectively verifiable data, although "a system based solely upon strict fair market value is not expressly required." *St. John II, 675 N.E.2d at 327.* The State Board argued to the Tax Court that the system adequately determines property wealth by the use of separate cost schedules for various classes of property and by measuring the "value in use" of assessed property.

The Tax Court found that the present system's separate cost schedules for different types of property prevented uniformity and equality. *St. John III, 690 N.E.2d at 377.* To the extent the Tax Court's determination may be understood to assert that different procedures or cost schedules can never be used, we disagree. The General Assembly may adopt different methods of assessment for different classifications of property in order to achieve uniformity and equality.... The use of different methods does not alone make the system unconstitutional. However, although different methods may be used, the classification of the differing properties cannot be arbitrary but rather must be based upon differences naturally inhering in the property.

As to the "value in use" claim, the Tax Court found that, under the applicable cost schedules, "it is the physical characteristics of an improvement, not its use, which governs reproduction costs" and that, therefore, the system does not measure use. *St. John III, 690 N.E.2d at 382.* The Tax Court did not prohibit the evaluation of property wealth based upon value in use but rather found that the present system was defective in its methodology. Id. As the Tax Court noted, the constitution does not require an assessment to be based upon the highest and best use of the property. *Id. at 379.* Focusing upon the taxpayer's actual use of land and improvements, rather than the possible uses which potential purchasers may choose, is an altogether appropriate way to evaluate property wealth for the purpose of assessment and taxation under the Property Taxation Clause. We find that property valuation for assessment based upon value in use is a reasonable measure of property wealth. A uniform and equal assessment of land or improvements accurately based upon value in use would not offend constitutional requirements.

However, while it is constitutionally permissible for the assessment system to apply different valuation methods for differing property classifications, including the assessment of some classifications based upon value in use rather than upon highest and best use, the Property Taxation Clause requires that the property wealth assessment methodologies result in general uniformity and equality across all the classifications.

Independent from its statements regarding the issues of value in use, separate cost schedules, mandatory use of standard market-value measurement methods, and entitlement to individual assessments based on property worth, the Tax Court further concluded that the "true tax value" system in general violated the uniformity and equality requirements of the Property Taxation Clause of the Indiana Constitution. The Tax Court found that the current assessment system as a whole fails to use "*any method* to determine property wealth," *id. at 381* (emphasis in original), and that the cost schedules "are arbitrary figures and formulas, determined by the State

Board and applied to property by local assessors with little or no reference to actual value or worth," *id. at 382.* The Tax Court explains that, because the "system eschews real world, objective data, no verification of either equality or uniformity of taxation based on property wealth is possible." *Id. at 376 n. 11.*

The State Board contends that the Tax Court's determination is clearly erroneous. It argues that the cost schedules were based upon a commercially available valuation manual modified to account for actual costs in Indiana.

Citing the Report of the Indiana Fair Market Value Study ("DeBoer Report"), conducted at the direction of the State Board and admitted as State Board Exhibit 64C, the Tax Court found that "the State Board assesses different types of property unequally," noting that residential property was assessed at 62%, commercial property at 81%, industrial property at 72%, and agricultural property at 54%, of market value. *Id. at 378 n. 17.* Citing supporting evidence, the Tax Court found that the State Board has not identified any way to measure equality of taxation under the present system except by using market information. *Id. at 379.* As discussed *supra*, although each individual assessment need not consist of a separate valuation of fair market value, the State Board's assessment regulations must be based on objectively verifiable data to enable review of the system and to ensure that it generally provides for uniformity and equality based on property wealth.

* * *

There exists evidence in the record to support the Tax Court's findings that the cost schedules lack sufficient relation to objectively verifiable data to ensure uniformity and equality based on property wealth, and to support its findings of significant lack of uniformity and equality across property classifications. The State Board has not demonstrated that these findings are clearly erroneous.

We affirm the Tax Court's determination that the existing cost schedules, lacking meaningful reference to property wealth and resulting in significant deviations from substantial uniformity and equality, violate the Property Taxation Clause of the Indiana Constitution. However, the Clause does not require the consideration of all property wealth evidence in individual assessments or appeals therefrom. It does not mandate the use of strict market value or the use of its three measurement standards. It does not prohibit the use of different assessment methodologies for differing property classifications, or assessment based on value in use, provided that the result is substantial uniformity and equality based on property wealth across all property classifications.

* * *

Conclusion

The judgment of the Tax Court is affirmed in part and reversed in part. We remand this cause to the Tax Court with instructions to modify its

Order and Judgment Entry of March 2, 1998, which remanded this cause to the State Board to consider "any real world evidence," *St. John IV, 691 N.E.2d at 1390,* and for further proceedings consistent with this opinion.

■ SULLIVAN, JUSTICE, concurring and dissenting.

* * *

I respectfully dissent from the court's conclusion in part 2 that the cost schedules for buildings and other improvements used by the Tax Board at the time relevant to this litigation are unconstitutional. The schedules were created by taking cost information from a national commercial appraisal guide for developing replacement costs, depreciated values and insurable values of buildings and other improvements. The cost data in the guide was then taken into the field where it was tested and validated against known construction costs here in Indiana. Based on the field testing and validation, the cost data was then adjusted if necessary to reflect actual costs in Indiana. The resulting cost schedules were then applied to all classes of property. See Record at 1144–1147 (testimony of consultant who developed cost schedules); Respondent's Exh. 5 (Marshall Valuation Service (valuation manual compiled by the firm of Marshall & Swift, Los Angeles, CA)). Contrary to the majority's conclusion, this approach appears to me to be based on objectively verifiable data (national cost data, adjusted for actual Indiana costs), applied uniformly across property classifications. I see no violation of *art. X, § 1, of the Indiana Constitution.*

Although I disagree with the majority's analysis of the cost schedules issue, I note that the Tax Board has advised us that its rules governing the next reassessment "will conceptually change Indiana's assessing system by adding market-value concepts." Brief of Appellant at 9. For this reason, I see the issue as effectively moot.

NOTES

1. *Questions on "Fair" Taxation.* Why isn't market value alone always appropriate as a measure of the "true tax value" of property? What other factors could a jurisdiction or board of taxation consider that would cause "true tax value" to deviate from market value? What would make cost schedules appropriate or inappropriate for measuring tax value? Would it matter that the schedules were updated on a regular basis? It would be possible to ensure taxation at fair market value by assessing each parcel within the jurisdiction on an annual basis. But the administrative costs of such a system would likely violate the condition that a good tax system should collect a significant amount of net revenue. If annual, individual assessment is not appropriate, however, some surrogate will be necessary. Any useful surrogate will be imperfect, but presumably its savings in administrative costs will offset its imperfections. Why wouldn't we believe that schedules derived and adjusted along the lines of the schedules used in Indiana constitute a "good enough," if imperfect, surrogate?

2. *Fractional Assessment.* Ideally, fair market valuation will provide a means by which the respective owners of any two parcels can easily compare their tax burdens, whether those parcels are within the same jurisdiction or in other jurisdictions. That process becomes more difficult if different jurisdictions use different measures of value, as the court in the principal case suggests occurred in Indiana. One source of interjurisdictional differences has been the practice of "fractional assessment." Under this procedure, localities assessed properties at a fraction of their fair market value, and different localities within the same state used different fractions. The practice in New York received a thorough critique in a series of cases decided in the past 30 years. As applied, fractional assessment resulted in intra-and inter-class variations in the assessment of similar properties, particularly where assessing residential properties at a lower percentage of current market value than commercial properties shifted the burden of real property taxation from residential to commercial property owners. In Matter of Hellerstein v. Assessor of Town of Islip, 332 N.E.2d 279 (N.Y. 1975), the court determined that a state statute required that all property be assessed at full value. Fractional assessments were, therefore, invalid.

What objection could there be to the practice, as long as the same fraction is applied to all property within the same jurisdiction? Assume, for instance, that a jurisdiction used a constant 60 percent ratio, so that a home with a fair market value of $120,000 was valued at $72,000 and a home with a fair market value of $100,000 was valued at $60,000. Why should it matter that the assessment was not based on full market value? How persuasive are the following arguments: (1) fractional assessments lull taxpayers into believing that their taxes are lower than they would be if full market assessment were used, and hence discourage taxpayers from challenging improper assessments; (2) fractional assessments make it more difficult to monitor assessment practices; (3) where fractional assessments are permitted, localities will engage in a "race to the bottom" to assess property as low as possible if state aid to localities is predicated on assessed valuation rather than fair market valuation. For a review of state practices on fractional assessment and classification, see Robert L. Beebe & Richard J. Sinnott, In the Wake of Hellerstein: Whither New York, 43 Alb. L. Rev. 203, 412, 777 (1979).

Hellerstein was statutorily overruled in 1981 as the New York Legislature recognized that full value reassessment would produce a dramatic shift in the local property tax burden away from nonresidential property owners to residential property owners. The statute permitted cities and towns to employ fractional assessment and differential rates for homestead and nonhomestead properties. The assessment formula of this statute was challenged in Foss v. City of Rochester, 480 N.E.2d 717 (N.Y. 1985), where the court found the assessment practices violated the equal protection clauses of the federal and state Constitutions because they permitted similarly situated properties to be taxed unequally. The statutory formula was determined to cause an unconstitutional disparity between assessments based on geography, because cities and towns within the same county employed unequal tax rates for homestead and nonhomestead properties. Moreover, because the municipalities used varying rates and different fractional assessment ratios, any attempt at countywide equalization was impossible.

The legislature responded to the *Foss* decision by enacting Real Property Tax Law article 19–A, Laws of 1985 (ch. 828), which shifted the responsibility for calculating the tax rate or rates and levying the tax on individual properties from the counties to the cities and towns. In Foss v. City of Rochester, 489 N.E.2d 727 (N.Y.1985), the Court of Appeals invalidated the new statute as violative of state and federal equal protection guarantees. The court concluded: "The imposition of demonstrably different county tax burdens, solely by reason of geographic location, continues unabated pursuant to chapter 828. Article 19–A makes no effort to provide interjurisdictional equality between taxpayers in different assessing units."

3. *Incidence of the Property Tax.* One of the major debates in the property tax literature concerns who bears the incidence and distributional consequences of the tax. In the first instance, of course, landowners pay the tax. Hence, it might be considered to be a relatively progressive tax, since those with relative wealth are likely to be landowners. To the extent that the tax is passed on to tenants, in the case of rental property, or to consumers, in the case of business property, however, the tax looks increasingly regressive. Regressivity also seems implicit in the imposition of the property tax on households, since housing expenditures tend to decline as a percent of income as income increases. For many years, this was the dominant view in the economics literature:

> The real property tax was treated as a tax on land and structures that causes increases in the prices of goods and services produced with the tax base. The burden of the property tax on structures was felt to be borne in proportion to consumption of such commodities. Following this logic, the tax was regressive, because consumption (especially of housing, in whose price the property tax is an especially large component) looms larger in the budgets of low-income families than of those of the well to do. The tax on land was alleged to be borne by landowners, and this component was seen as progressive.

Henry J. Aaron, Who Pays the Property Tax? 19–20 (1975). See also Helen F. Ladd, The Role of the Property Tax: A Reassessment, in Broad–Based Taxes: New Options and Sources 39 (Richard A. Musgrave ed., 1973). Notice that the regressive view of the property tax is also embraced in the above excerpt from Netzer.

In the mid–1970s, however, what has become known as the "new view" of the property tax emerged. On this theory, the property tax is what Aaron refers to as "a friend" of egalitarianism, insofar as it reflects more progressivity. Professor Edward Zelinsky has summarized this more charitable view of the property tax.

> Chief among the intellectual developments challenging this critique of the local property tax are two alternative claims now widely accepted by students of property taxation: that the property tax is, as an economic matter, a tax on capital income generally and that the property tax essentially purchases benefits received from municipal government. In the first case, the tax is progressive

in its economic incidence; in the second case, the tax has no net economic effect since the cost of the tax is offset by the benefits the tax purchases. While both views cannot be correct, together they erode the once widely-held belief that property taxation passes onto the consumers of housing and is thus regressive in its ultimate economic effect.

Central to the characterization of the real property tax as a levy on capital income generally is Professor Harberger's model of the corporate income tax and his conclusion that the corporate tax ultimately falls on all capital, corporate and noncorporate. For purposes of this discussion, Professor Harberger's basic insights are that the corporate levy is initially imposed on selective capital (i.e., capital invested in corporate solution), that capital for the long term is fungible and mobile between the corporate and noncorporate portions of the economy, and that the owners of corporate capital, to avoid selective taxation, will seek higher after-tax returns by shifting their investments from the (taxed) corporate sector to the (nontaxed) unincorporated sector. This shift of capital, in turn, contracts the corporate sector and expands the amount of capital invested noncorporately. The upshot is a lower rate of return for all owners of capital as the holders of corporate capital are taxed while the owners of noncorporate capital receive lower returns since the supply of noncorporate capital is increased by the tax-induced movement of resources into the unincorporated sector to avoid corporate taxation; the consequent increase of the supply of noncorporate capital depresses the rate of return to such capital.

The Harberger model is readily adaptable to the local property tax, which, like the corporate income tax, is a selective tax on one particular sector of capital investment, i.e., real property. To avoid this selective taxation, mobile capital will migrate to nontaxed sectors, i.e., forms of investment other than real property. Thus, the property tax turns out to be an impost on capital, imposed (directly) on capital held as real property and (indirectly) on all other capital, the supply of which is increased by the migration of capital avoiding real property taxation with an attendant decrease in the rate of return to non-real estate capital.

If the real property levy is conceived in this fashion as ultimately burdening capital in general, the distributional implications of the tax are more complex than the traditional critique suggests. To the extent the property tax is passed onto renters and less affluent homeowners, that critique retains force since lower- and middle-income families devote higher percentages of their budgets to housing costs than do affluent households and thus spend (via their rent and mortgage payments) higher percentages of their incomes on real property taxation than do more prosperous families.

However, to the extent that the property tax falls on the owners of capital generally, the tax is potentially progressive in its impact; indeed, the property tax resembles the kind of wealth impost favored by certain commentators. The characterization of the property tax as a potentially progressive levy on wealth is reinforced by the fact that the real property tax, conceived as a tax on the users of particular types of capital, falls directly, not just on homeowners, but on the holders of commercial and industrial real estate as well.

The alternative challenge to the traditional wisdom, premised on the seminal writings of Charles Tiebout, views the property tax as a wash: the payment of property taxes purchases offsetting benefits in the form of government services. In a Tieboutian world, if a particular taxpayer does not desire the package of taxes and services offered by the community in which he resides,

> he will change his residence to a locality furnishing a set of taxes and services more to his liking. Thus, each individual's property tax payments ultimately purchase for him a bundle of local government services which, in the individual's judgment, are worth the property tax cost.
>
> Of course, this model is not without its limitations and qualifications. In any given metropolitan area, there may not in practice be enough municipalities to offer every individual the particular package of taxes and services he considers optimal; relocation from locality to locality may not be as easy as the Tiebout model assumes.
>
> Nevertheless, with all of the necessary limitations and qualifications, the benefits perspective on the local property tax contains an important insight: local property taxes can plausibly be characterized as, in large measure, the price paid for a particular bundle of government services. To that extent, the tax expended is offset by the municipal benefits received.

Edward A. Zelinsky, The Once and Future Property Tax: A Dialogue with My Younger Self, 23 Cardozo L. Rev. 2199, 2203–06 (2002). For an argument that the complexity of administering and defining the incidence of a property tax are best addressed by a system that allows reassessment only on sale, subject to a retrospective tax adjustment, payable by the seller, to compensate for the seller's low assessment during the period of ownership, see Stewart E. Sterk and Mitchell L. Engler, Property Tax Reassessment: Who Needs It?, 81 N.D.L. Rev. 1037 (2006).

The new view of the property tax depends on certain assumptions that prevent owners of taxed property from being able to shift burdens to users and consumers. These assumptions include a sufficient amount of competition, a mobile workforce, and a desire by property owners to maximize returns on their capital. As a result of these assumptions (as well as issues such as whether residential housing should be considered as a capital investment or a good that is consumed), the debate over the incidence of the property tax continues. For technical treatments, see, e.g., Oskar Ragnar Harmon, A New View of the Incidence of the Property Tax: The Case of New Jersey, 17 Pub. Fin. Q. 323 (1989); Paul Hobson, The Incidence of Heterogeneous Residential Property Taxes, 29 J. Pub. Econ. 29 (1986).

4. If the property tax were applied as the *St. Johns* court suggests it ought to be, would it more closely resemble a benefits-based tax or a redistributive tax based on ability to pay? Note that because a benefits-based tax would impose payment obligations on individuals roughly equal to the value of the service each individual receives, the exaction reflects the price the service would bring in the private market. Hence, government plays a purely allocative role when providing goods paid for through benefit-based taxes. Government provision may be required to overcome collective action problems, but the goods are basically those that residents would choose to purchase anyway. Thus, if we believe, for example, that individuals obtain benefits from municipal removal of snow from sidewalks roughly proportionate to the amount of taxable property they own, then if that service were paid for through property taxes, we might conclude that, at least in part, the property tax is benefit-based. On the other hand, if we believe that property taxes are used primarily to pay for services (such as public schools) used relatively equally by both wealthy and poorer residents or services (such as municipal day-care) that are disproportionately utilized by lower-income residents, then we might conclude that the property tax is primarily based on ability to pay and, therefore, redistributive.

Either of these justifications for the property tax is defensible. On the other hand, if officials use tax revenues without regard to either of these justifications, property taxes may serve neither to provide benefits that residents actually desire nor to redistribute wealth. Instead, the goods and services funded with the tax may either be inefficiently supplied or may not satisfy residents' preferences. Of course, this could not happen in a world that met all the Tiebout assumptions. However:

> The major fundamental challenge to the Tiebout literature comes from a group of economists ... who argue that the coercive power of government imbues it with an element of monopoly power, which is frequently if not generally used to enhance the utility of the elected at the expense of the electorate. The argument is that officials have objectives which differ from those of the electorate, and that they have sufficient monopoly power to pursue these objectives, at least to some degree....
>
> The divergence of officials' objectives from those of the electorate can take one of three forms—(1) efficient provision of public services beyond that level demanded by the public; (2) explicit diversion of tax revenues to private use, via expense account padding, and the like; and (3) ... a setting in which bureaucrats desire to maximize the size of their bureaucracies, and are able to do so by using resources inefficiently....

Bruce W. Hamilton, A Review: Is the Property Tax a Benefit Tax?, in Local Provision of Public Services: The Tiebout Model after Twenty–Five Years 85, 96 (George R. Zodrow ed., 1983).

One would anticipate that when property taxes are perceived as serving the objectives identified by Hamilton above, rather than such "legitimate" objectives as funding desired services or redistributing wealth to the needy, pressures will arise to limit government's capacity to impose and collect taxes. Indeed, local residents who oppose redistributive taxes, or at least decentralized redistributive taxes, might wish to limit state or local taxation in order to minimize the redistributive expenditures made by those governments. Consider whether the provisions at issue in the following case can be explained as an attempt to restrict the capacity of local governments to provide more than basic services for residents.

Amador Valley Joint Union High School District v. State Board of Equalization

583 P.2d 1281 (Cal. 1978).

■ RICHARDSON, JUSTICE.

In these consolidated cases, we consider multiple constitutional challenges to an initiative measure which was adopted by the voters of this state at the June 1978 primary election. This measure, designated on the ballot as

Proposition 13 and commonly known as the Jarvis–Gann initiative, added article XIII A to the California Constitution. Its provisions are set forth in their entirety in the appendix to this opinion. As will be seen, the new article changes the previous system of real property taxation and tax procedure by imposing important limitations upon the assessment and taxing powers of state and local governments....

The new article contains four distinct elements. The first imposes a limitation on the tax rate applicable to real property: "The maximum amount of any ad valorem tax on real property shall not exceed one percent (1%) of the full cash value of such property...." (§ 1, subd. (a).) (This limitation is made specifically inapplicable, under subdivision (b), to property taxes or special assessments necessary to pay prior indebtedness approved by the voters.) The second is a restriction on the assessed value of real property. Section 2, subdivision (a), provides: "The full cash value means the County Assessors valuation of real property as shown on the 1975–76 tax bill under 'full cash value,' or thereafter the appraised value of real property when purchased, newly constructed, or a change in ownership has occurred after the 1975 assessment...." Subdivision (b) permits a maximum 2 percent annual increase in "the fair market value base" of real property to reflect the inflationary rate.

The third feature limits the method of changes in state taxes: "From and after the effective date of this article, any changes in State taxes enacted for the purpose of increasing revenues collected pursuant thereto whether by increased rates or changes in methods of computation must be imposed by an Act passed by not less than two-thirds of all members ... of the Legislature, except that no new ad valorem taxes on real property, or sales or transaction taxes on the sales of real property may be imposed." (§ 3.) The fourth element is a restriction upon local taxes: "Cities, Counties and special districts, by a two-thirds vote of the qualified electors of such district, may impose special taxes on such district, except ad valorem taxes on real property or a transaction tax or sales tax on the sale of real property within such City, County or special district." (§ 4.) (The remaining sections relate to the effective dates (§ 5) and severability (§ 6) of the provisions of the new article).

We examine petitioners' specific contentions....

3. Equal Protection of the Laws

Petitioners' equal protection argument against article XIII A is directed at two aspects of the article. They contend that (1) the "rollback" of assessed valuation (§ 2, subd. (a)) assertedly will result in invidious discrimination between owners of similarly situated property, and that (2) the two-thirds voting requirement for enacting "special taxes" by local agencies (§ 4) unduly discriminates in favor of those voters casting negative votes. As will appear, we hold that neither contention has merit.

a.) 1975–1976 Assessment Date. As we have noted, section 2, subdivision (a), of article XIII A provides that "The full cash value (to which the 1 percent maximum tax applies) means the County Assessors valuation of real property as shown on the 1975–76 tax bill under 'full cash value,' or thereafter, the appraised value of real property when purchased, newly constructed, or a change in ownership has occurred after the 1975 assessment. All real property not already assessed up to the 1975–76 tax levels may be reassessed to reflect that valuation." (Section 2, subdivision (b), permits an annual 2 percent maximum increase on the "fair market value base" of property, to reflect the inflationary rate.) Petitioners emphasize that, by reason of the "rollback" of assessed value to the 1975–1976 fiscal year, two substantially identical homes, located "side-by-side" and receiving identical governmental services, could be assessed and taxed at different levels depending upon their date of acquisition. Such a disparity in tax treatment, petitioners claim, constitutes an arbitrary discrimination in violation of the federal equal protection clause (amend. XIV, § 1)....

* * *

The general principles applicable to the determination of an equal protection challenge to state tax legislation were recently summarized by the United States Supreme Court as follows: "We have long held that '(w)here taxation is concerned and no specific federal right, apart from equal protection, is imperiled, the States have large leeway in making classifications and drawing lines which in their judgment produce reasonable systems of taxation.' (Citation.) A state tax law is not arbitrary although it 'discriminate(s) in favor of a certain class ... if the discrimination is founded upon a reasonable distinction, or difference in state policy,' not in conflict with the Federal Constitution. (Citation.) This principle has weathered nearly a century of Supreme Court adjudication...." ...

Petitioners, in response, rely upon a line of cases which hold, as a general proposition, that the intentional, systematic undervaluation of property similarly situated with other property assessed at its full value constitutes an improper discrimination in violation of equal protection principles....

The foregoing cases, however, involved constitutional or statutory provisions which mandated the taxation of property on a current value basis. These cases do not purport to confine the states to a current value system under equal protection principles or to state an exception to the general rule accepted both by the United States Supreme Court and by us, as previously noted, that a tax classification or disparity of tax treatment will be sustained so long as it is founded upon some reasonable distinction or rational basis.

By reason of section 2, subdivision (a), of the article, except for property acquired prior to 1975, henceforth all real property will be assessed and taxed at its value at date of acquisition rather than at current value (subject, of course, to the 2 percent maximum annual inflationary increase provided for in subdivision (b)). This "acquisition value" approach to taxation finds reasonable support in a theory that the annual taxes which a property owner must pay should bear some rational relationship to the original cost of the property, rather than relate to an unforeseen, perhaps unduly inflated, current value. Not only does an acquisition value system enable each property owner to estimate with some assurance his future tax liability, but also the system may operate on a fairer basis than a current value approach. For example, a taxpayer who acquired his property for $40,000 in 1975 henceforth will be assessed and taxed on the basis of that cost (assuming it represented the then fair market value). This result is fair and equitable in that his future taxes may be said reasonably to reflect the price he was originally willing and able to pay for his property, rather than an inflated value fixed, after acquisition, in part on the basis of sales to third parties over which sales he can exercise no control. On the other hand, a person who paid $80,000 for similar property in 1977 is henceforth assessed and taxed at a higher level which reflects, again, the price he was willing and able to pay for that property. Seen in this light, and contrary to petitioners' assumption, section 2 does not unduly discriminate against persons who acquired their property after 1975, for those persons are assessed and taxed in precisely the same manner as those who purchased in 1975, namely, on an acquisition value basis predicated on the owner's free and voluntary acts of purchase. This is an arguably reasonable basis for assessment. (We leave open for future resolution questions regarding the proper application of article XIII A to involuntary changes in ownership or new construction.)

In addition, the fact that two taxpayers may pay different taxes on substantially identical property is not wholly novel to our general taxation scheme. For example, the computation of a sales tax on two identical items of personalty may vary substantially, depending upon the exact sales price and the availability of a discount. Article XIII A introduces a roughly comparable tax system with respect to real property, whereby the taxes one pays are closely related to the acquisition value of the property.

In converting from a current value method to an acquisition value system, the framers of article XIII A chose not to "roll back" assessments any earlier than the 1975–1976 fiscal year. For assessment purposes, persons who acquired property prior to 1975 are deemed to have purchased it during 1975. These persons, however, cannot complain of any unfair tax treatment in view of the substantial tax advantage they will reap from a return of their assessments from current to 1975–1976 valuation levels. Indeed, the adoption of a uniform acquisition value system without some "cut off" date reasonably might have been considered both administratively unfeasible and incapable of producing adequate tax revenues. The selection of the 1975–1976 fiscal year as a base year, although seemingly arbitrary, may be considered as comparable to utilization of a "grandfather" clause wherein a particular year is chosen as the effective date of new legislation, in order to prevent inequitable results or to promote some other legitimate purpose.

Petitioners insist, however, that property of equal current value must be taxed equally, regardless of its original cost. This proposition is demonstrably without legal merit, for our state Constitution itself expressly contemplates the use of "a value standard other than fair market value. . . ." (Art. XIII, § 1, subd. (a).) Moreover, the Legislature is empowered to grant total or partial exemptions from property taxation on behalf of various classes (e.g., veterans, blind or disabled persons, religious, hospital or charitable property; see art. XIII, § 4), despite the fact that similarly situated property may be taxed at its full value. In addition, homeowners receive a partial exemption from taxation (art. XIII, § 3, subd. (k)) which is unavailable to other property owners. As noted previously, the state has wide discretion to grant such exemptions. . . .

Finally, no compelling reason exists for assuming that property lawfully may be taxed only at current values, rather than at some other value, or upon some different basis. As the United States Supreme Court has explained, "The State is not limited to ad valorem taxation. It may impose different specific taxes upon different trades and professions and may vary the rate of excise upon various products. In levying such taxes, the State is not required to resort to close distinctions or to maintain a precise, scientific uniformity with reference to composition, use or value." . . . We cannot say that the acquisition value approach incorporated in article XIII A, by which a property owner's tax liability bears a reasonable relation to his costs of acquisition, is wholly arbitrary or irrational. Accordingly, the measure under scrutiny herein meets the demands of equal protection principles. . . .

■ BIRD, CHIEF JUSTICE, concurring and dissenting

I

Consider these facts. John and Mary Smith live next door to Tom and Sue Jones. Their houses and lots are identical with current market values of $80,000. The Smiths bought their home in January of 1975 when the market value was $40,000. The Joneses bought their home in 1977 when the market value was $60,000. In 1977, both homes were assessed at $60,000, and both couples paid the same amount of property tax. However, under Article XIII A in 1978, the Joneses will pay 150 percent of the taxes that the Smiths will pay. Should a third couple buy the Smiths' home in 1978, that couple would pay twice the taxes that the Smiths would have paid for the same home had they not sold it. Today, this court holds that such disparity is not only equitable, but that it does not violate the equal protection clause of the Constitution.

The basic problem with this position is that it upholds the adoption of an assessment scheme that systematically assigns different values to property of equal worth. By pegging some assessments to the value of property at its date of purchase and other assessments to the value of property as of March 1, 1975, article XIII A creates an irrational tax world where people living in homes of identical value pay different property taxes. Thus, instead of establishing an assessment scheme with one basis by which all property owners are taxed, article XIII A utilizes two bases, acquisition date and 1975 market value, to impose artificial distinctions upon equally situated property owners.

Article XIII A divides the property tax-paying public into two classes, pre– and post–1975 purchasers. Section 2(a) rewards those owners who purchased their property before March 1, 1975, by constitutionally fixing their tax assessments at lower figures than those who buy property of similar or identical value at a later date. This "roll back" provision confers substantial benefits upon one group of property owners not shared by other similarly situated owners. This provision raises the ugly specter of a race for tax savings in which the players start at different points, weighed down by different "handicaps."

Inequalities in state taxation have been held to be constitutional so long as they "rest upon some ground of difference having a fair and substantial relation to the object of legislation. . . ."

However, even minimal scrutiny requires that the statutes of the Legislature and the initiatives of the people be defensible in terms of a shared public good, not merely in terms of the purposes of a special group or class of persons. (See Tribe, American Constitutional Law (1978) p. 995.) The law should be something more than just the handmaiden of a special class; it must ultimately be the servant of justice.

Respondents fail to establish the general public benefit to be found in giving some, but not all, individuals a "roll back" to 1975 assessments. To be eligible for the full "roll back," article XIII A requires that an individual have owned continuously his or her property since a date prior to March of 1975. This requirement makes it literally impossible for persons purchasing property in 1978 or thereafter to qualify for benefits granted fully to pre–1975 owners (and less fully to 1975–78 owners). In so doing, article XIII A transgresses the constitutional guarantee of equal protection under the law.

Respondents defend the rationality of the 1975 date by characterizing it as a cut-off date or "grandfather" clause. Although its arbitrariness is conceded, they argue that it is defensible as a matter of administrative convenience. This contention lacks merit. It merely acknowledges that "it is difficult to be just, and easy to be arbitrary." (Stewart Dry Goods Co. v. Lewis (1935) 294 U.S. 550, 560, 55 S. Ct. 525, 529, 79 L. Ed. 1054.) Administrative convenience is wholly inadequate to warrant preferred treatment of a closed class of property owners. This court has previously refused to accept administrative convenience as a sufficient explanation of "great" differences in tax rates among similarly situated individuals. (Haman v. County of Humboldt (1972) 8 Cal. 3d 922, 927–928, 106 Cal. Rptr. 617, 506 P.2d 993; cf. Toomer v. Witsell (1948) 334 U.S. 385, 398–399, 68 S. Ct. 1156, 92 L. Ed. 1460.) In *Haman*, this court rejected the contention that administrative convenience justified a 23 percent spread in the rate at which California-registered and out-of-state registered fishing vessels were taxed. Article XIII A may in individual cases cause a disparity in taxes which is much greater than 23 percent. This is especially true in those cases where the effect of inflation and appreciation on real property values has been acute. . . .

* * *

Once it is understood that article XIII A systematically imposes different assessments on property of similar worth, a long line of Supreme Court cases becomes relevant. Those cases support the proposition that a person is denied equal protection of the law when his property is assessed at a higher value than property of equal worth in the same locale. "The purpose of the equal protection clause of the Fourteenth Amendment is to secure every person within the State's jurisdiction against intentional and arbitrary discrimination, whether occasioned by express terms of a statute or by its improper execution.... And it must be regarded as settled that intentional systematic undervaluation by state officials of other taxable property in the same class contravenes the constitutional right of one taxed upon the full value of his property."

In *Sioux City Bridge*, supra, the Supreme Court held it to be a violation of the equal protection clause to assess one company's property at 100 percent of its market value while other real estate in the same district was generally assessed at only 55 percent of the market value. Section 2(a) of article XIII A authorizes the same kind of discrimination as that condemned in Sioux City Bridge. Initially, properties purchased in earlier years will be undervalued in comparison with other properties (though they may be identical in current fair market value) purchased, constructed, or transferred in later years. Then, as the years go by, the skewed nature of the tax world created by article XIII A will become even more pronounced as each successive generation of purchasers will have their property overvalued in comparison to their neighbors or predecessor owners. For example, consider the condominium complex where each unit, though of identical fair market value, receives a different tax assessment simply because purchased in a different year. Consider the plight of the military family required by circumstances to change residence periodically. In 1979, that family may sell a house purchased in 1975, and buy a new house of identical current cash value. However, their tax bill will take a quantum leap upward, as their assessment jumps from 1975 to 1979 levels. Conversely, the family allowed by circumstances to remain in one house for long periods of time will reap substantial tax benefits simply because of the length of their residency.

Consider further the plight of the family which "newly constructs" their house after a natural disaster such as fire or flood. Article XIII A, section 2(a) penalizes them by reassessing the value of their house to market value at the time of the new construction. What is the possible rationale for allowing natural disasters to trigger an increase in property tax obligations? Surely a truly rational tax world would consider such families for tax relief. Finally, consider the reassessment to current market value mandated by section 2(a) for "changes in ownership" brought about by divorce or death. Did those who voted so overwhelmingly for article XIII A's general tax relief also intend to penalize those families who experience such family crises? ...

Respondents would seek to deny that those who pay more for property are in reality "similarly situated" with those who paid less for property of the same value in earlier years. The premise of this argument is that the later purchaser is better able to afford a high tax since (1) he paid more for his property to begin with and (2) he knew from the beginning he was buying a highly assessed piece of property.

The fact that a purchaser presently pays $80,000 for a home which someone else bought for $40,000 in 1975 may tell us nothing more than that inflation has been rampant and property values on the rise. In fact, the higher mortgage payments that new homeowners pay as compared to earlier purchasers forewarns us against any cavalier assumption that later purchasers are able to bear heavier taxes.

Section 2(a) mandates reassessment to current market value not only for voluntary purchasers but any time there is a "change in ownership." Thus, as previously noted, the person who inherits the family home or the spouse who gains title to property after a divorce may find that the assessment on the property suddenly skyrockets for property tax purposes. There is no rationality to the jump in valuation that accompanies these occurrences. Similarly, those persons who must move often because of the nature of their employment (for example, military families) will find that section 2(a)'s mandated reassessments bear little relation to their financial situation. Even more perplexing is the situation of persons who find that new construction must be done to their property after a natural disaster. Section 2(a) once more requires reassessment to "full cash value." The arbitrariness of article XIII A's assessment scheme could not be more apparent....

* * *

NOTES

1. *Differential Tax Rates and the Federal Constitution.* Florida and Michigan also use acquisition value as the basis for property taxes. In Nordlinger v. Hahn, 505 U.S. 1 (1992), the Supreme Court upheld Proposition 13 against an equal protection challenge under the federal constitution. In an 8–1 decision, the Court held that an acquisition-value property tax system need only pass rational basis review as it did not implicate a fundamental right or classify taxpayers on the basis of an inherently suspect characteristic. The Court discerned two legitimate state interests that satisfied the rational basis criterion. First, the California system discouraged rapid turnover in the ownership of homes and businesses, thus promoting the state's interest in local neighborhood preservation, continuity, and stability. Second, the system safeguarded existing homeowners against prohibitive tax increases. The Court also sustained exceptions to the reassessment requirement for persons over age 55 and for transfers between parents and children.

The Court distinguished Allegheny Pittsburgh Coal Co. v. Webster County, 488 U.S. 336 (1989). That case concerned the application of a provision of the West Virginia Constitution that establishes a general principle that all real and personal property be taxed proportionately to its value. Petitioners challenged a system by which the assessor of Webster County determined property value on the basis of the most recent purchase price and did not make major modifications once that value had been established. The result, as with the California system under Proposition 13, was gross disparities in the assessed value of comparable properties. In *Allegheny Pittsburgh*, the Supreme Court concluded that petitioners had no constitutional complaint simply because their property was assessed at less than its fair market value, so that fractional assessment, standing alone, was not suspect. But the Court did find an equal protection violation in petitioner's comparative claim that other property was assessed at a substantially lower fraction of its fair market value. The county sought to demonstrate that its two-tier method of assessment—assessment on transfer with subsequent adjustments "based on some perception of the general change in area property values"—was rationally related to reducing the administrative costs of the system. The Court opined that, while the need for transitional delays could justify a failure to equalize assessments, the extreme and longstanding disparities in assessed values for comparable properties in the county could not be explained by that rationale. The Court concluded that the procedures followed by the county appeared to have been in conflict with procedures endorsed by the state tax commission. In *Nordlinger*, the Court noted that the practice in Webster County had not been implemented pursuant to a state-authorized scheme of acquisition-based valuation, but had been defended as consistent with the state requirement that property taxes be based on fair market value. Nothing in *Allegheny Pittsburgh*, therefore, precluded upholding an acquisition-based valuation scheme where mandated by state law.

In Columbus–Muscogee County Consol. Government v. CM Tax Equalization, Inc., 579 S.E.2d 200 (Ga. 2003), the Georgia Supreme Court upheld a local amendment to the state constitution that froze homestead valuations at acquisition value for purposes of county ad valorem property taxes. The court concluded that the same policies that the Supreme Court noted in *Nordlinger* applied to the county's imposition of a freeze on valuation. Plaintiffs had complained that the freeze would place a disproportionate burden on the working poor, the young, and racial minorities, presumably because taxes would increase for new purchasers, and these groups had traditionally been unable to purchase homes. The court concluded that there was insufficient evidence that the amendment adversely affected these groups, or of racial motivation for, or disparate impact resulting from, the legislation.

2. *Proposition 13 and Community Stability.* The results in *Amador Valley* and *Nordlinger* may be consistent with the communitarian vision of local government in ways that suggest the anti-communitarian nature of the Tiebout model. Recall that under the assumptions in Tiebout, those who are dissatisfied with the level of public goods and services can costlessly gravitate to more congenial jurisdictions. Hence, mobility replaces communal efforts to compromise and accommodate competing interests. For a follower of the Tiebout model, homeowners who are unable or unwilling to pay taxes that have increased because of higher property values should sell their homes and move to jurisdictions that permit residents to pay a lower tax price for services. Proposition 13 can be considered as endorsing a different solution. Rather than embracing mobility, an acquisition-value based property tax system creates substantial *disincentives* to moving. It encourages individuals to remain in their current residences, which is an essential element to the creation of a stable community and of an environment in which individuals who have varying degrees of wealth, but who share other values, can pursue their common vision of the good life. Proposition 13, therefore, promotes the value of residences and commercial property as places in which to live and interact with others, what Logan and Molotch, in the excerpt in Chapter 1, analyzed as the "use value" of property, over its "exchange value," which favors transfer of property to those who value it primarily for its ability to generate a favorable return on capital. See, in this context, Pa. Const. art. 8, § 2(b)(v), which provides that the legislature may:

> (v) Establish standards and qualifications by which local taxing authorities in counties of the first and second class may make uniform special real property tax provisions applicable to taxpayers who are longtime owner-occupants as shall be defined by the General Assembly of residences in areas where real property values have risen markedly as a consequence of the refurbishing or renovating of other deteriorating residences or the construction of new residences.

3. Where property taxes are based on current fair market value do they correlate with ability to pay, with benefits received, or with neither? If ownership of taxable property is a good surrogate for wealth, then one might argue that property taxes reflect ability to pay. Hence, if A owns a home worth $50,000 and B owns a home worth $100,000, and if A and B can take equal advantage of a nearby public park, we might justify using property taxes to maintain the park on the theory that B has greater ability to pay and hence should pay more for the park, even though B obtains no greater benefit from the park than A. On the other hand, it may be that we believe that those with more taxable property are also greater users of local goods and services, so that ownership of taxable property is a good surrogate for benefits received. For instance, those who have more children in the school system may have larger (more expensive) homes and those with larger lots may receive more police and maintenance services. But if you believe that ownership of taxable property is not a very good surrogate for either ability to pay or benefits received, on what theory is the property tax defensible?

4. *Temporal Externalities.* To this point, our discussion of externalities has involved situations in which residents of one geographical area sought to obtain certain spatial benefits and impose the costs related to those benefits on those outside the benefited area. As indicated above, much of incorporation and annexation law can be explained as an attempt to prohibit the externalization of costs, and many judicial decisions in those areas are best understood as part of that process. *Amador Valley* arguably deals with a related issue. Homeowners who voted in the initiative stood to gain much from the adoption of Proposition 13. They would be able to freeze their property taxes in time (apart from the nominal allowable increase), regardless of subsequent increases in fair market value of their property. Costs of municipal services, therefore, would be borne disproportionately by subsequent purchasers. This disparity would likely become greater over time. Imagine, for instance, owners of similar homes, one of whom purchased in 1975 and one of whom purchased in 2000. Given increases in real estate values, these individuals are likely to pay greatly divergent property taxes. In short, homeowners who voted for the initiative are able to externalize costs to future generations. Thus, Proposition 13 arguably permitted homeowners to impose costs on future residents—a case of temporal rather than geographical or spatial externalities. Should the courts be as concerned with these issues as they are with the extrajurisdictional imposition of costs? One way to think about that issue is to determine whether future generations of home buyers were represented in the initiative. Persons who were not residents of California at that time but who might subsequently move to and purchase homes in that state certainly would not have had a voice in the process. Arguably tenants who lived in the state at the time of the initiative and someday hoped to own homes there would have served as surrogates for nonresidents. But those same tenants might have voted for the Proposition on the theory that lower property taxes would translate into lower rents today, even if it meant higher property taxes for them when they became homeowners in the (possibly distant) future. A final group that might have opposed the Proposition would be current homeowners who hoped to move into another home in the future or who wanted to ensure that they could sell their homes at favorable prices. Presumably, the higher taxes that new purchasers pay will reduce housing prices, so current owners would bear some of the costs of Proposition 13 when they sell their homes. But this group, too, would have to trade off current savings against future costs. The further in the future a homeowner contemplated selling his or her home, the less likely the homeowner would be to consider the effects of Proposition 13 on sales prices.

5. Proposition 13 was passed at a time when a great many states were the targets of citizen "tax revolts" against municipal reliance on property taxes. See Mildred Wigfall Robinson, Difficulties in Achieving Coherent State and Local Fiscal Policy at the Intersection of Direct Democracy and Republicanism: The Property Tax as a Case in Point, 35 U. Mich. J. L. Reform, 511, 533, 539–40 (2002). If taxes were higher than the value of the goods that residents were obtaining for their payments, then limits on the capacity of governments to raise taxes should increase local property values. In November 1980, Massachusetts voters adopted "Proposition 2½," which was projected to reduce property taxes by 40 percent. See Mass. Gen. L. Ann. ch. 59, § 21C. The law prohibits property taxes from exceeding 2.5 percent of the fair market value of the local tax base and limits annual increases in the property tax levy to the same percentage. A recent study concludes that the tax limitation does constrain local government spending, but that those constraints can prevent localities from maximizing the total property values of the locality. The result is that the locality may fail to provide an optimal level of services. See Katharine L. Bradbury, Christopher J. Mayer, & Karl E. Case, Property Tax Limits, Local Fiscal Behavior, and Property Values: Evidence from Massachusetts under Proposition 2½?, 80 J. Pub. Econ. 287 (2001).

6. *The Fiscal Consequences of Tax Limitations.* One objective of tax limitations is to reduce the discretion of officials to spend funds on projects that their constituents do not want. If local officials have limited funds, presumably they will continue to finance those projects most preferred by constituents and have less funds left for projects that serve personal, rather than civic, objectives. But tax limitations are obviously imperfect ways of accomplishing this. David Figlio and Arthur O'Sullivan find some evidence for the proposition that local governments manipulate service cuts in order to persuade voters of the need to vote in favor of tax overrides. David N. Figlio & Arthur O'Sullivan, The Local Response to Tax Limitation Measures: Do Local Governments Manipulate Voters to Increase Revenues?, 44 J.L. & Econ. 233 (2001). They find that officials of cities that face fiscal pressures who cannot increase taxes without a popular vote tend to cut a relatively large share of service inputs relative to administrative inputs. The authors hypothesize that officials adopt this strategy in order to encourage tax limit override votes.

Some studies suggest that tax caps shift burdens to other fiscal tools, such as user fees. See Richard F. Dye & Therese J. McGuire, The Effect of Property Tax Limitation Measures on Local Government Fiscal Behavior, 66 J. Pub. Econ. 469 (1997). This shift is not necessarily invidious, since, as I suggested above, user fees can provide beneficial means of gauging preferences and increasing efficiency. But user fees may also be regressive in ways that property taxes are not, and the shift to benefit-based finance surely reduces flexibility to engage in redistributive spending. Other studies, moreover, purport to demonstrate that tax caps have had a selective restraining effect on the growth of government. For instance, one study suggests that the tax limitation in Illinois had a restraining effect on school district operating expenditures, but no effect on school district instructional spending. Richard F. Dye and Therese J. McGuire, The Effect of Property Tax Limitation Measures on Local Government Fiscal Behavior, 66 J. Pub. Econ. 469 (1997). Still other studies indicate that limitations on property taxes significantly constrain spending, but that those reductions are accompanied by increases in property values only if the locality is able to find non-tax mechanisms to avoid reductions in school spending. Katharine L. Bradbury, Christopher J. Mayer, and Karl E. Case, Property Tax Limits, Local Fiscal Behavior, and Property Values: Evidence from Massachusetts Under Proposition 2½, 80 J. Pub. Econ. 287 (2001).

Limitations on property taxes should also induce localities to encourage development that will generate other taxes and that can currently be taxed at fair market value. For an argument that local governments have responded by imprudently competing for business that will generate sales taxes at the expense of land use, environmental and fiscal planning, see Jonathan Schwartz, Prisoners of Proposition 13: Sales Taxes, Property

Taxes, and the Fiscalization of Municipal Land Use Decisions, 71 S. Cal. L. Rev. 183 (1997).

If property taxes are truly benefit taxes, then one might imagine that homeowners would oppose tax limitations. The taxes they pay would reflect valuable public goods from which they benefit and that increase the value of their homes. Thus, homeowner support for tax limitations may indicate that property taxes are being used for redistributive purposes that homeowners oppose. This possibility has sparked a debate about whether explicit redistribution through property taxes increases support for tax limitations. In an influential article, Professor William Fischel contended that court decisions requiring state-wide equalization of school financing that had previously been funded at differential local levels through local property taxes was a major motivating force for Proposition 13. William A. Fischel, Did *Serrano* Cause Proposition 13?, 42 Nat'l Tax J. 465 (1989). For continuation of this debate, see William A. Fischel, The Homevoter Hypothesis (2001); Kirk Stark and Jonathan Zasloff, Tiebout and Tax Revolts: Did *Serrano* Really Cause Proposition 13?, 50 U.C.L.A.L. Rev. 801 (2003); William A. Fischel, Did John Serrano Vote for Proposition 13? A Reply to Stark and Zasloff's "Tiebout and Tax Revolts: Did *Serrano* Really Cause Proposition 13?," 51 UCLA L. Rev. 887 (2004).

Allegro Services, Ltd. v. Metropolitan Pier and Exposition Authority

665 N.E.2d 1246 (Ill. 1996).

■ JUSTICE NICKELS delivered the opinion of the court:

This appeal represents our second encounter with the program of taxes imposed by defendant, the Metropolitan Pier and Exposition Authority (Authority), to finance the renovation and expansion of McCormick Place and related infrastructure improvements. [McCormick Place is a convention center in Chicago managed by the Authority—EDS.] In *Geja's Cafe v. Metropolitan Pier & Exposition Authority*, 153 Ill.2d 239, 180 Ill. Dec. 135, 606 N.E.2d 1212 (1992), this court upheld a retailers' occupation tax imposed by the Authority on certain food and beverage sales. In the instant case we consider the constitutionality of an airport departure tax imposed by the Authority on providers of ground transportation services from Chicago's O'Hare and Midway Airports. The trial court entered judgment on the pleadings or summary judgment in the Authority's favor on each of the counts in plaintiffs' class action complaint....

In 1992, the General Assembly enacted Public Act 87–733, eff. July 1, 1992, amending the Metropolitan Pier and Exposition Authority Act (Act) (70 ILCS 210/1 et seq. (West 1994)) to provide for a project to renovate and expand McCormick Place (the expansion project). The expansion project includes plans for the renovation of McCormick Place's existing facilities and the construction of a new exhibition hall with a concourse to the existing facilities. It is anticipated that the expanded and improved McCormick Place facilities will lead to a significant increase in tourism to Chicago, thereby boosting certain sectors of the local and regional economy.

To finance the expansion project, the Authority was granted power to issue bonds in an amount not to exceed $937 million. 70 ILCS 210/13.2 (West 1994). In turn, under section 13 of the Act (70 ILCS 210/13 (West 1994)) the Authority is directed to levy a series of local taxes in order to repay the bonds. Section 13(f) provides that "[b]y ordinance the Authority shall . . . impose an occupation tax on all persons, other than a governmental agency, engaged in the business of providing ground transportation for hire to passengers in the metropolitan area. . . ." 70 ILCS 210/13(f) (West 1994). The tax is collected at rates specified in the Act from commercial vehicles departing from Chicago's O'Hare Airport and Midway Airport with passengers for hire. . . .

The Authority enacted an ordinance imposing the airport departure tax in accordance with section 13(f), and plaintiffs brought this lawsuit as a class action seeking, inter alia, a declaratory judgment that the airport departure tax is invalid. The trial court conditionally certified four classes of plaintiffs who provide airport transportation service exclusively to destinations outside the City of Chicago. Classes A and C consist of operators of taxicabs or limousines based in Illinois (Class A) or outside the State (Class C) that, from time to time, depart from the airports with passengers for hire, but are not licensed by the City of Chicago to operate within its city limits. Class E consists of all operators of buses or vans regulated by the Interstate Commerce Commission that provide scheduled service from the airports with no destinations within the City of Chicago. Class F consists of bus and van operators providing charter or other unscheduled passenger service from the airports to destinations outside the City of Chicago. Vehicle operators with vehicle licenses issued by the City of Chicago who pay the tax are not included in the plaintiff classes. . . .

I. Uniformity and Equal Protection

Plaintiffs first contend that the trial court erred in denying their summary judgment motion and granting the Authority's motion on those counts alleging that the airport departure tax violates the equal protection clause of the United States Constitution (U.S. Const., amend. XIV) and the uniformity clause of the Illinois Constitution (Ill. Const. 1970, art. IX, § 2). The uniformity clause provides:

> "In any law classifying the subjects or objects of non-property taxes or fees, the classes shall be reasonable and the subjects and objects within each class shall be taxed uniformly. Exemptions, deductions, credits, refunds and other allowances shall be reasonable." Ill. Const. 1970, art. IX, § 2.

The uniformity clause imposes more stringent limitations than the equal protection clause on the legislature's authority to classify the subjects and objects of taxation. "If a tax is constitutional under the uniformity clause, it inherently fulfills the requirements of the equal protection clause." *Geja's Cafe*, 153 Ill.2d at 247, 180 Ill. Dec. 135, 606 N.E.2d 1212. Accordingly, we need only consider the validity of the airport departure tax under the uniformity clause.

A

To survive scrutiny under the uniformity clause, a nonproperty tax classification must be based on a real and substantial difference between the people taxed and those not taxed, and the classification must bear some reasonable relationship to the object of the legislation or to public policy. Searle Pharmaceuticals, Inc. v. Department of Revenue, 117 Ill.2d 454, 468, 111 Ill. Dec. 603, 512 N.E.2d 1240 (1987). The uniformity requirement, as traditionally understood, may be violated by classifications which are either "underinclusive" or "overinclusive." See G. Braden & R. Cohn, The Illinois Constitution: An Annotated and Comparative Analysis 416 (1969) ("where the legislature defines and levies ... [a nonproperty tax] upon a class, ... the class as defined must include only those properly within it and not exclude those reasonably a part of it"). Although the uniformity clause imposes a more stringent standard than the equal protection clause, the scope of a court's inquiry under the uniformity clause remains relatively narrow. *Geja's Cafe*, 153 Ill.2d at 248, 180 Ill. Dec. 135, 606 N.E.2d 1212. Statutes bear a presumption of constitutionality, and broad latitude is afforded to legislative classifications for taxing purposes. *Geja's Cafe*, 153 Ill.2d at 248, 180 Ill. Dec. 135, 606 N.E.2d 1212. One challenging a nonproperty tax classification has the burden of showing that it is arbitrary or unreasonable, and if a state of facts can reasonably be conceived that would sustain the classification, it must be upheld. *Geja's Cafe*, 153 Ill.2d at 248, 180 Ill. Dec. 135, 606 N.E.2d 1212.

In the case at bar, the common characteristic linking the vehicle operators in the plaintiff classes—and forming the basis of plaintiffs' uniformity clause challenge—is that although they provide ground transportation service departing from the airports, they do not transport airport passengers for hire into the City of Chicago. Some of the class members are prohibited by Chicago's ground transportation licensing ordinance from transporting passengers from the airports to destinations in Chicago. Under the ordinance, a Chicago vehicle license is required to provide transportation service wholly within the city. See Chicago Municipal Code §§ 9–112–020, 9–112–030 (1990). Other class members provide scheduled airport service along routes which do not include destinations in the City of Chicago. Plaintiffs maintain that in terms of the economic impact of the McCormick Place expansion project, there is a real and substantial difference between the vehicle operators in the plaintiff classes and their city-licensed counterparts, because only the operators of city-licensed vehicles enjoy the opportunity to transport passengers from the airports to McCormick Place or nearby downtown hotels. Plaintiffs contend that any positive economic impact from the expansion project for class members is too indirect to support taxing them in the same manner as those operators providing airport transportation to destinations in Chicago, who enjoy a direct benefit by virtue of an increased demand for transportation to McCormick Place and nearby hotels.

Plaintiffs rely on *Geja's Cafe*, where, as previously noted, this court upheld the food and beverage tax imposed by the Authority in connection with the McCormick Place expansion project. The tax applied to certain types of food and beverage sales within a geographic subdistrict in Chicago. One of the arguments raised by its opponents was that pursuant to the uniformity requirement, the tax should have been imposed on food and beverage sales throughout Cook County. This court rejected the argument, finding that "[t]he General Assembly could reasonably conclude that the direct beneficiaries [of the expansion project's economic impact] would be those within the taxing subdistrict, and plaintiffs have not produced anything to suggest that narrowing the taxed area in this fashion was unreasonable." *Geja's Cafe*, 153 Ill.2d at 250–251, 180 Ill. Dec. 135, 606 N.E.2d 1212. Plaintiffs contend that, like the food and beverage tax in *Geja's Cafe*, the Authority's airport departure tax should also be limited to the subclass of vehicle operators who benefit most directly from the expansion project.

In response, the Authority notes that in *Geja's Cafe* this court merely held that it was *permissible* to limit the tax to the geographic subdistrict; the court did not hold or suggest that a more broadly applicable tax would necessarily be unconstitutional. The Authority's observation underscores a basic flaw in plaintiffs' analysis. Plaintiffs' argument rests largely on their understanding that a "real and substantial difference" between the vehicle operators in the plaintiff classes and those who transport passengers from the airports into Chicago would necessarily be fatal to a tax scheme imposing the same taxes on both groups of operators. While *Geja's Cafe* and other decisions under the uniformity clause hold that there must be a real and substantial difference between *the people taxed and those not taxed*, we are aware of no authority for a converse rule that there may be no real and substantial difference *among those taxed*. As this court observed in *Geja's Cafe*, "[t]he uniformity clause was not designed as a straitjacket for the General Assembly. Rather, the uniformity clause was designed to enforce *minimum standards of reasonableness and fairness* as between groups of taxpayers." (Emphasis added.) *Geja's Cafe*, 153 Ill.2d at 252, 180 Ill. Dec. 135, 606 N.E.2d 1212. Accordingly, the "real and substantial difference" standard merely represents the *minimum* level at which the differences among groups are of a sufficient magnitude to justify taxing the groups differently. However, just because the differences between groups reach this minimum level, it does not follow that identical tax treatment would necessarily be unreasonable.

To apply the real and substantial difference test in the manner plaintiffs propose would transform the uniformity requirement from a minimum standard of reasonableness and fairness to a precise formula for drawing tax lines. Under the analysis that plaintiffs advocate, the relative tax treatment of any two groups of potential taxpayers would be preordained by the existence or nonexistence of a real and substantial difference between the groups. Under such an analysis, the taxing body would be deprived of any range of options in the formulation of tax classifications. We reject such a rigid rule. Instead, we adhere to the view that the existence of a real and substantial difference between groups of taxpayers only establishes that differential taxation may be permissible, not that it is constitutionally essential....

We agree with plaintiffs that at some point the differences among taxpayers may be so profound that taxing them as a single class would violate the uniformity requirement. In our view, however, this limitation is embraced within the uniformity clause test's second and more general requirement that tax classifications must bear some reasonable relationship to the object of the legislation or to public policy. See *Searle*, 117 Ill.2d at 468, 111 Ill. Dec. 603, 512 N.E.2d 1240. In other words, the relevant question here is not whether the differences among vehicle operators serving the airports are "real and substantial," but whether the differences are so great that the General Assembly's decision to tax all such operators as a single class bears no reasonable relationship to the object of the tax. We turn to that question below.

B

The parties agree that in enacting the scheme of taxation to finance the McCormick Place expansion project, the General Assembly sought to impose the tax burden on certain industries that could be expected to realize significant economic benefits from the large number of visitors the project is expected to bring to the Chicago area. The Authority contends that while not all ground transportation providers who serve the airports will necessarily benefit in precisely the same way or to the same extent, it was still reasonable for the General Assembly to treat all providers as a single class for tax purposes based on anticipated benefits flowing to the class as a whole. The Authority maintains that by focusing exclusively on a limited sector of the market for ground transportation services—the market for transportation from the airports to downtown Chicago—plaintiffs have ignored the broader positive economic impact for the industry in general resulting from the expansion project. Plaintiffs respond that the specific benefits the Authority claims the vehicle operators in the plaintiff classes will enjoy are either nonexistent or "drastically attenuated" and do not support industrywide taxation.

As a prelude to consideration of these arguments, we digress briefly to address certain procedural matters. First, we note that in *Geja's Cafe*, this court clarified the burdens borne by the parties in litigation involving a uniformity clause challenge. While a classification will be upheld if a state of facts can reasonably be conceived to sustain it, the opponent of a tax is not required to come forward with any and all conceivable explanations for the tax and then prove each one to be unreasonable. *Geja's Cafe*, 153 Ill. 2d at 248, 180 Ill. Dec. 135, 606 N.E.2d 1212. Rather, upon a good-faith uniformity challenge, the taxing body bears the initial burden of producing a justification for the classifications. *Geja's Cafe*, 153 Ill. 2d at 248, 180 Ill. Dec. 135, 606 N.E.2d 1212. Once the taxing body has provided a sufficient justification, the opponent has the burden of persuading the court that the justification is unsupported by the facts. *Geja's Cafe*, 153 Ill. 2d at 248–249, 180 Ill.Dec. 135, 606 N.E.2d 1212.

We also take note of the procedural posture of this case, which is before us on the trial court's ruling in favor of the Authority on the parties' cross-motions for summary judgment.... Accordingly, in the present case, to the extent the Authority has produced a legally sufficient justification for its tax classification, plaintiffs would then be required to present a factual basis negating the asserted justification to survive defendant's motion for summary judgment. Conversely, if the Authority has failed to produce a legally sufficient justification for the classification, plaintiffs would be entitled to a judgment as a matter of law.

Applying these principles, we conclude that the Authority has submitted a legally sufficient justification for imposing the airport departure tax on the members of the plaintiff classes who operate taxicab or limousine services from the airports to destinations outside the City of Chicago (Classes A and C). First, the Authority notes that while suburban and out-of-state operators are precluded from making trips into Chicago, Chicago-licensed operators are permitted to operate outside the city. Hence, both categories of operators compete for the business in taking travellers from the airports to suburban and out-of-state destinations. The Authority maintains that the generally increased demand for transportation from the airports into the city owing to the McCormick Place expansion project will take many city-licensed operators out of competition for the suburban/out-of-state market, thereby increasing the share of this market served by suburban and out-of-state taxicab and limousine operators. In other words, the increased demand for the city market will allow operators without Chicago licenses to take up the slack in the market for airport transportation to destinations outside the city.

Second, the Authority contends that the demand for downtown hotel rooms during major McCormick Place events is likely to divert other visitors to hotels in the suburbs, thereby increasing the demand for transportation from the airports to those hotels. The Authority notes the findings of a marketing study conducted by the firm of KPMG Peat Marwick in conjunction with the McCormick Place expansion project:

> A poorly documented but real effect is the ripple effect. When a large event comes to Chicago, demand currently accommodated in an area may be displaced into outlying areas. A convention oriented hotel which has a strong commercial base may displace regular corporate demand to outlying hotels. Meeting events in Chicago regularly have room in the O'Hare, Oak Brook and Rosemont areas. As delegates stay in these hotels, regular business may be displaced to further outlying areas. In this way the outlying areas are getting demand associated with McCormick Place, but it is not from visitors attending McCormick Place events directly.

Plaintiffs contend that their own informal survey shows that, at present, visitors attending McCormick Place events rarely stay in suburban hotels. However, plaintiffs have offered no evidence contradicting the assertion that McCormick Place events displace other visitors to outlying areas. Nor have plaintiffs offered any evidence to refute the Authority's theory that suburban and out-of-state taxicab and limousine operators will benefit from decreased competition in the market they serve. In essence, plaintiffs simply protest that these benefits are too indirect in comparison with the benefits to city-licensed operators. Be that as it may, the benefits identified are nonetheless tangible and would appear to represent reasonable conclusions about the dynamics of related market forces in the local economy. In this regard, we agree with the observation of our appellate court in Forsberg v. City of Chicago, 151 Ill. App.3d 354, 365, 104 Ill. Dec. 20, 502 N.E.2d 283 (1986), cited by the Authority, that "not all persons burdened by a tax must be benefited in the same way." We cannot say as a matter of law that the inclusion of these vehicle operators bears no reasonable relationship to the object of the tax....

Accordingly, the trial court properly granted the Authority's motion for summary judgment on the counts brought under the uniformity and equal protection clauses.

[The discussion of plaintiffs' other contentions is omitted.—EDS.]

NOTES

1. *Uniformity Clauses and Classification of Property.* All states impose a requirement that taxation be uniform throughout the taxing jurisdiction. In all states other than New York and Connecticut, where judicial decisions fill the gap, the requirement is imposed through a constitutional provision. See John M. Payne, Intergovernmental Condemnation as a Problem in Public Finance, 61 Tex. L. Rev. 949, 970 n.79 (1983). Uniformity clauses restrict the ability of taxing officials to exercise discretion in the valuation of property. Hence, they prevent officials from favoring some parcels, either by failing to assess them on the same basis as similarly situated property, or by carving out particular classes of property for special treatment. Uniformity clauses, therefore, can be seen as analogous to prohibitions on special legislation. At the same time, there may be reasons why localities (or the state) would desire to give favorable treatment to an entire class of property, such as farmland, residential land, or open spaces. For instance, a locality that sought to encourage the creation of an undeveloped wilderness area might believe that incentives in the form of lower property taxes would bring about the desired result.

Some state constitutions avoid this conflict by expressly authorizing property classifications. See, e.g., Ill. Const. art. IX, §§ 2, 4(b) (permitting classification for nonproperty taxes and for property taxes in counties with populations in excess of 200,000); Mass. Const. pt. 2, ch. 1, § 1, art. 4. Other state constitutional provisions permit differential taxation of specific types of property. See, e.g., Mo. Const. art. 10, § 7 (forest lands); Pa. Const. art. 8, § 2 (forest reserves, property owned by those in need of special provisions); Wash. Const. art. 7, § 11 (agricultural lands, timber lands).

In Senior Corp. v. Board of Assessment Appeals, 702 P.2d 732 (Colo. 1985), the court upheld a differential tax rate that purported to link millage rates to the level of service provided by a water and sewer district. The taxpayer claimed that the uniformity clause precluded any right of legislative classification. The court concluded that the legislature could exercise such a power absent an express constitutional prohibition. Why doesn't the uniformity clause itself serve as a sufficiently express prohibition?

Most courts apply traditional equal protection tests to the question of classifications. Thus, legislative classifications must bear a reasonable relationship to a legitimate government purpose. Consistent with views that economic legislation receive minimal scrutiny, however, courts have not examined the alleged rational relationships very rigorously. In In re Property of One Church Street, 565 A.2d 1349 (Vt. 1989), the court validated a city taxation scheme, authorized by the legislature, that imposed a higher rate of taxation on some forms of nonresidential property. The legislature indicated that the function of the differential was to raise revenue in order to compensate for lost federal revenues. The court found this a sufficiently rational choice, and sufficiently related to its express purpose, to uphold the classification scheme, notwithstanding a constitutional uniformity clause that, on its face, did not permit exceptions.

Nevertheless, in City of Harrisburg v. School District of the City of Harrisburg, 710 A.2d 49 (Pa. 1998), the court invalidated a tax imposed by the school district on the leasing of tax-exempt real property. The school district contended that rates paid by lessees of nonexempt property already incorporated the taxes paid by the lessor; hence, a tax imposed solely on lessees of exempt property effectively equalized tax burdens. The court, however, opined that nonuniformity in certain taxes could not be offset by nonuniformity in others. The court also concluded that, in a competitive market, a comparison of the rental rates for nonexempt and exempt property did not necessarily reflect the tax difference payable by lessors of taxable property.

For other cases upholding legislative classifications in the face of uniformity clauses, see Kottel v. State, 60 P.3d 403 (Mont. 2002) (upholding state tax for vocational-technical colleges imposed only in those counties in which such colleges are located); Youngblood v. State, 388 S.E.2d 671 (Ga. 1990) (differential tax rates on public accommodations imposed by special districts within county); City of Ann Arbor v. National Center for Manufacturing Sciences, Inc., 514 N.W.2d 224 (Mich. Ct. App. 1994) (differential property tax rates for state-funded and privately funded research facilities).

2. *Defining the Class*. Although the court in the principal case permits significant differences among those within a taxed class, some degree of uniformity within the class is required. In Minnegasco, Inc. v. County of Carver, 447 N.W.2d 878 (Minn. 1989), a utility challenged a county assessment that treated the utility's personal property differently from commercial and industrial real property. The utility relied on a statute that appeared to consider utility property and commercial or industrial real property as lying within the same class. The court determined that the statute expressed a legislative intent to treat the personal property of a utility as a unique case, and thus permitted differential taxation.

In Gillis v. Yount, 748 S.W.2d 357 (Ky. 1988), however, a divided court invalidated a statute that classified unmined coal separately from other real property. Interests in unmined coal were taxed at a rate of one-tenth of

1per $100 of assessed valuation, while all other real property interests were taxed at a rate of 31–1/2on each $100 of value. The court determined that the classification violated the requirement that all property within the same class be taxed at the same rate, since unmined coal could not be distinguished rationally from other forms of property. In a candid assessment of the need to apply constitutional restrictions to grants of special benefits from the legislature, the court implied that the preferential tax rate for unmined coal was a result of legislative deference to special interests, rather than an expression of a "reasonable" (i.e., publicly interested), classification.

> The Revenue Cabinet's Brief claims: "The politics and issues of Kentucky in 1890 are as foreign to this generation as the intrigues of ancient Rome. The revenue provisions of the Constitution shackled the hand of the legislature to keep it from embracing the corrupt and polluting grasp of wealthy corporations. Today there is no need to tighten those shackles to prevent the legislature from extending a benevolent hand to . . . others [presumably the owners of unmined coal—EDS.] who honor their debt to the Commonwealth in ways worthy of legislative consideration."
>
> The record is not convincing that circumstances today are so different that constitutional restrictions on the power of the General Assembly with regard to property taxes are no longer viable. With special interests and pressure groups seemingly better organized, better financed and more powerful than ever before, we can hardly take judicial notice that the General Assembly should be free from constitutional restraint to manipulate the tax structure to extend "a benevolent hand" to those "who honor their debt to the Commonwealth in ways worthy of legislative consideration." The proponents of the special tax treatment for unmined coal in KRS 132.020(5) have yet to provide any hard information in the record or in briefs as to how this statute benefits anyone but the coal owners. The best that has been offered is an argument that it is part of an overall scheme for taxing the coal industry in which the severance tax paid by coal producers "more than makes up" for any potential loss of revenue. Even if we were inclined to accept as fact that the people of Kentucky no longer need protection from the "corrupt and polluting grasp of wealthy corporations" (or the power of today's special interest groups), we are not free to strike the constitutional mandate. We have no power to ignore the plain meaning of the Constitution when we believe it expedient to do so.

748 S.W.2d at 359–360. Not to be outdone, the dissent suggested that it was the attack on the classification, rather than the classification itself, that was motivated by special interests, to wit, domestic interests that sought to undo benefits that had been obtained by foreign corporations:

> The engine that has driven this lawsuit from the beginning to the majority opinion is that out-of-state corporations own large tracts of coal and pay a minimal tax on such property. I am sure that if it was possible to tax the landholding corporations at a high rate and leave alone the thousands of relatively small-holding coal owners, we would not have the hue and cry over unmined coal taxes.

Id. at 370 (Stephenson, J., dissenting). Since exemption from property taxes is permissible in Kentucky, why wouldn't the advocates of the nominal one mill rate have sought an express constitutional exemption rather than a differential tax rate? For an argument that tax incentives to provide affordable housing could be implemented by classifying eligible housing and allowing it to be taxed at a lower rate, see Richard A. Newman & Phil T. Feola, Housing Incentives, A National Perspective, 21 Urb. Law. 307 (1989).

3. *Uniformity Clauses, Frequency of Assessment, and Denial of Equal Protection.* As is evident from the New York and California experiences, where reassessments occur only on sale or improvement of property, disparities in assessed value among comparable properties may become substantial. That disparity, standing alone, may be sufficient to violate the state uniformity clause or the federal Equal Protection Clause. Recall that in Allegheny Pittsburgh Coal Co. v. Webster County, 488 U.S. 336 (1989), the Supreme Court invalidated a procedure under which assessments were made on sale of property, with only minor adjustments thereafter. In Township of West Milford v. Van Decker, 576 A.2d 881 (N.J. 1990), the court concluded that the practice of making "spot assessments" of only properties that were the subject of a recent sale, known as the "welcome stranger" pattern, violated the uniformity clause of the New Jersey Constitution and the Equal Protection Clause of the Fourteenth Amendment.

4. *The Scope of Uniformity Requirements.* In Senior Corp. v. Board of Assessment Appeals, 702 P.2d 732 (Colo. 1985), discussed in Note 1 supra, the Colorado Supreme Court interpreted a state constitutional provision that "[a]ll taxes shall be uniform upon each of the various classes of real and personal property located within the territorial limits of the authority levying the tax." The court stated that the provision "is applicable only to ad valorem property taxes." 702 P.2d at 738. Is that what the clause says? Some state constitutions limit the uniformity clause to property taxes by virtue of specific provisions that permit graduated taxes in other areas, such as income taxes. See, e.g., Alabama Const. amend. no. 25; Wisc. Const. art. VIII, 1. In other states, uniformity clauses have been limited to property taxes through judicial construction. See, e.g., Miles v. Department of Treasury, 199 N.E. 372 (Ind. 1935), appeal dismissed, 298 U.S. 640 (1936).

2. Special Assessments

PROBLEM XIX

The Phylon Flood Control District has been created by an act of the state legislature "to provide for the control of flood and storm waters in the district, to conserve waters in the district for beneficial and useful purposes and to protect from damage from flood or storm waters the harbors, waterways, public highways, and property in the district." The district possesses both the power to tax and to levy "on land benefited by acts of the district special assessments necessary to pay in whole or part" for any improvements made. Assessments are levied by the district in proportion to the benefit obtained from local improvements. The district contains several separate and unconnected watersheds, a considerable area of mountainous land (much of which lies above the plain of any anticipated floods), and some land that is beyond the historic flood plain.

Chauncey and Benedict are residents of the district who have brought an action to contest special assessments that have been imposed on them for district functions. Chauncey claims that his land lies beyond any area subject to inundation by flood waters over the past 100 years, that he maintains his own supply of water, and that his land is sufficiently remote from other settled areas that it would be impracticable for the district to supply stored water to him through any existing or contemplated water delivery system.

Benedict is a resident of an area of the district that is subject to frequent inundation by flood and storm waters. He claims, however, that the improvements the district creates confer a benefit on the entire area by ensuring the physical and economic well being of its residents. Benedict points out that even those who do not live in the area subject to inundation depend on that area for jobs, shopping, or revenue generated by commercial activity within the area. Thus, Benedict contends, the district must raise revenues through taxation rather than through special assessment.

Both plaintiffs move for summary judgment. What result?

City of Seattle v. Rogers Clothing for Men

787 P.2d 39 (Wash. 1990).

■ ANDERSEN, JUSTICE.

Facts of Case

In this case we consider whether a Seattle city ordinance establishing a special assessment area in downtown Seattle exceeded its statutory basis or violated the Constitution of the State of Washington. We hold that the ordinance is constitutional and that Seattle did not exceed its statutory authority by enacting it.

In 1971, the Legislature enacted RCW 35.87A allowing municipalities to establish "Parking and Business Improvement Areas." This statute authorizes a city to establish such an area after a petition is submitted by the businesses responsible for 60 percent of the assessments within the area.

In 1986, Seattle passed Seattle City Ordinance 113015 which established the "Downtown Seattle Retail Core Business Improvement Area" (Business Improvement Area) extending from Second Avenue to Seventh Avenue and from Stewart Street and Olive Way to Union Street. The ordinance was enacted pursuant to authority provided by RCW 35.87A. In accordance with that chapter (RCW 35.87A.010(1)), a petition had been signed by more than 60 percent of the businesses within the designated Business Improvement Area. The trial court found and concluded that the ordinance reflects and follows the initiating petition.

The ordinance at issue imposes special assessments to be used for two programs, a "Marketing Program" and a "Common Area Maintenance Program." The Marketing Program promotes the retail core area by such services as decorating and beautifying public places in the Business Improvement Area, maintaining informational and directional signing for pedestrians, and improving public relations. The Maintenance Program maintains the appearance of the Business Improvement Area by such services as sweeping sidewalks, cleaning and erasing graffiti, maintaining flowers and greenery, providing litter receptacles and providing security. The ordinance provides that all such activities are supplemental to, and not replacements of, regular city maintenance.

Rogers Clothing for Men, Inc., and Grand Furniture Company, Inc. (hereafter referred to as the petitioning store owners) are retailers located within the Business Improvement Area. The City of Seattle brought this action in municipal court to collect the special assessments levied against these petitioning store owners pursuant to the ordinance. . . .

During the 1986–87 fiscal year, the [Downtown Seattle Association, which managed the program for the Business Improvement Area] carried out a number of programs. It contracted with the YMCA to hire youth to sweep sidewalks in the Business Improvement Area every weekday. It arranged for advertising and conducted a number of activities, celebrations and events in the Business Improvement Area. The Association entered into contracts with the Municipality of Metropolitan Seattle (METRO) and the City.

The trial court found that during the 1986–87 program-year revenues to downtown Seattle businesses generally increased 4.7 percent over the preceding year, and that this increase reflected the advertising, activities and cleanup work done by the Association. The record reflects this study was not confined solely to businesses within the Business Improvement Area. However, the economist who conducted the study testified that the 4.7 percent increase was indicative of retail sales of small businesses in the Business Improvement Area. The petitioning store owners offered no retail figures, nor did they offer any figures on the value of their respective properties.

The court found that METRO and the City are engaged in major construction projects in downtown Seattle which have an adverse effect on downtown shopping. In early 1986 the City's economist had projected that without business promotion the construction would cause a major slowdown in business revenues.

Some activities conducted by the Association included events scheduled outside the Business Improvement Area. The programs also had some spillover value to businesses outside the Business Improvement Area. The court found, however, that the Association had apportioned the costs among its own funds, the Business Improvement Area funds and its contracts with METRO and the City, and had charged to Business Improvement Area funds only so much of the costs as it deemed were reflective of activities within the Business Improvement Area and advertising that benefited the Business Improvement Area. The court found that the store owners had not shown the apportionment was unreasonable.

The trial court found that the Business Improvement Area program had produced an opportunity to benefit well in excess of the assessments for each store owner. It found Rogers and Grand had benefited from the sidewalk cleaning outside their stores, that they could take advantage of the extended parking hours program and benefited from the increased downtown pedestrian traffic from the Business Improvement Area program.

The amount of assessments is based upon type of use and square footage. The ordinance divides business space into a number of classifications: (a) developed ground floor business space; (b) individual commercial retail sales space at the basement level or on the second or third floors; (c) major multilevel retail stores with more than 100,000 square feet under single ownership; (d) parking garages and surface parking lots; and (e) other uses (hotels, theaters). Then each classification is assessed separately for the Marketing Program and the Common Area Maintenance Program. All classes are assessed for ground floor per square foot. Class (b) is assessed for basement, second and third floors while class (c) is assessed for ground floor and the "next" floor. The effect of this is that the large multilevel department stores are assessed for their ground floor footage and one other floor, while other retailers (with less than 100,000 square feet) are assessed for all floors. Additionally, there is a dollar amount ceiling of $28,000 for any one business. . . .

Issue One

CONCLUSION. The city ordinance at issue does not exceed the City's statutory authority under RCW 35.87A.

Article 7, section 9 of the Constitution of the State of Washington states in relevant part:

> The legislature may vest the corporate authorities of cities, . . . with power to make local improvements by special assessment, or by special taxation of property benefited.

As this provision makes clear, the power of the city in this regard is dependent upon authority delegated to it by the Legislature. The power to tax does not exist in a municipality absent a legislative grant of authority. Therefore, the threshold issue is whether the city ordinance violated or exceeded the State's statutory grant of authority. . . .

The petitioning store owners further argue that by calculating assessments based on square footage, the ordinance violates the statute by failing to indicate factors showing the special benefit. . . .

. . . The store owners' argument is without merit. This statute enables the city to classify property based upon a list of factors and the factors in the list are expressed in the disjunctive. The statute does not say that the ordinance must explicitly state that the factors are related to the benefit received.

This statute (RCW 35.87A.080) authorizes the City to make a reasonable classification of businesses, "giving consideration to various factors such as ... square footage of the business ... or any other reasonable factor relating to the benefit received." The ordinance did classify businesses within the Business Improvement Area into a number of classifications based upon type of use and square footage. The statute also provides that "[t]he special assessments need not be imposed on different classes of business, as determined pursuant to RCW 35.87A.080, on the same basis or the same rate. . . ." The ordinance tracks the statute by classifying property pursuant to RCW 35.87A.080 based upon type of use and square footage and then proceeds under RCW 35.87A.090 to apply different rates to the different classifications of property. The type of use (hotel, parking lot, retail business) is a reasonable factor relating to the benefits received from the maintenance and the marketing programs. Apportionment of special assessments based upon square footage of property has often been upheld.

We conclude that the ordinance carefully follows the authorizing statute, does not exceed its delegated power and does not violate it.

Issue Two

CONCLUSION. The purposes delineated in the ordinance, for which the assessments in this case were levied, are a "benefit" to businesses within the meaning of article 7, section 9 of the Constitution of the State of Washington.

Const. art. 7, § 9 provides that property must be "benefited" in order to be subjected to special assessment. Petitioning store owners challenge the nature of the benefits afforded by the Business Improvements Area ordinance. They argue that because the benefits are derived from services rather than capital improvements they are not "benefits" within the meaning of Const. art. 7, 9.

The petitioning store owners have cited no case law to support the proposition that services cannot be considered "benefits" under article 7, section 9. They instead rely on language in Heavens v. King Cy. Rural Library Dist., 66 Wash. 2d 558, 563, 404 P.2d 453 (1965) which states that "[a]ll such assessments have one common element: they are for the construction of local improvements that are appurtenant to specific land and bring a benefit substantially more intense than is yielded to the rest of the municipality. The benefit to the land must be actual, physical and material and not merely speculative or conjectural." *Heavens*, however, does not lend support to the store owners' argument on this issue. *Heavens* involved the issue of whether a library was a general benefit to the entire municipality rather than a special benefit to a smaller area within the taxing jurisdiction; it did not address whether "benefits" were confined to permanent capital improvements. . . .

Whether RCW 35.87A and Seattle City Ordinance 113015 supply the proper kind of benefits for special assessment purposes is primarily a legislative question, at least so long as the assessment does not exceed the benefit to the property. A municipal corporation having the power to make local improvements by special assessment or taxation has the implied power to declare what are local improvements, where such a declaration is not made arbitrarily or unreasonably, or without reference to benefits.

The store owners also rely upon *Heavens* for the proposition that benefits must be actual, physical and material and not merely speculative or conjectural. The ordinance before us provides for decorating and beautifying public places in the retail core area, sponsoring public events, advertising, maintaining information and directional signing for pedestrians, improving public relations, sweeping and cleaning sidewalks, cleaning and erasing graffiti, maintaining flowers and greenery, providing and cleaning litter receptacles and providing additional security. The trial court found that the Business Improvement Area had hired young people to sweep sidewalks in the Business Improvement Area every weekday, had conducted a series of programs involving advertising, and various activities, celebrations, and other events in the Business Improvement Area. Although not all of these services are permanent, they are actual, physical and material as opposed to speculative or conjectural. . . .

Issue Three

CONCLUSION. The benefits delineated by the challenged ordinance are "special" benefits to the assessed property within the Business Improvement Area rather than benefits which inure to all property within the taxing jurisdiction.

It is the petitioning store owners' position that the benefits conferred in this case inured to the community at large rather than to the assessed property. It is, of course, essential that a special assessment be based upon an improvement which is local in character as opposed to general. 14 E. McQuillin, Municipal Corporations § 38.11, at 77 (3d rev. ed. 1987) explains this distinction:

> Laws recognize a distinction between public improvements which benefit the entire community, and those local in their nature which benefit particular real property or limited areas. The property benefited is usually required to pay the expense of the latter. A local improvement is a public improvement which, although it may incidentally benefit the public at large, is made primarily for the accommodation and convenience of the inhabitants of a particular locality, and which is of such a nature as to confer a special benefit upon the real property adjoining or near the improvement. On the other hand, if its primary purpose and effect are to benefit the public, it is not a local improvement, although it may incidentally benefit property in a particular locality.
>
> Whether an improvement is local is a question of fact rather than one of law, to be determined from its nature and object. (Footnotes omitted.)

The petitioning store owners maintain that the improvements in the ordinance do not "specially benefit" the assessed property in that other businesses outside the Business Improvement Area also benefit as do downtown shoppers and workers. The store owners again rely on *Heavens* where it was held that a library did not specially benefit the property around the library, but rather generally benefited all the property in the taxing district and should, therefore, have been funded out of general taxes. The *Heavens* majority mentioned other improvements which should be funded by general taxation rather than by special assessment such as public auditoriums, war memorials, courthouses and public school buildings and the dissent added post offices to the list. Both the *Heavens* majority and dissent agreed that a public park could be the subject of a special assessment. The improvements delineated in the Business Improvement Area ordinance are distinguishable from a public library. The ordinance provides decorating, landscaping, cleaning, litter receptacles, security, advertising and promotion directly to the area within the Business Improvement Area.

We have held repeatedly, and recently, that whether a property has been "specially" benefited by the improvement (as distinguished from providing a general benefit to the entire district) is ordinarily a question of fact. In the case before us the trial court found that in order to carry out the common area maintenance program the Downtown Seattle Association had contracted with the YMCA for sidewalk cleaning in the Business Improvement Area. The trial court also found that while the advertising and availability of parking for extended hours had some spillover value to businesses outside the Business Improvement Area, the City had taken this into account and had apportioned the costs of programs between city funds and Business Improvement Area funds. The trial court further found that the City had charged the Business Improvement Area funds only so much of the overall costs as the Downtown Seattle Association deemed to reflect activities that took place within, and advertising that benefited, the Business Improvement Area. Similarly, the trial court found that the stores did not show that the apportionment was unreasonable....

Since the determination of whether an improvement is special or general is ordinarily a question of fact, and since the trial court determined that the assessments specially benefited property within the Business Improvement Area, we conclude the assessments were local in nature rather than general. The fact that improvements had some spillover benefit to the community at large does not change the character of special benefits in this case.

Issue Four

CONCLUSION. The petitioning store owners had the burden of proving that the assessment against them substantially exceeded their benefit and failed to sustain their burden of proof in this regard....

In arguing that the City failed to demonstrate that the benefit conferred upon the store owners' businesses exceeded the amount of the assessments on those properties, petitioners do not recognize the presumptions applicable where the amount of a special assessment is challenged. A series of cases spell out the presumptions when property owners challenge the amount they have been assessed under a special assessment scheme. The presumptions relevant to this case include: (1) the burden is upon the one challenging the assessment to prove its incorrectness as it is presumed the City has acted properly and legally; (2) the assessment is presumed to be a benefit; (3) the assessment is presumed to be no greater than the benefit; (4) it is presumed that an assessment is equal or ratable to an assessment upon other property similarly situated and that the assessment is fair; and (5) evidence of appraisal values and benefits is necessary to rebut these presumptions. Appellate review of such cases does not permit an independent evaluation of the merits....

It is presumed that a local improvement benefits property unless the challenging party produces competent evidence to the contrary. The burden of proof shifts to the City only after the challenging party presents expert appraisal evidence showing that the property would not be benefited by the improvement. Thus petitioning store owners had the burden of establishing that the assessments exceeded the benefit but they did not present evidence on the issue. It follows that the petitioning store owners' claims, absent supporting evidence of appraisal values, are inadequate to overcome the presumption that the improvements were a benefit and that the assessments were no greater than the benefits.

Petitioners also argue that the trial court failed to find a "benefit" because it only found an "opportunity to benefit." First, this ignores the presumption of benefit, and secondly, courts have not required benefit measured only by the property's present use. As Professor Trautman explains, "[p]roperty cannot be relieved from the burden of an assessment simply because its owner has seen fit to devote it to a use which presently may not be specifically benefited by the improvement." Trautman, Assessments in Washington, 40 Wash. L. Rev. 100, 119 (1965). Inherent in this concept of benefit based upon a different use of the property is the idea that "benefit" includes the "opportunity to benefit" from the improvement so long as the opportunity is not merely speculative.

Although petitioners argue that the benefit to their properties has not been calculated and the amount has not been determined, they fail to recognize that apportionment based upon square footage of property is a routinely upheld method of calculating a benefit. Petitioners also exceed their argument on the ordinance's alleged unconstitutionality and instead embark into the issue of properness of and amount of assessments to which, of course, the presumptions previously discussed must attach.

For the foregoing reasons, we conclude that the municipal court and the Superior Court correctly decided that Seattle City Ordinance 113015 properly follows RCW 35.87A and is constitutional.

Affirmed.

NOTES

1. As demonstrated in the principal case, special assessments constitute exactions based on benefits received by the payor. In an excellent article tracing the development of special assessments in the United States, Professor Stephen Diamond distinguishes special assessments from property taxes in three respects, at least in theory. First, in the case of a special assessment, revenue received by the government is linked to a distinct expenditure, rather than contributed to the general treasury. Second, the assessment is imposed on those whose property lies within an area benefited by the expenditure, rather than within preexisting political boundaries. Third, assessments are based on determinations of benefit to individual lots, rather than on individuals. See Stephen Diamond, The Death and Transfiguration of Benefit Taxation: Special Assessments in Nineteenth-Century America, 12 J. Legal Stud. 201, 201–202, 239–240 (1983). Diamond contends that early enthusiasm for special assessments was predicated on a belief that they would prevent private parties from receiving windfalls subsidized by the general taxpaying public, most of whom received little or no benefit from the expenditure. Diamond concludes, however, that special assessments in the United States have not had that effect, as meaningful measurement of benefits became difficult and formulas for allocating payment obligations invited corruption. Instead, use of special assessments has been limited to certain improvements, such as street development, and has never attained the status claimed for it as a "quasi-scientific, rational, neutral, apolitical, and enforceable rule by which to evaluate public actions and to apportion their burdens." Id. at 239. Does the principal case suggest either recapture of private benefits or broader possible uses for special assessments?

2. In theory, special assessments may induce better monitoring of municipal improvements, since assessments are linked to specific projects and individual payors can more readily determine whether they are getting their "money's worth" than is the case with taxes that can be spent for multiple projects. Thus, the use of the special assessment may be justified as a mechanism for controlling municipal expenditures. Nevertheless, special assessments represent a less important source of local revenue and capital improvements today than was the case in the nineteenth century. One explanation for this phenomenon lies in the aftermath of the Depression in the 1930s. Numerous municipal projects had been financed by the issuance of bonds, payment of which was secured by a pledge of special assessment revenues. When property values and homeowner income fell, municipalities that had issued such bonds were unable to collect assessments in amounts sufficient to pay bondholders. The subsequent defaults made the investment community wary of special assessment financing, so that by 1940, special assessment revenues fell to one-tenth of their pre-Depression level. See Alan A. Altshuler & José A. Gómez–Ibàñez, Regulation for Revenue: The Political Economy of Land Use Exactions 17 (1993).

3. Special assessments typically consist of capital improvements that increase the value of neighboring property. Thus, plaintiffs in *Rogers* contended that benefits supported by assessments must be "actual, physical, and material." Is there a reason why improvements supportable by assessments should be restricted to capital improvements rather than extended to services such as improving public relations, sweeping and cleaning sidewalks, cleaning litter, and removing graffiti? In 2nd Roc–Jersey Associates v. Town of Morristown, 731 A.2d 1 (N.J. 1999), the court approved assessments for similar projects. The court concluded that "the core of the definition of a special assessment ... is not that the benefit necessarily or primarily consists of physical improvements that are permanent.... Rather, the special assessment is used to provide a combination of services and improvements that are intended and designed to benefit particular properties and demonstrably enhance the value and/or the use or function of the properties that are subject to the special assessment." 731 A.2d at 9.

NOTE ON BUSINESS IMPROVEMENT DISTRICTS

The assessment at issue in *Rogers* was imposed to support a Business Improvement Area, which was composed of businesses within the designated area. Several states have allowed the creation of such business improvement districts, known as BIDs, to finance and provide services within the defined district. Those services, which may include police protection, street and sidewalk maintenance, sanitation, and capital improvements, are similar to those that we traditionally attribute to local government. In effect, the BID becomes a subunit of private government within the locality with a unique tax structure and service package. See Richard Briffault, The Rise of Sublocal Structures in Urban Governance, 82 Minn. L. Rev. 503 (1997).

The extra services and improvements provided within the BID are funded through additional taxes or assessments imposed by the cities on businesses within BID boundaries. Thus, many states permit the formation of BIDs only with the consent of businesses within the proposed district. See, e.g., Ida. Code, § 50–1703A (5). Note, for instance, the 60 percent requirement discussed in *Rogers*. Some states, however, allow the city to create the BID, but provide some form of veto for the landowners or businesses within the district. See, e.g., Or. Rev. Stat. § 223.117(2)(c).

BIDs are typically governed by a board composed of representatives from the businesses within the district and elected local officials, with the latter chosen by local government and community organizations. See, e.g., La. Rev. Stat. Ann. § 33:2740.3.D(1) (providing for nomination by the Chamber of Commerce and mayor and approval by the city council). Some BIDs, however, allow the business community within the district to elect all board members, providing only general guidelines for membership. See, e.g., N.Y. Gen. Mun. Law § 980–m(b) (allowing for election by members but requiring that owners constitute the majority and that tenants be represented). One court has held that BIDs are not bound by the "one-person—one-vote" principle that applies to general purpose municipalities, and thus can elect board members by giving property owners, rather than residents, majority control. See Kessler v. Grand Central Dist. Mgmt. Ass'n, 158 F.3d 92 (2d Cir. 1998). One commentator has concluded that BIDs are democratically accountable in the sense that BID officials are accountable to stakeholders in BID activities in proportion to the extent to which BID activities affect those stakeholders. See Brian R. Hochleutner, BIDs Fare Well: The Democratic Accountability of Business Improvement

Districts, 78 N.Y.U.L. Rev. 374 (2003). He finds that BID formation and governance procedures inherently respond to the interests of property owners within the BID, residents within the BID, and city residents outside of the BID through a series of voting mechanisms, procedural safeguards, and audit requirements.

Cities generally monitor BIDs by determining their boundaries, approving their annual budgets and financial strategies, and evaluating the provision of services. See generally, Lawrence O. Houstoun, Jr., Betting on BIDs, Urban Land 13–18 (June 1994). A 1996 study of BIDs in the United States and Canada estimated that between 1,000 and 2,000 of these districts had been formed in North America. See Lawrence O. Houstoun, Jr., Business Improvement Districts, 20 Econ. Dev. Commentary 4, 5 (1996).

Most BIDs supplement services provided by the city. BIDs may also more directly engage in activities designed to generate and retain business, drawing customers through expenditures on capital projects, public relations and marketing, and social services. Many BIDs sponsor capital improvements for better lighting, sidewalks, and parking structures. BIDs often organize festivals and produce advertising campaigns. Social services provided by BIDs tend to facilitate causes which fight homelessness. The Times Square BID in New York City, for example, provides services to the homeless.

Even these seemingly publicly interested movements, however, have generated criticism. See, in addition to Professor Briffault's analysis, Robert Ellickson, Controlling Chronic Misconduct in City Spaces: Of Panhandlers, Skid Rows, and Public–Space Zoning, 105 Yale L. J. 1165 (1996). As sublocal governmental structures, BIDs arguably come nearer to fulfilling the Tiebout model than their larger local government counterparts, and can enhance local autonomy and choice of services within the locality. Like their residential counterparts, homeowners associations, they allow business owners to obtain collectively more of a service, such as security or sidewalk maintenance, than the municipal government would provide. In theory, at least, they require only beneficiaries of these improvements to pay for them, although the principal case reveals the difficulty of measuring "benefit." But Professor Briffault suggests that BIDs may also exhibit unattractive features of the Tiebout model. By allowing some residents to obtain a higher level of service than others, BIDs increase the inequalities in service provision within the city and could decrease the willingness of district members to participate in the funding of services to poorer communities. Members of BIDs who could afford their own services could conceivably lobby to reduce public expenditures on similar services in order to make their district more attractive than an area containing competitive businesses that could not afford to tax themselves. But would members of BIDs always have the incentive to reduce municipal expenditures? Since they have to pay the full cost of services they provide, but only a pro rata share of the cost of services that the municipality provides, BID members may prefer to have a high level of services provided by the city so there is less need for them to obtain "extra" services. For a discussion of when this might be the case, see Clayton P. Gillette, Opting Out of Public Provision, 73 Den. U.L. Rev. 1185, 1209 (1996).

Other courts have followed *Rogers* in rejecting challenges to BID assessments as invalid taxes. See, e.g., Zimmerman v. City of Memphis, 67 S.W.3d 798 (Tenn. App. 2001); Howard Jarvis Taxpayers Assn. v. City of San Diego, 84 Cal.Rptr.2d 804 (Cal. App. 1999) (holding assessment is neither a special tax nor an assessment imposed on real property and thus subject to a state constitutional voting requirement); 2nd Roc–Jersey Associates v. Town of Morristown, 731 A.2d 1 (N.J. 1999) (uniformity clause inapplicable to BID assessments).

city down

City of Boca Raton v. State

595 So.2d 25 (Fla. 1992).

■ GRIMES, JUSTICE.

This is an appeal from a final judgment which declined to validate special assessment improvement bonds proposed to be issued by the City of Boca Raton. We have jurisdiction under article V, section 3(b)(2) of the Florida Constitution, and chapter 75, Florida Statutes (1989).

In an effort to revitalize its downtown area, the City of Boca Raton (the City) determined to construct a wide range of specifically enumerated improvements in the infrastructure. The estimated cost of the improvements was $44,000,000. The City determined to obtain a portion of the money to pay the cost from the issuance of bonds in an amount not to exceed $21,000,000. The bonds were to be repaid from special assessments levied over a period of years against the downtown property to be benefitted by the improvements. The City's effort to validate the bonds was opposed by the State pursuant to chapter 75, Florida Statutes (1989), as well as by several property owners. At the trial, the issues devolved into (1) whether the City had the authority to levy special assessments to pay the bonds, and (2) even if such authority existed, whether this proposal met the legal requirements of a proper special assessment.

Following the presentation of testimony, the trial judge held that the City did not have the authority to impose special assessments to fund the bonds....

[The court first recounted the scope of home rule in Florida in order to determine whether Boca Raton had authority to impose a special assessment. The court concluded that the city could levy the assessment unless expressly prohibited by law or expressly preempted by the state or county.—EDS.]

In this respect, those opposing the bond issue make two arguments. First, they contend that the special assessment is really a tax, which the City may not impose because of the language of article VII, section 1(a) of the Florida Constitution, which provides:

> (a) No tax shall be levied except in pursuance of law. No state ad valorem taxes shall be levied upon real estate or tangible personal property. All other forms of taxation shall be preempted to the state except as provided by general law.

However, a legally imposed special assessment is not a tax. Taxes and special assessments are distinguishable in that, while both are mandatory, there is no requirement that taxes provide any specific benefit to the property; instead, they may be levied throughout the particular taxing unit for the general benefit of residents and property. On the other hand, special assessments must confer a specific benefit upon the land burdened by the assessment. City of Naples v. Moon, 269 So. 2d 355 (Fla. 1972). As explained in Klemm v. Davenport, 100 Fla. 627, 631–34, 129 So. 904, 907–08 (1930):

> A tax is an enforced burden of contribution imposed by sovereign right for the support of the government, the administration of the law, and to execute the various functions the sovereign is called on to perform. A special assessment is like a tax in that it is an enforced contribution from the property owner, it may possess other points of similarity to a tax but it is inherently different and governed by entirely different principles. It is imposed upon the theory that that portion of the community which is required to bear it receives some special or peculiar benefit in the enhancement of value of the property against which it is imposed as a result of the improvement made with the proceeds of the special assessment. It is limited to the property benefited, is not governed by uniformity and may be determined legislatively or judicially.
>
> ... [I]t seems settled law in this country that an ad valorem tax and special assessment though cognate in immaterial respects are inherently different in their controlling aspects....

There are two requirements for the imposition of a valid special assessment. First, the property assessed must derive a special benefit from the service provided. Atlantic Coast Line R.R. v. City of Gainesville, 83 Fla. 275, 91 So. 118 (1922). Second, the assessment must be fairly and reasonably apportioned among the properties that receive the special benefit. South Trail Fire Control Dist. v. State, 273 So. 2d 380 (Fla.1973). Thus, a special assessment is distinguished from a tax because of its special benefit and fair apportionment. We do not believe that the special assessment proposed by the City constitutes a tax which would be prohibited by article VII, section 1(a) of the Florida Constitution....

We now turn to the legality of the special assessment which underlies the bond issue proposed by the City of Boca Raton. The opponents' primary contention is that the special assessments are not directly proportional to and less than the special benefits to be provided each parcel. They also argue that certain properties are improperly excluded from the assessments. At the outset, we note that the City made specific findings that the improvements would constitute a special benefit to the subject property, that the benefits would exceed the amount of the assessments, and that the benefits would be in proportion to the assessments. The apportionment of benefits is a legislative function, and if reasonable persons may differ as to whether the land assessed was benefitted by the local improvement, the findings of the city officials must be sustained. Rosche v. City of Hollywood, 55 So. 2d 909 (Fla. 1952).

To better understand the opponents' position, it is necessary to discuss the manner in which the proposed assessments will be made. The City's ordinance permits and its resolution provides that the special assessments are to be apportioned among the benefitted properties in relation to the property values of the various tracts as determined by the latest available real property assessment roll prepared by the county tax appraiser. Robert J. Harmon, the City's urban economic consultant, testified that his analysis showed that the subject properties "would at least on a cumulative basis receive $7 of benefit for every $1 that they were paying in assessments." He expressed the opinion that the use of ad valorem values in making special assessments, which has been nationally recognized for at least twenty years, was the most equitable method that could be employed for the City's project. He gave an example of what he called the self-correcting mechanism of the ad valorem method when he stated:

> If a property, for example, initially represented one percent of the entire tax base of downtown Boca Raton, they would pay one percent of the assessment. If over ten years the assessed value of that particular property, if it did not benefit to the same degree as the rest of downtown, their percentage of the total assessment would go down proportionally.
>
> And the reverse would be also true. If a property benefitted more in its total percentage of the total assessed value of downtown increased, as will be the case with particularly the large developments, their percentage of the total assessment increases.

He added that if in any given year a property owner felt that his benefit was inequitable there was an appeal process in place by which he could seek to have his assessment adjusted. When asked how an improved property could receive the same proportional benefit as a vacant lot, he explained that while improved property would initially pay a higher assessment, over a period of time the cumulative payments would tend to equalize because the vacant properties as they were developed would ultimately carry higher assessments due to increased construction costs.

Mr. Harmon also testified that the small number of residential properties in the downtown area as well as churches had been excluded from the assessment because they would receive much less benefit from the project than business properties. However, he pointed out that should those properties be changed to a business use, they would then be subject to the assessment.

The trial court found against the bond opponents on these issues. From our review of the record, we conclude there is competent substantial evidence to support these findings. The City was not required to specifically itemize a dollar amount of benefit to be received by each parcel. See Cape Dev. Co. v. City of Cocoa Beach, 192 So. 2d 766 (Fla. 1966). Moreover, we reject the contention that the assessment cannot be sustained because it will be applied on an ad valorem basis. In fact, in an early case this Court upheld a special assessment for local improvements which was imposed upon an ad valorem basis. Richardson v. Hardee, 85 Fla. 510, 96 So. 290 (1923); see also City of Naples v. Moon, 269 So. 2d 355 (Fla. 1972) (approving special assessment based in part upon assessed values). As we explained in Meyer v. City of Oakland Park, 219 So. 2d 417, 419–20 (Fla. 1969):

> Many elements enter into the question of determining and prorating benefits in a case of this kind. They are physical condition, nearness to or remoteness from residential and business districts, desirability for residential or commercial purposes, and many other peculiar to the locality where the lands improved are located. As stated by the Court in City of Ft. Myers v. State of Florida and Langford, 95 Fla. 704, 117 So. 97, 104:
>
> > No system of appraising benefits or assessing costs has yet been devised that is not open to some criticism. None have attained the ideal position of exact equality, but, if assessing boards would bear in mind that benefits actually accruing to the property improved in addition to those received by the community at large must control both as to benefits prorated and the limit of assessments for cost of improvement, the system employed would be as near the ideal as it is humanly possible to make it.

While front foot or square foot methodologies for apportioning costs of special improvement projects are more traditional, other methods are permissible. As we stated in South Trail Fire Control District v. State, 273 So. 2d 380, 384 (Fla.1973):

> The manner of the assessment is immaterial and may vary within the district, as long as the amount of the assessment for each tract is not in excess of the proportional benefits as compared to other assessments on other tracts.

We do not believe that Fisher v. Board of County Commissioners, 84 So. 2d 572 (Fla. 1956), mandates a contrary result. In that case, there was no credible evidence that the amount of the benefit was related to the property valuation.

We reverse the final judgment and remand with directions that the bond issue be approved.

It is so ordered.

■ OVERTON, BARKETT, KOGAN and HARDING, JJ., concur.

■ MCDONALD, J., concurs in part and dissents in part with an opinion, in which SHAW, C.J., concurs.

■ MCDONALD, JUSTICE, concurring in part and dissenting in part.

I concur with the holding that Florida municipalities possess the constitutional and statutory power to impose special assessments by ordinance and that the City of Boca Raton could lawfully impose a valid special assessment. I part company with the majority and the trial judge where they conclude that the proposal under scrutiny is a valid special assessment. Reviewing the evidence in the light most favorable to the City, I fail to find any special benefits to the assessed properties or its owners. There is a general benefit to all the citizens of the City. Hence, I believe that the project can only be paid by taxes, which requires a referendum and assessment against all taxpayers. I would therefore disapprove the bonds.

■ SHAW, C.J., concurs.

NOTES

1. *Assessments versus Taxes.* Public officials may prefer special assessments to payment through property taxes because nontax exactions typically are not subject to voting requirements or tax limitations, such as Proposition 13, discussed in *Amador Valley*. For the same reason, however, those who must pay the assessment may want to reclassify it as a tax. In addition, the distributional consequences of a tax may vary from those of an assessment, because different groups will bear the burden depending on which payment mechanism is used. The court in *Boca Raton* applies the standard rule that an exaction can be classified as an assessment only if those who pay it enjoy some special benefit that is not shared by others in the locality. See, e.g., Stephen Diamond, Constitutional Limits on the Growth of Special Assessments, 6 Urb. L. & Pol'y 311 (1984). Assume that an exaction is imposed on owners and operators of underground storage tanks in order to provide revenue sufficient to support financing of a system to prevent leaks from such facilities. Does the system benefit the owners and operators of the storage tanks, as opposed to the victims of such leaks, sufficiently to characterize the exaction as an assessment? See State ex rel. Petroleum Underground Storage Tank Release Compensation Board v. Withrow, 579 N.E.2d 705 (Ohio 1991).

In Sarasota County v. Sarasota Church of Christ, Inc., 667 So.2d 180 (Fla. 1995), the court concluded that a special assessment for stormwater services was valid. The assessment was imposed on developed property, but not on undeveloped property. Religious organizations that were exempt from ad valorem property taxes, and thus would not have had to pay for stormwater treatment services supported by taxes, contended that the entire community benefited from stormwater services. Thus, they claimed, property taxes alone should be used to finance the services. The court determined that the county could properly conclude that all developed property, including churches, received a special benefit from stormwater treatment "because those are the properties with impervious surfaces that contribute the polluted stormwater to be treated by the system." The court also found that the county had apportioned fees according to the way in which developed property was used and that the apportionment reflected the contributions to runoff from different uses. The majority suggested that it was irrelevant that the assessment was imposed throughout the community, a conclusion that a dissenting judge indicated would make the distinction between a tax and an assessment "illusory."

In Collier County v. State, 733 So.2d 1012 (Fla. 1999), however, the court invalidated an "Interim Governmental Services Fee Ordinance" as an impermissible tax. The ordinance authorized the county to impose an assessment on property owners who had made improvements after the state placed a moratorium on the collection of property taxes with respect to such improvements. The county claimed that the assessment was valid because it was not based on the value of the property, but rather on the increased cost of providing certain "growth-sensitive" services as a result of the improvement. These services included the sheriff's office, elections, code enforcement, libraries, animal control, parks and recreation, and public health. The court concluded that the assessed property did not receive any special benefit from the services financed with the assessment, as required by *Boca Raton*. The fact that the assessment was rationally related to an increased demand for county services or was used for services that were sensitive to population size was insufficient to constitute a special benefit. For additional discussion of the distinction between taxes and assessments, see Zahner v. City of Perryville, 813 S.W.2d 855 (Mo. 1991) (special assessment for street improvements not a tax).

2. *Motives for Using Assessments.* The above cases demonstrate the substantial latitude that courts give to municipal decisions about the imposition and calculation of special assessments. Where a jurisdiction pays for an improvement through a special assessment rather than a broader-based property tax, one might analyze the propriety of the assessment from either of two presumptions. First, one might contend that special assessments tend to be used by officials who would prefer to impose a larger burden on a small group of constituents rather than to impose a small burden on all constituents on the theory that this device minimizes the number of people who will express concern about increased costs of residence. Alternatively, one might contend that special assessments tend to be used by officials who believe that the improvements only benefit a discrete segment of the community and do not want to impose these costs on the community at large. If one believes that special assessments tend to be of the first category, then one might be reluctant to defer to municipal decisions to use this mechanism. One might be less deferential to measurement techniques used by the locality or to a local determination that there exists a special benefit sufficient to support a special assessment. See Goodger v. City of Delavan, 396 N.W.2d 778 (Wis. Ct. App. 1986). If one believes that special assessments tend to be of the second category, however, one might be more deferential to local decisions and less sympathetic to judicial intervention.

3. *Calculating Differential Benefits.* The propriety of judicial intervention may also reflect the extent to which one believes there is a single, accurate mechanism for determining the amount and value of benefit that any resident receives from a local improvement. The courts in the above cases agree that a special assessment can only be imposed on those who receive a special benefit from the improvement. How can the amount of the benefit be measured?

Assume that you had unlimited resources to measure the amount of benefit that each resident received from an improvement such as street paving. You might measure the value of each abutting home before and after the improvement and define the difference as the proper amount of the special assessment. But even this procedure would not capture all the benefits of the improvement. Nonabutting users might substantially benefit from the improvement if they drove on the street with great frequency. Thus, you might dedicate some resources to capturing the benefit enjoyed by those individuals, e.g., by setting up a toll booth at each end of the street. In the absence of an unconstrained budget, some surrogate must be found for these more precise, but expensive, measurements. The Florida court agrees that the mechanism suggested in *Rogers*, the front-footage method, serves as a useful surrogate for the proportionate increase in market value of the property that benefits from the improvement. Under some circumstances, this assumption seems appropriate. Assume, for instance, a series of lots that have the following configuration along a recently paved street for which the locality seeks reimbursement through special assessment: Lots A, B, C, and D may increase in value in proportion to their front footage. But there is no reason to believe that the same can be said with respect to lots E, F, G, and H. Thus, the accuracy of the front-footage method will depend on whether lots are generally configured in such a manner that front footage reflects total lot size.

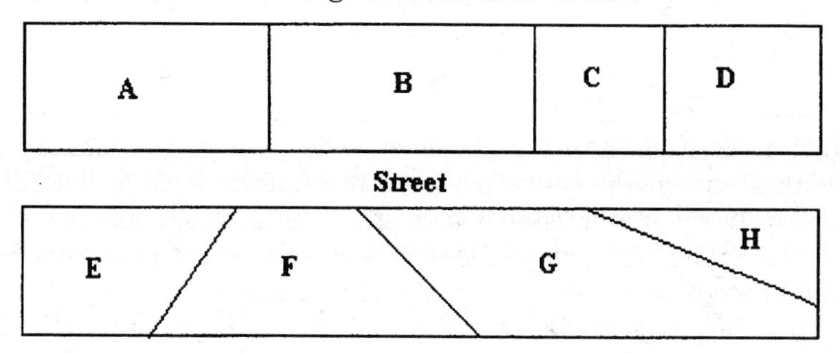

In City of Waukegan v. De Wolf, 101 N.E. 532 (Ill. 1913), the court upheld a decision that special assessments could not be used to pay the cost of constructing a viaduct. The improvement was necessary to restore the main street of the city, which had become severed by the closing of a dilapidated structure. All land in the city was subjected to the special assessment. The amount of the assessment for each parcel, however, depended on how much benefit the improvement provided to the area of the city in which the parcel was located. Assessments among zones ranged from $5 per front foot on lands contiguous to the improvement, to 4 cents per front foot on lands most remote from it. The court concluded that although all benefit zones differentiated among beneficiaries, the effect of this particular improvement was to benefit the public, and not to benefit adjoining property. Hence, the improvement was not local or special and could not be financed through assessments.

In Concerned Taxpayers Coalition v. Town of Scarborough, 576 A.2d 1368 (Me. 1990), residents subject to an assessment contended that the sole permissible measure of benefit was the increased market value of the assessed properties attributable to the improvement. The court rejected that proposition, holding: "In order to support the assessment it is not necessary for the Town to measure precisely the benefit to each piece of property or to calculate exactly how much of the improvement is for the public and how much is for the special benefit of those assessed. Under the statutes quoted above, it need only estimate the benefit." 576 A.2d at 1369–1370. Does this mean that the locality need make no effort to distinguish among beneficiaries? Assume that a locality constructs a waste water treatment plant and seeks to pay for it by imposing an equal lump-sum "special assessment" on each parcel without regard to use. Would such an exaction satisfy the requirements of linking benefits to burdens? Would it matter that measurement of use is rendered difficult by the fact that some of the parcels are used as full-time residences, some as summer homes, some as seasonal commercial enterprises, and some as full-time businesses? See Village of Egg Harbor v. Mariner Group, Inc., 457 N.W.2d 519 (Wis. Ct. App. 1990).

Boca Raton suggests that even less precise measures of benefit will be acceptable. Is there reason to doubt that the benefits paid for by the assessment in that case will be reflected in real property values? Assume that the owner of a parcel within the downtown area makes improvements that are not funded by the bonds at issue, such as better lighting within the store or a repaved parking lot. As a result, the property taxes on that parcel will increase, as will its pro rata share of the entire tax base of the downtown area. Does it make sense to allocate a proportionately larger share of the assessment costs to that owner as well? In 2nd Roc–Jersey Associates v. Town of Morristown, 731 A.2d 1 (N.J. 1999), the court upheld an assessment on all property within a business improvement district and imposed on the basis of .105% of the property's assessed value for local real property tax purposes. Plaintiffs complained that real property tax assessments could not be the basis for determining special assessments. They asserted that various properties in the district were used for different purposes, such as hotels, offices, and retail space; that properties with different land uses received different benefits from the improvements; and that those benefits should be reflected in the assessment. The court upheld the assessment. It concluded:

> It is not unreasonable for Morristown to select one of the simpler methods of valuing benefits during the initial phase of the SID. The tax system offers several advantages in that it is updated periodically and provides property owners with a basis to challenge erroneous tax assessments and the derivative SID assessments. Although a more complex method might yield a fairer apportionment, it would be substantially more expensive and difficult to employ in the early stages of the SID.

731 A.2d at 10.

4. Note the court's insistence in *Rogers* that the test of an assessment is not the actual benefit obtained by the landowner, but the "opportunity to benefit." Thus, the existence of a benefit is not tested by reference to the present use of the improved land, but by reference to whether the improvement enhances potential uses of the property. A town, for instance, may consider as a benefit the effect that a sewer improvement will have on undeveloped land should the land subsequently be developed for residential purposes. See Baglivi v. Town of Highlands, 537 N.Y.S.2d 552 (N.Y. App. Div. 1989); Vail v. City of Bandon, 630 P.2d 1339 (Or. Ct. App. 1981).

How far does this principle permit a locality to go in imposing costs on property owners whose current use makes the improvement superfluous? In Owatonna v. Chicago, Rock Island & Pacific R. Co., 450 F.2d 87 (8th Cir. 1971), the court reversed a district court decision that had upheld an assessment against a railroad whose tracks abutted a newly paved road. The city that imposed the assessment also erected a drainage ditch on the railroad's property. The court found that the ditch detracted from the property's potential transformation to residential use. Since the railroad, which owned only an easement on a substantial portion of the real property over which its right of way ran, did not receive any direct benefit from the road paving or the drainage ditch, and could not readily transform its property to alternative uses that might benefit from the improvements, the court concluded that the municipality's assessment was "demonstrably wrong."

Is *Owatonna* a case in which a municipality imposes a disproportionate burden on a readily available nonresident who cannot easily exit? After all, if we take seriously the argument that local officials might prefer to impose a substantial burden on a small minority of individuals rather than a small burden on a large number of individuals, the most advantageous decision for an official who must subsequently seek re-election is to impose the greatest burden on those who have no vote. That seems to call for imposing assessments on some entity or person, like the railroad, for whom exit costs (the costs of rerouting the tracks) likely far exceed the assessment. Or is there some more benign explanation for the municipality's action? The district court, which had upheld the assessment, concluded that accepting the railroad's argument "would result in exempting all property used for railroad purposes as a right of way from any special assessments.... Such would not in this court's opinion be a just result." The court noted that railroads were exempted by state legislation from paying other taxes that might redound to the benefit of communities through which their lines run. If that legislation was passed because railroads were able to exercise disproportionate influence with the legislature, could the assessment be considered an appropriate means of requiring the railroad to pay its fair share for municipal services? How easily can a court determine whether the malign or benign explanation for the municipality's action more accurately reflects what happened?

5. Assume that a municipality seeks to impose a special assessment for street paving on 10 abutters of the improvement and that each abutter owns an identical lot. Assume that the improvement costs $5,000 and that the assessor determines that the market value of each lot has been increased by $400 as a result of the improvement. Can the abutters be charged a pro rata share of the cost of the improvement ($500) or only the amount by which the value of their lots has been increased? Given that the underlying theory of special assessment is to recapture the benefit conferred by the improvement, the $400 figure would appear appropriate.

What if the assessor determines that the value of each lot has been increased by $600? Can the municipality recover the full benefit or only $500? Courts tend to use cost as a ceiling on special assessments. The increased value of the lot, however, should also be reflected in higher property taxes that the locality is able to collect, so that the locality may ultimately recover its costs. See Mullins v. City of El Dorado, 436 P.2d 837 (Kan. 1968).

NOTE ON OTHER REVENUE SOURCES

Local government sales and income taxes follow property taxes as the second and third largest sources of local revenue. According to the Advisory Commission on Intergovernmental Relations, by 1994 the sales tax was used by 6,579 local governments in 50 states. See 1 ACIR, Significant Features of Fiscal Federalism: Budget Processes and Tax Systems 27 (1995). In 1995, local government sales taxes generated almost $27.9 billion, providing 6.7 percent of these local governments' own-source revenue. U.S. Bureau of the Census, United States State & Local Government Finances by Level of Government: 1994–95, <http://www.census.gov/govs/estimate/95stlus.txt>. The sales tax, however, is not used uniformly throughout the country. A large number of the jurisdictions using sales taxes are located in Texas (1,318). Local income taxes, used by 4,111 governments in 14 states, generated $12.3 billion in 1995. See 1 ACIR, at 21. However, 2,830 of these local governments are located in Pennsylvania and 523 are located in Ohio. In those jurisdictions that raise revenue in this manner, income taxes yield an average of 12.3 percent of total own-source local revenues.

In general, the use of sales and income taxes by general purpose local governments requires state authorization and frequently a voter referendum. These taxes, however, may also be authorized by home rule charter or local ordinance. In Louisiana and Missouri, enabling legislation that creates special purpose districts frequently allows financing of operations through sales or income taxes.

Only eight states authorize local governments to levy both sales and income taxes. Some, like Iowa, authorize sales taxes for one form of local government, and reserve income taxes for another. See, e.g., Iowa Code Ann. 298.14, 422B.1. Ohio, for example, authorizes cities to impose an income tax, Ohio Rev. Code Ann. 718.01 (Anderson 1993), and counties to impose a sales tax, Ohio Rev. Code Ann. 5739.06. The number of jurisdictions using local sales taxes peaked in 1989 as localities shifted to other forms of taxation. The bulk of this shift occurred in Texas and Illinois. Use by other states remains stable. See 1 ACIR, at 27.

The tax rate for municipal sales taxes ranges substantially. The ACIR found sales taxes imposed from 0.4 percent in Albuquerque, New Mexico, to 5.75 percent in Washington, D.C. The majority of cities, however, tax sales at 1 or 2 percent. See 1 ACIR, at 28. Enactment of sales taxes is not always a local government choice. Cities and counties in Virginia and counties in

California are required by the state to enact sales taxes at the rates of 1 percent and 1.25 percent, respectively. Two other states, New Mexico and Tennessee, require sales taxes but allow local governments to choose the rate from a specified range.

Sales taxes may impose significant costs on local businesses in two ways. If neighboring localities do not impose a similar tax, consumers may attempt to avoid the tax by shopping outside the locality, hence reducing revenues for the taxing jurisdiction and the local businesses. In addition, local administration of the sales tax may be costly to businesses that must collect and account for tax receipts. State administration of local sales taxes may ease the burden in jurisdictions where state and local taxes provide for the same exemptions. See John F. Due and John L. Mikesell, Sales Taxation 265–318 (1983).

Income taxes are more likely to be used by local governments if the state does not require voter approval. Only four states require such approval. One of these, Georgia, also prohibits local governments from enacting both sales and income taxes. As a result, there are no local income taxes in Georgia.

Fourteen states authorize local income taxes. In most of these jurisdictions, the tax takes the form of a flat rate imposed on wage or payroll income. Other local governments tax local incomes at a percentage of federal or state taxes. These rates typically are below 4 percent of the taxpayer's wages. Many cities and counties also employ different rates for residents and nonresidents. New York City's income tax is unique in that it employs a definition of income similar to that of the federal government, but applies its own progressive rates and allows for deductions patterned on the state law. Wage or payroll taxes are normally collected through payroll withholding, facilitating administration and making taxpayer filings unnecessary.

Wage income taxes face criticism as regressive, since they rarely allow for exemptions or deductions, and are imposed only on wage earnings, which may be more applicable to middle and lower income taxpayers. Thus, incomes such as rental, interest, and self-employment escape taxation. Taxes based on federal adjusted gross income or state tax liability are more progressive as they tax all forms of income.

Lotteries have also become an important part of state and local government financing. In 1994, the 40 states that have state lotteries generated $11.4 billion in net proceeds. 2 ACIR, Significant Features of Fiscal Federalism: Revenues & Expenditures 59 (1995). The revenue generated is used to fund state and local interests such as parks, recreation, and economic development. Especially prevalent is the use of state lottery revenues to fund education. Although the lotteries are typically administered by the states, the revenue is also used by some states to finance various local government activities. In Massachusetts, the $2.3 billion generated by that state's lottery in 1994 was shared with localities. For example, the Massachusetts State Lottery Fund provides annual distributions to a Local Aid Fund, used to assist cities, towns, and districts with expenses; another lottery allocation through the State Arts Lottery Fund provides revenue to be distributed to cities and towns for use by local cultural councils, with each city or town eligible to receive an annual minimum of $1000. (Mass. Gen. Laws Ann. ch. 29 2C 1/2; ch. 58 18C; ch. 10 57). In Arizona, some of the revenues are dedicated to local transportation assistance and county assistance. (Ariz. Rev. Stat. Ann. 5–522). Some of the money generated in Maryland and Washington state lotteries provides funding for stadium authorities. (Md. State Gov't § 9–120.1; Wash. Rev. Code § 67.70.024–040). The Nebraska County and City Lottery Act (Neb. Rev. St. §§ 9–601 to 9–653) gives localities the authority to conduct lotteries for community betterment purposes. Notwithstanding their financial success, lotteries have been criticized as a regressive form of taxation insofar as lower-income groups spend a higher percentage of their income on lottery tickets than do higher-income groups. See, e.g., Todd A. Wyett, State Lotteries: Regressive Taxes in Disguise, 44 Tax Law. 867 (1991). For an interesting discussion of whether lottery ticket purchases by low-income groups are nevertheless rational, see Edward J. McCaffery, Why People Play Lotteries and Why It Matters, 1994 Wis. L. Rev. 71.

Finally, the federal government serves as a significant source of state and local revenue. In 1994, the federal government provided $215.4 billion to state and local governments, contributing approximately 19.5 percent of their total revenue. 2 ACIR, Significant Features of Fiscal Federalism: Revenues and Expenditure 47 (1995). Of this $215.4 billion, states received $191 billion (or 27.7 percent of total state revenue) and local governments received $24 billion (or 4 percent of total local revenue). Localities also benefit from federal revenue initially directed at states, as some of this funding is channelled back to localities.

3. User Fees and Service Charges

PROBLEM XX

Crystal Lake lies completely within Merchants County. The county maintains a small patrol force that enforces boating safety regulations promulgated by the county and that rescues boaters who are either stranded (as when they inopportunely run out of gas or meet inclement weather) or endangered. To this point, the county has always paid for the patrol force out of its general revenues. Recently, however, tax protests have mounted and county officials are attempting to augment their fiscal base with "nontax" revenues. One official has recommended that the patrol force be financed with fees rather than through taxes. She has suggested that fees could be imposed on all users of the lake. Other officials have endorsed the idea of fees, but have expressed a preference for having the fee imposed only on all boaters. Another official has suggested that the fee only be imposed on boaters who are actually assisted by the patrol force, in the form of a "rescue fee." You serve as legal advisor to the county. You have been asked to consider each of these proposals, to indicate what you believe would be the effects of each, and to recommend the one most consistent with the objective of imposing a user fee. How will you respond?

PROBLEM XXI

You have been asked to advise the newly incorporated Town of Hume about appropriate methods for financing local services. The town proposes to keep property taxes low by charging user fees for a variety of services. The plan includes the following:

(1) Charge each family a fee for each child attending the local schools. The fee would likely not cover the full cost of teaching the student, and "scholarships," funded through property taxes, would be available to families that met a needs test. Hence, it is anticipated that no resident child will be denied the ability to attend the local schools for financial reasons.

(2) Charge a user fee for garbage collection. Garbage would be collected once a week. Each household would pay the same amount, regardless of the number of household members or amount of garbage the household generated.

(3) Charge a user fee for certain police details. Police services would generally be available, and payable from property taxes, for general matters such as traffic control. Any request for a specific response (e.g., a call relating to a specific home or a request for police assistance), however, would require the caller to pay a fee.

(4) Charge a user fee for a municipal day-care center. Any resident could leave preschool children at a municipally operated day-care center. Daily rates would be charged to defray the costs of rent, caretakers, and supplies. Rates would presumably be less than those at private day-care centers, as the town would not seek to make a profit from the service.

(5) Charge a user fee for a municipal golf course. Any resident could sign up to use the golf course, but would be required to pay a fee in an amount necessary to defray a pro rata share of the expected costs of labor and maintenance. Rates would presumably be less than those at private country clubs, as the town would not seek to make a profit from the golf course.

Clayton P. Gillette & Thomas D. Hopkins, Federal User Fees: A Legal and Economic Analysis

67 B.U. L. Rev. 795, 800, 805–811 (1987).

A. A Definition of User Fees and a Standard for Evaluation

A user fee is a price charged by a governmental agency for a service or product whose distribution it controls. A user fee is, at least in theory, a benefit-based source of revenue whose logic is simple. Payment of a user fee reflects receipt of a valued service in return, a quid pro quo. By contrast, federal income taxation is generally not benefit-based; rather, it imposes burdens that reflect complex Congressional judgments about, among other things, a taxpayer's ability to pay. . . .

B. User Fees and Economic Efficiency

Efficient pricing exists if one is deterred from consuming additional units of public service only when the benefits of that consumption are less than its costs to society. As the above discussion suggests, there are many situations in which a user fee can successfully ration limited supplies of currently available goods and services to more highly valued uses, signal whether particular output levels should increase or decrease, avert wasteful usage, and encourage use of more suitable substitutes. In this sense, a user fee is essentially a mechanism available to link the service with the potential consumer of a scarce resource. It is an alternative to first-come, first-served, to lotteries, and to administrative judgment. The central task is to determine those circumstances in which a user fee will be the most satisfactory choice of rationing mechanisms....

If there are no significant externalities associated with a particular service that warrants public provision, then user fees constitute an efficient rationing mechanism. If the government is producing goods that could be provided at least as well by the market, user fees certainly are appropriate. In both these situations, a user fee can be relatively successful in encouraging the most productive use of the service, barring possible accounting and managerial complexities.

With the user fee, the potential beneficiary of a government service is the one who must pay the opportunity cost of the service—that is, the additional cost that society will incur in providing an increment of service.

There are two important results if the beneficiary freely decides how much, if any, of the service to utilize. First, the consumer for whom the service holds little value automatically will be deterred from its use. Second, persuasive willingness-to-pay evidence will be yielded indicating whether the government should increase or decrease its provision of the service. The former is conducive to maximizing society's material well-being over the short-term; the latter facilitates the same result over the long run.

For a user fee to have these desirable consequences, setting the amount of the fee is quite important. As a general matter, "the costs that should be recovered are the opportunity costs sacrificed at any time." Application of this principle, however, may require attention to varying factors, depending on the specific situation. Consider four possible scenarios:

1. The government can increase or decrease its output of a particular service that is not available elsewhere. The inputs used have known market values, and per unit costs do not decline as more is produced (for example, inspection services). In this situation, marginal cost pricing keyed to full recovery of incremental production costs will be efficient. The opportunity cost will be the personnel and support costs incurred by government in providing the service.

2. A particular service can be characterized exactly as in Example 1 except that it also can be obtained from private firms through market transactions (for example, certain postal delivery services). Assuming con-

tinued governmental provision is warranted—a privatization issue—an efficient user fee may properly exceed incremental agency production costs, and instead reflect the service's market value. This conclusion, however, requires some judgment about whether private suppliers are pricing and producing efficiently and whether the government enjoys artificial cost advantages, such as tax exemption.

3. The government is allocating a good or service—grazing rights, for example—that entails little if any current costs of production, the service has scarcity value in that not all who want the service can be accommodated, and more of the service cannot be produced. In this situation, the opportunity cost associated with providing an increment of service to an additional beneficiary is the value forgone by shifting the service away from the next most interested potential consumer. Where identified—through auction, bidding, or private markets for comparable services—this value should serve as the amount of the user fee if efficiency is to be achieved. This user fee may exceed actual out-of-pocket costs incurred by the government.

4. Considerable past (one-time) cost has been incurred relative to the level of ongoing production costs (for example, dam construction). Sunk costs or historical costs as a general rule should not be factored into user fees; that is, historical cost recovery and efficient user fees are not always compatible objectives. This is an example of a natural monopoly that poses a well-known efficiency dilemma between short-run allocation and long-run replacement decisions. To the extent that user fee revenues fall short of recouping the total costs borne by the government, the gap must be filled with general tax revenues. Then, "[t]he efficiency questions should be concerned with the possible adverse effects of these taxes upon resource allocation versus the adverse effects of the levy of beneficiary charges that might return historical costs but still be inefficient." Moreover, if replacement costs are likely to be encountered at some point, efficiency is not well-served by restricting user fees to the recovery of current production costs alone.

We have thus far focused on situations in which consumption is voluntary. For some, the voluntary use of the good serves as an additional justification for a user fee. Even if there is a degree of coercion in the decision to use the service, however, a user fee may have important efficiency advantages. For example, assume a statute directs each member of a certain group to take a personal safety training course offered only by the federal government. As a general matter, the short-term allocative efficiency objective would not likely be particularly well-served by a user fee, still assuming no externalities. However, suppose further a statute accurately reflects plausibly paternalistic motives and unambiguously indicates both what groups should be directed to make use of the service and how much they should use. If the statute is based on solid benefit-cost reasoning, a user fee may be superior on efficiency grounds to other means of finance, because it will not burden those who neither use nor benefit from this service, and thus not influence their actions. On the other hand, should the statute have little to commend it on benefit-cost grounds, it is still arguable that a user fee would have favorable longer-term efficiency consequences. The payer would be more inclined to insist on prudent service delivery and to press for closer scrutiny of the levels and terms of service continuation.

To summarize, in the absence of both externalities and mandated usage, user fees are likely to have attractive efficiency attributes in allocating access to the service in the short run as well as in guiding governmental decisions about levels and types of service to provide in the longer run. Moreover, regardless of whether usage is mandated, user fees probably will have desirable efficiency effects in financing service provision. Directly placing the production cost burden on the recipient of the service rather than on other taxpayers will likely limit the excess burden associated with all revenue sources.

Once we relax the assumption that governmental services produce no externalities, the efficiency, and hence desirability, of user fees changes markedly. User fees may be associated with external effects in either of two ways. As our discussion of public goods reveals, where each recipient who pays for a governmental service simultaneously confers benefits on nonpayers, a user fee may induce underuse of the service from a societal perspective. Alternatively, where recipients of a governmental service are not otherwise required to incur the corresponding costs of the service, imposition of a user fee may forestall overuse.

Consider first the situation in which partaking of a governmental service by one party necessarily confers benefits on a third party who contributes nothing to the cost of the service, as in the case of spillover benefits or positive externalities. An apt example would be a municipality that offers and charges a fee for, but does not require, weekly garbage collection. Residents who do not accept the municipal service may either remove their own garbage or may contract with private collectors. Those persons unwilling to pay the user fee may find less frequent disposal more consistent with their own preferences. Nevertheless, the resulting accumulation of garbage may impose adverse effects on neighbors. More frequent collection, therefore, would confer a benefit on the neighbors, even though they bear none of the commensurate costs. The neighbors (who effectively wish to free ride by changing the collection practices of the infrequent disposer) play no role, however, in determining how much collection will be undertaken by the infrequent disposer. Similarly, the infrequent disposer has no incentive to factor third party benefits into his decision about making use of the service. Consequently, an individual resident will ignore external benefits when deciding whether to use the service. Measured from a societal perspective, underuse of the service will likely result. Elimination or reduction of the user fee to reflect the external benefits might reduce the cost of frequent collection sufficiently to induce the infrequent disposer to take advantage of the governmental service. In other words, user fees that place full costs of service on only a subset of service beneficiaries have an efficiency drawback. . . .

Unlike the garbage collection example, in which full cost recovery through user fees may induce underuse, there are other instances in which user fees can avoid overuse. For example, when the government supplies goods or services at a charge less than the cost of supplying the service, the recipient necessarily receives a subsidy from others. An individual recipient who can reap the benefits of the service while imposing the corresponding costs on others has an incentive to overuse the governmental resources. One such situation of public "bads," perhaps best referred to as the tragedy of the commons, is likely to arise where scarce property is held in common—public parkland or fishing areas, for example—so that each individual has a claim to use. As each individual exercises that claim, however, the resource may be overused from a societal perspective. Nevertheless, no individual has an incentive to moderate his or her personal use, notwithstanding that joint use generates a net social loss. User fees may be particularly appropriate insofar as they discourage overuse by requiring users to bear some of the costs of maintaining the public property or to recognize the costs imposed on others through private use. As a mechanism for pricing access to the commons, user fees provide an alternative to direct government rationing or grants by government to private parties of monopoly rights in the public property.

Quite apart from such commons effects, other types of adverse consequences, such as pollution, often are imposed on nonusers. Failure of the producer to recognize all the costs of its activity is likely to generate overinvestment in the activity. An additional user fee may play an important efficiency role in restraining this excess. Indeed, charges in excess of marginal costs may be justified where the service is receiving some benefit from expenditures made through the general treasury. For instance, if a locality is providing waste treatment and charging a user fee for the service, it may be appropriate for the locality to charge a fee that exceeds the capital and operating costs of the facility and to return the "profit" to the local treasury. This result could be appropriate if the excess charge reflects the costs incurred by the locality in providing police and fire services to the facility, as those services generally will be financed through local taxation.

NOTES

1. The authors suggest that a user fee is appropriate if the users of the service capture enough of the benefit from providing the service to avoid the risks of free riding and undersupply, that is, the threats of Prisoner's Dilemmas and Chicken Games. Conversely, user fees would appear to be inappropriate where providing the service generates too many beneficial effects for those who are not required to pay. In that case, each potential beneficiary would be induced to await action by others in order to receive benefits without incurring the related costs. But if we are dealing with a situation in which the benefits of the service are, in fact, "internalized" to the person paying for them, we do not seem to be dealing with public goods at all. Instead, we seem to be dealing with a situation in which private markets would be able to provide a satisfactory amount of the service. Thus, why is there a need for government intervention at all? See the discussion of privatization at pages 654–673 infra.

2. Discussions of user fees in the economics literature can be found in Charles J. Goetz, The Revenue Potential of User–Related Charges in State and Local Governments, in Broad–Based Taxes: New Options and Sources 113 (Richard A. Musgrave ed., 1973); M. Z. Kafoglis, Local Service Charges: Theory and Practice, in State and Local Tax Problems 164 (H. L. Johnson ed., 1969).

Silva v. City of Attleboro

908 N.E.2d 722 (Mass. 2009).

■ COWIN, J.

In this case, we are asked to consider whether a charge assessed by certain municipalities for the issuance of a burial permit is a lawful fee or an unlawful tax. The Appeals Court, applying our decision in *Emerson College v. Boston,* 391 Mass. 415, 462 N.E.2d 1098 (1984) (*Emerson College*), held that the burial permit charge was an unlawful tax. We conclude that it is a valid regulatory fee.

Background. General Laws c. 114, § 45, requires that any funeral director seeking to dispose of the body of a deceased person must obtain a burial permit from the board of health or the clerk of the municipality in which the decedent died. The statute requires that a person seeking the burial permit must present both a death certificate and "a satisfactory written statement containing the facts required by law to be returned and recorded" in order for the burial permit to issue. The municipality must issue the burial permit upon receipt of the statement and certificate required by the statute. See id. Some municipalities, including the defendants, exact a monetary charge to issue these burial permits. These amounts are deposited in each of the defendants' general revenue funds. The amounts constitute a relatively small portion of the budget of each defendant's board of health, and are roughly proportional to the cost of compensating municipal employees for their time in receiving and examining the death certificates, issuing the burial permits, and record-keeping associated with the process.

The plaintiff is a licensed funeral director operating his business in the city of Fall River and surrounding communities throughout Bristol County. He brought this action seeking declaratory and injunctive relief against the defendants, claiming that the burial permit fees are illegal taxes. After a jury-waived trial, a Superior Court judge ruled for the defendants. Applying the Appeals Court's decision in *Silva v. Fall River,* 59 Mass.App.Ct. 798, 807, 798 N.E.2d 297 (2003), the judge concluded that the burial permit charges are not exacted in exchange for any particularized benefit that is not also provided to other members of the community. He also decided that payment of the charges was mandatory rather than voluntary. The judge found, however, that the defendants "incurred significant expenses in issuing, processing and regulating burial permits," and that "the fee charged is reasonable and is used to cover these expenses." He therefore concluded that the burial permit charges were permissible fees intended to defray costs associated with the permit process and were not unlawful taxes.

As stated, the Appeals Court reversed. That court determined that the judge had given improper weight to the fact that the burial permit charges were reasonably proportional to the costs incurred by the defendants. Because "the issuance of burial permits has a shared public benefit and ... the services provided are involuntary in a way that is distinct from the typical regulatory fee," the Appeals Court held that the burial permit charges were not valid regulatory fees but improper taxes. Id. We granted further appellate review. We affirm the Superior Court judgment.

Discussion. ... "A municipality does not have the power to levy, assess, or collect a tax unless the power to do so in a particular instance is granted by the Legislature." *Commonwealth v. Caldwell,* 25 Mass.App.Ct. 91, 92, 515 N.E.2d 589 (1987). See *Opinion of the Justices,* 378 Mass. 802, 810 n. 10, 393 N.E.2d 306 (1979), citing art. 2 of the Amendments to the Massachusetts Constitution, as appearing in art. 89, §§ 1, 6 and 7 ("Cities and towns have no independent power of taxation"). The plaintiff has the burden of proving the invalidity of the exaction. Although we give some deference to the defendants' classification of the burial permit charge as a fee, "[u]ltimately" the nature of a monetary exaction "must be determined by its operation rather than its specially descriptive phrase." *Emerson College, supra* at 424, 462 N.E.2d 1098, quoting *Thomson Elec. Welding Co. v. Commonwealth,* 275 Mass. 426, 429, 176 N.E. 203 (1931).

In distinguishing fees from taxes, we have noted that fees tend to share common traits. Fees, unlike taxes, "are charged in exchange for a particular governmental service which benefits the party paying the fee in a manner 'not shared by other members of society.'" *Emerson College, supra,* quoting *National Cable Television Ass'n v. United States,* 415 U.S. 336, 341, 94 S.Ct. 1146, 39 L.Ed.2d 370 (1974). Fees "are paid by choice, in that the party paying the fee has the option of not utilizing the governmental service and thereby avoiding the charge." *Emerson College, supra* at 424–425, 462 N.E.2d 1098. Finally, the charges "are collected not to raise revenues but to compensate the governmental entity providing the services for its expenses." Id. at 425, 462 N.E.2d 1098. Valid fees fall into one of two categories: "user fees, based on the rights of the entity as proprietor of the instrumentalities used ... or regulatory fees (including licensing and inspection fees), founded on the police power to regulate particular businesses or activities." Id. at 424, 462 N.E.2d 1098, citing *Opinion of the Justices,* 250 Mass. 591, 597, 602, 148 N.E. 889 (1925).

The plaintiff argues that the burial permit charges are not fees, but are rather taxes that the defendants lack statutory or constitutional authority to levy. Relying on *Emerson College, supra* at 424–425, 462 N.E.2d 1098, and *Silva v. Fall River,* 59 Mass.App.Ct. 798, 807, 798 N.E.2d 297 (2003), the plaintiff argues that the burial permit fees lack the essential characteristics of fees because, according to the analysis prescribed in the *Emerson College* decision, the charges are not exacted in exchange for a particular governmental service that benefits the permit seeker in a manner not shared by other members of society; they are not voluntarily incurred because a burial permit is required for the plaintiff to dispose of a body in a lawful manner; and they are not charged in order to compensate the municipalities for their expenses, but rather are intended to raise general revenue because the proceeds are deposited into the general fund of each of the defendants.

We do not agree. Although a municipality has no independent power of taxation, it may assess, levy, and collect fees when the Legislature has authorized it to do so, provided that those fees are reasonable and proportional. Here, the defendants are required to issue the burial permits in question pursuant to G.L. c. 114, § 45, and are authorized, pursuant to G.L. c. 40, § 22F, to defray these expenses by charging a reasonable fee. In pertinent part, the latter statute provides:

"Any municipal board or officer empowered to issue a license, permit, certificate, or to render a service or perform work for a person or class of persons, may, from time to time, fix reasonable fees for all such licenses, permits, or certificates issued pursuant to statutes or regulations wherein the entire proceeds of the fee remain with such issuing city or town, and may fix reasonable charges to be paid for any services rendered or work performed by the city or town or any department thereof, for any person or class of persons. . . ."

court reasoning

statute

G.L. c. 40, § 22F. The trial judge found that the defendants incur significant expenses in issuing said permits, and the evidence supports his finding. The parties stipulated in their statements of agreed facts that the amounts charged by the defendants for the issuance of burial permits are reasonably proportional to the amounts expended by their boards of health in administering the permit process. All the statutory conditions required under G.L. c. 40, § 22F, have therefore been satisfied.

In addition, the reasoned application of the factors discussed in *Emerson College,* and subsequent cases demonstrates that the burial permit charges are valid regulatory fees, not taxes. As to the first factor, we are not persuaded that funeral directors who pay the burial permit charges receive no special benefit that other members of society do not. We have long held that the Legislature may authorize a municipality to impose a reasonable fee to defray the cost of issuing a license that the municipality lawfully requires for one to engage in a particular activity. The Appeals Court's analysis in this case overlooks a crucial distinction between proprietary fees and regulatory fees, i.e., that the particularized benefit provided in exchange for the latter is the existence of the regulatory scheme whose costs the fee serves to defray. Regulatory fees are founded on the State's police power to regulate a particular activity or business, *Emerson College, supra* at 424, 462 N.E.2d 1098, and serve regulatory purposes either "directly by, for example, deliberately discouraging particular conduct by making it more expensive," or indirectly by defraying an agency's regulation-related expenses.

The burial permit charges are regulatory fees, not proprietary fees. These charges are founded upon the State's police power to regulate the disposal of dead bodies in a manner that preserves the public health, safety and welfare. They are not exacted in exchange for the use of the defendants' property, but are "imposed by an agency upon those subject to its regulation." In exchange for payment of the burial permit charges, funeral directors and their clients (on whose behalf the former act) receive particularized benefits in the form of a well-regulated industry for the disposal of human remains. The administration of the burial permit process by municipal boards of health provides assurances that the decedent's body is disposed of properly. The process also helps to police the industry by allowing the board of health to ensure that funeral directors have complied with applicable regulations governing the disposition of human remains and to take action against those who do not. Law-abiding funeral directors are thus spared from having to compete at a disadvantage against those who flaunt the rules governing their profession.

We turn our attention to the second *Emerson College* factor, voluntariness. *Emerson College, supra* at 424–425, 462 N.E.2d 1098. We conclude that the Appeals Court erred in applying this criterion to the present case, and that the role of the voluntariness factor in *Emerson College* is limited to the particular factual context of that case. The *Emerson College* decision dealt with purported proprietary fees in the form of assessments of certain large buildings for augmented fire services. See id. at 419–423, 425, 462 N.E.2d 1098. The burial permit charges at issue here, however, are regulatory rather than proprietary in nature. The second factor of the *Emerson College* decision should not be understood as having described the essential characteristics shared by all fees, both regulatory and proprietary. Nothing in that case suggests that whether a charge is incurred voluntarily is relevant in the regulatory fee context.

Massachusetts cases decided since *Emerson College* have consistently given less weight to the voluntariness factor. Other jurisdictions have abandoned it as unhelpful in determining whether a charge is a fee or a tax, in part because "citizens routinely incur different levels of compulsory taxation based on the voluntary choices they make." *Hill v. Kemp,* 478 F.3d 1236, 1252–1253 (10th Cir. 2007), cert. denied, 552 US. 1096, 128 S.Ct. 873, 884, 169 L.Ed.2d 725 (2008). An alternative test to that discussed in *Emerson College* focuses instead on "whether the charge (1) applies to the direct beneficiary of a particular service, (2) is allocated directly to defraying the costs of providing the service, and (3) is reasonably proportionate to the benefit received." *State v. Medeiros,* 89 Hawai'i 361, 367, 973 P.2d 736 (1999). We need not consider whether to follow the courts of these jurisdictions with respect to proprietary charges. We decide only that, although relevant in the context of proprietary fees, the question whether a regulatory charge is voluntarily incurred is of no relevance in determining whether that charge is a fee or a tax.

Finally, the plaintiff argues, as mentioned, that the burial permit charges lack the third characteristic of permissible fees described in *Emerson College,* i.e., that the charges are revenue-raising rather than compensatory because the proceeds are deposited into each defendant's general fund. That the amounts collected from the receipt of burial permit charges are deposited in a general fund instead of a fund for a particular purpose "is of weight in indicating that the charge is a tax," but it is "not decisive." Id. at 427, 462 N.E.2d 1098, quoting P. Nichols, Taxation in Massachusetts 7 (3d ed. 1938). However, "the critical question is whether the [burial permit] charges [are] reasonably designed to compensate" the board of health for its anticipated regulation-related expenses. *Southview, supra* at 404, 486 N.E.2d 700. As discussed previously, the evidence in the record clearly supports the conclusion that the amounts of the burial permit charges are reasonably proportional to those expended by the boards of health in administering the permit process. The Appeals Court correctly concluded that "there is ample evidence in the present case to show that the charges collected were for compensation and not for the general raising of revenue." *Silva v. Attleboro,* 72 Mass.App.Ct. 450, 453, 892 N.E.2d 792 (2008).

Judgment affirmed.

State v. City of Port Orange

650 So.2d 1 (Fla. 1994).

■ WELLS, JUSTICE.

We have on appeal a decision of the trial court declaring that a proposed bond issue is valid. We have jurisdiction. Art. V, 3(b)(2), Fla. Const ....

The City of Port Orange (the City) enacted a "Transportation Utility Ordinance," City of Port Orange Ordinance No. 1992–11, creating a "Transportation Utility" of the City and adopting a "transportation utility fee" relating to the use of city roads. The fee is imposed upon the owners and occupants of developed properties within the City. No fees are imposed on undeveloped property. Any unpaid fee becomes a lien upon the property until such fee is paid. The costs to be defrayed by the fee are the City's expenses relating to the operation, maintenance, and improvement of the local road system. The circuit court limited these costs to capital projects.

The ordinance requires that city-maintained roads be classified as arterial, collector, or local roads, and the cost of constructing and maintaining such roads be allocated separately. Because arterial and collector roads provide mobility and facilitate traffic movement to and from all properties, the ordinance requires that costs incurred by the City on those roads be allocated to all developed properties within the city.

The function of local roads, it was determined, is to provide access to abutting properties. The ordinance requires the City to allocate costs incurred on local roads to developed properties fronting those roads. None of the costs of local roads are allocated to properties fronting private subdivision roads.

The City is required by the ordinance to estimate the amount of usage of the local roads by the owners and occupiers of developed properties through a mixture of actual traffic counts and the use of a "Trip Generation Manual" developed by the Institute of Traffic Engineers. The City allocates the costs for each class of roads to the users of that class of road in proportion to the number of trips generated by each user. The ordinance states that the fees collected from any property need not be in close proximity to such property or provide a special benefit to such property that is different in type or degree from benefits provided to the community as a whole.

The City further authorized the issuance of Transportation Utility Bonds, City of Port Orange Ordinance No. 1992–28, to finance the costs of constructing, renovating, expanding, and improving certain city transportation facilities. Such bonds are to be paid by a pledge of the transportation utility fees.

Subsumed within the inquiry as to whether the public body has the authority to issue the subject bond is the legality of the financing agreement upon which the bond is secured. GRW Corp. v. Department of Corrections, 642 So.2d 718 (Fla. 1994). Integral to the financing agreement here under review is the pledge of what the bond ordinance labels "transportation utility fees." Thus, we must determine whether the pledge of the transportation utility fees is a pledge of tax revenue or is a pledge of user charges or fees. Because a tax must be authorized by general law, the City agrees that if the transportation utility fee is a tax, even broad home rule powers granted to municipalities do not authorize it.

The circuit court ruled that the transportation utility fee is a valid user fee, not a tax, and the City is authorized under municipal home rule powers to impose and collect the fee. We do not agree. We reverse the decision of the circuit court. We hold that what is designated in the bond ordinance as a transportation utility fee is a tax which must be authorized by general law.

This Court has held that taxation by a city must be expressly authorized either by the Florida Constitution or grant of the Florida Legislature. "Doubt as to the powers sought to be exercised must be resolved against the municipality and in favor of the general public." City of Tampa v. Birdsong Motors, Inc., 261 So.2d 1, 3 (Fla. 1972). It is our view that the power of a municipality to tax should not be broadened by semantics which would be the effect of labeling what the City is here collecting a fee rather than a tax.

In City of Boca Raton v. State, 595 So.2d 25 (Fla. 1992), this court noted that a tax is an enforced burden imposed by sovereign right for the support of the government, the administration of law, and the exercise of various functions the sovereign is called on to perform. Funding for the maintenance and improvement of an existing municipal road system, even when limited to capital projects as the circuit court did here, is revenue for exercise of a sovereign function contemplated within this definition of a tax.

User fees are charges based upon the proprietary right of the governing body permitting the use of the instrumentality involved. Such fees share common traits that distinguish them from taxes: they are charged in exchange for a particular governmental service which benefits the party paying the fee in a manner not shared by other members of society, National Cable Television Assn. v. United States, 415 U.S. 336, 341, 94 S.Ct. 1146, 1149, 39 L.Ed.2d 370 (1974); and they are paid by choice, in that the party paying the fee has the option of not utilizing the governmental service and thereby avoiding the charge. Emerson College v. City of Boston, 391 Mass. 415, 462 N.E.2d 1098, 1105 (1984) (citing City of Vanceburg v. Federal Energy Regulatory Comm'n, 571 F.2d 630, 644 n. 48 (D.C. Cir. 1977), cert. denied, 439 U.S. 818, 99 S.Ct. 79, 58 L.Ed.2d 108 (1978)). The above concept of user fees was approved by this Court in City of Daytona Beach Shores v. State, 483 So.2d 405 (Fla. 1985). The City's transportation utility fee falls within our definition of a tax, not our definition of a user fee.

The circuit court found this transportation utility fee to be similar to the concept of impact fees which this Court has approved. Impact fees imposed by a municipality were upheld in Contractors and Builders Association v. City of Dunedin, 329 So.2d 314 (Fla. 1976). However, in that case, impact fees were clearly limited:

> Raising expansion capital by setting connection charges, which do not exceed a pro rata share of reasonably anticipated costs of expansion, is permissible where expansion is reasonably required, if use of the money collected is limited to meeting the costs of expansion. Users "who benefit expecially [sic], not from the maintenance of the system, but by the extension of the system . . . should bear the cost of that extension." Hartman v. Aurora Sanitary District, [23 Ill.2d 109, 177 N.E.2d 214, 218 (Ill. 1961)]. On the other hand, it is not "just and equitable" for a municipally owned utility to impose the entire burden of capital expenditures, including replacement of existing plant, on persons connecting to a water and sewer system after an arbitrarily chosen time certain.
>
> The cost of new facilities should be borne by new users to the extent new use requires new facilities, but only to that extent. When new facilities must be built in any event, looking only to new users for necessary capital gives old users a windfall at the expense of new users.

Id. at 320–321 (footnote omitted).

Thus, the impact fee in *Contractors and Builders Association v. City of Dunedin* was a valid user fee because it involved a voluntary choice to connect into an existing instrumentality of the municipality. The Port Orange fee, unlike Dunedin's impact fee, is a mandatory charge imposed upon those whose only choice is owning developed property within the boundaries of the municipality.

The circuit court cites to storm-water utility fees as being analogous to the transportation utility fee. However, storm-water utility fees are expressly authorized by section 403.031, Florida Statutes (1993). Similarly, various municipal public works and charges for their use are authorized by chapter 180, Florida Statutes (1993). However, the City's transportation utility fee is not authorized by chapter 180, Florida Statutes.

What the City's transportation utility fee does is convert the roads and the municipality into a toll road system, with only owners of developed property in the city required to pay the tolls. We find no statutory or constitutional authority for such tolls by a municipality.

Finally we recognize the revenue pressures upon the municipalities and all levels of government in Florida. We understand that this is a creative effort in response to the need for revenue. However, in Florida's Constitution, the voters have placed a limit on ad valorem millage available to municipalities, art. VII, 9, Fla. Const.; made homesteads exempt from taxation up to minimum limits, art. VII, 9, Fla. Const.; and exempted from levy those homesteads specifically delineated in article X, section 4 of the Florida Constitution. These constitutional provisions cannot be circumvented by such creativity.

The issuance by the City of transportation utility revenue bonds in an aggregate principal amount not to exceed $500,000, pursuant to Ordinance No. 1992–28, is not authorized and is hereby invalidated. The circuit court's judgment is reversed.

It is so ordered.

NOTES

1. *User Fees and Voluntariness.* Why does the court in *Silva* reject the use of "voluntariness" to draw the tax/fee distinction, while the court in *Port Orange* makes it such a relevant part of the inquiry? Is one of these positions more justifiable? The court in *Port Orange* concludes that the fee in the *Dunedin* case was valid because it involved a voluntary choice to connect into an existing instrumentality of the municipality, while the only choice of Port Orange residents was "owning developed property within the boundaries of the municipality." Why is one act more or less voluntary than the other? If a locality chooses to require that all garbage be collected by licensed garbage collectors and then pays for garbage collection through a user fee, should the fact that the service is mandatory make the user fee invalid? What about employing user fees to pay for water and sewer service in an area that is not suitable for well water or septic tanks, so that individuals have little alternative to using publicly supplied water and sewer systems? If the function of user fees is to induce efficient supply and use of a service, or to match benefits and burdens, is the inquiry into voluntariness useful?

2. *When Does a Fee Become a Tax?* In Holman v. City of Dierks, 233 S.W.2d 392 (Ark. 1950), a resident appealed from a fine for nonpayment of an "annual sanitation tax" of $4.00 for each business, house, and dwelling in the city to be used for spraying the city with insecticide. He contended that the tax exceeded the constitutional tax limit of the municipality and was therefore illegal. The court concluded that the charge "is actually not a tax but a charge for services to be rendered. The city proposes to spray the property of its citizens and to charge the cost of this operation against those who receive its benefits. Such a fee for the performance of a service is not taxation. Cooley on Taxation (3d Ed.), p. 5." Were all payors of the fee receiving a benefit sufficiently similar to justify the identical charge? Assume that one dwelling housed a family of eight, while another dwelling housed a single individual. Should both dwellings pay the same amount to avoid disease that might be alleviated by the city's spraying? Do businesses and residential dwellings enjoy sufficiently similar benefits from such programs to justify the identical charge?

This is not to say that the service funded with the fee cannot confer any public benefit. In State ex rel. Petroleum Underground Storage Tank Release Compensation Board v. Withrow, 579 N.E.2d 705 (Ohio 1991), the court upheld the validity of an exaction imposed on owners and operators of underground storage tanks. The fees were to be used to repay bonds issued to capitalize a compensation fund for alleviation of environmental hazards created by leaking tanks. State constitutional provisions permitted issuance of such bonds only if they were not secured by moneys raised by "taxation." The court rejected arguments that the fees should be classified as taxes because the public was benefited by the program. The court determined that the exactions were intended for regulatory purposes related to the activities of the payors, rather than revenues placed in the general fund for support of general governmental activities. Since the exactions were used to fund a system of insuring owners and operators against liability for environmental damage, the benefit they received was sufficient to bring the scheme within the category of fees.

As the city appears to have recognized when it designed the "transportation utility fee" in *Port Orange*, a fee may be more justifiable when the benefit conferred by the service to be paid for with the fee varies with each user. Under those circumstances, one would expect the amount payable to vary with individual use if the exaction is truly a fee. In Building Owners & Managers Assoc. v. City of Kansas City, 231 S.W.3d 208 (Mo. Ct. App. 2007), the court invalidated ordinances that required businesses and multi-family dwellings to pay fees for annual fire inspection certificates. Plaintiffs contended that the fees had been imposed in violation of a provision of the state constitution that required a vote of the electorate for any increases in fees that were tantamount to taxes. The court applied a five-factor test that investigated the timing of the fee (was the payment obligation triggered by the provision of service or just the passage of time), the identity of the payer (all residents or only users of the fee or service), whether the amount of the fee depended on the level of goods or services provided, the nature of the service, and the relationship of the service to historical governmental functions. The court concluded that the charge was an invalid fee, in part because the amount payable was capped at $100, so that large properties paid the same as smaller properties, even though inspection of the former would take additional time.

3. *The Consequences of Fees.* Are there reasons why local officials, given the choice of paying for a particular service through either a fee or a tax, would select one over the other? Fees may make the costs of a particular service more transparent, in that they indicate precisely what an exaction is used for. It is plausible that fees will cause more efficient delivery of fee-based services, both because willingness to pay fees signals local officials about the preferences of constituents, and because political pressure to keep fees low discourages excessive costs. On the other hand, fees may make it more difficult for residents to determine their entire fiscal burden, because they would have to calculate the fees they pay for each service and then add it to the taxes they pay for other services. Fees also have fewer distributive consequences insofar as they are linked to the costs imposed or benefit conferred on the payer of the fee, whereas taxes may be related to ability to pay and thus require some residents to subsidize services received by others. Of course, some services cannot easily be paid for through fees. Some services are deliberately redistributive, such as municipal housing shelters. Paying for other services through fees would cause rather perverse effects. For instance, if a fee is imposed for calling the police, residents would be discouraged from calling for assistance unless their own safety or property was at stake. But with the exception of those situations, would it be better if local expenditures were paid for by a series of fees or by one overall tax? Would you prefer to pay one sum for your law school education that included tuition, all books, and copying services, or to pay separately for tuition, books, and copying services? For a critique of local reliance on fees, see Laurie Reynolds, Taxes, Fees, Assessments, Dues and the "Get What You Pay For" Model of Local Government, 56 Fla. L. Rev. 373 (2004).

4. *Market Prices and Fees.* A fee would presumably be valid if it reflects the cost of the service provided. But what if government enjoys certain advantages, such as a tax exemption or different labor costs, that reduce the costs of providing the service below those that would be charged by private providers of equivalent services? May the government provider charge a fee that reflects the higher costs of alternative providers? Would those charges distort demand for the service in the way that Gillette and Hopkins suggest is inappropriate? In Harris v. City of Little Rock, 40 S.W.3d 214 (Ark. 2001), a city proposed to issue bonds to construct a presidential library. The bonds were to be secured in part by fees charged by the city for recreational facilities that the city provided. Plaintiffs claimed that increases in fees, necessary to support the bonds, constituted illegal exactions because the increased fees bore no relationship to the service provided. The court disagreed:

> [T]he chancellor found that the increases are fair and reasonable in light of the studies conducted by the city comparing its fees to those charged at similar facilities. The user fees for the fitness center were raised from $33.00 per month to $35.00 per month. In comparison, the fees for the YMCA were $46.00 per month, while those for a local gym were $90.00 per month. The fees for the city's zoo were raised from $3.00 to $5.00, after comparing the fees charged in

> other zoos in the southern region, such as Atlanta and Memphis. Lastly, the fees for eighteen holes of golf at the city's three courses were raised from $8.50 to $10.50 on weekdays, and from $10.50 to $12.50 on weekends. These fees were compared to those of $17.00 or $18.00 charged to play golf at the Country Club of Arkansas. The chancellor also noted that North Little Rock had similarly raised its user fees for its golf course at Burns Park. Accordingly, we cannot say that the chancellor erred in determining that the increase in user fees at the city's recreational facilities is fair and reasonable and bears a reasonable relationship to the benefits conferred on those persons who use the facilities. We thus affirm the chancellor's ruling on this issue.

40 S.W.3d at 222.

5. *Transportation Financing and Fees.* In Bloom v. City of Fort Collins, 784 P.2d 304 (Colo. 1989), the court concluded that a "transportation utility fee" imposed on owners or occupants of developed lots of land within the city in order to fund street maintenance was not a property tax, but was a special fee and thus not subject to the constitutional uniformity requirement. The fee for each landowner was based on a formula that took into account front footage and the amount of traffic "generated by the property," a factor that led to distinctions among single-family, multi-family, and business properties. The court distinguished fees from taxes:

> Unlike a tax, a special fee is not designed to raise revenues to defray the general expenses of government, but rather is a charge imposed upon persons or property for the purpose of defraying the cost of a particular governmental service.... The amount of a special fee must be reasonably related to the overall cost of the service.... Mathematical exactitude, however, is not required, and the particular mode adopted by a city in assessing the fee is generally a matter of legislative discretion.... An ordinance creating a special service fee, therefore, generally will be upheld as long as the ordinance is reasonably designed to defray the cost of the particular service rendered by the municipality....
>
> A special fee, however, might be subject to invalidation as a tax when the principal purpose of the fee is to raise revenues for general municipal purposes rather than to defray the expenses of the particular service for which the fee is imposed. See Zelinger [v. City and County of Denver,] 724 P.2d 1356 (Colo. 1986), (city ordinance creating a storm drainage service charge not a tax, since sole objective of ordinance was to raise funds to pay expenses attributable to municipal storm drainage activities and not to raise revenues for general municipal purposes).

784 P.2d at 308–309. The court concluded that the involuntary nature of the exaction was not a barrier to its classification as a fee rather than a tax.

The court did, however, invalidate a part of the fee ordinance that permitted the city to transfer to other parts of the city treasury amounts collected in excess of what was necessary for streets. The court concluded:

> The transfer of a substantial amount of money generated by the transportation utility fee to some other city fund would be tantamount to requiring the class of persons responsible for the fee—the owners or occupants of developed lots fronting city streets—to bear a disproportionate share of the burden of providing revenues to defray general governmental expenses unrelated to the

> purpose for which the fee is imposed. The effect of such a transfer would be to render the transportation utility fee the functional equivalent of a tax.

784 P.2d at 311. Two judges dissented. They claimed that a fee has three characteristics: It is imposed in return for a specific governmental service; it is voluntary, in that the payor has requested the service for which payment was made; and the payor receives a direct benefit from the service. In the view of the dissent, road maintenance expenditures are traditional governmental expenditures that benefit the public at large rather than specific individuals, the fee at issue was not restricted to providing maintenance on any particular streets fronting the property of the payors, and there was no direct benefit derived by a property owner upon whom the fee is imposed that was not shared by other members of society. For a case upholding the use of transportation fees imposed on new developments, but only to the extent that all expenditures were made for improvements within, or in areas immediately adjacent to, the area from which expended monies were collected, see Northern Illinois Home Builders Association, Inc. v. County of Du Page, 649 N.E.2d 384 (Ill. 1995).

6. *Fees in Excess of Cost.* User fees are justified on the theory that they defray the costs of services as well as send signals to government about the proper level of service to provide. What are the consequences of this justification for the amount of the user fee? Several courts have indicated that fees imposed in excess of the cost of service constitute a tax. See, e.g., State ex rel. Waterbury Development Co. v. Witten, 387 N.E.2d 1380 (Ohio Ct. App. 1977), aff'd, 377 N.E.2d 505 (Ohio 1978); Ross v. City of Geneva, 373 N.E.2d 1342 (Ill. 1978); King County Water District No. 75 v. City of Seattle, 577 P.2d 567 (Wash. 1978) (semble). See 12 Eugene McQuillin, The Law of Municipal Corporations 35.38 (1970).

PROBLEM XXII

Norwell owns a lot in downtown Boomtown that she wishes to improve with a high-rise office building. When fully occupied, the building will house more than 2,000 workers and will likely attract more than 200 business visitors daily. Boomtown has passed an ordinance that requires the owners of new commercial buildings in the downtown area to pay a fee of $5 per square foot of new office space. Proceeds of the fee are dedicated to three purposes: (1) construction of parking garages in the downtown area; (2) funding of day-care opportunities in the downtown area; and (3) maintenance of roads within and leading into the downtown area. The city council argued, in passing the ordinance, that the increase in downtown traffic and workforce attributable to office buildings created the need for parking spaces and child care for workers, and was generating a faster than anticipated deterioration of downtown streets.

Norwell has retained you to investigate the validity of the ordinance. You have discovered that the city council is authorized to pass ordinances with respect to "fees and service charges in amounts reasonably related to the costs of providing municipal services," but that the city cannot impose any new "tax" without the approval of the electorate. What arguments will you inform Norwell are available to her if she opposes the fee? What responses can you anticipate from the city?

New Jersey Builders Assn. v. Mayor and Township Committee of Bernards Township

528 A.2d 555 (N.J. 1987).

■ STEIN, J.

The narrow issue that we address in this appeal is whether Bernards Township's Ordinance 672 is a valid exercise of the authority conferred upon municipalities by the Municipal Land Use Law (MLUL), specifically N.J.S.A. 40:55D–42. We hold that that portion of the ordinance that requires new developers to pay their pro-rata share of the Township's long term, twenty-million dollar road improvement plan exceeds the Township's authority under the MLUL and is therefore invalid. Accordingly, we affirm the judgment of the Appellate Division.

I

. . . Bernards Township, bisected by Interstate Highways 78 and 287, is a rapidly-developing municipality in northern Somerset County. During the late 1970's, and in response to the impact of new and increased development, the Township authorized a consulting firm to undertake a comprehensive transportation and traffic study of the entire Township. The study summarized the existing traffic conditions in the community, made traffic projections based on current and projected development in accordance with the zoning ordinance, and set forth road improvements deemed necessary to accommodate current and anticipated development throughout the Township. The result of the study was a Transportation Management Plan that was substantially incorporated into the circulation element of the Township's Master Plan. See N.J.S.A. 40:55D–28b(4). Reflecting the consultant's recommendations, the Master Plan proposed an extensive roadway improvement program involving improvements to twenty-two township roads, seventeen intersections, seven county roads, two county bridges, and off-street commuter parking facilities. It was anticipated that the improvements would be constructed over a twenty-year period at an estimated cost of twenty million dollars.

As recommended by the Master Plan, Ordinance 672 was adopted to provide a mechanism for allocating the cost of the road improvement program between the Township and its residential and commercial developers. The premise underlying Ordinance 672 is that all new development within the Township contributes to the need for Township-wide road improvements. Thus, allocating the cost of such roadway improvements, on the basis of "trip generation" forecasts, between the Township—to reflect the impact of existing development—and new developers was a reasonable and appropriate exercise of the Township's regulatory authority under the MLUL.

Judge D'Annunzio carefully summarized the cost-allocation formula set forth in Ordinance 672:

> Utilizing the Trip Generation Handbook published by the Institute of Transportation Engineers the appendix to the ordinance establishes trip generation rates for six basic uses: single family, multi-family, senior citizen, general office, professional office and retail. For example, a single-family residence will generate 1.1 P.M. peak hour trips. Specifically it will generate 0.7 arrivals and 0.4 departures. Similarly, a general office will generate 1.63 P.M. peak-hour trips per 1,000 square feet. A development of 100 single-family residences will generate 110 P.M. peak hour trips. The township determined that at full development 23,700 P.M. peak-hour trips per day will be generated. It was further determined that development in place in 1982 generated 7,450 P.M. peak-hour weekday trips. Utilizing simple mathematics the township determined that the share of the cost of the roadway improvement program to be borne by general township revenues is 31.4% and the share to be borne by future developers is 68.6%. The estimated cost for the improvement of municipal roads is $14,800,000. The general revenue share, i.e., the share allocated to existing development is 31.4% or $4,547,000. The balance of $9,933,000 is allocated to new development as is the entire projected cost of improvements to county roads which are to be made by the township in the amount of $5,520,000. Therefore, the total cost to be borne by future development is $15,453,000. Dividing that amount by the 16,250,000 P.M. peak hour trips to be generated by all future development yields an assessment of $951 per trip generated by all new development. The developer of 100 single-family homes resulting in 110 trips must pay Bernards Township $104,610 as his share of the cost of the transportation network improvement program. This assessment would be in addition to the cost of off-tract improvements necessitated or required by the new development where no other property owners receive a special benefit. In a non-residential context the builder of four retail stores of 1,000 square feet each would pay an assessment of $54,770.60 because each 1,000 square feet of retail space generates 14.40 P.M. peak-hour trips.

211 N.J. Super. at 292–93, 511 A.2d 740....

II

Although our disposition of this appeal is controlled by what we discern to be the intended scope of N.J.S.A. 40:55D–42, a broader context is indispensable to a full understanding of the implications of the issue before us. We acknowledge that our experience with municipal attempts to charge developers for off-site improvements has heretofore been limited to the cost of facilities closely related to needs generated by the specific development. See, e.g., Divan Builders v. Township of Wayne, 66 N.J. 582, 334 A.2d 30 (1975) (municipality sought contribution toward improvement of drainage basin serving subdivision and adjacent area); ordinances adopted by state Longridge Builders v. Planning Bd. of Princeton Township., 52 N.J. 348, 245 A.2d 336 (1968) (municipality required developer to pave dedicated right-of-way from subdivision boundary to public street); cf. Daniels v. Point Pleasant, 23 N.J. 357, 129 A.2d 265 (1957) (municipality enacted invalid ordinance amendment increasing building permit fees for the purpose of raising revenue to meet increased school costs). In other states, local governments have attempted to impose a variety of indirect capital costs on new developers, a trend that appears to have gained momentum during the past decade....

There is wide variation in the types of exactions that governmental entities impose on developers. The most common are those that require dedication of land within the subdivision for public purposes and the construction of improvements such as streets, sidewalks, and water and sewer lines. Connors & High, "The Expanding Circle of Exactions: From Dedication to Linkage," Law & Contemp. Probs., Winter 1987, at 70. Another common type of exaction requires developers to construct off-site improvements, usually on property adjacent to the subdivision for road or drainage purposes....

Less common but frequently sustained are requirements for dedication of land for recreational purposes, or payments in lieu of dedication, where the purpose of the dedication or payment is primarily, but not exclusively, to benefit the residents of the new development. Connors & High, supra at 71; see also City of College Station v. Turtle Rock Corp., 680 S.W.2d 802 (Tex. 1984) (upholding ordinance requiring dedication of one acre of land for each 133 housing units, or payment of fee in lieu of dedication, to be used for neighborhood park purposes); Aunt Hack Ridge Estates v. Planning Commn., 160 Conn. 109, 273 A.2d 880 (1970) (sustaining ordinance requiring dedication of area equal to 4% of subdivision, but not less than 10,000 square feet, for recreational use); Jenad, Inc. v. Village of Scarsdale, 18 N.Y.2d 78, 218 N.E.2d 673, 271 N.Y.S.2d 955 (1966) (upholding ordinance requiring dedication of land, or payment of fee of $250 per lot, for park purposes); Jordan v. Village of Menomonee Falls, 28 Wis. 2d 608, 137 N.W.2d 442 (1965) (upholding ordinance requiring payment of $200 per lot, or dedication of land of equal value, for school, park, and recreational purposes). But cf. Pioneer Trust v. Village of Mt. Prospect, 22 Ill. 2d 375, 176 N.E.2d 799 (1961) (invalidating municipal ordinance requiring dedication of one acre per sixty housing units for public use).

Another type of municipal exaction, typified by the Bernards ordinance and by ordinances challenged in a series of Florida cases, is the impact fee, described generally as a "charge[ ] against new development for the purpose of raising money to defray the costs of basic services local government provides to its citizens." Currier, "Legal and Practical Problems Associated with Drafting Impact Fee Ordinances," 1984 Institute on Planning, Zoning and Eminent Domain at 273–74. Impact fees are described as a cost-shifting device that contribute to "the efforts of local governments to cope with the economic burdens of population growth such as the need for new roads, schools, parks, and sewer and water treatment facilities." Juergensmeyer & Blake, "Impact Fees: An Answer to Local Governments' Capital Funding Dilemma," 9 Fla. St. U. L. Rev. 415, 417 (1981). They are justified on the theory that "it is possible to allocate to each development its proportionate share of the future cost of providing public services...." Smith, supra, at 16.

In Contractors & Builders Assn. v. City of Dunedin, 329 So. 2d 314, 318 (1976), the Florida Supreme Court concluded that a city had the authority under Florida's constitution and statutory law to impose an impact fee to defray the capital cost of improving the city's water and sewerage system to meet the increased demand created by new development. The Court concluded that such an ordinance is valid "where expansion is reasonably required, *if use of the money collected is limited to meeting the cost of expansion*." Id. at 320....

Recently, some municipalities, such as San Francisco and Boston, have enacted "linkage" ordinances that condition the right to develop commercial properties on construction of or contribution to the cost of low-and moderate-income housing. See Smith, supra, 25–28; Connors & High, supra, 77–83. See generally Kayden & Pollard, "Linkage Ordinances and Traditional Exactions Analysis: The Connection Between Office Development and Housing," Law & Contemp. Probs., Winter 1987, at 127 (asserting that ordinances linking housing needs with office development are sustainable under "reasonable relationship" test used by courts to analyze development exactions).

The variety of governmental devices used to impose public facility costs on new development reflect a policy choice that higher taxes for existing residents are less desirable than higher development costs for builders, and higher acquisition costs for new residents. An obvious concern is that the disproportionate or excessive use of development exactions could discourage new development or inflate housing prices to an extent that excludes large segments of the population from the available market. See generally Nicholas, "Impact Exactions: Economic Theory, Practice, and Incidence," Law & Contemp. Probs., Winter 1987 at 85 (arguing for more restricted use of developer exactions). The complex legal and policy issues affecting both the decision to authorize impact-fee-type ordinances, and if authorized, their sustainable limits, are not before us in this case. We are convinced that when the Legislature enacted the MLUL, it did not authorize the exaction imposed on developers by Bernards Township's Ordinance 672.

III

... Our evaluation of the validity of Bernards Township's Ordinance 672 depends on whether the power to enact it is expressly conferred by, or may fairly be inferred from, the relevant provisions of the MLUL. It is fundamental that laws concerning municipal corporations are to be "liberally construed in their favor," N.J. Const. of 1947 art. IV, sec. 7, para. 11, and the MLUL expressly requires that its provisions be broadly construed. N.J.S.A. 40:55D–92. Nevertheless, in determining the legislative intent, we are constrained by the plain language of N.J.S.A. 40:55D–42 and are informed by decisional law concerning municipal subdivision regulation that preceded the statute's enactment.

The predecessor to N.J.S.A. 40:55D–42 was N.J.S.A. 40:55–1.21 (repealed), a section of the Municipal Planning Act of 1953 that authorized municipalities to require construction of on-site improvements in connection with subdivision approval, but contained no reference to off-site improvements. See Divan Builders v. Township of Wayne, supra, 66 N.J. at

595, 334 A.2d 300. Prior to the Divan decision, municipal authority to compel installation of or payment for off-site improvements had not been established....

It was not until Divan Builders v. Township of Wayne, supra, that the issue of a municipality's power to require off-site improvements was definitively resolved. There the developer's building site was substantially covered by a pond, and the preliminary subdivision plan contemplated draining the pond and "construct[ing] a conduit to pipe the water from its upstream source through the development and into an existing drainage facility on the downstream border of the site." 66 N.J. at 587, 334 A.2d 30. Subsequent to the grant of preliminary subdivision approval, the governing body amended the subdivision ordinance to establish procedures authorizing the construction of off-site improvements as a condition of subdivision approval. The planning board's recommendation for final approval of the subdivision included the condition that the applicant contribute to the township the sum of $20,000 as its "share of improving the downstream conditions of the stream which carries the drainage from the subdivision." Id. at 589, 334 A.2d 30. One other developer was also required to contribute to the cost of the drainage improvement.

The primary issue in *Divan* was the authority of the planning board, pursuant to the Municipal Planning Act of 1953, to require the developer to contribute to the cost of an off-site improvement. Acknowledging that the statute was silent with regard to off-site improvements, the court concluded that recognition of a municipality's authority to require construction of or contribution to the cost of off-site improvements "comports with the overall legislative purpose to require developers in the first instance to assume the legitimate expenses of subdivision." Id. at 597, 334 A.2d 30....

It is against this rather sparse backdrop of New Jersey case law considering municipal power to require off-site improvements that we assess the Legislature's intent in adopting N.J.S.A. 40:55D–42. We note counsels' concurrence that although the MLUL became effective in August 1976, more than a year after the decision in *Divan*, the drafting of the MLUL was substantially completed before the opinion in *Divan* was published. Nevertheless, when the Legislature enacted the MLUL in 1976, it is presumed to have had knowledge of the relevant judicial decisions. See Barringer v. Miele, 6 N.J. 139, 144 (1951). Had its intent been to expand significantly municipal power to require contribution for off-site improvements, we are confident that this intention would have been manifested in the legislative history of the MLUL. In its absence, we construe N.J.S.A. 40:55D–42 in a manner consistent with the rationale expressed in our decisions in *Divan* and *Longridge Builders*.

Thus, the critical language of the statute permits a municipality to require a developer "to pay his pro rata share of the cost of providing only *reasonable and necessary street improvements* and water, sewerage and drainage facilities, and easements therefor, located outside the property limits of the subdivision or development *but necessitated or required by construction or improvements within such subdivision or development*.["]

N.J.S.A. 40:55D–42 (emphasis added). We conclude that the plain meaning and obvious legislative intent was to limit municipal authority only to improvements the need for which arose as a direct consequence of the particular subdivision or development under review. The phrase "necessitated or required by construction ... within such subdivision or development" precludes the more expansive statutory interpretation urged upon us by counsel for Bernards Township.

It is indisputable that subdivisions and development applications, in addition to their direct impact on municipal facilities in the surrounding area, have a cumulative and wide-ranging impact on the entire community. We cannot fault the logic or the foresight that induces a municipality such as Bernards Township to consider the long-term impact of permitted development on municipal resources and public facilities. But as yet the Legislature has not delegated to municipalities the far-reaching power to depart from traditionally authorized methods of financing public facilities so as to allocate the cost of substantial public projects among new developments on the basis of their anticipated impact.

For the reasons stated, we hold that Ordinance 642 is an invalid exercise of municipal authority. We are in accord with the Appellate Division's conclusion that the invalidation of the ordinance should not be limited to prospective application only. 219 N.J. Super. at 539, 530 A.2d 1254.

The judgment of the Appellate Division is affirmed.

Raintree Homes, Inc. v. Village of Long Grove

906 N.E.2d 751 (Ill. App. 2009).

■ JUSTICE JORGENSEN delivered the opinion of the court:

Plaintiffs, Raintree Homes, Inc., and Raintree Builders, Inc. (collectively, Raintree), filed a one-count amended complaint against defendant, the Village of Long Grove (Village), seeking: (1) a declaratory judgment as to the validity of Village ordinances requiring the payment of impact fees to the Village as a condition of obtaining building permits; and (2) a refund of the impact fees it paid to the Village for 19 homes it built there between 1993 and 1997. Following a bench trial, the trial court found the Village's ordinances unenforceable and rejected the Village's affirmative defenses. Accordingly, it entered judgment in Raintree's favor and awarded Raintree $114,700. The Village appeals from that order.

* * *

Section 4–1–4(B) of the Village's code sets forth that, "as a condition of the issuance of a building permit for the construction of a dwelling unit, the building permit applicant shall be required to donate monies to the Village." Long Grove Municipal Code § 4–1–4(B) (amended June 25, 1996). The monies, or impact fees, are for the benefit of the school districts and for the acquisition, maintenance, preservation, and operation of open space in the Village. Long Grove Municipal Code § 4–1–4(B) (amended June 25, 1996).

* * *

Raintree filed its amended complaint on July 14, 2000. Raintree alleged that, between February 1993 and August 1997, it entered into contracts to build homes in the Village, a non-home-rule municipal corporation. To obtain the building permits, Raintree was required to pay certain impact fees. Between August 15, 1988, and March 24, 1997, Raintree obtained 43 building permits from the Village. In its complaint, Raintree sought a refund of the impact fees it paid for 19 permits issued to it by the Village from August 1993 through March 1997. Pursuant to the Village's code, the impact fees between March 1993 and June 24, 1994, were $4,300 per permit. Raintree paid the fees and obtained eight building permits from the Village. Between June 26, 1994, and February 1998, the Village's impact fees were $7,300 per permit. Raintree paid the fees and obtained 11 permits.

* * *

1. Validity of Ordinances

In its appeal, the Village argues first that it did not exceed its authority under section 11–12–5 of the Illinois Municipal Code when it enacted a series of ordinances requiring the payment, upon issuance of a building permit, of impact fees for schools and open spaces. The Village contends that the trial court erred in finding that its school and open space impact fees were invalid and asserts that the court misapplied the rules governing statutory and ordinance construction.

* * *

"American local government law and civic culture has increasingly privatized development costs that had previously been carried as general societal expenses. * * * Increasingly, local governments combine their traditional land use regulatory powers with their authority to impose land development conditions." R. Rosenberg, *The Changing Culture of American Land Use Regulation: Paying for Growth with Impact Fees,* 59 SMU L. Rev. 177, 181 (2006). Impact fees, or development exactions, are utilized by rapidly growing municipalities in an attempt to "bridge the gap between the increased demand for services brought on by rapid growth and the stagnant or shrinking amount of revenue available from traditional sources." *Thompson v. Village of Newark,* 329 Ill.App.3d 536, 539, 263 Ill.Dec. 775, 768 N.E.2d 856 (2002). However, non-home-rule municipalities possess only those powers that are specifically conveyed to them by the Illinois Constitution or by statute. Impact fees may not be imposed without legislative authority. Absent such authority, a municipal enactment is void.

Section 11–12–5 of the Illinois Municipal Code describes the general powers of municipal plan commissions and planning departments, including the preparation of a comprehensive plan for development or redevelopment of a municipality. Specifically, the plan "*may include reasonable requirements* with reference to streets, alleys, *public grounds,* and other improvements hereinafter specified." (Emphases added.) Furthermore:

"*[The] plan may be implemented by ordinances* (a) establishing reasonable standards of design for subdivisions and for resubdivisions of unimproved land and of areas subject to redevelopment in respect to public improvements as herein defined; (b) *establishing reasonable requirements governing* the location, width, course, and surfacing of public streets and highways, alleys, ways for public service facilities, curbs, gutters, sidewalks, street lights, *parks,* playgrounds, *school grounds,* size of lots to be used for residential purposes, storm water drainage, *water supply and distribution,* sanitary sewers, and sewage collection and treatment * * *." (Emphases added.)

The statutory provisions with respect to reasonable requirements for streets and public grounds are based upon the theory that "the developer of a subdivision may be required to assume those costs which are specifically and uniquely attributable to [the developer's] activity and which would otherwise be cast upon the public" (*Rosen* test) (*Rosen v. Village of Downers Grove,* 19 Ill.2d 448, 453, 167 N.E.2d 230 (1960)). In *Pioneer Trust & Savings Bank v. Village of Mount Prospect,* 22 Ill.2d 375, 176 N.E.2d 799 (1961), the supreme court explained the *Rosen* test as follows:

> "If the requirement is within the statutory grant of power to the municipality and if the burden cast upon the subdivider is specifically and uniquely attributable to [the subdivider's] activity, then the requirement is permissible; if not, it is forbidden and amounts to a confiscation of private property in contravention of the constitutional prohibitions rather than reasonable regulation under the police power." *Pioneer Trust,* 22 Ill.2d at 380, 176 N.E.2d 799.

(a) School Impact Fees

As to the school impact fees, the trial court found that the Illinois Municipal Code prohibits cash donations for general school operations, as opposed to school grounds. The court also found that the Village's school impact fees were not specifically and uniquely attributable to a development, because they applied to every house and were not adjusted based on a developer's activity.

The Village asserts that its ordinances do not refer to general operations but, rather, specify that the impact fees are used to reimburse the school districts for expenditures made on behalf of new pupils from new Village residences. According to the Village, new pupils from new residences present new demands on schools and satisfy the *Rosen* test. The Village further argues that its ordinances do not expressly require impact fees to be used for general operations and that there was no evidence that the fees were used for any improper purpose. The Village reasons that, given the presumption of the validity of municipal ordinances and Raintree's failure to meet its burden of showing improper expenditures, the school impact fee provisions should have been upheld.

Raintree responds that the Village's school impact fees are not limited to land acquisition (*i.e.,* school grounds) for schools, but are for the schools' general operation funds to reimburse the schools for expenditures made on behalf of new pupils. Raintree asserts that the schools did not receive all of the impact fees, because portions of the fees, as determined by formula, were retained by the Village. In Raintree's view, since the school impact fees can be utilized for purposes other than land acquisition for schools, the trial court did not err in finding that they are unauthorized. Finally, Raintree argues that the impact fees did not satisfy the *Rosen* test, because they applied to every house under construction and, thus, did not assess each structure's unique impact on the schools.

We agree that the school impact fees were improper. The Village's code provides that school impact fees, "(as adjusted by the formula on file with the Village Administrator)," are "forwarded by the Village to the appropriate" elementary or high school district "*for its general operation fund* at the time of issuance of a certificate of occupancy. This payment is designed *to partially reimburse the school districts* for expenditures made on behalf of new pupils from new residences within the Village." (Emphases added.) Long Grove Municipal Code § 4–1–4(B) (amended June 25, 1996). Section 11–12–5(1)(b) of the Illinois Municipal Code provides that a municipality may implement its development plan via ordinances "establishing reasonable requirements governing * * * *parks* * * * [and] *school grounds.*" (Emphases added.) 65 ILCS 5/11–12–5(1)(b) (West 2000).

In *Thompson v. Village of Newark,* 329 Ill.App.3d 536, 263 Ill.Dec. 775, 768 N.E.2d 856 (2002), the Village of Newark, a non-home-rule municipality, passed an ordinance imposing school construction impact fees on new development within the village. The plaintiffs, landowners, sought, *inter alia,* a declaratory judgment that the impact fee ordinance was not authorized by section 11–12–5 of the Illinois Municipal Code. The trial court granted the village summary judgment. On appeal, this court reversed the trial court, holding that the village lacked the statutory authorization to impose impact fees for school construction and, to the extent that it did so, its ordinance was invalid. Rejecting the village's argument that the statutory term "school grounds" is broad enough to encompass capital improvements, this court concluded that the plain meaning of the term "school grounds" is land surrounding a school building and does not include the building itself. We further held that the remainder of the statute is primarily concerned with traditional planning concepts such as the location of streets and other improvements and that to read the statute "to also authorize the village to collect revenue to undertake massive capital improvements reads the statutory authority too broadly."

We hold that the Village exceeded its authority when it enacted ordinances assessing school impact fees. Contrary to the Village's assertion, its ordinances do provide that school impact fees are forwarded to the appropriate elementary or high school district "for its general operation fund." Long Grove Municipal Code § 4–1–4(B) (amended June 25, 1996). The restriction in section 11–12–5 of the Illinois Municipal Code specifies that ordinances implementing redevelopment plans may establish reasonable requirements governing only "school grounds." The plain meaning of the term "school grounds," even under its more expansive definition effective as of 2003, is not, in our view, so broad as to encompass a "general operation fund." There is no language in the ordinances to limit expenditures of school districts' general operation funds to expenditures for school buildings and the land surrounding school buildings. Thus, we cannot conclude that the impact fees that partially reimburse school districts for expenditures on new pupils from new residences are limited to expenditures for school buildings and land.

We also reject the Village's argument that the ordinances' limitation that the fees are "designed to partially reimburse the school districts for expenditures made on behalf of new pupils from new residences within the Village" satisfies the *Rosen* test and, therefore, transforms the ordinances into valid enactments. As the supreme court has explained, to satisfy the *Rosen* test, the requirements must be: (1) within the statutory grant of power to the municipality; and (2) specifically and uniquely attributable to the developer's activity. *Pioneer Trust,* 22 Ill.2d at 380, 176 N.E.2d 799. Here, the Village's ordinances fail the first part of the supreme court's test.

(b) Open Space Impact Fees

Turning to the Village's open space impact fees, the Village's code requires payment of impact fees to the Village's general fund that are "designed to enable the Village, with these moneys, to acquire, maintain, and preserve open space in the Village." Long Grove Municipal Code § 4–1–4(B)(3) (1993). A portion of the impact fees is allocated to the Long Grove Park District "to assist in the acquisition, maintenance, and preservation of open space within the Village, and for the general operational expenses relating thereto." Long Grove Municipal Code § 4–1–4(B)(3) (1993). Again, section 11–12–5(1)(b) of the Illinois Municipal Code provides that a municipality may implement its development plan via ordinances "establishing reasonable requirements governing * * * *parks* * * * [and] *school grounds.*" (Emphases added.)

The trial court found that the Village's open space fees were solely revenue oriented and that there was no evidence that the Village considered anything individual to the construction at issue in order to satisfy the requirement that the fees be specifically and uniquely attributable to Raintree's activity. Further, the court found impermissible the ordinances' provisions concerning the maintenance and preservation of open space. It interpreted the statute as prohibiting cash fees for the maintenance and preservation of existing open space, reasoning that existing open space is not specifically and uniquely attributable to current development activity.

The Village contends that the Illinois Municipal Code uses terms that are synonymous with "open space," where it authorizes municipalities to adopt and implement ordinances to provide for "public grounds," "parks," and "playgrounds," all of which are recreational land uses, and asserts that the ordinances' purpose is proper. Furthermore, the Village asserts that the term "open space" is a term of art used to define active and passive recreational lands serving its residents. Open space, according to the Village, encompasses parks, ball fields, public grounds, and unimproved land.

Next, addressing the *Rosen* test, the Village argues that it is a given that new residents from newly constructed homes will have an impact on the Village's finite open space and, therefore, open space fees are a reasonable measure of the specific and unique impact of new residents on the limited open space within the Village. Moreover, the Village argues that the trial court erred by inserting the word "existing" into the ordinances when it found that the open space fees were unauthorized because the Illinois Municipal Code does not permit cash fees for the maintenance and preservation of existing open space. Finally, the Village asserts that there was no evidence that its fees were excessive.

Raintree argues that the Village's open space impact fees are void because the term "open space" is not contained in section 11–12–5 of the Illinois Municipal Code. Alternatively, Raintree contends that, even if the Village had the statutory authority to adopt reasonable design standards for open space, its ordinances are void because the impact fees are not limited to land acquisition for open space. Furthermore, Raintree argues that there was no evidence that the funds were used solely for open space purposes, because impact fees were deposited into the Village's general operation fund. Finally, Raintree adopts the trial court's findings that the ordinances are not specifically and uniquely attributable to developer activity.

Assuming, without deciding, that the term "open space" in the Village's code comes within the terms "public grounds," "parks," and "playgrounds" in section 11–12–5 of the Illinois Municipal Code (625 ILCS 5/11–12–5(1)(b) (West 2000)), we conclude that section 11–12–5 does not authorize a municipality to require payment of impact fees to the municipality's general fund that are designed to enable it "to acquire, maintain, and preserve open space" therein, where the ordinance does not prohibit use of the funds to maintain and preserve existing open space. The phrasing "to acquire, maintain, and preserve open space" can encompass, as the trial court found, not only newly acquired but also existing open space. The ordinances, therefore, fail to satisfy the *Rosen* test's requirement that a developer may assume only those costs that are "specifically and uniquely attributable to [the developer's] activity * * *." We agree with the trial court that the Village exceeded its statutory authority because the Village's ordinances do not limit the use of impact fees to only newly acquired open space. Accordingly, the ordinances are void.

In summary, we hold that the Village, as a non-home-rule municipality, did not have the statutory authority to impose these impact fees for schools and open space, and, to the extent that they do so, its ordinances (and corresponding code provisions) imposing such fees are invalid.

III. CONCLUSION

For the foregoing reasons, the judgment of the circuit court of Lake County is affirmed.

Affirmed.

NOTES ON IMPACT FEES

1. Attempts by municipalities to impose fees on developers for the off-site impacts allegedly created by the development have met with mixed success. In Albany Area Builders Association v. Town of Guilderland, 546 N.E.2d 920 (N.Y. 1989), the New York Court of Appeals struck down a local ordinance that imposed a fee for improvements to off-site roads on "applicants for building permits who seek to make a change in land use that will generate additional traffic." The court held that any attempt to impose a transportation fee was pre-empted by substantial state legislation concerning highway fees. In the absence of an explicit legislative statement of pre-emption, is the need for uniformity in paying for highways so significant as to justify a finding of pre-emption? See also Kamhi v. Town of Yorktown, 547 N.E.2d 346 (N.Y. 1989), in which the same court struck down the imposition of a recreation fee on developers.

In Russ Building Partnership v. City & County of San Francisco, 234 Cal.Rptr. 1 (Cal. Ct. App. 1987), the court upheld an ordinance that imposed a fee on owners of buildings that contained newly developed office space. The ordinance required the owners to pay a transit fee that was designed to provide revenue for a mass transit system to offset the anticipated increased costs to accommodate new riders during peak commuter hours generated by the new office space. The court concluded that the fee did not constitute a tax, which could only be enacted by a supermajority of the electorate, because it only reflected the reasonable cost of providing the service for which the fee was charged. The court relied on the fact that the fees were not earmarked for general revenue purposes and were not compulsory, but were exacted only if the developer "voluntarily chooses" to create new office space. "Developers have been required to pay for streets, sewers, parks and lights as a condition for the privilege of developing a particular parcel. There is little difference between these public improvements and the benefit to the public from the increased transit services paid for by the transit fee." 234 Cal.Rptr. at 5. Can you distinguish among these exactions? Does it matter whether the development fees are for improvements within the development or whether, as in *Russ*, the fee finances an improvement that is used by the general public? The court in *Russ* also found that the fee did not violate due process or amount to double taxation. The court did, however, determine that the fee could not be imposed retroactively.

In Holmdel Builders Association v. Township of Holmdel, 583 A.2d 277 (N.J. 1990), the New Jersey Supreme Court upheld the statutory authority of municipalities to impose fees on development of commercial and residential properties in order to fund low-income housing. Such fees were considered essential in satisfying the court's prior rulings that required each locality within the state to create opportunities for the construction of low-income housing. See Southern Burlington County, NAACP v. Township of Mount Laurel, 336 A.2d 713 (N.J.), appeal dismissed and cert. denied, 423 U.S. 808 (1975). The court, however, invalidated fees that had been imposed prior to the promulgation of standards and guidelines for such fees by the state Council on Affordable Housing.

Impact fees, as all user fees, must be sufficiently related to the activities of the payor as to be distinguishable from taxes. In Idaho Building Contractors Ass'n v. Coeur d'Alene, 890 P.2d 326 (Idaho 1995), the court invalidated a fee imposed on developers of single family housing, the proceeds of which were to be used for capital improvements to public facilities, including libraries, police, fire, and streets. The court concluded that the fee could not be related to increased demand for these services from newcomers, reasoning: "the fact that the fee is collected every time a building permit is applied for illustrates the error in this argument. Under the City's ordinance, a Coeur d'Alene resident of forty years, who chooses to build a new house, is assessed this fee. The fee is collected despite the fact that the resident already uses the public facilities, and is not increasing the demand on them. This is clearly a revenue raising measure, not a regulation." Since the revenue was to be used for public services generally rather than to cover the cost of a particular service provided to the payor, the fee constituted a tax and, as such, was unauthorized by state statutes. See also City of Tarpon Springs v. Tarpon Springs Arcade Ltd., 585 So.2d 324 (Fla. Dist. Ct. App. 1991) (ordering refund of impact fees where method used to calculate payments was "arbitrary and capricious" and had no logical relationship to impact).

2. *Fees and Development.* The New Jersey court identifies as an "obvious" concern about impact fees the possibility that "disproportionate or excessive use of development exactions could discourage new development or inflate housing prices to an extent that excludes large segments of the population from the available market." Why is this a concern at all? If developers are required to pay fees that reflect the costs that their developments impose on the community, but cannot profitably sell houses at prices that include those fees, does that suggest that the development should not occur? In short, isn't there some point at which "new development" is undesirable? Is so, are market forces (i.e., the unwillingness of potential new residents to migrate to the area and the willingness of current residents to emigrate) capable of revealing when that point has been reached? If so, are impact fees a useful way of allowing the market for housing or commercial development to identify that point? To what extent does competition among localities for development constrain the ability to impose unjustified fees? See Vicki Been, "Exit" as a Constraint on Land Use Exactions: Rethinking the Unconstitutional Conditions Doctrine, 91 Colum. L. Rev. 473 (1991).

Nevertheless, is there a more basic concern about the use of impact or linkage fees? As the New Jersey court suggests, these fees have been used by localities to defray the costs of large-scale social problems (child care, overcrowded parking areas) by charging a small subset of the community (developers) and future residents (occupants of the development) who have little opportunity for complaint. What reason is there to believe that it is appropriate to select these individuals to bear the costs of development? Recall the discussion earlier about rent control. One traditional attack on rent control is that it requires one subset of society (landlords) to subsidize solutions to a society-wide problem—insufficient affordable housing. Are there reasons to distinguish between landlords and developers for purposes of this argument?

3. *Fee Payers v. Non–Fee Payers.* Assume that the schools in Long Tree are, indeed, overcrowded so that new schools are necessary. Who has contributed to the overcrowding? Only the residents of new development? If the pre-existing residents did not have children in the public schools, presumably the existing schools would be sufficient to accommodate new residents. So why should new residents be paying more for schools than existing residents? Assume that a pre-existing resident and a resident of a new development live in essentially identical homes and send their children to the same schools. Only the new resident will pay an fee, presumably factored into the sale price of her home, that reflects the impact of her children on the school system. What arguments exist for making that distinction?

4. *Reasonableness of Fees.* Is it reasonable to impose a fee on a developer at the time a home is constructed, rather than on the homeowner at the time of hookup to a municipal water or sewer system? In the early and important case of Banberry Development Corp. v. South Jordan City, 631 P.2d 899 (Utah 1981), the court concluded that an exaction imposed on developers prior to the time a home was occupied did not necessarily constitute a tax rather than a fee. The court reasoned that

> [w]hen the subdivision is connected to the city's water and sewer systems, the city must be prepared to perform its services on demand, and from that fact the subdividers receive immediate benefit. The provision of standby capacity to a subdivision requires the commitment of substantial capital. The city does not have to wait until someone turns on a tap or flushes a toilet before it requires participation in the cost of providing its services.

Id. at 902. The court also articulated standards by which to measure the reasonableness of a fee that purported to divide costs of municipal services between new and existing residents.

> To determine the equitable share of the capital costs to be borne by newly developed properties, a municipality should determine the relative burdens previously borne and yet to be borne by those properties in comparison with the other properties in the municipality as a whole; the fee in question should not exceed the amount sufficient to equalize the relative burdens of newly developed and other properties.
>
> Among the most important factors the municipality should consider in determining the relative burden already borne and yet to be borne by newly developed properties and other properties are the following, suggested by the well-reasoned authorities cited below: (1) the cost of existing capital facilities;

(2) the manner of financing existing capital facilities (such as user charges, special assessments, bonded indebtedness, general taxes, or federal grants); (3) the relative extent to which the newly developed properties and the other properties in the municipality have already contributed to the cost of existing capital facilities (by such means as user charges, special assessments, or payment from the proceeds of general taxes); (4) the relative extent to which the newly developed properties and the other properties in the municipality will contribute to the cost of existing capital facilities in the future; (5) the extent to which the newly developed properties are entitled to a credit because the municipality is requiring their developers or owners (by contractual arrangement or otherwise) to provide common facilities (inside or outside the proposed development) that have been provided by the municipality and financed through general taxation or other means (apart from user charges) in other parts of the municipality; (6) extraordinary costs, if any, in servicing the newly developed properties; and (7) the time-price differential inherent in fair comparisons of amounts paid at different times.

Id. at 903–04. How would these factors apply to the construction of a new facility made necessary by the new development rather than the extension of existing facilities? Is it permissible to impose the entire cost of the new facility on the new development?

5. *Impact Fees and the Federal Constitution*. Governmental restrictions on land use are subject to limitations under the Takings Clause of the federal Constitution. Since linkage fees similarly impose conditions on land use, they may similarly be constrained by the same constitutional restrictions.

In Nollan v. California Coastal Commission, 483 U.S. 825 (1987), the Supreme Court found that a condition the California Coastal Commission had placed on the acquisition of a development permit which required the owner who sought the permit to allow the public an easement to cross their beachfront property constituted a violation of the Takings Clause of the Fifth Amendment, as incorporated by the Fourteenth Amendment. The public easement sought by the commission in *Nollan* would have connected two public beaches that were separated by the Nollans' property. The city asserted that the easement was imposed to promote the legitimate state interest of reducing the "blockage to the view of the ocean" which would be caused by the Nollans' construction of a larger house. The Court decided that this desire to protect against the psychological effects of an obstructed view was not reasonably related to the condition placed on the Nollans' land. Hence, there was no "essential nexus" between the permit condition and the governmental objective advanced as the justification for the requirement. Imposition of the condition under these circumstances could not be treated as an exercise of the police power, but instead constituted an exercise of the eminent domain power that would have to be compensated. The Court, however, did not reach the question of the required degree of connection between the legitimate state interest and the permit condition.

Seven years later, in Dolan v. City of Tigard, 512 U.S. 374 (1994), the Court found that a city's condition that a landowner dedicate portions of her property to the city for improvement of a storm drainage system and for a bicycle/pedestrian pathway in order to obtain a building permit violated the Takings Clause of the Fifth Amendment. Justice Rehnquist, writing for the majority, set out to clarify the court's position in *Nollan*, declaring that a two-part analysis was required. The Court's first question was "whether the 'essential nexus' exists between the 'legitimate state interest' and the permit condition exacted by the city." 512 U.S. at 386. A second inquiry required the Court to determine whether the degree of exactions demanded by the city was reasonably related, or "roughly proportionate," to the projected impact of the development proposed by the landowner. The Court held that both of the City of Tigard's conditions met the essential nexus test. Neither one, however, met the proportionality standard. The court found the city had not articulated a reason for requiring a public greenway for storm water drainage when a private condition already existed, and the city had failed to demonstrate that the additional vehicle and bicycle trips generated by the proposed development were reasonably related to the pedestrian/bicycle pathway easement.

Subsequently, the California Supreme Court considered whether *Nollan* and *Dolan* applied to conditions for development permits that involve a fee rather than a dedication of property. In Ehrlich v. City of Culver City, 911 P.2d 429 (Cal.), cert. denied, 519 U.S. 929 (1996), the court concluded that, under the circumstances of the case before it, *Nollan* and *Dolan* applied to a monetary exaction. The city had imposed exactions as a condition of rezoning real property to permit the construction of a multi-unit residential building in an area previously zoned for private recreational use. The first exaction was to be used to construct additional recreational facilities in the city. The second was to be used for the city art fund. In a series of opinions by individual justices, a majority of the court first found that the heightened standards of *Nollan* and *Dolan* applied to exactions that do not involve possession of land, at least as long as the exactions constitute development fees imposed "neither generally nor ministerially, but on an individual and discretionary basis." 911 P.2d at 444. The majority believed that the presence of those circumstances indicated a higher risk that the locality was seeking to impose conditions on development while avoiding the obligation to pay just compensation. A majority of the court concluded that there was a sufficient nexus between the rezoning and the imposition of a monetary exaction to be expended to support recreation elsewhere in the city. The majority concluded, however, that the city had not demonstrated that its recreation fee was proportionate to the projected impact of the development, as there were no individualized findings to support the relationship between the exaction and the loss of the parcel for recreational use. Finally, the majority determined that the art ordinance was more of a design regulation, similar to setback provisions and landscaping requirements, than a development exaction of the type susceptible to *Nollan/Dolan* analysis.

Other state courts have tended to follow the *Ehrlich* decision by limiting heightened scrutiny to cases in which localities make individualized decisions about exactions. In Krupp v. Breckenridge Sanitation Dist., 19 P.3d 687 (Colo. 2001), for instance, the court concluded that a "plant investment fee" imposed on townhouse developers to defray the costs of expanding infrastructure to meet increased demand for the District's services was a valid, legislatively established fee that was reasonably related to the interest in accommodating new development. The court accepted distinction between legislative and adjudicative determinations, and refused to apply heightened scrutiny to the District's plan, which involved the imposition of generally applicable legislatively and administratively formulated fees rather than ad hoc determinations. The court noted that the Supreme Court had further signaled that *Nollan/Dolan* should receive narrow construction in City of Monterey v. Del Monte Dunes at Monterey, Ltd., 526 U.S. 687 (1999). In *Monterey*, the Court had rejected application of *Nollan/Dolan* where a city had denied permission for development after imposing additional requirements on the developer. The Court noted that it had not extended the rough proportionality test of *Dolan* "beyond the special context of exactions—land-use decisions conditioning approval of development on the dedication of property to public use," a condition that seemed to exclude pure monetary exactions. See also Home Builders Ass'n of Cent. Arizona v. City of Scottsdale, 930 P.2d 993, 1000 (Ariz. 1997). The Ohio Supreme Court, however, has applied the *Nollan/Dolan* test to exactions in Home Builders Ass'n of Dayton v. City of Beavercreek, 729 N.E.2d 349 (Ohio 2000). That case concerned the constitutionality of a system of impact fees payable by developers of real estate to aid in the cost of new roadway projects. The court concluded that the fees were legitimate, but only after determining (1) that there was a reasonable connection between the need for additional capital facilities and the growth in population generated by the subdivision; and (2) that there was a reasonable connection between the impact fee imposed on the developer and the benefits accruing to the subdivision.

6. In the principal case, the New Jersey court indicated that some cities, such as San Francisco and Boston, have enacted "linkage" ordinances that require developers to make payments to offset additional demands for housing and social services that are deemed to be attributable to development. A 1983 ordinance passed by the Boston City Council required developers to make payments to the city to be used for affordable housing, job training, park restoration, and athletics. Although one factor that motivated the campaign for linkage was the replacement of affordable housing with a proposed luxury residence and shopping area, no study was undertaken to demonstrate a direct relationship between the consequences of development and the use of the fees exacted from developers. A lower court invalidated the fee after concluding that it was a tax that the city was not authorized to enact under the state constitution. The Massachusetts Supreme Judicial Court subsequently reversed the decision on procedural grounds. See Bonan v. City of Boston, 496 N.E.2d 640 (Mass. 1986). The legislature, however, authorized Boston to collect taxes for linkage purposes from developers. That legislation has not been subjected to any constitutional challenge. See Alan A. Altshuler & José A. Gómez–Ibàñez, Regulation for Revenue: The Political Economy of Land Use Exactions 43 (1993); Donald L. Connors & Michael E. High, The Expanding Circle of Exactions: From Dedication to Linkage, 50 L. & Contemp. Probs. 69 (Winter 1987).

7. For discussions of the issues involved in linkage and impact fees, see Rachelle Alterman, Evaluating Linkage and Beyond: Letting the Windfall

Recapture Genie Out of the Exactions Bottle, 34 Wash. U. J. Urb. & Contemp. L. 3 (1988); Symposium: Land–Use, Zoning and Linkage Requirements Affecting the Pace of Urban Growth, 20 Urban Lawyer 513 (1988); Symposium, Exactions: A Controversial New Source for Municipal Funds, 50 Law & Contemp. Probs. 1 (1987). For a critical appraisal of the distinction between monetary and nonmonetary exactions, see J. David Breemer, The Evolution of the "Essential Nexus": How State and Federal Courts Have Applied *Nollan* and *Dolan* and Where They Should Go from Here, 59 Wash. & Lee L. Rev. 373 (2002). For a more sympathetic view of the distinction, see Robert H. Freilich & David W. Bushek, Thou Shall Not Take Title Without Adequate Planning: The Takings Equation After *Dolan v. City of Tigard*, 27 Urb. Law. 187, 190 (1995).

E. DEBT LIMITATIONS AND THEIR AVOIDANCE

PROBLEM XXIII

The City of Marion and the Marion Improvement Board have proposed to the state legislature a statutory scheme that would permit the City to finance construction of a convention center and sports arena in the City's downtown area. The City has received a feasibility study that indicates a dramatic increase in tourism and related economic activity if the project is completed. Most of the economic activity would be generated by convention participants and nonresident spectators at sporting events. The proposed legislation would grant the City and Board authority to issue bonds to obtain construction funds and to levy certain excise taxes. The excise taxes would consist of (1) a 1 percent tax on the sale of food and beverages sold for immediate consumption at retail establishments in the City; (2) a 5 percent tax on admissions to professional sporting events to be held in the convention center and arena; and (3) a 10 percent use tax on all hotel and motel room charges. Revenues collected under these taxes, along with the operating revenues of the convention center and arena would be placed in a trust fund that is pledged to the holders of the bonds. These would be the only funds available to pay bondholders. The City and Board estimate that they will have to issue approximately $47 million in bonds to complete the project.

The constitution of the state in which Marion is located contains the following provision in Article VII:

> Section 3. Debt Limit. No municipal corporation shall become indebted in any manner or for any purpose to an amount, in the aggregate, exceeding two percent of the value of the taxable property within such corporation, to be ascertained by the last assessment for State and local taxes, previous to the incurring of such indebtedness. All bonds or obligations in excess of such amount given by such corporations shall be void.

The total assessed valuation of the City is currently $3.8 billion. Two percent of that total is $76 million. The City currently has outstanding indebtedness in the amount of $53 million. You serve as legislative counsel to the state legislature. You have been asked whether the City's proposal would constitute a lawful obligation of the City under Article VII, Section 3 of the state constitution. How will you respond?

PROBLEM XXIV

In order to realize economies of scale, 80 municipalities in three states have joined together to finance a large nuclear power plant that will (hopefully) generate sufficient energy to satisfy all their electricity needs. The plant is to be constructed by the Washington Municipal Power Authority (WMPA), which will issue bonds to obtain the capital necessary to construct the massive plant. Each municipality will contract to purchase from WMPA a specific proportion of the energy to be generated from the plant, so that the total shares add up to 100 percent of plant capacity. The WMPA bonds are to be secured by the promise of the 80 municipalities to charge their residents electricity rates sufficient to allow each municipality to pay WMPA an amount necessary for debt service (principal and interest) on the bonds that bears the same relationship to total debt service as the municipality's energy share bears to total energy capacity of the plant. The municipalities, however, are obligated to make these payments only out of revenues they receive in the form of user fees for supplying electricity to their residents. They are under no obligation to impose taxes on their residents in order to make payments to WMPA. In order to induce potential bond purchasers to make the investment, however, each municipality will contract to charge its residents electricity rates high enough to pay its proportionate share of WMPA debt service even if the municipality does not receive the full amount (or any) of the energy for which it contracts and even if the plants are neither operative nor operating. Participating municipalities will impose these charges even though they ultimately obtain electricity from some alternative source and must pass the costs of that electricity on to their residents as well. You are the corporation counsel to one of the municipalities that is considering entering into a contract with WMPA. If this scheme constitutes "debt" for purposes of the state debt limitation, the total obligations that your municipality will incur far exceed that limitation and the contract with WMPA will be void. Thus, you must decide whether these terms create constitutional "debt." How will you respond? Compare Asson v. City of Burley, 670 P.2d 839 (Idaho 1983) (debt), with DeFazio v. Washington Public Power Supply System, 679 P.2d 1316 (Or. 1984) (not debt).

Lennox Moak & Albert Hillhouse, Local Government Finance

274–280 (1975).

Constitutional and Statutory Limitations on Local Government Borrowing

For more than a century the states have sought to impose suitable legal limits upon local government borrowing and to regulate borrowing methods and debt management. In a majority of the states some of the basic provisions are incorporated in the constitutions; in a minority statutory law has been widely used. The main features of these regulatory provisions may be summarized as follows:

1. Limitation of the amount of debt that may be outstanding
2. Voter approval of bond authorizations
3. Mandatory levy of annual taxes sufficient for the payment of principal and interest
4. Establishment of certain principles of debt management
5. Prohibition of the gift or loan of money or credit to individuals and private associations and corporations (and, in some cases, to public corporations). . . .

The Debt-to-Property Ratio. The device used almost universally by the states as a measure of permitted local borrowing is to establish a maximum amount of outstanding "tax-supported" debt that a local government may have in relation to the value of taxable property—usually measured by the local assessed valuation, the market value, or the state equalized valuation of taxable property. This method of control, which seemed quite logical when most local government revenue came from the general property tax, had its origin in the 1850s. Having no inherent long-term borrowing power, local governments looked to the state legislatures for authorization to incur debt; and, in this period, the taxpayers in some states became convinced that the legislatures could not be trusted with this responsibility and demanded constitutional restrictions on local borrowing. In 1857, Iowa placed in its constitution a limitation of five percent of the local assessed valuation on the debt that any local government could incur; but, it was not until the peak of local financial troubles in the 1870s that such action became widespread. . . .

[Limitations on the power of local governments to issue long-term, general obligation bonds are found in the constitutions of many states, supplemented by statutory requirements in a large number of these. Solely statutory limitations are found in other states, and some of these limitations are restricted to only one class of local government. No limitations exist in a very small number of states.—EDS.]

The legal device of limiting a local government's borrowing power to some percentage of the property tax base still carries great authority and prestige, but it has serious defects. Dependence on this device to permit local governments to use their credit adequately, but not excessively, is a demonstration of misdirected confidence in many jurisdictions. The defects tend to be greatest in those states which have made no real effort to modernize ancient formulae to take into account contemporary needs and contemporary assessment practices. Constitutions are difficult to amend; but, even in the minority of states that have worked assiduously to make their constitutional or statutory debt limit provisions meaningful and constructive, there remain certain deficiencies that may be inherent. The nature of the defects most commonly ascribed to the debt-to-property ratio indicates that some of them are easily remediable; others, only with great difficulty, if at all.

1. Percentages Are Arbitrary and Unrealistic. Although some states adjust the debt ceiling to allow for the varying needs of different classes and sizes of local governments, other states make no such distinctions or the adjustments are perfunctory. When the ratio for cities ranges among the states from one percent to 20 percent, and for school districts from one-half of one percent to 25 percent, there is no reason to believe that these divergent ratios are the product of careful study and analysis of the needs and fiscal abilities of local governments.

There is the additional complication that borrowing requirements vary not only among classes but also within classes of local governments, depending on rate of growth, population density, topography, and other economic, geographic, and demographic factors. Some states maintain rigid limiting ratios with no allowances for such factors, necessitating various makeshift arrangements. In many states, on the other hand, legal borrowing power is given considerable flexibility by such devices as two-level limits, with borrowing in the upper level requiring a popular referendum; provision, in a few instances ... to exceed the debt limit by a special majority popular vote and approval by a state administrative agency; and exemption from the limit of debt incurred for revenue-producing undertakings, reflecting the traditional concept that debt limits are primarily for the protection of property taxpayers. In some states, self-sustaining debt is automatically exempt or is given additional range because of the basic importance of the purpose. There would appear to be ample justification for exemption of the self-supporting debts of basic municipally-owned utilities which might, alternately be privately owned; but, when it is extended to the debts of an increasing variety of public functions whose support has been shifted from taxes to service charges, the effectiveness of the limit is weakened. Debt does not vanish because of a change in the means of its financial support. As noted earlier, the exemption of general obligation special assessment debt in some states has caused trouble in the past.

2. Assessed Value Offers An Unreliable Guide. The measurement base to which the limiting ratio is applied, usually the most recent assessed valuation of taxable property, is unreliable because of the general practice of underassessment—in varying degrees. The law requires that property be assessed at its full value or at some specified fraction of full value; but, local assessors commonly set the level much lower than these standards and on a go-as-you-please basis that varies the level among local assessing districts in the same state. . . .

3. The Single Year Base is Inappropriate. Use of the assessed valuation of a single year as a measurement base opens the door to manipulation of borrowing power by quick inflation of the base—an artifice that occasionally has played a disconcerting role in municipal debt history. There is also the shortcoming that, since assessed valuations tend to expand in boom periods and contract in depressed periods, local governments may be induced to over-borrow in periods of inflation and may be unable to borrow

in time of deflation. A few states ... try to minimize these defects by using a moving average of the assessed valuations of the last three or five years as a measurement base....

4. Failure to Apply Limits to Overlapping Local Governments. Debt limits tend to be misleading and ineffective because they are applied to the debts of individual local governments rather than to the aggregate debt of the overlapping local governments serving a community. In the relatively few states where the structure of local government is simple, the formulation of a satisfactory debt limit should not be difficult; but, when the local public debt that must be supported by the same group of taxpayers and ratepayers is incurred by several layers of separate local governments, there is the problem of how to place a reasonable ceiling on the aggregate debt and apportion this overall limit among the component governmental units in line with their respective responsibilities and needs....

5. Outdated Limitations. The failure of some states, mainly those with constitutional debt limits, to provide realistic limits that protect, but do not suppress, has led to methods of evasion that are costly; detrimental to local government structure, administrative organization, and fiscal management; and contributory to the weakening of fiscal responsibility. One aspect of this development is that constitutional debt limitations are rapidly losing jurisdiction over local government debt. Vast amounts and confusing varieties of local debt are being created throughout a large part of the country which the courts have held not to be debt in a constitutional sense. But, all local government debt, regardless of the source of revenue for its payment, has an impact on the local community that needs to be evaluated as to its equity and economic effect.

6. Lack of Limits Related to Needs. Some of the criticisms of the prevailing method of restricting local government borrowing go beyond the defects in application of the debt-to-property ratio and question the validity of the method itself. What has troubled a number of critics is the emphasis placed on arbitrary limitation and the lack of attention to the appropriate use of borrowing. The point is often made, too, that the capacity to incur debt is measured by existing resources, although the ability to meet interest and repay principal must depend on future resources. The prospect for future economic growth, stagnation, or decline is clearly a vital consideration in planning the incurrence of debt, but would be difficult to include in any legal measurement formula. There is a frequently voiced belief that the value of property subject to ad valorem taxation is not a good measure of fiscal resources for the support of debt. While one can readily agree that it is a far from ideal index of a community's fiscal ability, it is the only annually recurrent measurement standard presently available for virtually all local governments....

The Referendum as a Means of Debt Control

The desirability of mandatory referenda for the authorization of borrowing is to be questioned. The use of this device shifts responsibility from elected representatives, who should be required to make, instead of evade, important decisions. And, too, it is a deterrent to the advancement of comprehensive, well integrated budgeting for capital and current expense purposes, which calls for versatile financing of programs rather than sporadic decisions on bond issues. That voters often give perfunctory attention to bond referenda is indicated by low voter participation, and the assumption that their understanding of the validity of the proposed borrowing is more profound than that of the responsible officials is doubtful.

NOTES ON MUNICIPAL DEBT FINANCE

1. *The Time Dimension in Municipal Debt Finance.* Much of the law that we have studied to this point can be understood as efforts to control the ability of one locality to impose burdens on nonresidents, while capturing the benefits of projects for residents. The issuance of debt poses an analogous but slightly different problem. Localities usually issue debt to construct projects that require a substantial capital infusion and that have a long useful life. Think of a city hall or library, a power plant, or a sewer system in this regard. These examples suggest that projects do not necessarily have significant geographic external effects. Hence, the justification of local government law as a constraint on the imposition of external burdens does not easily apply.

These projects, however, have other unique characteristics that make the use of debt financing appropriate. The benefits of these projects will be conferred on future residents as well as current ones. Therefore, it makes sense to pay for them by incurring an obligation (long-term debt) that is repaid during the project's useful life. In this way, all who benefit from the project now and in the future also bear some of the burden of financing it. If current residents had to bear the entire cost of the project, e.g., through current tax revenues, they would bear a disproportionately high amount of the financial burden, while future residents who receive substantial benefit from the project would be subsidized.

For the same reason that debt finance is useful to make temporal benefits and burdens coincide, however, local officials have incentives to overutilize debt. Local officials can obtain immediate benefits by constructing capital projects. These improvements create jobs, generate a sense of progress, and instill civic pride, all of which redound to the immediate benefit of the officials in place at the time of construction. Should the project subsequently prove unnecessary or unsuccessful (e.g., a new power plant that is subsequently terminated because expected growth in population or demand for energy does not materialize), the official who decided to undertake the project may be out of office or may be able to avoid responsibility for his or her decision because intervening events becloud the circumstances under which the initial decision was made. Thus, officials who decide whether to issue debt for a project from which their constituents will benefit today, and for which those officials will receive credit, are likely to apply a significant discount to future costs.

The claim that local officials have incentives to favor capital projects helps to counter the argument that debt limits are inherently anti-democratic, in that they prevent local residents from obtaining the goods and services that they desire. Whether these limits advance or retard democracy depends on whether one believes that the decision to incur debt is made in an environment that encourages participation by all affected parties. One justification for debt limits is that, in their absence, the tendencies of officials to overissue debt would be exacerbated as supporters of any proposed project would be able to dominate any debate about the desirability of the project. Supporters are likely to be able to receive intense and discrete benefits from governmental financing that makes their participation in the approval process worthwhile. Think, for instance, of projects as diverse as sewer systems, sports stadiums, multi-family housing, a new municipal library, and a toll bridge. Who would incur the costs of organizing and lobbying for approval of each project? Contractors, developers, tenants, bond underwriters, users of the facility? Who would incur the costs of organizing and lobbying against? If you can identify numerous groups in the first category and fewer groups in the second, the likelihood of a municipality issuing "too much" debt (measured by whatever metric you like) is rather high. Debt limitations, however, make projects compete with each other, so that groups that favor one project may oppose alternate uses of the locality's limited borrowing power. The result, in theory at least, is that any proposed project receives a more thorough hearing.

Against this background, constitutional debt limitations may be understood as an effort to prevent temporal externalities the same way much of the law we have already considered may be seen as an effort to prevent geographical externalities. Debt limitations prevent officials from investing as much in capital projects as they might otherwise prefer. Thus, a limitation that initially seems quite anti-democratic, insofar as it prevents current residents from obtaining the goods and services they prefer, begins to look like a useful mechanism for ensuring that the desires of a population that includes future residents are satisfied.

For the history of debt limitations and a discussion of debt elections as constraints on legislative vulnerability to particular interests that would benefit from debt financing of capital projects, see Stewart E. Sterk & Elizabeth S. Goldman, Controlling Legislative Shortsightedness: The Effectiveness of Constitutional Debt Limitations, 1991 Wis. L. Rev. 1301.

2. *The Effect of Debt Elections*. One of the objectives of debt limitations is obviously to reduce the amount of debt that a state or locality incurs. There is some evidence that these debt limitations are effective, although the form of the debt limitations apparently matters. Debt elections apparently have a significant effect in reducing government expenditures. See, e.g., D. Roderick Kiewiet & Kristin Szakaly, Constitutional Limitations on Borrowing: An Analysis of State Bonded Indebtedness, 12 J.L. Econ. & Org. 62 (1996); John G. Matsusaka, Fiscal Effects of the Voter Initiative: Evidence from the Past 30 Years, 103 J. Pol. Econ. 587 (1995). But is this necessarily a good thing? Moak and Hillhouse suggest that debt elections have low turnout and that most voters pay little attention to bond referenda. If that is the case, who will likely end up dominating the elections—those who favor the project proposed at the election, or those who wish to keep their taxes low and thus disfavor government spending and indebtedness generally? Although approval rates at debt elections vary, ranging from 41.7 percent to 84.2 percent between 1983 and 2002, in an average year during that period 71.6 percent of state and municipal bond referendums (measured by amount of debt proposed, not by number of elections) passed. See The Bond Buyer, Annual Bond Referendums Results at http://www.bondbuyer.com/msa_displayquickreport.html?prod=Vote_history.

Is it conceivable that debt elections could actually increase the amount of debt that a state or locality incurs? Notice that the structure of the debt election separates the function of proposing a change in the status quo from the function of adopting such a change. Officials can propose to fund a project with a specific amount of debt; electors can only accept or reject the proposal—they cannot amend it. The result is that proposing officials who prefer to increase their capital budgets have incentives to propose a higher amount of debt than the majority of voters in the jurisdiction prefer. To see why this is the case, imagine that both officials and a majority of voters agree that a municipality needs a new library. The majority believe that the ideal expenditure for such a library would be $10 million. Officials, however, may propose a $12 million library, perhaps because they wish to build a more grandiose monument that they can point to, or to provide more funds to contractors who will be supporters in future elections. If the electorate could amend the proposal, they would do so, reducing it to $10 million. But the debt election provides them only with the choice of approving a $12 million library or retaining the status quo. If the value of having a new library rather than the status quo exceeds the $2 million "overexpenditure," then the electorate is likely to approve the bond issue, even though they would prefer an alternative. For theoretical and empirical evidence that local officials take advantage of the structure of debt elections to increase capital budgets, see Thomas Romer & Howard Rosenthal, Bureaucrats Versus Voters: On the Political Economy of Resource Allocation by Direct Democracy, 93 Q. J. Econ. 563 (1979).

3. *The Range of Debt Limitations.* As the reading from Moak and Hillhouse indicates, there is little uniformity among states or their political subdivisions in establishing a formula for the optimal level of debt. State debt limits are frequently imposed in flat amounts that have gone unamended since their original passage. Thus, the state debt limit in Arizona is $350,000, Ariz. Const. art. IX, § 5, while the California state debt limit is $300,000, Calif. Const. art. XVI, § 1. Rhode Island has had a state debt limit of $50,000 since 1842. See R.I. Const. art. XXXI, § 1. Some states have moved away from flat amounts to debt limits that are related to revenues. For instance, Pennsylvania restricts total outstanding debt to an amount that does not exceed 1–3/4 times the average annual tax revenues of the previous five years. See Pa. Const. art. VIII, § 7. See also Haw. Const. art. VII, § 13. Illinois, on other hand, links debt financing to appropriations rather than revenues and limits state debt to an amount not exceeding 15 percent of state appropriations for that fiscal year. Ill. Const. art. IX, § 9. See also N.J. Const. art. VIII, § 2.

As Moak and Hillhouse suggest, debt limits for political subdivisions more commonly are based on assessed valuation. The range is quite significant. Indiana restricts each locality to debt equal to 2 percent of the value of its property assessments, Ind. Const. art. XIII, § 1, while Virginia permits its localities to incur debt up to 10 percent of assessed valuation. Va. Const. art. VII, § 10. For additional information on the range of debt limits, see Robert S. Amdursky & Clayton P. Gillette, Municipal Debt Finance Law: Theory and Practice § 4.2 (1992).

NOTE ON VOTING REQUIREMENTS FOR DEBT ELECTIONS

As Moak and Hillhouse suggest, many debt limitations are subject to electoral overrides. See, e.g., Haw. Const. art. 7, § 13; Iowa Const. art. 7, §§ 2, 5; Kan. Const. art. 11, § 6–7. Various criteria for voting in a bond referendum or approving the issuance of bonds have recently faced constitutional challenge. The Supreme Court has applied a "strict scrutiny" analysis under the Fourteenth Amendment Equal Protection Clause to require that a compelling state interest support any limitation on the right to vote in such elections, whether the bonds at issue are supported by the issuer's taxing power or a more limited fund.

In Cipriano v. City of Houma, 395 U.S. 701 (1969), the Court invalidated a provision of Louisiana law that gave only "property taxpayers" the right to vote in revenue bond elections. Revenue bonds are payable only from revenues generated by operation of the facility financed by bond proceeds. These bonds are distinguished from general obligation bonds, which are payable from any tax or revenue-creating power that the bond issuer possesses. The proceeds of the bond issue in *Cipriano* were to be used to improve a municipally owned utility system and the bonds were to be payable out of the operations of the facility, not out of property taxes. The Court held that a state statute may grant the right to vote in a limited purpose election to some otherwise qualified voters and deny it to others only if the exclusion is necessary to promote a compelling state interest. The Court held that exclusion of nonproperty taxpayer users of the facility not only failed to promote such an interest but also disenfranchised a class of voters who were as substantially affected and directly interested in the matter upon which was voted as those allowed to vote. Although the Court appeared to assume that property taxpayers might have an additional interest in protecting property values through sponsorship of an efficient utility system, the exclusion of nonproperty taxpayers failed to satisfy the constitutional standards necessary to uphold selective distribution of the franchise.

The Supreme Court followed this decision in City of Phoenix v. Kolodziejski, 399 U.S. 204 (1970), where it held that a state could not limit to property owners the right to vote in elections for general obligation bonds, although state law required property taxes to be levied in an amount sufficient to service the bonds. The Court reasoned that all residents had an interest in the various municipal improvements to be financed with bond proceeds and that even if the bonds were payable exclusively from property taxes, nonproperty owning lessees share the burden of property taxes through higher rents.

In Hill v. Stone, 421 U.S. 289 (1975), the Court invalidated a scheme that permitted bonds to be issued only on concurrent majority votes of two overlapping groups: (1) property taxpayers and (2) an aggregate of property taxpayers and nonproperty taxpayers. Relying on *Phoenix* and *Cipriano*, the Court held that this general obligation bond issue was a matter of general interest and the classification served no compelling state interest. Thus the state could not enforce a classification based on property ownership. Such a classification would in effect disenfranchise those who had not rendered their property for taxation by permitting a majority of property taxpayers to veto the will of a majority of all those interested in the issue.

State and lower federal courts have relied upon these decisions to invalidate franchise restrictions on bond issue elections for failure to establish a compelling state interest. See Wright v. Town Board of Carlton, 342 N.Y.S.2d 577 (N.Y. App. Div. 1973); Light v. MacKenzie, 356 N.Y.S.2d 991 (N.Y. Sup. Ct. 1974); Stewart v. Parish School Board, 310 F.Supp. 1172 (E.D. La.), aff'd, 400 U.S. 884 (1970).

In Southern California Rapid Transit District v. Bolen, 822 P.2d 875 (Cal.), cert. denied sub nom. Atchison, Topeka & Santa Fe Ry. v. Southern California Rapid Transit Dist., 505 U.S. 1220 (1992), the California Supreme Court upheld a statute conditioning the right to vote on the ownership of real property. The voting scheme permitted only owners of commercial real property located in a proposed district to vote in a referendum on the propriety of creating the district. In addition, votes in the referendum were to be weighted on the basis of the assessed value of real property owned by the voter. The court explained that the beneficial impact of the assessment districts—funding of rapid transit—on nonvoting residents was indistinguishable from the impact on residents of the service area outside of the benefit districts. Since nonresidents were not entitled to vote on the district's creation, residents who received no greater benefit than nonresidents could also constitutionally be excluded from the franchise. Additionally, since rapid transit improvements within the district were to be funded by the issuance of municipal bonds payable only from assessments imposed on owners of commercial property within the district, the economic burden of the assessments fell disproportionately on those to whom the vote was granted. Finally, the court approved the allocation of votes in accordance with property valuation on the grounds that "the Legislature was entitled to assume that within . . . relatively small benefit assessment districts, assessed valuation bears a rough relationship to lot or building size and that the vote allotment and assessment formulas are thus not unreasonably disproportionate for equal protection purposes."

The Supreme Court has, moreover, upheld requirements that bonds be approved by more than a simple majority of voters, unless the supermajority requirements discriminate against an insular minority. In Gordon v. Lance, 403 U.S. 1 (1971), the Court rejected a challenge to provisions of the West Virginia Constitution and certain state statutes that required the approval of 60 percent of the voters to incur bonded indebtedness. The challengers, who supported bond issues that had won the approval of a majority—but less than 60 percent—of those voting, claimed that the supermajority requirement impermissibly diluted their voting power and gave disproportionate influence to the minority. The Court, citing provisions of the Federal Constitution in which simple majority votes are insufficient, concluded that supermajority provisions are a valid means of safeguarding against fiscal overextension of municipalities. Thus, as long as the supermajority requirements do not discriminate or authorize discrimination against any identifiable class, they do not violate the Equal Protection Clause of the Fourteenth Amendment. State and lower federal courts have followed this pattern. See Bogert v. Kinzer, 465 P.2d 639 (Idaho 1970), appeal dismissed, 403 U.S. 914 (1971); Tiews v. Timberland Regional School District, 273 A.2d 680 (N.H. 1971).

Supermajority requirements may be perceived as an additional protection for the future generations who arguably constitute the persons intended to be protected by debt limits. Since future residents will bear the burden of paying for capital projects, but cannot easily be represented in the decision to construct the projects, supermajority requirements may be explained as a filtering mechanism to ensure that only projects that enjoy substantial popularity will be financed with municipal assets. This popularity may be considered a surrogate for the likelihood that there is a substantial need for the project and that it does not satisfy the desires of only a small segment of residents. Alternatively, debt limits may be seen as paternalistic devices intended to prevent current residents from incurring debt beyond their capability. On this reading, debt should be incurred only when support for the underlying project is so widespread that there is relative certainty that those who favor the project are not acting whimsically.

Harris v. City of Little Rock

40 S.W.3d 214 (Ark. 2001).

■ CORBIN, JUSTICE.

This is a suit brought by a taxpayer, Appellant Nora Harris, against Appellee City of Little Rock, challenging the city's issuance of revenue bonds that will, in part, finance the acquisition of land for the William Jefferson Clinton Presidential Park. On March 17, 1998, the city, through its board of directors, passed Ordinance No. 17,690, authorizing the city to issue and sell capital-improvement revenue bonds in the amount of $16,500,000 to fund park and recreational improvements. In addition to the Presidential Park, the bonds would also provide improvements to the city's zoo and its three public golf courses. Appellant challenged the ordinance under Amendment 65 to the Arkansas Constitution on the grounds that it pledged as repayment user fees other than those generated from the particular projects being funded by the bonds, and that it indirectly pledged tax revenues as repayment.

* * *

I. Repayment of Bonds by Project Revenues

Appellant first argues that the Presidential Park will not generate revenues and that, therefore, the ordinance issued by the city fails to comply with the requirements of Amendment 65. Appellant asserts that Amendment 65 mandates that if user fees are pledged as repayment of revenue bonds, those fees must be generated by the particular project being funded. We disagree....

Section 1 of Amendment 65 provides in part:

> [A]ny governmental unit, pursuant to laws heretofore or hereafter adopted by the General Assembly, may issue revenue bonds for the purpose of financing all or a portion of the costs of capital improvements of a public nature, facilities for the securing and developing of industry or agriculture, and for such other public purposes as may be authorized by the General Assembly.

Section 3(a) defines the term "revenue bonds" as:

> [A]ll bonds, notes, certificates or other instruments or evidences of indebtedness the repayment of which is secured by rents, user fees, charges, or other revenues (other than assessments for local improvements and taxes) derived *from the project or improvements financed* in whole or in part by such bonds, notes, certificates or other instruments or evidences of indebtedness, *from the operations of any governmental unit, or from any other special fund or source other than assessments for local improvements and taxes.* [Emphasis added.]

Section 3(b) of Amendment 65 defines the term "governmental unit" as including any municipality and its agencies, boards, commissions, or other instrumentalities.

The Revenue Bond Act of 1987, enacted under Amendment 65, defines "bonds" or "revenue bonds" as "all bonds or other obligations, the repayment of which are secured by rents, loan payments, user fees, charges, or other revenues derived from any special fund or source other than assessments for local improvements and taxes[.]" *See* Ark.Code Ann. § 19–9–604(1) (Repl.1998). Similarly, the Local Government Capital Improvement Revenue Bond Act of 1985, which was passed prior to Amendment 65, defines "revenues" as:

> project revenues or any other special fund or source other than taxes or assessments for local improvements including, without limitation, any acquired with bond proceeds and the revenues to be derived from them, and any other user fees, charges or revenues derived from the operations of any municipality or county and any agency, board, commission, or instrumentality thereof[.]

See Ark.Code Ann. § 14–164–402(12) (Repl.1998).

It is clear from the plain language of Amendment 65 and the foregoing statutes that revenue bonds may be repaid with rents, user fees, charges, or other revenues, other than tax revenues, derived from three sources: (1)

the project or improvement financed by the bonds; (2) the operations of any governmental unit; or (3) any other special fund or source other than assessments for local improvement and taxes. Here, the city's ordinance specifically provides that the bonds are not general obligations of the city, "but shall be special obligations payable solely from fees derived from the operation of the parks and recreational facilities owned or operated by the City[.]" The city's Parks and Recreation Department is certainly an agency, board, commission, or instrumentality of the city. Thus, the user fees pledged to repay the bonds are revenues from the operation of any governmental unit. Accordingly, the ordinance is in compliance with Amendment 65.

II. Costs for Maintenance and Operation of the City's Recreational Facilities

Appellant next argues that Ordinance No. 17,690 is unconstitutional because it indirectly pledges tax revenues to repay the revenue bonds. This argument is premised on a provision in Section 2 of the ordinance, wherein the city has covenanted "to appropriate sufficient funds to insure the efficient operations and maintenance of the park and recreational activities of the City[.]" The exhibits offered below showed that the recreational facilities consistently operated at a loss. In other words, the user fees did not cover the expenses. The city has, however, historically made up the difference from its general revenues. Appellant asserts that by pledging the facilities' user fees to repay the revenue bonds, the city will have to contribute even more money from its general revenues to insure the efficient operations and maintenance of the facilities for the life of the bonds, which extend through the year 2023. Thus, Appellant argues, by using general revenues to subsidize these parks, while the user fees are pledged to repay the bonds, the city is circumventing the prohibition in Amendment 65 that revenue bonds may not be repaid from taxes.

The City, on the other hand, argues that Amendment 65 prohibits it from pledging general revenues, or taxes, to repay the revenue bonds, but does not prohibit it from using general revenues to fund the operation and maintenance of its parks and recreational facilities. The City relies on the holding in *Rankin v. City of Fort Smith*, 337 Ark. 599, 990 S.W.2d 535 (1999). There, the appellants argued that the city had illegally exacted funds from its general revenues to help pay for bonds issued by the city for the construction of a parking deck. The appellants sought to establish the existence of an illegal exaction by alleging that the city unlawfully used its general funds to pay revenue-bond indebtedness in violation of Amendment 65. The appellants contended that the revenues were transferred to the parking deck's fund specifically to meet alleged shortfalls in the fund's debt-service obligation for the revenue bonds. The city, however, produced an affidavit demonstrating that for each year in question, the parking facilities' revenues exceeded the debt-service obligation. This court affirmed the ruling in favor of the city based on the appellants' failure to offer countervailing proof. Here, the City asserts that *Rankin* is determinative of the issue at hand. We disagree.

The issue in *Rankin* concerned the allegation that the city was *directly* paying its debt-service obligation for the parking deck with general revenues. The appellants argued that the city had taken money from its general funds to make up shortfalls on the debt-service obligations. Clearly, Amendment 65 forbids such action. *Rankin* did not, however, involve the allegation that the city was *indirectly* paying debt service with general revenues by making up shortfalls in the operation and maintenance of the parking facilities. That is the issue to be resolved here.

We believe that Amendment 65 prohibits a city from doing indirectly that which it cannot do directly. Because Amendment 65 forbids repaying revenue bonds with assessments from local improvements or taxes, it correspondingly forbids pledging tax revenues to fill the gaps left by using other sources of monies to repay the bonds. In short, using tax revenues to offset losses caused by pledging revenues from user fees to cover bond indebtedness is indirectly using tax revenues to secure repayment of the bonds, which is prohibited conduct. The question then is whether the city has done so in this case. Based on the record before us, we cannot say that it has.

The only evidence presented by Appellant on this issue came from City Manager Cy Carney. He testified that the city's board of directors will make the decision as to whether and how the city will provide any additional funds to replace the user fees now pledged to the repayment of the bonds. Carney stated that he had asked the various department heads for recommendations as to how budget cuts could be made. Carney explained that he was considering proposing to the board that the shortfalls in the parks' operation be made up by budgeting cuts, such as reducing salary expenses. Appellant's attorney attempted a number of times, to no avail, to get Carney to state that the shortfalls would be supplied by the city's general fund, which is mostly comprised of tax revenues. The City objected to that line of questioning on the grounds that Carney had no authority to speak for the board, and that the decision as to whether and how to make the up the shortfalls would be up to the board. The chancellor sustained the City's objections. Appellant's attorney only succeeded in getting Carney to state, hypothetically, that if he were to make such a proposal to the board, it would involve monies from the general fund.

Appellant did not call any board members as witnesses, nor did she present any other proof on this issue. Indeed, she acknowledges in her brief that nothing in the ordinance, the bond documents, or the testimony given below identifies the source of the funds to be appropriated for the efficient operation and maintenance of the city's parks. Appellant simply assumes that "[t]he reason the source is not identified is that there is only one such source—the General Fund." This is an assumption that we are not willing or able to make. This court has consistently refused to issue advisory opinions based on facts not in evidence and events that have not yet occurred. "[C]ourts do not sit for the purpose of determining speculation and abstract questions of law or laying down rules for the future conduct [.]" *Baker Car & Truck Rental, Inc. v. City of Little Rock,* 325 Ark. 357,

363, 925 S.W.2d 780, 784 (1996). We thus concur with the chancellor that "[t]he Court must base its findings on evidence admitted at trial, and not on assumptions as to what will happen in the future."

To make a decision on this issue, we would have to assume that (1) the City's recreational facilities will continue to operate at a loss, even after improvements to those facilities are made; (2) the City's board of directors will elect to make up the difference in any shortfalls to insure the efficient operation and maintenance of the facilities; and (3) the shortfalls will necessarily be made up from funds derived from taxes. Moreover, we would have to speculate about the effect that periodic increases in the user fees would have on the recreational facilities' revenues. Bryan Day, Director of the City's Parks and Recreation Department, testified that effective January 1, 1998, the City had increased its user fees by $2.00 at the golf courses, the fitness center, and the zoo. The data presented below only went through 1997, the year before the increases took effect.

* * *

On its face, Ordinance No. 17,690 complies with the repayment provisions of Amendment 65. The ordinance reflects that the city "will pledge the fees from the park and recreational facilities owned or operated by the City more specifically defined hereinafter to secure the payment of the principal of and interest on the Bonds." The ordinance reflects further:

> The Bonds shall not be general obligations of the City, but shall be special obligations payable solely from fees derived from the operation of the parks and recreational facilities owned or operated by the City (specifically including, but not limited to, amounts deposited by the City into the enterprise funds for the zoo, golf, and War Memorial Fitness programs of the City established pursuant to Resolution No. 10,040 of the City adopted August 5, 1997), and any other fees designated and pledged by the City to such purpose[.]

The foregoing language demonstrates that the city has not pledged for repayment of the bonds any monies from taxes assessed or collected by the city. Furthermore, it is not evident from the city's covenant to operate and maintain its parks and recreational facilities at efficient levels that the city has pledged or will otherwise be required to use general revenues to offset the lost user fees. Thus, the ordinance is not, on its face, in violation of Amendment 65.

Additionally, we point out that the covenant contained in the ordinance is only to provide sufficient funds to insure the *efficient* operations and maintenance of the city's recreational facilities. The covenant does not specifically require the city to maintain those facilities at their current rate. Thus, it is speculation as to whether the city will need to increase the amounts that it currently provides to satisfy its covenant to insure the efficient operations and maintenance of the facilities. Accordingly, because this issue depends on a state of facts that is future, contingent, or uncertain, it would be premature and advisory to render a decision at this time. We note, however, that our opinion today should not be construed to prohibit Appellant from challenging any future action taken by the city that is inconsistent with this opinion.

* * *

■ GLAZE, JUSTICE, concurring in part; dissenting in part.

I agree in part and dissent in part with the majority opinion. The City of Little Rock agrees that Amendment 65 to the Arkansas Constitution prohibits the City from using monies from its general funds to pay the revenue bonds it authorized in order to acquire land for the William Jefferson Clinton Presidential Park. This is so because Amendment 65 and the Revenue Bond Act of 1987 clearly provide the bonds must be paid from revenues from sources *other than taxes* or assessments. Thus, unless the voters approved a tax to pay for the land in question, the City cannot use tax proceeds for such purpose. No such election or approval has occurred here. Significantly, the City's general fund is largely comprised of sales tax proceeds the voters approved for other purposes.

* * *

The majority opinion correctly reflects the City's attempt to circumvent the plain terms of Amendment 65, but it stops there. The opinion states that, while general funds or tax monies cannot be used to replace the user fees pledged to secure the revenue bonds, it is premature to so hold because it has not yet been shown if the City will be required to use its general or tax funds to offset the user fees pledged for revenue bond purposes. I disagree.

In oral argument, the City was asked repeatedly whether its general fund would be used to pay this increased deficit sustained by its zoo, parks, and recreation facilities, and caused by the City redirecting the user fees revenue. The City implicitly and explicitly agreed in the responses it made in oral argument:

City's counsel said, "[I] do not deny that the general fund will continue to support the parks department. . . ." . . .

City's counsel answered, "Right" to the question, "[You] are creating a tremendous deficit in the use or in the facilities such as the zoo, and the fitness center, and the golf courses, and you are going to have to make up that deficit with general revenues." . . .

After being asked, "If [the City] had not had the general revenues available to repay the user fees that were used to secure this bond, could the City have issued those bonds," the City's counsel said, *"[I]f you are asking if,* because of the use of the user fees, *the [City] had to use general revenues to support a department* such as the parks department in a manner that *it didn't have to because it used* to collect (*sic*) *user fees,* then I think *the answer to that question is yes* . . . as long as the [City] doesn't engage in deficit spending."

From the foregoing, the City was quite candid that general funds (containing tax monies) would be used to reimburse the user fees pledged to secure the revenue bonds. However, the City simply sees no wrong in switching or redirecting these funds. Instead, the City responds, stating it has always used general funds to make up deficits incurred by its programs; that is true, but Amendment 65 was not involved then and its programs' user fees were not being diverted to secure revenue bonds.

Obviously, general tax funds can be used to supplement the City's zoo, parks, and recreation programs, but those tax funds cannot indirectly be used to secure Amendment 65 revenue bonds. Unlike the conclusion reached by the majority opinion, the City's counsel's remarks reflect an honest assessment that general revenues must be used to improperly replace its user fees. The city manager, Cy Carney, acknowledged that past deficits in its programs, such as the zoo, golf courses, and fitness center, have been paid by the general fund. He further admitted pledges of user fees from these programs will create a need for additional revenues to make up those program deficits. Where will the City get those needed monies? Mr. Carney identified reducing the number of city employees. Of course, this would give the City additional revenues to spend from general funds, since such salaries are paid from those funds. Mr. Carney's answer merely confirms the source or revenue stream it looks to in order to pay the debts incurred by its programs. The City's evidence merely reveals the obvious—general revenues are and will continue to be those used to meet the City's increasing program deficits. For that reason, I would reverse the chancellor's decision....

■ BROWN, JUSTICE, concurring.

* * *

I write ... to emphasize that the question of the general fund subsidy is left open for judicial determination at a later time. Stated differently, in my judgment the doctrine of *res judicata* would not foreclose future resolution of this point. My reason for concluding as I do is that the issue of the general fund subsidy could not have been litigated at the first trial because city officials (Mr. Carney and Mr. Day) never acknowledged that the general fund would subsidize the affected park facilities to the extent of the debt service and no other proof was offered by Ms. Harris on this point. Because this issue was not one that could have been decided in the first trial, *res judicata* does not prevent a later determination. *See Linn v. NationsBank,* 341 Ark. 57, 14 S.W.3d 500 (2000); *Baltz v. Security Bank of Paragould,* 272 Ark. 302, 613 S.W.2d 833 (1981).

The case of *Rankin v. City of Fort Smith,* 337 Ark. 599, 990 S.W.2d 535 (1999), bears some similarities to the facts in this case but does not meet the subsidy issue head on or resolve it. The *Rankin* case involved a commingling of garage fees, parking meter revenues, and general fund dollars in the Parking Facilities Fund which was used to pay off revenue bonds issued to build the parking garage. Garage fees and other parking fees were pledged to pay off the bonded indebtedness. The general fund was used to subsidize maintenance and operations at the parking garage. We held in that case that the general fund was not being used to pay the bond indebtedness directly because city financial statements showed that the garage fees and other parking fees were sufficient to meet the debt service. The question never raised to, or addressed by, this court in *Rankin* was whether the general fund was being used indirectly to meet the bonds' debt service in light of the fact that tax dollars were replacing garage fees and parking revenues diverted from the maintenance and operation of that facility. That is the crucial issue that looms before us in the Nora Harris lawsuit and remains to be answered.

* * *

■ IMBER, JUSTICE, concurring.

I concur in the result but do so for different reasons than those expressed in the majority opinion.

This court's construction of Amendment 65 is of utmost importance because, as Section 4 of the Amendment states, "[t]his amendment *shall be the sole authority* required for the authorization, issuance, sale, execution and delivery of revenue bonds authorized hereby[.]" (Emphasis added.) The majority opinion interprets Amendment 65 to allow for the repayment of revenue bonds with rents, user fees, charges, or other revenues (other than tax revenues) derived from the operations of "any governmental unit," including municipalities and their instrumentalities. The plain language of Amendment 65 lends itself to no other reading. Accordingly, I wholeheartedly agree with the majority's conclusion in Part I of the opinion that "the ordinance is in compliance with Amendment 65." However, I must disagree with Part II of the majority opinion which interprets Amendment 65 as prohibiting the use of general revenues to offset losses caused by pledging revenues from user fees to cover bond indebtedness:

> Because Amendment 65 forbids repaying revenue bonds with assessments from local improvements or taxes, *it correspondingly forbids pledging tax revenues to fill the gaps left by using other sources of monies to repay the bonds. In short, using tax revenues to offset losses caused by pledging revenues from user fees to cover bond indebtedness is indirectly using tax revenues to secure repayment of bonds, which is prohibited conduct.*

(Emphasis added.)

As the majority points out in Part I of the opinion, Amendment 65, by its broad and plain language, allows revenue bonds to be repaid with user fees or revenues derived from *the operations of any instrumentality of the City.* Nothing in the language of Amendment 65 limits the use of such revenues to (a) revenues that have never been produced before, or (b) revenues that exceed operating expenses. Indeed, the use of revenues derived from the operations of any governmental unit to repay revenue bonds will inevitably leave "gaps" in operating funds. The record in this case shows that in previous years, the City has subsidized the operations of its parks and recreational facilities with money from the City's general fund because those facilities do not generate sufficient revenues to support themselves. Although the City's authority to subsidize the operations of its parks and recreational facilities with general revenue funds is not questioned, the majority opinion would nonetheless require the City to refrain from increasing that subsidy by so much as one dime once the bonds are issued. These revenue bonds were issued in 1998. Thus, pursuant to the majority opinion, the City's subsidy of its parks and recreational facilities can never exceed the amount of the 1997 subsidy; that is, the maximum amount of the subsidy from the general fund will be frozen in time. Such a result is absurd because future subsidy increases may be necessitated by outside economic forces over which the City has no control, such as an increase in the minimum wage. Under the majority's reasoning, the City Board's hands will be tied from making the financial decisions that it must make to account for such unforseen [sic] circumstances.

Furthermore, such an interpretation of Amendment 65 creates a moving target, whereby the constitutionality of this bond issue will depend upon how much money the City Board appropriates each year from the general fund to subsidize its parks and recreational facilities. The constitutionality may also depend upon the source of the revenue that the City Board appropriates each year. However, the City Board's ability to increase the subsidy to its parks and recreational facilities by appropriating funds from sources other than tax revenues will also be limited by the majority's interpretation of Amendment 65 because tax revenues can never be used to offset losses caused by such an appropriation.

In effect, the majority has engrafted two words onto Amendment 65. Henceforth, the revenues that can be used to secure repayment of revenue bonds must be *new* revenues or *net* revenues. In the future, governmental units will rarely, if ever, be able to issue revenue bonds "for the purpose of financing all or a portion of the costs of capital improvements of a public nature . . . and for such other public purposes as may be authorized by the General Assembly." Ark. Const. amend. 65, § 1.

I must also disagree with the majority's conclusion that our decision in *Rankin v. City of Fort Smith,* 337 Ark. 599, 990 S.W.2d 535 (1999), is not determinative of the issue at hand. The bond financing arrangement presented in *Rankin,* which we upheld, is no different than the one now before this court. In *Rankin,* the city issued revenue bonds to fund the building of a parking garage. In order to repay those bonds, the city pledged the revenues collected from *all* parking facilities owned and operated by the city, including those unrelated to the parking garage. Id. Therefore, just as in this case, the city was taking revenue from existing instrumentalities of the city in order to repay bonds for a new project. In addition to the revenue collected from the parking facilities, the City of Fort Smith paid over $500,000 from its general fund to the parking facilities fund between 1992 and 1996. Id. These general fund monies were specifically appropriated for use in the maintenance and operation of the facilities. Id. Again, like this case, the bond financing arrangement approved in *Rankin* left "gaps" in operating funds for the city's parking facilities. In upholding the appropriation of general funds in *Rankin,* we relied upon the undisputed proof that the parking facilities' revenue exceeded the bond debt service obligation. Id.

Likewise, the record in this case shows that the maximum payment required to meet principal and interest payments on these revenue bonds in any one year is $1,294,112.50 in the year 2002. The record also reveals that for the years 1988 through 1997, the last year for which there is a financial statement, the total annual revenue for the City's parks and recreational facilities was never less than $1,485,186, in 1988. Since that time, revenue has increased every year, with the exception of one, and, for the year 1997, revenue collections totaled $3,273,919. Clearly, revenue collections for the City's parks and recreational facilities have historically exceeded the debt service requirements on these revenue bonds, just as they did in *Rankin*. The burden of proof was on the appellant to show otherwise, which Ms. Harris failed to do. *Rankin v. City of Fort Smith, supra.*

* * *

I fear that the majority's construction of Amendment 65 in Part II of the opinion has entangled the political issues involved in this case with the legal issues presented to this court. It may be that the City Board made an unwise political decision in passing the ordinance in question, which divests the City's parks and recreational facilities of their revenue in order to finance the acquisition of land for the Presidential Park and fund capital improvements to the City's zoo and its three public golf courses. If the citizens of Little Rock disagree with that decision, political consequences will surely follow. However, that is not for us to decide. We must only determine whether Amendment 65, as the sole authority for the revenue bonds at issue, allows the City Board to do what it has done here. I conclude that it does.

■ [The opinion of SPECIAL JUSTICE KLAPPENBACH is omitted.—EDS.]

NOTES

1. *Debt and Risk of Project Failure.* At the time that debt limits were initially placed in state constitutions, most governmental debts consisted of general obligations payable from ad valorem taxes These same property taxes were almost the exclusive source of municipal income from which debts could be paid. See M. David Gelfand, Seeking Local Government Financial Integrity Through Debt Ceilings, Tax Limitations, and Expenditure Limits: The New York City Fiscal Crisis, the Taxpayers' Revolt, and Beyond, 63 Minn. L. Rev. 545 (1979). For this reason, some courts have determined that only debts secured by pledges of property tax revenues fall within the debt limitation. One might contend that the drafters of these provisions were concerned more with the total amount of debt that a locality incurred rather than the source from which the locality was going to pay the debt. But if that is the case, then why should revenue bond debt be exempt? Does the following commentary explain any of the skepticism about the financing in *Harris*?

> [T]raditional revenue bonds do not offend debt limits when payable from revenues generated solely by operation of the project for which the bonds were

> sold. The rationale for the decisions that reach this conclusion appears to be that, but for the project, those revenues would not have been available at all. Since the project is the sine qua non of the revenues, and no other municipal revenues are put at risk by the arrangement, the fear of supporting failed projects—the fear that generated passage of debt limits—seems not to be entangled with traditional revenue bonds. The negative implication, however, is that when municipal revenues are put at risk by the project, "debt" within the meaning of the constitutional limit does exist. The appearance of "debt," then, depends more on who bears the risk of the project's failure than on what the issuer denominates as the source of payment.

Clayton P. Gillette, Risk of Project Failure and the Definition of "Debt," 6 Mun. Fin. J. 311 (1985). Under this "risk analysis," revenue bonds properly fall outside debt limits when the public treasury is not exposed in the event that the project financed with bond proceeds turns out to be unworkable or otherwise fails to produce sufficient revenues to service the debt.

Even if one accepts this rationale, it may be difficult to determine which revenues are sufficiently linked to the project that they can properly be considered as placing the risk of project failure on bondholders. In Long v. Napolitano, 53 P.3d 172 (Ariz. App. 2002), plaintiffs contended that a pledge of funds diverted from state revenues to secure bonds issued to construct a new football stadium for a professional football team would create a debt of the state in excess of the constitutional limit. The revenues consisted of transaction privilege taxes paid by person conducting businesses at the stadium; transaction privilege taxes paid by persons constructing the stadium, and income taxes paid by the football team, its employees, and their spouses. The court determined that debts payable from ad valorem property taxes were subject to the constitutional limit, but so were taxes that had an insufficient relationship to the project being financed with the bonds. If the relationship between the funded project and the pledged taxes was "sufficiently direct and apparent that the taxes may be effectively treated as revenues of the project or otherwise related to its purpose," however, the debt limitation was not implicated. The court believed that this test was appropriate because such a relationship would connect the success of the project to the likelihood that the bondholders would be paid and whether the general taxing authority of the state was placed at risk. The court then concluded that the privilege taxes were properly pledged because they would not have been collected at all if the stadium had not been constructed. (Would those who constructed or worked at the stadium otherwise have been unemployed?) The court also found that income taxes from the team and its employees could be pledged without violating the debt limitation. The court, however, concluded that no sufficient nexus existed between the stadium and income taxes paid by employees and their spouses from sources unrelated to professional football. The court believed that such income would have been earned either by those individuals or by other persons even if no football stadium existed. See also Terry v. Mazur, 362 S.E.2d 904 (Va. 1987) (bonds secured by pledge of "highway user revenues" fell within constitutional debt where those revenues included funds unrelated to the project financed with bond proceeds and the revenues would have been available for other state purposes if not dedicated to repayment of these bonds).

2. *The Special Fund Doctrine.* The "risk analysis" approach to the definition of debt is inconsistent with broad readings of the special fund doctrine. A narrow conception of the special fund doctrine excludes an obligation from constitutional debt only if the obligation is payable from a revenue stream that would otherwise be unavailable to defray other municipal expenses. There need only be a sufficient nexus between the revenue source and the project financed with the debt. Hence, bonds issued by a state liquor control board payable only from a fund consisting of license and permit fees and penalties were deemed to be outside the realm of debt, Ajax v. Gregory, 32 P.2d 560 (Wash. 1934); gasoline taxes have been considered special funds when pledged to the payment of bonds issued for roads and bridges, Arizona State Highway Commn. v. Nelson, 459 P.2d 509 (Ariz. 1969); delinquent railroad property taxes and excise taxes on railroad equipment have been considered a special fund for payment of bonds issued by a railroad finance authority, Train Unlimited Corp. v. Iowa Ry. Finance Auth., 362 N.W.2d 489 (Iowa 1985); and bonds issued to construct an extraterritorial water line were excluded from debt where secured solely from revenues of the entire system, Baker v. City of Richmond, 709 S.W.2d 472 (Ky. Ct. App. 1986). Where, however, bonds issued to construct a hospital were to be repaid from revenues unrelated to hospital operations, such as cigarette taxes and parking meter fees, the special fund doctrine could not remove the obligation from the scope of debt. See City of Trinidad v. Haxby, 315 P.2d 204 (Colo. 1957). The Alabama Supreme Court disallowed use of monies earned on state investments to be used to pay bonds proposed to support a Mercedes–Benz plant in the state. See Opinion of the Justices, 665 So.2d 1357 (Ala. 1995).

Broader readings of the special fund doctrine do exist, however. On these readings, the funds set aside for payment of the obligation need not be generated by operation of the facilities financed with bond proceeds. Instead, once revenues, regardless of their source, are earmarked as the exclusive fund for payment of the obligation, the bonds are removed from the debt limitation. The only caveat is that the bonds not be payable from ad valorem property taxes. See, e.g., State v. City of Tampa, 72 So.2d 371 (Fla. 1954). Does this doctrine encourage officials to avoid debt limits by dividing revenue streams into a series of funds, each of which can be used to finance a discrete project? See Naftalin v. King, 90 N.W.2d 185 (1958).

3. *Tax Increment Financing.* One popular form of incurring indebtedness by creating a special fund that allegedly removes the obligation from constitutional debt limits in tax increment financing. Under one common structure, bonds are issued to redevelop a blighted area within a municipality. The value of the redeveloped property is assessed prior to the redevelopment and used as a base to determine the taxes that the property would generate without the improvement. Properties within the area are reassessed after redevelopment has occurred. Subsequent increases in property value in the area are attributed to the improvement. Thus, any "increment" in tax revenues above what would have been collected without the improvement is similarly attributed to the improvement alone. The assumption is that those revenues would not have materialized without the bond issue. As a result, bonds secured solely by the incremental property tax revenues allegedly fall outside the debt limitation. Most states have upheld these arrangements. See, e.g., Fults v. City of Coralville, 666 N.W.2d 548 (Ia. 2003). Recently, however, other courts have invalidated these arrangements as obligations subject to the state's constitutional debt limitations. See, e.g., Oklahoma City Urban Renewal Authority v. Medical Technology and Research Authority of Oklahoma, 4 P.3d 677 (Okla. 2000); State ex rel. County Com'n of Boone County v. Cooke, 475 S.E.2d 483 (W. Va. 1996).

4. *A Debt Is a Debt Is a Debt?* Various other types of obligations of governmental units will not be considered in calculating the debt limitation. In State ex rel. Keck v. City of Sunnyside, 43 P.2d 621 (Wash. 1935), the defendant city refused to pay installments due to a drainage district over a 14–year period on the grounds that the city was already indebted in excess of its debt limitation. The court held that while the obligation to pay the district constituted a debt, it would not be a "debt" within the meaning of the limitation if it was incurred in the performance of "mandatory duties" or for expenditures "necessary to corporate existence." The court affirmed a judgment of the trial court that because the improvements that led to incurrence of the obligation were not undertaken out of compulsion by court order or as a result of any emergency, the obligation did fall within the constitutional limit and mandamus would not lie to force city officials to levy taxes for payment of the overdue installments.

Debts frequently excluded from the limitation also include current expenses, e.g., salaries of municipal employees, debts incurred in anticipation of revenues to be collected within the fiscal year, obligations payable from special assessments, emergency expenses, and debts incurred in the purchase of specific property to be paid exclusively from income generated by use of that property. See 14 Eugene McQuillin, The Law of Municipal Corporations § 41.17 (1970).

If the location of the risk of the project's failure is the standard by which to measure the existence of debt, one would imagine that no constitutional debt exists where localities can extricate themselves from payment obligations should they find that the goods or services originally contracted for are no longer necessary. This is consistent with the "service contract" exception to debt limits, under which long-term agreements to pay only for services provided, and only as they are provided, will not constitute "debt," even though the agreement is to remain in place for several years. See, e.g., State ex rel. Council of City of Charleston v. Hall, 441 S.E.2d 386 (W. Va. 1994); Concerned Residents of Gloucester County v. Board of Supervisors, 449 S.E.2d 787 (Va. 1994).

Montano v. Gabaldon

766 P.2d 1328 (N.M. 1989).

■ SCARBOROUGH, CHIEF JUSTICE.

This suit involves a constitutional question arising out of the decision of the Board of County Commissioners of Valencia County to enter into a

Lease with Option to Purchase Agreement (lease) with a private corporation for the use of a new jail facility to be constructed on county-owned land. Valencia County voters have twice voted down referendums to finance a new jail. Plaintiff-appellant and County Commissioner Salomon Montano brought this declaratory judgment action questioning the legality of the lease given the restrictions in Article IX, Section 10 of the New Mexico Constitution. That provision requires the approval of county voters prior to the creation of county indebtedness for the purpose of erecting public buildings. The district court granted summary judgment in favor of defendants-appellees, finding that the lease did not create an unconstitutional debt. This appeal follows. We reverse and hold that the lease creates indebtedness within the meaning of Article IX, Section 10 of the New Mexico Constitution.

The lease in question requires Valencia County to make semi-annual payments, denominated as rent, for the use of a new facility which is to be built by a private contractor on county-owned land. Certificates of Participation would be issued by the contractor and sold to private investors to raise the costs of construction ($3,100,000). The private contractor would hold title to the "project," which is defined as the land, the improvements, and the fixtures, until and unless the County exercised its purchase option. The option to purchase the facility could be exercised during the twenty-year term of the lease by payment according to an amortization schedule included in the lease. Or, should the County continue to make the scheduled rental payments for the entire twenty-year term, the County would acquire ownership of the facility, and reacquire ownership of the land, after the final payment on July 1, 2008.

The lease also contains a "non-appropriation" provision which allows for termination of the lease at the end of any fiscal year should the Board of County Commissioners not appropriate sufficient funds to pay the rent. In addition, the lease defines a number of conditions in which the County may be declared in default, including failure to make a scheduled payment for a period of ten business days, failure to observe certain covenants, or filing of voluntary bankruptcy by the County. If the County exercised its termination rights, or if the private contractor terminated the lease upon default by the County, the contractor or its assigns would acquire permanent title to the land and the jail facility.

Article IX, Section 10 of the New Mexico Constitution provides in pertinent part as follows:

> No county shall borrow money except for the following purposes:
>
> A. erecting, remodeling and making additions to necessary public buildings . . .
>
> In such cases, indebtedness shall be incurred only after the proposition to create such debt has been submitted to the qualified electors of the county and approved by a majority of those voting thereon.

N.M. Const. art. IX, § 10 (Cum. Supp. 1988).

This Court will assume that the framers were familiar with similar constitutional provisions from other states and their judicial interpretation when they drafted the New Mexico Constitution. Jaramillo v. City of Albuquerque, 64 N.M. 427, 430, 329 P.2d 626, 628 (1958). It is apparent from the cases cited in 1 J. Dillon, Law of Municipal Corporations, §§ 193–200 (5th ed. 1911) [hereinafter Dillon], that the courts at the turn of the century were familiar with the basic issues involved here. In fact, these constitutional provisions were primarily a response to the heavy borrowing, and subsequent default, engaged in by many states prior to 1840. In re Constitutionality of Chapter 280, Oregon Laws 1975, 276 Or. 135, 554 P.2d 126 (1976). Accordingly, indebtedness provisions such as ours were generally given an expansive definition. Dillon writes: "What are debts? In defining these terms it has been declared that the language of the Constitution is exceedingly broad, and should not receive a narrow or strained construction...." Dillon § 193 at 349. When a local government pledged property as security for repayment of a debt, this was usually held to constitute the creation of indebtedness. Id. § 199.

In keeping with the intent of the framers, a broad interpretation of the debt limitation has long been favored in New Mexico. Regardless of whether an agency of government is bound in personam to pay a debt, a borrowing has been deemed to take place within the prohibition of Article IX, Section 10 of the Constitution when, by transfer of legal title and/or the payment of money, the agency of government obtains an equitable interest in property which is subject to forefeiture in the event future periodic payments are not made as agreed. See, e.g., Palmer v. City of Albuquerque, 19 N.M. 285, 142 P. 929 (1914). An agreement that commits the county to make payments out of general revenues in future fiscal years, without voter approval, violates the New Mexico Constitution even if that obligation is merely an "equitable or moral" duty, State ex rel. Capitol Addition Building Commission v. Connelly, 39 N.M. 312, 318, 46 P.2d 1097, 1100 (1935) (quoting Seward v. Bowers, 37 N.M. 385, 24 P.2d 253 (1933)), or a "contingent" duty, State Office Building Commission v. Trujillo, 46 N.M. 29, 45, 120 P.2d 434, 444 (1941) (quoting City of Santa Fe v. First National Bank, 41 N.M. 130, 138, 65 P.2d 857, 862 (1937)).

The appellees argue no unconstitutional debt is created by this lease because there is no legal obligation either to continue the lease from year to year or to purchase the facility. However, we are of the opinion that once the County accepted this lease, it would be obligated to continue making rental payments in order to protect a growing equitable interest in the facility, as well as to protect the County's interest in the title to County land.[1] This is the type of future economic commitment that requires the arrangement be approved by the voters.

---

1. The lease divides rental payments into "principal" and "interest" according to a twenty-year amortization schedule. At any time during the lease the County could exercise its purchase option by payment of the initial cost of construction ($3,100,000) less accrued payment of principal. Thus, the lease in question is significantly different from a lease

Additionally, consistent with our conclusion that the obligation in question falls within the intended broad interpretation of indebtedness, we find the lease-purchase agreement to be a "lease" in form only. If an option price is nominal or nonexistent, a purported lease may be treated as a sale. See Springer Corp. v. American Leasing Co., 80 N.M. 609, 611, 459 P.2d 135,137 (1969); Transamerica Leasing Corp. v. Bureau of Revenue, 80 N.M. 48, 53, 450 P.2d 934, 939 (Ct. App. 1969). In this case, the County acquires ownership of the facility simply by making the agreed rental payments over the twenty-year term; however, it loses all interest in the project if it exercises its termination rights or defaults. The only method by which the County may redeem its investment is by tendering the full purchase price of the facility, plus interest. Accordingly, each semi-annual "rental" payment represents more than just a present debt for the use of the facility for a six month period. The arrangement is in essence an installment-purchase agreement for the acquisition of a public building, with outside financing and payments spread over twenty years, and as such it requires voter approval.

Local governments have no authority under our Constitution to borrow money or issue bonds absent a delegation by the legislature of all or part of the legislature's plenary authority to create debts. See Board of Commrs. v. State, 43 N.M. 409, 411, 94 P.2d 515, 516 (1939). In the present context, the legislature has provided that counties may enter into lease-purchase agreements. NMSA 1978, 6–6–12. We recognize that county governments may have entered into lease-purchase agreements similar to the agreement under consideration here, in which the option purchase price is nominal or nonexistent, in reliance upon a 1976 Attorney General's Opinion which misconstrued the language of our decisions in *Connelly* and *Trujillo*. See AG Op. No. 20 (1976). For this reason, this ruling shall have modified prospective effect only. See Hicks v. State, 88 N.M. 588, 592–94, 544 P.2d 1153, 1157–59 (1975), as well as the dissent of Montoya, J., id. at 595–96, 544 P.2d at 1160–61, for a discussion of prospective versus modified prospective application of a new rule of law.

The order of the district court finding that the lease will not violate Article IX, Section 10 of the New Mexico Constitution, and granting summary judgment in favor of defendants-appellees, is reversed, and the case is remanded for action consistent with this opinion.

It is so ordered.

Dieck v. Unified School District of Antigo

477 N.W.2d 613 (Wis. 1991).

■ ABRAHAMSON, JUSTICE. . . .

---

purchase agreement where the option price is tied to the actual fair market value of the facility at the time the option is exercised. We do not accept the appellees' argument that the amortization schedule merely reflects an estimate of the fair market value of the jail facility as it depreciates over time. If the facility were adequately designed and maintained it would be unreasonable to assume that after two decades of use it would have a market value of zero.

.... The relevant facts are not in dispute. The plaintiffs, taxpayers residing within the boundaries of the Unified School District of Antigo, filed a class action suit seeking a declaratory judgment and injunctive relief against the Unified School District of Antigo and others. This suit challenged the District's authority to enter into a lease purchase agreement, executed on June 12, 1989, with the Antigo School Board Leasing Corporation, to finance the acquisition of land and the construction of a new high school. The Leasing Corporation is a chapter 181 not-for-profit corporation.

According to the lease purchase agreement, the Leasing Corporation (the lessor) will acquire the site, construct the new building, and hold title to the property. The District (the lessee), however, will act as the Leasing Corporation's agent to select the site and oversee the design and construction of the building. Under the lease purchase agreement the District may lease the building from the Leasing Corporation for twenty years, paying rent annually from annual appropriations.

The lease purchase agreement incorporates and approves the terms of a Mortgage and Indenture of Trust between the Leasing Corporation and the First Wisconsin Trust Company (the trustee). The District has no direct contractual relationship with the Trust Company. The Leasing Corporation has assigned its rights to rental payments to the Trust Company. Thus the District makes payments directly to the Trust Company, which maintains all accounts created under the lease purchase agreement.

If the District rents the school for the duration of the twenty-year lease period, it has the option to purchase the property for ten dollars. The Trust Company holds in escrow a deed from the Leasing Corporation to the District.

As we explained previously, the District has the right under the nonappropriation option to terminate the lease purchase agreement by electing not to appropriate funds for the following fiscal year's payment. If the District exercises this nonappropriation option it will not be obligated to make any future payments under the lease purchase agreement but forfeits its right to future use of the school building and all the monies that it has appropriated. No funds of the District are jeopardized beyond the current fiscal year.

The Leasing Corporation will acquire the $9,725,000 necessary to buy the site and construct the school from the sale of certificates of participation. These certificates entitle the registered owners to receive a portion of the rent the Trust Company receives from the District. The District has no direct contractual relationship with the certificate owners....

This lease purchase agreement, according to the plaintiffs, circumvents chapters 67 and 120, Stats. 1989–90, and contravenes the wishes of the electorate who, over the past 20 years, have rejected eight referenda for the issuance of general obligation bonds to fund school construction. The last vote occurred on September 13, 1988, when over 53 percent of the voters opposed the issuance of bonds.

II

We first address the plaintiffs' claim that the lease purchase agreement violates art. XI, secs. 3(2) and (3), of the Wisconsin Constitution. Article XI, secs. 3(2) and (3), limit the power of school districts to become indebted. Article XI, sec. 3(2), states:

(2) No county, city, town, village, school district, sewerage district or other municipal corporation may become indebted in an amount that exceeds an allowable percentage of the taxable property located therein equalized for state purposes as provided by the legislature. In all cases the allowable percentage shall be 5 percent except as specified in pars. (a) and (b)....

Section 3(3) requires a school district that incurs indebtedness under art. XI, sec. 3(2), to collect a direct annual tax sufficient to pay the interest on the debt as it falls due and also to pay and discharge the principal of the debt within 20 years from the time the debt was contracted. Article XI, sec. 3(3), states:

(3) Any county, city, town, village, school district, sewerage district or other municipal corporation incurring any indebtedness under sub. (2) shall, before or at the time of doing so, provide for the collection of a direct annual tax sufficient to pay the interest on such debt as it falls due, and also to pay and discharge the principal thereof within 20 years from the time of contracting the same.

At issue in this case is whether, by its execution of the lease purchase agreement with a nonappropriation option, the District will become indebted or incur any indebtedness, as those words are used in art. XI, secs. 3(2) and (3). If the District becomes indebted or incurs indebtedness under art. XI, secs. 3(2) and (3), by executing the lease purchase agreement, it violates art. XI, sec. 3(3), because the District has failed to provide for a direct annual tax sufficient to pay the interest on such debt and to pay and discharge the principal within 20 years. If the District does not become indebted or incur indebtedness under art. XI, secs. 3(2) and (3), by executing the lease purchase agreement, then the District need not comply with the tax levy provisions of art. XI, sec. 3(3), and the lease purchase agreement is constitutional.

The history of the Wisconsin constitutional provisions concerning municipal debt manifests both an abhorrence of public debt and a willingness to increase the debt limit, particularly for school purposes. The purpose of art. XI, secs. 3(2) and (3), is to prevent the creation of excessive municipal debt and the consequent burdensome taxation. The constitutional restrictions seek to assure that the burden of paying off the debt is imposed upon those who contracted the obligations. The court has said that "the purpose of the constitutional provision was to limit the burden which those who contract obligations may place upon posterity." School District No. 6 v. Marine National Exchange Bank, 9 Wis. 2d 400, 407, 101 N.W.2d 112 (1960).

The court has interpreted the phrases "become indebted" and "incurring any indebtedness" in art. XI, secs. 3(2) and (3), according to the purposes underlying the constitutional provisions. The court has interpreted the word "indebtedness" as referring to a voluntary and absolute undertaking to pay a sum certain. No indebtedness exists if the municipal body may avoid its obligation or if conditions precedent exist. Indebtedness under this constitutional provision thus means, according to our cases, that the municipal body has assumed "legally enforceable obligations." State ex rel. La Follette v. Reuter, 33 Wis. 2d 384, 398, 407, 147 N.W.2d 304 (1967); State ex rel. Thomson v. Giessel, 265 Wis. 185, 199, 60 N.W.2d 873 (1953) (quoting State ex rel. Wisconsin Dev. Auth. v. Dammann, 228 Wis. 147, 197, 280 N.W. 698 (1938)). The undertaking must be enforceable by the creditor against the municipal body or its assets.

The test established in our cases for indebtedness in art. XI, secs. 3(2) and (3), is not whether the municipal body unit will probably pay or whether the municipal body would be foolish not to pay. The test is whether the municipal body is under an obligation to pay and the creditor has a right to enforce payment against the municipal body or its assets. No indebtedness is incurred "where payments are to be made solely at the government's option." State ex rel. Thomson v. Giessel, 271 Wis. 15, 40, 72 N.W.2d 577 (1955). When the governmental unit has no binding obligation to pay rent for the full term of the lease, it has not incurred any indebtedness under art. XI, secs. 3(2) and (3). *Giessel*, supra 271 Wis. at 37, 72 N.W.2d 577.

Thus according to our cases, if a municipal body can acquire property without incurring indebtedness, that is, without incurring legally enforceable obligations, neither the spirit nor the letter of the constitution has been violated. "For it must be kept in mind that the purpose of a debt limitation is not to prevent the municipality from acquiring buildings or public works, but to place a limitation on the extent to which it may pledge its credit and hence burden the taxpayers." *Giessel*, supra 271 Wis. at 36, 72 N.W.2d 577 (quoting 71 A.L.R. 1326 (1931)). The court of appeals captured the theme of the cases when it stated that the constitutional restrictions in art. XI, secs. 3(2) and (3) "guard against indebtedness, not creative financing." *Dieck*, supra 157 Wis. 2d at 143, 458 N.W.2d 565. Applying this longstanding interpretation of art. XI, secs. 3(2) and (3), to the lease purchase agreement with a nonappropriation option in this case leads to one conclusion: The District has not incurred any indebtedness under art. XI, sec. 3(2).

The District can terminate the lease purchase agreement at any time by refusing to appropriate funds to meet the annual rental payment. The nonappropriation option allows the District to pay rent solely at its own option, even though the District may envision leasing the building for twenty years and then exercising its option to purchase. Payments under the lease purchase agreement are made solely from current year budget expenditures. Future rental payments are conditioned on the District's voting future appropriations. Certificate holders have no recourse against the District for rental payments in future years. Applying *Giessel*, supra 271 Wis. at 37, 72 N.W.2d 577, we must conclude that "since there is no binding obligation ... to pay rent for the full terms of the lease, it is inconceivable that a debt is incurred. . . ."

Our conclusion that this lease purchase agreement with the nonappropriation option does not create indebtedness under art. XI, sec. 3(2), effectuates the purpose and maintains the integrity of the constitutional debt limitations. A nonappropriation option preserves for each successive legislative body the responsibility of reviewing the wisdom of the lease and of deciding whether to continue it and shield taxpayers from burgeoning debt. Future generations are not burdened by past decisions. While their decisions are not binding on us, most other state courts considering the constitutionality of lease purchase agreements with nonappropriation clauses have upheld the transactions as not being debt under their constitutions.

The plaintiffs advance arguments to convince the court that this case differs from prior cases in which the court held the transactions constitutional. We are not persuaded by plaintiffs' arguments. The plaintiffs argue first that this lease purchase agreement is a subterfuge designed by the District to avoid compliance with the Wisconsin Constitution. The plaintiffs contend that the lease purchase agreement is a disguised installment purchase plan with the construction costs amortized over the twenty-year lease period and thus creates indebtedness under art. XI, secs. 3(2) and (3).

The court has faced similar substance-over-form arguments in previous cases. In response to these arguments the court has stated that it is not an illegal evasion of the constitution "to accomplish a desired result, lawful in itself, by finding a legal way to do it." *Giessel*, supra 271 Wis. at 42, 72 N.W.2d 577 (citation omitted). Leasing a new school building is the desired, lawful objective in this case. The issue is whether the District has found a legal way to accomplish this lawful objective. We conclude it has. . . .

. . . The essence of constitutional indebtedness is that the governmental unit has an absolute obligation to make future payments. In this case the District has the option to stop rental payments, cancel the lease purchase agreement, and not acquire title to the property. Even though the District's present intention is to make all the payments, and perhaps the District would be wise to do so, the lease purchase agreement will not result in the District's having any legally binding obligations.

We conclude that the District has found a legal way to accomplish its lawful objective. This argument of the plaintiffs fails. . . .

For the reasons set forth, we conclude that when the District entered into the lease purchase agreement with the nonappropriation clause it did not incur indebtedness under art. XI, secs. 3(2) and (3).

NOTES

1. Do the transactions in *Montano* and *Dieck* have different or similar structures? In each, a governmental entity (the county; the school district) leases a building for a public facility. In each, the facility is constructed by another entity (a private contractor) and leased to the government. In each, the contractual arrangements contain a "nonappropriation clause" that permits the government to avoid its payment obligations by failing to appropriate sufficient funds to make lease payments. In each, the case turns on whether the debt incurred by the other entity to construct the facility can be attributed to the government. What justifies the different results? Or is the difference between the cases simply one of judicial style, that is, the willingness of the New Mexico Supreme Court to transcend the language of the constitutional provision and apply its purposes to somewhat unorthodox transactions versus the Wisconsin Supreme Court's desire to adhere closely to the formal language of the constitution?

The practice of including a nonappropriation clause in a lease-purchase agreement in order to avoid debt limitations has met with mixed success. Most courts have shared the Wisconsin court's view that the clause effectively removes any legal obligation to make payments over the full lease term, and hence takes the lease outside of the scope of constitutional debt. See, e.g., Colleton County Taxpayers Ass'n v. School Dist. of Colleton County, 638 S.E.2d 685 (S.C. 2006); Moschenross v. St. Louis County, 188 S.W.3d 13 (Mo. Ct. App. 2006) ("The agreement in the present case was merely to request annual appropriations for repayment of the bonds, subject to the approval of the county council. Therefore, the performance of the contract depends upon action by the county council before any unconditional indebtedness arises. This is distinguishable from an absolute agreement to incur debt, which has been determined to violate the debt-limitation provisions of Article VI, section 26 of the constitution."); Fults v. City of Coralville, 666 N.W.2d 548 (Ia. 2003). In other cases, however, courts have adopted the New Mexico court's position that, as a practical matter, the locality will necessarily make payments throughout the lease term, so that, pragmatically speaking, the clause is a nullity. Hence, the contractual obligation to make payments should be treated as legally binding with the result that it constitutes debt. See, e.g., Brown v. City of Stuttgart, 847 S.W.2d 710 (Ark. 1993).

In Lonegan v. State, 809 A.2d 91 (N.J. 2002), the New Jersey Supreme Court scheduled further arguments on the state's use of nonappropriation debt after deciding a challenge to the use of such financing to fund renovation of the state's urban schools. The court upheld nonappropriation financing for schools because it had previously required the legislature to fulfill constitutional requirements of equalizing school systems in urban and nonurban districts. But the legislature had authorized nonappropriation debt in a much wider range of situations. A separate opinion noted that in 2001 the state had outstanding $3.5 billion in general obligation debt, but $10.8 billion of nonappropriation debt, and that the bond markets treated the two kinds of obligation as essentially equivalent, notwithstanding the absence of a legal obligation to pay the latter. After the rehearing, however, a majority of the court upheld the use of nonappropriation debt on the grounds that "the unambiguous and clear language" of the state constitution made the existence of debt contingent only on whether the state faced a legal obligation to make payments. Lonegan v. State, 819 A.2d 395 (N.J. 2003). Why did the court schedule the rehearing if the language was so clear?

How realistic is the concern that seems to underlie the court's decision in *Montano*, that is, the possibility that a debtor jurisdiction will continue to make discretionary payments even if it no longer needs the financed facility? In State ex rel. Charleston Building Commission v. Dial, 479 S.E.2d 695 (W. Va. 1996), the court upheld a financing arrangement for a public building, in part because of a non-appropriation clause. Amici who opposed the plan contended that the state would be unwilling to terminate payments even if the project proved unnecessary. The court's opinion includes the following footnote:

> Amici Curiae describe, in detail, a similar lease-purchase agreement whereby the State, as lessee, obtained office space at the Morris Square building for the Workers' Compensation Division. After leasing the building for eight years of the twenty-year lease term, the State seemingly vacated the premises due to the building's deterioration. Owing approximately one million dollars in rental payments under the remaining, unexpired term of the lease, the State decided not to terminate the agreement, apparently fearing such cancellation would negatively impact its national bond rating. Consequently, Amici Curiae direct the Court's attention to this scenario in support of its position that the State should not be permitted to enter into the proposed lease-purchase agreement with the Commission.

479 S.E.2d at 710n.18.The court proceeded to uphold the arrangement without further comment on its practical effect.

Note that in both *Montano* and *Dieck*, the lease-purchase arrangements were entered into after the government failed to obtain voter approval for general obligation financing of the project. Should the fact that the voters have already indicated that they do not want to pay for these projects enter into the determination of whether the funding arrangements constitute debt? Recall Madison's admonition in Federalist No. 10 that the function of representatives is to "refine," not simply to reflect, the views of their constituents. The proposed project in *Montano* was a jail; in *Dieck* it was a school. Is there reason to believe that voters' views needed more "refinement" in one case than the other? Up to this point, one concern with the use of debt has been tendencies for overuse because those who favor a project are likely to work for its adoption, while those who oppose it have diffuse, small interests and are unlikely to work against it. Does that mean that where projects are voted down, there should be a presumption that the project served no net social benefit? Is there more reason to believe this conclusion in either *Montano* or *Dieck*? See Clayton P. Gillette, Direct Democracy and Debt, 13 J. Contemp. Legal Issues 365 (2004).

2. The New Mexico court's concern with the practical implications of the financial arrangement has an analogue in bonds that are supported by what has become known as a "moral obligation."

> Under the typical moral obligation procedure, the issuer, usually a public authority, is statutorily enabled to issue revenue bonds and use the proceeds to

> construct projects that the authority is permitted to finance. Simultaneously, the issuer creates a capital reserve fund, into which are deposited bond proceeds or grants from the state and the use of which is restricted to payment of principal and interest on bonds. The capital reserve fund is intended to be maintained at a level that ensures an adequate sum will be available to pay debt service on the bonds in forthcoming years. Should the fund fall below that point, an official of the state—typically the governor—is authorized or required to request the legislature to appropriate a sum of money sufficient to replenish the fund. The legislature, however, is specifically exempted from any legal obligation to comply with the request. In effect, the state recognizes that it has no legal obligation to aid the issuer, but acknowledges its "moral obligation" to do so.

Robert S. Amdursky & Clayton P. Gillette, Municipal Debt Finance Law: Theory and Practice 201 (1992). Most states have held that a state's "moral" commitment to appropriate funds necessary to pay debt service on outstanding bonds does not transform the bonds into "debt" since no legal obligation to pay the bonds exists. See In re Interrogatories by Colorado State Senate, 566 P.2d 350 (Colo. 1977); California Housing Finance Agency v. Elliott, 551 P.2d 1193 (Cal. 1976); Massachusetts Housing Finance Agency v. New England Merchants National Bank of Boston, 249 N.E.2d 599 (Mass. 1969); Wein v. City of New York, 331 N.E.2d 514 (N.Y. 1975). In Witzenberger v. State ex rel. Wyoming Community Development Authority, 575 P.2d 1100 (Wyo. 1978), however, the court took a more skeptical view of the practice. The state had enacted a statute establishing the Wyoming Community Development Authority. The Authority was to issue revenue bonds that were secured in part by state funds. Among the challenged provisions was an authorization for the legislature, within its discretion, to appropriate and pay to the Authority a sufficient amount to pay principal and interest due to the Authority's bondholders. The court concluded that such discretion created a debt that fell within the election requirement of art. XVI, § 2:

> The expression on the bonds and in the Act that the bonds are "not an indebtedness of the state" does not reflect their true status. The other compelling provisions of the Act contradict and overwhelm such a conclusion. Any discretion of the legislature has been lost in the shuffle.
>
> The provisions of the Act, creating what is referred to as a "moral obligation" are misleading to those of the public who would invest their money. If they were not intended as an attraction, a sales gimmick, and if they had no significance, there would be no reason for their existence as a part of the Act. We question the ethics of a government utilizing such a merchandising technique. Principles of justice and honesty fundamentally apply to individuals, municipalities, states and the Nation alike, and should be applied alike....
>
> Furthermore, it is an intrusion on the spirit of the Wyoming Constitution. A court will not ignore the general spirit of the Constitution or its jurisdiction. Schaefer v. Thomson, D.C. Wyo., 1964, 240 F.Supp. 247. Section 2, Article XVI, prohibits the legislature from in "any manner" binding its successors. The moral obligation provision, § 9–839(d), is contrary to the spirit of 2 and is a nullity in that it does in a "manner" attempt to impose some pressure, by furnishing the procedure to do so, and provide a lever for others to exert

> pressure upon some future legislature of the state to make payment on a debt it has authorized its own legislatively-constructed instrumentality to create and for which it attempts to impose future responsibility.

575 P.2d 1129. Why is a statement of moral obligation necessary? Couldn't a state always intervene to assist one of its political subdivisions in fiscal distress? If so, what additional assurance does the bondholder receive from an explicit statement to that effect in the documents underlying the bond issue? See Robert S. Amdursky & Clayton P. Gillette, Municipal Debt Finance Law: Theory and Practice 4.10 (1992); Janice C. Griffith, "Moral Obligation" Bonds: Illusion or Security?, 8 Urb. Law. 54 (1976).

NOTE ON PUBLIC AUTHORITIES

One tool that state and local governments have utilized to circumvent debt limitations has been the creation of a separate entity that incurs debt to construct capital projects or perform other functions that might otherwise be performed by the state or locality. If the debt incurred by that entity is not attributed to the government that created it, states and local governments can effectively increase their borrowing authority notwithstanding debt limits. In one popular example, states created "building authorities" to borrow money and construct office buildings that were then nominally leased to the state to house governmental offices. Essentially, these authorities serve as conduits for transferring payments from the general government that uses the facilities to bondholders who provide the funds with which the facilities are constructed. Courts have varied on the question of whether these "building authorities" had a separate existence from the state or local government that created them. See C. Robert Morris, Jr., Evading Debt Limitations with Public Building Authorities: The Costly Subversion of State Constitutions, 68 Yale L.J. 234 (1958); Jon Magnusson, Lease–Financing by Municipal Corporations as a Way Around Debt Limitations, 25 Geo. Wash. L. Rev. 377 (1957). Although upheld in some jurisdictions, see, e.g., Clayton County Airport Authority v. State, 453 S.E.2d 8 (Ga. 1995), they have proven unpopular with other courts. The Oregon Supreme Court, confronted with a plan to have a building authority issue bonds, payable from state revenues, and to construct state offices with bond proceeds, but to exclude the bonds from state debt, denounced the scheme as an attempt to create a "gutless intermediary" that " 'would fool only a lawyer.' " In the Matter of the Constitutionality of Chapter 280, Oregon Laws, 1975, 554 P.2d 126, 131 (Or. 1976).

Other than building authorities, states and local governments have employed the public authority structure to fund activities such as sports stadiums, multi-family housing, and educational finance. Judicial responses to the use of public authorities to circumvent debt limits tend to uphold the "separate entity" theory. In Train Unlimited Corp. v. Iowa Ry. Finance Auth., 362 N.W.2d 489 (Iowa 1985), the state had created an authority to increase railway lines and facilities in the state. The enabling legislation provided that the Authority's obligations were not to be a debt or liability of the state. Nevertheless, those obligations were payable from taxes imposed by the state and unrelated to the Authority's operations. The court concluded that the Authority's obligations were not debt of the state for purposes of the constitutional limitation because any obligations owed to bondholders were those of "an autonomous public authority," and the general treasury of the state was unavailable to the Authority's bondholders. That the state had earmarked for the Authority revenues that would otherwise have been available to the state was apparently irrelevant. See also City of San Diego v. Rider, 55 Cal.Rptr.2d 422 (Cal. App. 1996); Schulz v. State, 639 N.E.2d 1140 (N.Y. 1994), cert. denied, 513 U.S. 1127 (1995). Courts have also upheld arrangements in which general governments lease facilities funded by an authority if the lease payments are "subject to appropriation." See, e.g., Enourato v. New Jersey Bldg. Auth., 448 A.2d 449 (N.J.1982).

Public authorities raise a variety of issues. For present purposes, the most important issue involves the use of authorities to circumvent debt limitations. If debt incurred by an authority is not attributed to the state or political subdivisions in which it operates, then residents within its jurisdiction will be required to pay the debt of overlapping jurisdictions, the general purpose jurisdiction and the special authority. This arguably exposes those residents to greater financial obligations than debt limitations were intended to permit. Perhaps the existence of such entities can nevertheless be justified as a means of financing the greater involvement of government with costly infrastructure than may have been anticipated at the time that debt limitations were placed in state constitutions. See, e.g., Comment, An Analysis of Authorities: Traditional and Multicounty, 71 Mich. L. Rev. 1376 (1973).

Apart from the issue of whether states use public authorities to circumvent debt limitations, there is significant debate about whether these entities can more efficiently provide public goods than the states or political subdivisions that create them. States and political subdivisions may use authorities to perform particular functions such as highway construction, operation of ports, or construction and maintenance of sewer or water plants. These authorities are frequently useful because they perform functions that cross jurisdictional lines and thus cannot readily be delegated to a single municipality. For instance, a port authority or transportation authority may be able to conduct activities that involve multiple jurisdictions without requiring costly negotiations among the affected localities. Authorities, therefore, may develop expertise in a particular area that allows more efficient delivery of the services they provide. In addition, the fact that public authorities only provide a single service arguably makes them more susceptible to monitoring than general purpose municipalities. Arguably it is easier to supervise public officials who only have one objective, e.g., operation of a highway or public zoo, than it is to supervise public officials who have many tasks, some of which conflict, e.g., operate a school system, a fire department, and a public works department.

Nevertheless, one of the major criticisms of public authorities involves their lack of accountability. See, e.g., Annmarie Hauck Walsh, The Public's

Business (1978); Robert H. Bowmar, The Anachronism Called Debt Limitations, 52 Iowa L. Rev. 863 (1957). Officials of public authorities tend to be appointed rather than elected. In theory, this should not matter too much, because public authorities typically lack taxing power. In order to obtain funds necessary to construct projects, they must rely on user fees charged for the services they render and must retain access to capital markets in order to fund capital projects. As we saw in the discussion of user fees, payers may be more attentive to a fee for a service than they are to taxes that are used for multiple services. Thus, dependence on user fees arguably make public authorities accountable to the users of the projects the authorities finance. The need to access capital markets requires that authorities be able to survive the scrutiny of bond rating agencies, underwriters, and sophisticated investors in municipal bonds. The very fact that the authority has a single function may render its financial situation and the success of its operations far more transparent than those of a general purpose municipality.

Practice, however, may deviate from theory. For reasons that should now be familiar, users of facilities are unlikely to monitor the fees they are charged with great care. This is especially true with respect to facilities that are used by transients, such as toll bridges, though commuters who use mass transit facilities financed by authorities may be sufficiently interested in the fees they are charged that they are attentive to the way that an authority conducts it business. While those who underwrite or who purchase bonds issued by authorities have incentives to ensure their efficient operation, the interests of the investment community do not necessarily coincide with those of the customers whom the authority is supposed to serve. For instance, investors may prefer that the risk of their investments be minimized, that "safe" projects be favored, and that the issuing authority maintain a high level of flexibility to ensure continued access to the bond market. While economic theory suggests that investors will be neutral about the level of risk as long as it is properly reflected in the interest rate they are paid, very risky projects, such as low-income housing, may be difficult to market under any circumstances. Consequently, issuers must choose projects or repayment devices that make bonds more marketable by financing projects that are more likely to be self-sustaining or that are less likely to default. Yet the high risk of low-income housing—and consequent reluctance of the private market to invest in such projects—may have been precisely why the issuance of tax-exempt bonds are considered appropriate. Thus, those who make decisions for the authority may be responsive to a group whose concerns are inconsistent with those that led to the authority's creation. See Alberta M. Sbragia, Debt Wish 135–162 (1996); Clayton P. Gillette, Fiscal Federalism and the Use of Municipal Bond Proceeds, 58 N.Y.U. L. Rev. 1030, 1065–1066 (1983); William J. Quirk & Leon E. Wein, A Short Constitutional History of Entities Commonly Known as Authorities, 56 Cornell L. Rev. 521 (1971).

Finally, the efficiency claim about public authorities must also confront the fact that authorities add to the fragmentation of local governments. It is unclear whether that fragmentation interferes with efficient operations, by creating multiple governments that must allocate responsibilities and that may sometimes provide overlapping services, or increases efficiency, by creating competition and assigning separate tasks to different governmental units.

F. PRIVATIZATION

To this point, we have assumed in this course that local government is both the provider and the producer of local public goods that are offered to residents. That is, local government not only ensures that these goods are provided, but does so through the use of its own employees. Local government not only makes garbage collection available, for instance, but does so through a Department of Sanitation. Local government, of course, does not fully produce all the services it provides; it does not, for instance, manufacture the garbage trucks used by the Department of Sanitation. Instead, it purchases those goods from private producers, either by making purchases in the marketplace or by contracting with a manufacturer for a unique good. But if government can compensate for market failure by contracting with private firms to provide equipment, then perhaps it can also contract with private firms to provide personnel who perform the service. Indeed, the possibility that private firms will arise to contract with government suggests that groups of individuals may be able to contract without governmental intervention. In short, once we realize that private provision is available, the question arises as to whether government is necessary or only useful in overcoming the collective action problem.

Even if government is unnecessary to provide a service, privatization may be debatable on other grounds. If we believe that government, especially local government, provides a means of creating community or ensures access to services, or if we believe that privatization would create conflict among members of the community with respect to the allocation of public goods, then we might desire government provision, even if private supply were more efficient. Alternatively, we might support one form of privatization over another, as the term "privatization" encompasses an array of governmental involvements. For instance, government may play a significant role in garbage collection by selecting a private provider of that service. This process of contracting out would avoid the need for individual residents to make their own collection arrangements. Or, government could withdraw from the function entirely, perhaps selling assets previously used by the government to private firms that fill the gap. This form of privatization, evident where individual residents make their own arrangements for garbage collection, has been advocated for certain federal operations, such as Amtrak, low-income housing, and the Postal Service. See Privatization: Toward More Effective Government, Report of the President's Commission on Privatization (1988).

Finally, some privatization efforts take the form of expanding consumer choice to include both private and public providers of the same good. Of course, education has long fallen into this category, with public and private schools competing for students and teachers. Recent efforts to increase the supply of educational providers have included issuing vouchers that could be redeemed at either a public or private educational institution and deregulating private entities that compete with public ones. We have already seen some examples of how privatized providers of public goods can expand the range and level of services available to some residents of a community. Homeowners associations that provide public goods to their residents, such as security, road maintenance, and recreation, essentially serve as private providers of public goods that would otherwise be provided to those residents by the local government. Business improvement districts similarly constitute private providers of public goods traditionally associated with local government. Of course, whether we want to embrace that expanded choice may depend on whether we believe that those who select the private alternative impose significant costs on those who either do not or cannot. Our reaction to private education, for instance, may depend on whether we believe private schools will draw the most desirable students from the public schools. (Of course, we might think that the possibility of such a result will stimulate competition that ultimately improves *all* schools.) Similarly, we may fear that residents of homeowners associations who can afford their own police protection will be less supportive of publicly funded police protection in the rest of the locality. See, in this regard, Note on Business Improvement Districts at pages 570–572 supra.

Konno v. County of Hawai'i

937 P.2d 397 (Hawaii 1997).

■ RAMIL, JUSTICE.

The central issue addressed in these cases is the privatization of public services. The United Public Workers and its officers (collectively the UPW) challenge the validity of a contract entered into by the County of Hawai'i (the County) to privatize the operation of a landfill at Pu'uanahulu on the island of Hawai'i. In No. 18203, the UPW argues that the County violated civil service laws and merit principles by privatizing the landfill worker positions in question. In No. 18236, the UPW argues that the County violated collective bargaining laws by privatizing without participating in mandatory negotiations with the UPW. For the reasons discussed below, we hold that the County violated civil service laws and merit principles but did not violate collective bargaining laws. The contract between the County and Waste Management of Hawai'i, Inc. (WMI) is void as a violation of public policy to the extent that it provides for the private operation of the Pu'uanahulu landfill....

I. Facts

Prior to the events at issue in this opinion, the County owned and operated two landfills on the island of Hawai'i: one in Kealakehe, Kona, and the other in Hilo. The Department of Public Works employed thirty-eight workers, consisting of equipment operators, landfill attendants, and transfer station attendants, to operate the landfills. These workers were traditionally recruited and employed through the merit system pursuant to civil service laws. The UPW is a labor union and has long been the exclusive representative of landfill workers in the state of Hawai'i.

In 1991, Mayor Lorraine Inouye began to consider the possibility of having a private contractor construct and operate a new landfill at Pu'uanahulu. The new landfill would be a replacement for the Kealakehe landfill, which had reached capacity and was plagued by subterranean fires. Another concern was that the Environmental Protection Agency (EPA) had issued new federal regulations on solid waste management that contained strict standards for landfill construction. Mayor Inouye met with UPW officials to discuss the privatization proposal. The UPW did not oppose the private construction of the new landfill but did strenuously object to the private operation of the landfill. In the summer of 1992, Mayor Inouye agreed not to privatize the operation of the landfill.

Subsequent to her decision not to privatize the landfill, Mayor Inouye won the endorsement of the UPW in the 1992 primary election. This was an extremely close race, and Mayor Inouye lost to Stephen Yamashiro by a thin margin. Shortly after assuming office in December 1992, Mayor Yamashiro announced that the County would be privatizing not only the construction of the Pu'uanahulu landfill, but its operation as well. In March 1993, bids were received from WMI and Browning Ferris Industries. On March 25, 1993, County officials informed WMI that the County intended to award WMI the contract....

A contract with WMI, dated April 21, 1993, was executed by Mayor Yamashiro on April 30, 1993. Under the terms of the contract, WMI assumed responsibility for the construction, operation, and closure of the new landfill. The County was to pay WMI based on the amount of waste received. WMI also agreed to assume liability for claims arising from the landfill and to carry environmental and liability insurance....

Ten workers at the Kealakehe landfill were directly affected by the County's privatization efforts. Workers at Kealakehe were given the option of relinquishing their civil service status and working for WMI at Pu'uanahulu or being reassigned to other civil service positions. The actual work performed by the workers at the new landfill is virtually identical to the work performed at the old landfill. The only difference is that equipment operators who formerly spent half their time trucking and half bulldozing waste now spend their entire time trucking waste....

On May 6, 1993, the UPW filed a complaint in the Third Circuit Court, claiming, inter alia, that the County had violated constitutionally mandated merit principles and civil service statutes. The complaint requested damages, as well as declaratory and injunctive relief. WMI was subsequently allowed to intervene in the action....

II. DISCUSSION

1. Background Information.

Before addressing the County's privatization effort in the present dispute, useful background information can be obtained by examining the policies behind privatization, the policies behind the civil service, and the approaches taken by other states.

The term "privatization" is a broad term that has been used to describe a wide range of activity. See generally Ronald A. Cass, Privatization: Politics, Law, and Theory, 71 Marq. L. Rev. 449, 451 (1988). "Privatization refers to the shift from government provision of functions and services to provision by the private sector." George L. Priest, Introduction: The Aims of Privatization, 6 Yale L. & Pol'y Rev. 1, 1 (1988). In countries other than the United States, privatization usually refers to the selling of government owned and operated businesses to private enterprise. Cass, supra, at 450. However, another type of privatization, which is at issue in the present dispute, is known as "contracting out." This activity can be defined as "the transfer by governmental entities of responsibility for the performance of desired functions, mostly of a personal service (i.e., administrative) nature, to private institutions" or "the replacement of members of [a] bargaining unit by the employees of an independent contractor performing the same work under similar conditions of employment." Timothy P. Dowling, Note, Civil Service Restrictions on Contracting Out by State Agencies, 55 Wash. L. Rev. 419, 419 n.3 (1980).

The purported policy behind privatization is to increase governmental efficiency. Id. at 425–426. Services can often be provided more efficiently by private entities than by civil servants. Id. The productivity of civil servants can be enhanced in that the threat of privatization serves as an incentive to improve performance. Id. at 426. Privatization may also give public employers increased leverage in labor negotiations, thus avoiding costly labor disputes. Id.

In contrast to privatization, the purpose of the civil service is not just to foster efficiency but to implement other policies as well. Craig Becker, With Whose Hands: Privatization, Public Employment, and Democracy, 6 Yale L. & Pol'y Rev. 88, 94–99 (1988). One obvious policy is the elimination of the "spoils system," which awarded jobs based on political loyalty. Id. at 95. The civil service also embodies positive principles of public administration such as openness, merit, and independence. Id. at 95–96. Openness is served through public announcement of job vacancies, clear articulation of qualifications, open application to all persons, and selection according to objective criteria. Id. at 96. Merit is served through a system of competitive examinations and qualification standards aimed at identifying competent candidates. Id. Independence is served through the job security provided by civil service laws; because civil servants can be terminated only for just cause, they are more likely to speak out against unlawful activities occurring in their agencies. Id. at 98. Justice William O. Douglas called the civil service system " 'the one great political invention' of nineteenth century democracy." United Public Workers v. Mitchell, 330 U.S. 75, 121, 67 S.Ct.

556, 580, 91 L.Ed. 754 (1947) (Douglas, J., dissenting in part) (quoting G. Wallas, Human Nature in Politics 263 (2d ed.)).

Insofar as a job position that is privatized is, by definition, removed from the civil service system, there is a tension between privatization and the civil service. There are three basic approaches that other states have taken in dealing with this tension. See Becker, supra, at 99–103. The first approach has been called the "nature of the services" test. According to this approach, services that have been "customarily and historically provided by civil servants" cannot be privatized, absent a showing that civil servants cannot provide those services. Washington Fed'n of State Employees, AFL–CIO v. Spokane Community College, 90 Wash. 2d 698, 585 P.2d 474, 477 (1978) (en banc). In *Spokane*, a state community college attempted to contract out custodial services for a new administration building. Id. 585 P.2d at 476. Custodial services had been historically provided by civil service employees of the college. Id. Despite the fact that the contract would have reduced the cost of custodial services substantially, the Washington Supreme Court held that the contract violated state civil service statutes. Id. The court noted that privatization contravenes the basic policy and purpose of the civil service statutes and held the contract to be void. Id. 585 P.2d at 476–477....

The second approach is known as the "functional inquiry" test. Under this test, the focus shifts from the type of services to be performed to the particular state program or function involved. New state programs performing new functions are not constrained by civil service laws. Thus, new programs may contract out services even if those services are of a type that can be performed by civil servants. See Department of Transp. v. Chavez, 7 Cal. App. 4th 407, 9 Cal. Rptr. 2d 176 (1992); California State Employees' Ass'n v. Williams, 7 Cal. App. 3d 390, 86 Cal. Rptr. 305, reh'g denied, 86 Cal. Rptr. 312 (Cal. Ct. App. 1970).

The third approach can be called the "bad faith" test. Under this approach, privatization violates civil service laws only if the employer acts in "bad faith" or with intent to circumvent the civil service laws. This test reduces the protection of civil service laws to its narrowest degree. Under this approach, a public employer whose motive is economic efficiency is generally considered to act in "good faith." However, efficiency is almost always the justification given for privatization. Therefore, civil service laws are effective against privatization only in the rare instances in which there is actual proof of improper intent/motive....

2. Analysis

... On appeal, the UPW argues that the circuit court erred in granting summary judgment because: (1) the County violated constitutionally mandated merit principles in privatizing the Pu'uanahulu landfill; (2) the County violated civil service statutes in privatizing the landfill; and (3) Mayor Yamashiro's alleged political motivation behind his privatization decision was a genuine issue of material fact.

Regarding constitutionally mandated merit principles, article XVI, section 1 of the Hawai'i Constitution provides: "The employment of persons in the civil service, as defined by law, of or under the State, shall be governed by the merit principle." By its express terms, this provision simply means that the civil service, however defined, is to be governed by merit principles. It does *not* define the precise scope of the civil service, i.e., the particular job positions that are within the civil service. Instead, article XVI, section 1 expressly refers to other sources for a definition of "civil service." It states: "civil service, *as defined by law*...." (Emphasis added.) Thus, in order to determine the scope of the term "civil service," we must examine statutory law and case law. For these reasons, we hold that the Hawai'i Constitution does not establish an independently enforceable right to the protection of merit principles.

In defining "civil service," the statute most relevant is HRS § 76–77:

> **Civil service and exemptions**. The civil service to which this part applies comprises all positions in the public service of each county, now existing or hereafter established, and embraces all personal services performed for each county, except the following:....
>
> (7) Positions filled by persons employed by contract where the personnel director has certified and where the certification has received the approval of the commission that the service is special or unique, is essential to the public interest, and that because of the circumstances surrounding its fulfillment, personnel to perform the service cannot be recruited through normal civil service procedures; provided that no contract pursuant to this paragraph shall be for any period exceeding one year;....
>
> (10) Positions specifically exempted from this part by any other state statutes[.]

HRS § 76–77 (1993).

In interpreting statutes, this court has long held that

> the fundamental starting point is the language of the statute itself. The interpretation of a statute is a question of law which this court reviews *de novo*. Moreover, where the language of the statute is plain and unambiguous, our only duty is to give effect to its plain and obvious meaning. When construing a statute, our foremost obligation is to ascertain and give effect to the intention of the legislature, which is to be obtained primarily from the language contained in the statute itself. And we must read statutory language in the context of the entire statute and construe it in a manner consistent with its purpose.
>
> When there is doubt, doubleness of meaning, or indistinctiveness or uncertainty of an expression used in a statute, an ambiguity exists. Put differently, a statute is ambiguous if it is capable of being understood by reasonably well-informed people in two or more different senses.
>
> In construing an ambiguous statute, the meaning of the ambiguous words may be sought by examining the context, with which the ambiguous words, phrases, and sentences may be compared, in order to ascertain their true meaning. Moreover, the courts may resort to extrinsic aids in determining the legislative intent. One avenue is the use of legislative history as an interpretive tool.

State v. Toyomura, 80 Hawai'i 8, 18–19, 904 P.2d 893, 903–904 (1995) (quoting Housing Finance & Dev. Corp. v. Castle, 79 Hawai'i 64, 76–77, 898 P.2d 576, 588–589 (1995)) (internal quotation marks, citations, ellipses, and brackets omitted). Furthermore, "[s]tatutory construction dictates that an interpreting court should not fashion a construction of statutory text that effectively renders the statute a nullity or creates an absurd or unjust result." Dines v. Pacific Ins. Co., Ltd., 78 Hawai'i 325, 337, 893 P.2d 176, 188 (1995) (Ramil, J., dissenting) (citing Richardson v. City & County of Honolulu, 76 Hawai'i 46, 60, 868 P.2d 1193, 1207, reconsideration denied, 76 Hawai'i 247, 871 P.2d 795 (1994)).

HRS § 76–77 states that the civil service encompasses "all positions in the public service of each county, now existing or hereafter established, and embraces all personal services performed for each county." Clearly, the language "*all* positions" and "*all* personal services" indicates that "civil service" was meant to be read broadly. (Emphases added.) Nevertheless, we must not read the term so broadly as to lead to absurdity. For example, one could read "all positions in the public service" as literally meaning any position that provides a service to the public. However, such an interpretation would encompass employees of businesses such as Hawaiian Electric (electrical service), GTE Hawaiian Tel (telephone service), or even Bank of Hawai'i (financial services). It would clearly be absurd to suddenly and radically expand the civil service system to include employees of these organizations. Furthermore, we cannot read "civil service" as only including those employees who are paid regular salaries by the government. Such an interpretation would allow the state or the counties to avoid civil service coverage simply by reducing the size of their official payroll. This would elevate form over substance and effectively render HRS § 76–77 a nullity. Because of these difficulties in interpreting the statute, we look to the three approaches utilized by other states for guidance.

Under the nature of the services test, the protection of civil service laws extends to those services that have been customarily and historically provided by civil servants. This approach has a number of advantages. First, it is the broadest of the three approaches and is therefore consistent with the broad coverage suggested by the language of the statute. Second, by limiting coverage to those types of services that have been customarily and historically performed by civil servants, it does not risk being applied so broadly as to lead to absurdity. Third, and most importantly, the nature of the services test focuses on the types of services performed rather than the particular programs or governmental functions involved or the intent or motive underlying the decision. This focus on services is consistent with the statutory language "all personal *services* performed in each county." (Emphasis added.)

Under the functional inquiry test, new state programs performing new functions are not subject to civil service laws. The problem with this approach is that it is inconsistent with the statutory language of HRS § 76–77. The statute provides that the civil service includes "all positions

... now existing *or hereafter established.*" (Emphasis added.) Thus, the Hawai'i statute clearly encompasses new programs as well as old.

Under the bad faith test, civil service laws are violated only if the employer acts in bad faith or with intent to circumvent the civil service laws. The problem with this approach is that it is very narrow and therefore inconsistent with the broad statutory language of HRS § 76–77. Furthermore, the test focuses on the intent or motive underlying the privatization effort. Nothing in HRS § 76–77 indicates that intent or motive is relevant to civil service coverage at all.

Therefore, we deem the nature of the services test to be most consistent with the language of our statute. We hold that the civil service, as defined by HRS § 76–77, encompasses those services that have been customarily and historically provided by civil servants.

In the present dispute, the landfill worker positions at Pu'uanahulu are essentially the same positions as at Kealakehe. The actual work performed is basically the same except for a minor change in the duties of equipment operators. At Kealakehe, these positions were civil service positions, and Pu'uanahulu is a replacement landfill for Kealakehe. Furthermore, the landfill workers at Hilo also held civil service positions. Thus, the landfill workers at Pu'uanahulu are performing a service that has been customarily and historically provided by civil servants. They are therefore within the civil service unless one of the exceptions enumerated in HRS § 76–77 applies.

Only two of the exceptions in HRS § 76–77 even remotely apply to the facts of the present dispute. Under HRS § 76–77(7), persons employed by contract are not within the civil service if the county personnel director certifies (with the approval of the civil service commission) that the service is special or unique, is essential to the public interest, and that personnel cannot be recruited through normal civil service procedures. However, in the present dispute, the County made no effort to seek certification.

HRS § 76–77(10) provides that positions are not within the civil service if they are specifically exempted by other state statutes. The County and WMI rely on HRS § 46–85 as one such statute. If HRS § 46–85 does indeed include a specific exemption to civil service coverage, then clearly HRS § 76–77(10) would require us to hold that the landfill worker positions are not within the civil service.

HRS § 46–85 provides:

> **Contracts for solid waste disposal.** Any other law to the contrary notwithstanding, a county is authorized from time to time to contract with users or operators of a project for the abatement, control, reduction, treatment, elimination, or disposal of solid waste, whether established or to be established under chapter 48E or as a public undertaking, improvement, or system under chapter 47 or 49, or otherwise. The contract may be included in an agreement, may be for such periods as agreed upon by the parties, and, without limiting the generality of the foregoing, may include:

> (1) Provisions for the delivery to the project of minimum amounts of solid waste and payments for the use of the project based on the delivery of the minimum amounts (which payments the political subdivision may be obligated to make, whether or not such minimum amounts are actually delivered to the project);
>
> (2) Unit prices, which may be graduated; and
>
> (3) Adjustments of the minimum amounts and the unit price.
>
> The payments, unit prices, or adjustments need not be specifically stated in the contract but may be determined by formula if set forth in the contract. The contract may include provisions for the arbitration and reasonable restrictions against other disposal by the county or by other public or private entities or persons over which the county shall have jurisdiction of the substances covered by the contract while the contract is in force and disposal under the contract is practicable.

HRS § 46–85 (1993). This statute clearly authorizes the County to enter into contracts relating to disposal of solid waste; however, it mentions nothing about the civil service. HRS § 76–77(10) expressly states that to avoid civil service coverage, the positions must be "*specifically* exempted" by another state statute. (Emphasis added.) Inasmuch as HRS § 46–85 mentions nothing about civil service positions, it does not include a specific exemption. Therefore, under the plain meaning of HRS § 76–77(10) and 46–85, the landfill worker positions are still within the civil service....

In summary, under HRS § 76–77, the landfill worker positions at Pu'uanahulu are within the civil service. Accordingly, they are governed by merit principles under article XVI, section 1 of the Hawai'i Constitution. As civil service positions, they are also subject to the civil service statutes contained within HRS chs. 76 and 77. Therefore, privatization of the operation of the new landfill deprived civil servants of the protections guaranteed in article XVI, section 1 and HRS chs. 76 and 77. Thus, the County violated constitutionally mandated merit principles and civil service statutes. We emphasize that nothing in this opinion should be interpreted as passing judgment, one way or the other, on the wisdom of privatization. Whether or not, as a policy matter, private entities should be allowed to provide public services entails a judgment ordinarily consigned to the legislature. Our decision today merely applies the civil service laws of this state to the example of privatization at issue in the present appeal.

As we have discussed above, privatization involves two important, but potentially conflicting, policy concerns. On the one hand, privatization purportedly can improve the efficiency of public services. On the other hand, privatization can interfere with the policies underlying our civil service, i.e., elimination of the spoils system and the encouragement of openness, merit, and independence. Given the importance of these policy concerns and the potential conflict between them, clear guidance from the legislature is indispensable.

The Colorado Supreme Court invalidated an attempt to privatize highway services because neither the legislature nor administrative agencies had directly addressed the competing policy concerns underlying privatization. In Colorado Association of Public Employees v. Department of Highways, 809 P.2d 988 (Colo. 1991) (en banc), the court held:

> The scope and characteristics of any plan of privatization and means by which such a plan is to be implemented require careful consideration. Legislation, rules, or some combination thereof establishing standards will be necessary to ensure that privatization does not subvert the policies underlying the state personnel system as a whole, rather than a case specific consideration of the effect of a particular privatization plan of a single state agency on individual employees.... At the time relevant to the present case, however, no one had analyzed whether or under what circumstances positions within the state personnel system can be eliminated consistent with the civil service protections in order to obtain the same services by contract with private sector providers. The legislature has not spoken concerning privatization, and no regulatory criteria or guidelines had been adopted by which an executive agency could determine whether privatization is permissible and, if so, under what circumstances. Because privatization so directly implicates both the personnel system as a whole and the specific protections accorded state personnel system employees under [the Colorado Constitution], standards regulating privatization must be established by legislation, regulation, or some combination of the two.

Id. at 994–995. See also Horrell v. Department of Admin., 861 P.2d 1194 (Colo. 1993) (en banc); Moore v. State Dep't of Transp., 875 P.2d 765, 774–775 (Alaska 1994) (Rabinowitz, J., dissenting).

In the present dispute, there is no statute that expressly addresses privatization of public landfills. Although the County and WMI attempt to rely on HRS § 46–85, neither that statute nor its legislative history directly address the issue. In contrast, our statutes, and indeed our state constitution, strongly support the policies underlying the civil service. Because the only unequivocal support in our statutes is in favor of civil service policies, we must decide the present dispute in favor of civil service policies and against privatization.

We note that the legislature has expressly excluded many positions from civil service coverage in the past. For example, HRS § 76–16 is the equivalent of HRS § 76–77 for the state civil service. HRS § 76–16(13) expressly excludes positions held by prisoners from civil service coverage. Thus, programs that involve prisoners providing services to the state do not violate our civil service laws. HRS § 76–16(13) reflects a policy decision by our legislature—the policies behind prisoner work programs supersede the policies behind the civil service. In contrast to prisoner work programs, privatization does not have an express exclusion, and we believe that it would be improper for this court to usurp the legislature's role by making our own policy decision in favor of privatization....

In conclusion, we hold that the County violated civil service statutes and the Hawai'i Constitution when it privatized the operation of the Pu'uanahulu landfill. The County was not entitled to judgment as a matter of law, and the circuit court erred in granting summary judgment in favor of the County. Instead, summary judgment should be granted in favor of the UPW. Although the UPW never filed its own motion for summary judgment, a court may enter judgment for the non-moving party on a motion for summary judgment where there is no genuine issue of material fact and the non-moving party is entitled to judgment as a matter of law. Flint v. MacKenzie, 53 Haw. 672, 501 P.2d 357 (1972) (per curiam). In the present case, the material facts are not in dispute and, in accordance with our discussion of the legal issues above, the UPW was entitled to judgment as a matter of law.

Privatization may, or may not, be a worthy idea; we do not, and indeed should not, express an opinion in this regard. But if privatization is attempted by the government, it must be done in accordance with the laws of this state. The privatization effort of the County of Hawai'i simply did not comply with our laws.

[Discussion of whether the county violated collective bargaining laws is omitted—EDS.]

NOTES

1. *Privatization and the Justifications for Civil Service.* The court in the principal case suggests that the civil service system was intended to protect merit, independence, and openness, and that the need for this protection constrains the state's ability to privatize. What reason is there to believe that these factors will be less relevant in the hiring and retention process in private firms than in governmental entities with a civil service system? After all, if the motivation for privatization is a desire for greater efficiency in the delivery of public services, doesn't that translate into retention of the most meritorious workers? To the extent that "openness" is a desirable substitute for the "spoils system" that the court believes the civil service system was intended to avoid, why wouldn't market pressures provide the proper level of "openness" for private firms?

The retention of a merit system has been a rationale for limiting privatization in other jurisdictions. In Professional Engineers in California Government v. Department of Transportation, 936 P.2d 473 (Cal. 1997), the court determined that privatization is forbidden if the services at issue are of a kind that persons selected through civil service could perform "adequately and competently." Again, ensuring that the public received service from employees of high quality provided the justification for the decision. See also Moore v. State, Dep't of Transportation and Public Facilities, 875 P.2d 765 (Alaska 1994).

The preference for using civil service employees to operate governmentally owned facilities was also an issue in Civil Service Comm'n of New Orleans v. City of New Orleans, 854 So.2d 322 (La. 2003). The city had entered into an agreement with a private entity for the operation of the city's cultural center, which had theretofore been operated by a department of the city and had employed 19 civil service employees. Ten of those employees accepted employment with the private operator and the remainder took new jobs with the city. The Civil Service Commission, a constitutionally created body that was intended to ensure selection of classified employees on the basis of merit and preclude their discriminatory dismissal or discipline, filed an action to enjoin implementation of the agreement on the grounds that it violated a rule of the Commission requiring the city to obtain Commission approval prior to privatizing a government operation. The court concluded that the Commission did not have explicit authority to draft rules involving privatization that would trump the decisions of a home rule municipality such as New Orleans. Nevertheless, the court determined that it was necessary to provide the Commission with a limited ability to review such agreements in order to effectuate "the objectives and purposes of civil service." Thus, the court upheld the Commission's right to review privatization agreements to permit determination of whether civil servants would be involuntarily displaced, and, if so, whether the contract was motivated by reasons of efficiency and economy or as a pretext for the discriminatory dismissal of civil servants.

Other courts have upheld the privatization of governmental services, at least where it is justified by cost savings and not inconsistent with constitutional or statutory mandates. See, e.g., Oklahoma Public Employees Ass'n v. Oklahoma Dept. of Central Services, 55 P.3d 1072 (Okla. 2002); Vermont State Employees' Ass'n v. Vermont Criminal Justice Training Council, 704 A.2d 769 (Vt. 1997).

2. *Privatization and Efficiency.* The recent surge of interest in privatization has largely been motivated by a concern that government has become too pervasive and performs its tasks less efficiently than private firms. See John Donahue, The Privatization Decision (1989); Ronald A. Cass, Privatization: Politics, Law and Theory, 71 Marq. L. Rev. 449 (1988). Courts have similarly alluded to the possibility that privatization could reduce costs and increase the efficiency of governmental operations. See Civil Service Comm'n of New Orleans v. City of New Orleans, 854 So.2d 322 (La. 2003); Moore v. State Dep't of Transportation and Public Facilities, 875 P.2d 765 (Alaska 1994).

Why would privatization create greater efficiency? Consider the arguments set forth below, from Michael H. Schill, Privatizing Federal Low Income Housing Assistance: The Case of Public Housing, 75 Cornell L. Rev. 878, 881–887 (1990) (footnotes omitted).

> Privatization typically refers to the shift of functions from the state to the private sector. Importantly, privatization need not result in a reduction in government expenditure for social services. Privatization proposals are sometimes categorized according to whether the state continues to fund production. "Government load-shedding" occurs when the state divorces itself from both the financing and the production of goods and services; "empowerment of mediating institutions" refers to situations in which the state continues to finance public goods and services, but leaves their delivery and production to the private sector.
>
> The most frequent justification for privatization is the utilitarian concern of efficiency. According to this view, a primary, if not overriding, objective of public policy is the maximization of aggregate individual utility. To the extent that resources currently being utilized one way can instead be used differently so as to increase aggregate utility or output, the former use is inefficient. A large number of empirical studies that compare public and private sector

provision of goods and services conclude that the private sector is the more efficient provider. Two reasons commonly offered to explain the apparent inefficiency of the public sector are the absence of transferable property rights in government enterprise and the belief that the structure of the political process tends to give special interest groups disproportionate influence and leads elected officials and bureaucrats to maximize their personal utility rather than the utility of the public.

A major difference between the private and public sectors is the existence in the private sector of transferable property rights in the residuum of the enterprise. The existence of such profits, in theory, provides a strong incentive for private entrepreneurs to minimize costs and maximize productivity. In addition, in instances where the ultimate owners of an enterprise delegate management to agents, as in a corporation, the existence of property rights creates an incentive for the owners to monitor carefully the activities of managers to ensure that they are profit-maximizing. Even where individual property owners fail to monitor, the existence of a market for corporate control provides a safeguard against inefficient management. Similar incentives for cost reduction and careful monitoring do not exist or exist in only an attenuated fashion in the public sector. Individual taxpayers do not have a direct claim to the surplus created by government. In addition, because a taxpayer's interest in the government is not freely transferable, no market for control exists to monitor efficiency.

A second approach to explaining why government seems to act in an inefficient manner examines how individual choices are aggregated in majority rule, democratic political systems and the nature of the incentives that motivate elected officials and bureaucrats. Due to collective action problems, narrow self-interested groups, frequently referred to as special interest groups, have an advantage over diffuse majorities in influencing government. Individual voters who favor a government policy or program benefitting a large number of citizens often lack the incentive to organize and expend resources in collecting information and lobbying public officials. Typically, the costs associated with organizing large numbers of only moderately interested voters are enormous. Because benefits cannot be limited to those who organize, but instead must be shared among a large number of citizens, each individual voter has an incentive to leave the expensive and time consuming task of political organization to others and "free ride" on their efforts. Small groups of intensely interested citizens, however, have much lower organizational costs and are likely to have an impact on the legislative process that is disproportionate to their numbers. Special interest groups can use this organizational advantage to influence the political process and increase their wealth at the expense of the majority. This rent-seeking behavior results in inefficiencies associated both with the resources the interest groups expend in their efforts to influence public officials as well as their successful diversion of public resources to private interests.

In addition to rent-seeking, political economists have argued that the public sector tends to be inefficient because elected representatives and administrative officials face strong incentives to act inefficiently. Based on their assumption that a legislator's primary motivation is to win reelection, these theorists predict that public programs will be designed to confer concentrated benefits on legislative districts rather than to deal with public problems in an efficient manner. In addition, administrative officials are thought to pursue their private goals rather than the public interest by maximizing the size and scope of their bureaus.

The indictments of the public sector offered by property rights and public choice theorists are themselves subject to criticism. Even though taxpayers do not possess freely transferable property rights in government enterprise, they nonetheless have an interest in efficient government operation. To the extent that government operates more efficiently, their tax burdens will be reduced. Property rights theorists also tend to have an idealized model of the private sector. Private sector enterprises, however, are observed to engage in inefficient behavior which is often unchecked by the market for corporate control. Public choice theorists, in turn, may overstate the self-interest of voters and public officials. Little room is left for altruistic or public-regarding behavior on behalf of either group.

Nevertheless, significant empirical evidence indicates that, on the whole, the public sector does tend to be a less efficient provider of goods and services than the private sector. The reasons offered by property rights and public choice theorists seem to explain at least part of the cause of this differential. However, most economists and political scientists would also agree that, at times, government action is necessary not only to achieve efficiency, but also to attain other objectives, such as the society's consensus of distributive fairness. The private sector may be unable to realize efficiency due to market failures. Among the most commonly mentioned causes of market failure are the existence of monopolies, public goods, externalities, incomplete markets and imperfect information. Where a market failure exists, it may be necessary for the public sector to correct it, using its powers of taxation, spending and regulation. Furthermore, even in instances where no market failure exists, the public sector has a role in achieving objectives that may have little to do with economic efficiency. For example, although the strength of the conviction ebbs and flows over time, most people would say that a legitimate role for government is the redistribution of wealth. The coercive power of government is usually thought to be necessary to achieve this objective.

Many people committed to objectives other than economic efficiency, such as income redistribution, tend to view the advocates of privatization with a mixture of skepticism and hostility. Clearly, the property rights and public choice theorists paint a somewhat bleak picture of the public sector and may call into question the ability of government to achieve worthwhile social objectives. In addition, advocates of redistribution may, at least in some cases, justifiably suspect that proponents of privatization have a political agenda that goes beyond efficient delivery of social services to shrinking the level of government intervention in all facets of society. Some may also suspect that there exists an ideological bias in privatization to benefit the wealthy at the expense of the poor.

Nevertheless, it would be shortsighted for those who believe, as I do, in redistribution of income to reject out of hand the insights of those advocating privatization based on a suspicion of ulterior motives. To the contrary, proponents of privatization provide us with the tools to analyze how social services can best be delivered.

Consider Professor Schill's suggestions that the chance for residual profits gives officials of private firms incentives for efficiency that is not replicated in the public sector, and that officials of private firms are more easily monitored. Is it clear that shareholders of firms have a more intense interest in monitoring their officials than constituents of a municipality? Is it clear that those shareholders who do monitor officials of firms have the same objectives as those who do not monitor? Are there proxies for non-monitoring constituents? For instance, does the local press have incentives to monitor the performance of public employees? What about potential political opponents of the current administration?

What is efficient in theory may turn out differently in practice. Nevertheless, the literature on services supplied in both public and private sectors does indicate an edge for private sector provision if the criterion for success is efficiency. For a summary, see Dennis C. Mueller, Public Choice II 261–266 (1989) (concluding that of the more than 50 studies of similar service provision by public and private firms, public firms were found to be more efficient than their private counterparts in only two). There is some evidence, however, that efficiency is more related to the presence of competition than to the public or private identity of the service provider. See John D. Donahue, The Privatization Decision 57–78 (1989).

Do these potential gains in efficiency nevertheless conflict with conceptions of government's role in the society? In Council of the City of New York v. Giuliani, 710 N.E.2d 255 (N.Y. 1999), plaintiffs challenged the validity of an attempted sublease of a hospital owned by the New York City Health and Hospitals Corporation, a governmental entity created to operate the city's municipal hospitals, to a private, for-profit entity. The city claimed that the sublease was necessary to reduce spiraling costs of providing service. The proposed sublessee would have been obligated to provide specified services "to substantially the same degree" as the hospital currently provided. The sublease also contained a non-compete clause for the private entity and required the sublessee to increase the amount of charity care to the immediate community, to make capital improvements, and to assume the debt of the hospital. The statute that created the Corporation permitted it to lease or sublease its properties, but only "for its corporate purposes." The court concluded that those "purposes" did not include transferring operation of the hospital to a private entity. While the court concluded that this conclusion was mandated by the "clear and well-defined statutory purposes and legislative intent," it seemed more concerned with a perceived inconsistency between the objectives of the Corporation and the proposed sublessee:

> We are also troubled by the inherent conflict between HHC's statutory mission and the profit-maximizing goals of a private, for-profit corporation. This clash of missions precludes the transfer of total operational control over a public hospital to a for-profit entity. A public benefit corporation like HHC is "organized to construct or operate a public improvement wholly or partly within the state, the profits from which inure to the benefit of this or other states, or to the people thereof". In contrast, a private, for-profit corporation exists to provide maximum economic returns to its shareholders. This inherent conflict between HHC's public purpose and the goals of a health care institution run by a private, for-profit entity was recognized by experts evaluating the public hospital system more than 30 years ago, and played a significant role in the Legislature's decision to create a public benefit corporation to run the municipal hospital system.

710 N.E.2d at 614. Given the contractual constraints on the sublessee, is there reason to doubt that public provision of hospital care will be superior to that of a private entity? Are there additional contractual constraints that would reduce the conflict? Or is the court suggesting that there are no circumstances in which a private entity could satisfy the purposes for which the legislature created the Corporation?

3. *Privatization and Democracy.* Even if privatization creates greater efficiency in the delivery of municipal services, are there reasons why it should be disfavored? It might be that some municipal functions are quite appropriate for privatization, since municipal involvement in these functions serves only to compensate for some failure in the private market. Once government corrects that failure, e.g., by contracting for a service that might otherwise go unprovided as a result of collective action problems, it is not necessary that the government be the actual provider of the service. Think about contracting for provision of electrical or water service in these terms. But other government functions may entail more than simply compensating for market failure. Here, some believe that privatization is more problematic, because it delegates governmental functions to parties who are not accountable to the electorate and are motivated by a quest for profits that may require reducing services to constituents in order to maximize returns to the private firm's shareholders. These concerns often center on the possibility that private firms that are employed to provide social services will seek efficiencies that adversely affect the ability of some recipients to obtain governmental benefits because some intended beneficiaries are expensive to serve. See, e.g., David A. Super, Privatization, Policy Paralysis, and the Poor, 96 Calif. L. Rev. 393 (2008); Wendy A. Bach, Welfare Reform, Privatization, and Power, 74 Brook. L. Rev. 275 (2009).

Other critiques of privatization focus on the capacity of constituents to participate in democratic decision making where the relevant actor is a private firm. Consider the following excerpt from Frank I. Michelman, Conceptions of Democracy in American Constitutional Argument: Voting Rights, 41 Fla. L. Rev. 443, 487–488 (1989).

> It is possible that the country stands at the brink of a wave of "privatization" that, especially should it occur without sustained resistance, will further and irreversibly depoliticize American life for a long time to come. One arresting example: The Commonwealth of Massachusetts recently adopted a statute authorizing the City of Chelsea to execute a contract with Boston University providing a ten-year takeover by the University of "authority and responsibility for the management, supervision, and oversight" of Chelsea's public primary and secondary education. One result for Chelsea residents will be devotion to Chelsea educational services of a quantity of monetary and other resources available to the University, but not otherwise to Chelsea. Another will be to single out Chelsea from all other Massachusetts school districts for a uniquely depoliticized form of public education governance. By comparison with everyone else in the state, individual Chelsea residents stand to be substantially deprived for a period of ten years (half of a Jeffersonian generation and five-sixths of a normal journey from first grade through high school) of whatever personal "rights" one may think they have to political self-government in a realm of obvious high democratic significance. (Footnotes omitted.)

What reason is there to believe that Chelsea residents will be less political in their monitoring of Boston University's performance than they were of their city officials? After all, the reason for the contract was a widely held belief that the public school system as operated by the city had failed substantially to educate its residents. Maybe Professor Michelman is more concerned with the responsiveness of the University than with the demands made on it. Is there reason to believe that the University will be less attentive to the demands of Chelsea residents than city officials would be? The initial inclination is to say "Yes," because city officials must run for election and University officials do not. But if the contract (1) provides the city with oversight responsibilities or opportunities, (2) allows the city to set specific input or output requirements for the private party's performance, and (3) permits the city to terminate the contract at any time with or without cause, is there less reason to believe that the University will deviate from the residents' interest more than local officials would? In short, it would seem that the ultimate objective of nondelegation is to ensure that decisionmakers consider the public's interest, rather than only the decisionmaker's self-interest, in deciding on a course of action. How could privatized educational programs be structured in a way to accomplish that objective? Even if they could be, are there competing objectives for education that make privatization inappropriate in this area? Regardless of these concerns, there appears to be growing interest in some form of private involvement in the operation of public schools. For an account of some recent efforts to privatize public schools and the scope of their success, see Lewis D. Solomon, Edison Schools and the Privatization of K–12 Public Education: A Legal and Policy Analysis, 30 Fordham Urb. L.J. 1281 (2003).

Professor Jack Beermann suggests that at least some forms of privatization raise substantial accountability problems. He maintains that the public may have greater difficulty identifying parties responsible for problems in the operation of the privatized entity and that privatized enterprises may be able to avoid procedures that make governmental activities more transparent to the public. He questions the extent to which public bodies will be able to regulate private firms to whom public services are contracted, especially in areas, such as prison services, that do not attract widespread public interest. Nevertheless, Professor Beermann concludes that there may be circumstances in which the contracting government provides sufficiently detailed, comprehensive instructions, and retains sufficient responsibility for the success or failure of the private firm that any loss in political accountability can be offset by "market accountability." See Jack Beermann, Privatization and Public Accountability, 28 Fordham Urb. L.J. 1507 (2001). For more optimistic speculation that privatization may induce the introduction of public norms into the private sector, see Jody Freeman, Extending Public Law Norms Through Privatization, 116 Harv. L. Rev. 1285 (2003).

4. *Privatization and Distribution.* Consider some of the distributional consequences of privatization of municipal services. The possibility of privatization (where that term means total governmental departure from contracting for or providing the service) raises the possibility that at least some members of the community can more substantially opt into the services that they prefer and avoid governmentally imposed exactions for services they do not utilize. This possibility brings residents closer to the Tiebout ideal of living in a jurisdiction that offers local public services preferred by its constituents. At the same time, if only some individuals have access to a full range of privatized services, while those further removed from the Tiebout assumptions have less ability to obtain their preferred mix of goods and services, broad-ranging privatization may limit the ability of the latter group to obtain local public goods at all. Does this possibility affect the selection of services that should be privatized?

Privatization may also have distributional consequences if those who privatize services fail to support similar publicly supported service for those who cannot or do not take advantage of the privatized alternative. The degree of support may depend on whether the privatized service completely substitutes for the publicly provided service or simply augments it. For instance, those who send their children to private schools in search of a more religious education than the locality provides may be less willing to support public schools because their children receive all their education at the private school. Parents who hire private tutors for their children, on the other hand, presumably would continue to support a high level of spending on the public schools, because improving public schools could reduce their need to make the incremental expenditure on tutoring. See Clayton P. Gillette, Opting Out of Public Provision, 73 Den. U.L. Rev. 1185, 1206–1216 (1996).

5. Are there some functions that government *cannot* turn over to the private sector? It is difficult to imagine a task that must be provided by government. Given that the state is often seen as providing some minimum level of protective services, one might think that policing functions could not be abandoned. In 515 Associates v. City of Newark, 623 A.2d 1366 (N.J. 1993), the city had enacted an ordinance requiring public and private owners of housing buildings to provide security guards. Plaintiffs, owners of apartment buildings, alleged that the ordinance improperly delegated the city's obligation to provide police protection. While the court agreed that the city did have such a nondelegable obligation, it concluded that the city could compel private parties to assist it in the performance of that obligation, as long as the city did not make a "wholesale transfer" of its public duty to private entities.

Is the transfer of the policing function to private entities appropriate? One might claim that some residents (those who owned or lived in housing covered by the ordinance) were required to provide a service (crime reduction) that benefits all residents, so all residents should be required to pay by having public police, paid for with tax revenues, perform the service. If, however, the addition of protective services in some residential buildings does not diminish the total amount of crime in the city, but only moves it to other areas of the city not covered by the ordinance, then it might be appropriate to impose the cost of those additional services on the residential units enjoying the reduction in crime in their neighborhood.

6. *Private Actors and Governmental Immunity*. Once a service has been privatized, the employees of the private entity continue to provide services that are supervised by public officials or that serve public functions. To what extent should these employees share the liabilities and immunities available to public employees? In Richardson v. McKnight, 521 U.S. 399 (1997), a prison inmate brought a civil rights action against two guards in a Tennessee prison that the state had privatized. If the guards had been state employees, they could have defended against the lawsuit by asserting qualified immunity. See pp. 693–711 infra. This defense would have required the prisoner to prove that the guards violated clearly established rights. The Tennessee guards, employees of a private firm, claimed the same immunity.

In an opinion for the Court, Justice Breyer concluded that the guards could not invoke the qualified immunity available to government employees, even if they had acted under "color of state law." Justice Breyer relied in part on the historical evolution of immunity, but also maintained that immunity for government officials and employees encouraged "principled and fearless" decisionmaking, discouraged "unwarranted timidity" in the conduct of the traditional functions of government, and overcame the reluctance of talented candidates to enter public service due to fear of lawsuits. Justice Breyer concluded that immunity was unnecessary to achieve these same objectives for employees of private firms. Instead, competition among firms would create incentives for managers to instill the necessary work ethic in employees. Firms face marketplace pressures to retain the governmental contract and thus have an incentive to encourage sound decisionmaking and overcome tendencies toward excessive timidity in employees who feared personal liability. Because firms did not have to contend with civil service restrictions on employee discipline and discharge, they could offer employees inducements (both carrots and sticks) unavailable to government actors. Hence, personal immunity would not improve the quality of decisions made by these firms and their agents.

The incentive structure, Justice Breyer suggested, is very different for "government employees . . . [who] work within a system that is responsible through elected officials to voters who, when they vote, rarely consider the performance of individual subdepartments or civil servants specifically or in detail. And that system is often characterized by multidepartmental civil service rules that, while providing employee security, may limit the incentives or the ability of individual departments or supervisors flexibly to reward, or to punish, individual employees." 521 U.S. at 410–11. These distinctions, Justice Breyer argued, warranted extending immunity to workers in the public sector, but not to those employed by private firms, even though they might perform identical functions. The majority proceeded at some length to delineate the extent to which the private prison management firm involved in *Richardson* could limit the risk of underperformance, obviating the need for immunity. Higher compensation and the availability of indemnification could overcome personal reservations about appropriate action and allow the private firm to respond to market pressures through rewards and penalties that "operate directly on its employees."

A vigorous dissent, authored by Justice Scalia, disagreed with the incentive structure suggested by the majority. Justice Scalia instead suggested that if threat of liability induced underperformance of the actor's public functions, then society would do better by immunizing the actor, even if that meant relaxing liability, regardless of the actor's private status. The dissenters concluded that market pressures would be insufficient to produce optimal decisionmaking by private actors because those pressures were inadequate in areas "where public officials are the only purchaser, and other people's money the medium of payment." 521 U.S. at 418–19. To the extent that politicians pay attention to either cost or quality, Justice Scalia speculated that cost would dominate. This implied (at least in the private governance of prisons) that firms would underperform from a social perspective to avoid disciplinary functions that might entail costly lawsuits. Finally, Justice Scalia observed that neither the availability of liability nor freedom from civil service rules necessarily distinguished private contractors from government employees. For further analysis, see Clayton P. Gillette and Paul B. Stephan, *Richardson v. McKnight* and the Scope of Immunity after Privatization, 8 Sup. Ct. Econ. Rev. 103 (2000).

Courts have limited the holding of *Richardson* to cases in which state supervision over the private entity was not pervasive. Thus, in Bartell v. Lohiser, 12 F.Supp.2d 640 (E.D. Mich. 1998), the court allowed a private foster home contractor and private social workers who had contracted to provide services to the state to invoke a qualified immunity defense. The court concluded that, unlike prison guards in *Richardson*, the defendants operated under the close supervision of government officials, were not susceptible to competitive pressures, and could be biased in their recommendations about parental rights to care and custody of children if they were faced with the prospect of legal liability. Similarly, in Mejia v. City of New York, 119 F.Supp.2d 232 (E.D.N.Y. 2000), the court held that the rationale articulated in *Richardson* for extending qualified immunity to public employees warranted the application of immunity to private actors who had been enlisted by governmental officials in making an arrest that was ultimately determined to be unlawful (although the private party in that case was determined to have acted so unreasonably as to preclude a claim of immunity).

G. LOCAL ECONOMIC DEVELOPMENT

In the view of some commentators, the primary objective of local government is to enhance the local economy. On this theory, local governments cannot easily redistribute goods and cannot engage in macroeconomic policies. What they can do is increase the tax base for their constituents and thus generate revenues to provide a greater array of services that current and prospective residents prefer. As Paul Peterson, one of the primary advocates of this position, has argued,

> [t]he interests of local government require that it emphasize the economic productivity of the community for which it is responsible. Because they are open systems [i.e., exit is relatively easy—Eds.] local governments are particularly sensitive to external changes. To maintain their local economic health, they must maintain a local efficiency that leaves little scope for egalitarian concerns. These limits on local government ... require that local governments concentrate on developmental as against redistributive objectives.

Paul E. Peterson, City Limits 69 (1981).

But subsidies that promote local economic development can be controversial, both within the municipality and from the broader social perspective. First, attracting firms to one jurisdiction often means enticing them away from another jurisdiction. Interlocal competition for firms may produce a race to the top, insofar as firms migrate to areas where they are likely to be most productive. But there is also a fear that interlocal competition will create a race to the bottom in which localities vie for firms by reducing tax burdens and thus lowering the quality and quantity of public goods to some residents, or by using revenue raising methods that regressively favor firms and wealthy residents. This effect is arguably exacerbated if the gains to the locality that "wins" the competition are offset by losses to the locality from which the firm exits. For some commentators, the resulting downward spiral in which localities compete for the lowest tax burden can only be stopped by centralized prohibitions on the local use of business incentives. See Peter D. Enrich, Saving the States from Themselves: Commerce Clause Constraints on State Tax Incentives for Business, 110 Harv. L. Rev. 377 (1996); Walter Hellerstein and Dan T. Coenen, Commerce Clause Constraints on State Business Development Incentives, 81 Cornell L. Rev. 789 (1996). For a more skeptical view of these restrictions, see Clayton P. Gillette, Business Incentives, Interstate Competition, and the Commerce Clause, 82 Minn. L. Rev. 447 (1997).

Second, localities often attract firms through abatements or other programs that reduce the tax burden of the firms that are attracted. Abatements raise a variety of issues. They are less transparent than subsidies, because they do not involve an explicit expenditure from the city budget. It is difficult to calculate whether the benefits related to an abatement offset the amount of the abatement. And, abatements can create a competitive imbalance if other firms in the jurisdiction are required to bear a tax burden from which the new entrant is relieved. This suggests that "mobile capital" will be able to obtain tax relief, and that relatively "immobile capital" will bear a disproportionate burden of the cost of local public goods. See Richard C. Schragger, Mobile Capital, Local Economic Regulation, and the Democratic City, 123 Harv. L. Rev. 483 (2009). In DaimlerChrysler Corp. v. Cuno, 547 U.S. 332 (2006), taxpayers of Toledo, Ohio, alleged that state and local tax benefits intended to attract new investment increased their tax burdens and violated the Commerce Clause.

The United States Court of Appeals for the Sixth Circuit concluded that a municipal property tax exemption for new investment did not violated the Commerce Clause, but that a state franchise tax credit for new investment did. The Supreme Court avoided the issue on the merits. Instead, it held that plaintiffs had no standing, either as municipal taxpayers or as state taxpayers, to challenge the credit. Are there reasons to believe that relatively "immobile capital" will be able to protect itself against exploitation by the city?

Third, the emphasis on local economic development necessarily entails the concern found in Logan and Molotch, supra at pages 24–27, that exchange value will dominate use value. Economic development typically means that land will be made available for its highest economic use. But there may be uses that are not easily reflected in economic terms and that will be subordinated to the search for additional tax dollars. For instance, an area that contains restaurants and shops used primarily by residents in the immediate neighborhood may have a higher economic value if those restaurants and shops can be transformed into uses that attract tourists or shoppers who live outside the immediate neighborhood. This frequently means displacing locally owned storefronts that service the immediate neighborhood with branches of popular national chain stores. The resulting increase in tax receipts may make the locality as a whole better off financially, and lower prices offered by national chains may benefit even local shoppers. But the transformation may also diminish what was a focal point of neighborhood activity. Local resistance to the incursion of national stores has frequently been intensive. See William Simon, The Community Economic Development Movement (2002).

Fourth, and perhaps most controversially, inducing firms to locate within a jurisdiction often requires finding space in which the firms can locate. This may require the use of eminent domain in order to overcome the difficulties of assembling a large number of contiguous plots of land that can be used by private firms. Eminent domain may be relatively uncontroversial where the government condemns land in order to create a public space or a governmental building. But it has proven far more contentious where it is used to condemn private land that is then used by or leased to a private enterprise.

In Kelo v. City of New London, 545 U.S. 469 (2005), the Supreme Court held that the use of eminent domain to condemn private land for economic development did not violate the Takings Clause of the federal Constitution, at least where the locality was proceeding pursuant to a "carefully considered" development plan that served a public purpose. The *Kelo* decision led to a substantial reaction within the states. Many state legislatures subsequently adopted prohibitions or restrictions on the use of eminent domain for economic development. See, e.g., Ilya Somin, The Limits of Backlash: Assessing the Political Response to *Kelo*, 93 Minn. L. Rev. 2100 (2009); Patricia Salkin, Eminent Domain Legislation Post *Kelo*: A State of the States, 36 Envtl. L. Rep. 10864 (2006). Where the ability to exercise eminent domain for economic development was predicated on alleviating "blight," some legislatures defined that condition in ways that precluded condemnation of buildings, land, or neighborhoods unless they displayed substantial decay. The following materials reveal the nature of the debate that these decisions produce.

Goldstein v. New York State Urban Development Corp.

921 N.E.2d 164 (N.Y. 2009).

■ LIPPMAN, CHIEF JUDGE.

We are asked to determine whether respondent's exercise of its power of eminent domain to acquire petitioners' properties for purposes of the proposed land use improvement project, known as Atlantic Yards, would be in conformity with certain provisions of our State Constitution. We answer in the affirmative.

On December 8, 2006, respondent Empire State Development Corporation (ESDC) issued a determination pursuant to Eminent Domain Proceedings Law (EDPL) § 204, finding that it should use its eminent domain power to take certain privately owned properties located in downtown Brooklyn for inclusion in a 22–acre mixed-use development proposed, and to be undertaken, by private developer Bruce Ratner and the real estate entities of which he is a principal, collectively known as the Forest City Ratner Companies (FCRC).

According to the record upon which the ESDC determination was based and by which we are bound, the development will extend eastward from the junction of Atlantic and Flatbush Avenues, and include blocks now occupied by the subgrade Vanderbilt Rail and MTA bus yards as well as certain blocks bordering the yards to the south. The project is to involve, in its first phase, construction of a sports arena to house the NBA Nets franchise, as well as various infrastructure improvements-most notably reconfiguration and modernization of the Vanderbilt Yards rail facilities and access upgrades to the subway transportation hub already present at the site. The project will also involve construction of a platform spanning the rail yards and connecting portions of the neighborhood now separated by the rail cut. Atop this platform are to be situated, in a second phase of construction, numerous high rise buildings and some eight acres of open, publicly accessible landscaped space. The 16 towers planned for the project will serve both commercial and residential purposes. They are slated to contain between 5,325 and 6,430 dwelling units, more than a third of which are to be affordable either for low and or middle income families.

The project has been sponsored by respondent ESDC as a "land use improvement project" within the definition of Urban Development Corporation Act (McKinney's Uncons Laws of NY) § 6253(6)(c), upon findings that the area in which the project is to be situated is "substandard and insanitary" or, in more common parlance, blighted. It is not disputed that the project designation and supporting blight findings are appropriate with respect to more than half the project footprint, which lies within what has, since 1968, been designated by the City of New York as the Atlantic Terminal Urban Renewal Area (ATURA). To the south of ATURA, however, and immediately adjacent to the Vanderbilt Rail Yard cut, are two blocks and a fraction of a third which, although within the project footprint, have not previously been designated as blighted. FCRC has purchased many of the properties in this area, but there remain some that it has been unsuccessful in acquiring, whose transfer ESDC now seeks to compel in furtherance of the project, through condemnation. In support of its exercise of the condemnation power with respect to these properties, some of which are owned by petitioners, ESDC, based on studies conducted by a consulting firm retained by FCRC, has made findings that the blocks in which they are situated possess sufficient indicia of actual or impending blight to warrant their condemnation for clearance and redevelopment in accordance with a section 6253(6)(c) land use improvement plan, and that the proposed land use improvement project will, by removing blight and creating in its place the above-described mixed-use development, serve a "public use, benefit or purpose" in accordance with the requirement of EDPL § 204(B)(1).

* * *

Turning now to the merits, petitioners first contend that the determination authorizing the condemnation of their properties for the Atlantic Yards project is unconstitutional because the condemnation is not for the purpose of putting their properties to "public use" within the meaning of article I, § 7(a) of the State Constitution-which provides that "[p]rivate property shall not be taken for public use without just compensation"-but rather to enable a private commercial entity to use their properties for private economic gain with, perhaps, some incidental public benefit. The argument reduces to this: that the State Constitution has from its inception, in recognition of the fundamental right to privately own property, strictly limited the availability of condemnation to situations in which the property to be condemned will actually be made available for public use, and that, with only limited exceptions prompted by emergent public necessity, the State Constitution's takings clause, unlike its federal counterpart, has been consistently understood literally, to permit a taking of private property only for "public use," and not simply to accomplish a public purpose.

Even if this gloss on this State's takings laws and jurisprudence were correct—and it is not—it is indisputable that the removal of urban blight is a proper, and, indeed, constitutionally sanctioned, predicate for the exercise of the power of eminent domain. It has been deemed a "public use" within the meaning of the State's takings clause at least since *Matter of New York City Housing Authority v. Muller* (270 N.Y. 333 [1936]) and is expressly recognized by the Constitution as a ground for condemnation.... Pursuant to article XVIII [of the State Constitution], respondent ESDC has been vested with the condemnation power by the Legislature and has here sought to exercise the power for the constitutionally recognized public purpose or "use" of rehabilitating a blighted area.

Petitioners, of course, maintain that the blocks at issue are not, in fact, blighted and that the allegedly mild dilapidation and inutility of the property cannot support a finding that it is substandard and insanitary within the meaning of article XVIII. They are doubtless correct that the conditions cited in support of the blight finding at issue do not begin to approach in severity the dire circumstances of urban slum dwelling described by the *Muller* court in 1936, and which prompted the adoption of article XVIII at the State Constitutional Convention two years later (*see* Constitutional Convention Committee, Reports and Studies, Vol. VI, Part II, p. 636–639 [1938]). We, however, have never required that a finding of blight by a legislatively designated public benefit corporation be based upon conditions replicating those to which the Court and the Constitutional Convention responded in the midst of the Great Depression. . . .

It is important to stress that lending precise content to these general terms has not been, and may not be, primarily a judicial exercise. Whether a matter should be the subject of a public undertaking-whether its pursuit will serve a public purpose or use-is ordinarily the province of the Legislature, not the Judiciary, and the actual specification of the uses identified by the Legislature as public has been largely left to quasi-legislative administrative agencies. It is only where there is no room for reasonable difference of opinion as to whether an area is blighted, that judges may substitute their views as to the adequacy with which the public purpose of blight removal has been made out for that of the legislatively designated agencies; where, as here, "those bodies have made their finding, not corruptly or irrationally or baselessly, there is nothing for the courts to do about it, unless every act and decision of other departments of government is subject to revision by the courts".

It is quite possible to differ with ESDC's findings that the blocks in question are affected by numerous conditions indicative of blight, but any such difference would not, on this record, in which the bases for the agency findings have been extensively documented photographically and otherwise on a lot-by-lot basis, amount to more than another reasonable view of the matter; such a difference could not, consonant with what we have recognized to be the structural limitations upon our review of what is essentially a legislative prerogative, furnish a ground to afford petitioners relief.

It may be that the bar has now been set too low—that what will now pass as "blight," as that expression has come to be understood and used by political appointees to public corporations relying upon studies paid for by developers, should not be permitted to constitute a predicate for the invasion of property rights and the razing of homes and businesses. But any such limitation upon the sovereign power of eminent domain as it has come to be defined in the urban renewal context is a matter for the Legislature, not the courts. Properly involved in redrawing the range of the sovereign prerogative would not be a simple return to the days when private property rights were viewed as virtually inviolable, even when they stood in the way of meeting compelling public needs, but a re-weighing of public as against private interests and a reassessment of the need for and public utility of what may now be out-moded approaches to the revivification of the urban landscape. These are not tasks courts are suited to perform. They are appropriately situated in the policy-making branches of government.

The dissenter, after thoughtful review of the evolution of the concept of public use-an evolution that even he acknowledges has sapped the concept of much of its limiting power-urges that there remains enough left in it to require that this case be decided differently. We cannot agree. The Constitution accords government broad power to take and clear substandard and insanitary areas for redevelopment. In so doing, it commensurately deprives the Judiciary of grounds to interfere with the exercise.

While there remains a hypothetical case in which we might intervene to prevent an urban redevelopment condemnation on public use grounds-where "the physical conditions of an area might be such that it would be irrational and baseless to call it substandard or insanitary,"-this is not that case. The dissenter looks at the "Blight Study" contained in the administrative record and sees only a "normal and pleasant residential neighborhood," but others, it would appear not irrationally, have come to very different conclusions. This is not a record that affords the purchase necessary for judicial intrusion. The situation in the end is remarkably like that presented in *Kaskel* where Judge Desmond, writing for the Court said:

> "Plaintiff does not dispute with defendants as to the condition of these properties or of the whole area. He is simply opposing his opinion and his judgment to that of public officials, on a matter which must necessarily be one of opinion or judgment, that is, as to whether a specified area is so substandard or insanitary, or both, as to justify clearance and redevelopment under the law. It is not seriously contended by anyone that, for an area to be subject to those laws, every single building therein must be below civilized standards. The statute (and the Constitution), like other similar laws, contemplates that clearing and redevelopment will be of an entire area, not of a separate parcel, and, surely, such statutes would not be very useful if limited to areas where every single building is substandard. A glance at the photographs, attached to the city's affidavit on these motions, shows that a considerable number of buildings in this area are, on a mere external inspection, below modern standards because of their age, obsolescence and decay. The other exhibits confirm this."

Here too, all that is at issue is a reasonable difference of opinion as to whether the area in question is in fact substandard and insanitary. This is not a sufficient predicate for us to supplant respondent's determination....

Accordingly, the order of the Appellate Division should be affirmed, with costs.

■ SMITH, J.(dissenting).

* * *

Article I, § 7(a) of the State Constitution says: "Private property shall not be taken for public use without just compensation."

The words "public use" embody an important protection for property owners. They prevent the State from invoking its eminent domain power as a means of transferring property from one private owner to another who has found more favor with state officials, or who promises to use the land in a way more to the State's liking. They do not require that all takings result in public ownership of the property, but they do ordinarily require that, if the land is transferred to private hands, it be used after the taking in a way that benefits the public directly. A recognized exception permits the transfer of "blighted" land to private developers without so strict a limitation on its subsequent use, but that exception is applicable only in cases in which the use of the land by its original owner creates a danger to public health and safety.

These principles are established by two centuries of New York cases. A line of 19th century decisions made clear that the State could not use the eminent domain power to transfer property from one private owner to another, unless the use to which the second owner put the property would be "public" in some meaningful sense. In the 20th century-an era friendlier to government, and less friendly to private property-this rule was diluted, but our cases do not justify the conclusion that the public use limitation was abandoned or rendered trivial. Rather, the 20th century cases created what may be called a "blight exception" to the public use limitation. The critical question on this appeal is whether that exception applies, a question that can be better understood after a more detailed description of the way our "public use" law has developed.

* * *

The majority does not wholly reject what I have said in section I of this dissent. Indeed, the majority seems to accept the premise that the Eminent Domain Clause of the New York Constitution has independent vitality, and may offer more protection to property owners than its federal counterpart. I am pleased that the majority does not follow the Supreme Court's decisions in *Berman, Midkiff* and *Kelo,* which equate "public use" in the Constitution with public purpose, thus leaving governments free to accomplish by eminent domain any goal within their general power to act. Where I part company with the majority is in its conclusion that we must defer to ESDC's determination that the properties at issue here fall within the blight exception to the public use limitation.

It is clear to me from the record that the elimination of blight, in the sense of substandard and unsanitary conditions that present a danger to public safety, was never the bona fide purpose of the development at issue in this case. Indeed, blight removal or slum clearance, which were much in vogue among the urban planners of several decades ago, have waned in popularity, vindicating the comment of Judge Van Voorhis, dissenting in *Cannata,* that "[t]he public theorists are not always correct". It is more popular today to speak of an "urban landscape"—the words used by Bruce Ratner to describe his "vision" of the Atlantic Yards development in a public presentation in January 2004 (Powell, *For Brooklyn, a Celebration or a Curse?,* Washington Post, January 26, 2004, section A, at 3).

According to the petition in this case, when the project was originally announced in 2003 the public benefit claimed for it was economic development-job creation and the bringing of a professional basketball team to Brooklyn. Petitioners allege that nothing was said about "blight" by the sponsors of the project until 2005; ESDC has not identified any earlier use of the term. In 2005, ESDC retained a consultant to conduct a "blight study." In light of the special status accorded to blight in the New York law of eminent domain, the inference that it was a pretext, not the true motive for this development, seems compelling.

It is apparent from a review of ESDC's blight study that its authors faced a difficult problem. Only the northern part of the area on which Atlantic Yards is to be built can fairly be described as blighted. As the majority opinion explains, the northern part has long been included in the Atlantic Terminal Urban Renewal Area (ATURA), and is afflicted by deteriorating conditions perhaps attributable to the presence of the Vanderbilt Yards. But the southern part of the project area, where petitioners live, has never been part of ATURA and appears, from the photographs and the descriptions contained in ESDC's blight study, to be a normal and pleasant residential community.

ESDC's consultants did their best. Proceeding lot by lot through the area in which petitioners live, they were able to find that a number of buildings were not in good condition; petitioners claim that this results in large part from the fact that Ratner's plan to acquire the properties and demolish the buildings had been public knowledge for years when the blight study was conducted. Choosing their words carefully, the consultants concluded that the area of the proposed Atlantic Yards development, taken as a whole, was "characterized by blighted conditions." They did not find, and it does not appear they could find, that the area where petitioners live is a blighted area or slum of the kind that prompted 20th century courts to relax the public use limitation on the eminent domain power.

The majority opinion acknowledges that the conditions ESDC relies on here "do not begin to approach in severity the dire circumstances of urban slum dwelling" contemplated by the cases that developed the blight exception (majority op at 14). The majority concludes, however, that determining whether the area in question is really blighted is not "primarily a judicial exercise" (id. at 16, 227 N.Y.S.2d 903, 182 N.E.2d 395). In doing so, I think, the majority loses sight of the nature of the issue.

The determination of whether a proposed taking is truly for public use has always been a judicial exercise-as the cases cited in section I of this dissent, from *Bloodgood* in 1837 through *Yonkers Community Development* in 1975, demonstrate. The right not to have one's property taken for other than public use is a constitutional right like others. It is hard to imagine any court saying that a decision about whether an utterance is constitutionally protected speech, or whether a search was unreasonable, or whether a school district has been guilty of racial discrimination, is not primarily a judicial exercise. While no doubt some degree of deference is due to public agencies and to legislatures, to allow them to decide the facts on which constitutional rights depend is to render the constitutional protections impotent.

The whole point of the public use limitation is to prevent takings even when a state agency deems them desirable. To let the agency itself determine when the public use requirement is satisfied is to make the agency a judge in its own cause. I think that it is we who should perform the role of judges, and that we should do so by deciding that the proposed taking in this case is not for public use.

Kaur v. New York State Urban Development Corporation

892 N.Y.S.2d 8 (N.Y. App. Div. 2009).

■ CATTERSON, J.

* * *

The exercise of eminent domain power by the New York State Urban Development Corporation d/b/a Empire State Development Corporation (hereinafter referred to as "ESDC") to benefit a private elite education institution is violative of the Takings Clause of the U.S. Constitution, article 1, § 7 of the New York Constitution, and the "first principles of the social contract." The process employed by ESDC predetermined the unconstitutional outcome, was bereft of facts which established that the neighborhood in question was blighted, and ultimately precluded the petitioners from presenting a full record before either the ESDC or, ultimately, this Court. In short, it is a skein worth unraveling.

THE TAKING OF MANHATTANVILLE

This case involves the acquisition, by condemnation or voluntary transfer, of approximately 17 acres in the Manhattanville area of West Harlem for the development of a new campus for Columbia University, a not for profit corporation (hereinafter referred to as "The Project"). The Project, referred to as the Columbia University Educational Mixed Used Development Land Use Improvement and Civic Project, would consist of a total of approximately 6.8 million gross square feet in up to 16 new buildings, a multi-level below-grade support space, and the adaptive re-use of an existing building. In addition, the Project would purportedly create approximately two acres of publicly accessible open space, a market along Twelfth Avenue, and widened, tree-lined sidewalks.

The Project site is bounded by and includes West 125th Street on the south, West 133rd Street on the north, Broadway and Old Broadway on the east, and Twelfth Avenue on the west, as well as certain areas located beneath City streets within this area and beneath other City streets in the Project site. The estimated acquisition and construction cost for the Project is $6.28 billion, and will be funded by Columbia without any contribution from any municipal entity.

In 2001, Columbia, together with numerous other organizations, began working with the New York City Economic Development Corporation (hereinafter referred to as "EDC") to redevelop the West Harlem area. In August 2002, the EDC issued a West Harlem Master Plan (hereinafter referred to as the "Plan") describing the economic redevelopment plan. In the Plan, the EDC contended that the area was "once denser, livelier and a waterside gateway for Manhattan," and that "[a] renewed future seem[ed] possible." The EDC stated that it hoped to "revitaliz[e] [...] a long-forsaken waterfront," provide transportation, develop "a vibrant commercial and cultural district," and support academic research. The EDC noted that the current land use was "auto-related or vacant," with several "handsome, mid-rise buildings [...] interspersed with parking lots and partially empty industrial buildings." According to data prepared for the Plan by Ernst & Young, 54 of the 67 lots were in "good," "very good" or "fair" condition.

In 2000, Columbia owned only 2 properties in the Project area. In 2002, Columbia began purchasing property in the area in order to effectuate its own plan to expand its facilities. By early October 2003, Columbia controlled 51% of the property in the Project area–33% of which was still privately owned....

In August 2004, EDC issued a "Blight Study" of the West Harlem/Manhattanville Area which was prepared by a consultant, Urbitran Associates, Inc. The study concluded that the area was "blighted."

In December 2004, the ESDC, not content to rest on the Urbitran study, noted that it would have to make its own "blight findings" in connection with the Project. In an e-mail dated January 7, 2005, Columbia's Project Manager, Lorinda Karoff of Karen Buckus and Associates, indicated that Columbia's attorneys "and also possibly AKRF (who has already reviewed the document once at EDC's offices), wished to see the draft blight study." Karoff noted that the draft study "may change or even be completely replaced as ESDC uses different standards than the City."

In or about September 2006, ESDC retained Columbia's consultant AKRF to evaluate the conditions at the Project site. AKRF in turn retained Thornton Tomassetti, Inc., an engineering firm, to inspect and evaluate the physical condition of each existing structure at the Project site.

On November 1, 2007, AKRF issued its Manhattanville Neighborhood Conditions Study (hereinafter referred to as "AKRF's study"). The study noted that as of April 30, 2007, Columbia owned or had contracted to purchase 48 of the 67 tax lots (72 percent) in the study area. The study found that "48 of the 67 lots in the study area (or 72 percent of the total lots) have one or more substandard condition, including poor or critical physical lot conditions, a vacancy rate of 25 percent or more, or site utilization of 60 percent or less." In addition, the study found that "34 of the 67 lots in the study area (or 51 percent of the total lots) were assessed as being in poor or critical condition." According to the study, "[t]he presence of such a high proportion of properties with multiple substandard conditions suggests that the study area has been suffering from a long-term trend of poor maintenance and disinvestment." The study concluded that the Project area was "substantially unsafe, unsanitary, substandard, and deteriorated."

* * *

[ESDC retained Earth Tech, Inc., an engineering and environmental consultant, to "audit, examine and evaluate" AKRF's study.]

According to the Earth Tech study, Earth Tech's "independently arrived at findings substantially confirm[ed] those of AKRF and Thornton Tomasetti." However, Earth Tech found that certain buildings had "further deteriorated since the prior inspections." In particular, while the AKRF report had found that 34 lots (51%) were in critical or poor condition, Earth Tech found that 37 sites (55%) were in critical or poor condition. In addition, Earth Tech found a "long-standing lack of investor interest in the neighborhood," demonstrated by, among other things, the paucity of new buildings constructed since 1961, as well as "the extended neglect of building maintenance" and extensive Building Code violations. In particular, Earth Tech found that, as of July 2006, "there were 410 open violations" with respect to 75% of the lots in the Project site. Accordingly, Earth Tech concluded that a majority of the buildings and lots in the Manhattanville area exhibited "substandard and deteriorated conditions" creating "a blighted and discouraging impact on the surrounding community." ...

ESDC issued its determination and findings authorizing the acquisition of certain real property for the Project. In particular, ESDC found that "[t]he Project qualifies as both a Land Use Improvement Project and separately and independently as a Civic Project pursuant to the New York State Urban Development Corporation Act."

On February 20, 2009, two petitions were filed in this Court challenging the determination and findings. The petitioners Tuck–It–Away, Inc., Tuck–It–Away Bridgeport, Inc., Tuck–It–Away at 133rd Street, Inc. and Tuck–It–Away Associates, L.P. are owners of storage facilities located at 3261 Broadway, 614 West 131st Street, 655 West 125th Street, and 3300 Broadway. Petitioners Parminder Kaur and Amanjit Kaur are the owners of a gasoline service station located at 619 West 125th Street, and petitioner P.G. Singh Enterprises, LLP is the owner of a gasoline service station located at 673 West 125th Street. It is uncontested that the petitioners' property is within the Project site and thus is subject to condemnation.

* * *

ESDC's determination that the project has a public use, benefit or purpose is wholly unsupported by the record and precedent. A public use or benefit must be present in order for an agency to exercise its power of eminent domain. *See*U.S. Const. 5th amend; NY Const. art. I, § 7; EDPL 204[B][1]. "[T]he term 'public use' broadly encompasses any use [...]

which contributes to the health, safety and general welfare of the public." *See Matter of C/S 12th Ave. LLC v. City of New York,* 32 A.D.3d 1, 10–11, 815 N.Y.S.2d 516, 525 (1st Dept.2006). If an adequate basis for the agency's determination is shown, and the petitioner cannot show that the determination was corrupt or without foundation, the determination should be confirmed.

The UDCA [the state "Urban Development Corporation Act"—Eds.] defines a "civil project" as: "[a] project or that portion of a multi-purpose project designed and intended for the purpose of providing facilities for educational, cultural, recreational, community, municipal, public service or other civic purposes." Uncons. Laws of N.Y. § 6253(6)(d) (UDCA 3(6)(d)).

At the outset, it is important to note that as late as May 18, 2006, 2 1/2 years into ESDC's participation project planning, the draft GPP still identified the project only as the "Manhattanville in West Harlem Land Use Improvement Project" even though there was no arguably independent blight study until May 2008. It was not until September 2006 that the project had "and Civic Project" added to its title, fully two years after Columbia agreed to wholly underwrite the project.

THE *KELO* DOCTRINE MANDATES

Any analysis of the constitutionality of ESDC's scheme for the development of Manhattanville must necessarily begin with a discussion of the most recent Taking Clause exposition by the U.S. Supreme Court in *Kelo v. City of New London.* 545 U.S. 469, 125 S.Ct. 2655, 162 L.Ed.2d 439 (2005).

* * *

The *Kelo* plurality reaffirmed the broad deference accorded to the legislature in determining what constitutes a valid public use as first enunciated in *Berman.* However, Justice Kennedy, in a concurring opinion, pointed out the obligations of any court faced with challenges such as presented by ESDC's scheme to redevelop Manhattanville. He wrote specifically and separately on the issue of improper motive in transfers to private parties with only discrete secondary benefits to the public.

This is precisely the issue presented by the instant case. Justice Kennedy placed particular emphasis on the importance of the underlying planning process that ultimately called for the exercise of the power of eminent domain, and laid out in detail the elements of the New London plan that ensured against impermissible favoritism:

1. The city's awareness of its depressed economic condition, by virtue of a recent closing of a major employer and the state's designation of the city as a distressed municipality.

2. The formulation of a comprehensive development plan meant to address a serious citywide depression. Id. at 493,

3. The substantial commitment of public funds to the project before most of the private beneficiaries were known. Id. at 491–492.

4. The city's review of a variety of development plans.

5. The city's choice of a private developer from a group of applicants rather than picking out a particular transferee beforehand.

6. The identities of most of the private beneficiaries being unknown at the time the city formulated its plan.

7. The city's compliance with elaborate procedural requirements that facilitate the review of the record and inquiry into the city's purposes.

Justice Kennedy specifically acknowledged that "[t]here may be private transfers in which the risk of undetected impermissible favoritism of private parties is so acute that a presumption (rebuttable or otherwise) of invalidity is warranted under the Public Use Clause." *Id.*, 125 S.Ct. at 2670, 162 L.Ed.2d at 460. Although he declined to conjecture as to what sort of case might justify a more demanding standard of scrutiny, beyond finding the estimated benefits there "not *de minimis*", it was the specific aspects of the New London planning process that convinced him to side with the plurality in deference to the legislative determination. *See Id.*

The contrast between ESDC's scheme for the redevelopment of Manhattanville and New London's plan for Fort Trumbull could not be more dramatic. Initially, it must be noted that unlike Fort Trumbull, Manhattanville or West Harlem as a matter of record was not in a depressed economic condition when EDC and ESDC embarked on their Columbia-prepared-and-financed quest. The 2002 West Harlem Master Plan stated that not only was Harlem experiencing a renaissance of economic development, but that the area had great development potential that could easily be realized through rezoning. Again, its bears repeating that the only purportedly unbiased or untainted study that concluded that Manhattanville was blighted, and thus in need of redevelopment, was not completed until 2008; the point at which the ESDC/ Columbia steamroller had virtually run its course to the fullest.

Unlike the City of New London, EDC, in conjunction with ESDC, did not endeavor to produce a comprehensive development plan to address a Manhattanville-wide economic depression. Furthermore, no municipal entity in New York committed any public funds for the redevelopment of Manhattanville. Indeed, Columbia underwrote *all* of the costs of studying and planning for what would become a sovereign sponsored campaign of Columbia's expansion. This expansion was not selected from a list of competing plans for Manhattanville's redevelopment. Indeed, the record demonstrates that EDC committed to rezoning Manhattanville, not for the goal of general economic development or to remediate an area that was "blighted" before Columbia acquired over 50% of the property, but rather solely for the expansion of Columbia itself. . . .

Thus, the record makes plain that rather than the identity of the ultimate private beneficiary being unknown at the time that the redevelopment scheme was initially contemplated, the ultimate private beneficiary of the scheme for the private annexation of Manhattanville was the progenitor of its own benefit. The record discloses that every document constituting the plan was drafted by the preselected private beneficiary's attorneys and consultants and architects, from the General Project Plan, the Special District Zoning Text, the City Map Override Proposal, and the Land Use Restrictions to all phases of the environmental review. Even the blight study on which ESDC originally proposed to base its findings was prepared by Columbia's consultant AKRF, nominally retained by ESDC for the purpose, but which retention and use by ESDC was roundly condemned by this Court in *Tuck-it-Away I.*

In *Kelo,* the plurality assumed that the redevelopment in question was itself a public purpose. No such assumption should be made in the instant case despite the Columbia sponsored finding of blight.

THERE IS NO INDEPENDENT CREDIBLE PROOF OF BLIGHT IN MANHATTANVILLE

Under the UDCA, the ESDC is empowered to acquire property for a land use improvement project if it finds, in pertinent part, that "the area in which project is to be located is a substandard or insanitary area, or is in danger of becoming a substandard or insanitary area and tends to impair or arrest the sound growth and development of the municipality." Uncons. Laws 6260[c][1] (UDCA 10(c)(1)). The statute states, in relevant part, that "[t]he term 'substandard or insanitary area' shall mean and be interchangeable with a slum, blighted, deteriorated or deteriorating area, or an area which has a blighting influence on the surrounding area." Uncons. Laws 6253[12] (UDCA 3[12]). The statute's statement of legislative findings and purposes lists various "substandard, insanitary, deteriorated or deteriorating conditions" including, among other things:

> "obsolete and dilapidated buildings and structures, defective construction, outmoded design, lack of proper sanitary facilities or adequate fire or safety protection, excessive population density, illegal uses and conversions, inadequate maintenance, [and] buildings abandoned or not utilized in whole or substantial part[.]" Uncons. Laws § 6252 (UDCA 2).

It is important to note that the record before ESDC contains no evidence whatsoever that Manhattanville was blighted prior to Columbia gaining control over the vast majority of property therein. Only that evidence which was part of ESDC's record before it was closed on December 18, 2008 can be properly considered on the question of blight....

It is critical to recognize that EDC's 2002 West Harlem Master Plan which was created prior to the scheme to balkanize Manhattanville for Columbia's benefit found no blight, nor did it describe any blighted condition or area in Manhattanville. Instead, as described above, the Plan noted that West Harlem had great potential for development that could be jump-started with re-zoning. It was only after the Plan was published in July 2002 that the rezoning of the "upland" area was essentially given over to the unbridled discretion of Columbia. In little more than a year from publication of the Plan, EDC joined with *Columbia* in proposing the use of eminent domain to allow Columbia to develop Manhattanville for Columbia's sole benefit.

This ultimately became the defining moment for the end game of blight. Having committed to allow Columbia to annex Manhattanville, the EDC and ESDC were compelled to engineer a public purpose for a quintessentially private development: eradication of blight.

From this point forward, Columbia proceeded to acquire by lease or purchase a vast amount of property in Manhattanville. It is apparent from the record that ESDC had no intention of determining if Manhattanville was blighted prior to, or apart from Columbia's control of the area. Though ESDC staff expressed concern about the sufficiency of the Urbitran study as early as December 15, 2004, it made no move towards independently ascertaining conditions in the area until late March 2006. Indeed, ESDC only commissioned a new study on September 11, 2006. From its first meeting with Columbia in September 2003, ESDC received regular updates about Columbia's property acquisitions in the area. On August 1, 2005, ESDC solicited reports about the parcels that were not owned by Columbia. Throughout this time Columbia not only purchased or gained control over most of the properties in the area, but it also forced out tenant businesses, ultimately vacating, in 17 buildings, 50% or more of the tenants. The petitioners clearly demonstrate that Columbia also let water infiltration conditions in property it acquired go unaddressed, even when minor and economically rational repairs could arrest deterioration. Columbia left building code violations open, let tenants use premises in violation of local codes and ordinances by parking cars on sidewalks and obstructing fire exits, and maintaining garbage and debris in certain buildings over a period of years.

Thus, ESDC delayed making any inquiry into the conditions in Manhattanville until long after Columbia gained control over the very properties that would form the basis for a subsequent blight study. This conduct continued when ESDC authorized AKRF to use a methodology biased in Columbia's favor. Specifically, AKRF was to "highlight" such blight conditions as it found, and it was to prepare individual building reports "focusing on characteristics that demonstrate blight conditions."

This search for distinct "blight conditions" led to the preposterous summary of building and sidewalk defects compiled by AKRF, which was then accepted as a valid methodology and amplified by Earth Tech. Even a cursory examination of the study reveals the idiocy of considering things like unpainted block walls or loose awning supports as evidence of a blighted neighborhood. Virtually every neighborhood in the five boroughs will yield similar instances of disrepair that can be captured in close-up technicolor....

THERE IS NO CIVIC PURPOSE TO THIS USE OF EMINENT DOMAIN

The use of eminent domain should also be rejected on the grounds that Columbia's expansion is not a "civic project." *See* Uncons Laws § 6253(6)(d) (UDCA 3(6)(d)). ESDC states that the project will be used by Columbia for "education related uses," and thus the project serves a civic purpose. The petitioners correctly contend that within the definition of Uncons. Laws § 6253(6)(d) (UDCA 3(6)(d)), a private university does not constitute facilities for a "civic project." The statutory definition does refer to educational uses, but the final clause "or other civic purposes," clearly restricts the educational purposes qualifying for a civic project to only such educational purposes as constitute a "civic purpose."

There is little precedent on precisely this question, and what there is to guide us augurs powerfully against the respondent. In *Matter of Fisher* (287 A.D.2d 262, 263, 730 N.Y.S.2d 516, 517 (1st Dept.2001)), this Court affirmed the condemning agency's findings that the condemnation of a building for the construction of new New York Stock Exchange facilities would "result in substantial public benefits, among them increased tax revenues, economic development and job opportunities as well as preservation and enhancement of New York's prestigious position as a worldwide financial center." Here, Columbia is virtually the sole beneficiary of the Project. This alone is reason to invalidate the condemnation especially where, as here, the public benefit is incrementally incidental to the private benefits of the Project.

Although, as the petitioners note, there does not appear to be any New York case involving the condemnation of property for the purpose of expanding a private university, a California court held that a private university could acquire private land under its power of eminent domain for the purpose of landscaping and "beautify[ing]" the grounds surrounding a newly constructed university library. *See University of S. California v. Robbins,* 1 Cal.App.2d 523, 525, 37 P.2d 163, 164 (1934), *cert. denied,*295 U.S. 738, 55 S.Ct. 650, 79 L.Ed. 1685 (1935). The California court reasoned that "[t]he higher education of youth in its largest implications is recognized as a most important public use, vitally essential to our governmental health and purposes." *Robbins,* 1 Cal.App.2d at 530, 37 P.2d at 166. However, this case offers little support for the respondent's position. In *Robbins,* the grant of eminent domain power to a tax-exempt educational institution was a creature of state law. No such legislative grant is present in the instant case. Furthermore, neither ESD nor ESDC based the use of eminent domain on Columbia's tax exempt status....

Were we to grant civic purpose status to a private university for purposes of eminent domain, we are doing that which the Legislature has explicitly failed to do: as in California and Connecticut, that decision is solely the province of the state legislature.

* * *

Many commentators have noted that "[f]ew policies have done more to destroy community and opportunity for minorities than eminent domain. Some three to four million Americans, most of them ethnic minorities, have been forcibly displaced from their homes as a result of urban renewal takings since World War II." Belito and Somin, *Battle Over Eminent Domain is Another Civil Rights Issue,* Kansas City Star, Apr. 27, 2008. The instant case is clear evidence of that reality. The unbridled use of eminent domain not only disproportionately affects minority communities, but threatens basic principles of property as contained in the Fifth Amendment....

It is not necessary to reach the position that *Kelo* was wrongly decided to invalidate the proposed takings in this case. The sharp differences between this case and the careful plan drafted by New London and described by the *Kelo* plurality could not be more compelling.

Accordingly, the petitions brought in this Court pursuant to Eminent Domain Procedure Law § 207 challenging the determination of respondent New York State Urban Development Corporation d/b/a Empire State Development Corporation, dated December 18, 2008, which approved the acquisition of certain real property for the project commonly referred to as the Columbia University Educational Mixed Use Development Land Use Improvement and Civic Project, should be granted, and the determination annulled.

■ All concur except RICHTER, J. who concurs in a separate Opinion and TOM, J.P. and RENWICK, J. who dissent in an Opinion by TOM, J.P.RICHTER, J. (concurring).

NOTES

1. The New York State Appellate Division decided *Kaur* about ten days after the Court of Appeals, the highest court in the state, decided *Goldstein*. Do you think that the Appellate Division neglected to read *Goldstein*? Or are the cases distinguishable?

2. The requirement that property suffer from "blight" in order to be vulnerable to eminent domain for economic development is obviously sufficiently vague to be open to substantial interpretation. Where a legislative body or municipal authority has made a determination of blight, what are the circumstances under which a court should reverse that finding? What were the reasons offered by the Appellate Division for intervening in the determination? To the extent that there was concern that an entity with significant political influence was able to dominate the decision making process in *Kaur*, what determinations would have to be made to justify similar judicial intervention in *Goldstein*? Does the Court of Appeals believe that the requisite level of judicial investigation into the political process is appropriate?

In Goldstein v. Pataki, 516 F.3d 50 (2d Cir. 2008), the same plaintiff had challenged the Atlantic Yards project on federal constitutional grounds. Plaintiff contended that *Kelo* permitted the court to determine whether the "public purpose" rationale for a proposed condemnation served simply as a "pretext" for bestowing a private benefit on the private user of the condemned property. Plaintiff suggested that judicial investigation into the motivations of the officials who approved the Atlantic Yards project would reveal just such a motivation. The Second Circuit declined the invitation. The court concluded:

> We do not read *Kelo*'s reference to "pretext" as demanding, as the appellants would apparently have it, a full judicial inquiry into the subjective motivation of every official who supported the Project, an exercise as fraught with conceptual and practical difficulties as with state-sovereignty and separation-of-power concerns. Beyond being conclusory, the claim that the "decision to take Plaintiffs' properties serves only one purpose" defies both logic and experience. "Legislative decisions to invoke the power to condemn are by their nature political accommodations of competing concerns." *Brody v. Vill. of Port Chester,* 434 F.3d 121, 136 (2d Cir. 2005). And as Justice Scalia observed in words, if anything, more pertinent in this case:
>
> > [W]hile it is possible to discern the objective "purpose" of a statute (i.e., the public good at which its provisions appear to be directed).... discerning the subjective motivation of [a legislative body] is, to be honest, almost always an impossible task. The number of possible motivations, to begin with, is not binary, or indeed even finite.... To look for *the sole purpose* of even a single legislator is probably to look for something that does not exist.
>
> Edwards v. Aguillard, 482 U.S. 578, 636–37, 107 S.Ct. 2573, 96 L.Ed.2d 510 (1987) (Scalia, J., dissenting) (emphasis in original).

516 F.3d at 63.

3. *Just Compensation for Economic Development Condemnations.* One issue that affects the use of eminent domain for economic development is the question of just compensation, which must be paid to landowners whose property is condemned. As a general matter, just compensation is predicated on the market value of the property at the time of condemnation. But the underlying purpose of the condemnation is to transform the property to more productive uses that will generate more tax revenues. The concern that underlies at least some of the resistance to the use of eminent domain in these circumstances is that local officials are overly optimistic in predicting the increase in revenues, either as a result of political capture by those benefited by condemnation or overconfidence about the economic future. Presumably, officials will be less attentive to the risk that the project for which property is condemned will be unsuccessful, because that risk will only materialize in the future and officials can gain the benefits of funding the project immediately. Are there ways to reduce the likelihood that officials will overestimate the benefits of local economic development? Some commentators have suggested that the present value of the expected future revenue stream be provided to condemnees or that compensation to condemnees otherwise be adjusted in a manner that causes officials to incur present costs from their estimates of increased tax benefits and thus to be more realistic about projecting future benefits from the sponsored project. See, e.g., Clayton P. Gillette, *Kelo* and the Political Process, 34 Hofstra L. Rev. 13 (2005); James E. Krier and Christopher Serkin, Public Ruses, 2004 Mich. St. L. Rev. 859; Amnon Lehavi and Amir N. Licht, Eminent Domain, Inc., 107 Colum. L. Rev. 1704 (2007); Christopher Serkin, The Meaning of Value: Assessing Just Compensation for Regulatory Takings, 99 Nw. U. L. Rev. 677 (2005).

CHAPTER 6

The Community's Relationship with Its Residents—Municipal Liabilities

A. Municipal Tort Liability Under State Law

PROBLEM XXV

The city of Harneyville operates a municipal swimming pool for its residents. Each resident may obtain an annual pass that entitles the holder to free admission. Nonresidents may use the pool only if accompanied by a resident, and nonresidents must pay $1.00 per day even when so accompanied.

Traditionally, the municipal pool has been attended at all times by two lifeguards. For financial reasons, the city council recently reduced by one-half the number of lifeguards at the pool. Hortense Hitchcock, a qualified lifeguard, was hired by the city to serve at the pool.

Hortense always placed herself at the shallow end of the pool since it was in that area that small children and nonswimmers tended to congregate. On the day in question, Hortense was on duty and in her usual position when she saw the plaintiff's decedent, Barton Beaumont, struggling in the deep end of the pool. Barton seemed to be crying for help, but had already been sapped of his strength by struggling to stay afloat, and could not cry out. Hortense ran toward the deep end of the pool, dove in and swam to Barton's side. By the time she pulled him out of the water, however, Barton had drowned.

Barton's survivors have now brought an action against the city, claiming negligence in the assignment of only one lifeguard to the pool, and against Hortense, claiming she acted negligently in placing herself at one end of the pool instead of along one side.

The state in which Harneyville is located has long held to the doctrine of immunity of municipal corporations from suit for tortious conduct. Nevertheless, the legislature has statutorily abrogated immunity for park districts, school districts, and hospital districts in the state and for tortious conduct of police officers and fire fighters. The judiciary is edgy about the state's continuing immunity policy, given abrogation of the doctrine in other jurisdictions.

You serve as legal advisor to the city. How will you address the following issues: (1) the desirability of maintaining immunity, (2) the limits of municipal liability if immunity is abolished, and (3) the capacity of the court to abolish immunity? If the judiciary abrogates total immunity in this case, how will you argue that the city still avoids liability?

Ann Judith Gellis, Legislative Reforms of Governmental Tort Liability: Overreacting to Minimal Evidence

21 Rutgers L.J. 375, 384–386, 398 (1990).

The effect of tort liability on the government's pocketbook is twofold. It not only diverts current funds from other public services, but also interferes with future allocations. In order to avoid further liability, the government diverts funds from other competing uses which government managers may consider higher priorities. Tort immunity maximizes a government's ability to allocate resources in furtherance of its political agenda by preventing judicial second guessing of the costs and benefits of government decisions. . . .

Unrestrained judicial review of government decisions poses other concerns for the political well-being of the community in addition to concern for the separation of powers between the branches of government. At least one function of tort liability is to create incentives to prevent injuries by forcing the internalization of the costs of carelessness. Underlying the continued acceptance of some immunity for government acts are assumptions about government actors and organization which suggests that these incentives do not get properly translated into government decision-making processes.

Fearing liability, bureaucrats who are already risk averse may become more so, and the pool of talented persons willing to forego private advantage to serve in the public sector may be reduced.

. . . A government decision to provide a good which is either unavailable in, or inadequately supplied by, the private sector involves various subdecisions relating to the provision of that good: how much to produce, who should receive the good, how to finance it, and how to structure delivery of the good. These decisions are complicated political decisions, quite apart from the political nature of the budgetary process. Moreover, the indivisibility of "public goods" (i.e., exclusion is not feasible) makes it more difficult to measure government's productivity or effectiveness in managing resources. Thus, the argument in favor of sovereign immunity is not only that judicial second guessing is inappropriate in our democratic society in terms of who makes decisions as to resource allocation, but that the complexity of the decision-making process as to the entire output makes it far less certain that the judiciary has the information necessary to second guess as to any one decision. . . .

However imperfect the translation of deterrence incentives from court decisions might be, the absence of liability reduces significantly the chances that government decisionmakers will account for these costs in making their decisions ex ante. The result is a less efficient decision-making process and one which is less responsive to consumer preferences....

There are other factors which suggest government officials will not consider the true costs of negligent delivery of public services. Politicians are under constant pressure to provide increased public goods and services.... Visible, tangible delivery of public services enhances their stature for the next election....

Regardless of the causes of the liability insurance industry crisis of the mid-eighties ... the evidence is overwhelming that the effect on local governments as a group was particularly severe. Premium increases of 200%–400% accompanied by lower coverage and higher deductibles were the norm. Moreover, widespread policy cancellations and withdrawals of companies from the municipal liability insurance market often made insurance unavailable at any cost. Dozens of states organized task forces during this period to investigate the causes of the liability insurance crisis. One task force, the Cuomo Commission, found that the types of activities singled out by the insurance industry as uninsurable risks tended to be publicly supplied services, such as hazardous waste removal, recreation activities, mass transit and child care centers.

NOTES

1. We could make either of the following assumptions about what motivates local officials when they decide how much care to take in delivering goods and services to the public: (1) they are primarily motivated by the public's total welfare and thus take into consideration the public's safety and the fiscal burden placed on their constituents by increasing safety; (2) they are primarily motivated by their own welfare and thus seek to deliver a level of care that will increase their own leisure time, or their own election, or their own advancement, regardless of how well that objective fits with the public welfare. Gellis implies that if we subscribe to the former position, it is difficult to see why judicial intervention to impose tort liability on officials who, by definition, are already seeking to advance public welfare, will be useful. Instead, judicial second-guessing will interfere with decisions made by political decisionmakers with the interests of their constituents in mind. If we subscribe to the second position, however, judicial intervention may serve as an effective check to enforce a decision that might be preferred by constituents who have few other forms of redress against recalcitrant public officials. For a detailed examination of these motivations, see Ronald A. Cass & Clayton P. Gillette, The Government Contractor Defense: Contractual Allocation of Public Risk, 77 Va. L. Rev. 257 (1991). Which assumption do you believe better reflects the motives of local officials? What is the effect on these motivations of infrequent elections or common benefits for public employees such as rigid pay scales and civil service protections? If you believe that public employees do not necessarily fit the first assumption, are there mechanisms other than liability that might encourage publicly interested conduct?

2. Immunity for all acts of public officials would tend to underdeter negligent behavior unless those officials perfectly seek to advance the public interest. On the other hand, as Gellis suggests, the total abrogation of sovereign immunity could well overdeter public officials. Courts have long sought to balance these considerations to develop a useful test for sovereign immunity. As you read the following cases, think about how successful the courts have been.

Campbell v. State of Indiana

284 N.E.2d 733 (Ind. 1972).

■ ARTERBURN, CHIEF JUSTICE.

These cases were consolidated for the purposes of appeal. The facts in the two cases are somewhat different, but the outcome of both is dependent on the same question of law. The cases were decided separately in the Court of Appeals and were consolidated upon transfer to the Supreme Court. See opinions of the Appellate Court reported in 269 N.E.2d 765 and 274 N.E.2d 400.

In the Campbell case the appellants sustained personal injuries as a result of a head-on collision with an automobile traveling in appellant's lane of traffic upon a state-maintained highway. In their complaint appellants alleged negligence on the part of the state in that, after repaving the highway, it failed to: (a) mark with a yellow line the aforesaid State Road 221 where it is unsafe to pass; and (b) carelessly and negligently failed to install no passing signs along Road 221 or any other signs indicating to the traveling public that the public highway was unsafe for passing. Appellants also contended that the road as maintained constituted a nuisance.

In the Knotts case, the appellant sued the City of Indianapolis and the State of Indiana complaining that he sustained $100,000 in damages because of personal injuries incurred as the result of a fall on a crosswalk in Indianapolis. Appellant alleged that the injuries were the result of the negligent state of repair of the crosswalk. The fall occurred on the crosswalk at the intersection of Market Street and Monument Circle in Indianapolis. Monument Circle is a part of the state highway system and as such, the State of Indiana is responsible for its care and maintenance. In both Campbell and Knotts the state filed a motion to dismiss in the trial court alleging that there was no basis upon which relief could be granted premised upon the doctrine of sovereign immunity. In both cases the trial court sustained the motion and the Court of Appeals affirmed the rulings. Thereafter, both appellants petitioned this court for transfer to resolve the status of the doctrine of sovereign immunity in Indiana.

Both the Campbell and Knotts briefs raise the issue of whether the State of Indiana still recognizes the common law doctrine of sovereign immunity. The doctrine in its present form is a far cry from the original common law principle which exempted the sovereign from liability in court on the basis that "the king could do no wrong." The doctrine has been amended and eroded until the most that remains is an abstract and confusing principle which finds literally no continuity between jurisdictions. The purpose for which the doctrine was created has long since vanished and it is now time to finally reexamine the basis of the rule.

The original adoption of the doctrine in America following the Revolutionary War was founded on the premise that the new government was not financially secure enough to face claims of negligence in its governmental activities. Therefore, the English Common Law was adopted and the same immunity which protected the King from liability was adopted to protect the states. The first inroad in Indiana to limit the doctrine occurred in the case of City of Goshen v. Myers (1889), 119 Ind. 196, 21 N.E. 657, where the court held that:

> In our opinion, it was the duty of the city of Goshen to keep the bridge under consideration in repair. The public bridges within the limits of the cities of the state, located upon the streets and public highways of the cities ... and such cities, where they take charge of the same, are liable to persons suffering injury or loss ...

Id. at 199, 21 N.E. 658–659.

Out of early forms of municipal liability grew the current governmental-proprietary standard which has been applied to the state and its subdivisions. This is in essence a court-made distinction as to the types of activities which governmental bodies perform, created to ameliorate the harshness of total governmental immunity. It is generally held that if a governmental body is negligent in performing a proprietary function, it will be liable for its negligence; while, if its activity is classified as governmental, the defense of sovereign immunity shall apply.

Exactly what constitutes a proprietary function as opposed to a governmental function has never been clearly enunciated by the courts, and this failure to establish a criteria has led to the generally confused state of the bench and bar in the application of the doctrine of sovereign immunity. Deciding on useful guidelines between rather obscure, whimsical notions enunciated by the appellate courts throughout the country has caused enormous conflicts in the courts in the past decade. However, the fact that the doctrine is beyond the scope of explicit definition has not halted its application....

Further erosion of the doctrine followed in the case of Brinkman v. City of Indianapolis (1967), 141 Ind. App. 662, 231 N.E.2d 169, transfer denied; in which the appellate court abolished the right of a city to claim the defense of sovereign immunity regardless of whether the nature of the act was governmental or proprietary. The court reasoned:

> The governmental-proprietary rule, however, often produces legalistic distinctions that are only remotely related to the fundamental considerations of municipal tort responsibility. As for example, it does not seem to be good policy to permit the chance that a school building may or may not be producing rental

> income at the time, determine whether a victim may recover for a fall into a dark and unguarded basement stairway or elevator shaft. Neither does it seem to be good policy to find that a municipal garbage truck is engaged in a nonimmune proprietary function when enroute from a wash rack to the garage while the same truck is engaged in an immune governmental function when enroute to a garbage pickup.... The extent to which a municipal corporation should be held liable for torts committed by its officers or employees in the course of the employment is a perplexing problem that has been the subject of litigation on many occasions. There has been a general apprehension that fraud and excessive litigation would result in unbearable cost to the public in the event municipal corporations were treated as ordinary persons for purposes of tort liability. On the other hand the unfairness to the innocent victim of a principle of complete tort immunity and the social desirability of spreading the loss—a trend now evident in many fields—have been often advanced as arguments in favor of extending the scope of liability. It is doubtful whether the purposes of tort law are well served by either the immunity rule or its exceptions. After careful consideration we are of the opinion that the doctrine of sovereign immunity has no proper place in the administration of a municipal corporation.

Id. at 665–666, 231 N.E.2d 171–172.

The next logical step was taken in the case of Klepinger v. Board of Commissioners (1968), 143 Ind. App. 155, 239 N.E.2d 160, transfer denied. The court abrogated immunity for all counties in Indiana. In the aftermath of Klepinger all that remained was immunity to the state. The court in Klepinger made it clear that the governmental-proprietary distinction was to be completely disregarded in cases involving city or county immunity.

In Perkins v. State (1969), 252 Ind. 549, 251 N.E.2d 30, the Supreme Court utilized the governmental-proprietary function to limit the application of the doctrine on the state level. In Perkins, the appellants fell ill due to the contamination of a lake with raw sewage. They had rented a lakeside cottage in a state park for which the maintenance thereof was the duty of the state. The trial court sustained the state's motion to dismiss on the ground that the court did not have jurisdiction due to the sovereign immunity of the state. The Supreme Court reversed, holding that such operation was a proprietary activity, and, therefore, the state could not avail itself of the immunity privilege. Following the holding in Perkins, all that remained of sovereign immunity was immunity on the part of the state from negligent acts occurring while the state was in performance of a solely "governmental function." Exactly what a governmental function constituted was not yet clearly defined. However, this court in Perkins recognized that municipal corporations and county governments had been eliminated from the scope of sovereign immunity as to tortious acts.

With only a mere fraction of the original doctrine remaining, we are faced with the task of attempting to eliminate the confusion surrounding the doctrine.

The argument has been presented that elimination of the doctrine of sovereign immunity will impose a disastrous financial burden upon the state. Assuming there is any relevancy to this contention, we point out that

Laws Ann. 691.1403 (2010). Some of these acts have been interpreted as abolishing the distinction between governmental and proprietary acts for purposes of liability; see, e.g., Sadler v. New Castle County, 565 A.2d 917, 921 (Del. 1989); or expressly abrogate the distinction, see, e.g., Iowa Code 670.2 (2010); Minn. Stat. 466.02 (2009). Some state statutes, however, purport to preserve the distinction. See, e.g., Tex. Civ. Prac. & Rem. Code 101.0215 (2009); Mich. Comp. Laws. Ann. 691.1407(1) (2010). And some courts have read state immunity acts as applying only to governmental activities, see, e.g., Jones v. Village of Willow Springs, 608 N.E.2d 298 (Ill. Ct. App. 1992). For a review of some general provisions of state tort claims acts, see Ann Judith Gellis, Legislative Reforms of Governmental Tort Liability: Overreacting to Minimal Evidence, 21 Rutgers L.J. 375 (1990).

In the absence of statute, some courts continue to apply the governmental/proprietary distinction to the question of immunity. See, e.g., Anderson v. Andrews, 492 S.E.2d 385 (N.C.App. 1997); State ex rel. Board of Trustees v. Russell, 843 S.W.2d 353 (Mo. 1992); Hambel v. Bohemia Fire Dept., 601 N.Y.S.2d 654 (N.Y. Sup. Ct. 1993); Stokes v. Kemper County Bd. of Supervisors, 691 So.2d 391 (Miss. 1997); Town of Brunswick v. Hyatt, 605 A.2d 620 (Md. Ct. Spec. App. 1992).

2. *Insurance and Immunity*. Some courts have interpreted the purchase of liability insurance by a municipality as an implicit waiver of immunity. See, e.g., Stryker v. City of Atlanta, 738 F.Supp. 1423 (N.D. Ga. 1990); Dugger v. Sprouse, 364 S.E.2d 275 (Ga. 1988). But see Sadler v. New Castle County, 565 A.2d 917 (Del. 1989). Are there reasons why a municipality might purchase such a policy other than as an expression of an intent to waive immunity?

3. *Indemnification*. Many jurisdictions permit or require localities to indemnify officers and employees for costs and damages incurred as a result of claims of tortious or criminal activity in the course of duty. See, e.g., Conn. Gen. Stat. Ann. § 53–39a (2010), which provides:

> Whenever, in any prosecution of an officer of . . . a local police department for a crime allegedly committed by such officer in the course of his duty as such, the charge is dismissed or the officer found not guilty, such officer shall be indemnified by his employing governmental unit for economic loss sustained by him as a result of such prosecution, including the payment of any legal fees necessarily incurred.

Similarly, Wis. Stat. Ann. § 895.46(1)(a) (2010) provides in part:

> If the defendant in any action or special proceeding is a public officer or employee and is proceeded against in an official capacity or is proceeded against as an individual because of acts committed while carrying out duties as an officer or employee and the jury or the court finds that the defendant was acting within the scope of employment, the judgment as to damages and costs entered against the officer or employee . . . in excess of any insurance applicable to the officer or employee shall be paid by the state or political subdivision of which the defendant is an officer or employee. Agents of any department of the state shall be covered by this section while acting within the scope of their agency. Regardless of the results of the litigation the governmental unit, if it does not provide legal counsel to the defendant officer or employee, shall pay

reasonable attorney fees and costs of defending the action, unless it is found by the court or jury that the defendant officer or employee did not act within the scope of employment.

The issue of whether a particular act has been committed "in the course of duty" may raise difficult issues of when an employee's conduct diverges from assigned obligations and whether the legislature intended to provide indemnity in such situations. See, e.g., Rawling v. City of New Haven, 537 A.2d 439 (Conn. 1988). What if the damages for which the municipality is obligated or authorized to indemnify its employee exceed the damage limitation for which the municipality can itself be sued? See Kelley v. City of St. Paul, 285 N.W.2d 671 (Minn. 1979).

Even where municipal corporations have not been granted express power to indemnify officers and employees, courts (including courts purporting to adhere to Dillon's Rule) have concluded that municipalities have common law authority of indemnification. See Washington Hospital Liability Insurance Fund v. Public Hospital District No. 1, 795 P.2d 717 (Wash. 1990).

Chandler v. District of Columbia

404 A.2d 964 (D.C. Ct. App. 1979).

■ KERN, ASSOCIATE JUDGE:

Appellant, administratrix and legal representative of her two deceased children, brought an action against the District of Columbia under the survival and wrongful death statutes. The children had been killed by smoke inhalation when a fire broke out in their home on September 8, 1976.

Prior to that time the District, for financial reasons, had instituted a program closing a number of fire stations on a random, rotating basis. Appellant alleged that on the day of the fire the station nearest her home was closed pursuant to this program; that this closure constituted negligence on the part of the District, its agents and instrumentalities; and, that the closure was the direct and proximate cause of the deaths of the two children.

On the District's motion, the trial judge dismissed the suit for failure to state a claim for which relief could be granted on the grounds that the District is immune from civil suit for the results of the discretionary decisions of its officials. Whether the court correctly granted this motion is the issue on appeal.

Appellant concedes that the District now enjoys immunity if the actions in question were "discretionary," Wade v. District of Columbia, D.C. App., 310 A.2d 857 (1973) (en banc).[1] Appellant admits that the action

1. According to the current standard, "the District is immune from suit only if the act complained of was committed in the exercise of a discretionary function; if committed in the exercise of a ministerial function the District must respond." Wade v. District of Columbia, supra at 860.

she alleges to have been negligent, viz., the decision regarding the fire station closure program, was "discretionary." Yet she urges this court to abolish the "ministerial-discretionary" test in the situation when a litigant alleges a "discretionary" governmental action is so unreasonable as to be arbitrary and capricious. For several reasons we reject appellant's argument and affirm.

First, this panel would not abolish the settled doctrine of sovereign immunity even if its survival in its present state was of questionable merit. Neither Wade, supra, nor Urow v. District of Columbia, 114 U.S. App. D.C. 350, 316 F.2d 351 (1963), may be overruled by a division of this court. See M. A. P. v. Ryan, D.C. App., 285 A.2d 310 (1971). Moreover, the decisions concerning sovereign immunity in this jurisdiction have stressed circumspection in according changes in the doctrine, See, e.g., Spencer v. General Hospital of District of Columbia, 138 U.S. App. D.C. 48, 53, 425 F.2d 479, 484 (1969), undoubtedly in acknowledgement that the doctrine as it now stands forms a tentative dividing line between the legislative and judicial functions; and this appropriate caution is an additional consideration compelling the conclusion that a re-examination of the doctrine is a matter for the full court.

Even assuming that we were free to redefine the doctrine of sovereign immunity, the revision suggested by appellant is not appealing. One rationale for distinguishing discretionary functions is what defines them, viz., activities "of such a nature as to pose threats to the quality and efficiency of government in the District if liability in tort were made the consequence of negligent act or omission." Spencer v. General Hospital, supra, 138 U.S. App. D.C. at 51, 425 F.2d at 482. Thus, to prevent an unhealthy stasis in policy choices and decision-making, government bodies are immune from suits aimed at the results of those decisions. Appellant cites in rebuttal King v. Seattle, 84 Wash. 2d 239, 525 P.2d 228 (1974). She argues that so long as individual officials, as distinguished from the government unit for which they perform, are immune from suit, governmental decisions will not be "chilled." However, an official whose actions ultimately result in judgments against his employer does not remain "immune" and cannot remain unaffected in his decision-making by the potential liability of the government for which he works.

Appellant's second argument has superficial appeal but does not overcome the other rationale for the continued vitality of sovereign immunity. Specifically, appellant reasons that since the implementation of policy decisions, or "ministerial" functions, is in fact subject to liability in order to encourage conscientious performance, then imposing some liability for "arbitrary and capricious" exercise of government discretion would also encourage reasonable decision-making. However, one of the purposes of imposing tort liability in the first place is to influence decisions so that their real social costs are taken into consideration when made even by public officials. See, e.g., Rieser v. District of Columbia, 183 U.S. App. D.C.

375, 563 F.2d 462 (1977). Appellant's argument fails to recognize that there are certain decisions made in the exercise of the discretionary functions of government for which there is no reason to believe a jury would render a sounder decision than those officials chosen, qualified, and prepared to make them. It is these that are labeled "discretionary" and which constitute policy decisions deemed immune from suit because there is no legal standard by which a judge or jury could gauge their arbitrariness and capriciousness or lack thereof.

As the court in Griffin v. United States, 500 F.2d 1059, 1064 (3d Cir. 1974), applied this test to the Federal Tort Claims Act "to determine the applicability of the discretionary function exception, ... we must analyze not merely whether judgment was exercised but also whether the nature of the judgment called for policy considerations." If policy considerations were involved and no statutory or regulatory requirements limited the exercise of policy discretion, the court explained, immunity would bar suit. Here, since appellant concedes that the station closure program was an action taken by government decision-makers who were prompted by policy considerations, and no statute or regulation was applicable, we conclude that her action is removed from the court's jurisdiction because of the District's immunity.

Finally, the District urged on appeal that we affirm on the alternate ground that no tort liability can lie in this suit because no duty of care was owed this appellant by the District. As was pointed out by the federal appellate court in Rieser v. District of Columbia, supra, 183 U.S. App. D.C. at 391, 563 F.2d at 478, the questions of immunity and duty owed require separate analysis in this jurisdiction due to the "ministerial-discretionary" test for immunity. Immunity revolves around the necessity or desirability of freeing policy decisions from jury speculation; a duty of care, on the other hand, concerns foreseeability.

The difficulties of defining what duty of care is owed individuals by the District confronted the court in Westminster Investing Corp. v. G. C. Murphy Co., 140 U.S. App. D.C. 247, 434 F.2d 521 (1970). Drawing aside the veil of sovereign immunity and finding no such common law tort as a failure to prevent losses due to riots, the court refused to create such a tort. This decision that the provision of or failure to provide services does not define a duty of care reflects the general rule.

There are exceptions. These exceptions follow from the doctrine that the duty of care encompasses foreseeable consequences. Thus, when a special relationship develops between an agent of the government and a private individual, a duty of care may be found. Rieser v. District of Columbia, supra. Similarly, when services are provided for private use, liability may ensue from injury to the private user. E.g., Johnson v. Municipal University of Omaha, 184 Neb. 512, 169 N.W.2d 286 (1969). Neither of these exceptions is applicable here and hence, in our view, there is no definable tort upon which appellant's suit can rest because the essential element of a duty of care owed this appellant by the District is missing.

Therefore, the order dismissing the suit is affirmed.

NOTES

1. The *Ministerial/Discretionary Distinction.* In distinguishing between ministerial and discretionary functions, the Court in *Chandler* appears to be concerned about the capacity of the judiciary to make decisions about the allocation of municipal resources. Is the reason for this skepticism rooted in concern about democratic decisionmaking bodies and electoral accountability or in the relative institutional capabilities of the legislature and the judiciary? What reasons are there to believe that the judiciary is less capable than the local legislature of making those decisions? Assume that the District of Columbia had insufficient funds to maintain all local services at current levels. Can an adjudicative proceeding provide an appropriate forum for deciding which services should be cut? Now assume that the decision has been made to cut fire-fighting services. A variety of means to implement those cuts are possible. The rotation plan described in *Chandler* might be adopted; or some fire stations might be closed permanently; or all fire stations might remain open, but be staffed by fewer personnel; or [insert here your favorite alternative]. Given the various means to limit fire-fighting expenditures, what advantages does the judiciary have in choosing among them? If you can't think of any, what does that tell you about the desirability of having the judiciary (in tort suits against the municipality) second-guess the political process through which the decision is made? Does this type of decisionmaking raise the issues of polycentricity that posed difficulty for claims that the judiciary should intervene in allocating municipal budgets? See the discussion at pages 403–405 supra.

What other kinds of decisions fall into the category covered by the ministerial/discretionary distinction?

2. The ministerial/discretionary distinction may survive even statutory abrogation of sovereign immunity. In 1961, the Washington legislature adopted RCW 4.92.090 (2010), which provides: "The state of Washington, whether acting in its governmental or proprietary capacity, shall be liable for damages arising out of its tortious conduct to the same extent as if it were a private person or corporation." Notwithstanding the apparent reach of the statute, the Washington courts have concluded that the statute does not affect the traditional immunity for discretionary activities of state employees. See, e.g., Petersen v. State, 671 P.2d 230 (Wash. 1983). In that case, the court explained the rationale underlying the distinction as ensuring "that courts refuse to pass judgment on policy decisions in the province of coordinate branches of government." 671 P.2d at 240. See also Santangelo v. State, 426 N.Y.S.2d 931 (N.Y. Ct. Cl. 1980), aff'd, 474 N.Y.S.2d 995 (N.Y. App. Div. 1984). Other statutes specifically retain immunity for discretionary acts, see, e.g., Alaska Stat. 09.65.070(d)(2) (2010); Minn. Stat. Ann. 3.736(3)(b) (2009); Or. Rev. Stat. 30.260 to 30.300 (2009). The same rationale may be applied to actions for personal liability against public officials. In Susla v. State, 247 N.W.2d 907 (Minn. 1976), the court determined that the state was liable for acts committed in a proprietary capacity, but not for acts committed in a governmental capacity. (The issue in the case dealt with manufacturing of products by prisoners in state correctional institutions. Receipts from sale of the products were dedicated to operation of correctional facilities. Is this a governmental or a proprietary activity?) Even where the state was liable in its proprietary capacity, however, individual public officials would not be: "It is settled law in Minnesota that a public official charged by law with duties which call for the exercise of his judgment or discretion is not personally liable to an individual for damages unless he is guilty of a willful or malicious wrong." 247 N.W.2d at 912. The legislature subsequently abrogated sovereign immunity in most tort cases, regardless of whether the state had acted in a governmental or proprietary capacity. See Minn. Stat. § 3.736 (2009).

3. To the extent that statutory immunity is limited to the state or its political subdivisions, and not extended to public employees, tort immunity might seem to produce an anomaly. Why should it be the case that employees, who are unlikely to be sued given their limited wealth, should be deemed liable, while their wealthier public employers, who supervise and monitor their activities, are immunized? The New Jersey Supreme Court addressed the realities of this apparent incongruity in an action brought against employees of a city public works department after plaintiff suffered injuries when a pickup truck hit a large hole in a city street. Note, however, that the New Jersey court interprets the state legislature to have reached a very different balance on the ministerial/discretionary distinction explored above:

> In determining the issues posed by this appeal, we rely on the New Jersey Tort Claims Act, N.J.S.A. 59:1–1 to :12–3 (Act), which governs claims against public entities and public employees. We emphasize initially that the Act reestablishes sovereign immunity for public entities, but does not similarly shield public employees. A public entity is deemed "not liable for an injury" except as provided in the Act. In contrast, a public employee "is liable for injury" except as otherwise provided. Thus, the analysis for determining public-employee liability differs markedly from the analysis for determining public-entity liability. That differential treatment of public employees and entities by the Tort Claims Act reflects longstanding legal principles in the State and explains in large part the apparent anomaly that public employees may be exposed to greater liability than their public employers. While some may be surprised that public employees and employers are treated differently for tort purposes, the distinctions are readily explainable given the evolution of tort law in New Jersey. Moreover, it should be emphasized that the apparent harshness of exposing employees to greater liability under certain limited circumstances is just that—apparent. In practice, the longstanding policy of indemnifying public employees shields them from ruinous tort penalties.
>
> We now hold that under the Tort Claims Act and relevant common law jurisprudence public employees owe a duty to members of the public to protect against the dangerous condition of public property and that such employees are not immune from suit under the "inspection" immunities of the Act. With respect to protecting against the dangerous condition of public property, we

> determine that the standard of care applicable to public employees depends on the nature of their duties. If those duties are ministerial and non-discretionary, public employees may be found liable if they failed to use reasonable care. If those duties require the exercise of discretion or policy decisions, public employees may be found liable if their failure to use care was palpably unreasonable. These rules insure that innocent victims are not left with the financial burden imposed on them by other persons' negligence while at the same time safeguarding the legitimate policy-making functions of local government.

Chatman v. Hall, 608 A.2d 263, 267–268 (N.J. 1992) (citations omitted). In 1994, the New Jersey legislature amended the state's Tort Claims Act to provide immunity for any public employee where the public entity is immune for the same injury. See N.J.S.A. § 59:3–1 (c) (2010).

4. Recall that Professor Gellis is primarily concerned with judicial reallocation of resources after democratic processes have led to a particular allocation of the municipal budget. This concern seems consistent with the court's rejection in *Chandler* of the proposition that juries will "render a sounder decision than those officials chosen, qualified, and prepared to make them." Now consider the Court's role in Crosland v. New York City Transit Authority, 498 N.E.2d 143, 143 (N.Y. 1986), in which the question presented was "whether a public carrier whose employees allegedly stood by and did nothing while one of its passengers [a student at the High School of Music and Art] was beaten to death by hoodlums should be immune from all civil liability."

> There were no police in the [125th Street subway] station. [The decedent's] friends claimed there had almost always been officers in that station in the past. Allegedly, several track workers witnessed the incident and did nothing to summon aid. As the attack progressed, the complaint also stated, at least two trains, whose personnel were able to observe the attack, passed through the station, and these employees also did nothing.
>
> Recovery was sought against the Transit Authority on three separate theories: that the defendant breached its special duty of care to the decedent because it failed to maintain "around-the-clock police presence" at the 125th Street station though it knew that station was the site of previous youth gang attacks on [High School of] Music and Art students; that the defendant's employees breached a duty to [the decedent] by failing to "take every precaution to prevent ... injuries to persons," as required by the Authority's rule 85; and that defendant failed to meet the standard of care owed by common carriers to their passengers....
>
> This court has held that the allocation of police resources implicates a governmental function for which a publicly owned carrier cannot be held liable, even though a private carrier could be held liable for a similar failure to allocate security personnel if that failure proximately resulted in a patron's sustaining injury at the hand of a third party (Weiner v. Metropolitan Transp. Auth., 55 N.Y.2d 175, [448 N.Y.S.2d 141, 433 N.E.2d 124 (N.Y. 1982)]). In the two cases decided under the *Weiner* caption, it must be stressed, the plaintiffs were attacked at stations where no police were present, and they argued, without success, that police should have been put there because of prior incidents at the

> stations. To the extent the complaint in the present action alleges a failure to properly allocate police resources, therefore, it too must fail....
>
> Whether any act or failure to act of a Transit Authority employee alleged in the complaint can be the basis for an actionable claim against the Authority depends upon whether it is within or without the boundaries of the policy-based governmental immunity established in [*Weiner*]. Because the complaint alleges that an employee seeing the injury being inflicted unreasonably failed to summon aid although he could have done so without risk to himself, we hold such failure to act beyond the boundary of the *Weiner* immunity. Watching someone being beaten from a vantage point offering both safety and the means to summon help without danger is within the narrow range of circumstances which could be found to be actionable....

498 N.E.2d at 144–145 (citations omitted). Does the court's decision in *Crosland* mean that municipal resources will have to be reallocated in order to avoid future liability? Consider that the meritorious allegation in this case was not that the municipality failed to assign a sufficient number of employees to protect users of the transit system; rather, the meritorious allegation was that the employees assigned did nothing during the fatal attack. In short, the judiciary agreed to enforce the political deal struck by the responsible officials rather than to recreate the deal. What about the response that the decision in *Crosland* requires the transit authority to hire better employees, and hence to allocate more resources to protection of transit system users?

5. The court in *Chandler* concludes with recognition that liability may be imposed on a locality where it has created a special relationship with a particular individual. The court in *Campbell* seems to recognize the same principle when it contends that "in order for one to have standing to recover in a suit against the state there must have been a breach of duty owed to a private individual." What is the justification for this exception once the court has decided to confer immunity on a locality? And how does the court determine whether the requisite relationship exists? Under New York law,

> A special relationship can be formed in three ways: (1) when the municipality violates a statutory duty enacted for the benefit of a particular class of persons; (2) when it voluntarily assumes a duty that generates justifiable reliance by the person who benefits from the duty; or (3) when the municipality assumes positive direction and control in the face of a known, blatant and dangerous safety violation.

Pelaez v. Seide, 810 N.E.2d 393 (N.Y. App. 2004) (citing Garrett v. Holiday Inns, Inc., 447 N.E.2d 717, 721 (N.Y. App. 1983)).

In Raucci v. Town of Rotterdam, 902 F.2d 1050 (2d Cir. 1990), the United States Court of Appeals for the Second Circuit outlined the test under New York law for the second type of special relationship listed in *Pelaez* above. In *Raucci*, the estranged husband of the plaintiff repeatedly threatened and physically beat her. With police assistance, plaintiff obtained an order of protection and taped telephone conversations in which the husband threatened her life. When plaintiff played the tapes for the police, they delayed the effort to arrest the husband. When he was arrested after continuing threats, the police failed to inform the judge of the nature of the husband's threats and he was released from custody. Ultimately, the husband followed the plaintiff, shot her and killed their son. Plaintiff brought actions against the town under federal and state law. In upholding a jury verdict in favor of the plaintiff on the state claims, the court summarized New York law on local tort liability for failure to protect:

> Generally, a municipality is not liable under New York law for failing to provide an individual with police protection. "[I]n order for liability to be imposed upon a municipality . . . there must be proof of a 'special relationship' between that person and the municipality." The "special duty" imposed by that relationship is recognized only in a "narrow class of cases." The reason for limiting this exception is that a municipality's duty to provide police protection is owed to the public at large rather than to any individual or class of citizens, and questions of resource allocation, such as how much protection a municipality must provide to an individual or class, are left to the discretion of the municipal policy makers.
>
> The elements of the special relationship are
>
> (1) an assumption by the municipality, through promises or actions, of an affirmative duty to act on behalf of the party who was injured;
>
> (2) knowledge on the part of the municipality's agents that inaction could lead to harm;
>
> (3) some form of direct contact between the municipality's agents and the injured party; and
>
> (4) that party's justifiable reliance on the municipality's affirmative undertaking.
>
> Once the special relationship is found to exist between the municipality and the injured person, the actions of the municipality's agents will be subject to a reasonableness standard. "Whether a special duty has been breached is generally a question for the jury to decide," and "whether the municipality has acted reasonably depends upon the circumstances of the particular case."
>
> **A. Assumption of Duty**
>
> Defendants assert that there was no evidence of Rotterdam assuming a duty to act through promises or actions of the Rotterdam Police Department. They contend that they fulfilled any obligation they had to Ms. Raucci by arresting her husband on June 23.
>
> The evidence, however, supports the verdict as to this first element. Deputy Chief DeCarlo told Ms. Raucci that the police "could do more" than what she had requested of them and suggested the taping of the harassing telephone calls. The Rotterdam Police trained her to record these calls. Despite the acknowledgment that the tapes provided sufficient evidence for a charge of aggravated harassment, and despite the fact that they evidenced the lethal character of Mr. Raucci's threats, the police did nothing with them. The June 23 information the police drafted for Ms. Raucci merely referred to "numerous telephone calls" by Mr. Raucci but only as background for the charge arising from the incident that took place on that day. Neither the tapes nor their contents were presented to Justice O'Connor during Raucci's arraignment. DeCarlo said on June 28 that he was still working on the tapes, implying that the June 23 arrest was not the end of the police department's role. The police

also knew, beginning in late May, that Ms. Raucci had an order of protection (having suggested that she obtain the order) and that these harassing telephone calls constituted violations of the order. "[W]hen the police are made aware of a possible violation [of an order of protection], they are obligated to respond and investigate, and their actions will be subject to a 'reasonableness' review in a negligence action."

B. Knowledge That Inaction Would Lead to Harm

Defendants claim that the record is barren of any proof that the Rotterdam Police Department knew that Mr. Raucci was a violent person or otherwise harmful and therefore they were unaware that inaction would lead to harm. The Rotterdam Police Department, however, was well aware of Mr. Raucci's threats against Ms. Raucci's life: from her statements to them; from the recorded telephone conversations which revealed that Mr. Raucci was armed and threatening; and from physical injuries which corroborated her allegations. At the suggestion of Officer Bethmann, Ms. Raucci obtained an order of protection against Mr. Raucci, and she reminded the Rotterdam Police Department of this order whenever she contacted them concerning Raucci's harassment. An order of protection evinces a preincident legislative and judicial determination that its holder should be accorded a reasonable degree of protection from a particular individual. It is presumptive evidence that the individual whose conduct is proscribed has already been found by a court to be a dangerous or violent person and that violations of the order's terms should be treated seriously.

The police thus were aware of Mr. Raucci's dangerousness....

C. Direct Contact With Rotterdam's Agents

... One reason for the direct contact requirement is to provide a rational limit on the number of citizens "to whom the municipality's 'special duty' extends." Cuffy, 69 N.Y.2d at 261, 505 N.E.2d at 940, 513 N.Y.S.2d at 375. "[T]he proper application of the 'direct contact' requirement depends on the peculiar circumstances of each case, all of which must be considered in light of the policies underlying the narrow 'special duty' doctrine." ...

In this case, Ms. Raucci initially approached the Rotterdam Police Department with Chad. She obtained an order of protection which, under Sorichetti and its progeny, extended to her children insofar as her contacts with the Rotterdam Police Department were concerned. Officers of the Rotterdam Police Department had seen Chad and knew who he was. They also knew from the tapes and from observing Mr. Raucci in the police station on June 28 that Chad was the object of a custody dispute between the couple. The district court did not err in determining that the element of direct contact was established as to Chad as well as his mother.

D. Justifiable Reliance on Rotterdam's Affirmative Assumed Duty

... The reliance element is "critical in establishing the existence of a 'special relationship' " because it provides "the essential causative link between the 'special duty' assumed by the municipality and the alleged injury." Defendants' contention rests on the fact that Ms. Raucci did not change her routine for the seven days between Mr. Raucci's release on bail and the shooting. According to defendants, Ms. Raucci had to avoid Mr. Raucci in order to establish reliance on the Rotterdam Police Department's assurances. The district court found, to the contrary, that the failure of Ms. Raucci to change her routine was a true indicator of her reliance on a perceived promise of police

> protection. On June 28, DeCarlo told Ms. Raucci that he was still working on the tapes, implying that the case was not closed with the police after Raucci's arrest and release as far as the police were concerned. Obviously, the tapes would have been key evidence in any further proceeding against Mr. Raucci. Ms. Raucci relied on DeCarlo's statement, believed that the police either would arrest Mr. Raucci again or would otherwise protect her, and was "lulled ... into a false sense of security" by DeCarlo's statement.
>
> Based on the foregoing, there was sufficient evidence of all of the elements of a special relationship between Ms. Raucci and Rotterdam not to grant judgment notwithstanding the verdict. Further, the court correctly found that the verdict was not against the weight of the evidence.

902 F.2d at 1055–1058 (citations omitted). For a far less rigorous test of a special relationship that imposes liability on a public officer for failure to intervene, see Burdette v. Marks, 421 S.E.2d 419 (Va. 1992). In that case, plaintiff claimed that defendant, a uniformed police officer, failed to protect plaintiff after seeing a third party beat plaintiff after a traffic accident. The court concluded that a public official only had a duty enforceable in tort to protect persons with whom he had a special relation. That relation, however, could be inferred in this case from the fact that defendant was present and on duty as a deputy sheriff when plaintiff was under attack, and that defendant had the capacity to subdue the attacker without being subjected to undue danger.

6. Claims against localities for negligent failure to perform duties have increased dramatically in recent years. One can characterize many of these cases as involving claims similar to that raised in *Crosland*, where the locality had agreed to undertake a service and rendered it negligently. See, e.g., A.L. v. Commonwealth, 521 N.E.2d 1017 (Mass. 1988) (negligent supervision of convict by probation officer); De Long v. County of Erie, 457 N.E.2d 717 (N.Y. 1983) (negligent response to 911 emergency call); Emig v. State, Dept. of Health and Rehabilitative Services, 456 So.2d 1204 (Fla. Dist. Ct. App. 1984) (negligent failure to prevent escape from confinement).

What if instead the locality expressly refuses to undertake an obligation? In Riss v. City of New York, 240 N.E.2d 860 (N.Y. 1968), for example, a woman who had been terrorized for months by a rejected suitor repeatedly, and unsuccessfully, asked the police for protection. After a threatening phone call from the suitor, and yet another unsuccessful plea to the police for help, the plaintiff was blinded in one eye, lost a good portion of her vision in the other, and had her face permanently scarred by a thug hired by the suitor to throw lye in the plaintiff's face. In dismissing her complaint, the N.Y. Court of Appeals reasoned:

> [T]his case involves the provision of a governmental service to protect the public generally from external hazards and particularly to control the activities of criminal wrongdoers.... The amount of protection that may be provided is limited by the resources of the community and by a considered legislative-executive decision as to how those resources may be deployed. For the courts to proclaim a new and general duty of protection in the law of tort, even to those who may be the particular seekers of protection based on specific hazards, could

> and would inevitably determine how the limited police resources of the community should be allocated and without predictable limits....
>
> ... Quite distinguishable, of course, is the situation where the police authorities undertake responsibilities to particular members of the public and expose them, without adequate protection, to the risks which then materialize into actual losses....

240 N.E.2d at 860–861. Is this distinction—between instances in which the locality agreed to undertake a service and rendered it negligently, and those in which the locality expressly refused to undertake an obligation—useful in trying to determine whether the judiciary should intervene in what are initially local decisions about hiring, training, and implementing policies?

B. MUNICIPAL LIABILITY UNDER FEDERAL CIVIL RIGHTS LAW

42 U.S.C. § 1983

> Every person who, under color of any statute, ordinance, regulation, custom, or usage, of any State or Territory or the District of Columbia, subjects, or causes to be subjected, any citizen of the United States or other person within the jurisdiction thereof to the deprivation of any rights, privileges, or immunities secured by the Constitution and laws, shall be liable to the party injured in an action at law, suit in equity, or other proper proceeding for redress....

PROBLEM XXVI

On March 21, at 11:15 P.M., Elwood Black drove his 1976 Cadillac Coupe de Ville to pick up his wife who was finishing work in the city of Allentown. On the way home, the Blacks stopped for a red light in the westbound lane of Lehigh Street at the intersection of 8th Avenue. Wayne Stephens, on duty as a plainclothes detective, is employed by the City of Allentown. What transpired next is the subject of much dispute.

According to the Blacks, when the traffic light turned green, Mr. Black proceeded through the intersection at a reasonable rate of speed. After crossing the intersection, Detective Stephens suddenly raced up from behind and passed the Black's vehicle by crossing the double yellow line on Lehigh Street. Black was startled by Stephens' recklessness and remarked to his wife about the driver.

After passing the Black's car, Stephens stopped at the intersection of 10th and Lehigh. Black stopped about 6 feet behind Stephens in the outside westbound lane. At this point, Stephens jumped out of his car and, without identifying himself, approached the Black's car and started screaming that Mr. Black was a "rotten driver." Stephens was wearing slacks, an open collared shirt, and a nylon windbreaker. After arguing with Stephens for a moment, Black said: "Why am I even bothering with you. Your car is in the way; it is blocking traffic; will you move your car so I can move mine and get out of here." Black then put his car in drive and attempted to pull around to the left of the approaching Stephens. At this point, Stephens pulled out his service revolver and aimed it directly at Black's head. Mrs. Black, sitting in the right rear seat, was in the precise line of fire. With gun drawn, Stephens screamed that Black had driven onto his foot and threatened to shoot if Black did not move the car. Black alleges that his car was nowhere near Stephens' foot, but he backed up and drove around the right of Stephens' vehicle and continued west on Lehigh Street.

Terribly shaken by their encounter with the as of yet unidentified gunman, the Blacks continued toward their home. As they approached 29th and Lehigh, however, they saw flashing red lights and encountered a police roadblock. They stopped at the roadblock and were arrested for aggravated assault by Officer Shoemaker of the Allentown police force.

Detective Stephens' version of the events is, predictably, much different. According to his pre-trial testimony, Stephens first noticed the Blacks' vehicle as he pulled behind their car at the intersection of 8th and Lehigh. When the light changed, the Blacks' car, originally in the outside westbound lane of the street, started to swerve into the inside lane. As Stephens began to pass, the Blacks' vehicle swerved back and forced Stephens over the double yellow line, into the eastbound lane. Stephens stopped for a red light at 10th and Lehigh and the Blacks' car screeched to a halt a few inches behind him. Stephens, worried that the driver might be intoxicated or that something was amiss, got out of his car and walked toward the Blacks' vehicle. Stephens inquired if there was anything wrong and Black screeched that Stephens was a "rotten driver." At this point, the Blacks' car lurched directly at him and the left front tire rolled onto Stephens' foot. He screamed in vain for Black to get off his foot. Finally, because of the excruciating pain, Stephens drew his revolver and ordered Black to remove his car. Black then backed up and swung to the right through the intersection.

A high-speed chase ensued. Stephens radioed for help and Officer Shoemaker set up the road block at which the arrest was made.

The parties agree that at 1:00 A.M. Stephens filed a criminal complaint against Black. While filling out the complaint, Stephens testified that Black was extremely upset and had promised to complain to Police Chief Gable and the Mayor of Allentown.

Black returned to the police station on March 23 to register a complaint about Stephens. He spoke with Chief of Police Gable, but was informed that no investigation of Stephens' conduct would commence until the charge against Black was resolved. Chief Gable cited a police regulation, contained in the official police manual, that stated: "Please Note: Where a complaint alleging misconduct on the part of an officer arises from an incident where the officer made an arrest, disciplinary proceedings (against the officer) will not take place until the arrest charges are finally adjudicated."

On March 24, Chief Gable met with Stephens and informed him of Black's complaint about his conduct during the incident. Thereafter, Stephens filed three additional charges against Black based on the March 21 episode: reckless endangerment, carrying a concealed deadly weapon, and terroristic threats. The latter two charges were subsequently dropped and Black was found not guilty on the reckless endangerment charge. Black was later found guilty of simply assault, but on appeal this conviction was vacated and remanded for a new trial. The record is silent as to the present status of this case.

The Blacks have now consulted you concerning the possibility of bringing a civil rights action against the city and Stephens under 42 U.S.C. § 1983. What charges should be alleged in the complaint? What would you hope to prove against each defendant in order to be successful?

Owen v. City of Independence

445 U.S. 622 (1980).

■ MR. JUSTICE BRENNAN delivered the opinion of the Court.

Monell v. New York City Dept. of Social Services, 436 U.S. 658, 98 S. Ct. 2018, 56 L. Ed. 2d 611 (1978), overruled Monroe v. Pape, 365 U.S. 167, 81 S. Ct. 473, 5 L. Ed. 2d 492 (1961), insofar as *Monroe* held that local governments were not among the "persons" to whom 42 U.S.C. § 1983 applies and were therefore wholly immune from suit under the statute. *Monell* reserved decision, however, on the question whether local governments, although not entitled to an absolute immunity, should be afforded some form of official immunity in § 1983 suits. 436 U.S., at 701, 98 S. Ct., at 2041. In this action brought by petitioner in the District Court for the Western District of Missouri, the Court of Appeals for the Eighth Circuit held that respondent city of Independence, Mo., "is entitled to qualified immunity from liability" based on the good faith of its officials: "We extend the limited immunity the district court applied to the individual defendants to cover the City as well, because its officials acted in good faith and without malice." 589 F.2d 335, 337–338 (1978). We granted certiorari. 444 U.S. 822, 100 S. Ct. 42, 62 L.Ed.2d 28 (1979).

We reverse. . . .

II

Petitioner named the city of Independence, City Manager Alberg, and the present members of the City Council in their official capacities as defendants in this suit. Alleging that he was discharged without notice of reasons and without a hearing in violation of his constitutional rights to procedural and substantive due process, petitioner sought declaratory and injunctive relief, including a hearing on his discharge, backpay from the date of discharge, and attorney's fees. The District Court, after a bench trial, entered judgment for respondents. 421 F. Supp. 1110 (1976).

The Court of Appeals initially reversed the District Court. 560 F.2d 925 (1977). Although it agreed with the District Court that under Missouri law petitioner possessed no property interest in continued employment as

Police Chief, the Court of Appeals concluded that the city's allegedly false public accusations had blackened petitioner's name and reputation, thus depriving him of liberty without due process of law. That the stigmatizing charges did not come from the City Manager and were not included in the official discharge notice was, in the court's view, immaterial. What was important, the court explained, was that "the official actions of the city council released charges against [petitioner] contemporaneous and, in the eyes of the public, connected with that discharge." Id., at 937.

Respondents petitioned for review of the Court of Appeals' decision. Certiorari was granted, and the case was remanded for further consideration in light of our supervening decision in Monell v. New York City Dept. of Social Services, 436 U.S. 658, 98 S. Ct. 2018, 56 L. Ed. 2d 611 (1978). 438 U.S. 902, 98 S. Ct. 3118, 57 L. Ed. 2d 1145 (1978). The Court of Appeals on the remand reaffirmed its original determination that the city had violated petitioner's rights under the Fourteenth Amendment, but held that all respondents, including the city, were entitled to qualified immunity from liability. 589 F.2d 335 (1978).

Monell held that "a local government may not be sued under § 1983 for an injury inflicted solely by its employees or agents. Instead, it is when execution of a government's policy or custom, whether made by its lawmakers or by those whose edicts or acts may fairly be said to represent official policy, inflicts the injury that the government as an entity is responsible under § 1983." 436 U.S., at 694, 98 S. Ct., at 2038. The Court of Appeals held in the instant case that the municipality's official policy was responsible for the deprivation of petitioner's constitutional rights: "[T]he stigma attached to [petitioner] in connection with his discharge was caused by the official conduct of the City's lawmakers, or by those whose acts may fairly be said to represent official policy. Such conduct amounted to official policy causing the infringement of [petitioner's] constitutional rights, in violation of section 1983." 589 F.2d, at 337.

Nevertheless, the Court of Appeals affirmed the judgment of the District Court denying petitioner any relief against the respondent city, stating:

> The Supreme Court's decisions in Board of Regents v. Roth, 408 U.S. 564 [92 S. Ct. 2701, 33 L. Ed. 2d 548] (1972), and Perry v. Sindermann, 408 U.S. 593 [92 S. Ct. 2694, 33 L. Ed. 2d 570] (1972), crystallized the rule establishing the right to a name-clearing hearing for a government employee allegedly stigmatized in the course of his discharge. The Court decided those two cases two months after the discharge in the instant case. Thus, officials of the City of Independence could not have been aware of [petitioner's] right to a name-clearing hearing in connection with the discharge. The City of Independence should not be charged with predicting the future course of constitutional law. We extend the limited immunity the district court applied to the individual defendants to cover the City as well, because its officials acted in good faith and without malice. We hold the City not liable for actions it could not reasonably have known violated [petitioner's] constitutional rights.

Id., at 338 (footnote and citations omitted).

We turn now to the reasons for our disagreement with this holding....

III

Because the question of the scope of a municipality's immunity from liability under § 1983 is essentially one of statutory construction, see Wood v. Strickland, 420 U.S. 308, 314, 316, 95 S. Ct. 992, 996, 998, 43 L. Ed. 2d 214 (1975); Tenney v. Brandhove, 341 U.S. 367, 376, 71 S. Ct. 783, 788, 95 L. Ed. 1019 (1951), the starting point in our analysis must be the language of the statute itself. Andrus v. Allard, 444 U.S. 51, 56, 100 S. Ct. 318, 322, 62 L. Ed. 2d 210 (1979); Blue Chip Stamps v. Manor Drug Stores, 421 U.S. 723, 756, 95 S. Ct. 1917, 1935, 44 L. Ed. 2d 539 (1975) (Powell, J., concurring). By its terms, § 1983 "creates a species of tort liability that on its face admits of no immunities." Imbler v. Pachtman, 424 U.S. 409, 417, 96 S. Ct. 984, 988, 47 L. Ed. 2d 128 (1976). Its language is absolute and unqualified; no mention is made of any privileges, immunities, or defenses that may be asserted. Rather, the Act imposes liability upon "*every person*" who, under color of state law or custom, "subjects, or causes to be subjected, any citizen of the United States ... to the deprivation of any rights, privileges, or immunities secured by the Constitution and laws." And *Monell* held that these words were intended to encompass municipal corporations as well as natural "persons."

Moreover, the congressional debates surrounding the passage of 1 of the Civil Rights Act of 1871, 17 Stat. 13—the forerunner of § 1983—confirm the expansive sweep of the statutory language....

However, notwithstanding § 1983's expansive language and the absence of any express incorporation of common-law immunities, we have, on several occasions, found that a tradition of immunity was so firmly rooted in the common law and was supported by such strong policy reasons that "Congress would have specifically so provided had it wished to abolish the doctrine." Pierson v. Ray, 386 U.S. 547, 555, 87 S. Ct. 1213, 1218, 18 L. Ed. 2d 288 (1967). Thus in Tenney v. Brandhove, supra, after tracing the development of an absolute legislative privilege from its source in 16th-century England to its inclusion in the Federal and State Constitutions, we concluded that Congress "would [not] impinge on a tradition so well grounded in history and reason by covert inclusion in the general language" of § 1983. 341 U.S., at 376, 71 S. Ct., at 788.

Subsequent cases have required that we consider the personal liability of various other types of government officials. Noting that "[f]ew doctrines were more solidly established at common law than the immunity of judges from liability for damages for acts committed within their judicial jurisdiction," Pierson v. Ray, supra, 386 U.S., at 553–554, 87 S. Ct., at 1217, held that the absolute immunity traditionally accorded judges was preserved under § 1983. In that same case, local police officers were held to enjoy a "good faith and probable cause" defense to § 1983 suits similar to that which existed in false arrest actions at common law. 386 U.S., at 555–557, 87 S. Ct., at 1218–1219. Several more recent decisions have found immunities of varying scope appropriate for different state and local officials sued under § 1983. See Procunier v. Navarette, 434 U.S. 555, 98 S. Ct. 855, 55 L. Ed. 2d 24 (1978) (qualified immunity for prison officials and officers); Imbler v. Pachtman, 424 U.S. 409, 96 S. Ct. 984, 47 L. Ed. 2d 128 (1976) (absolute immunity for prosecutors in initiating and presenting the State's case); O'Connor v. Donaldson, 422 U.S. 563, 95 S. Ct. 2486, 45 L. Ed. 2d 396 (1975) (qualified immunity for superintendent of state hospital); Wood v. Strickland, 420 U.S. 308, 95 S. Ct. 992, 43 L. Ed. 2d 214 (1975) (qualified immunity for local school board members); Scheuer v. Rhodes, 416 U.S. 232, 94 S. Ct. 1683, 40 L. Ed. 2d 90 (1974) (qualified "good-faith" immunity for state Governor and other executive officers for discretionary acts performed in the course of official conduct).

In each of these cases, our finding of § 1983 immunity "was predicated upon a considered inquiry into the immunity historically accorded the relevant official at common law and the interests behind it." Imbler v. Pachtman, supra, at 421, 96 S. Ct., at 990. Where the immunity claimed by the defendant was well established at common law at the time § 1983 was enacted, and where its rationale was compatible with the purposes of the Civil Rights Act, we have construed the statute to incorporate that immunity. But there is no tradition of immunity for municipal corporations, and neither history nor policy supports a construction of § 1983 that would justify the qualified immunity accorded the city of Independence by the Court of Appeals. We hold, therefore, that the municipality may not assert the good faith of its officers or agents as a defense to liability under § 1983.[18]

A

Since colonial times, a distinct feature of our Nation's system of governance has been the conferral of political power upon public and municipal corporations for the management of matters of local concern. As *Monell* recounted, by 1871 municipalities—like private corporations—were treated as natural persons for virtually all purposes of constitutional and statutory analysis. In particular, they were routinely sued in both federal and state courts. See 436 U.S., at 687–688, 98 S. Ct., at 2034. Cf. Cowles v. Mercer County, 7 Wall. 118, 19 L. Ed. 86 (1869). Local governmental units were regularly held to answer in damages for a wide range of statutory and constitutional violations, as well as for common-law actions for breach of contract. And although, as we discuss below, a municipality was not subject to suit for all manner of tortious conduct, it is clear that at the time § 1983 was enacted, local governmental bodies did not enjoy the sort of "good-faith" qualified immunity extended to them by the Court of Appeals.

---

18. The governmental immunity at issue in the present case differs significantly from the official immunities involved in our previous decisions. In those cases, various government officers had been sued in their individual capacities, and the immunity served to insulate them from personal liability for damages. Here, in contrast, only the liability of the municipality itself is at issue, not that of its officers, and in the absence of an immunity, any recovery would come from public funds.

As a general rule, it was understood that a municipality's tort liability in damages was identical to that of private corporations and individuals. . . .

[I]n the hundreds of cases from that era awarding damages against municipal governments for wrongs committed by them, one searches in vain for much mention of a qualified immunity based on the good faith of municipal officers. Indeed, where the issue was discussed at all, the courts had rejected the proposition that a municipality should be privileged where it reasonably believed its actions to be lawful. . . .

To be sure, there were two doctrines that afforded municipal corporations some measure of protection from tort liability. The first sought to distinguish between a municipality's "governmental" and "proprietary" functions; as to the former, the city was held immune, whereas in its exercise of the latter, the city was held to the same standards of liability as any private corporation. The second doctrine immunized a municipality for its "discretionary" or "legislative" activities, but not for those which were "ministerial" in nature. A brief examination of the application and the rationale underlying each of these doctrines demonstrates that Congress could not have intended them to limit a municipality's liability under § 1983.

The governmental-proprietary distinction owed its existence to the dual nature of the municipal corporation. On the one hand, the municipality was a corporate body, capable of performing the same "proprietary" functions as any private corporation, and liable for its torts in the same manner and to the same extent, as well. On the other hand, the municipality was an arm of the State, and when acting in that "governmental" or "public" capacity, it shared the immunity traditionally accorded the sovereign. But the principle of sovereign immunity—itself a somewhat arid fountainhead for municipal immunity—is necessarily nullified when the State expressly or impliedly allows itself, or its creation, to be sued. Municipalities were therefore liable not only for their "proprietary" acts, but also for those "governmental" functions as to which the State had withdrawn their immunity. And, by the end of the 19th century, courts regularly held that in imposing a specific duty on the municipality either in its charter or by statute, the State had impliedly withdrawn the city's immunity from liability for the nonperformance or misperformance of its obligation. See, e.g., Weightman v. The Corporation of Washington, 1 Black 39, 50–52, 17 L. Ed. 52 (1862); Providence v. Clapp, 17 How. 161, 167–169, 15 L. Ed. 72 (1855). See generally Shearman & Redfield §§ 122–126; Note, Liability of Cities for the Negligence and Other Misconduct of their Officers and Agents, 30 Am. St. Rep. 376, 385 (1893). Thus, despite the nominal existence of an immunity for "governmental" functions, municipalities were found liable in damages in a multitude of cases involving such activities.

That the municipality's common-law immunity for "governmental" functions derives from the principle of sovereign immunity also explains why that doctrine could not have served as the basis for the qualified privilege respondent city claims under § 1983. First, because sovereign immunity insulates the municipality from unconsented suits altogether, the presence or absence of good faith is simply irrelevant. The critical issue is whether injury occurred while the city was exercising governmental, as opposed to proprietary, powers or obligations—not whether its agents reasonably believed they were acting lawfully in so conducting themselves. More fundamentally, however, the municipality's "governmental" immunity is obviously abrogated by the sovereign's enactment of a statute making it amenable to suit. Section 1983 was just such a statute. By including municipalities within the class of "persons" subject to liability for violations of the Federal Constitution and laws, Congress—the supreme sovereign on matters of federal law—abolished whatever vestige of the State's sovereign immunity the municipality possessed....

In sum, we can discern no "tradition so well grounded in history and reason" that would warrant the conclusion that in enacting 1 of the Civil Rights Act, the 42d Congress *sub silentio* extended to municipalities a qualified immunity based on the good faith of their officers. Absent any clearer indication that Congress intended so to limit the reach of a statute expressly designed to provide a "broad remedy for violations of federally protected civil rights," Monell v. New York City Dept. of Social Services, 436 U.S., at 685, 98 S. Ct., at 2033, we are unwilling to suppose that injuries occasioned by a municipality's unconstitutional conduct were not also meant to be fully redressable through its sweep.

B

Our rejection of a construction of § 1983 that would accord municipalities a qualified immunity for their good-faith constitutional violations is compelled both by the legislative purpose in enacting the statute and by considerations of public policy. The central aim of the Civil Rights Act was to provide protection to those persons wronged by the " '[m]isuse of power, possessed by virtue of state law and made possible only because the wrongdoer is clothed with the authority of state law.' " Monroe v. Pape, 365 U.S., at 184, 81 S. Ct., at 482 (quoting United States v. Classic, 313 U.S. 299, 326, 61 S. Ct. 1031, 1043, 85 L. Ed. 1368 (1941)). By creating an express federal remedy, Congress sought to "enforce provisions of the Fourteenth Amendment against those who carry a badge of authority of a State and represent it in some capacity, whether they act in accordance with their authority or misuse it." Monroe v. Pape, supra, 365 U.S., at 172, 81 S. Ct., at 476.

How "uniquely amiss" it would be, therefore, if the government itself—"the social organ to which all in our society look for the promotion of liberty, justice, fair and equal treatment, and the setting of worthy norms and goals for social conduct"—were permitted to disavow liability for the injury it has begotten. See Adickes v. Kress & Co., 398 U.S. 144, 190, 90 S. Ct. 1598, 1620, 26 L. Ed. 2d 142 (1970) (opinion of Brennan, J.). A damages remedy against the offending party is a vital component of any scheme for vindicating cherished constitutional guarantees, and the importance of assuring its efficacy is only accentuated when the wrongdoer is the institution that has been established to protect the very rights it has transgressed. Yet owing to the qualified immunity enjoyed by most government officials, see Scheuer v. Rhodes, 416 U.S. 232, 94 S. Ct. 1683, 40 L. Ed. 2d 90 (1974), many victims of municipal malfeasance would be left remediless if the city were also allowed to assert a good-faith defense. Unless countervailing considerations counsel otherwise, the injustice of such a result should not be tolerated.

Moreover, § 1983 was intended not only to provide compensation to the victims of past abuses, but to serve as a deterrent against future constitutional deprivations, as well. See Robertson v. Wegmann, 436 U.S. 584, 590–591, 98 S. Ct. 1991, 1995, 56 L. Ed. 2d 554 (1978); Carey v. Piphus, 435 U.S. 247, 256–257, 98 S. Ct. 1042, 1048–1049, 55 L. Ed. 2d 252 (1978). The knowledge that a municipality will be liable for all of its injurious conduct, whether committed in good faith or not, should create an incentive for officials who may harbor doubts about the lawfulness of their intended actions to err on the side of protecting citizens' constitutional rights. Furthermore, the threat that damages might be levied against the city may encourage those in a policymaking position to institute internal rules and programs designed to minimize the likelihood of unintentional infringements on constitutional rights. Such procedures are particularly beneficial in preventing those "systemic" injuries that result not so much from the conduct of any single individual, but from the interactive behavior of several government officials, each of whom may be acting in good faith. Cf. Note, Developments in the Law: Section 1983 and Federalism, 90 Harv. L. Rev. 1133, 1218–1219 (1977).[36]

Our previous decisions conferring qualified immunities on various government officials, see supra, at 1408–1409, are not to be read as derogating the significance of the societal interest in compensating the innocent victims of governmental misconduct. Rather, in each case we concluded that overriding considerations of public policy nonetheless demanded that the official be given a measure of protection from personal liability. The concerns that justified those decisions, however, are less compelling, if not wholly inapplicable, when the liability of the municipal entity is at issue.

In Scheuer v. Rhodes, supra, 416 U.S., at 240, 94 S. Ct., at 1688, the Chief Justice identified the two "mutually dependent rationales" on which the doctrine of official immunity rested:

> (1) the injustice, particularly in the absence of bad faith, of subjecting to liability an officer who is required, by the legal obligations of his position, to exercise discretion; (2) the danger that the threat of such liability would deter

36. In addition, the threat of liability against the city ought to increase the attentiveness with which officials at the higher levels of government supervise the conduct of their subordinates. The need to institute system-wide measures in order to increase the vigilance with which otherwise indifferent municipal officials protect citizens' constitutional rights is, of course, particularly acute where the front-line officers are judgment-proof in their individual capacities.

his willingness to execute his office with the decisiveness and the judgment required by the public good.

The first consideration is simply not implicated when the damages award comes not from the official's pocket, but from the public treasury. It hardly seems unjust to require a municipal defendant which has violated a citizen's constitutional rights to compensate him for the injury suffered thereby. Indeed, Congress enacted § 1983 precisely to provide a remedy for such abuses of official power. See Monroe v. Pape, 365 U.S., at 171–172, 81 S. Ct., at 475–476. Elemental notions of fairness dictate that one who causes a loss should bear the loss.

It has been argued, however, that revenue raised by taxation for public use should not be diverted to the benefit of a single or discrete group of taxpayers, particularly where the municipality has at all times acted in good faith. On the contrary, the accepted view is that stated in Thayer v. Boston—"that the city, in its corporate capacity, should be liable to make good the damage sustained by an [unlucky] individual, in consequence of the acts thus done." 36 Mass., at 515. After all, it is the public at large which enjoys the benefits of the government's activities, and it is the public at large which is ultimately responsible for its administration. Thus, even where some constitutional development could not have been foreseen by municipal officials, it is fairer to allocate any resulting financial loss to the inevitable costs of government borne by all the taxpayers, than to allow its impact to be felt solely by those whose rights, albeit newly recognized, have been violated. See generally 3 K. Davis, Administrative Law Treatise 25.17 (1958 and Supp. 1970); Prosser § 131, at 978; Michelman, Property, Utility, and Fairness: Some Thoughts on the Ethical Foundations of "Just Compensation" Law, 80 Harv. L. Rev. 1165 (1967).

The second rationale mentioned in *Scheuer* also loses its force when it is the municipality, in contrast to the official, whose liability is at issue. At the heart of this justification for a qualified immunity for the individual official is the concern that the threat of personal monetary liability will introduce an unwarranted and unconscionable consideration into the decisionmaking process, thus paralyzing the governing official's decisiveness and distorting his judgment on matters of public policy. The inhibiting effect is significantly reduced, if not eliminated, however, when the threat of personal liability is removed. First, as an empirical matter, it is questionable whether the hazard of municipal loss will deter a public officer from the conscientious exercise of his duties; city officials routinely make decisions that either require a large expenditure of municipal funds or involve a substantial risk of depleting the public fisc. See Kostka v. Hogg, 560 F.2d 37, 41 (CA 1 1977). More important, though, is the realization that consideration of the *municipality's* liability for constitutional violations is quite properly the concern of its elected or appointed officials. Indeed, a decisionmaker would be derelict in his duties if, at some point, he did not consider whether his decision comports with constitutional mandates and did not weigh the risk that a violation might result in an award of damages from the public treasury. As one commentator aptly put it: "Whatever other concerns should shape a particular official's actions, certainly one of them should be the constitutional rights of individuals who will be affected by his actions. To criticize section 1983 liability because it leads decision-makers to avoid the infringement of constitutional rights is to criticize one of the statute's *raisons d'etre.*"

IV

In sum, our decision holding that municipalities have no immunity from damages liability flowing from their constitutional violations harmonizes well with developments in the common law and our own pronouncements on official immunities under § 1983. Doctrines of tort law have changed significantly over the past century, and our notions of governmental responsibility should properly reflect that evolution. No longer is individual "blameworthiness" the acid test of liability; the principle of equitable loss-spreading has joined fault as a factor in distributing the costs of official misconduct.

We believe that today's decision, together with prior precedents in this area, properly allocates these costs among the three principals in the scenario of the § 1983 cause of action: the victim of the constitutional deprivation; the officer whose conduct caused the injury; and the public, as represented by the municipal entity. The innocent individual who is harmed by an abuse of governmental authority is assured that he will be compensated for his injury. The offending official, so long as he conducts himself in good faith, may go about his business secure in the knowledge that a qualified immunity will protect him from personal liability for damages that are more appropriately chargeable to the populace as a whole. And the public will be forced to bear only the costs of injury inflicted by the "execution of a government's policy or custom, whether made by its lawmakers or by those whose edicts or acts may fairly be said to represent official policy." Monell v. New York City Dept. of Social Services, 436 U.S., at 694, 98 S. Ct., at 2038.

Reversed.

■ MR. JUSTICE POWELL, with whom THE CHIEF JUSTICE, MR. JUSTICE STEWART, and MR. JUSTICE REHNQUIST join, dissenting. . . .

[T]he Court holds that municipalities are strictly liable for their constitutional torts. Until two years ago, municipal corporations enjoyed absolute immunity from § 1983 claims. Monroe v. Pape, 365 U.S. 167, 81 S. Ct. 473, 5 L. Ed. 2d 492 (1961). But Monell v. New York City Dept. of Social Services, supra, held that local governments are "persons" within the meaning of the statute, and thus are liable in damages for constitutional violations inflicted by municipal policies. 436 U.S., at 690, 98 S. Ct., at 2035. *Monell* did not address the question whether municipalities might enjoy a qualified immunity or good-faith defense against § 1983 actions. 436 U.S., at 695, 701, 98 S. Ct., at 2038, 2041; id., at 713–714, 98 S. Ct., at 2047 (POWELL, J., concurring).

After today's decision, municipalities will have gone in two short years from absolute immunity under § 1983 to strict liability. As a policy matter, I believe that strict municipal liability unreasonably subjects local governments to damages judgments for actions that were reasonable when performed. It converts municipal governance into a hazardous slalom through constitutional obstacles that often are unknown and unknowable.

The Court's decision also impinges seriously on the prerogatives of municipal entities created and regulated primarily by the States. At the very least, this Court should not initiate a federal intrusion of this magnitude in the absence of explicit congressional action. Yet today's decision is supported by nothing in the text of § 1983. Indeed, it conflicts with the apparent intent of the drafters of the statute, with the common law of municipal tort liability, and with the current state law of municipal immunities....

The Court today abandons any attempt to harmonize § 1983 with traditional tort law. It points out that municipal immunity may be abrogated by legislation. Thus, according to the Court, Congress "abolished" municipal immunity when it included municipalities "within the class of 'persons' subject to liability" under § 1983. Ante, at 1414.

This reasoning flies in the face of our prior decisions under this statute. We have held repeatedly that "immunities 'well grounded in history and reason' [were not] abrogated 'by covert inclusion in the general language' of § 1983." Imbler v. Pachtman, supra, at 418, 96 S. Ct., at 989, quoting Tenney v. Brandhove, supra, at 376, 71 S. Ct., at 788. See Scheuer v. Rhodes, supra, at 243–244, 94 S. Ct., at 1689–1690; Pierson v. Ray, supra, at 554, 87 S.Ct., at 1217. The peculiar nature of the Court's position emerges when the status of executive officers under § 1983 is compared with that of local governments. State and local executives are personally liable for bad-faith or unreasonable constitutional torts. Although Congress had the power to make those individuals liable for all such torts, this Court has refused to find an abrogation of traditional immunity in a statute that does not mention immunities. Yet the Court now views the enactment of § 1983 as a direct abolition of traditional municipal immunities. Unless the Court is overruling its previous immunity decisions, the silence in § 1983 must mean that the 42d Congress mutely accepted the immunity of executive officers, but silently rejected common-law municipal immunity. I find this interpretation of the statute singularly implausible.

Important public policies support the extension of qualified immunity to local governments. First, as recognized by the doctrine of separation of powers, some governmental decisions should be at least presumptively insulated from judicial review. Mr. Chief Justice Marshall wrote in Marbury v. Madison, 1 Cranch 137, 170, 2 L. Ed. 60 (1803), that "[t]he province of the court is ... not to inquire how the executive, or executive officers, perform duties in which they have a discretion." Marshall stressed the caution with which courts must approach "[q]uestions, in their nature political, or which are, by the constitution and laws, submitted to the executive." The allocation of public resources and the operational policies of the government itself are activities that lie peculiarly within the competence of executive and legislative bodies. When charting those policies, a local official should not have to gauge his employer's possible liability under § 1983 if he incorrectly—though reasonably and in good faith—forecasts the course of constitutional law. Excessive judicial intrusion into such decisions can only distort municipal decisionmaking and discredit the courts. Qualified immunity would provide presumptive protection for discretionary acts, while still leaving the municipality liable for bad faith or unreasonable constitutional deprivations.

Because today's decision will inject constant consideration of § 1983 liability into local decisionmaking, it may restrict the independence of local governments and their ability to respond to the needs of their communities. Only this Term, we noted that the "point" of immunity under § 1983 "is to forestall an atmosphere of intimidation that would conflict with [officials'] resolve to perform their designated functions in a principled fashion." Ferri v. Ackerman, 444 U.S. 193, 203–204, 100 S. Ct. 402, 409, 62 L. Ed. 2d 355 (1979).

The Court now argues that local officials might modify their actions unduly if they face personal liability under § 1983, but that they are unlikely to do so when the locality itself will be held liable. Ante, at 1418. This contention denigrates the sense of responsibility of municipal officers, and misunderstands the political process. Responsible local officials will be concerned about potential judgments against their municipalities for alleged constitutional torts. Moreover, they will be accountable within the political system for subjecting the municipality to adverse judgments. If officials must look over their shoulders at a strict municipal liability for unknowable constitutional deprivations, the resulting degree of governmental paralysis will be little different from that caused by fear of personal liability. Cf. Wood v. Strickland, 420 U.S., at 319–320, 95 S. Ct., at 999; Scheuer v. Rhodes, 416 U.S., at 242, 94 S. Ct., at 1689.

In addition, basic fairness requires a qualified immunity for municipalities. The good-faith defense recognized under § 1983 authorizes liability only when officials acted with malicious intent or when they "knew or should have known that their conduct violated the constitutional norm." Procunier v. Navarette, 434 U.S., at 562, 98 S. Ct., at 860. The standard incorporates the idea that liability should not attach unless there was notice that a constitutional right was at risk. This idea applies to governmental entities and individual officials alike. Constitutional law is what the courts say it is, and—as demonstrated by today's decision and its precursor, *Monell*—even the most prescient lawyer would hesitate to give a firm opinion on matters not plainly settled. Municipalities, often acting in the utmost good faith, may not know or anticipate when their action or inaction will be deemed a constitutional violation.

The Court nevertheless suggests that, as a matter of social justice, municipal corporations should be strictly liable even if they could not have known that a particular action would violate the Constitution. After all, the Court urges, local governments can "spread" the costs of any judgment across the local population. Ante, at 1417. The Court neglects, however, the fact that many local governments lack the resources to withstand substantial unanticipated liability under § 1983. Even enthusiastic proponents of municipal liability have conceded that ruinous judgments under the statute could imperil local governments. E.g., Note, Damage Remedies Against Municipalities for Constitutional Violations, 89 Harv. L. Rev. 922, 958 (1976). By simplistically applying the theorems of welfare economics and ignoring the reality of municipal finance, the Court imposes strict liability on the level of government least able to bear it. For some municipalities, the result could be a severe limitation on their ability to serve the public....

Today's decision also conflicts with the current law in 44 States and the District of Columbia. All of those jurisdictions provide municipal immunity at least analogous to a "good faith" defense against liability for constitutional torts. Thus, for municipalities in almost 90% of our jurisdictions, the Court creates broader liability for constitutional deprivations than for state-law torts.

Twelve States have laws creating municipal tort liability but barring damages for injuries caused by discretionary decisions or by the good-faith execution of a validly enacted, though unconstitutional, regulation. Municipalities in those States have precisely the form of qualified immunity that this Court has granted to executive officials under § 1983. Another 11 States provide even broader immunity for local governments. Five of those have retained the governmental/proprietary distinction, while Arkansas and South Dakota grant even broader protection for municipal corporations. Statutes in four more States protect local governments from tort liability except for particular injuries not relevant to this case, such as those due to motor vehicle accidents or negligent maintenance of public facilities. In Iowa, local governments are not liable for injuries caused by the execution with due care of any "officially enacted" statute or regulation.

Sixteen States and the District of Columbia follow the traditional rule against recovery for damages imposed by discretionary decisions that are confided to particular officers or organs of government. Indeed, the leading commentators on governmental tort liability have noted both the appropriateness and general acceptance of municipal immunity for discretionary acts. See Restatement (Second) of Torts § 895C(2) and Comment *g* (1979); K. Davis, Administrative Law of the Seventies § 25.13 (1976); W. Prosser, Law of Torts 986–987 (4th ed. 1971). In four States, local governments enjoy complete immunity from tort actions unless they have taken out liability insurance. Only five States impose the kind of blanket liability constructed by the Court today....

NOTES

1. Justice Brennan identifies a series of justifications for imposing municipal liability under § 1983. Do these justifications also support the distinction between allowing a good faith defense for municipal employees, but not extending that defense to the municipality itself? Consider, for example, Justice Brennan's discussion of the deterrence function of liability. He suggests that liability is inappropriate where municipal employees are involved because they might be overdeterred by fear of personal liability. But Justice Brennan does not indicate that he believes that employees not exposed to liability have incentives to act in the public interest. Rather, he indicates that the municipality will have to supervise its employees and prevent them from acting in a self-interested manner, through internal procedures such as denial of promotions, suspension of pay, etc. The municipality, Justice Brennan suggests, will have incentives to impose these internal penalties in order to reduce or eliminate its own exposure to liability. See footnote 36 of the opinion and accompanying text. From the perspective of overdeterrence, how does the imposition of internal sanctions on employees who commit constitutional torts differ from the imposition of liability through the tort system? Is there reason to believe that employees will be overdeterred less by threat of the former than the latter? Indeed, to the extent that employees will receive indemnification for judgments rendered against them as a result of the performance of their duties, it would seem that internal sanctions will be more likely to deter than nominally external (judicially imposed) sanctions. Given Justice Brennan's reasoning, do you agree with his statement that "[t]he inhibiting effect [of liability] is significantly reduced, if not eliminated, however, when the threat of personal liability is removed"?

Consider the following arguments for allowing a "good faith" immunity for individuals, but not for the locality:

(a) Ultimately, we want to induce localities to change a custom or policy that violates federally protected rights, even if that custom or policy was implemented in good faith. A locality is likely to make the desired change only if failure to do so will result in liability. Unless prospective plaintiffs can recover from the locality, they have no incentive to bring an action that would inform the locality of the illegal nature of its policies and induce the desired change. Thus, denying the locality the benefit of qualified immunity is necessary to provide an incentive to sue.

(b) There will be some situations in which liability that is initially imposed on the locality will not translate into internal sanctions being imposed on individual officials. For instance, where an official has acted in good faith, there is no reason for the locality to impose a formal sanction. In the absence of a formal sanction, the official will not be overdeterred, except to the extent that he fears informal sanctions, e.g., being passed over for promotion because of an affiliation with an episode that led to liability against the city. Thus, imposing strict liability on localities may induce localities to train officials to prevent wrongful conduct, but not necessarily to reprimand, and thus overdeter, individual officers.

(c) Municipal liability, unlike personal liability imposed on individual officials, is likely to enhance the political process by which municipal resource allocations are made. If this result occurs, then the objectives of leaving the allocation decision to politically responsible actors, rather than to judges, is not necessarily frustrated. Enhancement of the political process presumably occurs when residents are required to bear the social costs of depriving individuals of their federally protected rights. To the extent that tort damages are reflected in local taxes, residents will have incentives to monitor the conduct of local officials and to lobby for "cheaper" local customs and policies, i.e., those that do not violate federally protected rights. Thus, it is important that those who enjoy the benefit of the customs and policies also bear the burdens. Does this rationale swallow up all immunities?

(d) Perhaps we simply want to compensate victims injured by official action and find that the cheapest way to accomplish this is through transfer payments from the municipality rather than from individual officials.

2. *The Scope of Immunity.* As the majority opinion indicates, the Supreme Court held in Monell v. Department of Social Services of City of New York, 436 U.S. 658 (1978) that municipalities constitute "persons" to whom 42 U.S.C. § 1983 applies. That decision overruled a contrary decision in Monroe v. Pape, 365 U.S. 167 (1961). States enjoy broader immunity. In Will v. Michigan Department of State Police, 491 U.S. 58 (1989), the Court held that a state is not a person for purposes of § 1983. See also Arizonans for Official English v. Arizona, 520 U.S. 43 (1997). The majority in *Will* found no congressional intent in § 1983 to subject the states to liability, to disturb the states' Eleventh Amendment immunity for violations of civil rights, or to override well-established immunities available to the sovereign under common law. The Court applied the same immunity to state officials when sued for damages in their official capacities. State officials sued in their official capacity for injunctive relief, however, are "persons" under § 1983, as such actions are not considered to be actions against the state. *Will*, 491 U.S. at, 71 n.10.

The Supreme Court has assigned absolute immunity to some officials "whose special functions or constitutional status requires complete protection from suit." Harlow v. Fitzgerald, 457 U.S. 800, 807 (1982). These officials include state prosecutors involved in the initiation of criminal proceedings, Imbler v. Pachtman, 424 U.S. 409 (1976); state prosecutors who appear for the state in a probable cause hearing, Burns v. Reed, 500 U.S. 478 (1991); state prosecutors who appear in court to present evidence in support of a search warrant application, Kalina v. Fletcher, 522 U.S. 118 (1997); state prosecutors involved in supervision or training of trial prosecutors or involved in information-system management, Van de Kamp v. Goldstein, 129 S.Ct. 855 (2009); state legislators, Tenney v. Brandhove, 341 U.S. 367 (1951); regional legislators, Lake Country Estates, Inc. v. Tahoe Regional Planning Agency, 440 U.S. 391 (1979); local legislators, Bogan v. Scott–Harris, 523 U.S. 44 (1998); witnesses at trial, Briscoe v. LaHue, 460 U.S. 325 (1983); and judges, Pierson v. Ray, 386 U.S. 547 (1967). Only qualified immunity applies, however, to a prosecutor for giving legal advice to the police, Burns v. Reed, 500 U.S. 478 (1991); to a prosecutor making statements to the press, Buckley v. Fitzsimmons, 509 U.S. 259 (1993); to a peace officer when obtaining an arrest warrant, Malley v. Briggs, 475 U.S. 335 (1986); to state public defenders, Tower v. Glover, 467 U.S. 914 (1984); to state executive officers, Scheuer v. Rhodes, 416 U.S. 232 (1974); or to private outside counsel employed by a city, Cullinan v. Abramson, 128 F.3d 301 (6th Cir. 1997), cert. denied, 523 U.S. 1094 (1998).

Under current law, an official who is entitled to qualified immunity under § 1983 can be held liable only if he or she violates "clearly established statutory or constitutional rights of which a reasonable person would have known." Harlow v. Fitzgerald, 457 U.S. 800 (1982); Anderson v. Creighton, 483 U.S. 635 (1987). This standard replaced the common law subjective standard of good faith.

Certain actors may enjoy immunity from § 1983 claims, even if their actions otherwise satisfy the conditions of liability. In Bogan v. Scott–Harris, 523 U.S. 44 (1998), a former director of the city's social services department brought a § 1983 action against the city and city officials, alleging that the city's passage of an ordinance eliminating the director's position violated her First Amendment rights. The Supreme Court held that local legislators are absolutely immune from suit under § 1983 for their legislative activities, that legislative immunity attaches to all actions of local officials taken in the sphere of legitimate legislative activity, and that the legislative character of an act depends on its nature rather than the motive of the legislator in committing it. Thus, the act of voting in favor of the ordinance was legislative and the mayor's act of preparing a budget and signing the ordinance that eliminated the position was legislative, regardless of motive.

Are there more reasons to grant legislative immunity to city councilors than to state legislators? What do you make of the following arguments in favor of absolute immunity?

> Legislatures themselves possess effective internal mechanisms for countering misbehavior in the give-and-take of public debate and deliberation. Also, legislative action in a multi-member body requires coalition-building among individual legislators, which acts as a further check on arbitrary or extreme conduct. Many local legislatures have internal disciplinary powers as well. In this case, for example, members of the Common Council may be removed from the legislature for "official misconduct" by either a two-thirds vote of the council or by the circuit court of Kanawha County. Public scrutiny through the press also exposes and deters legislative action that crosses permissible lines.

Berkley v. Common Council of City of Charleston, 63 F.3d 295, 310 (4th Cir. 1995) (Wilkinson, J., dissenting) (citations omitted), cert. denied, 516 U.S. 1073 (1996). See also McMillian v. Monroe County, 520 U.S. 781 (1997) (Alabama sheriffs represent state when executing their law enforcement duties and, therefore, are not county "policymakers" for purposes of county liability under § 1983). For discussion of issues involving legislative and official immunity, see Alan K. Chen, The Facts about Qualified Immunity, 55 Emory L.J. 229 (2006); Caryn J. Ackerman, Fairness or Fiction: Striking a Balance Between the Goals of § 1983 and the Policy Concerns Motivating Qualified Immunity, 85 Or. L. Rev. 1027 (2006).

3. *Persons under § 1983.* In Hafer v. Melo, 502 U.S. 21 (1991), the Court concluded that state officials sued in their individual capacities are "persons" for purposes of § 1983. The action taken by the official that serves as the basis for the claim must, of course, be action "under color of state law" if § 1983 is to apply. The official in such a case has a broader range of immunities than those available to the governmental entity by which the official is employed. "While the plaintiff in a personal-capacity suit need not establish a connection to governmental 'policy or custom,' officials sued in their personal capacities ... may assert personal immunity defenses such as objectively reasonable reliance on existing law." Id. at 25. The Court extended the availability of such defenses to officials sued in their personal capacity in the prior case of Kentucky v. Graham, 473 U.S. 159 (1985). A claim brought against a public servant "in her official capacity" imposes liability on the entity that she represents rather than on her personally. Brandon v. Holt, 469 U.S. 464 (1985). The plaintiff in such a case must, however, provide the entity with notice and an opportunity to respond. An individual sued in an official capacity will only be able to assert those immunities available to the governmental entity that the official represents. Are Justice Brennan's concerns about overdeterring state officials through liability less compelling when the plaintiff has a remedy against the official in his or her personal rather than official capacity?

4. Punitive damages are not available in an action brought against a municipality under § 1983. See Newport v. Fact Concerts, Inc., 453 U.S. 247 (1981); cf. Jefferson v. City of Tarrant, 522 U.S. 75, 79 (1997). They may be recovered in a § 1983 action brought against an official in his or her personal capacity. See Smith v. Wade, 461 U.S. 30 (1983).

5. What constitutes "good faith" conduct that will immunize officials from liability? In Williams v. City of Albany, 936 F.2d 1256 (11th Cir. 1991), the court ruled that police officers had acted in good faith sufficient to support immunity where the officers had submitted evidence from a witness to a grand jury, even though they suspected that the witness lacked credibility and knew that any grand jury indictment might be barred by the statute of limitations. The court applied the rationale adopted by the Supreme Court in Harlow v. Fitzgerald, 457 U.S. 800 (1982), that qualified immunity is not available where the official knew or should have known that his actions would violate the constitutional rights of the plaintiff. The Supreme Court has indicated that this test creates an objective standard, Anderson v. Creighton, 483 U.S. 635 (1987), and courts have applied it as such by stating that good faith does not exist where the public official's actions violate clearly established constitutional rights. See, e.g., Hudgins v. City of Ashburn, 890 F.2d 396, 404–407 (11th Cir. 1989). In Coleman v. McHenry, 735 F.Supp. 190 (E.D. Va. 1990), aff'd, 945 F.2d 398 (4th Cir. 1991), the court determined that, since the right to be free from racial discrimination was well recognized, a supervisor who allegedly engaged in acts of racial discrimination and retaliation against a subordinate was not entitled to assert a good faith immunity defense.

6. *Owen* makes clear that a municipality will not be liable under § 1983 for acts of its officials and employees on a respondeat superior theory. See also Board of County Commissioners of Bryan County v. Brown, 520 U.S. 397, 403 (1997). In Jett v. Dallas Independent School District, 491 U.S. 701 (1989), the Court addressed the issue of whether a locality can be held vicariously liable under 42 U.S.C. § 1981. That provision grants all persons within the jurisdiction of the United States "the full and equal benefit of all laws and proceedings for the security of persons and property as is enjoyed by white citizens." Jett claimed that he was improperly removed from his duties and brought actions under 42 U.S.C. § 1981 and § 1983. The Court concluded that § 1983 constituted the exclusive federal remedy for violation of the rights guaranteed by § 1981, so that the limitations on respondeat superior implicit in § 1983 applied with equal force to § 1981 actions.

7. Some courts have displayed a clear antipathy toward § 1983 actions against localities and their officials by imposing a "heightened pleading requirement" that allows defendant municipalities and officials to secure summary judgment unless allegations against them are pleaded with sufficient specificity. See, e.g., Palmer v. San Antonio, 810 F.2d 514 (5th Cir. 1987); Hunter v. District of Columbia, 943 F.2d 69 (D.C. Cir. 1991); and cases cited in Elliott v. Perez, 751 F.2d 1472, 1479 n.20 (5th Cir. 1985).

In 1993, however, the U.S. Supreme Court in Leatherman v. Tarrant County Narcotics Intelligence and Coordination Unit, 507 U.S. 163 (1993), rejected the Fifth Circuit's heightened pleading requirement in a § 1983 action alleging municipal liability. The Court held that such a standard was "impossible to square" with the "liberal system of 'notice pleading' set up by the Federal Rules [of Civil Procedure]." Id. at 168.

The Court in *Leatherman* also expressly stated, however, that "[w]e . . . have no occasion to consider whether our qualified immunity jurisprudence would require heightened pleading in cases involving individual government officials." Id. at 166–167. In declining to extend its holding to suits against individual officers, the Court emphasized that "unlike various government officials, municipalities do not enjoy immunity from suit—either absolute or qualified—under § 1983." Id. at 166. Thus, at least some courts have continued to apply a heightened pleading requirement in cases concerning individual government officials. See, e.g., Breidenbach v. Bolish, 126 F.3d 1288, 1292 n.2 (10th Cir. 1997); Schultea v. Wood, 47 F.3d 1427, 1430 (5th Cir. 1995) (en banc); Jordan by Jordan v. Jackson, 15 F.3d 333, 338–41 (4th Cir. 1994).

City of St. Louis v. Praprotnik

485 U.S. 112 (1988).

■ JUSTICE O'CONNOR announced the judgment of the Court and delivered an opinion, in which CHIEF JUSTICE REHNQUIST, JUSTICE WHITE, and JUSTICE SCALIA join.

[In *Praprotnik,* 485 U.S. 112 (1988), the Court set forth the legal standard for determining when isolated decisions by municipal officers or employees may expose the municipality itself to liability under 42 U.S.C. § 1983. The plaintiff-respondent was an architect working for the city who was suspended for 15 days in 1980 because he accepted outside employment without prior approval, in violation of a requirement of his city employment. He successfully appealed the suspension to the city's Civil Service Commission and, two years later, was transferred from the city's Community Development Agency to its Heritage and Urban Design Division. After an unsuccessful appeal of his transfer, Plaintiff filed suit in federal court alleging, in part, that his First Amendment rights had been violated through retaliatory actions taken in response to his successful appeal of the 1980 suspension. The jury exonerated the individual defendants, but found the city liable. The Court of Appeals for the Eighth Circuit affirmed the jury verdict.—EDS.]

Monell's rejection of respondeat superior, and its insistence that local governments could be held liable only for the results of unconstitutional governmental "policies," arose from the language and history of § 1983....

In the years since *Monell* was decided, the Court has considered several cases involving isolated acts by government officials and employees. We have assumed that an unconstitutional governmental policy could be inferred from a single decision taken by the highest officials responsible for setting policy in that area of the government's business. See, e.g., Owen v. City of Independence, supra; Newport v. Fact Concerts, Inc., supra. Cf. *Pembaur*, supra, 475 U.S., at 480, 106 S. Ct., at 1298–1299. At the other end of the spectrum, we have held that an unjustified shooting by a police officer cannot, without more, be thought to result from official policy....

Two terms ago, in *Pembaur*, [475 U.S. 469 (1986)], we undertook to define more precisely when a decision on a single occasion may be enough to establish an unconstitutional municipal policy. Although the Court was unable to settle on a general formulation, Justice Brennan's plurality opinion articulated several guiding principles. First, a majority of the Court agreed that municipalities may be held liable under § 1983 only for acts for which the municipality itself is actually responsible, "that is, acts which the municipality has officially sanctioned or ordered." 475 U.S., at 480, 106 S. Ct., at 1298. Second, only those municipal officials who have "final policymaking authority" may by their actions subject the government to § 1983 liability. Id., at 483, 106 S. Ct., at 1300. Third, whether a particular official has "final policymaking authority" is a question of state law. Ibid. Fourth, the challenged action must have been taken pursuant to a policy adopted by the official or officials responsible under state law for making policy in that area of the city's business. Id., at 482–483, and n.12, 106 S. Ct., at 1299–1300, and n.12....

C

Whatever refinements of these principles may be suggested in the future, we have little difficulty concluding that the Court of Appeals applied an incorrect legal standard in this case....

The city cannot be held liable under § 1983 unless respondent proved the existence of an unconstitutional municipal policy. Respondent does not contend that anyone in city government ever promulgated, or even articulated, such a policy. Nor did he attempt to prove that such retaliation was ever directed against anyone other than himself. Respondent contends that the record can be read to establish that his supervisors were angered by his 1980 appeal to the Civil Service Commission; that new supervisors in a new administration chose, for reasons passed on through some informal means, to retaliate against respondent two years later by transferring him to another agency; and that this transfer was part of a scheme that led, another year and a half later, to his lay off. Even if one assumes that all this was true, it says nothing about the actions of those whom the law established as the makers of municipal policy in matters of personnel administration. The mayor and aldermen enacted no ordinance designed to retaliate against respondent or against similarly situated employees. On the contrary, the city established an independent Civil Service Commission and empowered it to review and correct improper personnel actions. Respondent does not deny that his repeated appeals from adverse personnel decisions repeatedly brought him at least partial relief, and the Civil Service Commission never so much as hinted that retaliatory transfers or lay offs were permissible. . . .

Accordingly, the decision of the Court of Appeals is reversed, and the case is remanded for further proceedings consistent with this opinion.

It is so ordered.

■ JUSTICE KENNEDY took no part in the consideration or decision of this case.

■ JUSTICE BRENNAN, with whom JUSTICE MARSHALL and JUSTICE BLACKMUN join, concurring in the judgement. . . .

Municipalities, of course, conduct much of the business of governing through human agents. Where those agents act in accordance with formal policies, or pursuant to informal practices "so permanent and well settled as to constitute a 'custom or usage' with the force of law," Adickes v. S.H. Kress & Co., 398 U.S. 144, 167–168, 90 S. Ct. 1598, 1613–1614, 26 L. Ed. 2d 142 (1970), we naturally ascribe their acts to the municipalities themselves and hold the latter responsible for any resulting constitutional deprivations. *Monell*, which involved a challenge to a city-wide policy requiring all pregnant employees to take unpaid leave after their fifth month of pregnancy, was just such a case. Nor have we ever doubted that a single decision of a city's properly constituted legislative body is a municipal act capable of subjecting the city to liability. See, e.g., Newport v. Fact Concerts, Inc., 453 U.S. 247, 101 S. Ct. 2748, 69 L. Ed. 2d 616 (1981) (city council canceled concert permit for content-based reasons); Owen v. City of Independence, 445 U.S. 622, 100 S. Ct. 1398, 63 L. Ed. 2d 673 (1980) (city council passed resolution firing police chief without any pretermination hearing). In these cases we neither required nor, as the plurality suggests, assumed that these decisions reflected generally applicable "policies" as that term is commonly understood, because it was perfectly obvious that the actions of the municipalities' policymaking organs, whether isolated or not, were properly charged to the municipalities themselves. And, in *Pembaur* we recognized that "the power to establish policy is no more the exclusive province of the legislature at the local level than at the state or national level," 475 U.S., at 480, 106 S. Ct., at 1298, and that the isolated decision of an executive municipal policymaker, therefore, could likewise give rise to municipal liability under § 1983.

In concluding that Frank Hamsher was a policymaker, the Court of Appeals relied on the fact that the City had delegated to him "the authority, either directly or indirectly, to act on [its] behalf," and that his decisions within the scope of this delegated authority were effectively final. 798 F.2d, at 1174. In *Pembaur*, however, we made clear that a municipality is not liable merely because the official who inflicted the constitutional injury had the final authority to act on its behalf; rather, as four of us explained, the official in question must possess "final authority to establish municipal policy with respect to the [challenged] action." 475 U.S., at 481, 106 S. Ct., at 1299. Thus, we noted, "[t]he fact that a particular official—even a policymaking official—has discretion in the exercise of particular functions does not, without more, give rise to municipal liability based on an exercise of that discretion." Id., at 481–482, 106 S. Ct., at 1299. By way of illustration, we explained that if, in a given county, the Board of County Commissioners established county employment policy and delegated to the County Sheriff alone the discretion to hire and fire employees, the county itself would not be liable if the Sheriff exercised this authority in an unconstitutional manner, because "the decision to act unlawfully would not be a decision of the Board." Id., at 483, n.12, 106 S. Ct., at 1300, n.12. We pointed out, however, that in that same county the Sheriff could be the final policymaker in other areas, such as law enforcement practices, and that if so, his or her decisions in such matters *could* give rise to municipal liability. Ibid. In short, just as in *Owen* and *Fact Concerts* we deemed it fair to hold municipalities liable for the isolated, unconstitutional acts of their legislative bodies, regardless of whether those acts were meant to establish generally applicable "policies," so too in *Pembaur* four of us concluded that it is equally appropriate to hold municipalities accountable for the isolated constitutional injury inflicted by an executive final municipal policymaker, even though the decision giving rise to the injury is not intended to govern future situations. In either case, as long as the contested decision is made in an area over which the official or legislative body could establish a final policy capable of governing future municipal conduct, it is both fair and consistent with the purposes of § 1983 to treat the decision as that of the municipality itself, and to hold it liable for the resulting constitutional deprivation....

NOTES

1. What are the implications of considering wrongs committed under 42 U.S.C. § 1983 to be "constitutional torts?" Does it alter the analysis for determining liability from what would exist under state tort law? In a subsequent case, the Supreme Court has required that, where the challenged policy is facially lawful, plaintiffs "must demonstrate that the municipal action was taken with 'deliberate indifference' as to its known or obvious consequences. A showing of simple or even heightened negligence will not suffice." Board of County Commissioners of Bryan County v. Brown, 520 U.S. 397 (1997).

2. Assume that we live in a system in which there is no liability for causing injuries to others. Public officials would still have some incentive to avoid actions that cause injury to their constituents. Elected officials would fear that a reputation for creating or implementing policies that cause injury would affect their chances for reelection. Nonelected officials would fear that creating or implementing policies that cause injury would affect their chances for promotion or for adequate salary increases. If these incentives are substantial, then the need for judicial supervision of official conduct is reduced; indeed, given the possibility for judicial error—juries might impose liability where there has been no misconduct or fail to impose liability where there has been misconduct—judicial supervision of officials could not only be superfluous, but could create a worse situation than "political" supervision standing alone. Are there reasons to believe that these incentives are not adequate to the task and must be supplemented by the threat of civil suit? If civil service laws reduce the probability of firing and limit the flexibility that would otherwise exist to use salaries as carrots (and sticks), then judicial supervision is not necessarily redundant. Similarly, if we believe that most voters will not base their votes on policies such as those involved in cases like *Owen* and *Praprotnik*, but on the broader success or failure of local officials, then some external (judicial) check on official conduct may be necessary. How does this affect the policies underlying § 1983? state tort liability?

Cases like *Praprotnik* involve alleged deprivations of the rights of employees rather than of constituents. Does this mean that the argument about political process as an alternative to judicial intervention works less well? Are the interests of employees less likely to be served than those of service recipients? Even if the political process does not serve employees, are there alternatives to judicial intervention that does serve their interests?

PROBLEM XXVII

Assume that in Problem XXVI, page 711 supra, the chief of police had prior knowledge that Officer Stephens acted erratically and abusively towards citizens, but had not undertaken any efforts to reprimand Officer Stephens or to provide additional counseling and training to him. Would this omission properly serve as the basis of a § 1983 lawsuit?

Collins v. City of Harker Heights

503 U.S. 115 (1992).

■ JUSTICE STEVENS delivered the opinion of the Court....

In Canton [v. Harris, 489 U.S. 378 (1989),] we held that a municipality can, in some circumstances, be held liable under § 1983 "for constitutional violations resulting from its failure to train municipal employees." ...

... [W]e concluded that if a city employee violates another's constitutional rights, the city may be liable if it had a policy or custom of failing to train its employees and that failure to train caused the constitutional violation. In particular, we held that the inadequate training of police officers could be characterized as the cause of the constitutional tort if—and only if—the failure to train amounted to "deliberate indifference" to the rights of persons with whom the police come into contact. Id., at 388, 109 S. Ct., at 1204....

III

Petitioner's constitutional claim rests entirely on the Due Process Clause of the Fourteenth Amendment....

Neither the text nor the history of the Due Process Clause supports petitioner's claim that the governmental employer's duty to provide its employees with a safe working environment is a substantive component of the Due Process Clause....

Petitioner's submission that the city violated a federal constitutional obligation to provide its employees with certain minimal levels of safety and security is unprecedented. It is quite different from the constitutional claim advanced by plaintiffs in several of our prior cases who argued that the State owes a duty to take care of those who have already been deprived of their liberty.... Petitioner cannot maintain, however, that the city deprived [Petitioner's deceased husband] of his liberty when it made, and he voluntarily accepted, an offer of employment.

We also are not persuaded that the city's alleged failure to train its employees, or to warn them about known risks of harm, was an omission that can properly be characterized as arbitrary, or conscience-shocking, in a constitutional sense. Petitioner's claim is analogous to a fairly typical state law tort claim: The city breached its duty of care to her husband by failing to provide a safe work environment. Because the Due Process Clause "does not purport to supplant traditional tort law in laying down rules of conduct to regulate liability for injuries that attend living together in society," Daniels v. Williams, 474 U.S., at 332, 106 S. Ct., at 665, we have previously rejected claims that the Due Process Clause should be interpreted to impose federal duties that are analogous to those traditionally imposed by state tort law, see, e.g., id., at 332–333, 106 S. Ct., at 665–666; Baker v. McCollan, 443 U.S. 137, 146, 99 S. Ct. 2689, 2695, 61 L. Ed. 2d 433 (1979); Paul v. Davis, 424 U.S. 693, 701, 96 S. Ct. 1155, 1160, 47 L. Ed. 2d 405 (1976). The reasoning in those cases applies with special force to claims asserted against public employers because state law, rather than the Federal Constitution, generally governs the substance of the employment relationship....

Our refusal to characterize the city's alleged omission in this case as arbitrary in a constitutional sense rests on the presumption that the administration of Government programs is based on a rational decision-making process that takes account of competing social, political, and economic forces. Cf. Walker v. Rowe, 791 F.2d 507, 510 (CA7 1986). Decisions concerning the allocation of resources to individual programs, such as sewer maintenance, and to particular aspects of those programs, such as the training and compensation of employees, involve a host of policy choices that must be made by locally elected representatives, rather than by federal judges interpreting the basic charter of Government for the entire country. The Due Process Clause "is not a guarantee against incorrect or ill-advised personnel decisions." Bishop v. Wood, 426 U.S. [341, 350 (1976)], 96 S. Ct., at 2080. Nor does it guarantee municipal employees a workplace that is free of unreasonable risks of harm....

In sum, we conclude that the Due Process Clause does not impose an independent federal obligation upon municipalities to provide certain minimal levels of safety and security in the workplace and the city's alleged failure to train or to warn its sanitation department employees was not arbitrary in a constitutional sense. The judgment of the Court of Appeals is therefore affirmed.

It is so ordered.

NOTES

1. The penultimate paragraph of the opinion suggests that courts should be reluctant to translate harmful activity into constitutional claims where doing so would require localities to reallocate resources. What kinds of judicial decisions under § 1983 do not require second-guessing state or local resource allocations? If the answer is "none," then does the rationale in Collins effectively eliminate § 1983 liability? Or is the Court suggesting that the desire for judicial restraint can be overcome where the governmentally imposed injury is sufficiently egregious? Are your answers to any of these questions affected by the fact that one scholar has shown that variations over time in cities' expenditures on legal services seem to bear no relationship to important changes in the law, such as the Supreme Court's decision in *Monell*, which extended liability for constitutional torts to cities? See Charles R. Epp, Exploring the Costs of Administrative Legalization: City Expenditures on Legal Services, 1960–1995, 34 Law & Soc'y Rev. 407, 426 (2000). This finding is underscored by Epp's further finding that although the laws of different states expose cities to significantly different levels of tort liability, patterns in legal department expenditures bear no relationship to these variations in state laws. Id. at 426–27. How do you explain these findings? Is it possible that the increased threat of litigation has encouraged cities to adopt reforms that have minimized the likelihood of liability? See also Theodore Eisenberg & Stewart Schwab, The Reality of Constitutional Tort Litigation, 72 Cornell L. Rev. 641 (1987);

2. In DeShaney v. Winnebago County Department of Social Services, 489 U.S. 189 (1989), the Court declined to impose affirmative duties of assistance on governmental entities under § 1983. In that case, employees of the defendant had knowledge of child abuse by plaintiff's father and failed to take protective action. The child was subsequently beaten into a life-threatening coma and brain damaged. The Court found no violation of the Due Process Clause, and hence no remediable right under § 1983, in the state's failure to protect an individual against private violence. The Court also concluded that where the state had not taken an individual into custody, and hence limited the ability of an individual to act on his or her own behalf, no special relationship existed between the state and the individual sufficient to create an affirmative duty of care on the state. The majority held that the Due Process Clause was intended to protect the people from the state, not to impose obligations of protection on the state. Any such obligation could be created under state law through the political process, but was not, in the Court's view, a proper subject for federal judicial imposition under the guise of the Fourteenth Amendment. Justice Brennan, in dissent, agreed that the function of the Due Process Clause was to protect the people from the state, but contended that state-imposed harms could be found where the state had created a system to protect potential victims (those injured by child abuse), hence lulling potential private rescuers into inaction, and then failed to implement the system properly. Such an omission, Justice Brennan concluded, was as oppressive as direct state action.

What was the likelihood that the political process would respond to the needs of abused children? Who would be adversely affected by additional regulation of child abuse? Would those individuals be likely to oppose the allocation of additional public resources to assist victims of child abuse? Who would be affirmatively affected by such regulation? Would they be likely to lobby for additional funding? Does this comparison suggest that judicial intervention in favor of child abuse victims is unnecessary because child abuse victims are sufficiently protected in the budget allocation process? Or do the facts of *DeShaney* imply an administrative failure properly to utilize funds that had been made available to protect against the very harms that materialized?

In Town of Castle Rock v. Gonzales, 545 U.S. 748 (2005), the Supreme Court held that a Colorado domestic violence restraining order did not give the holder a property interest in police enforcement of that order, and that the holder therefore had no § 1983 claim against the town when the police failed to enforce the restraining order. The restraining order at issue, obtained by the mother, required the father to remain 100 yards from the family home at all times and commanded him further not to "disturb the peace of [the mother] or of any child." Id. at 751. When the father nonetheless abducted the three daughters from outside the family home, the mother repeatedly contacted the Castle Rock police seeking the return of the children and the enforcement of the restraining order, but the police declined to respond. The three children were eventually found murdered in the cab of the father's truck. Id. at 752–754. A majority of the Court held that "[a]lthough the underlying substantive interest is created by 'an independent source such as state law,' federal constitutional law determines whether that interest rises to the level of a 'legitimate claim of entitlement' protected by the Due Process Clause." Id. at 757. The majority went on to interpret Colorado law not to make enforcement of restraining orders mandatory because a "well established tradition of police discretion has long coexisted with apparently mandatory arrest statutes." Id. at 760. Thus, the majority concluded that "respondent did not, for purposes of the Due Process Clause, have a property interest in police enforcement of the restraining order against her husband," and that it was therefore not necessary to reach the § 1983 claim. Id. at 768. The majority ended its opinion with this observation:

> In light of today's decision and that in *DeShaney,* the benefit that a third party may receive from having someone else arrested for a crime generally does not trigger protections under the Due Process Clause, neither in its procedural nor in its "substantive" manifestations. This result reflects our continuing reluctance to treat the Fourteenth Amendment as " 'a font of tort law,' " *Parratt v. Taylor,* 451 U.S. 527, 544, 101 S.Ct. 1908, 68 L.Ed.2d 420 (1981) (quoting *Paul v. Davis,* 424 U.S., at 701, 96 S.Ct. 1155), but it does not mean States are powerless to provide victims with personally enforceable remedies. Although the framers of the Fourteenth Amendment and the Civil Rights Act of 1871, 17 Stat. 13 (the original source of § 1983), did not create a system by which police departments are generally held financially accountable for crimes that better policing might have prevented, the people of Colorado are free to craft such a system under state law. Cf. *DeShaney,* 489 U.S., at 203, 109 S.Ct. 998.

545 U.S. at 768–769.

For discussion of the state-created danger doctrine, see Laura Oren, Safari into the Snake Pit: The State–Created Danger Doctrine, 13 Wm. & Mary Bill of Rts. J. 1165 (2005); Jeremy Daniel Kernodle, Policing the Police: Claifying the Test for Holding the Government Liable under 42 U.S.C. § 1983 and the State–Created Danger Theory, 54 Vand. L. Rev. 165 (2001). For discussion of *Town of Castle Rock*, see, e.g., Leading Cases: Scope of Procedural Due Process Protection—Property Interests in Police Enforcement, 119 Harv. L. Rev. 208 (2005); Tritia L. Yuen, No Relief: Understanding the Supreme Court's Decision in *Town of Castle Rock v. Gonzales* through the Rights/Remedies Framework, 55 Am. U. L. Rev. 1843 (2006).

For a critical view of *DeShaney*, see, e.g., Jack M. Beermann, Administrative Failure and Local Democracy: The Politics of *DeShaney*, 1990 Duke L.J. 1078; Susan Bandes, The Negative Constitution: A Critique, 88 Mich. L. Rev. 2271 (1990); David A. Strauss, Due Process, Government Inaction, and Private Wrongs, 1989 Sup. Ct. Rev. 53. For an opposing view, see Barbara E. Armacost, Affirmative Duties, Systemic Harms, and the Due Process Clause, 94 Mich. L. Rev. 982 (1996).

C. LIABILITY UNDER FEDERAL ANTITRUST LAWS

Municipal activities and regulations may frequently limit permissible activity in ways that appear to run afoul of social interests in competition. For instance, municipalities may limit the number of providers of cable services or may zone out providers of certain services. These regulations might seem to permit the kind of monopolization that federal antitrust laws purport to prohibit. The role of federal antitrust liability is limited, however, by immunities that the courts have conferred on governmental entities and by statutory restrictions on damages where those immunities do not apply. Taking the latter point first, the Local Government Antitrust Act of 1984, 15 U.S.C. §§ 34–36, precludes awards of damages, interest, costs, or attorney's fees against any local government, or official or employee thereof acting in an "official capacity" where the claim is based on violation of the antitrust laws. Damages from a suit against any private individual engaged in "official action directed by a local government, or official or employee thereof" are also precluded. Declaratory or injunctive relief, however, may still be obtained. See, e.g., Thatcher Enterprises v. Cache County Corp., 902 F.2d 1472 (10th Cir. 1990).

The scope of municipal immunity from federal antitrust laws is derived from Supreme Court doctrine concerning the immunity of states from similar liability. In Parker v. Brown, 317 U.S. 341 (1943), the Court held that the Sherman Act, which prohibits anticompetitive activity, does not apply to "state action." As the following excerpt indicates, successive opinions have wrestled with the interpretation of that phrase and the proper scope of municipal immunity from antitrust liability.

> Antitrust doctrine currently uses a formal rule to mediate the perceived conflict between the federal policy favoring competition and the notion (based in federalism or anti-Lochnerism) that state and local governments should be free to regulate in ways that interfere with competitive markets. Founded on the seminal case of Parker v. Brown, which declared that the Sherman Act does not apply to "state action," this formal rule provides that anticompetitive restraints are immune from antitrust scrutiny if they are attributable to an act of "the State as sovereign." In a series of cases, the Supreme Court and, to an even greater extent, the lower courts have struggled with the problem of defining the degree of state or local government involvement necessary to confer this state action immunity.
>
> As it has evolved, antitrust state action doctrine employs three different tiers of immunity. The applicable level of immunity turns on which actor is deemed responsible for the challenged restraint. An anticompetitive restraint is deemed a direct act of the state as sovereign, and thus per se immune from antitrust scrutiny, if it represents the act of the state legislature, the highest state court acting legislatively, or (probably) the governor. [Hoover v. Ronwin, 466 U.S. 558, 567–69 (1984).] At the other extreme, anticompetitive restraints by "private" persons are, under the two-prong test announced in California Retail Liquor Dealers Association v. Midcal Aluminum, Inc. [445 U.S. 97 (1980)], immune only if clearly authorized and actively supervised by the state.
>
> Intermediate immunity applies to the restraints of public entities that are subordinate to the top levels of state government. The restraints of municipalities and state agencies are not deemed direct acts of "the State as sovereign," and thus do not receive absolute immunity. [See Southern Motor Carriers Rate Conference, Inc. v. United States, 471 U.S. 48, 60–61, 62–63 (1985); Town of Hallie v. City of Eau Claire, 471 U.S. 34, 38–40 (1985); Hoover, 466 U.S. at 568–569; Community Communications Co. v. City of Boulder, 455 U.S. 40, 50–

54 (1982).] Rather, one of the entities that acts directly for the state (such as the state legislature, supreme court, or governor) must clearly authorize a restraint, even if embodied in a municipal ordinance or agency regulation, for the restraint to enjoy antitrust immunity. In contrast to private parties, however, municipalities and (probably) state agencies need not show active supervision by the state [see *Hallie*, 471 U.S. at 46–47 & n.10], and apparently can themselves supply the active supervision needed to immunize private restraints that the state as sovereign has clearly authorized. [See Patrick v. Burget, 486 U.S. 94, 101–103 (1988).] . . .

. . . [T]he current three-tiered structure of immunity has, under the conflict paradigm, been subject to a simple but powerful critique: that neither the federal interest in competition nor notions of federalism or anti-Lochnerism offer any grounds (1) for distinguishing between the regulatory restraints of state legislatures and the regulatory restraints of lower-level state entities or local governments, or (2) for distinguishing between clearly authorized restraints that the state has chosen to supervise actively and those it has chosen not to supervise. The critics emphasize three points. First, they argue that the federal interest in competition cannot justify distinguishing anticompetitive restraints issued by high versus low levels of government, with clear versus unclear authorization, and with active versus inactive supervision, because restraints with any of these pedigrees can equally obstruct competition. Indeed, state statutes or regulations may merely make anticompetitive cartels more reliable and durable. Second, the critics argue that requiring local governments to seek state authorization for each type of regulatory restraint confounds principles of local autonomy and federalism. In fact, the doctrine leads to results that seem perverse from a federalism perspective. Home rule local governments, which states intended to endow with the broadest authority, have no immunity because the doctrine deems home rule provisions too general to provide sufficient state authorization. [See Community Communications Co. v. City of Boulder, 455 U.S. 40, 54–56 (1982).] Meanwhile, special local government units, which states intended to constrain narrowly, often enjoy immunity because their authority is, by nature, detailed with more specificity. The third point made by critics is that requiring clear authorization and (for private restraints) active supervision embodies a policy of limiting intrastate delegation that cannot be squared with federalism and anti-Lochnerism because differences in the degree of delegation do not correspond to any real differences in a state's regulatory interest. Indeed, federalism and anti-Lochnerism seem offended rather than furthered by an active supervision requirement that restricts a state's regulatory options and by a clear authorization requirement that turns antitrust courts into adjudicators of what are essentially issues of state administrative law.

Einer Richard Elhauge, The Scope of Antitrust Process, 104 Harv. L. Rev. 667, 672–676 (1991). Professor Elhauge contends that the proper scope of the state action doctrine should be viewed in terms of whether the entity imposing the anticompetitive restriction had reasons to make a decision inconsistent with the public interest. Hence, municipalities should not benefit from immunity for anticompetitive restrictions that impose costs primarily on nonresidents and hence give municipalities a financial interest in making decisions about anticompetitive restrictions. In Town of Hallie v. City of Eau Claire, 471 U.S. 34 (1985), the city refused to provide sewage treatment service to outlying unincorporated areas unless they first agreed to be annexed to the city. The Court held that the city's action was immune from antitrust attack as it was the "foreseeable result" of the state's statutory authorization for the city to provide sewage services and to determine the areas to be served. Id. at 42.

Given that the effects of the city regulation were imposed on nonresidents, one might think that the city was peculiarly vulnerable to the decisionmaking distortions that would make antitrust immunity inappropriate, unless some surrogate, e.g., the state, represented the nonresidents. Nevertheless, it was in *Hallie* that the Court discarded the requirement that the state actively supervise any municipal activity for which a state action exemption is successfully claimed. As Elhauge indicates, private parties who seek to take advantage of the state action exemption must still satisfy that requirement. There has been a significant debate about the desirability of the "active supervision" requirement. Its abandonment in *Hallie* was predicated on the contention that local officials were less in need of supervision to pursue public interest than were officials of private firms. Does that analysis seem appropriate? To the extent that it does not, should the requirement be retained or abandoned for both municipalities and firms? For summaries of the debate, see Robert P. Inman & Daniel L. Rubinfeld, Making Sense of the Antitrust State–Action Doctrine: Balancing Political Participation and Economic Efficiency in Regulatory Federalism, 75 Tex. L. Rev. 1203 (1997); William H. Page, State Action and "Active Supervision": An Antitrust Anomaly, 35 Antitrust Bull. 745 (1990).

Concerns about anticompetitive conduct do not involve only the external effects of local government decisionmaking. Anticompetitive effects may also be an indication that some local group has captured the local political process in ways that have adverse consequences for other local businesses. Nevertheless, the Supreme Court has refused to authorize investigations into the motives of local decisionmaking to determine whether something like capture has occurred. In City of Columbia v. Omni Outdoor Advertising, Inc., 499 U.S. 365 (1991), the city enacted a zoning ordinance restricting the construction of new billboards shortly after a new entrant to the market began placing its billboards in and around the city. An existing local business, which controlled 95 percent of the relevant market and which had contributed funds and free billboard space to the campaigns of city officials, had been instrumental in the enactment of the ordinance. The Supreme Court held that the new firm's antitrust claim was barred by *Parker* immunity. The Court reiterated its position in *Hallie* that the "clear articulation" requirement underlying municipal antitrust liability could be satisfied if suppression of competition was a "foreseeable result" of the authorizing statute, and no more explicit authorization from the state was necessary. The Court then repudiated any "conspiracy" exception to *Parker* that would have imposed antitrust liability on municipalities that enacted regulations to assist private anticompetitive activity rather than to further the public interest. The Court concluded that such investigation "would require the sort of deconstruction of the governmental process and probing of the official 'intent' that we have consistently sought to avoid." 499 U.S. at 377.

Justice Stevens, joined by Justices White and Marshall, dissented. They opposed broad municipal antitrust immunity on the grounds that "[u]nlike States, municipalities do not constitute bedrocks within our system of federalism. And also unlike States, municipalities are more apt to promote their narrow parochial interests...." The dissenters believed that the zoning authority had been delegated to the city by the state as a general welfare measure, but had been used by the city to displace competition through economic regulation. Thus, the dissenters concluded, the state statutes did not satisfy the immunity test of clearly articulating a state policy to permit anticompetitive regulations.

The court applied this analysis in Electrical Inspectors, Inc. v. Village of East Hills, 320 F.3d 110 (2d Cir.), cert. denied, 540 U.S. 982 (2003). A village required building owners to obtain approval from a not-for-profit New York Board of Fire Underwriters before securing a certificate of occupancy. A rival of that organization challenged the requirement on antitrust grounds. Using the *City of Columbia* analysis, the court inquired into whether the municipality had the authority to regulate the act in question and whether the municipality had the authority to suppress the competition. The court concluded that although the Village did not have an explicit grant of authority to impose the requirement, the power was within the state's broad grant of power. Additionally, the court pointed out that the nature of a uniform fire code makes it more efficient to have one organization perform the inspections.

Nevertheless, some courts have intimated that the state action doctrine would not apply where municipal officials have acted fraudulently or illegally. See, e.g., Classic Communications, Inc. v. Rural Tel. Serv. Co., Inc., 956 F.Supp. 896 (D. Kan. 1996). Assume that a city council refuses to approve industrial development bonds to finance a shopping mall because a council member owns a pharmacy that would be in competition with a pharmacy proposed to be located within the mall. Does this conduct deprive the municipality of its immunity? See Fisichelli v. City Known as Town of Methuen, 956 F.2d 12 (1st Cir. 1992) (state action immunity applied).

For a view that broad antitrust immunity for municipalities is more likely to serve the diversification that federalism seeks to foster, see Glen O. Robinson, The Sherman Act as a Home Rule Charter: Community Communications Co. v. City of Boulder, 2 Sup. Ct. Econ. Rev. 131 (1983). For a similar effort to justify antitrust immunity as a means of fostering political participation, see Robert P. Inman & Daniel L. Rubinfeld, Making Sense of the Antitrust State–Action Doctrine: Balancing Political Participation and Economic Efficiency in Regulatory Federalism, 75 Tex. L. Rev. 1203 (1997).

A sympathetic reading that would allow localities to share the state's antitrust immunity without clear authorization to engage in anticompetitive conduct is found in John Shepard Wiley, Jr., A Capture Theory of Antitrust, 99 Harv. L. Rev. 713 (1986). Wiley contends that decentralized decisionmaking—local autonomy—itself serves the interests of consumer autonomy that the antitrust laws are intended to foster. For a response, see

William H. Page, Interest Groups, Antitrust, and State Regulation: Parker v. Brown in the Economic Theory of Legislation, 1987 Duke L.J. 618, 639–640. Professor Page concludes:

> Even if we were to accept that populist goals are somehow reflected in the antitrust laws, that concession would imply only a preference for small economic units; it would say nothing about the sources of regulatory control. The federalism justification for displacing national norms, based as it is on respect for traditional Madisonian legislative processes, is far stronger than a generalized preference for local autonomy, which carries with it little assurance of particular processes of lawmaking.

The debate continues (though with less attention to the implications for local decision making), in Jim Rossi, Antitrust Process and Vertical Deference: Judicial Review of State Regulatory Inaction, 93 Iowa L. Rev. 185 (2007); C. Douglas Floyd, Plain Ambiguities in the Clear Articulation Requirement for State Action Antitrust Immunity: The Case of State Agencies, 41 B.C. L. Rev 1059, 1131 (2000); Matthew L. Spitzer, Antitrust Federalism and Rational Choice Political Economy: A Critique of Capture Theory, 61 S. Cal. L. Rev. 1293 (1988); John Shepard Wiley, Jr., A Capture Theory of Antitrust Federalism: Reply to Professors Page and Spitzer, 61 S. Cal. L. Rev. 1327 (1988); and William H. Page, Capture, Clear Articulation, and Legitimacy: A Reply to Professor Wiley, 61 S. Cal. L. Rev. 1343 (1988).

CHAPTER 7

THE COMMUNITY'S RELATIONSHIP WITH ITS RESIDENTS—CITIZEN PARTICIPATION

A. THE BASES FOR CITIZEN PARTICIPATION IN GOVERNMENT

Peter Bachrach, Interest, Participation, and Democratic Theory

NOMOS XVI: Participation in Politics 39–43 (1975).

The primary challenge for the student of democracy ... is to explore how the democratic system itself can be reformed to combat its own deficiencies. To do so, a difficult question must be confronted at the outset: if indeed a large number of people have real but unexpressed political demands, how can a democratic system respond to such demands?

Certainly democratic theory provides no justification for political elites to determine where the shoe pinches as well as how the pinch should be eased. (Democratic principles aside, if the past is any indication, elites have neither the commitment nor the insight to do this job.) In a democracy, the task of determining the latent interests of the inarticulate rests exclusively with the inarticulate themselves. If the underlying assumption of this paper is sound—that a man becomes aware of his political interests only as he becomes a communicative being—this cycle can be broken only if the polity as a whole develops democratic structures that facilitate political reflection and action by people from all groups in society.

In other words, the time has come for the underbelly of society to acquire the democratic and constitutional protection upper parts of the social body have traditionally enjoyed. For example, freedom of speech is indeed an inviolable right, but a right exercised only by those who can express opinions and who have the opportunity for discussion and dialogue. How can this basic right be made relevant and useful to individuals who have no opinions? That is the problem.

Persons who in their everyday life—in their clubs, professional organizations, and social activity—have the opportunity of formulating and honing their opinions are in a position to determine where their interests lie. It is the political equivalent of these organizational structures and activities, lacking in the lower-class subculture, that the political sector must provide.

It is not until socially disadvantaged groups become involved in structuring their own channels of communication and their own decision-making forums that they will begin to gain self-awareness. And it is only through self-awareness that they can identify their political interests. In short, political participation plays a dual role: it not only catalyzes opinion but also creates it.

In this context, the Office of Economic Opportunity (OEO) antipoverty program was instrumental. As the now-famous "maximum feasible participation" principle was implemented and took effect, inarticulate and passive representatives of the poor, sitting on various boards and commissions, were invariably transformed into angry, articulate, and concerned individuals. By its very nature, their participation, contrary to the anticipation of most government officials, was destined to "get out of control" as it evolved from a cooptative instrumentality to genuine involvement. . . .

The second assumption underlying pluralist theory is that the American political system is essentially an open one—that political demands, spearheaded by legitimate groups, are convertible into issues that are seriously considered in an appropriate decisionmaking arena. With this assumption, one can focus on the process by which issues are converted into public policy. Evidence of vigorous competition and a dispersion of power among political elites, directly or indirectly participating in the decision-making process, will permit the pluralist to conclude that the democratic system is alive and well.

An important inference can be drawn from the pluralist interpretation of the democratic process. Not only is the system responsive to the articulated interests of the people, but the responsiveness is elicited by minimum exertion on the people's part. To exercise control over the leaders and to insure their continuing responsiveness, it is essential that a significant portion of the electorate vote. Also, to protect their private interest, they must occasionally air their views to their appropriate representative. In this view, democracy is conceived as a method that affords maximum output (policy decision) from leaders with minimum input (participation) on the citizen's part.

Pluralists fail to consider the possibility that all political systems, including democracies, are shaped by the interests of the constellations of elites that regularly share power within the polity. The exclusion of this possibility prevents pluralists from examining the extent of the power and influence elites exercise to sustain the biased system. The hard fact is that the unorganized, the poor, and the weak are more or less excluded from the political system. Even when they mount a political protest, they usually cannot generate a conflict of sufficient magnitude to influence decision makers. Their failure to convert demands into issues is, to a considerable degree, a function of their powerlessness. But it also has been shown that their failure has been perpetuated through the exercise of power by elites intent upon keeping them outside the political system.

Demands for community control and decentralization in decision making are clearly a reaction to the malfunctioning of the democratic system.

Barred by gatekeepers from established political channels, the excluded have begun to construct their own decision-making forums. Again, practice has outpaced theory. Despite the difficult, and as yet unresolved, problems that this movement has created for democratic theorists, it is essential on democratic grounds that it be legitimated and nurtured in its growth.

Joseph Schumpeter, Capitalism, Socialism and Democracy

260–262 (3rd ed. 1950).

Now this comparative definiteness of volition and rationality of behavior does not suddenly vanish as we move away from those concerns of daily life in the home and in business which educate and discipline us. In the realm of public affairs there are sectors that are more within the reach of the citizen's mind than others. This is true, first, of local affairs. Even there we find a reduced power of discerning facts, a reduced preparedness to act upon them, a reduced sense of responsibility. We all know the man—and a very good specimen he frequently is—who says that the local administration is not his business and callously shrugs his shoulders at practices which he would rather die than suffer in his own office. High-minded citizens in a hortatory mood who preach the responsibility of the individual voter or taxpayer invariably discover the fact that this voter does not feel responsible for what the local politicians do. Still, especially in communities not too big for personal contracts, local patriotism may be a very important factor in "making democracy work." Also, the problems of a town are in many respects akin to the problems of a manufacturing concern. The man who understands the latter also understands, to some extent, the former. The manufacturer, grocer or workman need not step out of his world to have a rationally defensible view (that may of course be right or wrong) on street cleaning or town halls.

Second, there are many national issues that concern individuals and groups so directly and unmistakably as to evoke volitions that are genuine and definite enough. The most important instance is afforded by issues involving immediate and personal pecuniary profit to individual voters and groups of voters, such as direct payments, protective duties, silver policies and so on. Experience that goes back to antiquity shows that by and large voters react promptly and rationally to any such chance. But the classical doctrine of democracy evidently stands to gain little from displays of rationality of this kind. Voters thereby prove themselves bad and indeed corrupt judges of such issues, and often they even prove themselves bad judges of their own long-run interests, for it is only the short-run promise that tells politically and only short-run rationality that asserts itself effectively.

However, when we move still farther away from the private concerns of the family and the business office into those regions of national and international affairs that lack a direct and unmistakable link with those private concerns, individual volition, command of facts and method of inference soon cease to fulfill the requirements of the classical doctrine. What strikes me most of all and seems to me to be the core of the trouble is the fact that the sense of reality is so completely lost. Normally, the great political questions take their place in the psychic economy of the typical citizen with those leisure-hour interests that have not attained the rank of hobbies, and with the subjects of irresponsible conversation. These things seem so far off; they are not at all like a business proposition; dangers may not materialize at all and if they should they may not prove so very serious; one feels oneself to be moving in a fictitious world.

This reduced sense of reality accounts not only for a reduced sense of responsibility but also for the absence of effective volition. One has one's phrases, of course, and one's wishes and daydreams and grumbles; especially, one has one's likes and dislikes. But ordinarily they do not amount to what we call a will—the psychic counterpart of purposeful responsible action. In fact, for the private citizen musing over national affairs there is no scope for such a will and no task at which it could develop. He is a member of an unworkable committee, the committee of the whole nation, and this is why he expends less disciplined effort on mastering a political problem then he expends on a game of bridge.

The reduced sense of responsibility and the absence of effective volition in turn explain the ordinary citizen's ignorance and lack of judgment in matters of domestic and foreign policy which are if anything more shocking in the case of educated people and of people who are successfully active in non-political walks of life than it is with uneducated people in humble stations. Information is plentiful and readily available. But this does not seem to make any difference. Nor should we wonder at it. We need only compare a lawyer's attitude to his brief and the same lawyer's attitude to the statements of political fact presented in his newspaper in order to see what is the matter. In the one case the lawyer has qualified for appreciating the relevance of his facts by years of purposeful labor done under the definite stimulus of interest in his professional competence; and under a stimulus that is no less powerful he then bends his acquirements, his intellect, his will to the contents of the brief. In the other case, he has not taken the trouble to qualify; he does not care to absorb the information or to apply to it the canons of criticism he knows so well how to handle; and he is impatient of long or complicated argument. All of this goes to show that without the initiative that comes from immediate responsibility, ignorance will persist in the face of masses of information however complete and correct. It persists even in the face of the meritorious efforts that are being made to go beyond presenting information and to teach the use of it by means of lectures, classes, discussion groups. Results are not zero. But they are small. People cannot be carried up the ladder.

Thus the typical citizen drops down to a lower level of mental performance as soon as he enters the political field. He argues and analyzes in a way which he would readily recognize as infantile within the sphere of his real interests. He becomes a primitive again. His thinking becomes associative and affective. And this entails two further consequences of ominous significance.

First, even if there were no political groups trying to influence him, the typical citizen would in political matters tend to yield to extra-rational or irrational prejudice and impulse. The weakness of the rational processes he applies to politics and the absence of effective logical control over the results he arrives at would in themselves suffice to account for that. Moreover, simply because he is not "all there," he will relax his usual moral standards as well and occasionally give in to dark urges which the conditions of private life help him to repress. But as to the wisdom or rationality of his inferences and conclusions, it may be just as bad if he gives in to a burst of generous indignation. This will make it still more difficult for him to see things in their correct proportions or even to see more than one aspect of one thing at a time. Hence, if for once he does emerge from his usual vagueness and does display the definite will postulated by the classical doctrine of democracy, he is as likely as not to become still more unintelligent and irresponsible than he usually is. At certain junctures, this may prove fatal to his nation.

NOTES

1. The chapter of Schumpeter's work from which the above excerpt is taken is entitled "Human Nature in Politics." Are the defects of democracy that make Schumpeter so skeptical endemic in the human condition? Or are there institutions that could be created to counter the ability of particular groups to pursue their self-interest, enhance political debate beyond the superficiality of "commercial advertising," and induce citizens to overcome "irrational prejudice and impulse"?

2. *The Costs and Benefits of Political Activity.* Bachrach's reaction to politics is obviously quite different from that of Schumpeter, and far more optimistic. Is this view founded on a different view of human nature, or does Bachrach's view also depend on the ability to harness particular institutional structures that permit the electorate to participate in particular ways? Recall Hannah Arendt's claim, at pages 12–14 supra, that widespread political participation can lead people to think of their own interests in light of the interests of others. It was this objective that led Arendt to endorse the Jeffersonian desire to "turn the counties into wards."

Opportunities for political participation, however, may seem quite limited. For instance, the most obvious form of participation, casting votes on election day, appears to be significantly underutilized, and turnout at elections for local candidates or on local matters such as bond issues is typically lower than turnout at elections for national offices. One explanation for low voter turnout is that voting is costly—voters must stand in line at the polling booth, must consider for whom to vote, and must take off time from other activities to get to the polling place. These costs may be considered too high, given that the payoff to the individual voter is quite low. What, for instance, is the probability that my vote will determine the winner of the election? If my vote is irrelevant to the outcome, and is costly to cast, why shouldn't I just free ride off the votes of others?

If rational individuals do not vote because the costs of the exercise exceed its expected benefits, then encouraging additional forms of involvement in the political process would seem to be self-defeating. Compared to voting, the costs of other political acts by members of the electorate—participating in a campaign for a candidate or an initiative proposition, lobbying legislators, organizing like-minded neighbors—all involve significantly more effort than the relatively simple act of voting. Thus, unless the expected benefits of the activity are high, one would not expect many members of the electorate to participate in these efforts.

But maybe this image of participation miscasts the function that political activity plays (or, at least, can play) in the life of the electorate. Political participation should, perhaps, be viewed not as a cost, but as a benefit. Those who engage in political activity receive substantial benefits, if not in the form of single-handedly determining the outcome of the election, in the very process of participating. If, for example, voting is seen as an affirmative act of civic duty, then the voter can view herself, and be viewed by others, as a participant in a socially important activity, wholly apart from the outcome of the election. Voters may share in the pleasures of the victory of their favored candidate or commiserate with others over a defeat. As Professor Albert O. Hirschman has said, summarizing the issue in economic terms, considering political participation as a consumption good, rather than as a cost, allows the individual to define the benefit of political participation as "not the difference between the hoped-for result and the effort furnished by him or her, but the *sum* of these two magnitudes." Albert O. Hirschman, Shifting Involvements: Private Interest and Public Action 86 (1982) (emphasis in original).

If participation creates benefits for those who participate, then it follows that, at least to some point, benefits increase as the amount of political activity increases. If that is correct, then those who engage in political activity that requires more effort than voting (again—campaigning, lobbying, organizing) will obtain significantly more benefits than those whose only political activity consists of occasionally casting a vote.

Although put in economic terms, this argument appears to have much in common with Arendt's argument that participation by the populace is necessary to the pursuit of the public good. If political participation holds out the promise of providing benefits, and if participation increases the possibility that the public good can be realized (that is, if our vision of those who would participate is closer to that of Bachrach than to that of Schumpeter), then it may be useful to create institutional structures in which participation can occur. Recall that, for Arendt, the appropriate amount of participation could only occur at the local level: It was the failure of the founders that "[o]nly the representatives of the people, not the people themselves, had an opportunity to engage in those activities of 'expressing, discussing and deciding' which in a positive sense are the activities of freedom." See page 12 supra. What is necessary, therefore, is to create an environment in which the electorate has opportunities to engage in political activity. On this optimistic assumption, the more political activity that is available to individuals, the more they will take advantage of those opportunities because the benefits are substantial (again, wholly apart from the results obtained), and the more participation, the greater the possibility for overcoming private interests that might otherwise dominate the political process.

Of course, one might respond that citizens currently have opportunities to participate through campaigning, lobbying, and organizing, but do not take advantage of these opportunities. Does this mean that the "consumption benefits" explanation of political activity has no force? Or does it mean that there are insufficient structures for individuals to engage in political activity? What kinds of decisionmaking processes would enable the electorate better to capture these benefits? What are the risks of trying to design such structures?

B. INITIATIVE AND REFERENDUM

M. Dane Waters, The Initiative and Referendum Almanac

11, 6–8, 31, 36 (2003).

Initiatives are when the citizens, collecting signatures on a petition, place advisory questions, memorials, statutes or constitutional amendments on the ballot for the citizens to adopt or reject. Twenty-four states have the initiative process.... Of the 24 states, 18 have the constitutional initiative process. Twenty-one of the 24 states have the statutory initiative process....

In many of the same states the citizens have the ability to reject laws or amendments proposed by the state legislature. This process is commonly referred to as the referendum process.... Popular referendum, which is available in 24 states ... is when the people have the power to refer, by collecting signatures on a petition, specific legislation that was enacted by the legislature for the people to either accept or reject. Legislative referendum, which is possible in all states, is when the state legislatures, an elected official, state appointed constitutional revision commission or other government agency or department submits propositions (constitutional amendments, statutes, bond issues, etc.) to the people for their approval or rejection....

In the United States, the initiative process is used much more frequently than the popular referendum process and is considered by many the more important and powerful of the two processes....

There is little doubt that in recent years the initiative process has become one of the most important mechanisms for altering and influencing public policy at the local, state and even national level. In the last decade alone, utilizing the initiative process, citizens were heard on affirmative action, educational reform, term limits, tax reform, campaign finance reform, drug policy reform and the environment....

Clearly, reforms have been enacted that represent different ideologies—conservative, liberal, libertarian and populist agendas. This typifies the initiative process—individuals of all different political persuasions use it. Furthermore, because of the diversity of issues that have been placed on the ballot, voters in states with an initiative on the ballot have been more likely to go to the polls than voters in states without an initiative on the ballot. In election after election, no matter what election cycle is analyzed, voter turnout in states with an initiative on the ballot has been usually 3% to 8% higher than in states without an initiative on the ballot....

The 2002 election cycle continues to show that the use of the initiative process is declining—perhaps showing the success that legislatures have had in restricting the public's use of the initiative process. On Election Day 2002, voters cast their ballots on 202 statewide ballot measures in 40 states.... Fifty-three were placed on the ballot by the people, and 149 were placed on the ballot by the state legislatures. Of the measures placed on the ballot by the people, 45% were approved. This number is a little higher than the 100-year average of 41%. In looking at the measures placed on the ballot by the state legislatures, the voters continued the trend of passing those at a higher percentage than citizen measures by adopting almost 66% of them....

The bright glare of statewide ballot propositions sometimes makes the local initiative and referendum (I & R) process seem almost invisible. Yet far more Americans have access to I & R in their local government than have access in their state government....

- Most large cities provide for the initiative, including 15 of the 20 largest.
- One-third to one-half of American cities provide for initiatives.
- Approximately 61 to 71 percent of citizens have the initiative available in their cities.
- Almost 75 percent of citizens have either state or local initiatives available.
- Large cities are more likely to have the initiative than small cities.

American Bar Association, Tort and Insurance Practice Section Task Force on Initiatives and Referenda, The Challenge of Direct Democracy in a Republic

4–7 (1993).

While [initiatives and referenda] grow out of the populist movements and antipathy towards organized government in the late 19th century, they have an importance to the overall political process and democratic governance that transcends their effect on particular laws. Individuals tend to become engaged in campaigns on ballot propositions in ways that are not found in electoral campaigns for individual officials. The issues that are the subject of the campaign may hold an especially intense interest for certain individuals and entice them into political action. Thus, wholly apart from the benefit they confer as a check on legislative excess or inaction, initiatives and referenda possess the potential to foster a level of participation that is highly desirable in a democratic state. They permit individuals to go beyond the role of citizens who are "represented" in the lawmaking process and instead to become lawmakers, even if their involvement is limited to single issues and for short periods of time.

Initiatives and referenda simultaneously serve as a check on representative democracy. In theory, representatives enact the will of the represented. Representatives, however, may deviate from that role. They may fail to enact popularly preferred legislation for fear of offending particular interest groups who can provide financial or other support during election campaigns, or because the proposed measures run counter to the personal interests of legislators. Conversely, representatives may enact legislation considered detrimental by a majority but preferred by particular interests who have greater access to and more influence with lawmakers or who can benefit legislators seeking re-election or higher office. Proponents of the initiative and referendum thus perceive legislators as captives of interest groups or as overly attentive to action that will ensure personal welfare rather than the welfare of their constituents. On this view, legislators will sacrifice long-term benefits for immediate ones whenever they fear retaliation at the polls. Similarly, proponents of the initiative contend that the need to obtain a majority vote will avoid divisive or radical proposals in favor of more moderate ones and that individual voters will take sufficient responsibility to engage in deliberation and fact-seeking sufficiently similar to that of the average state legislator. In all of these cases, the initiative and referendum provide a potential check on legislative disregard of popular will.

At the same time, the initiative and referendum have recently been the object of dissatisfaction. At the center of most of these criticisms has been an explicit or implicit suggestion that lawmaking by the electorate is inferior to legislative lawmaking. Legislators are viewed by some as better able to deliberate and more likely to do so, since they are accountable for their decisions in ways that individual voters, who need only register their preferences in the privacy of a voting booth, are not. In addition, legislators are perceived as more attentive to the overall public interest in ways that the electorate, voting on a single issue, will not be. Legislators, for instance, may be considered more responsive to the long-term consequences of legislation than individual voters. Finally, the legislative process may be considered to have institutional advantages over the plebiscite, even if the two share a common view of the public interest. Legislators can form committees, convene hearings, and obtain information in ways that exceed the capabilities of the average voter. Further, legislators—small in number and constantly in contact with one another—can work with each other in ways not available to the electorate at large to reach compromises and engage in informed debate. For instance, the legislative process facilitates the correction of drafts of proposed law and permits amendments that are foreclosed by the binary choice of total acceptance or rejection that is available to the electorate.

Additional criticisms suggest that, process aside, the subject matter of initiatives is likely to contravene popular conceptions of the public interest. Commentators have suggested that special interests may resort to the initiative where they are unable to win a majority of representatives and believe that they can more readily persuade the electorate to support their position. Underlying this concern is a view about who, within the electorate, is most likely to participate. Those who have an intense interest in the outcome of a question—members of the special interest group to be benefited—certainly have incentives to become involved in advocating its passage. As with all political action, however, most people will avoid involvement in lobbying or supporting a ballot proposition since these efforts are costly and time consuming, and even silent supporters of a measure will obtain its benefits without incurring any costs if those who participate are successful. Hence, only those to whom the personal benefits of involvement exceed the costs are likely to participate. Critics of ballot propositions fear that special interests will foresee sufficiently unique benefits to make it worth their while to dominate the process. If this occurs, the level of participation falls far short of what is envisioned in the ideal description of direct democracy.

There have also been suggestions that ballot issues are decided by large expenditures of money, that issues are deliberately stated in an obtuse fashion to confuse voters, that the multitude of ballot propositions at a given election make intelligent voting on any of them difficult, and that minority interests are ignored in the initiative process. Indeed, one frequent criticism of the plebiscite is that it is sometimes used as a direct attack on minorities.

One criticism of initiatives and referenda in recent years has been that they have proliferated in numbers that exceed their utility. There are two concerns that underlie this criticism. The first is that the referendum and initiative process was originally intended only as a check on legislative excess or inaction rather than a replacement for legislative lawmaking. On this theory, plebiscites should be used only when there is evidence of a substantial gap between the legislature and the electorate. Frequent use of the initiative process may indicate that legislators are avoiding controversial issues on which votes may offend constituents. The second concern is related to the issue of voter competence. If ballot propositions are too numerous, then voters may be unable or unwilling to devote sufficient attention to the issues, so that they will be resolved by a minority of residents with an intense interest in a particular outcome that may deviate from the interests of the public at large.

NOTES

1. The Report of the ABA Task Force was limited to statewide initiatives and referenda. Many of the same criticisms of the plebiscite, however, can be directed at decision-making by the local electorate. Are the differences between states and their political subdivisions sufficient to make an initiative or referendum appropriate for one, while it would be inappropriate for the other? Do you think there are differences in decisionmaking by large versus small groups? If so, does that affect your view as to whether direct democracy is more appropriate at the state or local level? For a general discussion of small-versus large-group decisionmaking, see Jane Mansbridge, Beyond Adversary Democracy 282–296 (1983). Local initiatives and referenda are frequently restricted in ways that do not apply at the state level. Nevertheless, all electoral lawmaking serves as an alternative to legislative lawmaking. Under what circumstances would the former be more likely to produce legislation that is consistent with the public interest (however one might to define that term)? To answer that question, one must determine the relative ability of the electorate and the legislature to participate, to reflect the preferences of constituents, to avoid the kinds of interest group pressure that might cause decisionmaking to be skewed away from the public interest, and to achieve compromise and consensus necessary to effective government. Obviously, Bachrach and Schumpeter have very different visions of the relative capacities of legislators and the electorate. The more one agrees with Bachrach's vision of political participation, the more one might trust active political forms, such as initiative and referendum campaigns, as true expressions of popular will. The more one considers electoral politics as susceptible to Schumpeter's "dark urges" or manipulation by interests, the less one will want to rely on the electorate for a trustworthy political process. As you read the following materials, consider how the courts envision the relative capabilities of the populace and politicians. Are the tests that the courts articulate for determining the proper scope of initiative and referendum accurate measures of those situations in which there is particular reason to trust that popular lawmaking reflects "the public interest"? See Alan Hirsch, Direct Democracy and Civic Maturation, 29 Hastings Const. L.Q. 185 (2002); Frank I. Michelman, "Protecting the People from Themselves," or How Direct Can Democracy Be?, 45 UCLA L. Rev. 1717 (1998); Hans A. Linde, Practicing Theory: The Forgotten Law of Initiative Lawmaking, 45 UCLA L. Rev. 1735 (1998); Symposium: Initiatives, 34 Willamette L. Rev. 391 (1998); Symposium: Perspectives on Direct Democracy, 4 U. Chi. L. Sch. Roundtable 1 (1997); Lynn A. Baker, Constitutional Change and Direct Democracy, 66 U. Colo. L. Rev. 143 (1995); Lynn A. Baker, Direct Democracy and Discrimination: A Public Choice Perspective, 67 Chi.-Kent L. Rev. 707 (1991); Julian N. Eule, Judicial Review of Direct Democracy, 99 Yale L.J. 1503 (1990); Clayton P. Gillette, Plebiscites, Participation, and Collective Action in Local Government Law, 86 Mich. L. Rev. 930, 974–988 (1988).

2. Prerequisities to qualifying a proposition for the ballot may be adjusted to facilitate or frustrate efforts to hold an initiative or referendum election.

For instance, states require that proponents of an initiative election procure signatures from a specified number of electors before the proposition is placed on the ballot. Even where states use the same base of voters, e.g., the number of votes cast in the last gubernatorial election, the required percentage ranges from 5 to 10. Five and ten percent appear to be common percentages. There is some evidence that there is an inverse relationship between the percentage of signatures required and the number of plebiscites held. See David Magelby, Direct Democracy 42 (1984). Demonstrating the correlation between signature requirements and number of initiatives does not, of course, respond to the normative question of whether decisionmaking by initiative is desirable. It may be that jurisdictions with high signature requirements have "too few" initiatives, or that those with low signature requirements have "too many." In addition, some states require that ballot titles and language be subjected to preelection administrative or judicial review. See, e.g., Ark. Stat. Ann. 7–9–107; Colo. Rev. Stat. 1–40–105. Other states impose a requirement that there be a particular geographical distribution of signatures on initiative petitions. Missouri, for instance, requires petitions for statewide initiatives to be signed by 5 percent of the voters in each of two-thirds of the state's congressional districts. Mo. Const. Art. III, 50. The Massachusetts Constitution provides that no more than one quarter of the signatories on a statewide petition may be registered voters in the same county. See Mass. Const. Amend. Art. 48, Pt. 2. These requirements presumably make it more difficult for parochial initiatives of limited interest to get on the ballot. A similar geographical distribution requirement would have a lesser effect on municipal initiatives, since the cost of complying would be significantly lower. Does this mean that other cost-raising measures should be imposed in order to prevent "overutilization" of the local initiative? What would such cost-raising measures look like? See, e.g., Kenneth P. Miller, Constraining Populism: The Real Challenge of Initiative Reform, 41 Santa Clara L. Rev. 1037 (2001); Richard B. Collins & Dale Oesterle, Structuring the Ballot Initiative: Procedures That Do and Don't Work, 66 U. Colo. L. Rev. 47 (1995); David B. Magleby, Let the Voters Decide?: An Assessment of the Initiative and Referendum Process, 66 U. Colo. L. Rev. 13 (1995).

3. *Are Initiatives "Publicly Interested"?* Do initiatives serve as correctives to local legislators who want to circumvent their constituents' preferences? Or do they serve as an instrument by which special interests can circumvent publicly-interested legislators? In an empirical study of the use of initiatives at the state and local level, John Matsusaka concluded that availability of initiatives had three major policy effects: (1) reducing total government spending, (2) shifting spending from state to local governments, and (3) shifting the sources of revenue from taxes to user fees and service charges. Matsusaka then analyzed opinion data to assess what voters thought about these policies. He concludes that a majority of people preferred the policies brought about by the initiative. Matsusaka concludes that, at least with respect to fiscal policy, it is "hard to escape the conclusion that the initiative promoted the interests of the many and not the few." John G. Matsusaka, For the Many or the Few 71 (2004). The fact that people prefer these policies does not necessarily mean that they are ideal policies from some metric other than preference satisfaction. For instance, it is possible that the initiative causes underspending rather than overspending, or that presence of the initiative causes state governments to impose unfunded mandates on local governments. Matsusaka also concludes that these changes were consistent with the preferences of most voters, so the initiative, at least on fiscal issues, does not appear to be a tool of special interests. See also Lars P. Feld & Gebhard Kirchgässner, Does Direct Democracy Reduce Public Debt? Evidence from Swiss Municipalities, 109 Public Choice 347 (2001) (direct democracy procedures appear to reduce public debt more than special procedural rules for incurring debt).

Other studies suggest that government officials may fail to implement programs enacted by initiative or otherwise attempt to frustrate the objectives of the initiative through funding decisions or bureaucratic delay. See, e.g., Elisabeth R. Gerber, et al., Stealing the Initiative: How State Government Responds to Direct Democracy (2001).

PROBLEM XXVIII

You serve as clerk to the Chief Judge of the supreme court in a state with a constitution that provides: "The powers of initiative and referendum are reserved to the qualified voters of each municipality and district as to all local, special, and municipal legislation of every character in or for their municipality or district." Dissatisfaction with inertia in local legislative bodies has recently led to the filing of a spate of petitions for initiatives in municipalities throughout the state. Each of the following petitions has been challenged by opponents of the initiative as falling outside the constitutional grant. The Chief Judge has asked you to prepare a memorandum indicating which of these proposals is permissible under the constitutional prerogative. To the extent that there is doubt, please indicate the factors that make any of these proposals particularly appropriate or inappropriate for electoral decisionmaking.

1. A petition to adopt a specific budget for the following fiscal year in City A. The proposed budget establishes property tax rates and allocates revenues.

2. A petition that requires the police department of City B to spend at least $100,000 of its budget on school crossing guards.

3. A petition that directs the city council of City C to adopt a plan to desegregate the city's schools. City C contains a population that is 10 percent black, but 95 percent of the black schoolchildren attend schools with a population that is at least 80 percent black.

4. A petition to permit a nuclear waste dump within City D.

5. A petition to change the zoning ordinance of City E to permit professional offices in residences.

6. A petition to recommend to City F's congressional delegation that they use all their delegated powers to seek an Article V convention to consider an amendment to the U.S. Constitution providing for congressional term limits.

Kaiser Hawaii Kai Development Co. v. City and County of Honolulu

777 P.2d 244 (Hawaii 1989).

■ WAKATSUKI, JUDGE.

In this case, the majority of this court filed an order affirming the decision of the circuit court on May 17, 1989. The basis of the affirmance is the following opinion.

I

Bishop Estate is the fee owner of a tract of land divided into two segments, which are designated as Golf Course 5 and Golf Course 6, in the Kalama Valley area in East Honolulu. Kaiser Hawaii Kai Development Company (Kaiser) has the legal right to possess and develop this land. This land has been zoned for residential use since 1954. A portion of the land falls within the Shoreline Management Area. See Chapter 205A, Hawaii Revised Statutes (HRS) (1985 & Supp. 1988). Before Kaiser could proceed with its planned residential housing project on this tract, it had to obtain a special management area use permit from the City and County of Honolulu (City).

A

The permit application drew the attention of a number of citizens who protested that the housing development would severely impact the beach area known as Sandy Beach which is on the opposite side of Kalanianaole Highway from the proposed development area. The citizens voiced their concerns relative to the housing development in a series of public meetings and hearings before the City Department of Land Utilization, the Hawaii Kai Neighborhood Board, and the City Council. But Kaiser was eventually granted a permit to proceed with its plan for the housing development.

A group of citizens formed The Save Sandy Beach Coalition (Coalition) to prevent the housing development. The Coalition circulated an initiative petition which proposed to amend the designation of the tract from residential to preservation on both the City's land use development plan and zoning maps. The Coalition, in accordance with Article III, Chapter 4 of the Revised Charter of the City and County of Honolulu 1973 (1984 ed.) (Charter), gathered the necessary signatures to place the initiative proposals on the ballot for vote by the electorate of the City on November 8, 1988.

B

Kaiser, by initiating this suit prior to the election, sought, inter alia, a declaration that the initiative process was an improper procedure to downzone the tract of land from residential use to preservation. Bishop Estate joined with Kaiser. The circuit court agreed with Kaiser and Bishop Estate, and thereby enjoined the placement of the initiative proposals on the ballot.

This court, upon motion by the Coalition, stayed the circuit court's injunction, thus permitting a vote on the initiative proposals on the November 8, 1988 general election ballot. The order staying the injunction expressly noted that the court did not determine the merits of the appeal.

At the general election, the initiative proposals were approved by the electorate.

II

The issue before this court is whether the initiative proposals adopted by the electorate of the City on November 8, 1988 validly amended the land use development plan and zoning maps of the City. We answer in the negative.

In view of our holding herein, we deem it unnecessary to determine the issue of whether appellees' constitutional rights to due process have been violated by the initiative process.

A

The duty of this court in interpreting statutes is to ascertain and give effect to the intention of the legislature. Reefshare, Ltd. v. Nagata, 70 Haw. ___, ___, 762 P.2d 169, 174 (1988). In view of legislative history, it is abundantly clear that the legislature in its wisdom established a public policy of not effectuating land use zoning through the initiative process.

The counties of our state derive their zoning powers from HRS § 46–4(a) (Supp. 1988), referred to as the Zoning Enabling Act. It states in pertinent part:

> Zoning in all counties shall be accomplished within the framework of a long range, comprehensive general plan prepared or being prepared to guide the overall future development of the county. *Zoning shall be one of the tools available to the county to put the general plan into effect in an orderly manner*. . . .
>
> The powers granted herein shall be liberally construed in favor of the county exercising them, and in *such a manner as to promote the orderly development of each county or city and county in accord with a long range, comprehensive, general plan, and to insure the greatest benefit for the State as a whole.* (Emphasis added).

The language of the Zoning Enabling Act clearly indicates the legislature's emphasis on comprehensive planning for reasoned and orderly land use development. This emphasis on planning was reiterated in the statement of policy adopted as part of the legislation enacting the Zoning Enabling Act. There, the legislature stated:

> The pressure of a rapidly increasing population in the Territory of Hawaii requires an orderly economic growth within the various counties and the conservation and development of all natural resources. Adequate controls must be established, maintained and enforced by responsible agencies of government to reduce waste and put all of our limited land area, and the resources found thereon, to their most beneficial use. It is the intent and purpose of the legislature, by means of zoning ordinances and regulations enacted by or under this act, and in accord with a long range, comprehensive general plan, to promote the health, safety, convenience, order, welfare and prosperity of the present and future inhabitants of the Territory.

§ 1, Act 234, 1957 Session Laws of Hawaii.

B

Zoning by initiative is inconsistent with the goal of long range comprehensive planning, and "[i]t seems unlikely that the Legislature intended the possible frustration of comprehensive zoning through the initiative process." Smith v. Township of Livington, 106 N.J. Super. 444, 457, 256 A.2d 85, 92 (1969).

In Township of Sparta v. Spillane, 125 N.J. Super. 519, 525–526, 312 A.2d 154, 157 (1973), a New Jersey Superior Court stated:

> Zoning is intended to be accomplished in accordance with a comprehensive plan and should reflect both present and prospective needs of the community. [ ] Among other things, the social, economic, and physical characteristics of the community should be considered. The achievement of these goals might well be jeopardized by piecemeal attacks on the zoning ordinances if referenda were permissible for review of any amendment. Sporadic attacks on a municipality's comprehensive plan would tend to fragment zoning without any overriding concept. That concept should not be discarded because planning boards and governing bodies may not always have acted in the best interest of the public and may not, in every case, have demonstrated the expertise which they might be expected to develop. (Citations omitted.)

Similarly, the Washington Supreme Court stated in Leonard v. City of Bothell, 87 Wash. 2d 847, 852, 557 P.2d 1306, 1309–1310 (1976) (quoting Kelley v. John, 162 Neb. 319, 323–324, 75 N.W.2d 713, 716 (1956)):

> The uniformity required in the proper administration of a zoning ordinance could be wholly destroyed by referendum. A single decision by the electors by referendum could well destroy the very purpose of zoning where such decision was in conflict with the general scheme fixing the uses of property in designated areas.... It would permit the electors by referendum to change, delay, and defeat the real purposes of the comprehensive zoning ordinance by creating the chaotic situation such ordinance was designed to prevent.

We are cognizant that both *Spillane* and *Leonard* involved referenda. Nevertheless, we agree with the reasoning and statements made by the respective courts as applied to the process of zoning by initiative....

IV

In view of legislative history and clear legislative intent, we declare that the amendments which downzoned the tract of land designated as Golf Course 5 and Golf Course 6 from residential to preservation through the initiative process are invalid.

■ NAKAMURA JUSTICE, dissenting.

When the Supreme Court of Hawaii divests the people of the City and County of Honolulu of a right granted under the City's charter, it owes them a logical explanation for the action. The opinion of the majority, however, does not tell us exactly why the employment of a process designed to give the people a voice on important questions of policy is per se incompatible with a statutory requirement that zoning "shall be accomplished [by ordinance] within the framework of a long-range, comprehensive general plan prepared ... to guide the overall future development of the county." HRS § 46–4. Rather than a reasoned exegesis of the relevant provisions of HRS § 46–4, the opinion offers the fears of the majority that the objectives of planning would be jeopardized if the people were given the opportunity to effect zoning changes through the process. Because I neither share the majority's distrust of democracy nor subscribe to the notion that political decisions rendered directly by the electorate invariably are devoid of civic virtue, a fair reading of HRS § 46–4 reveals it does not forbid zoning amendments by initiative, and zoning amendments are subject to judicial review for consistency with general plans, I dissent....

II

The issue on appeal being one of statutory interpretation, my analysis begins as it must with the statute in question, HRS § 46–4.

The genesis of HRS § 46–4 is traceable to 1957 when the Territorial Legislature found "[t]he pressure of a rapidly increasing population ... require[d] an orderly economic growth within the various counties, and the conservation and development of all natural resources." Session Laws of Hawaii (Haw. Sess. Laws) 1957, c. 234, § 1. "Adequate controls," it said, "must be established, maintained and enforced by responsible agencies of government to reduce waste and put all of our limited land area, and the resources found thereon, to their most beneficial use." Id. The legislature therefore passed an act designed, "by means of zoning ordinances and regulations enacted by and under [the] act, and in accord with a long range, comprehensive general plan, to promote the health, safety, convenience, order, welfare and prosperity of the present and future inhabitants of [Hawaii]." Id.

The section of the act relating to county zoning provided in part that "[z]oning in all counties shall be accomplished within the framework of a long range, comprehensive, general plan prepared or being prepared to guide the overall future development of the county[,]" and "[z]oning shall be one of the tools available to the county to put the general plan into effect in an orderly manner." 1957 Haw. Sess. Laws, c. 234, § 9. "The zoning power granted [under the act was to] be exercised by ... ordinance...." Id. And the granted powers, which included the power of enforcement, were to "be liberally construed in favor of the county or city and county exercising them, and in such a manner as to promote the orderly development of each county or city and county in accord with a long range, comprehensive general plan, and to insure the greatest benefit for [Hawaii] as a whole." The provisions of the section, furthermore, were not to "be construed to limit or repeal any powers [then] possessed by any county to achieve such ends through zoning and building regulations except insofar as forest and water reserve zones are concerned." Id.

As the majority notes, the Zoning Enabling Act "was enacted in substantially the same form it exists today." A fair reading of its relevant language ineluctably leads to a conclusion that the legislature recognized zoning was primarily a matter of county concern and imposed a modicum of restraints on the exercise of the power by the counties. For the plain language of HRS § 46–4 only compels a county to accomplish zoning by ordinance within the framework of a long range, comprehensive general plan designed to guide its overall future development.

"The intention of the legislature," we have said, "is to be obtained primarily from the language contained in the statute itself." In re Hawaiian Tel. Co., 61 Haw. 572, 577, 608 P.2d 383, 387 (1980). And "where the language of the law in question is plain and unambiguous, construction by this court is inappropriate and our duty is only to give effect to the law according to its plain and obvious meaning." Id. at 577–78, 608 P.2d at 387. The circuit court erred by engaging in construction where none was required and concluding that zoning is a power to be exercised exclusively by the county's legislative body. This court also subjects the plain language of HRS § 46–4 to construction and concludes the statute "established a public policy of not effectuating land use zoning through the initiative process." I have searched the statute in vain for anything that even intimates either conclusion is justified. Reading the language of the statute as written by the legislature and construing the powers granted therein "liberally ... in favor of the county ... exercising them" as directed by HRS § 46–4(a), I conclude the statute does not divest the people of the City and County of Honolulu of a political right granted them by the City's charter.

The holding of the majority in essence is that its notion of what constitutes good planning, which is nowhere stated in the statute, must prevail over a decision made by the people of the City and County of Honolulu when they adopted the City charter that a zoning ordinance could be passed by the direct vote of the people. But "[c]harter provisions with respect to a political subdivision's executive, legislative and administrative structure and organization [are] superior to statutory provisions, subject to the authority of the legislature to enact general laws allocating and reallocating powers and functions." Haw. Const. art. VIII, § 2. Because the City's legislative structure includes the people and their power to enact legislation through popular vote and the legislature has not exercised its authority to pass a general law reallocating this power where zoning amendments are concerned, I conclude too that the Home Rule provisions of the State Constitution dictate a reversal of the trial court.

Unlike the majority, I am not deterred by the possibility that a zoning amendment effected by initiative may be inconsistent with the City's long range, comprehensive general plan. There is, of course, no certainty that a popular vote will reflect the objectives and policies of the plan. Yet, there is no certainty too that the City Council's zoning amendments will always reflect these objectives and policies. "[T]here is no more advance assurance that a legislative body will act by conscientiously applying consistent standards than there is with respect to voters." Eastlake v. Forest City Enters., Inc., 426 U.S. 668, 675 n.10, 96 S. Ct. 2358, 2363 n.10, 49 L. Ed. 2d 132 (1976). . . .

NOTES

1. In City of Eastlake v. Forest City Enterprises, Inc., 426 U.S. 668 (1976), the United States Supreme Court held that the enactment of zoning changes through referendum does not violate due process under the federal Constitution. Thus, a referendum could be held to overturn zoning changes voted by a local legislative body since the power of referendum is reserved to the people of Ohio in its constitution. For an argument that the decision represented a victory for "raw majoritarianism" over the claim for "a deliberative tribunal between the public will and individuals who stand to suffer unjustly from legislative enactments," see Lawrence G. Sager, Insular Majorities Unabated: *Warth v. Seldin* and *City of Eastlake v. Forest City Enterprises, Inc.*, 91 Harv. L. Rev. 1373 (1978). Professor Sager's critique suggests that the electorate is inherently less deliberative than a representative body. There may be some reasons to support that proposition. After all, representatives are small in number; meet frequently for the very purpose of debate; and—as repeat players—can become familiar with issues that affect deliberation, such as the expertise and reliability of the speaker. Additionally, representatives vote in public. Thus, they cannot vote their "dark urges" without fear that they will be required to explain their actions. The electorate does not share these characteristics. Does the fact that the electorate does not meet as a whole mean that its members do not engage in deliberation before voting? Might there be surrogates for single meeting places that facilitate deliberation by the local electorate? In addition, the model of a deliberative legislature may be somewhat romantic, especially once one considers representative bodies other than the national legislature. See, e.g., Ethan J. Leib, Toward a Practice of Deliberative Democracy: A Proposal for a Popular Branch, 33 Rutgers L.J. 359 (2002); Richard Briffault, Distrust of Democracy, 63 Tex. L. Rev. 1347 (1985) (book review); Bruno S. Frey, Direct Democracy: Politico–Economic Lessons from Swiss Experience, 84 Am. Econ. Rev. Pap. & Proc. 338 (1994); Gregory Schmid, Reviving Athenian Democracy in California, 8 Notre Dame J.L., Ethics & Pub. Pol'y 499 (1994). For arguments for and against the proposition that direct democracy is inconsistent with the Guarantee Clause of the U.S. Constitution, see Symposium: Guaranteeing a Republican Form of Government, 65 Colo. L. Rev. 709 (1994); Robert G. Natelson, A Republic, Not a Democracy? Initiative, Referendum, and the Constitution's Guarantee Clause, 80 Tex. L. Rev. 807 (2002); Catherine Engberg, Taking the Initiative: May Congress Reform State Initiative Lawmaking to Guarantee a Republican Form of Government?, 54 Stan. L. Rev. 569 (2001); James M. Fischer, Plebiscites, the Guarantee Clause, and the Role of the Judiciary, 41 Santa Clara L. Rev. 973 (2001); Catherine A. Rogers & David L. Faigman, "And to the Republic for Which It Stands": Guaranteeing a Republican Form of Government, 23 Hast. Const. L.Q. 1057 (1996).

One theme of these materials with which the student should be familiar by this time is that governmental decisions should be made by the decisionmaker that is most likely to enact laws that are consistent with the public interest. We have seen throughout these materials that much of local government law can be defended or attacked for the way in which it allows the lawmaking process to be immunized from or susceptible to special interests. One possible downside to the representative assembly is that it provides a stable target for interests that seek favors through legislation. It may be easier or less costly to lobby a majority of local legislators to support a proposal than it is to convince the electorate. But before accepting this proposition too readily, consider whether proponents of an initiative really seek to convince a majority. If parochial initiatives receive little publicity, those who will obtain benefits from it may vote in favor of it, while those who bear the cost may find it not worthwhile either to discover the effects of the measure or to organize against its passage. Thus, it may be in the interests of those who favor an initiative that is intended to provide private benefits to limit the exposure that the initiative receives. Alternatively, proponents might cast the initiative in broad, popular terms. For instance, an initiative to create favorable tax treatment for farmland might be advertised as a proposal to "save the family farm," even if the primary beneficiaries are large, corporate farms. See Daniel Lowenstein, Political Bribery and the Intermediate Theory of Politics, 32 U.C.L.A. L. Rev. 784 (1985). Is this traditional form of collective action more likely to affect the electorate than legislators?

2. In Atlantic City Housing Action Coalition v. Deane, 437 A.2d 918 (N.J. Super. Ct. 1981), the court considered whether a city clerk could prevent a "People's Ordinance" relating to urban development from being placed on the ballot as inappropriate for submission to the voters under state legislation regulating use of the initiative. The ordinance would have required the Atlantic City Housing Authority and Redevelopment Agency to agree with the Coalition on a redevelopment plan that would include substantial low-income housing. The court determined that state law provisions permitting use of the initiative for any ordinance really meant "any ordinance except such as to which a contrary legislative purpose may be discerned." The court then concluded that myriad state statutes relating to redevelopment were intended as a limitation on an initiative campaign that would interfere with the comprehensive redevelopment process. The court depended in large part on the rationale stated in a law review article:

> Louis J. Sirico, Jr., in "The Constitutionality of the Initiative and Referendum," 65 Iowa L. Rev. 637, 654–656 (1980), elucidates how a plebiscite must not pretend to the role of an alternate administrative agency.
>
> [A]lthough agencies do not serve primarily as checks or lawmakers, they do perform a different ancillary function—implementing the directives of the legislature. When the agency acts outside its mandate, it becomes an alternative lawmaking body, disrupts the Constitution's structural arrangement, and invites attack under the delegation doctrine. (Footnote omitted.) The doctrine's dormancy as a judicially enforced constitutional rule (footnote omitted) does not negate its conceptual validity. Rather, the doctrine admits a shaky trust in the legislature to hold its own creature accountable. The administrative system's autonomous proclivities draw frequent fire and trigger demands to tighten the legislative and judicial reins. (Footnote omitted.) The concerns underlying the delegation doctrine thus continue to prompt vigilance. Like the agency, the

> plebiscite must remain in its respective ancillary role and not pretend to the role of an alternative legislature. . . .
>
> The heart of the problem lies with the plebiscite's method of performing its ancillary role. The agency implements legislative mandates and makes no formal pretense to be the legislature's equal. When the agency's conduct constitutes independent lawmaking, judicial and legislative checks become operative. The plebiscite, however, performs its role by serving as a competitive source of lawmaking. The plebiscite's check is extremely potent because it can actually override the representative legislature on specific issues. (Footnote omitted.) In the case of the initiative, a ballot vote can even decree an alternative course of conduct. Thus, a paradox exists: the plebiscite operates by assuming the function of the body that it is designed to check.

437 A.2d at 922–923. Are there advantages that a plebiscite has over an administrative agency with respect to execution of the legislative will? How does the legislative will properly become defined if not through consideration of what legislators' constituents would prefer? But even if we were to assume that the plebiscite is a poor mechanism for measuring legislative will, are there offsetting benefits that would be produced by use of the plebiscite? Return to the reading from Hannah Arendt, pages 12–14 supra. Recall that Arendt was concerned about the distance that could exist between representatives and the represented. In what kinds of cases is the plebiscite a means of closing that gap? See, e.g., Elisabeth R. Gerber, et al., Stealing the Initiative: How State Governement Responds to Direct Democracy (2001); Sherman J. Clark, A Populist Critique of Direct Democracy, 112 Harv. L. Rev. 434 (1998); Lynn A. Baker, Preferences, Priorities, and Plebiscites, 13 J. Contemp. Legal Issues 317 (2004); Sherman J. Clark, The Character of Direct Democracy, 13 J. Contemp. Legal Issues 341 (2004); Glen Staszewski, Rejecting the Myth of Popular Sovereignty and Applying an Agency Model to Direct Democracy, 56 Vand. L. Rev. 395 (2003); Eric A. Posner & Adrian Vermeule, Legislative Entrenchment: A Reappraisal, 111 Yale L.J. 1665 (2002); Philip P. Frickey, The Communion of Strangers: Representative Government, Direct Democracy, and the Privatization of the Public Sphere, 34 Willamette L. Rev. 421 (1998); Lynn A. Baker, "They the People": A Comment on U.S. Term Limits, Inc. v. Thornton, 38 Ariz. L. Rev. 859 (1996); Elisabeth R. Gerber, Legislative Response to the Threat of Popular Initiatives, 40 Am. J. Pol. Sci. 99 (1996); Michael Klarman, Majoritarian Judicial Review: The Entrenchment Problem, 85 Geo. L.J. 491 (1997); Kris W. Kobach, Rethinking Article V: Term Limits and the Seventeenth and Nineteenth Amendments, 103 Yale L.J. 1971 (1994); Lisa O. Monaco, Give the People What They Want: The Failure of "Responsive" Lawmaking, 3 U. Chi. L. Sch. Roundtable 735 (1996); Nathaniel A. Persily, The Peculiar Geography of Direct Democracy: Why the Initiative, Referendum and Recall Developed in the American West, 2 Mich. L. & Pol'y Rev. 11 (1997).

What does Professor Sirico (and, by extension, the court) mean when he suggests that the plebiscite plays an "ancillary role" to legislation adopted by a representative legislature? Does this characterization suggest that local legislation adopted through initiative is entitled to less judicial deference than legislative enactments? Perhaps the "ancillary" nature of the plebiscite is intended to suggest that its use is extraordinary, that we continue to rely on the legislature as the primary source of lawmaking, and that the initiative should be reserved for instances in which the legislature has failed, in some dramatic way, to bend to popular preferences. Are there reasons to limit the initiative to such situations?

3. Zoning through popular vote remains a volatile issue on the grounds that it threatens to interfere with comprehensive planning. In Griswold v. City of Homer, 186 P.3d 558 (Alaska 2008), the court rejected an initiative that altered an ordinance enacted by the city council and that would have limited the floor areas of stores within the city to between 20,000 and 45,000 square feet, depending on the zoning district. The proposed initiative would have increased the allowable space to 66,000 square feet. The court concluded that the ordinance impermissibly bypassed the city advisory planning commission, which was required by the city's comprehensive plan to be involved in development issues. A dissent would have permitted the initiative, since the state constitutional provision created broad authority for its use, unconstrained by the limits imposed on legislatures. In Garvin v. Ninth Judicial District Court ex rel. County of Douglas, 59 P.3d 1180 (Nev. 2002), the Nevada Supreme Court overruled an earlier decision and concluded that an initiative concerning zoning was permitted by the state constitution. The initiative in question, which had passed at the time the court reviewed its constitutionality, limited the number of dwelling units that could be built annually in the county. The court found that the state constitution's broad adoption of the initiative power was intended to permit direct citizen action with respect to "legislation of every kind," including zoning legislation. The fact that the county had previously adopted a zoning policy without provisions of the sort included in the initiative did not remove that power from the voters. The court concluded that the initiative process contained protections that are generally equivalent to statutory notice and hearing requirements that are intended to protect property when they are affected by legislation. See also Marcilynn A. Burke, The Emporer's New Clothes: Exposing the Failures of Regulating Land Use Through the Ballot Box, 84 N.D.L. Rev. 1453 (2009); Daniel P. Selmi, Reconsidering the Use of Direct Democracy in Making Land Use Decisions, 19 UCLA J. Envt'l L. & Pol'y 293 (2002); David G. Anderson, Urban Blight Meets Municipal Manifest Destiny: Zoning at the Ballot Box, the Regional Welfare, and Transferable Development Rights, 85 Nw. U.L. Rev. 519 (1991); David C. Callies, Nancy C. Neuffer & Carlito P. Caliboso, Ballot Box Zoning: Initiative, Referendum and the Law, 39 J. Urb. & Contemp. L. 53 (1991).

Buckeye Community Hope Foundation v. City of Cuyahoga Falls

697 N.E.2d 181 (Ohio 1998).

ON MOTION FOR RECONSIDERATION

Appellant Buckeye Community Hope Foundation ("Buckeye Hope"), a nonprofit Ohio corporation, develops housing for individuals through the use of state grants and tax credits. Buckeye Hope is affiliated with Cuyahoga Housing Partners, Inc. and Buckeye Community Three L.P. ("Buckeye Three"), also appellants herein.

In 1995, Buckeye Three purchased a tract of land in Cuyahoga Falls for the purpose of building a seventy-two unit apartment complex. The land was zoned for multifamily use. Subsequently, the Cuyahoga Falls Planning Commission unanimously approved a site plan concerning the proposed complex. Pursuant to Section 1.7, Article VIII of the Charter of Cuyahoga Falls, the plan was then submitted to the City Council of Cuyahoga Falls for its approval.

On April 1, 1996, the city council ratified the decision of the planning commission by passing Ordinance No. 48–1996. The ordinance provided, in part, that "City Council approves the plan for development of land situated in an R–17 Medium Density Multiple Family zoning district in accordance with such district and zoning regulations as stipulated in the Codified Ordinances of the City of Cuyahoga Falls and as approved by the Planning Commission * * *."

Following passage of the ordinance, a group of residents of Cuyahoga Falls filed referendum petitions with the clerk of city council. The petitions sought a referendum to approve or reject Ordinance No. 48–1996, pursuant to Section 2, Article IX of the municipal charter, which provides, in relevant part, that the citizens of Cuyahoga Falls "have the power to approve or reject at the polls *any ordinance or resolution passed by the Council* * * *." (Emphasis added.) The Summit County Board of Elections then certified that the petitions contained a sufficient number of valid signatures to be placed on the November 1996 ballot.

On May 1, 1996, the appellants filed a complaint against the appellees in the Court of Common Pleas of Summit County, requesting injunctive relief and a declaration that the ordinance could not be challenged by referendum because its passage by the city council was an administrative, rather than legislative, action. Appellants claimed that Section 1f, Article II of the Ohio Constitution did not grant powers of referendum to citizens of municipalities on administrative actions taken by municipal legislative bodies.

The trial court denied the appellants' request for injunctive relief. The court also determined that the Charter of Cuyahoga Falls permitted the residents of the city to exercise powers of referendum on any action taken by the city council, regardless of whether the action taken was legislative or administrative in nature.

Appellants appealed the decision of the trial court to the Court of Appeals for Summit County. The court of appeals affirmed the judgment of the trial court, holding that Section 1f, Article II of the Ohio Constitution does not limit the referendum powers of charter municipalities such as Cuyahoga Falls.

Pursuant to the allowance of a discretionary appeal, this court affirmed the judgment of the court of appeals. *Buckeye Community Hope Found. v. Cuyahoga Falls* (1998), 81 Ohio St.3d 559, 692 N.E.2d 997.

The cause is now before this court upon a motion for reconsideration filed by the appellants. . . .

■ MOYER, CHIEF JUSTICE

. . . For the reasons that follow, we grant the appellants' motion for reconsideration and reverse the judgment of the court of appeals.

I

Section 3, Article XVIII of the Ohio Constitution grants powers of local self-government to municipalities by providing, "Municipalities shall have authority to exercise all powers of local self-government and to adopt and enforce within their limits such local police, sanitary and other similar regulations, as are not in conflict with general laws." In exercising those powers, municipalities may choose to govern themselves by charter in accordance with Section 7, Article XVIII of the Ohio Constitution: "Any municipality may frame and adopt or amend a charter for its government and may, subject to the provisions of section 3 of this article, exercise thereunder all powers of local self-government."

It is well settled that although the Ohio Constitution grants broad powers of local self-government to municipalities, the scope of those powers is not without limits. In *Canton v. Whitman* (1975), 44 Ohio St.2d 62, 73 O.O.2d 285, 337 N.E.2d 766, this court interpreted Section 3, Article XVIII as follows: "This section, adopted in 1912, preserved the supremacy of the state in matters of 'police, sanitary and other similar regulations,' while granting municipalities sovereignty in matters of local self-government, *limited only by other constitutional provisions.*" (Emphasis added.) Id. at 65, 73 O.O.2d at 287, 337 N.E.2d at 769. . . .

In *Bazell v. Cincinnati* (1968), 13 Ohio St.2d 63, 42 O.O.2d 137, 233 N.E.2d 864, . . ., we articulated the limits of charter government by stating that "a charter city has all powers of local self-government *except to the extent that those powers are taken from it or limited by other provisions of the Constitution* or by statutory limitations on the powers of the municipality which the Constitution has authorized the General Assembly to impose." (Emphasis added.) More recently, we stated that "[a] municipality that chooses to adopt a charter does so in order to manage its own purely local affairs without interference from the state, *with the understanding that these local laws will not conflict with the Constitution and general laws.*" (Emphasis added.) *Rispo Realty & Dev. Co. v. Parma* (1990), 55 Ohio St.3d 101, 102, 564 N.E.2d 425, 426–427.

The City Charter of Cuyahoga Falls provides that voters may exercise powers of referendum on any ordinance or resolution passed by the city council. The appellants contend that this provision conflicts with Section 1f, Article II of the Constitution,. . . .

Section 1f, Article II provides initiative and referendum powers only on those questions that municipalities "may now or hereafter be authorized by law to control by legislative action." We have interpreted this phrase to exclude, from referendum proceedings, administrative actions taken by a city council. In *Myers v. Schiering* (1971), 27 Ohio St.2d 11, 56 O.O.2d 6, 271 N.E.2d 864, we held that "[u]nder Section 1f of Article II of the Ohio Constitution, municipal referendum powers are limited to questions which municipalities are 'authorized by law to control by legislative action.' ".... There, we determined that the passage of a resolution "granting a permit for the operation of a sanitary landfill, pursuant to an existing zoning regulation, constitutes administrative action and is not subject to referendum proceedings." Id.....

The section of the Charter of Cuyahoga Falls providing that voters may exercise powers of referendum on any ordinance or resolution passed by the city council is constitutionally invalid. Voters of Cuyahoga Falls may exercise powers of referendum on any ordinance or resolution that constitutes legislative action. Section 1f, Article II does not authorize the residents of Cuyahoga Falls to initiate referendum proceedings on an action taken by the city council that is not legislative in nature....

II

The remaining question for our determination is whether the approval of the site plan by the city council constituted administrative or legislative action.

The city argued that the approval of the site plan was a legislative action because the action was taken by adopting an ordinance. In support of its position, the city cited *Donnelly v. Fairview Park* (1968), 13 Ohio St.2d 1, 42 O.O.2d 1, 233 N.E.2d 500, ..., which states that "[t]he test for determining whether the action of a legislative body is legislative or administrative is whether the action taken is one enacting a law, ordinance or regulation, or executing or administering a law, ordinance or regulation already in existence."

The question presented to this court in *Donnelly* was whether the action of a city council in failing to approve the recommendation of the city's planning commission for a resubdivision of a parcel of real estate constituted legislative or administrative action. Id. at 3, 42 O.O.2d at 2, 233 N.E.2d at 501. This court determined that the action was administrative. Id. at 4, 42 O.O.2d at 3, 233 N.E.2d at 502. In arriving at that conclusion, the court stated, " 'The crucial test for determining that which is legislative from that which is administrative or executive is whether the action taken was one already making a law, or executing or administering a law already in existence.' * * * If, then, the action of a legislative body *creates a law, that action is legislative, but if the action of that body consists of executing an existing law, the action is administrative.*" (Emphasis added.) Id. at 4, 42 O.O.2d at 2–3, 233 N.E.2d at 502, citing *Kelley v. John* (1956), 162 Neb. 319, 321, 75 N.W.2d 713, 715. Therefore, ... *Donnelly* established that the test requires an examination of the nature of the action taken, rather than the mere form in which it is taken. Accordingly, the city's position that the approval of the site plan was a legislative action because the council took action via an ordinance (rather than by resolution or other means) is in error.

Additionally, the city argued that the ordinance approving the site plan constituted legislative action because city law stated that decisions made by the city council relating to approvals of site plans "shall be considered as legislative rather than administrative actions." Cuyahoga Falls Zoning Ordinance No. 1171.03(c). This argument also is without merit. The city council cannot designate an action as legislative simply because it desires the action to be legislative. *Donnelly* requires that the nature of the action taken determines whether it is legislative or administrative, *i.e.*, whether the action creates or establishes law, or whether the action merely applies existing law to a given situation. *Donnelly* at 4, 42 O.O.2d at 2, 233 N.E.2d at 502. Additionally, it is our constitutional duty, in interpreting the words of Section 1f, Article II, to independently analyze whether the action by the city is a legislative action.

The action taken by the city council here was clearly administrative in nature. Ordinance No. 48–1996 passed by the city council approved a plan for the "development of land * * * in accordance with such district and zoning regulations as stipulated in the Codified Ordinances of the City of Cuyahoga Falls and as approved by the Planning Commission * * *." The ordinance merely approves the planning commission's application of existing zoning regulations to the plan submitted by the appellants. The ordinance has no general, prospective application such that the action taken would fit within the usual and customary meaning of the phrase "legislative action" contained in Section 1f, Article II. See Black's Law Dictionary (6 Ed.1990) 899 (defining "legislative act" as "[l]aw * * * passed by legislature in contrast to court-made law. One which prescribes what the law shall be in future cases arising under its provisions."). Rather, the city council determined the rights of the appellants by applying existing law to the site plan submitted by the appellants. Accordingly, adoption of Ordinance No. 48–1996 was an administrative act, and therefore was not a legislative action that could be subjected to referendum proceedings pursuant to Section 1f, Article II.

Therefore, we hold that pursuant to Section 1f, Article II of the Ohio Constitution, actions taken by a municipal legislative body, whether by ordinance, resolution, or other means, that constitute administrative action, are not subject to referendum proceedings. The passage by a city council of an ordinance approving a site plan for the development of land, pursuant to existing zoning and other applicable regulations, constitutes administrative action and is not subject to referendum proceedings.

NOTES

1. The *Buckeye* litigation did not end with the 1998 decision of the Ohio Supreme Court. While the state-court litigation was still pending, respondents filed suit in federal court against the City and several city officials, seeking an injunction ordering the City to issue the building permits, as well as declaratory and monetary relief. Buckeye alleged, *inter alia*, that "in allowing a site plan approval ordinance to be submitted to the electors of Cuyahoga Falls through a referendum and in rejecting [its] application for building permits," the City and its officials violated the Equal Protection and Due Process Clauses of the Fourteenth Amendment. The case made its way through the federal courts, and the United States Supreme Court granted certiorari to determine whether the Sixth Circuit erred in ruling that respondent's suit against the City could proceed to trial. The Supreme Court found no merit in either the Equal Protection or Due Process claim. City of Cuyahoga Falls, Ohio v. Buckeye Community Hope Foundation, 538 U.S. 188 (2003). With regard to the claim that "the City's submission of an administrative land-use determination to the charter's referendum procedures constituted *per se* arbitrary conduct," id. at 1396, the Court held that such a "theory of liability has no basis in our precedent":

> As a matter of federal constitutional law, we have rejected the distinction that respondents ask us to draw, and that the Ohio Supreme Court drew as a matter of state law, between legislative and administrative referendums. In *Eastlake v. Forest City Enterprises, Inc.*, 426 U.S. at 672, 675, 96 S.Ct. 2358, we made clear that because all power stems from the people, "[a] referendum cannot ... be characterized as a delegation of power," unlawful unless accompanied by "discernible standards." The people retain the power to govern through referendum " 'with respect to any matter, legislative or administrative, within the realm of local affairs.' " *Id.*, at 674, n. 9, 96 S.Ct. 2358. Cf. *James v. Valtierra,* 402 U.S., at 137, 91 S.Ct. 1331. Though the "substantive result" of a referendum may be invalid if it is "arbitrary and capricious," *Eastlake v. Forest City Enterprises, supra,* at 676, 96 S.Ct. 2358, respondents do not challenge the referendum itself. The subjection of the site-plan ordinance to the City's referendum process, regardless of whether that ordinance reflected an administrative or legislative decision, did not constitute *per se* arbitrary government conduct in violation of due process.

2. Notwithstanding the holding of the U.S. Supreme Court in *Buckeye*, the administrative/legislative distinction appears to be well accepted in state-court decisions concerning the scope of the municipal initiative. See, e.g., Garvin v. Ninth Judicial District Court ex rel. County of Douglas, 59 P.3d 1180 (Nev. 2002); State ex rel. Hazel v. Cuyahoga County Bd. of Elections, 685 N.E.2d 224 (Ohio 1997); Town of Hilton Head Island v. Coalition of Expressway Opponents, 415 S.E.2d 801 (S.C. 1992); Wennerstrom v. City of Mesa, 821 P.2d 146 (Ariz. 1991). At the same time, different courts have set forth quite different guidelines to be used in drawing the distinction. Compare, for example, the test articulated in *Buckeye* above with the following:

> The central inquiry is whether the proposed legislation announces new public policy or is simply the implementation of a previously declared policy. Two "tests" or guidelines are used to resolve the issue in most cases. First, actions that relate to subjects of a permanent or general character are legislative, while those that are temporary in operation and effect are not. *Witcher*, 716 P.2d at

> 449; *Margolis*, 638 P.2d at 303; *Zwerdlinger*, 194 Colo. at 196, 571 P.2d at 1077. "In this connection an ordinance which shows an intent to form a permanent *rule of government* until replaced is one of permanent operation." 5 E. McQuillin, Municipal Corporations § 16.55, at 194 (3d ed. 1981) (emphasis added) (footnote omitted). Second, acts that are necessary to carry out existing legislative policies and purposes or which are properly characterized as executive are deemed to be administrative, while acts constituting a declaration of public policy are deemed to be legislative....

City of Idaho Springs v. Blackwell, 731 P.2d 1250, 1254 (Colo. 1987). Which test is more attractive to you? Why?

After reviewing a variety of tests employed by different state courts in drawing the administrative/legislative distinction, the Nevada Supreme Court concluded, "From all of these cases and others like them, one overarching principle may be derived: regardless whether an initiative proposes enactment of a new statute or ordinance, or a new provision in a constitution or city charter, or an amendment to any of these types of laws, it must propose policy—it may not dictate administrative details." Citizens for Public Train Trench Vote v. City of Reno, 53 P.3d 387, 392 (Nev. 2002). The Nevada court thus concluded that an initiative to prohibit a particular project that would lower the railroad tracks through downtown Reno below street level did not qualify as legislative, since it was "of very special character, not of general character." A dissenting judge objected:

> The decision to proceed with the train trench project constitutes a decision unlike any the City has ever before made. It is unique in the financial burden it will impose on the taxpayers, possibly for generations to come. The City estimates that the project will cost an additional $260 million. To many observers, this figure appears to be conservative. The City has acknowledged that project expenses could run much higher, as the builders have a design and build contract. It thus appears that the builders have what almost amounts to a blank check. The City concedes that it has already spent $15 million on the project, including $300,000 to reimburse *unsuccessful* design/build proposers. The City is now poised to spend projected tax revenue—and probably more—on what it refers to as a transportation project....
>
> The cost of this single project is more than the City's total 1999–2000 annual budget. The funds to pay for this project will be derived from various sources, including money from room and sales taxes, grants, bonds, loans, and the City's general fund, and bonded indebtedness will be repaid over a period of forty years. The magnitude of this undertaking is more than a mere administrative decision by the City's elected officials.

53 P.3d at 395–96.

3. A case might also be made, consistent with both the explicit statement by the court in *Idaho Springs* and the implicit debate between the majority and dissent in *Citizens for Public Train Trench Vote* that a "proposed ordinance's classification as legislative or administrative is largely an ad hoc determination." See *Idaho Springs*, 731 P.2d.at 1254 (citing Witcher v. Canon City, 716 P.2d 445, 459 (Lohr, J., dissenting)). For example, in Moore v. School Committee of Newton, 378 N.E.2d 47 (Mass. 1978), the Supreme Judicial Court of Massachusetts determined that a decision by the city's school committee to close two elementary schools was legislative and therefore subject to referendum. The committee had argued that while its prior decision to close schools because of decreasing enrollment was legislative in nature, the subsequent selection of the particular schools in question was merely administrative implementation of that prior policy decision. The court disagreed. It concluded:

> The line between executive and legislative actions is sometimes difficult to delineate and in some instances may be completely obliterated. See Selectmen of Milton v. District Court of E. Norfolk, 286 Mass. 1, 5, 189 N.E. 607 (1934). Such is not the case here. The votes to close the Hamilton and Emerson Schools involved a policy determination common to legislative action. Before voting to close and consolidate, the school committee weighed the social costs of the closing on the pupils and community against the economic savings and other gains to be realized. The prior approval of the guidelines was merely a statement to the public of the factors which the school committee considered relevant when voting to close a school, and thus did not constitute final legislative action.

378 N.E.2d at 50.

In Foster v. Clark, 790 P.2d 1, 5–7 (Or. 1990), the court determined that a proposed initiative to rename Martin Luther King, Jr. Boulevard in the city of Portland as Union Avenue was simply an implementation of the city's policy for renaming streets, and hence was not "municipal legislation" under a state constitutional provision that granted local residents initiative power over "all local, special and municipal legislation." The court reasoned that the city had previously adopted a complete scheme for changing Portland city street names, including rules on petition forms, fees, review by various city officials, and final consideration by the city council. The ordinance enacting this scheme represented the policy decision of the city. "Acts of renaming streets under the policies embodied in the plan thereafter become administrative acts, not legislation." Id. at 7. Had the city's procedure for street naming involved only the passage of ordinances for each street on an individual basis, rather than a procedure dictated by a general "policy" for street naming, the court suggested, the initiative might have been permitted.

In each of these cases, can you construct an argument for the theory that proposed ballot proposition should have be classified in the category opposite from the one applied by the court? If the administrative/legislative distinction is so malleable, then is it an appropriate test at all? If so, does it serve as a surrogate for some other concerns that might be addressed more directly?

4. Some state courts have rejected the administrative/legislative distinction on the grounds that it is not contained in the constitutional or statutory provision authorizing local initiatives and referenda. See Albert v. Town of Fairfield, 597 A.2d 1353 (Me. 1991) (rejecting distinction in favor of an interpretation that permits initiative for municipal, rather than state, affairs); Christianson v. City of Bismarck, 476 N.W.2d 688 (N.D. 1991) (expansive reading of provision permitting initiative on "any" matter within capacity of local legislature).

5. Even if one rejects the administrative/legislative distinction as inherently ambiguous and susceptible to manipulation, it might be possible to defend it as a surrogate for more detailed examinations into whether an initiative is more or less likely to reflect the public interest than a decision made by a representative body. The possibility that representatives will make decisions in a manner consistent with the interests of their constituents will depend on such factors as the opportunities for deliberation, the capacity to compromise or engage in logrolling (recall that it is unclear whether logrolling results in positive or negative trades), accountability, and the susceptibility of the decisionmaker to discrete interest groups that might have an advantage in organizing or lobbying to influence the decision. On the relative ability of interest groups to influence representatives or the electorate as a whole, consider the following:

> Not all grass-roots movements for plebiscites emerge from public interest, of course. A desire by one group to expropriate the wealth of another may also underlie attempts to alter the status quo. The proposed closing of a neighborhood school, for instance, may impose substantial costs on parents who would be required to transport their children elsewhere and who fear the disintegration of other aspects of their neighborhood. While these expected costs may be insufficient to overcome the substantial barriers to exit, they may be sufficient to induce organized behavior, including petitioning for a referendum. Nevertheless, there is little reason to believe that groups formed in this manner are attempting to vindicate any broader interests than those of their own neighborhood. These groups, therefore, do not vary in perspective from more traditional interest groups that represent the financial interests of their membership. Yet even if these groups have the resources necessary to gain access to plebiscitary processes, that avenue becomes a source of concern only if the plebiscite is more susceptible to interest groups than is the legislature.
>
> Certainly, a rich literature suggests that legislative action is systematically undertaken at the behest of special interest groups rather than in furtherance of the public interest. The explanation for this phenomenon lies in an understanding of legislators as rational self-interested actors rather than pure altruists. As in any relationship between a principal and a self-regarding agent, there is likely to be some divergence of interest between legislators and their constituencies. Ideally, any divergence is minimized by a legislator's desire to retain electoral support or attain higher office. Outside the realm of the ideal, however, there remain situations in which representatives can ignore the interests of constituents with relative impunity.
>
> The first such situation is where free riding will be prevalent in the electorate. As noted above, only those most interested in a particular piece of legislation—those to whom the costs of expressing preferences and seeking legislative approval are worth the benefits—will actually engage in the lobbying efforts necessary to secure passage. Legislators seeking electoral support presumably will be attentive to lobbying efforts, as the lobby has evidenced its willingness to advance or withhold support in the legislators' subsequent efforts to retain or advance in public office. Legislation procured in this manner, of course, need not coincide with public interest, but only with the interest of the particular group involved in lobbying. Nevertheless, a legislator who votes based on the entreaties of lobbies will not necessarily adversely affect his or her prospects of reelection. If the adverse public effects of the legislation are

diffuse, contesting the legislation will not be worthwhile to any adversely affected individual, even if aggregate costs outweigh aggregate benefits. Nor will support of a particular piece of special interest legislation necessarily cost the legislator much support in the voting booth, even among those who identify the conduct as a defalcation. Representatives must be voted for on the basis of the package of programs they support; voters cannot pick and choose among the various issues for which a legislator stands. Thus, a vote on any particular piece of special interest legislation is unlikely to offend sufficient numbers of voters to affect chances at reelection.

Secondly, some legislators are beyond simple electoral control. Most obviously, this phenomenon occurs when a politician is serving what is anticipated to be his or her "last" term and thus need not account to the electorate for actions taken during the period. This is not to say that even self-interested legislators will consistently ignore the public interest. Exogenous constraints may prevent wholly self-interested conduct by the representative even during an ultimate term: fear of conviction may dissuade bribery or blatant conflicts of interest; concern for reputation or (more likely at the national level) a "place in history," or expectation of nonelectoral rewards such as appointive office for good last-term performance, may encourage attention to public concerns. The problem of nonaccountability, however, does indicate that plebiscites are not unique in their vulnerability to special interests.

Finally, incumbents may have opportunities to manipulate voter preferences in order to avoid penalties for self-interested behavior. In a jurisdiction with voters who have heterogeneous preferences, Ferejohn suggests [John Ferejohn, Incumbent Performance and Electoral Control, 50 Pub. Choice 5, 10 (1986)—EDS.], the incumbent may play off voters against each other, so that a majority will not form to remove the representative from office. Alternatively, representatives may act in a more publicly interested manner as elections approach and avoid the invective of a myopic electorate for earlier defalcations.

Both representatives and the electorate, then, are vulnerable to special interests, to the concept of "capture" that has been used to explain administrative behavior inconsistent with public interest. If capture is possible at the legislative as well as the plebiscitary level, however, one might sensibly ask, in which forum is it more likely to occur? The focus of some commentators on campaign finance implies that the electorate is disproportionately susceptible to unreasoned media campaigns, so that well-financed interest groups have less difficulty persuading voters to share their position than do poorly financed grassroots organizations. Nevertheless, even the evidence mustered in support of campaign finance reform is, at best, ambiguous on the issue of electoral susceptibility to confusion and dishonesty.

Much of our understanding of collective action suggests a contrary conclusion—that capture would be facilitated by creation of a decisionmaking body like a legislature. Collective action theory suggests that groups are more likely to coalesce in ways that solve problems of free riding where they are small and insular, thereby facilitating efforts to monitor members' activities and to appeal to unified interest. These same features, however, should tend to make small, discrete groups whose members share a common objective (e.g., reelection) more susceptible to the influence of interest groups than atomized individuals. Unlike the electorate (diffuse and relatively disinterested in the benefits that an interest group has to offer), the legislature constitutes a body small in number, easily reachable, and (according to capture theory) seriously interested in the (electoral) benefits that an interest group can offer. Lobbyists are likely to have repeated contacts with legislators, to know their views on a variety of subjects, and to have access that cannot be replicated in the case of individual voters. While few within the population may vote, lobbyists cannot, ex ante, distinguish voters from nonvoters and must direct their appeals to all. Thus, to the extent that interest groups engage in lobbying as a means of influencing legislation, they appear to have greater opportunities for success if they need only lobby a discrete and relatively fixed segment of the population—representatives—as opposed to the voting population at large. Representatives may also be more susceptible to entreaties from lobbyists, as interest groups are able to affect opportunities for reelection and advancement. Lobbyists have no comparable threat against the electorate. Therefore, decisions made by legislators may be far more susceptible to interest group pressure than plebiscitary ones. Indeed, the survival in state courts of doctrines long abandoned by federal courts, e.g., substantive conceptions of "public purposes" for which governmental expenditures may be made and the nondelegation doctrine, reveals a relatively low judicial opinion of the capacity of legislatures to ignore the entreaties of special interests.

Clayton P. Gillette, Plebiscites, Participation, and Collective Action in Local Government Law, 86 Mich. L. Rev. 930, 978–982 (1988). See also Elisabeth R. Gerber, The Populist Paradox: Interest Group Influence and the Promise of Direct Legislation (1999); David S. Broder, Democracy Derailed: Initiative Campaigns and the Power of Money (2000).

State ex rel. Rhodes v. Board of Elections of Lake County

230 N.E.2d 347 (Ohio 1967).

■ PER CURIAM.

This is an action in mandamus originating in this court. By this action, relators seek to compel the respondent Board of Elections of Lake County to place the following resolution proposed by initiative petition on the ballot:

> Be it resolved by the people of the Village of Willoughby Hills, Ohio, that:
>
> The President of the United States should bring all American troops home from Vietnam now so that the Vietnamese people can settle their own affairs.

Section 1f, Article II, of the Ohio Constitution, provides for municipal initiative and reads as follows:

> The initiative and referendum powers are hereby reserved to the people of each municipality on all questions which *such municipalities may* now or hereafter *be authorized by law to control by legislative action*; such powers shall be exercised in the manner now or hereafter provided by law. (Emphasis added.)

The initiative petition in the instant case does not contain any question which a municipality is authorized by law to control by legislative action.

Writ denied.

NOTES

1. *Matters Within Municipal Legislative Control.* In the *Board of Elections of Lake County* case, the court concluded that the municipality was not authorized to control the issue at hand by legislative action. Did the court believe that the petition had been offered in an attempt to control the conduct of the Vietnam war? Is that what the petition says? Could the local legislature of Lake County have passed a resolution in praise of a local Little League team that won the state championship? If so, could an initiative petition to the same effect be placed on the ballot? Could the local legislature of Lake County have passed a resolution that it was the sense of that body that American troops should be brought home from Vietnam? Would such a "sense of the county" resolution constitute an effort to "control" the conduct of the war? If the county legislature could have passed such a resolution, could an initiative petition to the same effect be placed on the ballot? What if the initiative in the Board of Elections of Lake County had instead established a new municipal office to be known as the "Anti Vietnam War Coordinator," with the following powers and duties:

> (a) to publicly demand at appropriate times and places the immediate withdrawal of United States troops from Vietnam.
>
> (b) to make studies and periodic public reports on how money spent on war in Vietnam could be used for such social benefits as school and housing construction, and improved hospital and medical facilities for the people of [the Village of Willoughby Hills].
>
> (c) to take other appropriate actions to support the immediate withdrawal of United States Troops from Vietnam.

See Silberman v. Katz, 283 N.Y.S.2d 895 (N.Y. Sup. Ct.), aff'd, 284 N.Y.S.2d 836 (N.Y. App. Div. 1967).

2. In an area as fraught with conflicting views and public exposure as the Vietnam war, is there reason to believe that the electorate will enter the voting booth without careful consideration of the issues? Or consider the issue of abortion. Public opinion seems both deeply held and widely split on this issue. Does this mean that restrictions on abortion are an appropriate or inappropriate subject for an initiative petition? See Arkansas Women's Political Caucus v. Riviere, 677 S.W.2d 846 (Ark. 1984). What is the likelihood that one side of the issue will participate in the initiative campaign or vote in numbers disproportionate to their actual strength in the electorate? If this does occur, is it problematic?

3. Citizen groups have attempted to use the initiative to express the sense of the electorate on a political issue, rather than to change an explicit law, in other contexts at both the local and state level. In Southeastern Michigan Fair Budget Coalition v. Killeen, 395 N.W.2d 325 (Mich. Ct. App. 1986), the court dismissed a petition for a writ of mandamus to require the county clerk to place on the ballot "advisory questions" concerning military spending and United States military assistance to Central America. The Detroit City Council had passed resolutions authorizing the questions to appear on the ballot. The court determined that although the legislature could empower "subordinate governmental entities" to place advisory questions on the ballot, the legislature had not exercised that power. Nor, the court concluded, was the power to place such questions on the ballot included within the home rule charter of the city of Detroit. The court determined that since the initiative, by statute, extended only to matters "within the scope of" municipal powers, and foreign policy fell outside the municipal mandate, these resolutions fell outside the city's statutory authority. Is the power to conduct foreign policy the same as the power to comment on foreign policy?

In State ex rel. City of Upper Arlington v. Franklin County Board of Elections, 895 N.E.2d 177 (Ohio 2008), the court held that the Ohio constitutional grant of initiative power for legislative actions did not extend to a proposed initiative that expressed the view that residents "do not desire" privatization of trash-collection services, "want" to continue the preexisting trash-collection method, and "don't want" the city to enter into a contract with a private corporation. For other initiatives that may be construed as merely advisory, see League of Women Voters of Maine v. Gwadosky, 966 F.Supp. 52 (D. Me. 1997) (holding that state initiative directing state's U.S. congressional delegation and state legislators to use their powers to promote a term limits amendment to the U.S. Constitution violates Article V); Donovan v. Priest, 931 S.W.2d 119 (Ark. 1996), cert. denied, 519 U.S. 1149 (1997) (same); Saggio v. Connelly, 709 P.2d 874 (Ariz. 1985) (holding that proposed municipal initiative seeking opinion of electorate on whether the city of Apache Junction should be dissolved is impermissible because it does not present any proposed law or ordinance); State of Nebraska ex rel. Brant v. Beermann, 350 N.W.2d 18 (Neb. 1984) (rejecting as improper subject for an initiative a nonbinding expression of public opinion on a nuclear freeze to be forwarded to those in power in the U.S. and the Soviet Union). But see Farley v. Healey, 431 P.2d 650, 652 (Cal. 1967) (upholding initiative measure stating "policy" of the people of San Francisco regarding Vietnam war, pursuant to charter provision stating that "[a]ny declaration of policy may be submitted to the electors in the manner provided for the submission of ordinances"); Kimble v. Swackhamer, 439 U.S. 1385 (1978) (holding permissible under Article V a purely advisory referendum requested by Nevada state legislature regarding proposed equal rights amendment to U.S. Constitution).

4. *Initiatives and the "Single–Subject" Rule.* Recall the discussion of the single-subject requirement in state legislation at pages 278–281 supra. Many jurisdictions impose the same requirement on initiatives. See Rachel Downey, Michelle Hargrove, and Vanessa Locklin, A Survey of the Single Subject Rule as Applied to Statewide Initiatives, 13 J. Contemp. Legal Issues 579 (2004). Should the phrase "single subject" be defined identically for purposes of legislation enacted through representatives and through initiatives? Consider that the function of the requirement is to prevent logrolling or the building of coalitions among minority interests to pass legislation, no part of which is favored by a majority of the voters. Is it easier to build coalitions in representative assemblies than in the electorate? If so, then it might be desirable to have more cogent obstacles to coalition building (for instance, a narrower construction of single subject) in the legislature than in initiatives. On the other hand, logrolling may occur in the legislature by vote trading on separate bills. Since voters do not convene in one location to discuss issues, and since they vote privately so there can be no monitoring of the "deal," logrolling among voters can only occur when all provisions being traded are considered simultaneously. This suggests a need for a stronger check on logrolling in the electorate. For an argument that application of the single-subject rule in initiatives depends on the extent to which the different components of a proposal on separable in the minds of voters, see Michael D. Gilbert and Robert D. Cooter, A Theory of Direct Democracy and the Single Subject Rule, 110 Colum. L. Rev. 687 (2010).

In Advisory Opinion to the Attorney General, 778 So.2d 888 (Fla. 2000), the Florida Supreme Court reviewed proposed initiatives that would have added civil rights provisions to the Florida Constitution prohibiting discriminatory practices based on race, color, ethnicity, national origin, and (in one initiative) sex in public education, employment, and contracting. The court concluded that the proposed amendments violated the state's single-subject requirement because it applied to "diverse areas of governmental operation which, in themselves, are multifaceted," and failed to indicate the effect that the proposals would have on existing constitutional protections, such as those based on religion and physical disability.

The Oregon Supreme Court reached a similar result in League of Oregon Cities v. State, 56 P.3d 892 (Or. 2002). Voters had approved a statewide initiative that amended the state constitution in order to require governments to compensate real property owners for the cost of regulations that reduced real property values, unless the regulations prohibited the use of property for purposes of selling pornography. The court concluded that the initiative effectively amended both the state's eminent domain powers and a constitutional provision involving freedom of expression. Thus, the initiative violated the state's version of a single-subject requirement for constitutional amendments.

In Chemical Specialties Manufacturers Ass'n, Inc. v. Deukmejian, 278 Cal.Rptr. 128 (Cal. App. 1991), the court considered a statewide initiative that proponents contended dealt with the single subject of the peoples' "right to know." The initiative contained provisions involving notices about the effects of disposal of toxic products, disclosure on contract provisions for health insurance, disclosure by corporations about investment in South Africa, a rating system for insurance companies, and advertising. Employing a test that an initiative could be said to contain a single subject if all its provisions were "reasonably germane" to each other, the court invalidated the initiative.

For cases in which a proposed initiative was invalidated under a state's "single subject" requirement, see, e.g., Amalgamated Transit Union Local 587 v. State, 11 P.3d 762 (Wash. 2000); In re Proposed Initiative 1996–4 v. Pool, 916 P.2d 528 (Colo. 1996); Missourians to Protect the Initiative Process v. Blount, 799 S.W.2d 824 (Mo. 1990); Evans v. Firestone, 457

So.2d 1351 (Fla. 1984). For cases in which a proposed initiative was sustained under a state's "single subject" requirement, see, e.g., Manduley v. Superior Court, 41 P.3d 3 (Cal. 2002); State ex rel. Caleb v. Beesley, 949 P.2d 724 (Or. 1997); State v. Thorne, 921 P.2d 514 (Wash. 1996); Wyoming National Abortion Rights Action League v. Karpan, 881 P.2d 281 (Wyo. 1994); Raven v. Deukmejian, 801 P.2d 1077 (Cal. 1990). For academic commentary on "single subject" requirements, see, e.g., Daniel H. Lowenstein, Initiatives and the New Single Subject Rule, 1 Election L.J. 35 (2002); Daniel H. Lowenstein, California Initiatives and the Single–Subject Rule, 30 UCLA L. Rev. 936 (1983); Clayton P. Gillette, Expropriation and Institutional Design in State and Local Government Law, 80 Va. L. Rev. 625, 664–670 (1994).

Equality Foundation of Greater Cincinnati, Inc. v. City of Cincinnati

128 F.3d 289 (6th Cir. 1997), cert. denied, 525 U.S. 943 (1998).

■ KRUPANSKY, CIRCUIT JUDGE.

This court previously disposed of this cause in Equality Foundation of Greater Cincinnati, Inc. v. City of Cincinnati ("Equality Foundation I"), 54 F.3d 261 (6th Cir. 1995), vacated, 518 U.S. 1001, 116 S.Ct. 2519, 135 L.Ed.2d 1044 (1996). It has been remanded for reconsideration by the United States Supreme Court consequent to its decision in Romer v. Evans, 517 U.S. 620, 116 S.Ct. 1620, 134 L.Ed.2d 855 (1996).

... [D]efendant/appellant the City of Cincinnati ("the City"), and intervening defendants/appellants Equal Rights Not Special Rights ("ERNSR") [and three individuals] (collectively denominated "the defendants"), challenged the lower court's invalidation of an amendment to the City Charter of Cincinnati ("the Charter") for purported constitutional infirmities, and its permanent injunction restraining implementation of that measure. As a result of an initiative petition, the subject amendment had appeared on the November 2, 1993, local ballot as "Issue 3" and was enacted by 62% of the ballots cast, thereby becoming Article XII of the Charter (hereinafter "the Cincinnati Charter Amendment" or "Article XII"). Article XII read:

> NO SPECIAL CLASS STATUS MAY BE GRANTED BASED UPON SEXUAL ORIENTATION, CONDUCT OR RELATIONSHIPS.
>
> The City of Cincinnati and its various Boards and Commissions may not enact, adopt, enforce or administer any ordinance, regulation, rule or policy which provides that homosexual, lesbian, or bisexual orientation, status, conduct, or relationship constitutes, entitles, or otherwise provides a person with the basis to have any claim of minority or protected status, quota preference or other preferential treatment. This provision of the City Charter shall in all respects be self-executing. Any ordinance, regulation, rule or policy enacted before this amendment is adopted that violates the foregoing prohibition shall be null and void and of no force or effect.

Defendant ERNSR had drafted and initiated Issue 3 in response to the prior adoption by the Cincinnati City Council ("Council") of two city ordinances. On March 13, 1991, Council enacted Ordinance No. 79–1991, commonly known as the "Equal Employment Opportunity Ordinance," which mandated that the City could not discriminate in its own hiring practices on the basis of

> classification factors such as race, color, sex, handicap, religion, national or ethnic origin, age, *sexual orientation*, HIV status, Appalachian regional ancestry, and marital status.

(Emphasis added.)

Subsequently, Council on November 25, 1992, adopted Ordinance No. 490–1992 (commonly referred to as the "Human Rights Ordinance") which prohibited private discrimination in employment, housing, or public accommodation for reasons of sexual orientation. The opening paragraph of the Human Rights Ordinance expressed the intent of this legislation as:

> PROHIBITING unlawful discriminatory practices in the City of Cincinnati based on race, gender, age, color, religion, disability status, *sexual orientation*, marital status, or ethnic, national or Appalachian regional origin, in *employment, housing, and public accommodations* by ordaining Chapter 914, Cincinnati Municipal Code.

(Emphases added.) The new law created a complaint and hearing procedure for seeking redress from purported sexual orientation discrimination, and exposed offenders to civil and criminal penalties....

On May 12, 1995, this reviewing court reversed the lower court's judgment, vacated its injunction, and vacated its award of costs and attorneys' fees to the plaintiffs, concluding that the Cincinnati Charter Amendment offended neither the First nor the Fourteenth Amendments to the United States Constitution and accordingly could stand as enacted by the Cincinnati voters. *Equality Foundation I*, 54 F.3d 261 (6th Cir. 1995)....

On May 20, 1996, the United States Supreme Court decided Romer v. Evans, 517 U.S. 620, 116 S.Ct. 1620, 134 L.Ed.2d 855 (1996). In that decision, the Court invalidated an amendment to the Colorado constitution ("Colorado Amendment 2") enacted by a statewide plebiscite as an infringement of the Equal Protection Clause of the Fourteenth Amendment to the United States Constitution. Colorado Amendment 2 recited:

> No Protected Status Based on Homosexual, Lesbian, or Bisexual Orientation. Neither the State of Colorado, through any of its branches or departments, nor any of its agencies, political subdivisions, municipalities or school districts, shall enact, adopt or enforce any statute, regulation, ordinance or policy whereby homosexual, lesbian or bisexual orientation, conduct, practices or relationships shall constitute or otherwise be the basis of or entitle any person or class of persons to have or claim any minority status, quota preferences, protected status or claim of discrimination. This Section of the Constitution shall be in all respects self-executing.

Id. at 624, 116 S.Ct. at 1623.

Although the United States Supreme Court in *Romer* affirmed the Colorado Supreme Court's decision striking down Colorado Amendment 2, it rejected the reasoning of that court which had posited the existence of a fundamental constitutional right to participate in the political process and then concluded that, under "strict scrutiny" review, Colorado Amendment 2 deprived homosexuals in Colorado of that fundamental right. *Romer*, at 625–626, 116 S.Ct. at 1624 (citing Evans v. Romer, 854 P.2d 1270 (Colo. 1993) and Evans v. Romer, 882 P.2d 1335 (Colo. 1994)). By contrast, the United States Supreme Court did not assess Colorado Amendment 2 under "strict scrutiny" or "intermediate scrutiny" standards, but instead ultimately applied "rational relationship" strictures to that enactment and resolved that the Colorado state constitutional provision did not invade any fundamental right and did not target any suspect class or quasi-suspect class. See *Romer*, at 631–632, 116 S.Ct. at 1627....

Nonetheless, the *Romer* court invalidated Colorado Amendment 2 because it was deemed invidiously discriminatory and not rationally connected to the advancement of any legitimate state objective. *Romer*, at 632–635, 116 S.Ct. at 1627, 1629....

Although this circuit, in *Equality Foundation I*, and the Supreme Court, in *Romer*, each applied "rational relationship" scrutiny to a popularly enacted measure which negatively impacted the interests of homosexuals, this court concluded that the Cincinnati Charter Amendment withstood a constitutional equal protection attack, whereas the Supreme Court resolved that Colorado Amendment 2 did not. An exacting comparative analysis of *Romer* with the facts and circumstances of this case disclose that these contrary results were reached because the two cases involved substantially different enactments of entirely distinct scope and impact, which conceptually and analytically distinguished the constitutional posture of the two measures. As developed herein, the salient operative factors which motivated the *Romer* analysis and result were unique to that case and were not implicated in *Equality Foundation I.*

The *Romer* Court, prior to undertaking the conventional "rational relationship" equal protection inquiry, initially characterized Colorado Amendment 2 as facially objectionable because it removed municipally legislated special legal protection from gays and precluded the relegislation of special legal rights for them at every level of state government[].... The Court elaborated:

> Sweeping and comprehensive is the change in legal status effected by this law.... Homosexuals, by state decree, are put in a solitary class with respect to transactions and relations in both the private and the governmental spheres. The amendment withdraws from homosexuals, but no others, specific legal protection from the injuries caused by discrimination, and it forbids reinstatement of these laws and policies.

Id. at 627, 116 S.Ct. at 1625....

The Court additionally observed that Colorado Amendment 2 could be read to divest homosexuals of all state law government protection available to all other citizens:

> Amendment 2's reach may not be limited to specific laws passed for the benefit of gays and lesbians. It is a fair, if not necessary, inference from the broad language of the amendment that it deprives gays and lesbians even of the protection of general laws and policies that prohibit arbitrary discrimination in governmental and private settings.

Romer, at 630, 116 S.Ct. at 1626. However, the *Romer* Court did not rely upon that potential universally exclusive effect to invalidate the measure, but instead ultimately construed Colorado Amendment 2 only to remove and prohibit special legal rights for homosexuals under state law[]....

The more restricted reach of the Cincinnati Charter Amendment, as compared to the actual and potential sweep of Colorado Amendment 2, is noteworthy....

... [T]he language of the Cincinnati Charter Amendment, read in its full context, merely prevented homosexuals, as homosexuals, from obtaining special privileges and preferences (such as affirmative action preferences or the legally sanctioned power to force employers, landlords, and merchants to transact business with them) from the City. In stark contrast, Colorado Amendment 2's far broader language could be construed to exclude homosexuals from the protection of every Colorado state law, including laws generally applicable to all other Coloradans, thus rendering gay people without recourse to any state authority at any level of government for any type of victimization or abuse which they might suffer by either private or public actors. *Romer*, at 627–631, 116 S.Ct. at 1625–1627. Whereas Colorado Amendment 2 ominously threatened to reduce an entire segment of the state's population to the status of virtual non-citizens (or even non-persons) without legal rights under any and every type of state law, the Cincinnati Charter Amendment had no such sweeping and conscience-shocking effect, because (1) it applied only at the lowest (municipal) level of government and thus could not dispossess gay Cincinnatians of any rights derived from any higher level of state law and enforced by a superior apparatus of state government, and (2) its narrow, restrictive language could not be construed to deprive homosexuals of all legal protections even under municipal law, but instead eliminated only "special class status" and "preferential treatment" for gays as gays under Cincinnati ordinances and policies, leaving untouched the application, to gay citizens, of any and all legal rights generally accorded by the municipal government to all persons as persons.

At bottom, the Supreme Court in *Romer* found that a state constitutional proviso which deprived a politically unpopular minority, but no others, of the political ability to obtain special legislation at every level of state government, including within local jurisdictions having pro-gay rights majorities, with the only possible recourse available through surmounting the formidable political obstacle of securing a rescinding amendment to the state constitution, was simply so obviously and fundamentally inequitable, arbitrary, and oppressive that it literally violated basic equal protection values. Thus, the Supreme Court directed that the ordinary three-part equal protection query was rendered irrelevant. See *Romer*, at 631–632, 116

S.Ct. at 1627 (noting that Colorado Amendment 2 "defies" conventional equal protection analysis).

This "extra-conventional" application of equal protection principles can have no pertinence to the case sub judice. The low level of government at which Article XII becomes operative is significant because the opponents of that strictly local enactment need not undertake the monumental political task of procuring an amendment to the Ohio Constitution as a precondition to achievement of a desired change in the local law, but instead may either seek local repeal of the subject amendment through ordinary municipal political processes, or pursue relief from every higher level of Ohio government including, but not limited to, Hamilton County, state agencies, the Ohio legislature, or the voters themselves via a statewide initiative.

Moreover, unlike Colorado Amendment 2, which interfered with the expression of local community preferences in that state, the Cincinnati Charter Amendment constituted a direct expression of the local community will on a subject of direct consequences to the voters. Patently, a local measure adopted by direct franchise, designed in part to preserve community values and character, which does not impinge upon any fundamental right or the interests of any suspect or quasi-suspect class, carries a formidable presumption of legitimacy and is thus entitled to the highest degree of deference from the courts. Cf. Hunter v. Erickson, 393 U.S. 385, 89 S.Ct. 557, 21 L.Ed.2d 616 (1969) (commanding that a municipal charter amendment adopted by initiative cannot stand if it facially discriminates along suspect lines of race, color, religion, and national origin); James v. Valtierra, 402 U.S. 137, 140–141, 91 S.Ct. 1331, 1333–1334, 28 L.Ed.2d 678 (1971).

As the product of direct legislation by the people, a popularly enacted initiative or referendum occupies a special posture in this nation's constitutional tradition and jurisprudence. An expression of the popular will expressed by majority plebiscite, especially at the lowest level of government (which is the level of government closest to the people), must not be cavalierly disregarded. See, e.g., City of Eastlake v. Forest City Enterprises, Inc., 426 U.S. 668, 679, 96 S.Ct. 2358, 2364–2365, 49 L.Ed.2d 132 (1976) (explaining that the referendum process is "a basic instrument of democratic government"); *James*, 402 U.S. at 141–143, 91 S.Ct. at 1333–1334 (exalting the referendum as manifesting "devotion to democracy, not to bias, discrimination, or prejudice" and as constituting a "procedure [which] ensures that all the people of a community will have a voice in a decision ... that will affect the future development of their own community."); accord Southern Alameda Spanish Speaking Organization v. Union City, 424 F.2d 291, 294 (9th Cir. 1970) ("A referendum ... is far more than an expression of ambiguously founded neighborhood preference. It is the city itself legislating through its voters—an exercise by the voters of their traditional right through direct legislation to override the views of their elected representatives as to what serves the public interest.") (citing

Spaulding v. Blair, 403 F.2d 862, 863 (4th Cir. 1968) ("The referendum procedure ... is a fundamental part of the State's legislative process.")).[9]

In any event, *Romer* should not be construed to forbid electorates the authority, via initiative, to instruct their elected city council representatives, or their elected or appointed municipal officers, to withhold special rights, privileges, and protections from homosexuals, or to prospectively remove the authority of such public representatives and officers to accord special rights, privileges, and protections to any non-suspect and non-quasi-suspect group. Such a reading would disenfranchise the voters of their most fundamental right which is the very foundation of the democratic form of government, even through the lowest (and most populist) organs and avenues of state government, to vote to override or preempt any policy or practice implemented or contemplated by their subordinate civil servants to bestow special rights, protections, and/or privileges upon a group of people who do not comprise a suspect or a quasi-suspect class and hence are not constitutionally entitled to any special favorable legal status. *Romer* dealt with a statewide constitutional amendment that denied homosexuals access to every level and instrumentality of state government as possible sources of special legal protection. *Romer* supplied no rationale for subjecting a purely local measure of modest scope, which simply refused special privileges under local law for a non-suspect and non-quasi-suspect group of citizens, to any equal protection assessment other than the traditional "rational relationship" test....

In essence, the high Court resolved that a state constitutional amendment which denied homosexuals any opportunity to attain state law protec-

---

9. This court underscores that the constitutional concerns which anchor *Romer* are not implicated when previously adopted special legal protection at the local level is rescinded, and its reinstatement precluded, irrespective of whether the prohibition is enacted by the voters directly, by the city's elected representatives, or by some other competent instrumentality such as a local department supervisor. Unlike a state government, which is composed of discrete and quasi-independent levels and entities such as cities, counties, and the general state government, a municipality is a unitary local political subdivision or unit comprised, fundamentally, of the territory and residents within its geographical boundaries. See, e.g., Mumford v. Basinski, 105 F.3d 264, 267–268 (6th Cir. 1997) (distinguishing Ohio municipalities and counties as creatures of state law constituting "bodies politic and corporate" from the state government and its arms, officers, and instrumentalities), [cert. denied, 522 U.S. 914 (1997)]....

No logically sound construction of the components of a municipal polity could compartmentalize the City's citizens, elected representatives, and administrative departments into conceptually separate levels of local government, in the way that municipalities and other local entities are distinct levels of state government as compared to the state entity itself. Hence, it would be irrational to argue that the adoption of a gay rights regulation by a municipal department could not constitutionally be eliminated, and its reintroduction barred, by the city council or the city's voters, on the theory that it would be more difficult for proponents of gay rights to lobby the city council or the city's electorate than to lobby the pertinent department chief, because the city's voters, elected council, and departments and employees are all components, with varying degrees and spheres of authority, of the same (municipal) level of state government. Stated differently, it would be illogical to conclude that city council would be powerless to void a rule or regulation promulgated by one of the city's departments or department heads on the theory that it would be more difficult to lobby council for a change than the department administrators.

tion, even from municipalities or other local entities within that state which desired to accord them special legal rights, could not be justified by the proffered public interests purportedly advanced by that state enactment, namely enhancement of the associational liberty of the state's residents and the conservation of public resources, because the citizens of the affected subordinate bodies politic had elected, or otherwise would elect, to forgo those identified public interests in favor of guaranteeing, through local governmental instrumentalities, nondiscriminatory treatment of the gay citizens of their local governmental units.

A state law which prevents local voters or their representatives, against their will, from granting special rights to gays, cannot be rationally justified by cost savings and associational liberties which the majority of citizens in those communities do not want. Clearly, the financial interests and associational liberties of the citizens of the state as a whole are not implicated if a municipality creates special legal protections for homosexuals applicable only within that jurisdiction and implements those protections solely via local governmental apparatuses. For this reason, the justifications proffered by Colorado for Colorado Amendment 2 insufficiently supported that provision, and implied that no reason other than a bare desire to harm homosexuals, rather than to advance the individual and collective interests of the majority of Colorado's citizens, motivated the state's voters to adopt Colorado Amendment 2.

In contradistinction, as evolved herein, the Cincinnati Charter Amendment constituted local legislation of purely local scope. As such, the City's voters had clear, actual, and direct individual and collective interests in that measure, and in the potential cost savings and other contingent benefits which could result from that local law. Beyond contradiction, passage of the Cincinnati Charter Amendment was not facially animated solely by an impermissible naked desire of a majority of the City's residents to injure an unpopular group of citizens, rather than to legally actualize their individual and collective interests and preferences. Clearly, the Cincinnati Charter Amendment implicated at least one issue of direct, actual, and practical importance to those who voted it into law, namely whether those voters would be legally compelled by municipal ordinances to expend their own public and private resources to guarantee and enforce nondiscrimination against gays in local commercial transactions and social intercourse.

Unquestionably, the Cincinnati Charter Amendment's removal of homosexuals from the ranks of persons protected by municipal antidiscrimination ordinances, and its preclusion of restoring that group to protected status, would eliminate and forestall the substantial public costs that accrue from the investigation and adjudication of sexual orientation discrimination complaints, which costs the City alone would otherwise bear because no coextensive protection exists under federal or state law. Moreover, the elimination of actionable special rights extended by city ordinances, and prevention of the reinstatement of such ordinances, would effectively advance the legitimate governmental interest of reducing the exposure of the City's residents to protracted and costly litigation by eliminating a municipally-created class of legal claims and charges, thus necessarily saving the City and its citizens, including property owners and employers, the costs of defending against such actions. Although the *Romer* Court never rejected associational liberty and the expression of community moral disapproval of homosexuality as rational bases supporting an enactment denying privileged treatment to homosexuals, it concluded that under the facts and circumstances of *Romer*, the state's argument in support of Colorado Amendment 2 was not credible. Because the valid interests of the Cincinnati electorate in conserving public and private financial resources is, standing alone, of sufficient weight to justify the City's Charter Amendment under a rational basis analysis, discussion of equally justifiable community interests, including the application of associational liberty and community moral disapproval of homosexuality, is unnecessary to sustain the Charter Amendment's viability.

In summary, the Cincinnati Charter Amendment did not disempower a group of citizens from attaining special protection at all levels of state government, but instead merely removed municipally enacted special protection from gays and lesbians. Unlike Colorado Amendment 2, the Cincinnati Charter Amendment cannot be characterized as an irrational measure fashioned only to harm an unpopular segment of the population in a sweeping and unjustifiable manner.

Accordingly, the judgment below is hereby REVERSED, and the district court's permanent injunction against implementation and enforcement of the Cincinnati Charter Amendment (Article XII) is hereby VACATED. The lower court's award of costs (including attorney's fees) to the plaintiffs is also VACATED. This case is hereby REMANDED to the district court for entry of judgment in favor of the defendants, and for such further necessary and appropriate proceedings and orders as are consistent with this decision.

NOTES

1. In November 2004, Cincinnati voters, by 54 percent to 46 percent, repealed the Article XII provision that the Sixth Circuit upheld. In 2006, the Cincinnati City Council voted 8–1 to modify the provisions of the City Municipal Code to "prohibit discrimination against individuals based on their sexual orientation or transgendered status."

As *Equality Foundation of Greater Cincinnati* indicates, initiatives and referenda are subject to federal constitutional constraints in the same way that legislatively enacted laws are. What effect does the possibility of judicial review for constitutional defects have on the claim that the electorate, by virtue of its ability to vote in secret and without the benefit of open deliberation, will be more likely than legislators to vote in a manner that offends the rights of a minority? How do you explain the fact that the Cincinnati City Council, an elected body, enacted two ordinances prohibiting discrimination on the basis of sexual orientation that were overturned by 62 percent of those voting in an initiative election held shortly thereafter? In Crawford v. Board of Education, 458 U.S. 527 (1982), the Court upheld an amendment to the California constitution adopted by the voters to limit state court-ordered busing for desegregation purposes. The amendment was proposed after a California state court had ordered busing of students to remedy segregation in the Los Angeles school district. The amendment limited state court-ordered busing for desegregation purposes to those instances in which a federal court would order busing to remedy a Fourteenth Amendment violation. The Court held that the California amendment did not employ a racial classification and that there was sufficient evidence that the amendment was not enacted for a discriminatory purpose. Finally, the Court determined that a state is not precluded from restricting its antidiscrimination policies to those required by the Fourteenth Amendment, even if it previously undertook a broader obligation.

In Washington v. Seattle School District No. 1, 458 U.S. 457 (1982), the Court invalidated a statute, adopted by initiative, that prohibited school boards from requiring any student to attend a school other than the school geographically nearest or next nearest his place of residence. The statute then excepted from its restrictions out-of-area assignments of students for virtually all purposes required by school board policies other than racial desegregation. The Court concluded that the initiative altered the decision-making structure of integration decisions in a manner that burdened racial groups, and was not simply an attempt to resolve an ongoing political debate. For an example of a referendum that was valid notwithstanding disparate impact on racial groups, see Arthur v. City of Toledo, 782 F.2d 565 (6th Cir. 1986).

For discussion of whether initiatives and referenda are more likely than legislative enactments to affect racial and other minorities adversely, and should therefore be subject to heightened judicial scrutiny, see, e.g., Lynn A. Baker, Direct Democracy and Discrimination: A Public Choice Perspective, 67 Chi.-Kent L. Rev. 707 (1991); Derrick A. Bell, The Referendum: Democracy's Barrier to Racial Equality, 54 Wash. L. Rev. 1 (1978); Robin Charlow, Judicial Review, Equal Protection and the Problem with Plebiscites, 79 Cornell L. Rev. 527 (1994); William N. Eskridge, Jr., Democracy, Kulturkampf, and the Apartheid of the Closet, 50 Vand. L. Rev. 419 (1997); Julian N. Eule, Judicial Review of Direct Democracy, 99 Yale L.J. 1503 (1990); Barbara S. Gamble, Putting Civil Rights to a Popular Vote, 41 Am. J. Pol. Sci. 245 (1997); Mark Tushnet, Fear of Voting: Differential Standards of Judicial Review of Direct Legislation, 1996 Ann. Surv. Am. L. 373; Sylvia R. Lazos Vargas, Judicial Review of Initiatives and Referendums in which Majorities Vote on Minorities' Democratic Citizenship, 60 Ohio St. L.J. 399 (1999); Elizabeth R. Leong, Ballot Initiatives & Identifiable Minorities: A Textual Call to Congress, 28 Rutgers L.J. 677 (1997); John F. Niblock, Anti–Gay Initiatives: A Call for Heightened Judicial Scrutiny, 41 UCLA L. Rev. 153 (1993).

For discussion of the special problems of interpretation posed by ballot initiatives, see, e.g., Philip P. Frickey, Interpretation on the Borderline: Constitution, Canons, Direct Democracy, 1996 Ann. Surv. Am. L. 477; John Copeland Nagle, Direct Democracy and Hastily Enacted Statutes, 1996 Ann. Surv. Am. L. 535; Jane S. Schacter, The Pursuit of "Popular Intent": Interpretative Dilemmas in Direct Democracy, 105 Yale L.J. 107 (1995); Michael M. O'Hear, Statutory Interpretation and Direct Democracy: Lessons from the Drug Treatment Initiatives, 40 Harv. J. Legis. 281 (2003); Stephen Salvucci, Say What You Mean and Mean What You Say: The Interpretation of Initiatives in California, 71 S. Cal. L. Rev. 871 (1998).

2. In footnote 9 of its opinion, the court in Equality Foundation explicitly underscored its view "that the constitutional concerns which anchor *Romer* are not implicated when previously adopted special legal protection at the local level is rescinded, and its reinstatement precluded. . . ." 128 F.3d at 298 n.9. To be sure, those seeking to prohibit discrimination on the basis of sexual orientation in a single Colorado locality after the adoption of the statewide initiative at issue in *Romer*, face the barrier of first needing to amend the state constitution. But it is similarly noteworthy that the Cincinnati initiative did not merely repeal in relevant part the two antidiscrimination ordinances that the City Council had previously adopted. Instead, it amended the city Charter to prohibit "[t]he City ... and its various Boards and Commissions" from enacting any such ordinance in the future. Thus, those seeking to prohibit discrimination on the basis of sexual orientation in the city of Cincinnati after the adoption of this local initiative face the additional barrier of first needing to amend the city Charter. Should the level of government—i.e., state versus local—at which the initiative is enacted be the crucial variable for assessing its constitutionality as the court in *Equality Foundation* suggests? Should it also (or instead) matter how high a legal process barrier the initiative imposes on those who would repeal it, so that, for example, an initiative amending the state Constitution is subject to greater judicial scrutiny than one adopting or repealing a state statute, and an initiative amending a city Charter is analogously subject to greater judicial scrutiny than one adopting or repealing a local ordinance? Does the following observation of the *Equality Foundation* court merely beg the latter question?

> Although Cincinnati's interest in conserving public and private resources might have been served by a mere repeal of the sexual orientation clauses of the Human Rights Ordinance and Equal Employment Opportunity Ordinance, *we do not think it irrational* for Cincinnati to advance this interest by means of a charter amendment. Cincinnati voters may have doubted that the city council would exercise the fiscal restraint the voters themselves valued, and they may, therefore, have feared that the Council would respond to a simple repeal by reenacting the two sexual orientation clauses.

128 F.3d at 301 n.13 (emphasis added). Is the following argument, put forth by Justice Scalia (joined by Justice Thomas and Chief Justice Rehnquist) in dissenting from the Court's 1996 decision to remand *Equality Foundation* to the Sixth Circuit for further consideration in light of *Romer*, more or less persuasive than the Equality Foundation court's observation above?

> The consequence of [*Romer's*] holding is that homosexuals in a city (or other electoral subunit) that wishes to accord them special protection cannot be compelled to achieve a state constitutional amendment in order to have the benefit of that democratic preference. [*Equality Foundation*], by contrast, involves a determination by what appears to be the lowest electoral subunit that it does not wish to accord homosexuals special protection. It can make that determination effective, of course, only by instructing its departments and agencies to obey it—which is what the Cincinnati Charter Amendment does. Thus, the consequence of holding this provision unconstitutional would be that nowhere in the country may the people decide, in democratic fashion, not to accord special protection to homosexuals.

Equality Foundation, 116 S.Ct. 2519, 2519 (mem). (Scalia, J., dissenting).

3. After the Sixth Circuit handed down its decision upon remand by the U.S. Supreme Court, a petition for rehearing en banc was filed but did not garner favorable votes of a majority of the judges. The petition did, however, give all of the then-active judges of the Sixth Circuit the opportunity to express their views on the case.

How persuasive do you find the following portions of the dissent from the denial of hearing en banc, which was signed by six of the Circuit's judges?

> The panel [in the decision at issue in the petition for rehearing] then noted that the Supreme Court struck down Amendment 2 because the only avenue through which homosexuals could seek redress after Amendment 2 was by "the formidable political obstacle of securing a rescinding amendment to the state constitution." 128 F.3d. at 297. Because homosexuals could "seek local repeal [of Issue Three] through ordinary municipal political processes," the panel declared Issue Three did not impose as onerous a burden as Amendment 2. Id. at 297. This distinction is unpersuasive, however, given that the Supreme Court expressly declined to rest its holding on the political restructuring cases, such as *Hunter v. Erickson,* where such distinctions are normally used. *Romer,* 116 S.Ct. at 1624. Therefore, the fact that it is easier for a group to seek the repeal of a city charter amendment as opposed to a state constitutional amendment is of no consequence as far as the essential rationale of *Romer* is concerned....
>
> Finally, the panel makes the sweeping statement that "[i]n any event, *Romer* should not be construed to forbid local electorates the authority, via initiative, to instruct their elected ... representatives ... to withhold special rights." *Equality Foundation,* 128 F.3d at 298. *Romer,* however, was decided on equal protection grounds, which applies to local as well as state governmental action. Therefore, the fact that Issue Three is a local as opposed to a state measure is of no controlling significance for purposes of the Equal Protection Clause. *See City of Cleburne v. Cleburn Living Ctr.,* 473 U.S. 432, 105 S.Ct. 3249, 87 L.Ed.2d 313 (1985).
>
> Whether or not we agree with the majority decision in *Romer,* we are of course obligated by law to give rulings of the Supreme Court full force and effect. We believe the panel decision in this case draws "distinctions without a difference" and fails to abide by the key ruling in *Romer* that "A law declaring that in general it shall be more difficult for one group of citizens than for all others to seek aid from the government is itself a denial of equal protection of the laws in the most literal sense." 116 S.Ct. at 1628.

Equality Foundation, 1998 WL 101701, *3 (Gilman, J., dissenting).

Is Judge Boggs' concurrence in the denial of hearing en banc, excerpted below, more or less persuasive to you than the above excerpt from the dissent? Why?

> I write separately to point out that, contrary to the view expressed by my dissenting colleagues, *Romer* said nothing about whether a city like Cincinnati could choose to foreclose the enactment of possibly salutary, but also possibly insidious, gay-rights ordinances. *Romer's* holding is simple: a state may not, by constitutional amendment, prohibit a municipal government from enacting ordinances conferring benefits or protections on gay residents. *See Romer,* 116 S.Ct. at 1626. As explained below, nothing about this holding calls into question the judgment of the panel in this case, and I therefore concur in the court's denial of the petition for rehearing en banc.
>
> The federal Constitution contemplates only two sovereigns: the United States itself, on the one hand, and the respective states, on the other. *Romer,* along with evidence from the Constitutional text itself (for example, the Guaranty Clause, *see* U.S. CONST. art. IV, § 4), at most arguably suggests that *state* government may not be structured so as to uniquely burden the ability of gays (or members of other non-suspect classes) to participate in the political life of the sovereign absent a demonstrable, rational reason for doing so. Even this limited principle, however, does not apply to *cities,* which are not constitutionally cognizable political sovereignties and which, therefore, vary widely in their forms of government. Perhaps more so than states, "[c]ities ... [are] laboratories for political experiments in public participation." Joseph P. Tomain, *On Local Autonomy: Discontinuity and Convergence,* 55 U. CIN. L. REV. 399, 418 (1986). Indeed, one of the rationales for Ohio's home-rule statute is that "home rule permits cities and counties to serve as laboratories for innovations in government, a role for which their limited size is ideally suited." Stephen Cianca, *Home Rule in Ohio Counties: Legal and Constitutional Perspectives,* 19 U. DAYTON L. REV. 533, 534 (1994).
>
> In my opinion, Cincinnati's Issue 3 merely reflects the kind of social and political experimentation that is such a common characteristic of city government. Cincinnati (unlike other cities in Ohio) has made a political judgment, expressed by plebiscite, that its city council will not enact ordinances that confer legal status or benefits based on sexual orientation. It is not the case that this judgment deprives anyone of their right to participate in the political life of the sovereign (*i.e.,* the State of Ohio). Unlike gays in Colorado after the passage of Amendment 2, gay residents of Cincinnati are not even arguably deprived of their rights under the state civil rights laws, nor are they deprived of their right to seek redress in the state legislature. In this respect, gays in Cincinnati are in a situation essentially similar to Colorado gays who happen not to reside in Aspen, Boulder, or Denver (the three cities whose gay-rights ordinances would have been nullified by Amendment 2). In short, if in *Romer* the Supreme Court held that cities may choose to enact gay-right ordinances without nullification by state constitutional amendment, it did not hold that cities *must* choose to do so. It is not constitutionally offensive that over time some cities (*e.g.,* Aspen, Boulder, and Denver) will pass such ordinances, while others (*e.g.,* Cincinnati) will not.
>
> Since Issue 3 does not implicate the same kind of political-process concerns identified by the Supreme Court in *Romer,* it remains only to consider whether

> there was a rational reason for Cincinnati voters to approve the change in the city charter....
>
> In *Romer,* the Supreme Court said that "[a] State cannot ... deem a class of persons a stranger to its laws." *Romer,* 116 S.Ct. at 1629. In the present case, no state has done so. Instead, a *city* has made a political judgment that it will not enact gay-rights measures of the sort adopted in Aspen, Boulder, or Denver. Because the *Romer* Court's special concern that no group be excluded from the political life of the sovereign does not apply here, this court was obligated to uphold Issue 3 as long as it was a rational means of achieving some permissible state interest.... Issue 3 satisfies this test.

Id. at *1 (Boggs, J., concurring in the denial of the suggestion for rehearing en banc).

4. When the Supreme Court denied the petition for a writ of certiorari in *Equality Foundation*, Justice Stevens, joined by Justices Souter and Ginsburg, issued a rare, explanatory opinion. He observed that "the Sixth Circuit held that the city charter 'merely removed' municipally enacted special protection from gays and lesbians," while petitioners in the case would "construe the charter as an enactment that 'bars antidiscrimination protections only for gay, lesbian and bisexual citizens.'" 525 U.S. 943 (1998). Noting that "[t]his Court does not normally make an independent examination of state law questions that have been resolved by a court of appeals," he concluded that "the confusion over the proper construction of the city charter counsels against granting the petition for certiorari." Id.

CHAPTER 8

THE COMMUNITY'S RELATIONSHIP WITH ITS NEIGHBORS

A. INTERLOCAL COOPERATION

Unfortunately, the ideal boundaries for the creation of a community or the provision of public goods do not always coincide with municipal boundaries. Issues of local government, therefore, may best be addressed through cooperation among localities. The desire to foster cooperation may emerge from either of two circumstances. First, the problem at issue may not be confined to a single locality. In Chapter 3 we saw that local problems that generate external effects may best be resolved at the state level. Some issues, however, may generate effects that extend beyond local boundaries, but that are not sufficiently widespread to warrant state intervention. Instead, resolution of the problem may best occur through action at an intermediate level. The intermediary may be some new entity, created for the purpose of addressing the problem and having jurisdiction co-extensive with the effects of the problem. This solution may require either the legislative creation of a new governing entity, a special district, or regional government that encompasses the entire affected area, or a legal structure that permits the existing localities to cooperate with one another. (Why can't localities simply agree to cooperate even in the absence of a statutory authorization?) A third possible resolution is to permit one locality to exercise authority beyond its boundaries. This last alternative is likely to create opportunities for conflict, rather than cooperation, and will be discussed in the next section.

The second motivation for interlocal cooperation arises where the problem at issue can be resolved intramurally, but a better solution can be achieved if a cooperative effort is undertaken. These additional rewards are generally realized where the solution to the problem at issue is susceptible to economies of scale. For instance, it may be possible for each locality in a metropolitan area to produce its own electrical energy, but the sum of the costs of numerous small electrical generating plants might be much greater than the cost of a single large electrical generating plant that could service the entire area. Services such as sewage treatment, mass transit, and water supply may also be efficiently provided by joint action.

Theoretically, mutual cooperation should be relatively easy to obtain, since each participant receives benefits that are not otherwise available. If all localities would gain from a power plant that produces energy at a lower cost to all concerned, one would imagine that few would oppose its construction. Nevertheless, there are reasons to believe that interlocal arrangements will be underutilized. Where free riding is possible, for instance, in the case of pollution control, each potential participant may avoid making a contribution, either to take advantage of the contributions of others or out of fear that others will free ride on that participant's efforts. A locality that considers a new regional airport useful may still prefer that another locality incur the costs associated with construction and operation. In the absence of mutual agreement, the result may be mutual forbearance.

Even where free riding is not a major threat, interlocal cooperation is likely to face difficulties of governance that lead otherwise willing localities to avoid cooperative solutions. Organizational structures that permit localities to act together necessarily impinge on the autonomy of each of them. The interests of the cooperating localities will rarely be identical, and some hierarchy among them will be necessary if conflicts are to be resolved. All the difficulties we have encountered to this point concerning the inability of residents to monitor their officials are exacerbated when those agents are neither electorally accountable to the residents nor identical to them in the interests they are pursuing. This problem may be familiar from the study of how privately owned firms are organized and governed. Contemporary literature suggests that the structure of a firm may be related as much to problems of internal governance that go by the name of "agency costs" (the ability to monitor employees, the ability to offer incentives that induce employees to identify their personal interests with the interests of the firm) as to the nature of the market for the goods or services that the firm produces. See, e.g., Ronald Coase, The Nature of the Firm (1939); Eugene Fama, Agency Problems and the Theory of the Firm, 88 J. Pol. Econ. 288 (1980); Michael Jensen & William Meckling, Theory of the Firm: Managerial Behavior, Agency Costs and Ownership Structure, 3 J. Fin. Econ. 305 (1976); Paul H. Rubin, The Theory of the Firm and the Structure of the Franchise Contract, 21 J.L. & Econ. 223 (1978); Frank Easterbrook & Daniel Fischel, The Economic Structure of Corporate Law (1991). The result is that there may be situations in which joint ventures among private firms would otherwise be desirable but are not used because the individuals cannot resolve questions about how to cooperate while still protecting their individual interests. To what extent does the fact that the "firms" with which we are concerned are municipal corporations rather than private firms exacerbate the problem of agency costs?

N.Y. Const. art. I

1. Bill of rights for local governments

> Effective local self-government and intergovernmental cooperation are purposes of the people of the state. In furtherance thereof, local governments shall have the following rights, powers, privileges and immunities in addition to those granted by other provisions of this constitution: ...
>
> (c) Local governments shall have power to agree, as authorized by act of the legislature, with the federal government, a state or one or more other governments within or without the state, to provide cooperatively, jointly or by

contract any facility, service, activity or undertaking which each participating local government has the power to provide separately. Each such local government shall have power to apportion its share of the cost thereof upon such portion of its area as may be authorized by act of the legislature.

Minn. Stat. Ann. § 453.53. Municipal power agencies: incorporation

Subdivision 1. Two or more cities, resolution. (a) Any two or more cities may form a municipal power agency by the execution of an agency agreement authorized by a resolution of the governing body of each city.

(b) The agency agreement shall state:

(1) That the municipal power agency is created and incorporated under the provisions of sections 453.51 to 453.62 as a municipal corporation and a political subdivision of the state, to exercise thereunder a part of the sovereign powers of the state;

(2) The name of the agency, which shall include the words "municipal power agency";

(3) The names of the cities which have approved the agency agreement and are the initial members of the municipal power agency;

(4) The names and addresses of the persons initially appointed by the resolutions approving the agreement to act as the representatives of the cities, respectively, in the exercise of their powers as members;

(5) Limitations, if any, upon the terms of representatives of the respective member cities, provided that such representatives shall always be selected and vacancies in their offices declared and filled by resolutions of the governing bodies of the respective cities;

(6) The names of the initial board of directors of the municipal power agency, who shall be not less than five persons who are representatives of the respective member cities, selected by the vote of a majority of such representatives; or the agreement may provide that the representatives of the member cities from time to time shall be and constitute the board of directors;

(7) The location by city, town, or other community in the state, of the registered office of the municipal power agency;

(8) That the cities which are members of the municipal power agency are not liable for its obligations; and

(9) Any other provision for regulating the business of the municipal power agency or the conduct of its affairs which may be agreed by the member cities, consistent with sections 453.51 to 453.62.

Utah County v. Ivie

137 P.3d 797 (Utah 2006).

■ Durrant, Justice:

¶ 1 This is the second case in which Appellants (collectively "Spring Canyon") have appeared before us to challenge local governments' attempts to condemn Spring Canyon property for the construction of a road. The road would connect two Provo City streets over an island of unincorporated Utah County. In the first case, *Provo City v. Ivie,* we held that Provo City did not have the statutory or constitutional power necessary to condemn Spring Canyon's property because the property is located in unincorporated Utah County. 2004 UT 30, ¶ 18, 94 P.3d 206. In this case, Spring Canyon disputes Utah County's action to condemn the same property and the district court's decision to grant Utah County immediate occupancy. During the pendency of the appeal in *Provo City,* Utah County contracted with Provo City ("the Agreement") and agreed to condemn Spring Canyon's property if Provo City would pay the expenses.

¶ 2 In this interlocutory appeal, Spring Canyon makes three main claims: first, that the condemnation action should be dismissed because the Agreement either exceeded the contracting parties' authority or evidenced a bad faith attempt to circumvent our decision in *Provo City;* second, that the district court improperly granted immediate occupancy because Spring Canyon was deprived of due process when Utah County failed to give notice of its factual basis for seeking immediate occupancy and the district court refused to allow discovery of that basis; and third, that the district court improperly granted immediate occupancy because Utah County's proof of necessity was inadequate.

¶ 3 Addressing these issues in turn, we first hold that Utah County and Provo City had authority to enter the Agreement, that this authority was not abrogated by the Interlocal Cooperation Act, and that the Agreement does not demonstrate bad faith. Second, we do not consider Spring Canyon's claim under the state constitution because Spring Canyon failed to adequately brief it, and we conclude that the federal constitution is satisfied where, as here, there is an adequate mechanism for obtaining compensation. Third, we affirm the district court's order of immediate occupancy because Spring Canyon has not demonstrated that the district court abused its broad discretion in weighing the equities in this case.

BACKGROUND

¶ 4 In 1970, Utah County and Provo City first planned to, at some point, build a collector street between Provo Canyon Road at 4525 North and University Avenue at 4800 North. In June of 2002, traffic congestion in the area was such that Provo City instituted a condemnation action to acquire the property needed to build the road. Although the proposed road would connect two Provo City streets, it would cross over an island of unincorporated Utah County land owned by Appellants Kay J. Ivie, Devon R. Ivie, Kristine J. Lee, Edward R. Lee, Spring Canyon Limited Partnership, and Canyon Acres Limited Partnership (collectively "Spring Canyon"). The district court in that case originally granted an order of immediate occupancy, but, following an interlocutory appeal, we reversed the order and held that Provo City did not have the power to condemn land outside its corporate boundaries because (1) Provo is not a charter city and could therefore not avail itself of the extraterritorial condemnation power granted in article XI, section 5(b) of the Utah Constitution, and (2) no other then-existing statute granted them the power to do so.

¶ 5 In May of 2003, during the pendency of its appeal, Provo City entered into an agreement with Utah County purportedly under the Interlocal Cooperation Act, Utah Code Ann. §§ 11–13–101 to –314 (2003 & Supp. 2005) (the "ICA"). The Agreement provided that Utah County would condemn the necessary property, and Provo City would pay all expenses required to do so. In May of 2004, following the Court's decision in *Provo City v. Ivie,* Utah County filed the condemnation complaint and motion for order of immediate occupancy that are at issue in this case. Spring Canyon subsequently filed a motion to dismiss based on the theory that Utah County was unlawfully "lend[ing] its condemning powers to Provo City." Prior to the September 1, 2004 hearing, Spring Canyon also filed a motion to allow discovery and an objection to the district court's consolidating the hearings for the motion to dismiss and the motion for order of immediate occupancy. On September 14, 2004, the district court denied Spring Canyon's motion to dismiss and issued an order of immediate occupancy in favor of Utah County. Spring Canyon then requested and was granted leave to file this interlocutory appeal to challenge both the denial of its motion to dismiss and the order of immediate occupancy.

* * *

ANALYSIS

I. UTAH COUNTY'S AGREEMENT WITH PROVO CITY DOES NOT LIMIT ITS POWER TO CONDEMN SPRING CANYON'S PROPERTY

¶ 8 Spring Canyon's appeal of the district court's denial of its motion to dismiss depends entirely on the effect, if any, that the Agreement between Utah County and Provo City has on Utah County's condemnation power. We will first discuss the validity of the Agreement and whether it limits Utah County's condemnation power. We will then discuss whether Utah County satisfied the requirements for exercising its condemnation power under Utah Code section 78–34–4, and specifically whether the existence of the Agreement mandates a finding of bad faith that undermines Utah County's condemnation authority.

A. Utah County and Provo City Were Authorized to Enter into the Agreement Pursuant to Their General Contracting Power

¶ 9 Spring Canyon argues that because Provo City lacks the power to condemn the subject property, both the Agreement and the exercise by Utah County of its eminent domain power pursuant to the Agreement were unlawful and invalid under the ICA. Spring Canyon's primary argument is that the ICA requires that all parties to an agreement have the power to do everything contemplated by the agreement. We conclude that local governments have authority to enter into agreements pursuant to their general contracting powers so long as each entity does not exceed its individual power, and, although the ICA provides for contracting only where all parties to an interlocal agreement have the power to do all acts under the agreement, the ICA does not abrogate local governments' general contracting power.

¶ 10 We first examine the limits of local governments' general contracting power. Before the Legislature passed the ICA in 1965, local governments had the power to contract with one another under general powers granted by the state constitution and various statutes. *See Bair v. Layton City Corp.,* 6 Utah 2d 138, 307 P.2d 895, 902 & 902 n. 8 (1957) (citing various constitutional and statutory provisions that conferred authority for Layton City to contract with North Davis County Sewer District); Utah Code Ann. § 10–1–202 (2003) ("Municipalities may . . . enter into contracts. . . ."); id. § 17–50–302(1)(b) (2005) ("A county may . . . provide services, exercise powers, and perform functions that are reasonably related to the safety, health, morals, and welfare of their inhabitants, except as limited or prohibited by statute."). The limit on these general contracting powers was presumably that no governmental party to a contract could exceed its individual powers in fulfilling its obligation under the contract. Thus, two governmental entities of unequal power could contract in their areas of inequality so long as neither exceeded its own powers in performing the contract.

¶ 11 The Agreement in this case does not require any performance by either Utah County or Provo City that is beyond the individual authority of that entity. The terms of the Agreement material to this appeal require Utah County to condemn the property for the road and Provo City to pay the expenses of condemnation, installation, and maintenance of the road. Utah County has authority to condemn property under Utah Code section 17–50–302(2)(a)(ii). Provo City has authority "to appropriate money for any purpose that, in the judgment of the municipal legislative body, provides for the safety, health, prosperity, moral well-being, peace, order, comfort, or convenience of the inhabitants of the municipality." Id. § 10–8–2(3) (Supp. 2005). Paying for the construction and for the maintenance of a public road certainly falls within Provo City's authority under this provision. Thus, absent the ICA, the Agreement is a valid exercise of both Utah County's and Provo City's general contracting powers. We are called upon to determine, however, whether the ICA operates to limit these general contracting powers.

¶ 12 Spring Canyon argues that because the ICA, specifically Utah Code section 11–13–212(1)(a), allows for interlocal agreements only where each party has the power to do all acts contemplated in the agreement, it must also preclude all other agreements between local governmental entities. Utah County counters that Spring Canyon's proposed interpretation would lead to logically inconsistent results because a local government could condemn property for a street if a private party paid the expenses, *see* 7 Patrick J. Rohan & Melvin A. Reskin, *Nichols on Eminent Domain,* § 5.02[3] (3d ed.2006), but could not do the same where another local government pays the expenses. We conclude that although the ICA does not provide a source of power for cooperative action between local governments of unequal power in their area of inequality, it also does not preclude local governments from contracting with each other in these areas under their general contracting power.

¶ 13 It is true that Utah Code section 11–13–212 only allows agencies to contract with one another "to perform any service, activity, or undertaking which each public agency ... is authorized by law to perform." Utah Code Ann. § 11–13–212(1)(a) (2003). We further stated in *CP National Corp. v. Public Service Commission* that "the intent of the [ICA] appears to be to allow the municipalities collectively to exercise powers which they already possess individually." 638 P.2d 519, 521 (Utah 1981). But while these sources support Spring Canyon's argument that the ICA only authorizes contracting among local governments of equal power, they do not support the argument that the ICA precludes all other contracts between local governments. Spring Canyon offers no evidence that the Legislature intended the ICA to have that effect.

¶ 14 Indeed, the ICA's stated purpose is "to permit local governmental units to make the most efficient use of their powers by enabling them to cooperate with other localities on a basis of mutual advantage" and also "to provide the benefit of economy of scale." Utah Code Ann. § 11–13–102 (2003). This purpose statement demonstrates that the Legislature intended the ICA to expand rather than limit local governments' ability to cooperate. Additionally, we can find no provision of the ICA that removes existing powers from local governments. Where the Legislature has not clearly limited the general contracting powers of local governments, we construe those powers broadly. *State v. Hutchinson,* 624 P.2d 1116, 1126–27 (Utah 1980). Thus, the ICA does not abrogate local governments' power to contract among themselves under their general contracting power.

¶ 15 In sum, although the ICA did not empower Utah County and Provo City to enter into the Agreement, the Agreement is nevertheless valid under their general contracting powers. *See* Utah Code Ann. § 10–1–202; id. § 17–50–302(1)(b). Having determined that the ICA does not invalidate the Agreement, we now discuss whether the agreement evidences bad faith such that we must dismiss Utah County's condemnation action.

B. Utah County Satisfied the Elements of Section 78–34–4

¶ 16 Spring Canyon argues that even if the condemnation is not precluded by the ICA, the Agreement shows bad faith, and we should therefore dismiss the condemnation action on that basis. In addition to the requirement that the entity have the authority to condemn property, Utah Code section 78–34–4 requires that "the use to which [the property] is to be applied is a use authorized by law ... [and] the taking is necessary to such use." Utah Code Ann. § 78–34–4(1), (2) (2002); *see also Utah State Rd. Comm'n v. Friberg,* 687 P.2d 821, 832 (Utah 1984). Utah County has authority to condemn property under Utah Code section 17–50–302(2)(a)(ii). Further, a public street is clearly "a use authorized by law," as specifically set forth in Utah Code section 78–34–1(3). Therefore, only the question of necessity remains at issue. Spring Canyon contends that the taking is not necessary because Utah County is exercising its power of eminent domain in bad faith.

¶ 17 In *Bountiful v. Swift,* we noted that the "necessity ... in opening a public street is a political question and in absence of fraud, bad faith, or abuse of discretion[,] action of [local governments] will not be disturbed by the courts." 535 P.2d 1236, 1238 (Utah 1975). From this statement, Spring Canyon argues that bad faith precludes a finding that a taking is necessary. We are not convinced that *Swift* establishes that premise. Rather, *Swift* merely stands for the proposition that, on evidence of bad faith, a court need not defer to the legislative body on the question of necessity. Id. But even were we to accept Spring Canyon's interpretation, the district court specifically found that Utah County did not condemn the property in bad faith, and it is entitled to deference on that finding. Indeed, we can only reverse the district court's finding that Utah County did not act in bad faith if it is clearly erroneous. *Warner v. DMG Color, Inc.,* 2000 UT 102, ¶ 21, 20 P.3d 868 ("[I]t is within the discretion of the trial court to determine whether an action is asserted in bad faith, and we therefore review such a determination under the clearly erroneous standard.").

¶ 18 In this case, there is both scant evidence of bad faith and ample evidence of good faith. Spring Canyon argues that Utah County's motive in bringing this action was only to help Provo City circumvent our decision in *Provo City v. Ivie.*While circumventing that decision was clearly an objective of the *Agreement,* it was not the only objective of the *condemnation action.* Utah County has a substantial interest in minimizing traffic congestion within its boundaries. Citizens of Utah County, as well as Provo City, will benefit from the road. The fact that Utah County waited until Provo City discovered it could not condemn the property, and the fact that Provo City will be paying the expenses are more indicative of prudent fiscal management than bad faith. It would be folly for the county to have its taxpayers pay to condemn and construct this road where Provo City is ready and willing to cover that expense. As there is evidence that Utah County had legitimate reasons for condemning the property at issue, we affirm the district court's finding that there was no bad faith. Accordingly, Utah County's legislative finding that this condemnation is necessary "will not be disturbed." *Swift,* 535 P.2d at 1238.

¶ 19 Because the ICA did not prohibit Utah County and Provo City from entering into the Agreement, and because Utah County satisfied the statutory requirements to condemn the property, we hold that the district court correctly denied Spring Canyon's motion to dismiss.

* * *

CONCLUSION

¶ 29 We affirm the district court on all three issues before us. First, the Agreement between Provo City and Utah County does not give cause to disturb Utah County's exercise of its eminent domain power because the Agreement is valid under the entities' general contracting authority and does not evidence bad faith. Thus, the district court's denial of Spring

Canyon's motion to dismiss was appropriate. Second, we conclude that, where a local government has authority to condemn, the federal constitution requires only that a property owner have an adequate mechanism for obtaining compensation. There is such a mechanism here. We decline to address Spring Canyon's state constitutional claim because it was inadequately briefed. Third, we affirm the district court's order of immediate occupancy because Utah County presented prima facie evidence of the elements of section 78–34–9(2) and Spring Canyon has not shown that the district court abused its broad discretion in weighing the equities under that section. We affirm and remand for further proceedings in accordance with this opinion.

Goreham v. Des Moines Metropolitan Area Solid Waste Agency

179 N.W.2d 449 (Iowa 1970).

■ LARSON, JUSTICE.

This is a declaratory judgment action involving the validity of a contract and the constitutionality of chapter 28E, Code of Iowa 1966, and chapter 236, Acts of the Sixty-third General Assembly, submitted upon an agreed stipulation of facts.

Plaintiffs, who are residents, property owners, and taxpayers of the cities of Des Moines and West Des Moines, Iowa, brought this action at law against the Des Moines Metropolitan Area Solid Waste Agency (hereafter called the Agency) and its members asking an interpretation of chapter 28E, Code of Iowa 1966, and chapter 236, Acts of the Sixty-third General Assembly, First Session, with reference to the power and authority of the Agency under those laws. The vital question presented is whether under these statutes and the Iowa Constitution the Agency can issue bonds to finance the planned functions of the Agency in the collection and disposition of solid waste, and pay the interest and principal from fees legally collectible from its members for this service. The trial court held that the Agency was properly created, that due authority was properly delegated to it, that the submitted agreement between the members was valid, and that it could issue such revenue bonds and fix and collect fees from those using these services including interest and principal on the bonds, but held the participation by Polk County was limited to disposition of solid waste only and did not permit participation in collection costs. Plaintiffs appeal as to the creation of the Agency, the propriety of the authority delegated, and the legality of the agreement, and defendants cross-appeal as to the limited participation by Polk County. Due to the importance of this issue, special attention is given this problem.

The object or purpose of the involved legislation is clearly stated and relates to the health, safety and welfare of the people, involves a service and facility needed, and directs a liberal construction to accomplish a worthy purpose. After careful study and research, we conclude neither the legislation nor the contract involved are violative of the Iowa Constitution....

Appellants further contend that the defendant Agency is invalid and has no legal character as a "public body corporate and politic" for the reason that chapter 28E of the 1966 Code of Iowa and Senate File 482 (also known as chapter 236, Acts of the 63rd General Assembly, First Session) under which said Agency was created is in violation of Article III, Section 1, of the Constitution of the State of Iowa, as an improper delegation of legislative authority, and that as a result the creation of said Agency by the "Intergovernmental Agreement, Exhibit A", is *ultra vires* and of no force and effect, and that as a consequence thereof said defendant Agency is without authority to issue revenue bonds pursuant to Senate File 482 enacted by the 63rd General Assembly of Iowa.

Fairly summarized, the Stipulation of Facts filed herein on March 30, 1970, states as follows:

> On August 8, 1966, the City Manager of the defendant City of Des Moines, by memorandum to the City Council, informed it that the city was confronted with a serious problem relating to the collection and disposal of solid waste, in that the solid waste facility operated by the City of Des Moines was fast filling up. The impact of the report was heightened by the fact that the local units of government in the near metropolitan Des Moines area were using the Des Moines dump to a greater extent for the disposition of some or all of their solid waste and were using local dumps in the area surrounding Des Moines to a lesser extent for the disposition of a portion of their solid waste. The memorandum proposed a study and demonstration project for the metropolitan area which contained approximately 430 square miles. The manager recommended that the communities in the metropolitan area engage in a cooperative effort in disposing of their solid waste....

Subsequent thereto the defendant municipalities entered into an agreement based upon the form suggested by the study, Exhibit D, which said intergovernmental agreement created the Metropolitan Area Solid Waste Agency.

Pursuant to said agreement the Agency was duly organized, officers were elected and a director was hired to manage the affairs of the Agency under the direction of the Agency board which was composed of one representative from the governing body of each member of the Agency, each having one vote for every 50,000 or fraction thereof population in his area of representation....

Specifically, appellants contend (1) that chapter 28E, Code of Iowa 1966, is unconstitutional because the legislature is without power to delegate to political subdivisions of the state the power to create a new quasi municipality for the purpose of exercising functions delegated by the legislature to it; (2) that chapter 28E is unconstitutional because it endeavors to delegate legislative power without providing a suitable legislative policy which sufficiently defines and limits the powers granted; (3) that the quasi municipality purported to be created has no power to issue general revenue bonds; that the bonds issued by the Agency, if valid, constitute general obligations of the participating political entities because the "special-fund" doctrine is not applicable for the reason that the agreement provides the Agency has the power to collect fees as assessed from each of its members as payment for providing the services of collection and disposal of waste; (4) that defendant Polk County has no authority from the legislature to participate in the operation of the defendant Agency; and (5) that the agreement creating the Agency is contrary to public policy to the extent that it provides that the governing board of the Agency will be comprised of an elected representative of the governing body of each participating governmental jurisdiction or his designated substitute.

I. Perhaps before discussing these contentions we should set out the provisions of the law in question.

Chapter 28E entitled "Joint Exercise of Governmental Powers" purports to authorize any political subdivision of the State of Iowa and certain agencies of the state or federal government to join together to perform certain public services and by agreement create a separate legal or administrative entity to render that service. Its worthy purpose is clearly expressed in section 28E.1. Section 28E.2 provides definitions, and section 28E.3 purports to define the limitations upon the participants as follows:

> 28E.3. Joint exercise of powers. Any power or powers, privileges or authority exercised or capable of exercise by a public agency of this state may be exercised and enjoyed jointly with any other public agency of this state having such power or powers, privilege or authority, and jointly with any public agency of any other state or of the United States to the extent that laws of such other state or of the United States permit such joint exercise or enjoyment. Any agency of the state government when acting jointly with any public agency may exercise and enjoy all of the powers, privileges and authority conferred by this chapter upon a public agency.

Sections 28E.4 and 28E.5 provide for the agreement and its contents as follows:

> 28E.4. Agreement with other agencies. Any public agency of this state may enter into an agreement with one or more public or private agencies for joint or co-operative action pursuant to the provisions of this chapter, including the creation of a separate entity to carry out the purpose of the agreement. Appropriate action by ordinance, resolution or otherwise pursuant to law of the governing bodies involved shall be necessary before any such agreement may enter into force.
>
> 28E.5. Specifications. Any such agreement shall specify the following:
>
> 1. Its duration.
>
> 2. The precise organization, composition and nature of any separate legal or administrative entity created thereby together with the powers delegated thereto, provided such entity may be legally created.
>
> 3. Its purpose or purposes.
>
> 4. The manner of financing the joint or co-operative undertaking and of establishing and maintaining a budget therefor.

5. The permissible method or methods to be employed in accomplishing the partial or complete termination of the agreement and for disposing of property upon such partial or complete termination.

6. Any other necessary and proper matters.

II. Although appellants contend the creation of a separate legal entity or public body is solely a function of the legislature, we find no unconstitutional delegation of legislative power involved in this law providing for the creation of the Des Moines Metropolitan Area Solid Waste Agency. It is not the mere establishment or creation of such an agency or entity that causes trouble, but the functions to be performed by that agency in the legislative field which must be examined closely to determine whether there has been an unlawful delegation of legislative authority. . . .

In this connection it must also be noted that administrative agencies may be delegated certain legislative functions by the legislature when properly guidelined, and that when this is done, the distinction between such agencies and public bodies, corporate and politic, which have been delegated proper legislative functions, has largely disappeared. Ordinarily the latter body is created by an act of the legislature and the former by an already-established public body with legislative authority. However, the power and authority of each must be measured by the legality of the delegation thereof. If such power is derived from the State Legislature, is adequately guidelined, and does not violate the separation-of-powers provision of the State Constitution set forth in Article III, Section 1, the exercise thereof should be sustained.

Thus, our primary problem here is whether the authority provided in chapter 28E of the 1966 Code and chapter 236, Acts of the Sixty-third General Assembly, constitutes a lawful delegation of legislative power.

III. Regularly-enacted statutes are presumed to be constitutional, and courts exercise the power to declare such legislation unconstitutional with great caution. It is only when such conclusion is unavoidable that we do so. Lee Enterprises, Inc. v. Iowa State Tax Comm., Iowa, 162 N.W.2d 730; State v. Rivera, supra, 260 Iowa 320, 149 N.W.2d 127; Cook v. Hannah, 230 Iowa 249, 297 N.W. 262. Also see Farrell v. State Board of Regents, Iowa, 179 N.W.2d 533, decided September 2, 1970.

Thus, while the provisions of section 28E of the 1966 Code leave much to be desired as to the extent of the authority granted to such a newly-created entity, the presumption of constitutionality operates strongly in its favor.

It is also well to remember that our function is not to pass upon the feasibility or wisdom of such legislation, but only to determine whether the power here exercised exceeds that which the legislature could or did delegate to the newly-created entity. Green v. City of Mt. Pleasant, 256 Iowa 1184, 131 N.W.2d 5, and authorities cited.

In this regard it is also well to note the importance of the expressed or recognized purpose or policy to be achieved by the legislation. Generally, when the legislature has adequately stated the object and purpose of the legislation and laid down reasonably-clear guidelines in its application, it may then delegate to a properly-created entity the authority to exercise such legislative power as is necessary to carry into effect that general legislative purpose. See Schmidt v. Department of Resources Development, 39 Wis. 2d 46, 158 N.W.2d 306, 313; Chicago & North Western Ry. Co. v. Public Service Comm., 43 Wis. 2d 570, 169 N.W.2d 65, 69; 1 Davis, Administrative Law Treatise, pp. 75–76, 2.01.

The purpose of this legislation, as recognized in chapter 28E, is to provide a solution to the growing problems of local government including the problem of collection and disposal of solid wastes by public bodies and to cooperate with the Office of Solid Waste of the United States Department of Health, Education and Welfare to accomplish that purpose by joint efforts. We further observe that this purpose may soon be made a legal requirement for all communities throughout the entire land under federal law. We are satisfied that this is health and general welfare legislation and that the legislative policy and purpose for chapter 28E is sufficiently stated. It amounts to this, that public agencies or governmental units may cooperate together to do anything jointly that they could do individually.

True, if chapter 28E is examined without reference to the powers granted the various governmental units by other legislation, the factors constituting sufficient guidelines might well be said to be insufficient. But this legislation must be interpreted with reference to the power or powers which the contracting governmental units already have. The pre-existing powers contain their own guidelines. The legal creation of a new body corporate and politic to jointly exercise and perform the powers and responsibilities of the cooperating governmental unit would not be unconstitutional so long as the new body politic is doing only what its cooperating members already have the power to do. This would be true under the above-recognized general rule that a statute is presumed to be constitutional until shown otherwise beyond a reasonable doubt.

Chapter 28E does not attempt to delineate the various governmental or proprietary functions which the individual governmental units may be implementing. While such a broad approach may be unwise, as appellants argue, it is not unconstitutional so long as the cooperating units are not exercising powers they do not already have.

With this in mind, it appears that chapter 28E supplies sufficient guidelines for the purposes necessary to the chapter. That is, the units are authorized to handle what might be called the mechanical details of implementing the joint project either by the creation of a separate entity or by using a joint administrator or board for the purpose of implementing the agreement reached. The agreement itself, of whatever nature, must have its specific contents delineated in section 28E.5 and specifically prohibits governmental units being involved in the new entity, except insofar as the new entity is in fact performing the same responsibilities as the units involved.

Thus, when the entire chapter is examined, it would appear that the delegations of power to the governmental units made by the legislature in chapter 28E are constitutional....

IX. Appellants further contend that the agreement creating the Agency is contrary to public policy to the extent that it permits elected officials of the member municipalities to serve on the governing board of the Agency. They argue that the integrity of representative government demands that the administrative officials should be able to exercise their judgment free from the objectionable pressure of conflicting interests. We agree with that proposition, but do not believe it appears here that these members of the Agency board are in such a position. It is conceded that here there is nothing to indicate a personal pecuniary interest of those representatives is involved such as appears in Wilson v. Iowa City, Iowa, 165 N.W.2d 813, 820.

Although the members of the board understandably will want to keep the rates their constituents must pay as low as possible, they are well aware that rates must be maintained sufficient to meet the Agency's cost for such services. This is not such a conflict of interest as to be contrary to public policy or fatal to the agreement.

In passing on this question the trial court said, "Inasmuch as each representative is on the board primarily to serve as spokesman for the particular municipality or political subdivision he represents, (it could) ... see no conflict of interest such as would likely affect his individual judgment by virtue of his status as an elected official." It pointed out no compensation is provided for such service and the representative serves at the pleasure of his municipality or political subdivision. We agree with the trial court.

In the recent case of Wilson v. Iowa City, supra, we discussed the issue of conflict of interest and held, where it appeared the official had a personal interest, either actual or implied, he would be disqualified to vote on a municipal project—in that case, urban renewal. No such interest would appear in connection with this project unless some litigation would occur between the municipality he represents and the Agency, in which event the contract itself provides for arbitration procedures. We conclude there is no merit in this assignment.

X. Having found no reversible error in the trial court's judgment except as to the participation of the county in the project prior to the enactment of Senate File 1232, Acts of the 63rd General Assembly, Second Session, which objection has now been resolved, we affirm its decision holding both chapter 28E of the 1966 Code and chapter 236, Acts of the 63rd General Assembly, are constitutional and that the contract entered into pursuant thereto, except as to county participation thereunder, is valid.

Modified and affirmed.

NOTES

1. Why did the localities in *Goreham* create a new entity in order to implement their desire to cooperate on waste disposal? Why didn't they simply contract with one another as a group of individual localities the way the governments involved in *Ivie* did? The laws of 42 states currently permit localities to create interlocal service agreements. See U.S. Advisory Comm'n on Intergovernmental Relations, State Law Governing Local Government Structure and Administration 26–27 (1993). But creating legal authority for governments may not be enough. What obstacles may prevent interlocal agreement even among localities that are permitted to enter into contracts? Does it matter that multiple localities are involved, so that the costs of attaining agreement may be higher than if only two parties are involved? For theoretical rationales for the scarcity of cooperation Richard Briffault, The Local Government Boundary Problem in Metropolitan Areas, 48 Stan. L. Rev. 1115, 1147 (1996). If you think that interlocal agreement could displace the need for more centralized levels of government, what legal rules would help overcome the obstacles to contract? See Clayton P. Gillette, The Conditions of Interlocal Cooperation, 21 J. L. & Politics 365 (2005); Kurt Thurmaier and Curtis Wood, Interlocal Agreements as an Alternative to Consolidation, in Jered B. Carr and Richard C. Feiock (eds.), City–County Consolidation and Its Alternatives 113 (2004).

2. What is the source of the nondelegation doctrine? The court does not point to any constitutional language that bars the legislature from delegating authority to political subdivisions of the state. At most the court refers to a provision of the Iowa Constitution, article III, § 1, that divides the government of the state into legislative, executive, and judicial branches and requires separation of those branches. In this case, however, the state legislature is delegating power to local legislatures to join interlocal agreements. In the absence of a more specific prohibition on intrabranch delegation, why isn't the legislature free to delegate, given the standard interpretation that a state constitution is a document of limitation, not a document of grant? See Sanitation Dist. No. 1 of Shelby County v. Shelby County, page 244 supra.

3. The court in *Goreham* implies that a constitutionally proper delegation from the state to a political subdivision must contain legislative guidelines about the tasks that the delegate is to perform. Nevertheless, those guidelines, at least in the statute at issue in *Goreham*, appear relatively vague. It would, of course, be possible to impose a more stringent requirement of specificity. Would that be desirable? Consider the following commentary on the role of delegation.

> There are, however, reasons for restraining one's enthusiasm for state legislative standards. The statehouse does not provide the ideal vantage point from which to identify and cure all problems of local government; city hall may often provide a better one. And local governments and local conditions vary widely enough to indicate that courts should hesitate to force the resolution of all problems into the mold of a single statutory framework. Legislative standards limiting the discretion of the cities may achieve control at the cost of

> rigidity. They run counter to a general modern consensus on the desirability of according the cities broad powers to govern without explicit statutory authorization. A system favoring statutory standards would inhibit creative government at the local level by increasing the cities' dependence upon the legislature for authorization....
>
> Sometimes the legislators merely tack on platitudinous requirements that the delegate advance the public interest or the public health, safety, and welfare. Of course, the presence or absence of explicit statutory statements of policy should not be determinative; the structure or the legislative history of a statute may provide a court ample means to determine the policy that the delegate is to follow.... The absence of policy may be due to political impasse or to a legislative judgment that it is unwise or impossible to set policy in advance of experience....
>
> The case law applying the delegation doctrine thus reveals that legislative standards requirements have always proved difficult to enforce, and have sometimes seemed unwise. In local government cases, legislative standards are unnecessary unless there is a need for statewide policy; otherwise, they tend overly to restrict local discretion.... It is the principal recommendation of this Article that the state courts concentrate on requirements for locally adopted standards and procedures, and that only when a need for statewide statutory policy renders these insufficient to control the local exercise of power should the courts invalidate statutes delegating power to the cities for the insufficiency of legislative standards.

Harold H. Bruff, Judicial Review in Local Government Law: A Reappraisal, 60 Minn. L. Rev. 669, 681–682 (1976).

In Newport Court Club Associates v. Town Council of the Town of Middletown, 800 A.2d 405 (2002), users of a town sewage system contended that a legislative grant of authority that permitted the town to charge sewer users for the cost of debt service and capital improvements related to the system unconstitutionally delegated "unbridled discretion" to the town to decide whether to impose those charges on all taxpayers or only on sewer users. The court noted that the nondelegation doctrine serves two functions: to protect citizens against discriminatory and arbitrary actions of public officials, and to assure that "duly authorized, politically accountable officials make fundamental policy decisions." The court then concluded that the fact that the town council would make decisions about sewer charges eliminated the concern about accountability, and the statutory requirement that any charges be "just and reasonable" and be applied to all users constituted a standard that constrained the discretion of the town council.

4. *Goreham* addresses the question of delegation from the legislature to the Agency. But it ignores an additional delegation problem lurking in the structure of the Agency's decisionmaking. According to the opinion, the Agency board is to be composed of one representative from the governing body of each member and each member is to have one vote for every 50,000 constituents. The result could be that more populated participating localities can outvote less populated ones. In effect, outvoted localities will have delegated decisionmaking to other Agency members. Is this a more difficult issue than the delegation of state legislative power to the Agency? Why should a locality be entitled to authorize another locality to decide crucial issues of public policy simply because it has had its say about the desirable outcome? Certainly we would look askance at the proposition that Locality A could set a budget for Locality B as long as officials from Locality B were entitled to make nonbinding recommendations. So why is the fact that one locality is heard before being outvoted sufficient to authorize interlocal cooperation?

5. In Frank v. City of Cody, 572 P.2d 1106 (Wyo. 1977), localities had joined together under a Joint Powers Act, similar to Chapter 28E in the *Goreham* case, to form an Agency that would participate in the construction of an electrical generation plant. Plaintiffs claimed that the grant of authority from the member localities to the Agency violated a constitutional prohibition against delegation. The court noted that member localities would be represented on the board of the Agency. Nevertheless, the rationale of the court appeared to depend less on the nature of each participant's representation than on the underlying function of the Agency. Here, the court reverted to the governmental/proprietary distinction. The court concluded: "[w]hen the details of a 'proprietary' transaction [such as operating an electric utility] only are involved, there is no unconstitutional delegation of powers because the constitutional provision relates only to 'purely' municipal or governmental functions of a city." Id. at 1110.

The court in *Goreham* notes that the authorizing statute allows localities to do cooperatively what they could do individually. Plaintiffs in Roberts v. City of Maryville, 750 S.W.2d 69 (Mo. 1988), faced with a similar provision, challenged a proposed revenue bond issue on the grounds that proceeds would be used in a cooperative project, parts of which involved flood control on lands outside the city's boundaries. Since the city had no authority to engage in extraterritorial flood control, plaintiffs claimed, it could not cooperate in an enterprise with other governments to provide such services, although the other participants were authorized to provide those services. The bond proceeds at issue were to be used only for parts of the project that would directly benefit the city. Nevertheless, plaintiffs contended that the city could not enter into an agreement that obligated other contracting entities to undertake functions outside the range of purposes that the city alone could undertake. The court rejected this argument:

> The General Assembly, by enacting § 70.220, is deemed to have acted with an intent to conform and further the constitutional purpose.... It seems readily apparent the wholesome purpose of all this is to allow government within the framework of the law to provide better service at less cost and in this instance the cooperating governmental entities have agreed to a plan designed to fit that purpose. Each participating entity could separately plan and construct its discrete portion of the project, but at a total cost exceeding that of the joint effort. The pooling of resources not only promotes cooperation among governmental agencies, it permits cost saving and avoids duplication of facilities.

Id. at 71–72.

PROBLEM XXIX

Spring Garden Township, a township of the third class, and the City of York, a city of the third class, have entered into an agreement permitting the township to have its sewage conveyed to and treated by the city. The agreement provides that no connection may be made to the sanitary sewage system of the township and no plumbing fixtures may be installed in any property in the township unless a permit has been obtained from the city. The city is bound to apply the same rules and regulations to permit requests from the township as it applies to applications for such connections and installations within the city. A city ordinance permits the issuance of permits only to plumbers who possess a certain level of experience and who have passed an examination. Smith is a plumber by trade who has applied to the city for permits to do plumbing work in the township. The city has refused his requests because he does not possess the required experience and has not passed the required examination. Smith has consulted you to determine whether the township can permit the city to set standards for one who performs work within the township. He suggests to you that it sounds like the township has "completely abdicated its responsibility to be accountable for the welfare of its citizens. The city is just allowing its plumbers to monopolize the work in this area." How will you respond? See Smith v. Spring Garden Township, 34 D. & C.2d 54 (Pa. Commw. Pleas 1964).

Vermont Department of Public Service v. Massachusetts Municipal Wholesale Electric Co.

558 A.2d 215 (Vt. 1988), cert. denied, 493 U.S. 872 (1989).

■ ALLEN, CHIEF JUSTICE.

In 1979, four Vermont municipalities and two electric cooperatives contracted with the Massachusetts Municipal Wholesale Electric Company (MMWEC) for shares of the power generating potential of its Project No. 6. This project consisted of a 6.001 percent ownership interest in two nuclear power plants to be built in Seabrook, New Hampshire. In 1985, the Vermont Department of Public Service (Department) filed a complaint in Washington Superior Court, alleging that the Vermont utilities had violated statutory and common law in executing the contracts with MMWEC. The superior court granted summary judgment for defendants, and this appeal ensued. We reverse and hold that the contracts were void ab initio.

Although the underlying litigation was designated formally as a complex action under the provisions of V.R.C.P. 16.1, only a brief summary of the procedural history is necessary here. The Department filed its complaint, seeking declaratory and injunctive relief, on October 18, 1985. The Village of Stowe intervened shortly thereafter as a plaintiff, and the Vermont Electric Cooperative (VEC), originally a defendant, was denominated a plaintiff after accepting plaintiffs' position. The defendants include

MMWEC and the Villages of Ludlow, Lyndonville, Morrisville, and Northfield, as well as the Washington Electric Cooperative (WEC).

MMWEC is a joint planning and action agency, incorporated under the terms of special enabling legislation in Massachusetts, through which municipal electric systems may finance and acquire supplies of electrical power or power sources. Its membership comprises thirty-four Massachusetts municipalities; it is governed by a board of nine directors, two appointed by the Governor and seven elected by the Massachusetts-member municipalities. There is no provision for representation of the Vermont municipalities or cooperatives on the MMWEC Board.

In 1976, MMWEC began development of a bulk power supply system consisting of ownership interests in various existing and planned electric power facilities. Included among the planned facilities were Seabrook nuclear plants No. 1 and No. 2. MMWEC obtained a fractional ownership interest in the two plants and designated this interest as Project No. 6. The contracts at issue here relate to this project.

The basic theory under which the parties operate is as follows: MMWEC finances its construction and other costs by issuing bonds; in return, the participants commit a sufficient portion of their utility revenues to cover MMWEC's monthly debt service on the bonds. To this end, MMWEC and public utilities from several states, including the Vermont participants, executed "power sales agreements" (PSAs) regarding Project No. 6.

Under the agreements, which became effective upon the execution and delivery of PSAs covering 100 percent of the project, participants purchased shares of "project capability." "Project capability" is defined in the PSAs as "the amounts of electric capacity and energy, if any, which the Project is capable of producing at any particular time (including times when the Project is not operable or operating or the operation thereof is suspended, interrupted, interfered with, reduced or curtailed, in each case in whole or in part for any reason whatsoever), less Project station use and losses. . . ."

Each month, the participants are required to pay their proportional shares of MMWEC's costs relating to the project, including debt service; an additional ten percent of the debt service figure is paid monthly for deposit in a reserve and contingency fund. MMWEC is empowered to fix these monthly payments so as to provide revenues sufficient to meet its obligations. The participants are not required to make payments from any source other than revenues derived from their electric departments or systems, but they are obligated to fix their rates in amounts at least sufficient to meet their obligations under the PSAs. Participants also agree to pay any unrelated debts or amounts which might otherwise constitute a charge or a lien upon their revenues, and, except in certain circumstances, they forego the right to issue any of their own revenue bonds without first providing for the payment of all operating expenses and the monthly payments to MMWEC. Further, the agreements include a so-called "step-up" provision, under which each participant's monthly obligation will increase proportionately to cover MMWEC's costs should any participant default.

The participants must make the scheduled monthly payments to MMWEC without regard to whether the project is completed, operating, or even undertaken. Such provisions are known variously as "take-or-pay" or "hell or high water" because of the unconditional nature of the obligation imposed. Here, the monthly payments are required in their full amounts, even if no electricity is ever produced. Participants do not acquire any ownership interest in the physical plant.

The agreements provide further that MMWEC, acting in good faith and in accordance with the tenets of "Prudent Utility Practice" (a term defined in the agreements), will use its best efforts to arrange for the financing, planning, engineering, design, acquisition, construction, operation and maintenance of the project; obtain all necessary permits and rights; and issue revenue bonds to finance all costs. While the Vermont participants share in the costs and risks of the project, they retain no decision-making power with respect to the incurrence of debt, plant construction, or operation.

In the superior court, the parties filed an extensive stipulation of facts, a procedural stipulation, and subsequent motions and cross-motions for summary judgment. After hearing, the court granted summary judgment in favor of defendants. The judgment was entered pursuant to V.R.C.P. 54(b) on the cross-claims for summary judgment.

Three principal questions are presented on appeal. First, plaintiffs contend that the lower court erred in concluding that the Vermont utilities had statutory authority to enter into contracts that include take-or-pay provisions. Second, we must determine whether the PSAs are void, in any event, because the participants attempted to transfer all decision-making authority with regard to the project to MMWEC, thereby violating the fundamental principle of nondelegation. Finally, plaintiffs maintain that the municipal utilities could not legally incur the financial obligations at issue without obtaining voter approval and that the cooperatives were required to obtain the approval of the Public Service Board....

II

Under the provisions of the PSAs, all decision-making power with regard to the project rests with MMWEC; the Vermont participants retain no voice in decisions to incur debt, to commence operation of the plant, or to decommission the plant. They have abdicated all management responsibility for and have obtained no ownership interest in the project. Plaintiffs maintain that these provisions constitute an impermissible delegation of authority to MMWEC. We agree.

A

Our analysis begins with the agreements executed by the municipal participants. This Court has long adhered to the "deep-rooted principle of law that the delegate of power from the sovereign cannot without permission recommit to another agent or agency the trust imposed upon its judgment and discretion." Thompson v. Smith, 119 Vt. 488, 501, 129 A.2d 638, 647 (1957). In Wabash Railroad v. City of Defiance, 167 U.S. 88, 17 S. Ct. 748, 42 L. Ed. 87 (1897), the United States Supreme Court stated that "the legislative power vested in municipal bodies is something which cannot be bartered away in such manner as to disable them from the performance of their public functions." Id. at 100, 17 S. Ct. at 752. In other words, "when authority to exercise the police power within a defined sphere is delegated by the state to a municipal or other public corporation, the authority is inalienable in the corporation, and it cannot in any manner be contracted away or otherwise granted, delegated, diminished, divided, or limited by the corporation." 6A E. McQuillin, Municipal Corporations § 24.41, at 116–17 (3d ed. rev. 1988).

Such authority is in the nature of a public trust conferred upon the legislative body of the corporation for the public benefit, and it cannot be exercised by others. Arkansas–Missouri Power Co. v. City of Kennett, 78 F.2d 911, 920 (8th Cir. 1935). Therefore, if a public corporation enters into a contract that barters away or otherwise restricts the exercise of its legislative or police powers, then the contract is *ultra vires* and void *ab initio*. Byrd v. Martin, Hopkins, Lemon & Carter, P.C., 564 F. Supp. 1425, 1428 (W.D. Va. 1983), aff'd, 740 F.2d 961 (4th Cir. 1984); see also *Arkansas–Missouri Power Co.*, 78 F.2d at 922 ("any contract whereby legislative authority or duty is attempted to be delegated by a city is absolutely null and void.") and 6A E. McQuillin, Municipal Corporations, at 117 ("contracts ... which embarrass in any degree the municipal power of regulation of public affairs are *ultra vires*. . . .").

In executing the agreements at issue here, the Vermont municipalities violated the nondelegation doctrine in at least two ways. First, each of the participants attempted to redelegate one of the most fundamental of its legislative powers: the spending power. Second, the municipalities' agreements regarding other liens on their revenues impermissibly restricted the future exercise of discretion and judgment by their legislative bodies.

"[U]nits of local government cannot by contract or otherwise barter away or surrender their essential legislative or police powers. . . ." *Byrd*, 564 F. Supp. at 1428; see also Northwest Natural Gas Co. v. City of Portland, 300 Or. 291, 304–06, 711 P.2d 119, 128 (1985) (municipality's power to act for the public's general welfare cannot be bargained away to a public utility). Here, each Vermont participant was presented with an opportunity to obtain—without capital investment—exclusive rights to a percentage of potentially available, inexpensive, electrical energy. But, as part of the substantial consideration required for this bargain, the participants bartered away the ability to exercise judgment and discretion regarding energy costs. "Where the exercise of judgment and discretion and the power to burden the public treasury have been so vested [in the municipality] by the Legislature, they may not be delegated wholesale." Syrtel Buildings, Inc. v. City of Syracuse, 78 Misc. 2d 780, 782, 358 N.Y.S.2d 627, 630 (Sup. Ct. 1974).

The express component of the municipalities' attempted delegation of spending authority is found in paragraph 3(a) of the uniform PSAs, which provides that:

> MMWEC, in good faith and in accordance with Prudent Utility Practice, shall ... use its best efforts: (i) to arrange for the financing, planning, engineering, design, acquisition, construction, operation and maintenance of the Project; ... and (iii) to issue and sell Bonds to finance the Costs of Acquisition and Construction of the Project, and to finance the costs of any necessary renewals, extraordinary repairs, replacements, modifications, additions and betterments for the Project....

The purported delegation was made complete by the participants' failure to retain any vestige of control over decisions to incur debt. Under the provisions of the PSAs and the bond resolution, MMWEC has the sole power to establish budgets, revise those budgets, and fix the amount of the participants' monthly payments. Further, the authority to issue bonds resides in MMWEC alone, whether the bonds be for the costs of plant construction, operation, termination, or of "renewals, extraordinary repairs, replacements, modifications, additions and betterments...." In sum, MMWEC makes all decisions to incur, or to refrain from incurring, project debt. Hence, MMWEC is given exclusive control over the magnitude of the participants' monthly payments and over the duration of these payments.

Defendants argue, in effect, that the attempted contractual delegation is permissible because MMWEC has substantial obligations to each of the participants under the PSAs. They note that MMWEC's duties to the Vermont participants are no different than its duties to Massachusetts participants and that MMWEC is obligated to act in accordance with prudent utility practice. This reasoning is flawed because no degree of contractual consideration—even an agreement to assume substantial obligations—can render a municipality's abdication of legislative power permissible. We also note that the Massachusetts participants have elected representatives on MMWEC's board of directors, while the Vermont participants retain no voice whatsoever in the management of the project.

The parameters of permissible redelegation by public corporations can be illustrated by contrasting two cases. In Arkansas–Missouri Power Co. v. City of Kennett, 78 F.2d 911, the Eighth Circuit considered the legality of a municipality's loan agreement with the federal government that would enable the city to construct an electric power plant. Under the terms of the agreement, the federal government obtained a large amount of discretion and control over plans for the plant, labor contracts, and the use of materials. The court stated that:

> The building of an electric light plant obviously requires the exercise of judgment and discretion.... The duty to exercise that judgment is imposed upon the council of the city. We think that it may not contract that duty away or share it with others. That does not mean that it may not have plans and specifications prepared by architects and engineers, or that, when such plans have been finally approved by it, it may not let a general contract for the doing of the work and the furnishing of the materials. It does mean that in selling its bonds or otherwise financing the project, it may not delegate to the person who

> furnishes the money any substantial discretion with respect to the selection of labor or material to be furnished, or share with that person the authority to direct and control the construction.

Id. at 922. Because the federal government had retained "sufficient control ... to insure that the money furnished would be spent in the way that the government thought it should be spent, whether that was in accord with the ideas of the city council or not," the court held that the city had impermissibly delegated its authority to build the plant. Id. at 923.

By way of contrast, the Supreme Court of Washington found no unlawful delegation of legislative or discretionary functions in Roehl v. Public Utility Dist. No. 1, 43 Wash. 2d 214, 239–40, 261 P.2d 92, 105 (1953). There, a consortium of five public utility districts employed an independent consulting engineer to assist them in operating a joint power supply system. In the course of dismissing an argument that the district commissioners had unlawfully delegated their powers, the court noted that the engineer was given no authority to make policy decisions of a legislative character and that he was not free to ignore the basic policies formulated by the commissioners. Instead, the engineer was to act as a consultant, prepare budgets, perform inventories and valuations, and act as an impartial fact-finder as between the individual districts. Although these duties required the exercise of judgment, the court concluded that they were administrative in character and that no violation of the nondelegation principle had occurred. Id. at 241–42, 261 P.2d at 106.

The case at hand is closer to *Arkansas–Missouri Power* than it is to *Roehl*. As in the construction of a generating plant, arrangements aimed at ensuring long-term supplies of power require the ongoing exercise of legislative judgment and discretion. This is especially true where, as here, it is contemplated that the attempted arrangements may fail but where long-term financial obligations will be incurred nonetheless. The duty to exercise that judgment and discretion lies with the legislative bodies of the municipalities, and they cannot legally contract this duty away. The authority to spend the municipalities' revenues and the power to limit those expenditures must always be available for use in order that present and future needs may be met. See Ericksen v. City of Sioux Falls, 70 S.D. 40, 52–54, 14 N.W.2d 89, 95 (1944); 6A E. McQuillin, Municipal Corporations, at 117.

The participants also violated the nondelegation doctrine by agreeing to restrictions upon their power to make expenditures with regard to other projects or purchases. Paragraph 5(f) of the PSAs provides that:

> The Participant shall not issue bonds, notes or other evidences of indebtedness payable from and secured by a lien on the revenues derived from the ownership or operation of its electric system without providing for the payment of operating expenses (including Monthly Power Costs hereunder) from such revenues ahead of debt service on such bonds, notes or other evidences of indebtedness unless an independent consulting engineer ... certifies that the facilities, for the financing of which the bonds, notes or other evidences of indebtedness are being issued, are ... reasonably expected to properly and advantageously contribute to the conduct of the business of the electric system

of the Participant in an efficient and economical manner consistent with prudent management.

Under an important corollary to the nondelegation principle, a public corporation may not enter into a contract that purports to restrict the future exercise of its legislative authority. See *Byrd*, 564 F. Supp. at 1428–29; Illinois Power & Light Corp. v. City of Centralia, 11 F. Supp. 874, 885 (E.D. Ill. 1935), rev'd on other grounds, 89 F.2d 985 (7th Cir. 1937); Barton v. Atkinson, 228 Ga. 733, 744, 187 S.E.2d 835, 843 (1972); and City of Louisville v. Fiscal Court of Jefferson County, 623 S.W.2d 219, 224 (Ky. 1981); cf. Pierce Oil Corp. v. City of Hope, 248 U.S. 498, 501, 39 S. Ct. 172, 173, 63 L. Ed. 381 (1919) (where public welfare is involved, a contract not to legislate would have no effect). By agreeing to the contractual provisions above, the participants have fettered the future exercise of the authority granted to them under the provisions of 24 V.S.A. § 1822 and other municipal utility financing statutes. In the not unlikely event that a participant should wish to commit a portion of its revenues to acquire energy supplies or facilities in the future, it would have to either: (1) give priority to the monthly payment to MMWEC, or (2) obtain the certification of an independent engineering consultant regarding the advisability of the acquisition. The first option would hinder any prospective financial arrangement because of MMWEC's priority, and either option would deny the free exercise of legislative discretion.

The assignment of proprietary functions, such as plant operation, to MMWEC may be permissible, but the effective transfer of the municipalities' spending power and the restrictions upon their ability to incur other debts constitute impermissible attempts to redelegate legislative authority. Therefore, the municipalities' execution of the PSAs was *ultra vires*, and these contracts were void *ab initio*. . . .

The superior court's grant of defendants' motions for summary judgment is reversed and judgment for plaintiffs is entered.

NOTES

1. Should it matter that the power of the Vermont municipalities was delegated to a political subdivision of another state? What if the same power had been delegated to the Vermont attorney general; what concerns of the Vermont Supreme Court would be eliminated? Would any concerns remain? See Thompson v. Smith, 129 A.2d 638 (Vt. 1957).

2. Would the case have come out differently if the state legislature had passed a statute explicitly authorizing the arrangements in *MMWEC*? The court notes that the authority initially delegated to localities "is in the nature of a public trust conferred upon the legislative body of the corporation for the public benefit, and it cannot be exercised by others." This statement suggests an absolute bar to any redelegation. But recall the statement by the Vermont Supreme Court that "the delegate of power from the sovereign cannot without permission recommit to another agent or agency the trust imposed upon its judgment and discretion." This statement suggests that the delegate (the municipality) of legislative power could redelegate if it had the legislature's permission to do so. But the source of the nondelegation doctrine appears to be constitutional rather than legislative. If the constitutional prohibition on nondelegation admits of no exception for delegations permitted by the legislature, why does the court think that legislative authorization would solve the problem?

3. *Representation versus Control.* The Vermont court seems rather categorical in its denunciation of delegation where the delegating municipality does not retain control over the actions of the delegate. What if the Vermont municipalities had been full voting members of MMWEC, but could be outvoted by other members? Assume, for instance, that there were 35 full voting members of MMWEC and they voted 34–1 to terminate construction of the nuclear power plant. Would the one dissenting locality be deemed to have delegated power impermissibly to those who voted in the majority? If that is the result that the Vermont court intends, then interlocal cooperation through joint agencies can exist only when all participants agree. Unanimity implies that no jurisdiction is able to impose the costs of its decisions on other jurisdictions without making some form of compensation. But unanimity rules are subject to the criticism that they induce each voter to hold out its consent in order to extract more than its pro rata share of the benefits from other voters who need to secure the holdout vote. The result, as in the Chicken Game, is to deprive all potential beneficiaries of gains from trade as each voter holds out to extract additional gains from others. But if the Vermont court wants to avoid the consequences of a unanimity rule, and thus would approve the result of the 34–1 vote, how can it maintain that the dissenting municipality retained the requisite "control" over MMWEC decisions? On unanimity rules, see James M. Buchanan & Gordon Tullock, The Calculus of Consent 84–96 (1962).

In Municipality of Metropolitan Seattle v. City of Seattle, 357 P.2d 863 (Wash. 1960), the city of Renton had been included in a metropolitan municipal corporation created by a regional vote to dispose of sewage. Residents of Renton had overwhelmingly voted against the proposal. Plaintiff complained that the new municipality was entitled to impose real property taxes upon the taxpayers of Renton through a governing board, composed of 15 officials from the metropolitan area, that was not entirely elected by the people of Renton. Plaintiff contended that such a scheme constituted taxation without representation and a deprivation of property without due process. The court rejected the claim: "Through the democratic processes of the ballot, Renton has become a part of a regional area for the purpose of sewage disposal. The governing body is the Metro council, as ordained by the electorate residing within the newly formed regional municipality." 357 P.2d at 869. The court concluded that since Renton would be represented on the Metropolitan council by an elected official of Renton, and since that representative would be directly responsible to Renton citizens, any constitutional obligation to have a representative form of government was satisfied.

4. What authority must the alleged "delegatee" have in order to constitute an improper delegation? Will municipal action be invalid if the locality simply employs standards developed by the original delegate? In Turner v. Woodruff, 689 S.W.2d 527 (Ark. 1985), the state had created a student loan authority and permitted it to issue revenue bonds to provide low-interest loans to college students. The authority, however, could only make loans to students who met standards created by the federal Higher Education Act of 1965. Plaintiff contended that the incorporation of the federal standard in the state enabling act constituted an impermissible delegation of legislative power to the federal government. The court rejected the claim:

> The basic rule of law . . . is:
>
> > [T]he functions of the Legislature must be exercised by it alone. That power cannot be delegated to another authority. [Cites omitted.]
>
> However, non-legislative powers are delegable by the legislature.
>
> > Thus, the rule is that in order that a court may be justified in holding a statute unconstitutional as a delegation of legislative power, it must appear that the power involved is purely legislative in nature—that is, one appertaining exclusively to the legislative department. It is the nature of the power, and not the liability, its use or the manner of its exercise, which determines the validity of its delegation.
>
> *Arkansas S & L Ass'n Bd.*, supra. . . .
>
> > In *Arkansas S & L Ass'n Bd.* we held the statute requiring savings and loan associations chartered by the state to have their savings accounts insured by the Federal Savings and Loan Insurance Corporation (FSLIC) or other federal agency was not an unconstitutional delegation of legislative power. . . . There the FSLIC had denied the West Helena Savings and Loan Association's application for insurance. Thereafter, the Association's charter was cancelled . . . and the Association filed suit. Our decision rested upon the findings that the FSLIC was not required to do anything under the statute and that the Federal Housing Loan Bank Board, which conducted hearings on applications for insurance with FSLIC, was not mentioned in the statute. . . .
> >
> > Similarly in the case at bar, the Student Loan Act does not require any action on the part of the Secretary of Education or any other federal agent or agency. The Act anticipates interest payments from the federal government, but an anticipation is far short of a delegation. The Act does not mention any function to be performed by the federal government.

689 S.W.2d at 530.

5. In Chemical Bank v. Washington Public Power Supply System, 666 P.2d 329 (Wash. 1983), the court invalidated an arrangement similar to that in the *MMWEC* case. Municipalities throughout the Pacific Northwest had entered into Participants' Agreements with the Washington Public Power Supply System to purchase Project Capability from two nuclear power plants. The participants were obligated to make payments to the System in amounts sufficient to permit the System to pay its bondholders. Payments were due whether or not the plants were operating or operable. Unlike the *MMWEC* case, in which participants had no formal role in agency decisions, participants in the System were members of a Participants' Committee that had authority to disapprove certain decisions made by the System. Decisions not explicitly disapproved were deemed to have been accepted. The court found this level of control over the construction financing and operation of the plants insufficient to avoid claims of improper delegation. The court concluded:

> Considering the complexity of the various budgetary items, construction decisions and financing arrangements involved in a project of this scope, it seems unlikely that a part-time committee of representative participants could provide significant input to the management of the projects with such rigid procedural requirements. It appears to this court that such limited involvement in project management does not satisfy the type of ownership control envisioned in the statutes.
>
> It should be noted that we recognize the necessity and propriety of establishing representative committees to manage and oversee joint development projects.... Our concern is not with the use of such committees in general; it is with the structuring of such committee procedures in a way that does not allow sufficient participant involvement in project management to control their risk.

666 P.2d at 337.

The nuclear power plants whose construction was to be financed through payments from the power sales agreements in the *Chemical Bank* case had run into substantial difficulties at the time the case arose. Cost overruns had dramatically increased the originally predicted price of the project, and the expected demand for energy that would have required the plants had not materialized. It appeared, at the time of the lawsuit, that neither of the plants would ever generate any electrical energy. Similarly, in the *MMWEC* case, the power plant in Seabrook, New Hampshire had suffered substantial cost overruns at the time the case was heard, and it was uncertain whether the plant would ever be completed or would receive an operating license from the Nuclear Regulatory Commission. Thus, in both cases, it appeared that municipalities that sought to avoid the contracts would never have obtained any energy in return for their payments. Should this be relevant to the court's decision? If so, which way should it cut? Can the decisions be read as efforts by judges to impose the costs of failed or failing projects on out-of-state entities? Are there reasons to reject this interpretation? Given your study of municipal debt finance, what would you have recommended at the time these contracts were signed in order to avoid the problems of validity that subsequently arose?

6. In Mount Spokane Skiing Corporation v. Spokane County, 936 P.2d 1148 (Wash. Ct. App. 1997), a private firm that had been involved in the operation of a skiing facility challenged the county's creation of a public authority to operate a competing public facility. The company asserted that the legislature had granted authority over recreation directly to the county commissioners, and the county's creation of the authority constituted an unlawful redelegation. By state statute, municipalities could create a public authority to "perform any lawful public purpose or public function" in an effort to "improve the general living conditions in the urban areas of the state." The court held that no unconstitutional delegation had occurred because the county acted in pursuit of a public purpose, did not act in an arbitrary or capricious manner, and there was no express limitation preventing the county from carrying out its authority in this manner. If nondelegation is an independent constitutional principle, why should it matter whether the delegated function satisfies a public purpose?

NOTE ON METROPOLITAN GOVERNMENT AND REGIONALISM

Existing local boundary lines may be inappropriate to address local government action or inaction that imposes significant external effects. Regional solutions that transcend local boundaries may be necessary if problems such as pollution, transportation, and fiscal equity are to be confronted at a suitable scale. Indeed these occasions may suggest that the current organization of local government is unsuited to the needs of the region. A broader scope of cooperation might be required. Nevertheless, local government law has been heavily criticized for its failure to provide more incentives or requirements for intergovernmental cooperation within a metropolitan area. See, e.g., Richard Briffault, The Local Boundary Problem in Metropolitan Areas, 48 Stan. L. Rev. 1115 (1996); Richard Thompson Ford, Beyond Borders: A Partial Response to Richard Briffault, 48 Stan L. Rev. 1173 (1996); Jerry Frug, The Geography of Community, 48 Stan. L. Rev. 1047 (1996).

To understand the difficulties of achieving metropolitan cooperation, consider two different types of services that might best be provided at a regional level. Cooperation may be relatively easy to obtain where metropolitan or regional provision would allow all parties to realize economies of scale or to coordinate services that all participants desire to provide. For instance, we could easily imagine localities agreeing on regional provision of ambulance services or road construction. In these situations, everyone wins from cooperation, so the only issue is who will decide the point around which all parties will coordinate. Nevertheless, we would imagine that even in these situations, localities will be reluctant to abandon their right to make decisions independent of the decisions of other localities. Thus, the desire for local autonomy could interfere with regional decisionmaking even where it is most obviously preferable.

The problem becomes more difficult where the service at issue requires significant redistribution from one area within the region to another. Examples include affordable housing and the siting of undesirable land uses, such as landfills and prisons. In true Prisoner's Dilemma fashion, even if all localities within the region desire that these services be provided, each locality may prefer that some other locality incur the redistributive burden. We discuss legal means of distributing this burden among localities in Section C below. For the moment, however, it is useful to recognize that one way to deal with this issue is by moving the decision to a more centralized level by forming regional or metropolitan governments.

We begin by describing successful efforts to achieve metropolitan cooperation. These ventures require more formal arrangements, and more statutory authority, than cooperative efforts that involve only a single service. The most successful forms of metropolitan governments to date (setting aside the possibility of annexation of an unincorporated area into a municipal corporation) involve city-county consolidations, federations of governments, and councils of governments, or COGs. We then turn to issues of using metropolitan governments to achieve interlocal equity. Both the need for regional solutions to questions of distribution and possible solutions are addressed in the excerpt from the article by Scott A. Bollens at the end of this Note.

Single Government Forms of Government

A federation or consolidation of governments is the most complex and most infrequently employed method of metropolitan government formation. A central characteristic of the formation process is the transfer of local government power to a regional body. Perhaps the most important such transfer was the creation of a new New York City in 1898 by the consolidation of five boroughs and elimination of other municipal governments such as that of the city of Brooklyn. The resulting metropolitan government takes one of two forms: single-tiered government or two-tiered government.

City–County Consolidation

A single-tier consolidation may be legislatively authorized through a process that unites two or more governments. Frequently, the single government is an enlarged version of an existing government that results from the consolidation or merger of counties and cities. Unlike the annexation of an unincorporated area by an existing municipality, this method requires the establishment of a new governmental entity that exercises the powers previously conferred on the former incorporated areas. This method, for instance, was used in Louisiana to consolidate Baton Rouge with East Baton Rouge Parish, and in Florida to consolidate the City of Jacksonville with Duval County. See Jay S. Goodman, The Dynamics of Urban Government and Politics 195 (1980). However, in recent years the number of states authorizing city-county consolidation has decreased.

Generally, proposals for the consolidation of governments must receive electoral, as well as legislative, approval. Where electoral approval is necessary, the requirement serves as a major barrier to consolidation. See David Rusk, Cities Without Suburbs 97–98 (1993). Consolidation proposals that do reach the electorate are rejected three times as frequently as they are accepted. See Nelson Wikstrom, Councils of Government 6 (1977).

City–County Consolidation: The Nashville and Indianapolis Examples

Two exceptions to this trend against city-county consolidation include the consolidation of the City of Nashville and Davidson County, Tennessee, and the creation of Unigov, merging the City of Indianapolis and Marion County, Indiana. The consolidation of the City of Nashville and Davidson County, Tennessee, eliminating longstanding county-city competition for services and tax revenues, presents one of the earliest successful attempts at overcoming the electoral obstacle. Each government alleged that the other was unfairly using its services without paying a fair share of the cost. Most county residents who worked in the city paid taxes only to their resident communities. They resented the city's attempts to charge them for use of the city's services by imposing a commuter tax and charging them for water and electricity provided by the city. The battle between the city and county government was so strong that some streets, divided down the center by the city-county border, had two speed limits, one for each direction. See David A. Booth, Metropolitics: The Nashville Consolidation (1963), and Governor's Interagency Council on Growth Management, Governor's Office of Planning and Research Models of Regional Government 3–5 (1991).

After the General Assembly passed legislation allowing city-county consolidation, Tenn. Code Ann. § 7–1–101, county voters passed a charter consolidating the region's 12 governments: Davidson County, the City of Nashville, its six suburbs, and four special districts. The current "Metro" government is governed by an elected metropolitan mayor and a legislature comprising a mix of district-based and at-large elected officials. The mix is designed to ensure that both individual and regional views are represented. The charter created two special tax districts: a general services district that covers the entire county and provides areawide services such as jails, schools, and parks, and an urban services district that is limited in area and provides only urban needs such as additional police protection, trash collection, and street lighting. Different tax rates apply to each area, and sections of the county are free to join the urban services district on approval of local residents and payment of the additional taxes.

Judicial interpretations of the enabling legislation permit participating jurisdictions to determine the powers transferred to the new government, Glasgow v. Fox, 383 S.W.2d 9 (Tenn. 1964); Metropolitan Gov't v. Poe, 383 S.W.2d 265 (Tenn. 1964). The legislation that authorized the consolidation of Nashville and Davidson County has been held to have merged the governments, but not to have extended municipal powers to the entire consolidated area. Rather, different services, such as fire and police protection and garbage collection, are provided by an "urban services district" within the consolidated area. Those within the urban services district pay a higher tax rate. Thus, urban area districts are likely to be created only when an area is undergoing substantial urbanization. See Templeton v. Metropolitan Gov't, 650 S.W.2d 743 (Tenn. Ct. App. 1983).

The Indiana General Assembly united the City of Indianapolis and Marion County, Indiana, into Unigov (short for "unified government") in 1969 without voter approval. Under Unigov, the city and county councils combined to form a 29–member city-county council. A Unigov mayor is also elected countywide. Five executive departments absorb some of the functions of prior special-purpose corporations. In Dortch v. Lugar, 266 N.E.2d 25 (Ind. 1971), the Supreme Court of Indiana held that the act was a valid delegation of authority, was not an impairment of obligations of contracts, did not constitute special legislation, and did not deprive citizens of voting rights. Some have argued that Unigov is not a comprehensive city-county obligation, contending that it functions like a structure of overlapping districts containing interior, independent cities rather than a unified regional government. See John Kincaid, "Regulatory Regionalism in Metropolitan Areas: Voter Resistance and Reform Persistence," 13 Pace L. Rev. 449, 461 (1993). The Unigov configuration excluded four municipalities and six special-purpose corporations from its jurisdiction. The legislation was also approved without facing the obstacle of local voter approval.

Two–Tiered Government: Federations of Governments and Urban Counties

Metropolitan federations, often called "two-tier" governments, consist of regional bodies created to address areawide concerns, such as sewerage and police protection, and a layer of local governments with authority over more local concerns. Such an arrangement can take the form of a "federation" of governments or an "urban-county" government. The two forms are essentially similar, the difference being that the creation of an urban-county government involves the transfer of local powers to an existing government, whereas a federation requires the establishment of a new government that receives the powers of the participating areas. Creation of metropolitan governments can be accomplished under specific or general legislative acts.

The extent of the metropolitan government created through such legislative acts can be as small as the merger of a city and a county or as large as the federation of several counties and hundreds of local governments. For example, Michigan has authorized any combination of two or more local governments to create a metropolitan council, to prescribe the council's powers and duties, and to levy a property tax. See Mich. Comp. Laws Ann. ch. 124. Kentucky has enacted extensive legislation addressing the formation and powers of urban-county governments. See Ky. Rev. Stat. Ann. ch. 67A. These provisions of Kentucky law permit creation of an urban-county government after petition and approval by county voters. The resulting entity has the power to enact ordinances to provide for the "health, education, safety, welfare and convenience of the inhabitants of the county and for the effective administration of the urban-county government" as long as the ordinances do not conflict with general state statutes. Ky. Rev. Stat. Ann. § 67A.070(1). These provisions have been upheld against the claim that they are unconstitutional special legislation. Conrad v. Lexington–Fayette Urban County Government, 659 S.W.2d 190 (Ky. 1983), appeal dismissed sub. nom. Cox v. Lexington–Fayette Urban County Government, 466 U.S. 919 (1984).

Federations of Governments: Grand Rapids Example

In 1990, the Michigan state legislature enacted the Metropolitan Council Act (Mich. Comp. Laws Ann. § 124.651–124.685) authorizing limited two-tier governments. The statute permits a metropolitan area, defined as a group of two or more cities with a combined population of less than 1 million, to create a metropolitan council. The creation of such a metropolitan council is subject to a referendum on the petition of 5 percent of the registered electors. (§ 124.663). The Grand Rapids metropolitan area has formed the only metropolitan federation to date in Michigan. The Grand Rapids Metropolitan Council provides water and sewer, transportation, economic development, and land and water development services.

Urban Counties: The Miami–Dade Example

The Miami–Dade urban-county was created primarily to provide more efficient service delivery to the one-third of the county's population that resided in unincorporated areas. Service to these areas had been provided through informal agreements with incorporated localities. With the country's rapid increase in population, the services became increasingly difficult and expensive. Governor's Interagency Council on Growth Management, supra, at 6–8.

Incorporated areas were relieved from this burden in 1957 when voters approved an amendment to the county charter that created Metro, a two-tiered urban-county government. The first tier, the county level, possesses ultimate responsibility for coordinating services such as public transportation, regional planning, water supply, and waste disposal for the unincorporated areas, Miami, and surrounding suburbs. The county creates minimum standards for services provided by local governments. On the second level, the City of Miami retains control over local matters such as police protection and zoning. Incorporated areas outside of Miami retain similar powers, including the right to alter their boundaries and to regulate the sale of alcoholic beverages. Municipalities are prevented from adopting provisions that directly conflict with the county charter.

This urban-county approach has met with little acceptance in other areas of the country, although some counties have become de facto urban counties as the counties have acquired sufficient municipal powers. Lest one believe that such metropolitanism will necessarily be successful, it is worth noting that the Miami–Dade Commission received significant criticism following massive hurricane destruction in 1992. Many blamed relaxed construction standards enacted by the Commission for much of the damage suffered. See Kincaid, supra, at 465. Local critics argued that the Commission had "simply outgrown the weak form of government called Metro Dade that was devised to encourage growth with minimum regulation." See Larry Rohter, "Local Government Is Taken to Task as Florida Hurricane Cleanup Drags," New York Times, B12, Oct. 20, 1992. The authority of the county's elected chief executive has subsequently been strengthened through the grant of a veto power in an effort to address that concern.

Councils of Governments

Councils of Governments (COGs) are voluntary associations that link local governments. COGs have been the most widespread effort to create forms of metropolitan government. They currently operate as advisory bodies designed to allow members to discuss regional concerns. These councils typically consist of elected officials from each of the member governments. COGs lack independent political authority and the power to levy taxes. As laid out in the North Carolina statute authorizing the creation of COGs, "[o]nce created, a council does not become a municipality, or a political or governmental subdivision of the State in the same sense as a city, town or county. A council may take on some of the attributes and functions of a political subdivision, but does not possess the powers which municipalities are said to possess." N.C. Gen. Stat. Ann. 160A–470.

COGs had been encouraged by federal programs that either required that federal funds be allocated to bodies addressing regional concerns or specifically granted COGs additional power to evaluate federal grant applications for a region. Throughout the 1960s and 1970s, COGs served as clearinghouses for federal grant applications involving federal housing, mass transit, and urban development programs. COGs thus played a significant role in regional planning. However, in the 1980s, President Reagan abolished federal regional councils and abandoned most of the federally funded programs for which regional planning had been required. COGs ceased to serve an important planning function as their clearinghouse role declined. Today COGs serve as advisors, providing information and services to their affiliated local governments "on such matters as local government payroll management, landfills, police firing ranges, fingerprint and ID systems, street maintenance, purchase and operation of snow-removal equipment, counseling services, and emergency communications," but they lack any real authority. See Kincaid, supra, at 473; see also Briffault, supra, at 1148.

Councils of Governments: The Allegheny County Example

Allegheny County, Pennsylvania, is home to eight established COGs whose benefits extend to all regions of the county. There exist over 300 general and special governments in the county, which includes the metropolitan area around the City of Pittsburgh. 1987 Census of Governments, Volume 1: Government Organization, No. 1: Government Organization, p. 66, Table 23; U.S. Advisory Commission on Intergovernmental Relations, Metropolitan Organization: The Allegheny County Case 5 (1992). Most of the municipalities in Allegheny County belong to one of eight COGs that serve the area. Most of these COGs are governed by a general assembly, which consists of all elected officials in the COG area, and a board of directors, which consists of one elected official from each member government. Operating funds may be obtained through membership dues, county and state funding, or revenues from the provision of services. Each COG has developed functions that address particular needs of the member governments. These functions include a payroll and accounting service, utility billing service, emergency dispatch service, police firing range, traffic sign manufacturing, street sweeping, credit union, purchasing council, and finance manager. Cooperation between COGs has led to the development of a surplus property auction and multi-municipality public works teams.

These interlocal arrangements are primarily directed at the efficient delivery of services within a metropolitan area. They do not, however, necessarily entail an additional function of addressing financial disparities among regional localities and their residents. It is at this point that cries of local autonomy and the desire to keep local revenues within local boundaries may be most vocal. Recall the reading from Nancy Rosenblum in

Chapter 1 in this regard. The following reading addresses the possibility that metropolitan governmental structures can address issues of equity as well as efficiency.

Scott A. Bollens, Concentrated Poverty and Metropolitan Equity Strategies

8 Stan. L & Pol'y Rev. 11, 15–18 (1997).

Concentrated poverty and racial segregation have become indelible parts of the American metropolitan landscape. In 1990, about 2800 census tracts (out of 45,000 total) had poverty rates in excess of forty percent of the tract population, compared to about 1000 in 1970. Eight and one-half million people live in these areas of concentrated poverty, compared to 4.2 million people in 1970. People of color comprise the majority of residents in these areas. Of the 8.2 million people living in areas of concentrated poverty, one-half are African American, one-fourth are Hispanic, and one-fourth are non-Hispanic whites. Fully thirty-three percent of the African–American poor in the United States live in these high-poverty neighborhoods, and 800 of the poorest census tracts have populations that are at least ninety percent African–American. Segregation and concentrated poverty are products of institutional discrimination and individual prejudice and constitute significant sources of future disadvantage and relative deprivation. Location of households and individuals in segregated, poverty-stricken neighborhoods significantly influences the quality of their schools, the level of municipal services, tax burdens, access to work, and level of safety. As poverty concentrates, the physical fabric of neighborhoods deteriorates, oppositional behaviors take over the streets, and communities are spatially and psychologically separated from good urban jobs, education, and amenities. Because racial segregation concentrates poverty and systematically builds deprivation into the residential structure of black communities, Douglas Massey and Nancy Denton have deemed it "the principal feature of American Society that is responsible for the creation of the urban underclass." . . .

An increased interest in, and redefinition of, regional governance is occurring in the United States. Two factors have stimulated public, private, and nonprofit sector interest in multi-jurisdictional governance. First, international economic competitiveness is focusing our attention on the urban economic region, not simply individual municipal units, as the proper scale of intervention. Regions or "city-states" competing in an international economy may not be able to afford the costs of internal divisions (such as central city-suburbs) that dampen overall regional health. Second, infrastructure deficiencies and gridlock produced by local citizen and government opposition ("Not In My Back Yard" or NIMBYism) call for the creation of more decisive regional entities able to site and finance region-serving NIMBY facilities such as highways, airports, and sewage disposal. Thus, international market pressures and the obstacles raised by local governments to the efficient allocation of resources contribute to the increasing interest in regional governance.

Contemporary discussions concerning regionalism also focus on collaborative efforts as opposed to comprehensive models. Policymakers must develop less intrusive types of metropolitan collaboration that are more effective than comprehensive forms of metropolitan government.

In the face of function-specific and fragmented approaches to regional governance in America, how might regionalism be re-created so that it can deal more effectively with the social and economic challenges of contemporary metropolitan life? To the extent that intra-metropolitan disparities are self-defeating in an internationally competitive economy, introducing social equity policies to help alleviate concentrated poverty would be consistent with the pursuit of economic self-interest. In order to overcome these challenges, regional governance must assume multiple and qualitatively different public functions so that it can make tradeoffs across policy areas and political borders within the metropolitan area. For example, a multifunctional regional agency with authority to site affordable housing, waste disposal facilities, and other locally unwanted land uses (LULUs) could assure that no local government is burdened with multiple or concentrated LULUs. In contrast, contemporary regional agencies are often restricted to narrow policy fields and single constituencies. In the cases where a regional body, such as a council of government, is responsible for multiple policy fields, the governing body's mission and voluntary nature limit its power to affect regional and local development policy. The resulting metropolitan landscape consists of fragmented regional interests each pursuing their own goals in an uncoordinated and competitive arena.

Metropolitan and regional governance must transcend the traditional focus on systems-maintenance, or "things" regionalism in an effort to encompass life-style, or "people" regionalism. They can play an instrumental role in alleviating the growing number of neighborhoods of concentrated poverty, both through community development of poor neighborhoods and the metropolitan deconcentration of poverty. By virtue of its appropriate geographic reach and closer ties to local sentiment than state or national agencies, regional governance is in a unique position to address the issue of the inter-municipal distribution of poor and minority individuals.

Racial and income desegregation of urban regions constitutes an important step in alleviating urban poverty. Increasing the socioeconomic integration of metropolitan America is important for several reasons. Desegregation of the urban poor can provide better access to urban opportunities. Secondly, equitable distribution of the poor would sustain metropolitan property values and tax bases more than if one or two cities absorb a disproportionate share of the region's poor. Integration also combats the deleterious social, psychological, and behavioral consequences that segregation fosters. Segregation creates structural conditions that precipitate the emergence of an oppositional culture and urban underclass. Often, this segregated culture devalues work, schooling, and marriage, and instead fosters attitudes and behaviors antithetical and often hostile to success in the larger economy. Involuntary or institutional segregation, like that in South Africa, may inflict profound social-psychological damage because it "manufactures an inward, group-oriented consciousness which, in turn, is one basis for race-based political mobilization and inter-group conflict."

The following ... initiatives, each a regional planning strategy to help alleviate concentrated poverty in metropolitan America, when taken together, might constitute a comprehensive metropolitan equity program. These proposals reflect ideas of both the in-place and mobility approaches to alleviating concentrated poverty in urban regions.

A. *Channel Federally–Assisted Housing Expenditures to Lessen Racial Concentration*

Pursuant to Executive Orders 12372 and 12416, regional agencies, such as councils of governments (COGs) are to perform intergovernmental review of proposed federal financial assistance and federally directed development activities. This authority provides regional agencies with the capacity to channel federally-assisted housing expenditures toward lessening concentrated poverty across the metropolitan landscape. Relevant precedents forbid the use of public money to perpetuate increased concentrations of minorities and the poor.... To channel federal expenditures to increase desegregation, metropolitan governments need to develop similar site selection criteria and regularly monitor racial and socioeconomic concentrations in its neighborhoods, cities, and sub-regions....

B. *Establish a Regional Government Campaign Against Residential Segregation*

Metropolitan governments could help establish and support non-profit fair housing organizations. In an effort to increase desegregation, these community organizations provide housing information on a metropolitan-wide basis and pursue legal action when necessary. Metropolitan governments could take more direct action by each creating their own Division of Housing Opportunity. This agency's advocates could promote affirmative real estate marketing programs, file fair housing complaints, and engage in ongoing monitoring of metropolitan housing opportunities....

C. *Limit Regional Suburban Sprawl*

Urban analysts commonly associate suburban sprawl with excessive land consumption and destruction of natural resources and farmland. Suburban sprawl also results in region-wide inefficiencies in public facilities and infrastructure and places unnecessary fiscal pressure on suburban governments. Its greatest effect, however, may be its facilitation of metropolitan-level income segregation. Suburbs attract higher-income residents through the provision of large lots, high quality housing, and community amenities. To counter the pattern of segregation produced by contemporary urbanization and suburban sprawl, state and regional governments could define minimum density standards to diversify housing types and sizes offered throughout the urban region....

D. Require "Fair–Share" Affordable Housing Obligations

Regional governments have a key role in opening the suburbs to low-and moderate-income housing. An important report sponsored by HUD partially attributed the shortage of affordable housing in suburban areas to local regulatory barriers that drive up the cost of housing or limit the building of low-and moderate-income housing. Several state and metropolitan governments have intervened to promote the development of affordable housing on a more fairly distributed basis.

In New Jersey, state actions have included both judicial displacement of local growth authority and the more recent enactment of fair housing and planning legislation. Subsequent to the *Mt. Laurel II* decision [456 A.2d 390 (N.J. 1983) (prohibiting exclusionary zoning and requiring local governments to make affordable housing available to low-income residents)], the New Jersey Supreme Court established a three-judge panel to assure that each growing city in the state provides its "fair share" of affordable housing. . . .

In California, all local governments and regional councils of governments must engage in a "regional housing needs assessment" (RHNA) process. Each local government must plan for its share of the regional housing need. While an RHNA must contain a plan for meeting existing and projected housing needs, it must also contain a plan for reducing "the concentration of lower income households in jurisdictions where they are disproportionately represented relative to their representation in the whole regional market." . . .

E. Encourage Balanced Distribution of Jobs and Housing

In many metropolitan regions, the spatial disparity grows between residents' homes and jobs. This disparity affects the inner-city poor who are distant from growing suburb job opportunities, and urban fringe poor who are far from urban core opportunities. Primarily in response to federal air quality standards, regional transportation and air quality authorities seek ways to equalize jobs/housing ratios across their metropolitan areas. The intended result is the reduction of region-wide commuting distances and air pollution. At the same time, jobs-housing balance policies resulting from an integration of transportation planning and air quality management can affect social equity goals relating to job accessibility for lower income communities and households.

F. Target Regional Transportation and Redevelopment Strategies

The Intermodal Surface Transportation Efficiency Act (ISTEA) of 1991 [23 U.S.C. 134] mandates that regional governments play a greater role in regional transportation improvements. ISTEA requires metropolitan transportation organizations to consider "[t]he overall social, economic, energy, and environmental effects of transportation decisions." Investment in regional transportation has a significant social cost which must now be considered when making policy decisions. Innovative planners could document that continued highway funding in outer suburban areas may exacerbate sprawl, metropolitan income segregation, and inner-city disinvestment as new suburban areas open for development. These same planners may argue for increased and flexible bus schedules, including the establishment and enhancement of routes, from cities to suburbs, aimed at increasing the inner-city poor's access to job-rich areas.

Metropolitan governments can also play an instrumental role in channeling additional resources to areas of concentrated poverty. They can restrict the use of redevelopment authority and tax-increment financing for revitalizing commercial or residential areas, which captures property value increases, to the most distressed neighborhoods. . . .

H. Site LULUs Based on Equity Criteria

While regional economic and demographic forces adversely affect inner-city communities of poverty and color, public policies may also facilitate the over-concentration of noxious and troublesome "locally unwanted land uses." High concentrations of homeless shelters, regional waste disposal facilities, major polluting industries, or government-assisted and public housing contribute to the destabilization of poor and minority communities. The commonly fragmented form of regionalism in the United States obstructs the analysis of cumulative LULU impacts and poor neighborhoods pay the price. In contrast, multi-functional and multi-jurisdictional regional governments can assure a more equitable distribution of controversial facilities across the metropolitan landscape. . . .

J. Attack Root Fiscal Reasons Behind Ineffective Municipal Planning

Increased concentrations of poor and minority communities parallel the continued restrictive practices of suburban communities protective of their fiscal strength and socioeconomic character. As long as the fiscal capacity of suburban cities is tied to the amount and type of development within their borders, suburbs will continue resisting metropolitan equity strategies that create fiscal strains on their local budgets. Metropolitan tax-base sharing policies counter the "fiscalization" of land use imperatives. Since 1971, the Minnesota legislature has required that every local government in the seven-county Minneapolis–St. Paul area deposit forty percent of its commercial and industrial tax base growth into a region-wide pool created to remedy inter-jurisdictional fiscal disparities. Another legislative method for countering inter-suburban competition is the development of stricter municipal incorporation requirements and more lenient central city annexation rules arbitrated by regional boundary commissions.

B. INTERLOCAL CONFLICT

Township of Washington v. Village of Ridgewood

141 A.2d 308 (N.J. 1958).

■ WEINTRAUB, C.J.

The Chancery Division of the Superior Court entered a judgment directing the Village of Ridgewood to dismantle and remove an elevated steel water tower it erected upon Van Emburgh Avenue, partially within the village and partially within the Borough of Ho–Ho–Kus. 46 N.J. Super. 152, 134 A.2d 345 (1957). Ridgewood appealed and we certified the appeal on our own motion prior to consideration of it by the Appellate Division.

Ridgewood operates a water supply system serving itself, the Boroughs of Glen Rock and Midland Park and the Township of Wyckoff, and meeting the needs of the inhabitants and municipalities, including fire fighting. The water is obtained from deep-rock wells. There are no reservoirs; storage to meet the increased demands of certain days or portions thereof is provided by tanks.

The pressure being inadequate, Ridgewood engaged a consulting engineer, Mr. Crew, to devise a plan for additional storage. He recommended three tanks, all elevated, one at the Van Emburgh site here involved, another on Goffle Road in Ridgewood, and the third on the Cedarhill site in Wyckoff. The anticipated total cost was $1,701,000.

In view of the sum involved, Ridgewood solicited the opinion of another expert, Mr. Capen. Mr. Capen, then some 1,200 miles away, was familiar with the Goffle site, and on the basis of his recollection of it, said in his report:

> In areas where elevated tanks have been established (and particularly where such installation has been made prior to nearby residential developments) repetition of the practice may well be in order. A very serious question is raised, however, in regard to placing an elevated tank in the Goffle area, near Goffle Road. There are a number of substantial residences in the vicinity which will probably be adversely affected in value by such a structure. It is therefore recommended that the entire matter of this storage be carefully reviewed and that an underground or ground level storage tank be substituted. This procedure is not a new trend but has been adopted in various residential communities.

This recommendation was explored and a decision made to shift from the Goffle site to another on Lafayette Avenue in Wyckoff, where a tank could be installed partially below ground level. The change was profitable. Instead of the Goffle tank, designed to provide storage of two million gallons at an estimated cost of $499,000, Ridgewood obtained storage of 2 1/4 million gallons at Lafayette at a cost of $243,672.84.

With respect to the proposed Cedarhill tank, the Board of Adjustment of Wyckoff refused approval because of objections to an elevated structure. Ridgewood thereupon selected another site where as of the time of trial a ground level tank was to be installed without increase in cost and with an increase in capacity from one million to 2 ¼ million gallons.

Thus as to two of the sites, objections to elevated tanks led to their abandonment in favor of tanks at or below ground level.

Mr. Capen's report was received in February 1955. In September 1955 Mr. Crew approached the governing body of Ho–Ho–Kus with respect to the

Van Emburgh improvement. The testimony is not harmonious, but it is clear that the officials of Ho–Ho–Kus understood the tank would be at ground level, the same as the existing water tanks of Ho–Ho–Kus, and as such would be shielded by trees. In the light of Mr. Capen's report, Mr. Crew should have been explicit, but was not. The board of adjustment and planning board approved, and a permit issued. The approvals were granted informally; Ridgewood concedes that the statutory requirements for a variance or exception were not met, and that if the zoning ordinance of Ho–Ho–Kus applies, it can claim no benefit from the wholly irregular grant.

When the work got under way, it was realized that an elevated structure was involved. It in fact would tower to the height of 160 feet. Ho–Ho–Kus immediately adopted a resolution rescinding the permit, and Ho–Ho–Kus and the abutting Township of Washington and residents affected instituted these actions promptly. About 75 to 85% of the structure itself was completed by the time of trial, representing a cost of some $80,000.

Three issues are involved: (1) whether the improvement violates the zoning ordinance of Ridgewood; (2) whether it violates the zoning ordinance of Ho–Ho–Kus; and (3) whether the action of Ridgewood in any event constitutes an unreasonable and arbitrary exercise of delegated power.

I

We are satisfied that neither zoning ordinance applies.

In Thornton v. Village of Ridgewood, 17 N.J. 499, 111 A.2d 899 (1955), a question involved was whether Ridgewood could acquire property within its one-family district for use as an administrative building and assembly hall. It was held that the zoning statute does not restrain the power of a municipality to determine where to locate municipal facilities within its borders, and hence the issue became whether the zoning ordinance itself accomplished a restriction. As the ordinance then read, "any governmentally owned or operated building" was authorized in the one-family district. It was concluded that the proposed use came within the quoted phrase.

In the course of *Thornton*, it was indicated that the phrase "governmentally owned or operated" would "seem to bar governmental buildings devoted to industrial or proprietary use" (17 N.J. at page 514, 111 A.2d at page 906). For the obvious purpose of meeting that view, Ridgewood amended its ordinance to substitute "Any municipally owned or operated building, structure or use" for the phrase quoted above. There can be no doubt that the amendatory expression embraces the storage tank, and hence there is no violation by Ridgewood of its own ordinance.

With respect to so much of the site as is situated in Ho–Ho–Kus, it is conceded that the zoning ordinance of that municipality by its terms forbids the improvement and, as pointed out above, that the informal variance cannot be sustained. The issue accordingly is whether Ridgewood is bound by the ordinance of Ho–Ho–Kus in the use of property as part of a water supply system. We think it is not.

We see no difference between this case and Aviation Services, Inc. v. Board of Adjustment of Hanover Township, 20 N.J. 275, 119 A.2d 761, 765 (1956), in which it was held that a municipality's power to establish and maintain an airport was not subject to the zoning ordinance of another municipality in which the airport was situate. In *Aviation Services*, the municipality was authorized to acquire and establish airports "within or without" its boundaries, with power to condemn. Here R.S. 40:62—49, N.J.S.A., provides:

> Any municipality may provide and supply water, or an additional supply of water, . . . in any one or more of the following methods:
>
> (g) Any municipality may purchase, condemn or otherwise acquire the necessary lands, and rights or interests in lands, water rights and rights of flowage or diversion, within or without the municipality, for the purpose of a water supply, or an additional water supply, and for the connection thereof with the municipality, and in case of highway or other public or quasi public structures, may require the same to be abandoned as far as necessary for such purposes, and to be relaid, if necessary, by some other route or in some other location. . . .

The lands necessary for "a water supply" must include lands necessary for facilities required to meet the needs of the consumer.

The consent of such other municipality is required only with respect to the laying of pipes or mains "in and under any and all streets, highways, alleys and public places" in that municipality, subject to the power of the Superior Court to direct the terms of such laying if consent should be refused. N.J.S.A. 40:62–65.

This result has a baneful potential, but so does a contrary holding. The problem invites a legislative solution committing the final decision to a body other than the interested municipalities themselves, but if *Aviation Services* correctly found the legislative will in that case, the same considerations dictate the same answer here.

Plaintiffs urge that the supply of water is a "proprietary" rather than a "governmental" function and hence should be subject to the Ho–Ho–Kus ordinance.

We cannot agree that the distinction between governmental and proprietary functions is relevant to this controversy. The distinction is illusory; whatever local government is authorized to do constitutes a function of government, and when a municipality acts pursuant to granted authority it acts as government and not as a private entrepreneur. The distinction has proved useful to restrain the ancient concept of municipal tort immunity, not because of any logic in the distinction, but rather because sound policy dictated that governmental immunity should not envelop the many activities which government today pursues to meet the needs of the citizens. Cloyes v. Delaware Township, 23 N.J. 324, 129 A.2d 1, 57 A.L.R.2d 1327 (1957). We see no connection between that classification and the problem before us. Surely the supply of water cannot be deemed to be a second-class activity in the scheme of municipal functions. Nor is it significant that the municipality serves areas in addition to its own, for from the nature of the subject, cooperative action among municipalities is imperative and consonant with the governmental nature of the activity.

II

But Ridgewood was required to act reasonably in the exercise of its authority, *Aviation Services*, supra (20 N.J. at page 285, 119 A.2d at page 766), and the circumstance that its own interests conflicted with those of Ho–Ho–Kus and Washington emphasized that obligation. Among the considerations which Ridgewood should have weighed but in fact ignored were the zoning schemes of the municipal plaintiffs and the land uses abutting and near the site.

Mr. Crew was concerned solely with the engineering aspects. Despite Mr. Capen's caveat and the confirmation of it by experience with respect to the Goffle and Cedarhill sites recited above, Ridgewood made no effort to re-evaluate its plan for an elevated tank on the Van Emburgh property. The testimony shows without contradiction that the residential development there was equal or superior to that at either of the other sites and that Mr. Capen had not adverted to the interest of property owners at the Van Emburgh location only because he was not aware of that development.

Mr. Crew and Mr. Capen agreed a ground level tank could be used at Van Emburgh Avenue if pumping facilities were added. Mr. Crew stated that a gravity flow system would yield a better quality of water, but conceded that a satisfactory, wholesome supply would be furnished by ground level storage tanks. Mr. Capen made no reference to that subject and in fact had suggested pumping at the Goffle site if a ground level tank were used. The difference between the two approaches is one of cost. If the elevated tank should be used, the estimated cost for the complete installation is $226,026, whereas if the tank is placed at ground level the pumping facilities would increase the outlay to a total of $272,700. Mr. Capen would prefer to add an inlet pipe costing another $60,000 but agreed the improvement could be engineered to operate without it. The annual bill for pumping would be $5,000, less a saving of the higher maintenance costs of an elevated structure.

It appears further that immediately before trial consideration was given to alternate sites, and that one permitting a ground level tank with gravity flow operation is available at an estimated expenditure of $292,600. This exceeds the original proposal by some $66,000, part of which is attributable to the increase in costs in the intervening period (and perhaps also to the inclusion of land costs; it is not clear whether the figure of $226,026 for the elevated tank installation includes the value of the land which Ridgewood had acquired back in 1940).

Hence Ridgewood could have placed the tank at ground level, either at the Van Emburgh site or the alternate site. The difference is one of cost described above. Under the circumstances, Ridgewood should have assumed that cost rather than visit the burden of an elevated structure of 160 feet upon the other municipalities. We agree with the trial court's finding that Ridgewood acted arbitrarily.

The judgment is accordingly affirmed....

■ HEHER, J. (for affirmance)....

There is no showing, none whatever, that Ridgewood's lands in Ho–Ho–Kus are "necessary for facilities required to meet the needs of the consumer." It does not matter that Ridgewood is now the owner of the lands in Ho–Ho–Kus. If it were not in such ownership, on what principle could Ridgewood condemn this particular piece of land in Ho–Ho–Kus for water storage purposes, notwithstanding the zoning limitation? R.S. 40:62–49(g), N.J.S.A., authorizes a municipality to purchase, condemn or otherwise acquire "the necessary lands, and rights or interests in lands, and water rights and rights of flowage or diversion, within or without the municipality, for the purpose of a water supply, or an additional water supply, and for the connection thereof with the municipality,...."

This provision by its own terms has to do with water rights and rights of flowage or diversion for the purpose of a water supply and connection thereof with the municipality; and, without undertaking a more specific delineation of the terms, it is enough to say that they patently do not include the use of Ridgewood's lands in Ho–Ho–Kus for the erection of a water tower contrary to local use-zoning, to serve the inhabitants of three nearby municipalities as well as its own, and the land, if in other proprietorship, could not in this context have been condemned for such use. The condemnation statute has no such sweep. There is no showing of need for land in Ho–Ho–Kus for the given purpose, much less the land in question; presumably, the motivating consideration is the economic advantage of using land now in Ridgewood's ownership, even though in part beyond its borders in an area restricted against such use. R.S. 40:62–65, N.J.S.A., requiring the consent of the other municipality for the extension of pipes and mains, is significant in this regard. Why this particular provision if there be the claimed broad power to condemn? Can it be that, though consent be required for the mere extension of pipes and mains, Ridgewood may, *ex proprio vigore*, store and distribute water to other municipalities through a plant maintained in Ho–Ho–Kus' highest class residence district? It is to be borne in mind that Ho–Ho–Kus has no interest whatever in the operation; neither it nor its inhabitants are to have water service from Ridgewood. Ridgewood may undertake to supply water to other municipalities, but not by subverting Ho–Ho–Kus' zone plan, and thus to lay the burden on its neighbor, *in invitum*. Simple justice so ordains....

I submit that there is no jurisdiction in equity, nor at law, for that matter, to enjoin submission by Ho–Ho–Kus (and such is a postulate of the majority opinion) to this invasion of its first-class residence zone by an alien use deemed by the court to be "reasonable" in its exercise as compared with other more conspicuous means of accomplishing the same end. And if the given use of its lands in Ho–Ho–Kus is not subject to the established use-restrictions, then is it reasonable thus to outlaw a much less expensive mechanism, both as to capital outlay and cost of operation, and in the face of expert opinion evidence that "a gravity flow system would yield a better quality of water"? Compare Wallerstein v. Westchester

Joint Water Works, 166 Misc. 34, 1 N.Y.S.2d 111 (Sup. Ct. 1937). There, also, the water tower had been almost completed. And if the whole of the land so used were situated in Ridgewood, could the gravity-flow use be enjoined in equity as arbitrary on the hypothesis that since the ground-level mechanism is feasible, Ridgewood "should have assumed (the greater) cost rather than visit the burden of an elevated structure of 160 feet upon the municipalities"? The choice of means would then rest in the discretion and judgment of the local authority. It is, I would suggest, the zoning restriction established by Ho–Ho–Kus that alone restrains Ridgewood's use of the lands in question.

We have here the problem of a local political boundary dividing an expanse of land area peculiarly suitable for the highest residence use, and so zoned by the adjoining municipalities save that in one a variant use is allowable that is denied in the other, a border conflict involving something more than the mere nonconforming use of Ridgewood's land in Ho–Ho–Kus. Ho–Ho–Kus may assert its sovereignty over lands within its limits, except as otherwise ordained by the Legislature, but it cannot oppose a different use of adjacent lands in Ridgewood unless such use constitutes a nuisance—a clash of interests that suggests the wisdom of coordinate inter-municipal action for the essential common good.

I would affirm the judgment and remand the cause with direction to stay execution until plaintiff is afforded an opportunity to take such further action in the light of the foregoing considerations as it may be advised.

■ PROCTOR, J., joins in this opinion.

NOTES

1. How does the court know that Ridgewood's construction of the elevated water storage tank was "unreasonable"? The court suggests that the elevated tank saved Ridgewood $66,000 and delivered a better quality of water. How can a system that provides these benefits be deemed unreasonable? Assume that the only adverse effect generated by the tower was that six homes in Ho–Ho–Kus had less attractive views and their homes diminished in value $12,000 each. Would construction of the elevated tank be unreasonable? What if the diminution in value was $10,000 per home? Now would the construction be unreasonable? The court suggests that in each case, the answer must be "Yes," because Ho–Ho–Kus received none of the benefit of the facility and thus should have to bear none of the burden. Is there an alternative conception of "reasonableness" that might lead to a different result? Finally, assume that each of the six homes diminished in value by $100 as a result of construction of the tower. Again, that burden would be imposed on Ho–Ho–Kus residents who received none of the benefits.

These three possibilities (diminution in value by $12,000, $10,000, and $100) suggest different approaches to the question of when it is "reasonable" for one locality to impose costs on another. Given that localities have incentives to capture for themselves the benefits of their activities and to impose the costs of those activities on others, it may be useful to consider what kinds of constraints are placed on localities by each of these interpretations. In the first situation, Ridgewood will have incurred a benefit of $66,000 (considering cost savings as the only relevant benefit for the time being), but will have done so only by imposing costs of $72,000 on others. This appears to be the most blatant sort of expropriation from nonresidents, in that, from a social perspective, it creates waste by imposing total costs in excess of total benefits. Assuming that the political process worked in Ridgewood, the Village would not have erected a water tower within its own boundaries if the project created costs in excess of benefits, and the court may be read as refusing to allow Ridgewood to treat nonresidents worse than it treats its own residents.

But now assume the second situation, i.e., that the benefits to Ridgewood residents exceed the costs to nonresidents. It is still the case that nonresidents receive no benefit, but—from the social perspective—their losses are outweighed by the gains to Ridgewood. Is this sufficient to render the action of Ridgewood "reasonable"? Is this what the court means by "reasonable"? Or would the court invalidate any plan that imposed costs on nonresidents who received no benefit from the activity, regardless of how many benefits were obtained by residents of the locality that initiated the activity? To test this latter proposition, consider whether the court would or should have found Ridgewood's conduct unreasonable if the savings to Ridgewood of $66,000 had required losses of $100 to each of six nonresidents, or a total of $600. If you take seriously the court's proposition that Ridgewood should not be able to impose any costs on nonresidents who do not benefit from the project, even these relatively small costs should be sufficient to offset substantial benefits. Yet that result would seem counterproductive from the social perspective. Maybe the court is suggesting that both the imposition of costs on nonbeneficiaries *and* the presence of benefits in excess of costs should be factors in the determination of reasonableness, but that neither, standing alone, should be conclusive. In that case, it might matter *by how much* internal benefits exceed external costs.

Of course, one way to address the problem would be to require Ridgewood to compensate the nonresidents for their losses. Presumably, Ridgewood would then internalize the full effects of their activity and would engage in the activity only if benefits exceeded costs. At the same time, those who were burdened in order to make Ridgewood better off would at least receive some offsetting monetary benefit. The problem with this scenario is that the statute does not appear to authorize compensation. Indeed, it is unclear that compensation would be desirable insofar as it raises questions of valuation and administrative costs that might be so difficult and costly as to deter otherwise socially useful activities.

Finally, consider the extent to which it is possible to quantify the full effects of municipal activities for purposes of determining whether a proposed project is "reasonable" or not under the social cost accounting definition used in the previous paragraphs. Construction of some municipal projects, such as airports, or roadway construction, may disrupt neighborhoods or communities in ways that are difficult to evaluate or compensate. How, for instance, does one evaluate the loss of a community when a neighborhood is bisected by a major highway that makes access to former neighbors more difficult? In these situations, efforts to use cost and benefit calculations may be unavailing. Given that localities have incentives systematically to obtain benefits for residents and to impose costs on nonresidents, do the difficulties of evaluation and compensation raise questions about the propriety of the court's presumption that a municipality is not bound by the host municipality's zoning ordinances?

2. What role is the court playing in *Village of Ridgewood*? Assume that all the adverse effects of the water tower had been visited on Ridgewood residents. Would you anticipate the same level of intervention by the court? Why?

3. As might be anticipated at this point in the course, the ability of a municipality to exercise extraterritorial jurisdiction is governed by statute. The extent to which a municipality must involve residents of the outlying jurisdiction in any decision affecting their welfare is discussed below. See Holt Civic Club v. City of Tuscaloosa, page 136 supra. Constitutional limitations only become an issue, however, when localities have received the appropriate state legislative authority. A survey of these statutes reveals that a few states grant complete police powers over contiguous unincorporated areas. See, e.g., N.D. Cent. Code. § 40–06–01(2). Most states that permit the exercise of extraterritorial powers do so on a far more limited scale. Several states permit central cities to regulate activities ranging from land use to forms of entertainment, explosives, and health-related activities (garbage, cemeteries, or pollutants). See Comment, The Constitutionality of the Exercise of Extraterritorial Powers by Municipalities, 45 U. Chi. L. Rev. 151 (1977).

City of Everett v. Snohomish County

772 P.2d 992 (Wash. 1989).

■ ANDERSEN, JUSTICE.

Facts of Case

This "sibling rivalry" case involves a zoning dispute between a county and city. Snohomish County claims its zoning authority is paramount and the City of Everett claims it is not. It is the City's argument that the statutes empowering the City to dispose of its sewage sludge and solid waste, together with the City's general eminent domain power, establish its authority to locate a disposal facility in the County even though it does not comply with the County's zoning regulations.

The City of Everett owns and operates a sewage treatment plant on Smith Island in the estuary of the Snohomish River. At this facility the City discharges treated domestic, commercial and industrial wastes into the

Snohomish River. It does so subject to effluent limitations and monitoring and reporting requirements imposed by a state permit.

In September 1985, the United States Environmental Protection Agency (EPA) found that the City had violated the permit requirements by allowing the accumulation of sewage sludge or solid wastes in the facility's treatment lagoons, thereby reducing that facility's treatment capacity. The EPA ordered the City to submit a plan and schedule for removal and disposal of the excess sludge. In its effort to comply with the EPA order, the City formulated a sludge management program which entailed removal of the sludge to a 952–acre site on nearby Ebey Island. This site, on another island in the Snohomish River, lies outside the City and within unincorporated Snohomish County.

The City then acquired an option to purchase the Ebey Island property and applied to the Snohomish Health District for a sludge utilization permit. The health district agreed to issue this permit on condition that the City first obtain a zoning code conditional use permit from the County. The City applied for a permit, but a Snohomish County hearing examiner denied the application. In so doing, the examiner found that the sludge exhibited high levels of heavy metals and that the property was characterized by low soil pH, flooding and a high water table. It was the examiner's conclusion that the City's proposed use of the site was incompatible with the use of surrounding property for agricultural purposes. The Snohomish County Council upheld the decision.

The City thereupon brought this action against Snohomish County and the Snohomish County Council, hereinafter collectively referred to as the County. The City moved for summary judgment in its favor on the siting dispute and the Superior Court granted it.

The County petitioned this court for direct review. We granted review and address the critical issue in the case.

Issue

Are the land use activities of an intruding subunit of government (the City) immune from the zoning regulations of the host subunit of government (the County)?

Decision

CONCLUSION. Legislative intent determines whether the intruding subunit of government (the City) is immune from the zoning regulations of the host subunit (the County). In reviewing the statutes empowering the pertinent activities of both subunits of government in this case, it is apparent that the intent of the Legislature is that the City be required to comply with the County's zoning regulations in establishing a sewage sludge and solid waste disposal site in the County.

The problem presented in this case is but illustrative of the broader problem of an almost unlimited range of potential controversies that can develop when push comes to shove between various subunits of government. Where all else fails, it is incumbent upon the courts to determine which subunit of government, if any, has the paramount authority in a given situation. A review of the numerous cases on the subject nationwide suggests that the most vexing of such problems are those involving the siting of unpopular but essential facilities such as sewage treatment, sewage sludge and solid waste disposal, penal and certain health care institutions. It is very clear, particularly in the case of sewage and solid waste disposal facilities, that while everyone contributes to the problem, no one wants to be part of the solution.

Since this case involves a zoning dispute, it is appropriate to note one preliminary matter. This is, that while it has sometimes been declared to be a general rule that zoning regulations or restrictions of a subunit of government do not apply to the State, its agencies and subunits of government, unless the Legislature has manifested a contrary intent, this court has declined to adopt any such blanket rule of governmental immunity from local zoning ordinances.

In past years, in deciding controversies involving zoning conflicts between subunits of government, particularly before the present day profusion of municipal corporations and state and local agencies, courts tended to resort to four traditional "tests."

One such test is the superior sovereignty test. Under this test, where one governmental unit seeks immunity from the zoning restrictions of another governmental unit, the unit which is higher in the governmental hierarchy will be held to prevail. The difficulty with this test is that " 'superior authority' in the political hierarchy does not necessarily imply superior ability in allocating land uses."[7]

A second of these traditional tests is the governmental-proprietary test. Using this test, a subunit of government will be deemed immune from conflicting zoning regulations when it performs governmental functions, but will be subject to such regulations when it acts in a proprietary capacity. A review of the cases applying this test, however, demonstrates that different courts often reach entirely different conclusions on similar facts.

A third test used is the eminent domain test. Under the eminent domain test, any governmental unit with condemnation authority may be considered automatically immune from zoning restrictions. This test, however, is susceptible to being used as a bludgeon to allow an intruding subunit of government to locate an offensive facility, such as a sewage treatment plant, anywhere in a host subunit's area that it wants to, even, for example, in a single family residential neighborhood. Nor is there anything in the constitutional requirement that eminent domain powers be exercised only when there is a finding that property is being taken for a "public use" that offers protection in such cases. This, in turn, is in disregard of the State's expressed concern for planned environments. As

---

7. Note, Governmental Immunity from Local Zoning Ordinances, 84 Harv. L. Rev. 869, 878 (1971).

one commentator observes, "when eminent domain power automatically immunizes a governmental unit from zoning regulation, there is no institutional incentive to comply with local zoning ordinances and no sanction other than adverse public opinion for irresponsible land-use decisions."

Yet a fourth test is the balancing of interests test, which has been favored by some commentators and courts dissatisfied with the other tests noted. This more recent test calls for taking into consideration the nature of the governmental unit seeking immunity, the land use involved and its effects as well as the public interest served by such use. Attractive as this particular test appears to some who find the other tests unsatisfactory, it is an approach which has now been rejected by some courts which consider it to be discredited. The Supreme Court of Pennsylvania, for example, calls the test too uncertain, pointing to the inevitable litigation that results from the knowledge that the next court might "balance" differently from the last. The Supreme Court of Georgia, in turn, finds this balancing test to be "too nebulous and judicially unmanageable."

Considerable dissatisfaction with all four of these traditional tests and combinations thereof has been evinced by numerous courts and commentators for a variety of reasons, including the reasons noted in connection with the preceding enumeration of the tests. They have been variously described as simplistic abstractions, unhelpful epithets, ritualistic, enigmatic and as leading to the proliferation of inconsistent results.

As one court cogently explains, "[t]he question of what governmental units or instrumentalities are immune from municipal land use regulations, and to what extent, is not one properly susceptible of absolute or ritualistic answer. Courts have, however, frequently resolved such conflicts in perhaps too simplistic terms and by the use of labels rather than through reasoned adjudication of the critical question of which governmental interest should prevail in the particular relationship or factual situation."

An example of what is wrong with simply applying one of the four labels and letting the results fall where they may is illustrated by a case argued by counsel herein, and in which case the facility of the intruding sewer district was ruled immune from the County's zoning regulations. That case was South Hill Sewer Dist. v. Pierce Cy., 22 Wash. App. 738, 591 P.2d 877 (1979). There, the Court of Appeals had before it a situation, to use the court's terminology, where Pierce County had "repudiated" its previous approval of the siting of a sewage treatment facility in Pierce County, or "[b]luntly put, they reneged, . . ." The Court of Appeals applied the eminent domain test to justify striking down the county's action and to allow siting the facility in the county. To follow the eminent domain test in *South Hill* was one thing, but to follow it here, or, for example, to use it to justify placement of a sewage treatment or waste disposal facility in a residential neighborhood, are entirely different propositions indeed.

The crux of the matter, as we see it, and the real determinant in cases such as this, is legislative intent. As one court has aptly summarized in the context of a sibling rivalry zoning dispute,

> [the] common thread running through these cases, although not clearly stated in some, is an attempt to determine the intent of the Legislature when deciding whether a governmental unit is subject to a municipal zoning ordinance. We hold today that the legislative intent, where it can be discerned, is the test for determining whether a governmental unit is immune from the provisions of local zoning ordinances.

We agree with this statement of the law and so hold in this case. This succinct statement of principle fully accords with the views this court has previously expressed in analogous cases. While it is true that the analysis of statutory law to discern legislative intent is often difficult, particularly where the legislative design is complex, it is nevertheless a judicial function which courts are both capable of and experienced at performing.

This principle is essentially predicated on the proposition that under our state constitutional system, it is the Legislature which not only enacts statutes enabling municipalities to adopt zoning ordinances, but which also enacts the statutes which authorize state agencies and other subunits of government to undertake governmental functions. By the same measure, the Legislature is also the body empowered to prescribe by statute the extent to which state facilities should be subject to local land use controls, as well as to confer authority upon subunits of government and to establish priorities between them.

A situation was before this court in Edmonds School Dist. 15 v. Mountlake Terrace, 77 Wash. 2d 609, 465 P.2d 177 (1970) which was similar in many respects to the one now before us. There, the dispute was between a school district, which had the authority to build, operate and maintain public schools, and a city, which had the authority to adopt and enforce its own building code.

In *Edmonds*, after discussing the sources of the authority of the school district and the city, we observed that

> the state, in delegating to school districts power to build, maintain and operate public schools, has not prescribed minimum standards for street offsets, nor directed that building permits be waived in the construction of public school buildings or additions. It has left its subordinate municipalities free to regulate each other in those activities which traditionally are thought to lie within their particular competence and are more proximate to their respective functions.

Edmonds, at 613, 465 P.2d 177. Then, after reviewing other similar cases, we concluded:

> There is little doubt that the State of Washington . . . has the constitutional power to prescribe standards for and regulate school construction, and may, as an attribute of its sovereignty, deprive municipalities of any voice in these matters. But the state has not thus far exercised this power nor prohibited cities from exacting a building permit fee, nor relieved school districts within the corporate limits of a city from paying such fee or complying with the setback provisions of the municipal building code. Unless the state has, so to speak, preempted the field of building standards or specifically ousted the municipality of jurisdiction over school construction, we think the school district is obliged to comply with the minimum standards set forth in the city's building code.

Edmonds, at 614, 465 P.2d 177.

So it is here that the Legislature, in empowering cities to acquire property within and without their corporate limits and to acquire, construct and operate sewage and solid waste disposal systems, did not provide detailed standards to guide them in selecting sites to dispose of their sewage sludge and solid wastes. Nor did the Legislature purport to preempt the field of zoning regulations or otherwise oust the counties from their zoning authority. Thus, as we perceive the intent of the Legislature through a careful examination of the statutory authority extended by the Legislature to both the City and the County in the matters before us, the City was obliged to comply with the County's zoning code. Accordingly, we conclude that the trial court erred in ruling to the contrary. Further, to the extent that the substances the City seeks to dispose of in this case may be deemed solid waste, as we believe they can be, compliance with pertinent zoning requirements is mandated by statute.

Just as one subunit of government cannot intrude its unpopular facilities upon a host subunit of government any place it desires simply because it has the power of eminent domain, neither may the host subunit of government erect an impenetrable barrier against intrusions by other subunits of government just because it possesses the zoning power.... In the case before us, the County has provided a number of areas where the zoning is appropriate for solid waste disposal.

Furthermore, zoning ordinances of one subunit of government do not necessarily conflict with another governmental subunit's authority to condemn; reasonable zoning ordinances limit but do not necessarily eliminate another governmental subunit's power to locate its facilities through its eminent domain power.

The parties inform us that most disputes of this kind are resolved amicably between the subunits of government involved. This is as it should be and is a practice to be earnestly commended. As one court has observed in a similar situation, "[o]ur burgeoning population and the rapidly diminishing available land make it all the more important that the use of land be intelligently controlled. This can only be done by a cooperative effort between interested parties who approach their differences with an open mind and with respect for the objectives of the other." Such cooperation is particularly appropriate where, as here, the differences are between governmental subunits, both dedicated to serving the public.

In the trial court, the City argued to the effect, as it again does here, that the Court of Appeals decision in South Hill Sewer Dist. v. Pierce Cy., 22 Wash. App. 738, 591 P.2d 877 (1979) stands for the proposition that the City's power of eminent domain exempts it from obtaining a County conditional use permit. As discussed above, that is incorrect. In this case, the experienced trial court found that view of *South Hill* difficult to accept, but ultimately did accept it while at the same time inviting the County to appeal and seek review of that issue. To the extent that *South Hill* does not accord with our decision herein, it is overruled. The remaining issues referred to in the briefs are nonmeritorious.

Reversed and remanded.

NOTES

1. *Legislative Intent and Extraterritorial Authority.* By this point in the course, it should be obvious that the search for legislative intent at the state level is fraught with difficulty. But that task is made more problematic by the court's assumption that, in the absence of a finding of intent to the contrary, the proper presumption is that the legislature intended that the host jurisdiction's zoning regulations prevail. Why should this be the presumption? Why not presume that, in the absence of a finding of intent to the contrary, the invading jurisdiction may ignore the host jurisdiction's zoning regulations? Given that explicit statements of legislative intent will likely be rare, so that the default rule we choose will typically be the rule that governs the case, why should one presumption be favored over the other? For a broader interpretation of legislative grants of extraterritorial power, see Village of Schiller Park v. City of Chicago, 186 N.E.2d 343 (Ill. 1962). In that case, the village sought to restrain Chicago from condemning land within the village to construct an airport. The village claimed that a statute authorizing Chicago to condemn land within or without corporate limits for airport purposes restricted the extraterritorial condemnation power to unincorporated land. The court disagreed:

> We are unable to accept appellants' arguments. The statute is clear in authorizing the taking for airport purposes of "any land either within or outside" the municipality. No exception is expressed for land within some other municipality, nor do we think such an exception can be implied from the statute as a whole. The intent is evident to encourage and facilitate the establishment of airports, and to delegate broad authority in determining the amount and location of land to be taken for such purpose.

186 N.E.2d at 344. Can you defend an alternative construction of the legislature's intent?

2. *The Standard for Immunity.* As the above cases reveal, there is substantial disparity in the way that jurisdictions handle issues of intergovernmental immunity from zoning. The results can obviously be dramatically different. In Hayward v. Gaston, 542 A.2d 760 (Del. 1988), the court held that a state agency that desired to operate a residential treatment center for emotionally disturbed juveniles in an area zoned single-family residential was subject to county zoning regulations under a balancing of interests test. In Edelen v. County of Nelson, 723 S.W.2d 887 (Ky. Ct. App. 1987), the court determined that a county, as an instrumentality of the state, had statutory authority to construct a jail without regard to local zoning regulations. The Ohio Supreme Court tried to split the difference in Taylor v. State, Dept. of Rehabilitation and Correction, 540 N.E.2d 310 (Ohio Ct. App. 1988). There the court held that there was no ironclad requirement that the state comply with a local zoning ordinance, but did require the state to exercise its "best efforts" to accommodate local land-use restrictions. The state was not required, however, to comply with city procedures for obtaining a variance. For a general discussion, see Laurie Reynolds, The

Judicial Role in Intergovernmental Land Use Disputes: The Case Against Balancing, 71 Minn. L. Rev. 611 (1987).

3. *State Immunity from Local Zoning Ordinances.* The state, being a superior of its political subdivisions, is not subject to local zoning ordinances in the absence of a contrary statute. See Morse v. Vermont Division of State Buildings, 388 A.2d 371 (Vt. 1978), where the court permitted the state to construct a sewer project for a state-operated facility without obtaining a permit that was required under local zoning regulations. The definition of the "state" for these purposes, however, may be narrowly construed. In Incorporated Village of Nyack v. Daytop Village, Inc., 583 N.E.2d 928 (N.Y. 1991), the New York Court of Appeals held that the fact that a state had oversight of the location and operation of a substance abuse facility and the licensing of the operator did not preempt local zoning laws. Thus, the operator of the facility had to comply with applicable local zoning laws.

4. *Intergovernmental Condemnation and Compensation.* Similar conflicts arise where one locality seeks to condemn property owned by another and each locality alleges that it desires to dedicate the property to a public use. In City of New Haven v. Town of East Haven, 402 A.2d 345 (Conn. Super. Ct. 1977), the latter town had instituted eminent domain proceedings to take three parcels of land located within its boundaries, but which were owned by New Haven and which were held for future expansion of an airport located in both localities. East Haven desired to develop the land as an industrial park. The court granted that both proposed uses constituted "public uses" sufficient to justify government ownership. It also determined that New Haven's holding property for future use did not diminish the public use of the property. On these premises, the court concluded that the prior public use of the property by New Haven precluded East Haven from exercising its eminent domain powers to condemn the property. On the prior use doctrine, see Condemnation Of Public Entity's Land, 35 A.L.R.3d 1293.

What if the City of New Haven wanted to condemn an existing industrial park in East Haven in order to expand the airport? Presumably, since both uses would be public uses, this dispute would be resolved in favor of maintaining the industrial park. Does it make sense to settle these issues by reference to a first-in-time, first-in-right standard? There was some language in the court's opinion that East Haven could have used other land for an industrial park. Is there reason to favor a nonrelocatable use over a relocatable one? Does your answer depend on whether you think that East Haven is acting strategically, that is, whether East Haven is less concerned about losing an industrial park than it is about gaining a larger airport as a neighbor with all the attendant problems of noise and traffic? To what extent should we credit East Haven's desire to avoid being a "dumping ground" for the airport? After all, New Haven may well have placed the airport at the edge of its own boundaries for the very purpose of externalizing noise and traffic problems.

Condemnation poses a threat of majoritarian ganging up because the interests of so many can outweigh the interests of the few. In condemnations involving takings of private property, this possibility is mitigated by the requirement that just compensation be paid. The expected result is that the majority, who must pay the compensation, will only authorize the exercise of eminent domain where the benefits of the acquisition outweigh the costs borne by the condemnor. See Frank I. Michelman, Property, Utility, and Fairness: Comments on the Ethical Foundations of "Just Compensation" Law, 80 Harv. L. Rev. 1165 (1967). But the constitutional requirement that just compensation be paid applies (literally, at least) only where government condemns private property. Condemnation of public property in another jurisdiction, therefore, does not necessarily trigger a claim for compensation. Some courts resort to the dubious governmental/proprietary distinction to require compensation when the condemned public property is deemed to be held in a proprietary capacity. This distinction has been applied both when the state condemns municipal property, see, e.g., Proprietors of Mt. Hope Cemetery v. City of Boston, 33 N.E. 695 (Mass. 1893); City of Cambridge v. Commissioner of Public Welfare, 257 N.E.2d 782 (Mass. 1970), and when one municipality condemns property of another, see, e.g., Town of Winchester v. Cox, 26 A.2d 592 (Conn. 1942). If extraterritorial condemnation is permitted without compensation, what is to prevent the condemnor from acting in a manner that adversely affects the condemnee, notwithstanding the absence of offsetting benefits to anyone? Is it relevant that extraterritorial eminent domain powers must be specifically granted by statute? If the legislative process achieves the same objective of allowing intergovernmental condemnation only when the interests of the condemnor exceed those of the condemnee (perhaps the equivalent of what some courts consider to be a "higher use" of the property), then an award of compensation might be superfluous. Given the costs associated with valuing the property and adjudicating just compensation claims, legislative determination can be an attractive substitute for compensation. Are there reasons to believe that the legislative process will pay insufficient attention to the question of whether the proposed condemnation returns net benefits? For a general discussion of intergovernmental condemnation, see John M. Payne, Intergovernmental Condemnation as a Problem in Public Finance, 61 Tex. L. Rev. 949 (1983).

There exist alternative justifications for compensation of private property takings. One is to prevent an unfair distribution of the burdens of government onto those whose property is condemned. Another is to minimize risks that might otherwise discourage investment. Does either of these rationales require compensation where intergovernmental takings are involved? For a negative answer (although endorsing compensation to prevent "fiscal illusion" and exploitation by dominant political factions), see Michael H. Schill, Intergovernmental Takings and Just Compensation: A Question of Federalism, 137 U. Penn. L. Rev. 829 (1989).

When the federal government condemns property owned by a state or political subdivision (a right that exists under the supremacy clause of the federal Constitution), just compensation must be paid. The amount of compensation that is "just" is not necessarily measured by the condemnee's cost of obtaining a substitute facility, but must be calculated in the same manner as compensation to private condemnees. See United States v. 50 Acres of Land, 469 U.S. 24 (1984).

5. *Intergovernmental Conflict Over Undesirable Land Uses.* As the *Snohomish County* case indicates, one area of increasing interlocal conflict involves the siting of activities that promote social welfare generally, but that impose a disproportionate burden on the area immediately surrounding the activity. These "locally undesirable land uses" include waste disposal facilities, homeless shelters, treatment centers, and half-way houses, as well as more traditional uses such as airports and prisons. The debate about the siting of these activities (which involves both interlocal and intralocal decisions) has intensified with allegations that siting decisions tend to place a disproportionate number of these uses in areas that are inhabited by the poor or by racial minorities. Claims of "environmental racism" have spurred both caselaw and legal commentary. See, e.g., Kristin Shrader–Frechette, Environmental Justice (2002); Regina Austin & Michael Schill, Black, Brown, Poor & Poisoned: Minority Grassroots Environmentalism and the Quest for Eco–Justice, 1 Kan. J.L. Pub. Poly. 69 (1991); Richard J. Lazarus, Pursuing "Environmental Justice": The Distributional Effects of Environmental Protection, 87 Nw. U.L. Rev. 787 (1993); R.I.S.E., Inc. v. Kay, 768 F.Supp. 1144 (E.D. Va. 1991), aff'd, 977 F.2d 573 (4th Cir. 1992); Coalition of Bedford–Stuyvesant Block Assn., Inc. v. Cuomo, 651 F.Supp. 1202 (E.D.N.Y. 1987). The likelihood of success for these claims in the federal arena has been reduced by recent court decisions. In Alexander v. Sandoval, 532 U.S. 275 (2001), the Supreme Court held that citizens could not bring a cause of action to compel compliance with federal regulations designed to remedy disparate impact discrimination. The Third Circuit applied the rationale of that decision to deny any private right of action under 42 U.S.C. § 1983 for citizens to enforce disparate impact regulations. South Camden Citizens in Action v. New Jersey Department of Environmental Protection, 274 F.3d 771 (3d Cir. 2001). See Sten–Erik Hoidal, Note, Returning to the Roots of Environmental Justice: Lessons from the Inequitable Distribution of Municipal Services, 88 Minn. L. Rev. 193 (2003).

Siting of undesirable land uses is problematic because it raises conflicts between distributional concerns and efficiency concerns. As a matter of efficiency, it may make sense to place certain land uses in relatively poor areas. Facilities that tend to service the poor, such as homeless shelters, might not provide optimal levels of service if they were located in neighborhoods far from the intended beneficiaries. More controversially, some might claim that, to the extent that governmental or social resources are dedicated to purchase property and convert it to undesirable uses, low-value property should be utilized. Otherwise, both the price of the facilities and the costs related to their adverse effects will be higher than is necessary. As a result, fewer governmental or social resources will be available for other public goods and services.

As a matter of distributional justice, however, these efficiency justifications, even if true, pose serious problems. Certainly it seems unjust, from a redistributional perspective, to place the most burdensome land uses in the same area, particularly where that area already suffers other social burdens such as poverty. This may be true even where undesirable land uses generate some benefits, such as employment opportunities and an economic base for the immediate neighborhood. Given current distributions of wealth and the immobility of those who prefer not to live around undesirable land uses, it cannot be said that those who desire to take advantage of the benefits of these uses can do so, while those who desire to escape are similarly able to satisfy their preferences. Indeed, claims of redistribution suggest that these burdensome land uses should disproportionately be located in relatively wealthy areas. Such claims, however, run headlong into the efficiency argument that placing undesirable uses in wealthy areas creates excess costs.

For an excellent review and analysis of the arguments surrounding the siting of undesirable land uses and the difficulties inherent in efforts to calculate a fair distribution of these burdensome, but necessary, activities, see Vicki Been, What's Fairness Got to Do With It? Environmental Justice and the Siting of Locally Undesirable Land Uses, 78 Cornell L. Rev. 1001 (1993); Symposium on Urban Environmental Justice, 21 Ford. Urb. L.J. 431–856 (1994).

C. SHARING THE "BURDEN" AMONG COMMUNITIES

Throughout these materials there has been a constant tension between the desire for municipalities to achieve some level of autonomy that allows residents to define and satisfy their own preferences for public goods or services and their view of the "good life," and the demands of the larger community that the residents of a particular community might prefer to avoid. As we saw in Chapter 2, this tension sometimes arises because one locality seeks to promote a particular lifestyle or identity that is less pluralistic than that of the society at large and incompatible with the desires of some prospective residents. On other occasions, however, tension arises because one locality seeks to avoid certain burdens, often redistributive ones, because the related benefits will tend to accrue to nonresidents.

The question of burden sharing may be addressed either at the state level or the regional level. In some instances, courts have imposed on the state an obligation to provide a good or service to all state residents. Thus, if the court finds that local governments fail to provide an appropriate level of the good or service, the state may be required to take control. This might entail either financing the activity at the state rather than the local level, mandating local allocations of the good or service, or both.

Alternatively, burden sharing may be limited to regional issues. These issues often arise in discussions about the relationship between central cities and their suburbs. For some, suburbs are viewed as attracting individuals who can afford to move away from the fiscal and social problems identified with central cities, but who still take advantage of central cities as places of work or entertainment. Unless some legal mechanism can be created to require suburbs to contribute to the relatively poor central cities, it is alleged, the relatively wealthy will be able to seize on legal doctrines such as the concept of local autonomy to insulate themselves from regional problems.

In the material that follows, we examine both forms of interlocal burden sharing. We explore the issue of statewide financing of schools as an example of the first form. We then turn to the relationship between cities and suburbs to investigate the extent to which localities in the same region have obligations to assist each other and, to the extent that they do, the extent to which legal intervention is necessary to overcome tendencies to avoid those obligations.

1. SCHOOL FINANCE

After the United States Supreme Court rejected (largely on the grounds that wealth is not a suspect classification) a federal constitutional equal protection challenge to the property tax system of financing education, San Antonio Independent School District v. Rodriguez, 411 U.S. 1 (1973), the debate about local control over public education financing shifted to the states. Numerous state supreme courts have struck down financing schemes on state constitutional grounds. The following excerpt from an article by Professor Richard Briffault describes some of the issues that have dominated the debate. Among the most critical issues in this debate, often addressed only implicitly, is whether "fair" financing of education requires only that each locality have access to an "adequate" level of financing, above which any locality may spend, or whether each locality within a state is constrained to provide only an "equal" level of financing, above which it may not spend even if it has available resources. For further reflections on the role of the concept of "local autonomy" in determining the desirability of a statewide financing system for public schools, see Richard Briffault, The Role of Local Control in School Finance Reform, 24 Conn. L. Rev. 773 (1992); Eric P. Christofferson, *Rodriguez* Reexamined: The Misnomer of "Local Control" and a Constitutional Case for Equitable Public School Funding, 90 Geo. L.J. 2553 (2002).

As you read the following materials, consider what other services fall into the same category as education for purposes of equalization. Why is it appropriate to have different levels of garbage collection or police protection among localities if it is inappropriate to have different levels of educational funding? Does the answer lie in the "fundamental" nature of the need for education or in the positive externalities generated by an educated populace? Does it lie in the possibility that one service is less susceptible to the kinds of market variations that the Tiebout hypothesis assumes would cause different groups of people to prefer different levels of service? Or is it that there is greater variance in the demand for education, so people will have difficulty moving to a jurisdiction that offers their desired level of schooling, but they will not have similar difficulty moving to a jurisdiction that offers their desired level of other services? Finally, is education in particular an issue on which we are willing to impose a certain standard regardless of people's preferences because we believe that people will otherwise underinvest in education? If this is the explanation, how does it differ from fire protection, road paving, or mosquito spraying?

Richard Briffault, Our Localism, Part I: The Structure of Local Government Law

90 Colum. L. Rev. 1, 24–30 (1990).

Courts in twenty-four states have considered state constitutional challenges to the local property tax system of financing public schools. The school finance reform plaintiffs usually based their claims on two state constitutional provisions—state equal protection clauses, and state constitutional articles directing legislatures to provide for free public school systems. In fourteen states, the courts sustained the traditional school financing system, rejecting both state equal protection and education article claims. In six states, the courts found the existing school finance systems invalid under the state education articles, although they rejected or declined to reach equal protection claims. In four states, the courts determined that the traditional finance system violates state equal protection clauses. An underlying concern in most of the school finance cases was the impact on local autonomy of a legal requirement that would force interlocal equalization of school spending. Even in the decisions invalidating the traditional school finance systems local control was an important concern, as courts troubled by the consequences of limited local tax bases for educational quality in poorer districts sought to reconcile a greater fiscal role for the state with the preservation of local school autonomy.

For many of the state courts upholding the existing local property tax-based system of financing public schools, their decisions reflected a background assumption of local self-government which implicitly requires local control of the funding and provision of basic government services. They treated local control of education, in particular, as essential to the existence of effective local self-government. The local public school was proclaimed "the center of community life, and a pillar in the American conception of freedom in education and in local control of institutions of local concern." Schools were seen as the focal points of local communities, and local control of education deemed critical to local autonomy. The state constitutional provisions directing the state legislatures to provide for the "maintenance and support" of public schools did not bar the delegation of the administration and funding of education to localities. Rather, many courts read their constitutional traditions to mandate the preservation of local control.

Most of these courts candidly acknowledged the existence of substantial spending differences among school districts, which they recognized were largely attributable to differences in local taxable wealth. But they held that interlocal wealth and spending differences did not undermine the legitimacy of the state delegation of responsibility for the provision and funding of basic public services to local governments. Instead, unequal levels of local services and taxation were deemed characteristic of the American system of local government. "We are all aware," observed the Arizona Supreme Court, "that the citizens of one county shoulder a different tax burden than the citizens of another and also receive varying degrees of governmental service." Differences in the cost and quality of services were seen as inherent in the structure of the local government system.

Plaintiffs did not challenge the value of local control, but rather contended that true local control for all districts required reformation of the finance system and a greater fiscal role for the state, since poorer districts lacked the taxable wealth to support the educational programs their residents desired. They asserted that local administrative authority could be preserved even if fiscal responsibility were shifted to the state. Typically, plaintiffs did not call for full state funding of education, centralized state determination of educational needs and allocation of resources, or the interdistrict equalization of spending. Instead, plaintiffs usually sought only to equalize local fiscal capacity.

To combine the benefits of local administrative authority with state fiscal support for poorer districts, school finance reformers advanced the "district power equalization" concept. Under district power equalization, local school districts would continue to set the local tax rate, determine the portion of local revenues allocated to education and, within the school budget, fix local spending priorities. However, the states would have to guarantee all districts an equal fiscal capacity for school programs. Spending differences could still result, but they would be due to local decisions concerning the level of taxation and the share of local budgets to be devoted to schools, not to differences in tax base.

The state courts that sustained the traditional school finance system generally rejected the idea that local control could be separated from local fiscal responsibility. The New York Court of Appeals, for example, concluded that there was "a direct correlation" between the implementation of local interests and local control of school budgets. Only through control of the school budget could local residents "exercise a substantial control over the educational opportunities made available in their districts." Local fiscal responsibility was an incentive to community involvement, and it enabled district residents to decide the size of the school budget and the allocation of funds among school programs. Thus, local fiscal control was deemed essential for local administrative control.

These courts considered district power equalization to be inconsistent with local control. Given the enormous interlocal wealth differences, guaranteeing the poorest school district the same fiscal capacity as the richest would be prohibitively expensive for the states. The only way to make district power equalizing fiscally feasible would be to limit spending by the richer districts. The richer districts strenuously opposed any such limitation on the use of their tax bases for their schools. Many state courts agreed. The New York Court of Appeals indicated that a basic element of local autonomy was the right of individual school districts to spend more than the state requires or more than their neighbors can afford: "Any legislative attempt to make uniform and undeviating the educational opportunities offered by the several hundred local school districts ... would inevitably work the demise of the local control of education available to students in the individual districts."

Indeed, judicial commitment to local control led the Wisconsin Supreme Court in Buse v. Smith to invalidate state legislation that would have equalized interdistrict spending in part by limiting the power of wealthier communities to outspend poorer ones. The Wisconsin plan provided a guaranteed tax base for poorer districts and required that districts with spending or assessed valuation per capita above a certain level make payments, euphemistically styled "negative aid," into a state fund. The "negative aid" payments would supplement the state's revenues for "positive aid" to poorer districts while restricting the capacity of rich districts to outspend the poor. The Wisconsin Supreme Court declared "negative aid" an unconstitutional infringement upon the autonomy of the richer districts.

The *Buse* court invoked the traditional doctrine that school districts, like all other political subdivisions, are "but arms of the state, carrying out state duties." Nonetheless, the court treated the districts as autonomous entities and placed local rights on a par with state power. Although the Wisconsin Constitution obligated the state legislature to provide for free public schools "which shall be as nearly uniform as practicable," the text of the constitution referred to "district schools." Based on that language, the Wisconsin Supreme Court held the local interest in administering and funding schools to be of constitutional magnitude. Rather than giving the state plenary power over local districts, the court found a "state-local control dichotomy" to be "part and parcel of the constitution." Thus, the court concluded, "[l]ocal districts retain the control to provide educational opportunities over and above those required by the state and they retain the power to raise and spend revenue '... for the support of common schools therein.'" Local autonomy meant that the state could neither limit district spending in the name of interlocal equality nor require one school district to contribute to the support of a poorer neighbor.

Edgewood Independent School District v. Kirby [Edgewood I]

777 S.W.2d 391 (Tex. 1989).

Opinion

■ MAUZY, JUSTICE.

At issue is the constitutionality of the Texas system for financing the education of public school children. Edgewood Independent School District, sixty-seven other school districts, and numerous individual school children and parents filed suit seeking a declaration that the Texas school financing system violates the Texas Constitution. The trial court rendered judgment to that effect and declared that the system violates the Texas Constitution, article I, section 3, article I, section 19, and article VII, section 1. By a 2–1 vote, the court of appeals reversed that judgment and declared the system constitutional. 761 S.W.2d 859 (1988). We reverse the judgment of the court of appeals and, with modification, affirm that of the trial court.

The basic facts of this case are not in dispute. The only question is whether those facts describe a public school financing system that meets the requirements of the Constitution. As summarized and excerpted, the facts are as follows.

There are approximately three million public school children in Texas. The legislature finances the education of these children through a combination of revenues supplied by the state itself and revenues supplied by local school districts which are governmental subdivisions of the state. Of total education costs, the state provides about 42 percent, school districts provide about fifty percent, and the remainder comes from various other sources including federal funds. School districts derive revenues from local ad valorem property taxes, and the state raises funds from a variety of sources including the sales tax and various severance and excise taxes.

There are glaring disparities in the abilities of the various school districts to raise revenues from property taxes because taxable property wealth varies greatly from district to district. The wealthiest district has over $14,000,000 of property wealth per student, while the poorest has approximately $20,000; this disparity reflects a 700 to 1 ratio. The 300,000 students in the lowest-wealth schools have less then 3 percent of the state's property wealth to support their education while the 300,000 students in the highest-wealth schools have over 25 percent of the state's property wealth; thus the 300,000 students in the wealthiest districts have more than eight times the property value to support their education as the 300,000 students in the poorest districts. The average property wealth in the 100 wealthiest districts is more then twenty times greater than the average property wealth in the 100 poorest districts. Edgewood I.S.D. had $38,854 in property wealth per student; Alamo Heights I.S.D., in the same county, has $570,109 in property wealth per student....

Because of the disparities in district property wealth, spending per student varies widely, ranging from $2,112 to $19,333. Under the existing system, an average of $2,000 more per year is spent on each of the 150,000 students in the wealthiest districts than is spent on the 150,000 students in the poorest districts.

The lower expenditures in the property-poor districts are not the result of lack of tax effort. Generally, the property-rich districts can tax low and spend high while the property-poor districts must tax high merely to spend low. In 1985–86, local tax rates ranged from $.09 to $1.55 per $100 valuation. The 100 poorest districts had an average tax rate of 74.5 cents and spent an average of $2,978 per student. The 100 wealthiest districts had a average tax rate of 47 cents and spent an average of $7,233 per student. In Dallas County, Highland Park I.S.D. taxed at 35.16 cents and spent $4,836 per student while Wilmer–Hutchins I.S.D. taxed at $1.05 and spent $3,513 per student. In Harris County, Deer Park I.S.D. taxed at 64.37 cents and spent $4,846 per student while its neighbor North Forest I.S.D. taxed at $1.05 and yet spent only $3,182 per student. A person owning an $80,000 home with no homestead exemption would pay $1,206 in taxes in the east Texas low-wealth district of Leveretts Chapel, but would pay only $59 in the west Texas high-wealth district of Iraan–Sheffield. Many districts have become tax havens. The existing funding system permits "budget balanced districts" which, at minimal tax rates, can still spend above the statewide average; if forced to tax at just average tax rates, these districts would generate additional revenues of more than $200,000,000 annually for public education.

Property-poor districts are trapped in a cycle of poverty from which there is no opportunity to free themselves. Because of their inadequate tax base, they must tax at significantly higher rates in order to meet minimum requirements for accreditation; yet their educational programs are typically inferior. The location of new industry and development is strongly influenced by tax rates and the quality of local schools. Thus, the property-poor districts with their high tax rates and inferior schools are unable to attract new industry or development and so have little opportunity to improve their tax base.

The amount of money spent on a student's education has a real and meaningful impact on the educational opportunity offered that student. High-wealth districts are able to provide for their students broader educational experiences including more extensive curricula, more up-to-date technological equipment, better libraries and library personnel, teacher aides, counseling services, lower student-teacher ratios, better facilities, parental involvement programs, and drop-out prevention programs. They are also better able to attract and retain experienced teachers and administrators.

The differences in the quality of educational programs offered are dramatic. For example, San Elizario I.S.D. offers no foreign language, no pre-kindergarten program, no chemistry, no physics, no calculus, and no college preparatory or honors program. It also offers virtually no extracurricular activities such as band, debate, or football. At the time of trial, one-third of Texas school districts did not even meet the state-mandated standards for maximum class size.

The great majority of these are low-wealth districts. In many instances, wealthy and poor districts are found contiguous to one another within the same county.

Based on these facts, the trial court concluded that the school financing system violates the Texas Constitution's equal rights guarantee of article I, section 3, the due course of law guarantee of article I, section 19, and the "efficiency" mandate of article VII, section 1. The court of appeals reversed. We reverse the judgment of the court of appeals and, with modification, affirm the judgment of the trial court.

Article VII, section 1 of the Texas Constitution provides:

> A general diffusion of knowledge being essential to the preservation of the liberties and rights of the people, it shall be the duty of the Legislature of the State to establish and make suitable provision for the support and maintenance of an efficient system of public free schools.

The court of appeals declined to address petitioners' challenge under this provision and concluded instead that its interpretation was a "political question." Said the court:

> That provision does, of course, require that the school system be "efficient," but the provision provides no guidance as to how this or any other court may arrive at a determination of what is efficient or inefficient. Given the enormous complexity of a school system educating three million children, this Court concludes that which is, or is not, "efficient" is essentially a political question not suitable for judicial review.

761 S.W.2d at 867. We disagree. This is not an area in which the Constitution vests exclusive discretion in the legislature; rather the language of article VII, section 1 imposes on the legislature an affirmative duty to establish and provide for the public free schools. This duty is not committed unconditionally to the legislature's discretion, but instead is accompanied by standards. By express constitutional mandate, the legislature must make "suitable" provision for an "efficient" system for the "essential" purpose of a "general diffusion of knowledge." While these are admittedly not precise terms, they do provide a standard by which this court must, when called upon to do so, measure the constitutionality of the legislature's actions. See Williams v. Taylor, 83 Tex. 667, 19 S.W. 156 (1892). We do not undertake this responsibility lightly and we begin with a presumption of constitutionality. See Texas Public Bldg. Authority v. Mattox, 686 S.W.2d 924, 927 (Tex. 1985). Nevertheless, what this court said in only its second term, when first summoned to strike down an act of the Republic of Texas Congress, is still true:

> [W]e have not been unmindful of the magnitude of the principles involved, and the respect due to the popular branch of the government.... Fortunately, however, for the people, the function of the judiciary in deciding constitutional questions is not one which it is at liberty to decline.... [We] cannot, as the legislature may, avoid a measure because it approaches the confines of the constitution; [we] cannot pass it by because it is doubtful; with whatever doubt, with whatever difficulties a case may be attended, [we] must decide it, when it arises in judgment.

Morton v. Gordon, Dallam 396, 397–398 (Tex. 1841). If the system is not "efficient" or not "suitable," the legislature has not discharged its constitutional duty and it is our duty to say so.

The Texas Constitution derives its force from the people of Texas. This is the fundamental law under which the people of this state have consented to be governed. In construing the language of article VII, section 1, we consider "the intent of the people who adopted it." Director of Dept. of Agriculture and Envt. v. Printing Indus. Assn., 600 S.W.2d 264, 267 (Tex. 1980); see also Smissen v. State, 71 Tex. 222, 9 S.W. 112, 116 (1888). In determining that intent, "the history of the times out of which it grew and to which it may be rationally supposed to have direct relationship, the evils intended to be remedied and the good to be accomplished, are proper subjects of inquiry." Markowsky v. Newman, 134 Tex. 440, 136 S.W.2d 808, 813 (1940). However, because of the difficulties inherent in determining the intent of voters over a century ago, we rely heavily on the literal text. We seek its meaning with the understanding that the Constitution was ratified to function as an organic document to govern society and institutions as they evolve through time. See generally *Printing Indus.*, 600 S.W.2d at 268–269.

The State argues that, as used in article VII, section 1, the word "efficient" was intended to suggest a simple and inexpensive system. Under the Reconstruction Constitution of 1869, the people had been subjected to a militaristic school system with the state exercising absolute authority over the training of children. See Tex. Const. art. VII, § 1, interp. commentary (Vernon 1955). Thus, the State contends that delegates to the 1875 Constitutional Convention deliberately inserted into this provision the word "efficient" in order to prevent the establishment of another Reconstruction-style, highly centralized school system.

While there is some evidence that many delegates wanted an economical school system, there is no persuasive evidence that the delegates used the term "efficient" to achieve that end. See Journal of the Constitutional Convention of the State of Texas 136 (Oct. 8, 1875); S. McKay, Debates in the Texas Constitutional Convention of 1875, at 107, 217, 350–351 (1930). It must be recognized that the Constitution requires an "efficient," not an "economical," "inexpensive," or "cheap" system. The language of the Constitution must be presumed to have been carefully selected. Leander Indep. School Dist. v. Cedar Park Water Supply Corp., 479 S.W.2d 908 (Tex. 1972); Cramer v. Sheppard, 140 Tex. 271, 167 S.W.2d 147 (Tex. 1943). The framers used the term "economical" elsewhere and could have done so here had they so intended.

There is no reason to think that "efficient" meant anything different in 1875 from what it now means. "Efficient" conveys the meaning of effective or productive results and connotes the use of resources so as to produce results with little waste; this meaning does not appear to have changed over time. E.g., IV Oxford English Dictionary 52 (1971); Webster's Third New International Dictionary 725 (1976). One dictionary used by the framers defined efficient as follows:

> Causing effects; producing results; actively operative; not inactive, slack or incapable; characterized by energetic and useful activity....

N. Webster, An American Dictionary of the English Language 430 (1864). In 1890, this court described "efficient" machinery as being "such as is capable of well producing the effect intended to be secured by the use of it for the purpose for which it was made." Maxwell v. Bastrop Mfg. Co., 77 Tex. 233, 14 S.W. 35, 36 (1890).

Considering "the general spirit of the times and the prevailing sentiments of the people," it is apparent from the historical record that those who drafted and ratified article VII, section 1 never contemplated the possibility that such gross inequalities could exist within an "efficient" system. See Mumme v. Marrs, 120 Tex. 383, 40 S.W.2d 31, 35 (1931). At the Constitutional Convention of 1875, delegates spoke at length on the importance of education for all the people of this state, rich and poor alike. The chair of the education committee, speaking on behalf of the majority of the committee, declared:

> [Education] must be classed among the abstract rights, based on apparent natural justice, which we individually concede to the State, for the general welfare, when we enter into a great compact as a commonwealth. I boldly assert that it is for the general welfare of all, rich and poor, male and female, that the means of a common school education should, if possible, be placed within the reach of every child in the State.

S. McKay, Debates in the Texas Constitutional Convention of 1875 198 (1930). Other delegates recognized the importance of a diffusion of knowledge among the masses not only for the preservation of democracy, but for the prevention of crime and for the growth of the economy. See, e.g., id. at 199–200, 216–217, 335.

In addition to specific comments in the constitutional debates, the structure of school finance at the time indicates that such gross disparities were not contemplated. Apart from cities, there was no district structure for schools nor any authority to tax locally for school purposes under the Constitution of 1876. B. Walker and W. Kirby, The Basics of Texas Public School Finance 5, 86 (1986). The 1876 Constitution provided a structure whereby the burdens of school taxation fell equally and uniformly across the state, and each student in the state was entitled to exactly the same distribution of funds. See Tex. Const. art. VII, § 5 (1876). The state's school fund was initially apportioned strictly on a per capita basis. B. Walker and W. Kirby at 21. Also, a poll tax of one dollar per voter was levied across the state for school purposes. Id. These per capita methods of taxation and of revenue distribution seem simplistic compared to today's system; however they do indicate that the people were contemplating that the tax burden would be shared uniformly and that the state's resources would be distributed on an even, equitable basis.

If our state's population had grown at the same rate in each district and if the taxable wealth in each district had also grown at the same rate, efficiency could probably have been maintained within the structure of the present system. That did not happen. Wealth, in its many forms, has not appeared with geographic symmetry. The economic development of the state has not been uniform. Some cities have grown dramatically, while their sister communities have remained static or have shrunk. Formulas that once fit have been knocked askew. Although local conditions vary, the constitutionally imposed state responsibility for an efficient education system is the same for all citizens regardless of where they live.

We conclude that, in mandating "efficiency," the constitutional framers and ratifiers did not intend a system with such vast disparities as now exist. Instead, they stated clearly that the purpose of an efficient system was to provide for a "*general* diffusion of knowledge." (Emphasis added.) The present system, by contrast, provides not for a diffusion that is general, but for one that is limited and unbalanced. The resultant inequalities are thus directly contrary to the constitutional vision of efficiency.

The State argues that the 1883 constitutional amendment of article VII, section 3 expressly authorizes the present financing system. However, we conclude that this provision was intended not to preclude an efficient system but to serve as a vehicle for injecting more money into an efficient system. James E. Hill, a legislator and supporter of the 1883 amendment, argued:

> If [article VII, section 1] means anything, and is to be enforced, then additional power must be granted to obtain the means "to support and maintain" an efficient system of public free schools. What is such a system, then? is the question. I have examined the laws of the older States of this Union, especially those noted for efficient free schools, and not one is supported alone by State aid, but that aid is supplemented always by local taxation.... When a man tells me he favors an efficient system of free schools, but is opposed to local taxation by districts or communities to supplement State aid, he shows that he ignores the successful systems of other States, or he is misleading in what he says.

Galveston Daily News, August 10, 1883, at 3, col. 9 (interview with Hon. James E. Hill). Governor O. M. Roberts also gave strong support to the 1883 amendment. In his address to the 18th Legislature, Governor Roberts directed the legislature's attention to the efficiency standard set by article VII, section 1 and said: "The standard fixed in law is certainly high enough to enable the masses of people generally, who receive the benefit of it, to have that general diffusion of knowledge...." Speech of Gov. O. M. Roberts, S. J. of Tex., 18th Leg., Reg. Sess. 15 (1883). He then explained the need for the amendment by stating that the practical remedy for the attainment of the objective of efficiency was the formation of school districts with the power of taxation. Thus, article VII, section 3 was an effort to make schools more efficient and cannot be used as an excuse to avoid efficiency. See also 761 S.W.2d at 874 (further discussing the historical context of the amendment).

In the context of article VII, section 1, the legislature has expressed its understanding of the term "efficient" for a long time even though it has never given the term full effect. Sixty years ago, the legislature enacted the Rural Aid Appropriations Act with the express purpose of "equalizing the educational opportunities afforded by the State...." 1929 Tex. Gen. Laws, ch. 14 at 252 (3rd called session). Again, in creating the Gilmer–Aikin Committee to study school finance, the legislature indicated an awareness of this obligation when it spoke of "the foresight and evident intention of the founders of our State and the framers of our State Constitution to provide equal educational advantages for all." Tex. H. Con. Res. 48, 50th Leg. (1948). Moreover, section 16.001 of the legislatively enacted Education

Code expresses the state's policy that "a thorough and efficient system be provided ... so that each student ... shall have access to programs and services ... that are substantially equal to those available to any similar student, notwithstanding varying economic factors." Not only the legislature, but also this court has previously recognized the implicit link that the Texas Constitution establishes between efficiency and equality. In Mumme v. Marrs, 40 S.W.2d at 37, we stated that rural aid appropriations "have a real relationship to the subject of equalizing educational opportunities in the state, and tend to make our system more efficient...."

By statutory directives, the legislature has attempted through the years to reduce disparities and improve the system. There have been good faith efforts on the part of many public officials, and some progress has been made. However, as the undisputed facts of this case make painfully clear, the reality is that the constitutional mandate has not been met.

The legislature's recent efforts have focused primarily on increasing the state's contributions. More money allocated under the present system would reduce some of the existing disparities between districts but would at best only postpone the reform that is necessary to make the system efficient. A band-aid will not suffice; the system itself must be changed.

We hold that the state's school financing system is neither financially efficient nor efficient in the sense of providing for a "general diffusion of knowledge" statewide, and therefore that it violates article VII, section 1 of the Texas Constitution. Efficiency does not require a per capita distribution, but it also does not allow concentrations of resources in property-rich school districts that are taxing low when property-poor districts that are taxing high cannot generate sufficient revenues to meet even minimum standards. There must be a direct and close correlation between a district's tax effort and the educational resources available to it; in other words, districts must have substantially equal access to similar revenues per pupil at similar levels of tax effort. Children who live in poor districts and children who live in rich districts must be afforded a substantially equal opportunity to have access to educational funds. Certainly, this much is required if the state is to educate its populace efficiently and provide for a general diffusion of knowledge statewide.

Under article VII, section 1, the obligation is the legislature's to provide for an efficient system. In setting appropriations, the legislature must establish priorities according to constitutional mandate; equalizing educational opportunity cannot be relegated to an "if funds are left over" basis. We recognize that there are and always will be strong public interests competing for available state funds. However, the legislature's responsibility to support public education is different because it is constitutionally imposed. Whether the legislature acts directly or enlists local government to help meet its obligation, the end product must still be what the constitution commands—i.e., an efficient system of public free schools throughout the state. See Lee v. Leonard Indep. School Dist., 24 S.W.2d 449, 450 (Tex. Civ. App.–Texarkana 1930, writ ref'd). This does not mean that the state may not recognize differences in area costs or in costs associated with providing an equalized educational opportunity to atypical students or disadvantaged students. Nor does it mean that local communities would be precluded from supplementing an efficient system established by the legislature; however any local enrichment must derive solely from local tax effort.

Some have argued that reform in school finance will eliminate local control, but this argument has no merit. An efficient system does not preclude the ability of communities to exercise local control over the education of their children. It requires only that the funds available for education be distributed equitably and evenly. An efficient system will actually allow for more local control, not less. It will provide property-poor districts with economic alternatives that are not now available to them. Only if alternatives are indeed available can a community exercise the control of making choices.

Our decision today is not without precedent. Courts in nine other states with similar school financing systems have ruled those systems to be unconstitutional for varying reasons.[6] DuPree v. Alma School Dist. No. 30, 279 Ark. 340, 651 S.W.2d 90 (1983); Serrano v. Priest, 5 Cal. 3d 584, 96 Cal. Rptr. 601, 487 P.2d 1241 (1971); Horton v. Meskill, 172 Conn. 615, 376 A.2d 359 (Conn. 1977); Rose v. Council for Better Educ. [790 S.W. 2d 186 (Ky. 1989)]; Helena Elementary School Dist. No. 1 v. State, 769 P.2d 684 (Mont. 1989); Robinson v. Cahill, 62 N.J. 473, 303 A.2d 273, cert. denied, 414 U.S. 976, 94 S. Ct. 292, 38 L. Ed. 2d 219 (1973); Seattle School Dist. No. 1 v. State, 90 Wash. 2d 476, 585 P.2d 71 (1978); Pauley v. Kelly, 162 W. Va. 672, 255 S.E.2d 859 (1979); Washakie County School Dist. No. 1 v. Herschler, 606 P.2d 310 (Wyo.), cert. denied, 449 U.S. 824, 101 S. Ct. 86, 66 L. Ed. 2d 28 (1980). . . .

Although we have ruled the school financing system to be unconstitutional, we do not now instruct the legislature as to the specifics of the legislation it should enact; nor do we order it to raise taxes. The legislature has primary responsibility to decide how best to achieve an efficient system. We decide only the nature of the constitutional mandate and whether that mandate has been met. Because we hold that the mandate of efficiency has not been met, we reverse the judgment of the court of appeals. The legislature is duty-bound to provide for an efficient system of education, and only if the legislature fulfills that duty can we launch this great state into a strong economic future with educational opportunity for all.

---

6. But see Shofstall v. Hollins, 110 Ariz. 88, 515 P.2d 590 (1973); Lujan v. Colorado State Bd. of Educ., 649 P.2d 1005 (Colo. 1982); McDaniel v. Thomas, 248 Ga. 632, 285 S.E.2d 156 (1981); Thompson v. Engelking, 96 Idaho 793, 537 P.2d 635 (1975); Hornbeck v. Somerset County Bd. of Educ., 295 Md. 597, 458 A.2d 758 (1983); Board of Educ., Levittown v. Nyquist, 57 N.Y.2d 27, 453 N.Y.S.2d 643, 439 N.E.2d 359 (1982), appeal dism'd, 459 U.S. 1138, 103 S. Ct. 775, 74 L. Ed. 2d 986 (1983); Board of Educ. v. Walter, 58 Ohio St. 2d 368, 390 N.E.2d 813 (1979), cert. denied, 444 U.S. 1015, 100 S. Ct. 665, 62 L. Ed. 2d 644 (1980); Fair School Finance Council of Oklahoma, Inc. v. Oklahoma, 746 P.2d 1135 (Okla. 1987); Olsen v. State, 276 Or. 9, 554 P.2d 139 (1976); Danson v. Casey, 484 Pa. 415, 399 A.2d 360 (1979); Richland County v. Campbell, 294 S.C. 346, 364 S.E.2d 470 (1988).

Because of the enormity of the task now facing the legislature and because we want to avoid any sudden disruption in the educational processes, we modify the trial court's judgment so as to stay the effect of its injunction until May 1, 1990. However, let there be no misunderstanding. A remedy is long overdue. The legislature must take immediate action. We reverse the judgment of the court of appeals and affirm the trial court's judgment as modified.

NOTES

1. *Subsequent History*. Note that in its 1989 *Edgewood* decision the Texas Supreme Court assigned primary responsibility for developing a constitutional means of financing the Texas public schools to the legislature and stayed the trial court's injunction on the existing system until such time as the court believed the legislature could reasonably act.

It was not until 1995, however, that the Texas Supreme Court was able to find constitutional one of the legislature's several enactments reforming the state's education finance system. See Edgewood Independent School District v. Meno, 917 S.W.2d 717 (Tex. 1995) [*Edgewood IV*]. And even then the Court cautioned that "the challenge to the school finance law based on inadequate provision for facilities fails only because of an evidentiary void. Our judgment in this case should not be interpreted as a signal that the school finance crisis in Texas had ended." Id. at 725.

The court in *Edgewood IV* summarized the legislative plan that it was approving as follows:

> Like the systems reviewed in our previous opinions, Senate Bill 7 provides a two-tiered education finance structure known as the Foundation School Program. The stated purpose of Tier 1 is to guarantee "sufficient financing for all school districts to provide a basic program of education that meets accreditation and other legal standards." Tex. Educ. Code § 16.002(b). For each student in average daily attendance, a district is entitled to a basic allotment of $2,300, which is subject to various adjustments and special allotments to reflect variations in actual cost. Tex. Educ. Code § 16.101. To be eligible for the program, a district must raise its local share of funding, defined as the amount produced when an effective tax rate of $0.86 per $100 valuation is applied to the taxable value of property in the district for the prior tax year. Tex. Educ. Code § 16.252. To the extent that an $0.86 effective tax rate fails to produce the adjusted allotment from the district's own tax base, the State makes up the difference. Tex. Educ. Code § 16.254.
>
> Tier 2 comprises a guaranteed yield system, the stated purpose of which is "to provide each school district with the opportunity to supplement the basic program at a level of its own choice and with access to additional funds for facilities." Tex. Educ. Code § 16.301.[5] For every cent of additional tax effort beyond the $0.86 required for Tier 1, the State guarantees a yield of $20.55 per

5. See also Tex. Educ. Code § 16.002(b) ("The second tier provides a guaranteed yield system of financing to provide all school districts with substantially equal access to funds to provide an enriched program and additional funds for facilities.").

weighted student.[6] Tex. Educ. Code § 16.302. To the extent that an additional cent of tax effort fails to yield that amount from the district's own tax base, the State makes up the difference. Tex. Educ. Code § 16.254. The yield guarantee applies only to $0.64 of tax effort beyond the $0.86 required for Tier 1, so no Tier 2 funds are provided for any effective tax rates exceeding $1.50. Tex. Educ. Code § 16.303.

While this two-tiered structure is, for the most part, carried forward from prior systems, Senate Bill 7 does contain a significant new feature: it imposes a cap on a school district's taxable property at a level of $280,000 per student. Tex. Educ. Code § 36.002....

In addition to reforming the financing system, Senate Bill 7 makes significant educational reforms in Chapter 35 of the Texas Education Code, entitled "Public School System Accountability." In this Chapter, the Legislature defines the contours of its constitutional duty to provide a "general diffusion of knowledge" by articulating seven public education goals.[7] These goals emphasize academic achievement. Most notably, the Legislature envisions that all students will have access to a high quality education and that the achievement gap between property-rich and property-poor districts will be closed. The Legislature has established a system of student assessment and school district accreditation to measure each district's progress toward meeting these goals. Tex. Educ. Code § 35.021–.121. Districts that chronically fail to maintain accreditation standards are subject to penalties, including dissolution of the offending school district and its annexation to another district. Tex. Educ. Code §§ 35.041, .062, .121.

917 S.W.2d at 727–729.

---

6. The Tier 2 allotment is based on a district's weighted students in average daily attendance (WADA). Based on the evidence at trial, a district's WADA roughly equals 1.3 times its average daily attendance.

7. The goals of public education are:

GOAL A: All students shall have access to an education of high quality that will prepare them to participate fully now and in the future in the social, economic, and educational opportunities available in Texas.

GOAL B: The achievement gap between educationally disadvantaged students and other populations will be closed. Through enhanced dropout prevention efforts, the graduation rate will be raised to 95 percent of students who enter the seventh grade.

GOAL C: The state shall demonstrate exemplary performance in comparison to national and international standards for student performance.

GOAL D: A well-balanced and appropriate curriculum will be provided to all students.

GOAL E: Qualified and effective personnel will be attracted and retained. Adequate and competitive compensation commensurate with responsibilities will be ensured. Qualified staff in critical shortage areas will be recruited, trained, and retained.

GOAL F: The organization and management of all levels of the education system will be productive, efficient, and accountable.

GOAL G: Instruction and administration will be improved through research that identifies creative and effective methods. Demonstration programs will be developed and local initiatives encouraged for new instructional arrangements and management techniques. Technology will be used to increase the equity, efficiency, and effectiveness of student learning, instructional management, staff development, and administration.

Tex. Educ. Code 35.001.

In holding constitutional the financing plan established by Senate Bill 7, the court observed that:

> Under the system established by Senate Bill 7, [the disparities in school districts' ability to raise revenue have] changed dramatically. Instead of a 700–to–1 ratio between the richest and poorest districts, there is now a 28–to–1 ratio. Furthermore, the $20.55 yield guarantee within Tier 2 effectively reduces this ratio further. The State meets its constitutional duty to provide a general diffusion of knowledge through funding provided by Tiers 1 and 2, and the disparity in access to funds within these tiers is 1.36–to–1. Children who live in property-poor districts and children who live in property-rich districts now have substantially equal access to the funds necessary for a general diffusion of knowledge. Thus, we hold that Senate Bill 7 is efficient under article VII, section 1 of the Texas Constitution.

Id. at 730–731.

In 2003, four Texas school districts argued to the Texas Supreme Court that the existing school finance plan violated Article VIII, section 1–e of the Texas Constitution, which states that "No State ad valorem taxes shall be levied upon any property within this State." West Orange–Cove Consolidated I.S.D. v. Alanis, 107 S.W.3d 558 (Tx. 2003) [*West Orange–Cove I*]. The plaintiff school districts contended "that they and other districts have been forced to tax at maximum rates set by statute in order to educate their students. These taxes, they say, have become indistinguishable from a state ad valorem tax prohibited by article VIII, section 1–e." Id. at 562. Both the trial court and the court of appeals dismissed the case on the pleadings, but for different reasons. Id. at 562–63. The Texas Supreme Court, however, reversed the judgment of the court of appeals, and remanded the case to the trial court for further proceedings not inconsistent with its opinion.

On remand, the district court, after a five-week bench trial, found in favor of the school districts and enjoined the state from continuing to fund the public schools. West Orange–Cove Consolidated I.S.D. v. Neeley, 176 S.W.3d 746, 753–54 (Tx. 2005) [*West Orange–Cove II*]. The district court issued its judgment on November 30, 2004, but stayed the effect of its injunction until October 1, 2005 " 'to give the Legislature a reasonable opportunity to cure the constitutional deficiencies in the finance system.' " Id. at 754. Although the legislature was not able to enact legislation by the end of August 2005, the district court's injunction was stayed by the State's appeal to the Texas Supreme Court.

In its November 22, 2005 decision, the Texas Supreme court postponed the effective date of the district court's injunction to June 1, 2006, id. at 799, and stated, id. at 754:

> We now hold, as did the district court, that local ad valorem taxes have become a state property tax in violation of article VIII, section 1–e, as we warned ten years ago they inevitably would, absent a change in course, which has not happened. Although the districts have offered evidence of deficiencies in the public school finance system, we conclude that those deficiencies do not amount to a violation of article VII, section 1. We remain convinced, however, as we were sixteen years ago, that defects in the structure of the public school finance

> system expose the system to constitutional challenge. Pouring more money into the system may forestall those challenges, but only for a time. They will repeat until the system is overhauled.

By mid–May 2006, both the Texas House and Senate had passed legislation aimed at remedying the "state property tax" that the Court had held unconstitutional. The official Enrolled Bill Summary, http://www.legis.state.tx.us/BillLookup/BillSummary.aspx?LegSess=793&Bill=HB, stated in relevant part:

> Property Tax Relief and Public School Funding:.... The bill includes provisions for the commissioner of education to compute the amount to which each district is entitled, taking into account a variety of specified factors; [and] appropriates $3.825 billion to the Texas Education Agency for distribution to school districts in accordance with these provisions;....
>
> The bill replaces the fixed dollar amounts currently specified for the Tier 1 basic allotment, the Tier 2 guaranteed yield level, and the Chapter 41 equalized wealth level (currently $2,537 per pupil, $27.14 per pupil per penny of tax effort above $0.86, and $305,000 per pupil, respectively) and sets those at varying amounts based on the level of school district tax effort. The basic allotment is set at the per-pupil amount that would be available to the district at the 88th percentile of per-pupil wealth at a tax rate of $0.86 per $100 valuation (estimated to be $2,748 for the 2006–2007 school year). The guaranteed yield level is set at varying amounts based on a district's tax effort....

For discussion of the two post–*Edgewood I* plans for redesigning school finance that the legislature passed but that the Texas Supreme Court found unconstitutional, see Carrollton–Farmers Branch Independent School District v. Edgewood Independent School District, 826 S.W.2d 489 (Tex. 1992) [*Edgewood III*] (although legislature reduced financing disparities by requiring property taxes collected from wealthy school districts to be redistributed to poorer school districts within newly consolidated county districts, legislation created unconstitutional ad valorem tax; effect of ruling would be delayed to permit plan to be created by 1993–1994 school year); Edgewood Independent School District v. Kirby, 804 S.W.2d 491 (Tex. 1991) [*Edgewood II*] (statute that guaranteed revenue per student per each cent of local tax effort over specified minimum and that required periodic adjustments to minimize distinctions failed to remedy major causes of wide opportunity gaps between rich and poor school districts and hence was unconstitutional; statute failed to comprehensively restructure school finance system, as evidenced by failure to change district boundary lines to consolidate wealthy and poor districts).

2. *The Relationship Between Educational Inputs and Outputs.* In each of the first four *Edgewood* decisions, the Texas Supreme Court relied in large part on the difference in dollar inputs among school districts and the difference in programs available in different districts to indicate differences in educational quality. Similarly, the Supreme Court of New Jersey, in invalidating that state's school finance legislation, specified in great detail the differences among programs and physical facilities to establish that poor, urban school districts provided a significantly inferior quality of education. Abbott v. Burke, 575 A.2d 359 (N.J. 1990) [*Abbott II*]. The New

Jersey court indicated that poorer urban districts lacked the quality of science laboratories, foreign language programs, computer facilities, music programs, art programs, industrial arts programs, and physical amenities (e.g., heating, lighting, and lunch rooms) that existed in wealthier districts. The court concluded that the constitutional standard in New Jersey, which required the state to provide a "thorough and efficient" system of education, must be interpreted by reference to the ability of the educational system to prepare students to "compete in the marketplace" and to "take their fair share of leadership and professional positions." The court concluded that the programmatic disparities among districts precluded the urban poor from obtaining an education that would satisfy the standard. See also Abbott v. Burke, 643 A.2d 575 (N.J. 1994) [*Abbott III*] (finding Quality Education Act of 1990 unconstitutional as applied to the special needs districts (SNDs) because it failed to ensure parity of educational spending); Abbott v. Burke, 693 A.2d 417 (N.J. 1997) [*Abbott IV*] (finding financing system unconstitutional as applied to the SNDs because it failed to guarantee sufficient funds to enable students in those districts to achieve the requisite academic standards, and mandating, as an interim remedy, that the State provide parity funding for each SND for the 1997–1998 school year); Abbott v. Burke, 710 A.2d 450, 454 (N.J. 1998) [*Abbott V*] (explaining "remedial measures that must be implemented in order to ensure that public school children from the poorest urban communities receive the educational entitlements that the Constitution guarantees them"); Abbott v. Burke, 751 A.2d 1032, 1034 (N.J. 2000) [*Abbott VI*] (clarifying that *Abbott V* holds that "[t]he State is required to fund all of the costs of necessary facilities remediation and construction in the Abbott districts").

The relationship between local tax revenues and spending on education is uncontrovertible. Does low level of spending necessarily translate into low quality of education? Are there factors that account for educational quality that cannot be remedied by injecting more funds into the educational system? See, e.g., Michael Heise, The Courts, Education Policy, and Unintended Consequences, 11 Cornell J.L. & Pub. Pol'y 633, 656 n.148 (2002) (collecting sources debating whether money matters); William S. Koski & Rob Reich, When "Adequate" Isn't: The Retreat from Equity in Education Law and Policy and Why It Matters, 56 Emory L.J. 545, 547 (2006) (contending that relative educational quality may matter more than absolute educational quality). Studies to date reveal some, but small, improvement in student test performance subsequent to school finance reform. See, e.g., Thomas Downes, School Finance Reform and School Quality: Lessons from Vermont, in John Yinger (ed.), State Aid and the Pursuit of Educational Equity 283 (2004); David A. Card and A. Abigail Payne, School Finance Reform, the Distribution of School Spending, and the Distribution of Student Test Scores, 83 J. Pub. Econ. 49 (2002).

3. *Remedies for Unconstitutional School Finance.* The New Jersey Court in *Abbott II*, like the Texas Supreme Court in *Edgewood I*, did not seek to specify a plan that would pass constitutional muster. Rather, the court left to the legislature the obligation of filling in the details in accordance with the constitutional standard devised by the court. In New Jersey, the court mandated that any plan assure that educational funding for poorer urban districts is "substantially equal" to that of wealthy districts, where "assure" means that funding may not rely on local budgeting and taxing decisions. 575 A.2d at 408. Among the possible mechanisms that the court suggested the legislature might use was mandating the local share of the school district budget or determining a proper division between state aid and local funding. Id. at 408–12. For discussions of various possible remedies, see also, e.g., Comment, Private School Voucher Remedies in Education Cases, 62 Univ. of Chi. L. Rev. 795 (1995); Peter Enrich, Leaving Equality Behind: New Directions in School Finance Reform, 48 Vand. L. Rev. 101 (1995); Molly S. McUsic, The Future of *Brown v. Board of Education*: Economic Integration of the Public Schools, 117 Harv. L. Rev. 1334 (2004); Laurie Reynolds, Uniformity of Taxation and the Preservation of Local Control in School Finance Reform, 40 U.C. Davis L. Rev. 1835 (2007); James E. Ryan, Charter Schools and Public Education, 4 Stan. J. Civ. Rts. & Civ. Liberties 393 (2008); James E. Ryan & Michael Heise, The Political Economy of School Choice, 111 Yale L.J. 2043 (2002); James E. Ryan, Schools, Race, and Money, 109 Yale L.J. 249 (1999); Aaron Saiger, Disestablishing Local School Districts as a Remedy for Educational Inadequacy, 99 Colum. L. Rev. 1830 (1999).

If wealthy localities are constrained from using local taxes to support education in amounts well in excess of funding available from local taxes in poorer districts, does it necessarily follow that spending for education will become equalized? Are there other mechanisms that residents of wealthy school districts, or schools within those districts, will be able to use to continue a pattern of inequality? Might wealthy districts rely on private funds from residents to operate programs that would otherwise be eliminated when property taxes are redistributed to poorer districts? If so, would that simply replicate, at least in part, the inequalities that occur through local public financing? See John Schomberg, Equity v. Autonomy: The Problems of Private Donations to Public Schools, 1998 Ann. Surv. Am. L. 143.

4. *The Role of the Courts.* In some states, court challenges to property-tax-based school finance have become an effective means of reform. In addition to the various *Abbott* decisions, see supra and the nine cases cited in *Edgewood I*, 777 S.W.2d at 398, see supra page 858, see the cases cited in *West Orange–Cove II*, 176 S.W.3d 746, 780–781 n.183 (Tex. 2005), and Roosevelt Elementary School Dist. v. Bishop, 877 P.2d 806 (Ariz. 1994) (calling into doubt Shofstall v. Hollins, 515 P.2d 590 (Ariz. 1973)); DeRolph v. State, 677 N.E.2d 733 (Ohio 1997), clarified in 678 N.E.2d 886 (Ohio 1997) (per curiam); Tennessee Small Sch. Systems v. McWherter, 851 S.W.2d 139 (Tenn. 1993); Brigham v. State, 692 A.2d 384 (Vt. 1997). See also School Money Trials: The Legal Pursuit of Educational Adequacy (Martin R. West & Paul E. Peterson eds., 2007); Equity and Adequacy in Education Finance (Helen Ladd et al. eds., 1999); Karen Swenson, School Finance Reform Litigation: Why Are Some State Supreme Courts Activist and Others Restrained?, 63 Alb. L. Rev. 1147, 1148–49 (2000) (observing that while 17 state courts of last resort have invalidated local property tax-based school finance systems, that 26 state high courts have upheld their state's school funding system); John Dayton, *Serrano* and Its Progeny: An Analysis of 30 Years of School Funding Litigation, 157 Ed. Law Rep. 447 (2001).

Why should the judiciary become involved if state legislatures have been unwilling to intervene? Are there reasons why majoritarian decision-making is a questionable process for deciding how to fund education? Consider the following.

> The *Robinson* cases suggest that the inadequacy of particular school finance remedies may arise from two features of the legislative process that lead to systematic underrepresentation of the school finance plaintiff's interests. First, the disproportionate influence of property-rich districts in state legislatures often impedes the efforts of citizens of poorer districts to secure satisfactory legislative remedies. Although imperfect, the correlation between property wealth and political influence is significant enough to cast doubt upon the underlying premise of representative democracy that all citizens have equal access to the legislative arena. The New Jersey legislature's preservation of numerous provisions in the 1975 Act favoring property-rich districts reflected the power exercised by those districts....
>
> Second, collective action problems arising from voter unwillingness to pay for the higher taxes associated with school finance remedies also increase the difficulty of securing an adequate remedy. Assuming that a better-educated citizenry is a collective good produced by school finance reform, cooperation among taxpayers to finance the reform would enhance the political feasibility of a legislative remedy. However, the asymmetry of benefits for two subgroups of taxpayers—those with children in low-wealth school districts and all other taxpayers—undermines the prospects for cooperation. A low-wealth district parent gains her share of the collective good as well as a noncollective benefit, her child's improved education. In contrast, other taxpayers are likely to underestimate the collective benefit because the benefits of a better-educated citizenry are widely dispersed over time. Even if all taxpayers can maximize their welfare by cooperative support of the remedy, undervaluation of the collective benefit leads to self-interested behavior and a collective action problem. Moreover, the most concerned parents often have availed themselves of a substitute good for the noncollective benefit, such as schools in costlier suburbs or private schools, thereby further diminishing the possibility for collective action. The undervaluation of the collective benefit and the availability of substitute goods lead to taxpayer and legislative unwillingness to support a constitutionally adequate remedy.
>
> Additionally, some taxpayers without low-wealth district children may correctly perceive that their individual cost will outweigh their share of the collective gain, even if the collective benefit will produce a net societal gain. This group may reject higher taxes as well as the collective benefits generated by reform that is optimal for society as a whole. In the wake of *Abbott*, for example, the tax package needed to finance the new remedy stirred deep opposition to the reform itself among some New Jersey voters. Thus, the asymmetry of benefits can also create a collective action problem arising from a subgroup's rejection of the collective good.

Note, Unfulfilled Promises: School Finance Remedies and State Courts, 104 Harv. L. Rev. 1072, 1078–1081 (1991) (citations omitted). See also James E. Ryan, Standards, Testing, and School Finance Litigation, 86 Tex. L. Rev.

1223, 1225 (2008) (observing that "using standards and tests to define a court-enforced right to funding creates perverse incentives for legislatures to dilute standards and lower expectations. One way to make education cheaper, after all, is to lower the goals").

5. *A Nonjusticiable Political Question?* Several state supreme courts have declined to hear constitutional challenges to public school finance on the ground that the claims raise nonjusticiable political questions. See, e.g., the cases cited in *West Orange–Cove II*, 176 S.W.3d 746, 780 n.182 (Tex. 2005). These courts have held, inter alia, that the relevant constitutional provision does not provide a judicially manageable standard, see, e.g., Lobato v. State of Colorado, 216 P.3d 29, 39 (Colo. App. 2008), and that "ongoing judicial review of the school finance system under the [state constitution] raises the spectre of lengthy and potentially unending litigation," id. at 40. See also Nebraska Coalition for Educational Equity and Adequacy v. Heineman, 731 N.W.2d 164, 179, 183 (Neb. 2007) (holding that "there are no qualitative, constitutional standards for public schools that this court could enforce," and concluding that the "landscape is littered with courts that have been bogged down in the legal quicksand of continuous litigation and challenges to their states' school funding systems ... [and] we refuse to wade into that Stygian swamp").

Consider the response to such arguments by the Texas Supreme Court, which ultimately concluded "that the separation of powers does not preclude the judiciary from determining whether the Legislature has met its constitutional obligation to the people to provide for public education," *West Orange–Cove II*, 176 S.W.3d at 780–781:

> Nor do we agree with the State defendants that the constitutional standards of adequacy, efficiency, and suitability are judicially unmanageable. These standards import a wide spectrum of considerations and are admittedly imprecise, but they are not without content.... The judiciary is well-accustomed to applying substantive standards the crux of which is reasonableness....
>
> The State defendants argue that if the standards of article VII, section 1 had judicially manageable content, litigation over the constitutionality of the public education system would not have lasted as long as it has. It is true, of course, as this case illustrates, that disagreements over the construction and application of article VII, section 1 persist. But such disagreements are not unique to article VII, section 1; they persist as to the meanings and applications of due course of law, equal protection, and many other constitutional provisions. Indeed, those provisions have inspired far more litigation than article VII, section 1, which has been at the heart of only a few lawsuits in two decades. Moreover, the continued litigation over public school finance cannot fairly be blamed on constitutional standards that are not judicially manageable; the principal cause of continued litigation, as we see it, is the difficulty the Legislature has in designing and funding public education in the face of strong and divergent political pressures.

Id. at 778–779. Do you find the above arguments of the Texas Supreme Court persuasive?

6. Why should education be treated differently than other goods and services that are provided at the local level? Assume that residents of a relatively poor locality claim they are receiving a lower level of police services than residents of relatively wealthy localities. These residents may make claims very similar to those made in the school finance cases—police services are financed primarily from local taxes, wealthier areas can spend more on new technologies for police, can hire more officers per capita, and can afford more and better equipment than is found in poorer localities. In the presence of such a claim, should the logic of the school finance decisions be extended to police services? Recall that although the Texas Supreme Court relied on a specific clause in the state constitution requiring an "efficient" level of education, many of the school finance cases have relied on more general state equal protection clauses. Are there other services about which similar claims might be made?

School finance litigation represents attempts to use existing legal doctrine to achieve some measure of burden-sharing among localities of differing wealth in the provision of a particular service. Even the cases such as *Edgewood I* in which the courts have ordered some degree of redistribution in the financing of public schools, however, have provided no resolution to the many other areas of conflict that currently exist between central cities and their suburbs. In recent years, several commentators have offered broad structural proposals intended to facilitate broader burden-sharing between cities and suburbs and, in some cases, intended also to alter the very character and identity of both types of communities. See, e.g., Governance and Opportunity in Metropolitan America (Alan Altshuler et al. eds. 1999); Andres Duany, et al., Suburban Nation (2000); Gerald E. Frug, City Making: Building Communities Without Building Walls (1999); Reflections on Regionalism (Bruce J. Katz, ed., 2000); Emel Gokyigit Wadhwani, Achieving Greater Inter–Local Equity in Financing Municipal Services: What We Can Learn from School Finance Litigation, 7 Tex. F. on Civ. Lib. & Civ. Rights 91 (2002).

2. THE CITY-SUBURB RELATIONSHIP

The relationship between cities and their suburbs is complicated and controversial. Since suburban residents often use the central city as a place for work, shopping, or culture, but pay taxes only to their place of residence, there is a tendency to think of the relationship as one in which suburbs exploit the central city. If true, the relationship might be altered by the imposition of commuter taxes, regional government, or fees that fall disproportionately on nonresidents (e.g., meal taxes or entertainment taxes). But nonresidents who work, shop, and play in the central city obviously generate significant economic activity, and some claim that they therefore already confer central city benefits in excess of the cost of the services that they use (e.g., use of the streets and police services). See, e.g., David F. Bradford & Wallace E. Oates, Suburban Exploitation of Central Cities and Governmental Structure, in Redistribution through Public Choice 43 (Harold M. Hochman & George E. Peterson eds., 1974). Nevertheless, to the extent that central cities and suburbs must fund activities from internally generated revenues, it seems clear that wealthy communities will have greater opportunities to provide an array of goods and services not available to poorer communities. In addition to having a larger per capita tax base, wealthy communities will have to spend far fewer of their revenue dollars to relieve social burdens related to poverty and will thus have more leeway to fund activities that might be considered luxuries in poorer communities. Thus, claims to share burdens are likely to arise from poorer communities, and relatively wealthy communities are equally likely to resist by resorting to claims of local autonomy. In addition, the relationship between some cities and suburbs has a racial element as well as a fiscal one. See Sheryll D. Cashin, Localism, Self–Interest, and the Tyranny of the Favored Quarter: Addressing the Barriers to the New Regionalism, 88 Geo. L.J. 1985 (2000).

The debate is perhaps less contentious if one views the relationship between cities and suburbs as one of interdependence rather than of competition. If suburbs and cities rely on each other, then one would anticipate that they would have incentives to cooperate rather than to exploit each other, at least in areas where cooperation would benefit all parties. There is some reason to believe that suburbs depend on the fiscal health of and quality of life in central cities. There exists significant evidence that even suburbs with a robust commercial base remain in a strongly interdependent relationship with central cities. First, city employment offers advantages that cannot readily be displaced by suburban employment. This phenomenon is related to the concept of "agglomeration economies," the benefits that entities such as firms or localities can realize by being situated near other entities and that could not be realized if they were geographically distant. For instance, firms that locate close to other firms in the same industry reduce the costs of interfirm communication and can readily share inputs in production and consumption. But agglomeration economies can also be realized between firms in different industries that are located in the same geographic area. Transportation systems, infrastructure, labor markets, and legal and financial services originally developed to support one industry will simultaneously be able to support new industries, thus reducing costs to new firms. Leaders within each of these industries will have greater access to each other and be better able to interact within a centralized community. To the extent that suburbs cannot accommodate the infrastructure and range of businesses necessary to realize these benefits, firms and suburban residents will continue to be attracted to central cities as a place to work, and thus will have incentives to ensure the city's fiscal health.

Additionally, some studies suggest that population density (which is likely to be greater in cities) accelerates the rate of human capital accumulation, simply because individuals have more interactions with each other. See Edward Glaeser, Are Cities Dying?, 12 J. Econ. Persp. 139, 140 (1998). Hence, profit-maximizing firms will continue to see advantages to location within cities, notwithstanding that many of the employees of those firms reside elsewhere. City economies may be more specialized in a manner that requires more workers from higher-paid occupational ranks. Some evidence of this can be inferred from the relative effect of urban and suburban employment growth on suburban house prices. Recent studies suggest that an increase in city jobs translates into an increase of suburban house values, but that suburban employment growth, however, has little effect on house prices. Similarly, city growth in income, population, and housing values tends to correlate with suburban growth of the same variables. Richard Voith, Do Suburbs Need Cities, 38 J. Reg. Sci. 445 (1998); Richard Voith, The Suburban Housing Market: The Effects of City and Suburban Growth, Federal Reserve Bank of Philadelphia Business Review 13, 19 (November/December 1996). These data do suggest (if, as seems likely, commuters make possible the higher average earnings in the city) that financially healthy cities continue to provide substantial employment opportunities to nonresidents, thus creating incentives for those nonresidents to support the city economy. Some recent studies that attempt to quantify the benefits that cities confer on suburban residents thus suggest that the average suburban homeowner should be willing to pay a significant amount to reduce the adverse effects of weak city financial performance. See Andrew F. Haughwout, Regional Fiscal Cooperation in Metropolitan Areas: An Exploration, 18 J. Pol'y Analysis & Mgmt. 579, 592–93 (1999).

There is some countervailing evidence that questions the interdependence thesis, and there is little doubt that, at least to some extent, cities and their suburbs compete for residents, labor, and tax base. See Edward W. Hill, Harold L. Wolman, & Coit Cook Ford III, Can Suburbs Survive Without Their Central Cities, 31 Urb. Aff. Rev. 147 (1995). But much of the data do suggest that financially healthy cities continue to provide substantial employment opportunities to nonresidents, thus creating incentives for those nonresidents to support the city economy. Conversely, some studies suggest that the presence of a large poor, unskilled population will impose drag either on the economy directly or on social interactions that necessarily implicate economic growth. See, e.g., Paul D. Gottlieb, The Effects of Poverty on Metropolitan Area Economic Performance: A Policy-Oriented Research Review, in Rosalind Greenstein and Wim Wiewel, Urban-Suburban Interdependencies 21 (2000).

If one believes that cities and suburbs are interdependent, and that suburbs therefore have both an incentive and an obligation to assist their central cities, then two questions arise. First, why don't we see more burden sharing between cities and suburbs? Second, what should burden sharing programs look like? The first question, of course, assumes that we don't currently have a significant amount of burden sharing. It may be that existing programs already provide a means of transferring suburban wealth to central cities, if not from a regional tax, than from more targeted taxes, such as parking taxes and commuter taxes, that are directed at individuals who use city services. But it is unlikely that those taxes would capture the full benefit that the city confers on suburbs. Certainly it is rare, though not unheard of, to find instances in which cities and their suburbs agree to a plan of regional taxation or in which suburbs make direct financial contributions to cities. One explanation for this takes us back to the Prisoner's Dilemma. In an area comprising one central city and multiple suburbs, it may serve the interests of each suburb to minimize its contributions to regional welfare, by minimizing transfers to the central city, as long as other suburbs are willing to contribute. The effect is that each suburb will refrain from making contributions in the hope that others will fill the gap. But there are alternative explanations. Suburbs may not want to make contributions to the central city if they cannot control the expenditures that will be made with the funds. Suburbanites may fear that the city will spend the funds in a manner that does not increase regional welfare. Thus, suburban residents may only be willing to make contributions targeted towards specific objectives that the city might not otherwise fund. See Clayton P. Gillette, Regionalization and Interlocal Bargains, 76 N.Y.U. L. Rev. 190 (2001).

The second issue depends on one's answer to the first. If one believes that suburbs fail to contribute to central cities either out of narrow self-interest or a failure to comprehend the benefits that cities confer, then it is necessary to design some mechanism by which to remedy the situation. The readings that follow introduce some possibilities. One is to create regional institutions that permit better matching of the costs and benefits of regional activity. Professor Gerald Frug, for instance, argues for a deemphasis on traditional local boundaries and for the encouragement of "a form of metropolitan life in which people across the region learn to recognize, and make policy on the basis of, their interactions with each other." Jerry Frug, Decentering Decentralization, 60 U. Chi. L. Rev. 253, 336 (1993). Professor Vicki Been suggests that regionalism may be less effective than proposals in that direction suggest. Finally, two economists, Andrew Haughwout and Robert Inman, suggest that programs that are tailored to specific objectives may best induce suburbs to consider the regional consequences of their actions, while simultaneously preserving decentralization and the current degree of local autonomy.

Jerry Frug, Decentering Decentralization

60 U. Chi. L. Rev. 253, 279–281, 294–299 (1993).

By allocating power principally to individual cities or the state, current local government law treats as irrelevant the fact that localities are situated within a region. Legal decisionmaking therefore oscillates between increasing the centralized power of the state government and empowering localities in a way that affects their neighbors without the neighbors' participation in the decisionmaking process. It is time to create another option.

Of course, many states have already created public authorities to deal with specific issues on a regional basis (such as transportation, natural resources, and parks) and, in a few parts of the country, regional governments have assumed a considerable share of local political power. But neither of these regional forms fosters inter-local relationships; each simply replaces the city's version of the centered subject with its own. Public authorities centralize power in a corporate-style bureaucracy. They are structured more like businesses than like government: their managers are appointed not elected, they are exempted from many limits placed on governmental entities, their authority is defended in terms of expertise, and they replace rather than involve local democratic decisionmakers. Regional governments, by contrast, centralize power in yet another form of sovereignty. They are sub-state governments with qualities intermediate between those of the state and cities: like the state, they can exercise power across the region; like cities, they are subservient to state power. Although both of these entities decrease the authority of city governments, neither transforms the subjectivity of the region's localities in any way.

New forms of regional organization have to be created to foster a situated conception of local identity. One possibility would be to decentralize authority from the federal and state governments to localities under a system of rules established by a regional legislature authorized to allocate entitlements to the area's cities and suburbs. The purpose of such a regional legislature would not be to act as a regional government or ape the powers of the state. Instead, it would be a democratic version of the idea of regional planning embodied in federal legislation of the 1960s and 1970s. These federal statutes sought to inject a regional voice into local decisionmaking by requiring local decisions to be consistent with a regional plan; Congress hoped that such a requirement would overcome the selfish pursuit of local self-interest by forcing each locality to consider the impact of their actions on the region as a whole. But the effect of these federal statutes was limited. They made regional considerations relevant only in the context of allocating federal grants; they created as many different regional planning agencies as there were subject matters to plan for; they concentrated on requiring agencies to prepare a written plan rather than on an ongoing process of regional negotiations; and they relied on existing political boundaries in the organization of the regional planning process. Nevertheless, the germ of the idea was sound. The object was not to have regional bodies replace local decisionmaking but to require localities, when making their decisions, to take the interests of other localities within the region into account.

As just mentioned, the task of the regional legislature would be to perform one specific function of the state legislature (and the state courts): the allocation of entitlements to local governments. An example of such an allocation is the articulation of standards—such as the *Mt. Laurel* standard—that describe the extent to which localities must accommodate the interest of others in the region when they decide their land-use policies. But there are also countless other entitlement issues facing local governments—What portion of the funds derived from the property tax can a locality use solely for its own schools? Can a locality exclude a facility the region needs (a waste dump)? What incentives can a locality offer a business in a neighboring jurisdiction to move across the border? Are stricter gun control laws more appropriate in one area of the region than elsewhere? Current local government law has clearly established that the kinds of entitlement questions I have just proposed cannot be distinguished "in principle" from substantive local decisionmaking. One could frame every issue as an entitlement question and thereby eliminate city decisionmaking altogether (and frame every issue as suitable for local resolution and thereby eliminate regional decisionmaking altogether). What, then, is the distinction that I am making between the entitlement allocation function of a regional legislature and a regional government?

The answer to this question must be found not in an analytical distinction between entitlement allocation and governance but in the way the regional legislature is organized. The regional legislature itself (and not the courts or the cities) should have the power to determine which questions it (rather than the localities) can decide, but the legislature should be structured to encourage its members not to exercise power themselves but to turn the legislature into a forum for inter-local negotiations about how to decentralize power. The best chance of doing so, in my view, lies in electing representatives from neighborhoods rather than from the city or the suburbs. By organizing the legislature on the basis of the subdivisions of the city and the suburbs to which people feel most attached, its members would be sufficiently connected to their communities that they would be under constant pressure to decentralize power. But they could not achieve such a goal without convincing fellow legislators that decentralization was a good idea. The members of the legislature would thus regularly experience the conflict between attachment to their neighborhood and the pull of the larger community, a conflict that parallels the struggle between the attachment to the self and to others embodied in the notion of the situated self. The contradictory pulls of the situated self—between particularism and universalism, between immanence and transcendence—would thereby become the structure of decisionmaking about decentralizing power. To be sure, additional institutional innovations might well be necessary to prevent legislators from becoming so enamored of their own power that they attempt to transform the regional legislature into a regional government. Requiring legislators to appear regularly before neighborhood meetings to report on legislative activity, allowing those at the meeting to vote on the kinds of compromises that the legislators are authorized to make, enabling neighborhood residents to control legislative salaries and perks, establishing term limits for those serving in the legislature—ideas such as these, from sources as varied as the history of New England towns and Marx's analysis of the Paris Commune, suggest that regional legislatures can be organized to frustrate the dynamic of centralization. Localities will not be able to get everything they want from such a structure, but they are likely to be able to gain more power than they now have or than they would have if they ceded authority to a regional (or state) government....

Once cities and suburbs learn, through battles in the regional legislature, what the regional impact of their decisions are, they can begin to internalize this perspective. They can improve their own "capacity for reflexively critical reconsideration ... by reaching for the perspectives of other and different persons." Considerable authority could then be delegated to cities, suburbs and neighborhoods; the review (and potential review) by the regional legislature would help overcome the fear of the centered subject that has limited the possibility of decentralizing power in America. There surely would no longer be much reason to prefer state over local decisionmaking. Regions are as diverse as states, and they therefore can serve the purpose of protection against parochialism usually advanced for state power. Moreover, little democratic participation in their decisionmaking is possible because of the size of most states (and of most state legislative districts). Indeed, many regions in America cross state boundaries, and state decisionmaking is likely to increase the fragmentation of metropolitan regions rather than solve it. Decentralizing power to cities, suburbs, and neighborhoods thus seems a far better alternative than state decisionmaking, as long as regional views are incorporated into their decisionmaking.

Vicki Been, Comment on Professor Jerry Frug's *The Geography of Community*

48 Stan. L. Rev. 1109, 1109–1114 (1996).

[I start] from the premise that Professor Frug is absolutely right to want to replace cities and suburbs that are highly segregated by race, class, ethnicity, and life-style with something different—a "new urbanism" that draws the best from the past, perhaps, or some other approach to urban design that makes people get out of their cars and get into watching, interacting with, learning from, and learning to appreciate, others.

My concerns . . . are not about Professor Frug's goals, but about his understanding of what lies behind the evils that need to be remedied, and about the remedies he suggests. . . . [I]n assessing why people move to suburbs, where single family detached houses with unusable front yards are separated from all other forms of life, stratified rigidly by the income, and even more rigidly by the race of the occupants, Professor Frug focuses on people's desire to avoid strangers who are "others." He argues that "[t]he most important contemporary distinction between central cities and at least some suburbs is heterogeneity," and draws on both psychology and sociology to show us that many, perhaps most, people fear, and seek to avoid, the challenge heterogeneity poses. That fear is especially acute when the "other" is the poor African American who is inextricably linked in people's minds to the city, or at least to the "inner" or "center" city.

. . . I would like to reemphasize the aspects of the move to the suburbs that don't directly relate to fear of others, or to the desire for racial, ethnic, and life-style homogeneity. It is important to do so because solutions primarily aimed at issues of racism or other "isms" won't necessarily work for the other factors that pull or push people to the suburbs.

The factors I want to focus on are economic factors. There are two major ways in which economics have mattered in shaping our landscape. First, economics drives many people to move to the suburbs. When I talk to the mothers and fathers of my children's friends about their inevitably impending move to the suburbs, they talk about the higher standard of living they can enjoy there—the increased space they can get for the same housing dollar, the savings of writing one check for property taxes rather than one for property taxes and another for the private school tuition, the lower tax rates in the suburbs, and the cheaper child care options available in the suburbs. Some of the economic calculations are naive—they undervalue the cost of the time spent commuting, for example, or are overly optimistic about the viability of having only one car in the suburbs. But the calculations are honest, and are a large part of the basis of people's decisions. Of course, even realistic economic calculations wouldn't come out the way they do if the government did not subsidize so much of life in the suburbs, or if sufficient numbers of the better off stayed in the city and worked together to improve the public schools. But ending the subsidies and revitalizing the cities present an enormous collective action challenge, not to mention a transition problem.

So personal economics pulls people to the suburbs, or pushes them out of the city. Once the idea of moving to help one's budget starts to work its way into the subconscious, it leads people inexorably to a particular kind of suburb. To get the most bang for the buck out of the move to the suburbs, one needs to move to a suburb in which one's property tax payments are no higher than a fee for service, or even better, are a bargain for the services received because clean industry or other "good ratables" are subsidizing the service. So economics, or more precisely a desire to avoid the redistribution of one's income, leads people to income-stratified suburbs. Suburbs are able to offer the economic advantages of income homogeneity because they can engage in fiscal or exclusionary zoning—zoning that ensures that everyone who lives in the town pays taxes at least equal to the cost of the services they draw.

This is, of course, the theory of fiscal zoning, generalized from the Tiebout hypothesis that local governments compete for residents, who vote with their feet to select a community that offers the public service package they desire at the least cost. There is a vast literature about the fiscal zoning thesis that provides evidence that fiscal motivations are one of the important reasons that people move to the suburbs and choose income-homogeneous communities when they make that move.

Why do fiscal motivations warrant more attention than Professor Frug gives them? Because a solution needs to fit the problem, and I'm not sure the solution Professor Frug offers fits the problem of fiscal motivations. As I understand his vision, he wants land use reformed to allow for the type of development that goes by the name "new urbanism," a form of development he believes would contribute significantly to community building by forcing people to engage with others, and thereby come to appreciate whatever it is that makes the others different. He suggests that the mechanism for achieving such reforms would be a regional legislature that does not itself exercise land use powers, but rather serves as a forum in which local governments would renegotiate, and thereby restructure, land use powers. Will those solutions successfully dismantle fiscal zoning?

I fear not. It's not at all clear that the new urbanism will lead to a greater tolerance for redistribution, and thereby change people's demand for fiscal zoning. Getting people out of their cars and into the streets is a great accomplishment, for all kinds of reasons. But mixing uses, reverting back to grid street patterns, allowing granny or in-law flats, and reinventing the city commons won't guarantee that the pedestrians will see people very different from themselves. One way of assessing the likelihood of greater diversity would be to look to the towns that are the showcases for the new urbanism—are they more economically (or even racially) diverse than their Euclidean-zoned, cul-de-saced counterparts? Some of them, like Windsor, Florida, are unabashedly very upscale communities. The literature about others, like the showcase Seaside, Florida, is conspicuously silent about the demographics of the town's residents.

Even if changing land use regulations to allow urban designs like those proposed by the new urbanists does result in greater diversity on the streets, will that diversity lead residents to be willing to pay more in taxes so that the others they see—people who would pay lower taxes and present different public service needs—can live there as well? Professor Frug references evidence that city folks are more tolerant of other lifestyles and viewpoints than suburbanites. But there is much anecdotal evidence that points in the other direction. Many very diverse cities have been at the forefront of exclusionary, expulsive, and fiscal zoning. The history of urban renewal, of public housing siting in cities, of gentrification, and most recently, of the siting of homeless shelters and other social service facilities, makes clear that diversity within many cities hasn't promoted a greater compassion for the poor or for "others," or a greater willingness to share wealth with others. Indeed, many cities have found over the last decade that day to day exposure to the poor may lead to compassion fatigue, and make people even less willing to pay higher taxes to help the poor.

But let's assume that better urban design would lead to greater diversity, and that greater diversity would lead to increased tolerance and all the advantages of tolerance. Can we get there from here through the vehicle of Professor Frug's regional legislature?

As I understand his proposal, the regional legislature wouldn't be a centralized regional government in the traditional sense, but would instead be a forum in which the authority to engage in land use controls and other local government activities would be renegotiated. Legislators would be elected, in one version, at a neighborhood level by people whose votes were not constrained by boundaries—people would be given five votes, for example, to use in any local election or elections they wanted. Given the unbounded nature of their constituency, regional legislators will come to realize during the renegotiation process that fiscal zoning is a tragedy of the commons, in which each town's pursuit of self-interest will eventually lead to ruin for all. They will therefore begin to cooperate, and restructure land use (among other things) so that every local government shoulders its fair share of the burden of low and moderate income housing....

... I agree with Professor Frug that regional legislators who believe their constituency is broader than a local government's are likely to structure entitlements in a way that will lead to greater redistribution. But as the regional contribution agreements that are the end result of *Mt.*

Laurel show us, one can effect redistribution without achieving any greater integration. Why then should we trust that the regional legislators will *both* integrate and redistribute? Indeed, it could be the case that those goals come to be in some tension. The beneficiaries of greater redistribution could prefer more redistribution to more integration. If that's the outcome, will the regional legislature have achieved its goals? . . .

[Moreover, h]ow will the regional legislature separate good land use controls from bad ones? One way would be to legislate through broad standards: "Thou shalt not engage in fiscal or exclusionary zoning." Almost all zoning could be characterized as fiscal or exclusionary because it raises the price of housing. How then would a community prove that its preference for cul-de-sacs rather than a grid system, for example, meets the standard? Could it prove that it was currently well integrated and therefore could not have exclusionary intentions?

Because of the problems of interpreting, applying, and enforcing broad standards, I fear that the regional legislature might succumb to the temptation to instead legislate by rules: "Thou shall not impose minimum lot size requirements that exceed X feet." But then the regional legislature will be a regional government, and threaten the autonomy of local governments in very fundamental ways. The end result may be a uniformity that is just as, or even more, stultifying than the current predictability in suburban design. The grid-pattern may become the standard, rather than the cul-de-sac, but the opportunity to improve upon both grid-patterns and cul-de-sacs through the "laboratory" of multiple local governments will be lost.

Lastly, I'm concerned that the regional legislature will be unable to do the job Professor Frug envisions because it will be forced to work within an existing system of state and federal powers, and will be able to bump the level of redistribution up, at most, to a regional level. Unless regional legislatures are imposed across the board in all states, wealthier people will be able to escape to other income-stratified tax avoidance havens, although it will be harder to do so. And unless all local government powers are strictly controlled, the impetus behind fiscal zoning will lead local governments stripped of land use powers to invent other ways to allow individuals to sort themselves into anti-redistributive groupings. Or private land use restrictions and private residential community associations, both of which would be beyond the power of the regional legislature, will step in to fill the void.

Andrew F. Haughwout & Robert P. Inman, Should Suburbs Help Their Central City?

Brookings–Wharton Papers 2002, 45, 77–79.

Because of natural competitive advantages or simply economic history, U.S. central cities are important production and consumption centers favored by significant agglomeration economies. Unfortunately, our current institutions of local public finance impose redistributive burdens on mobile city firms and middle- and upper-income households that undermine the efficiency advantages of city production. Unfunded poverty mandates, monopoly unions, redistributive local taxation, and weak city governance each strengthen the ability of lower income households, public employees, and neighborhoods to extract fiscal resources from productive but mobile firms and households. The exit of these firms and households undermines city agglomeration economies, resulting in economic losses for the average city and suburban resident.

Can we reorganize central city public finance so that all parties to the city's redistribution game—city and suburban landowners *and* the current winners from city redistribution—might be made better off? The answer is potentially yes. Comparing our earlier estimates of the average transfer paid per city resident by redistributive fiscal institutions to the maximal gain to suburbanites of removing those institutions as reported in table 6 suggests that sufficient compensation can be found to facilitate institutional reform. The above comparison suggests suburbanites will gain $2 to $4 annually for every $1 of suburban aid. Suburban aid must be tied to successful institutional reforms, however. Four reforms seem particularly promising.

First, poverty mandates should be fully funded, and revenues lost through poverty's direct effect on the city tax base should be replaced by a residential tax base equalization grant. Second, efforts should be made to encourage the competitive provision of city services, either by relaxing strong duty-to-bargain rules or by passing laws that allow cities to contract out for the provision of cities services. The state of Pennsylvania's recent takeover of city school management, requiring the city to accept bids from private providers to manage the city's worst schools, is an example of such reform. Third, cities losing tax base because of demographic shifts and structural declines in their manufacturing job base should be given transition aid tied to business tax relief to prevent further declines in the business tax base. Even more aggressive reforms would replace the city's general property tax by a resident-based property tax or a resident-based income tax and exempt business property, but would allow cities to impose user fees for city-provided business services. To the extent city businesses use city infrastructure that cannot be priced through user fees—roads are the prime example—the city should be given matching infrastructure grants tying funding to new construction or maintenance. Fourth, ward-based city politics should be replaced by at-large politics and by requiring cities to elect an at-large mayor. The elected mayor should be given broad agenda setting and veto powers.

Each of these institutional reforms may require compensation of the reform's losers in order to achieve passage at the state or metropolitan level. This is where suburban-to-city aid plays a useful role. First, suburban or state aid should be given to fully fund all poverty mandates imposed upon the city budget. Further, a city-suburban tax base equalization aid program equalizing the residential component of local tax bases should be adopted to remove the adverse tax price effects of large poverty concentrations in central cities. Second, suburban aid can be made available to local governments that adopt competitive bidding for core city services. Such aid should be sufficient to compensate the current median-aged public employee, paid perhaps through targeted pensions or early retirement payments; once that worker retires with her fully funded pension, however, aid should stop. Third, suburban-funded transition aid should be given to cities for their loss of revenues from the reform of city business taxes, perhaps most easily done as part of a general reform of local property taxation. We recommend that local property taxation be restricted to the taxation of resident property. Alternatively, a resident-only income or wage tax could be used. Fourth, suburban aid should be given, as above for private contracting reforms, to current city workers released by cutbacks in neighborhood services because of the adoption of more efficient strong mayoral politics. Each of these four aid programs can be financed and administered at either the state or metropolitan level.

NOTES

1. Professor Frug is not the only commentator who has recently offered a broad, structural proposal to mitigate the various tensions in the city-suburb relationship. See, e.g., Richard Briffault, Our Localism, Part I and II, 90 Colum. L. Rev. 1, 346 (1990); Stephen Goldsmith, The Twenty–First Century City: Resurrecting Urban America (1997); David Rusk, Cities without Suburbs (2d ed. 1995); Myron Orfield, Metropolitics (Rev. ed. 1997); Richard Briffault, Localism and Regionalism, 48 Buff. L. Rev. 1 (2000); Sheryll D. Cashin, Localism, Self–Interest, and the Tyranny of the Favored Quarter: Addressing the Barriers to the New Regionalism, 88 Geo. L.J. 1985 (2000); Richard Thompson Ford, The Boundaries of Race: Political Geography in Legal Analysis, 107 Harv. L. Rev. 1841 (1994); Clayton P. Gillette, Regionalization and Interlocal Bargains, 76 N.Y.U. L. Rev. 190 (2001); Janice C. Griffith, Regional Governance Reconsidered, 21 J.L. & Pol. 505 (2005); Georgette C. Poindexter, Collective Individualism: Deconstructing the Legal City, 145 Pa. L. Rev. 607 (1997); Laurie Reynolds, Intergovernmental Cooperation, Metropolitan Equity, and the New Regionalism, 78 Wash. L. Rev. 93 (2003); Laurie Reynolds, Local Governments and Regional Governance, 39 Urb. Law. 483 (2007).

Commentaries on Professor Frug's proposal, excerpted supra, in addition to that of Professor Been, excerpted supra, include Richard Briffault, The Local Government Boundary Problem, 48 Stan. L. Rev. 1115 (1996); Ford, supra; Poindexter, supra; See also Gerald E. Frug, City Making: Building Communities Without Building Walls (1999); and the various reviews of the book: Sheryll D. Cashin, Building Community in the Twenty–First Century: A Post–Integrationist Vision for the American Metropolis, 98 Mich. L. Rev. 1704 (2000); Roderick M. Hills, Jr., Romancing the Town: Why We (Still) Need a Democratic Defense of City Power, 113 Harv. L. Rev. 2009 (2000); Martha A. Lees, Expanding Metropolitan Solutions through Interdisciplinarity, 26 N.Y.U. Rev. L. & Soc. Change 347 (2000–2001).

2. Why do Haughwout and Inman suggest that ward-based politics be replaced by at-large elections? What assumptions are they making about the behavior of elected officials? Even if they are correct, are there reasons to oppose at-large elections? Assume that minority populations tend to congregate in certain sections of the city, either as a result of discrimination or a conscious desire to live together. Ward-based politics may still ensure some representation by that group in the governance of the city. That advantage, however, would be diluted in at-large politics that made minority representation more difficult. This observation applies not only with respect to racial or ethnic minorities, but also with respect to socio-economic minorities (e.g., the wealthy), who tended to congregate in one section of the city.

3. Is it possible that the two goals of increased residential integration (whether economic, racial, ethnic, or class-based) and of redistribution to achieve greater equality of service provision are inherently incompatible? What if those with greater wealth, and therefore greater choices when deciding where to live, are likely to support increased fiscal redistribution only if doing so would permit them to live in an economically homogeneous community (a suburb, say) rather than a more economically diverse one? Or, what if those with greater wealth are willing to live in a more economically diverse community (the city rather than a suburb, for example) only if the public schools and other services in their part of town are of a better quality than those provided their less wealthy neighbors within that community? Consider the following:

> For better or worse, some persons live closer to the Tiebout world than others. Moreover, people with relative, if not perfect, mobility are likely to be on the subsidizing side of redistributive local public goods. At some point, mobile and self-interested actors who bear the burdens of subsidizing these goods will adopt the Tiebout solution of voting with their feet. Should they do so, those less able to pay for services will have more difficulty receiving them.
>
> Viewed in this way, inequality of services becomes a bribe, a mechanism for cooptation, an inducement to the middle and upper classes not to abandon the non-Tiebout city. Those in a position to subsidize goods and services that come close to the "necessities of life" may be more willing to do so if they receive more amenities than their less wealthy neighbors. This argument permits those in a position to do so to pay the price for the services that are best provided collectively but that may vary in quality in accordance with price, such as education, fire and police protection, and open space.
>
> We are left, then, in a quandary. To provide equal services in an environment of underlying inequality requires either increasing the portion of the municipal budget dedicated to services, reallocating the existing services, or financing those services on a nonredistributive basis, such as through user fees or service charges. The first two choices induce marginal residents to take advantage of their mobility and seek communities that better satisfy their preferences for services at a cost reflecting less economic redistribution. The third choice introduces a level of regressivity that, while theoretically making

> services available to all, would leave the relatively dispossessed without the means to take advantage of their new-found equality of opportunity. Not surprisingly, no easy answer exists....

Clayton P. Gillette, Equality and Variety in the Delivery of Municipal Services, 100 Harv. L. Rev. 946, 961–962 (1987). What does Professor Gillette's analysis suggest about the likely support for, and therefore real-world feasibility of, Professor Frug's regional legislature? Must one conclude, with Professor Edward Zelinsky, that "the issue, in the final analysis, is not the need to recast the structure of municipal government, but the need to revise the preferences of the American people ..."? Edward A. Zelinsky, Metropolitanism, Progressivism, and Race, 98 Colum. L. Rev. 665, 668 (1998) (book review). If so, how might these preferences be altered within the existing structure of local government?

D. THE COMMUNITY'S RELATIONSHIP WITH NONRESIDENTS

1. PARTICIPATION BY NONRESIDENTS

PROBLEM XXX

The City of Baxter supplies waste disposal service to both residents and nonresidents who live in a neighboring unincorporated area. Both residents and nonresidents pay for the service through the payment of user fees. Fees are set in an amount sufficient to cover the costs of collecting and treating waste. The city is now planning construction of a new waste disposal plant. The plant is to be constructed with the proceeds of bonds that the City of Baxter will issue. Debt service on the bonds is payable exclusively from user fees, which will be set in an amount sufficient to pay principal and interest on the bonds issued to finance the new plant. State law requires that issuance of the bonds be preceded by a bond election. Baxter proposes to permit only residents to vote in the election. You represent a group of nonresidents who oppose construction of the new plant. Your clients desire the opportunity to vote in the bond election. What arguments can you make on their behalf? What responses do you anticipate from Baxter?

Holt Civic Club v. City of Tuscaloosa

439 U.S. 60 (1978).

[The text of the Opinion and Notes thereto begin on page 136.]

2. PROVIDING SERVICES TO NONRESIDENTS

Melton v. City of Wichita Falls

799 S.W.2d 778 (Tex. Ct. App. 1990).

■ JOE SPURLOCK, II, JUSTICE.

... The appeal is from a judgment denying Melton a permanent injunction against the City of Wichita Falls by which he sought to establish permanent water service to his residence located outside the city limits. There had been a temporary injunction entered in his favor in November of 1988, establishing the water service at the residence located at 3101 Old Windthorst Road from a twelve inch main which belonged to the city and existed south of the city limits along that road. Water and sewer service is currently being furnished to the residence, but the city is prohibited from discontinuing such service until the appeals have been exhausted.

Melton complains of certain findings of fact made by the trial court as a result of the hearing on the request for permanent injunction. In point of error number one, Melton complains that the court had either no evidence or alternatively insufficient evidence to support its finding of fact ... that he, Melton, was not similarly situated to other non-residents who were granted service before the adoption of the City of Wichita's resolution number 69–86. That resolution, adopted on May 20, 1986, repealed a previous resolution number 10–57 and prohibited any connections for water service outside the corporate limits of the City of Wichita Falls. Almost two years after the adoption of resolution 69–86 Melton made his request for water service from the city. He asserts that he is similarly situated to other non-residents who receive water service under the old resolution 10–57, and therefore should have been connected to water service when he applied after the new ordinance went into effect.

Under section 402.001 of the Local Government Code the powers of the city are listed in regards to the operation of the water system. These powers include specifically the power to purchase, construct or operate a utility system inside or outside the municipal boundaries and to regulate the system in a manner that protects the interest of the municipality. The city notes that the section provides the power to contract with persons outside its boundaries to permit them to connect with the utility system on terms that the municipality considers to be in its best interest. Tex. Local Gov. Code Ann. sec. 402.001 (Vernon 1988). The city argues that the evidence established that the new ordinance 69–86 as passed, approved and repealed resolution 10–57 and prohibited any new connections for water service for any persons outside the corporate limits of the town. The city argues this was the purpose of the ordinance and the major effect of its passage. The appellant's request, almost two years after passage of 69–86, was treated the same as all other requests for new service from persons similarly situated at that time. That is, no one outside the city limits not already connected to the system before the adoption of resolution 69–86 was thereafter connected to the system.

The city concludes, and, by implication, the trial court found, that the operation of ordinance 69–86 is a reasonable exercise of the express power granted to the city. The exercise of such power is legislative in nature and will not be regulated by the courts unless the exercise by the city is clearly an abuse of its power. The law presumes that city officials act within the limits of their authority, in good faith, and in the best interest of the city they serve. Kimbrough v. Walling, 371 S.W.2d 691, 692 (Tex. 1963).

Testimony by the witness for the city was that the adoption of the resolution was an attempt by the city to protect the interest of the municipality by controlling improper growth on its periphery and by encouraging the development of land within its corporate limits. There was no showing of any bad faith in the adoption of the ordinance, nor any favoritism shown to any affected by it. We agree with the city that the evidence is clearly sufficient to support the trial court's finding that appellant was not similarly situated to other non-residents outside the city who made applications for water service before the adoption of the new ordinance. He was treated alike with other non-residents who applied after the ordinance went into effect. We overrule point of error one.

In his second point of error Melton complains that the city failed to demonstrate a reasonable basis to differentiate between those persons who were granted water service under the old resolution 10–57 and those who were denied water service after the adoption of resolution 69–86. In this connection he complains that there was either no evidence or in the alternative only insufficient evidence to support the court's finding of fact that a reasonable basis existed.

Melton argues that the evidence at trial showed that non-residents received water under the old resolution 10–57, if their property was contiguous to the city limits or to a city water line. The new resolution was passed to provide that no connection would be allowed outside the city limits of Wichita Falls. Melton does not argue that on its face the resolution is unreasonable in denying connection. He does not argue that the city officials acted in bad faith, or that their action in passing the ordinance was a clear abuse of their power to act. However, he argues that in practice the ordinance has been applied in an unreasonable and discriminatory fashion. To support his argument he points out that no connections existing outside the city limits were discontinued upon the passage of resolution 69–86. He argues in essence that people outside the city limits are therefore treated in an arbitrary fashion depending upon whether or not they had service by a certain date.

He additionally argues that the city did give a new water meter to an existing customer outside the city limits for a sprinkler system after the passage of resolution 69–86. Further, Jerry Gross, the Utilities Manager for the city, testified that there was no substantial difference between Melton's property on Windthorst Road and other properties on Windthorst Road which were receiving water service from the city at the time that the new ordinance went into effect. Melton concludes that he was similarly situated to those who were receiving service at the time the ordinance went into effect. Nevertheless, the city refused to provide service to Melton.

The city counters that the evidence considered by the trial court also showed that a stated purpose for passage of the ordinance was to prevent improper development along the periphery of the city. One way to accomplish this desired purpose of the city was to refuse to provide any new water connections to persons along the periphery of the city. The city had recently installed a major water system line which extended outside the city limits and created a substantial potential for uncontrolled growth if resolution 10–57 were not repealed. For that reason it was repealed. Testimony showed that the main ingredient for development either within or without the city is water, and that the purpose for the adoption of resolution 69–86 was to promote development within the corporate limits of the city as there was a considerable amount of vacant and undeveloped land lying therein. Clearly, controlling development is a legitimate goal of the city and resolution 69–86 was reasonably calculated to achieve that goal.

Just as clearly, resolution 69–86 is non-discriminatory both on its face and in its application, for it is prospective only in its application and treats all persons within the same circumstances (or class) as Melton, alike. The appellee notes that in finding of fact number six the trial court found that the appellee had denied water service to all non-resident applicants, including Melton, who applied for service after the passage of resolution 69–86. As appellant has not challenged this finding of fact, it therefore is conclusive and binding on appellant and on this appeals court. See Jack v. State, 694 S.W.2d 391 (Tex. App.–San Antonio 1985, writ ref'd n.r.e.).

Appellant was not treated differently from those in a similar situation. There are clear, non-discriminatory, reasonable distinctions between those who already had service, and those who will not get it. If you already had it, you kept it. If you did not have it, for the protection of the growth of the city and promotion of interests of the city, you will not get the service. The city concludes, therefore, and we agree, that there is sufficient evidence to support the trial court's finding. Point of error number two is overruled.

In point of error number three, Melton complains that there is either no evidence or only insufficient evidence to support finding of fact number four that the passage of both resolutions was an effort by the city to control proper development on the periphery of the city and that the attempts by the city to control that growth are logical and reasonable. We have reviewed the arguments of appellant and find that they are without substance, that the previous testimony discussed under point of error number two is sufficient to establish the court's finding of fact in this regard. We believe, as the city argues, that one way to control the problem of improper growth around the periphery of the city, and to promote the development and growth within vacant land in the city, is to prohibit any new connections for water service beyond the city's boundary, because water is a main ingredient for the development of a city. The exercise of the power by the city officials to provide a suitable water supply rests largely in their discretion. In the exercise of that discretion, they may oppose those activities that are detrimental to the present or future water supply they are required to provide for the inhabitants of the city. See *Kimbrough*, 371 S.W.2d at 693. Accordingly we overrule point of error number three....

The judgment of the court is affirmed.

City of Attalla v. Dean Sausage Co.

889 So.2d 559 (Ala. Civ. App. 2003).

■ PITTMAN, JUDGE.

The City of Attalla ("the City") and its mayor and city council appeal from a trial court's judgment requiring them to provide sewer service to certain nonresidents and businesses located in the City's police jurisdiction but outside its corporate limits.

On January 29, 2002, Dean Sausage Company, Inc.; Machine Products Company, Inc.; and Trambeam, Inc. (hereinafter referred to collectively as "the businesses") filed an action requesting a temporary restraining order and a permanent injunction to prevent the City and its mayor and its city council members (hereinafter referred to collectively as "the City defendants") from terminating sewer service to those businesses....

On April 15, 2002, AAA Plumbing Pottery, Inc. ("AAA") filed a separate action requesting a temporary restraining order and a permanent injunction to prevent the City defendants from terminating sewer service to AAA. On that same day, the trial court issued a temporary retraining order that prevented the City defendants from terminating sewer service to AAA. The City defendants answered AAA's complaint and counterclaimed for a declaratory judgment that the City defendants owed no duty to provide sewer service in the City's police jurisdiction; the City defendants also requested that the trial court issue an order requiring AAA to disconnect from the City's sewer system. On April 19, 2002, the trial court consolidated the two actions.

All of the parties' claims were tried on June 12 and 13, 2002. Charles O'Rear, the City's mayor, testified at length about the City's sewer problems. O'Rear stated that on February 1, 2002, the City had been notified by the Alabama Department of Environmental Management ("ADEM") that the City's sewer system had been found to be in violation of the Alabama Water Pollution Act because the system contained more than the maximum permissible amounts of Biochemical Oxygen Demand ("BOD") concentrations and Total Suspended Solids ("TSS") and because the system had had an inordinate amount of sewer overflows....

O'Rear also described the events leading to the present litigation. When the City engineers determined that most, if not all, of the blood and grease contained in the overflows occurring in many residents' homes was coming from the businesses located in the City's police jurisdiction, the City requested a meeting with business representatives to discuss options for solving the sewer problems. At that meeting in August 2001, O'Rear discussed several lawsuits that had been filed by City residents seeking damages for injuries caused by blood and grease backflows, as well as the ongoing problems caused by AAA and the businesses' use of the City's sewer system; he requested that the businesses consider annexation of their property into the City to help provide funds to pay for a solution to the City's sewer problems. O'Rear stated that the business representatives were very aloof and unconcerned by the City's problems; one representative told O'Rear that if the City needed to fix the sewer, the City should raise the rates paid by its residents, and another representative told the City to "go away and leave us alone."

* * *

The City alleges that the trial court erred: (1) in holding that the City has a duty to provide sewer service for the health and safety of nonresidents, i.e., those located in the police jurisdiction and not within the City's corporate limits; (2) in allowing the businesses and AAA the option of staying connected to the City's sewer system or building their own sewage-treatment facilities; (3) in holding that the City's adoption of Ordinance 758(01) (terminating sewer service in the police jurisdiction) was arbitrary and capricious; and (4) in denying the City defendants's request for an injunction requiring the businesses and AAA to disconnect from the City's sewer system and their request for declaratory relief.

* * *

Police jurisdictions in Alabama are created by statute. *See* § 11–40–10, Ala.Code 1975. "The police jurisdiction in cities having 6,000 or more inhabitants shall cover all adjoining territory within three miles of the corporate limits, and in cities having less than 6,000 inhabitants and in towns, such police jurisdiction shall extend also to the adjoining territory within a mile and a half of the corporate limits of such city or town." Id. ... Municipalities have no options regarding the existence of police jurisdictions; they exist as a function of a city's having the minimum population specified in § 11–40–10.

* * *

In certain limited situations, nonresidents may benefit from municipal services that are provided within a municipality's police jurisdiction. On occasion, municipal water and sewer service has been extended into a city's police jurisdiction in order to assist the development and growth of a municipality. Other municipal services have been extended into municipal police jurisdictions over the years at varying costs to Alabama cities; the concept of recouping some of the costs of those services from persons located in those police jurisdictions developed over a period of time. As early as 1917, our Supreme Court held that a municipality in the exercise of its police powers could impose a reasonable license tax on a manufacturing company located in its police jurisdiction and doing business in the municipality....

Existing side by side with those cases detailing the method of recouping the cost of municipal services in police jurisdictions is a line of cases discussing municipal provision of services generally. Among the more important recent decisions in this line of cases are *State Department of Revenue v. Reynolds Metals Co.,* 541 So.2d 524 (Ala.1988), and *City of Prattville v. Joyner,* 698 So.2d 122 (Ala.1997) ("*Joyner II*"). In *Reynolds Metals,* our Supreme Court established the principle that municipal regulatory taxes levied and collected within a police jurisdiction pursuant to § 11–

45–1 are valid so long as they do not exceed one-half the tax or fee charged to similar businesses within a city's corporate limits and they are reasonably related to the provision of municipal services to persons in the police jurisdiction. In *Joyner II,* our Supreme Court reaffirmed the holding in *Reynolds Metals* and concluded that any municipal ordinance levying a license fee on persons in a police jurisdiction that was limited to one-half the fee charged to residents within a city's corporate limits would be presumed reasonable. Reviewing the facts of this case in light of *Joyner II,* we conclude that trial court erred when it found that the City had a duty to provide sewer service in its police jurisdiction.

AAA cites *Reynolds Metals* for the proposition that a municipality has a *duty* to provide municipal services in its police jurisdiction. This is an incorrect statement of Alabama law. In *Joyner II,* Justice Houston, the author of *Reynolds Metals,* wrote specially to clarify his position on that issue:

> "If a municipality collects taxes from the businesses within its police jurisdiction, that municipality must provide within the police jurisdiction services that cost the municipality the amount of the tax collected there. *Holt Civic Club v. City of Tuscaloosa,* 439 U.S. 60, 99 S.Ct. 383, 58 L.Ed.2d 292 (1978). I referred to this as a *duty* in the majority opinion in *State Department of Revenue v. Reynolds Metals Co.,* 541 So.2d 524 (Ala.1988), where I was primarily expressing how a municipality's obligation to provide such services could be fulfilled. 541 So.2d at 531. If a municipality is providing within the police jurisdiction services the cost of which exceeds the amount of taxes collected there, then I believe *the municipality has the right to curtail those services that the governing body of the municipality in its reasonable discretion elects to curtail.*"

Joyner II, 698 So.2d at 127 (Houston, J., concurring specially) (emphasis added). *Joyner II* ultimately held that a municipality may provide services to and collect taxes from residents of its police jurisdiction so long as the funding principles set out in *Reynolds Metals* are applied. Conversely, *Joyner II* implies that a municipality is not required to provide any specific services to persons in its police jurisdiction so long as no taxes are collected from persons in the police jurisdiction. That proposition also derives support from *Board of Water & Sewer Commissioners of Mobile v. Yarbrough,* 662 So.2d 251 (Ala.1995). In *Yarbrough,* our Supreme Court expressly held that a municipality did not have a duty to provide a source of water to nonresidents located in its police jurisdiction. "[A]lthough the city may have a duty based on its police powers to provide a source of treated and purified water to its residents, it does not owe such a duty to persons outside the city limits, to whom providing such a service greatly increases its costs." *Yarbrough,* 662 So.2d at 254.

The evidence in this case clearly shows that no municipal taxes of any kind are collected by the City in its police jurisdiction. The City's provision of municipal services in the police jurisdiction has been gratuitous, subject only to a connection fee and a monthly user fee. Based on those facts and the cases cited above, we conclude that if a municipality has no duty to provide services, such as water service, to nonresidents, it also has no duty to provide sewer service to nonresidents. We conclude that the trial court erred when it determined that the City had a duty to provide municipal sewer service in the police jurisdiction.

Our analysis with respect to the first issue raised by the City defendants leads naturally to the City defendant's third issue—whether Ordinance 758(01) is arbitrary and capricious. . . .

In 1983 the City adopted Ordinance 546, pursuant to § 11–45–1 and § 11–50–1, establishing guidelines that all users of the City's sewer system must obey. AAA cites that ordinance, which requires all *residents* of the City to connect to the City's sewer system, as evidence that the passage in December 2001 of Ordinance 758(01), terminating sewer service in the City's police jurisdiction, was arbitrary and capricious. We disagree.

Article III, § 4 of Ordinance 546 states, in pertinent part:

> "The owner(s) of all houses, buildings, or *properties situated within the City and abutting on any street, alley, or right-of-way in which there is now located or may be located in the future a public sanitary or combined sewer* of the City, is hereby required at the owner(s)' expense to install suitable toilet facilities therein, and to connect such facilities directly to the [City's sewer system]. . . ."

(Emphasis added.)

AAA contends that this ordinance requires businesses located in the City's police jurisdiction to connect to the City's sewer system. However, we read the provision to require the owners of all properties located within the City's *corporate limits* that abut any street, alley, or right-of-way where sewer lines are placed to connect to the City's sewer system. The fact that the City requires its residents to be connected to the City's sewer system does not in any way vitiate the City's decision not to provide sewer service in the City's police jurisdiction as reflected in Ordinance 758(01).

The testimony at trial clearly shows that the City, if it continues to provide sewer service to persons or businesses in its police jurisdiction, will be in an untenable position. Mayor O'Rear testified regarding the recurring backflows of blood and grease into the homes of the City's residents that have given rise to numerous lawsuits asserting damage claims against the City. O'Rear then discussed the ADEM fines and the consent order that required the City to spend over $3,000,000 to upgrade the municipal sewer system. Doug Waldrup, the City's consulting civil engineer, discussed the ADEM consent order at length and anticipated that another $426,000 would have to be spent in the police jurisdiction to begin to combat the problems caused by the businesses' noncompliant effluents that entered the City's system and created backflows and clogs. Sharron Jones, the City's clerk, testified that since 1995 the City's sewer system had operated at a loss.

The testimony from the City defendants, AAA, and the businesses indicated that at no time did the businesses consider voluntary annexation into the City in order to help the City secure the appropriate tax revenues needed to rehabilitate the sewer system as currently constituted. Eventually, the businesses asked the City to apply for a state or federal environmental grant for rehabilitation of the sewer lines in the police jurisdiction;

however, the City rejected that request, believing that its municipal credit and income should be spent on underwriting and retiring the $3,000,000 debt for the sewer upgrades being performed for its residents.

The businesses and AAA seem to argue that because the City has legislative authority under which it *may* levy certain taxes and fees in the police jurisdiction, the City's possession of that taxing authority *requires* the City to provide whatever services that nonresidents require. That contention is simply incorrect; pursuant to Ala.Code 1975, § 11–45–1, the City must provide municipal services to its residents, but is not required to provide the same services to nonresidents. *See Joyner II, supra,* and *Yarbrough, supra.*

The record is clear that the City has been providing sewer service to the residents of the police jurisdiction for a number of years; however, this service has not been provided pursuant to any agreement or contract, written or oral. The businesses and AAA essentially present an equitable-estoppel argument. Our Supreme Court's decision in *Joyner II* precludes the application of equitable estoppel in this situation. Quoting *State Highway Department v. Headrick Outdoor Advertising, Inc.,* 594 So.2d 1202, 1204–05, the court in *Joyner II* stated:

> " 'Equitable estoppel is to be applied against a governmentality only with extreme caution or under exceptional circumstances. *First Nat'l Bank of Montgomery v. United States,* 176 F.Supp. 768 (M.D.Ala.1959), aff'd, 285 F.2d 123 (5th Cir. 1961); *Ex parte Fields,* 432 So.2d 1290 (Ala.1983).' "
>
> " 'Under the settled law, equitable estoppel ... must be predicated upon the conduct, language, or silence of the party against whom it is sought to be invoked. Said conduct, language, or silence must amount to the representation or concealment of a material fact or facts. *The representation must be as to the facts and not as to the law....*' " (Emphasis added [in *Headrick Outdoor Advertising*]). 176 F.Supp. at 772, quoting *Automobile Club of Michigan v. Commissioner,* 353 U.S. 180, 182, 77 S.Ct. 707, 709, 1 L.Ed.2d 746 (1957).

698 So.2d at 126. The underlying rationale of *Joyner II* is that residents in a municipal police jurisdiction acquire no vested interest or entitlement to the continued provision of municipal services by reliance or estoppel. Thus, any municipal services being provided in a police jurisdiction without a formal contract or agreement " 'may be prospectively altered in scope or terminated, after appropriate prior public notice.' " *Joyner II,* 698 So.2d at 125. Applying those principles in this case, we conclude that equitable estoppel does not apply.

In this case, the City met with the businesses and AAA before passing Ordinance 758(01). Additionally, Ordinance 758(01) contained extension provisions whereby the mayor was empowered to grant employers or other persons affected by the termination of sewer service in the police jurisdiction good-faith extensions of up to 30 days, with no limit as to the number of extensions that could be granted at the mayor's discretion. The fact that the City recognized that terminating sewer service in the police jurisdiction was a drastic remedy to a grave problem and still provided a means of "phasing in" the effective date of the termination militates against the proposition that the City's adoption of the ordinance was arbitrary and capricious. We conclude that in light of the evidence of record that showed that the City was faced with a financial catastrophe and that Ordinance 758(01) represented a reasonable (if desperate) measure to alleviate an overburdened sewer system, the trial court erred when it determined that the City's adoption of Ordinance 758(01) was arbitrary and capricious.

* * *

Based on the foregoing facts and authorities, we conclude that the trial court's judgment in favor of the businesses and AAA was erroneous. We reverse the trial court's judgment and remand the case for the entry of a judgment consistent with this opinion.

REVERSED AND REMANDED WITH INSTRUCTIONS.

NOTES

1. Provision of extraterritorial service appears to be a quintessential example of a service that does not involve solely a "municipal affair." Thus, with the exception of some interpretations of the National League of Cities model of home rule, localities will require legislative authorization to provide these services. See, e.g., City of Little Rock v. Chartwell Valley Limited Partnership, 772 S.W.2d 616 (Ark. 1989); Quality Water Supply, Inc. v. City of Wilmington, 388 S.E.2d 608 (N.C. Ct. App.), review denied, 393 S.E.2d 882 (N.C. 1990).

2. In each of these situations, the city seems to be using its authority to provide or withhold services to accomplish some ulterior motive. In *Melton*, the court suggests that denial of service to nonresidents is an effective means of controlling "improper development." If residents are willing to pay for the service, what makes the development "improper"? In *Attalla*, the court appears sympathetic to the claim that the nonresidents did not exercise an option of becoming annexed to the city. Is it appropriate for a city to use the granting or withholding of services to affect such issues as extramural development and to induce annexation? Are these examples of cities attempting to do indirectly what they could not do directly? Why do you think that the businesses in *Attalla* did not want to annex themselves to the city?

3. The court in *Attalla* asserts that the fact that a locality may provide service to nonresidents does not mean that it is required to do so. This appears to be an accepted legal principle. See Burger v. City of Beatrice, 147 N.W.2d 784 (Neb. 1967). Under what circumstances may a municipality refuse to provide services to nonresidents? As a general matter, service to nonresidents is considered contractual, and thus subject to conditions agreed to by the parties, just as if private individuals alone were involved. The sole constraints on this principle are constitutional and statutory immunities and limitations. In Andres v. City of Perrysburg, 546 N.E.2d 1377 (Ohio Ct. App. 1988), the court permitted a city to enforce a contractual provision that required nonresidents who desired municipal sewer services to sign an annexation petition. The court concluded that the city could not be required to provide services extraterritorially, so that the city could impose any conditions that are not "unreasonable, arbitrary, or capricious." Neither contractual defenses of distress nor constitutional claims of equal protection prohibited the city from enforcing the annexation condition, even though it had previously extended sewer service to nonresidents without any similar requirement. See also Colorado Springs v. Kitty Hawk Dev. Co., 392 P.2d 467 (Colo. 1964), *cert. denied*, 379 U.S. 647 (1965).

4. Some states prohibit a municipality from discontinuing extraterritorial service once it has been undertaken, even though the original provision of the service was not mandatory. See, e.g., Ariz. Rev. Stat. § 9–516(C), which provides:

> A city or town acquiring the facilities of a public service corporation rendering utility service without the boundaries of such city or town, or which renders utility service without its boundaries, shall not discontinue such service, once established, as long as such city or town owns or controls such utility. A city or town which renders utility service outside of its boundaries as prescribed by this subsection shall not be prohibited from selling a part of its utility operation to another utility which operates under regulations prescribed by law.

City of Texarkana v. Wiggins

246 S.W.2d 622 (Tex. 1952).

■ SMITH, JUSTICE.

Respondents, all nonresidents of the City of Texarkana, Texas, filed this suit against petitioner, the City, seeking to enjoin it in the operation of its municipally-owned water and sewer systems from charging nonresidents higher water and sewer rates than those paid by persons residing within the corporate limits of the city.

The trial court rendered judgment for petitioner, the judgment reciting that the court heard sufficient evidence to determine the case on its merits. This judgment was reversed and the cause remanded by the Court of Civil Appeals. 239 S.W.2d 212. The case is before us on writ of error.

Prior to August, 1948, the City of Texarkana, Texas, and surrounding territory, was served by the American Water Works, Inc., a privately-owned utility corporation. At that time the petitioner purchased from this utility corporation all its property serving the city and surrounding territory, payment being made with proceeds derived from the sale of revenue bonds previously authorized by vote of the citizens of the city. An ordinance of the city, enacted on August 27, 1948, adopted for the municipally owned utility the schedule of rates theretofore charged by the American Water Works; this schedule of rates remained in effect until August 8, 1950. The system of rates charged by the American Water Works was, of course, nondiscriminatory in that both residents and nonresidents were charged the same rate for service.

On August 8, 1950, petitioner passed an ordinance providing that water service to nonresident consumers would be furnished at one and one-half times the rate which applied within the corporate limits of the city. The ordinance further provided that sewer service to nonresident users would be furnished "at a rate double the rate applying within the city limits." A water tapping charge for all connections to the water system for residential use outside the city was fixed at $50; the water tapping charge for users within the city was set at $10 on unpaved streets, and $15 on paved streets.

Respondents are all residents of the City of North Texarkana, Texas, which adjoins the petitioner on the north. The east-west streets in the City of Texarkana, Texas, are numbered consecutively, beginning with 1st Street in the business district of the City of Texarkana, Texas, and continuing to 36th Street in the City of North Texarkana. The line marking the corporate limits of the City of Texarkana, Texas, lies in the center of 29th Street. The north-south streets, which continue through both cities, bear the same names throughout their entire lengths. In short, the geographical line upon which the rate differentiation is based is an arbitrary line marking the limits of a political subdivision.

Petitioner contends that it is under no legal duty to furnish water and sewage disposal service to the respondents; that if it does furnish such service to respondents it is under no legal duty to charge the respondents the same rate as is charged residents, but that it may make such charge as appears to be for the best interest of the City of Texarkana, Texas. This latter contention is based upon the provisions of Article 1108, section 3, R.C.S. of Texas, Vernon's Ann. Civ. St. art. 1108, subd. 3, which provides:

> Any town or city in this State which has or may be chartered or organized under the general laws of Texas, or by special Act or charter, and which owns or operates waterworks, sewers, gas or electric lights, shall have the power and right:
>
> 3. To extend the lines of such systems outside of the limits of such towns or cities and to sell water, sewer, gas, and electric light and power privileges or service to any person or corporation outside of the limits of such towns or cities, or permit them to connect therewith under contract with such town or city under such terms and conditions as may appear to be for the best interest of such town or city; provided that no electric lines shall, for the purposes stated in this section, be extended into the corporate limits of another incorporated town or city.

Respondents contend that the city in operating its water and sewer systems is acting in its proprietary capacity, that it is subject to the same rules and regulations as privately-owned utility corporations engaged in the same or similar business, and that the rates established by the ordinance of August 8, 1950, being discriminatory, are void and their collection should be enjoined.

We cannot agree with petitioner's contention that this statute is sufficient to authorize it to charge a discriminatory rate for utilities furnished to nonresidents than to its residents. Under the facts in this case, the city has dealt with the residents and nonresidents as one class or unit. The ordinance under consideration recites that the city has purchased and is now maintaining and operating within and without the limits of said city a municipal water system. Since 1948 the same rates have been charged consumers living within and without the city. No other utility exists within the area to furnish water and sewer service.

The common-law rule that one engaged in rendering a service affected with a public interest or, more strictly, what has come to be known as a utility service, may not discriminate in charges or service as between persons similarly situated is of such long standing and is so well recognized that it needs no citation of authority to support it. The economic nature of the enterprise which renders this type service is such that the courts have imposed upon it the duty to treat all alike unless there is some reasonable basis for a differentiation. Statutes have been enacted in almost every state making this common-law rule a statutory one. Pond, Public Utilities (4th. ed. 1932) sections 270–275. Hence, the American Water Works was required to, and did, render service to respondents at the same rate as was charged within the corporate limits of petitioner.

It is settled in this state that the petitioner, upon the purchase by it of the property of the privately-owned utility, was subject to this same rule prohibiting unreasonable or unjustified discrimination in rates and service. . . .

Admittedly these cases do not settle the particular question before us; they announce the broad common-law principle that a municipality may not unreasonably discriminate in rates and charges and they do not determine the further question whether or not different rates based on nothing more than the limits of a municipal corporation are unreasonably discriminatory. These cases are authority, however, for at least this much: in the absence of (1) a showing that the discrimination has a reasonable basis or (2) a statute to the contrary, a municipality may not discriminate in charges or service as between those similarly situated. Many decisions have transported the concept of proprietary capacity, as distinguished from governmental capacity, from the cases involving the liability of a governmental unit for the torts of its agents to these decisions involving the duty of a municipality to offer its utility service at nondiscriminatory rates and have found in this concept a basis for the rule set out above. The concept of proprietary capacity is, however, hardly helpful in this situation. The real reason for the rule that, in so far as treatment of consumers is concerned, the municipally-owned utility is no different from the privately-owned utility is that the economic nature of the business has not changed; it remains a monopoly in spite of the change in ownership.

The change from private to public ownership may, in theory at least, eliminate or lessen the profit motive, but the consumer of utility services still cannot pick and choose his supplier of water as he does his grocer. The utility consumer is thus at the mercy of the monopoly and, for this reason, utilities, regardless of the character of their ownership, should be and have been, subjected to control under the common-law rule forbidding unreasonable discrimination.

We do not pass upon the question whether the petitioner is under a legal duty to serve respondents with water and sewage disposal, nor do we pass on the question whether the rates charged by petitioner, whether within or without its corporate limits, are required to be "reasonable" as that term is understood in public utility parlance (i.e., a "reasonable" rate yields "a fair return on fair value"). But assuming that petitioner has no duty to serve, it does not follow, under the common-law rule at least, that having elected to serve it may do so on such terms as it chooses to impose. The contention that the petitioner, being under no legal obligation to serve, may do so on such terms as it chooses to impose brings before us a familiar argument in a new guise. It is the old, and logically appealing, argument that the greater includes the lesser power, that a governmental unit having the greater power of granting or withholding a privilege or service it perforce must have the lesser power of offering the privilege or service on whatever terms it may impose. That this is not necessarily true is demonstrated in the doctrine of unconstitutional conditions....

The petitioner being subject to the rule prohibiting unjustified discrimination between consumers of utility service, the question presents itself whether there is in fact any justification for treating the respondents differently than the residents of the petitioner city. The ordinance complained of contains, on its face, no such justification. The difference in rates, so far as is shown by the ordinance, is based entirely upon the location of the corporate limits. The petitioner does not contend that the costs of supplying the service to respondents vary so as to justify the difference in charges and the record is devoid of any evidence upon which to base such a contention. As was pointed out by the Court of Civil Appeals in its opinion below, the discrimination cannot be justified on the ground that the residents of the City of Texarkana, Texas, are liable to taxation to pay for acquisition of the water system. We are brought again, then, to what is apparent from the record of this case: the only difference between consumers who pay more and those who pay less for petitioner's utility service lies in the fact that the former reside north of 29th Street while the latter reside south of 29th Street. The limits of a municipal corporation, of themselves, do not furnish a reasonable basis for rate differentiation....

The case of City of Montgomery v. Greene, supra (180 Ala. 322, 60 So. 902), which was cited with approval in the case of Dallas Power & Light Co. v. Carrington, supra, was decided by the Supreme Court of Alabama on facts very similar to the present case. The Court there said:

> It may be stated, as a general proposition of law, that a corporation or municipality, authorized to supply water or lights to the inhabitants of a municipality, may not discriminate as to the rates charged, at least among those of the same class. State ex rel. Ferguson v. Birmingham Water Works, 164 Ala. 586, 51 So. 354, 27 L.R.A.,N.S., 674, and note. "The acceptance by a water company of its franchises carried with it the duty of supplying all persons along its mains, without discrimination, with the commodity which it was organized to furnish. All persons are entitled to have the same service on equal

> terms and uniform rates." City of Mobile v. Bienville Co., 130 Ala. (379), 384, 30 So. (445), 447. The service cannot be arbitrarily limited to such consumers as are technically residents of the municipality, although the right of persons living within the city or beyond may depend upon the sufficiency of the supply and the contiguity or remoteness of such persons from the mains....

Under the common-law rules, then, the ordinance is void. But the petitioner contends that all this has been changed by the statute referred to above. The petitioner asserts that "the crux of this case in its final analysis rests upon a construction of section 3, Article 1108, R.C.S. of Texas." This article has been set out above. We find nothing in this language which would authorize the city to discriminate, at its pleasure, between its patrons. The first part of the section merely gives the city the right to extend its service to persons residing beyond the corporate limits of the city. This the city has done....

We think the effect of the statute is that when a city decides to exercise this power to provide its utility service to customers outside the city limits it may then fix such service charges as it decides the situation requires; if it requires a higher charge than is fixed against residents of the city for the same service, the city may exact the higher rate. But whatever it fixes, a rate status between the city and its outside customers is thereby established and the city cannot thereafter arbitrarily change the rate so as to discriminate, or further discriminate, between them and customers residing in the city. This conclusion is certainly in line with well-established principles of public utility law.

For these reasons we hold that the statute did not change the common-law rule prohibiting unreasonable discrimination. The ordinance is therefore void unless the petitioner can show, on another trial of the cause, that there is some reasonable basis for the difference in rates which it establishes. In order that the petitioner may have an opportunity to make such a showing the judgment of the Court of Civil Appeals reversing and remanding the cause is affirmed.

■ SMEDLEY, GARWOOD, GRIFFIN and CALVERT, JJ., dissent.

■ CALVERT, JUSTICE.

I dissent.

The conclusion reached by the majority is contrary to the overwhelming weight of authority as evidenced by the decisions in those states in which the question has been decided under applicable common law rules.... Typical of the reasoning of all the courts is the language of the Kentucky Court of Appeals in the Davisworth case (311 Ky. 606, 224 S.W.2d 651). The City of Lexington had for years permitted non-resident suburban citizens to connect with the city sewer system without charge. In 1935 the City enacted as ordinance levying a charge for non-resident use which ordinance was upheld in the Jones case, supra, and in 1948 another ordinance was passed increasing the non-resident use charges from a range of from $4.20 to $9 per year to a range of from $25 to $200 per year. The validity of the ordinance was attacked on the ground that it was discriminatory against non-residents. The Court said:

> Approaching the heart of our particular problem, we may ask: Where the City has permitted non-residents to use its sewer system for a number of years, may it require them to discontinue such use? The query is answered by posing a counterquestion: Why not? The City's essential duties are owed to its inhabitants. Non-residents have no lawful claim upon any city service. Any use of city facilities by non-residents is wholly permissive (in the absence of contract or estoppel) and not based upon legal right. In this case Lexington has done no more than acquiesce in what would be, without its permission, a trespass upon its property by appellants and those similarly situated. The latter became mere licensees, and acquired no prerogative claim to a continuance of such license. It follows that the City's consent could be withdrawn at will.... If then, the City may discontinue the service altogether, it clearly may fix in its own discretion the charges to be paid by those who wish its continuance.

... The citizens of North Texarkana do not occupy the same relationship toward the City of Texarkana as do its own citizens. "The primary purpose of a municipal corporation is to contribute towards the welfare, health, happiness, and public interest of the inhabitants of such city, and not to further the interests of those residing outside of its limits." City of Sweetwater v. Hamner, Tex. Civ. App., 259 S.W. 191, 195. The City of Texarkana owes to its own citizens a duty to see that their health and welfare are protected through the continuing availability of water and sewer lines and facilities. It owes no such duty to the citizens of North Texarkana. It may furnish water and sewer services and facilities to residents of North Texarkana so long and only so long as the residents of that municipality contract for such services and the authorities of that municipality permit; but being under no duty to furnish in the first instance it may discontinue such services, on reasonable notice, with or without cause. Being entitled to discontinue the services according to its want, it follows that the City can continue them on its own terms and conditions. This was its common law right. It is now its statutory right....

NOTES

1. The assumption of the majority seems to be that nonresidents stand in no better position to ensure fair pricing than a consumer who faces a monopoly provider of a private good. Is the analogy apt? Even if officials who set prices for utilities are not electorally accountable to nonresidents, might there be other constraints on their ability (or desire) to externalize costs? What would these constraints look like? Are they sufficiently significant that we would want to embrace a rule of judicial deference to local decisions?

2. The majority indicates that differential rates for residents and nonresidents could be justified under some circumstances. What would those justifications look like? Does it matter, for instance, that the city obtained the plant through the issuance of revenue bonds that are repaid through user fees imposed on both resident and nonresident customers of the system? Would it have made a difference if the city had built the plant itself by issuing general obligation bonds and was repaying bondholders with general revenues including property taxes? What about an argument that all customers who are served by the municipal utility enjoy subsequent increases in the value of their property, but the municipality only captures the benefit of those increases (through property taxes) from residents; hence, higher fees serve as a mechanism for allowing municipalities to capture part of the benefit they visit on nonresidents? See Faxe v. City of Grandview, 294 P.2d 402 (Wash. 1956). In Bleick v. City of Papillion, 365 N.W.2d 405 (Neb. 1985), the court explicitly endorsed the dissent in Texarkana. Although the court suggested that discriminatory pricing would be justified by the fact that residents of the municipality had borne the cost of establishing or financing the system, the opinion did not appear to require that any such justification be shown. Rather, the decision appeared to rely on the "business" relationship between the city and the district that contracted for the services on behalf of the nonresidents. See also LCM Enterprises, Inc. v. Town of Dartmouth, 14 F.3d 675 (1st Cir. 1994) (upholding a town's higher harbor usage fees for nonresidents against a Fourteenth Amendment challenge on the ground that the higher fee merely balances the disproportionate burden on residents whose real estate and fire district taxes fund the municipal services provided the harbor.)

3. To the extent that municipal providers of services are monopolists, they also share the capacity of private providers to engage in other monopolistic behavior. For instance, they can "tie" unwanted services to desired services on an "all-or-nothing" basis, and hence enhance their monopoly position by making provision of the monopoly good contingent on purchase of another good over which the municipality has no monopoly. In order to prevent this type of tying, one would anticipate that judges would include within the realm of "unreasonable" any contractual terms that required nonresidents to accept another service along with the one for which they preferred to contract. See, e.g., Edris v. Sebring Utilities Commission, 237 So.2d 585 (Fla. Dist. Ct. App.), cert. denied, 240 So.2d 643 (Fla. 1970). Nevertheless, one could imagine situations in which two services are sufficiently intertwined as to render extraterritorial provision economically feasible only if they are both provided. In such a situation, supply of either service might properly be contingent on supply of the other. See, e.g., Sebring Utilities Commission v. Home Savings Association, 508 So.2d 26 (Fla. Dist. Ct. App.), rev. denied, 515 So.2d 230 (1987).

3. Favoring Residents in the Allocation of Resources

PROBLEM XXXI

The Town of Easton has constructed tennis courts in its public park. Although the park is open to the public at large, only Easton residents may use the tennis courts. Construction of the courts was financed with the proceeds of a general obligation bond issued by Easton for various improvements, installation of lighting at a public ballpark, repairs to the junior high school, and repaving a public parking lot. Residents pay $3.00 per hour for use of the courts. This fee completely defrays the cost of town employees who work at the tennis courts, with enough left over that a significant amount of the fee is returned to the city treasury. A nonresident is allowed to play with a resident, and no additional fee is charged to the nonresident. The tennis courts are constantly occupied during the summer months, and are quite crowded during the spring and fall months.

Longwood is a resident of Weston. Weston had not constructed any public tennis courts, and the closest courts available to Longwood are those in Easton. Longwood has attempted to play with other nonresidents at the Easton courts, but has always been denied access when she has been unable to show proof of residence. She has offered to pay the fee charged by Easton, and has even suggested a willingness to pay an additional charge. Since all her efforts have proven unsuccessful, she has consulted you to advise her whether she has any recourse against Easton. "After all," she tells you, "it's not like they're paying more to use the courts than I'd be willing to pay. I don't see why I should have to move to Easton just to play a game of tennis."

You have examined the statutes and discovered that Easton, which is not a home rule locality, has received statutory authority to "construct and operate parks and recreational facilities" and to pass ordinances that "regulate the use of such facilities." What advice do you have for Longwood?

Localities may favor residents in ways other than offering lower rates on municipal services. Residents may be given an advantage (or an exclusive right) with respect to jobs, access to publicly owned land, or public goods provided by the locality. At one level, these advantages seem quite natural and acceptable, given the financial support that residents provide to the locality through their tax dollars. Additionally, if we seek to advance forms of community, there must be times when the community is allowed to set itself apart from outsiders.

On further reflection, however, the benefits that one community can allocate often seem less a reflection of resident contributions or preferences than of good fortune. Do those who live in an area with a beachfront necessarily prefer access to beaches more than those who live in a landlocked locality? To the extent that nonresidents would be willing to pay a user fee that accurately reflects the cost of their use of the beach, is there reason to deny them access on the grounds of nonresidency?

Denial of access to nonresidents does not necessarily raise federal constitutional issues. In Arlington County Board v. Richards, 434 U.S. 5 (1977), the Court upheld a county ordinance that restricted parking to residents of areas that were deemed to suffer an influx of traffic from commercial and industrial districts. The ordinance explained the function of the limitation as "to reduce hazardous traffic conditions resulting from the use of streets within areas zoned for residential uses for the parking of vehicles by persons using districts zoned for commercial or industrial uses . . .; to protect those districts from polluted air, excessive noise, and trash and refuse caused by the entry of such vehicles; to protect the residents of those districts from unreasonable burdens in gaining access to their residences; to preserve the character of those districts as residential districts; to promote efficiency in the maintenance of those streets in a clean and safe condition; to preserve the value of the property in those districts; and to preserve the safety of children and other pedestrians and traffic safety, and the peace, good order, comfort, convenience and welfare of the inhabitants of the County." In vacating a Virginia court decision that invalidated the ordinance, the Court determined that these were appropriate municipal purposes that were rationally related to regulations that inherently discriminated against nonresidents. Since discrimination against nonresidents did not trigger heightened scrutiny of the regulation, this relationship was sufficient to survive a Fourteenth Amendment challenge.

Courts, however, continue to look askance at regulations that discriminate against nonresidents. In New York State Public Employees Federation v. City of Albany, 527 N.E.2d 253 (N.Y. 1988), the court considered a parking ordinance based on the one that the Supreme Court had approved in Arlington County Board that favored residents. The court invalidated the ordinance on the grounds that state statutes incorporated the traditional principle that roadways are open to the public at large. Hence, abrogation of that principle by a municipality would require specific authorization by the legislature. The court was unwilling to find any such authority in the existing powers of the City of Albany. See also People v. Speakerkits, Inc., 633 N.E.2d 1092 (N.Y. 1994).

Do the following cases provide a basis for a general theory about the circumstances in which localities are entitled to favor their residents?

Zaroogian v. Town of Narragansett

701 F.Supp. 302 (D.R.I. 1988).

■ FRANCIS J. BOYLE, CHIEF JUDGE.

The Plaintiffs in this action seek to have declared as violating the Equal Protection Clause of the United States Constitution an ordinance of the Town of Narragansett which seeks to provide exclusive use of some of its beach facilities to residents of the town only. This is the sole issue in this action.

The Town of Narragansett is located on the westerly shore of Narragansett Bay and nature has blessed the community with a substantial sandy beach front. When the great hurricane of 1938 destroyed the privately owned buildings on the beach, the Town sought and obtained authorization from the State of Rhode Island to carry on a general beach and bathhouse business, to acquire land for beach purposes through a bond issue and to construct and maintain buildings and accommodations for bathers, to charge fees for the use of such facilities and to make reasonable rules and regulations for the use of the facilities. This legislation took form in Chapter 764 of the Public Laws of Rhode Island 1939. As authorized, the Town acquired a natural sand beach located in approximately the center of the Town, 437,300 square feet in area at the present time, combining private beaches which had been known by such names as "Palmers" "Sherry's" and the "Clambake Club."

With funds obtained by the bonds authorized by the State of Rhode Island, the Town constructed two bathhouses, one known as the "Town Pavilion" and another known as the "Canonchet Pavilion" and moved a house onto the property near the present Canonchet Pavilion to serve as a clubhouse. As a result of another hurricane in 1954 these buildings were destroyed. Following the 1954 hurricane the Town built eleven free-standing beach facilities structures and four separate paved parking lots on the property. There are in effect two separate municipal beach operations, one known as the Narragansett Beach and the other known as the Canonchet Beach maintained by the Town. The beach area is itself available for use by anyone willing to pay a uniform entrance fee whether they are residents or non-residents of the Town.

There is one building and three parking lots which are associated with the Town Pavilion. This building contains 297 rental lockers that have changing rooms with or without showers, a lifeguard office, a concession stand, storage areas and offices for the beach management. Historically the lockers at the Town Pavilion had been leased both to non-residents and to persons who either reside in or pay taxes to the Town of Narragansett. Lessees of the Town Pavilion facilities are also provided a parking space in the Town lot reserved for that purpose.

The Canonchet Beach facility consists of eleven buildings, one called the Canonchet Pavilion, one called the Canonchet Clubhouse and nine buildings which comprise the cabanas. This area has available two parking lots. The pavilion has 256 changing rooms, suites and shower rooms. It also has a concession area and beach chair and umbrella storage areas. The nine buildings which comprise the cabanas house a total of 72 cabana units, each of which contains a shower, a dressing room and shares a joint storage area and deck with an adjoining unit. There were a total of 328 cabana units, suites, shower rooms and changing rooms in the Canonchet Pavilion. The Canonchet Clubhouse, another building, houses a meeting room, which is leased to the public on occasion, storage areas, kitchen areas, available for use by the public, rest room facilities, and a porch and a deck area which are also available for use by the public. Other than the changing rooms, shower rooms and cabana units, all of the Canonchet Beach land and buildings have been open to use by the general public and no distinction is made between residents and non-residents of the Town.

In all, the Town Beach and Canonchet Beach had 625 individual beach facilities available through the 1987 season. From 1954 until approximately 1978, the Town leased these individual beach facilities at both the Town Beach and the Canonchet Beach to residents and non-residents on a first-come, first-serve basis. It was the practice of the Town to first notify those who had leased facilities the previous year that they had the first opportunity to renew. This practice changed in 1981. A waiting list has been maintained since 1981, on which the Town has separately listed residents and non-residents. No non-resident has been offered a facility from the waiting list since this distinction has been made.

The Town Building Inspector condemned the Town Pavilion for the 1988 summer season because of an asbestos inspection, with the result that it became necessary to make some provision for the lessees of the 297 rental lockers at the Town Pavilion. The Town's solution to this problem was to adopt a policy of giving residents of the Town who had leased facilities at Canonchet and the Town Pavilion, 176 at Canonchet and 112 at Town Pavilion, the first opportunity to enter into leases for the Canonchet facilities for the year 1988 and giving other residents of the Town the first opportunity to lease any then remaining available facilities. Not only did this action prompt dismay from persons who for many years, although non-residents, had maintained cabanas at Canonchet Beach, it prompted this litigation.

Although the Plaintiffs initially raised a number of issues, it is now stipulated that there is but one issue and that is, whether or not the action of the Town in denying to nonresidents the opportunity to lease facilities at Canonchet Beach has violated the Equal Protection Clause of the United States Constitution. The Plaintiffs argue that because a State law authorizes the funding and maintenance of a beach facility for the benefit of the public, the denial of the opportunity to use the facilities by non-residents by the Town's action constitutes a violation of the Equal Protection rights of the public and the parties and requires a determination that the Town's policy is unconstitutional and therefore invalid.

The State law at issue is Chapter 764, the 1939 Enabling Act which authorized the Town of Narragansett to

> carry on a general beach and bathhouse business at said town, to purchase ... lands within said town, and purchase, construct, maintain and operate or lease thereon buildings, piers, walks, parking facilities and swimming pools; to furnish bathing accommodations and facilities to the public; and to make reasonable rules and regulations for the use of the same, and charge reasonable fees therefore.

1939 R.I. Pub. Laws, ch. 764, Sec. 1. In the absence of ambiguity, the language of a statute must be given its plain meaning. K Mart Corp. v. Cartier, Inc., 486 U.S. 281, 108 S. Ct. 1811, 1817, 100 L. Ed. 2d 313 (1988) (reviewing court must determine that challenged regulation is consistent with enabling statute). "If the statute is clear and unambiguous 'that is the end of the matter....' " Id. While the word "public" can be defined as "the community at large, without reference to geographical limits," it can also refer to "the inhabitants of a particular place" or "the people of the neighborhood." To the extent that the statute's use of the word "public" can be regarded as ambiguous, this Court finds that the Town of Narragansett is authorized by virtue of its delegated authority to regulate the use to include or exclude non-residents from its definition as circumstances require. The Act specifies only that the "bathing accommodations and facilities" be furnished to the public, not the leased bathhouse facilities. The bathing facilities—beach and some parking areas, rest rooms, etc.—are and always have been available to the public.

Plaintiffs contend that the legislative intent of the 1939 General Assembly can be ascertained, not by reading the plain language of the statute, but by reading the contents of a letter submitted as a part of the effort to obtain passage of the Enabling Act. This letter, from the Town Council of Narragansett to the General Assembly, urges passage of the Enabling Act "so that the Town ... may be ready to receive the people of the State of Rhode Island and other States during the summer of 1939...." Plaintiffs view this wording as requiring that each of the facilities at Narragansett be made available to all Rhode Island and, indeed, all the world. The Court disagrees. The beach and other areas of the facilities are open to the world. However, use of the leased facilities—lockers, shower and changing rooms, and cabanas—by virtue of their finite number must be restricted. It can hardly be argued otherwise that the use of these facilities demands privacy.

That the Town policy restricts the use so as to give priority to residents does not contravene the Enabling Act. The Act itself purports to protect the rights of town residents:

> [N]o rights of the inhabitants of said town ... shall be destroyed or substantially impaired by this act ... though the exercise of any rights may be regulated or reasonably restricted under this act so as to secure the most equitable enjoyment of such rights by said inhabitants....

1939 R.I. Pub. Laws, ch. 764, Sec. 9. The resident priority policy of the Town acts to secure an equitable enjoyment of the individual beach facilities for the Town's inhabitants. A plain reading of the statute, coupled with the facts, compel the conclusion that the state did not intend that all the facilities of the beach and bathhouse business in Narragansett must be open to all the public under all circumstances.

Where a classification is not inherently suspect and does not involve a fundamental right, the proper test to use in determining whether it violates the equal protection clause is the rational basis test. Cleburne v. Cleburne Living Center, Inc., 473 U.S. 432, 440, 105 S. Ct. 3249, 3254, 87 L. Ed. 2d 313 (1985). Social or economic legislation enacted by states is especially given "wide latitude" in relation to the equal protection clause. Id. Accord Plyler v. Doe, 457 U.S. 202, 216, 102 S. Ct. 2382, 2394, 72 L. Ed. 2d 786 (1982) (classification must bear "fair relationship to a legitimate public purpose"); Bankers Life & Casualty Co. v. Crenshaw, 486 U.S. 71, 108 S. Ct. 1645, 1653, 100 L. Ed. 2d 62 (1988) (legislation need only be "rationally related to ... legitimate interests"). The Supreme Court upheld Montana's increased elk-hunting license fees for non-residents of the state, determining that "a chance to engage temporarily in a recreational activity" is "not fundamental." Baldwin v. Fish & Game Commn. of Montana, 436 U.S. 371, 377, 98 S. Ct. 1852, 1857, 56 L. Ed. 2d 354 (1978). By its very nature, use of beach facilities is a recreational activity and therefore not entitled to heightened scrutiny. In examining a resident-only parking ordinance, the Court found "distinctions between residents and non-residents of a local neighborhood [not] to be invidious," so long as they "rationally promote the regulation's objectives." County Bd. of Arlington County, Va. v. Richards, 434 U.S. 5, 7, 98 S. Ct. 24, 26, 54 L. Ed. 2d 4 (1977). So here, the distinction between residents and non-residents rationally promotes the Town's legitimate objectives.

The Enabling Act authorizes the Town to operate beach and bathhouse facilities for the benefit of the public. The Town does this. The beach itself is open to the public without limitation or exclusion. Further, the meeting room, concession areas, rest rooms, kitchen areas and porch and deck areas are available to the public.

Only the changing rooms, shower rooms, and cabana units are restricted primarily to residents. The condemnation of the Town Pavilion decreased the number of these individual facilities from 625 to 358 for the 1988 season. The resident priority policy is a "reasonable rule and regulation," as allowed by the Enabling Act, of the use of the facilities which rationally furthers the aim of the Town to allocate the limited number of rental facilities in the conduct of its beach and bathhouse business. The rationing of this scarce resource is based on a rational premise. The very nature of the use requires exclusion. As such, the limitation does not violate Plaintiffs' constitutional guarantees to equal protection of the laws.

Therefore, Judgment will be entered for Defendants for costs.

NOTE

The Connecticut Supreme Court relied on a First Amendment analysis to invalidate a town ordinance that limited access to a town park that had beachfront access. Leydon v. Town of Greenwich, 777 A.2d 552 (Conn. 2001). The ordinance restricted use of the park to residents and their guests. The court concluded that the park constituted a public forum that had to be open to all speakers in the absence of a compelling state interest. While reasonable time, place, or manner restrictions on nonresidents were plausible, a virtual ban was not. The court found that similar analysis precluded enforcement of the ordinance under the state constitution. Similarly, the court found that any agreement between the town and a private association that had an easement on the property was invalid where the agreement restricted use of the easement to town residents and their guests.

In Matthews v. Bay Head Improvement Association, 471 A.2d 355 (N.J.), cert. denied, 469 U.S. 821 (1984), the New Jersey Supreme Court expanded on a series of its prior decisions concerning public access to beachfront property. The Association, which had been formed to protect and improve the beachfront of the Borough of Bay Head, owned six properties along the shore. The Association hired lifeguards, patrolled the beaches, and restricted access. Between 10:00 A.M. and 5:30 P.M. during summer months, access to the dry sand area of the beach was restricted to

Association members, and membership was itself restricted to borough residents. Exceptions were granted to hotel and motel guests, borough employees, and certain public servants. In prior cases, the court had held that the public trust doctrine required that access to the beach and ocean be made available to all persons on equal terms and that a municipality could not limit access to its dry sand beaches. In Matthews, the court declared that the public also had a right to access privately owned dry-sand beaches. The court noted that the public trust doctrine required access both for passage to the ocean and for rest and relaxation, and that there was no distinction for these purposes between municipally owned and privately owned property. Thus, public access was required where "reasonably necessary" to accomplish these objectives. The court's holding, however, did not lead to the conclusion that all private property owners had to open their property to the public. Rather, the court focused on the relationship between the Association and the borough. The borough had contributed to the cost of jetties, had provided the Association free office space, exempted certain Association property from taxation, and had included Association activities under borough insurance policies. In return, the Association's activities typically approximated those made available by a governmental entity. The result was that, "[w]hen viewed in its totality—its purposes, relationship with the municipality, communal characteristic, activities, and virtual monopoly over the Bay Head beachfront," the Association took on the character of a "quasi-public" entity. Id. at 368. The court required the Association to open its membership to the general public and to provide a reasonable number of seasonable and daily badges to nonresidents. Restrictions on access could be imposed to ensure safety, and the Association could impose fees to cover its costs. Fees, however, could not be set in a manner that discriminated between residents and nonresidents.

For discussion of the public trust doctrine, see Joseph D. Kearney & Thomas W. Merrill, The Origins of the American Public Trust Doctrine: What Really Happened in *Illinois Central*, 71 U. Chi. L. Rev. 799 (2004); Carol Rose, The Comedy of the Commons: Custom, Commerce, and Inherently Public Property, 53 U. Chi. L. Rev. 711 (1986).

United Building and Construction Trades Council v. Mayor of Camden

465 U.S. 208 (1984).

■ Justice Rehnquist delivered the opinion of the Court.

A municipal ordinance of the city of Camden, New Jersey requires that at least 40% of the employees of contractors and subcontractors working on city construction projects be Camden residents. Appellant, the United Building and Construction Trades Council of Camden and Vicinity (the Council), challenges that ordinance as a violation of the Privileges and Immunities Clause, Article IV, 2, of the United States Constitution. The Supreme Court of New Jersey rejected appellant's privileges and immunities attack on the ground that the ordinance discriminates on the basis of *municipal*, not state, residency. The court "decline[d] to apply the Privileges and Immunities Clause in the context of a municipal ordinance that has identical effects upon out-of-state citizens and New Jersey citizens not residing in the locality." 88 N.J. 317, 342, 443 A.2d 148, 160 (1982). We conclude that the challenged ordinance is properly subject to the strictures of the Clause. We therefore reverse the judgment of the Supreme Court of New Jersey and remand the case for a determination of the validity of the ordinance under the appropriate constitutional standard.

On August 28, 1980, the Camden City Council, acting pursuant to a state-wide affirmative action program, adopted an ordinance setting minority hiring "goals" on all public works contracts. Ordinance MC 1650, Pet., at A36. The ordinance also created a hiring preference for Camden residents, with a separate one-year residency requirement triggering eligibility for that preference. Id., at I(5), Pet., at A38.... Since the Council filed its appeal ... the Court decided White v. Massachusetts Council of Const. Employers, 460 U.S. 204, 103 S. Ct. 1042, 75 L. Ed. 2d 1 (1983), which held that an executive order of the Mayor of Boston, requiring that at least 50% of all jobs on construction projects funded in whole or part by city funds be filled by bona fide city residents, was immune from scrutiny under the Commerce Clause because Boston was acting as a market participant rather than as a market regulator. In light of the decision in *White*, appellant has abandoned its Commerce Clause challenge to the Camden ordinance. ...

[T]he only question left for our consideration is whether the Camden ordinance, as now written, violates the Privileges and Immunities Clause. We first address the argument, accepted by the Supreme Court of New Jersey, that the Clause does not even apply to a municipal ordinance such as this. Two separate contentions are advanced in support of this position: first, that the Clause only applies to laws passed by a *State* and, second, that the Clause only applies to laws that discriminate on the basis of *state* citizenship.

The first argument can be quickly rejected. The fact that the ordinance in question is a municipal, rather than a state, law does not somehow place it outside the scope of the Privileges and Immunities Clause. First of all, one cannot easily distinguish municipal from state action in this case: the municipal ordinance would not have gone into effect without express approval by the State Treasurer....

More fundamentally, a municipality is merely a political subdivision of the State from which its authority derives. City of Trenton v. New Jersey, 262 U.S. 182, 187, 43 S. Ct. 534, 536, 67 L. Ed. 937 (1923). It is as true of the Privileges and Immunities Clause as of the Equal Protection Clause that what would be unconstitutional if done directly by the State can no more readily be accomplished by a city deriving its authority from the State.... Thus, even if the ordinance had been adopted solely by Camden, and not pursuant to a state program or with state approval, the hiring preference would still have to comport with the Privileges and Immunities Clause.

The second argument merits more consideration. The New Jersey Supreme Court concluded that the Privileges and Immunities Clause does not apply to an ordinance that discriminates solely on the basis of *municipal* residency. The Clause is phrased in terms of state citizenship and was designed "to place the citizens of each State upon the same footing with citizens of other States, so far as the advantages resulting from citizenship in those States are concerned." Paul v. Virginia, 8 Wall. 168, 180, 19 L. Ed. 357 (1869)....

Municipal residency classifications, it is argued, simply do not give rise to the same concerns.

We cannot accept this argument. We have never read the Clause so literally as to apply it only to distinctions based on state citizenship. For example, in Mullaney v. Anderson, 342 U.S. 415, 419–420, 72 S. Ct. 428, 431–432, 96 L. Ed. 458 (1952), the Court held that the Alaska Territory had no more freedom to discriminate against those not residing in the Territory than did any State to favor its own citizens. And despite some initial uncertainty, ... it is now established that the terms "citizen" and "resident" are "essentially interchangeable," ... for purposes of analysis of most cases under the Privileges and Immunities Clause....

Given the Camden ordinance, an out-of-state citizen who ventures into New Jersey will not enjoy the same privileges as the New Jersey citizen residing in Camden. It is true that New Jersey citizens not residing in Camden will be affected by the ordinance as well as out-of-state citizens. And it is true that the disadvantaged New Jersey residents have no claim under the Privileges and Immunities Clause.... But New Jersey residents at least have a chance to remedy at the polls any discrimination against them. Out-of-state citizens have no similar opportunity, ... and they must "not be restricted to the uncertain remedies afforded by diplomatic processes and official retaliation." Toomer v. Witsell, 334 U.S. 385, 395, 68 S. Ct. 1156, 1162, 92 L. Ed. 1460 (1948). We conclude that Camden's ordinance is not immune from constitutional review at the behest of out-of-state residents merely because some in-state residents are similarly disadvantaged....

Application of the Privileges and Immunities Clause to a particular instance of discrimination against out-of-state residents entails a two-step inquiry. As an initial matter, the court must decide whether the ordinance burdens one of those privileges and immunities protected by the Clause. Baldwin v. Montana Fish and Game Commn., 436 U.S. 371, 383, 98 S. Ct. 1852, 1860, 56 L. Ed. 2d 354 (1978). Not all forms of discrimination against citizens of other States are constitutionally suspect....

Certainly, the pursuit of a common calling is one of the most fundamental of those privileges protected by the Clause.... Public employment, however, is qualitatively different from employment in the private sector; it is a subspecies of the broader opportunity to pursue a common calling. We have held that there is no fundamental right to government employment for purposes of the Equal Protection Clause.... And in *White*, 103 S. Ct., at 1046, n.7, we held that for purposes of the Commerce Clause everyone employed on a city public works project is, "in a substantial if informal sense, 'working for the city.' "

It can certainly be argued that for purposes of the Privileges and Immunities Clause everyone affected by the Camden ordinance is also "working for the city" and, therefore, has no grounds for complaint when the city favors its own residents. But we decline to transfer mechanically into this context an analysis fashioned to fit the Commerce Clause. Our decision in *White* turned on a distinction between the city acting as a market participant and the city acting as a market regulator. The question whether employees of contractors and subcontractors on public works projects were or were not, in some sense, working for the city was crucial to that analysis. The question had to be answered in order to chart the boundaries of the distinction. But the distinction between market participant and market regulator relied upon in *White* to dispose of the Commerce Clause challenge is not dispositive in this context. The two Clauses have different aims and set different standards for state conduct.

The Commerce Clause acts as an implied restraint upon state regulatory powers. Such powers must give way before the superior authority of Congress to legislate on (or leave unregulated) matters involving interstate commerce. When the State acts solely as a market participant, no conflict between state regulation and federal regulatory authority can arise.... The Privileges and Immunities Clause, on the other hand, imposes a direct restraint on state action in the interests of interstate harmony.... This concern with comity cuts across the market regulator-market participant distinction that is crucial under the Commerce Clause. It is discrimination against out-of-state residents on matters of fundamental concern which triggers the Clause, not regulation affecting interstate commerce. Thus, the fact that Camden is merely setting conditions on its expenditures for goods and services in the marketplace does not preclude the possibility that those conditions violate the Privileges and Immunities Clause.

In Hicklin v. Orbeck, 437 U.S. 518, 98 S. Ct. 2482, 57 L. Ed. 2d 397 (1978), we struck down as a violation of the Privileges and Immunities Clause an "Alaska Hire" statute containing a resident hiring preference for all employment related to the development of the State's oil and gas resources. Alaska argued in that case "that because the oil and gas that are the subject of Alaska Hire are *owned* by the State, this ownership, of itself, is sufficient justification for the Act's discrimination against nonresidents, and takes the Act totally without the scope of the Privileges and Immunities Clause." Id., at 528, 98 S. Ct., at 2489. We concluded, however, that the State's interest in controlling those things it claims to own is not absolute. "Rather than placing a statute completely beyond the Clause, a State's ownership of the property with which the statute is concerned is a factor—although often the crucial factor—to be considered in evaluating whether the statute's discrimination against noncitizens violates the Clause." ... Much the same analysis, we think, is appropriate to a city's efforts to bias private employment decisions in favor of its residents on construction projects funded with public monies. The fact that Camden is expending its own funds or funds it administers in accordance with the terms of a grant is certainly a factor—perhaps the crucial factor—to be considered in evaluating whether the statute's discrimination violates the Privileges and Immunities Clause. But it does not remove the Camden ordinance completely from the purview of the Clause.

In sum, Camden may, without fear of violating the Commerce Clause, pressure private employers engaged in public works projects funded in whole or in part by the city to hire city residents. But that same exercise of power to bias the employment decisions of private contractors and subcontractors against out-of-state residents may be called to account under the Privileges and Immunities Clause. A determination of whether a privilege is "fundamental" for purposes of that Clause does not depend on whether the employees of private contractors and subcontractors engaged in public works projects can or cannot be said to be "working for the city." The opportunity to seek employment with such private employers is "sufficiently basic to the livelihood of the Nation," ... as to fall within the purview of the Privileges and Immunities Clause even though the contractors and subcontractors are themselves engaged in projects funded in whole or part by the city.

The conclusion that Camden's ordinance discriminates against a protected privilege does not, of course, end the inquiry. We have stressed in prior cases that "[l]ike many other constitutional provisions, the privileges and immunities clause is not an absolute." ... It does not preclude discrimination against citizens of other States where there is a "substantial reason" for the difference in treatment....

The city of Camden contends that its ordinance is necessary to counteract grave economic and social ills. Spiralling unemployment, a sharp decline in population, and a dramatic reduction in the number of businesses located in the city have eroded property values and depleted the city's tax base. The resident hiring preference is designed, the city contends, to increase the number of employed persons living in Camden and to arrest the "middle class flight" currently plaguing the city. The city also argues that all non-Camden residents employed on city public works projects, whether they reside in New Jersey or Pennsylvania, constitute a "source of the evil at which the statute is aimed." That is, they "live off" Camden without "living in" Camden. Camden contends that the scope of the discrimination practiced in the ordinance, with its municipal residency requirement, is carefully tailored to alleviate this evil without unreasonably harming nonresidents, who still have access to 60% of the available positions.

Every inquiry under the Privileges and Immunities Clause "must ... be conducted with due regard for the principle that the states should have considerable leeway in analyzing local evils and in prescribing appropriate cures." ... This caution is particularly appropriate when a government body is merely setting conditions on the expenditure of funds it controls. See supra, at 1028....

Nonetheless, we find it impossible to evaluate Camden's justification on the record as it now stands. No trial has ever been held in the case. No findings of fact have been made. The Supreme Court of New Jersey certified the case for direct appeal after the brief administrative proceedings that led to approval of the ordinance by the State Treasurer. It would not be appropriate for this Court either to make factual determinations as an initial matter or to take judicial notice of Camden's decay. We, therefore, deem it wise to remand the case to the New Jersey Supreme Court. That court may decide, consistent with state procedures, on the best method for making the necessary findings.

The judgment of the Supreme Court of New Jersey is reversed, and the case is remanded for proceedings not inconsistent with this opinion.

Reversed and remanded.

■ JUSTICE BLACKMUN, dissenting. . . .

While the Framers thus conceived of the Privileges and Immunities Clause as an instrument for frustrating discrimination based on state citizenship, there is no evidence of any sort that they were concerned by intrastate discrimination based on municipal residence. The most obvious reason for this is also the most simple one: by the time the Constitution was enacted, such discrimination was rarely practiced and even more rarely successful. Even had attempts to practice the kind of economic localism at issue here been more widespread, moreover, there is little reason to believe that the Framers would have devoted their limited institutional resources to bringing such conduct within the ambit of the Privileges and Immunities Clause. . . .

The Court recognizes, as it must, that the Privileges and Immunities Clause does not afford state residents any protection against their own State's laws. . . . When this settled rule is combined with the Court's newly-fashioned rule concerning municipal discrimination, however, it has the perverse effect of vesting non-New Jersey residents with constitutional privileges that are not enjoyed by most New Jersey residents themselves. This result is directly contrary to the Court's longstanding position that the Privileges and Immunities Clause does not give nonresidents "higher and greater privileges than are enjoyed by the citizens of the state itself." . . . When judicial alchemy transmutes gold into lead in this fashion, it is time for the Court to re-examine its reasoning.

Finally, the Court fails to attend to the functional considerations that underlie the Privileges and Immunities Clause. The Clause has been a necessary limitation on state autonomy not simply because of the self-interest of individual States, but because state parochialism is likely to go unchecked by state political processes when those who are disadvantaged are by definition disenfranchised as well. The Clause remedies this breakdown in the representative process by requiring state residents to bear the same burdens that they choose to place on nonresidents; "by constitutionally tying the fate of outsiders to the fate of those possessing political power, the framers insured that their interests would be well looked after."

J. Ely, Democracy and Distrust 83 (1980). As a practical matter, therefore, the scope of the Clause may be measured by asking whether failure to link the interests of those who are disadvantaged with the interests of those who are preferred will consign the former group to "the uncertain remedies afforded by diplomatic processes and official retaliation." . . .

Contrary to the Court's tacit assumption, discrimination on the basis of municipal residence is substantially different in this regard from discrimination on the basis of state citizenship. The distinction is simple but fundamental: discrimination on the basis of municipal residence penalizes persons within the State's political community as well as those without. The Court itself points out that while New Jersey citizens who reside outside Camden are not protected by the Privileges and Immunities Clause, they may resort to the State's political processes to protect themselves. Ante, at 1027. What the Court fails to appreciate is that this avenue of relief for New Jersey residents works to protect residents of other States as well; disadvantaged state residents who turn to the state legislature to displace ordinances like Camden's further the interests of nonresidents as well as their own.

NOTES

1. In White v. Massachusetts Council of Construction Employers, 460 U.S. 204 (1983), discussed in the *Camden* case, the Court considered a Commerce Clause challenge to the constitutionality of an executive order issued by the mayor of Boston, requiring that at least 50 percent of the employees for any construction project financed in whole or in part with city funds, or with funds which the city had the authority to administer, be Boston residents. The majority began its analysis by indicating that the Commerce Clause would not apply if the city was acting as a "market participant" rather than a "market regulator," since the Commerce Clause responds primarily to state taxes and regulatory measures that impede private trade in the national marketplace. Without sharply distinguishing when a locality was operating in each sphere, the Court concluded that where construction funding came only from city funds, the city was acting as a market participant, and thus was exempt from Commerce Clause review. The majority further held that "[w]here state or local government action is specifically authorized by Congress, it is not subject to the Commerce Clause even if it interferes with interstate commerce. Thus, if the restrictions imposed by the city on construction projects financed in part by federal funds are directed by Congress then no dormant Commerce Clause issue is presented." Id. at 213 (citations omitted). Finally, the Court concluded, the projects at issue in Boston were undertaken under federal programs intended to encourage economic revitalization that affirmatively authorized the type of parochial favoritism implicit in the mayor's order.

Justice Blackmun dissented. He argued that the mayor's order was subject to the Commerce Clause insofar as it involved activities that were not specifically authorized by Congress. Here, the imposition by the city of requirements on private firms required analysis of whether those restrictions constituted an impermissible burden on interstate commerce.

The Seventh Circuit applied the principles of *White* in J. F. Shea Co. v. City of Chicago, 992 F.2d 745 (7th Cir. 1993), where a nonresident contractor challenged a local preference rule that gave the bids of local businesses competing for contracts with the City of Chicago a 2 percent advantage over the bids of nonlocal businesses. The Court determined that White authorized such a preference where the locality was using its own funds for the project and was a party to the contract at issue. Hence, the preference did not prevent the contractor from submitting bids on city projects or on projects with private parties in the city. The sole effect of the preference was to award contracts to resident bidders unless the nonresident contractor submitted a bid that was at least 2 percent lower than the lowest resident contractor's bid.

2. In a series of cases involving environmental protection, the Supreme Court has limited the capacity of localities and states to restrict the private importation of waste. In Fort Gratiot Sanitary Landfill, Inc. v. Michigan Dept. of Natural Resources, 504 U.S. 353 (1992), the Court held that a state may not prohibit private landfill operators from accepting solid waste that originates outside the county in which their facilities are located. This case followed the decision in City of Philadelphia v. New Jersey, 437 U.S. 617 (1978), that prevented a state from prohibiting private landfill operators from accepting waste from other states. The Court has held that similar standards apply to restrictions on the exportation of waste. C & A Carbone, Inc. v. Town of Clarkstown, 511 U.S. 383 (1994) (invalidating under the Commerce Clause a "flow control" ordinance that required all solid waste to be delivered to a particular private processing facility before leaving the municipality, on the ground that it deprived competitors, including out-of-state firms, of access to a local market). But see United Haulers Ass'n, Inc. v. Oneida–Herkimer Solid Waste Management Auth., 550 U.S. 330, 334 (2007) (limiting the *Carbone* holding to situations in which a flow control ordinance requires haulers to deliver waste to a particular *private* processing facility, and holding that the Commerce Clause is not violated by laws that require haulers to deliver waste to particular *state-created public benefit corporations*).

In Swin Resource Systems, Inc. v. Lycoming County, 883 F.2d 245 (3d Cir. 1989), cert. denied, 493 U.S. 1077 (1990), however, the Third Circuit upheld regulations authorizing a county-owned and operated solid waste processing facility to charge a lower rate for disposal of waste generated within that county and nearby counties than for waste generated outside that area, on the ground that the county was acting as a market participant rather than as a market regulator and was therefore not subject to the constraints of the Commerce Clause. En route to this holding the court observed that "If a city may constitutionally limit its trucks to collecting garbage generated by city residents, we see no constitutional reason why a city cannot also limit a city-operated dump to garbage generated by city residents.... [A]pplication of the market participant doctrine enables 'the people [acting through their local government] to determine as conditions demand ... what services and functions the public welfare requires.' " 883 F.2d at 251.

INDEX

References are to Pages

†